R. Gupta's®

Popular Master Guide

Joint CSIR-UGC (NET)

Junior Research Fellowship and Eligibility for Lectureship

Earth, Atmospheric, Ocean and Planetary Sciences

PART B & C

By

Dr. Surender Kumar

Ph.D., JNU; M.Phil., JNU

&

RPH Editorial Board

2027
EDITION

RAMESH PUBLISHING HOUSE, NEW DELHI

Published by

O.P. Gupta *for* Ramesh Publishing House

Admin. Office

12-H, New Daryaganj Road, Opp. Officers Mess,
New Delhi-110002 ✆ 23275224, 23245124

E-mail: info@rameshpublishinghouse.com

For Online Shopping: www.rameshpublishinghouse.com

Showroom

- Balaji Market, Nai Sarak, Delhi-110006 ✆ 23282525 📱 9354373464
- 4457, Nai Sarak, Delhi-110006

Book Code: R-1277

ISBN: 978-81-7812-978-5

Price: ₹ 690

Printed at: Deepak Offset, Delhi

Contents

Previous Years' Paper

Joint CSIR-UGC NET/JRF

Earth, Atmospheric, Ocean & Planetary Sciences

DECEMBER-2025

(Exam held on 18-12-2025, Conducted by NTA)

PART-A

1. Consider the following information regarding a 3-digit PIN.

6	8	9	→ One number is correct and correctly placed
7	3	8	→ Nothing is correct
9	0	6	→ Two numbers correct but wrongly placed
6	1	5	→ One number is correct but wrongly placed
7	8	0	→ One number is correct but wrongly placed

The correct PIN is:
1. 059
2. 601
3. 590
4. 859

2. Numbers of seats for Mathematics, Physics and Biology in a college are in the ratio 2:3:4. What will be the respective ratio if the seats for each subject are increased by 50%?
1. 1:1:1
2. 2:3:4
3. 4:3:2
4. 3:2:4

3. With only one match, between teams B and C, remaining in a tournament where each win fetches two points and a loss none, team A observes that they will become champions with more points than any other team if B wins, but not necessarily if B loses. Then
1. A is leading B by one point
2. B is leading C by one point
3. B is leading C by at least two points
4. A is leading C by at most two points

4. Sachin sees one-fourth of his body (height) when he stands in front of a vertical mirror at a distance of 20 cm from it. How much of his body will he see if he steps back and stands 40 cm from the mirror?
1. half
2. one-fourth
3. one-eighth
4. full

5. A box contains 20 black, 22 white, and 24 red socks. If a person draws socks at random one by one without looking, what is the minimum number of socks she must pick to be certain of having at least one pair of black socks?
1. 3
2. 4
3. 44
4. 48

6. The unit's place digit is half the ten's place digit in a two-digit number N. If we swap the digits, the number gets reduced by 18. The number N is ________ .
1. 24
2. 42
3. 48
4. 84

7. Suppose a tap mixes hot water and cold water in a ratio that depends linearly on the proportion of opening. Water out of the tap has temperature 40°C when the tap is half-open, and 30°C when it is three-fourths open. To get water at 50°C, the tap should be ________.

1. one-eighth open
2. one-fourth open
3. three-eighths open
4. five-eighths open

8. The pie charts show placement percentages of graduates of five different subjects out of the total campus placements for two consecutive years.

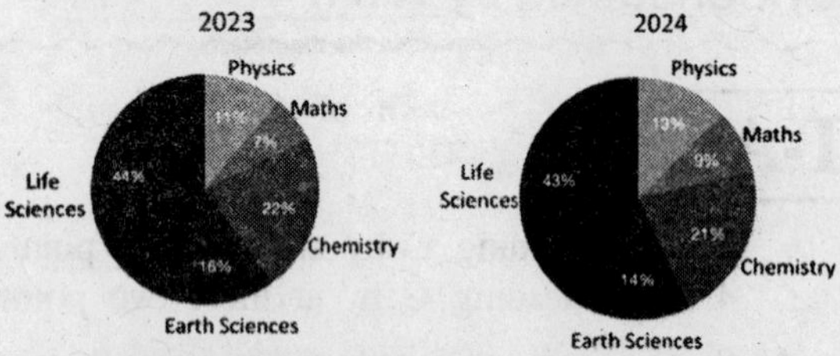

In the year 2024, the number of Maths students who got placed was the double that of the previous year. Which of the following is the closest to the percentage change in the number of Life Sciences students placed in the year 2024?

1. decreased by 1%
2. increased by 50%
3. decreased by 50%
4. increased by 20%

9. The following bus schedule is seen at a bus stop located somewhere in between town A and town B.

Town A: 00:10, then every 20 mins

Town B: 00:15, then every 20 mins

If a person arrives at this bus stop at some random time, the probability that the next bus is for town B is

1. 1/2 2. 1/4
3. 1/3 4. 3/4

10. There is an increase of 30% in the number of people coming to a theatre after reducing the entry fee by 25% per person. How much change is expected in the total earnings?

1. 2.5% increase 2. 2.5% decrease
3. Nil 4. 7.5% increase

11. The following ternary figure shows the marks obtained by students A, B and C in an exam of 100 marks. Here, C received 10 marks in Physics, 50 marks in Chemistry and 40 marks in Mathematics.

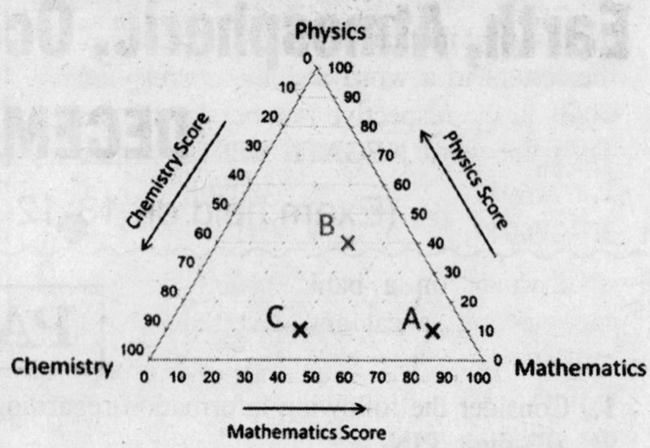

Which one of the following is CORRECT?

1. A's marks in Chemistry are more than C's marks in Physics
2. B has scored equal in Mathematics and Physics
3. A has scored 20 in Chemistry
4. A has scored 80 in Chemistry

12. A cellphone tower with signals reaching up to 500 m is set up on a conical hill of height 1.5 km and base radius 2 km. Assuming the tower's height to be negligible compared to the hill, the area served by the tower in km^2 is (the area of the curved surface of a right circular cone is $\pi \times$ base radius $\times$ slant height)

1. 0.2π 2. 0.25π
3. 4π 4. 5π

13. Restaurants A, B, C, and D give the following offers:

A. one mocktail free for every two purchased
B. one mocktail free for every three purchased
C. two mocktails free for every six purchased
D. 30% discount on each mocktail

If all of the restaurants have the same marked price for each mocktail, in which restaurant would you pay the least if you drank eight mocktails?

1. A 2. B
3. C 4. D

14. Suppose the words GATE, FAST, SAND and READ can be written in numbers as 2938, 6921, 0798 and 5917, but not necessarily in that order. The positions of the letters in a word and the corresponding digits in the respective number are the same. Then the word NEGATE will be written as

1. 716921 2. 380798
3. 375917 4. 891217

15. A boatman on a bank of a river has to carry a dog, a cat and a container full of milk to the other bank in a boat, one at a time. The cat cannot be left alone with the milk or with the dog on either bank. What is the minimum number of times the boatman has to cross the river to carry all to the other bank?

1. 3 2. 5
3. 7 4. 8

16. A person borrowed ₹ 2500/- for 2 years, and ₹ 2000/- for 3 years, with the same simple interest rate. If he paid a total of ₹ 550/- as interest, then the annual rate of interest was

1. 10% 2. 2%
3. 5% 4. 8%

17. An auditorium has 8 seats in the first row, with every row to follow having 4 more seats than its preceding row. The total capacity is 416. What is the minimum number of rows needed to seat 150 people?

1. 8 2. 5
3. 3 4. 2

18. A father said to his son, "I was as old as you are when I became your father." If the current age of father is 52 years, the age of son after 10 years will be ______.

1. 26 years 2. 36 years
3. 20 years 4. 40 years

19. With a certain set of diameters, a tractor's front wheels make 2 revolutions (revs) for every 1 revolution of the rear wheels. The effect of changing wheel diameter(s) is shown in the following plot.

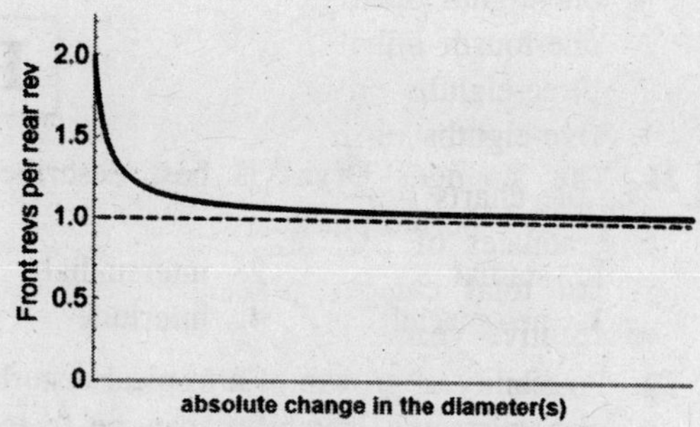

In this context, which of the following statements is CORRECT?

1. Only the rear wheel diameter is decreased
2. Both the rear and front wheel diameters are decreased equally
3. Both the rear and front wheel diameters are increased equally
4. The rear wheel diameter decreased, and the front wheel diameter increased equally

20. The Sankey diagram shows food preferences of males and females. The widths of the bands are proportional to numbers of persons opting for a given food item.

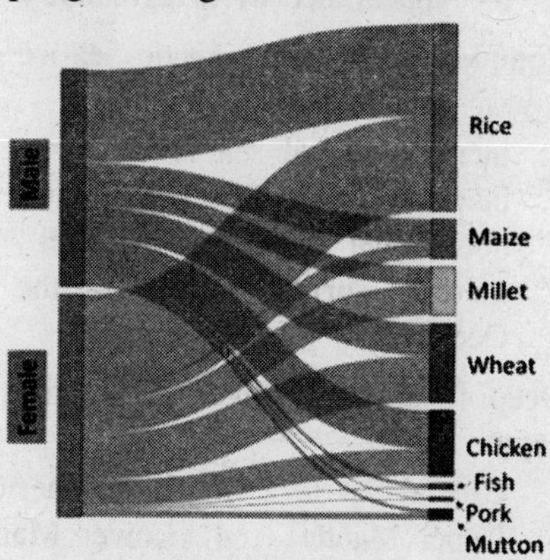

Which one of the following is an INCORRECT statement about the food preferences?

1. Chicken is the second most preferred food in males.
2. As compared to males, more females prefer wheat.
3. As compared to males, more females prefer mutton and millet.
4. Fewer females prefer rice than the total number of males preferring maize and millet.

PART-B

21. The Younger Dryas is best described as .... period/phase.

1. stadial
2. interstadial
3. neo-glacial
4. interlude

22. Possibility of growth of a tropical disturbance via barotropic instability can be tested by examining the ....

1. Latitudinal variation of zonal wind
2. Longitudinal variation of meridional wind
3. Vertical variation of zonal wind
4. Longitudinal variation of zonal wind

23. The 410 km discontinuity primarily represents ....

1. a change in bulk chemical composition
2. the change of olivine to wadsleyite
3. the change of olivine to ringwoodite
4. the appearance of bridgmanite

24. Complete melting of Arctic sea-ice within a year will immediately ....

1. increase global sea level
2. increase Arctic Sea level only
3. not change the global sea level
4. increase surface salinity of the Arctic Ocean

25. Deep focus earthquakes occur at .... depth.

1. Crustal
2. Lithospheric
3. Upper Mantle
4. Lower Mantle

26. In a Mohr's circle, the radius represents ....

1. mean stress
2. differential stress
3. shear stress
4. lithostatic stress

27. Which component of the geomagnetic field is primarily affected by equatorial electrojet?

1. East-West and vertical component
2. North-South and vertical component
3. Vertical component only
4. All components affected equally

28. Which one of the following statements is NOT true about the mid-latitude wave cyclones?

1. They generally travel eastward
2. They are embedded within the larger general circulation
3. Warm air ascends at a lower angle of slope along warm front compared to that along cold front
4. They decay as they move into an area of increasing upper air absolute vorticity

29. The seismic phase which is recorded in the P-shadow zone is ....

1. P
2. S
3. PcP
4. PKiKP

30. What is the major source of heat in the Earth's continental crust?

1. Primordial heat
2. Plate tectonics
3. Radioactive decay
4. Convection currents

31. Which one of the following relates to the management of soil erosion?

1. Stone line
2. Log line
3. Tree line
4. Shrub line

32. Inselbergs are most common on ....

1. sandstones and limestones
2. mudstones and syenites
3. limestones and granites
4. granites and gneisses

33. The Curie point is defined as the temperature above which a .... material becomes ....

1. Ferromagnetic, Paramagnetic
2. Paramagnetic, Ferromagnetic
3. Ferromagnetic, Ferrimagnetic
4. Ferromagnetic, Diamagnetic

34. The Earth's magnetic field can be approximately modelled by which source field?

1. Quadrupole 2. Tripole
3. Dipole 4. Monopole

35. Which one of the following features record the location of past ice-walled or subglacial streams or channels?

1. Moulins 2. Kames
3. Eskers 4. Kettle holes

36. The sediments deposited in the delta region of the Ganga-Brahmaputra rivers at a depth of 50 m (compared to modern sea level), during the last glacial maximum will contain ....

1. both marine and terrestrial fractions
2. only marine classic fraction
3. only terrestrial fraction
4. only marine authigenic fraction

37. A 1-in-25-yr flood has a ....% probability of occurring in any one year.

1. 2.5 2. 25
3. 4 4. 40

38. Which one of the following elements remain largely conserved in the ocean?

1. Lead 2. Thorium
3. Silicon 4. Molybdenum

39. Which one of the following satellite data is used to predict potential fishery zones?

1. Fish
2. Zooplankton
3. Phytoplankton
4. Chlorophyll

40. In the Indian Ocean, the oxygen isotopic composition ($\delta^{18}O$) of calcareous benthic foraminifera at 2500 m water depth is .... than that of the planktic foraminifera because of the difference in ....

1. higher, temperature
2. lower, temperature
3. higher, pressure
4. lower, pH

41. In the Northern Hemisphere, the major ocean currents tend to curve to the right due to ....

1. Cyclonic eddies
2. Wind shear
3. Density gradient
4. Coriolis Force

42. Under similar situations, remote sensing using longer wavelength typically corresponds to ....

1. enhanced spatial detail
2. more number of grey shades
3. reduced field of view
4. broader spectral bands

43. What generally happens during a warm phase of ENSO?

1. Indian summer monsoon rainfall decreases
2. Tropical east Pacific water becomes colder
3. Indian summer monsoon rainfall increases
4. Somali jet becomes stronger

44. The correct sequence of increasing thermal maturity of coal is ....

1. Lignite, Anthracite, Bituminous, Peat
2. Peat, Bituminous, Lignite, Anthracite
3. Peat, Lignite, Graphite, Bituminous
4. Peat, Lignite, Bituminous, Anthracite

45. What will be the final temperature of an air parcel initially at 295 K and 900 hPa if it is lifted dry adiabatically to 700 hPa?

(Given: Specific gas constant for dry air $R_d = 287$ J kg^{-1}K^{-1}; Specific heat at constant pressure for dry air $C_p = 1004$ J kg^{-1}K^{-1})

1. 265 K 2. 274 K
3. 280 K 4. 284 K

46. If the Sun lost half of its mass, but the orbital radius of the Earth remained the same, then the orbital period of the Earth would increase by a factor of ....

1. 2 2. 4
3. $\sqrt{2}$ 4. $\sqrt[3]{2}$

47. Banded iron-formation formed during the Precambrian because of ....

1. conversion of Fe^{2+} to Fe^{3+} during chemical weathering
2. formation of stable cratons
3. conversion of Fe^{3+} to Fe^{2+} in the water column
4. conversion of Fe^{2+} to Fe^{3+} in the water column

48. 'Standing stock' is a term used to represent the productivity of the ocean. Which of the following represents standing stock?

1. Total weight of all organisms in a given area or volume of water
2. Number of organisms per unit area or per unit volume of water
3. Total number of phytoplankton in unit area or unit volume of water
4. Total number of zooplankton in unit area or unit volume of water

49. Which one of the following properties is essential for the existence of large-scale atmospheric waves?

1. Compressibility
2. Buoyancy
3. Viscosity
4. Planetary vorticity

50. Which one of the following rock types would be of interest for a Lithium-exploration program?

1. Komatiites
2. Metabasalt in greenstone belt
3. Granitic pegmatite
4. Banded iron-formations

51. Which one of the following sub-horizon distinctions is observed in the B horizon of a soil profile in an arid region?

1. B_g 2. B_k
3. B_h 4. B_o

52. Conditions A and B show two positions of the solstices on the Earth. The approximate time interval between conditions A and B is ....

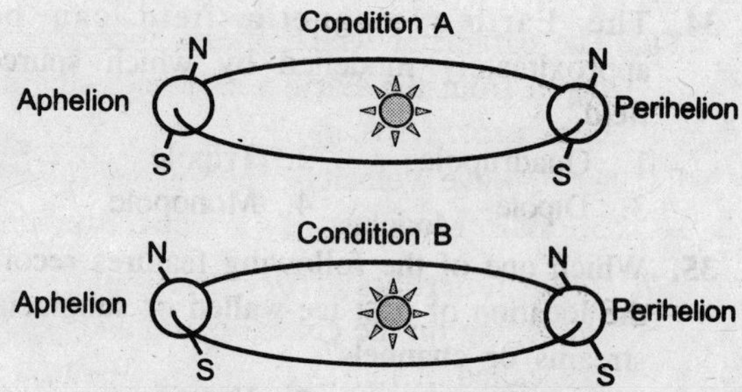

1. 11,000 yrs 2. 23,000 yrs
3. 40,000 yrs 4. 100,000 yrs

53. When an air parcel is lifted from a humid boundary layer into a conditionally unstable atmosphere, which statement about the Lifting Condensation Level (LCL), the Level of Free Convection (LFC), and the Equilibrium Level (EL) is always correct?

1. The LCL is the highest altitude a parcel can reach without external lifting, since condensation begins at this level
2. The LFC is the first level above the LCL where the parcel becomes positively buoyant compared to the environment
3. The EL is the altitude where condensation ends because the air parcel can no longer hold liquid water
4. The LCL and LFC coincide whenever the environment is conditionally unstable

54. Which of the following metamorphic facies best represents a low-T, high-P metamorphism at a convergent margin setting?

1. Granulite
2. Eclogite
3. Albite-epidote hornfels
4. Blueschist

55. Which one of the following is an example for strong and direct air-sea coupling?

1. Jet stream
2. Quasi-Biennial Oscillation (QBO)
3. Tropical cyclone
4. Thunderstorm

56. The parameter which always increases with depth from the Earth's surface to the inner core is ....

1. P-wave velocity 2. S-wave velocity
3. Bulk Modulus 4. Shear Modulus

57. Tidal currents from the open ocean impinging on the coastal ocean and estuaries are called ....

1. Amphidromes
2. Co-oscillation Tides
3. Lunar Equilibrium Tides
4. Semidiurnal Tides

58. Which among the following is unique to wind action?

1. Suspension 2. Saltation
3. Abrasion 4. Deflation

59. Which Cephalopod suture is characterized by rounded saddles and angular lobes?

1. Ceratitic 2. Goniatitic
3. Ammonitic 4. Nautiloid

60. If τ is the surface wind stress vector, then the expression $\left[\frac{\nabla \times \tau}{\rho f}\right]$ represents ....

[ρ = density of seawater, f = Coriolis parameter]

1. Potential Vorticity
2. Baroclinic Vorticity
3. Ekman Pumping
4. Ekman Transport

61. Which one of the following best describes the turbulent fluid flow (TFF)?

1. TFF is associated with low Reynolds number flow
2. TFF has multiple scales of motion
3. TFF is irrotational
4. TFF is a steady flow

62. Which one of the following reactions dominantly produces ^{14}C in the Earth's atmosphere?

1. $^{12}C + 2n = {}^{14}C$
2. $^{13}C + n = {}^{14}C$
3. $^{14}N + n = {}^{14}C + p$
4. $^{15}N + p + 2n = {}^{14}C + {}^{4}He$

63. The centrifugal force due to the rotation of the Earth causes ....

1. maximum decrease in gravity at the equator
2. maximum decrease in gravity at the poles
3. no change in gravity
4. maximum decrease in gravity at 45° latitude

64. Boussinesque approximation on density CANNOT be applied to study ....

1. Dry gravity waves
2. Boundary layer turbulence
3. Thunderstorms
4. Tsunami waves

65. The term 'carat' used in context of diamond is a ....

1. unit of clarity, with higher carat implying less inclusions
2. unit of colour, ranging from Yellow for low carat diamonds to colourless for higher carat diamonds
3. unit of weight with one carat approximately being equal to 200 milligrams
4. unit of purity with lower carat having mixing of other material

66. Cooler average night temperature in a tropical land region indicates that ....

1. it is a densely forested area
2. it is a densely populated area with extensive urbanization
3. mean atmospheric humidity is low
4. overcast cloud condition exists

67. Which one of the following sequences is correctly arranged in decreasing order of accretion/growth rates?

1. Coral reef, Polymetallic nodule, Cobalt crust
2. Cobalt crust, Coral reef, Polymetallic nodule
3. Polymetallic nodule, Coral reef, Cobalt crust
4. Cobalt crust, Polymetallic nodule, Coral reef

68. A mountain of 5 km height and density 2.67 g/cm^3 is isostatically compensated according to Airy's model. If the average thickness of crust is 35 km and density of mantle is 3.3 g/cm^3, then the depth of the isostatic Moho beneath the mountain is ....

1. 50.2 km
2. 52.2 km
3. 54.2 km
4. 56.2 km

69. Which one of the following DOES NOT represent a type of drainage network pattern?

1. Pinnate
2. Anabranching
3. Annular
4. Barbed

70. Which one of the following is LEAST likely to increase ocean productivity?

1. Upwelling
2. Convective mixing
3. Cyclonic eddies
4. Anticyclonic eddies

PART-C

71. Permeability of coal bed changes with methane production primarily because ....

1. coal contains several impurities
2. coal cleats experience matrix swelling and shrinkage
3. coal cleats have a tortuous fluid flow path
4. gas content in coal varies based on the Langmuir isotherm

72. $2KAlSi_3O_8 + 9H_2O + 2H^+ = Al_2Si_2O_5(OH)_4 + 2K^+ + 4H_4SiO_4$

The above reaction of weathering of K-feldspar to form kaolinite indicates that:

1. higher activity of silicic acid enhances weathering
2. a higher water-to-rock ratio will maintain the equilibrium between K-feldspar and kaolinite.
3. lower water-to-rock ratio and high silicic acid activity restrict weathering
4. K-feldspar can never form from kaolinite

73. Which one of the following waves has a phase speed that does not vary with its wavelength under dry shallow-water fluid conditions?

1. Inertio-gravity wave
2. Mixed Rossby-gravity wave
3. Kelvin wave
4. Rossby wave

74. Choose the correct statement about a mid-latitude weather disturbance exhibiting characteristic horizontal velocity, horizontal and vertical length scales of 10 m/s, 1000 km, and 10 km, respectively.

1. Maximum vertical velocity of the disturbance is 10 mm/s
2. Maximum vertical velocity of the disturbance is 10 cm/s
3. The disturbance is in hydrostatic balance, and hence the vertical motion is not allowed
4. The disturbance follows cyclostrophic balance

75. Match the landform feature in Column I with the process/structure in Column II

Column I (Landform feature)	Column II (Process/Structure)
A. Damodar valley	(*i*) Headward erosion
B. Dhala impact structure	(*ii*) Unloading anticline
C. Tista River	(*iii*) Rift basin
D. Nohkalikai falls	(*iv*) Inversion of relief
	(*v*) Ingrown meander

Choose the correct option:

	A	B	C	D
1.	(*iii*)	(*iv*)	(*ii*)	(*i*)
2.	(*i*)	(*iii*)	(*iv*)	(*ii*)
3.	(*iv*)	(*ii*)	(*v*)	(*iii*)
4.	(*v*)	(*i*)	(*iii*)	(*iv*)

76. Choose the statement that DOES NOT correctly describe the Manning's equation (v = velocity)

1. v is inversely proportional to the Manning's roughness coefficient.
2. v increases with two-thirds power of flow depth.
3. v increases with the square root of channel slope.
4. v is directly proportional to the product of hydraulic radius and flow depth.

77. Match column I with column II:

Column I	Column II
A. Ombrothermic diagram	P. Wet bulb temperature (°F) and relative humidity (%)
B. Climograph	Q. 12-sided polygon constructed by joining points representing temperature (°C) and rainfall (mm)
C. Hythergraph	R. Identification of wet, dry and excess of water seasons in relation to a climate type.
D. Hyetograph	S. Rainfall intensity over time

Choose the correct option:

1. A–P; B–S; C–R; D–Q
2. A–R; B–P; C–S; D–Q
3. A–R; B–P; C–Q; D–S
4. A–Q; B–S; C–P; D–R

78. Match the following columns:

Column I (Drainage Basin Properties)	Column II (Relation with Stream Order)
A. Number of streams of each order	X. Approximates a direct geometric series
B. Mean length of streams of each order	Y. Approximates an inverse geometric series
C. Mean area of the basin of each order	
D. Mean gradient of streams of each order	

Choose the correct option:

1. A–X; B–X; C–Y; D–Y
2. A–X; B–Y; C–Y; D–X
3. A–Y; B–X; C–X; D–Y
4. A–Y; B–Y; C–X; D–X

79. If the vector field (A) is represented as $A = \nabla\phi + \nabla \times \psi$, where ϕ, and ψ are the scalar and vector potentials, respectively, then the divergence of A is given by ....

1. $\nabla^2\phi - \nabla^2\psi$
2. $\nabla^2\phi$
3. $-\nabla^2\psi$
4. 0

80. Match the EM methods in Column I with the associated quantities in Column II.

Column I	Column II
P. INPUT EM method	A. Rotary field
Q. VLF method	B. Dip angle measurement
R. Airborne EM method	C. Static shift
S. MT method	D. Early and late time apparent resistivity

Choose the correct option:

1. P–B; Q–C; R–D; S–A
2. P–D; Q–B; R–A; S–C
3. P–C; Q–A; R–B; S–D
4. P–A; Q–D; R–C; S–B

81. Cloud X forms over land, while Cloud Y forms over the ocean with the same amount of liquid water content. It is very likely that ....

1. number of cloud droplets in X < Y
2. average size of cloud droplet in X > Y
3. collection efficiency in X > Y
4. number of cloud droplets in X > Y

82. In the following diagram, alphabets represent strata and the symbols indicate fossils.

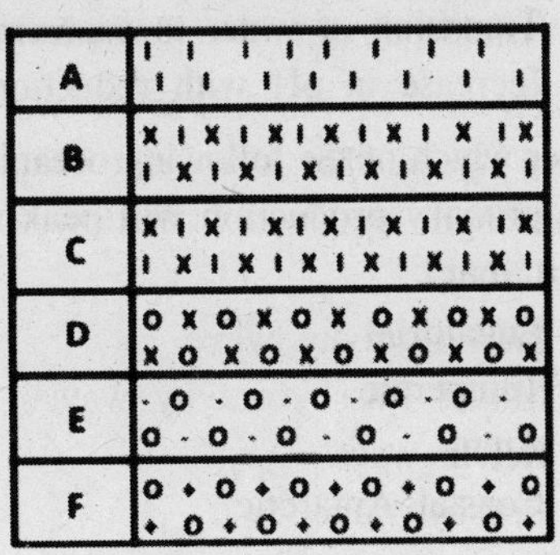

Match the First and Last Appearance Datum (FAD & LAD, respectively) of the fossils in Column I with the respective strata in Column II.

Column I	Column II
P. FAD of -	T. B
Q. LAD of x	U. C
R. FAD of l	V. D
S. LAD of o	W. E

Choose the correct option:
1. P–T; Q–W; R–V; S–U
2. P–W; Q–T; R–U; S–V
3. P–V; Q–U; R–T; S–W
4. P–U; Q–V; R–W; S–T

83. In the given Eh-pH diagram at ambient surface conditions, the upper stability limit of water indicates ....

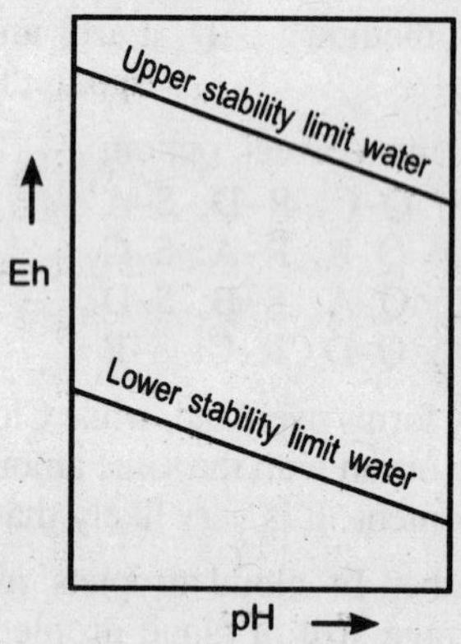

Choose the correct option:
1. Breakdown of water to release electrons
2. Breakdown of water to consume electrons
3. Transition of water to supercritical fluid
4. Increase in pH with reduction in Eh

84. Over which of the following oceanic regions, the primary production will peak two times in a year?
1. Equatorial
2. Temperate
3. Arctic
4. Coastal Antarctic

85. Match the magmatic activity in column I with its approximate age in column II.

Column I	Column II
A. Panjal Traps	Q. 1700 Ma
B. Malani volcanics	R. 116 Ma
C. Sylhet Traps	S. 65 Ma
D. Dalma Lavas	T. 745 Ma
E. Amba Dongar carbonatites	V. 285 Ma

Choose the correct option:
1. A–Q; B–T; C–R; D–V; E–S
2. A–S; B–V; C–T; D–R; E–Q
3. A–V; B–T; C–R; D–Q; E–S
4. A–R; B–S; C–Q; D–T; E–V

86. How could the high ambient salinity affect the buoyancy of pelagic organisms?
1. Organisms spend less energy to avoid sinking in water of high salinity.
2. Higher salinity will help the animals to develop larger appendages.
3. Higher salinity will help prevent loss of body fluids and gases to the environment.
4. Higher salinity will induce production of gas vacuoles in the body fluids.

87. Assertion (A): Sand-bed rivers braid at lower slopes than gravel-bed rivers of similar discharge.

Reason (R): Sand is more easily entrained.

Choose the correct option:
1. A is true, but R is false
2. Both A and R are true, but R is not the correct explanation of A
3. Both A and R are true, and R is the correct explanation of A
4. A is false, but R is true

88. The order of accuracy of the centered finite difference approximation

$$\left.\frac{df}{dx}\right|_{x=x_0} = \frac{f(x_0+h)-f(x_0-h)}{2h} \text{ is } \ldots\ldots\ldots .$$

1. $O(h)$
2. $O(h^2)$
3. $O(h^3)$
4. $O(h^4)$

89. A sediment rating curve represents the relationship between ....

1. sediment load and bedload
2. suspended sediment concentration and water discharge
3. suspended sediment yield and catchment area
4. sediment grain size and flow velocity

90. What will be the coefficient of electrical anisotropy for two horizontally stratified layers having resistivity 10 Ωm and 20 Ωm and thicknesses 10 m each?

1. 1.06 2. 1.11
3. 1.14 4. 1.18

91. A listric normal fault flattens to 15° near the base of a sedimentary cover. If the vertical throw at the surface is 120 m, what is the approximate heave?

1. 200 m 2. 630 m
3. 460 m 4. 560 m

92. What is the approximate thickness of an atmospheric layer between 1000 hPa and 700 hPa, given its pressure-weighted virtual temperature is 285 K?

(Given: Gas constant for dry air, R_d = 287 $Jkg^{-1}K^{-1}$; Acceleration due to gravity g = 9.81 ms^{-2})

1. 2650 m
2. 3125 m
3. 2975 m
4. 2145 m

93. The 1-D Schlumberger sounding data corresponding to seven subsurface layers is given in the figure below. According to the principle of equivalence, which is the correct statement regarding ambiguity in the interpretation of this data?

(h_i and ρ_i are the interpreted thickness and resistivity of individual layers)

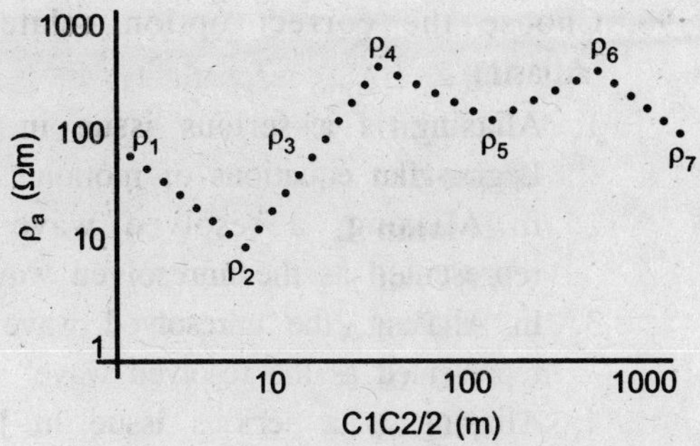

1. Second and fifth layers will exhibit h/ρ = constant type Equivalence
2. Second and fifth layers will exhibit $h \times \rho$ = constant type Equivalence
3. Fourth and sixth layers will exhibit h/ρ = constant type Equivalence
4. Third and sixth layers will exhibit $h \times \rho$ = constant type Equivalence

94. Which of the following statements best describes the behaviour of the saturated adiabatic lapse rate Γ_s in the Earth's troposphere?

1. Γ_s is nearly fixed at about 6.5 K km^{-1}
2. Γ_s becomes smaller in warm and moist air due to strong latent heating and approaches the dry-adiabatic lapse rate in cold and dry air aloft
3. Γ_s remains equal to the dry-adiabatic lapse rate just above the LCL until the parcel reaches the LFC, after which latent heating reduces the lapse rate
4. Γ_s is always larger than the observed environmental lapse rate, under a conditionally unstable atmosphere

95. According to the Irvine model of chromite crystallization, which one of the following processes CANNOT lead to significant formation of chromite seams?

1. mixing of less-evolved magma with evolved magma
2. contamination by olivine
3. contamination by silica
4. higher initial chromium concentration in the melt

96. Choose the correct option related to 'Aliasing'.

1. Aliasing is a serious issue in fully Lagrangian equations of motion
2. In Aliasing, a resolved wave gets represented as the unresolved wave
3. In Aliasing, the unresolved wave gets represented as the resolved wave
4. Aliasing is a serious issue in linear equations of motion

97. The tidal acceleration of a fluid parcel at the "sublunar point" is given as $\frac{2GMa}{r^3}$ where G is the gravitational constant, M is mass of the moon, a is radius of the earth, and r is the centre-to-centre distance between the earth and the moon. What is the approximate tidal acceleration at antipodal point?

1. $-\frac{4GMa}{r^3}$ 2. $-\frac{2GMa}{r^3}$
3. $-\frac{GMa}{r^3}$ 4. $-\frac{GMa}{2r^3}$

98. Match the lunar landform feature in Column I with its process of formation in Column II:

Column I (Feature)	Column II (Process of formation)
A. Maria	(*i*) Gravity slide
B. Sinuous rilles	(*ii*) Bolide impact
C. Rays	(*iii*) Flood volcanism
D. Boulder tracks	(*iv*) Lava tubes
	(*v*) Desiccation shrinkage

Choose the correct option:

1. A–(*ii*); B–(*i*); C–(*v*); D–(*iv*)
2. A–(*i*); B–(*ii*); C–(*iv*); D–(*iii*)
3. A–(*iii*); B–(*iv*); C–(*ii*); D–(*i*)
4. A–(*iv*); B–(*v*); C–(*i*); D–(*iii*)

99. Which of the following statements are correct for effluent streams?

A. They lose water to the saturated zone.
B. The surface of these streams coincides with the water table.
C. The water table slopes away from these streams.
D. Discharge of these streams increases downstream.
E. These streams occur in humid regions.

Choose the correct option:

1. A and C only 2. B and D only
3. B, D, and E only 4. A, C, and D only

100. Fishes with accessory respiratory organs are often seen in which of the following intertidal habitats?

1. Rocky shore 2. Muddy shore
3. Sandy shore 4. Estuary

101. One of the reasons for the relatively poor development of coral reefs off the west coast of Australia and South America is due to the presence of ....

1. fresh water inputs by large rivers
2. high coastal water turbidity due to river-derived sediments
3. cold ocean currents and upwelling of cold water
4. high rate of sea floor sedimentation

102. Choose the correct option regarding the Regular High and Anomalous High system in the Northern Hemisphere.

1. Both systems have the same sense of anti-clockwise rotation
2. Both systems have the same sense of clockwise rotation
3. For both systems, the resultant of the Centrifugal force and the Coriolis force balances the horizontal pressure gradient force
4. For both systems, the resultant of horizontal pressure gradient force and Coriolis force balances the Centrifugal force

103. The number of non-zero singular values for an $m \times n$ matrix A ($m \neq n$) with full rank is equal to ....

1. $m + n$ 2. $m - n$
3. min (m, n) 4. max (m, n)

104. Which one of the following statements about the internal gravity wave is INCORRECT?

1. Fluid elements of internal gravity waves propagate parallel to the direction of their phase propagation
2. The phase and group velocity of the internal gravity waves are in opposite directions
3. The frequency of internal gravity waves has an upper limit
4. The phase of the internal gravity waves exhibits a tilt with the horizontal axes

105. Consider the following statements:

Statement A: Inclusion of the frictional force in the geostrophic balance results in a cross-isobaric flow with a component towards lower pressure in the northern hemisphere.

Statement B: Inclusion of the frictional force in the geostrophic balance results in a cross-isobaric flow with a component towards higher pressure in the southern hemisphere.

Choose the correct option:

1. Statement A is incorrect; statement B is correct
2. Statement A is correct; statement B is incorrect
3. Both statements are correct
4. Both statements are incorrect

106. The given schematic diagram shows the nitrogen cycle processes for oxic and anoxic waters in the ocean. Identify the processes A, B, C, and D correctly in the figure.

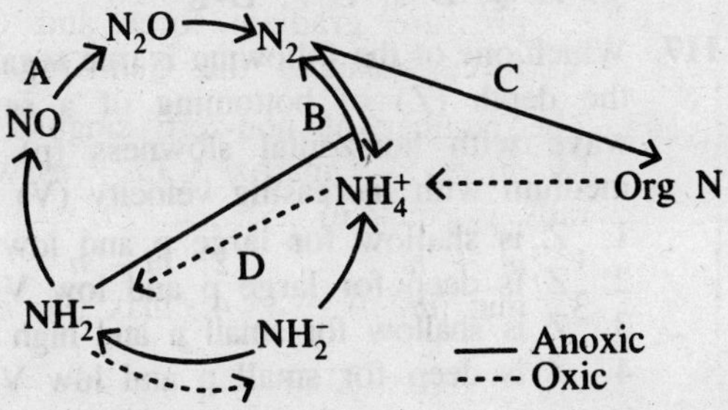

1. A–Denitrification, B–N_2 fixation, C– Anammox, D–Nitrification
2. A–N_2 fixation, B–Anammox, C–Denitrification, D–Nitrification
3. A–Denitrification, B–Anammox, C–Nitrification, D–N^2 fixation
4. A–Denitrification, B–Anammox, C–N_2 fixation, D–Nitrification

107. If slope height doubles, keeping other soil properties constant, factor of safety for frictional slope causing landslide ....

1. doubles
2. halves
3. remains the same
4. slightly decreases

108. Choose the correct option related to the following vorticity equation applied in the northern hemisphere

$$\frac{D_h}{D_t}(\zeta+f) = -(\zeta+f)\left(\frac{\partial u}{\partial x}+\frac{\partial v}{\partial y}\right)$$

where $\frac{D_h}{D_t}(\,) = \frac{\partial}{\partial t}(\,) + u\frac{\partial}{\partial x}(\,) + v\frac{\partial}{\partial y}(\,)$,

ζ, f are the relative vorticity and planetary vorticity, respectively, and $\left(\frac{\partial u}{\partial x}+\frac{\partial v}{\partial y}\right)$ is the horizontal divergence.

1. The above equation is valid for planetary-scale motion
2. The above equation conserves absolute vorticity for divergent motions
3. The above equation represents Baroclinic conditions
4. The above equation indicates the reason for cyclonic systems to be more intense than anticyclonic systems

109. A heavy mineral bearing clean sandstone bed is distinguished from a shaly sandstone bed by which one of the following log combinations?

1. Neutron log and gamma ray log
2. Density log and S.P. log
3. Gamma ray spectroscopy and gamma ray log
4. Density log and gamma ray log

110. An FFT (Fault-Fault-Trench) triple junction is ....

1. always stable
2. always unstable
3. stable only if the trench and one of the transform faults have the same trend
4. stable only if both the transform faults have the same trend

111. Outside corridor stacking in VSP data processing is a technique used to ....

1. eliminate ground roll
2. perform seismic migration
3. suppress internal multiples
4. estimate the seismic wavelet

112. A sand aquifer is 10 m thick, 200 m wide, and has a hydraulic conductivity of 2×10^{-5} m/s. If the head difference between two points 500 m apart is 4 m, the total ground water flow volume per day through a cross section of the aquifer as per Darcy's law will be ....

1. 4.32 m^3/day   2. 43.2 m^3/day
3. 27.6 m^3/day   4. 2.76 m^3/day

113. Identify the type of channel changes.

(Arrow shows the direction of the present flow)

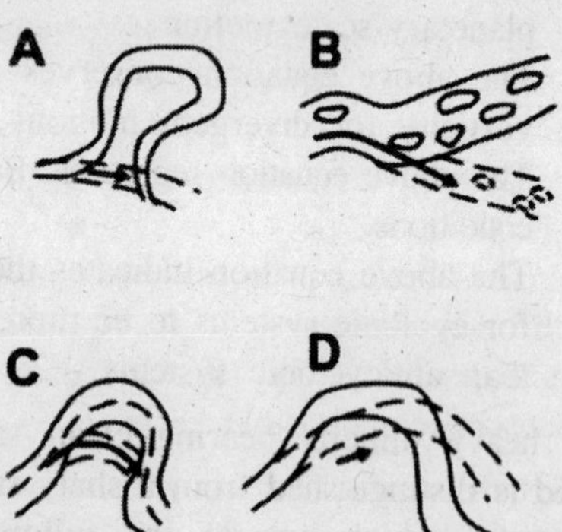

Choose the correct option:

1. A- Neck cutoff; B- Avulsion; C- Chute cutoff; D- Meander shift
2. A- Chute cutoff; B- Avulsion; C- Neck cutoff; D- Meander migration
3. A- Neck cutoff; B- Chute cutoff; C- Avulsion; D- Meander shift
4. A- Meander shift; B- Chute cutoff; C- Neck cutoff; D - Avulsion

114. Which one of the following mineral assemblages typically represents the high-P, low-T belt in a paired metamorphic belt?

1. Garnet + Sillimanite + K-feldspar
2. Glaucophane + Lawsonite + Jadeite
3. Omphacite + Sillimanite + Jadeite
4. Garnet + Lawsonite + Spinel

115. Following faulting, streams flowing towards the uplift block and streams flowing towards the downthrown side, respectively, experience ....

1. impoundment and rapid downcutting
2. impoundment and aggradation
3. rapid downcutting and impoundment
4. rapid downcutting and lateral erosion

116. Match the column I with column II:

Column I	Column II
A. IPCC Assessment Report 3	P. Vulnerability is a function of exposure, sensitivity, and adaptive capacity
B. IPCC Assessment Report 4	Q. Year 2001
C. IPCC Assessment Report 5	R. Shared Socioeconomic Pathways
D. IPCC Assessment Report 6	S. Disaster Risk is a function of hazard, exposure, and vulnerability

Choose the correct option:

1. A–P; B–S; C–R; D–Q
2. A–P; B–Q; C–S; D–R
3. A–Q; B–P; C–S; D–R
4. A–Q; B–S; C–P; D–R

117. Which one of the following is true regarding the depth (Z) of bottoming of a seismic wave with horizontal slowness (p) in a medium with increasing velocity (V)

1. Z is shallow for large p and low V
2. Z is deep for large p and low V
3. Z is shallow for small p and high V
4. Z is deep for small p and low V

118. The observed strength of Indian summer monsoon circulation is primarily attributed to ....

1. land-ocean temperature gradient
2. rotation of the Earth
3. release of latent heat due to condensation
4. sensible heating by land

119. Assuming the Earth's magnetic field to be purely dipolar, what is the ratio of its radial to tangential components at 30° magnetic latitude on the Earth's surface?

1. $1:\sqrt{3}$
2. $\sqrt{3}:1$
3. $2:\sqrt{3}$
4. $\sqrt{3}:2$

120. A bulk mixed layer (50 m) of the ocean undergoes heat loss of 400 W/m^2 for one-day. If the initial temperature of the mixed layer is 25°C, what would be the final temperature after one-day?

(Assume water density = 1000 kg/m^3, specific heat capacity of water is 4000 J/kg/K and one day = 10^5 seconds)

1. 20.4 °C
2. 24.8 °C
3. 22.8 °C
4. 25 °C

121. If deep water had historically formed in the North Pacific instead of North Atlantic, which one of the following changes in ocean chemistry would most likely to have occurred?

1. Pacific deep water would acquire higher nutrient concentrations due to increased biological productivity.
2. The North Atlantic would become oxygen rich due to enhanced vertical mixing.
3. Pacific deep water would acquire higher oxygen concentration due to younger water masses
4. Global ocean chemistry would remain unaffected

122. Match the column I with column II:

Column I (Process)	Column II (Diagnostic that remains conserved)
I. Unsaturated, dry adiabatic, reversible ascent/descent	A. Moist Static Energy
II. Saturated pseudoadiabatic ascent (condensate immediately removed)	B. Potential Temperature
III. Saturated reversible ascent (condensate retained)	C. Total Water Mixing Ratio
IV. Deep convective plume with steady entrainment of environmental air (condensate retained)	D. Equivalent Potential Temperature

Choose the correct option:

1. I-C, II-A, III-D, IV-B
2. I-D, II-C, III-B. IV-A
3. I-A, II-D, III-B, IV-C
4. I-B, II-D, III-A, IV-C

123. In the warm clouds, growth of droplets ....

1. increases rapidly with time by condensation from the vapour phase
2. increases rapidly with time initially, but the growth rate decreases with the increase in radius
3. decreases due to an increase in collisions with other droplets
4. decreases due to the increase in coalescence with other droplets

124. The higher organic carbon content in the continental slope sediments on the eastern and western margins of India is facilitated by ....

1. higher fine grain fraction, low dissolved oxygen
2. higher fine grain fraction, high dissolved oxygen

3. lower fine grain fraction, high dissolved oxygen
4. higher coarse grain fraction, high dissolved oxygen

125. Match the sedimentary structure in column I with the corresponding depositional environment in column II:

Column I	Column II
A. Low-angled reverse-graded planar laminae	P. Fluvial
B. Curve-crested dune in poorly sorted sandstone	Q. Tidal
C. Herringbone cross-strata sandstone	R. Continental Slope
D. Profoundly normally graded bed with scoured base	S. Aeolian

Choose the correct option:
1. A–Q; B–P; C–R; D–S
2. A–P; B–S; C–Q; D–R
3. A–S; B–P; C–Q; D–R
4. A–Q; B–R; C–S; D–P

126. At a given location in the ocean, new production is 10 mmol N m^{-2} d^{-1} and *f* ratio is 0.2. Which of the following CANNOT be concluded based on this data?
1. Primary production is 330 mmol C m^{-2} d^{-1}
2. Regenerated production is 40 mmol N m^{-2} d^{-1}
3. External nitrogen nutrients support 10 mmol N m^{-2} d^{-1} productivity
4. 66 mmol C is deposited in the ocean sediment per day

127. Match the tracers (Column - II) that are used to identify/quantify ocean properties/processes (Column - I)

Column I	Column II
A. Ventilation	P. ^{226}Rn
B. Export C Flux	Q. Cd/Al
C. Paleo Productivity	R. ^{234}Th
D. Water Masses	S. ^{3}He
E. Gas Exchange	T. ε_{Nd}

Choose the correct option:
1. A–P; B–Q; C–R; D–S; E–T
2. A–S; B–R; C–Q; D–T; E–P
3. A–R; B–Q; C–P; D–S; E–T
4. A–S; B–R; C–P; D–T; E–Q

128. Numerical weather prediction is limited to about two weeks, while climate can be predicted months in advance because ..... .
1. the governing equations for the evolution of the atmosphere for weather and climate modelling are different
2. weather prediction is primarily an initial value problem; climate prediction is primarily a boundary value problem
3. lack of a dense observation network
4. computational resources are not adequate

129. Cross correlation of the vibroseis pilot sweep signal with seismic data produced from the same source ....
1. results in a random signal
2. removes the phase of the vibroseis sweep
3. recovers the Earth's impedance response
4. results in a zero signal

130. Which among the following is the dispersion relation of a surface gravity wave if water depth < < wavelength?
[k = wave number, ω = frequency, H = depth of the fluid]
1. $\omega^2 = gk^2H$
2. $\omega^2 = gk$
3. $\omega = gkH$
4. $\omega = gkH^2$

131. Choose the correct option related to invoking the Reynolds averaging procedure to the conservation of mass and momentum equations for a three-dimensional viscous incompressible fluid to obtain the mean turbulent equations of motion.
1. No additional terms arise in the zonal mean momentum equation

2. No additional terms arise in the meridional mean momentum equation
3. No additional terms arise in the vertical mean momentum equation
4. No additional terms arise in the conservation of mass equation

132. Which one of the following statements is NOT TRUE about image displacement due to relief (RD) in aerial photography?
1. RD increases with increasing distance from nadir point and image of the top of the object
2. RD is proportional to the height of the object
3. RD decreases with decreasing height of the flight altitude
4. RD is radial from the plumb point

133. What will be the hydrostatic pressure exerted on an animal living at an ocean depth of 4000 m?
1. 40 bar
2. 4 bar
3. 400 bar
4. 4000 bar

134. The bulk composition of three medium-grade metapelitic rocks (1, 2 and 3) is shown on the AFM diagram given below. Which one of the following minerals will be stable in all three rocks?

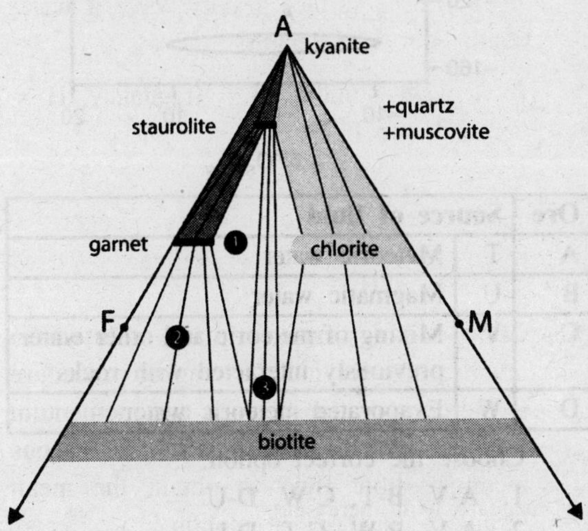

1. Kyanite
2. Garnet
3. Staurolite
4. Biotite

135. What is the atomic $^{87}Rb/^{86}Sr$ ratio of a rock sample containing Rb = 100 ppm and Sr = 200 ppm? Given that the atomic weights of Rb and Sr are 85.46 amu and 87.6 amu, respectively. Isotopic abundances of ^{87}Rb and ^{86}Sr are 27.83% and 10%, respectively.
1. 0.5
2. 14.3
3. 1.43
4. 0.722

136. Statement (A): The rating curve of a river gauging station located in the lower course usually shows a concave profile.

Statement (R): The channel becomes less efficient at carrying water as flood occurs.

Choose the correct option.
1. Both A and R are true, and R is the correct explanation of A
2. Both A and R are true, but R is not the correct explanation of A
3. A is true, but R is false
4. A is false, but R is true

137. Which one of the following best defines the Shannon-Wiener Biodiversity Index?
1. Uncertainty of predicting the species of a randomly selected individual
2. Probability that two randomly selected individuals from a sample belong to the same species
3. Total probability of selecting individuals of the same species from multiple samples
4. Uncertainty in predicting the species of two randomly selected individuals from two different samples

138. A morning sounding shows a pronounced warm layer (cap) between 800 hPa and 750 hPa. The surface-based CAPE is moderate, but the CIN is large. Which single change would most effectively reduce CIN and make convective initiation easier, while causing the least change to CAPE?

1. Warming the entire boundary layer by 2-3 K
2. Increasing the surface dewpoint by 2-3 K with little change to temperature
3. Cooling the mid-troposphere by 2-3 K
4. Decreasing the surface dewpoint by 2-3 K with little change to temperature

139. **Assertion (A):** Following reclamation of its marginal areas, a macrotidal estuary would respond by channel sedimentation to reduce its depth.

Reasoning (R): Positive feedback drives a system away from equilibrium.

Choose the correct option.
1. Both A and R are true, and R is the correct explanation of A
2. Both A and R are true, and R is not the correct explanation of A
3. A is true, but R is false
4. A is false, but R is true

140. A buried chromite ore body produces a maximum gravity anomaly of 5 mGal. The horizontal distance between the points on the profile where the anomaly is half of its maximum value is 1000 m. Assuming the ore body is spherical, what is the excess mass of the ore body?
1. 3.2×10^{10} kg
2. 3.2×10^{11} kg
3. 3.2×10^{12} kg
4. 3.2×10^{13} kg

141. The Antarctic Circumpolar Current (ACC) formed around .... My ago, due to the .... of ...., and lead to the .... of Antarctica.
1. 65, closure, Tethys seaway, warming
2. 34, closure, Tasmanian and Drake passage, warming
3. 65, opening, Tethys seaway, cooling
4. 34, opening, Tasmanian and Drake passage, cooling

142. Match the Quaternary events/periods in column I with their ages in column II

Column I	Column II
A. Younger Dryas	P. 14700-12900 yr BP
B. Bronze Age	Q. 5500-3200 yr BP
C. Bolling-Allerod	R. 9500-5500 yr BP
D. Holocene climate optimum	S. 12900-11600 yr BP

Choose the correct option:
1. A–S; B–P; C–Q; D–R
2. A–Q; B–S; C–P; D–R
3. A–R; B–Q; C–S; D–P
4. A–S; B–Q; C–P; D–R

143. The figure shows oxygen and hydrogen isotopic compositions of hydrothermal fluid associated with ore deposits A, B, C, and D. Match the deposit with its source of hydrothermal fluid.

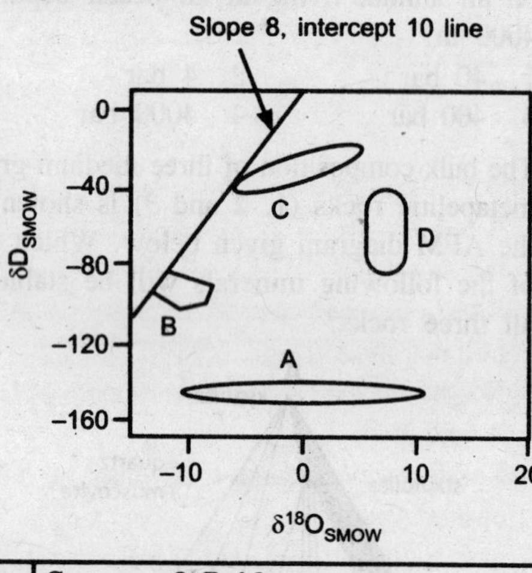

Ore	Source of fluid	
A	T	Meteoric water
B	U	Magmatic water
C	V	Mixing of meteoric and other water previously interacted with rocks
D	W	Evaporated meteoric water

Choose the correct option:
1. A-V, B-T, C-W, D-U
2. A-V, B-W, C-T, D-U
3. A-W, B-T, C-U, D-V
4. A-W, B-U, C-V, D-T

144. Which of the following regions in the Indian Ocean is best suited to retrieve turbidite free cores with high calcareous microfossils?
1. Continental slope of the western Bay of Bengal
2. Central Indian Ocean basin deeper than 5500 m
3. Central Arabian Sea deeper than 2000 m and shallower than 3500 m
4. Southern Bay of Bengal deeper than 4000 m

145. The hypothetical conditions of circulations in two identical ocean basins, A and B, are given in the following figure.

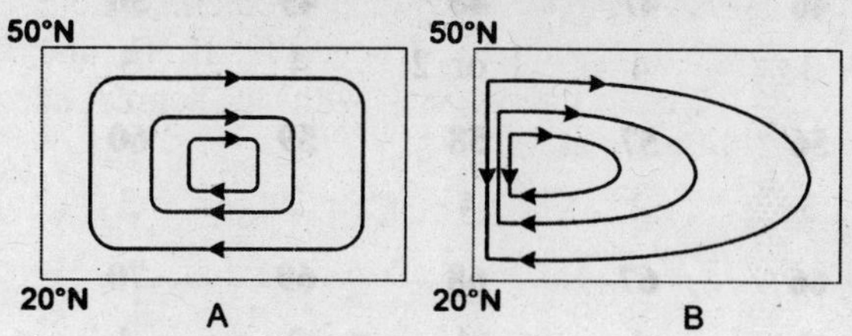

Choose the correct option:
1. Rossby waves can develop in basin A but not in B
2. Rossby waves can develop in basin B but not in A
3. Rossby waves can develop in both basins A and B
4. Rossby waves cannot develop in both basins A and B

146. What is the dilatation produced by three normal stresses of 150 GPa each, acting on a cuboid which is a Poisson's solid having a Youngs modulus of 15 GPa?

1. 5 2. 10
3. 15 4. 20

147. The magnetic anomaly over a dyke is represented by $e^{-|x|}$, where x is the distance along the profile. The upward continued magnetic anomaly at height (h) in the Fourier domain is represented by .... (where k is wave number)

1. $\frac{e^{-|k|h}}{1+k}$ 2. $\frac{2e^{-|k|h}}{1+k}$
3. $\frac{e^{-|k|h}}{1+k^2}$ 4. $\frac{2e^{-|k|h}}{1+k^2}$

148. The slopes of the Wadati plots corresponding to an earthquake each in region A and B are 1 and 0.5, respectively. Assuming, that the pairs $\{T(A)_P$ and $T(B)_P\}$ and $\{T(A)_{S-P}$ and $T(B)_{S-P}\}$ represent P travel times and S-P travel time differences, respectively at stations located at same hypocentral distance in regions A and B, which one of the following is correct?
1. $T(A)_{S-P} > T(B)_{S-P}$ and $T(A)_P > T(B)_P$
2. $T(A)_{S-P} < T(B)_{S-P}$ and $T(A)_P < T(B)_P$
3. $T(A)_{S-P} = T(B)_{S-P}$ and $T(A)_P < T(B)_P$
4. $T(A)_{S-P} > T(B)_{S-P}$ and $T(A)_P < T(B)_P$

149. In magnetotelluric measurements, ρ_{xy}, ρ_{yx} are the apparent resistivities and ϕ_{xy}, ϕ_{yx} are phases computed at various time periods. The correct expressions for the average apparent resistivity (ρ_{av}) and average phase (ϕ_{av}) computed for 1-D interpretation are ....
1. $\rho_{av} = \frac{\rho_{xy}+\rho_{yx}}{2}$ and $\phi_{av} = \frac{\phi_{xy}+\phi_{yx}}{2}$
2. $\rho_{av} = \sqrt{\rho_{xy}\cdot\rho_{yx}}$ and $\phi_{av} = \frac{\phi_{xy}+\phi_{yx}}{2}$
3. $\rho_{av} = \sqrt{\rho_{xy}\cdot\rho_{yx}}$ and $\phi_{av} = \sqrt{\phi_{xy}\cdot\phi_{yx}}$
4. $\rho_{av} = \frac{\rho_{xy}+\rho_{yx}}{2}$ and $\phi_{av} = \sqrt{\phi_{xy}\cdot\phi_{yx}}$

150. The angle of internal friction of a rock is 30°, and cohesion is 20 MPa. What is the approximate shear stress required for failure at a normal stress of 50 MPa using Mohr-Coulomb failure criteria?

1. 30.1 MPa 2. 48.9 MPa
3. 60.5 MPa 4. 90 MPa

ANSWERS

1	2	3	4	5	6	7	8	9	10
1	2	4	2	4	2	2	2	2	2
11	**12**	**13**	**14**	**15**	**16**	**17**	**18**	**19**	**20**
2	1	4	3	3	3	1	2	3	4
21	**22**	**23**	**24**	**25**	**26**	**27**	**28**	**29**	**30**
1	1	2	3	3	3	2	4	4	3
31	**32**	**33**	**34**	**35**	**36**	**37**	**38**	**39**	**40**
1	4	1	3	3	3	3	4	4	1
41	**42**	**43**	**44**	**45**	**46**	**47**	**48**	**49**	**50**
4	4	1	4	2	3	4	1 or 2	4	3
51	**52**	**53**	**54**	**55**	**56**	**57**	**58**	**59**	**60**
2	1	2	4	3	3	2	4	2	3
61	**62**	**63**	**64**	**65**	**66**	**67**	**68**	**69**	**70**
2	3	1	3	3	3	1	4	2	4
71	**72**	**73**	**74**	**75**	**76**	**77**	**78**	**79**	**80**
2	3	3	2	1	2 or 4	3	3	2	2
81	**82**	**83**	**84**	**85**	**86**	**87**	**88**	**89**	**90**
4	2	1	2	3	1	3	2	2	1
91	**92**	**93**	**94**	**95**	**96**	**97**	**98**	**99**	**100**
3	3	1	2	2	3	2	3	3	2
101	**102**	**103**	**104**	**105**	**106**	**107**	**108**	**109**	**110**
3	2	3	1	2	4	3	4	2	3
111	**112**	**113**	**114**	**115**	**116**	**117**	**118**	**119**	**120**
3	3	1	2	1	3	1	3	3	2
121	**122**	**123**	**124**	**125**	**126**	**127**	**128**	**129**	**130**
3	4	2	1	3	4	2	2	2	1
131	**132**	**133**	**134**	**135**	**136**	**137**	**138**	**139**	**140**
4	3	3	4	3	1	1	2	2	2
141	**142**	**143**	**144**	**145**	**146**	**147**	**148**	**149**	**150**
4	4	1	3	2	3	4	4	2	2

EXPLANATORY ANSWERS

1. From 738, none is correct, so 7, 3, 8 are not in the PIN.

   From 780, only one number is correct but wrongly placed. Since 7 and 8 are already absent, the correct digit is 0, and it is not in the 3rd place.

   From 689, one number is correct and correctly placed. Since 8 is absent, either 6 is correct in the 1st place or 9 is correct in the 3rd place.

   From 906, two numbers are correct but wrongly placed. One of them is already 0, so the other must be 9 or 6. If 6 were correct in the 1st place, then in 615 it would be correctly placed, but that clue says one number is correct but wrongly placed. So 6 cannot be in the PIN. Hence 9 is correct and is in the 3rd place.

   Now 0 is in the PIN, not in 2nd place from 906, and not in 3rd place from 780, so 0 must be in the 1st place.

   From 615, one number is correct but wrongly placed. Since 6 is absent, the correct digit is 5 or 1. The only empty place is the 2nd place. If 1 were correct, it would already be correctly placed in 615, which is not allowed. Therefore 5 must be the digit, and it goes to the 2nd place. So the PIN is 059.

2. Let the original numbers of seats be $2x, 3x, 4x$. After increasing each by 50%,

   $$2x \rightarrow 2x \times \frac{3}{2} = 3x$$

   $$3x \rightarrow 3x \times \frac{3}{2} = \frac{9x}{2}$$

   $$4x \rightarrow 4x \times \frac{3}{2} = 6x$$

   So the new ratio is $3x : \frac{9x}{2} : 6x$

   Multiplying by 2,

   $6x : 9x : 12x = 2:3:4$

   Hence, the ratio remains unchanged.

3. Let the present points of teams A,B,C be a, b, c. If B wins the only remaining match, final points become:

   $$A = a,\ B = b + 2,\ C = c$$

   Given that A then becomes champion with more points than any other team,

   $a > b + 2$ and $a > c$

   If B loses, then C wins. Final points become:

   $$A = a,\ B = b,\ C = c + 2$$

   Now A is not necessarily champion, so C can reach or cross A:

   $$c + 2 \geq a$$

   Thus, $a - c \leq 2$

   So A is leading C by at most two points.

4. In a plane mirror, the fraction of the body visible depends on the size of the mirror, not on the distance of the person from the mirror.

   So if Sachin sees $\frac{1}{4}$ of his height at 20 cm, then after moving to 40 cm, the visible portion remains the same.

   Hence, he will still see $\frac{1}{4}$ of his body.

5. To be certain of getting at least one pair of black socks, consider the worst possible case. A person may first pick all the non-black socks:

   $$22 + 24 = 46$$

   Then she may pick only one black sock:

   $$46 + 1 = 47$$

   Even now, there is no pair of black socks. The next sock, that is the 48th sock, must be black, because black socks still remain in the box. So at 48 socks, she is certain to have at least two black socks, that is, one pair of black socks.

6. Let the tens digit be t. Then unit digit $= \frac{t}{2}$.

   Number $= 10t + \frac{t}{2}$

   Reversed number $= 10 \cdot \frac{t}{2} + t = 5t = 5t + t = 6t$

Given decrease = 18:

$$\left(10t+\frac{t}{2}\right)-6t = 18$$

$$\frac{20t+t-12t}{2} = 18$$

$$\frac{9t}{2} = 18$$

$$9t = 36$$

$$\Rightarrow \quad t = 4$$

Unit digit = 2.

Number = 42.

7. Let opening = x, temperature T = $ax + b$.

Given, $40 = a\cdot\frac{1}{2}+b$

$$30 = a\cdot\frac{1}{2}+b$$

Subtract, $-10 = a\left(\frac{3}{4}-\frac{1}{2}\right)=a\cdot\frac{1}{4}$

$$a = -40$$

Now, $40 = -40\cdot\frac{1}{2}+b$

$$\Rightarrow \quad 40 = -20 + b$$

$$\Rightarrow \quad b = 60$$

So, $T = -40x + 60$

For T = 50:

$$50 = -40x + 60$$

$$-40x = -10 \Rightarrow x = \frac{1}{4}$$

Thus, tap is one-fourth open.

8. Let total placements in 2023 be T.

Maths (2023) = 7% = 0.07T.

Let total placements in 2024 be T_2.

Maths (2024) = 9% = $0.09T_2$.

Given Maths students doubled:

$$0.09\ T_2 = 2 \times 0.07T$$

$$0.09\ T_2 = 0.14\ T$$

$$T_2 = \frac{0.14}{0.09}T \approx 1.56T$$

Now Life Sciences:

2023 = 44% = 0.44T

2024 = 43%

$$= 0.43T_2$$

$$= 0.43 \times 1.56T$$

$$\approx 0.671T$$

Percentage change:

$$\frac{0.671T-0.44T}{0.44T} \approx \frac{0.231T}{0.44T} \approx 0.525 \approx 52.5\%$$

Closest value = 50%.

9. Buses for town A arrive at 00:10,00:30,00:50,... and for town B at 00:15,00:35,00:55,....

Consider one cycle of 20 minutes between two A buses:

From 10 to 15 minutes → next bus is B → duration = 5 minutes

From 15 to 30 minutes → next bus is A → duration = 15 minutes

Total interval = 20 minutes

$$\text{P(next bus is B)} = \frac{5}{20}=\frac{1}{4}$$

10. Let initial fee = 100, people = 100

Initial earning: 100 × 100 = 10000

New fee after 25% reduction:

100 → 75

New people after 30% increase:

100 → 130

New earning: 75 × 130 = 9750

Change: 10000 - 9750 = 250

$$\frac{250}{10000}\times 100 = 2.5\%$$

Hence earnings decrease by 2.5%.

11. In a ternary diagram, each vertex represents 100% of one subject, and any point inside represents proportional distribution summing to 100.

Point B lies approximately along the line where Mathematics ≈ Physics, indicating both scores are equal.

Point A is close to the Mathematics corner, so it has high Maths and low Chemistry; its Chemistry is clearly not as high as 80 and not significantly greater than C's Physics (which is 10).

Given C = (Physics 10, Chemistry 50, Mathematics 40), comparison shows A's Chemistry is not more than 10 significantly.

Thus, only the statement about B having equal Mathematics and Physics scores matches the diagram accurately.

12. Height of hill = 1.5 km, base radius = 2 km.

Slant height of the hill:

$$l = \sqrt{(1.5)^2 + (2)^2}$$

$$= \sqrt{2.25+4}$$

$$= \sqrt{6.25}$$

$$= 2.5 \text{ km}$$

Signal range = 500 m = 0.5 km, so the served part is a smaller similar cone on the curved surface with slant height 0.5 km.

By similarity,

$$\frac{r}{2} = \frac{0.5}{2.5} = \frac{1}{5}$$

$$r = \frac{2}{5} = 0.4 \text{ km}$$

$$\text{Area served} = \pi r l$$

$$= \pi \times 0.4 \times 0.5$$

$$= 0.2\pi$$

13. Let marked price of one mocktail = M.

For 8 mocktails:

Restaurant A: one free for every two purchased.

Need minimum purchased x such that

$$x + \left[\frac{x}{2}\right] \geq 8$$

For $x = 5$,

$$5 + \left[\frac{5}{2}\right] = 5 + 2$$

$$= 7$$

For, $x = 6$,

$$6 + \left[\frac{6}{2}\right] = 6 + 3$$

$$= 9$$

So payment = 6M.

Restaurant B: one free for every three purchased.

$$x + \left[\frac{x}{3}\right] \geq 8$$

For, $x = 6$,

$$6 + \left[\frac{6}{3}\right] = 6 + 2$$

$$= 8$$

So payment = 6M.

Restaurant C: two free for every six purchased.

For 6 purchased, total received = 8.

So payment = 6M.

Restaurant D: 30% discount on each mocktail.

$$8 \times 0.7\text{M} = 5.6\text{M}$$

Since $5.6\text{M} < 6\text{M}$

Restaurant D is cheapest.

14. Since letter A appears in all four words, its digit must be common in all four numbers. That common digit is 9. So,

A = 9

Now READ has A in the third position. Among the given numbers, only 0798 has 9 in the third place. So,

READ = 0798

Hence, R = 0, E = 7, A = 9, D = 8

Now GATE shares A and E with READ. So its code must contain digits 9 and 7. That matches 5917.

GATE = 5917

Thus, G = 5, T = 1

Now FAST shares A and T with GATE, so its code must contain 9 and 1. That matches 6921.

FAST = 6921

Thus, F = 6, S = 2

The remaining word is

SAND = 2938

So, N = 3

Therefore,

NEGATE = N E G A T E

= 3 7 5 9 1 7

= 375917

15. Let the three things be Dog (D), Cat (C), and Milk (M).

The cat cannot be left with the dog or with the milk on either bank.

So the crossings must be:

1. C goes across
2. Boatman returns alone
3. D goes across
4. C is brought back
5. M goes across
6. Boatman returns alone
7. C goes across

Now all three are safely on the other bank.

Hence the minimum number of crossings is 7.

16. Using simple interest,

$$SI = \frac{P \times R \times T}{100}$$

Total interest is

$$\frac{2500 \times R \times 2}{100} + \frac{2000 \times R \times 3}{100} = 550$$

$$\frac{5000R}{100} + \frac{6000R}{100} = 550$$

$$50R + 60R = 550$$

$$110R = 550$$

$$R = 5$$

So the annual rate of interest is 5%.

17. Number of seats per row forms an AP with

$$a = 8,\ d = 4$$

Sum of first n rows:

$$S_n = \frac{n}{2}[2a + (n-1)d]$$

$$= \frac{n}{2}[16 + 4(n-1)]$$

$$= \frac{n}{2}(4n + 12) = 2n(n+3)$$

For seating 150 people:

$$2n(n + 3) \geq 150$$

$$n(n+3) \geq 75$$

Check: $n = 7$

$\Rightarrow$ $7 \times 10 = 70 < 75$

$n = 8$

$\Rightarrow$ $8 \times 11 = 88 \geq 75$

Minimum rows required = 8.

18. Let present age of son = x.

When father became father, his age = son's present age = x.

Time since son's birth: $52 - x$

This equals son's present age:

$$x = 52 - x$$

$$2x = 52$$

$$\Rightarrow \quad x = 26$$

After 10 years:

$$26 + 10 = 36$$

So son's age after 10 years = 36 years.

19. Number of revolutions is inversely proportional to diameter, so

$$\text{Front revs per rear rev} = \frac{D_r}{D_f}$$

Initially, $\dfrac{D_r}{D_f} = 2$

If both diameters are increased by the same amount x, new ratio becomes

$$R = \frac{D_r + x}{D_f + x}$$

As x increases, $R \to 1$

This matches the graph: the ratio starts at 2 and gradually decreases towards 1 without crossing it.

Other cases:

Only decreasing rear diameter would increase the ratio.

Decreasing both would make ratio unstable or increase.

Rear decreasing and front increasing would reduce the ratio rapidly and may go below 1, which is not shown.

Thus, only equal increase in both diameters produces the smooth asymptotic approach to 1 as shown in the graph.

20. From the Sankey diagram, the band from Female to Rice is quite broad. If we compare it with the combined male bands going to Maize and Millet, that combined male width is still smaller. So the statement saying that fewer females prefer rice than those males is not correct.

The other three statements match the figure reasonably well: for males, Rice is the largest and Chicken appears to be the next thicker preference band, the female-to-Wheat band is wider than the male-to-Wheat band, and for both Millet and Mutton, the female bands are wider than the male bands.

Hence, the incorrect statement is option 4.

21. The Younger Dryas is best described as a stadial period because it was a short, cold climatic phase that interrupted the general warming trend after the Last Glacial Maximum. A stadial represents a colder interval within a broader glacial or deglacial sequence. The Younger Dryas was marked by a return to near-glacial conditions, especially in the North Atlantic region. It occurred after the warmer Bølling–Allerød interstadial and before the beginning of the Holocene. Therefore, the term "stadial" fits the question most accurately.

22. The possibility of growth of a tropical disturbance through barotropic instability is tested by examining the latitudinal variation of zonal wind. Barotropic instability depends on the horizontal shear of the basic flow, especially how the zonal wind changes with latitude. The relevant condition involves the meridional gradient of absolute vorticity, which is directly related to latitudinal changes in the zonal wind. Vertical variation of zonal wind is more relevant to baroclinic processes, not purely barotropic instability. Therefore, latitudinal variation of zonal wind is the best fitting answer.

23. The 410 km discontinuity primarily represents the mineral phase transformation of olivine into wadsleyite. This discontinuity occurs near the boundary between the upper mantle and the mantle transition zone. It is not mainly a change in bulk chemical composition, but a pressure-induced change in mineral structure. Olivine is the dominant mineral in the upper mantle, and at around 410 km depth it transforms into the denser wadsleyite phase. Therefore. the correct explanation is the change of olivine to wadsleyite.

24. Complete melting of Arctic sea-ice within a year will immediately not change the global sea level because Arctic sea ice is already floating on ocean water. According to the principle of displacement, floating ice has already displaced a volume of seawater equivalent to its mass. When it melts, it simply becomes water that occupies nearly the same displaced volume. This is different from melting land ice, such as glaciers or ice sheets, which adds new water to the ocean. Therefore, the immediate global sea-level change from melting floating Arctic sea ice would be essentially zero.

25. Deep focus earthquakes occur at upper mantle depths, generally between about 300 km and 700 km. These earthquakes are mostly associated with subducting slabs within the mantle transition zone. The crust and lithosphere are too shallow for deep focus earthquakes. The lower mantle begins below about 660–700 km, while most deep focus earthquakes are confined above or around this transition depth. Therefore, "Upper Mantle" is the most appropriate option among the given choices.

26. In a Mohr's circle, the radius represents the maximum shear stress acting on the material. Mathematically, the radius of the circle is equal to $(\sigma_1 - \sigma_3)/2$, where σ_1 and σ_3 are the maximum and minimum principal stresses. The full difference $(\sigma_1 - \sigma_3)$ is the differential stress, but the radius is only half of that value. Therefore, the radius does not directly represent differential stress; it represents maximum shear stress. Hence, option 3, shear stress, is the correct answer.

27. The equatorial electrojet is an intense eastward electric current flowing in the ionospheric E-region near the magnetic equator. Its magnetic effect is seen mainly in the horizontal component of the geomagnetic field, especially the north-south or H component. The vertical component may also be affected, particularly away from the centre of the electrojet belt. The east-west component is not the primary affected component in the standard geomagnetic signature of the equatorial electrojet. Therefore, the north-south and vertical components best fit the question.

28. This statement is NOT true about mid-latitude wave cyclones. Mid-latitude cyclones generally travel eastward and are embedded within the larger westerly general circulation. In these cyclones, warm air rises gently over the warm front, while uplift along the cold front is steeper. Increasing upper-air absolute vorticity or positive vorticity advection is generally favourable for upward motion and cyclone development, not decay. Therefore, saying that they decay in an area of increasing upper-air absolute vorticity is the incorrect statement.

29. The seismic phase recorded in the P-shadow zone is PKiKP. The P-shadow zone occurs because direct P waves are strongly refracted by the liquid outer core and are absent over a certain angular distance range. However, core-related phases can still be recorded within this region because they travel through or interact with the core. PKiKP is a P-wave phase that travels through the mantle and outer core and reflects from the inner-core boundary. Hence, among the given options, PKiKP is the most suitable phase recorded in the P-shadow zone.

30. The major source of heat in the Earth's continental crust is radioactive decay. Continental crust is enriched in heat-producing radioactive elements such as uranium, thorium, and potassium. Their decay releases heat over geological time and contributes significantly to crustal heat production. Primordial heat is important for the Earth as a whole, but in the continental crust radioactive heat production is the dominant source. Plate tectonics and convection currents redistribute heat but are not the major heat source within the continental crust.

31. Stone line relates to the management of soil erosion because stones are arranged along contours across a slope to reduce the speed of surface runoff. When runoff slows down, soil particles carried by water are trapped behind the stone barriers. This helps in reducing sheet erosion and also supports moisture conservation in the soil. Stone lines are a recognized soil and water conservation measure, especially in dry and semi-arid regions. Therefore, option 1, stone line, is the correct answer.

32. Inselbergs are most common on granites and gneisses because these rocks are massive, resistant, and often form isolated residual hills after prolonged weathering and erosion. Granitic and gneissic terrains commonly undergo deep chemical weathering followed by stripping of the weathered material. The remaining resistant rock masses stand above the surrounding low-relief surface as inselbergs. Such landforms are especially common in tropical and subtropical crystalline shield regions. Therefore, granites and gneisses best fit the occurrence of inselbergs.

33. The Curie point is the temperature above which a ferromagnetic material becomes paramagnetic. Below the Curie temperature, magnetic domains in a ferromagnetic substance can remain aligned and produce strong magnetization. Above this temperature, thermal agitation destroys the ordered alignment of magnetic moments. The material does not become diamagnetic or ferrimagnetic after crossing the Curie point; it loses ferromagnetic ordering and behaves paramagnetically. Therefore, the correct combination is ferromagnetic to paramagnetic.

34. The Earth's magnetic field can be approximately modelled by a dipole source field. A magnetic dipole has two magnetic poles and produces a field pattern broadly similar to the observed geomagnetic field at the Earth's surface. Although the real geomagnetic field has non-dipole components and changes with time, the dipole component is dominant in first-order approximation. Monopoles are not physically observed magnetic sources, and quadrupole or higher components are secondary refinements. Therefore, dipole is the best answer.

35. Eskers record the location of past ice-walled or subglacial streams or channels. They are long, narrow, winding ridges made mainly of sand and gravel deposited by meltwater streams flowing within, beneath, or between ice walls. After the glacier melts away, these deposits remain as sinuous ridges on the landscape. Moulins are vertical shafts in ice, kames are irregular mounds of stratified drift, and kettle holes form from melting buried ice blocks. Therefore, eskers are the correct feature.

36. During the Last Glacial Maximum, global sea level was much lower than the modern sea level, roughly by about 120 m. Therefore, an area now lying at 50 m depth relative to modern sea level would have been exposed land or part of the fluvial-deltaic plain at that time. Sediments deposited there during the Last Glacial Maximum would mainly be supplied by riverine and terrestrial processes rather than by normal marine deposition. Since the site would not have been under open marine conditions at that time, marine fractions would not be expected as the dominant deposited component. Therefore, only terrestrial fraction is the correct answer.

37. A 1-in-25-year flood means a flood having a recurrence interval of 25 years. The annual probability of occurrence is calculated as 1/T, where T is the recurrence interval in years.

$$\text{Therefore, probability} = \frac{1}{25} = 0.04.$$

In percentage form, $0.04 \times 100 = 4\%$.

Thus, a 1-in-25-year flood has a 4% probability of occurring in any one year.

38. Molybdenum remains largely conserved in the ocean because it has a long residence time and behaves relatively conservatively in seawater. Conservative elements show nearly constant concentration ratios with salinity and are not rapidly removed by biological uptake or scavenging. Lead and thorium are particle-reactive and are removed efficiently from seawater. Silicon is strongly affected by biological uptake by organisms such as diatoms and is therefore nutrient-like rather than conservative. Hence, molybdenum is the correct answer.

39. Chlorophyll satellite data is used to predict potential fishery zones because chlorophyll concentration indicates phytoplankton abundance in the ocean. Phytoplankton forms the base of the marine food chain, so areas with higher chlorophyll often support higher biological productivity. Fish tend to aggregate near productive zones where food availability is greater. Satellite-derived chlorophyll maps, often combined with sea surface temperature data, are widely used for identifying potential fishery zones. Therefore, chlorophyll is the correct answer.

40. The $\delta^{18}O$ value of calcareous benthic foraminifera at 2500 m water depth is higher than that of planktic foraminifera mainly because of the difference in temperature. Benthic foraminifera live in deep ocean water, where temperature is much lower than the warm surface waters inhabited by planktic foraminifera. At lower temperature, calcium carbonate incorporates relatively more ^{18}O during shell formation, producing higher $\delta^{18}O$ values. Planktic foraminifera generally form their shells in warmer surface water, so their carbonate $\delta^{18}O$ is comparatively lower. Therefore, the correct combination is higher $\delta^{18}O$ due to temperature difference.

41. In the Northern Hemisphere, major ocean currents tend to curve to the right because of the Coriolis force. This apparent force arises due to the rotation of the Earth. Moving water masses are deflected to the right of their direction of motion in the Northern Hemisphere and to the left in the Southern Hemisphere. Wind, pressure gradients, and density differences can initiate or influence currents, but the systematic rightward curvature is due to Coriolis force. Therefore, Coriolis Force is the correct answer.

42. Under similar situations, remote sensing using longer wavelength typically corresponds to broader spectral bands. Longer wavelength regions, such as thermal infrared and microwave, generally use wider wavelength intervals than visible bands. This is because energy levels, detector response, and practical sensor design commonly require broader bands at longer wavelengths. Longer wavelength does not usually mean enhanced spatial detail; in fact, spatial detail commonly decreases for the same sensor aperture. Therefore, broader spectral bands is the best fitting answer.

43. During the warm phase of ENSO, that is El Niño, the tropical eastern and central Pacific Ocean becomes warmer than normal. This warming alters the Walker circulation and weakens the normal atmospheric circulation pattern over the Indo-Pacific region. As a result, Indian summer monsoon rainfall generally tends to decrease, although the relation is not perfect every year. The Somali jet also generally weakens rather than strengthens during such conditions. Therefore, Indian summer monsoon rainfall decreases is the correct answer.

44. The correct sequence of increasing thermal maturity of coal is peat, lignite, bituminous, and anthracite. Peat is the earliest stage, formed from partially decomposed plant material with low carbon content. With increasing burial, compaction, temperature, and pressure, peat changes into lignite. Further increase in thermal maturity produces bituminous coal, and the highest rank among the listed coal types is anthracite. Therefore, Peat, Lignite, Bituminous, Anthracite is the correct sequence.

45. $$T_2 = T_1\left(\frac{p_2}{p_1}\right)^{R_d/C_p}$$

$$= 295\left(\frac{700}{900}\right)^{287/1004}$$

$$= 295(0.7778)^{0.2859}$$

$$\approx 295 \times 0.930$$

$$\approx 274.4 \text{ K}.$$

Therefore, the final temperature is closest to 274 K.

46. $$T^2 = \frac{4\pi^2 r^3}{GM}$$

For the same orbital radius,

$$T \propto \frac{1}{\sqrt{M}}$$

If the Sun's mass becomes half,

$$T' \propto \frac{1}{\sqrt{\frac{M}{2}}}$$

$$\frac{T'}{T} = \sqrt{2}$$

Therefore, the orbital period of the Earth would increase by a factor of $\sqrt{2}$.

47. Banded iron-formations formed during the Precambrian mainly because dissolved ferrous iron, Fe^{2+}, present in ancient oceans was oxidized to ferric iron, Fe^{3+}. Ferric iron is much less soluble than ferrous iron, so it precipitated as iron oxides and hydroxides. This oxidation occurred in the water column as oxygen became available, especially due to early photosynthetic activity. The repeated precipitation of iron-rich layers along with silica-rich layers produced the banded character of these formations. Therefore, conversion of Fe^{2+} to Fe^{3+} in the water column is the correct answer.

48. Total weight of all organisms in a given area or volume of water; Number of organisms per unit area or per unit volume of water: Standing stock or standing crop means the quantity of living organisms present in a given area or volume of water at a particular time. This quantity can be expressed either as biomass, that is, total weight of organisms, or as abundance, that is, number of organisms per unit area or unit volume. Therefore, option 1 is correct when standing stock is expressed in terms of biomass, while option 2 is also correct when standing stock is expressed in terms of numerical abundance or density. Since both weight-based and number-based measures are valid ways of representing standing stock, the question does not have a single unambiguous answer. Options 3 and 4 are incomplete because they restrict standing stock only to phytoplankton or zooplankton rather than all organisms.

49. Planetary vorticity is essential for the existence of large-scale atmospheric waves such as Rossby waves. These waves arise because the Coriolis parameter varies with latitude, producing the beta effect. This latitudinal variation of planetary vorticity provides the restoring mechanism required for large-scale wave motion in the atmosphere. Compressibility, buoyancy, and viscosity may influence some atmospheric processes, but they are not the essential condition for planetary-scale atmospheric waves. Therefore, planetary vorticity is the correct answer.

50. Granitic pegmatite is the rock type of major interest in a lithium-exploration program. Lithium commonly occurs in minerals such as spodumene, lepidolite, petalite, and amblygonite, which are characteristically associated with rare-element granitic pegmatites. These pegmatites form from highly evolved, volatile-rich granitic melts capable of concentrating incompatible elements such as lithium. Komatiites, metabasalts in greenstone belts, and banded iron-formations are not the standard primary targets for hard-rock lithium exploration. Therefore, granitic pegmatite is the correct answer.

51. The sub-horizon distinction observed in the B horizon of a soil profile in an arid region is Bk. The suffix "k" denotes accumulation of carbonates, especially calcium carbonate, within the soil horizon. In arid and semi-arid regions, limited leaching allows carbonate to accumulate in the subsurface B horizon. This produces a calcic or carbonate-rich B horizon, commonly written as Bk. Bg is related to gleying under wet conditions, Bh to humus accumulation, and Bo is not the appropriate arid-region B-horizon carbonate notation.

52. The two conditions show opposite arrangements of solstice positions with respect to perihelion and aphelion. This change is controlled by axial precession, which shifts the seasonal positions around the Earth's orbit. A full precessional cycle is about 23,000 years, but reversal from one solstice arrangement to the opposite solstice arrangement takes about half of that time. Half of about 23,000 years is approximately 11,000 years. Therefore, the approximate time interval between conditions A and B is 11,000 years.

53. In a conditionally unstable atmosphere, an air parcel lifted from a humid boundary layer first reaches the LCL, where saturation and condensation begin. The LCL is not the highest level the parcel can reach without external lifting; it is simply the condensation level. Above the LCL, latent heat release can reduce the parcel's cooling rate and may eventually make it warmer than the surrounding air. The LFC is the first level at which the lifted parcel becomes positively buoyant and can rise freely without further forced lifting. Therefore, the statement about the LFC is the always correct one.

54. Blueschist facies best represents low-temperature and high-pressure metamorphism at a convergent margin setting. Such conditions are typical of subduction zones, where cold oceanic lithosphere is carried rapidly to high pressure before it can heat up strongly. Blueschist facies rocks commonly contain minerals such as glaucophane, which are characteristic of high-pressure, low-temperature metamorphism. Granulite represents high-temperature metamorphism, and hornfels facies is related to contact metamorphism. Eclogite is also high-pressure, but blueschist is the classic low-temperature, high-pressure convergent-margin facies.

55. A tropical cyclone is an example of strong and direct air-sea coupling. It obtains energy from warm ocean water through evaporation, latent heat release, and intense exchange of heat, moisture, and momentum between the ocean and atmosphere. The ocean surface strongly controls cyclone development, intensification, and maintenance. In turn, the cyclone affects the sea surface through strong winds, waves, mixing, and cooling. Jet stream, QBO, and thunderstorm do not represent such direct large-scale air-sea coupling as clearly as a tropical cyclone.

56. Bulk modulus is the parameter that always increases with depth from the Earth's surface to the inner core. It measures resistance to compression, and as pressure increases strongly with depth, Earth materials become progressively less compressible. P-wave velocity does not always increase because it drops sharply at the core-mantle boundary on entering the liquid outer core. S-wave velocity and shear modulus also do not always increase because the liquid outer core cannot transmit S-waves and has effectively zero shear rigidity. Therefore, bulk modulus is the correct answer.

57. Tidal currents from the open ocean that enter or impinge on the coastal ocean, bays, gulfs, and estuaries are called co-oscillation tides. These tides are not generated independently within the small basin itself; rather, the basin oscillates in response to tidal forcing from the adjoining open ocean. Estuaries and coastal seas commonly experience tides as forced oscillations linked to oceanic tidal waves. Amphidromes are points or systems around which tidal waves rotate, while lunar equilibrium tides are ideal theoretical tides. Therefore, co-oscillation tides is the correct answer.

58. Deflation is unique to wind action because it refers specifically to the removal and lifting away of loose, dry, fine-grained particles by wind. Suspension, saltation, and abrasion can occur in more than one geomorphic agent, including rivers, waves, glaciers, and wind. Deflation, however, is a characteristic aeolian erosional process and is directly associated with wind erosion in deserts and dry regions. It can produce desert pavements, deflation hollows, and other wind-eroded surfaces. Therefore, deflation is the correct answer.

59. Goniatitic cephalopod sutures are characterized by simple rounded saddles and angular or pointed lobes. This is the typical simple suture pattern seen in many Paleozoic ammonoids. In contrast, ceratitic sutures have rounded saddles but the lobes are serrated or denticulate rather than merely angular. Ammonitic sutures are still more complex, with highly frilled saddles and lobes. Therefore, for the description "rounded saddles and angular lobes," the correct answer is Goniatitic.

60. The expression $\left[\dfrac{\nabla\times\tau}{\rho f}\right]$ represents Ekman pumping velocity. Here, τ is the surface wind stress vector, so $\nabla \times \tau$ gives the curl of wind stress. When this wind-stress curl is divided by seawater density ρ and the Coriolis parameter f, it gives the vertical velocity associated with convergence or divergence of Ekman transport. Positive or negative wind-stress curl causes upward or downward motion at the base of the Ekman layer. Therefore, the given expression represents Ekman pumping, not Ekman transport itself.

61. Turbulent fluid flow is best described as flow having multiple scales of motion. In turbulence, large eddies transfer energy to progressively smaller eddies, producing a wide range of interacting length and time scales. Turbulent flow is generally associated with high Reynolds number, not low Reynolds number. It is also rotational, irregular, fluctuating, and unsteady rather than irrotational or steady. Therefore, the statement that turbulent fluid flow has multiple scales of motion is the correct answer.

62. Radiocarbon ^{14}C, is dominantly produced in the Earth's atmosphere when cosmic-ray-generated neutrons react with atmospheric nitrogen. The main nuclear reaction is $^{14}N(n,p)\ ^{14}C$, meaning nitrogen-14 captures a neutron and emits a proton to form carbon-14. Nitrogen is abundant in the atmosphere, so this reaction is the principal natural source of atmospheric radiocarbon. The other listed reactions are not the dominant atmospheric production pathway of ^{14}C.

63. The centrifugal force due to Earth's rotation causes an apparent decrease in gravity. This centrifugal effect is maximum at the equator because the distance from the rotation axis is greatest there. At the poles, the distance from the rotation axis is zero, so the centrifugal effect is absent. Therefore, the reduction in effective gravity is greatest at the equator and least at the poles. Hence, maximum decrease in gravity at the equator is the correct answer.

64. The Boussinesq approximation assumes that density variations are small and can be neglected except where they produce buoyancy. This approximation is suitable for many shallow, low-Mach-number flows such as boundary-layer turbulence, water waves, and many small-scale gravity-wave problems. Thunderstorms involve strong buoyancy, deep vertical development, moist processes, latent heat release, and significant thermodynamic density variations over large vertical distances. Because these conditions violate the simple Boussinesq density assumption more strongly, the approximation cannot be generally applied to study thunderstorms. Therefore, thunderstorms are the correct answer.

65. In the context of diamonds, carat is a unit of weight or mass. One metric carat is equal to 200 milligrams, or 0.2 grams. It does not measure clarity, colour, or purity of a diamond. Clarity refers to inclusions and blemishes, colour refers to the colour grading scale, and purity is not what diamond carat denotes. Therefore, the correct answer is that carat is a unit of weight with one carat approximately equal to 200 milligrams.

66. Cooler average night temperature in a tropical land region indicates that mean atmospheric humidity is low. Water vapour is an important greenhouse gas and helps retain outgoing longwave radiation during the night. When humidity is low, nocturnal radiative cooling becomes stronger, so the land surface and near-surface air cool more efficiently. Dense forests, urbanized regions, and overcast cloud conditions generally reduce night-time cooling and tend to keep nights warmer. Therefore, low mean atmospheric humidity is the correct answer.

67. The correctly arranged decreasing order of accretion or growth rates is coral reef, polymetallic nodule, and cobalt crust. Coral reefs have the fastest growth because biological carbonate production can build reef structures at relatively high rates. Polymetallic nodules grow extremely slowly on the deep-sea floor, but their growth rate is generally higher than that of many hydrogenetic cobalt-rich crusts. Cobalt crusts commonly grow at very slow rates on exposed hard substrates in the deep ocean. Therefore, the decreasing order is coral reef, polymetallic nodule, and cobalt crust.

68. $$r = \frac{\rho_c h}{\rho_m - \rho_c}$$

$$r = \frac{2.67 \times 5}{3.3 - 2.67}$$

$$r = \frac{13.35}{0.63}$$

$$r = 21.19 \text{ km}$$

Depth of isostatic Moho

$$= 35 + 21.19$$

$$= 56.19 \text{ km}$$

Depth of isostatic Moho $\approx$ 56.2 km

69. Anabranching does not represent a type of drainage network pattern. It refers to a river channel pattern in which a stream splits into two or more channels that later rejoin downstream. Drainage network patterns describe the overall arrangement of streams in a basin, such as dendritic, trellis, radial, annular, pinnate, or barbed patterns. Pinnate, annular, and barbed can be treated as drainage network patterns. Therefore, anabranching is the option that does not represent a drainage network pattern.

70. Anticyclonic eddies are least likely to increase ocean productivity. In general, anticyclonic eddies are associated with convergence and downwelling in the upper ocean. This tends to depress the nutricline and reduce the upward supply of nutrients into the sunlit surface layer. Upwelling, convective mixing, and cyclonic eddies generally help bring nutrient-rich deeper water toward the surface, thereby increasing productivity. Therefore, anticyclonic eddies are least likely to increase ocean productivity.

71. Permeability of a coal bed changes with methane production primarily because methane is stored by adsorption in the coal matrix. When methane is produced and reservoir pressure decreases, gas desorbs from the coal matrix. This desorption commonly causes matrix shrinkage, which can open cleats and increase permeability. However, changes in effective stress may also tend to close cleats, so permeability evolves through the interaction of cleat aperture and matrix shrinkage or swelling. Therefore, the primary reason is that coal cleats experience matrix swelling and shrinkage.

72. The given reaction shows weathering of K-feldspar to kaolinite, with potassium ion and silicic acid produced as products. If silicic acid activity becomes high, the reaction is shifted backward or the forward weathering reaction is suppressed. A lower water-to-rock ratio also restricts removal of dissolved products such as K^+ and H_4SiO_4, so these products accumulate in solution. Product accumulation reduces further breakdown of K-feldspar and therefore restricts kaolinite-forming weathering. Hence, lower water-to-rock ratio together with high silicic acid activity restricts weathering.

73. A Kelvin wave has a phase speed that does not vary with wavelength under dry shallow-water fluid conditions. In shallow-water theory, the Kelvin wave speed is $c = \sqrt{gH}$, where g is

gravitational acceleration and H is fluid depth. Since this expression does not include wavelength, the wave is nondispersive. Inertio-gravity waves, mixed Rossby-gravity waves, and Rossby waves generally have phase speeds that depend on wavenumber or wavelength. Therefore, Kelvin wave is the correct answer.

74. $U = 10\ ms^{-1}$

$L = 1000\ km = 10^6\ m$

$H = 10\ km = 10^4\ m$

$$W \sim U\frac{H}{L}$$

$$W \sim 10\times\frac{10^4}{10^6} = 10\times10^{-2} = 0.1\ ms^{-1}$$

$0.1\ ms^{-1} = 10\ cm\ s^{-1}$

Therefore, the maximum vertical velocity is 10 cm/s.

75. A. Damodar valley — (iii) Rift basin: Damodar valley is associated with a rift basin setting. It represents a tectonically controlled basin filled with Gondwana sediments.

B. Dhala impact structure — (iv) Inversion of relief: Dhala impact structure is matched with inversion of relief. Impact-modified resistant rocks may remain as positive relief after surrounding erosion.

C. Tista River — (ii) Unloading anticline: Tista River is matched with unloading anticline. River incision and removal of load can produce flexural or unloading-related anticlinal structures.

D. Nohkalikai falls — (i) Headward erosion: Nohkalikai falls is matched with headward erosion. Waterfall retreat commonly occurs by erosion at the head of the channel.

76. Manning's equation is $v = \frac{1}{n}R^{2/3}S^{1/2}$, where R is hydraulic radius, S is channel slope, and n is Manning's roughness coefficient. Therefore, velocity is inversely proportional to n, so option 1 is correct, and velocity increases with the square root of slope, so option 3 is also correct. Strictly, velocity increases with the two-thirds power of hydraulic radius, not necessarily flow depth, so option 2 is not generally correct unless a wide-channel approximation is assumed where R ≈ depth. Option 4 is definitely incorrect because Manning's equation does not make velocity directly proportional to the product of hydraulic radius and flow depth. Hence, if the question is interpreted strictly, both options 2 and 4 are incorrect; if the examiner assumes wide-channel approximation, then option 4 alone is the intended answer.

77. A. Ombrothermic diagram — R: Identification of wet, dry and excess of water seasons in relation to a climate type.

An ombrothermic diagram compares rainfall and temperature to identify humid and dry periods. It is especially used for recognizing seasonal water deficiency or excess in climatic classification.

B. Climograph — P: Wet bulb temperature (°F) and relative humidity (%).

A climograph represents climatic comfort conditions using wet-bulb temperature and relative humidity. This graphical method is used to compare climatic conditions in terms of human comfort or discomfort.

C. Hythergraph — Q: 12-sided polygon constructed by joining points representing temperature (°C) and rainfall (mm).

A hythergraph is drawn by plotting monthly temperature against monthly rainfall. The twelve monthly points are joined to form a polygon showing annual climatic character.

D. Hyetograph — S: Rainfall intensity over time.

A hyetograph represents rainfall distribution with respect to time. It is commonly used in hydrology to show variation of rainfall intensity during a storm event.

78. A. Number of streams of each order — Y: Approximates an inverse geometric series.

According to Horton's law of stream numbers, the number of streams decreases with increasing stream order. Therefore, stream number follows an inverse geometric relation with stream order.

B. Mean length of streams of each order — X: Approximates a direct geometric series.

According to Horton's law of stream lengths, mean stream length increases with increasing order. Thus, mean length of streams follows a direct geometric series.

C. Mean area of the basin of each order — X: Approximates a direct geometric series.

Mean basin area increases systematically with increasing stream order. Therefore, basin area follows a direct geometric progression with stream order.

D. Mean gradient of streams of each order — Y: Approximates an inverse geometric series.

Stream gradient generally decreases as stream order increases downstream. Therefore, mean gradient follows an inverse geometric relation with stream order.

79.

$$A = \nabla\phi + \nabla \times \psi$$

$$\nabla \cdot A = \nabla \cdot (\nabla\phi) + \nabla \cdot (\nabla \times \psi)$$

$$\nabla \cdot (\nabla\phi) = \nabla^2 \phi$$

$$\nabla \cdot (\nabla \times \psi) = 0$$

$$\nabla \cdot A = \nabla^2 \phi$$

80. P. INPUT EM method — D: Early and late time apparent resistivity.

The INPUT electromagnetic method is a time-domain EM method. Its response is commonly interpreted using early-time and late-time apparent resistivity behaviour.

Q. VLF method — B: Dip angle measurement.

The VLF method uses very low frequency electromagnetic fields from distant transmitters. Field interpretation commonly involves measuring dip angle or tilt of the resultant field.

R. Airborne EM method — A: Rotary field.

Airborne electromagnetic surveys commonly use moving transmitter-receiver systems. The associated EM field configuration may be described in terms of a rotary field response.

S. MT method — C: Static shift.

Magnetotelluric data are affected by near-surface resistivity inhomogeneities. This produces static shift, which distorts apparent resistivity curves without similarly shifting phase.

81. Cloud X forms over land, while Cloud Y forms over the ocean with the same liquid water content. Land areas generally have a higher concentration of cloud condensation nuclei because of dust, smoke, pollution, and other aerosols. Therefore, the same liquid water content is distributed among a larger number of smaller droplets in the continental cloud. Oceanic clouds usually have fewer but larger droplets because marine air has fewer condensation nuclei. Hence, the number of cloud droplets in X is greater than in Y.

82. P. FAD of - — W: E

The dash fossil first appears in the older part of the succession at stratum E. It is not present in F, and it continues upward into A, so its first appearance datum is E.

Q. LAD of x — T: B

The x fossil occurs in D, C, and B. Its last appearance datum is the youngest or uppermost occurrence, which is stratum B.

R. FAD of l — U: C

The vertical-line fossil occurs in C, B, and A. Its first appearance datum is the oldest or lowermost occurrence, which is stratum C.

S. LAD of o — V: D

The o fossil occurs in F, E, and D. Its last appearance datum is the youngest or uppermost occurrence, which is stratum D.

83. The upper stability limit of water in an Eh-pH diagram represents the oxidizing boundary beyond which water is no longer stable. Above this limit, water is oxidized to oxygen. The oxidation reaction may be written as $2H_2O \rightarrow O_2 + 4H^+ + 4e^-$. Since electrons are produced in this oxidation process, the upper stability limit indicates breakdown of water to release electrons. Therefore, option 1 is the correct answer.

84. Primary production peaks two times in a year in temperate oceanic regions. In temperate oceans, a strong spring bloom occurs when light increases and nutrients are still available after winter mixing. A second, smaller autumn bloom may occur when cooling and mixing again bring nutrients into the surface layer while enough light is still present. Equatorial regions may have more continuous productivity, while Arctic and Antarctic regions generally have a strong seasonal bloom controlled by light and ice conditions. Therefore, temperate oceanic regions show two productivity peaks in a year.

85. A. Panjal Traps — V: 285 Ma

Panjal Traps are associated with Permian magmatic activity. Their approximate age matches 285 Ma among the given options.

B. Malani volcanics — T: 745 Ma

Malani volcanics are Neoproterozoic volcanic rocks of northwestern India. Their approximate age corresponds to 745 Ma in the given list.

C. Sylhet Traps — R: 116 Ma

Sylhet Traps are Early Cretaceous volcanic rocks of northeastern India. Their approximate age is best matched with 116 Ma.

D. Dalma Lavas — Q: 1700 Ma

Dalma Lavas are Proterozoic volcanic rocks of the Singhbhum region. Their approximate age corresponds to 1700 Ma in the options.

E. Amba Dongar carbonatites — S: 65 Ma

Amba Dongar carbonatites are related to Deccan-age alkaline-carbonatite magmatism. Their approximate age is close to 65 Ma.

86. Higher ambient salinity increases the density of seawater. When seawater density increases, the buoyant support available to pelagic organisms also increases. This helps organisms remain suspended in the water column with less sinking tendency. Therefore, pelagic organisms need to spend less energy on swimming, flotation, or other mechanisms used to maintain their vertical position. Options related to larger appendages, gas vacuoles, or prevention of body-fluid loss do not directly give the general buoyancy effect of high salinity.

87. Sand-bed rivers braid at lower slopes than gravel-bed rivers of similar discharge because sand is more easily entrained than gravel. Since sand particles require lower shear stress for movement, sand-bed channels can transport sediment actively even at relatively lower gradients. Braiding develops when sediment supply and mobility are high relative to the transport capacity of the channel. For a similar discharge, gravel requires steeper slopes to become mobile and produce comparable braiding conditions. Therefore, both the assertion and reason are true, and the reason correctly explains the assertion.

88. $$f(x_0+h) = f(x_0) + hf'(x_0) + \frac{h^2}{2}f''(x_0) + \frac{h^3}{6}f'''(x_0) + 0(h^4)$$

$$f(x_0-h) = f(x_0) + hf'(x_0) + \frac{h^2}{2}f''(x_0) - \frac{h^3}{6}f'''(x_0) + 0(h^4)$$

$$f(x_0+h) - f(x_0-h) = 2hf'(x_0) + \frac{h^3}{3}f'''(x_0) + 0(h^5)$$

$$\frac{f(x_0+h) - f(x_0-h)}{2h} = f'(x_0) + \frac{h^2}{6}f'''(x_0) + 0(h^4)$$

Truncation error = $O(h^2)$

89. A sediment rating curve represents the relationship between suspended sediment concentration and water discharge. It is commonly used to estimate sediment transport from measured or predicted river discharge. In such a curve, discharge is usually plotted against suspended sediment concentration or suspended sediment load derived from concentration. The purpose is to describe how sediment carried by a river changes as streamflow increases or decreases. Therefore, the best fitting option is suspended sediment concentration and water discharge.

90. $\rho_1 = 10\ \Omega\text{m},\ \rho_2 = 20\ \Omega\text{m},\ h_1 = h_2 = 10$ m

$$\rho_l = \frac{\rho_1 h_1 + \rho_2 h_2}{h_1 + h_2}$$

$$= \frac{10\times 10 + 20\times 10}{20} = 15\ \Omega m$$

$$\rho_l = \frac{h_1 + h_2}{\frac{h_2}{\rho_1} + \frac{h_2}{\rho_2}}$$

$$= \frac{20}{\frac{10}{10}+\frac{10}{20}}$$

$$= \frac{20}{1+0.5}$$

$$= 13.33\ \Omega\ \text{m}$$

$$\lambda = \sqrt{\frac{\rho_t}{\rho_l}}$$

$$= \sqrt{\frac{15}{13.33}}$$

$$= \sqrt{1.125}$$

$$= 1.06.$$

91. Fault dip near base = 15°

Vertical throw = 120 m

$$\tan 15° = \frac{\text{vertical throw}}{\text{heave}}$$

$$\text{Heave} = \frac{120}{\tan 15°}$$

$$\text{Heave} = \frac{120}{0.268}$$

$$\text{Heave} \approx 448\ \text{m}$$

Nearest option = 460 m

92. $$\Delta z = \frac{R_d \overline{T}_v}{g} \ln\left(\frac{p_1}{p_2}\right)$$

$$= \frac{287 \times 285}{9.81} \ln\left(\frac{1000}{700}\right)$$

$$= \frac{81795}{9.81} \ln(1.4286)$$

$$= 8337.9 \times 0.3567$$

$$\approx 2974\ \text{m}$$

$$\approx 2975\ \text{m}$$

93. In a Schlumberger sounding curve, the principle of equivalence applies strongly to thin intermediate layers whose individual thickness and resistivity cannot be uniquely resolved. The second and fifth layers in the given curve are low-resistivity layers occurring between comparatively higher-resistivity layers. Such conductive intermediate layers commonly show longitudinal conductance equivalence, where S = h/ρ remains nearly constant. This means different combinations of h and ρ can give nearly the same sounding response if h/ρ is unchanged. Therefore, the second and fifth layers exhibit h/ρ = constant type equivalence.

94. The saturated adiabatic lapse rate is not fixed; it varies with temperature and moisture content. In warm, moist air, condensation releases a large amount of latent heat, so the rising saturated parcel cools more slowly and Γ_s becomes smaller. In cold and dry air aloft, much less water vapour is available for condensation, so latent heating becomes weak. Under such conditions, the saturated adiabatic lapse rate approaches the dry adiabatic lapse rate. Therefore, option 2 best describes its behaviour in the troposphere.

95. According to the Irvine model of chromite crystallization, significant chromite seam formation can be promoted by processes that drive magma into the chromite stability field. Mixing of less-evolved magma with evolved magma can produce such an effect. Silica contamination can also promote chromite saturation by changing melt composition. Higher initial chromium concentration in the melt can favour chromite crystallization. Contamination by olivine, however, does not effectively drive the melt toward significant chromite seam formation, so it is the process that cannot lead to significant formation of chromite seams.

96. Aliasing occurs when a wave or signal with wavelength shorter than the resolution of the sampling grid is falsely represented as a longer, resolved wave. This happens because the sampling interval is too large to represent the true high-frequency or short-wavelength variation. Therefore, the unresolved wave appears as a different lower-frequency wave within the resolved range. Aliasing is especially important in numerical modelling and spectral methods where insufficient resolution can distort wave representation. Hence, option 3 is the correct statement.

97. Tidal acceleration at sublunar point $= +\frac{2GMa}{r^3}$

At the antipodal point, the point lies on the opposite side of Earth from the Moon

The tidal acceleration is directed away from Earth's centre on the opposite side

Therefore, relative to the sublunar direction, its sign is negative

Magnitude is approximately the same to first order

Tidal acceleration at antipodal point $= -\frac{2GMa}{r^3}$

98. A. Maria — (iii) Flood volcanism

Lunar maria are broad, dark basaltic plains on the Moon. They formed mainly by extensive basaltic lava flooding of large impact basins.

B. Sinuous rilles — (iv) Lava tubes

Sinuous rilles are winding channel-like lunar features. They are commonly related to lava channels or collapsed lava tubes.

C. Rays — (ii) Bolide impact

Lunar rays are bright streaks of ejecta extending outward from impact craters. They are produced by bolide impact and dispersal of fresh excavated material.

D. Boulder tracks — (i) Gravity slide

Boulder tracks form when boulders roll or slide downslope under gravity. Their trails record downslope movement on lunar surfaces.

99. Effluent streams are gaining streams that receive water from the groundwater system. Their stream surface commonly coincides with, or is connected to, the water table. Since groundwater flows into the stream, the water table slopes toward the stream, not away from it. These streams gain water downstream, so their discharge generally increases downstream. They are commonly associated with humid regions where the water table is high enough to feed the stream channel.

100. Fishes with accessory respiratory organs are often seen in muddy shore intertidal habitats. Muddy shores and mudflats commonly experience low oxygen conditions, periodic exposure, and waterlogged fine sediment. Under such conditions, fishes may need accessory respiratory adaptations to survive outside water or in oxygen-poor water. Mudskippers and similar intertidal fishes are typical examples associated with muddy shores and mangrove mudflats. Therefore, muddy shore is the correct answer.

101. Coral reefs are poorly developed off the west coast of Australia and South America mainly because these margins are influenced by cold ocean currents and upwelling. Coral reefs require warm, clear, shallow tropical waters for good growth. Upwelling brings colder, nutrient-rich deep water to the surface, which lowers temperature and can also favour plankton growth that reduces water clarity. The west coast of South America is strongly affected by the cold Peru/Humboldt Current, while parts of western Australia are also influenced by relatively cooler eastern-boundary-type conditions. Therefore, cold ocean currents and upwelling of cold water is the correct answer.

102. In the Northern Hemisphere, both regular high and anomalous high systems are anticyclonic systems. Anticyclonic circulation around a high-pressure centre in the Northern Hemisphere is clockwise. The distinction between regular and anomalous highs is related to the relative roles and balance of pressure-gradient, Coriolis, and centrifugal forces in gradient-wind balance. However, both remain high-pressure circulations in the Northern Hemisphere and therefore have the same clockwise sense of rotation. Hence, option 2 is the correct answer.

103. For an $m \times n$ matrix with $m \neq n$, full rank means that the rank is the maximum possible rank of the rectangular matrix. The maximum possible rank of such a matrix is the smaller of the two dimensions, that is, $\min(m, n)$. The number of non-zero singular values of a matrix is always equal to its rank. Therefore, for a full-rank $m \times n$ matrix, the number of non-zero singular values is $\min(m, n)$.

104. This statement is incorrect for internal gravity waves. In internal gravity waves, particle motion is not simply parallel to the direction of phase propagation. The wave motion is strongly controlled by buoyancy and stable stratification, so particle displacement has a characteristic orientation relative to the wave vector and phase surfaces. Internal gravity waves also have an upper frequency limit controlled by the buoyancy frequency. Their phase surfaces commonly show a tilt with the horizontal. Therefore, option 1 is the incorrect statement.

105. Inclusion of friction in geostrophic balance reduces the wind speed below the ideal geostrophic value. Because the Coriolis force becomes weaker when the wind slows, it no longer fully balances the horizontal pressure-gradient force. The remaining pressure-gradient force drives a cross-isobaric component of flow toward lower pressure. This is true in both hemispheres, although the deflection direction differs between hemispheres. Therefore, statement A is correct, but statement B is incorrect because friction does not produce a cross-isobaric component toward higher pressure in the Southern Hemisphere.

106. **A. Denitrification:** The pathway from reduced/oxidized nitrogen intermediates such as NO and N_2O toward N_2 represents denitrification. This is mainly an anoxic process and converts fixed nitrogen species into molecular nitrogen.

B. Anammox: The pathway involving NH_4^+ and nitrite-type nitrogen leading to N_2 represents anaerobic ammonium oxidation. This process is called anammox and occurs under anoxic conditions.

C. N_2 fixation: The arrow from N_2 toward organic nitrogen represents conversion of molecular nitrogen into biologically usable fixed nitrogen. This is nitrogen fixation, by which N_2 enters the organic nitrogen pool.

D. Nitrification: The oxic dashed pathway involving ammonium oxidation toward nitrite/nitrate-type forms represents nitrification. Nitrification is an aerobic process that oxidizes reduced nitrogen species under oxic conditions.

107. For a frictional slope, the factor of safety is governed mainly by the ratio of resisting frictional force to driving shear force. In a purely frictional or cohesionless slope, both the resisting component and the driving component increase proportionally when slope height increases. Since both numerator and denominator scale in the same way, their ratio does not change. Therefore, doubling the slope height alone, while keeping the soil properties and slope angle constant, does not change the factor of safety. Hence, the correct answer is that it remains the same.

108. The given equation shows the stretching relation for absolute vorticity, where $\zeta + f$ is absolute vorticity. In the Northern Hemisphere, f is positive, so cyclonic relative vorticity adds to planetary vorticity and gives larger positive absolute vorticity. Convergence can strongly intensify cyclonic rotation through vortex stretching. Anticyclonic vorticity is limited because sufficiently strong negative ζ would reduce $\zeta + f$ toward zero, producing a dynamical constraint. Therefore, the equation supports why cyclonic systems can become more intense than anticyclonic systems.

109. A heavy-mineral-bearing clean sandstone bed can be distinguished from a shaly sandstone bed by using density log and S.P. log together. Heavy minerals increase the bulk density of a clean sandstone, so the density log helps identify the unusually high-density character. The S.P. log helps distinguish clean, permeable sandstone from shaly sandstone because clean sandstone generally gives a clearer spontaneous-potential deflection. A shaly sandstone may give a high gamma-ray response due to clay content, which can confuse it with radioactive heavy-mineral-bearing sandstone. Therefore, density log and S.P. log give the most appropriate distinction among the options.

110. An FFT triple junction contains two transform faults and one trench. Its stability depends on whether the geometry permits the triple junction to maintain the same boundary types as the plates continue moving. A transform boundary requires relative motion parallel to the fault, while a trench has its own convergence-related boundary condition. For this junction type, stability is achieved only under a special geometrical condition. That condition is that the trench and one of the transform faults have the same trend. Therefore, option 3 is the correct answer.

111. Outside corridor stacking in VSP data processing is used to suppress internal multiples. In VSP, corridor stacking enhances the primary reflected upgoing wavefield over a selected time corridor. Outside corridor stacking uses data outside the primary corridor to identify and attenuate multiple energy that may interfere with primary reflections. Internal multiples are a major type of unwanted coherent noise in VSP interpretation. Therefore, suppression of internal multiples is the correct purpose.

112. Q = KIA

$K = 2 \times 10^{-5}\ ms^{-1}$

$$I = \frac{\Delta h}{L} = \frac{4}{500} = 0.008$$

$A = 10 \times 200 = 2000\ m^2$

$Q = 2 \times 10^{-5} \times 0.008 \times 2000$

$Q = 3.2 \times 10^{-4}\ m^3s^{-1}$

$Q_{per\ day} = 3.2 \times 10^{-4} \times 86400 = 27.648\ m^3/day$

$Q \approx 27.6\ m^3/day$

113. A. Neck cutoff: A shows cutting across the narrow neck of a highly developed meander loop. This produces a shorter channel path and abandons the former loop as an oxbow-type feature.

B. Avulsion: B shows diversion of flow from an existing channel into a new course. This represents sudden abandonment or shifting of the main channel to another path.

C. Chute cutoff: C shows a shortcut channel across the inner side or point-bar area of a meander bend. Such a cutoff is called a chute cutoff because flow cuts through the chute across the bend.

D. Meander shift: D shows lateral shifting of the meander position from an earlier course to the present course. The dashed line indicates the former position, while the present flow has shifted laterally.

114. The high-pressure, low-temperature belt in a paired metamorphic belt is typically represented by blueschist-type mineral assemblages. Glaucophane is a diagnostic sodic amphibole of blueschist facies, and lawsonite is also characteristic of low-temperature, high-pressure subduction-zone metamorphism. Jadeite is another high-pressure mineral commonly associated with subduction-related metamorphic conditions. Garnet-sillimanite-K-feldspar assemblages represent high-temperature metamorphism, not high-pressure low-temperature conditions. Therefore, glaucophane + lawsonite + jadeite is the correct assemblage.

115. After faulting, streams flowing towards the uplift block are obstructed by the raised fault block, so they commonly experience impoundment. The uplifted side acts as a barrier and can pond water or sediment upstream. In contrast, streams flowing towards the downthrown side experience an increase in relative base-level fall and gradient. This promotes rapid incision or downcutting as the stream adjusts to the lowered block. Therefore, streams flowing towards the uplift block and downthrown side respectively experience impoundment and rapid downcutting.

116. A. IPCC Assessment Report 3 — Q: Year 2001

The IPCC Third Assessment Report corresponds to the year 2001.

Therefore, A matches with Q.

B. IPCC Assessment Report 4 — P: Vulnerability is a function of exposure, sensitivity, and adaptive capacity

The vulnerability framework using exposure, sensitivity, and adaptive capacity is associated with IPCC AR4.

Therefore, B matches with P.

C. IPCC Assessment Report 5 — S: Disaster Risk is a function of hazard, exposure, and vulnerability

IPCC AR5 emphasized the disaster-risk framework involving hazard, exposure, and vulnerability.

Therefore, C matches with S.

D. IPCC Assessment Report 6 — R: Shared Socioeconomic Pathways

IPCC AR6 prominently uses Shared Socioeconomic Pathways for climate scenario assessment.

Therefore, D matches with R.

117. In a medium where seismic velocity increases with depth, a seismic ray bottoms or turns where the ray becomes horizontal. The horizontal slowness is related to velocity by the turning condition $p = 1/V$. Therefore, a large value of p corresponds to a smaller velocity at the turning point. Since velocity is low at shallower levels and increases downward, a large p ray bottoms at shallow depth. Hence, Z is shallow for large p and low V.

118. The observed strength of the Indian summer monsoon circulation is primarily attributed to release of latent heat due to condensation. Land-ocean thermal contrast initiates the monsoon circulation, but the actual intensity of the observed monsoon is strongly amplified by deep convection and condensation heating. Latent heat release warms the atmospheric column and strengthens the large-scale pressure and circulation response. Sensible heating by land alone is not sufficient to explain the full observed strength of the monsoon. Therefore, latent heat release due to condensation is the best answer.

119.

$$B_r \propto 2 \sin \lambda$$

$$B_t \propto \cos \lambda$$

$$\lambda = 30°$$

$$\frac{B_r}{B_t} = \frac{2\sin 30°}{\cos 30°}$$

$$= \frac{2 \times \frac{1}{2}}{\frac{\sqrt{3}}{2}}$$

$$= \frac{1}{\frac{\sqrt{3}}{2}}$$

$$= \frac{2}{\sqrt{3}}$$

$$B_r : B_t = 2 : \sqrt{3}$$

120.

$$Q = 400 \times 10^5$$

$$= 4 \times 10^7 \text{ Jm}^{-2}$$

$$\rho C_p h = 1000 \times 4000 \times 50$$

$$= 2 \times 10^8 \text{ Jm}^{-2} \text{ K}^{-1}$$

$$\Delta T = \frac{Q}{\rho C_p h}$$

$$= \frac{4 \times 10^7}{2 \times 10^8} = 0.2°\text{C}$$

$$T_f = 25 - 0.2$$

$$= 24.8°\text{C}$$

121. If deep water had historically formed in the North Pacific instead of the North Atlantic, the newly formed Pacific deep water would have been relatively young and recently ventilated. Newly ventilated deep water carries more dissolved oxygen because it has recently been in contact with the atmosphere. In the present ocean, old deep waters generally accumulate nutrients and lose oxygen with time due to organic matter remineralization. Therefore, if the North Pacific were the main deep-water formation region, Pacific deep water would most likely have acquired higher oxygen concentration due to younger water masses.

122. I. Unsaturated, dry adiabatic, reversible ascent/descent — B: Potential Temperature

For dry adiabatic reversible motion, potential temperature remains conserved. This is the standard conserved thermodynamic variable for an unsaturated air parcel moving without heat exchange.

II. Saturated pseudoadiabatic ascent — D: Equivalent Potential Temperature

In pseudoadiabatic saturated ascent, condensate is removed immediately from the parcel. The diagnostic commonly treated as conserved for this process is equivalent potential temperature.

III. Saturated reversible ascent — A: Moist Static Energy

In saturated reversible ascent, condensate is retained and the parcel undergoes phase changes without precipitation loss. Moist static energy is the appropriate conserved energy-like diagnostic for this reversible moist adiabatic process.

IV. Deep convective plume with steady entrainment of environmental air — C: Total Water Mixing Ratio

For a convective plume with condensate retained, total water mixing ratio is the key conserved water variable during phase changes. Although entrainment mixes environmental air into the plume, the diagnostic associated with retained condensate is total water mixing ratio.

123. In warm clouds, droplet growth by condensation is rapid when droplets are very small. As the droplet radius increases, the same amount of vapour deposition produces a smaller increase in radius. Mathematically, condensational growth gives r^2 increasing approximately with time, so dr/dt decreases as r becomes larger. Therefore, droplet size increases with time, but the rate of increase in radius slows down. Hence, option 2 correctly describes warm-cloud droplet growth.

124. Higher organic carbon content in continental slope sediments on the eastern and western margins of India is facilitated by higher fine grain fraction and low dissolved oxygen. Fine-grained sediments have larger surface area and better ability to adsorb and preserve organic matter. Low dissolved oxygen reduces oxidation and decomposition of organic matter after deposition. Together, fine sediment texture and oxygen-poor bottom-water or pore-water conditions enhance organic carbon preservation. Therefore, higher fine grain fraction with low dissolved oxygen is the correct answer.

125. A. Low-angled reverse-graded planar laminae — S: Aeolian

Low-angle planar lamination with inverse or reverse grading is characteristic of wind-blown sand deposition. Aeolian grain-flow and grain-fall processes commonly produce such stratification.

B. Curve-crested dune in poorly sorted sandstone — P: Fluvial

Curved-crested dunes in poorly sorted sandstone are commonly produced by river-channel bedforms. Fluvial currents generate dunes and cross-stratification in sands with variable sorting.

C. Herringbone cross-strata sandstone — Q: Tidal

Herringbone cross-stratification forms due to alternating current directions. This is typical of tidal environments where flood and ebb currents reverse flow direction.

D. Profoundly normally graded bed with scoured base — R: Continental Slope

A deeply scoured base followed by strong normal grading is typical of turbidity-current deposits. Such turbidites are common in continental slope and deep-marine depositional settings.

126. $f = \dfrac{\text{new production}}{\text{total production}}$

$$0.2 = \frac{10}{\text{total production}}$$

total production $= 50$ mmol $\text{Nm}^{-2}\ \text{d}^{-1}$

regenerated production

$= 50 - 10 = 40$ mmol $\text{Nm}^{-2}\ \text{d}^{-1}$

Using Redfield ratio, 10 mmol N corresponds to about 66 mmol C, but that represents possible new/export production, not confirmed burial or deposition in sediment. Therefore, sediment deposition of 66 mmol C per day cannot be concluded from the given data.

127. A. Ventilation — S: ^{3}He

^{3}He is used as a tracer of ocean ventilation and water-mass spreading. It helps trace subsurface circulation and exchange processes in the ocean.

B. Export C Flux — R: ^{234}Th

^{234}Th is particle-reactive and is widely used to estimate export carbon flux. Its disequilibrium with uranium helps quantify removal of particles from surface waters.

C. Paleo Productivity — Q: Cd/Al

Cd/Al is used as a geochemical proxy connected with nutrient cycling and productivity. It helps reconstruct past ocean productivity from sedimentary records.

D. Water Masses — T: εNd

Neodymium isotopic composition, expressed as εNd, is used to identify water masses. Different source regions have distinct Nd isotopic signatures.

E. Gas Exchange — P: ^{226}Rn

^{226}Rn is useful in studying air-sea gas exchange because it is a naturally occurring radioactive gas. Its distribution can be used to estimate gas transfer across the sea surface.

128. Numerical weather prediction is limited to about two weeks mainly because weather depends strongly on the exact initial state of the atmosphere. Small errors in initial conditions grow rapidly due to the chaotic nature of atmospheric motion. Climate prediction, however, focuses more on statistics, averages, and responses to boundary forcing such as sea surface temperature, greenhouse gases, land surface, ice, and ocean conditions. Therefore, weather prediction is mainly an initial value problem, while climate prediction is mainly a boundary value problem. This is why climate anomalies may be predicted months ahead even though exact day-to-day weather cannot.

129. Cross-correlation of the vibroseis pilot sweep signal with seismic data produced from the same source removes the phase of the vibroseis sweep. The recorded vibroseis trace contains the Earth response combined with the long swept-frequency source signal. During correlation, the known pilot sweep is used to compress the sweep and cancel its phase effect, producing a correlated record with a Klauder-type wavelet. This process does not directly recover the true Earth impedance response, because the result still contains the autocorrelation wavelet of the sweep and requires further processing for true reflectivity or impedance recovery. Therefore, the correct answer is option 2.

130. For surface gravity waves, the general dispersion relation is $\omega^2 = gk \tan h(k\text{H})$. When water depth is much smaller than wavelength, the wave is a shallow-water wave and $k\text{H} << 1$. Under this condition, $\tan h\ (k\text{H}) \approx k\text{H}$.

Therefore, $\omega^2 = gk(k\text{H}) = gk^2\ \text{H}$.

Hence, the correct shallow-water dispersion relation is $\omega^2 = gk^2\ \text{H}$.

131. Reynolds averaging of the three-dimensional viscous incompressible equations produces additional turbulent stress terms in the mean momentum equations. These additional terms are the Reynolds stresses, which arise from correlations of velocity fluctuations. Therefore, the zonal, meridional, and vertical mean momentum equations all acquire extra turbulent transport terms. However, for an incompressible fluid, the continuity equation remains a divergence-free condition on the mean velocity field. Hence, no additional terms arise in the conservation of mass equation.

132. Relief displacement in aerial photography is given by the relation $d = \frac{rh}{\text{H}}$, where d is relief displacement, r is radial distance from the nadir or plumb point, h is object height, and H is flying height above the datum. Thus, relief displacement increases with increasing object height and increasing radial distance from the nadir point. It is also radial from the plumb point. Since d is inversely proportional to flight altitude H, relief displacement increases, not decreases, when flight altitude decreases. Therefore, option 3 is the statement that is NOT true.

133. $P = \rho g h$

$\rho \approx 1000\ \text{kg m}^{-3},\ g \approx 9.8\ \text{ms}^{-2},\ h = 4000\ \text{m}$

$P = 1000 \times 9.8 \times 4000$

$$P = 3.92 \times 10^7 \text{ Pa}$$

$$1 \text{ bar} = 10^5 \text{ Pa}$$

$$P = \frac{3.92 \times 10^7}{10^5} = 392 \text{ bar}$$

$$P \approx 400 \text{ bar.}$$

134. In the AFM diagram, all three bulk compositions 1, 2, and 3 lie within mineral assemblage fields that include biotite. Rock 1 lies in a field involving biotite along with higher-grade aluminous phases. Rock 2 also falls in a biotite-bearing field toward the Fe-rich side. Rock 3 lies directly in the biotite-bearing region near the lower central part of the diagram. Kyanite, garnet, and staurolite are not common to all three compositions, but biotite is stable in all three rocks.

135. $$^{87}\text{Rb} = \frac{100}{85.46} \times 0.2783$$

$$= 1.170 \times 0.2783$$

$$= 0.3256$$

$$^{86}\text{Sr} = \frac{200}{87.6} \times 0.10$$

$$= 2.283 \times 0.10$$

$$= 0.2283$$

$$\frac{^{87}Rb}{^{86}Sr} = \frac{0.3256}{0.2283}$$

$$= 1.426$$

$$\approx 1.43$$

136. The rating curve of a river gauging station in the lower course commonly shows a concave form because the hydraulic behaviour changes during high flow. In the lower course, floodwater spreads over floodplains and encounters higher roughness, storage, and backwater effects. This makes the river channel less efficient in carrying additional water during floods. Therefore, a given rise in stage does not produce the same proportional increase in discharge as in a more efficient confined channel. Hence, both the assertion and reason are true, and the reason correctly explains the assertion.

137. The Shannon-Wiener Biodiversity Index is based on the information or uncertainty associated with species identity. It measures how difficult it is to predict the species of an individual chosen randomly from a community. If a community has many species and individuals are evenly distributed, the uncertainty is high and the index value is high. If one species dominates, the uncertainty is low and the index value decreases. Therefore, option 1 is the correct definition.

138. Increasing the surface dewpoint raises the low-level moisture content and increases the equivalent potential temperature of the lifted surface parcel. This lowers the LCL and makes the parcel follow a warmer moist-adiabatic path after saturation, helping it overcome the warm cap between 800 hPa and 750 hPa. Hence, the negative buoyancy area, that is CIN, is reduced and convective initiation becomes easier. Since the environmental temperature profile is not changed and the modification is mainly in parcel moisture near the surface, it targets CIN more directly than mid-tropospheric cooling. Therefore, option 2 is the correct answer.

139. Reclamation of marginal areas in a macrotidal estuary reduces the tidal prism and decreases the volume of water exchanged during the tidal cycle. With reduced tidal flow, the existing channel becomes oversized relative to the new hydraulic conditions. The estuary therefore tends to adjust by sedimentation and reduction of channel depth. Thus, the assertion is true. The reason is also generally true because positive feedback drives a system away from equilibrium, but the sedimentation response described here is an adjustment toward a new equilibrium, so it is not the correct explanation of the assertion.

140. $$\Delta g(x) = \frac{GMz}{(x^2 + z^2)^{3/2}}$$

$$\Delta g_{\max} = \frac{GM}{z^2}$$

At half maximum,

$$\frac{\Delta g(x)}{\Delta g_{\max}} = \frac{z^3}{(x^2 + z^2)^{3/2}} = \frac{1}{2}$$

$$x = z\sqrt{2^{2/3}-1}$$
$$= 0.766z$$
$$2x = 1000 \text{ m}$$
$$\Rightarrow \quad x = 500 \text{ m}$$
$$z = \frac{500}{0.766} \approx 653 \text{ m}$$
$$M = \frac{\Delta g_{max} z^2}{G}$$
$$\Delta g_{max} = 5 \text{ mGal}$$
$$= 5 \times 10^{-5} \text{ ms}^{-2}$$
$$M = \frac{5\times10^{-5}\times(653)^2}{6.67\times10^{-11}}$$
$$M \approx 3.2 \times 10^{11} \text{ kg.}$$

141. The Antarctic Circumpolar Current formed around 34 million years ago. Its development is linked with the opening of the Tasmanian gateway and Drake Passage, which allowed circumpolar ocean circulation around Antarctica. This circulation thermally isolated Antarctica from warmer lower-latitude waters. The isolation promoted major Antarctic cooling and expansion of Antarctic glaciation. Therefore, the correct combination is 34 My ago, opening of Tasmanian and Drake passage, and cooling of Antarctica.

142. A. Younger Dryas — S: 12900–11600 yr BP

The Younger Dryas was a late-glacial cold stadial. Its age is approximately 12,900 to 11,600 years BP.

B. Bronze Age — Q: 5500–3200 yr BP

The Bronze Age falls broadly within the mid-to-late Holocene. Among the given choices, 5500–3200 yr BP is the correct match.

C. Bolling-Allerod — P: 14700–12900 yr BP

The Bølling-Allerød was a warm interstadial before the Younger Dryas. Its approximate age range is 14,700 to 12,900 yr BP.

D. Holocene climate optimum — R: 9500–5500 yr BP

The Holocene climate optimum corresponds to a relatively warm early-to-mid Holocene interval. Among the given options, 9500–5500 yr BP is the correct match.

143. A. A–V: Mixing of meteoric and other water previously interacted with rocks

A has very low δD, indicating a meteoric-water component. Its oxygen isotope composition is shifted to higher $\delta^{18}O$, which indicates interaction or mixing with rock-exchanged fluid.

B. B–T: Meteoric water

B lies on or very close to the meteoric water line. Its depleted δD and $\delta^{18}O$ values are characteristic of meteoric water.

C. C–W: Evaporated meteoric water

C is displaced to the right of the meteoric water line with enriched $\delta^{18}O$. Such enrichment relative to meteoric water is characteristic of evaporated meteoric water.

D. D–U: Magmatic water

D has relatively high $\delta^{18}O$ and moderately negative δD. This field corresponds to magmatic hydrothermal water.

144. The best region for retrieving turbidite-free cores with high calcareous microfossils is the central Arabian Sea between about 2000 m and 3500 m water depth. This depth range is deep enough for open-ocean pelagic sedimentation but still generally above the strong carbonate dissolution zone. Therefore, calcareous microfossils are better preserved than in very deep basins below the carbonate compensation depth. The Bay of Bengal margins and deeper Bengal fan regions are more affected by terrigenous input and turbidites. Hence, the central Arabian Sea at this intermediate depth is the best choice.

145. Basin B shows western intensification of circulation, which is the characteristic large-scale oceanic response associated with the planetary vorticity gradient and Rossby-wave dynamics. Rossby waves transmit adjustment westward in an ocean basin and help produce the strong western boundary current pattern shown in basin B. Basin A shows a more symmetric circulation without western intensification, which is not the circulation pattern expected when Rossby-wave adjustment is active. Therefore, Rossby waves can develop in basin B but not in basin A as represented in the given schematic.

146. $\nu = \frac{1}{4}$ for Poisson's solid

$$e = \frac{1-2\nu}{E}(\sigma_1 + \sigma_2 + \sigma_3)$$

$\sigma_1 = \sigma_2 = \sigma_3 = 150$ GPa

$\sigma_1 + \sigma_2 + \sigma_3 = 450$ GPa

$$e = \frac{1-2(1/4)}{15} \times 450$$

$$e = \frac{1/2}{15} \times 450$$

$$= 15.$$

147. $f(x) = e^{-|x|}$

$$F\{e^{-|x|}\} = \int_{-\infty}^{+\infty} e^{-|x|} e^{-ikx} dx$$

$$F\{e^{-|x|}\} = \frac{2}{1+k^2}$$

For upward continuation to height h, the Fourier-domain anomaly is multiplied by

$e^{-|k|h}$

$$F_h(k) = \frac{2}{1+k^2} e^{-|k|h}$$

$$F_h(k) = \frac{2e^{-|k|h}}{1+k^2}$$

148. Slope of Wadati plot $= \frac{T_s - T_p}{T_p} = \frac{V_p}{V_s} - 1$

For region A,

$$1 = \frac{V_p}{V_s} - 1$$

$$\frac{V_p}{V_s} = 2$$

For region B,

$$0.5 = \frac{V_p}{V_s} - 1$$

$$\frac{V_p}{V_s} = 1.5$$

Thus region A has the larger V_P/V_S ratio, giving comparatively smaller P-wave travel time and larger S-P time difference for the same hypocentral distance. Therefore,

$$T(A)_{S-P} > T(B)_{S-P}$$

$$T(A)_P < T(B)_P$$

149. In magnetotelluric measurements, for 1-D interpretation, the two orthogonal apparent resistivity components are commonly combined using the geometric mean. Therefore, the average apparent resistivity is

$$\rho_{av} = \sqrt{\rho_{xy}\,\rho_{yx}}$$

The phase is averaged arithmetically because phase is an angular response associated with the impedance components. Hence,

$$\phi_{av} = \frac{\phi_{xy} + \phi_{yx}}{2}$$

Therefore, option 2 gives the correct expressions for average apparent resistivity and average phase.

150. $\tau = c + \sigma_n \tan\phi$

$c = 20$ MPa, $\sigma_n = 50$ MPa, $\phi = 30°$

$\tau = 20 + 50 \tan 30°$

$\tan 30° = 0.577$

$\tau = 20 + 50(0.577)$

$\tau = 20 + 28.85 = 48.85$ MPa

$\tau \approx 48.9$ MPa.

Joint CSIR-UGC NET/JRF

Earth, Atmospheric, Ocean & Planetary Sciences

JULY-2025

(Exam held on 28-07-2025, Conducted by NTA)

PART-A

1. On a spherical balloon of 10 cm radius, a circular colour patch has an area of 25 cm^2. If the balloon is uniformly expanded to a sphere of 50 cm radius, the area of the colour patch in cm^2 would be:

1. 125 2. 625
3. 50 4. 500

2. Average age of 20 students of a class is 10 years. Average age of these students together with their five teachers is 14. The age of Ramesh Sir, one of their five teachers, is exactly the same as the average age of all their five teachers. The sum of the ages (in years) of all the students and Ramesh Sir is:

1. 214 2. 224
3. 230 4. 241

3. A pilgrim starts walking for a journey of 115 km. On the first day he covers 7 km, the next day 9 km, and likewise keeps adding 2 km everyday till he reaches 15 km per day which he maintains for the rest of the journey. How many days in all will he take to complete the journey?

1. 7 2. 8
3. 9 4. 10

4. A 2 cm wide wooden strip is to be fixed on a photo of 40 cm × 30 cm size all along its four sides. What is the minimum length of the wooden strip required?

1. 124 cm 2. 128 cm
3. 132 cm 4. 140 cm

5. The population of a town over the years 2000-2007 is shown in the given figure.

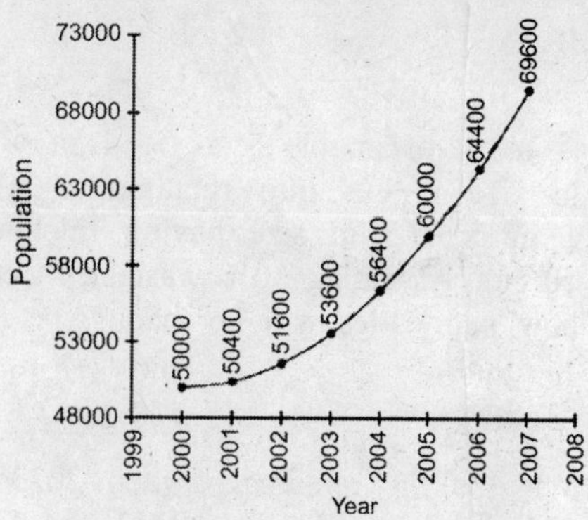

It can be inferred that during 2000-2007,

1. the population increased linearly
2. the rate of increase of the population increased linearly
3. the rate of increase of the rate of increase of the population increased linearly
4. the population increased exponentially

6. If any 9 papers are drawn from a both side printed book, the sum of their page numbers can NEVER be _____.

1. $\frac{9 \times (9+1)}{2}$ 2. divisible by 3
3. 179 4. 171

7. Which of the following is true?

1. $\pi^{\pi^\pi} < e^{e^e} < 3^{3^3}$ 2. $\pi^{\pi^\pi} < 3^{3^3} < e^{e^e}$
3. $3^{3^3} < e^{e^e} < \pi^{\pi^\pi}$ 4. $e^{e^e} < 3^{3^3} < \pi^{\pi^\pi}$

8. The areas (in km^2) under forests in four countries A, B, C and D for the years 2014 and 2024 are shown in the given bar chart:

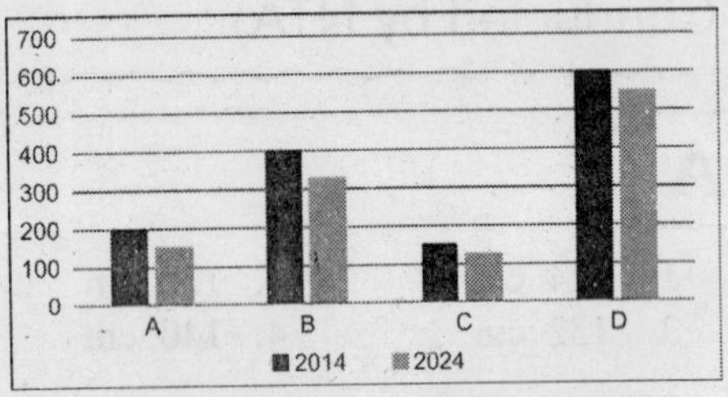

The minimum percentage of deforestation during 2014-2024 was in country:

1. A 2. B
3. C 4. D

9. A block of marble 5 m × 4 m × 2 m in size is cut into rectangular tiles of 1 m × 0.5 m size having thickness of 10 cm. Assuming 10% wastage in cutting, how many tiles will be made?

1. 240 2. 360
3. 480 4. 720

10. What is the remainder when $2023^{2024} + 2025^{2024}$ is divided by 2024?

1. 0 2. 2
3. 223 4. 2023

11. If there is rainfall in a village, flowers will bloom. If flowers bloom, celebrations will definitely take place. Flowers did not bloom. Which of the following is certain?

1. Celebrations took place
2. Celebrations did not take place
3. It did not rain
4. It rained too much

12. MAN is to CROWD is as TREE is to _____.

1. FOREST 2. FRUIT
3. BRANCH 4. ROOT

13. A man on a cycle is travelling on a terrain whose height (h) vs distance (d) can be described by a function $10\,d^4 - 5\,d^2$ in a certain unit (h can be negative). Starting at $d = 0$, the cycle will have the maximum velocity without pedaling at:

1. $d = 1/2$ 2. $d = 2$
3. $d = 1$ 4. $d = \sqrt{2}$

14. $\sqrt[3]{0.99}$ is closest to:

1. 0.33 2. 0.14
3. 0.99 4. 0.45

15. In a box there are 4 white balls and 6 black balls. A ball is drawn at random. If it is white, it is put back along with two more white balls in the box. If it is black, it is put back in the box and then two black balls are thrown out of the box. Now a ball is drawn again at random from the box. Then, what is the probability that it is black?

1. $\frac{1}{2}$ 2. $\frac{1}{3}$
3. $\frac{1}{4}$ 4. $\frac{1}{5}$

16. If a map is placed in such a manner that east becomes southeast, then what will northeast become?

1. North 2. East
3. West 4. South

17. The sixth largest three-digit odd number among those with all digits distinct is:

1. 989 2. 987
3. 973 4. 971

18. A fresh water tap fills a fish tank in 40 minutes. The same tank is filled by a salt water tap in 120 minutes. If both the taps are open, how many minutes will it take to fill the tank?

1. 45 minutes 2. 30 minutes
3. 25 minutes 4. 20 minutes

19. "Amit is a businessman, so he must be rich". From which of the following statements does the implication follow?

1. Only businessmen are rich.
2. If one is not a businessman, he cannot be rich.
3. All businessmen are rich.
4. Some businessmen are rich.

20. An empty plastic mug floats in a bucket of water. When a solid iron ball is kept in the mug it doesn't sink. When the ball is put in the water it sinks. Compared to when the ball is in water, the water level in the bucket when the ball is in the mug is:

1. the same
2. higher
3. lower
4. higher or lower depending on the surface area of the ball

PART-B

21. The energy required to remove a proton from the nucleus of an isotope ....

1. is the same as the energy required to remove a neutron from it.
2. is less than the energy required to remove a neutron from it.
3. is more than the energy required to remove a neutron from it.
4. depends on its electronic configuration.

22. In a sample, the number of atoms of a stable daughter isotope is three times the number of atoms of its radioactive parent. If the half-life of the parent isotope is 1.5 My, and if there were no atoms of the daughter isotope at the time of formation of the sample, then how old is the sample?

1. 1.5 Ma
2. 3.0 Ma
3. 4.5 Ma
4. 6.0 Ma

23. Continental crust is formed primarily at ....

1. mid-oceanic ridges
2. continental rifts
3. oceanic hotspots
4. subduction zones

24. Which of the following is a common essential symmetry element of the trigonal crystal system?

1. Three two-fold rotation axes, perpendicular to one another
2. One three-fold rotation axis
3. Four three-fold rotation axes at 70° 32′ to each other
4. One six-fold rotation axis

25. The correct hierarchy (highest to lowest) of the lithostratigraphic units: (*a*) Formation, (*b*) Supergroup, (*c*) Group, and (*d*) Member, is

1. *a, b, c, d*
2. *b, c, a, d*
3. *b, c, d, a*
4. *d, b, c, a*

26. The stability of a type of bedform varies with ....

1. mean flow velocity and sediment grain size
2. response of sediment substratum to flow shear
3. bedload and suspension load
4. low velocity and substrate condition

27. An antiformal syncline is a fold which:

1. closes upward on the profile section and has the oldest rock at the core of the fold
2. closes downward on the profile section and has the youngest rock at the core of the fold
3. closes upward on the profile section and has the youngest rock at the core of the fold
4. closes downward on the profile section and has the oldest rock at the core of the fold

28. Which one of the following ore deposit types generally does NOT form in continental settings?

1. Porphyry Cu-Mo
2. Volcanogenic massive sulfides
3. Granite-related Sn-W
4. Unconformity-related U

29. A very high T/P is characteristic of ....
(T = Temperature; P = Pressure)

1. burial metamorphism
2. shock metamorphism
3. orogenic metamorphism
4. contact metamorphism

30. Which one of the following mass extinction events is the largest?

1. Triassic-Jurassic
2. Permian-Triassic
3. Cretaceous-Palaeogene
4. Late Ordovician

31. .... terminates downstream against a steep slope at the foot of which the stream that carved the valley disappears underground into a cave system.

1. Beheaded valley 2. Bolson
3. Blind valley 4. Hanging valley

32. Barchans and transverse dunes generally form under .... sand-transporting wind regime.

1. Unimodal
2. Bimodal
3. Multimodal
4. Alternately reversing

33. Past high sea levels or shorelines CANNOT be inferred from ....

1. Marine terraces 2. Raised beaches
3. Strandlines 4. Sea stacks

34. Which one of the following indices quantifies how much a river deviates from a straight path in a plan view?

1. Stream gradient 2. Sinuosity
3. Braiding 4. Concavity

35. Which one of the following criteria is used to subdivide moist climates according to Thornthwaite's 1948 climate classification scheme?

1. Aridity Index
2. Humidity Index
3. Moisture efficiency
4. Hydric efficiency

36. Which one of the following soil types is NOT a 'pedalfer'?

1. Podzol 2. Chernozem
3. Red soils 4. Lateritic soils

37. Which one of the following terms best describes genetically different interfertile populations within the same species formed as inheritable, permanent, and irreversible adaptations to the local environment?

1. Ecotypes 2. Ecotopes
3. Ecads 4. Ecotones

38. Eskers are formed by ....

1. Ice wedging
2. Frost heaving
3. Sub-glacial streams
4. Fluvial deposition in outwash plain

39. Satellite altimetry data indicate that from 1993 to 2024, the global mean sea level has risen approximately by ....

1. 25 cm 2. 20 cm
3. 16 cm 4. 10 cm

40. Which one of the following carbonate rich materials often occurs within the soil profile?

1. Calcrete 2. Tufa
3. Aeolianite 4. Speleothem

41. The speed of the Earth in its orbit around the Sun, assuming a circular orbit, is about ...., given that the Sun-Earth distance is 150×10^9 m.

1. 20 km/s 2. 30 km/s
3. 40 km/s 4. 50 km/s

42. If 60000 nT is the magnitude of Earth's magnetic field at the geomagnetic North Pole, what will be its magnitude (in nT) at a height of 6371 km at the same location?

1. 60000
2. 30000
3. 15000
4. 7500

43. If the Earth had a uniform density from the surface to the center of the Earth, then the acceleration due to gravity 'g' would be maximum at ....

1. the Earth's surface
2. 35 km depth
3. 2900 km depth
4. 5200 km depth

44. Decrease in temperature within the mantle transition zone results in ....

1. deepening of both 410 km and 660 km discontinuities
2. shallowing of both 410 km and 660 km discontinuities
3. shallowing of 410 km and deepening of 660 km discontinuities
4. deepening of 410 km and shallowing of 660 km discontinuities

45. Which one of the following statements about earthquakes is CORRECT?

1. Intensity is measured using the Richter scale.
2. Deep earthquakes occur in the lower mantle.
3. Small earthquakes may have a negative magnitude.
4. The magnitude decreases with epicentral distance.

46. Presence of fluid in the Earth's core is indicated by ....

1. shadow zone of S wave
2. shadow zone of P wave
3. refraction of S wave from different boundaries within the Earth
4. refraction of P wave from different boundaries within the Earth

47. If the density of the medium is doubled keeping all elastic constants unchanged, then the ratio of P wave velocity to the S wave velocity will become .... the previous ratio.

1. $\frac{1}{\sqrt{2}}$ times
2. half of
3. the same as
4. twice

48. The mineral that is used in hydrophone for detecting pressure waves is ....

1. muscovite
2. olivine
3. calcite
4. quartz

49. The GPS derived ellipsoid height (*h*) and geoid undulation (N) at a location (A) in the Indian subcontinent are 250 m and –35.5 m, respectively. What would be the height of 'A' above the geoid?

1. 285.5 m
2. 214.5 m
3. – 285.5 m
4. – 214.5 m

50. A flux-gate magnetometer installed at a geomagnetic observatory has recorded the following readings, what would be its location?

N-S component; 27,000 nT

E-W component; 18,000 nT

Vertical component; 40,000 nT

1. North Pole
2. Northern mid-latitude
3. Southern mid-latitude
4. South Pole

51. .... in the atmospheric boundary layer is primarily caused by wind shear.

1. Convective turbulence
2. Mechanical turbulence
3. Laminar flow
4. Free convection

52. The atmosphere becomes conditionally unstable when ....

1. the environmental lapse rate is less than the dry adiabatic lapse rate but greater than the moist adiabatic lapse rate.

2. the environmental lapse rate is greater than both dry and moist adiabatic lapse rate.
3. the environmental lapse rate is less than both moist and dry adiabatic lapse rate.
4. the atmosphere is saturated, and the environmental lapse rate is lower than the moist adiabatic lapse rate.

53. Why do tropical cyclones rarely form within 5°N - 5°S?

1. High atmospheric moisture suppresses convection.
2. Sea surface temperatures are too warm in this region to allow the spin-up required for tropical cyclones.
3. The Coriolis force is too weak to support the development of relative vorticity.
4. Wind shear is the strongest near the equator.

54. Which of the following best describes the subtropical jet stream behaviour over South Asia during the summer monsoon season?

1. It shifts equatorward, enhancing convection.
2. It remains stationary over subtropics due to inadequate land heating.
3. It reverses direction and flows westward across the Indian subcontinent.
4. It shifts northward, allowing deep tropical convection to expand poleward.

55. Air parcels warmer than the environment ....

1. acquire acceleration upward.
2. acquire acceleration downward.
3. exhibit Brunt-Vaisala oscillation.
4. remain at the same location.

56. The spacing of isobars on a surface weather map gives an indication of the ....

1. wind direction
2. wind speed
3. temperature of the atmospheric column
4. stability of the atmosphere

57. What would be the centrifugal force due to rotation of the Earth experienced by an air parcel of mass 1 kg at the equator? (Given radius of the Earth is 6371 km)

1. 7 N
2. 0.5 N
3. 0.03 N
4. 0.006 N

58. The southwesterly winds in the lower troposphere during the Indian summer monsoon over the Arabian Sea are primarily due to ....

1. rotation of the Earth
2. latent heat release
3. land-ocean temperature contrast
4. moisture effect

59. Which of the following sequence of weather systems is from the largest to the smallest size?

1. Tropical cyclone, Extratropical cyclone, Thunderstorm, Tornado
2. Extratropical cyclone, Tropical cyclone, Thunderstorm, Tornado
3. Tropical cyclone, Extratropical cyclone, Tornado, Thunderstorm
4. Extratropical cyclone, Tornado, Tropical cyclone, Thunderstorm

60. Which one of the following conditions prevents air from rising freely in the atmosphere?

1. Surface air converging near a low-pressure zone
2. A deep layer of cumulonimbus clouds
3. A temperature inversion
4. Divergence of air aloft

61. The pristine organic matter of marine origin has .... C/N, and .... $\delta^{13}C$, as compared to those of C_4 plant-derived terrestrial organic matter.

1. lower, higher
2. lower, lower
3. higher, lower
4. higher, higher

62. The rainwater precipitating from clouds, formed by the evaporation of seawater, contains relatively

1. higher ^{18}O than that in the cloud, but lower than that in seawater
2. higher ^{16}O than that in the cloud, but lower than that in seawater
3. higher ^{18}O than that in both the cloud and seawater
4. higher ^{16}O than that in both the cloud and seawater

63. The surface sediments collected from a water depth of 6500 m in the central Indian Ocean will contain:

1. Foraminifera, Ostracodes, Pteropods
2. Ostracodes, Diatoms, Radiolaria
3. Diatoms, Radiolaria, Silicoflagellates
4. Radiolaria, Silicoflagellates, Foraminifera

64. The vertical profile of dissolved oxygen in the ocean is almost a mirror image of the profile of:

1. Temperature
2. Salinity
3. Argon
4. Phosphate

65. Which one of the following wavelength bands is referred to as Photosynthetically Active Radiation (PAR)?

1. 100 nm – 400 nm
2. 400 nm – 700 nm
3. 700 nm – 1000 nm
4. 1000 nm – 1300 nm

66. What would be the slope of a linear regression line between concentrations of NO_3^- (Y-axis) and PO_4^{3-} (X-axis) in the global ocean?

1. 1
2. 6
3. 16
4. 24

67. In the context of increasing CO_2 concentration and resultant 'Ocean Acidification', which one of the following group of organisms will be most affected in the marine environment?

1. Fish
2. Bivalve shellfish
3. Squid
4. Sea cucumber

68. Ocean color monitoring-based phyto-plankton pigments are used to identify potential fishing zones (PFZ). Which of the following satellites is used in the identification of PFZs?

1. INSAT-3DR
2. Oceansat 2
3. SARAL-ALtika
4. SCATSAT

69. With every 10 m increase in ocean water depth, pressure increases by ....

1. 100 mbar
2. 10000 mbar
3. 10 mbar
4. 1000 mbar

70. Which one of the following is more directly influencing the latent heat flux of the surface ocean?

1. Short-wave radiation
2. Thermocline of the ocean
3. Marine Boundary Layer Turbulence
4. Surface Ocean Chlorophyll-a

PART-C

71. If minerals of an igneous protolith are isotopically re-equilibrated during a short episode of metamorphism, its Rb-Sr mineral isochron will yield

1. age of metamorphism and lower initial Sr isotopic ratio than the protolith's initial Sr isotopic ratio.
2. age of metamorphism and higher initial Sr isotopic ratio than the protolith's initial Sr isotopic ratio.
3. age of protolith and the same initial Sr isotopic ratio as that of the protolith.
4. geologically meaningless age.

72. The meeting point of the Pacific, Philippine, and Eurasian Plates off central Japan is defined by what type of triple junction?

1. RRR
2. RTF
3. TTF
4. TTT

73. Match the characteristic mineral assemblage (Column-I) with the corresponding metamorphic condition (Column-II)

Column-I	Column-II
A. sapphirine + quartz + garnet	P. medium P, medium T
B. garnet + omphacite + coesite + rutile	Q. ultrahigh T
C. garnet + biotite + quartz + plagioclase	R. high P, low T
D. andalusite + quartz + plagioclase + biotite	S. ultrahigh P
	T. low P, medium T

Choose the correct option

1. A – T; B – P; C – S; D – Q
2. A – Q; B – S; C – R; D – P
3. A – Q; B – S; C – P; D – T
4. A – S; B – Q; C – P; D – T

74. A rock contains 60% olivine, 30% clinopyroxene and 10% orthopyroxene by weight, and has 150 ppm of a trace element X. What would be the concentration of X in the melt after 10% equilibrium melting? (Given: mineral-melt distribution coefficients of X for olivine, clinopyroxene and orthopyroxene are 0.006, 0.09 and 0.02, respectively)

1. 1160 ppm
2. 420 ppm
3. 11.6 ppm
4. 0.116 ppm

75. Consider the following reaction involving zinc-chloride complex in a hydrothermal fluid.

$$ZnCl_n^{2-n} + H_2S_{(aqueous)} \leftrightarrow ZnS_{(solid)} + 2H^+ + nCl$$

Which one of the following would NOT lead to precipitation of sphalerite?

1. The fluid passes through a region where bacterial sulfate reduction is occurring.
2. The fluid passes through limestone
3. The fluid mixes with the groundwater with low Cl content
4. The fluid mixes with brine.

76. Based on the structure depicted in the diagram, chose the correct statement.

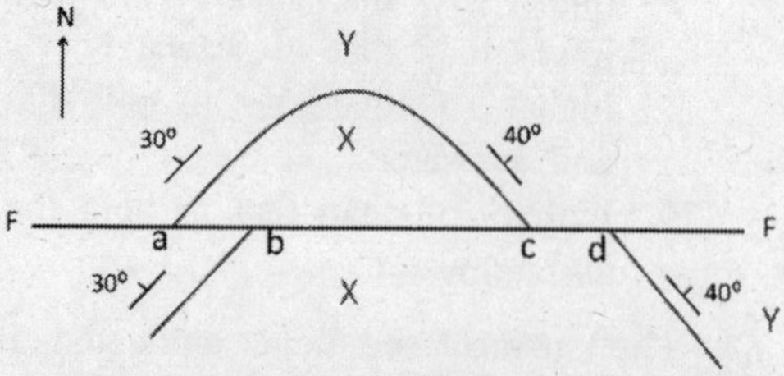

X, Y-lithounits, F-F:Fault plane trace, ab-cd, — Orientation of X-Y lithocontact

1. Dip-slip normal fault across an antiform with southern block is down thrown
2. Strike-slip fault across an antiform with sinistral (left lateral) sense of movement
3. Strike-slip fault across an antiform with dextral (right lateral) sense of movement
4. Reclined fold affected by a fault with sinistral sense of movement

77. How does the direction of fold hinge of early and late fold vary in type 1 superposed fold interference pattern across the axial plane?

1. Fold-hinge plunge directions of early and late folds will remain the same.
2. Plunge directions of early fold hinge changes across late fold axial plane, but direction of late fold hinge remains the same.
3. Plunge direction of early fold hinge remains the same but the plunge direction of the late fold hinge changes across the early fold axial plane.
4. Both early and late fold hinges change direction of plunge, when they cross each other's axial planes.

78. Match the columns.

Column-I	Column-II
A. Stasis	P. Biogeography
B. Disparity	Q. Morphology
C. Exaptation	R. Incompleteness
D. Biostratinomy	S. Punctuated Equilibrium
	T. Feathers

Choose the correct option.

1. A – S; B – Q; C – T; D – R
2. A – S; B – T; C – Q; D – R
3. A – P; B – Q; C – S; D – T
4. A – Q; B – R; C – T; D – P

79. Arrange the following geological events in chronological order (oldest to youngest):

A. Evolution of Ediacaran Fauna
B. Deposition of Banded Iron Formations
C. Appearance of Planktic foraminifera
D. Appearance of Fish
E. Rajmahal Traps

Choose the correct option.

1. A – E – B – D – C
2. B – A – D – C – E
3. A – B – C – D – E
4. B – A – E – C – D

80. A type of garnet ($Mg_3\ Al_2Si_3O_{12}$) has 160 atoms per unit cell. The structure of the garnet belongs to the space group Ia3d. The number of atoms in the motif are ....

1. 20
2. 80
3. 160
4. 40

81. Which one of the following techniques CANNOT be used to date Early Pleistocene mammalian teeth?

1. Amino Acid Racemization
2. U-series dating
3. Electron Spin Resonance dating
4. Radiocarbon dating

82. The stomatal density during interglacial periods, compared to that during glacial periods, was ....

1. lower due to higher temperature
2. higher due to higher temperature
3. lower due to higher CO_2 concentration
4. higher due to lower CO_2 concentration

83. Match the columns on the sequence stratigraphic events with surfaces.

Column-1 (Events)	Column-2 (Surfaces)
A. Onset of forced regression	P. Maximum flooding surface
B. End of forced regression	Q. Correlative conformity
C. End of normal regression	R. Basal surface of forced regression
D. End of trans-gression	S. Maximum regressive surface

Choose the correct option:

1. A – R; B – Q; C – S; D – P
2. A – Q; B – S; C – P; D – R
3. A – R; B – S; C – Q; D – P
4. A – P; B – Q; C – S; D – R

84. Match the sedimentary features in Column-I with their depositional regimes in Column-II.

Column-I (Features)	Column-II (Depositional regime)
A. Double mud drapes	P. Aeolian
B. Faceted pebble	Q. Tidal
C. Epsilon cross-strata	R. Glacial
D. Reverse graded cross-strata	S. Fluvial

Choose the correct option.

1. A – R; B – S; C – P; D – Q
2. A – Q; B – R; C – S; D – P
3. A – P; B – S; C – Q; D – R
4. A – Q; B – S; C – R; D – P

85. Which one of the following pairs of stratigraphic units and their corresponding characteristic properties is NOT correct?

1. Kurnool Group – Neoproterozoic siliciclastic-carbonate shelf deposits.
2. Semri Group – Mesoproterozoic mixed carbonate-siliciclastic shallow marine deposits
3. Bagh Group – Triassic continental fluvial siliciclastic deposits.
4. Barail Group – Palaeogene siliciclastic shallow marine-delta deposits

86. The given phase diagram represents a binary peritectic system at one atmospheric pressure. What are the degrees of freedom at points A, B, C, and D?

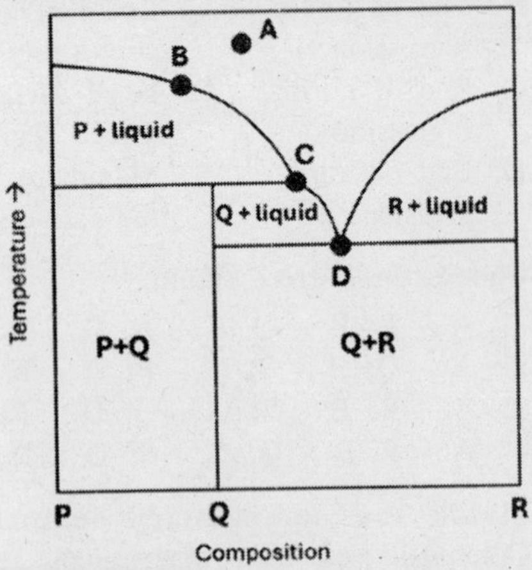

Choose the correct option.

1. A – 3; B – 2; C – 0; D – 0
2. A – 2; B – 1; C – 1; D – 0
3. A – 3; B – 2; C – 1; D – 0
4. A – 2; B – 1; C – 0; D – 0

87. Identify the MISMATCHED pair.

1. Ria – avulsion
2. Saltation – sediment grain transport
3. Riffle – depositional bar
4. Strath Terrace – rock-cut terrace

88. Consider the following statements (True or False) related to the Equilibrium Line (EL).

A. Net ablation generally increases down-glacier below the EL.
B. Net accumulation tends to increase up-glacier above the EL.
C. Net ablation generally increases up-glacier above the EL.
D. Net accumulation tends to increase down-glacier below the EL.

Choose the correct option.

1. A and B are True.
2. B and C are True.
3. C and D are True.
4. A and D are True.

89. Consider the following statements (True or False).

A. Waves with limited swash and stronger backwash withdraw sand and shingle to the nearshore zone.
B. Waves with limited backwash and stronger swash withdraw sand and shingle to the nearshore zone.
C. With a strong swash and lesser backwash, waves move sand and shingle laterally along the beach.
D. With a strong backwash and weaker swash, waves move sand and shingle up the beach.

Choose the correct option.

1. A and C are True.
2. B and C are True.
3. A and B are True.
4. B and D are True.

90. Identify the MISMATCHED pairs of geomorphic features.

A. Backswamp - Floodplain
B. Kame - Playa
C. Polje - Karst depression
D. Alveolus - Honeycomb weathering
E. Erg - River valley
F. Berm - Beach

Choose correct option

1. A and E
2. C and D
3. E and F
4. B and E

91. Match the columns.

Column-I	Column-II
A. Pediment	E. Streamlined wind-erosion forms
B. Playa	F. Predominantly wind deposited material dominated by silt
C. Yardang	G. A ridge or hill of sand deposited by wadi flow
D. Loess	H. At the base of a steep slope or mountain front
	I. Ephemeral lake in dryland

Choose the correct option

1. A – H, B – I, C – E, D – F
2. A – H, B – F, C – E, D – I
3. A – E, B – I, C – G, D – F
4. A – G, B – I, C – H, D – E

92. Consider the following statements about barchan dunes.

A. The horns of barchans point downwind, and barchans move in the downwind direction.

B. The horns of barchans point upwind, and barchans move in the upwind direction.

C. Barchans develop in areas of multi-directional winds and unlimited sand supply.

D. Barchans develop in areas of unidirectional winds and limited sand supply.

Choose the correct option.

1. A and B are incorrect
2. B and C are incorrect
3. C and D are incorrect
4. A and D are incorrect

93. **Statement A:** High values of hypsometric integral indicate a relatively large proportion of land at high elevation within the basin.

Statement B: Basins in which stream channels have incised deep valleys, leaving extensive areas of relatively high elevation, have low hypsometric integrals.

Based on the above statements, choose the correct option.

1. Both statements are incorrect.
2. Statement A is incorrect, but Statement B is correct
3. Statement A is correct, but Statement B is incorrect
4. Both statements are correct

94. Which one of the following sets includes landforms dominantly controlled by underlying lithology?

1. Cuestas – cockpits – hogbacks
2. Mesas – bajada – structural benches
3. Dyke ridges – shore platforms – spits
4. Knickpoints – natural levees – inselbergs

95. Which one of the following sets includes typical landforms/features of granitic terrains?

1. Bornhardt, inselberg, tors, tafoni
2. Inselberg, tarn, hogback, bornhardt
3. Tors, cuesta, uvala, tafoni
4. Inselberg, polje, mesa, bornhardt

96. Identify the type of doline in the given figure.

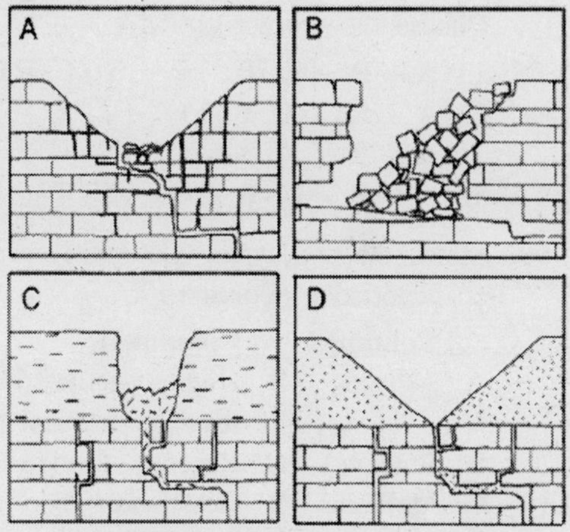

1. A–Suffusion; B–Solution; C–Dropout; D–Collapse
2. A–Dropout; B–Collapse; C–Suffusion; D–Solution
3. A–Collapse; B–Dropout; C–Suffusion; D–Solution
4. A–Solution; B–Collapse; C–Dropout; D–Suffusion

97. Which one of the following criteria is followed by India Meteorological Department to measure the intensity of tropical cyclone in the North Indian Ocean?

1. Estimated 3-minute maximum sustained winds
2. Estimated 10-minute maximum sustained winds
3. Estimated 3-second maximum wind gusts
4. Estimated 10-second maximum wind gusts

98. Match the columns.

List-I	List-II
A. Chinook	P. Rhone valley
B. Harmattan	Q. West Africa
C. Mistral	R. Eastern Slope of Rockies

List-III

X. Hot dry wind associated with air flow from subtropical highs

Y. Strong cold wind associated with regional low-pressure system

Z. Adiabatically warmed dry wind

Choose the correct option

1. A – R – Z; B – P – Y; C – Q – X
2. A – R – X; B – Q – Z; C – P – Y
3. A – R – Z; B – Q – X; C – P – Y
4. A – P – Z; B – Q – X; C – R – Y

99. Match the soil types (Column-I) and their characteristics (Column-II).

Column-I	Column-II
A. Alfisols	P. Highly weathered soils of the inter tropical regions
B. Entisols	Q. Recently formed soils
C. Mollisols	R. Grassland soils of steppes and prairies
D. Oxisols	S. High base status soils with argillic horizon

Choose the correct option.

1. A – S, B – Q, C – R, D – P
2. A – R, B – Q, C – P, D – S
3. A – S, B – P, C – R, D – Q
4. A – P, B – S, C – Q, D – R

100. Consider the following statements

A. At low pH, kaolinite's anion exchange capacity helps to reduce nitrogen loss from soils.

B. Phosphate availability is good in highly weathered soils.

C. Fixation of K^+ and NH_4^+ by high-charge smectites limits soil fertility.

D. Illite has a higher cation exchange capacity than smectite.

Choose the correct option

1. A and B are true; C and D are false
2. A and C are true; B and D are false
3. A, B and C are true; D is false
4. B, C and D are true; A is false

101. The below diagram presents different hypothetical biogeographic conditions in islands in the framework of Immigration-Extinction-Isolation-Area relationship.

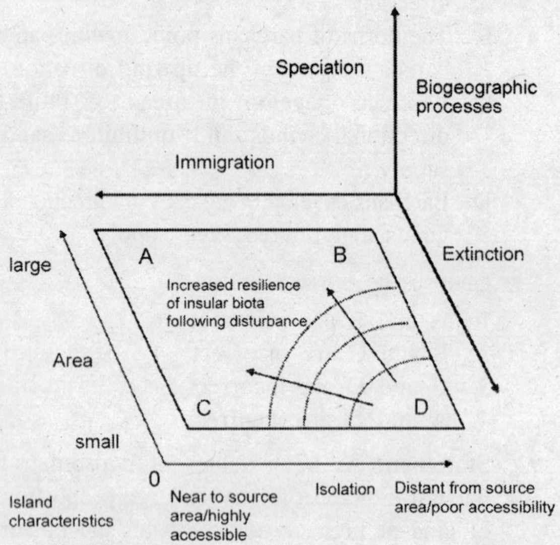

Which one of the following conditions represents region A in the above figure?

1. Low species richness, low endemicity and high turnover.
2. Moderate to high species richness, low endemicity and low turnover
3. Moderate to low species richness, low endemicity and high turnover
4. Moderate to high species richness, high endemicity and low turnover

102. Which of the following statements are NOT true about the UTM Grid co-ordinate of Sydney (33.8688°S, 151.0093°E)? (Given that Easting is 334368.63 and Northing is 6250948.35)

A. UTM zone for Sydney is 56

B. UTM band for Sydney is H

C. Sydney is located to the east of the zone central meridian
D. Distance of Sydney from the equator is 6250 km.

Choose the correct option.

1. A and B are not true
2. C and D are not true
3. A and C are not true
4. B and D are not true

103. In a resistivity survey, a pair of current electrodes (C_1 and C_2) and a pair of potential electrodes (P_1 and P_2) are located along a profile line at the following coordinates: P_1 at 0 m, C_1 at 40 m, C_2 at 60 m and P_2 at 100 m. The geometrical factor (in m) for this array will be ....

1. 60 π   2. 120 π
3. 180 π   4. 240 π

104. Consider the following statements about the induced polarization method.

Statement I: Electrode polarization is caused by the change in the mobility of ions in the electrolyte and electrons in metallic minerals.

Statement II: The chargeability is a dimensionless quantity.

Choose the correct option.

1. Both the statements are correct.
2. Statement I is correct and statement II is incorrect.
3. Statement I is incorrect and statement II is correct.
4. Both statements are incorrect

105. Consider the following statements about data processing in Magneto Telluric (MT) method.

Statement I: The rotation of impedance tensor Z in MT method gives the strike of the subsurface structures.

Statement II: In MT method the quantity $Z_D = |Z_{xx}Z_{yy}\text{-}Z_{xy}Z_{yx}|$ is not variable with rotation.

Choose the correct option.

1. Both statements are correct.
2. Statement I is correct and statement II is incorrect.
3. Statement I is incorrect and statement II is correct.
4. Both statements are incorrect.

106. The strike of a subsurface 2D conductor lies in N-S direction in a survey area. For VLF electromagnetic survey, four transmitters A, B, C and D are available in North, East, South and West directions, respectively. Which pair of transmitters will be the most suitable for VLF electromagnetic measurement over this conductor?

1. A and B   2. A and C
3. B and C   4. B and D

107. Zero-offset reflection seismic data are acquired over a subsurface consisting of a single dipping reflector with a true dip of 30 degrees. If the slope of the reflection event in the zero offset section is 0.5 s/km, the interval velocity above the reflector is .... km/s.

1. 0.5   2. 1.5
3. 2   4. 2.5

108. Which one of the following best describes a class 3 AVO response?

1. Strong positive amplitude at near-offset that decreases with offset
2. Small near-offset amplitude that decreases with offset
3. Strong negative amplitude at near-offset that becomes more negative with offset
4. Flat amplitude response with no offset dependence

109. In a geophysical experiment dealing with two model parameters, the data set d and Generalized matrix G are given as:

$$G = \begin{bmatrix} 2 & 3 \\ 1 & 1 \\ 1 & 2 \end{bmatrix} \qquad d = \begin{bmatrix} 1 \\ 2 \\ 3 \end{bmatrix}$$

Data resolution matrix for this case is ......

1. $\begin{bmatrix} 1 & 0 \\ 0 & 1 \end{bmatrix}$

2. $\begin{bmatrix} 1 & 0 & 0 \\ 0 & 1 & 0 \\ 0 & 0 & 1 \end{bmatrix}$

3. $\begin{bmatrix} 2/3 & 1/3 & 1/3 \\ 1/3 & 2/3 & -1/3 \\ 1/3 & -1/3 & 2/3 \end{bmatrix}$

4. $\begin{bmatrix} 2/3 & 1 \\ 0 & 1/3 \end{bmatrix}$

110. Which one of the following is the Z-transform of unit step function

$$u(n) = \begin{cases} 1 & \text{for } n \geq 0 \\ 0 & \text{for } n < 0 \end{cases} \; ?$$

1. $\dfrac{z}{1-z}$ 2. $\dfrac{z}{z-1}$
3. $\dfrac{z}{1+z}$ 4. $\dfrac{1}{1-z}$

111. The value of a signal $f(x, y)$ at (1, 0), (2, 0) and (3, 0) is obtained as 1, –1, 2, respectively. The value of first order numerical differentiation of this signal with respect to x axis at (2, 0) with minimum numerical error is:

1. 0.5 2. 3
3. –2 4. 2

112. Consider the following statements on Bouguer anomaly.

Statement-1: Bouguer gravity anomalies are typically negative over continental regions and generally positive over ocean basins.

Statement-2: The thicker continental crust exhibits a greater mass deficit relative to the reference ellipsoid, leading to negative Bouguer anomalies, while the thinner, denser, oceanic crust creates a relative mass excess, resulting in positive anomaly

Choose the correct option.

1. Both statement-1 and statement-2 are true, and statement-2 is the correct explanation for statement-1.
2. Both statement-1 and statement-2 are true, and statement-2 is not the correct explanation for statement-1.
3. Statement-1 is true, but statement-2 is false.
4. Statement-1 is false, but statement-2 is true.

113. An aeromagnetic survey was conducted at different altitudes over a buried iron orebody. The maximum vertical magnetic anomaly recorded was 50 nT at a flight altitude of 1500 m above sea level, and 15 nT at 3000 m above sea level. Assuming that the orebody can be approximated as a vertical magnetic dipole with a magnetic susceptibility contrast of 0.03, what is the approximate depth of the orebody (to the nearest integer)?

1. 825 m 1. 1561 m
3. 3300 m 4. 4950 m

114. In the Earth's magnetic field, the Nuclear Magnetic Resonance (NMR) frequency of proton varies from approximately 900 Hz near the magnetic equator to 4.2 kHz near the geomagnetic poles. Assuming the gyromagnetic ratio of proton is 0.042576 Hz/nT, what would be the approximate average rate of change of Earth's magnetic field strength between these two locations?

1. 7.75 nT/m 2. 7.75 nT/km
3. 48.69 nT/km 4. 48.69 nT/m

115. The residual Bouguer gravity anomaly values at five different stations along a profile over a landfill are – 0.025 mGal, – 0.125 mGal, – 0.25 mGal, – 0.15 mGal, and – 0.003 mGal. What would be the maximum thickness of the landfill assuming that the density contrast between the landfill and the bedrock is 300 kg/m^3? (Given: G = 6.6729 × 10^{-11} $kg^{-1}.m^3.s^{-2}$). (Roundoff to the nearest integer).

1. 2 m
2. 20 m
3. 200 m
4. 400 m

116. Given the scalar potential $\phi(x, t)$ and vector potential $\varphi(x, t)$, the displacement field $u(x, t)$ can be expressed as:

1. $u(x, t) = \nabla.\phi\{x, t) + \nabla \times \varphi(x, t)$
2. $u(x, t) = \nabla\phi\{x, t) + \nabla \times \varphi(x, t)$
3. $u(x, t) = \nabla.\phi\{x, t) + \nabla.\varphi(x, t)$
4. $u(x, t) = \nabla\phi\{x, t) + \nabla.\varphi(x, t)$

117. An earthquake occurring at a depth of 10 km at 00 hr : 00 min : 00s generates a P-wave which arrives at a surface station at 00hr : 00 min : 03s. Assuming the crust to be Poisson solid with a shear velocity of 3.0 km/s, the epicentral distance is .... km. (Roundoff to the nearest integer).

1. 15
2. 14
3. 12
4. 10

118. Consider the following statements on formation evaluation in petroleum exploration.

Statement-I: GR log and NGS log show high API values for a clean sandstone bed containing heavy minerals.

Statement-II: The clean sandstone bed contains shale.

Choose the correct option.

1. Statement-I is true and statement-II is false.
2. Statement-I is false and statement-II is true.
3. Both statement-I and statement-II are true.
4. Both statement-I and statement-II are false.

119. Assuming the Rossby number is 0.27, and the wind field is circular, with wind speed of 12 m/s at a distance of 500 km from the center, what would be the magnitude of Coriolis parameter (s^{-1})?

1. 8.88 × 10^{-6}
2. 8.88 × 10^{-5}
3. 8.88 × 10^{-4}
4. 8.88 × 10^{-3}

120. While deriving the phase speed of the external gravity wave, which one of the following assumptions is NOT made?

1. fluid is compressible
2. fluid is homogenous
3. fluid is hydrostatic
4. fluid is inviscid

121. What would be the phase speed of Rossby wave solution in the absence of background flow for a fluid of depth H = 10^4 m, zonal wavelength L = 10^6 m (assuming zero meridional wavelength), meridional variation of Coriolis parameter $\beta = 10^{-11} m^{-1} s^{-1}$, acceleration due to gravity g = 9.8 m/s^2?

1. 0.253 m/s
2. – 0.253 m/s
3. 2.53 m/s
4. – 2.53 m/s

122. A satellite sensor observes an outgoing radiance of 10 $W/m^2/Sr/\mu m$ at a wavelength of 10 μm in the thermal infrared region. What is the approximate brightness temperature of the emitting surface, given the Planck function

$$B_\lambda(\lambda, T) = \frac{2hc^2}{\lambda^5} \frac{1}{\exp\left(\frac{hc}{\lambda k T}\right) - 1}$$

$B_\lambda(\lambda, T)$ is the spectral radiance with respect to wavelength (λ) in units of $W/m^2/Sr/m$?

h = Planck's constant = 6.626 × 10^{-34}Js

c = Speed of light = 3.0 × 10^8 m/s

k = Boltzmann constant = 1.381 × 10^{-23} J/K

λ = Wavelength in m

T = Absolute temperature in K

1. 350 K
2. 320 K
3. 290 K
4. 300 K

123. Match the columns.

Column I Stability condition	Column II Meteorological Scenario
A. Absolutely Unstable	I. A moist layer overlying a dry surface with CAPE present
B. Conditionally Unstable	II. Cloudy skies with consistent mechanical turbulence
C. Neutral	III. A hot summer afternoon with strong surface heating
D. Absolutely Stable	IV. A winter morning with a surface-based radiation inversion

Choose the correct option.

1. A-I, B-III, C-IV, D-II
2. A-IV, B-II, C-I, D-III
3. A-II, B-IV, C-III, D-I
4. A-III, B-I, C-II, D-IV

124. Identify the CORRECT statement about the shallow water approximation in atmospheric/oceanic motions.

1. Horizontal pressure gradient is independent of height.
2. It does not permit vertical motion.
3. It removes pressure variation.
4. It linearizes the momentum equation.

125. Match the columns on atmospheric data filtering.

Column-I (Application)	Column-II (Filters)
A. Hydrostatic balance	P. Gravity waves
B. Assign the time derivative of horizontal divergence to zero	Q. Vertically propagating sound waves
	R. Horizontally propagating sound waves

Choose the correct option.

1. A-Q; B-P 2. A-R; B-P
3. A-P; B-Q 4. A-P; B-R

126. Match the columns on atmospheric numerical modelling.

Column-I (Solution Method)	Column-II (Application)
A. Relaxation method	P. One dimensional linear advection equation
B. Explicit time differencing method	Q. Laplace equation
C. Successive Correction method	R. Objective analysis

Choose the correct option.

1. A-P; B-R; C-Q 2. A-Q; B-P; C-R
3. A-R; B-P; C-Q 4. A-Q; B-R; C-P

127. **Statement A:** Raoult's law is invoked to derive Kelvin's equation

Statement B: In a mixed cloud, ice particles grow at the expense of supercooled water droplets, only if the temperature of the cloud is above the triple point temperature of water.

From the given statements, choose the correct option.

1. statement A is correct, statement B is incorrect.
2. statement A is incorrect, statement B is correct.
3. both statements A and B are correct.
4. both statements A and B are incorrect.

128. The appearance of Tropical easterly jet, observed only during the Indian summer monsoon, is a manifestation of ....

1. Geostrophic wind balance
2. Gradient wind balance
3. Cyclostrophic wind balance
4. Thermal wind balance

129. Which one of the following waves is observed only in the Tropics?

1. Mixed Rossby-Gravity wave
2. Rossby wave
3. Kelvin wave
4. Inertia-gravity wave

130. What would be the saturation vapor pressure (e_s) at 10°C, if e_s at 0°C is 611 Pa? (latent heat of vaporization, $L_v = 2.5 \times 10^6$ J/kg; Specific gas constant for water vapor, R_v = 461 J/kg/K)

1. 950 Pa
2. 1100 Pa
3. 1232 Pa
4. 1360 Pa

131. A dry air parcel at pressure level of 850 hPa has a temperature of 30°C. What would be its temperature if it is brought adiabatically to 1000 hPa? (Specific gas constant for dry air, R_d = 287 J/kg/K, specific heat of dry air at constant pressure (C_p) = 1005 J/kg/K)

1. 298 K
2. 318 K
3. 328 K
4. 308 K

132. Refer to the given diagram. Assuming the horizontal distance between two geopotential height contours on 500 hPa pressure-surface is 150 m, and Coriolis parameter is $10^{-4}s^{-1}$, where would you expect the difference between the speeds of the actual wind and the geostrophic wind to be the largest?

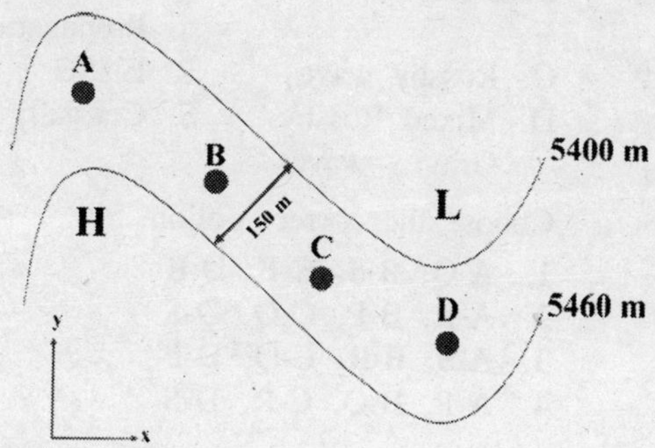

1. A
2. B
3. C
4. D

133. Match the columns on Tropical Cyclones (TC).

Column-I (TC features)	Column-II (Reason)
A. TC moves poleward	P. Conditional instability of second kind
B. Rapid intensification of TC	Q. Penetrative convection
C. TC forms over region of weak vertical wind shear	R. Conservation of absolute vorticity

1. A-P; B-Q; C-R
2. A-Q; B-R; C-P
3. A-R; B-P; C-Q
4. A-P; B-R; C-Q

134. **Statement-A:** Launching a satellite into a polar orbit requires a smaller launch vehicle as compared to that required to launch the same payload into a near-equatorial west to east orbit to the same altitude.

Statement-B: The angle of the Sun's rays on the Earth's surface remains constant for each satellite pass in a sun-synchronous orbit.

Based on the above statements, choose the correct option.

1. statement A is correct; statement B is incorrect
2. statement A is incorrect; statement B is correct
3. both statement A and statement B are correct
4. both statement A and statement B are incorrect

135. **Statement A:** Illite dominates the clays in the surface sediments of the northwestern Bay of Bengal, whereas smectite content is comparatively high in the southwestern Bay of Bengal.

Statement B: The catchment of Ganga and Brahmaputra rivers is mainly the Himalayas, whereas Krishna and Cauvery drain through the Peninsular India.

Based on the above statements, which of the following is correct?

1. Both A and B are incorrect.
2. A is correct and B is incorrect.
3. Both A and B are correct, and B explains A.
4. Both A and B are correct, but B does not explain A.

136. Match the following chronological tools with their age estimation suitability.

Chronological Tool	Age Limit
A. Radiocarbon	I. Ordovician to Triassic
B. $\delta^{18}O$ of foraminifera	II. Phanerozoic
C. Biostratigraphy	III. > 50,000 years
D. Conodonts	IV. Pliocene-Pleistocene

Choose the correct option.

1. A-III; B-I; C-IV; D-II
2. A-II; B-IV; C-III; D-I
3. A-III; B-IV; C-II; D-I
4. A-IV; B-III; C-I; D-II

137. Statement-A: *Globigerinoides ruber* is a mixed layer dweller, whereas *Neogloboquadrina dutertrei* thrives in thermocline waters.

Statement-B: The difference in shell composition of *G. ruber* and *N. dutertrei* is a proxy to reconstruct changes in water column stratification.

Based on the above statements, which of the following is correct?

1. Both A and B are correct, but A does not explain B.
2. Both A and B are incorrect.
3. A is correct and B is incorrect.
4. Both A and B are correct, and A explains B.

138. Statement A: The global sea level was ~100 m higher during the Last Glacial Maximum, as compared to present.

Statement B: $\delta^{18}O$ of foraminifera was lower by ~1.0% during the Meghalayan Stage as compared to that during the Last Glacial Maximum.

Based on the above two statements, choose the correct option.

1. A is incorrect and B is correct.
2. Both A and B are correct.
3. Both A and B are incorrect.
4. A is correct and B is incorrect.

139. What is the mixed layer cooling of an ocean in 10-days whose surface net heat flux is –50 W/m^2, with a mixed layer depth of 50 m? (Given: the density of water is 1000 kg/m^3, specific heat capacity is 4000 J/kg/K, and one day is equal to 10^5 seconds)

1. – 2.5°C
2. – 1.5°C
3. – 0.15°C
4. – 0.25°C

140. Match the columns on oceanographic phenomena.

Column-I	Column-II
A. Kelvin waves	P. Cross Equatorial transport
B. Delayed oscillator	Q. Westward Propagation
C. Rossby wave	R. ENSO
D. Mixed Rossby Gravity waves	S. Coastally trapped

Choose the correct option.

1. A-Q, B-S, C-P, D-R
2. A-R, B-P, C-Q, D-S
3. A-S, B-R, C-Q, D-P
4. A-P, B-Q, C-R, D-S

141. In the given diagram the values are depth-averaged currents in the ocean of 100 km × 100 km dimension. What is the rate of convergence to be added to make the flow geostrophic?

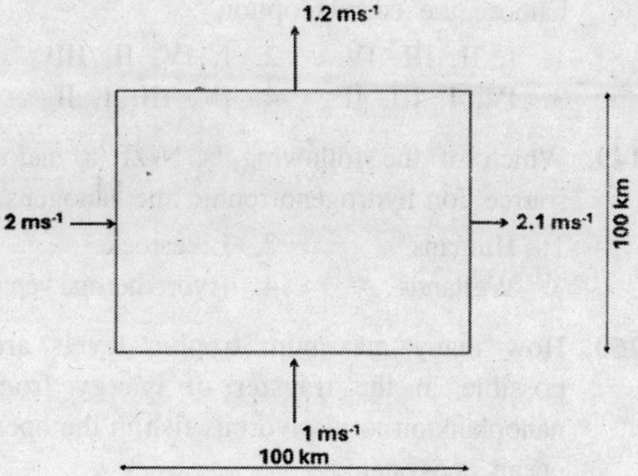

1. 3×10^{-5} s^{-1} 2. -3×10^{-5} s^{-1}
3. 0.3×10^{-5} s^{-1} 4. -0.3×10^{-5} s^{-1}

142. Match the columns on ocean currents.

Column-I	Column-II
A. Somali Current	P. Seasonally reversing
B. West India Coastal Current	Q. Eastward
C. Winter Monsoon Current	R. Western boundary current
D. Wyrtki Jet	S. Westward

Choose the correct option.
1. A-R, B-Q, C-P, D-S
2. A-R, B-P, C-S, D-Q
3. A-Q, B-P, C-R, D-S
4. A-P, B-Q, C-R, D-S

143. Match the columns for the contemporary ocean.

Column-I	Column-II	Column-III
A. Respiration	X Increases	P. Dissolved Inorganic Carbon (DIC)
B. Primary Production	Y Decreases	Q. Alkalinity
C. Biogenic carbonate production		R. Acidification

Choose the correct option.
1. A-Y-Q, B-X-P, C-Y-R
2. A-X-R, B-X-Q, C-Y-P
3. A-X-P, B-Y-Q, C-X-R
4. A-X-P, B-X-Q, C-Y-R

144. Which one of the following best represents [*x*] in the given figure of an ocean-water profile from an intense oxygen minimum zone?

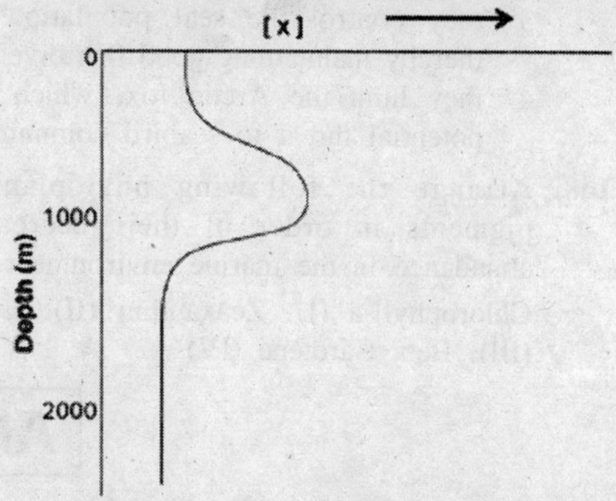

1. CO_2 2. O_2
3. N_2O 4. Chlorophyll

145. A. Sodium is more abundant in seawater than calcium, while reverse is true for rivers.

B. Calcium is used to form shells of marine organisms, while sodium remains largely unused.

Based on the above statements (A & R), which one of the following is CORRECT?
1. Both A and R are true; R explains A
2. Both A and R are true; R doesn't explain A
3. A is true and R is false
4. A is false, but R is true

146. The peak of primary production is shallower than the peak of chlorophyll in the tropical ocean water column profiles because
1. iron is high in the surface water.
2. deeper water is rich in dissolved inorganic carbon.
3. light and nutrients are optimum at shallower depth.
4. photosynthesis rate is high at the depth of chlorophyll maximum.

147. Polar bears are considered as "keystone species" in the Arctic ecosystem because:
1. they hunt the reindeer and reduce the grazing pressure on Tundra.
2. they stay in the Arctic during winter by undergoing hibernation.
3. they control the seal population and thereby maintaining good fish diversity.
4. they hunt the Arctic fox, which is a potential threat to seabird community.

148. Arrange the following phytoplankton pigments in order of their decreasing abundance in the marine environment.

Chlorophyll-a (I), Zeaxanthin (II), Lutein (III), Beta Carotene (IV)

Choose the correct option.

1. I, II, III, IV	2. I, IV, II, III
3. IV, I, III, II	4. IV, III, I, II

149. Which of the following is NOT a major source for hydrogenotrophic methanogens?

1. Humans	2. Livestock
3. Wetlands	4. Hydrothermal vents

150. How many maximum trophic levels are possible in the transfer of energy from nanoplankton to piscivorous fish in the open ocean ecosystem?

1. 4	2. 6
3. 3	4. 5

ANSWERS

1	**2**	**3**	**4**	**5**	**6**	**7**	**8**	**9**	**10**
2	3	3	3	2	1	4	4	4	2
11	**12**	**13**	**14**	**15**	**16**	**17**	**18**	**19**	**20**
3	1	1	3	1	2	3	2	3	2
21	**22**	**23**	**24**	**25**	**26**	**27**	**28**	**29**	**30**
2	2	4	2	2	1	3	2	4	2
31	**32**	**33**	**34**	**35**	**36**	**37**	**38**	**39**	**40**
3	1	4	2	1	2	1	3	4	1
41	**42**	**43**	**44**	**45**	**46**	**47**	**48**	**49**	**50**
2	4	1	3	3	1	3	4	1	2
51	**52**	**53**	**54**	**55**	**56**	**57**	**58**	**59**	**60**
2	1	3	4	1	2	3	1	2	3
61	**62**	**63**	**64**	**65**	**66**	**67**	**68**	**69**	**70**
2	1	3	4	2	3	2	2	4	3
71	**72**	**73**	**74**	**75**	**76**	**77**	**78**	**79**	**80**
2	4	3	1	4	2	4	1	2	2
81	**82**	**83**	**84**	**85**	**86**	**87**	**88**	**89**	**90**
4	3	1	2	3	4	1	1	1	4
91	**92**	**93**	**94**	**95**	**96**	**97**	**98**	**99**	**100**
1	2	3	1	1	4	1	3	1	2
101	**102**	**103**	**104**	**105**	**106**	**107**	**108**	**109**	**110**
2	2	2	2	1	2	3	3	3	2
111	**112**	**113**	**114**	**115**	**116**	**117**	**118**	**119**	**120**
1	1	2	2	2	2	3	1	2	1
121	**122**	**123**	**124**	**125**	**126**	**127**	**128**	**129**	**130**
2	4	4	1	1	2	4	4	1	3
131	**132**	**133**	**134**	**135**	**136**	**137**	**138**	**139**	**140**
2	1	3	2	3	3	4	1	4	3
141	**142**	**143**	**144**	**145**	**146**	**147**	**148**	**149**	**150**
4	2	2	3	1	3	3	2	4	2

Previous Years' Paper

Joint CSIR-UGC NET/JRF

Earth, Atmospheric, Ocean & Planetary Sciences

FEBRUARY-2025

(Exam held on 28-02-2025)

PART-A

1. If a map is placed in such a manner that southwest becomes east, then what will north become?

1. Northeast
2. Southwest
3. Northwest
4. Southeast

2. If water of pH 8 is diluted 100 times with neutral water (pH = 7) then it will:

1. become acidic.
2. remain basic.
3. become neutral.
4. become heavy.

3. Fifteen distinct points are randomly placed on the circumference of a circle. How many distinct straight lines at the most can be formed by pairs among these points?

1. 105 2. 455
3. 30 4. 210

4. In a population of microbial cells, the initial population is 50, and the growth rate is 0.1 per hour. If the population grows exponentially, what will the approximate size of the population be after 10 hours?

1. 51 2. 82
3. 136 4. 156

5. The given figure shows data points and a line fit by least squares method between profit in ice-cream business and mean temperature (T) for a city. Which one of the following inferences can definitely be drawn? (The correlation coefficient r is also given in the figure)

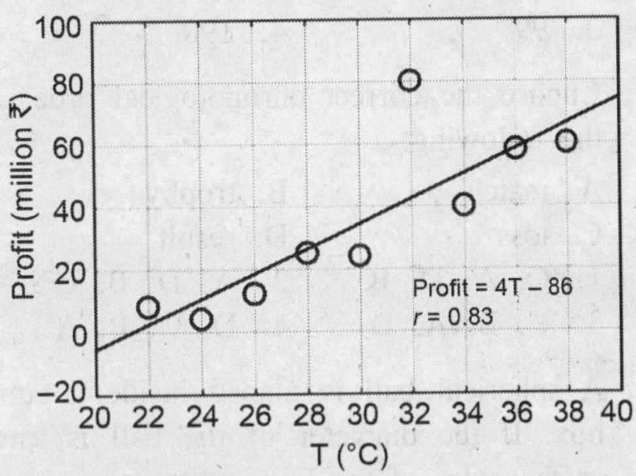

1. The sum of the squared values of differences between the observed and expected values of temperature is the minimum.
2. 83% of the variation in profit is explained by the variation in temperature.
3. Rise in temperature causes profit to increase.
4. At 25°C, estimated profit is ₹ 14 million.

1. 2 **2.** 2 **3.** 1 **4.** 3 **5.** 4

6. The average of seven numbers is 71. If we exclude one of these numbers, the average becomes 75. What is that number?

1. 75 2. 74
3. 73 4. 47

7. Choose the option to fill in the blank that will make the following statement logically correct:

THE NUMBER OF OCCURRENCES OF THE LETTER "N" IN THIS SENTENCE IS CORRECTLY COUNTED AS ....

1. SIX 2. SEVEN
3. EIGHT 4. NINE

8. In a board meeting of 20 directors, 6 shook everyone else's hands but the remaining 14 did not shake each another's. The total number of handshakes in the meeting was:

1. 26 2. 84
3. 99 4. 190

9. Choose the correct chronological order of the following:-

A. match B. trophy
C. toss D. result

1. C, A, D, B 2. A, D, B, C
3. C, B, A, D 4. D, C, B, A

10. A spherical ball is placed inside a cubic box. If the diameter of the ball is same as the sides of the box, what approximate percentage of volume will be empty?

1. 12% 2. 24%
3. 36% 4. 48%

11. If I walked east 100 metres, turned right and walked 60 metres, turned left and walked 150 metres and turned left again, I would be facing:

1. East 2. North
3. West 4. South

12. The words TEST, EXAM and EAST are coded as 1382, 2182 and 1937 but not necessarily in that order. How would the word MATE be coded?

1. 9321
2. 7321
3. 7312
4. 1982

13. All those who pass an entrance test take admission into a certain institute. Out of these, some graduate with a degree in 2 years while some fail and are removed, and all graduates from that institute get jobs in the same year. In 2022, no one took admission in that institute. Which of the following does NOT follow necessarily?

1. No one wrote the entrance test in 2022
2. No one passed the entrance test in 2022
3. No one graduated from the institute in 2024
4. No one got a job from the institute in 2024

14. Frank, Sam, Tom and David came first, second, third and fourth in a race but not necessarily in this order. Only one had first letter of position matching that of his name. If Tom came first and Sam did not come second then

1. David came third
2. Frank came fourth
3. David came fourth
4. Sam came fourth

15. In the fictional country of Numberia, which of the following provinces is the odd one out?

1. SONECON
2. CUGHUSTER
3. FATWOHUM
4. CAFIVENGUS

6. 4 **7.** 4 **8.** 3 **9.** 1 **10.** 4 **11.** 2 **12.** 2 **13.** 1 **14.** 2 **15.** 2

16. Which of the following pie-charts depicts the distribution of students in the five subjects such that physics and chemistry get equal number of students, 40% of the total go to the life sciences and remaining are equally divided into maths and earth sciences?

1. 
2. 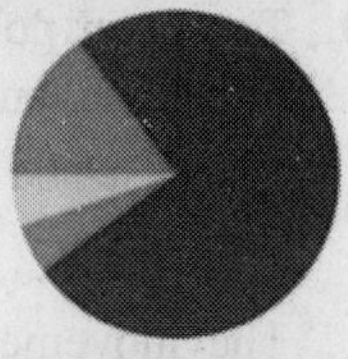
3. 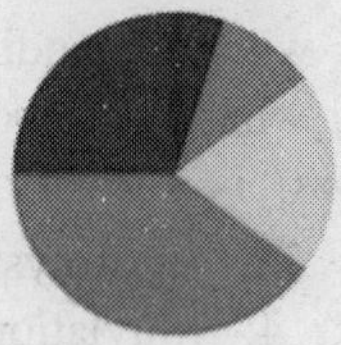
4. 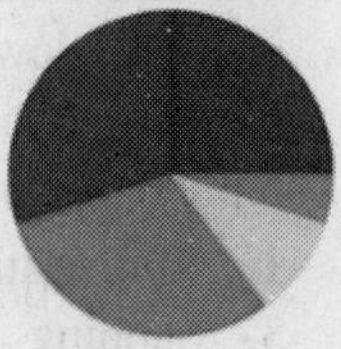

17. How many 4-digit numbers can be generated from the digits 1, 2, 3, 4, 5 such that no digit appears more than once, and digit 1 is always somewhere to the left of the digit 2?

1. 72 2. 36
3. 12 4. 6

18. Which one of the following Venn diagrams is NOT consistent with the following statements?

All A are B
No D is A
Some A are C

1. 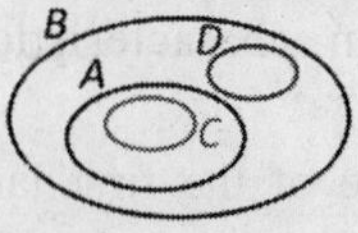

2. 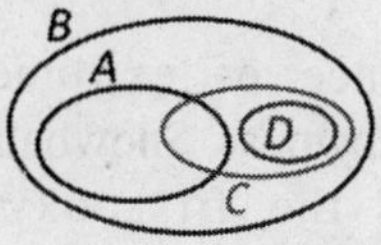

3. 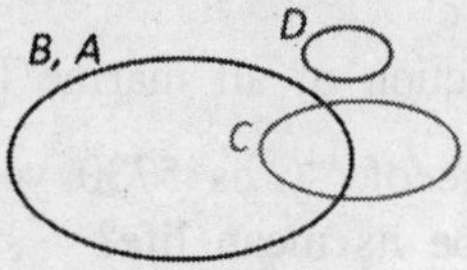

4. 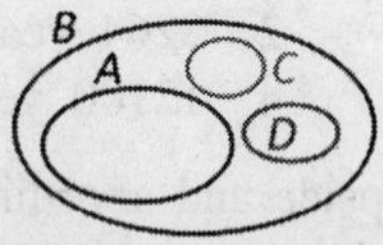

19. A square sheet of 10 cm sides is folded along its diagonal to form an isosceles right triangle, and then hypotenuses are folded successively two times to form isosceles right triangles. What is the length of each equal side after the third folding?

1. 0.625 cm 2. 1.25 cm
3. 2.5 cm 4. 5 cm

20. A water bottle costs ₹ 20 that includes cost of the bottle. If the water costs ₹ 15 more than the bottle, then what is the cost of the bottle?

1. ₹ 2.50 2. ₹ 5
3. ₹ 7.50 4. ₹ 10

PART-B

21. A hornblende bearing metamorphic rock formed very close to the surface, within the stability conditions of andalusite. This rock represents metamorphism.

1. Amphibolite facies
2. Hornfels facies
3. Granulite facies
4. Greenschist facies

22. When did the first multicellular life forms appear on the Earth?

1. ~541 Ma 2. ~635 Ma
3. ~2500 Ma 4. ~4500 Ma

16. 1	**17.** 2	**18.** 4	**19.** 4	**20.** 1	**21.** 2	**22.** 2

23. What is the main characteristic of the Cryogenian period?

1. The appearance of the first land plants and animals
2. The occurrence of extreme global glaciations known as Snowball Earth
3. The rise of the first oxygen-rich atmosphere
4. The extinction of all marine life

24. If the half life of ^{14}C is 5730 years, then what would be its mean life?

1. 16529 years 2. 8264 years
3. 4132 years 4. 12100 years

25. A mixture of diopside and anorthite begins to melt at a temperature of 1274°C at a fixed pressure of 0.1 MPa. The degree of freedom representing this system state is ....

1. 0
2. 2
3. 1
4. Non unique value

26. Kamacite and Taenite are dominant constituents of which group of meteorites?

1. Iron meteorite
2. Achondrite
3. SNC meteorite
4. Carbonaceous chondrite

27. The rake of slickenlines on a thrust fault plane 250°, 40° NW was measured to be 90°. The plunge amount of the slickenlines is ....

1. 10° 2. 20°
3. 30° 4. 40°

28. Which one of the following oil-fields belongs to the Cambay Basin?

1. Geleki 2. Lakwa
3. Charali 4. Kalol

29. Which one of the following sediments compact at the fastest rate during shallow burial?

1. Quartz arenite 2. Mudstone
3. Arkose 4. Grainstone

30. The Euler pole of the Cenozoic plate motion of the Indian plate is located in ....

1. Australia 2. India
3. Africa 4. North America

31. The movement of soluble and fine-grained material downward with descending water into soil B horizon, where re-deposition or reprecipitation occurs, is known as:

1. Rubification 2. Hydrolysis
3. Sapping 4. Illuviation

32. Under weathering-limited environment ....

1. thick saprolite develops
2. thick debris cover develops
3. no or little soil develops
4. soil formation takes place

33. Which one of the following is used in remote sensing to detect soil moisture?

1. Microwave
2. Optical
3. Thermal
4. Hyperspectral

34. The zoogeographic transition zone called Wallacea is bounded by ....

1. Wallace's line to the east and Weber's line to the west
2. Wallace's line to the west and Weber's line to the east
3. Wallace's line to the east and Lydekker's line to the west
4. Wallace's line to the west and Lydekker's line to the east

23. 2	**24.** 2	**25.** 1	**26.** 1	**27.** 4	**28.** 4
29. 2	**30.** 3	**31.** 4	**32.** 3	**33.** 1	**34.** 2

35. Which one of the following statements is INCORRECT about Coriolis force (CF)?
1. CF is the cross product between the rotational vector of the Earth and the velocity vector of the moving object
2. CF is the maximum for motions perpendicular to the Earth's axis
3. CF increases with increasing distance from the Earth's axis
4. CF affects west-east winds over the equator to deflect them in vertical direction

36. A transfer of westerly angular momentum takes place from the Earth's surface to the atmosphere in regions of surface ....
1. easterly 2. westerly
3. northerly 4. southerly

37. Water-layer weathering primarily occurs on ....
1. shore platforms 2. strath terraces
3. duricrust tops 4. stone pavements

38. A zone of coalescent deposition from adjacent prograding fans is known as ....
1. talus cone 2. bajada
3. megafan 4. erg

39. Which one of the following is the correct arrangement in up-slope order?
1. glacial table - kettle lake - bergschrund - firn
2. kettle lake- firn - bergschrund -glacial table
3. kettle lake- glacial table - firn - bergschrund
4. glacial table - firn - kettle lake- bergschrund

40. Which one of the following is the correct sequence of soil orders with increasing humid conditions?
1. vertisols > mollisols > spodosols > oxisols
2. mollisols > vertisols > spodosols > oxisols
3. vertisols > mollisols > oxisols > spodosols
4. mollisols > vertisols > oxisols > spodosols

41. The Earth's gravity field from surface to the centre:
1. decreases uniformly
2. increases in the mantle and decreases uniformly in the outer & inner core
3. increases in the mantle and decreases gently in the outer core and sharply in the inner core
4. decreases sharply in the mantle and gently in outer and inner core

42. Which one of the following combinations of radioisotopes produces the bulk of the heat generated within the Earth's continental crust?
1. ^{235}U, ^{14}C and ^{137}Cs
2. ^{238}U, ^{147}Sm and ^{240}Th
3. ^{238}U, ^{232}Th and ^{40}K
4. ^{235}U, ^{40}K and ^{234}U

43. If F, V and H are the Earth's magnetic field and its vertical and horizontal components, respectively at Colombo, then:
1. F > H > V 2. F > V > H
3. V > F > H 4. H > V > F

44. The declination of the Natural Remanent Magnetism of a rock unit is a measure of:
1. the latitude of the formation of the rock
2. its longitudinal movement
3. its latitudinal movement
4. amount of rotation about a vertical axis

45. The magnitude measured on a Richter scale ....
1. is valid for all epicentral distances
2. does not saturate
3. cannot be negative
4. underestimates the magnitude of Great earthquakes

35. 3 **36.** 1 **37.** 1 **38.** 2 **39.** 3 **40.** 2 **41.** 3 **42.** 3 **43.** 1 **44.** 4 **45.** 4

46. The orbital period of Mars is 687 Earth days. Then, the distance of Mars from the Sun in AU is ....

[1 AU = distance of the Earth from the Sun]

1. 1.5 2. 1.8
3. 2.2 4. 2.6

47. Choose the INCORRECT statement from the following

1. The geoid is an equipotential surface
2. The reference spheroid is an equipotential surface
3. The geoid is an undulating surface
4. The reference spheroid and geoid refer to the same surface

48. The S-wave velocity for a material with Poisson's ratio of 0.5 is ....

1. half of the P-wave velocity
2. equal to the P-wave velocity
3. twice the P-wave velocity
4. zero

49. Continent-continent collision zone is characterized by ....

1. shallow focus earthquakes
2. intermediate and deep focus earthquakes
3. shallow, intermediate and deep focus earthquakes
4. deep focus earthquakes

50. The seismic phase which reveals that the inner core of the Earth is solid is ....

1. PKP 2. SKIKP
3. SKJKS 4. PKIKP

51. In the absence of Earth's rotation, the flow of air in the lower atmosphere will be ....

1. parallel to isobars
2. parallel to isolines of pressure tendency
3. from high pressure to low pressure
4. from low pressure to high pressure

52. The magnitude of Rossby radius of deformation of atmosphere at 45°N latitude is ....

1. 300 km 2. 3000 km
3. 6000 km 4. 10000 km

53. In an incompressible atmosphere .... wave does not exist.

1. Kelvin 2. Rossby
3. Gravity 4. Acoustic

54. Which of the following is NOT a state function for a non-adiabatic process?

1. Enthalpy 2. Internal energy
3. Work 4. Entropy

55. Which one of the following factors could reduce the formation of groundlevel ozone in an urban atmosphere?

1. Increased emissions of nitrogen oxides (NO_x) from vehicles
2. Increased cloud cover during daytime
3. Higher concentrations of volatile organic compounds (VOCs) from industrial sources
4. Higher ambient temperature during daytime

56. A saturated air parcel rises in an environment with a lapse rate of 6.5 K/km. The parcel's lapse rate is 5 K/km. At 3 km, the parcel's temperature is 0°C. What is the temperature of the environment at 3 km?

1. –2.5°C 2. –4.5°C
3. –3.0°C 4. 0°C

57. What happens to moist air parcel rising adiabatically?

1. It cools due to expansion
2. It warms due to compression
3. It becomes drier
4. Its temperature does not change

58. Wavelength of an atmospheric disturbance that exhibits wavenumber 4 over the equatorial region is ....

1. 1000 km 2. 10000 km
3. 5000 km 4. 15000 km

46. 1	**47.** 4	**48.** 4	**49.** 1	**50.** 3	**51.** 3	**52.** 2
53. 4	**54.** 3	**55.** 2	**56.** 2	**57.** 1	**58.** 2	

59. Scale height of the Earth's atmosphere for a vertically averaged temperature 250 K is ....

1. 5.5 km 2. 7.3 km
3. 10.3 km 4. 6 km

60. Restoring force that supports the existence of gravity waves in the atmosphere is ....

1. buoyancy
2. compressibility
3. rotation of the earth
4. sphericity of the earth

61. How much phosphorus is required to sustain a primary productivity of 1272 mg C m^{-3} d^{-1}? (Assume Redfield ratio)

1. 1 mmol L^{-1} d^{-1} 2. 1 μmol L^{-1} d^{-1}
3. 1272 μg L^{-1} d^{-1} 4. 106 μmol L^{-1} d^{-1}

62. The difference between the *in-situ* temperature and the potential temperature in the ocean .... with depth.

1. is positive and remains constant
2. is negative and decreases
3. is positive and increases
4. is negative and increases

63. The solar radiation at a depth of 50 m in sea is 30% of surface radiation. In that case the extinction coefficient is ....

1. 0.05 m^{-1} 2. 0.48 m^{-1}
3. 0.25 m^{-1} 4. 0.024 m^{-1}

64. Opal concentration in the sediments is high in the ....

1. equatorial Pacific and Southern oceans
2. equatorial Atlantic and Arctic oceans
3. Indian Ocean
4. North Atlantic Ocean

65. Eastern boundary currents are colder because they ....

1. carry deeper water to the surface
2. carry water from high latitudes towards equator
3. cause convective mixing
4. are winter season currents

66. In the oceans, subsurface secondary nitrite maxima are generated by ....

1. nitrogen fixation
2. anaerobic ammonia oxidation
3. nitrification
4. denitrification

67. The thickness of sediment on seafloor at a place 200 km away from spreading center is 250 m. If the sedimentation rate in the area is 5 cm/10^3 year, the rate of seafloor spreading is ....

1. 4 cm/year 2. 5 cm/year
3. 20 cm/year 4. 2.5 cm/year

68. Precipitation of $CaCO_3$ from the ocean leads to ....

1. reduction in dissolved inorganic carbon and alkalinity
2. increase in dissolved inorganic carbon and alkalinity
3. reduction in dissolved inorganic carbon and increase in alkalinity
4. increase in dissolved inorganic carbon and decrease in alkalinity

69. Microbial respiration rates decrease in the ocean with increasing depth due to ....

1. low abundance of organic matter
2. influence of Antarctic bottom water
3. high pressure and low temperature
4. complete darkness

70. An ocean water sample has $[HCO^-_3]$ = 1700 μmol/kg and $[CO_3^{2-}]$ = 200 μmol/kg. How much is the carbonate alkalinity of this water?

1. 1700 μmol/kg 2. 1900 μmol/kg
3. 2100 μmol/kg 4. 2300 μmol/kg

59. 2	**60.** 1	**61.** 2	**62.** 3	**63.** 4	**64.** 1
65. 2	**66.** 4	**67.** 1	**68.** 1	**69.** 3	**70.** 3

PART-C

71. An unconfined aquifer has two horizontal isotropic layers. If the thicknesses of the two layers are 12 m and 15 m and their respective hydraulic conductivities are 8.6 m/day and 5.2 m/day, then what would be the approximate equivalent horizontal hydraulic conductivity?

1. 1.60 m/day
2. 1.01 m/day
3. 7.09 m/day
4. 6.71 m/day

72. If a body under a mean stress of 4 kbars requires a shear stress of 2.5 kbars for shear failure, the differential stress developed in the body is .... kbars.

1. 1.5
2. 2.0
3. 2.5
4. 3.0

73. Match the following:

Column-I (Wilson cycle stages)	Column-II (Examples)
A. Embryonic	P. Red Sea, Africa
B. Juvenile/young	Q. Arabian Sea
C. Mature	R. Mediterranean Sea
D. Terminal	S. Basin and Range Province, USA

1. A-S, B-P, C-Q, D-R
2. A-P, B-Q, C-R, D-S
3. A-Q, B-R, C-S, D-P
4. A-R, B-S, C-P, D-Q

74. In a pelitic bulk composition, biotite appears at 400° and 0.5 GPa. At what pressure, the rock will start metamorphosing under UHT conditions? Assume the thermal gradient of metamorphism to remain constant during the process.

1. 1.125 GPa
2. 11.25 GPa
3. 0.1125 GPa
4. 0.25 GPa

75. Match the critical metals with their ore minerals.

Critical Metal	Ore Mineral
A. Li	I. Bastnasite
B. U	II. Columbite
C. La	III. Pitchblende
D. Nb	IV. Spodumene

Choose the correct option:

1. A-II, B-IV, C-I, D-III
2. A-I, B-IV, C-II, D-III
3. A-III, B-IV, C-II, D-I
4. A-IV, B-III, C-I, D-II

76. Consider the five statements related to the figure depicting two Rb-Sr isochrons, one defined by three metaigneous rocks A, B, and C (Isochron-I), and the other by rock B and its minerals M_1 and M_2 (Isochron-II).

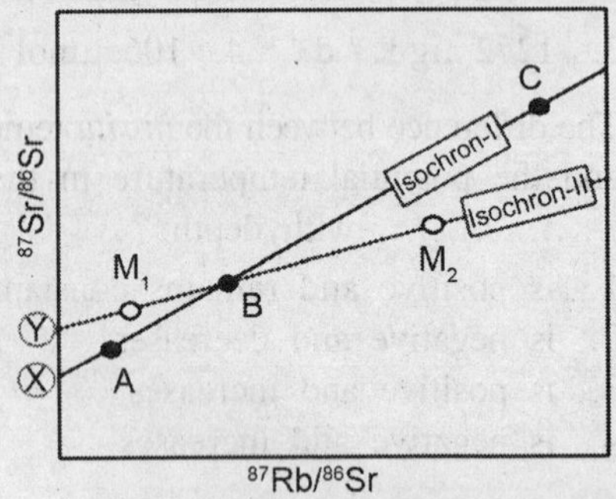

P. Isochron-I dates igneous emplacement while Isochron-II dates the metamorphic overprint

Q. Isochron-II dates igneous emplacement while Isochron-I dates the metamorphic overprint.

R. Intercept X is the $^{87}Sr/^{86}Sr$ ratio of the source.

S. Intercept Y is the $^{87}Sr/^{86}Sr$ ratio of the source.

T. Rock A may be mafic and rock C may be felsic in composition.

Identify the option that lists the correct statements.

1. P, R, T
2. Q, S, T
3. P, S
4. Q, R

71. 4 **72.** * **73.** 1 **74.** 1 **75.** 4 **76.** 1

77. A triangular block ABC is being explored for base metal mineralization. If AB = 25 m, BC = 30 m, and AC = 32 m and the thickness of the ore body intersected at A, B, and C are 4 m, 5 m and 8 m, respectively. What is the tonnage of the deposit (in metric ton) if the specific gravity of the ore is 4.95?

1. 162.8 mt
2. 16.28 mt
3. 52.35 mt
4. 523.5 mt

78. The following statements refer to two characteristic rock types of the Precambrian continental crust.

I. It is characterized by a texture defined by crisscrossing sheafs of acicular olivine crystals.
II. It is originated by partial melting of mantle at greater depth (> 100 km) and extruded on to the surface.
III. It may occur as layers in layered gabbroic intrusions or may form large massifs essentially composed of plagioclase.
IV. It commonly contains aluminous bronzite.

Given the above statements, choose the correct option.

1. I, II, and IV are about komatiite and III is about anorthosite
2. I and IV are about komatiite and II and III are about anorthosite
3. I and II are about komatiite and III and IV are about anorthosite
4. I is about komatiite and II, III and IV are about anorthosite

79. The given sketch shows the mineral assemblage and textural relations of a meta basic rock that experienced a single tectonothermal event.

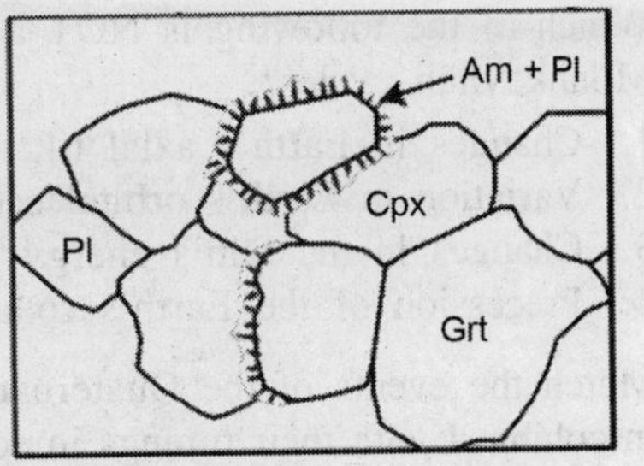

(Grt- garnet, Cpx- Clinopyroxene, Pl- plagiocase, and Am- amphibole)

Consider the following statements.

A. Grt + Cpx constitute the peak metamorphic assemblage
B. The rock experienced eclogite facies metamorphism
C. The Am + Pl reaction texture does not represent a symplectite texture
D. The Am + Pl reaction texture require hydration during its formation

Based on the above figure and statements, choose the correct option

1. Only statement A is correct
2. Statements A and B are correct
3. Statements A, C, and D are correct
4. Statements A and D are correct

80. Weathering of albite releases cations and anions in water as per the reaction given below:

$$2NaAlSi_3O_8 + 2CO_2 + 3H_2O = Al_2Si_2O_5(OH)_4 + 2Na^+ + 2HCO_3^- + 4SiO_2$$

Na^+ concentration in a water sample is measured to be 100 μmol/L. If 90% of it is derived from albite, how much albite is dissolved in 1 L of water? (Assume molecular weight of albite to be 262 g/mol)

1. 26.2 mg
2. 23.6 mg
3. 11.8 mg
4. 47.2 mg

77. * **78.** 3 **79.** 4 **80.** 2

81. Which of the following is NOT a cause of Milankovitch cycles?

1. Changes in Earth's axial tilt
2. Variation in Earth's orbital eccentricity
3. Changes in the Sun's energy output
4. Precession of the Earth's rotation axis

82. Match the events of the Quaternary period in column-I with their timings in column-II.

Column-I	Column-II
A. Last Glacial Maximum (LGM)	P. 300,000 - 200,000 years ago
B. Younger Dryas	Q. 1,170 - 770 years ago
C. Medieval Warming	R. 26,000 - 20,000 years ago
D. Appearance of modern Humans (Homo Sapiens)	S. 12,900 - 11,700 years ago

Choose the correct answer.

1. A-R, B-S, C-Q, D-P
2. A-S, B-R, C-P, D-Q
3. A-P, B-Q, C-R, D-S
4. A-Q, B-P, C-S, D-R

83. Which one of the following combinations of sedimentary structures do NOT occur together on a single bed?

1. Groove cast and convolute lamination
2. Prod mark and Wave ripple
3. Double mud drape and rain imprint
4. Desiccation crack and current ripple

84. Which one of the following formations listed below dominantly comprises of carbonate rocks?

1. Rohtas Formation
2. Srisailam Formation
3. Gulcheru Formation
4. Rabanapalli Formation

85. Which one of the following microfossils occurs exclusively in marine depositional environment?

1. Ostracoda
2. Diatom
3. Dinoflagellate
4. Radiolaria

86. A tunnel is to be excavated along the dip direction in a sandstone with bedding attitude of 30°, 270°.

Parameter	Rating
A. Strength of intact rock	7
B. RQD (%)	8
C. Joint Spacing	10
D. Condition of Joints	10
E. Groundwater	7

Given the ratings of the different parameters tabulated above, the rock mass rating (RMR) relevant for the tunnel excavation (including the tunnel adjustment) is:

1. 42
2. 40
3. 38
4. 36

87. Consider the following statements:

A. The mean velocity of flow in an open channel is directly related to the hydraulic radius but inversely related to channel gradient and roughness value.

B. Hydraulic radii is obtained by dividing the wetted perimeter of the channel by the cross-section area of the channel.

Choose the correct option:

1. Both A and B are true
2. Both A and B are false
3. A is false, but B is true
4. A is true, but B is false

88. Identify the INCORRECT pairs:

A. Till - glacial deposit
B. Tufa - limestone deposit
C. Ventifact - glacial erosion
D. Wind gap - Wind erosion
E. Yardang - streamlined by water erosion
F. Hamada - desert pavement

Choose the correct option

1. C, D and E
2. B, D and E
3. A, B and F
4. D, E and F

81. 3 **82.** 1 **83.** 3 **84.** 1 **85.** 4 **86.** 2 **87.** 2 **88.** 1

89. The following plot shows the relationship between stream order on X-axis and the number of streams, channel length (L), mean value of basin area (A) and gradient (G) on Y-axis.

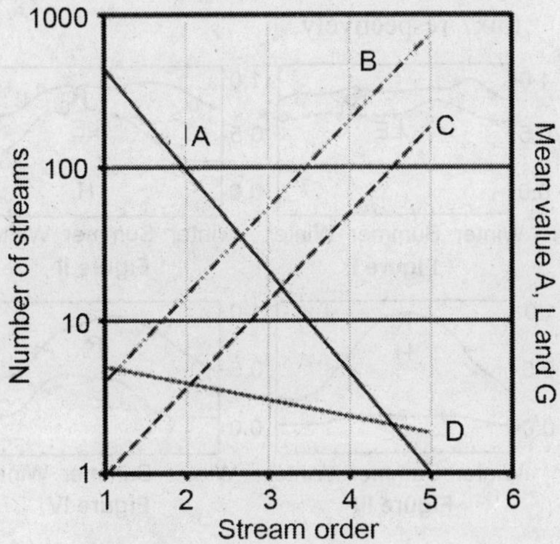

Identify the lines that correctly represent the relationship of stream order with number of streams and gradient, respectively

1. B and C
2. A and B
3. A and D
4. C and D

90. At-a-station hydraulic geometry equations of a river give values of 'b' and 'f' as 0.27 and 0.62. What is the expected value of 'm'?

1. 0.31
2. 0.21
3. 0.11
4. 0.01

91. Match the following:

Column-I	Column-II
A. Post-deposition changes in sediments	E. Speleogenesis
B. Soil formation	F. Orogenesis
C. Cave network development	G. Morphogenesis
D. Building of mountains by the forces of plate tectonics	H. Diagenesis
	I. Pedogenesis

Choose the correct option:

1. A-H, B-I, C-E, D-F
2. A-H, B-F, C-E, D-I
3. A-G, B-I, C-H, D-E
4. A-G, B-I, C-G, D-E

92. Which one of the following hypsographic curves represents a landscape with very low relief and a few isolated hills?

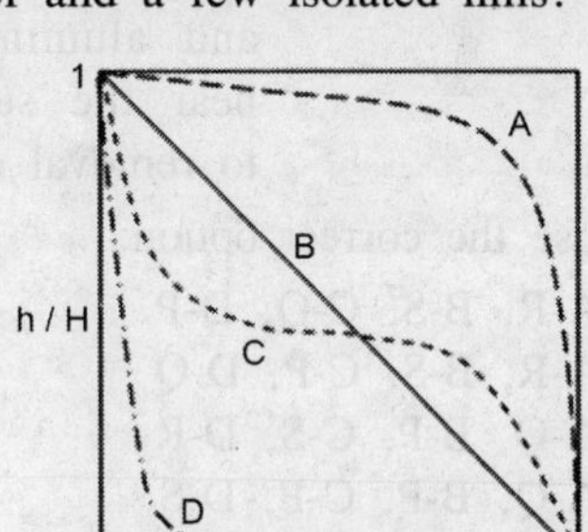

1. A
2. B
3. C
4. D

93. Consider the following assertion and reason

Assertion (A): Oligotrophic lakes in colder climate regions have high dissolved oxygen levels near the surface.

Reason (R): There is high productivity in oligotrophic lakes.

1. (A) and (R) are correct, (R) explains (A)
2. (A) and (R) are correct, (R) does not explain (A)
3. (A) is correct, (R) is incorrect
4. (A) is incorrect, (R) is correct

89. 3 **90.** 3 **91.** 1 **92.** 4 **93.** 3

94. Match the Column-I with Column-II.

Column-I	Column-II
A. Podzol	P. Thick and humus rich A horizon and accumulation of $CaCO_3$ in lower B or beneath B horizon
B. Laterite	Q. Accumulation of soluble salts
C. Chernozem	R. A_2 Horizon is light coloured due to removal of iron oxides and colloidal humus by leaching
D. Solonchak	S. Relative enrichment of sesquioxides of iron and aluminum at or near the surface due to removal of silica

Choose the correct option:

1. A-R, B-S, C-Q, D-P
2. A-R, B-S, C-P, D-Q
3. A-Q, B-P, C-S, D-R
4. A-Q, B-P, C-P, D-S

95. Match the Column-I with Column-II.

Column-I	Column-II
A. Heliophytes	P. Plants growing in acidic soils
B. Psammophytes	Q. Plants growing under direct sunlight
C. Chasmophytes	R. Plants growing in sandy soils
D. Oxilophytes	S. Plants growing in crevices of rocks

Choose the correct option:

1. A-P, B-S, C-Q, D-R
2. A-P, B-Q, C-R, D-S
3. A-Q, B-R, C-P, D-S
4. A-Q, B-R, C-S, D-P

96. Following figures depict the annual energy balance for 4 climatic types. The source energy flux density (on Y-axis) is normalized to the maximum radiation (Rn). Months of the year are shown on X-axis. H and LE refer to sensible heat flux and latent heat flux, respectively.

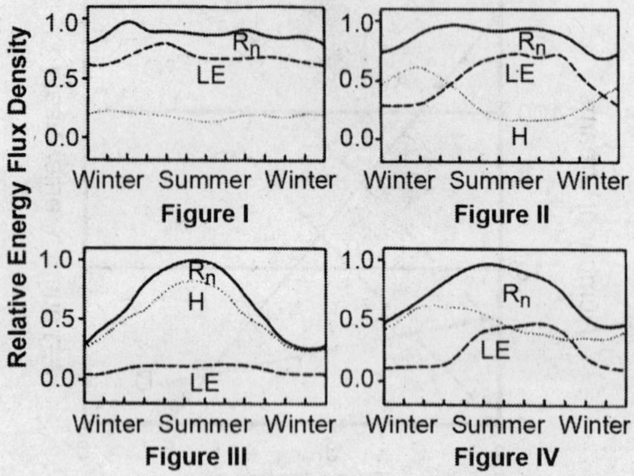

Match Column-I with Column-II:

Column-I	Column-II
A. Fig I	P. Warm steppe climate
B. Fig II	Q. Arid climate
C. Fig III	R. Tropical wet climate
D. Fig IV	S. Tropical wet summer and dry winter climate

Choose the correct option:

1. A-R, B-S, C-Q, D-P
2. A-R, B-S, C-P, D-Q
3. A-P, B-Q, C-R, D-S
4. A-P, B-Q, C-S, D-R

97. A and B are two stars of equal size and equidistant from the earth. The peak wavelengths coming from A and B are 965 nm and 482 nm, respectively. How many times brighter (in terms of energy) is the star B than star A?

1. 2
2. 4
3. 8
4. 16

94. 2 **95.** 4 **96.** 1 **97.** 4

98. **Assertion (A):** Upper section of a macrotidal estuary gets sedimented due to ebb dominance of tidal current.

Reason (R): Sediment entrainment and deposition depend on the speed of tidal currents.

Choose the correct option:

1. Both (A) and (R) are true and (R) is the correct explanation
2. Both (A) and (R) are true but (R) is not the correct explanation
3. (A) is true and (R) is false
4. (A) is false and (R) is true.

99. Which among the following shows the correct arrangement of landfall sites of the cyclonic storms from north to south since 2022?

1. Remal - Biparjoy - Asani - Dana - Mandous
2. Biparjoy - Remal - Dana - Asani - Mandous
3. Dana - Asani - Mandous - Biparjoy - Remal
4. Asani - Remal - Biparjoy - Mandous - Dana

100. Match the regions with the impact structures.

Region	Impact structure
A. Bundelkhand	L. Shiva
B. Kota Plateau	M. Luna
C. Arabian Sea shelf	N. Ramgarh
D. Buldhana	O. Dhala
	P. Lonar

Choose the correct option:

1. A-O, B-N, C-L, D-P
2. A-O, B-P, C-N, D-P
3. A-N, B-M, C-O, D-O
4. A-P, B-L, C-M, D-L

101. The correct sequence of bed forms, as the Froude Number decreases from >1 to <1, is:

1. Ripples - Dunes - Plane bed - Antidunes
2. Dunes - Ripples - Plane bed - Antidunes
3. Plane bed - Antidunes - Dunes - Ripples
4. Antidunes - Plane bed - Dunes - Ripples

102. Match Column-I with Column-II.

Column-I (DEM Product)	Column-II (Satellite)
A. ALOS	P. Endeavour
B. SRTM	Q. Terra
C. ASTER	R. TanDem X
D. Copernicus	S. Daichi
	T. Cartosat 3

Choose the correct option:

1. A-R, B-S, C-P, D-Q
2. A-T, B-Q, C-T, D-S
3. A-S, B-P, C-S, D-T
4. A-S, B-P, C-Q, D-R

103. Consider the following statements regarding Geoid, an equipotential surface.

Statement A: The gravity field denotes the rate of change of gravity potential.

Statement B: The gravity field on the geoid is everywhere zero.

Choose the correct option.

1. Both A and B are valid, B can be explained by A.
2. Both A and B are valid, but B cannot be explained by A
3. A is inaccurate, but B is valid
4. A is inaccurate and B is invalid

104. A magnetic anomaly profile across a dyke-like body records a maximum anomaly of 640 gammas and minimum anomaly of –320 gammas. The anomaly (in gammas) at a point above the position of the dyke is expected to be:

1. 480
2. 320
3. 0
4. –160

98. 4 **99.** 2 **100.** 1 **101.** 4 **102.** 4 **103.** 4 **104.** 2

105. (F_A, g_A) and (F_B, g_B) are the Free Air and Bouguer anomalies due to two isostatically compensated elevated masses of thicknesses 1.0 km and 2.0 km, respectively. Then:

1. $F_B = F_A$, $g_B = g_A$
2. $F_B = F_A$, $g_B = 2g_A$
3. $F_B = 2F_A$, $g_B = 2g_A$
4. $F_B = 2F_A$, $g_B = g_A$

106. From the position of the maximum anomaly, the gravity anomaly of a horizontal circular cylindrical body, at depth *z*, is reduced to one-third its maximum value at a distance of

1. Z 2. √3 Z/2
3. √2 Z 4. √3 Z

107. A seismic wave propagates through a medium with velocity perturbations (%) with respect to a reference velocity of 5 km/sec as shown in the figure. The travel time residual (%) at the receiver R is:

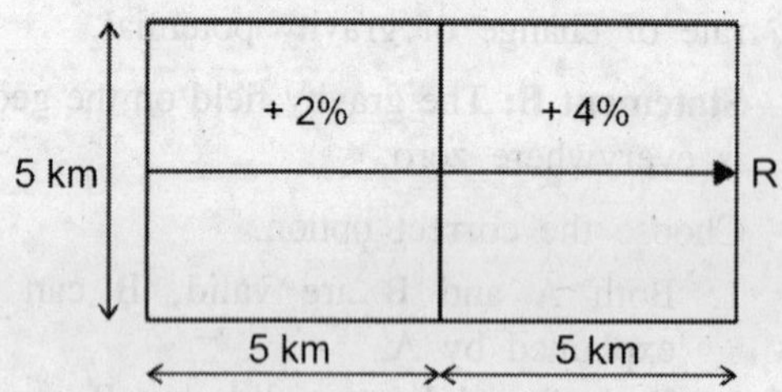

1. –0.5 2. –0.9
3. –1.9 4. –2.9

108. Match the well log observations in Column-A with their corresponding causes in Column-B.

Column-A	Column-B
P. Decrease in formation factor	1. Wet, shaly sandstone bed
Q. PSP	2. Presence of gas
R. Decrease in neutron porosity	3. Over pressured zone
S. Decrease in sonic velocity	4. Increase in permeability

Choose the correct option.

1. P-1, Q-4, R-3, S-2
2. P-4, Q-1. R-2, S-3
3. P-4, Q-1, R-3, S-4
4. P-1, Q-4, R-2, S-3

109. A near surface earthquake of magnitude 4.0 is recorded by broadband stations A, B and C which are located at local, regional and teleseismic distance. Assuming the recorded event duration at the stations A, B and C to be denoted as E_A, E_B and E_C, respectively, then

1. $E_A > E_B > E_C$
2. $E_A = E_B = E_C$
3. $E_A < E_B > E_C$
4. $E_A < E_B < E_C$

110. The P-wave time data corresponding to an earthquake are fit with two line segments having slopes p_1=0.5 s/km. p_2=0.33 s/km and intercepts times (delay times) $\tau_1 = 0$ s and $\tau_2 = 1.5$ s, respectively, leading to a two layered crust. Then, the thickness of the top layer is:

1. 0.5 km 2. 1 km
3. 1.5 km 4. 2 km

111. Frequency effect measured in Induced Polarization survey is 0.20. If the apparent resistivity computed at low frequency is 100 Ωm, then what will be the apparent resistivity at the high frequency measured in the survey?

1. 80 Ωm
2. 83.33 Ωm
3. 120 Ωm
4. 120.33 Ωm

105. 2	**106.** 3	**107.** 4	**108.** 2	**109.** 4	**110.** 4	**111.** 2

112. 'R' and 'T' are the reflection and transmission coefficients in electrical prospecting, then which is the correct sequence of minimum and maximum values of R and T given in corresponding brackets?

1. R (0, +1), T (0, +1)
2. R (–1, 0), T (0, +1)
3. R (–1, +1), T (0, +2)
4. R (0, +2), T (0, –1)

113. Consider the following statements about Very Low Frequency (VLF) EM method.

Statement I: VLF method has the highest depth of investigation among EM methods based on EM induction principle.

Statement II: VLF method uses the frequency range 5 kHz to 30 kHz.

Choose the correct option:

1. Both statements are correct.
2. Statement I is correct but statement II is incorrect.
3. Statement I is incorrect but statement II is correct.
4. Both statements are incorrect.

114. Which is the correct statement about the origin of signals used in natural source electromagnetic method?

1. Signals in frequency range ($1 - 10^4$ Hz) are generated by thunderstorm while signals in frequency range (10^{-4} – 1Hz) are generated by ionospheric current.
2. Signals in frequency range ($1 - 10^4$ Hz) are generated by ionospheric current while signals in frequency range (10^{-4} – Hz) are generated by thunderstorm activity.
3. Signals in the entire frequency range ($10^{-4} - 10^4$ Hz) are generated by ionospheric current.
4. Signals in the entire frequency range ($10^{-4} - 10^4$ Hz) are generated by thunderstorm activity.

115. A gas-sand layer is overlain by a shale layer. Both the acoustic impedance and Poisson's ratios for shale are higher than those for gas-sand. Then, the AVO class for the shale-gas-sand interface is:

1. Class 1
2. Class 2
3. Class 3
4. Class 4

116. Seismic diffractions appear in stacked sections as:

1. hyperbolae
2. parabolae
3. points
4. straight lines

117. If the S-wave vector potential is given by ψ, then which one of the following identities suggests that shear deformation preserves volume?

1. $\nabla \cdot (\nabla \times \psi) = 0$
2. $\nabla \cdot \psi = 0$
3. $\nabla \times \nabla \times \psi = 0$
4. $\nabla \times \psi = 0$

118. The auto correlation of a random signal with infinite length produces a:

1. random signal
2. unit step signal
3. unit sample signal [(δn)]
4. a signal that is identically zero

119. Consider a ring of air, initially at rest, around the equator moving poleward with a constant speed 15 m/s. What will be the approximate eastward speed when the air reaches 30°N? (Given the radius of the Earth is 6371 km)

1. 130 m/s
2. 150 m/s
3. 70 m/s
4. 30 m/s

120. What will be the approximate thickness of an atmospheric layer between two pressure levels namely, 1000 hPa and 900 hPa having a mean virtual temperature of 280 K (Given Rd = 287 J/kg K and $g = 9.8$ m/s^2)

1. 925 m
2. 760 m
3. 1000 m
4. 860 m

112. 3 **113.** 3 **114.** 1 **115.** 3 **116.** 1 **117.** 1 **118.** 3 **119.** 1 **120.** 4

121. The angle between the effective gravity force and the Newtonian gravitational force is maximum over:

1. Equator 2. North pole
3. South pole 4. 45° latitude

122. A tornado rotates with constant angular velocity (ω). Assuming constant temperature (T) in the tornado and pressure p_0 at a distance r_0 from the centre of tornado, what will be the pressure at the centre of the tornado? (R is specific gas constant for dry air)

1. $p_0 \exp\left(\frac{\omega^2 r_0^2}{2RT}\right)$
2. $p_0 \exp\left(\frac{\omega r_0^2}{2RT}\right)$
3. $p_0 \exp\left(-\frac{\omega^2 r_0^2}{2RT}\right)$
4. $p_0 \exp\left(-\frac{\omega^2 r_0}{2RT}\right)$

123. Consider 500 hPa geopotential field associated with a wavy disturbance in the westerlies in northern hemisphere.
Choose correct option related to advection of relative and planetary vorticity.

1. In the region upstream of 500 hPa trough, advection of relative vorticity tends to increase the local relative vorticity.
2. In the region upstream of 500 hPa trough, advection of planetary vorticity tends to increase the local relative vorticity.
3. In the region downstream of 500 hPa trough, advection of relative vorticity tends to decrease the local relative vorticity.
4. In the region downstream of 500 hPa trough, advection of planetary vorticity tends to increase the local relative vorticity.

124. A satellite sensor measures a radiance of 9.7 W m^{-2} μm^{-1} sr^{-1} at a wavelength of λ = 10 μm. Assuming the emissivity of the sea surface is ε = 0.98, what is the approximate value of sea surface temperature (SST) in Kelvin that will be retrieved from the measurement?

Given:

Planck constant, $\lambda = 6.626 \times 10^{-34}$ Js;

Boltzaman constant, $k = 1.38 \times 10^{-23}$ J/K;

Speed of light, $C = 3 \times 10^8$ m/s

1. 298 K
2. 288 K
3. 305 K
4. 278 K

125. What is the cross-isobaric wind induced vertical velocity at the top of the Ekman boundary layer at 45°N, provided that the geostrophic zonal wind varies by 10 m/s over 1000 km in latitudinal direction? (eddy viscosity coefficient, K_m = 5 m^2/s)

1. 2 mm/s
2. 0.5 m/s
3. 5 cm/s
4. 2 cm/s

126. Invoking potential vorticity conservation in northern hemisphere leads to:

1. manifestation of wave like pattern of easterly air current over an orographic barrier on the leeward side.
2. manifestation of purely zonal flow without any wavy pattern of westerly air current over an orographic barrier on the leeward side.
3. formation of gravity wave.
4. Sverdrup meridional transport.

121. 4 **122.** 3 **123.** 2 **124.** 1 **125.** 1 **126.** 4

127. While deriving the mean average Reynolds equation of motion for an incompressible turbulent fluid flow, identify the equation that does not have additional terms in the mean averaged Reynolds equation of motion.

1. Zonal momentum equation
2. Meridional momentum equation
3. Thermodynamic energy equation
4. Continuity equation

128. The maximum possible ratio of the normal anticyclonic gradient wind speed to the geostrophic wind speed for the same pressure gradient in the northern hemisphere is:

1. 8 2. 2
3. 4 4. 16

129. Consider a large ice sheet where surface temperature remains at the freezing point. What is the rate at which the thickness of the ice sheet decreases owing to the surface melting if the ice sheet were subjected to an additional downward heat flux of 5 Wm^{-2} from the atmosphere associated with global warming?

(Density of ice, $\rho_i = 0.9 \times 10^3$ kg m^{-3}; Latent heat of freezing ice, $L_f = 3.34 \times 10^5$ J kg^{-1})

1. 0.5 m/year 2. 0.2 m/year
3. 1 m/year 4. 0.01 m/year

130. Estimate the sea level rise due to the thermal expansion for a 2.5°C warming of a 4.5 km deep ocean.

(Thermal expansion coefficient is 1.5×10^{-4} $°C^{-1}$)

1. 1.3 m 2. 1.5 m
3. 1.7 m 4. 1.9 m

131. Assume that the sun is directly overhead and is at zenith. Choose the INCORRECT statement.

1. Single scattering albedo of the aerosols (w_o) is same over ocean and land
2. Albedo of the underlying surface (A_s) is same over ocean and land
3. Incident solar flux (F_0; Wm^{-2}) is same over ocean and land
4. Transmittance of the atmosphere (Ta) is same over ocean and land

132. "Aliasing" error occurs while solving the equation ....

1. $\frac{\partial^2 u}{\partial t^2} = c^2 \frac{\partial^2 u}{\partial x^2}$ (Wave equation)
2. $\frac{\partial u}{\partial t} = -u\frac{\partial u}{\partial x}$ (One dimensional advection equation)
3. $\frac{\partial u}{\partial t} = -Au$ (Dissipation equation with A as constant)
4. $\frac{\partial u}{\partial t} = -F$ (*x* component of Newtonian equation formation with F as external force)

133. Choose the INCORRECT option.

Spectral models are preferred over finite difference model due to:

1. handling of aliasing arising due to quadratic nonlinear term.
2. all higher derivatives are exact in spectral models
3. Polar singularity is automatically taken care of in the spectral models
4. Spectral models require less configuration time

134. The total wavenumber (m^{-1}) of a stationary barotropic Rossby wave at 45° N embedded in a westerly mean flow of speed 15 ms^{-1} is ....

1. 10^{-6} m^{-1} 2. 10^{-5} m^{-1}
3. 10^{-7} m^{-1} 4. 10^{-4} m^{-1}

127. 4 **128.** 2 **129.** 1 **130.** 3 **131.** 2 **132.** 2 **133.** 4 **134.** 1

135. Which one of the following is NOT correct regarding oxygen isotopic composition ($\delta^{18}O$) of foraminifera?

1. $\delta^{18}O$ of benthic foraminifera shows glacial-interglacial variability
2. The difference between $\delta^{18}O$ of planktic and benthic foraminifera is greater at high latitude
3. The difference between $\delta^{18}O$ of planktic and benthic foraminifera is greater at low latitude
4. The $\delta^{18}O$ of planktic foraminifera is more negative than that of benthic foraminifera

136. Unsorted sediments of large grain size variation without fabric are:

1. volcanic marine sediments.
2. turbidities.
3. windblown sediments.
4. ice-rafted sediments.

137. Which one of the following does NOT represent cold periods?

1. Dansgaard-Oeschger Events
2. Heinrich Events
3. Younger Dryas
4. Bond Events

138. Which one of the following values of oxygen isotopic composition ($\delta^{18}O$) is NOT possible?

1. 1500 ‰
2. −1500 ‰
3. 1×10^{99} ‰
4. −500 ‰

139. In the ocean, if the characteristic velocity and length scale are 10 cm/s and 100 km, respectively, then choose the correct option [given Coriolis parameter $f = 10^{-4}\ s^{-1}$, Angular velocity of Earth = Ω]

1. Rossby number is $10^{-1}\ \Omega$ and inertial force dominates the flow
2. Rossby number is 10^{-1} and inertial force dominates the flow
3. Rossby number is $10^{-2}\ \Omega$ and Coriolis force dominates the flow
4. Rossby number is 10^{-2} and Coriolis force dominates the flow

140. Observed current at an ocean mooring in the northern Bay of Bengal (18° N) shows 30-days periodicity. The mooring is located at the interior basin away from the boundary. Choose the correct option:

1. Kelvin wave forced at the equatorial Indian Ocean can contribute to the observed variability.
2. Rossby wave forced in the eastern part of the basin can contribute to the observed variability.
3. Both Kelvin wave and Rossby wave cannot influence variability at the location.
4. Rossby wave can influence, but Kelvin wave cannot at this location.

141. Assume westerly winds increase with latitude in an oceanic region in northern hemisphere and meridional wind is zero. Provided other conditions remain the same, choose the correct option.

1. Thermocline shallows and surface chlorophyll increases
2. Thermocline deepens and surface chlorophyll increases
3. Thermocline shallows and surface chlorophyll decreases
4. Thermocline deepens and surface chlorophyll decreases

135. 2	**136.** 4	**137.** 1	**138.** 2	**139.** 4	**140.** 1	**141.** 4

142. EICC (East India Coastal Current) is strongest and:

1. Poleward during Boreal Spring
2. Equatorward during Boreal Spring
3. Poleward during Boreal Summer
4. Equatorward during Boreal Summer

143. Consider the following statements about Ekman transport.

Statement A: Ekman transport is always 90° to the right of wind stress in the northern hemisphere, where the Coriolis parameter f is negative.

Statement B: Ekman transport can lead to upwelling and not downwelling.

Statement C: Ekman transport can give rise to upwelling through the blowing of winds near the equator.

Choose a correct option:

1. Only A is correct
2. Only B is correct
3. Only C is correct
4. All the three are correct

144. Based on the given statements, choose the correct option:

Statement A: Marine phytoplankton are controlled by nutrients, light, and vertical stability of the water column, but not by CO_2 concentration.

Statement B: The Biological pump does not sequester any anthropogenic carbon.

1. Both the statements are correct, but A does not explain B.
2. Both the statements are correct, and A explains B.
3. A is correct, B is incorrect.
4. A is incorrect, B is correct.

145. Considering similar physical states of the sea, which one of the following oxygen profiles indicates the highest primary production at the surface?

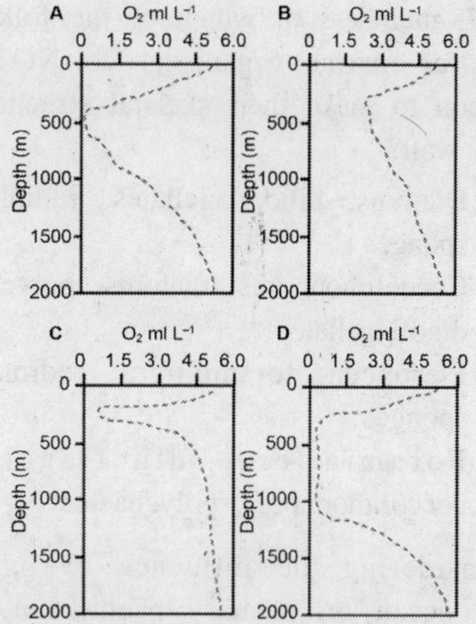

1. A
2. B
3. C
4. D

146. In the stratified temperate ocean, phytoplankton bloom progresses with seasonality. Below four different bloom scenarios are shown along with nutrient level (dashed orange line). Select the correct sequence of the bloom from winter to summer.

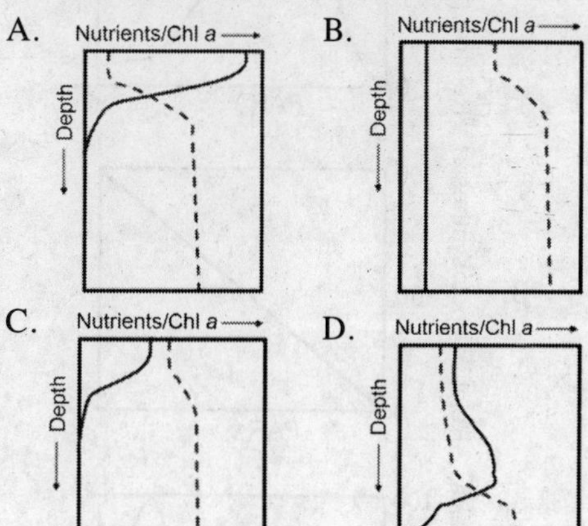

1. A → B → C → D
2. B → C → A → D
3. D → A → C → B
4. C → B → D → A

142. 1 **143.** 3 **144.** 3 **145.** 4 **146.** 2

147. ALL members of which of the following sets of marine organisms do NOT use silicon to make their skeletal structure on cell wall?

1. Diatoms, Silicoflagellates, radiolarian, sponges
2. Coccolithophores, diatoms, polychaeta, dinoflagellate
3. Pteropoda, foraminifera, radiolarian, sponges
4. Foraminifera, dinoflagellate, coccolithophores, polychaetes

148. Considering the influence of light in the ocean on primary production, how the responses of primary producers to increasing light level would be? (PAR: Photosynthetically Active Radiation)

A. 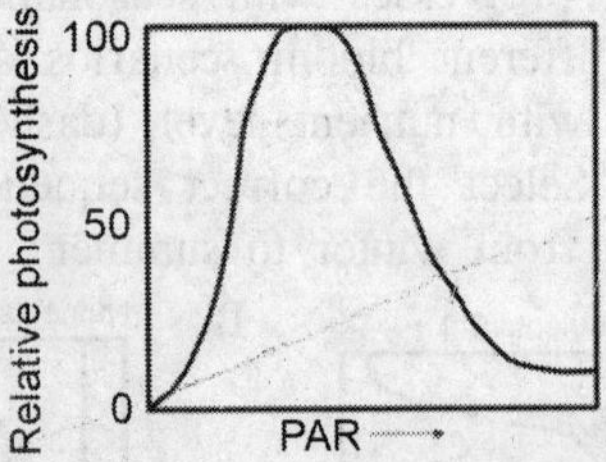

B. 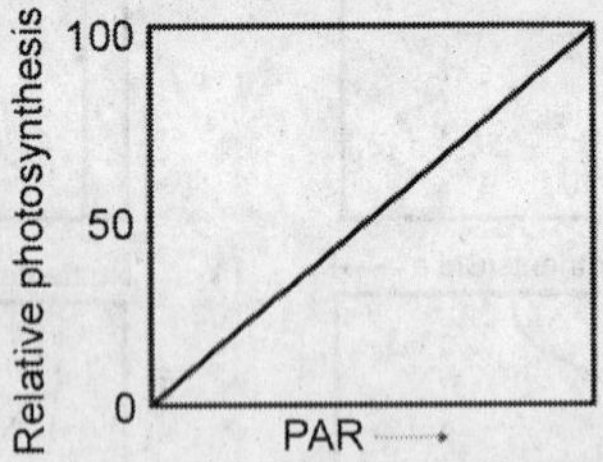

C. 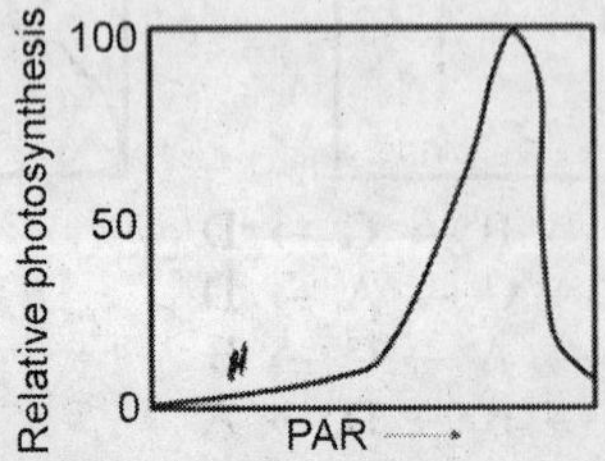

D. 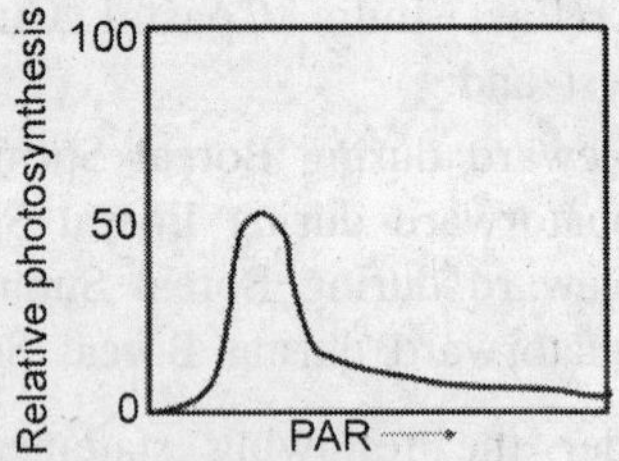

Choose the correct option:

1. A
2. B
3. C
4. D

149. Choose the right option showing the correct combination of various oceanic parameters (Column-I) and their respective measuring methods (Column-II).

A.

I	II
Phytopigments	ADCP
Phyto cell density	Flow cytometer
Ocean currents	HPLC
PAR	Radiometer

B.

I	II
Phytopigments	HPLC
Phyto cell density	Flow cytometer
Ocean currents	Radiometer
PAR	ADCP

C.

I	II
Phytopigments	HPLC
Phyto cell density	Flow cytometer
Ocean currents	ADCP
PAR	Radiometer

D.

I	II
Phytopigments	Radiometer
Phyto cell density	ADCP
Ocean currents	Flow cytometer
PAR	HPLC

1. A
2. B
3. C
4. D

150. Which of the following biological processes occurring in the ocean leads to the production of oxyluciferin?

1. Anaerobic ammonia oxidation
2. Methane oxidation
3. Bioluminescence
4. Nitrite oxidation

147. 4 **148.** 1 **149.** 3 **150.** 3

EXPLANATORY ANSWERS

1. We are told that Southwest (SW) becomes East (E). Let's analyze the direction angles on a compass:

- North (N) → 0°
- East (E) → 90°
- South (S) → 180°
- West (W) → 270°
- Southwest (SW) → 225°

Now, if SW (225°) is being placed at East (90°), the entire directional system must be rotated.

Determine the rotation:

To align SW (225°) to E (90°), we need to rotate the entire compass 135° counter-clockwise:

- 225° - 135° = 90° → SW aligns to East.

Now, where does North (0°) move?

Subtract the same 135° counter-clockwise rotation from North:

- North original position = 0°
- New position = 0° - 135° = -135°

But -135° is equivalent to +225°, because adding 360° to a negative angle normalizes it:

- -135° + 360° = 225°

225° corresponds to Southwest (SW).

Therefore: After rotating the map 135° counter-clockwise, North will point towards Southwest (SW).

2. Given water of pH = 8 is diluted 100 times with neutral water (pH = 7). We have to determine whether it becomes acidic, neutral, or remains basic.

- pH 8 water is weakly basic because pH > 7.
- Diluting basic water with neutral water will reduce its pH, but it will not immediately become neutral unless the dilution is sufficient to bring pH down to 7.

Here, diluting it 100 times will lower the concentration of OH^- ions but the pH will still stay slightly above 7, because pH is a logarithmic scale:

- pH = $-\log[H^+]$
- For pH to reach 7, we need the solution to be exactly neutral, which will not happen just by diluting once with neutral water.

Hence, the water will remain basic after dilution.

3. Fifteen distinct points are marked on the circumference of a circle. We are to find how many straight lines can be formed by joining pairs of these points.

Formula for number of lines from n points is $^nC_2$ (n choose 2).

Given $n = 15$:

- $^nC_2 = {}^{15}C_2 = (15 \times 14) / 2$
- Multiply: $15 \times 14 = 210$
- Divide by 2: $210 / 2 = 105$

Thus, 105 distinct straight lines can be formed.

4. Given:

- Initial population (N_0) = 50
- Growth rate (r) = 0.1 per hour
- Time (t) = 10 hours
- Population grows exponentially, so formula: $N = N_0 \times e^{(rt)}$

Step-by-step calculation:

1. Calculate exponent (rt):
   $rt = 0.1 \times 10 = 1$
2. Now compute $e^{(1)}$: $e \approx 2.718$
3. Compute population after 10 hours:
   $N = 50 \times e^1$
   $N = 50 \times 2.718 = 135.9$
4. Approximate to nearest whole number:
   $N \approx 136$

Thus, the population after 10 hours will be approximately 136.

5. The given graph shows the relationship between Profit (₹ million) and Temperature (T in °C), with a regression line fitted using the least squares method.

The regression equation is Profit = 4T - 86, and the correlation coefficient is $r = 0.83$, which indicates a strong positive correlation.

Let's examine each option:

Option 1: It states that the sum of squared differences between observed and expected values of temperature is minimized.

This is incorrect because in least squares regression, we minimize the sum of squared differences between observed and predicted values of the dependent variable (Profit), not the independent variable (Temperature).

Option 2: It claims that 83% of the variation in profit is explained by temperature variation. The given r = 0.83. The coefficient of determination (r^2) is:

$r^2 = (0.83)^2 = 0.6889 \approx 69\%$.

Thus, only 69% of profit variation is explained by temperature, not 83%. This option is incorrect.

Option 3: This option assumes that rising temperature causes profit to increase.

While the graph shows a positive correlation, correlation does not imply causation. The data only shows association, not a direct cause-effect relationship. Hence, this conclusion cannot be definitely drawn.

Option 4: It states that at T = 25°C, the estimated profit is ₹ 14 million.

Let's compute this using the given equation:

Profit = 4T – 86

Profit = 4 × 25 – 86

= 100 – 86 = ₹ 14 million.

This statement is mathematically correct.

Thus, Option 4 is the definite inference that can be drawn.

6. Given that the average of seven numbers is 71, their total sum is:

$$\text{Sum} = 71 \times 7 = 497.$$

When one number is excluded, the average becomes 75.

Thus, the sum of the remaining six numbers is:

$$\text{Sum of 6 numbers} = 75 \times 6 = 450.$$

Therefore, the excluded number is:

$$\text{Excluded number} = 497 - 450 = 47.$$

7. We are to determine which number-word correctly completes the sentence:

"THE NUMBER OF OCCURRENCES OF THE LETTER 'N' IN THIS SENTENCE IS CORRECTLY COUNTED AS ______."

First, count the number of 'N's in the sentence before the blank:

- NUMBER → 1
- OCCURRENCES → 1
- Letter "N" → 1
- IN → 1
- SENTENCE → 2
- COUNTED → 1

Total 'N's so far

= 1 + 1 + 1 + 1 + 2 + 1 = 7.

Now, test each option by inserting it into the blank and recalculate total 'N's:

- SIX → No 'N' → Total = 7
- SEVEN → 1 'N' → Total = 8
- EIGHT → No 'N' → Total = 7
- NINE → 2 'N's → Total = 7 + 2 = 9

The statement will be logically correct only when the total count of 'N's matches the number written in words.

Thus, filling the blank with NINE correctly matches the total count.

8. 6 directors shook hands with everyone else. Each of these 6 shakes hands with (20 – 1) = 19 people. But when A shakes hands with B, it's the same as B shaking hands with A, so we must avoid double-counting.

Among the 6 directors:

- Handshakes between themselves = ${}^6C_2$ = (6 × 5) / 2 = 15.

  Each of these 6 directors shakes hands with the remaining 14 directors (who don't shake with anyone else):
- Handshakes = 6 × 14 = 84.

  Total handshakes = Handshakes among 6 directors + Handshakes with the 14 directors = 15 + 84 = 99.

9. Correct chronological sequence of a cricket match event:

- First, toss (C) is conducted.
- Then, the match (A) is played.
- After that, the result (D) is declared.
- Finally, the trophy (B) is awarded.

Sequence: C → A → D → B.

10. Given that the diameter of the ball equals the side of the cube,

Let side of cube = d

Volume of cube = d^3

$$\text{Radius of sphere} = \frac{d}{2}$$

$$\text{Volume of sphere} = \frac{4}{3} \times \pi \times \left(\frac{d}{2}\right)^3 = \left(\frac{\pi d^3}{6}\right)$$

Empty volume = Cube volume – Sphere volume

$$= d^3 - \frac{\pi d^3}{6} = d^3\left(\frac{1-\pi}{6}\right)$$

Approximate value of π = 3.1416

Compute empty volume fraction:

$$\text{Empty fraction} = 1 - (3.1416/6) = 1 - 0.5236 = 0.4764.$$

Thus, percentage empty $\approx$ 47.64% $\approx$ 48%.

11. Let's trace the path step-by-step:

- Start facing East, walk 100 m.
- Turn right → now facing South, walk 60 m.
- Turn left → now facing East, walk 150 m.
- Turn left again → now facing North.

Thus, after the final turn, you are facing North.

12. We are given three words—TEST, EXAM, EAST—coded as 1382, 2182, and 1937 (order unknown). We are to find the code for MATE.

Step 1: Match Words to Codes

- TEST has a repeating letter 'T'. Among the codes, 2182 has a repeating digit '2'.
  Thus, TEST → 2182 → T is coded as 2.
- EAST contains the letter 'T', so its code must also contain '2'. Between the remaining codes (1382 and 1937), 1382 has a '2'.
  Thus, EAST → 1382.
- The remaining code 1937 corresponds to EXAM.

Step 2: Deduce Letter-to-Digit Mapping

From TEST → 2182:
T → 2, E → 1, S → 8.
From EAST → 1382:
E → 1, A → 3, S → 8, T → 2.
From EXAM → 1937:
E → 1, X → 9, A → 3, M → 7.
Thus, final mapping is:
E → 1, T → 2, A → 3, S → 8, M → 7, X → 9.

Step 3: Code for MATE

M → 7
A → 3
T → 2
E → 1

Therefore, MATE is coded as 7321.

13. Given:

- Only those who pass the entrance test take admission.
- All graduates from the institute get jobs in the same year.
- In 2022, no one took admission.

Now check which statement does NOT necessarily follow:

1. No one wrote the entrance test in 2022 → Not necessary. People might have written the test but failed.
2. No one passed the entrance test in 2022 → This follows since no one took admission.
3. No one graduated from the institute in 2024 → This follows, as no admissions in 2022 → no graduates in 2024.
4. No one got a job from the institute in 2024 → This follows because graduates get jobs in the same year and there are no graduates.

Thus, statement 1 does NOT necessarily follow.

14. Given:

- Only one person's name's first letter matches their position's first letter.
- Tom came first.
- Sam did not come second.

Positions:

- First (F)
- Second (S)
- Third (T)
- Fourth (F)

Tom is first → conflict (T $\neq$ F), so condition not satisfied yet.

Sam is not second, so possible positions left for Sam are: third or fourth.

If Sam is placed at fourth (S $\neq$ F) → still doesn't satisfy condition.

Try placing David third:

- David (D) at third (T) → no match.
- Frank (F) at second (S) → no match.
- Sam (S) at fourth (F) → no match.

Now try David fourth:

- David (D) at fourth (F) → no match.
- Frank (F) at second (S) → no match.
- Sam (S) at third (T) → no match.

Now place Frank fourth:

- Frank (F) at fourth (F) → match found.
- David (D) at second (S) → no match.
- Sam (S) at third (T) → no match.

This satisfies the condition that only one person's name matches their position's first letter (Frank-fourth).

Thus, Frank came fourth.

15. We are to identify the odd province out based on a hidden pattern in the names:

Analyze each province name for embedded number words:

1. **SONECON:** Contains letters O, N, E → Spells ONE completely.
2. **CUGHUSTER:** Intended to represent THREE, which requires letters T, H, R, E, E.

   Letters present: T, H, R, E, U, S, C, G. Problem: Only one 'E' is present, but spelling THREE requires two 'E's. Thus, CUGHUSTER is incomplete in spelling THREE.
3. **FATWOHUM:** Contains letters T, W, O → Spells TWO completely.
4. **CAFIVENGUS:** Contains letters F, I, V, E → Spells FIVE completely.

Thus, SONECON (ONE), FATWOHUM (TWO), CAFIVENGUS (FIVE) correctly embed number words, but CUGHUSTER fails to correctly encode THREE as it lacks a second 'E'.

16. We are to find the pie-chart that correctly represents the following distribution conditions:

1. Physics and Chemistry have an equal number of students.
2. Life Sciences gets 40% of the total students.
3. The remaining 60% is equally divided between Maths and Earth Sciences (i.e., 30% each).

Thus, the pie-chart must show:

- One sector of 40% (Life Sciences),
- Two smaller equal sectors (Physics and Chemistry),
- Two larger equal sectors (Maths and Earth Sciences).

Examining Pie-chart 1:

- One sector is distinctly larger and appears to cover 40% → this can represent Life Sciences.
- There are two smaller equal sectors → representing Physics and Chemistry.
- The remaining two medium-sized equal sectors can be Maths and Earth Sciences, each covering 30%.

This distribution perfectly matches all given conditions.

Examining Pie-charts 2, 3, and 4:

- **Pie-chart 2:** One sector is excessively large (over 50%), which violates the 40% Life Sciences condition.
- **Pie-chart 3:** Though it seems similar, the two medium sectors are not equal—violating the condition that Maths and Earth Sciences should be equally divided.
- **Pie-chart 4:** One sector is extremely large (about 50%)—exceeds the required 40% for Life Sciences and the remaining divisions are inconsistent.

Conclusion: Only Pie-chart 1 satisfies all the conditions given in the question.

17. We are to count how many 4-digit numbers can be formed using the digits {1, 2, 3, 4, 5} such that:

- No digit repeats.
- Digit 1 is always to the left of digit 2 (not necessarily adjacent).

Step 1: Total arrangements of 4 digits (without any condition)

We need to select 4 digits out of 5.

Number of ways to select 4 digits

$$= {}^5C_4 = 5 \text{ ways.}$$

For each selection, number of ways to arrange them $= 4! = 24$.

Total arrangements without restriction

$$= 5 \times 24 = 120.$$

Step 2: Apply the condition "1 is to the left of 2"

Among all these arrangements, for every arrangement where 1 is to the left of 2, there will be an arrangement where 2 is to the left of 1.

Thus, half of the total arrangements will have 1 to the left of 2.

So, number of valid numbers

$$= 120 \div 2 = 60.$$

Step 3: But wait! Do all arrangements include both digits 1 and 2?

No. We must ensure that both digits 1 and 2 are selected in the 4-digit number.

Thus:

- First, select the remaining 2 digits out of {3, 4, 5}.
- Number of ways $= {}^3C_2 = 3$ ways.

Now, arrange these 4 digits (including 1 and 2) in all possible ways:

Total arrangements $= 4! = 24$.

But we want only those arrangements where 1 is to the left of 2:

In half of them, 1 will be to the left of 2.

So, valid arrangements per selection

$$= 24 \div 2 = 12.$$

Total valid numbers $= 3 \times 12 = 36.$

18. Given Statements:

1. All A are B → Circle A must be completely inside circle B.
2. No D is A → Circle D must not overlap with A.
3. Some A are C → Circle A and C must partially overlap.

Let's analyze each diagram:

Diagram 1:

- A is completely inside B → ✓
- D is outside A → ✓
- C overlaps with A → ✓

Conclusion: Consistent.

Diagram 2:

- A is completely inside B → ✓
- D is outside A → ✓
- C overlaps with A → ✓

Conclusion: Consistent.

Diagram 3:

- A and B are merged ($A \subseteq B$) → ✓
- D is outside A → ✓
- C overlaps with A → ✓

Conclusion: Consistent.

Diagram 4:

- A is inside B → ✓
- D is outside A → ✓
- C is completely outside A and does not overlap with A → ✗ violates "Some A are C".

Conclusion: NOT Consistent.

Correct Answer: Diagram 4.

19. We are given a square sheet with side length 10 cm. It undergoes three successive foldings along its hypotenuse to form smaller isosceles right triangles each time. We are to find the length of each equal side (legs of the triangle) after the third folding.

Initially, the square has sides of 10 cm.

- **First Fold:** The square is folded along its diagonal, forming an isosceles right triangle. The legs are 10 cm each, and the hypotenuse (h_1) is calculated using Pythagoras' theorem:

$$h_1 = \sqrt{10^2 + 10^2}$$

$$= \sqrt{200} = 10\sqrt{2} \text{ cm.}$$

- **Second Fold:** Folding along hypotenuse h_1 creates a smaller isosceles right triangle where h_1 becomes the new hypotenuse. Let the new equal sides be s_2.

  Since hypotenuse = side $\times \sqrt{2}$, we have:

$$s_2 = \frac{h_1}{\sqrt{2}} = \frac{10\sqrt{2}}{\sqrt{2}} = 10 \text{ cm.}$$

  Thus, after the second fold, the side length remains 10 cm.

- **Third Fold:** Again, fold along the new hypotenuse.

  Hypotenuse $h_1 = s_2 \times \sqrt{2} = 10\sqrt{2}$ cm.

  Let the equal sides after this fold be s_3. Then:

$$s_3 = \frac{h_2}{\sqrt{2}} = \frac{10\sqrt{2}}{\sqrt{2}} = 5 \text{ cm.}$$

Thus, after the third folding, the length of each equal side is 5 cm.

20. Given:

- Total cost of water bottle = ₹ 20.
- Water costs ₹ 15 more than the bottle itself.
- Let cost of bottle = ₹ x.
- Then cost of water = ₹ $(x + 15)$.

Total cost equation:

$$x + (x + 15) = 20$$
$$2x + 15 = 20$$
$$2x = 20 - 15$$
$$2x = 5$$
$$x = 5 \div 2$$
$$x = 2.5$$

Thus, the cost of the bottle is ₹ 2.50.

21. The rock described is hornblende-bearing, formed very close to the surface, within the stability field of andalusite.

- Andalusite is stable at low pressure and moderate temperatures.
- Hornfels facies represents contact metamorphism occurring at low pressures and high temperatures near the surface.

Thus, the described rock represents Hornfels facies metamorphism.

22. The first multicellular life forms appeared during the Ediacaran period, which marks the end of the Proterozoic Eon.

- Approximate age: ~635 million years ago (Ma).

Thus, multicellular life appeared around 635 Ma.

23. The Cryogenian period (720–635 Ma) is primarily known for:

- Extreme global glaciations called Snowball Earth events, where ice possibly covered the entire planet.

Thus, the key characteristic is the occurrence of Snowball Earth glaciations.

24. Given:

- Half-life of 14C = 5730 years.
- Mean life (τ) is related to half-life ($t_{1/2}$) by:

$$\tau = \frac{t_{1/2}}{\ln(2)} = \frac{t_{1/2}}{0.693}$$

Compute: $\tau = \frac{5730}{0.693} \approx 8264$ years.

25. Given:

- A binary system of diopside and anorthite.
- At the eutectic point (melting begins), the system is invariant.
- By Gibbs Phase Rule:
  $F = C - P + 1$ (for constant pressure systems)
  $C = 2$ (components: diopside, anorthite)
  $P = 3$ (solid diopside + solid anorthite + liquid)
  $F = 2 - 3 + 1 = 0$.

Thus, the degree of freedom is 0.

26. Kamacite and Taenite are iron-nickel alloys found predominantly in Iron meteorites, also known as siderites.

- Kamacite has a low nickel content (4–7.5%), while Taenite is richer in nickel (20–50%).
- These two minerals intergrow to form structures like the Widmanstätten pattern, characteristic of iron meteorites.
- Achondrites, SNC meteorites, and Carbonaceous chondrites are primarily silicate-rich and lack significant amounts of metallic Fe-Ni phases like kamacite and taenite.

Thus, kamacite and taenite are the principal constituents of Iron meteorites.

27. Given:

- Fault plane orientation: Strike 250°, Dip 40° NW.
- Rake of slickenlines: 90°.

A rake of 90° indicates that the movement is pure dip-slip (the slip is along the dip direction). For a thrust fault, this means slickenlines plunge exactly down the dip of the fault plane at an angle equal to the dip of the plane.

Thus, the plunge of the slickenlines equals the dip of the fault plane, which is 40°.

28. Among the given options:

- Geleki, Lakwa, and Charali are oilfields located in the Assam-Arakan Basin of northeastern India.
- Kalol, however, is a significant oil field in the Cambay Basin, Gujarat.

The Cambay Basin is a rift basin known for its oil and gas production, whereas the others belong to the Assam fold belt.

29. Compaction rate of sediments during shallow burial depends on grain size, shape, and porosity:

- Mudstone is fine-grained (clay-sized particles), with high initial porosity due to water-filled pore spaces. These sediments compact rapidly as pore water is expelled under overburden pressure.
- Quartz arenite, Arkose, and Grainstone are coarser-grained sandstones or carbonates that have stronger grain frameworks resisting compaction.

Thus, Mudstone compacts at the fastest rate during shallow burial due to its high water content and fine grain size.

30. The Euler pole represents the point around which a tectonic plate rotates on the globe. For the Cenozoic motion of the Indian Plate, the Euler pole is located near Africa, specifically near the Somali Plate boundary in the Indian Ocean.

- This pole location explains the northward movement of the Indian Plate towards Eurasia, leading to the Himalayan orogeny.

Thus, the Euler pole of the Indian Plate's motion is positioned in Africa.

31. The process where soluble and fine-grained materials are transported downward from the upper soil horizons into the B horizon by percolating water is termed illuviation.

- This movement results in the accumulation of clay, iron, or organic matter in the B horizon.
- Rubification refers to reddening of soil due to iron oxidation.
- Hydrolysis is a chemical weathering process.
- Sapping involves the erosion of material due to seepage of groundwater.

Thus, the correct term for this downward translocation and deposition process is Illuviation.

32. In a weathering-limited environment, physical weathering exceeds chemical weathering due to arid or cold conditions.

- The rate of material removal (erosion) is higher than the rate of in-situ weathering.
- Therefore, there is little to no soil development, as weathered material is rapidly removed, preventing thick soil accumulation.

Thus, in weathering-limited environments, no or little soil develops.

33. To detect soil moisture through remote sensing, Microwave sensors are most effective because:

- Microwaves can penetrate through vegetation and soil surface layers.
- The dielectric properties of water in soil affect the microwave signal, making it sensitive to soil moisture content.
- Optical and thermal sensors are surface-based and less effective for sub-surface moisture detection.
- Hyperspectral sensors capture detailed surface reflectance data but are not effective for direct soil moisture measurement.

Thus, Microwave remote sensing is used for soil moisture detection.

34. The Wallacea region is a zoogeographic transitional zone between the Asian and Australian faunal realms.

- It is bounded by Wallace's Line to the west and Weber's Line to the east.
- Wallace's Line marks the western limit of Australasian species.
- Weber's Line indicates the eastern limit where Asian and Australasian species distributions blend.

Thus, Wallacea is bounded by Wallace's line to the west and Weber's line to the east.

35. Let's carefully analyze each statement regarding the Coriolis Force (CF), which is an apparent force experienced by objects in motion within a rotating reference frame like Earth.

1. **CF is the cross product between the rotational vector of the Earth and the velocity vector of the moving object.**
   This is true.
   Mathematically, Coriolis force is expressed as $F_n = -2m\ (\omega \times v)$, where ω is Earth's angular velocity vector and v is the velocity of the object.
   The direction of the Coriolis force is perpendicular to both ω and *v*.
2. **CF is maximum for motions perpendicular to the Earth's axis.**
   This is true.
   The Coriolis force depends on the sine of the latitude (sin ϕ).
   Maximum Coriolis acceleration occurs when the object's motion is perpendicular to Earth's rotational axis (i.e., purely horizontal motions at high latitudes).
3. **CF increases with increasing distance from the Earth's axis.**
   This is false.
   The horizontal component of the Coriolis force is zero at the equator (maximum distance from Earth's axis) and maximum at the poles (minimal distance from Earth's axis).
   Thus, CF decreases with increasing distance from Earth's axis.
4. **CF affects west-east winds over the equator to deflect them in vertical direction.**
   This is true.
   At the equator, the Coriolis force's horizontal component becomes zero.
   However, for east-west motions, the Coriolis force has a vertical component that slightly deflects the air parcel upward or downward, though this effect is usually negligible in large-scale atmospheric circulation.

Thus, statement 3 is incorrect.

36. The Earth's surface rotates from west to east, imparting westerly angular momentum.

- In regions where easterly surface winds blow (i.e., winds moving from east to west), the atmosphere moves slower than the Earth's surface rotation.

- Due to surface friction, a torque is applied by the faster-moving surface to the slower-moving atmosphere, resulting in a transfer of westerly angular momentum from Earth's surface to the atmosphere.
- Conversely, if surface winds are westerly (west to east), the atmosphere may transfer momentum back to Earth if the winds exceed the Earth's rotational speed.

Thus, transfer of westerly angular momentum from Earth's surface to the atmosphere happens in regions of surface easterlies.

37. Water-layer weathering is a physical weathering process where thin films of water on rock surfaces cause weathering due to hydration and temperature fluctuations.

- It is most effective on shore platforms, which are coastal erosional surfaces subject to tidal wetting and drying cycles.
- Strath terraces, duricrust tops, and stone pavements do not have the dynamic water-layer interaction like shore platforms.

Thus, water-layer weathering primarily occurs on shore platforms.

38. When adjacent alluvial fans merge laterally due to continuous sediment deposition from multiple sources, the resulting broad depositional plain is termed a bajada.

- A talus cone is an isolated cone-shaped debris accumulation at the base of cliffs.
- A megafan is a large alluvial fan but does not imply lateral coalescence.
- An erg is a vast desert sand sea.

Thus, a zone of coalescent deposition from adjacent prograding fans is called a bajada.

39. To arrange geomorphological features in up-slope order (from lower to higher elevation):

1. **Kettle lake** – depressions formed by retreating glaciers, found in lower areas.
2. **Glacial table** – boulders perched on ice pillars, typically found on glacier surfaces.
3. **Firn** – compacted snow between snow and glacial ice, found in higher accumulation zones.
4. **Bergschrund** – large crevasse at the uppermost part of a glacier, adjacent to the mountain face.

Thus, the correct up-slope sequence is:
Kettle lake → Glacial table → Firn → Bergschrund.

40. To arrange the soil orders in the correct sequence of increasing humid conditions, we must understand their typical climatic associations:

- **Mollisols:** Found mainly in temperate grasslands, mollisols are rich in organic matter but develop under moderate moisture conditions. They indicate semi-humid to sub-humid climates.
- **Vertisols:** These clay-rich soils expand and crack with moisture fluctuations. Though they need some rainfall, they are more common in semi-arid to sub-humid regions, slightly wetter than mollisols.
- **Spodosols:** Formed under cool, humid, and forested environments, spodosols experience significant leaching of organic matter and iron/aluminum oxides, indicating a higher humidity than vertisols and mollisols.
- **Oxisols:** These are the most weathered soils, found in tropical rainforests with extremely humid and hot climates. They represent the extreme end of the humid spectrum.

Thus, the correct ascending sequence in terms of increasing humid conditions is:
mollisols → vertisols → spodosols → oxisols.

41. The Earth's gravity field behaves differently in various layers:

- From the surface to the core-mantle boundary, gravity increases in the mantle due to increased mass beneath.
- In the outer core, gravity starts to decrease gently because though mass is still accumulating, it is distributed spherically around a point closer to the center.
- In the inner core, gravity decreases sharply towards the center, reaching zero at the very center of Earth due to symmetry (equal pull in all directions).

Thus, the gravity field increases in the mantle and decreases gently in the outer core and sharply in the inner core.

42. The primary sources of heat within the Earth's continental crust are:

- ^{238}U (Uranium-238)
- ^{232}Th (Thorium-232)
- ^{40}K (Potassium-40)

These isotopes undergo long-lived radioactive decay, generating most of the crustal radiogenic heat.

Other isotopes like ^{235}U, ^{14}C, and ^{137}Cs contribute negligibly to Earth's internal heat.

Thus, the correct combination is ^{238}U, ^{232}Th, and ^{40}K.

43. At Colombo (near the equator), Earth's magnetic field has:

- A strong horizontal component (H).
- A smaller vertical component (V) compared to H.
- The total magnetic field F is the resultant vector (F > H).

At equatorial regions:

- H > V.
- F > H.

Thus, the relation becomes F > H > V.

44. Declination of the Natural Remanent Magnetism (NRM) is the angle between the magnetic north and the horizontal component of the rock's magnetization.

- A change in declination indicates rotation of the rock unit about a vertical axis.
- It does not directly measure latitude or longitudinal shifts but rather horizontal rotational movement.

Thus, declination measures the amount of rotation about a vertical axis.

45. The Richter scale was designed for moderate-sized, nearby earthquakes.

- It tends to underestimate the magnitude of great earthquakes (M > 7) due to the saturation effect.
- Modern seismology uses the Moment Magnitude Scale (Mw) for larger quakes to avoid this issue.
- Richter magnitude is not universally valid for all epicentral distances and can give negative values for very small quakes.

Thus, the Richter scale underestimates the magnitude of great earthquakes.

46. Given:

Orbital period of Mars (T)

$= 687$ Earth days ≈ 1.88 Earth years.

Using Kepler's Third Law:

$T^2 \propto a^3$, where "a" is the semi-major axis in Astronomical Units (AU).

For Earth: T = 1 year, a = 1 AU.

For Mars: T = 1.88 years.

Compute: $a^3 = T^2 \rightarrow a^3 = (1.88)^2 = 3.5344$

$$a = \sqrt[3]{3.5344} \approx 1.52 \text{ AU}.$$

Thus, the distance of Mars from the Sun is approximately 1.5 AU.

47. Let's analyze each statement:

1. **The geoid is an equipotential surface** — *Correct*. The geoid represents the Earth's mean sea level extended under continents, where the gravitational potential is constant at every point. Gravity acts perpendicular to the geoid surface everywhere.
2. **The reference spheroid is an equipotential surface** — *Incorrect*. The reference spheroid (or ellipsoid) is a mathematically smooth, rotationally symmetric surface approximating Earth's shape. It is not an equipotential surface because it does not account for variations in Earth's gravitational field due to irregular mass distribution.
3. **The geoid is an undulating surface** — *Correct*. The geoid undulates above and below the reference spheroid, reflecting gravitational anomalies caused by mountains, ocean trenches, and varying Earth densities.
4. **The reference spheroid and geoid refer to the same surface** — *Incorrect*. While this statement is indeed wrong, statement 2 is the first incorrect one in the list. However, if the question explicitly asks for "Choose the INCORRECT statement", and option 4 is given, it is referring to the incorrect conceptual pairing of geoid and spheroid as the same surface.

Thus, although both option 2 and option 4 are incorrect in principle, the best choice for the intended incorrect statement is: (4) The reference spheroid and geoid refer to the same surface.

48. Given Poisson's ratio (σ) = 0.5, which indicates an incompressible material (e.g., perfect fluid). In such materials:

- S-waves (shear waves) cannot propagate because shear modulus is zero.

Thus, S-wave velocity is zero.

49. A continent-continent collision zone (e.g., Himalayas) is characterized by:

- Shallow focus earthquakes (within 70 km depth) occurring due to crustal shortening and thrust faulting.

- Unlike subduction zones, continent-continent collisions do not generate intermediate or deep-focus earthquakes.

Thus, such zones are primarily associated with shallow focus earthquakes.

50. The seismic phase that confirms the inner core of the Earth is solid is SKJKS. This phase involves an S-wave (shear wave) that travels through the Earth's inner core. Since S-waves can only propagate through solid materials and cannot pass through liquids, the detection of SKJKS waves is direct proof that the inner core is solid.

Here's how it works:

- The wave path of SKJKS involves an S-wave traveling through the mantle (S), converting to a P-wave in the outer core (K), becoming an S-wave again in the inner core (J), then repeating the path back through the outer core and mantle.
- The key evidence lies in the 'J' phase — S-waves reappearing in the inner core — which is only possible if the inner core is solid.

Other options:

- PKP and PKIKP are compressional P-waves. Since P-waves can travel through both solids and liquids, their paths do not confirm whether the inner core is solid.
- SKIKP involves an S-wave up to the core-mantle boundary, converting to a P-wave in the outer core, reflecting off the inner core boundary, but it does not involve S-wave propagation within the inner core itself.

Therefore, only SKJKS confirms the solid nature of the inner core.

51. If the Earth's rotation is absent, there would be no Coriolis force to deflect air movement.

- In such a scenario, air would move directly from high pressure to low pressure, following the pressure gradient force.
- There would be no geostrophic or gradient wind balancing, and no deflection parallel to isobars.

Thus, air in the lower atmosphere would flow from high pressure to low pressure.

52. The Rossby radius of deformation (L_0) is given by the formula:

$$L_0 = \frac{\sqrt{gH}}{f}$$

where g = gravity,

H = scale height of atmosphere (~ 10 km),

f = Coriolis parameter ($\sim 10^{-4}$ s^{-1} at 45°N).

Substituting approximate values, the atmospheric Rossby radius at 45° latitude is around 3000 km. Thus, the magnitude is 3000 km.

53. In an incompressible atmosphere, density is assumed constant, so Acoustic (sound) waves—which depend on compressibility and involve pressure-density perturbations—cannot propagate.

- Kelvin, Rossby, and Gravity waves are all permissible in incompressible fluid approximations.

Thus, Acoustic waves do not exist in an incompressible atmosphere.

54. A state function is a property that depends only on the current state of the system, not on how it got there.

- Enthalpy (H), Internal Energy (U), and Entropy (S) are all state functions.
- Work (W), however, is path-dependent; its value depends on the process path, especially in non-adiabatic processes.

Thus, Work is NOT a state function.

55. Ground-level ozone forms through photochemical reactions involving nitrogen oxides (NOx) and volatile organic compounds (VOCs) under sunlight.

- Increased NOx emissions → increases ozone formation.
- Higher VOC concentrations → increases ozone formation.
- Higher temperatures → accelerates ozone formation.
- Increased daytime cloud cover → reduces sunlight availability, thereby reducing ozone formation.

Thus, increased cloud cover during daytime reduces ground-level ozone formation.

56. Given:

- Environmental lapse rate = 6.5 K/km.
- Parcel lapse rate = 5 K/km.
- Parcel temperature at 3 km = 0°C.

Compute the environment temperature at 3 km: Since the environment cools faster than the parcel, the environment must be colder than the parcel.

Difference in lapse rates
$= 6.5$ K/km − 5 K/km = 1.5 K/km.
Over 3 km ascent:
Temperature difference = $1.5 \times 3 = 4.5$°C.
Thus, environment temperature at 3 km
= 0°C (parcel temp) − 4.5°C = −4.5°C.

57. When a moist air parcel rises adiabatically, it expands due to lower external pressure and hence:

- It cools due to expansion.
- This process involves condensation if saturation occurs, but temperature always decreases with ascent.

Thus, a moist parcel cools due to expansion when rising.

58. Wavenumber (n) is related to wavelength (λ) by:
λ = Circumference of Earth/n.
Earth's equatorial circumference ≈ 40000 km.
For wavenumber 4:

$$\lambda = \frac{40000}{4} = 10000 \text{ km.}$$

59. Scale height (H) is given by:

$$H = \frac{RT}{g}$$

where, $R = 287$ J/kg·K,
$T = 250$ K, $g = 9.8$ m/s^2.
Compute:

$$H = \frac{287 \times 250}{9.8} \approx \frac{7175}{9.8}$$

$$\approx 732.14 \times 10 \text{ m} = 7.3 \text{ km.}$$

Thus, the scale height is approximately 7.3 km.

60. Gravity waves in the atmosphere are supported by the buoyancy force, which restores displaced air parcels back to their equilibrium level.

- Buoyancy acts as the restoring force for vertical displacements, making oscillations possible.
- Compressibility affects acoustic waves.
- Earth's rotation supports Rossby waves, not gravity waves.

Thus, buoyancy is the restoring force for gravity waves.

61. The Redfield ratio (C:N:P) is 106:16:1 in moles.
Given primary productivity
= 1272 mg C m^{-3} d^{-1}.
Convert mg C to moles of C:

- Atomic weight of C = 12 g/mol.
- Moles of C = 1272 mg/12000 mg/mol = 0.106 moles C m^{-3} d^{-1}.

By Redfield ratio:
For every 106 moles of C, 1 mole of P is required.

$$\text{Thus, moles of P} = \frac{0.106}{106}$$

$$\approx 0.001 \text{ mol P m}^{-3} \text{ d}^{-1}$$

$$= 1 \text{ m mol m}^{-3} \text{ d}^{-1}.$$

Since, 1 m^3 = 1000 L,
this is equivalent to 1 μ mol L^{-1} d^{-1}.

62. In oceans:

- In-situ temperature is the actual measured temperature at depth.
- Potential temperature is the temperature the parcel would have if brought adiabatically to the surface.

Due to compression at depth, the in-situ temperature is slightly higher than the potential temperature:

- The difference ($T_{\text{in-situ}} - T_{\text{potential}}$) is positive and increases with depth due to increasing pressure.

63. Use Beer-Lambert's Law:
$I = I_0 \, e^{(-kz)}$, where k is the extinction coefficient.

Given: $\frac{I}{I_0} = 0.30$ at $z = 50$ m.

Thus, $0.30 = e^{(-k \times 50)}$
Take natural logarithm:

$$\ln(0.30) = -50k$$

$$-1.204 = -50k$$

$$k = \frac{1.204}{50} = 0.024 \text{ m}^{-1}.$$

64. High opal concentrations (biogenic silica from diatoms) are found in regions of high nutrient upwelling:

- Equatorial Pacific → strong upwelling.
- Southern Ocean → major diatom blooms.

Thus, opal-rich sediments are most abundant in the Equatorial Pacific and Southern Oceans.

65. Eastern Boundary Currents (EBCs), such as the California Current and Canary Current, are cold ocean currents flowing along the eastern margins of ocean basins. Their cold nature arises from two main factors:

1. **Equatorward Transport of Cold Water:** EBCs are part of the subtropical gyre circulation, where surface currents flow from higher latitudes (cooler regions) toward the equator.

   This transport of cooler water masses from polar or temperate regions into tropical zones is the primary reason for the persistently cold temperatures of EBCs.

2. **Coastal Upwelling (Secondary Factor):** Along EBCs, coastal upwelling occurs due to wind-induced Ekman transport, which moves surface waters offshore.

   This causes cold, nutrient-rich water from deeper layers to rise, reinforcing the coldness but is localized near coasts.

While upwelling enhances cold conditions locally, the dominant defining characteristic of EBCs is their role in carrying cold water from high latitudes towards the equator as part of large-scale gyre circulation.

Thus, Option 2 best represents the fundamental mechanism of EBC coldness.

66. The secondary nitrite maximum (SNM) is a subsurface feature observed in the oxygen minimum zones (OMZs) of the ocean, typically between depths of 100–1000 meters. In these low-oxygen layers, nitrite (NO_2^-) accumulates due to incomplete microbial processes.

There are two main processes contributing to SNM formation:

1. **Incomplete Nitrification:**
- Ammonia (NH_3) is oxidized to nitrite (NO_2^-).
- Due to low oxygen, the subsequent oxidation of nitrite to nitrate (NO_3^-) is inhibited, causing nitrite buildup.

2. **Partial Denitrification:**
- Denitrification is the anaerobic reduction of nitrate (NO_3^-) to nitrogen gas (N_2).
- The first step reduces nitrate to nitrite.
- If oxygen levels are very low but not zero, this step proceeds faster than the reduction of nitrite to nitrogen gas, leading to accumulation of nitrite.

Although both processes contribute, denitrification in OMZs is a dominant pathway for SNM formation in strongly oxygen-deficient waters.

Thus, denitrification is a valid and accepted explanation for the generation of secondary nitrite maxima.

67. Given:
- Distance from spreading center = 200 km = 200,000 m.
- Sediment thickness = 250 m.
- Sedimentation rate = 5 cm per 1000 years = 0.05 m per 1000 years.

Compute the age of the seafloor at this location:

$$\text{Age} = \frac{\text{Sediment thickness}}{\text{Sedimentation rate}}$$

$$\text{Age} = \frac{250 \text{ m}}{0.05 \text{ m per 1000 years}}$$

$$= 5000 \times 1000$$

$$= 5{,}000{,}000 \text{ years (5 Ma)}.$$

$$\text{Seafloor spreading rate} = \frac{\text{Distance}}{\text{Age}}$$

$$= \frac{200{,}000 \text{ m}}{5{,}000{,}000 \text{ years}}$$

$$= 0.04 \text{ m/year} = 4 \text{ cm/year}.$$

68. When $CaCO_3$ precipitates from seawater:
- It removes carbonate ions (CO_3^{2-}) and calcium ions (Ca^{2+}) from the solution.
- This results in a reduction of both dissolved inorganic carbon (DIC) and alkalinity, as each mole of $CaCO_3$ removes 2 equivalents of alkalinity.

Thus, precipitation leads to a reduction in both DIC and alkalinity.

69. Microbial respiration rates decrease in the ocean with increasing depth primarily because of high pressure and low temperature. As we go deeper, the hydrostatic pressure increases dramatically, which can affect microbial cellular structures like membranes and enzymes. Additionally, the temperature of deep ocean waters drops to near freezing levels, which reduces the kinetic energy of molecules and slows down enzymatic reactions critical for respiration. These two factors together significantly lower microbial metabolic activity, including respiration rates, in the deep ocean.

Other options:
- Low abundance of organic matter does impact microbial respiration since food availability declines with depth, but it is not

the principal factor. Microbes can adapt to low-nutrient environments, but the extreme pressure and cold temperatures universally suppress metabolic rates.

- Influence of Antarctic Bottom Water refers to the spreading of cold, dense water masses but this is a localized phenomenon and does not explain respiration rate decreases across all ocean depths.
- Complete darkness affects photosynthesis but not respiration. Microbial respiration is a biochemical process that doesn't require light, so darkness itself is not a limiting factor for microbial respiration.

Thus, the most comprehensive explanation involves the physical stress of high pressure and low temperature affecting microbial physiology at depth.

70. Carbonate alkalinity is the sum of bicarbonate ($[HCO_3^-]$) and twice the carbonate ion concentration ($[CO_3^{2-}]$):

$$\text{Alkalinity} = [HCO_3^-] + 2 \times [CO_3^{2-}]$$

Given:

$$[HCO_3^-] = 1700 \ \mu \text{ mol/kg}$$
$$[CO_3^{2-}] = 200 \ \mu \text{ mol/kg}$$

Compute:

$$\text{Alkalinity} = 1700 + 2 \times 200 = 1700 + 400 = 2100 \ \mu \text{ mol/kg.}$$

71. To find the equivalent horizontal hydraulic conductivity (Keq) of layered isotropic aquifers, we use the thickness-weighted arithmetic mean:

$$K_{eq} = \frac{K_1 \cdot b_1 + K_2 \cdot b_2}{b_1 + b_2}$$

Given: $K_1 = 8.6$ m/day, $b_1 = 12$ m

$K_2 = 5.2$ m/day, $b_2 = 15$ m

$$K_{eq} = \frac{(8.6 \times 12) + (5.2 \times 15)}{12 + 15} = \frac{103.2 + 78}{27} = \frac{181.2}{27} = 6.71 \text{ m/day.}$$

72. Given:

- Mean stress (σ_m) = 4 kbars
- Shear stress at failure (τ_{max}) = 2.5 kbars

We are to find the differential stress (σ_d) developed in the body.

Fundamental Relation:

The differential stress (σ_d) is defined as:

$$\sigma_d = \sigma_1 - \sigma_3$$

where:

- σ_1 = Maximum principal stress
- σ_3 = Minimum principal stress

The mean stress (σ_m) is:

$$\sigma_m = \frac{\sigma_1 + \sigma_3}{2}$$

The maximum shear stress (τ_{max}) is:

$$\tau_{max} = \frac{\sigma_1 - \sigma_3}{2} = \frac{\sigma_d}{2}$$

Step-by-Step Solution:

We are given: $\sigma_m = 4$ kbars and $\tau_{max} = 2.5$ kbars

From shear stress equation:

$$\tau_{max} = \frac{\sigma_d}{2}$$

$$\Rightarrow \quad \sigma_d = 2 \times \tau_{max} = 2 \times 2.5 = 5 \text{ kbars}$$

Thus: $\sigma_1 - \sigma_3 = 5$ kbars (Differential Stress)

Also: $\sigma_m = \frac{\sigma_1 + \sigma_3}{2} = 4$ kbars

$$\Rightarrow \quad \sigma_1 + \sigma_3 = 8 \text{ kbars}$$

Now, solving these two equations:

1. $\sigma_1 - \sigma_3 = 5$ 2. $\sigma_1 + \sigma_3 = 8$

Adding the two:

$$2\sigma_1 = 13 \Rightarrow \sigma_1 = 6.5 \text{ kbars}$$

Subtracting equation 1 from equation 2:

$$2\sigma_3 = 3 \Rightarrow \sigma_3 = 1.5 \text{ kbars}$$

Thus: $\sigma_d = \sigma_1 - \sigma_3 = 6.5 - 1.5 = 5$ kbars

Conclusion: The differential stress developed in the body is 5 kbars, but since 5 kbars is not among the given options, and the shear stress of 2.5 kbars is half of the differential stress, the question seems to expect the shear stress itself to be marked as the differential stress.

But strictly by definition, differential stress = 5 kbars. Thus, NONE of the given options (1.5, 2.0, 2.5, 3.0) is correct.

73. Matching Wilson cycle stages with examples:

- Embryonic – Basin and Range Province, USA (S)
- Juvenile/young – Red Sea, Africa (P)
- Mature – Arabian Sea (Q)
- Terminal – Mediterranean Sea (R)

Thus: A-S, B-P, C-Q, D-R.

74. Given biotite appears at 400°C and 0.5 GPa. UHT metamorphism typically refers to >900°C. If thermal gradient (T/P) is constant:

$$\frac{400}{0.5} = \frac{900}{P_{UHT}}$$

$$P_{UHT} = \frac{900 \times 0.5}{400} = \frac{450}{400} = 1.125 \text{ GPa.}$$

75. Matching critical metals with their ore minerals:
- Li – Spodumene (IV) • U – Pitchblende (III)
- La – Bastnasite (I) • Nb – Columbite (II)

Thus: A-IV, B-III, C-I, D-II.

76. Isochron-I is constructed using whole-rock samples A, B, and C. Whole-rock isochrons typically represent the time of igneous emplacement, hence Isochron-I dates the igneous event. Isochron-II is formed by minerals M_1 and M_2 from rock B. Mineral isochrons generally reflect isotopic re-equilibration during a metamorphic overprint; thus, Isochron-II represents the metamorphic event. Therefore, statement P is correct.

Intercept X is the point where Isochron-I meets the Y-axis at 87Rb/86Sr = 0. In Rb-Sr isochron diagrams, the intercept of the whole-rock isochron at 87Rb/86Sr = 0 represents the initial 87Sr/86Sr ratio of the source from which the rocks formed. Thus, statement R is correct.

Rock A lies towards the lower end of the 87Rb/86Sr axis, indicating a low Rb/Sr ratio, which is typical of mafic rocks. Rock C lies towards the higher end of the 87Rb/86Sr axis, indicating a high Rb/Sr ratio, typical of felsic compositions. Hence, statement T is correct.

Statement S is incorrect because intercept Y is associated with the mineral isochron (Isochron-II) and represents an isotopic resetting event during metamorphism, not the initial 87Sr/86Sr ratio of the igneous source.

77. Given: AB = 25 m, BC = 30 m, AC = 32 m

Ore thickness at A = 4 m, at B = 5 m, at C = 8 m; Specific Gravity (SG) = 4.95

Step 1: Calculate Area of Triangle ABC using Heron's Formula

Semi-perimeter (s):

$$s = \frac{AB + BC + AC}{2}$$

$$= \frac{25 + 30 + 32}{2} = \frac{87}{2} = 43.5 \text{ m}$$

Area (A) of triangle ABC:

$$A = \sqrt{s(s - AB)(s - BC)(s - AC)}$$

$$A = \sqrt{43.5 \times (43.5 - 25) \times (43.5 - 30) \times (43.5 - 32)}$$

$$A = \sqrt{43.5 \times 18.5 \times 13.5 \times 11.5}$$

Compute the product:

$$43.5 \times 18.5 = 804.75$$

$$804.75 \times 13.5 = 10864.125$$

$$10864.125 \times 11.5 = 124937.4375$$

$$A = \sqrt{124937.4375}$$

$$\approx 353.49 \text{ m}^2$$

Step 2: Average Thickness of Ore Body

$$\text{Average Thickness} = \frac{4 + 5 + 8}{3} = \frac{17}{3}$$

$$= 5.6667 \text{ m}$$

Step 3: Calculate Volume of Ore Body

Volume = Area of Triangle × Average Thickness

Volume = 353.49 × 5.6667 = 2003.98 m^3

Step 4: Calculate Tonnage

Tonnage (metric ton)

= Volume × Specific Gravity

Tonnage = 2003.98 × 4.95

= 9919.71 metric tons

None of given options match 9919.71 mt.

78. **Statement I:** Crisscrossing sheafs of acicular olivine → Komatiite

Statement II: Partial melting of mantle at >100 km, extruded to surface → Komatiite

Statement III: Layers in layered gabbroic intrusions, large massifs of plagioclase → Anorthosite

Statement IV: Contains aluminous bronzite → Anorthosite

Thus:
- I → Komatiite • II → Komatiite
- III → Anorthosite • IV → Anorthosite.

79. **Statement A:** Grt + Cpx constitute the peak metamorphic assemblage. → *Correct.*

The polygonal grain boundaries between Garnet and Clinopyroxene indicate equilibrium at peak metamorphic conditions, representing the stable high-pressure assemblage.

Statement B: The rock experienced eclogite facies metamorphism. → *Correct.*

The assemblage of Grt + Cpx, without Plagioclase at peak, is indicative of eclogite facies metamorphism formed under high-pressure conditions.

Statement C: The Am + Pl reaction texture does not represent a symplectite texture.

→ *Incorrect.* The formation of Amphibole + Plagioclase as reaction rims around Garnet and Clinopyroxene is a typical symplectitic texture, formed during decompression and hydration.

Statement D: The Am + Pl reaction texture requires hydration during its formation.

→ *Correct.* The retrograde reaction forming Amphibole (OH-bearing) and Plagioclase from Garnet + Clinopyroxene requires the addition of fluids, i.e., hydration.

Thus, statements A and D are correct.

80. Given Reaction:

$2NaAlSi_3O_8 + 2CO_2 + 3H_2O$

$\rightarrow Al_2Si_2O_5(OH)_4 + 2Na^+ + 2HCO_3^- + 4SiO_2$

Given Data:

- Na^+ concentration = 100 μ mol/L
- 90% of Na^+ is from albite dissolution
- Molecular weight of albite ($NaAlSi_3O_8$) = 262 g/mol
- Volume of water = 1 L

Step 1: Calculate moles of Na^+ derived from albite

Moles of Na^+ = 100 μ mol/L × 0.9
= 90 μ mol/L = 90×10^{-6} mol

Step 2: Determine moles of albite dissolved

From the reaction: 2 mol Albite → 2 mol Na^+

Thus, the molar ratio is 1:1.

Moles of Albite dissolved = 90×10^{-6} mol

Step 3: Calculate mass of albite dissolved

Mass of Albite = Moles × Molecular Weight

Mass = $90 \times 10^{-6} \times 262$
= 0.02358 g = 23.58 mg

Final Rounded Value: 23.6 mg.

81. Milankovitch cycles are caused by variations in Earth's orbital parameters, which include:

1. Changes in Earth's axial tilt (Obliquity)
2. Variation in Earth's orbital eccentricity
3. Precession of Earth's rotation axis

However, changes in the Sun's energy output are not a part of Milankovitch cycles. That pertains to solar activity cycles, not orbital mechanics.

82. Matching Quaternary Events:

A. Last Glacial Maximum (LGM) → R. 26,000 - 20,000 years ago

B. Younger Dryas → S. 12,900 - 11,700 years ago

C. Medieval Warming → Q. 1,170 - 770 years ago

D. Appearance of Modern Humans → P. 300,000 - 200,000 years ago

Correct matching sequence: A-R, B-S, C-Q, D-P.

83. Let's evaluate the combinations:

1. Groove cast and convolute lamination → Possible together (both found in turbidites)
2. Prod mark and wave ripple → Possible together (depositional structures in shallow marine environments)
3. Double mud drape and rain imprint → Not possible together
   Double mud drapes form in tidal environments.
   Rain imprints form on subaerially exposed surfaces.
   Both require different environmental settings.
4. Desiccation crack and current ripple → Possible together (found in fluvio-lacustrine environments)

Thus, combination 3 does not occur together.

84. Among the formations:

- Rohtas Formation → Dominantly carbonate rocks (limestone, dolostone)
- Srisailam Formation → Quartzites and shales
- Gulcheru Formation → Mainly quartzite
- Rabanapalli Formation → Mainly quartzite

Thus, Rohtas Formation is the carbonate-dominated unit.

85. Let's consider each:

- Ostracoda → Occur in both marine and freshwater
- Diatom → Occur in both marine and freshwater
- Dinoflagellate → Occur in both marine and freshwater
- Radiolaria → Exclusively marine, found in deep-sea pelagic deposits.

86. Given Ratings:

A. Strength of intact rock = 7

B. RQD = 8

C. Joint Spacing = 10

D. Condition of Joints = 10

E. Groundwater = 7

Sum of ratings (Basic RMR before adjustment):

RMR = 7 + 8 + 10 + 10 + 7
= 42

Since the tunnel is excavated along the dip direction of bedding planes (which is an unfavorable condition), an adjustment factor of –10 to –12 is typically applied.

However, in Bieniawski's RMR system, for a dip of 30° in sandstone, adjustment for unfavorable orientation is generally around –2 points.

Adjusted RMR = 42 – 2 = 40.

87. **Statement A:** Mean velocity in open channel flow (Manning's equation) is:

$$V = \frac{1}{n} R^{2/3} S^{1/2}$$

where V = velocity, n = Manning's roughness coefficient, R = hydraulic radius, S = channel slope (gradient). Thus, velocity is directly proportional to hydraulic radius and channel gradient (S), and inversely related to roughness (n). Therefore, Statement A is incorrect because it wrongly states "inversely related to gradient".

Statement B: Hydraulic radius (R) is defined as:

$$R = \frac{A}{P}$$

where A = cross-sectional area, P = wetted perimeter.

Statement B says R = P/A which is incorrect. It should be A/P.

Thus, Statement B is incorrect.

88. Let's analyze each pair:

A. Till – Glacial deposit → Correct

B. Tufa – Limestone deposit → Correct

C. Ventifact – Glacial erosion → Incorrect (Ventifacts are formed by wind abrasion)

D. Wind gap – Wind erosion → Incorrect (Wind gaps are erosional features formed by fluvial processes, not wind)

E. Yardang – Streamlined by water erosion → Incorrect (Yardangs are streamlined features formed by wind erosion)

F. Hamada – Desert pavement → Correct

Thus, C, D, and E are incorrect pairs.

89. Let's analyze the plot carefully:

- **Number of Streams vs Stream Order** → Number of streams decreases exponentially with increasing stream order (Horton's Law of Stream Numbers). This line will have a steep negative slope.
  → Line A is showing a steep negative slope.
- **Channel Length (L) and Basin Area (A) vs Stream Order** → Both increase exponentially with stream order.
  → Lines B and C are increasing trends, but B is steeper (likely basin area), C is more gradual (likely channel length).
- **Gradient (G) vs Stream Order** → Gradient decreases as stream order increases because higher-order streams have gentler slopes.
  → Line D shows a gentle decreasing trend, which is typical for gradient.

Thus:

- Number of Streams — Line A
- Gradient — Line D.

90. Given for at-a-station hydraulic geometry:

- b (width exponent) = 0.27
- f (velocity exponent) = 0.62
- Need to find m (depth exponent)

The relationship is based on the continuity equation:

$$Q = w \cdot d \cdot v$$

Where: w = width, d = depth, v = velocity.

In power-law form:

$$Q = a \cdot w^b \cdot d^m \cdot v^f$$

Since Q appears on both sides as a power function, the exponents must satisfy:

$$b + m + f = 1$$

Substitute given values:

$$0.27 + m + 0.62 = 1$$

$$m = 1 - (0.27 + 0.62) = 1 - 0.89 = 0.11.$$

91. Matching Column-I with Column-II:

A. Post-deposition changes in sediments → H. Diagenesis

B. Soil formation → I. Pedogenesis

C. Cave network development → E. Speleogenesis

D. Building of mountains by the forces of plate tectonics → F. Orogenesis

Correct matching sequence: A-H, B-I, C-E, D-F.

92. In a hypsographic (hypsometric) curve, the x-axis represents the relative area (a/A), and the y-axis represents the relative elevation (h/H).

For a landscape with very low relief and a few isolated hills:

- Most of the area will be at low elevation.
- Only a small portion of the area will have high elevation (isolated hills).

- The curve will stay close to the *x*-axis for most of its length and rise steeply near the end.

In the given plot:

- Curve D stays near the base (low elevation) for most of its length and rises abruptly near a/A = 1, indicating a flat lowland with a few isolated hills.

Thus, Curve D represents a landscape with very low relief and a few isolated hills.

93. **Assertion (A):** Oligotrophic lakes in colder climates have high dissolved oxygen near the surface — Correct, due to lower temperatures, oxygen solubility increases, and oligotrophic lakes have clear, oxygen-rich surface waters.

Reason (R): There is high productivity in oligotrophic lakes — Incorrect. Oligotrophic lakes are nutrient-poor and have low productivity.

Thus, (A) is correct but (R) is incorrect.

94. Matching soil types and characteristics:

A. Podzol → R. A2 horizon is light-colored due to removal of iron oxides and humus by leaching

B. Laterite → S. Relative enrichment of sesquioxides of iron and aluminum at or near the surface due to removal of silica

C. Chernozem → P. Thick and humus-rich A horizon and accumulation of $CaCO_3$ in lower B or beneath B horizon

D. Solonchak → Q. Accumulation of soluble salts

Correct matching: A-R, B-S, C-P, D-Q.

95. Matching plant types:

A. Heliophytes → Q. Plants growing under direct sunlight

B. Psammophytes → R. Plants growing in sandy soils

C. Chasmophytes → S. Plants growing in crevices of rocks

D. Oxilophytes → P. Plants growing in acidic soils

Correct matching: A-Q, B-R, C-S, D-P.

96. **Figure I** shows consistently high latent heat flux (LE) throughout the year with very low sensible heat flux (H), indicating abundant moisture availability year-round. This is characteristic of a Tropical wet climate, where evapotranspiration dominates the energy balance.

Figure II shows a distinct seasonal shift where LE is high during summer and drops significantly in winter, while H increases in winter. This represents a Tropical wet summer and dry winter climate, typical of monsoonal regions where moisture availability is seasonal.

Figure III shows a dominant sensible heat flux (H) throughout the year, especially in summer, while LE remains low. This pattern is typical of an Arid climate, where limited moisture suppresses latent heat flux.

Figure IV displays a balanced distribution of LE and H, with LE slightly increasing during summer. This is indicative of a Warm steppe climate, where moderate moisture availability leads to balanced energy fluxes.

Correct Matching:

A. Fig I → R. Tropical wet climate

B. Fig II → S. Tropical wet summer and dry winter climate

C. Fig III → Q. Arid climate

D. Fig IV → P. Warm steppe climate.

97. Given: Peak wavelengths:

- Star A: λ_a = 965 nm
- Star B: λ_b = 482 nm

Using Stefan-Boltzmann Law and Wien's Displacement Law, luminosity per unit area $\propto T_4$, and $T \propto 1/\lambda_{peak}$.

Thus, ratio of temperatures:

$$\frac{T_b}{T_a} = \frac{\lambda_a}{\lambda_b} = \frac{965}{482} \approx 2$$

Brightness ratio (energy emitted per unit area) is proportional to $(T_b/T_a)^4$:

$$\frac{E_b}{E_a} = \left(\frac{T_b}{T_a}\right)^4 = 2^4 = 16.$$

98. **Assertion (A)** claims that the upper section of a macrotidal estuary gets sedimented due to ebb dominance. This is incorrect because in ebb-dominant systems, the outgoing tidal current is stronger and tends to export sediments out of the estuary rather than deposit them in the upper reaches. Sedimentation in the upper part of an estuary is more typical of flood-dominant systems, where flood currents bring in sediments, and the weaker ebb currents are unable to carry them back out, resulting in deposition.

Hence, Assertion (A) is false.

Reason (R) states that sediment entrainment and deposition depend on the speed of tidal currents. This is a correct statement, as higher current velocities promote sediment entrainment (erosion and transport), while lower velocities favor deposition.

Thus, Reason (R) is true.

99. To arrange the landfall sites of the cyclonic storms from north to south since 2022, we need to consider the geographical locations where each cyclone made landfall:

- **Biparjoy:** Made landfall in the Kutch region of Gujarat, India, near the India-Pakistan border, making it the northernmost landfall among these storms.
- **Remal:** Struck the coastal areas of West Bengal, India, and Bangladesh. While still northern, its landfall was south of Biparjoy's.
- **Dana:** Cyclone Dana affected parts of Andhra Pradesh, placing its landfall further south than Remal.
- **Asani:** Made landfall along the Andhra Pradesh coast, slightly further south than Dana.
- **Mandous:** Landfall occurred in Tamil Nadu, near Chennai, making it the southernmost landfall site among the given cyclones.

Thus, the correct north-to-south arrangement of landfall sites is: Biparjoy → Remal → Dana → Asani → Mandous.

100. Match the impact structures:

A. Bundelkhand → O. Dhala

B. Kota Plateau → N. Ramgarh

C. Arabian Sea shelf → L. Shiva

D. Buldhana → P. Lonar

Correct match: A-O, B-N, C-L, D-P.

101. As the Froude Number (Fr) decreases from >1 to <1, the flow regime transitions from supercritical to subcritical, leading to the following bedform sequence:

- **Antidunes (Fr > 1):** Form under super-critical flow with upstream-migrating bedforms.
- **Plane Bed (Fr ≈ 1):** Transitional flat bedform as the flow becomes critical.
- **Dunes (Fr < 1):** Form under subcritical flow, migrate downstream.
- **Ripples (Fr << 1):** Small-scale bedforms forming at lower flow velocities.

Thus, the correct sequence is:

Antidunes → Plane bed → Dunes → Ripples.

102. Matching DEM products with their corresponding satellites:

A. ALOS (Advanced Land Observing Satellite) → S. Daichi: A Japanese satellite that produces high-resolution DEMs.

B. SRTM (Shuttle Radar Topography Mission) → P. Endeavour: SRTM was flown onboard the Space Shuttle Endeavour.

C. ASTER (Advanced Spaceborne Thermal Emission and Reflection Radiometer) → Q. Terra: ASTER sensor is onboard NASA's Terra satellite, producing DEMs.

D. Copernicus DEM → R. TanDEM-X: Copernicus DEM data is derived from the German TanDEM-X mission.

Correct matching: A-S, B-P, C-Q, D-R.

103. **Statement A:** The gravity field is defined as the gradient (rate of change) of the gravity potential. This is correct; gravity acceleration is the derivative of the potential.

Statement B: The gravity field on the geoid is zero — This is incorrect. The geoid is an equipotential surface, meaning the potential is constant, but the gravity field (gradient of potential) is not zero. Objects are still acted upon by Earth's gravity.

Thus, Statement A is correct, but Statement B is invalid.

104. Given data:

- Maximum magnetic anomaly = +640 gammas
- Minimum magnetic anomaly = –320 gammas
- The profile is across a dyke-like body, and we are to find the magnetic anomaly value directly above the dyke axis.

Geophysical Principle: For a dyke-like magnetic body, the anomaly profile shows:

1. A positive anomaly peak on one side.
2. A negative anomaly trough on the other side.
3. The anomaly value directly above the dyke is determined by the geometry of the body and the inclination of the Earth's magnetic field.

When the anomaly profile is asymmetric (i.e., maximum and minimum amplitudes are unequal as given here), the anomaly at the dyke axis will not be zero.

Instead, it will be closer to the smaller amplitude lobe's magnitude, because of the inclined inducing magnetic field.

Calculation Based on Known Dyke Anomaly Behavior:

- Maximum anomaly = +640 gammas
- Minimum anomaly = –320 gammas
- The anomaly directly over the dyke is typically around the value of the lower amplitude lobe, i.e., around + 320 gammas.

Thus, based on known dyke anomaly profiles, the anomaly directly over the dyke will be 320 gammas.

105. Given:

- Two isostatically compensated elevated masses with thicknesses 1 km (mass A) and 2 km (mass B).
- FA (Free Air anomaly) measures gravity at observation point; for isostatic compensation, FB = FA as surface elevation remains balanced.
- Bouguer anomaly (BA) accounts for subsurface mass; for a thicker compensated body, Bouguer anomaly is proportional to thickness.

Thus:

- FB = FA (Free Air anomaly remains constant for both masses)
- gB = 2 × gA (Bouguer anomaly doubles with thickness).

106. For a horizontal circular cylindrical body, the gravity anomaly (Δg) at a horizontal distance x from the center is given by:

$$\Delta g(x) = \frac{\Delta g_{max}}{1+\left(\frac{x}{z}\right)^2}$$

Where:

- Δg_{max} = Maximum gravity anomaly (at $x = 0$)
- z = Depth to the center of the cylinder
- x = Horizontal distance from the anomaly center

Given Condition:

At some distance x, the anomaly is reduced to one-third of its maximum value:

$$\Delta g(x) = \frac{\Delta g_{max}}{3}$$

Substitute into the equation:

$$\frac{\Delta g_{max}}{3} = \frac{\Delta g_{max}}{1+\left(\frac{x}{z}\right)^2}$$

Cancel Δg_{max} from both sides:

$$\frac{1}{3} = \frac{1}{1+\left(\frac{x}{z}\right)^2}$$

Invert both sides:

$$3 = 1+\left(\frac{x}{z}\right)^2$$

Solve for x/z:

$$\left(\frac{x}{z}\right)^2 = 3 - 1 = 2$$

$$\frac{x}{z} = \sqrt{2}$$

$$x = \sqrt{2}.z$$

Final Answer: $\sqrt{2}z$.

107. Given:

- Reference velocity V_0 = 5 km/sec
- First segment (5 km) velocity perturbation = +2%
- Second segment (5 km) velocity perturbation = +4%

Step 1: Calculate velocities in both segments

For the first 5 km segment:

$$V_1 = V_0 \times (1 + 0.02)$$
$$= 5 \times 1.02 = 5.10 \text{ km/sec}$$

For the second 5 km segment:

$$V_2 = V_0 \times (1 + 0.04)$$
$$= 5 \times 1.04 = 5.20 \text{ km/sec}$$

Step 2: Calculate travel times in each segment

Travel time through first segment:

$$T_1 = \frac{5}{5.10} = 0.9804 \text{ sec}$$

Travel time through second segment:

$$T_2 = \frac{5}{5.20} = 0.9615 \text{ sec}$$

Total travel time through perturbed medium:

$$T_{actual} = T_1 + T_2$$
$$= 0.9804 + 0.9615$$
$$= 1.9419 \text{ sec}$$

Step 3: Calculate travel time through reference medium

$$T_{ref} = \frac{10}{5} = 2.0 \text{ sec}$$

Step 4: Calculate travel time residual (%)

$$\text{Residual (\%)} = \frac{T_{actual} - T_{ref}}{T_{ref}} \times 100$$

$$= \frac{1.9419 - 2.0}{2.0} \times 100 = -2.905\%$$

Approximated to –2.9%.

108. Let's analyze the matching step-by-step:

P. Decrease in formation factor

- Formation factor decreases with increased permeability (because formation factor $F = a/\varphi^m$ where φ = porosity).
- Cause: Increase in permeability.

→ Match: 4

Q. PSP (Spontaneous Potential Log)

- PSP increases (shows deflection) in wet, shaly sandstone beds due to ionic exchange in clay minerals.

→ Cause: Wet, shaly sandstone bed.

→ Match: 1

R. Decrease in neutron porosity

- Neutron porosity logs respond to hydrogen content; presence of gas reduces hydrogen concentration, resulting in decreased neutron porosity readings.

→ Cause: Presence of gas.

→ Match: 2

S. Decrease in sonic velocity

- Sonic velocity decreases in over-pressured zones due to reduction in effective stress which slows down acoustic wave velocities.

→ Cause: Over-pressured zone.

→ Match: 3

Correct Matching:

- P → 4 • Q → 1 • R → 2 • S → 3.

109. Given:

- A near-surface earthquake of magnitude 4.0.
- Recorded by stations A (local), B (regional), and C (teleseismic).
- Event durations at these stations are EA, EB, and EC, respectively.

Explanation:

- **Local station (A):** Receives direct waves with minimal path dispersion, so the signal duration is short.
- **Regional station (B):** Waves undergo more path effects like scattering and multipathing, leading to longer signal duration than at A.
- **Teleseismic station (C):** At far distances, waves spread out even more due to dispersion and Earth's structure, leading to the longest signal duration.

Thus, event duration order: EA < EB < EC.

110. Given:

- Slope of direct wave $p_1 = 0.5$ s/km
- Slope of refracted head wave $p_2 = 0.33$ s/km
- Intercept time of head wave $\tau_2 = 1.5$ s

The thickness of the top layer in a two-layer seismic refraction model is calculated using the formula:

$$h = \frac{\tau_2}{\sqrt{\frac{1}{p_1^2} - \frac{1}{p_2^2}}}$$

Compute the terms:

$$\frac{1}{p_1^2} = \frac{1}{(0.5)^2} = \frac{1}{0.25} = 4$$

$$\frac{1}{p_2^2} = \frac{1}{(0.33)^2} = \frac{1}{0.1089} \approx 9.183$$

$$\frac{1}{p_1^2} - \frac{1}{p_2^2} = 4 - 9.183 = -5.183$$

But this gives a negative value, which is physically impossible. This suggests that we must use the correct formula involving the cosine of critical angle for refraction interface depth estimation, which is:

$$h = \frac{\tau_2 \times \sqrt{V_2^2 - V_1^2}}{2}$$

However, for slope-based formula in delay-time method, the correct formula is:

$$h = \frac{t_2}{2\sqrt{p_1^2 - p_2^2}}$$

Compute: $p_1^2 = (0.5)^2 = 0.25$

$$p_2^2 = (0.33)^2 = 0.1089$$

$$p_1^2 - p_2^2 = 0.25 - 0.1089 = 0.1411$$

$$\sqrt{0.1411} = 0.3756$$

$$h = \frac{1.5}{2 \times 0.3756} = \frac{1.5}{0.7512}$$

$$= 1.9968 \text{ km}$$

Thus, the thickness of the top layer is approximately 2 km.

111. Given:

- Frequency effect (FE) = 0.20
- Apparent resistivity at low frequency (ρ_{low}) = 100 Ωm

Frequency effect is defined as:

$$FE = \frac{\rho_{low} - \rho_{high}}{\rho_{high}}$$

Rearranging for ρ_{high}:

$$FE = \frac{100 - \rho_{high}}{\rho_{high}}$$

$$0.20 = \frac{100 - \rho_{high}}{\rho_{high}}$$

$$0.20 \times \rho_{high} = 100 - \rho_{high}$$

$$0.20\rho_{high} + \rho_{high} = 100$$

$$1.20\rho_{high} = 100$$

$$\rho_{high} = \frac{100}{1.20} = 83.33 \ \Omega\text{m}.$$

112. Reflection coefficient (R) in electrical prospecting ranges from –1 to +1.

Transmission coefficient (T) can range from 0 to +2.

Thus: R (–1, +1) and T (0, +2) is correct.

113. **Statement I:** *Incorrect* — VLF has a shallow depth of investigation (~30–50 m), not the highest among EM induction methods.

Statement II: *Correct* — VLF uses frequencies in the range 5 kHz to 30 kHz.

Thus: Answer. 3: Statement I is incorrect but Statement II is correct.

114. Frequency range 1 – 10^4 Hz signals are generated by thunderstorms (sferics).

Frequency range 10^{-4} – 1 Hz signals are generated by ionospheric currents (magnetotellurics).

Thus: Answer. 1: Signals in (1 – 10^4 Hz) are generated by thunderstorms, signals in (10^4 – 1 Hz) by ionospheric current.

115. Given:

- Shale has higher acoustic impedance and higher Poisson's ratio than gas-sand.
- AVO Class 1 occurs when both acoustic impedance and Poisson's ratio decrease across the interface.
- Class 3 occurs when gas-sand has much lower impedance and Poisson's ratio than shale, leading to strong negative reflection coefficient at zero offset with increasing amplitude with angle.

Since both parameters decrease from shale to gas-sand, the scenario corresponds to AVO Class 3.

116. Seismic diffractions in stacked seismic sections appear as hyperbolae because point diffractors scatter seismic waves in all directions, resulting in hyperbolic travel-time curves on seismic sections.

117. For S-waves, the displacement field is represented by the vector potential ψ, and shear deformation does not change volume. The identity that represents volume preservation (incompressibility) is:

$$\nabla\cdot(\nabla \times \psi) = 0$$

This identity holds for any vector field ψ because the divergence of a curl is always zero, representing volume preservation in shear waves.

118. The autocorrelation of a random signal with infinite length produces a unit sample signal ($\delta[n]$), which is an impulse function at zero lag.

119. Given:

- A ring of air initially at rest relative to Earth's surface at the equator.
- As the air moves poleward to 30°N, its radius of rotation decreases.
- Radius of Earth, R = 6371 × 10^3 m
- Angular velocity of Earth, Ω = 7.292 × 10^{-5} rad/s
- cos (30°) = 0.866

Step 1: Initial Angular Momentum (Equator)

At the equator, the air parcel's initial eastward velocity is Earth's rotational velocity:

$$v_1 = \Omega R$$
$$= 7.292 \times 10^{-5} \times 6371 \times 10^3$$
$$= 464.46 \text{ m/s}$$

Thus, initial angular momentum per unit mass:

$$L_1 = v_1 \times R = \Omega R^2$$

Step 2: Final Angular Momentum (at 30°N)

At latitude 30°N, the radius of rotation becomes:

$$r_2 = R \cos(30°)$$
$$= 6371 \times 10^3 \times 0.866$$
$$= 5516.6 \times 10^3 \text{ m}$$

Let the new absolute eastward velocity be v_2, then:

$$L_2 = v_2 \times r_2$$

By conservation of angular momentum:

$$L_1 = L_2$$

$$\Rightarrow \quad \Omega R^2 = v_2 \times R \cos(30°)$$

Solving for v_2:

$$v_2 = \frac{\Omega R^2}{R\cos(30°)} = \frac{\Omega R}{\cos(30°)}$$

$$= \frac{464.46}{0.866} = 536.3 \text{ m/s}$$

Step 3: Relative Eastward Speed w.r.t. Earth's Surface at 30°N

The Earth's rotational velocity at 30°N:

$$v_{earth} = \Omega \, R \cos(30°)$$

$$= 464.46 \times 0.866 = 402.4 \text{ m/s}$$

Thus, relative eastward velocity of the air parcel:

$$v_{rel} = v_2 - v_{earth}$$

$$= 536.3 - 402.4 = 133.9 \text{ m/s}$$

Thus, the relative eastward velocity is approximately 134 m/s, which is closest to the given option:

120. Given:

- Pressure levels:
  $p_1 = 1000$ hPa, $p_2 = 900$ hPa
- Mean virtual temperature $T_v = 280$ K
- $R_d = 287$ J/kg · K
- $g = 9.8$ m/s^2

Using the Hypsometric Equation:

$$Z = \frac{R_d \cdot T_v}{g} \cdot \ln\left(\frac{p_1}{p_2}\right)$$

Compute:

$$\ln\left(\frac{1000}{900}\right) = \ln(1.1111) = 0.1054$$

$$Z = \frac{287 \times 280}{9.8} \times 0.1054$$

$$= \frac{80360}{9.8} \times 0.1054$$

$$= 8200 \times 0.1054 \approx 864 \text{ m}$$

Thus, approximate thickness is: Answer. 4: 860 m.

121. The effective gravity force (g_{eff}) is the resultant of two forces:

1. Newtonian gravitational force (g_{Newton}) — acts radially towards Earth's center.
2. Centrifugal force (F_c) — due to Earth's rotation, acts outward, perpendicular to Earth's axis of rotation.

- **At the Equator (0° latitude):** Centrifugal force acts directly outward, opposite to the gravity vector, but since both forces are collinear, there is no angular deviation between effective gravity and Newtonian gravity.
- **At the Poles (90° latitude):** Radius of rotation becomes zero, so centrifugal force is zero. Hence, effective gravity equals Newtonian gravity, and there is no angular deviation.
- **At intermediate latitudes, centrifugal force has:**

  A vertical component (opposing gravity).

  A horizontal component (perpendicular to the gravity vector), which causes the plumb line (direction of effective gravity) to tilt.

The horizontal component of the centrifugal force is proportional to:

$$\sin\phi \cdot \cos\phi = \frac{1}{2}\sin(2\phi)$$

This expression reaches its maximum when $2\varphi = 90°$, i.e., at $\varphi = 45°$ latitude.

Therefore, the maximum angle between effective gravity and Newtonian gravitational force occurs at 45° latitude.

122. Given:

- Tornado with constant angular velocity ω
- Pressure at radius r_0
- Find pressure at the center of tornado ($r = 0$).
- Temperature T is constant.
- R is the specific gas constant for dry air.

Approach: The equation of motion in the radial direction for a rotating system is given by balancing the centrifugal force with the pressure gradient force:

$$\frac{dp}{dr} = \rho\omega^2 r$$

Where:

- ρ is the air density.
- $\omega^2 r$ is the centrifugal acceleration.

Using the ideal gas law:

$$\rho = \frac{p}{RT}$$

Substitute into the equation of motion:

$$\frac{dp}{dr} = \frac{p}{RT}\omega^2 r$$

Separate variables and integrate:

$$\frac{dp}{p} = \frac{\omega^2 r}{\text{RT}} dr$$

Integrating from $r = 0$ to $r = r_0$ and from $p = p_c$ (center pressure) to p_0:

$$\int_{p_c}^{p_0} \frac{dp}{p} = \frac{\omega^2}{\text{RT}} \int_0^{r_0} r\, dr$$

$$\ln\left(\frac{p_0}{p_c}\right) = \frac{\omega^2 r_0^2}{2\text{RT}}$$

Solving for p_c:

$$p_c = p_0 . \exp\left(-\frac{\omega^2 r_0^2}{2\text{RT}}\right).$$

123. In the Northern Hemisphere, planetary vorticity (Coriolis parameter, $f = 2\Omega \sin \phi$) increases with latitude. As air moves southward (equatorward) upstream of a trough, it moves into regions of lower planetary vorticity (f decreases).

To conserve absolute vorticity ($\zeta_{abs} = \zeta + f$), the relative vorticity (ζ) must increase (become more cyclonic). Hence, advection of planetary vorticity leads to an increase in local relative vorticity upstream of the trough.

124. Given:

- Radiance L = 9.7 W/m^2/μm/s
- Emissivity ε = 0.98
- λ = 10 μm
- Constants:
  $C_1 = 1.19104 \times 10^8$ W μm^4/m^2/sr,
  $C_2 = 1.4388 \times 10^4$ μm K

Compute: $\text{B} = \frac{\text{L}}{\varepsilon} = \frac{9.7}{0.98}$

$$\approx 9.898 \text{ W/m}^2/\mu\text{m/sr}$$

Planck's formula inversion for T:

$$\text{T} = \frac{C_2}{\lambda . \ln\left(1 + \frac{C_1}{\text{B}\lambda^5}\right)}$$

Compute: $\lambda^5 = 10^5 = 100000$

$$\frac{C_1}{\text{B}\lambda^5} = \frac{1.19104 \times 10^8}{9.898 \times 10^5} \approx 120.33$$

$$\ln(1 + 120.33) = \ln(121.33) \approx 4.80$$

$$\text{T} = \frac{14388}{10 \times 4.80} = \frac{14388}{48}$$

$$\approx 299.75\text{K}$$

Thus, SST ≈ 298 K.

125. Given:

- Latitude = 45°N → $f = 1.031 \times 10^{-4}$ s^{-1}
- Geostrophic wind shear:
  $\partial U_g/\partial_y = 10^{-5}$ s^{-1}
- Eddy viscosity $K_m = 5$ m^2/s

Compute Ekman layer depth (D_{Ek}):

$$D_{Ek} = \sqrt{\frac{2K_m}{f}} = \sqrt{\frac{2 \times 5}{1.031 \times 10^{-4}}}$$

$$= \sqrt{97000} \approx 311.4 \text{ m}$$

Ekman pumping vertical velocity at the top of boundary layer:

$$w_{Ek} = -\frac{D_{Ek}}{2} . \zeta_g = -\frac{311.4}{2} . (-10^{-5})$$

$$= 155.7 \times 10^{-5} = 0.001557 \text{ m/s}$$

Convert to mm/s:

$$w_{Ek} = 0.001557 \text{ m/s} \times 1000$$

$$= 1.56 \text{ mm/s}$$

Approximate to 2 mm/s.

126. In the Northern Hemisphere, conservation of Potential Vorticity (PV) governs large-scale atmospheric and oceanic circulations. As air parcels move meridionally (north-south), their planetary vorticity ($f = 2\Omega \sin\phi$) changes due to the variation in latitude (β-effect).

To conserve absolute vorticity ($\zeta + f$), adjustments through stretching, compression, or meridional motion must occur.

In large-scale geophysical flows like oceans and the mid-latitude atmosphere, this balance leads to Sverdrup meridional transport, where the meridional velocity of fluid parcels is determined by the curl of wind stress and the latitudinal change in planetary vorticity. Sverdrup transport is a planetary-scale manifestation of PV conservation. Options referring to wave-like patterns of easterlies or gravity waves over orography involve local effects and buoyancy oscillations, which are not direct consequences of PV conservation on a planetary scale.

Thus, the correct phenomenon directly resulting from potential vorticity conservation is Sverdrup meridional transport.

127. When deriving the Reynolds-averaged equations of motion for turbulent incompressible flow:

- Zonal, Meridional, and Energy equations acquire Reynolds stress terms.

- The Continuity equation ($\nabla \cdot u = 0$), when time-averaged, remains unchanged because it is linear in velocity.

Thus, correct answer: Continuity equation.

128. The gradient wind equation relates the wind to pressure gradient and curvature.

For anticyclonic flow (high pressure, curvature opposite to flow direction) in the Northern Hemisphere, the gradient wind speed can be up to twice the geostrophic wind speed for the same pressure gradient, beyond which no real solution exists (flow becomes unstable).

Thus, correct answer is 2.

129. Given:

- Additional heat flux (Q) = 5 W/m^2
- Density of ice, ρ_i = 0.9 × 10^3 kg/m^3
- Latent heat of fusion, L_f = 3.34 × 10^5 J/kg

Rate of ice thickness decrease (*dh*/*dt*) is given by:

$$\frac{dh}{dt} = \frac{Q}{\rho_i \cdot L_f}$$

Substitute values:

$$\frac{dh}{dt} = \frac{5}{0.9 \times 10^3 \times 3.34 \times 10^5}$$

$$= \frac{5}{3.006 \times 10^8}$$

$$\approx 1.664 \times 10^{-8} \text{ m/s}$$

Convert to m/year:

$$1.664 \times 10^{-8} \text{ m/s} \times 3.1536 \times 10^7 \text{ s/year}$$

$$\approx 0.525 \text{ m/year}$$

Thus, approximate answer: 1: 0.5 m/year.

130. Given:

- Ocean depth (H) = 4.5 km = 4500 m
- Temperature increase (ΔT) = 2.5°C
- Thermal expansion coefficient (α) = 1.5 × 10^{-4} °C^{-1}

Sea level rise (Δh) due to thermal expansion:

$$\Delta h = H \cdot \alpha \cdot \Delta T$$

$$= 4500 \times 1.5 \times 10^{-4} \times 2.5$$

Compute: $\Delta h = 4500 \times 3.75 \times 10^{-4}$

$$= 1.6875 \text{ m}$$

Approximate to closest option: 3: 1.7 m.

131. Given that the Sun is at the zenith, let's analyze each statement:

1. Single scattering albedo of aerosols (ω_0) is same over ocean and land → This is correct because ω_0 depends on aerosol properties, not surface type.
2. Albedo of the underlying surface (A_s) is same over ocean and land → This is incorrect because surface albedo varies significantly between ocean (low albedo) and land (higher albedo).
3. Incident solar flux (F_0) is same over ocean and land → Correct, since at zenith, F_0 is uniform.
4. Transmittance of the atmosphere (T_a) is same over ocean and land → Correct, assuming homogeneous atmospheric conditions.

Thus, the incorrect statement is: 2: Albedo of the underlying surface (A_s) is same over ocean and land.

132. Aliasing errors occur when high-frequency components are misrepresented as lower frequencies due to insufficient sampling (Nyquist theorem). This typically arises in advection equations due to nonlinearity and phase errors in numerical schemes.

Thus, the equation where aliasing is a problem is: $(\partial_u/\partial_t) = -u(\partial u/\partial x)$ — One-dimensional nonlinear advection equation.

133. Spectral models are preferred over finite difference models because:

1. They handle aliasing through dealiasing techniques.
2. Higher derivatives are computed exactly in spectral space.
3. Polar singularities can be handled using spherical harmonics.
4. However, spectral models require significant configuration and pre-processing time, especially for transforms and grid setups.

Thus, the incorrect statement is: Spectral models require less configuration time.

134. For a stationary barotropic Rossby wave, phase speed (c) = 0.

Rossby wave dispersion relation:

$$c = U - \frac{\beta}{k^2}$$

For stationary wave, $c = 0$

$$k^2 = \frac{\beta}{U}$$

Given:

- $\beta \approx 2 \times 10^{-11}$ m^{-1} s^{-1} (at 45°N)
- U = 15 m/s

Compute: $k^2 = \dfrac{2 \times 10^{-11}}{15} \approx 1.33 \times 10^{-12}$

$\Rightarrow \quad k = \sqrt{1.33 \times 10^{-12}}$

$\approx 1.15 \times 10^{-6}$ m^{-1}

Closest option: 1: 10^{-6} m^{-1}.

135. Oxygen isotopic composition (δ^{18}O) observations:

1. δ^{18}O of benthic foraminifera reflects glacial-interglacial cycles — Correct
2. δ^{18}O difference between planktic and benthic is greater at high latitudes — Incorrect. The difference is greater in low latitudes, where planktic foraminifera are more influenced by surface temperature.
3. δ^{18}O difference is greater at low latitudes — Correct
4. Planktic foraminifera δ^{18}O is more negative than benthic — Correct (due to warmer surface waters).

Thus, incorrect statement is: 2: The difference between δ^{18}O of planktic and benthic foraminifera is greater at high latitude.

136. Unsorted sediments with large grain size variations and lacking fabric (preferred orientation) are characteristic of ice-rafted sediments. These are deposited directly from melting icebergs and show poor sorting, large size variation, and lack of stratification.

137. Let's analyze:

1. **Dansgaard-Oeschger Events** — Rapid warming events during glacial periods, not cold periods.
2. **Heinrich Events** — Massive iceberg discharges causing cold conditions.
3. **Younger Dryas** — Cold reversal after the last glacial termination.
4. **Bond Events** — Periodic cold events during the Holocene.

Thus, Dansgaard-Oeschger events represent warmings, not cold periods.

138. The oxygen isotopic composition, δ^{18}O, is defined as:

$$\delta^{18}O = \left(\frac{(^{18}O/^{16}O)_{sample}}{(^{18}O/^{16}O)_{standard}} - 1\right) \times 1000\%$$

Where:

- The ratio (^{18}O/^{16}O) is always non-negative, because atomic quantities cannot be negative.
- The lowest possible ratio for a sample is zero (i.e., no ^{18}O atoms present).

If the sample has no ^{18}O atoms, the δ^{18}O value becomes:

$$\delta^{18}O = \left(\frac{0}{(^{18}O/^{16}O)_{standard}} - 1\right) \times 1000\%$$

$$= -1000 ‰$$

Thus, the minimum possible δ^{18}O value is –1000 ‰. Any value lower than –1000 ‰ (e.g., –1500 ‰) is physically impossible, as it would imply a negative ratio of oxygen isotopes, which is unrealistic.

Therefore:

- Values like +1500 ‰ or extreme positive values are theoretically possible (though not observed in natural systems).
- Values like –500 ‰ are also possible.
- But –1500 ‰ is physically impossible.

Answer. 2: –1500 ‰.

139. Given:

- Characteristic velocity (U) = 10 cm/s = 0.1 m/s
- Characteristic length (L) = 100 km = 1×10^5 m
- Coriolis parameter (f) = 1×10^{-4} s^{-1}

Rossby number (Ro) is:

$$Ro = \frac{U}{fL} = \frac{0.1}{(10^{-4} \times 10^5)} = \frac{0.1}{10}$$

$$= 0.01$$

Rossby number = 10^{-2}

Since Ro << 1, Coriolis force dominates.

140. The observed 30-day periodicity in ocean currents at a mooring located in the northern Bay of Bengal (18°N), away from the boundary, indicates intraseasonal variability likely linked to equatorial oceanic wave dynamics.

Explanation:

- **Kelvin Waves:** Equatorial Kelvin waves are generated in the equatorial Indian Ocean, often forced by atmospheric disturbances like the Madden-Julian Oscillation (MJO). These waves propagate eastward along the equator and, upon reaching the eastern Indian Ocean boundary (near Sumatra), convert into coastal Kelvin waves. These coastal Kelvin waves then propagate poleward along the coasts of Sumatra and into the Bay of Bengal, impacting the ocean dynamics even in the northern interior basin.

- The 30-day periodicity observed at the mooring site aligns with the intraseasonal timescales of equatorial Kelvin wave forcing, which is a dominant feature of variability in this region.
- **Rossby Waves:** These waves propagate westward and their influence becomes significant in the open ocean interior, but they typically take longer periods (months) to propagate across the basin, especially in tropical regions. For a mooring at 18°N in the interior Bay of Bengal, Rossby waves forced in the eastern basin are less likely to explain the observed 30-day variability.

Thus, Kelvin waves originating from the equatorial Indian Ocean are a plausible mechanism influencing the 30-day periodic variability at this location.

141. Given:

- Westerly winds increase with latitude in the Northern Hemisphere.
- Meridional winds are zero.
- We are to determine how thermocline and surface chlorophyll are affected.

Explanation:

The wind stress curl is defined as:

$$\text{curl}_z(\tau) = \frac{\partial \tau_y}{\partial x} - \frac{\partial \tau_x}{\partial y}$$

Since meridional wind (V) is zero, $\tau_y = 0$, and the first term becomes zero.

$$\text{curl}_z(\tau) = -\frac{\partial \tau_x}{\partial y}$$

Westerly winds (U) increase with latitude (y), so $\frac{\partial \tau_x}{\partial y} > 0$.

Thus, $\text{curl}_z(\tau)$ is negative.

Ekman pumping velocity at the base of the Ekman layer:

$$w_e = \frac{1}{\rho f}.\text{curl}_z(\tau)$$

Since $f > 0$ in the Northern Hemisphere and $\text{curl}_z(\tau) < 0$, the vertical velocity w_e becomes negative → downwelling.

Effects of Downwelling:

- Thermocline deepens as surface waters sink.
- Surface chlorophyll decreases due to suppressed nutrient upwelling.

142. Given:

- EICC (East India Coastal Current) seasonal behavior.

Explanation:

- **During Boreal Winter (Oct–Jan):** EICC flows equatorward due to northeast monsoon.
- **During Boreal Summer (June–Sept):** Though southwest monsoon winds dominate, EICC often weakens and can reverse direction depending on coastal Kelvin wave dynamics.
- **During Boreal Spring (Feb–May):** Poleward-propagating coastal Kelvin waves force a strong poleward flow, which is the strongest phase of EICC.

Thus, the correct statement is: 1: Poleward during Boreal Spring.

143. **Statement A:** Ekman transport is indeed 90° to the right of wind stress in the Northern Hemisphere.

However, it incorrectly mentions "where Coriolis parameter f is negative", which is wrong.

In the Northern Hemisphere, f is positive.

Hence, Statement A is incorrect.

Statement B: Ekman transport can cause both upwelling (divergence) and downwelling (convergence) depending on wind direction.

Therefore, Statement B is incorrect.

Statement C: At the equator, Ekman transport causes divergence of surface waters across the equator.

This results in equatorial upwelling, bringing cold, nutrient-rich water to the surface.

Thus, Only Statement C is correct.

144. **Statement A:** "Marine phytoplankton are controlled by nutrients, light, and vertical stability of the water column, but not by CO_2 concentration."

- Phytoplankton primary production is mainly limited by nutrient availability (like nitrate, phosphate, iron), light availability, and water column stability (stratification).

- CO_2 concentration in ocean surface waters is rarely a limiting factor because CO_2 is sufficiently dissolved in seawater for photosynthesis.

Thus, Statement A is correct.

Statement B: "The Biological pump does not sequester any anthropogenic carbon."

- This statement is incorrect.
- The biological pump is a key mechanism by which anthropogenic CO_2 is sequestered from the atmosphere to the deep ocean via biological processes (e.g., phytoplankton photosynthesis, sinking organic matter).

Therefore, Statement B is incorrect.

Logical Connection:

Option 2 states: "Both statements are correct, and A explains B."

But we found:

- Statement A is correct.
- Statement B is incorrect.

Thus, Option 2 cannot be correct because Statement B is factually wrong.

Correct Conclusion: Only Statement A is correct, and Statement B is incorrect.

Therefore, the correct option is: 3: A is correct, B is incorrect.

145. Primary production in the ocean is directly linked to photosynthesis by phytoplankton in the surface layer, which increases the concentration of dissolved oxygen (O_2) near the surface. The oxygen profile that shows the highest O_2 concentration at the surface will therefore indicate the region of highest primary productivity.

Analyzing the given profiles:

- **Profile A:** Low oxygen concentration at the surface.
- **Profile B:** Moderate oxygen concentration at the surface.
- **Profile C:** Slightly higher surface oxygen than A and B, but not the peak.
- **Profile D:** Shows a prominent oxygen maximum at the surface (close to 5.0 mL L^{-1}), higher than all other profiles.

This surface oxygen peak in Profile D indicates intense photosynthetic activity, hence highest primary production at the surface.

146. The seasonal sequence of phytoplankton blooms in a stratified temperate ocean follows the pattern of light availability, nutrient dynamics, and water column stratification.

Analyzing each profile:

- **B (Winter):** The profile shows high nutrient levels throughout the water column and low chlorophyll-a, indicating winter mixing with no significant bloom due to light limitation.
- **C (Spring Bloom):** Chlorophyll-a increases sharply near the surface as light availability improves. Nutrient depletion begins in surface layers due to phytoplankton uptake, marking the classic spring bloom.
- **A (Summer Stratification):** Nutrients are nearly exhausted at the surface due to strong stratification. Chlorophyll-a shows a subsurface maximum, typical of summer conditions where surface productivity declines.
- **D (Autumn Mixing/Bloom):** Slight mixing begins to bring nutrients up, and chlorophyll-a increases modestly at mid-depths, indicating a smaller secondary bloom before winter resets.

Thus, the correct seasonal sequence from winter to summer is: B → C → A → D.

147. We are to identify the set of marine organisms in which all members do NOT use silicon (Si) to build their skeletal structures or cell walls.

Option 1: Diatoms, Silicoflagellates, Radiolarians, Sponges

- Diatoms → Siliceous frustules (silicon-based).
- Silicoflagellates → Siliceous skeletons.
- Radiolarians → Siliceous skeletons.
- Sponges (Porifera, e.g., Hexactinellida) → Siliceous spicules.

→ All use silicon → Incorrect.

Option 2: Coccolithophores, Diatoms, Polychaeta, Dinoflagellates

- Coccolithophores → Calcareous plates (calcium carbonate, not silicon).
- Diatoms → Siliceous frustules → Use silicon.
- Polychaeta (worms) → Do not use silicon.
- Dinoflagellates → Cellulose plates (theca), no silicon.

→ Contains diatoms (which use silicon) → Incorrect.

Option 3: Pteropoda, Foraminifera, Radiolarians, Sponges

- Pteropoda (Sea butterflies) → Aragonite (calcium carbonate shells).
- Foraminifera → Calcareous (calcium carbonate) tests.
- Radiolarians → Siliceous skeletons.
- Sponges → Siliceous spicules (in some groups).

→ Contains Radiolarians & Sponges (which use silicon) → Incorrect.

Option 4: Foraminifera, Dinoflagellates, Coccolithophores, Polychaetes

- Foraminifera → Calcareous tests (calcium carbonate).
- Dinoflagellates → Cellulose plates (no silicon).
- Coccolithophores → Calcareous plates (calcium carbonate).
- Polychaetes → Soft-bodied, no siliceous skeletons.

→ None use silicon → Correct.

Final Answer: 4: Foraminifera, Dinoflagellates, Coccolithophores, Polychaetes.

148. We are asked how primary producers (like phytoplankton) respond to increasing light intensity (PAR: Photosynthetically Active Radiation).

Expected Photosynthesis vs. PAR Relationship:

- At low light intensities, photosynthesis increases rapidly with light (light-limited zone).
- At moderate light levels, photosynthesis reaches a saturation point where further increases in light do not significantly increase photosynthesis (light-saturated zone).
- At very high light levels, photoinhibition can occur where excessive light damages photosynthetic machinery, causing photosynthesis to decline.

Analysis of Given Graphs:

Graph A:

- Shows rapid increase at low PAR.
- Levels off at moderate PAR (saturation).
- Declines at very high PAR (photoinhibition).

→ This is the correct typical response curve of primary producers.

Graph B:

- Linear increase with PAR.

→ Unrealistic, as it ignores light saturation and photoinhibition.

Graph C:

- Sudden sharp peak and drop.

→ Unnatural; photosynthesis doesn't show a sudden spike after low PAR.

Graph D:

- Shows low maximum photosynthesis and drops to near-zero.

→ Incorrect; no realistic photosynthesis pattern follows this shape.

Correct Answer: 1: A.

149. Let's match the correct methods for measuring each oceanic parameter:

- Phytopigments → HPLC (High-Performance Liquid Chromatography)
  (Used for pigment analysis like chlorophylls and carotenoids)
- Phyto cell density → Flow Cytometer
  (Used for counting and sorting microscopic phytoplankton cells)
- Ocean Currents → ADCP (Acoustic Doppler Current Profiler)
  (Measures current velocities using the Doppler effect)
- PAR (Photosynthetically Active Radiation) → Radiometer
  (Measures light intensity in the PAR wavelength range)

Now, look at the options:

- Option A — Incorrect (wrongly associates ADCP with Phytopigments)
- Option B — Incorrect (swaps Radiometer and ADCP)
- Option C — All matches are correct.
- Option D — All parameter-method pairs are incorrect.

Answer. 3: C.

150. Oxyluciferin is produced as a result of the bioluminescence reaction in marine organisms. The reaction involves luciferin (substrate) being oxidized by luciferase (enzyme), producing oxyluciferin, light, and other products.

Thus, the biological process is: 3: Bioluminescence.

Previous Years' Paper

Joint CSIR-UGC NET/JRF

EARTH, ATMOSPHERIC, OCEAN & PLANETARY SCIENCES

JULY-2024

(Exam held on 25 July, 2024)

PART-A

1. The following dishes are offered in a restaurant.

Starter: Tomato Soup or Vegetable Salad or Chicken Soup

Main course: Chicken Biryani or Fish Biryani or Veg Biryani

Dessert: Gulabjamun or Rasagulla

A meal is prepared selecting one item from each category. What is the probability that a randomly drawn up menu is vegetarian?

A. 1/3 B. 5/8
C. 2/9 D. 1/2

2. Two vessels contain $\frac{3}{8}$ L and $\frac{2}{7}$ L of alcohol.

Water is added to both vessels to make each solution measure 1 L. When these solutions are mixed, the alcohol to water ratio would be approximately:

A. 16 : 21 B. 1 : 4
C. 1 : 2 D. 1 : 3

3. Beginning from April of a year, the rate at which a tree became taller increased linearly for 15 weeks when it was trimmed down. From then on, the rate decreased linearly for the next 15 weeks.

(*a*)

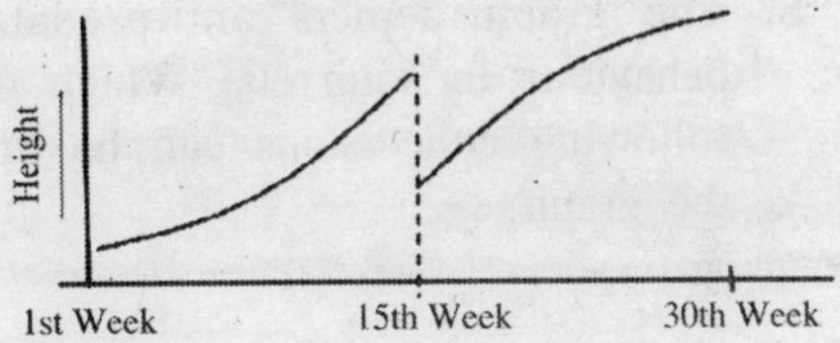

(*b*)

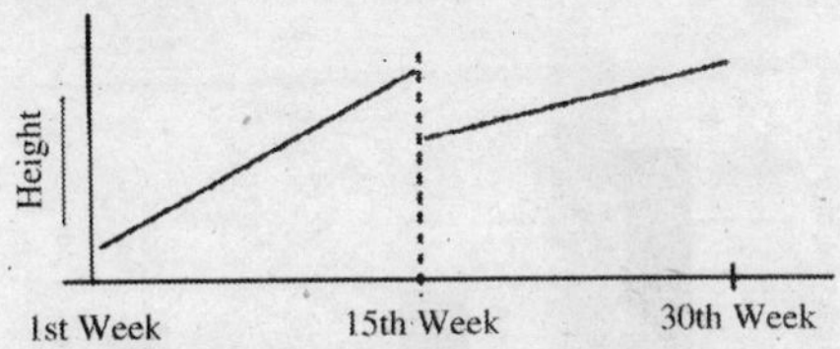

(*c*)

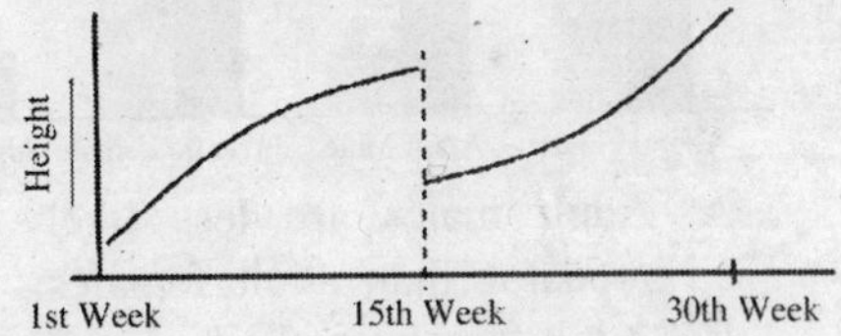

(*d*)

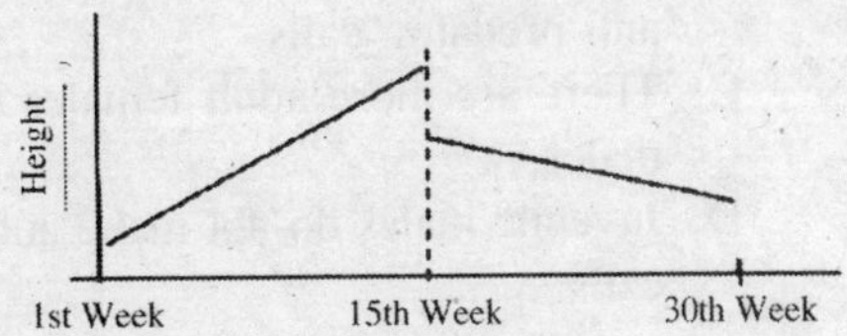

Which graph correctly shows the height of the tree against time during this period?

A. (*a*) B. (*b*)
C. (*c*) D. (*d*)

1. C **2.** C **3.** A

4. An eagle is sitting at the top of a 100 m high vertical cliff and a mouse is at the base of the cliff. The mouse starts running away from the cliff on a level ground in a straight line at a speed 10 m/s. The eagle spots the mouse and dives at 45° to the ground at a speed of 20 m/s and captures the mouse. The time at which the eagle started the dive is:

A. around 3 s after the mouse started running
B. around 5 s after the mouse started running
C. around 7 s after the mouse started running
D. the same at which the mouse started running

5. The graph depicts anti-predator calling behaviour in squirrels. Which one of the following conclusions can be drawn from the graph?

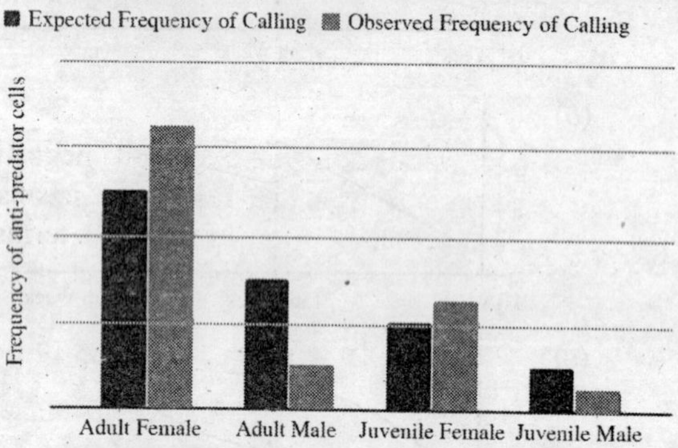

A. Adult males are less likely to see a predator than adult females.
B. Adult females make higher than expected anti-predator calls.
C. There are more adult females than adult males.
D. Juvenile males do not make anti-predator calls.

6. Two chords of a circle meeting at an angle 60° bisect each other. If the length of one chord is 10 cm, the length of the other chord (in cm) is:

A. $5\sqrt{3}$ B. $10/\sqrt{2}$
C. $10/\sqrt{3}$ D. 10

7. An ecologist catches 25 fish tags them and releases them back in the pond. She catches 30 fish on the next day, of which 10 carry the tag. Assuming that the fish in the pond remain unchanged and each fish has equal probability of being caught, what is the estimated number of fish in the pond?

A. 30   B. 75
C. 150   D. 300

8. In a five-floor building, a lawyer, a doctor, a teacher, an artist and an engineer occupy different floors. The artist has to go up three floors to meet the engineer, whereas the engineer has to come down four floors to visit the doctor. The lawyer lives just a floor above the teacher. The floors are occupied from the lowest to the topmost by:

A. artist, doctor, teacher, lawyer, engineer
B. artist, doctor, teacher, engineer, lawyer
C. doctor, artist, teacher, lawyer, engineer
D. doctor, artist, lawyer, teacher, engineer

9. A referendum on a proposal involved 3500 participants. Among the participants 1700 were men and the rest were women. 1450 participants, of whom 800 were men, voted against while 1500 participants voted in favour. 200 women abstained. How many women voted for the proposal?

A. 800   B. 650
C. 950   D. 550

10. A boy talking about his age said, "The day before yesterday I was 15, now I am 16 and next year I shall turn 18". Then:

A. he must have lied.
B. he was making the assertion on 29th February.
C. his birthday is on 29th February and he was making the assertion on 1st March.
D. his birthday is on 31st December and he was making the assertion on 1st January.

4. A **5.** B **6.** D **7.** B **8.** C **9.** C **10.** D

11. BOTANY is to PLANTS as PHILOSOPHY is to:

A. REGULATIONS B. RELIGIONS
C. IDEAS D. POLITICS

12. Two children A and B counted the number of chairs placed around a round table in the same direction, but starting at different chairs. As 5th chair was B's 9th, while B's 3rd was A's 12th. The number of chairs was:

A. 13 B. 14
C. 15 D. 21

13. Statistics of a certain test conducted to determine a disease are given in the table.

Category	Number of persons
True positive	8
False negative	3
False positive	2
True negative	12

The number of persons actually having the disease are:

A. 11 B. 8
C. 20 D. 3

14. In a family, A is the son of P and brother of V. N is the sister of V. S is the nephew of V and B is the daughter-in-law of A. M is the mother of N. B is related to M as the:

A. Granddaughter B. Daughter-in-law
C. Grandson's wife D. Mother

15. The addition of a three-digit number and the number with the same digits in reverse order, is 1089. The middle digit of that number must be:

A. 9 B. 8
C. 0 D. 4

16. The variation in the per carat price of diamond by caratage is shown in the graph.

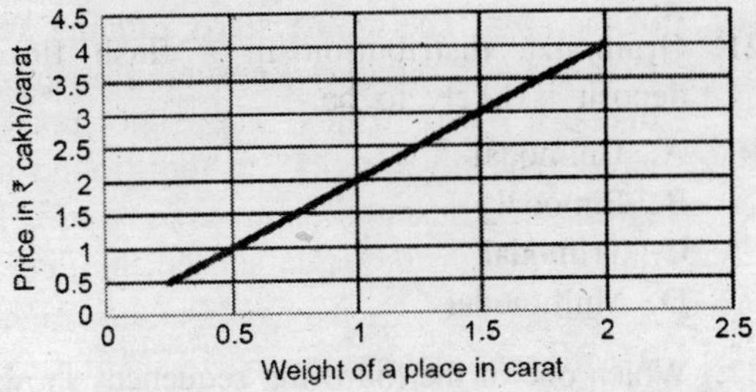

A person wants to buy 4 identical sized diamonds for ₹ 4.5 lakh. What is the largest size of one such diamond (in carat)?

A. 0.5 B. 0.75
C. 1.125 D. 0.625

17. Equality of which of the following quantities in two data sets of the **same size** will ensure equality of their standard deviations?

A. Their means.
B. The sums of positive and negative deviations from the respective means.
C. The averages of squares of all terms.
D. The averages of squares of all terms and their means.

18. In a leap year that began on a Tuesday, the third Saturday of March would fall on:

A. March 14 B. March 15
C. March 16 D. March 21

19. Which of the following can be a perfect square if X and Y are decimal digits?

A. 93XY215 B. 7XY0625
C. 613XY45 D. XY21375

20. A wholesale shopkeeper purchased 200 identical watches and sold the first 50 at 10% profit, the next 50 at 20% profit, the next 50 at 25% profit and the last 50 at 40% profit. If his total profit was ₹ 19000, at what total cost did he buy the watches?

A. ₹ 76000 B. ₹ 80000
C. ₹ 86000 D. ₹ 98000

11. C	12. A	13. A	14. C	15. A	16. B	17. D	18. B	19. B	20. B

PART-B

21. Grain-size distribution in a flash flood deposit is likely to be:

A. Unimodal
B. Bimodal
C. Trimodal
D. Multimodal

22. Which one of the following sequences shows the correct order of their first appearance in the geological record since Precambrian?

A. Land plants - Amphibians - Ediacaran biota
B. Ediacaran biota - Land plants - Amphibians
C. Land plants - Ediacaran biota - Amphibians
D. Ediacaran biota - Amphibians - Land plants

23. Which of the following is a FALSE statement about subtropical jet stream?

A. They form over subtropical high-pressure system at a height of about 12 km.
B. They satisfy geostrophic balance.
C. They are westerly winds.
D. They are stronger in the winter hemisphere as compared to the summer hemisphere.

24. LCL, EL and LFC stands for Lifting Condensation Level, Equilibrium Level and Level of Free Convection. Which of the following situations is not possible in our earth's atmosphere?

A. LCL = 900 hPa, EL = 400 hPa, LFC = 850 hPa
B. LCL = 850 hPa. EL = 300 hPa, LFC = 800 hPa
C. LCL = 800 hPa, EL = 400 hPa, LFC = 900 hPa
D. LCL = 900 hPa, EL = 450 hPa, LFC = 800 hPa

25. If the Earth starts rotating in opposite direction on its axis with the same period of rotation, then how will the length of day and night be affected at a particular place on the Earth's surface (say Delhi)?

A. Length of the day becomes longer but night shorter
B. Length of the night becomes longer but day shorter
C. There will be no significant change in the length of day and night
D. Lengths of the day and night both become shorter significantly

26. With increasing climate warming, the open ocean regions are expected to become:

A. eutrophic due to higher organic matter degradation at the surface
B. oligotrophic due to higher consumption of nutrients by plankton due to increasing temperature
C. eutrophic due to higher entrainment and mixing
D. oligotrophic due to higher thermal stratification and reduced mixing

27. Which one of these statements is NOT true for 'Till'?

A. Transported *en masse* by glacier.
B. May have deformation features such as folds.
C. Cannot be used to infer regional ice movement.
D. Are poorly sorted deposits.

28. If the Earth were to orbit around the Sun at twice its present distance, without any change in its rotational velocity, then a year on it would have:

A. 365 days
B. $365\sqrt{2}$ days
C. 730 days
D. $730\sqrt{2}$ days

21. D **22.** B **23.** B **24.** C **25.** C **26.** D **27.** C **28.** D

29. An imaginary line representing the first appearance of a particular metamorphic index mineral in the field is called an:

A. isopleth B. index line
C. isograd D. iso-facies line

30. In which one of the following towns, the magnetic needle in a dip circle deviates the most from the horizontal?

A. Thiruvananthapuram
B. Tirupati
C. Ujjain
D. Lucknow

31. Sphalerite is a major source of:

A. Zinc B. Copper
C. Aluminium D. Iron

32. Which one of the following defines steady state of materials in ocean?

A. inputs from rivers equal the particle flux out of the euphotic zone
B. concentration does not change with time
C. the removal flux must be proportional to the original amount
D. the river input equals the atmospheric input

33. Domestic waste water with gross faecal coliform contamination is called:

A. Grey water B. Black water
C. Red water D. Brown water

34. Scale height is the vertical distance over which the reference pressure changes to ______ of its original value.

A. e B. $\sqrt{e}$
C. $\frac{1}{e}$ D. $\frac{1}{\sqrt{e}}$

35. Which one of the following meteorite types is NOT derived from differentiated planetary bodies?

A. Iron meteorite
B. Shergottite
C. Eucrite
D. Carbonaceous chondrite

36. A cuboidal rock sample is subjected to purely shear stresses. Assuming an elastic regime, the change in volume of the rock sample is:

A. zero
B. proportional to bulk modulus
C. proportional to Young's modulus
D. proportional to Shear modulus

37. In Augite, how many O-atoms of each $[SiO_4]$ tetrahedron are shared with other tetrahedra?

A. 0 B. 2
C. 1 D. 4

38. Choose the correct sequence of rivers arranged in the order of increasing length.

A. Godavari, Kaveri, Mahanadi, Krishna
B. Kaveri, Mahanadi, Krishna, Godavari
C. Mahanadi, Krishna, Godavari, Kaveri
D. Krishna, Godavari, Kaveri, Mahanadi

39. Ekman layer in the atmosphere has the following three-way force balance between:

A. Pressure gradient force, Coriolis force and centrifugal force
B. Pressure gradient force, Coriolis force and turbulent drag force
C. Pressure gradient force, centrifugal force and turbulent drag force
D. Coriolis force, centrifugal force and turbulent drag force

40. In an urban polluted atmosphere, during what time of the day will the surface ozone concentration be the highest?

A. 5 AM to 7 AM B. 2 PM to 4 PM
C. 6 PM to 8 PM D. 9 AM to 11 AM

29. C **30.** D **31.** A **32.** B **33.** B **34.** C **35.** D **36.** A **37.** B **38.** B **39.** B **40.** B

41. Which one of the following minerals is NOT a part of the Bowen's discontinuous reaction series?

A. Olivine B. Amphibole
C. Enstatite D. Andesine

42. If the Green, Red, NIR and SWIR bands of the LISS-III sensor were designated as 1, 2, 3 and 4, respectively, then which of the following band combinations would render a standard FCC?

A. 1 → Blue, 3 → Green, 4 → Red
B. 2 → Blue, 3 → Red, 4 → Green
C. 1 → Red, 2 → Green, 3 → Blue
D. 1 → Blue, 2 → Green, 3 → Red

43. Which one of the following is the correct sequence of products of increasing weathering of orthoclase?

A. illite, kaolinite, hematite
B. kaolinite, illite, hematite
C. kaolinite, illite, gibbsite
D. illite, kaolinite, gibbsite

44. The horizontal wind in small-scale vortices such as tornadoes follows:

A. Geostrophic wind balance
B. Cyclostrophic wind balance
C. Inertial wind balance
D. Gradient wind balance

45. Activity of 14 mg of ^{14}C ($\lambda = 3.84 \times 10^{-12}\ s^{-1}$) in decays/second is approximately:

A. 6.023×10^{20} B. 2.31×10^{9}
C. 2.31×10^{12} D. 3.84×10^{11}

46. Which of the following is NOT true in the context of El Nino?

A. Weakening of the Walker circulation.
B. Surface pressure decreases at Tahiti and rainfall increases eastward over central equatorial Pacific Ocean.
C. The surface water off Western South America is colder than normal.
D. The Thermocline deepens in the eastern Pacific Ocean.

47. Which one of the following radioisotopes has the highest half life?

A. ^{232}Th B. ^{235}U
C. ^{238}U D. ^{234}Th

48. Which among the following seismic phases is never a first arrival?

A. Pg B. P^*
C. PmP D. Pn

49. In which of the following oceanic zones, the highest sediment deposition takes place?

A. Continental rise B. Continental slope
C. Shelf break D. Mid-oceanic ridge

50. If ρ_{PARCEL}, P_{PARCEL}, T_{PARCEL} and ρ_{ENV}, P_{ENV}, T_{ENV} are the density, pressure and temperatures of any air parcel and its surrounding environment, respectively, when will the air parcel have a positive buoyancy?

A. $\rho_{PARCEL} < \rho_{ENV}$
B. $\rho_{PARCEL} > \rho_{ENV}$
C. $T_{PARCEL} < T_{ENV}$
D. $P_{PARCEL} > P_{ENV}$

51. Which of the following types of ore deposits are NOT formed by magmatic or magmatic-hydrothermal processes?

A. Sudbury-type Ni-Cu deposits
B. Bushveld-type chromite deposits
C. Ironstone deposits
D. Porphyry-type Cu deposits

52. The pH of the ocean water and river is 8 and 4, respectively. What would be the dominant dissolved inorganic carbon species in the ocean and river, respectively?

A. $[CO_2]$, $[CO_3^{2-}]$ B. $[HCO_3^-]$, $[CO_3^{2-}]$
C. [HCO3$^-$], $[CO_2]$ D. $[CO_2]$, $[HCO_3^-]$

41. D **42.** D **43.** D **44.** B **45.** B **46.** C **47.** A **48.** C **49.** A **50.** A **51.** C **52.** C

53. Moving towards the Sun from outer space, the correct order of appearance of the following celestial objects/fields is:

A. Heliopause, Oort Cloud, Kuiper Belt, Asteroid Belt
B. Oort Cloud, Kuiper Belt, Heliopause, Asteroid Belt
C. Oort Cloud, Heliopause, Kuiper Belt, Asteroid Belt
D. Kuiper Belt, Oort Cloud, Asteroid Belt, Heliopause

54. What is the typical dip amount of unroofing joints?

A. 0°-15° B. 75°-90°
C. 25°-40° D. 30°-45°

55. The term "mineralization " in marine carbon cycle refers to the process where:

A. elements that have passed through the food web are recycled.
B. inorganic minerals are formed biologically.
C. inorganic minerals are incorporated into the food chain.
D. dissolution of biologically formed minerals at the sediment-water interface.

56. At a depth of 900 mm in a sedimentary core the ^{14}C activity is 1/16th of the surface activity. What is the average sedimentation rate (given ^{14}C half-life = 6000 years)?

A. 0.05 mm/year
B. 0.01875 mm/year
C. 0.0035 mm/year
D. 0.0375 mm/year

57. Which one of the following is the slowest hillslope process?

A. Mudflow B. Landslide
C. Earthflow D. Solifluction

58. Mass of water vapour per unit mass of dry air is called:

A. Specific humidity
B. Mixing ratio
C. Relative humidity
D. Vapour pressure

59. For an earthquake:

A. The magnitude and intensity decrease with epicentral distance
B. The magnitude and intensity increase with epicentral distance
C. The magnitude remains unchanged and intensity decreases with epicentral distance
D. The magnitude decreases with epicentral distance and intensity remains constant

60. Planetary Albedo depends on:

A. Amount of solar radiation reflected back to space by atmosphere
B. Amount of solar radiation reflected back to space by land surface of Earth
C. Amount of solar radiation reflected back to space by ocean surface
D. Amount of solar radiation reflected back to space by atmosphere, oceans and land

61. Which one of the following shows an ascending order of mixed layer depth in the oceanic regions?

A. Subtropical Pacific Ocean, Bay of Bengal, Polar oceanic region
B. Polar oceanic region, Subtropical Pacific Ocean, Bay of Bengal
C. Bay of Bengal, Polar oceanic region, Subtropical Pacific Ocean
D. Bay of Bengal, Subtropical Pacific Ocean, Polar oceanic region

62. The solubility of biogenic silica in seawater:

A. decreases with temperature and salinity
B. increases with temperature and salinity
C. decreases with temperature and increases with salinity
D. increases with temperature and decreases with salinity

53. C **54.** B **55.** A **56.** D **57.** D **58.** B **59.** C **60.** D **61.** D **62.** D

63. If the Earth were to be twice its present radius but with its density reduced to half its original value, then:

A. its mass and gravity field would remain the same
B. its mass would increase 4 times, but its gravity field would remain the same
C. its mass and gravity field would increase by 4 times
D. its mass would remain the same, but the gravity field would increase 4 times

64. The acceleration due to gravity, g, at sea level:

A. decreases with increasing latitude
B. increases with increasing latitude
C. remains constant at all latitudes
D. varies with longitude for a given latitude

65. Match the column-I and column-II assuming standard notations:

Column-I (Name of wave)	Column-II (Expression for wave speed)
A. Sound wave	P. $(gH)^{1/2}$
B. Shallow water gravity wave	Q. $-\beta/(k^2 + l^2)$
C. Barotrophic Rossby wave	R. $(C_p RT/C_v)^{1/2}$

Choose the correct option:

A. A-R; B-Q; C-P
B. A-P; B-Q; C-R
C. A-Q; B-P; C-R
D. A-R; B-P; C-Q

66. Compared to the epicenter of a shallow focus earthquake, the epicenter of a deep focus earthquake lies:

A. at the same level
B. deeper by not more than 30 km
C. deeper than 30 km, but shallower than 700 km
D. deeper than 700 km

67. The hypsometric curve of the earth's surface is shown. The area of the ocean floor covered above the carbonate compensation depth of 3250 m is:

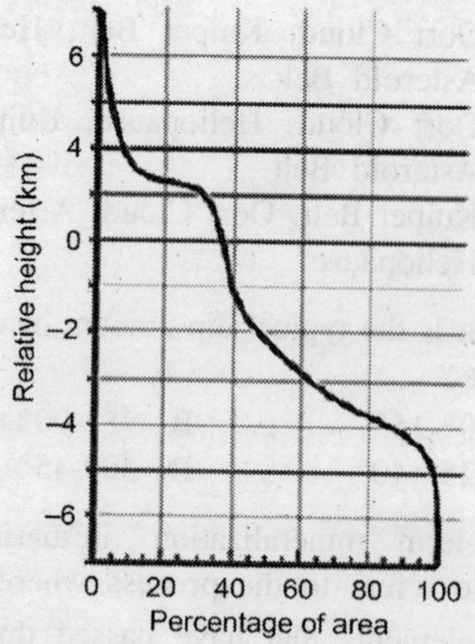

A. 20% B. 50%
C. 29% D. 40%

68. The process by which sediment grains, moved by wind or water, jump or hop along the surface is known as:

A. Deflation B. Suspension
C. Drag D. Saltation

69. North Pacific deep water has higher nutrient content, higher ΣCO_2 and lower dissolved O_2 than that in the North Atlantic because:

A. it is the farthest along deep circulation path.
B. of existence of more volcanoes along the margins of Pacific,
C. of larger area of the Pacific Ocean.
D. of deeper water depths of the Pacific Ocean.

70. Water having total dissolved solids (TDS) in the range of 10^3 – 10^4 mg/l is classified as:

A. Fresh B. Brackish
C. Saline D. Brine

63. B **64.** B **65.** D **66.** A **67.** A **68.** D **69.** A **70.** B

PART-C

71. Match the following:

List-I (Components of Earth's radiation budget)	List-II (% of total shortwave incoming solar radiation at top of atmosphere)
A. Long-wave Earth radiation directly from the surface to space	P. 107
B. Long-wave Earth radiation from surface to atmosphere	Q. 63
C. Long-wave radiation from atmosphere to the space	R. 30
D. Solar radiation reflected and scattered back to space by atmosphere and Earth surface	S. 7

Choose the correct option

A. A-P; B-Q; C-R; D-S
B. A-Q; B-R; C-S; D-P
C. A-S; B-P; C-Q; D-R
D. A-S; B-R; C-P; D-Q

72. What is the total Fe (wt%), approximately, in a garnet having FeO = 21.36 wt% and Fe_2O_3 = 1.96 wt%? (Given atomic weight of Fe = 56 amu and 0= 16 amu)

A. 16 B. 18
C. 20 D. 24

73. A discrete signal $x[n]$ is given as $x[n]= (1/2)^n u[n]$, where u is the unit step sequence and n takes integral values. If the unit sample sequence is given as $\delta[n]$, the inverse filter $h[n]$ for the signal $x[n]$ is:

A. $h[n] = \delta[n] - 1/2\ \delta[n - 1]$
B. $h[n] = (-1/2)^n\ u[n]$
C. $h[n] = 2^n\ u[n]$
D. $h[n] = \delta\ [n]$

74. The iron hypothesis was proposed:

A. based, in part, on evidence that Fe stimulated phytoplankton grew in lab experiments, especially of large diatoms.
B. to state that the trace metal Fe was a limiting nutrient in the coastal oceans.
C. based, in part, on evidence that pCO_2 in a Fe fertilized patch of ocean in the Equatorial Pacific, decreased rapidly.
D. based, in part, on evidence that $[NO_3^-]$ increased by a factor of two in the Fe-fertilized patch of ocean in the Equatorial Pacific.

75. Which one of the following is TRUE about ocean acidification?

A. It decreases carbonate ion concentration
B. It increases carbonate ion concentration
C. It decreases bicarbonate ion concentration
D. It decreases concentration of the dissolved CO_2

76. During break monsoon conditions the Tropical Easterly Jet moves:

A. northward up to 30° N
B. northward up to 20° N
C. southward up to 5° N
D. southward up to 10° N

77. Which one of the following statements does NOT represent a positive feedback in climate system?

A. When surface temperature increases, ice and snow cover decreases
B. Moisture content increases with increasing temperature
C. Surface cooling increases ice and snow cover leading to increased albedo
D. Increase in temperature increases the amount of cloud cover

71. C **72.** B **73.** A **74.** A **75.** A **76.** B **77.** D

78. Which of the statements is FALSE with respect to Quasi-Biennial Oscillation (QBO)?

A. One phase of QBO takes 12-15 months to reverse to another phase
B. It is a meridional circulation
C. It causes sudden stratospheric warming
D. Each wind regime (easterly/westerly) appears above 30 km and propagates downward at 1 km $month^{-1}$.

79. If f_0 is the Larmor frequency measured at a location on the magnetic equator, what is the Larmor frequency measured at a location of magnetic inclination 45°? Assume no anomalous bodies are present at the places of measurements.

A. $\left(\frac{2}{\sqrt{3}}\right) f_0$ B. $\left(\frac{\sqrt{2}}{2}\right) f_0$

C. $\sqrt{1.6} f_0$ D. $\sqrt{2.5} f_0$

80. Which one of the following is a FALSE statement about atmospheric Ekman layer?

A. The height at which winds equal geostrophic winds is called the top of the Ekman layer
B. Eddy viscosity coefficient is assumed constant over the entire Ekman layer
C. Within the Ekman layer, there is a component of wind which is directed towards high pressure
D. Height of atmospheric Ekman layer is about 1 km

81. The skin depth of a plane wave traveling vertically downward in a homogeneous medium is 100 m. At what depth, the amplitude of EM wave will become 25% of the amplitude at the Earth's surface?

A. 119 m B. 129 m
C. 139 m D. 149 m

82. Arrange the following dune types in relation to increasing sand supply and wind direction variability.

(*a*) Linear dunes (*b*) Transverse dunes
(*c*) Barchan (*d*) Star dunes

Choose the correct option

A. (*c*), (*b*), (*a*), (*d*) B. (*b*), (*c*), (*d*), (*a*)
C. (*a*), (*b*), (*c*), (*d*) D. (*d*), (*a*), (*b*), (*c*)

83. If the primary productivity off the Kerala coast during the upwelling becomes 400 g C m^{-2} yr^{-1} and Indian Oil Sardines are the major fish feeding on plankton, what would be the expected annual maximum yield of Oil Sardine in g C m^{-2} yr^{-1}, considering the average ecological efficiency of 10%?

A. 80 g C m^{-2} yr^{-1} B. 40 g C m^{-2} yr^{-1}
C. 8 g C m^{-2} yr^{-1} D. 4 g C m^{-2} yr^{-1}

84. Which of the following options is correct regarding nutrient-type elements in the ocean?

A. they are particle reactive, and thus have a short residence time in the ocean.
B. they include trace metals Cd and Zn.
C. they typically have lower concentrations in the deep Pacific Ocean compared to the deep Atlantic.
D. they are controlled primarily by salinity variations in the ocean.

85. In the electromagnetic wave equation $\nabla^2 E - k^2 E = 0$, the propagation constant 'k' for a sinusoidal EM wave propagating through subsurface will be:

A. $\pm\sqrt{j\omega\mu\sigma - \omega^2\mu\varepsilon}$ B. $\pm\sqrt{\omega\mu\sigma - j\omega^2\mu\varepsilon}$

C. $\pm\sqrt{j\omega\mu\sigma + \omega^2\mu\varepsilon}$ D. $\pm\sqrt{\omega\mu\sigma + j\omega^2\mu\varepsilon}$

(ω : Angular frequency; μ : magnetic permeability; σ : conductivity; ε : permittivity; j : complex representation)

78. B **79.** C **80.** C **81.** C **82.** A **83.** D **84.** B **85.** A

86. Match the following:

Column-I (Features)	Column-II (Zoogeographical realms)
A. Climate-limited region	P. Oriental and Australian
B. Main regions of the old-world tropics	Q. Oriental and Ethiopian
C. Barrier-limited regions	R. Palearctic and Nearctic
D. Wallace's Line	S. Neotropical and Australian

Choose the correct options:

A. A-Q, B-R, C-P, D-S
B. A-R, B-Q, C-S, D-P
C. A-P, B-S, C-Q, D-R
D. A-S, B-P, C-R, D-Q

87. Arrange the following types of volcanic eruptions in order of their increasing explosivity.

(*a*) Strombolian
(*b*) Plinian
(*c*) Vulcanian
(*d*) Hawaiian

Choose the correct option:

A. (*a*), (*d*), (*b*), (*c*)
B. (*d*), (*b*), (*c*), (*a*)
C. (*c*), (*b*), (*a*), (*d*)
D. (*d*), (*a*), (*b*), (*c*)

88. The distortion produced by the application of normal moveout (NMO) correction to seismic CMP gathers is termed as "NMO stretch." NMO stretch is more pronounced for:

A. shallower events and farther offsets
B. shallower events and nearer offsets
C. deeper events and farther offsets
D. deeper events and near offsets

89. If the concentration of an ion in a reservoir is diluted to 50% by adding pure water, and the rate of input of that cation to the reservoir doubled, the residence time of that ion in the reservoir would:

A. decrease by half
B. increase by half
C. decrease by factor of four
D. remains unchanged

90. What would be the concentration of CFC in seawater at equilibrium with its partial pressure of 300×10^{-12} atm at 25°C (given solubility coefficient of CFC at 25°C is 20.7×10^{-3} mol kg^{-1} atm^{-1})?

A. 6.2×10^{-12} mol kg^{-1}
B. 6.2×10^{-12} mmol kg^{-1}
C. 6.2×10^{-12} nmol kg^{-1}
D. 6.2×10^{-12} μmol kg^{-1}

91. Match column-I and column-II about subtropical westerly jet stream in northern hemisphere:

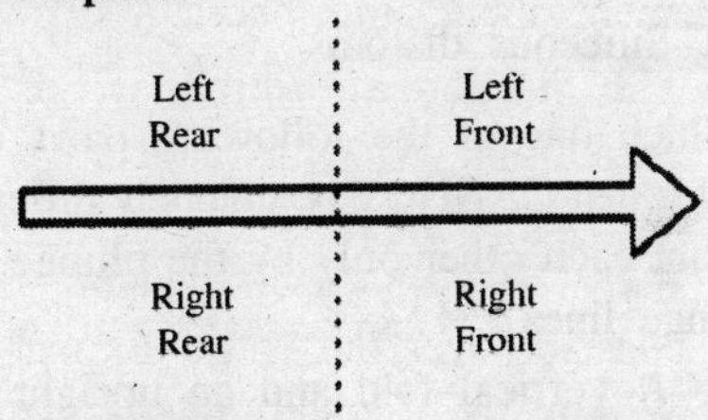

Column-I (Jet stream region)	Column-II (Convergence/ Divergence)
A. Left front	P. Convergence
B. Right front	Q. Divergence
C. Left rear	
D. Right rear	

Choose the correct option:

A. A-Q; B-P; C-P; D-Q
B. A-P; B-Q; C-Q; D-P
C. A-Q; B-P; C-Q; D-P
D. A-P; B-Q; C-P; D-Q

86. B	**87.** D	**88.** A	**89.** A	**90.** A	**91.** A

92. Consider the following sequence of genus/ species

Kandelia candel, Symbiodinium, Eucalanus elongatus, Synechococcus

What is the correct sequence of biota from the following options that corresponds to the above order?

A. Mangrove, Dinoflagellate, Copepod, Cyanobacteria
B. Cyanobacteria, Copepod, Mangrove, Dinoflagellate
C. Dinoflagellate, Copepod, Mangrove, Cyanobacteria
D. Mangrove, Dinoflagellate, Cyanobacteria, Copepod

93. The nutrient-rich coastal regions with high primary productivity are usually dominated by which of the following phytoplankton groups?

A. Heterotrophic dinoflagellate
B. Prokaryotic nitrogen fixers
C. Silicoflagellates
D. Siliceous diatoms

94. Which one of the following pairs contains folds that CANNOT be uniquely differentiated from each other only by the plunge of their hinge lines?

A. A vertical fold and an upright fold
B. A moderately plunging fold and a vertical fold
C. A recumbent fold and a vertical fold
D. A reclined fold and a recumbent fold

95. Consider the following statements.

Statement (A): The oceanic mesoscale eddies always rotate clockwise in the northern hemisphere.

Statement (B): A clockwise rotating mesoscale eddy in northern hemisphere has warmer water at its core compared to outside eddy.

Statement (C): A subtropical geostrophic gyre in the southern hemisphere always has counterclockwise circulation.

Select the CORRECT option

A. Statements (A) and (B) are True; Statement (C) is False
B. Statements (B) and (C) are True; Statement (A) is False
C. Statement (B) is True; Statements (A) and (C) are False
D. Statements (A), (B), and (C) are True

96. Which of the statement is FALSE about data assimilation in Numerical Weather Prediction (NWP)?

Data assimilation is:

A. a technique of bringing observational data into a regular grid.
B. a technique to generate initial condition for NWP model.
C. a technique to integrate the forecast equation in time.
D. based on a least square method.

97. In the given isobaric T-X phase diagram of olivine system at 1 atm pressure, a melt of composition 'A' starts cooling from a temperature of 1900°C. Assuming equilibrium crystallization to occur during the cooling process, how much melt (in %) will remain in the system at 1700°C?

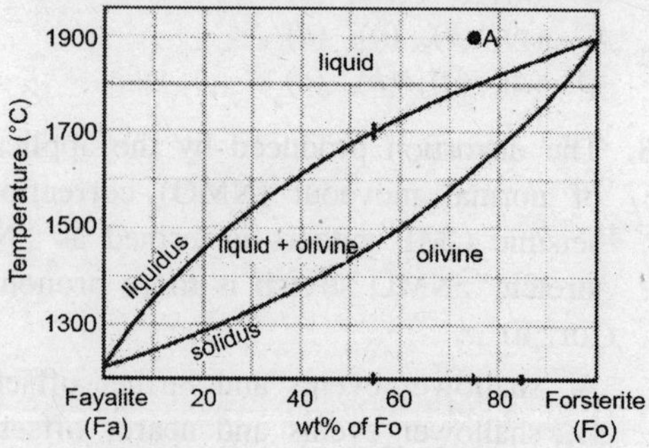

A. 66.7
B. 33.3
C. 20
D. 75

92. A	93. D	94. D	95. B	96. C	97. B

98. Which one of the source-receiver geometries in a seismic tomography experiment best resolves the model parameters (m_1, m_2) of the two horizontal layers?

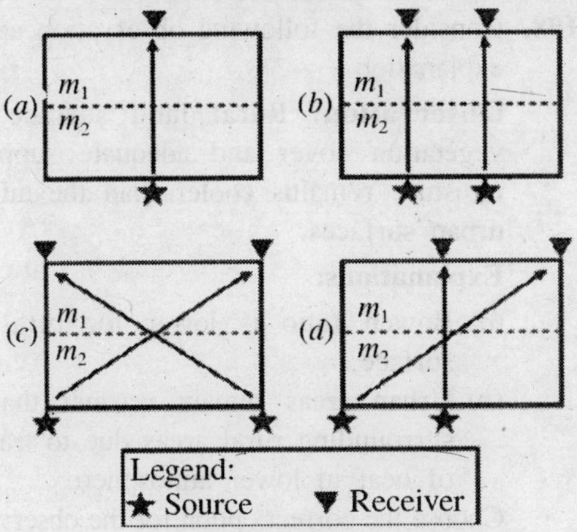

A. (*a*) B. (*b*)
C. (*c*) D. (*d*)

99. Which one of the following statements is TRUE about feedbacks in climate system?

A. Water vapour feedback is positive feedback in climate
B. Snow/ice albedo feedback is negative feedback in climate
C. Water vapour feedback is negative feedback in climate
D. Snow albedo has no effect on climate

100. A shallow water wave travels at a speed of V ms^{-1} in an ocean of depth 2500 m. What would be the depth of the ocean in which speed of this wave reduces to V/5 ms^{-1}?

A. 12.5 m B. 100 m
C. 250 m D. 500 m

101. A thick formation sandwiched between two thick shale beds, has a S.P. response varying from –50 mV to –20 mV and a uniform γ-ray response of 10 API. The formation is:

A. a shaly sandstone
B. a hydrocarbon bearing clean sandstone
C. a hydrocarbon bearing shaly sandstone
D. a water bearing clean sandstone

102. The facial suture which is NOT present along the ventral margin of cephalon of Trilobite is known as:

A. Proparian B. Hypoparian
C. Gonatoparian D. Opisthoparian

103. Consider the following sedimentary structures:

(*a*) Ripple (*b*) Gutter
(*c*) Antidune (*d*) Dune

What is the correct order of increasing velocity with constant grain-size?

A. (*b*), (*c*), (*d*), (*a*)
B. (*a*), (*d*), (*c*), (*b*)
C. (*a*), (*c*), (*b*), (*d*)
D. (*b*), (*d*), (*a*), (*c*)

104. Which one of the following statements is FALSE about atmospheric energetics? (Given E_I is internal energy, E_P is gravitation potential energy. $E_I + E_P$ is total potential energy, R is specific gas constant for dry air, C_P and C_V are specific heats at constant pressure and constant volume, respectively.)

A. $C_V E_P = R E_I$

B. $E_P + E_I = \left(\frac{C_P}{C_V}\right) E_I = \left(\frac{C_P}{R}\right) E_P$

C. Only 0.5% of the total potential energy is available for conversion to kinetic energy for the entire atmosphere

D. Out of the available potential energy, only about 20% is actually converted to kinetic energy

98. D **99.** A **100.** B **101.** B **102.** B **103.** B **104.** D

105. Match the following:

List-I (Dominant process)	List-II (Land form)
A. Vertical accretion	V. River meander
B. Lateral accretion	W. Abandoned delta front
C. Vertical erosion	X. Point bar
D. Lateral erosion	Y. Gully channel
	Z. Flood plain

Choose the correct option:

A. A-X; B-W; C-V; D-Y
B. A-W; B-Z; C-V; D-X
C. A-Z; B-W; C-Y; D-X
D. A-Z; B-X; C-Y; D-W

106. If the densities of freshwater and saltwater are 1000 kg/m^3 and 1020 kg/m^3 respectively, and the water table is at 2 m above sea level , then the freshwater-saltwater interface will be found at a depth of ....

A. 100 m B. 10 m
C. 80 m D. 8 m

107. The figure shows profiles of the parameter A in oceans P & Q. Which of the following statements is correct?

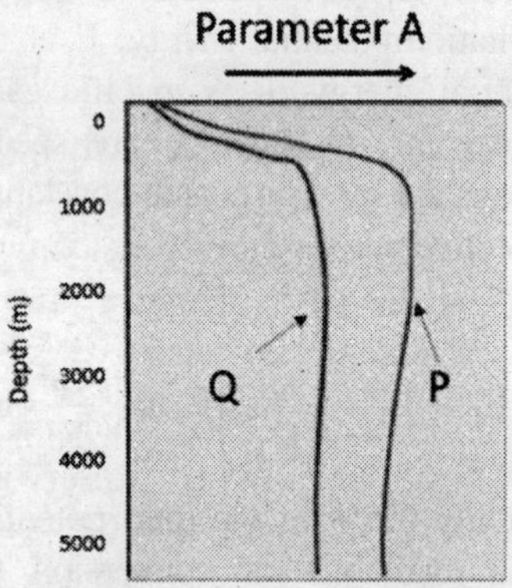

A. A is NO_3^-; P and Q represent Pacific and Atlantic oceans, respectively.
B. A is dissolved oxygen; P and Q represent Pacific and Atlantic oceans, respectively.
C. A is NO_3^-; Q and P represent Pacific and Atlantic oceans, respectively.
D. A is dissolved oxygen; Q and P represent Pacific and Atlantic oceans, respectively.

108. Consider the following observation and the explanation.

Observation: Rural land surface with vegetation cover and adequate supply of moisture remains cooler than the adjacent urban surfaces.

Explanations:

(*a*) Bowen ratio is lower for rural land surface.
(*b*) Urban areas remain warmer than the surrounding rural areas due to trapping of heat in lower atmosphere.

Choose the correct option for the observation.

A. Both (*a*) and (*b*) are correct explanations
B. Only (*a*) is the correct explanation
C. Only (*b*) is the correct explanation
D. None of (*a*) and (*b*) is a correct explanation

109. A real valued discrete time series has a duration of 0.5 seconds. If the sampling interval is 4 milliseconds, the possible range of frequencies in the time series is:

A. 0 Hz to 125 Hz B. 2 Hz to 125 Hz
C. 0 Hz to 2 Hz D. 0 Hz to 250 Hz

110. Identify the INCORRECT pair:

A. Isovels – velocity
B. Riffles – meander bends
C. Ripples – sand bedforms
D. Thalweg – deepest part of a channel

111. A dipping tabular ore body has a thickness of 24 m as measured in a vertical drill hole. If the true thickness of the ore body is 12 m. the dip of the ore body .... is degrees.

A. 30 B. 60
C. 90 D. 45

105. D	**106.** A	**107.** A	**108.** B	**109.** A	**110.** B	**111.** B

112. A mantle peridotite having 60% olivine, 30% clinopyroxene and 10% garnet undergoes equilibrium partial melting to produce a basaltic melt. If the fraction of melt produced is 10% of the original rock by weight, then what would the approximate concentration of La in the melt? Given that the concentration of La in the peridotite is 10 ppm and the mineral-melt partition coefficients (K_d) for olivine, clinopyroxene and garnet, respectively, are: 0.0002, 0.029 and 0.0014.

A. 596 ppm B. 59.6 ppm
C. 5.96 ppm D. 0.596 ppm

113. A is a gravity station at latitude 15° N. B and C are two other gravity stations at the same elevation, but B is 10 km east of A and C is 20 km north of A. If the gravity value measured at B is smaller than at A by 8.12 mgals, what would be the gravity value measured at C? (Assume no anomalous bodies are present at A, B or C)

A. Same as that at A
B. 4.06 mgals smaller than that at A
C. 8.12 mgals smaller than that at A
D. 4.06 mgals larger than that at A

114. A basement is repeatedly faulted resulting in the development of two horst-like structures A and B of limited thickness as indicated in the given figure. The average depth to the basement is $\sqrt{3}$ km. If the structure of A produces a maximum gravity anomaly of 4 mgals. then what would be the maximum gravity anomaly (in mgals) due to B?

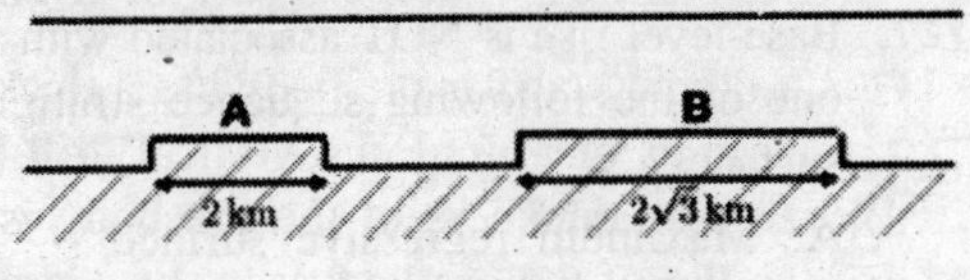

A. $4\sqrt{2}$ B. $4\sqrt{3}$
C. 6.0 D. $6\sqrt{2}$

115. A lower oxygen isotopic composition ($\delta\,^{18}O$) of planktic foraminifera compared to that of the benthic foraminifera at a given location in ocean indicates:

A. Warmer surface temperature
B. Cooler surface temperature
C. Cooler global temperature
D. Increased ice volume effect

116. If the mixing ratio and saturation mixing ratio of an air parcel are 3 g kg^{-1} and 6.5 g kg^{-1} respectively, then what is the relative humidity (RH) of this air parcel?

A. 26.2% B. 56.2%
C. 46.2% D. 36.2%

117. A wind wave at ocean surface has a wave height and wavelength of 5 m and 12 m, respectively. What would be its wave steepness (S) and wave energy per unit area (E. in J m^{-2})? (Given: Seawater density = 1030 kg m^{-3}, g = 9.8 ms^{-2})

A. S = 0.416; E = 31543
B. S = 2.40, E = 63086
C. S = 2.40, E = 6308
D. S = 0.416, E = 50470

118. Find the FALSE statement about a baroclinic atmosphere.

A. Isolines of density and pressure intersect.
B. No geostrophic vertical wind shear is present.
C. Large scale vertical velocity is present.
D. Isolines of pressure and potential temperature intersect.

119. If the present day $^{143}Nd/^{144}Nd$ and $^{147}Sm/^{144}Nd$ of Chondritic Uniform Reservoir (CHUR) are 0.512638 and 0.1967, respectively, then its $^{143}Nd/^{144}Nd$ at 2.5 Ga would have been .... (given decay constant of $^{147}Sm = 6.54 \times 10^{-12}\ y^{-1}$)

A. 0.515892 B. 0.501110
C. 0.509396 D. 0.499260

112. *	113. A	114. C	115. A	116. C	117. A	118. B	119. C

120. Arrange the following minerals in their ascending order of cation exchange capacity (CEC) at pH 7.

(*a*) Smectite (*b*) Feldspar
(*c*) Fe-Oxyhydroxides (*d*) Illite

Choose the correct option:

A. (*b*), (*a*), (*c*), (*d*) B. (*b*), (*c*), (*d*), (*a*)
C. (*d*), (*a*), (*b*), (*c*) D. (*a*), (*d*), (*c*), (*b*)

121. Statement (A): The relation between frequency and wavenumber is called dispersion relation.

Statement (B): Dispersive waves are waves for which phase speed does not vary with wavenumber.

Given the two statements, choose the correct option:

A. Statement (A) is incorrect and statement (B) is correct
B. Statement (A) is correct and statement (B) is incorrect
C. Both Statement (A) and statement (B) are incorrect
D. Both Statement (A) and statement (B) are correct

122. At a location in Australia, stromatolite length was 1.3 m, and considering there was no change in sea level and erosion, what would be its expected age?

A. 1300 years B. 3900 years
C. 5200 years D. 2600 years

123. The following figure shows a small part of a seafloor and its associated magnetic anomaly. Which of the following inferences is INVALID?

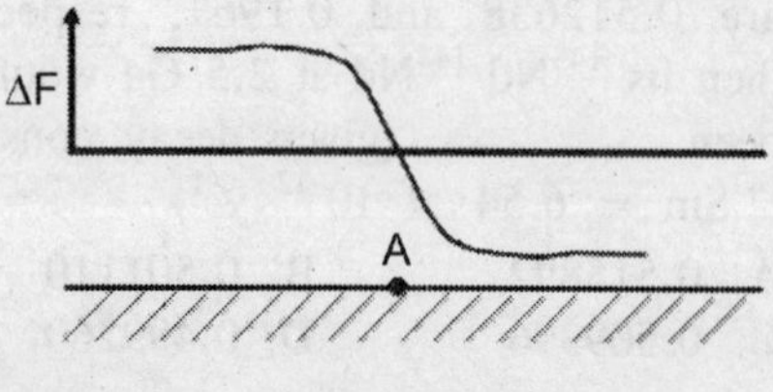

A. The seafloor is spreading about A
B. The seafloor spreading is caused by tectonic activity outside the area represented in the figure
C. The rocks on either side of A are magnetized in opposite directions
D. The sea floor represented in the figure witnessed a magnetic reversal during its formation

124. Identify the CORRECT pair:

A. Unconsolidated bank sediments → narrow, deep channel
B. Consolidated bank sediments wide → shallow channel
C. Unconsolidated bank sediments → high silt-clay ratio
D. Consolidated bank sediments → low channel width-depth ratio

125. A basaltic melt with Sr = 300 ppm mixes with a granitic melt having Sr = 150 ppm. If the hybrid melt has Sr = 200 ppm, what will be the fraction of the basaltic melt in the hybrid liquid?

A. 0.67 B. 0.50
C. 0.75 D. 0.33

126. Given a system of linear equations

$$2x + y + z = 0$$
$$2x + 3y + 2z = 0$$
$$2y + z = 0$$

The number of non-zero singular values associated with the above system is:

A. 0 B. 1
C. 2 D. 3

127. Base-level rise is NOT associated with which one of the following sequence stratigraphic surfaces?

A. Maximum regressive surface
B. Regressive surface of marine erosion
C. Ravinement surface (transgressive)
D. Maximum flooding surface

120. B **121.** B **122.** D **123.** A **124.** D **125.** D **126.** C **127.** B

128. Consider the given ridge-ridge-ridge (RRR) triple junction between plates A, B and C, and the relative vector velocities V_{BA}, V_{CB} and V_{AC} between them. If V_{BA} has azimuth 90° and magnitude 100 mm/y, V_{CB} has azimuth 200° and magnitude 80 mm/y, what will be the magnitude of V_{AC}?

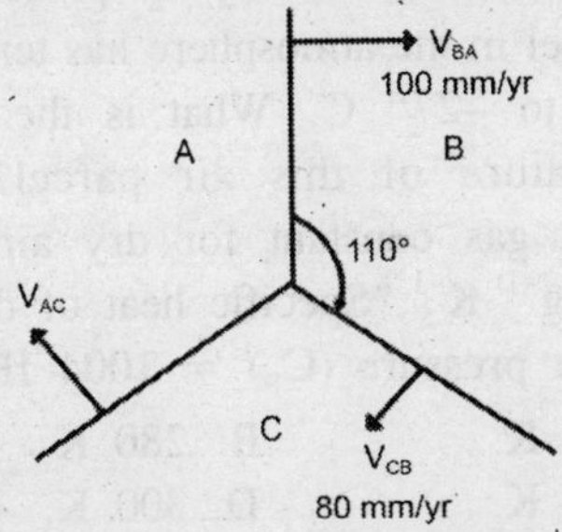

A. 90.4 mm/y B. 104.5 mm/y
C. 318.7 mm/y D. 212.3 mm/y

129. A single layered 35 km thick crust having a P-wave velocity of 6 km/s overlies a mantle having a velocity of 8 km/s. Then, the first arrival recorded at an epicentral distance of 120 km from an earthquake occurring at a depth of 10 km is:

A. Pg B. P^*
C. Pn D. PmP

130. Choose correct combination of the following statements for Equilibrium Line Altitude (ELA).

(*a*) It cannot be estimated using Cirque Floor altitude
(*b*) It represents a zone on glacier where accumulation is balanced by ablation.
(*c*) It can be estimated by minimum elevation of lateral moraines
(*d*) It can be estimated using toe-to-headwall ratio
(*e*) It can be estimated using ratio of accumulation area to the total glacier area

Choose the correct option:

A. (*a*), (*b*) and (*c*) B. (*b*), (*d*) and (*e*)
C. (*a*), (*d*) and (*e*) D. (*b*), (*c*) and (*d*)

131. Which one of the following is a reason for large movement over land (without weakening) of monsoon depression that crosses Head Bay of Bengal region?

A. Steered by easterly jet system
B. Move over land in an environment that is "marine-like"
C. Presence of strong vertical shear of horizontal winds
D. Reduced friction force during southwest Indian monsoon season

132. Consider the following statements

(*a*) Waves of shorter wavelengths have higher frequencies
(*b*) Waves of shorter wavelengths contain higher energy
(*c*) Waves of shorter wavelengths are emitted from objects with higher temperature
(*d*) The emitted radiation decreases with temperature.

Choose the correct option:

A. Only (*a*) is true
B. Only (*a*) and (*b*) are true
C. Only (*a*), (*b*) and (*c*) are true
D. Only (*a*), (*b*) and (*d*) are true

133. The Clapeyron equation gives a negative $\frac{dP}{dT}$ value for H_2O-saturated melting of albite at low pressure conditions [H_2O_{vap} + albite → $liquid_{aq}$]. This is due to:

A. large negative volume change associated with the reaction
B. large negative entropy change associated with the reaction
C. large negative change in both volume and entropy of the reaction
D. large positive volume change associated with the reaction

128. B	129. A	130. B	131. B	132. C	133. A

134. Find the correct match:

Isolines	Property
A. Isohaline	P. Lines of equal density
B. Isopycnal	Q. Lines of equal salinity
C. Isobath	R. Lines of equal depth
D. Isohyet	S. Lines of equal rainfall

Choose the correct option:

A. A-Q, B-P, C-R, D-S
B. A-S, B-R, C-P, D-Q
C. A-R, B-P, C-Q, D-S
D. A-Q, B-P, C-S, D-R

135. What is the minimum super-saturation level that is required for a cloud droplet with radius 0.04 μm to exist at an ambient temperature of 2°C in the absence of any aerosol? (Given surface tension of water $\sigma = 7.5 \times 10^{-2}$ Nm^{-1}, Specific gas constant for water R_V = 461 JK^{-1} kg^{-1}, Specific volume of water $\alpha_1 = 1 \times 10^{-3}$ m^3 kg^{-1})

A. 3% B. 1%
C. 5% D. 4%

136. The placer diamond is present within:

A. Kajrahat Limestone
B. Lower Rewa Sandstone
C. Upper Bhander Sandstone
D. Rohtas Limestone

137. The longitudinal resistivity of a rock, comprising of two horizontally stratified layers of resistivity ρ_1 and ρ_2 of 5 m thickness each, is 80 Ωm. If resistivity ρ_1 is 100 Ωm, then the resistivity ρ_2 will be close to:

A. 64 Ωm B. 67 Ωm
C. 70 Ωm D. 73 Ωm

138. Which one of the following statements is NOT true for Algoma-type banded iron formation?

A. They did not form at shallow continental shelves.
B. They formed laterally extensive units.
C. They are associated with submarine volcanic sequences.
D. They are occasionally associated with VMS deposits.

139. A 1.0 kg parcel of dry air present at 500 hPa level in the atmosphere has temperature equals to –27° C. What is the potential temperature of this air parcel? (Given specific gas constant for dry air (R_d) = 287 JKg^{-1} K^{-1}, Specific heat of dry air at constant pressure (C_P) = 1004 JKg^{-1} K^{-1})

A. 250 K B. 280 K
C. 320 K D. 300 K

140. An unsaturated air parcel originating at the surface of the earth (Z = 0 m has temperature of 25°C. What will be the temperature of this air parcel if it undergoes adiabatic displacement to the top of the mixed boundary layer and remains unsaturated (z = 800 m)?

A. 11.2°C B. 32.8°C
C. 17.2°C D. 21.2°C

141. Match the types of soil in Column-I with corresponding properties in Column-II.

Column-I	Column-II
A. Entisols	P. acidic soils in humid areas
B. Mollisols	Q. high content of expandable clay minerals
C. Vertisols	R. recently formed soil
D. Ultisols	S. base rich with high organic matter

Choose the correct option:

A. A-S, B-Q, C-R, D-P
B. A-R, B-S, C-Q, D-P
C. A-R, B-P, C-S, D-Q
D. A-P, B-S, C-Q, D-R

134. A **135.** A **136.** B **137.** B **138.** B **139.** D **140.** C **141.** B

142. A N-S striking 2-dimensional body, at a place of magnetic inclination 30°, generates an anomaly of 150 gammas in the total field at some point. What would be the magnetic anomaly, at the same location, in the vertical component?

A. It cannot be calculated with the given data
B. 75 gammas
C. $75\sqrt{3}$ gammas
D. 300 gammas

143. What will be the temperature change of an isolated air parcel of 100 kg due to a condensation of 100 g of water vapour (Given: Latent heat of condensation = 2.26 × 10^6 J/kg. Specific heat of air at constant pressure = 1004 Jkg^{-1} K^{-1})

A. 3.2°C B. 1.5°C
C. 2.3°C D. 4.2°C

144. Which of the following are described by the 'Rating curve'?

A. discharge and water stage
B. discharge and catchment area
C. sediment and solute concentrations and discharge
D. runoff and rainfall

145. The direct arrivals in a seismic shot gather have a linear moveout with a slope of 0.67 s/km. The slope of the corresponding event in the FK domain is:

A. 0 Hz/km^{-1} B. 0.33 Hz/km^{-1}
C. 0.67 Hz/km^{-1} D. 1.5 Hz/km^{-1}

146. Based on records from 1950 to 2020, the average precipitation received at Mawsynram is:

A. 12 – 14 m/y B. 10 – 12 m/y
C. 8 – 10 m/y D. 6 – 8 m/y

147. Consider the following statements:

(*a*) According to the definition, in-situ temperature is not a conservative property but potential temperature is.

(*b*) When it is not possible to measure the in-situ temperature, the potential temperature is measured instead.

(*c*) Both surface heating of the oceans and rainfall promote stability of surface layers.

Choose the correct option:

A. Only (*a*) and (*c*) are true
B. Only (*a*) and (*b*) are true
C. Only (*b*) and (*c*) are true
D. Only (*b*) is true

148. Which one of the following strain geometry patterns would correspond to a flexural flow fold?

A. Highest strain in the hinge zone
B. Uniform strain throughout the fold train
C. Lowest strain in the hinge zone
D. No strain in the fold train

149. On 10 October 2014, as cyclonic storm Hudhud approached Visakhapatnam, a buoy beneath the storm recorded a sea surface temperature of 29°C. At the same time a satellite measured cloud top temperature of –74°C. Assuming that the cyclonic storm Hudhud behaved like a Carnot cycle, how efficient was Hudhud as a heat engine?

A. 0.22 B. 0.34
C. 0.42 D. 0.54

150. Consider the following statements on the tidal flooding in an estuary

(*a*) It turns the estuary into a sedimentary source
(*b*) It turns the estuary into a sedimentary sink
(*c*) It represents operation of time-velocity asymmetry
(*d*) It represents equilibrium condition

Choose the correct option:

A. (*a*) and (*c*) are correct
B. (*a*) and (*d*) are correct
C. (*b*) and (*c*) are correct
D. (*b*) and (*d*) are correct

142. D **143.** C **144.** A **145.** D **146.** A **147.** A **148.** C **149.** B **150.** C

EXPLANATORY ANSWERS

1. **(C):** Total number of possible meals $= 3$ starters $\times$ 3 main courses $\times$ 2 desserts $= 18$.

   Vegetarian options:

   - Starters: 2 (Tomato Soup, Vegetable Salad)
   - Main Courses: 1 (Veg Biryani)
   - Desserts: 2 (Gulabjamun, Rasagulla)

   Total vegetarian meals = starters $\times$ main course $\times$ desserts $= 4$.

   Probability of a vegetarian meal $= \frac{4}{18} = \frac{2}{9}$.

2. **(C):** First vessel alcohol: $\frac{3}{8}$ L

   Second vessel alcohol: $\frac{2}{7}$ L

   Total alcohol: $\frac{3}{8} + \frac{2}{7} = \frac{37}{56}$ L

   Total solution volume after mixing: 2 L

   Alcohol concentration in mixture:

   $$\frac{\frac{37}{56}}{2} = \frac{37}{112}$$

   Alcohol to water ratio:

   $$\text{Alcohol} = \frac{37}{112}$$

   $$\text{Water} = 1 - \frac{37}{112} = \frac{75}{112}$$

   $$\text{Ratio} = \frac{37}{112} : \frac{75}{112} = 37 : 75$$

   Approximating $\frac{37}{75} \approx \frac{1}{2}$, so the ratio is approximately 1 : 2.

3. **(A):** The tree's height increased at an accelerating rate during the first 15 weeks, as the rate of growth increased linearly. After being trimmed at the 15th week, the rate of growth decreased linearly for the next 15 weeks. This means the height graph initially has a curve that becomes steeper, representing the increasing rate of growth, and then transitions into a curve that flattens, representing the decreasing rate of growth. Option (A) accurately represents this pattern of growth and trimming over the 30-week period.

4. **(A):** An eagle is sitting atop a 100 m high cliff. A mouse starts running away from the cliff at 10 m/s. The eagle spots the mouse and dives at a 45° angle with a speed of 20 m/s to capture it.

   First, calculate the time the eagle takes to reach the ground:

   - Vertical component of eagle's speed:
     $$v_y = 20 \times \cos(45°) \approx 14.14 \text{ m/s}$$
   - Time o descend:
     $$t_d = \frac{100}{14.14} \approx 7.07\,\text{s}$$
   - Horizontal distance covered by the eagle:
     $$x_{\text{eagle}} = 14.14 \times 7.07 \approx 100 \text{ m}$$

   Next, determine when the eagle must start its dive:

   - The mouse's position when caught:
     $$x_{\text{mouse}} = 10 \times (t_e + t_d)$$
   - Setting : $x_{\text{mouse}} = x_{\text{eagle}}$: $10 \times (t_e + 7.07) = 100$
   - Solving for : t_e : $t_e \approx 2.93$ s.

5. **(B):** The graph shows that the observed frequency of anti-predator calls for adult females is significantly higher than the expected frequency, indicating that adult females make more anti-predator calls than expected. This conclusion aligns with the data presented, where the observed frequency bar for adult females is taller than the expected frequency bar.

6. **(D)**: Given:

- Two chords of a circle intersect at point E and bisect each other.
- The angle between the chords at point E is 60°.
- One chord AB has a length of 10 cm, so each segment AE and EB is 5 cm.

Since the chords bisect each other, they form a parallelogram. The sides of the parallelogram are the halves of the chords.

Let:

- AE = EB = 5 cm (half of the known chord).
- CE = ED = x cm (half of the unknown chord).
- The angle between AE and CE is 60°.

Using the Law of Cosines in triangle AEC:

$$AC^2 = AE^2 + CE^2 - 2 \times AE \times CE \times \cos(60°)$$

Since cos (60°) = 0.5:

$$AC^2 = 5^2 + x^2 - 2 \times 5 \times x \times 0.5$$

$$AC^2 = 25 + x^2 - 5x$$

Similarly, in triangle BED, the angle between EB and ED is 120° (since adjacent angles in a parallelogram sum to 180°), and cos (120°) = –0.5:

$$BD^2 = EB^2 + ED^2 - 2 \times EB \times ED \times \cos(120°)$$

$$BD^2 = 5^2 + x^2 - 2 \times 5 \times x \times (-0.5)$$

$$BD^2 = 25 + x^2 + 5x$$

The sum of the squares of the diagonals in a parallelogram equals the sum of the squares of all sides:

$$AC^2 + BD^2 = 2(AE^2 + CE^2 + EB^2 + ED^2)$$

$$(25 + x^2 - 5x) + (25 + x^2 + 5x) = 2(5^2 + x^2 + 5^2 + x^2)$$

$$50 + 2x^2 = 2(50 + 2x^2)$$

$$50 + 2x^2 = 100 + 4x^2$$

Subtract $50 + 2x^2$ from both sides:

$$0 = 50 + 2x^2$$

Subtract 50 from both sides:

$$-50 = 2x^2$$

This leads to $x^2 = -25$, which is impossible since a square cannot be negative.

Conclusion: The only valid solution is when x = 5 cm, meaning the two chords are equal in length.

Therefore, the length of the other chord is:

$$CD = 2 \times x = 2 \times 5 = 10 \text{ cm}.$$

7. **(B)**: Using the capture-recapture method:

- Proportion of tagged fish in pond: $\frac{25}{N}$
- Proportion of tagged fish in sample: $\frac{10}{30} = \frac{1}{3}$
- Setting proportions equal: $\frac{25}{N} = \frac{1}{3}$
- Solving for N : N = 75.

8. **(C)**: Assigning floors based on clues:

1. Artist is on floor 2.
2. Engineer is on floor 5 (Artist's floor + 3).
3. Doctor is on floor 1 (Engineer's floor – 4).
4. Teacher is on floor 3.
5. Lawyer is on floor 4 (one floor above the teacher).

From lowest to topmost: Doctor, Artist, Teacher, Lawyer, Engineer.

9. **(C)**: Calculations:

Women who voted against:

1450 – 800 = 650

Women who abstained: 200

Women who voted for:

1800 – 650 – 200 = 950.

10. **(D)**: The boy's statements align if:

- Today is January 1st.
- His birthday is on December 31st.
- He was 15 on December 30, turned 16 on December 31, and will turn 18 next year on December 31.

His birthday is on December 31st, and he was making the assertion on January 1st.

11. (C): BOTANY is the study of PLANTS, so PHILOSOPHY is the study of IDEAS.

12. (A): Let N be the total number of chairs around the table. Since both A and B are counting chairs in the same direction, the difference in their counts remains constant modulo N.

Given:

1. A's 5th chair is B's 9th chair:
   $9 - 5 \equiv D \mod N \Rightarrow D \equiv 4 \mod N.$
2. B's 3rd chair is A's 12th chair:
   $12 - 3 \equiv D \mod N \Rightarrow D \equiv 9 \mod N.$

Setting the two equations: $4 \equiv 9 \mod N.$

$N = 13.$

13. (A): Total number of persons actually having the disease:

True positive + False negative

$= 8 + 3 = 11.$

14. (C): Constructing the family tree:

- A is son of P and sibling to V and N.
- M is mother of N (thus mother of A and V).
- S is nephew of V (child of A or N).
- B is daughter-in-law of A (married to A's son, S).
- Therefore, B is M's grandson's wife.

15. (A): Let the number be $100a + 10b + c$. Its reverse is $100c + 10b + a$.

Sum: $(100a + 10b + c) + (100c + 10b + a)$

$= 101(a + c) + 20b = 1089$

Solving: $101(a + c) + 20b = 1089$

$$= a + c = \frac{1089 - 20b}{101}$$

Trying $b = 9$:

$$a + c = \frac{1089 - 180}{101} = 9$$

Thus, middle digit, $b = 9$.

16. (B): From the graph, the price per carat increases linearly with the weight of the diamond. The equation of the price per carat is:

Price per carat = 2 × Weight (in carats).

The total cost of 4 diamonds is given as ₹ 4.5 lakh. The total cost can be expressed as:

4 × (Weight per diamond × Price per carat) = 4.5 lakh

Substitute the price per carat:

4 × (Weight × 2 × Weight) = 4.5.

Simplify:

$8 \times \text{Weight}^2 = 4.5.$

$$\text{Weight}^2 = \frac{4.5}{8} = 0.5625$$

$$\text{Weight} = \sqrt{0.5625} = 0.75 \text{ carats}$$

Hence, the largest size of one diamond is 0.75 carats.

17. (D): Equality of both the averages of squares of all terms and their means ensures equality of standard deviations.

The averages of squares of all terms and their means.

18. (B): A leap year starting on Tuesday means March 1st is a Saturday. Therefore, the third Saturday is on March 15th.

19. (B): If X = 6 and Y = 9, the number becomes $7690625 \approx 2773^2$, which is a perfect square.

20. (B): Let the cost price per watch be x.

Total profit:

$(50 \times 0.10x) + (50 \times 0.20x) + (50 \times 0.25x) + (50 \times 0.40x) = 47.5x$

$47.5x = 19000$

$x = 400$

Total cost:

$200 \times 400 =$ ₹ 80000.

21. **(D):** Flash floods are intense, short-duration events that can transport a wide range of sediment sizes simultaneously due to their high energy and rapid water flow. The grain-size distribution in flash flood deposits is often multimodal because:

- **Varied Sediment Sources:** Flash floods erode materials from diverse environments such as riverbanks, slopes, and soils, incorporating clays, silts, sands, gravels, and even boulders.
- **Lack of Sorting:** The rapid rise and fall of water levels prevent the natural sorting of sediments by size. There is insufficient time for finer particles to settle separately from coarser ones.
- **Multiple Energy Peaks:** Variations in flow velocity during the flood can create multiple peaks in sediment deposition, each representing different energy conditions.

As a result, the deposited sediments display a grain-size distribution with multiple peaks, characteristic of a multimodal distribution.

22. **(B):** The correct chronological order is:

1. **Ediacaran Biota:**

   Timeframe: Approximately 635 to 541 million years ago, during the Ediacaran Period at the end of the Precambrian.

   Significance: Represents some of the earliest known complex multicellular organisms.

2. **Land Plants:**

   Timeframe: First appeared around 470 million years ago during the Ordovician Period.

   Significance: The colonization of land by plants transformed Earth's ecosystems and paved the way for terrestrial life.

3. **Amphibians:**

   Timeframe: Emerged around 370 million years ago in the Late Devonian Period.

   Significance: Amphibians were the first vertebrates to live both in water and on land, marking a crucial step in vertebrate evolution.

Incorrect Options:

Option A & C: Incorrect because land plants did not appear before the Ediacaran biota.

Option D: Incorrect because amphibians did not precede land plants in the fossil record.

23. **(B): Option A (True):** The subtropical jet stream forms near the tropopause (~ 12 km altitude) above the subtropical highpressure zones around 30° latitude. It results from the conservation of angular momentum as air moves poleward from the equator.

Option B (False): While mid-latitude jet streams are largely geostrophic (balance between pressure gradient force and Coriolis force), the subtropical jet stream does not fully satisfy geostrophic balance. This is because:

- **Conservation of Angular Momentum:** The subtropical jet is significantly influenced by the conservation of angular momentum of air moving from the equator toward higher latitudes.
- **Ageostrophic Components:** The acceleration and curvature of the flow introduce ageostrophic motions that prevent full geostrophic balance.

Option C (True): The subtropical jet stream consists of westerly winds, flowing from west to east due to Earth's rotation and atmospheric circulation patterns.

Option D (True): The jet stream is stronger in the winter hemisphere because the temperature gradients between the equator and the poles are steeper during this season, intensifying the wind speeds.

24. (C):

- **Lifting Condensation Level (LCL):** The altitude (pressure level) where a parcel of air becomes saturated upon lifting and condensation begins.
- **Level of Free Convection (LFC):** The altitude where the parcel becomes warmer than the surrounding air and can rise freely due to buoyancy.
- **Equilibrium Level (EL):** The altitude where the parcel's temperature equals the environment's temperature again, and it stops rising.

Physical Relationship:

- The LCL occurs first as the parcel rises and cools to saturation.
- The LFC must be at a higher altitude (lower pressure) than the LCL because the parcel cannot rise freely before it becomes saturated.
- The EL is above the LFC.

Analysis of Option C:

- LCL at 800 hPa (higher altitude/lower pressure).
- LFC at 900 hPa (lower altitude/higher pressure).
- This scenario implies that the parcel would start rising freely (LFC) before it reaches saturation (LCL), which is not physically possible.

Other Options:

- In options A, B, and D, the LFC occurs at a pressure lower than the LCL, which is physically plausible.

25. (C):

- **Rotation Direction:** Reversing Earth's rotation would cause the Sun to appear to rise in the west and set in the east.
- **Period of Rotation:** The length of a day (24 hours) remains unchanged since the rotation period is the same.
- **Day and Night Lengths:** The durations of daylight and darkness are determined by Earth's axial tilt and orbit around the Sun.
- **Latitude Effects:** For any location (e.g., Delhi), the length of day and night varies seasonally due to the tilt, not the rotation direction.

Therefore, the reversal of Earth's rotation direction would not significantly affect the length of day and night at a particular place.

26. (D):

- **Thermal Stratification:** Warmer surface temperatures increase the temperature difference between surface and deeper waters, strengthening stratification.
- **Reduced Vertical Mixing:** Stronger stratification inhibits the upward movement of nutrient-rich deep waters to the surface.
- **Nutrient Availability:** With less mixing, surface waters become nutrient-poor (oligotrophic), limiting the growth of phytoplankton and reducing primary productivity.

Incorrect Options:

- **Option A & C (Eutrophic):** Eutrophication involves increased nutrient levels, which is unlikely under stronger stratification.
- **Option B:** While higher temperatures may increase metabolic rates, the limiting factor is nutrient availability, not consumption rate.

27. (C):

- **Option A (True):** Till is unsorted sediment deposited directly by glacial ice and is transported en masse by glaciers.
- **Option B (True):** Till can exhibit deformation features like folds and faults due to the stresses exerted by moving ice.

- **Option C (False Statement):** Till can be used to infer regional ice movement:

  Clast Orientation: The alignment of elongated rock fragments within till can indicate the direction of ice flow.

  Provenance Studies: Analyzing the composition of till can reveal the source areas and ice movement paths.

- **Option D (True):** Till is characteristically poorly sorted, containing a mix of particle sizes from clay to boulders.

28. (D): If the Earth were to orbit the Sun at twice its current distance without changing its rotational velocity (length of day remains 24 hours), we can calculate the new length of a year using Kepler's Third Law of planetary motion. Kepler's Third Law states that the square of the orbital period (T^2) is proportional to the cube of the semi-major axis of the orbit (R^3), expressed as:

$T^2 \propto R^3$

Let T_1 and R_1 be the original orbital period and radius, and T_2 and $R_2 = 2R_1$ be the new orbital period and radius. Applying Kepler's Third Law:

$$\left(\frac{T_2}{T_1}\right)^2 = \left(\frac{R_2}{R_1}\right)^3$$

$$\left(\frac{T_2}{T_1}\right)^2 = (2)^3 = 8$$

$$\frac{T_2}{T_1} = \sqrt{8} = 2\sqrt{2}$$

Since T_1 = 1 year (365 days), the new orbital period T_2 is:

$$T_2 = 2\sqrt{2} \times 365 \text{ days}$$

$$T_2 = 730\sqrt{2} \text{ days}$$

Thus, a year would have $730\sqrt{2}$ days.

29. (C): An isograd is an imaginary line on a geological map that represents the first appearance of a particular metamorphic index mineral in the field. It marks the boundary between different metamorphic zones, indicating a specific set of pressure-temperature conditions during metamorphism. Index minerals are minerals that form under specific conditions and are used to identify metamorphic grades. The appearance of a new index mineral signifies that the rocks have crossed into a higher grade of metamorphism. Therefore, an isograd is essential for mapping metamorphic terrains and understanding the metamorphic history of a region.

30. (D): The magnetic needle in a dip circle deviates most from the horizontal (i.e., has the highest magnetic dip or inclination) at locations closer to the magnetic poles. Magnetic dip increases with latitude, being zero at the magnetic equator and reaching 90 degrees at the magnetic poles. Among the given towns:

- **Thiruvananthapuram:** Approximately 8.5° N latitude.
- **Tirupati:** Approximately 13.6° N latitude.
- **Ujjain:** Approximately 23° N latitude.
- **Lucknow:** Approximately 26.8° N latitude.

Lucknow is the farthest north, closest to the Earth's magnetic pole among the options provided, resulting in the greatest deviation of the magnetic needle from the horizontal. Therefore, at Lucknow, the magnetic needle dips the most.

31. (A): Sphalerite is a mineral composed of zinc sulphide (ZnS) and is the primary ore of zinc. It often contains iron impurities, which can affect its color and properties, but its main economic value is as a source of zinc. Zinc extracted from sphalerite is used extensively for galvanizing iron and steel to prevent rusting, in making brass (an alloy of copper and zinc), and in various other applications such as batteries, die-casting alloys, and as a dietary mineral.

32. (B): The steady state of materials in the ocean refers to a condition where the concentration of a substance remains constant over time because the rates of input (sources) and output (sinks) are balanced. This means that, although materials are continuously being added to and removed from the ocean, the overall concentration does not change. Mathematically, this can be expressed as:

Rate of input = Rate of output

This concept is essential in oceanography for understanding the cycles of nutrients, trace elements, and other substances in marine environments.

33. (B): Black water is domestic wastewater that contains significant quantities of fecal matter and urine, hence gross fecal coliform contamination. It comes from toilets and includes sewage waste that can carry harmful pathogens and requires careful treatment before being released into the environment. In contrast, grey water refers to wastewater from sinks, showers, and washing machines, which does not contain sewage and is less contaminated.

34. (C): The scale height is the vertical distance over which the atmospheric pressure decreases to (approximately 36.8%) of its original value. It is a concept used in atmospheric physics to describe how pressure (or density) decreases with altitude in an isothermal atmosphere under the assumption of hydrostatic equilibrium. The mathematical expression for pressure variation with height is:

$$P(h) = P_0 e^{-h/H}$$

where:

- $P(h)$ is the pressure at height h,
- P_0 is the reference pressure at the surface,
- H is the scale height,
- e is the base of the natural logarithm (approximately 2.71828).

Thus, over a vertical distance equal to the scale height H, the pressure decreases to of $1/e$ of P_0.

35. (D): Carbonaceous chondrites are primitive meteorites that have not undergone differentiation. They are considered some of the oldest and most unaltered materials in the solar system, preserving the original composition of the solar nebula. Unlike iron meteorites, shergottites, and eucrites—which originate from differentiated planetary bodies where melting and segregation have occurred—carbonaceous chondrites come from undifferentiated bodies.

Therefore, they are not derived from differentiated planetary bodies.

36. (A): When a cuboidal rock sample is subjected to purely shear stresses in the elastic regime, it experiences a change in shape (distortion) without any change in volume. Shear stress causes angular deformation, but the overall volume remains constant because there is no net dilatation or compression occurring in the material. Hence, the change in volume of the rock sample is zero.

37. (B): Augite is a clinopyroxene mineral featuring a single-chain silicate structure. In this structure, each [SiO_4] tetrahedron shares two of its oxygen atoms with adjacent tetrahedra, forming continuous chains of linked tetrahedra. This sharing of two oxygen atoms per tetrahedron is characteristic of pyroxenes like augite and is responsible for their chain-like crystal structure.

38. (B): Kaveri, Mahanadi, Krishna, Godavari: The correct sequence of rivers in order of increasing length is:

- Kaveri (~800 km)
- Mahanadi (~860 km)
- Krishna (~1,400 km)
- Godavari (~1,465 km)

This arrangement starts with the shortest river, Kaveri, and progresses to the longest, Godavari. Thus, the sequence reflects the rivers arranged in increasing order of their lengths.

39. (B): Pressure gradient force, Coriolis force and turbulent drag force: The Ekman layer in the atmosphere involves a three-way force balance between the pressure gradient force, the Coriolis force, and the turbulent drag force (friction). In this layer near the Earth's surface, wind motion is affected by frictional forces due to turbulence, which modifies the balance between the pressure gradient and Coriolis forces present in geostrophic flow. This results in a spiral pattern of wind direction with altitude known as the Ekman spiral.

40. (B): In urban polluted atmospheres, surface ozone concentrations peak during the afternoon, typically between 2 PM and 4 PM. Ozone is a secondary pollutant formed through photochemical reactions involving sunlight, nitrogen oxides (NOx), and volatile organic compounds (VOCs). The intensity of sunlight is greatest during the early afternoon, accelerating these reactions and leading to the highest ozone levels at this time of day.

41. (D): Andesine is a plagioclase feldspar mineral that is part of the continuous reaction series in Bowen's Reaction Series, not the discontinuous series. The discontinuous series includes minerals like olivine, pyroxene (enstatite), amphibole, and biotite, which crystallize in a specific sequence as magma cools. Andesine, being a continuous solid solution between albite and anorthite, does not belong to the discontinuous reaction series.

42. (D): 1 → Blue, 2 → Green, 3 → Red: For a standard False Color Composite (FCC) using the LISS-III sensor bands designated as:

- Band 1: Green
- Band 2: Red
- Band 3: Near-Infrared (NIR)
- Band 4: Short-Wave Infrared (SWIR)

The standard FCC assigns:

- Band 1 (Green) to the Blue channel
- Band 2 (Red) to the Green channel
- Band 3 (NIR) to the Red channel

This combination enhances the visualization of vegetation, as healthy vegetation reflects strongly in the NIR band and appears red in the composite image. Therefore, option D provides the correct band assignments for a standard FCC.

43. (D): The correct sequence of products of increasing weathering of orthoclase is illite, then kaolinite, followed by gibbsite. Orthoclase, a potassium feldspar, undergoes chemical weathering processes where it first alters to illite, a mica-like clay mineral, under moderate weathering conditions. With increased weathering intensity, illite further alters to kaolinite, a clay mineral formed in acidic and humid environments. Under intense weathering, especially in tropical climates, kaolinite can decompose to form gibbsite, an aluminum hydroxide mineral, representing the most advanced stage of weathering in this sequence.

44. (B): In small-scale vortices such as tornadoes, the horizontal wind follows cyclostrophic wind balance. This balance occurs when the centrifugal force is balanced by the horizontal pressure gradient force, and the Coriolis force is negligible due to the small spatial scale and short time frame of these phenomena. Cyclostrophic balance explains the high wind speeds and tight circulation patterns observed in tornadoes, where the rapid rotation is maintained without significant influence from Earth's rotation.

45. (B): The activity of 14 mg of ^{14}C with a decay constant (λ) of 3.84×10^{-12} s^{-1} is approximately 2.31×10^9 decays per second.

To calculate this, first determine the number of atoms (N) in 14 mg of ^{14}C:

- Molar mass of ^{14}C = 14 g/mol
- Number of moles (n)
  = mass (m) / molar mass (M)
  = $(14 \times 10^{-3}$ g)/(14 g/mol)
  = 1×10^{-3} mol
- Number of atoms (N) = $n \times$ Avogadro's number (6.022×10^{23} mol^{-1})
  = 6.022×10^{20} atoms
- Activity (A) = λN
  = $(3.84 \times 10^{-12}$ s$^{-1}) \times (6.022 \times 10^{20})$
  $\approx 2.31 \times 10^9$ decays per second

46. (C): The statement "The surface water off Western South America is colder than normal." is NOT true in the context of El Niño. During an El Niño event, warmer-than-average sea surface temperatures occur in the central and eastern Pacific Ocean, including off the coast of Western South America.

This warming disrupts normal weather patterns, leading to decreased upwelling of cold, nutrient-rich water and impacting marine ecosystems and global climate patterns.

47. (A): Among the given radioisotopes, ^{232}Th (Thorium-232) has the highest half-life, approximately 1.405×10^{10} years. The half-lives of the other isotopes are:

- ^{235}U: $\sim 7.04 \times 10^8$ years
- ^{235}U: $\sim 4.468 \times 10^9$ years
- ^{235}Th: ~ 24.1 days

Thorium-232's significantly longer half-life means it remains radioactive for a much longer period compared to the other isotopes listed.

48. (C): PmP is never a first arrival among seismic phases. PmP is a phase that represents P-waves reflected off the Mohorovičić discontinuity (the Moho), which is the boundary between the Earth's crust and the mantle. Because PmP involves a longer travel path due to reflection, it arrives later than direct P-waves like Pg (crustal P-wave) and Pn (upper mantle refracted P-wave). Therefore, PmP cannot be the first seismic arrival on a seismogram.

49. (A): The highest sediment deposition takes place in the continental rise zone. The continental rise is located at the base of the continental slope and is characterized by a gentle incline formed by the accumulation of sediments. These sediments are transported from the continental shelf and slope by gravity-driven processes like turbidity currents. Over time, vast amounts of sediments build up in the continental rise, making it the area with the most significant sediment deposition in the ocean.

50. (A): An air parcel will have positive buoyancy when its density (ρ_{PARCEL}) is less than the density of the surrounding environment (P_{ENV}). Positive buoyancy causes the parcel to rise because the lower density means it is lighter than the surrounding air. This condition typically occurs when the air parcel is warmer than its environment, leading to convection and upward motion in the atmosphere.

51. **(C):** Ironstone deposits: Ironstone deposits are not formed by magmatic or magmatic-hydrothermal processes. They are typically sedimentary deposits formed through the chemical precipitation of iron minerals in ancient seas or lakes. Ironstones, such as banded iron formations (BIFs), result from the accumulation of iron-rich sediments deposited in layers, often indicating periods of high oxygen levels in Earth's early atmosphere.

In contrast, Sudbury-type Ni-Cu deposits, Bushveld-type chromite deposits, and porphyry-type Cu deposits are associated with magmatic or magmatichydrothermal activities involving the crystallization and differentiation of magma and the circulation of hydrothermal fluids.

52. **(C):** At a pH of 8, which is typical for ocean water, the dominant dissolved inorganic carbon species is bicarbonate ion ([HCO_3^-]). Bicarbonate constitutes the majority of inorganic carbon in seawater due to the ocean's slightly alkaline conditions. At a pH of 4, as in some river waters, the environment is acidic, and dissolved carbon dioxide ([CO_2]) becomes the dominant species. In acidic conditions, CO_2 remains in molecular form rather than dissociating into bicarbonate or carbonate ions.

53. **(C):** Moving towards the Sun from outer space, the order is:

- **Oort Cloud:** The most distant region, a spherical shell of icy bodies surrounding the solar system, extending up to 100,000 astronomical units (AU) from the Sun.
- **Heliopause:** The boundary where the solar wind is stopped by the interstellar medium, marking the edge of the heliosphere, located within the Oort Cloud.
- **Kuiper Belt:** A disk-shaped region beyond Neptune, spanning approximately 30 to 50 AU from the Sun, containing small icy bodies and dwarf planets like Pluto.
- **Asteroid Belt:** Located between Mars and Jupiter, about 2 to 3 AU from the Sun, consisting mainly of rocky and metallic asteroids.

This sequence reflects the correct order from the outermost region inward toward the Sun.

54. **(B):** The typical dip amount of unroofing joints is between 75° and 90°, indicating they are steeply dipping to vertical. Unroofing joints, also known as unloading joints, form due to the release of overburden pressure when overlying rocks are removed by erosion or uplift. This reduction in confining pressure causes the rock to fracture perpendicular to the least principal stress direction (which is horizontal), resulting in vertical or near-vertical joints. These steeply dipping joints play a crucial role in rock stability and influence geological processes such as weathering and groundwater flow.

55. **(A):** In the marine carbon cycle, "mineralization" refers to the decomposition of organic matter back into inorganic forms, such as carbon dioxide, water, and nutrients. This process recycles elements that have passed through the food web, making them available again for primary producers like phytoplankton. Mineralization occurs through microbial decomposition, respiration, and other biochemical processes, playing a crucial role in nutrient cycling and maintaining the productivity of marine ecosystems.

56. (D): Given that the ^{14}C activity at 900 mm depth is 1/16th of the surface activity, this indicates that four half-lives have elapsed (since $(1/2)^4 = 1/16$). With a half-life of 6000 years for ^{14}C, the total time elapsed is:

- Time = Number of half-lives × Half-life
  = 4 × 6000 years
  = 24,000 years

The average sedimentation rate is calculated by dividing the depth by the time:

- Sedimentation rate = Depth / Time
  = 900 mm / 24,000 years
  = 0.0375 mm/year

Therefore, the average sedimentation rate is 0.0375 millimeters per year.

57. (D): Solifluction is the slowest hillslope process listed. It involves the gradual, downslope flow of water-saturated soil and regolith, especially in regions underlain by permafrost or subject to freeze-thaw cycles.

The movement is typically on the order of millimeters to centimeters per year. In contrast, mudflows, landslides, and earthflows are faster mass-wasting events that can occur suddenly and move at much higher speeds, often meters per second.

58. (B): The mass of water vapour per unit mass of dry air is called the mixing ratio. It is a measure of the amount of moisture in the air and is used in meteorology to describe humidity independently of temperature and pressure changes. The mixing ratio is expressed in grams of water vapour per kilogram of dry air (g/kg). Specific humidity, on the other hand, is the mass of water vapour per unit mass of moist air (including the water vapour).

Relative humidity is the ratio of the current amount of water vapour in the air to the maximum amount it can hold at that temperature, expressed as a percentage. Vapour pressure is the partial pressure exerted by water vapour in the air.

59. (C): Earthquake magnitude is a measure of the total energy released at the earthquake source and is a fixed value for a given earthquake, regardless of where it is measured. Intensity refers to the strength of shaking and the effects of an earthquake at a specific location, which generally decrease with increasing distance from the epicenter. Therefore, while magnitude remains constant, intensity decreases with epicentral distance due to the attenuation of seismic waves as they travel through the Earth's crust.

60. (D): Planetary albedo is the fraction of incoming solar radiation that is reflected back into space by the entire Earth system, including the atmosphere (clouds, aerosols), ocean surfaces, and land surfaces (ice, vegetation, deserts). It depends on the combined reflectivity of these components. High albedo surfaces like ice and clouds reflect more solar radiation, while darker surfaces like oceans and forests absorb more. The overall planetary albedo influences Earth's energy balance and climate.

61. (D): The ascending order of mixed layer depth in the oceanic regions is Bay of Bengal (shallowest), Subtropical Pacific Ocean, and Polar oceanic region (deepest). The Bay of Bengal has a shallow mixed layer due to significant freshwater input from rivers and heavy rainfall, leading to strong stratification. The Subtropical Pacific Ocean has a moderately deep mixed layer influenced by subtropical gyres and thermal stratification. Polar oceanic regions have the deepest mixed layers because of intense cooling and wind-driven mixing, especially during winter, which deepen the mixed layer significantly.

62. (D): The solubility of biogenic silica in seawater increases with rising temperature because higher temperatures enhance the dissolution rate of silica.

Conversely, it decreases with increasing salinity because additional dissolved ions in seawater compete with silica molecules, reducing their solubility through ionic interactions.

63. (B): If Earth's radius doubles ($R_2 = 2R_1$) and its density halves ($\rho_2 = ½\rho_1$), the new mass (M_2) becomes four times the original mass:

$M_2 = \rho_2 \times \text{Volume}_2$

$$= \left(\frac{1}{2}\rho_1\right) \times \left(\frac{4}{3}\pi(2R_1)^3\right) = 4 \times M_1$$

The gravity field at the surface depends on $g = \dfrac{GM}{R^2}$. Substituting the new mass and radius:

$$g_2 = \frac{GM \times 4M_1}{(2R_1)^2} = \frac{GM_1}{R_1^2} = g_1$$

Thus, the mass increases fourfold, but the gravity field at the surface remains unchanged.

64. (B): The acceleration due to gravity at sea level increases from the equator towards the poles. This is because Earth is an oblate spheroid—bulging at the equator and flattened at the poles—resulting in a smaller radius and stronger gravitational pull at higher latitudes. Additionally, the centrifugal force caused by Earth's rotation is greatest at the equator, effectively reducing gravity there.

65. (D): The correct matching is:

- A (Sound wave): $R\left(\sqrt{\dfrac{C_pRT}{C_v}}\right)$:

  This is the speed of sound in a gas, where C_p and C_v are specific heats at constant pressure and volume, R is the gas constant, and is T temperature.

- B (Shallow water gravity wave): $P\left(\sqrt{gH}\right)$:

  This is the phase speed of gravity waves in shallow water, where g is the acceleration due to gravity and H is the water depth.

- C (Barotropic Rossby wave): $Q\left(-\dfrac{\beta}{k^2+l^2}\right)$:

  This is the phase speed of barotropic Rossby waves, where β is the variation of the Coriolis parameter with latitude, and k and l are the wave numbers in the x and y directions.

66. (A): The epicenter of an earthquake is the point on the Earth's surface directly above the focus (hypocenter).

Therefore, regardless of whether an earthquake is shallow-focus or deep-focus, the epicenter lies at the same level—that is, at the Earth's surface. The depth of the focus does not change the location of the epicenter in terms of elevation; it remains on the surface directly above the point of rupture.

67. (A): From the hypsometric curve, the carbonate compensation depth (CCD) is at 3250 m, corresponding to a relative height of approximately –3.25 km.

By observing the percentage of the Earth's surface above this depth, it is approximately 20%, which includes the land area and the ocean floor above the CCD.

68. (D): Saltation is the process by which sediment grains are transported in a series of short leaps or hops along the Earth's surface, propelled by wind or water.

Grains are lifted off the ground by the fluid flow, move forward, and then fall back to the surface, often dislodging other particles upon impact and causing them to move as well.

69. (A): North Pacific deep water has higher nutrient content, higher ΣCO_2, and lower dissolved O_2 compared to North Atlantic deep water because it is the oldest water mass, having traveled the longest path along the global thermohaline circulation. As deep water moves from the North Atlantic to the North Pacific, it accumulates nutrients and CO_2 from the decomposition of organic matter and consumes oxygen through respiration, leading to the observed differences.

70. (B): Water with total dissolved solids (TDS) in the range of $10^3 - 10^4$ mg/L is classified as brackish water.

Brackish water has higher salinity than freshwater (TDS < 1,000 mg/L) but is less saline than seawater or saline water (TDS > 10,000 mg/L).

It often occurs in estuaries where freshwater mixes with seawater.

71. (C):

- **A-S (7%):** Only a small portion (about 7%) of long-wave radiation emitted by Earth's surface escapes directly to space.
- **B-P (107%):** The surface emits long-wave radiation totaling approximately 107% of the incoming solar radiation due to additional energy from greenhouse effects.
- **C-Q (63%):** The atmosphere emits long-wave radiation to space amounting to about 63% of the incoming solar radiation.
- **D-R (30%):** About 30% of incoming solar radiation is reflected and scattered back to space by the atmosphere and Earth's surface (planetary albedo).

72. (B):

- **FeO (21.36 wt%):**

  Fe content is $\frac{56}{56+16} = \frac{56}{72} \approx 0.78\%$.

  Fe from FeO:

  $21.36\% \times 0.78\% \approx 16.62\%$.

- **Fe_2O_3 (1.96 wt%):** Fe content is $\frac{2\times 56}{2\times 56 + 3\times 16} = \frac{112}{160} = 0.7\%$.

  Fe from Fe_2O_3:

  $= 1.96\% \times 0.7\%$

  $\approx 1.37\%$

- **Total Fe wt%:**

  $16.62\% + 1.37\% \approx 17.99\%$

  approximately 18%.

73. (A):

- The inverse filter $h[n]$ satisfies $x[n] * h[n] = \delta[n]$
- Z-transform of $x[n]$: $X(z) = \dfrac{1}{1-\frac{1}{2}z^{-1}}$.
- Inverse filter $H(z)$:

  $H(z) = \dfrac{1}{X(z)} = 1 - \frac{1}{2}z^{-1}$

- Inverse Z-transform of $H(z)$:

  $h[n] = \delta[n] - \frac{1}{2}\delta[n-1]$.

74. (A): Based, in part, on evidence that Fe stimulated phytoplankton growth in lab experiments, especially of large diatoms:

- The iron hypothesis suggests that iron limitation controls phytoplankton growth in certain ocean regions.
- Laboratory experiments showed that adding iron stimulates the growth of phytoplankton, particularly large diatoms.

- This led to the proposal that iron fertilization could enhance biological productivity and affect atmospheric CO_2 levels.

75. (A): It decreases carbonate ion concentration:

- Ocean acidification is caused by the uptake of CO_2 from the atmosphere.
- Increased CO_2 forms carbonic acid, which releases H^+ ions.
- H^+ ions react with carbonate ions (CO_3^{2-}), reducing their concentration.

This process affects organisms that rely on carbonate ions for shell formation.

76. (B): Northward up to 20° N:

- During break monsoon conditions, the Tropical Easterly Jet (TEJ) weakens and shifts northward.
- The TEJ moves northward up to 20° N latitude.
- This northward movement is associated with a decrease in monsoon rainfall over the Indian subcontinent.
- The shift leads to a displacement of the monsoon trough and reduced convection over the region, contributing to break monsoon conditions.

77. (D): Increase in temperature increases the amount of cloud cover:

- Increased cloud cover can reflect more solar radiation back to space.
- This leads to a cooling effect, representing a negative feedback.
- The other options describe processes that amplify the initial change (positive feedback).

78. (B): It is a meridional circulation:

- The Quasi-Biennial Oscillation (QBO) is characterized by alternating easterly and westerly zonal (east-west) winds in the equatorial stratosphere.
- It is not a meridional (north-south) circulation.
- The wind regimes appear above 30 km and descend at about 1 km per month.
- The QBO influences phenomena like sudden stratospheric warming.

80. (C): Within the Ekman layer, there is a component of wind which is directed towards high pressure: This statement is false.

In the atmospheric Ekman layer, friction causes the wind to cross isobars from high to low pressure, resulting in a component directed towards low pressure, not high pressure.

81. (C): The amplitude of an EM wave decreases exponentially with depth z as

$$A(z) = A_0 e^{-z/\delta},$$

where δ is the skin depth (100 m). To find the depth where $A(z) = 0.25A_0$:

$$0.25A_0 = A_0 e^{-z/100}$$

$$\ln(0.25) = -\frac{z}{100}$$

$$z = 100 \times \ln(4)$$

$$\approx 100 \times 1.3863$$

$$= 138.63 \text{ m}$$

So, the depth is approximately 139 m.

82. (A): The dunes arranged in order of increasing sand supply and wind direction variability are:

(*c*) **Barchan:** Limited sand supply, unidirectional wind.

(*b*) **Transverse dunes:** Moderate sand supply, unidirectional wind.

(*a*) **Linear dunes:** Moderate to abundant sand, bidirectional winds.

(*d*) **Star dunes:** Abundant sand supply, multidirectional winds.

83. (D): With an average ecological efficiency of 10% per trophic level, and assuming Indian Oil Sardines feed on zooplankton (which feed on phytoplankton), the energy transfer is:

1. Primary Productivity (Phytoplankton):

   $400 \text{ g C m}^{-2} \text{ yr}^{-1}$

2. Zooplankton:

   $10\% \times 400 = 40 \text{ g C m}^{-2} \text{ yr}^{-1}$

3. Oil Sardines:

   $10\% \times 40 = 4 \text{ g C m}^{-2} \text{ yr}^{-1}$

Therefore, the expected annual maximum yield of Oil Sardine is $4 \text{ g C m}^{-2} \text{ yr}^{-1}$.

84. (B): They include trace metals Cd and Zn: Nutrient-type elements are biologically active and include trace metals like cadmium (Cd) and zinc (Zn).

These elements have nutrient-like profiles, being depleted at the surface due to biological uptake and enriched at depth due to remineralization.

85. (A): In a conducting medium, the electromagnetic wave equation is:

$$\nabla^2 E - k^2 E = 0$$

Where the propagation constant k is derived from Maxwell's equations:

$$k^2 = j\omega\mu\sigma - \omega^2\mu\epsilon$$

Therefore, the propagation constant k is:

$$k = \pm\sqrt{j\omega\mu\sigma - \omega^2\mu\epsilon}$$

This expression includes both the conduction term $j\omega\mu\sigma$ and the displacement term $-\omega^2\mu\epsilon$. Thus, the correct option is A.

86. (B): A-R, B-Q, C-S, D-P:

- **A. Climate-limited region matches with R. Palearctic and Nearctic:** These regions are limited by harsh climatic conditions, such as cold temperatures, which restrict species distribution.
- **B. Main regions of the old-world tropics matches with Q. Oriental and Ethiopian:** The Oriental and Ethiopian realms represent the tropical regions of Asia and Africa, respectively.
- **C. Barrier-limited regions matches with S. Neotropical and Australian:** These realms are separated by significant geographical barriers like oceans, limiting species dispersion.
- **D. Wallace's Line matches with P. Oriental and Australian:** Wallace's Line is a faunal boundary that separates the Oriental and Australian zoogeographical realms.

87. (D): The correct order is:

(*d*) **Hawaiian eruptions:** Least explosive, characterized by fluid basaltic lava flows.

(*a*) **Strombolian eruptions:** Mildly explosive, with intermittent explosive bursts ejecting cinders and lava bombs.

(*b*) **Plinian eruptions:** More explosive, producing high-altitude ash plumes and pyroclastic flows.

(*c*) **Vulcanian eruptions:** Most explosive, emitting dense ash clouds and viscous lava fragments.

The order from least to most explosive is Hawaiian, Strombolian, Vulcanian, Plinian.

88. (A): NMO stretch distortion is more pronounced for shallow seismic events recorded at far offsets. This is because the normal moveout correction varies rapidly with time for shallow events and larger source receiver distances, leading to stretching of seismic wavelets.

89. (A): The residence time (τ) of an ion in a reservoir is calculated as:

$$\tau = \frac{\text{Amount of ion in the reservoir}}{\text{Rate of input/output}}$$

Initial Conditions:

- Amount of ion in the reservoir: A
- Rate of input/output: R
- Residence time: $\tau = \frac{A}{R}$

After Changes:

- The concentration is diluted to 50% by adding pure water, but the total amount of ion (A) remains the same because no ion is removed.
- The volume of the reservoir increases, causing the concentration to decrease.
- The rate of input doubles: 2R

New Residence Time (τ'): $\tau' = \frac{A}{2R} = \frac{\tau}{2}$

Conclusion: The residence time decreases by half because the amount of ion remains the same while the rate of input/output doubles. Therefore, the correct answer is option A.

90. (A): Using Henry's Law: $C = k_H \times p$

$C = (20.7 \times 10^{-3} \text{ mol kg}^{-1} \text{ atm}^{-1}) \times (300 \times 10^{-12} \text{ atm})$

$= 6.21 \times 10^{-12} \text{ mol kg}^{-1}$

Approximately 6.2×10^{-12} mol kg^{-1}.

91. (A): In the context of the subtropical westerly jet stream in the Northern Hemisphere, the regions are associated with areas of rising or sinking air caused by convergence and divergence. This behaviour is influenced by the dynamics of the jet stream flow, specifically changes in wind speed and direction, which create areas of convergence (air coming together) and divergence (air spreading apart). Here is the explanation of each match:

1. **Left front (A - Divergence):** The left front region is where the jet stream accelerates, causing the air to spread out or diverge. This creates divergence (Q) in the upper atmosphere.
2. **Right front (B - Convergence):** In the right front region, the jet stream typically decelerates, causing air to converge or come together. This creates convergence (P).
3. **Left rear (C - Convergence):** The left rear region is also associated with deceleration, resulting in air convergence (P) in the upper atmosphere.
4. **Right rear (D - Divergence):** The right rear region is where the jet stream accelerates, leading to air spreading out or diverging. This creates divergence (Q).

Thus, the correct matches reflect how acceleration and deceleration in the jet stream influence the convergence and divergence patterns in each region.

92. (A):

- **Kandelia candel:** Mangrove species found in intertidal zones.
- **Symbiodinium:** Genus of dinoflagellates known for symbiotic relationships with coral.
- **Eucalanus elongatus:** Species of copepod, a type of zooplankton.
- **Synechococcus:** Genus of cyanobacteria, important photosynthetic microorganisms.

93. (D): Nutrient-rich coastal regions with high primary productivity are dominated by siliceous diatoms. These phytoplankton thrive in such environments due to abundant nutrients and contribute significantly to the marine food web.

94. (D): A reclined fold and a recumbent fold cannot be uniquely differentiated based solely on the plunge of their hinge lines because both can have hinge lines plunging in the direction of the dip of their axial planes. Additional structural analysis is required to distinguish between them.

95. **(B):** Statements (B) and (C) are True; Statement (A) is False:

- **Statement (A) is False:** Oceanic mesoscale eddies can rotate either clockwise or counterclockwise in the Northern Hemisphere.
- **Statement (B) is True:** A clockwise (anticyclonic) mesoscale eddy in the Northern Hemisphere often has warmer water at its core compared to the surrounding water.
- **Statement (C) is True:** Subtropical geostrophic gyres in the Southern Hemisphere have counterclockwise circulation due to the Coriolis effect.

96. **(C):** Data assimilation in Numerical Weather Prediction (NWP) is not a technique to integrate forecast equations in time. Instead, it involves incorporating observational data into models to generate accurate initial conditions.

The integration of forecast equations over time is performed by the numerical solver of the NWP model.

97. **(B):** To determine how much melt remains at 1700°C, follow these steps based on the phase diagram:

1. **Locate the initial composition and temperature:** The initial composition of the melt is labeled as point "A" in the diagram, which corresponds to approximately 70 wt% Forsterite (Fo). The starting temperature is 1900°C.
2. **Cooling process and equilibrium crystallization:** As the melt cools from 1900°C, it enters the liquid + olivine phase field. Crystals of olivine begin to form at the liquidus boundary. At 1700°C, the system is still in the liquid + olivine field. The proportions of melt and solid can be determined using the lever rule.
3. **Applying the lever rule:** At 1700°C, draw a horizontal tie line across the liquid + olivine field to connect the liquidus and solidus curves. The ends of the tie line correspond to the compositions of the liquid and solid phases at this temperature.

   From the diagram:

   Liquid composition at 1700°C $\approx$ 60 wt% Fo.

   Solid composition (olivine) at 1700°C $\approx$ 85 wt% Fo.

   Using the lever rule:

   Fraction of melt

   $$= \frac{\text{Solid composition} - \text{Initial composition}}{\text{Solid composition} - \text{Liquid composition}}$$

   Substituting values:

   $$\text{Fraction of melt} = \frac{85-70}{85-60} = \frac{15}{25}$$

   $$= 0.6.$$

4. **Convert to percentage:** The fraction of melt is 0.6, which means 60% of the system is melt. Therefore, the remaining melt at 1700°C is 33.3% (100 - 66.7%).

Hence, the correct answer is B (33.3%).

98. **(D):** In seismic tomography experiments, the resolution of model parameters (m_1, m_2) for two horizontal layers is best achieved when the ray paths adequately sample both layers with a combination of vertical and oblique paths. This ensures that variations in the properties of both layers are captured effectively.

In option D, the source-receiver geometry includes both vertical and diagonal ray paths, allowing comprehensive sampling of the layers. This geometry provides sufficient information to resolve the model parameters of the two horizontal layers effectively.

Thus, the correct geometry is D.

99. (A): Water vapour feedback is a positive feedback mechanism in the climate system. As global temperatures rise, the atmosphere can hold more water vapour, which is a potent greenhouse gas. Increased water vapour enhances the greenhouse effect, leading to further warming. This amplifies the initial temperature increase, making it a positive feedback.

100. (B): In shallow water waves, the wave speed V is proportional to the square root of the water depth H, expressed as $V = \sqrt{gH}$, where g is gravitational acceleration. If the wave speed reduces to V/5, then:

$$\frac{V}{V/5} = \frac{\sqrt{H_1}}{\sqrt{H_2}}$$

$$\Rightarrow \quad 5 = \sqrt{\frac{H_1}{H_2}}$$

$$\Rightarrow \quad H_2 = \frac{H_1}{25}$$

Given H_1 = 2500 m, the new depth H_2 = 2500 m/25 = 100 m.

101. (B): The low gamma-ray value of 10 API indicates a clean sandstone with minimal shale content. The spontaneous potential (SP) response ranging from –50 mV to –20 mV suggests reduced SP deflection, which can occur due to the presence of hydrocarbons suppressing the SP curve. Therefore, the formation is a hydrocarbon-bearing clean sandstone.

102. (B): In trilobites, the hypoparian suture is characterized by the absence of a facial suture along the ventral margin of the cephalon. Unlike proparian, gonatoparian, and opisthoparian sutures, which are present on various parts of the cephalon, the hypoparian suture does not appear on the ventral side.

103. (B): With constant grain size, the sedimentary structures form in order of increasing flow velocity. Ripples form at low velocities, dunes at moderate velocities, antidunes at high velocities in the upper flow regime, and gutter casts form due to very high velocities causing erosional scours. Therefore, the correct sequence is ripple, dune, antidune, gutter.

104. (D): Out of the available potential energy, only about 20% is actually converted to kinetic energy: This statement is false. In the atmosphere, only a small fraction—approximately 2%—of the available potential energy is converted into kinetic energy. The vast majority of the available potential energy remains unconverted. Therefore, stating that about 20% is converted into kinetic energy is incorrect, making option D false.

106. (A): Using the Ghyben-Herzberg relation for the freshwater-saltwater interface:

$$\text{Depth of interface} = \frac{\rho_{fresh}}{\rho_{salt} - \rho_{fresh}} \times h$$

$$= \frac{1000}{1020 - 1000} \times 2\,\text{m}$$

$$= 50 \times 2\ \text{m}$$

$$= 100\ \text{m}$$

Therefore, the interface is found at a depth of 100 m below sea level.

107. (A): The parameter represents nitrate concentration (NO_3^-), which increases with depth due to organic matter decomposition and remineralization. The profile labeled P corresponds to the Pacific Ocean, which has older water masses and thus higher nitrate concentrations. The profile labeled Q corresponds to the Atlantic Ocean, which has younger water masses and lower nitrate levels.

Thus:

- A is NO_3^-,
- P represents the Pacific Ocean,
- Q represents the Atlantic Ocean.

Therefore, the correct statement is A.

108. **(B):** The observation notes that rural land surfaces with vegetation and adequate moisture are cooler than adjacent urban surfaces. Explanation (*a*) is correct because a lower Bowen ratio in rural areas means more energy is used for latent heat (evapotranspiration) rather than sensible heat, leading to surface cooling. Explanation (*b*) is not the correct explanation for this observation because while urban areas are warmer due to various factors like reduced vegetation and heat absorption by buildings, the trapping of heat in the lower atmosphere is not the primary reason for rural areas being cooler. Therefore, only (*a*) is the correct explanation.

109. **(A):**

- Sampling interval (Δt):

  4 milliseconds (0.004 seconds)

- Sampling frequency (f_s):

$$f_s = \frac{1}{\Delta t} = \frac{1}{0.004\,\text{s}} = 250\,\text{Hz}$$

- Nyquist frequency:

$$f_{\text{Nyquist}} = \frac{f_s}{2} = 125\,\text{Hz}$$

The possible range of frequencies in the time series is from 0 Hz to 125 Hz.

110. **(B):** Riffles - meander bends:

- **Isovels - velocity:** Correct. Isovels are lines connecting points of equal velocity in a fluid flow.
- **Riffles - meander bends:** Incorrect. Riffles are shallow sections in a stream with fast, turbulent water, typically found between meander bends, not the bends themselves.
- **Ripples - sand bedforms:** Correct. Ripples are small-scale bedforms formed by the movement of sand in water or wind.
- **Thalweg - deepest part of a channel:** Correct. The thalweg is the line of the lowest elevation within a valley or watercourse, representing the deepest part of the channel.

111. **(B):** Given the apparent thickness (measured in a vertical drill hole) is 24 m and the true thickness is 12 m, the dip angle (θ) can be found using the formula:

$$\cos\theta = \frac{\text{True Thickness}}{\text{Apparent Thickness}}$$

$$\cos\theta = \frac{12\text{ m}}{24\text{ m}} = 0.5$$

$$\theta = \text{arc}\cos(0.5) = 60°$$

Thus, the dip of the ore body is 60 degrees.

112. **(*)** None of the options is correct: To find the concentration of La in the melt:

Mineral proportions and partition coefficients:

- Olivine: 60% (W_{ol} = 0.6), $K_d^{ol} = 0.0002$
- Clinopyroxene: 30% (W_{cpx} = 0.3), $K_d^{cpx} = 0.029$
- Garnet: 10% (W_{gt} = 0.1), $K_d^{gt} = 0.0014$

Bulk partition coefficient (D):

$$D = (0.0002 \times 0.6) + (0.029 \times 0.3) + (0.0014 \times 0.1)$$
$$= 0.00012 + 0.0087 + 0.00014$$
$$= 0.00896$$

Using the batch melting equation:

$$C_l = \frac{C_0}{D + F(1 - D)}$$

Where,

C_0 = 10 ppm,

F = 0.1

$$C_l = \frac{10}{0.00896 + 0.1 \times (1 - 0.00896)}$$

$$= \frac{10}{0.00896 + 0.099104} = \frac{10}{0.108064}$$

$\approx$ 92.5 ppm

Since 92.5 ppm is not among the given options, none of the options is correct.

113. (A): Gravity varies primarily with latitude and elevation. Since stations A and C are at the same elevation and C is directly north of A at the same latitude, the gravity difference due to latitude over a short distance (20 km) is negligible. The gravity change is minimal, and given that no anomalous bodies are present, the gravity at C would be effectively the same as that at A.

115. (A): Warmer surface temperature: A lower oxygen isotopic composition ($\delta^{18}O$) of planktic foraminifera compared to benthic foraminifera at a given location indicates a warmer surface temperature. Planktic foraminifera live near the ocean surface, while benthic foraminifera live on the ocean floor.

Lower $\delta^{18}O$ values in planktic foraminifera shells signify that they incorporated less heavy oxygen isotope (^{18}O) relative to the lighter isotope (^{16}O) during shell formation, which occurs at higher temperatures. Therefore, the difference suggests that the surface waters were warmer compared to the deep waters.

116. (C): The relative humidity (RH) is calculated using the formula:

$$RH = \left(\frac{\text{Mixing Ratio}}{\text{Saturation Mixing Ratio}}\right) \times 100\%$$

Substituting the given values:

$$RH = \left(\frac{3 \text{ g/kg}}{6.5 \text{ g/kg}}\right) \times 100\% = 46.15\%$$

Rounding to one decimal place, the relative humidity is 46.2%.

117. (A): Wave Steepness (S) is calculated as:

$$S = \frac{\text{Wave Height (H)}}{\text{Wavelength } (\lambda)} = \frac{5}{12} \approx 0.4167$$

So, S $\approx$ 0.416.

Wave Energy per Unit Area (E) is given by:

$$E = \frac{1}{8}\rho g H^2$$

Substituting the given values:

$$E = \frac{1}{8} 1030 \text{ kg/m}^3 \times 9.8 \text{ m/s}^2 \times (5\text{ m})^2$$

$$= \frac{1}{8} \times 1030 \times 9.8 \times 25$$

$$= \frac{1}{8} \times 252,350$$

$$= 31,543.75 \text{ J/m}^2$$

Therefore, E $\approx$ 31,543 J/m^2.

118. (B): No geostrophic vertical wind shear is present: This statement is false about a baroclinic atmosphere. In a baroclinic atmosphere, there are horizontal temperature gradients, causing the geostrophic wind to change with height, which is known as geostrophic vertical wind shear. The presence of thermal wind implies that geostrophic wind shear exists. Therefore, the statement that no geostrophic vertical wind shear is present is incorrect.

119. **(C):** To find the $^{143}Nd/^{144}Nd$ ratio of CHUR at 2.5 Ga ago:

Given:

Present-day $^{143}Nd/^{144}Nd = 0.512638$

Present-day $^{147}Sm/^{144}Nd = 0.1967$

Decay constant $(\lambda) = 6.54 \times 10^{-12}\ y^{-1}$

Time $(t) = 2.5 \times 10^9$ years

Calculate the amount of radiogenic ^{143}Nd produced over 2.5 Ga:

$$\Delta(^{143}Nd/^{144}Nd) = \left(\frac{^{147}Sm}{^{144}Nd}\right) \times \left(e^{\lambda t} - 1\right)$$

First, compute λt:

$$\lambda t = 6.54 \times 10^{-12}\ y^{-1} \times 2.5 \times 10^9\ y$$

$$= 0.01635$$

Compute $e^{\lambda t}$:

$$e^{0.01635} \approx 1 + 0.01635 + \frac{(0.01635)^2}{2} \approx 1.016484$$

Calculate $\Delta(^{143}Nd/^{144}Nd)$:

$$\Delta = 0.1967 \times (1.016484 - 1)$$

$$= 0.1967 \times 0.016484 \approx 0.003242$$

Determine the ratio 2.5 Ga ago:

$$(^{143}Nd/^{144}Nd)_{2.5\text{ Ga ago}}$$

$$= 0.512638 - 0.003242 \approx 0.509396.$$

120. **(B):** The ascending order of cation exchange capacity (CEC) at pH 7 is:

(*b*) **Feldspar:** Very low CEC

(*c*) **Fe-Oxyhydroxides:** Low to moderate CEC

(*d*) **Illite:** Moderate CEC

(*a*) **Smectite:** High CEC

Thus, the correct sequence is (*b*), (*c*), (*d*), (*a*).

121. **(B):** Statement (A) is correct and statement (B) is incorrect:

- **Statement (A):** Correct. The relationship between frequency (ω) and wavenumber (*k*) is called the dispersion relation, which describes how waves propagate through a medium.
- **Statement (B):** Incorrect. Dispersive waves are waves for which the phase speed varies with wavenumber. If the phase speed does not vary with wavenumber, the waves are non-dispersive.

122. **(D):** To estimate the age of the stromatolite:

- Assume a typical growth rate for stromatolites of 0.5 mm per year.
- Calculate the age:

$$\text{Age} = \frac{\text{Length}}{\text{Growth Rate}} = \frac{1.3\,\text{m}}{0.0005\,\text{m/year}}$$

$$= 2600 \text{ years}$$

Therefore, the expected age of the stromatolite is 2600 years.

123. **(A):**

- **A (INVALID):** The statement that "The seafloor is spreading about A" is invalid because the figure does not explicitly indicate symmetric seafloor spreading. While the magnetic anomaly may show some features related to tectonic activity, there is no direct evidence of symmetric spreading about point .
- **B (VALID):** Tectonic activity outside the area can influence seafloor spreading indirectly, making this statement plausible.
- **C (VALID):** The rocks on either side of A being magnetized in opposite directions is valid, as the magnetic anomaly pattern shows polarity changes associated with geomagnetic reversals.
- **D (VALID):** The magnetic anomaly indicates that the seafloor experienced magnetic reversals during its formation.

Thus, the INVALID inference is A.

124. (D): Consolidated bank sediments → low channel width-depth ratio: Consolidated bank sediments are resistant to erosion, leading to channels that are narrow and deep, which means they have a low width-depth ratio. The strong, cohesive nature of consolidated sediments prevents lateral erosion, resulting in narrower channels with greater depth.

125. (D): By applying a mass balance for strontium (Sr), the fraction of basaltic melt (x) in the hybrid melt is calculated using:

$$200 \text{ ppm} = x \times 300 \text{ ppm} + (1 - x) \times 150 \text{ ppm}$$

Solving for x:

$$200 = 300x + 150(1 - x)$$

$$200 = 300x + 150 - 150x$$

$$200 - 150 = 150x$$

$$50 = 150x$$

$$x = \frac{50}{150} = 0.33$$

Therefore, the fraction of basaltic melt in the hybrid liquid is 0.33.

126. (C): The system of equations results in a coefficient matrix of rank 2, indicating that there are two non-zero singular values. This is determined by reducing the matrix to its row-echelon form, revealing a dependency among the equations, and thus the solution space is one-dimensional.

127. (B): The regressive surface of marine erosion is formed during periods of base-level fall when sea level drops, exposing the seafloor to erosion processes. It is not associated with base-level rise. In contrast, the other sequence stratigraphic surfaces are formed during base-level rise associated with transgressive events.

128. (B):

1. Components of V_{BA} (magnitude 100 mm/yr, azimuth 90°):

$$V_{BA,\,x} = 0 \text{ mm/yr}$$

$$V_{BA,\,y} = 100 \text{ mm/yr}$$

2. Components of V_{CB} (magnitude 80 mm/yr, azimuth 200°):

$$V_{CB,\,x} = -75.18 \text{ mm/yr}$$

$$V_{CB,\,y} = -27.36 \text{ mm/yr}$$

3. Resultant components for V_{AC}:

$$V_{AC,\,x} = -75.18 \text{ mm/yr}$$

$$V_{AC,\,y} = 72.64 \text{ mm/yr}$$

4. Magnitude of V_{AC}:

$$V_{AC} = \sqrt{(-75.18)^2 + (72.64)^2}$$

$$\approx -104.54 \text{ mm/yr}$$

Thus, the correct magnitude of V_{AC} is 104.5 mm/yr, and the correct answer is B.

129. (A): At an epicentral distance of 120 km, the first seismic arrival is the Pg phase, which is the direct P-wave traveling through the crust at 6 km/s. Calculations show that the Pg travel time is shorter than that of other phases like Pn, making Pg the first recorded arrival at the given distance.

130. (B): Statements (*b*), (*d*), and (*e*) are correct regarding the Equilibrium Line Altitude (ELA):

(*b*) ELA represents the zone on a glacier where accumulation equals ablation.

(*d*) It can be estimated using the toe-to-headwall ratio method.

(*e*) It can be estimated using the ratio of accumulation area to total glacier area (Accumulation Area Ratio method).

131. (B): Move over land in an environment that is "marine-like": Monsoon depressions maintain their strength over land in the Head Bay of Bengal region because they move through an environment with abundant moisture and thermal characteristics similar to the ocean. This "marine-like" environment over land during the monsoon season supports the depression without significant weakening.

132. (C): Only (*a*), (*b*), and (*c*) are true:

(*a* True. Shorter wavelengths correspond to higher frequencies.

(*b*) True. Shorter wavelengths (higher frequencies) have higher energy per photon.

(*c*) True. Objects at higher temperatures emit radiation at shorter wavelengths (Wien's Law).

(*d*) False. The emitted radiation increases with temperature (Stefan-Boltzmann Law).

133. (A): The negative slope (dP/dT) in the Clapeyron equation for H_2O-saturated melting of albite at low pressures is due to a significant negative volume change (ΔV negative) when solid albite and water vapour react to form a liquid.

The positive entropy change (ΔS positive) and negative ΔV result in a negative dP/dT value.

134. (A): A-Q, B-P, C-R, D-S:

A. Isohaline matches with Q. Lines of equal salinity

B. Isopycnal matches with P. Lines of equal density

C. Isobath matches with R. Lines of equal depth

D. Isohyet matches with S. Lines of equal rainfall

135. (A): The minimum supersaturation required for a cloud droplet of radius 0.04 μm at 2°C is approximately 3%. Using the Kelvin equation:

$$S = \exp\left(\frac{2\sigma\alpha_1}{rR_vT}\right) - 1$$

Substituting the given values:

- Surface tension, $\sigma = 7.5 \times 10^{-2}\ \text{N m}^{-1}$
- Specific volume, $\alpha_1 = 1 \times 10^{-3}\ \text{m}^3\ \text{kg}^{-1}$
- Radius, $r = 0.04 \times 10^{-6}$ m
- Gas constant, $R_v = 461\ \text{JK}^{-1}\ \text{kg}^{-1}$
- Temperature, T = 275.15 K

Calculating S yields approximately 3%.

136. (B): Placer diamonds are present within the Lower Rewa Sandstone formation of the Vindhyan Supergroup in India. This formation is known for diamond-bearing conglomerates and sandstones, especially in the Panna region of Madhya Pradesh.

137. (B): The longitudinal resistivity ρ_L is calculated using:

$$\rho_L = \frac{h_1 + h_2}{\dfrac{h_1}{\rho_1} + \dfrac{h_2}{\rho_2}}$$

Given $\rho_L = 80\ \Omega\text{m}$, $\rho_1 = 100\ \Omega\text{m}$ and equal layer thicknesses $h_1 = h_2 = 5$ m, solving for ρ_2 yields:

$$\rho_2 = \frac{200}{3} \approx 66.67\ \Omega\text{m}$$

Thus, ρ_2 is approximately 67 Ωm.

138. (B): They formed laterally extensive units: This statement is not true for Algoma-type banded iron formations. Algoma-type BIFs are typically small, lenticular deposits associated with submarine volcanic sequences and are not laterally extensive. They contrast with Superior-type BIFs, which are extensive.

139. (D): The potential temperature θ is calculated using:

$$\theta = T\left(\frac{P_0}{P}\right)^k$$

Where:

- T = –27°C + 273.15 = 246.15 K

- P_0 = 1000 hPa
- P = 500 hPa
- $k = \frac{R_d}{C_p} = \frac{287}{1004} \approx 0.2857$

Calculating:

$$\theta = 246.15 \times \left(\frac{1000}{500}\right)^{0.2857}$$

$$= 246.15 \times 1.218$$

$$\approx 300 \text{ K.}$$

140. (C): The temperature decrease is:

$$\Delta T = -\Gamma_d \times \Delta z$$

$$= -9.8°C/km \times 0.8 \text{ km}$$

$$= -7.84°C$$

Thus, the temperature at 800 m is:

$$T = 25°C - 7.84°C$$

$$= 17.16°C$$

Approximately 17.2°C.

141. (B): A-R; B-S; C-Q; D-P:

A. Entisols match with R. recently formed soil

B. Mollisols match with S. base rich with high organic matter

C. Vertisols match with Q. high content of expandable clay minerals

D. Ultisols match with P. acidic soils in humid areas

142. (D): For a N-S striking 2D magnetic body, the relationship is:

$$\Delta T = \Delta Z \sin I$$

Given ΔT = 150 gammas and I = 30°:

$$\Delta Z = \frac{\Delta T}{\sin I} = \frac{150}{0.5}$$

$$= 300 \text{ gammas.}$$

143. (C): The temperature change of the air parcel is calculated using the formula:

$$\Delta T = \frac{\text{Heat released due to condensation}}{\text{Mass of air parcel} \times \text{Specific heat capacity}}$$

First, calculate the heat released:

- Mass of condensed water vapour: 100 g = 0.1 kg
- Latent heat of condensation (L): 2.26×10^6 J/kg
- Total heat released (Q): $0.1 \text{ kg} \times 2.26 \times 10_6$ J/kg = 226,000 J

Next, calculate the temperature change:

- Mass of air parcel (m): 100 kg
- Specific heat capacity of air (C_p): 1004 J/kg·K
- Temperature change (ΔT):

$$\Delta T = \frac{226{,}000 J}{100 \text{ kg} \times 1004 \text{ J/kg\textbackslash cdotpK}} \approx 2.5 K$$

Therefore, the temperature increase is approximately 2.25°C, corresponding to option C: 2.3°C.

144. (A): A rating curve illustrates the relationship between the water stage (height) of a river and its discharge (flow rate). It is essential for converting measured water levels into discharge values, aiding in flood forecasting and water resource management.

145. (D): The slope of direct arrivals in the time-distance (TX) domain is 0.67 s/km. In the frequency-wavenumber (FK) domain, the slope is inversely related to the TX slope and corresponds to the apparent velocity,

$$v = \frac{1}{0.67 \text{ s/km}} \approx 1.4925 \text{ km/s.}$$

Therefore, the slope in the FK domain is approximately 1.5 Hz/km^{-1}, matching option D.

146. (A): Mawsynram, based on records from 1950 to 2020, receives an average annual precipitation exceeding 12 meters per year. Estimates often range between 12 to 14 m/y, making option A correct.

147. (A): Only (*a*) and (*c*) are true:

- **Statement (*a*) is true:** In-situ temperature varies with pressure and is not conserved during adiabatic processes, whereas potential temperature is conserved and thus considered a conservative property.
- **Statement (*b*) is false:** Potential temperature is derived from measurements of in-situ temperature; if in-situ temperature cannot be measured, potential temperature cannot be determined.
- **Statement (*c*) is true:** Surface heating and rainfall both increase the stability of surface ocean layers by enhancing density stratification.

148. (C): In a flexural flow fold, strain distribution is such that the lowest strain occurs in the hinge zone, while the limbs experience higher strain due to layer-parallel shear. This pattern reflects deformation accommodated by flexural flow, making option C the correct choice.

149. (B): The efficiency (η) of the cyclonic storm as a heat engine is calculated using the Carnot efficiency formula:

$$\eta = 1 - \frac{T_c}{T_h}$$

Convert temperatures to Kelvin:

- Hot reservoir (sea surface temperature) $T_h = 29°C + 273.15 = 302.15$ K
- Cold reservoir (cloud top temperature) $T_c = -74°C + 273.15 = 199.15$ K

Calculate efficiency:

$$\eta = 1 - \frac{199.15}{302.15}$$

$$= 1 - 0.659 = 0.341$$

Therefore, the efficiency is approximately 0.34, corresponding to option B.

150. (C): (*b*) and (*c*) are correct:

- **Statement (*b*) is correct:** Tidal flooding brings sediments into the estuary, turning it into a sedimentary sink.
- **Statement (*c*) is correct:** Tidal flooding involves time-velocity asymmetry, where the difference in flood and ebb tide durations and velocities leads to net sediment deposition.

Statements (*a*) and (*d*) are incorrect in this context.

Previous Years' Paper

Joint CSIR-UGC NET/JRF

Earth, Atmospheric, Ocean & Planetary Sciences

DECEMBER-2023

(Exam held on 27-12-2023)

PART-A

1. The sum of the two positive integers is 14. Then their product CANNOT be divisible by

A. 12 B. 13

C. 14 D. 49

2. A letter is drawn at random from the following string of letters.

R A M U K Y A J N A S

What is the probability that it is NOT a vowel?

A. $\frac{1}{2}$ B. $\frac{6}{11}$

C. $\frac{7}{11}$ D. $\frac{8}{11}$

3. In the figure $\log_{10}y$ is plotted against $\log_{10}x$

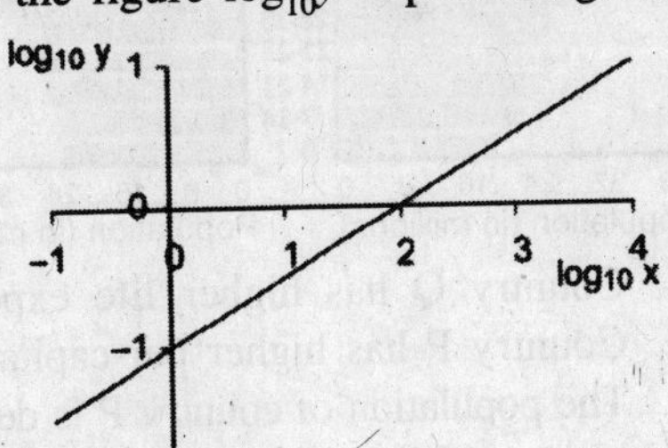

When y is plotted against x, then the plot in the provided range is

(*a*)

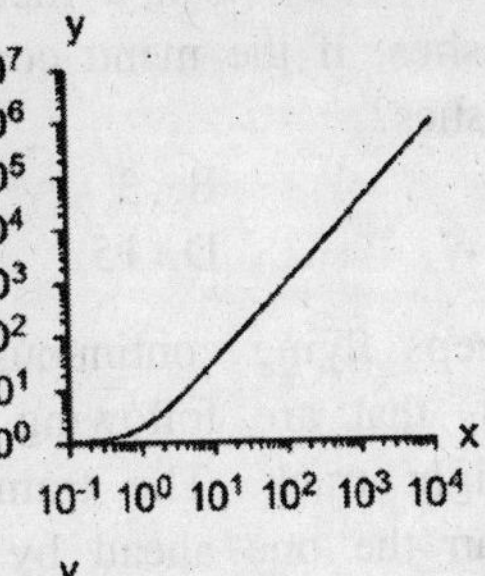

(*b*)

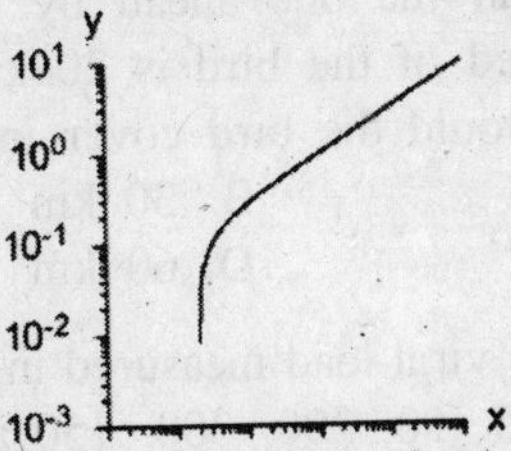

(*c*)

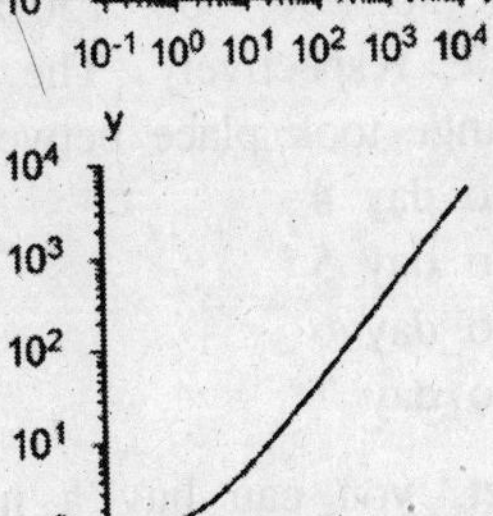

1. C **2.** C **3.** D

(*d*)

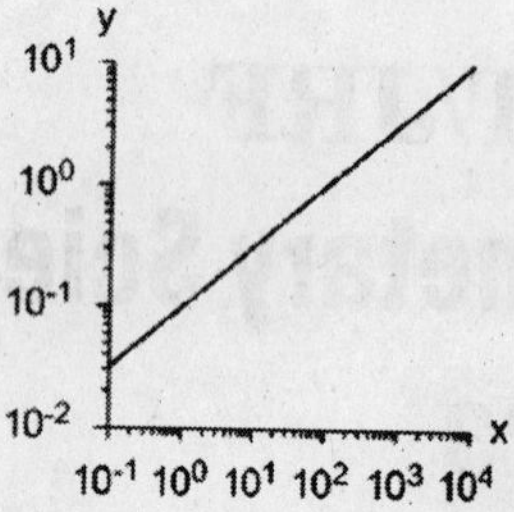

A. (*a*) B. (*b*)
C. (*c*) D. (*d*)

4. SCRIPT : DIRECTOR : : ?? : CHEF

Choose the most appropriate option from the following to fill the blank

A. MENU B. RECIPE
C. RESTAURANT D. MEAL

5. In how many ways can a menu be made from 5 dishes, if the menu contains either 3 or 4 dishes?

A. 2 B. 3
C. 7 D. 15

6. A bird keeps flying continuously between two trains, that are following each other on a straight track. The train behind is slower than the one ahead by 1.5 km/h. If the speed of the bird is 20 km/h, what distance would the bird cover in an hour?

A. 20 km B. 30 km
C. 50 km D. 60 km

7. A person's viral load measured in some unit was 15, 25, 50, 200, 300, 150 and 30 on days 1 to 7, respectively. The maximum relative change took place between:

A. day 3 to day 4
B. day 4 to day 5
C. day 5 to day 6
D. day 6 to day 7

8. In a market, you can buy a mango for ₹ 10, a lemon for Re 1 and 8 chillies for Re 1. How many of these items do you need to buy to get a mix of 100 items for exactly ₹ 100?

A. 6 mangoes, 22 lemons, 72 chillis
B. 7 mangoes, 21 lemons, 72 chillis
C. 1 mango, 9 lemons, 80 chillis
D. 8 mangoes, 12 lemons, 80 chillis

9. In 1979, Ramesh's age was the sum of the digits of his year of birth. In 2017, on his birthday, what was his age?

A. 49 B. 57
C. 60 D. 64

10. The figure shows age-wise bar graph of male and female population of two countries. Which one of the following is likely to be true?

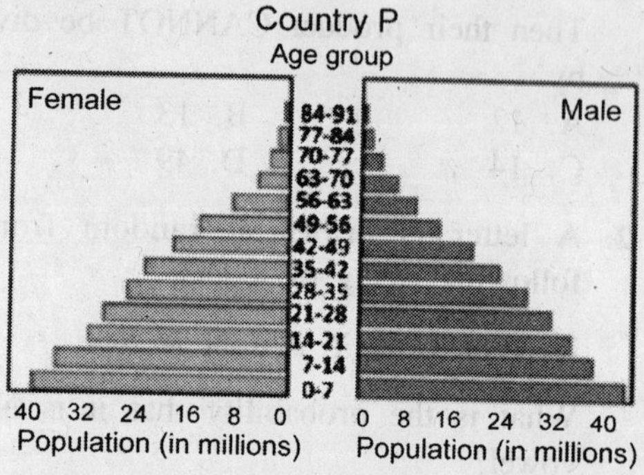

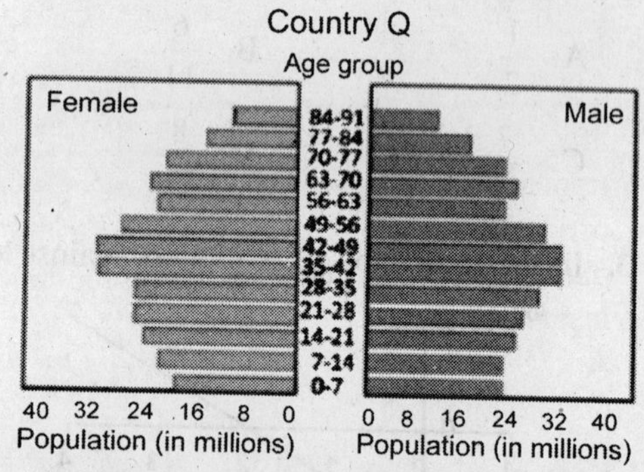

A. Country Q has higher life expectancy
B. Country P has higher per-capita income
C. The population of country P is decreasing more rapidly than Q
D. Country P has better health facilities

4. B **5.** D **6.** A **7.** A **8.** B **9.** C **10.** A

11. What is the value of x in the given magic square, (i.e., a square grid in which the sum of the numbers in rows, columns and diagonals is the same)?

x	$x-5$	8
$x+1$	y	$y-2$
2	9	4

A. 6 B. 4
C. 3 D. 1

12.

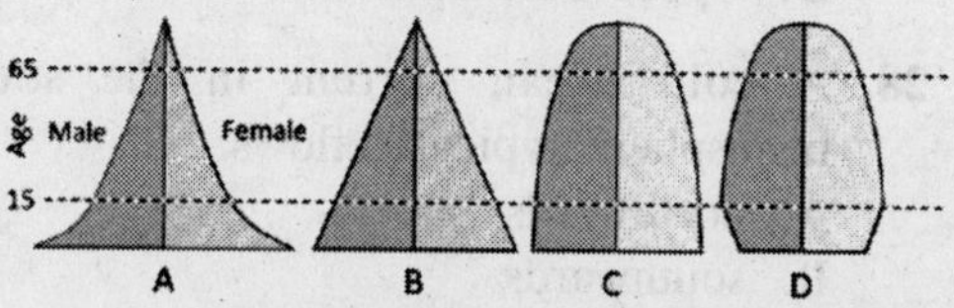

The above figures show population pyramids to four countries A, B, C and D. The country showing the most stable population is:

A. C B. A
C. B D. D

13. A truck from a post office is sent to collect post from a plane as per schedule. The plane lands ahead of schedule, therefore its contents are transported by a rickshaw. The rickshaw meets the truck 30 minutes after the arrival of plane, and the post is transferred. The truck returns to the post office 20 minutes early. How early did the plane arrive? (Assume all transactions are instantaneous.)

A. 10 minutes B. 20 minutes
C. 30 minutes D. 40 minutes

14. Radius of a sphere is measured with 5% uncertainty. What is the uncertainty in the volume, determined from this radius?

A. 5% B. 6.6%
C. 125% D. 15%

15. All the four entries in column A must be matched with all those in column B. Each correctly matched option gets one mark and no mark is awarded otherwise. Which of the following mark(s) CANNOT be scored?

A. 3 B. 1
C. 2 D. 4

16. Four children had 27 apples among them. No child had less than 5 apples. If no two children had the same number of apples, then which of the following could NOT be the number of apples a child had?

A. 5 B. 6
C. 8 D. 9

17. If $a < x < b$, then for which of the following relations does $0 < y < 1$ always hold?

A. $y = \frac{a-x}{b+a}$ B. $y = \frac{x-a}{b-a}$

C. $y = \frac{x-b}{b-a}$ D. $y = \frac{b-x}{a+b}$

18. What is the minimum number of pourings needed to get 4 litre of milk from a fully filled 8 litre can, using ungraduated empty 5 and 3 litre cans? No milk should be wasted.

A. 4 B. 5
C. 6 D. 8

19. The time seen in a mirror placed opposite a numberless analog (with hands) wall clock is 4 h 55 min. What approximately is the correct time?

A. 4 h 55 min B. 5 h 05 min
C. 7 h 05 min D. 1 h 35 min

20. For every 5 chocolates that Ramesh gets, Suresh gets 3 chocolates. Geeta gets 3 chocolates for every 2 chocolates that Suresh gets. If Geeta has 18 chocolates, then the sum of chocolates with Ramesh and Suresh is:

A. 16 B. 30
C. 32 D. 38

11. A **12.** A **13.** D **14.** D **15.** A **16.** C **17.** B **18.** C **19.** C **20.** C

PART-B

21. A crystal that has two perpendicular and one oblique crystallographic axes belongs to which of the following crystal systems?

A. tetragonal B. orthorhombic
C. monoclinic D. triclinic

22. The life history of an individual in a population is known as:

A. Biostratinomy B. Ontogeny
C. Paratype D. Phylogeny

23. Annular drainage pattern usually evolves on:

A. Stratovolcanoes B. Shield volcanoes
C. Bornhardts D. Structural domes

24. Chennai has reported an earthquake of magnitude 4 and intensity 6, simultaneously Guwahati reported an earthquake of magnitude 6 and intensity 4, which one of the following inferences is true?

A. Guwahati is closer to the epicenter than Chennai
B. Destruction around Guwahati is more than that at Chennai
C. Guwahati and Chennai recorded different earthquakes
D. Guwahati and Chennai recorded different core phases of the same earthquake

25. In an ocean water column of 4 km depth the speed of sound is minimum at:

A. a depth of about 1 km from sea surface
B. the bottom of water column.
C. the sea surface.
D. a depth equal to half of the total water column.

26. Which one of the following surface currents is generated by a westward (easterly) wind stress in the northern hemisphere?

A. Northwestward B. Westward
C. Northward D. Southwestward

27. Ozone concentration is the maximum in the:

A. Lower Stratosphere
B. Upper Stratosphere
C. Lower Mesosphere
D. Upper Mesosphere

28. A cold ocean current in the southern hemisphere typically flows:

A. northwards
B. southwards
C. eastwards
D. westwards

29. Which one of the following Large Igneous Provinces (LIPs) is the oldest?

A. Parana B. Karoo
C. Deccan D. Siberian

30. Which one of the following statements is NOT associated with the thermohaline circulation?

A. It plays a crucial role in meridional heat transport within and between the ocean basins.
B. It predominantly advects water mass zonally in the Atlantic Ocean.
C. It involves cold and dense water formation.
D. It involves deep descending motion of water followed by horizontal spreading at the deep sea.

31. The number of atoms of a radioactive element becomes half in 100 years, what is the average life expectancy of an atom of this element?

A. 100 years B. 144 years
C. 72 years D. infinity

21. C **22.** B **23.** D **24.** C **25.** A **26.** A **27.** A **28.** A **29.** D **30.** B **31.** B

32. During El Nino years the Walker cell shifts
A. northward B. eastward
C. southward D. westward

33. **Statement (A):** Deep convection is characterized by low outgoing longwave radiation (OLR).

Statement (B): Monsoon is characterized by bimodal air temperature.
A. (A) is correct; (B) is incorrect
B. (A) is incorrect; (B) is correct
C. Both (A) and (B) are correct
D. Both (A) and (B) are incorrect

34. The acceleration due to gravity (g) is the lowest at which discontinuity inside the Earth?
A. Conrad B. Mohrovicic
C. Gutenberg D. Lehmann

35. Which one of the following types of resolution of satellite images depends on the Instantaneous Field Of View (IFOV)?
A. Spatial B. Spectral
C. Radiometric D. Temporal

36. When there is a balance between the upward pressure gradient force and the downward force of gravity, the atmosphere is:
A. Geostrophic B. Hydrostatic
C. Baroclinic D. Barotropic

37. Most stable form of nitrogen in the oxygenated water is:
A. N_2O B. NO_3^-
C. NO_2^- D. N_2

38. Which of the following have/has more than 99% of the mass of the solar system?
A. The Outer Planets
B. The Inner Planets
C. The Comets and Kuiper belt objects
D. The Sun

39. Which one of the magnetic elements may be different at two locations situated on the same magnetic latitude?
A. F, the Earth's total field
B. V, its vertical component
C. H, its horizontal component
D. X, its N-S component

40. Which one of the following is used as a proxy of paleo-pH of the ocean?
A. $\delta^{18}O$ of foraminifera
B. $\delta^{13}C$ of corals
C. $\delta^{11}B$ of foraminifera
D. $^{87}Sr/^{86}Sr$ in black shale

41. Which one of the following leads to mineralogical maturity of a sandstone?
A. Short transportation and quick dumping
B. Erosion and quick dumping
C. Chemical weathering at source and quick dumping
D. Chemical weathering at source and long transportation

42. The eye of a tropical cyclone is warmer than its environment due to:
A. Adiabatic expansion of air parcel
B. Isothermal compression of air parcel
C. Adiabatic compression of air parcel
D. Isothermal expansion of air parcel

43. Which one of the following rocks commonly hosts Platinum Group Elements (PGE) ore deposits?
A. Felsic volcanic rock
B. Greywacke
C. Ultramafic igneous rocks
D. Mafic igneous rocks

44. Which one of the following forces is NOT involved in the balance of forces for an atmospheric Ekman layer?
A. Coriolis force
B. Pressure Gradient force
C. Viscous force
D. Centrifugal force

45. For a vertical fold, the dip of the profile plane is given by which one of the following values?
A. 0° B. 30°
C. 60° D. 90°

32. B	**33.** C	**34.** D	**35.** A	**36.** B	**37.** D	**38.** D
39. D	**40.** C	**41.** D	**42.** C	**43.** C	**44.** D	**45.** A

46. Barbed drainage pattern indicates:
A. reversal of drainage
B. evolution of drainage over plunging anticlines and synclines
C. presence of underlying en-echelon faults
D. channel incision

47. Which one of the following tectonic domains is characterized by the highest heat flow?
A. Craton
B. Mid Oceanic ridge
C. Collisional Mountain belt
D. Oceanic Trench

48. Statement (A): Turbulent flow is associated with high Reynolds number.

Statement (B): Turbulent flow is associated with strong mixing.
Choose the correct option:
A. (A) is correct; (B) is incorrect
B. (A) is incorrect; (B) is correct
C. Both (A) and (B) are correct
D. Both (A) and (B) are incorrect

49. Which waves of an earthquake are recorded last in a seismogram?
A. P B. S
C. Rayleigh D. Love

50. Which one of the following epochs was the warmest?
A. Pliocene B. Eocene
C. Oligocene D. Miocene

51. The magnitude of the magnetic field of the Moon is:
A. negligible compared to the Earth's magnetic field
B. equal to the Earth's magnetic field
C. half of the Earth's magnetic field
D. one fourth of the Earth's magnetic field

52. Which one of the following mid-oceanic ridges is exposed on land?
A. Carlsberg ridge
B. East Pacific rise
C. Southeast Indian ridge
D. Mid-Atlantic ridge

53. Which one of the following is NOT an ecosystem service?
A. Decomposition of organic matter
B. Pollination by winds
C. Soil formation
D. Sustaining biodiversity

54. Axis of monsoon depression is vertically tilted:
A. northward B. westward
C. southward D. eastward

55. Sea level does NOT increase due to the:
A. melting of sea-ice
B. warming of water
C. melting of continental ice
D. increase in river run-off

56. Which one of the following is a greenhouse gas?
A. N_2 B. O_2
C. H_2 D. H_2O

57. If the Earth were to be 20% farther from the Sun, then its gravity field would be:
A. same as the present
B. 14.14% smaller
C. 20% smaller
D. 28.3% smaller

58. The resistance of a wire of 1 meter length and 1 mm diameter is 1 ohm. The resistance of the wire of 50 cm length and 2 mm diameter, of the same material, is:
A. 1 ohm B. 2 ohm
C. 1/2 ohm D. 1/8 ohm

59. The most abundant mineral in the Earth's lower mantle is:
A. Bridgmanite B. Ringwoodite
C. Majorite D. Olivine

46. A	**47.** B	**48.** C	**49.** C	**50.** B	**51.** A	**52.** D
53. B	**54.** C	**55.** A	**56.** D	**57.** A	**58.** D	**59.** A

60. Which one of the following correctly represents the kinematic vorticity number for pure shear deformation?
A. 0 B. 0.5
C. 0.75 D. 1

61. Which one of the following plates has the lowest average plate-velocity?
A. Pacific B. Indian
C. African D. Eurasian

62. Assuming a standard Earth model, the P shadow zone can be increased by:
A. increasing the P-velocity in the inner core
B. decreasing the P-velocity in the inner core
C. increasing the radius of the outer core
D. decreasing the radius of the outer core

63. Temporal distribution of genesis of tropical cyclones over the north Indian ocean annually is:
A. Unimodal B. Bimodal
C. Trimodal D. Quadruple

64. Earth's energy budget is realized through:
A. radiative process only
B. radiative and latent heat processes
C. radiative and sensible heat processes
D. radiative, latent heat and sensible heat processes

65. Which one of the following is a gently sloping, concave rock cut surface with only a thin debris cover developed by erosional processes, at the base of a steep slope or mountain front?
A. Strath B. Peneplain
C. Etchplain D. Pediment

66. Which one of the following statements on eskers is incorrect?
A. They often show stratification.
B. They can be tens of kilometers long.
C. They do not show branching.
D. They form within glacial ice.

67. Which one of the following minerals indicates the highest degree of chemical weathering?
A. kaolinite B. chlorite
C. vermiculite D. illite

68. Tropical easterly jet is observed over the Indian region during:
A. December to February
B. October to November
C. June to September
D. March to May

69. In tropical ocean, the vertical thermal gradient is the lowest in the depth range of:
A. 100 - 200 m B. 200 - 500 m
C. 500 - 2000 m D. 2000 - 4000 m

70. A scratch or groove engraved on a hard rock surface by abrasive fragments frozen into moving ice, or trapped between sliding ice and the valley floor is known as:
A. Flute B. Striation
C. Ventifact D. Slickenside

PART-C

71. Statement (A): If a meander recurves until it intersects an upstream portion of a river channel, a neck cutoff occurs.

Statement (B): The abrupt shortening of a river channel length, locally increases the channel gradient and velocity.

Based on the given statements, choose the correct option?
A. (A) is correct, but (B) is incorrect
B. (A) is incorrect, but (B) is correct
C. Both (A) and (B) are correct and (B) is the correct explanation of (A)
D. Both (A) and (B) are correct and (A) is the correct explanation of (B)

60. A	**61.** D	**62.** C	**63.** B	**64.** D	**65.** D	**66.** C
67. A	**68.** C	**69.** D	**70.** B	**71.** D		

72. Match the paleoceanographic changes (Column I) with their approximately ages (Column II):

Column I	Column II
P. Opening of Andaman basin	(*a*) 34 Ma
Q. Opening of Red Sea rift	(*b*) 4 Ma
R. Opening of Drake Passage	(*c*) 20 Ma

Choose the correct option

	P	Q	R
A.	(*b*)	(*c*)	(*a*)
B.	(*c*)	(*b*)	(*a*)
C.	(*a*)	(*c*)	(*b*)
D.	(*b*)	(*a*)	(*c*)

73. If a framework silicate has Si:O ratio of 3:8, it implies that:

A. Si atom is replaced by Al in one out of every 4 tetrahedra
B. Si atoms are replaced by Al in three out of every 8 tetrahedra
C. tetrahedra sites are equal in number to the number of oxygen atoms in unit cell.
D. it has lattice defects

74. The relationship between mean oceanic depth (d in m) and lithospheric age (t in Ma) is given by $d = 2500 + 350\sqrt{t}$. If the ocean depth is 4700 m, at a distance of 1600 km from the Mid-Oceanic Ridge, then what is the approximate half spreading rate of the ridge?

A. 40 mm/y B. 40 cm/y
C. 80 mm/y D. 80 cm/y

75. $\delta^{18}O_{PDB}$ of benthic foraminifera in a deep-sea core increases from +0.2‰ to +2‰ from bottom to top. This compositional change, with time, is because of

A. increasing evaporation of sea water
B. decreasing surface temperature at depositional site
C. increasing melting of polar ice
D. combined effect of decreasing temperature and increasing accumulation of polar ice

76. How would the oxygen profile in modern tropical ocean look like if life were removed?

(*a*)
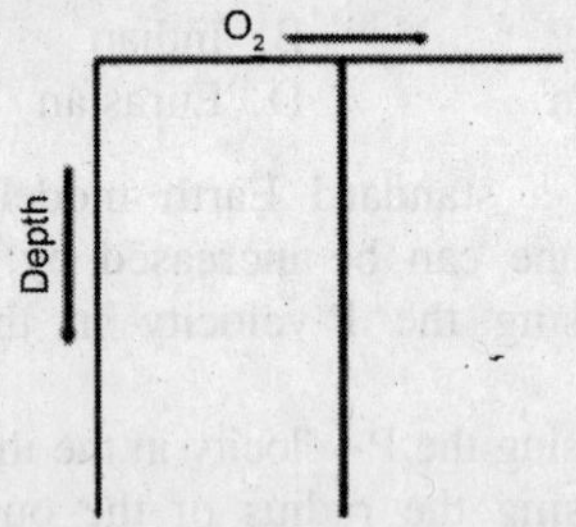

(*b*)
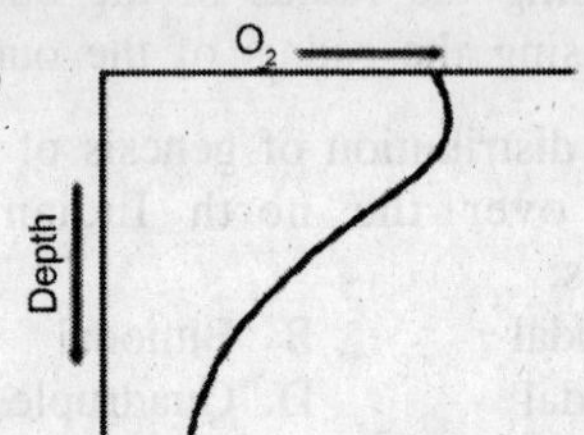

(*c*)
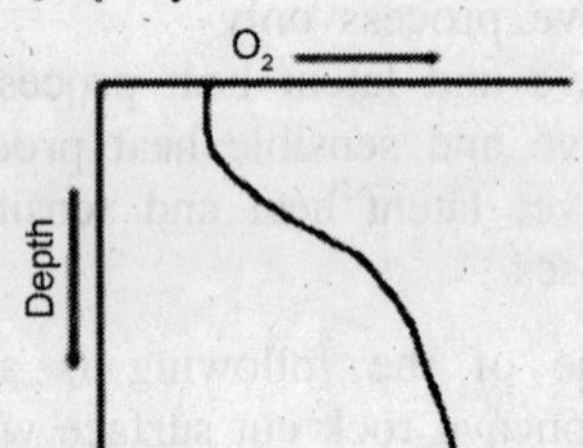

(*d*)
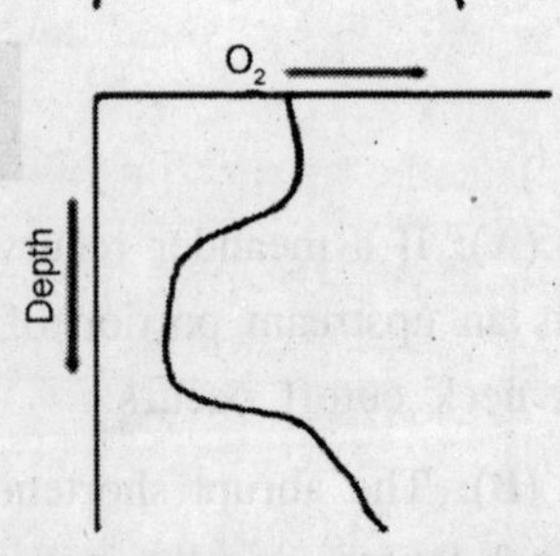

A. (*a*) B. (*b*)
C. (*c*) D. (*d*)

72. A **73.** A **74.** A **75.** D **76.** C

77. Match the modes of El-Nino southern oscillations in Column I with their associated conditions in Column II.

Column I	Column II
(*a*) El-Nino	P. Deeper thermocline in the east than in the west Pacific Ocean
(*b*) La-Nina	Q. Warmer than normal sea surface temperature in the eastern Pacific Ocean
	R. Warmer than normal sea surface temperature in the western Pacific Ocean
	S. Weaker than normal trade winds in the Pacific Ocean

Select the correct option:

A. (*a*) - P, Q, S; (*b*) - R
B. (*a*) - P, R; (*b*) - Q, S
C. (*a*) - Q, S; (*b*) - P, R
D. (*a*) - R, S; (*b*) - P, Q

78. Rain ratio in the ocean is the ratio between:

A. dust and organic matter
B. total rainfall and primary production
C. calcareous material and organic material
D. lithogenic and organic matter

79. Which one of the following remote sensing sensors includes a blue band?

A. LISS-II B. LISS-III
C. LISS-IV D. AWiFS

80. An earthquake is recorded at 3 stations with the P and S arrival times as given below. Calculate the crustal Poisson's ratio.

Station No.	P arrival time H : M : S	S arrival time H : M : S
1	10:00:01	10:00:05
2	10:00:05	10:00:13
3	10:00:09	10:00:21

Choose the correct option

A. 0.25 B. 0.275
C. 0.30 D. 0.33

81. For a given matrix $A = \begin{bmatrix} 2 & -1 & 1 \\ -1 & 3 & 2 \\ 1 & 2 & 1 \end{bmatrix}$ the ratio of its infinity norm and Euclidean norm is:

A. $3\sqrt{\frac{2}{13}}$ B. $7\sqrt{\frac{2}{13}}$

C. $2\sqrt{\frac{23}{5}}$ D. $7\sqrt{\frac{4}{15}}$

82. The fault plane AB in the given beach ball figure represents

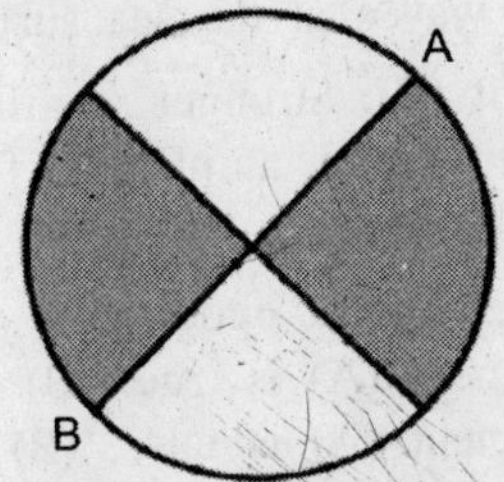

A. A normal fault striking N45°E
B. A thrust fault striking N45°E
C. A left lateral strike-slip fault
D. A right lateral strike-slip fault

83. Consider the following statements:

(*a*) A paraconformity does not involve erosion.
(*b*) Law of superposition is applicable only to deformed strata.
(*c*) Walther's law is applicable along the thrusted contact between strata.
(*d*) Angular unconformity involves long gap in sedimentation.

Which of the above statements are correct?

A. (*a*) and (*b*) B. (*a*) and (*c*)
C. (*a*) and (*d*) D. (*a*), (*b*) and (*c*)

77. A **78.** C **79.** A **80.** D **81.** A **82.** C **83.** C

84. Statement (A): Rossby number is a measure of importance of Earth's rotation.

Statement (B): Large scale motions in the atmosphere are associated with large Rossby number values.

Given the two statements, choose the correct option:

A. Statement (A) is incorrect; Statement (B) is correct
B. Statement (A) is correct; Statement (B) is incorrect
C. Both statements (A) and (B) are correct
D. Both statements (A) and (B) are incorrect

85. Consider the following statements

Statement (A): For a given wave generating force, internal waves have higher amplitude than the waves at the sea surface.

Statement (B): Stronger stratification leads to higher wave amplitude for a given generating force.

Select the correct option:

A. Statement (A) is true, (B) is false
B. Statement (A) is false, (B) is true
C. Both the statements are true, and (B) is the correct explanation of (A)
D. Both the statements are true, and (B) is not the correct explanation of (A)

86. Which one of the following is the most precise indicator of coal rank?

A. moisture content
B. color of spores
C. vitrinite reflection
D. volatile matter content

87. Match column I with II and choose the correct option

Column I	Column II
(*a*) Red tide	P. Viviparity
(*b*) Dimethyl Sulphide	Q. Fish
(*c*) Bombay Duck	R. Coccolithophores
(*d*) Mangals	S. Dinoflagellates

	(*a*)	(*b*)	(*c*)	(*d*)
A.	S	R	Q	P
B.	R	S	P	Q
C.	P	Q	R	S
D.	S	Q	P	R

88. Consider the following statement and the facts:

Statement: Urban surfaces generally exhibit higher value of Bowen Ratio compared to rural area.

Facts: (*a*) Higher proportion of impervious surfaces in urban areas.
(*b*) Lesser surface coverage under vegetation.
(*c*) Greater release of waste heat from air conditioners.

Which combination of facts explains the Statement?

A. (*a*) and (*b*)
B. (*b*) and (*c*)
C. (*a*) and (*c*)
D. (*a*), (*b*) and (*c*)

89. If the water from the oxygen minimum zone is brought to the surface ocean, then the rate of community respiration will

A. remain unchanged
B. reduce substantially
C. enhance drastically
D. cease completely

90. Bulk rock initial isotopic ratio of $^{87}Sr/^{86}Sr$ in an igneous rock sample is higher than the bulk silicate earth (BSE) and $^{143}Nd/^{144}Nd$ ratio is higher than the chondritic uniform reservoir (CHUR). It implies that the sample may have formed from

A. an incompatible element rich source
B. an incompatible element depleted source
C. mixed sources of incompatible element rich and depleted materials
D. a chondritic source

84. B **85.** A **86.** C **87.** A **88.** A **89.** C **90.** C

91. Identify the sand dune types

(*a*) These dunes are especially well-developed in the heart of Trade wind deserts and are huge landforms.

(*b*) Their crests are ridges roughly perpendicular to the effective wind and are common along coastline.

(*c*) These dunes occur on the windward side of a hill and move up the hillside.

Choose the correct option?

A. (*a*)-Longitudinal, (*b*)-Transverse, (*c*)-Star

B. (*a*)-Transverse, (*b*)-Climbing, (*c*)-Longitudinal

C. (*c*)-Longitudinal, (*b*)-Transverse, (*a*)-Climbing

D. (*a*)-Barchan, (*b*)-Parabolic, (*c*)-Climbing

92. Statement (A): The base-level is the lower limit in the landscape, represented by sea level, below which the rivers cannot erode.

Statement (B): In case of deflation basins, the water-table level or calcrete layer or armoured surface forms the base level.

Based on the given statements, choose the correct option:

A. Both (A) and (B) are True

B. (A) is True and (B) is False

C. Both (A) and (B) are False

D. (A) is False and (B) is True

93. Active and break cycle of south-west Indian monsoon are considered to be an oscillation of:

A. 1-5 days B. 5-10 days

C. 20-60 days D. 10-20 days

94. A gravity profile across a two-dimensional horizontal (cylindrical) body recorded a maximum anomaly value of 1.2 mgals. On upward continuation by one unit, the maximum anomaly value is reduced to 0.8 mgal. What would be the value of the maximum anomaly (in mgals) on downward continuation by 1 unit?

A. 1.6 B. 2.0

C. 2.4 D. 3.2

95. Match the factors (List-I) with corresponding processes or features (List-II):

List-I (Factors)	List-II (Processes/Features)
(*a*) Topographic Gradient	L. Extreme events
(*b*) Distance from water divide	M. Salinity incursion
(*c*) Geomorphic threshold	N. Topo sequence
(*d*) Dominance of flood tide	O. Creep
	P. Estuarine Sedimentation

	(*a*)	(*b*)	(*c*)	(*d*)
A.	P	L	N	M
B.	O	N	L	P
C.	O	M	N	P
D.	N	O	P	M

96. Statement (A): The asymmetry factor (AF) of a drainage basin is derived by $100 \times (A_T/A_R)$ where A_T is the total area of the basin and A_R is the area of the basin to the right (facing downstream) of the trunk river.

Statement (B): AF is an indication of possible tectonic tilt of a drainage basin.

Based on the given statements, choose the correct option:

A. (A) is correct, but (B) is wrong

B. (A) is wrong, but (B) is correct

C. Both (A) and (B) are correct

D. Both (A) and (B) are wrong

97. Arrange the following mineral deposits in the order of decreasing depth of formation.

(*a*) Porphyry type W deposit

(*b*) Porphyry type Cu deposit

(*c*) Bauxite deposit

(*d*) High-sulfidation Au deposits

Choose the correct option?

A. (*a*), (*b*), (*d*), (*c*) B. (*b*), (*a*), (*d*), (*c*)

C. (*d*), (*b*), (*a*), (*c*) D. (*a*), (*d*), (*c*), (*b*)

91. C **92.** A **93.** C **94.** C **95.** B **96.** B **97.** A

98. Which one of the following is the INCORRECT statement regarding Oxygen isotope stages

A. Interglacials are numbered backwards in time with odd numbers.

B. Ice ages are numbered backwards in time with even numbers.

C. The last ice age or Last Glacial Maximum is numbered as stage 2.

D. The last interglacial centered on ~125 ka is numbered as stage 3.

99. Which one of the following can be used to reconstruct Quaternary climate in a sediment core collected from the central Indian Ocean basin at a water depth >5000 m?

A. Diatoms, Radiolaria, Coccolithophores

B. Foraminifera, Coccolithophores, Ostracods

C. Diatoms, Radiolaria, Sillicoflagellates

D. Trilobites, Conodonts, Benthic foraminifera

100. If the surface air temperature increases towards north in the northern hemisphere, the direction of thermal wind will be

A. Northerly B. Easterly

C. Westerly D. Southerly

101. Statement (A): Turbidite deposits causing discontinuous sedimentary records are common in the eastern Bay of Bengal.

Statement (B): The narrow shelf, large terrigenous influx and steep slope facilitates turbidity flows.

From the given statements, which one of the following is correct?

A. Both statements are incorrect.

B. Statement (A) is correct and (B) is incorrect.

C. Both the statements are correct and (B) explains (A).

D. Both the statements are correct but (B) doesn't explain (A).

102. For the ocean to remain in a steady state, if the rate of input of a dissolved constituent increases then

(A) the rate of removal of that constituent increases.

(B) the residence time of that constituent remains unchanged.

A. Both (A) and (B) are correct.

B. Both (A) and (B) are incorrect.

C. (A) is correct and (B) is incorrect.

D. (A) is incorrect and (B) is correct.

103. Which situation among the following is more likely to cause Clear Air Turbulence?

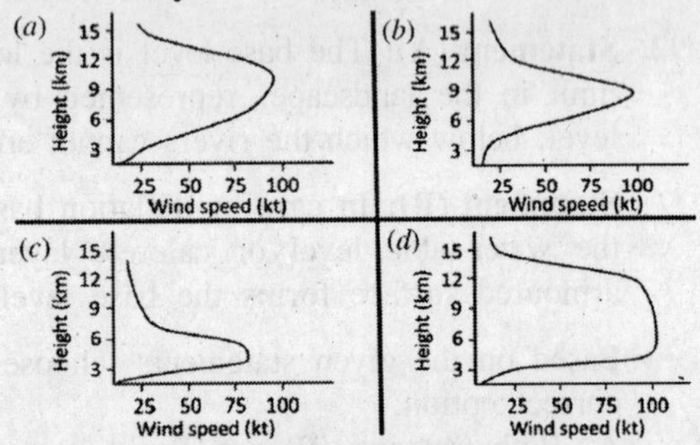

A. (*a*) B. (*b*)

C. (*c*) D. (*d*)

104. Match the EM methods given in Group 1 with their corresponding frequency ranges in Group 2:

Group 1	Group 2
P. Slingram	(*a*) 10^{-4} Hz-1Hz
Q. VLF	(*b*) 1 Hz-1000Hz
R. AFMAG	(*c*) 10 Hz-5000HZ
S. MT	(*d*) 5 KHz-30 KHz

Choose the correct option:

	P	Q	R	S
A.	(*d*)	(*a*)	(*c*)	(*b*)
B.	(*c*)	(*d*)	(*b*)	(*a*)
C.	(*b*)	(*a*)	(*d*)	(*c*)
D.	(*a*)	(*d*)	(*c*)	(*b*)

98. D **99.** C **100.** B **101.** C **102.** C **103.** B **104.** B

105. Tropical cyclones do not attain the maximum intensity during the Indian south-west monsoon period, due to:

A. high moisture availability
B. strong vertical wind shear
C. strong north-south temperature gradient
D. strong north-south pressure gradient

106. Match the igneous texture in Column I with the corresponding process in Column II:

Column I	Column II
(*a*) Porphyritic	P. Simultaneous crystallization
(*b*) Dendritic	Q. Exsolution
(*c*) Oscillatory zoning	R. Two-stage cooling
(*d*) Graphic	S. Magma mixing
(*e*) Antiperthite	T. Rapid cooling

	(*a*)	(*b*)	(*c*)	(*d*)	(*e*)
A.	R	T	S	P	Q
B.	R	S	Q	P	T
C.	T	S	P	Q	R
D.	T	P	R	Q	S

107. A, B, C, ... Y, Z, are 26 metal electrodes placed at 10 m interval each along a line over an inhomogeneous ground for electrical resistivity tomography survey. Assuming electrodes A to Z are arranged in series and a current flow of 1 Amp between electrodes A and B gives the potential difference of 500 μV between electrodes Y and Z, the calculated apparent resistivity for the above observation will be approximately:

A. 9 Ωm B. 22 Ωm
C. 69 Ωm D. 216 Ωm

108. Which one of the following is correct?

Statement I: Bright spots and dim spots represent amplitude lows and highs, respectively.

Statement II: V_S/V_P decreases in a gas saturated zone relative to a water saturated zone.

A. Both statements I and II are True
B. Statement I is True and Statement II is False
C. Statement I is False and Statement II is True
D. Both statements I and II are False

109. Assertion (A): Most sinuous rilles of the Moon were formed out of lava tubes.

Reason (R): Roofs of lava tubes often collapse to reveal their interiors.

A. Both (A) and (R) are true and (R) is the correct explanation of (A)
B. Both (A) and (R) are true and (R) is not the correct explanation of (A)
C. (A) is true, but (R) is false
D. (A) is false, but (R) is true

110. Which one of the following systems shows the shortest food chain in the ocean?

A. Oligotrophic gyre
B. Upwelling region
C. Downwelling region
D. Warm core eddies

111. Consider the following statements:

Statement (A): The magnitude of solar tide is about half to that of lunar tide.

Statement (B): The tidal acceleration is inversely proportional to the cube of the distance between Earth and tide generating body.

Select the correct option:

A. Statement (A) is true, (B) is false
B. Statement (A) is false, (B) is true
C. Both the statements are true and statement (B) explains statement (A)
D. Both the statements are true but statement (B) does not explain (A)

105. B	**106.** A	**107.** D	**108.** D	**109.** B	**110.** B	**111.** C

112. Match the column I with column II and choose the correct option:

Column-I	Column-II
(*a*) Glaciogenic deposit	P. Raniganj Formation
(*b*) Glossopteris flora	Q. Panchet Formation
(*c*) Dicroidium flora	R. Talchir Formation
(*d*) Ptilophyllum flora	S. Jabalpur Formation

	(*a*)	(*b*)	(*c*)	(*d*)
A.	R	P	S	Q
B.	Q	P	R	S
C.	R	P	Q	S
D.	S	R	Q	P

113. Which of the following features best defines the Weber's Line?

A. The line separating Australian and Asian fauna

B. The line of supposed 'faunal balance' between Oriental and Australian faunal regions

C. The western boundary between upper and lower mountain forest of New Guinea

D. The western boundary of strictly Australian fauna

114. Match the following aspects of south west monsoon over India and associated region from the table:

Region	Characteristics of southwest monsoon
(*a*) Rajasthan	P. Subtropical easterly jet
(*b*) Head Bay of Bengal	Q. Monsoon Depression
(*c*) Southern Peninsular region	R. Monsoon Heat Zone

Choose the correct option:

	(*a*)	(*b*)	(*c*)
A.	P	Q	R
B.	R	Q	P
C.	Q	R	P
D.	Q	P	R

115. Which one of the following is NOT true for the Boussinesq approximation in ocean?

A. Density remains constant except when it is multiplied by g (acceleration due to gravity) in calculation of pressure.

B. Background (reference) density is assumed to be function of height

C. Vertical accelerations are not neglected

D. Phase speed of ocean waves must be smaller than sound velocity in sea water

116. Moist convective processes are extremely important over the tropical regions. Which of the following is NOT true?

A. Tropical regions have higher air-temperature and plenty of moisture

B. Tropical regions have large amounts of latent heat of condensation energy release

C. Higher the air-temperature more moisture can be added until saturation is attained.

D. Change of saturation vapour pressure of air with temperature is linear function of air-temperature.

117. In ichnofossil assemblages, Fugichnia refers to:

A. Dwelling traces

B. Resting traces

C. Escape traces

D. Feeding traces

118. Which of the following statement is correct about the electromagnetic methods?

A. MT method is a time domain EM method

B. TURAM method measures the amplitude ratio and relative phase difference between two-receiver coils

C. AFMAG method gives amplitude and phase change information

D. Transient EM method cannot be applied for airborne EM survey

112. C **113.** B **114.** B **115.** C **116.** D **117.** C **118.** B

119. Computational stability in 1-dimensional Eulerian atmospheric model is controlled by which one of the following conditions? [where C is a phase speed, ΔT is the time step and Δx is the grid size]

A. $\frac{C\Delta T}{\Delta x} > \sqrt{3}$ B. $\frac{C\Delta T}{\Delta x} = 1$

C. $\frac{C\Delta T}{\Delta x} < 1$ D. $1 < \frac{C\Delta T}{\Delta x} < \sqrt{2}$

120. Match the Column I with Column II:

Column I: Atmospheric species	Column II: Peak absorption wavelength in μm
(a) CO_2	P. 9.6
(b) Water vapour	Q. 6.7
(c) Ozone	R. 15

Choose the correct option:

	(a)	(b)	(c)
A.	R	Q	P
B.	P	Q	R
C.	Q	P	R
D.	Q	R	P

121. Calculate the P wave velocity of a Poisson's solid having a bulk modulus of 120 GPa and density of 3 gm/cc.

A. 6.5 km/s B. 7.5 km/s
C. 8.5 km/s D. 9.5 km/s

122. With respect to surface currents in the Indian ocean during winter (December-February), Identify the currents in Column I with their predominant directions in Column II).

Column I	Column II
(a) Winter Monsoon Current (WMC)	R. Eastward
(b) East India Coastal Current	Q. Westward
(c) Somalia Current (SC)	R. Northward
(d) West India Coastal Current	S. Southward

	(a)	(b)	(c)	(d)
A.	Q	S	S	R
B.	S	R	S	Q
C.	Q	P	R	S
D.	P	S	R	Q

123. Which one of the following is used as boundary forcing in long-range (4 months & beyond) prediction by global atmospheric Numerical Weather Prediction (NWP) model?

A. Global surface wind
B. Global surface pressure
C. Global surface humidity
D. Global sea surface temperature

124. Which one of the following statements is TRUE for the Kathmandu 2015 Gorkha earthquake?

A. It originated along a strike-slip fault
B. It originated on the Main Himalayan Thrust
C. It was an in-sequence earthquake
D. It was a deep focus earthquake

125. Light absorbing aerosols in the atmosphere cause

A. surface warming and atmospheric cooling
B. surface cooling and atmospheric warming
C. surface warming and atmospheric warming
D. surface cooling and atmospheric cooling

126. The points with the maximum and minimum anomaly values along a total field magnetic anomaly profile over a single pole are separated by a distance of 120 m. If the horizontal component of the Earth's magnetic field in the area of survey is thrice its vertical component, the pole is located at a depth (in m) of:

A. 60 B. 60√2
C. 80 D. 80√2

119. C **120.** A **121.** C **122.** A **123.** D **124.** B **125.** B **126.** C

127. Which one of the following ligands forms the most stable complex with Cu in acidic hydrothermal fluid?

A. Cl^- B. OH^-

C. SO_4^{2-} D. HS^-

128. Match the column-I with the column-II:

Column-I	Column-II
(*a*) Density based spatial clustering	P. Performance of a classification algorithm
(*b*) Random forest	Q. Atmospheric correction of image
(*c*) Receiver Operating Characteristic curve	R. Supervised image classification
(*d*) Dark object subtraction	S. Unsupervised Learning method

	(*a*)	(*b*)	(*c*)	(*d*)
A.	Q	R	S	P
B.	S	R	P	Q
C.	S	R	Q	P
D.	R	Q	P	S

129. In a VLF electromagnetic survey, the primary magnetic field at an observation point is 20 units. If the secondary magnetic field at this location makes an angle of 120° with respect to the primary field and has a magnitude of 5 units, then the real anomaly in percentage will be approximately:

A. 10% B. 25%

C. 35% D. 45%

130. Match the following world climate types with the symbols that represent them, as proposed by Koppen.

Climate type	Symbol
(*a*) Tropical wet climate with no dry season	P. Cfb
(*b*) Mediterranean climate	Q. BWk
(*c*) Marine west coast type climate	R. Af
(*d*) Mid-latitude desert climate	S. Cs

	(*a*)	(*b*)	(*c*)	(*d*)
A.	P	S	R	Q
B.	S	R	Q	P
C.	R	S	P	Q
D.	Q	P	S	R

131. For clouds with fixed liquid water path cloud optical depth is

A. inversely proportional to the cloud droplet effective radius

B. directly proportional to the cloud droplet effective radius

C. directly proportional to the cube root of the cloud droplet effective radius

D. inversely proportional to the cube root of the cloud droplet effective radius

132. The following figure shows the positions of volcanic islands over an active tectonic plate. The numbers on them indicate their age in *My*. Consider the following inferences I_1 and I_2:

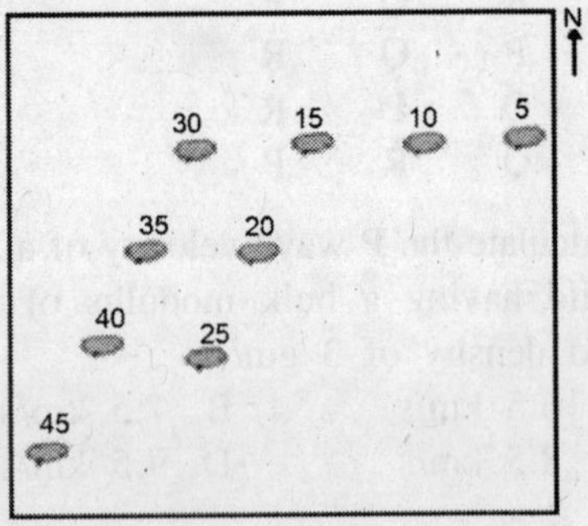

I_1 : The plate was moving towards NE up to 15 *My* then it started moving towards the east

I_2 : The plate encountered two hotspots, one becoming inactive at 30 *My* and other becoming active at 25 *My*

A. Inferences I_1 and I_2 are correct

B. Inference I_1 is correct, but I_2 is not correct

C. Inference I_1 is not correct, but I_2 is correct

D. Inferences I_1 and I_2 are not correct

127. A	**128.** B	**129.** B	**130.** C	**131.** A	**132.** C

133. Which of the following statements is NOT TRUE for the large-scale motion in the atmosphere?

A. Time scale is much smaller than the time scale of the rotating Earth

B. Ratio of relative vorticity to planetary vorticity is of the order of Rossby number

C. Ratio of horizontal divergence to relative vorticity is of the order of Rossby number

D. Ratio of horizontal divergence to planetary vorticity is of the order of square of Rossby number

134. Shear failure in rocks with pre-existing fractures under confining pressures greater than 300 MPa is governed by which one of the following laws?

A. Mohr-Coulomb Law

B. Byerlee's Law

C. Omori's Law

D. Amonton's Law

135. Two anomalous bodies A and B in the form of vertical sheets extend infinitely closest to the magnetic equator in the N-S and E-W directions, respectively. If neither body possesses remanence, then which of the following statements is valid with reference to their magnetic anomalies?

A. Their anomaly profiles are identical

B. Their anomaly profiles are similar, with the anomaly over B being stronger

C. Their anomaly profiles are similar, with the anomaly over A being stronger

D. Their anomaly profiles are dissimilar, with A producing little or no anomaly

136. A 2.0 km thick landmass with 9.0 km thick root at the Moho is associated with a Bouguer anomaly of –113 mgals and free-air anomaly of +113 mgals. What would be the free-air anomaly when the landmass undergoes subsidence to achieve a thickness of 1.1 km?

A. –56 mgals

B. 0 mgals

C. 56 mgals

D. 226 mgals

137. Assertion (A): Cheniers are linear beach ridges separated by low-lying swamps developed parallel to the coast.

Reason (R): Sequential transgression and regression of a coastal area leads to changes in littoral drifts that influence chenier development.

Choose a correct option:

A. Both (A) and (R) are true and (R) is the correct explanation of (A)

B. Both (A) and (R) are true and (R) is not the correct explanation of (A)

C. (A) is true, but (R) is false

D. (A) is false, but (R) is true

138. Match the mineral assemblages in Group-I with corresponding metamorphic facies in Group-II:

	Group-I	**Group-II**
P.	Garnet-muscovite-biotite-sillimanite-quartz	1. Granulite
Q.	Orthopyroxene-clinopy-roxeneplagioclase-garnet	2. Greenschist
R.	Glaucophane-lawsonite-albite-jadeite	3. Ambhibolite
S.	Chlorite-albite-epidote-actinolite	4. Blueschist

	P	Q	R	S
A.	4	1	3	2
B.	3	1	4	2
C.	2	4	1	3
D.	2	3	4	1

133. A	**134.** B	**135.** D	**136.** B	**137.** C	**138.** B

139. The normal log response (with spacing AM) for a high resistivity (R_1) formation with a thickness (H1 < AM) sandwiched between two thick (H = 10AM) low resistivity ($R_2 << R_1$) formations indicates which one of the following?

A. Larger (>H1) thickness with higher resistivity (>R1)

B. Smaller (<H1) thickness with higher resistivity (>R1)

C. Larger (>H1) thickness with lower resistivity (<R1)

D. Smaller (<H1) thickness with lower resistivity (<R1)

140. Statement (A): Sea breeze circulation is an example of barotropic circulation.

Statement (B): Sea breeze circulation can be explained using Bjerknes circulation theorem.

Given the two statements, choose the correct option.

A. Statement (A) is correct; Statement (B) is incorrect

B. Statement (A) is incorrect; Statement (B) is correct

C. Both statements (A) and (B) are correct

D. Both statements (A) and (B) are incorrect

141. Identify different geomorphic settings in the given schematic topographic profile.

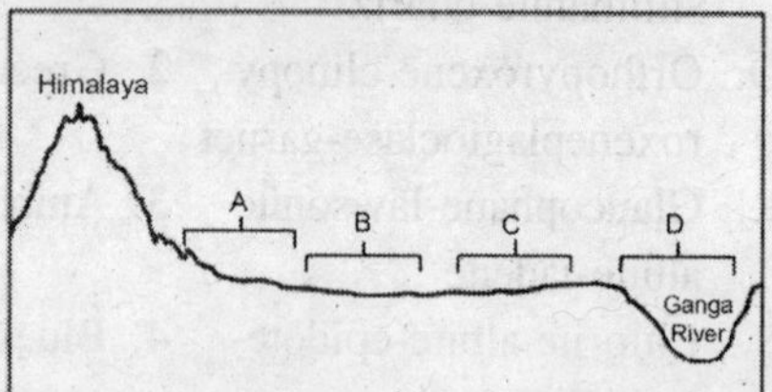

A. A-Bhangar, B-Terai, C-Khadar, D-Bhabhar

B. A-Bhabhar, B-Terai, C-Bhangar, D-Khadar

C. A-Bhabhar B-Bhangar C-Khadar, D-Terai

D. A-Bhangar, B-Khadar, C-Bhabhar, D-Terai

142. Which of the following is NOT responsible for the formation of oxygen minimum Zones (OMZ) in the ocean?

A. High Primary production

B. Denitrification

C. Slow Vertical Mixing

D. High respiration

143. How is vertical velocity computed in a hydrostatic model?

A. using zonal component of momentum equation

B. using thermodynamic energy equation

C. using continuity equation

D. using meridional component of momentum equation

144. Volcanogenic massive sulfide (VMS) deposits generally form because of mixing of magmatic hydrothermal fluid ($\delta^{34}S$ = 0‰) and seawater ($\delta^{34}S$ = +20‰). If a VMS deposit records $\delta^{34}S$ value of +12‰, what would have been the contribution of magmatic fluid?

A. 20% B. 30%

C. 40% D. 50%

145. Find out types of mass wasting represented by X, Y and Z in the given diagram.

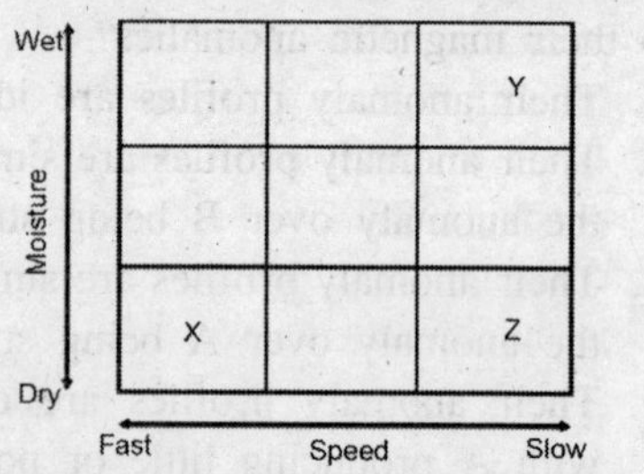

A. X - Landslide, Y - Mudflow, Z - Slump

B. X - Earthflow, Y - Solifluction, Z - Landslide

C. X - Rockfall, Y - Solifluction, Z - Creep

D. X - Mudflow, Y - Creep. Z - Solifluction

139. C 140. B 141. B 142. B 143. C 144. C 145. C

146. Which one of the following sedimentary features is observed on the vertical section of a bed?

A. flute cast B. dish and pillar
C. bounce mark D. prod cast

147. Sun-synchronous polar orbiting satellites pass over any given latitude:

A. at same local time during each pass with tilt of 98°
B. at different local time during each pass with tilt of 55°
C. at same local time during each pass with tilt of 55°
D. at different local time during each pass with tilt of 98°

148. Embayments are observed in which one of the following types of porphyroclasts in a mylonite?

A. σ-type B. δ-type
C. θ-type D. ϕ-type

149. Which one of the following is a FALSE statement about 'Ecosystem services'?

A. Soil formation constitutes 50% of the total value of ecosystem services
B. Four categories of ecosystem services were first documented in Global Environmental outlook 6
C. Pollination by winds is not an ecosystem service
D. Decomposition of organic matter is a regulating service

150. In a Time-domain induced polarization survey, chargeability is calculated as 500 msec. If the area under the transient decay curve is 5000 mV.sec, then what was the potential difference just before the current is switched off?

A. 500 mV B. 5 volts
C. 10 volts D. 50 volts

EXPLANATORY ANSWERS

1. (C): The sum of two positive integers that equals 14 can only produce a limited set of integer pairs: (1,13), (2,12), (3,11), (4,10), (5,9), (6,8), and (7,7). Multiplying these pairs, none of their products is divisible by 14 without resulting in a fraction, as 14 is a multiple of 7 and 2. None of the products of these pairs are multiples of 14, ensuring their indivisibility by 14, making it the correct answer.

2. (C): In the string "RAMUKYAJNAS," there are 11 letters, with 4 vowels (A, A, A, U) and 7 consonants (R, M, K, Y, J, N, S). The probability of drawing a letter that is not a vowel is determined by dividing the number of consonants by the total number of letters. Therefore, with 7 consonants out of 11 total letters, the probability is 7/11, which means the likelihood of drawing a consonant (not a vowel) is 7 out of 11 chances.

3. (D): The given plot shows $\log_{10}y$ plotted against $\log_{10}x$. The straight line with a positive slope through the origin suggests a power law relationship between x and y. Specifically, the fact that the line passes through the points where $\log_{10}x$ and $\log_{10}y$ are both 0 (corresponding to $x = 1$ and $y = 1$) and the point where $\log_{10}x=1$ and $\log_{10}y=3$ (corresponding to $x = 10$ and $y = 1000$) indicates that y is proportional to x^3. Therefore, when y is plotted against

146. B	147. A	148. B	149. B	150. C

x on a log-log scale, the slope of the line will be 3, which corresponds to the cube of x. Among the given options, D shows a cubic relationship where as x increases, y increases by the cube of x. The other plots do not match this relationship; they show either a linear relationship (A and C) or a more complex curve (B).

4. (B): A script is to a director what a recipe is to a chef. Just as a director uses a script as a foundational guide to shape a film or production, a chef uses a recipe as a fundamental guide to create a dish. Both are essential tools of their trades, providing the necessary instructions and steps to achieve their final products.

6. (A): The speed of the bird is 20 km/h, and it flies continuously for an hour between the two trains. The relative speed of the bird to the trains does not affect the distance it covers relative to the ground. Therefore, regardless of how it moves between the trains, it will cover 20 km in an hour because its speed is consistent at 20 km/h.

7. (A): To find the maximum relative change, we look for the greatest percentage change in viral load from one day to the next. Comparing the changes between the given days, the jump from 50 to 200 (day 3 to day 4) represents the most significant relative increase.

8. (B): The solution involves finding a combination of items that totals 100 items for exactly 100, balancing the cost and quantity. By systematically evaluating the options, the one that meets both criteria for quantity and cost involves buying 7 mangoes (70), 21 lemons (21), and 72 chillis (9), summing up to exactly 100 for 100 items.

10. (A): The age-wise bar graph for both countries shows a larger proportion of the population in the older age brackets for Country Q compared to Country P. Specifically, the population sizes for the 64-81 and 82+ age groups are noticeably larger in Country Q for both males and females, suggesting that a higher proportion of the population is reaching an older age. This is a strong indicator that Country Q has a higher life expectancy than Country P, as more people are living into older age. The other options are not directly supported by the data in the graph. For instance, per-capita income (B), the rate of population decrease (C), or the quality of health facilities (D) cannot be inferred from population age distribution alone.

11. (A): To determine the value of x in the magic square, where the sums of the numbers in rows, columns, and diagonals are equal, we can utilize the fact that the sum of the bottom row $(2 + 9 + 4)$ is 15. Thus, the sum of the numbers in any other row, column, or diagonal must also be 15. Looking at the top row, we have x, $x - 5$, and 8. Adding these together and setting them equal to 15 gives us the equation $x + (x - 5) + 8 = 15$. Solving this equation yields $x = 6$, meaning that the value of x that satisfies the condition of the magic square is 6. This aligns with the provided answer and confirms that the sums of numbers in any row, column, or diagonal indeed match.

12. (A): Population pyramids visually represent the age and sex distribution of a country's population. Country C's population pyramid is almost rectangular with a slightly tapered top, indicating that the number of people in each age group is relatively stable from the youngest to the oldest. This suggests low birth rates and low death rates, with a balance between the number of young and old people. The stable numbers across age groups imply that the population is neither growing rapidly nor declining, which is typically indicative of a developed country with consistent birth and death rates, and it suggests that the population size will remain relatively constant over time.

14. **(D):** The volume of a sphere is given by the formula $V = \frac{4}{3}\pi r^3$. The uncertainty in a measured quantity raised to a power is multiplied by that power. Thus, a 5% uncertainty in the radius (r) translates to a $3 \times 5\% = 15\%$ uncertainty in the volume (V), because the volume is directly proportional to the cube of the radius.

16. **(C):** Given that the total number of apples is 27 and no child had less than 5 apples, and all had a different number of apples, the only distribution that allows for no two children to have the same number of apples and for each to have at least 5 is to have a distribution that maximizes the difference between the numbers of apples each child has. With one child having 5 and another having 6, and considering the constraints, having a child with 8 apples becomes impossible to achieve the total without violating the conditions.

17. **(B):** To determine the relationship where $0 < y < 1$ always holds, given $a < x < b$, we examine option B: $y = \frac{x-a}{b-a}$. Since x is greater than a, the numerator $x - a$ is positive. Also, b is greater than a, making the denominator $b - a$ positive as well. This means y is a positive number because it is a division of two positive numbers. Now let's consider the maximum value of x, which is just less than b. In this case, $x - a$ will be less than $b - a$, making y less than 1. For the minimum value of x, which is just greater than a, $x - a$ approaches 0, making y approach 0 but never touch it. Therefore, as x varies between a and b, y will always be between 0 and 1, satisfying the condition.

18. **(C):** To achieve 4 liters using 5-liter and 3-liter cans without wasting milk involves a sequence of pourings and transfers:

Fill the 5-liter can from the 8-liter can. (8L can → 5L can, remaining in 8L can: 3L)

Pour from the 5-liter can into the 3-liter can. (5L can → 3L can, remaining in 5L can: 2L)

Empty the 3-liter can. (3L can emptied)

Transfer the remaining 2 liters from the 5-liter can to the 3-liter can. (5L can → 3L can, 3L can now has 2L)

Fill the 5-liter can again from the 8-liter can. (8L can → 5L can, 5L can full, 8L can empty)

Pour from the 5-liter can into the 3-liter can to fill it up. (5L can → 3L can, 3L can full, 5L can has 4L)

This sequence involves 6 steps, making the minimum number of pourings needed 6.

19. **(C):** The reflection of a clock showing 4:55 in a mirror would mean the actual time on the clock is the mirror image of that. Since a clock is circular and mirrors reverse left and right, the correct time would be approximately 7:05. This is because the mirror image of 4:55 would logically correspond to the hour hand nearing 7 and the minute hand at 5 minutes past the hour.

20. **(C):** If Geeta has 18 chocolates, and she gets 3 chocolates for every 2 chocolates Suresh gets, we can find Suresh's chocolates by setting up a ratio. Suresh would have $(18 \times 2) \div 3 = 12$ chocolates. Using the ratio between Ramesh and Suresh, where for every 5 chocolates Ramesh gets, Suresh gets 3, we can find Ramesh's chocolates by (12 × 5) % 3 = 20. Adding Ramesh's and Suresh's chocolates gives 20 + 12 = 32, indicating the sum of chocolates with Ramesh and Suresh is 32.

21. **(C):** A crystal with two perpendicular and one oblique crystallographic axes is characteristic of the monoclinic crystal system. This system is defined by three axes of unequal length, where two axes are perpendicular to each other, and the third axis is inclined, forming an oblique angle with one of the other axes. This arrangement distinguishes it from the orthorhombic, tetragonal, and triclinic systems, which have different configurations of their crystallographic axes.

22. **(B):** Ontogeny refers to the life history of an individual organism from fertilization to death, encompassing all the developmental processes in between. It includes stages such as embryonic development, maturity, and aging. This term contrasts with biostratinomy, which deals with the processes affecting organic remains post-mortem; paratype, a specimen related to the holotype in taxonomic description; and phylogeny, which concerns the evolutionary history and relationships among species.

23. **(D):** Annular drainage patterns are typically found on structural domes, where the rock strata are uplifted in the center to form a dome shape. Erosion and weathering processes preferentially remove the softer rocks in concentric patterns around the dome, leading to a circular or annular arrangement of streams. This pattern differs from the drainage systems on stratovolcanoes, shield volcanoes, and bornhardts, which are influenced by different geological structures and processes.

24. **(C):** The report indicates that Chennai and Guwahati recorded different earthquakes based on the discrepancy in magnitude and intensity measurements reported simultaneously. Magnitude measures the energy released at the source of the earthquake, while intensity measures the effects of the earthquake at a specific location. The inverse relationship between magnitude and intensity in the two locations suggests they were affected by separate seismic events, not variations in distance from a common epicenter or differences in seismic phases.

25. **(A):** In an ocean water column, the speed of sound reaches a minimum at a depth of about 1 km from the sea surface, known as the SOFAR (Sound Fixing and Ranging) channel or deep sound channel. At this depth, the decrease in temperature with depth reduces the speed of sound, before it begins to increase again due to rising pressure at greater depths. This phenomenon creates a zone where sound can travel long distances with little attenuation, unlike at the sea surface, bottom, or mid-water column where conditions are less favorable for sound transmission.

26. **(A):** Westward (easterly) wind stress in the Northern Hemisphere leads to the generation of a northwestward surface current due to the Coriolis effect. This force acts to the right of the direction of motion in the Northern Hemisphere, causing any movement (including wind-driven surface currents) to be deflected to the right of the initial direction. Hence, a westward-moving current will turn northwestward as it is influenced by this effect.

27. **(A):** The maximum concentration of ozone is found in the lower stratosphere. This region, known as the ozone layer, absorbs and scatters the solar ultraviolet radiation, playing a critical role in protecting life on Earth. The creation and destruction of ozone molecules primarily occur in this layer, with the highest concentrations typically found between about 15 to 35 kilometers above the Earth's surface.

28. (A): In the Southern Hemisphere, a cold ocean current typically flows northwards. This is due to the Coriolis effect, which causes moving objects (including water masses) to deflect to the left of their path of motion in the Southern Hemisphere. Therefore, cold currents flowing away from the polar regions towards the equator tend to be directed northward in this hemisphere.

29. (D): The Siberian Large Igneous Province (LIP) is the oldest among the options listed. It was formed during the late Permian and early Triassic periods, around 250 million years ago. This massive volcanic event is associated with one of the Earth's most significant extinction events, marking it as a critical point in geological and biological history.

30. (B): The statement that the thermohaline circulation "predominantly advects water mass zonally in the Atlantic Ocean" is not associated with the general characteristics of thermohaline circulation. Thermohaline circulation is driven by differences in water density, caused by variations in temperature and salinity, leading to vertical and meridional (north-south) movement of water masses. It is characterized by the deep descending motion of cold and dense water in polar regions, followed by its horizontal spreading across ocean basins and upwelling in other regions, rather than zonal (east-west) advection.

31. (B): The average life expectancy of an atom of a radioactive element, also known as its mean lifetime, can be calculated using the relation between the half-life (T½) and the mean lifetime (τ). The mean lifetime is given by τ = T½/ln(2), where ln(2) is the natural logarithm of 2 (approximately 0.693). Given that the half-life of the radioactive element is 100 years, the average life expectancy of an atom of this element can be calculated as 100/0.693, which results in approximately 144 years. This value reflects the average duration an atom of this element is expected to exist before undergoing radioactive decay.

32. (B): During El Niño years, the Walker circulation, which is an atmospheric circulation pattern in the tropical Pacific, typically shifts eastward. El Niño is characterized by warmer than average sea surface temperatures in the central and eastern Pacific Ocean. This warming leads to a disruption of the Walker circulation, which normally flows westward, bringing moist air and rainfall to the western Pacific. The shift eastward during El Niño results in decreased rainfall in the western Pacific and increased rainfall in the central and eastern Pacific regions.

33. (C): Both statements are correct. Deep convection in the atmosphere is characterized by the vigorous ascent of warm moist air, which cools and condenses to form clouds and precipitation. This process results in low outgoing longwave radiation (OLR) because the presence of thick clouds and moisture traps the radiation. Regarding monsoons, they are characterized by bimodal air temperature patterns, with significant temperature variations between the wet and dry seasons. The monsoon system brings about drastic changes in weather, including shifts in temperature, due to the seasonal reversal of wind patterns and the associated changes in precipitation.

34. (D): The acceleration due to gravity (g) is the lowest at the Lehmann discontinuity, which is a boundary within the Earth's interior, located near the base of the lower mantle, above the outer core. The variation in g throughout the Earth's interior is influenced by changes in density and compositional layers. At discontinuities like the Lehmann, transitions in material properties can affect the gravitational acceleration. However, the significant reduction in g is primarily because the force of gravity decreases with the increase in distance from the Earth's center, reaching its minimum at the core-mantle boundary, just above which the Lehmann discontinuity is situated.

35. (A): The spatial resolution of satellite images, which refers to the smallest object that can be detected by the satellite's sensor, is directly dependent on the Instantaneous Field Of View (IFOV) of the sensor. The IFOV is the angular cone of visibility of the sensor and determines the area on the Earth's surface that is seen in one pixel of the image. Therefore, the smaller the IFOV, the higher the spatial resolution of the image, allowing for smaller features to be discerned. This contrasts with spectral, radiometric, and temporal resolutions, which relate to the sensor's ability to discriminate in wavelength, intensity of electromagnetic radiation, and frequency of image acquisition, respectively.

36. (B): When the upward pressure gradient force is balanced by the downward force of gravity, the atmosphere is said to be in a hydrostatic equilibrium. This balance is crucial for understanding weather patterns and atmospheric stability. The pressure gradient force, which results from changes in air pressure over a distance, typically acts to move air from high to low pressure areas, while gravity tends to pull everything towards the Earth's center. The hydrostatic balance does not involve horizontal wind movements, distinguishing it from geostrophic balance, which involves the balance between Coriolis force and the horizontal pressure gradient force.

37. (D): In oxygenated water, the most stable form of nitrogen is N_2, or dinitrogen gas. This stability arises because N_2 is a diatomic molecule with a triple bond between the nitrogen atoms, making it relatively inert and less reactive compared to other nitrogenous compounds like nitrous oxide (N_2O), nitrate (NO_3^-), and nitrite (NO_2^-). In aerobic, or oxygen-rich, conditions, biological processes such as denitrification can convert more reactive nitrogen compounds back to N_2, which is then released into the atmosphere.

38. (D): The Sun holds more than 99% of the mass of the solar system. It is the central star around which all planets, dwarf planets, asteroids, comets, and other celestial bodies orbit. The massive gravitational pull of the Sun is what keeps the solar system together. The remaining mass, less than 1%, is distributed among all the planets, with the gas giants (Jupiter and Saturn) making up the bulk of that. This underscores the Sun's dominance in terms of mass and gravity within the solar system.

39. (D): The magnetic element that may be different at two locations situated on the same magnetic latitude is X, its N-S component. The Earth's magnetic field is a complex, dynamic system that can vary significantly from one location to another due to variations in the Earth's surface and the outer core's movements, where the magnetic field is generated. Two places at the same magnetic latitude can have different local geomagnetic conditions, affecting the N-S component of the magnetic field.

40. (C): The $\delta^{11}B$ (boron isotope ratio) of foraminifera is used as a proxy for the paleo-pH of the ocean. Boron has two stable isotopes, ^{11}B and ^{10}B, and their ratio in marine carbonates like foraminifera shells changes with the pH of seawater. This is because the absorption of ^{10}B and ^{11}B by foraminifera is influenced by the acidity of their environment. Therefore, the $\delta^{11}B$ of foraminifera can provide insights into past ocean acidity and, by extension, atmospheric CO_2 levels, contributing to our understanding of historical climate change.

41. (D): The mineralogical maturity of a sandstone refers to the composition and texture that result from processes affecting the sediment from its source to its final deposition site. Chemical weathering at the source breaks down less stable minerals into more stable ones, while long transportation distances allow for further sorting and rounding of the grains, as well as additional weathering. This combination results in sandstone composed primarily of stable minerals like quartz, which is considered mineralogically mature. Short transportation or quick dumping does not allow sufficient time for these processes to significantly alter the sediment.

42. (C): The eye of a tropical cyclone is warmer than its surrounding environment primarily due to adiabatic compression of air parcels. As air moves inward towards the cyclone's eye, it spirals upwards and outwards. This upward motion in the eyewall leads to cooling and condensation, releasing latent heat. The air then descends in the eye, warming up adiabatically (without heat exchange with the environment) due to compression. This process leads to a relatively warm and calm eye compared to the intense storm activity in the surrounding eyewall.

43. (C): Ultramafic igneous rocks commonly host Platinum Group Elements (PGE) ore deposits. These rocks are high in magnesium and iron and low in silica, and they form in settings that include the Earth's mantle and areas where mantle materials have been emplaced into the crust. The high mantle temperatures and pressures favour the formation of PGE minerals. Ultramafic rocks are commonly associated with large igneous provinces, layered mafic intrusions, and komatiite flows, all of which are potential hosts for significant PGE deposits.

44. (D): In the balance of forces for an atmospheric Ekman layer, the centrifugal force is not involved. The Ekman layer theory describes the flow of fluid under the influence of a uniform pressure gradient, Coriolis force, and viscous forces. This theory is often applied to oceanic and atmospheric circulations to explain the flow direction in the upper layer of the ocean or the lower layer of the atmosphere. The Coriolis force, pressure gradient force, and viscous force interact to produce a spiral effect in the flow, but the centrifugal force, which acts outwardly on a body moving in a circular path, is not a factor in this balance.

46. (A): Barbed drainage patterns indicate a reversal of drainage direction. This pattern is characterized by tributary streams that flow in a direction opposite to the main stream or river, suggesting a historical change in the flow direction due to uplift, tilting, or other geological processes. The "barbs" or hooks formed by the tributaries pointing upstream against the main river flow direction serve as evidence of this reversal, differentiating it from patterns formed by structural controls like faults or folding.

47. (B): Mid-oceanic ridges are characterized by the highest heat flow among the options provided. These underwater mountain ranges, where tectonic plates are diverging, are sites of significant volcanic activity and seafloor spreading. The process of seafloor spreading at mid-ocean ridges involves the upwelling of magma from the mantle to create new oceanic crust, which releases a substantial amount of heat. This heat flow is much higher than that found in cratons (stable interiors of continental plates), collisional mountain belts, or oceanic trenches (where one tectonic plate is subducted under another).

48. (C): Both statements are correct. Turbulent flow is indeed associated with high Reynolds numbers, a dimensionless quantity that helps predict flow patterns in different fluid flow situations. A high Reynolds number indicates that inertial forces dominate over viscous forces, leading to turbulence. Turbulent flow is also associated with strong mixing due to the erratic motion of fluid particles, enhancing the efficiency of momentum, heat, and mass transfer within the fluid.

49. (C): Rayleigh waves, a type of surface wave, are recorded last on a seismogram following an earthquake. Unlike body waves (P-waves and S-waves), which travel through the Earth's interior, Rayleigh waves travel along the Earth's surface and are slower than both P-waves and S-waves, as well as Love waves, another type of surface wave. The slower speed of Rayleigh waves means they arrive at seismic stations after the other types of earthquake waves.

50. (B): The Eocene epoch, part of the Paleogene Period, was the warmest of the epochs listed. The Early Eocene is particularly noted for the Eocene Optimum, a period characterized by significantly higher global temperatures than today. This warmth facilitated lush vegetation and the spread of warm-adapted species across much of the globe. The climate during the Eocene was so warm that even high latitudes experienced climates that supported dense forests, including areas that are now ice-covered.

51. (A): The magnitude of the magnetic field of the Moon is negligible compared to the Earth's magnetic field. The Moon's magnetic field is very weak in comparison, with certain regions possessing slight magnetism due to past magnetic activity. However, globally, the Moon lacks a significant magnetic field like Earth's, which is generated by its molten outer core dynamics. This makes the Moon's magnetic field strength substantially less than Earth's, contributing to a negligible overall magnetic effect.

52. (D): The Mid-Atlantic Ridge is exposed on land, notably in Iceland. This feature makes Iceland a unique place where the mid-oceanic ridge can be observed above sea level. The Mid-Atlantic Ridge is a tectonic plate boundary located along the floor of the Atlantic Ocean, where the Eurasian and North American plates are moving apart. In Iceland, this divergence is manifested on the surface, providing direct access to the processes of seafloor spreading and volcanic activity associated with the ridge.

53. (B): Pollination by winds is not considered an ecosystem service under the usual classifications. Ecosystem services are benefits humans receive from ecosystems, which include provisioning services (like food and water), regulating services (such as climate and disease control), supporting services (such as nutrient cycling and soil formation), and cultural services (like recreational, spiritual, and educational benefits). While pollination is indeed an ecosystem service, it is typically attributed to animal pollinators rather than abiotic factors like wind.

54. (C): The axis of monsoon depression is vertically tilted southward. In the Northern Hemisphere, monsoon depressions, which are areas of low atmospheric pressure associated with the seasonal monsoon, exhibit a southward tilt with height. This orientation is related to the structure and dynamics of the monsoon system, where the interaction of temperature gradients and atmospheric circulation patterns plays a crucial role.

55. (A): Sea level does not increase due to the melting of sea-ice. Sea-ice is already floating on the ocean's surface, and according to the principle of displacement, its melting does not contribute to a rise in sea level. This principle states that the water displaced by the ice is equal in volume to the water produced when the ice melts. In contrast, the melting of continental ice, the warming of water (thermal expansion), and an increase in river runoff contribute to sea-level rise by adding water to the ocean or increasing its volume.

56. (D): Water vapour (H_2O) is a significant greenhouse gas, contributing to the Earth's natural greenhouse effect. Greenhouse gases absorb and emit infrared radiation, warming the planet's surface and lower atmosphere. While other gases like carbon dioxide (CO_2) and methane (CH_4) are often highlighted for their roles in enhancing the greenhouse effect and climate change, water vapour is naturally abundant and plays a crucial role in regulating the Earth's temperature through feedback mechanisms.

57. (A): The gravity field of the Earth, or its gravitational force, would remain the same if the Earth were to be 20% farther from the Sun. Earth's gravity is determined by its mass and the distribution of that mass, not its distance from the Sun. While the Earth's orbit around the Sun is influenced by the Sun's gravity, the strength of Earth's own gravitational field is independent of its distance from the Sun.

58. (D): The resistance of a wire is given by the formula $R = \rho\frac{L}{A}$, where R is the resistance, ρ is the resistivity of the material, L is the length, and A is the cross-sectional area. Halving the length $\left(\frac{1}{2}L\right)$ and quadrupling the area (since the diameter is doubled, and area $\propto d^2$), the new resistance R′ becomes $\frac{1}{2}\times\frac{1}{4}R = \frac{1}{8}R$. Therefore, if the original resistance is 1 ohm, the new resistance would be 1/8 ohm.

59. (A): Bridgmanite is the most abundant mineral in the Earth's lower mantle. It is a high-density, high-pressure phase of magnesium iron silicate and was previously known as perovskite (Mg, Fe)SiO_3. This mineral was named bridgmanite in honor of the physicist Percy Bridgman, a pioneer in high-pressure research. The extreme conditions of the lower mantle, which spans from 660 to 2,900 kilometers below the Earth's surface, stabilize bridgmanite's structure, making it predominant in this region.

60. (A): The kinematic vorticity number (Wk) for pure shear deformation is 0. Pure shear is characterized by an equal and opposite stretching along two perpendicular axes, with no rotation of the material as a whole. In contrast, simple shear involves material rotation and has a kinematic vorticity number different from 0. The kinematic vorticity number quantifies the proportion of rotation (vorticity) to total deformation, with 0 indicating no rotational component, as is the case with pure shear.

61. (D): The Eurasian plate has the lowest average plate velocity among the options listed. Plate velocities vary widely, with some plates moving much faster than others. The Pacific Plate, for instance, is one of the fastest due to the amount of subduction occurring at its boundaries, while the Eurasian Plate, being larger and involved in complex interactions with several other plates, including the African and Indian plates, moves more slowly on average. This lower velocity can be attributed to the plate's interactions with adjacent plates and the resistance it encounters from the surrounding lithosphere and asthenosphere.

62. (C): Increasing the radius of the outer core can increase the P-wave shadow zone. The shadow zone results from the refraction (bending) of seismic waves as they pass through different layers of the Earth. P-waves are refracted by the liquid outer core, creating a zone on the Earth's surface where no P-waves are detected. Increasing the outer core's radius would cause a larger area of the Earth to fall within this shadow zone, as the bending of the P-waves would be more pronounced, further limiting the areas where these waves could be directly detected after an earthquake.

63. (B): The temporal distribution of the genesis of tropical cyclones over the North Indian Ocean annually is bimodal. This means there are two distinct periods each year when conditions are most favorable for cyclone formation. These periods typically occur before and after the summer monsoon season, with peaks in May-June and October-November. The bimodal pattern is influenced by sea surface temperatures, monsoonal winds, and atmospheric conditions, which vary seasonally and affect cyclone formation in the region.

64. (D): Earth's energy budget is realized through radiative, latent heat, and sensible heat processes. The energy budget describes how the Earth balances the energy it receives from the Sun with the energy it emits back into space. Radiative processes involve the absorption and emission of solar and terrestrial radiation. Latent heat processes are associated with phase changes of water (evaporation and condensation), affecting heat distribution. Sensible heat involves the transfer of energy between the surface and the atmosphere through conduction and convection. Together, these processes regulate the Earth's climate system and determine global temperature patterns.

65. (D): A pediment is a gently sloping, concave rock cut surface developed at the base of a steep slope or mountain front, characterized by only a thin debris cover. Pediments are formed through erosional processes, where bedrock is gradually worn down by water runoff, wind, and other mechanical and chemical weathering processes. They often extend from the base of mountains or hills, merging gradually into the adjacent basin or plain. This geomorphological feature is typical of arid to semi-arid environments where limited vegetation allows for the physical weathering processes to dominate, sculpting the landscape into these broad, sloping surfaces.

66. (C): The statement that eskers do not show branching is incorrect. Eskers are sinuous ridges of sand and gravel that form from sediment deposition within subglacial or englacial meltwater channels. They can indeed show branching where meltwater channels diverge, leading to a network of eskers that reflects the complex drainage patterns beneath or within the glacier. These features often exhibit stratification, can extend for many kilometers, and form as glaciers retreat, leaving behind the sediments carried by meltwater streams.

67. (A): Kaolinite indicates the highest degree of chemical weathering among the options given. It is a clay mineral resulting from the intense chemical alteration of silicate rocks, such as feldspar, through weathering processes involving water, which removes silica and leaves behind aluminum oxides and hydroxides. This process, known as leaching, is most effective in warm, wet climates and results in the formation of kaolinite, which is stable under these conditions. The presence of kaolinite in soils or sediments is thus a strong indicator of advanced chemical weathering.

68. (C): The Tropical Easterly Jet is observed over the Indian region during June to September. This jet stream forms over the Indian subcontinent and the Western Indian Ocean during the Northern Hemisphere summer, associated with the Asian monsoon system. It is driven by the temperature contrast between the heated landmass of Asia and the relatively cooler Indian Ocean, contributing to the monsoon circulation by enhancing the upward motion of air over the region, which in turn supports the development of monsoonal rains.

69. (D): In the tropical ocean, the vertical thermal gradient is the lowest in the depth range of 2000-4000 m. This layer, often referred to as the abyssal zone, experiences minimal temperature variations compared to the upper ocean layers. The upper layers, especially the first few hundred meters, are subject to seasonal and diurnal temperature changes. Below the thermocline (around 200-1500 m), where the temperature decreases rapidly with depth, the thermal gradient flattens out, leading to relatively stable conditions in the deep ocean.

70. (B): A striation is a scratch or groove engraved on a hard rock surface by abrasive fragments frozen into moving ice, or trapped between sliding ice and the valley floor. Striations are formed by the grinding action of glaciers as they move over bedrock, carrying with them rocks and sediments that act as abrasive tools. These features are parallel to the direction of glacier movement and provide important clues about the direction and extent of past glacial activity. They are distinct from flutes, ventifacts, and slickensides, which are formed by different geological processes.

71. (D): A neck cutoff occurs when a meander recurves so intensely that it intersects an upstream portion of the river channel, effectively shortening the river path. This abrupt change in the river's course results in a localized increase in the channel gradient and velocity because the river now has a steeper gradient to descend in a shorter distance. This process naturally increases water flow speed in the newly established channel segment, demonstrating how the mechanism described in (A) directly leads to the outcomes described in (B).

72. (A): The correct matches for the paleoceanographic changes with their approximate ages are: Opening of Andaman basin at around 4 million years ago (Ma) (*b*), opening of Red Sea rift at about 20 Ma (*c*), and opening of Drake Passage at approximately 34 Ma (*a*). The Andaman Basin, part of the complex tectonic interactions in the Southeast Asian region, formed relatively recently. The Red Sea rift, resulting from the separation of the Arabian Plate from the African Plate, began to open around 20 Ma. The opening of the Drake Passage, crucial for the establishment of the Antarctic Circumpolar Current, occurred around 34 Ma, significantly impacting global climate.

73. (A): If a framework silicate has a Si:O ratio of 3:8, it implies that an aluminum (Al) atom replaces a silicon (Si) atom in one out of every four tetrahedra. In the silicate tetrahedral structure, Si is typically surrounded by four oxygen atoms, creating a SiO_4 unit. A 3:8 ratio suggests that some Si atoms have been substituted by Al atoms, which also prefer a coordination number of four. This substitution alters the overall Si:O ratio from the typical 1:2 seen in unaltered tetrahedra. For every Al substitution, an extra oxygen is accommodated to maintain charge balance, slightly altering the stoichiometry to reflect the observed ratio.

75. (D): The increase in $\delta^{18}O_{PDB}$ of benthic foraminifera in a deep-sea core from +0.2‰ to +2‰ from bottom to top suggests a combined effect of decreasing temperature and increasing accumulation of polar ice over time. The $\delta^{18}O$ isotope ratio is a proxy for past environmental conditions, including temperature and ice volume. Higher values indicate cooler global temperatures and/or greater ice volumes, as ^{16}O is preferentially stored in ice. Thus, the observed increase in $\delta^{18}O$ values in the foraminifera shells reflects a period of cooling and ice accumulation, which would lower global sea levels and alter oceanic salinity and temperature, influencing $\delta^{18}O$ signatures in marine sediments.

76. (C): The correct graph depicting the oxygen profile in a modern tropical ocean if life were removed is option C. In the current state, marine life consumes oxygen at various depths, contributing to the observed oxygen minimum zone. If life were removed, the oxygen profile would be determined primarily by the physical processes of mixing and diffusion. Since sunlight warms the surface, causing it to mix with the atmosphere, the oxygen levels are higher at the surface. As depth increases, without biological consumption, the oxygen concentration would only slightly decrease due to the reduced mixing with the surface. The profile would not show a significant dip as seen in a system with biological activity. Thus, the graph in option C accurately shows a high surface oxygen concentration with a gentle decline with depth, reflecting the absence of biological consumption and the predominance of physical mixing processes.

77. (A): El Niño is characterized by P: Deeper thermocline in the east than in the west pacific Ocean; Q: Warmer than normal sea surface temperature in the eastern Pacific Ocean and S: Weaker than normal trade winds in the Pacific Ocean. These conditions lead to a reversal of the typical temperature gradient across the Pacific, with warmer waters and reduced upwelling in the east. This disrupts weather patterns globally. La-Nina, on the other hand, is represented by R: Warmer than normal sea surface temperature in the western Pacific Ocean, where the conditions are essentially opposite to those of El Niño, with strengthened trade winds and a deeper thermocline in the west indicating a strengthening of the normal climatic conditions.

78. (C): The rain ratio in the ocean is the ratio between calcareous material and organic material. This ratio is an important parameter in biogeochemical studies, reflecting the balance between inorganic (calcareous) and organic carbon deposition in marine sediments. A higher rain ratio indicates a predominance of calcareous material in the sediment, which can influence the ocean's carbon cycle and the sequestration of carbon in the deep sea.

79. (A): LISS-II is a type of remote sensing sensor that includes a blue band. The blue band is crucial for applications that require water body analysis, coastal studies, and vegetation differentiation. The inclusion of a blue band helps in distinguishing between different types of vegetation and in assessing water quality in aquatic ecosystems. This spectral band is sensitive to chlorophyll absorption, making it valuable for agricultural and forestry applications as well.

80. (D): The crustal Poisson's ratio can be estimated from the difference in arrival times of P (primary) and S (secondary) waves recorded by seismographs. The Poisson's ratio, a measure of the ductility or brittleness of Earth materials, can be calculated using the velocity of P and S waves, which in turn can be inferred from their travel times. Given the specified arrival times at three different stations, the calculated Poisson's ratio of 0.33 suggests a relatively elastic crustal composition. This value is consistent with typical crustal rocks and indicates a capacity for both elastic deformation and a degree of brittleness under stress.

82. (C): The beach ball diagram provided is a graphical representation of the type of stress and movement along a fault plane in geology. In this diagram, the shaded areas represent the regions that move upwards or towards the observer. For a left-lateral strike-slip fault, the movement along the fault plane is horizontal, and if one were to stand on one side of the fault and look across to the other side, that side would appear to have moved to the left. This is consistent with the diagram provided, where if we stand on side A and look towards side B, side B would have moved to the left. This movement does not match the vertical displacement seen in normal or thrust faults, and the direction of displacement is opposite to what would be expected in a right-lateral strike-slip fault. Therefore, the beach ball diagram matches the characteristics of a left lateral strike-slip fault, where side B has moved to the left relative to side A, matching option C.

83. (C): The correct statements are (*a*) A paraconformity does not involve erosion and (*d*) Angular unconformity involves a long gap in sedimentation. A paraconformity represents a type of unconformity where there is no apparent erosion but still signifies a significant hiatus in deposition, often identified by changes in fossil content rather than by physical evidence of erosion. Angular unconformity involves an observable angular difference between the orientations of younger sedimentary rocks and the older, tilted layers beneath them, indicating a substantial period during which deposition ceased, erosion occurred, and then deposition resumed. The Law of Superposition, which states that in any undeformed sequence of sedimentary rocks, each layer is older than the one above it and younger than the one below it, applies to all stratified rocks, not only to deformed strata. Walther's Law applies to the vertical succession of facies, indicating that environments that were once adjacent in a horizontal plane can come to lie atop one another in a vertical sequence of strata, not specifically along thrusted contacts.

84. (B): Statement (A) is correct; Rossby number is indeed a measure of the importance of Earth's rotation in the dynamics of atmospheric motions. It is defined as the ratio of inertial to Coriolis forces. A low Rossby number indicates that the Coriolis effect is significant in the flow pattern, characteristic of large-scale atmospheric motions, such as cyclones and anticyclones. Statement (B) is incorrect; large-scale motions in the atmosphere, such as those influenced significantly by the Earth's rotation, are associated with small Rossby number values, not large ones. Large Rossby numbers are typical of smaller-scale motions where the Coriolis effect is less significant.

85. (A): Statement (A) is true; internal waves, which occur within water bodies at interfaces of different densities, often have larger amplitudes than surface waves generated by the same force. This is due to the density stratification within the body of water that allows for the internal waves to propagate with less energy loss. Statement (B) is false; while stronger stratification can support the formation of internal waves, it doesn't necessarily lead to higher wave amplitudes for a given generating force. Stratification affects the speed and wavelength of internal waves but not directly their amplitude in the manner implied.

86. (C): Vitrinite reflectance is the most precise indicator of coal rank. It measures the percentage of light reflected from the surface of vitrinite particles in a polished specimen of coal. As coal matures, its vitrinite content becomes more reflective. This parameter is widely used in the coal industry to determine the rank of coal, which is a measure of the coal's carbon content and calorific value, and it indicates the stages of coal formation from peat through to anthracite. Vitrinite reflectance is preferred over moisture content, colour of spores, and volatile matter content for its accuracy and reliability.

87. (A): The correct matches are Red tide (*a*) with Dinoflagellates (S), as red tides, or harmful algal blooms, are often caused by the rapid proliferation of dinoflagellates, which can color the water red and have detrimental effects on marine life. Dimethyl sulphide (*b*) is associated with Coccolithophores (R), which are microscopic algae that can produce dimethyl sulfide, a compound that plays a role in cloud formation and climate regulation. Bombay Duck (*c*), known as a fish (Q), is not related to ducks but is a type of lizardfish commonly found in the waters around Mumbai (formerly Bombay), India. Mangals (*d*) are related to Viviparity (P), which is a reproductive strategy in coastal vegetation dominated by mangroves.

88. (A): The statement highlights that urban surfaces generally exhibit higher values of the Bowen Ratio compared to rural areas. This is explained by factors (*a*) and (*b*). Urban areas have a higher proportion of impervious surfaces, such as concrete and asphalt, which absorb and retain heat more efficiently than natural landscapes. This leads to higher sensible heat transfer in urban areas. Furthermore, the lesser coverage of vegetation in urban settings reduces latent heat fluxes because vegetation facilitates evapotranspiration, a process that cools the surface and increases moisture content in the air. Together, these factors contribute to a higher Bowen Ratio, indicating a higher proportion of sensible heat transfer over latent heat transfer in urban environments compared to rural areas.

89. (C): Bringing water from the oxygen minimum zone (OMZ) to the surface ocean would enhance the rate of community respiration drastically. OMZs are characterized by low oxygen concentrations due to the high rate of oxygen consumption by decomposing organic matter, which exceeds the supply of oxygen from the surface. When water from an OMZ is brought to the surface, the newly available oxygen facilitates increased biological activity, including the respiration of aerobic organisms. This results in an enhanced rate of community respiration as organisms take advantage of the increased oxygen availability to break down organic matter.

90. (C): The bulk rock initial isotopic ratio of $^{87}Sr/^{86}Sr$ being higher than the bulk silicate Earth (BSE) and the $^{143}Nd/^{144}Nd$ ratio being higher than the chondritic uniform reservoir (CHUR) implies that the igneous rock sample may have formed from mixed sources of incompatible element-rich and depleted materials. Higher ratios of $^{87}Sr/^{86}Sr$ suggest a contribution from older, crustal material that has had time to develop radiogenic Sr through the decay of ^{87}Rb. At the same time, a higher $^{143}Nd/^{144}Nd$ ratio than CHUR suggests a less radiogenic Nd isotopic signature, indicative of a depleted mantle source. The combination of these isotopic signatures points to a complex source that includes both enriched and depleted components, reflecting the mixing of mantle-derived magma with crustal materials or the melting of a heterogeneously enriched mantle.

91. (C): The correct identification of sand dune types based on their descriptions is as follows: (*a*) These dunes, described as huge landforms especially well-developed in the heart of trade wind deserts, are longitudinal dunes. They align parallel to the prevailing wind direction and can extend for great distances, forming continuous ridges that mirror the wind's direction. (*b*) Transverse dunes, whose crests are ridges roughly perpendicular to the effective wind direction, are common along coastlines where a consistent wind direction allows for the accumulation of sand in elongated forms perpendicular to the wind. (*c*) Climbing dunes, which occur on the windward side of a hill and move up the hillside, demonstrate the ability of wind to transport sand and form dunes in locations with significant topographic relief, such as hillsides or mountain fronts. This description corrects the previous mismatch by accurately associating each dune type with its characteristic formation and environmental setting.

92. (A): Both statements (A) and (B) are true, offering insight into the concept of base-level in geomorphology. Statement (A) accurately describes the base-level as the theoretical lower limit to which rivers can erode the landscape, commonly represented by sea level. This concept is fundamental in understanding river dynamics and landscape evolution, as it sets a limit to the downward erosion by streams and rivers. Statement (B) extends the concept of base-level to deflation basins, where not just the sea level, but also local factors such as the water-table level, calcrete layers, or armoured surfaces can act as a base level. In arid environments, these features create a physical barrier to further erosion, functioning effectively as the local base level and influencing the geomorphic processes.

93. (C): The active and break cycle of the South-West Indian monsoon are considered to be an oscillation of 20-60 days. This phenomenon, often associated with the Madden-Julian Oscillation (MJO), influences the variability of the monsoon. The MJO is characterized by an eastward progression of large regions of both enhanced and suppressed tropical rainfall, observed mainly over the Indian and Pacific Ocean. The cycle significantly affects the distribution and intensity of rainfall during the monsoon season, leading to periods of heavy rain (active phases) followed by intervals of reduced rainfall (break phases).

94. (C): The value of the maximum anomaly on downward continuation by 1 unit, after observing a reduction from 1.2 mgals to 0.8 mgals on upward continuation by one unit, would be 2.4 mgals. This calculation is based on the principle that the gravitational effect decreases with distance from the source. Upward continuation, moving away from the source, diminishes the anomaly, while downward continuation, moving closer, increases it. The change in anomaly value with continuation suggests a predictable pattern, where moving one unit closer to the source (downward continuation) after having moved one unit away (upward continuation) results in a larger increase in the anomaly value than the decrease observed with the upward continuation.

96. (B): The asymmetry factor (AF) of a drainage basin is indeed an indication of possible tectonic tilt of a drainage basin, making Statement (B) correct. However, Statement (A) inaccurately describes the formula for AF; the correct formula for calculating the asymmetry factor involves assessing the orientation of the drainage basin relative to a defined direction, not simply dividing the total area by the area to the right of the trunk river. Therefore, while the concept of using AF to infer tectonic activity is valid, the formula provided in Statement (A) is incorrect.

97. (A): Arranging the following mineral deposits in the order of decreasing depth of formation would be: (*a*) Porphyry type W deposit, (*b*) Porphyry type Cu deposit, (*d*) High-sulfidation Au deposits, (*c*) Bauxite deposit. Porphyry deposits, associated with intrusive igneous activities, typically form at significant depths within the Earth's crust. Among these, porphyry Cu and W deposits are known for their deep-seated origins. High-sulfidation Au deposits, also associated with hydrothermal systems, usually occur slightly shallower than porphyry deposits but still at considerable depths. Bauxite deposits, resulting from the weathering of aluminum-rich rocks under tropical conditions, form at or near the surface, making them the shallowest in this sequence.

98. (D): The incorrect statement regarding Oxygen isotope stages is that the last interglacial centered on ~125 ka is numbered as stage 3. In fact, interglacials are numbered with odd numbers, and the last interglacial, which occurred around 125,000 years ago, is correctly identified as stage 5. Oxygen isotope stages are a systematic way to number the alternating periods of cold (glacials) and warm (interglacials) climates throughout Earth's history, primarily during the Quaternary period. The Last Glacial Maximum, which is the most recent and extensive glaciation within the current Ice Age, occurring approximately 21,000 years ago, is accurately numbered as stage 2. This systematic numbering helps in studying and understanding the sequence and timing of Earth's climate changes.

99. (C): To reconstruct Quaternary climate in a sediment core collected from the central Indian Ocean basin at a water depth greater than 5000 meters, Diatoms, Radiolaria, and Silicoflagellates can be used. These microorganisms are part of the ocean's planktonic community and contribute to the marine sediment record. Their shells, made of silica, preserve well in deep-sea sediments and can be analyzed to infer past oceanic conditions, including water temperature, productivity, and circulation patterns. Their abundance and species composition vary with changes in climate, making them valuable proxies for reconstructing past oceanic conditions. This method excludes organisms not suited for deep-water environments or those not present in Quaternary periods, such as Trilobites and Conodonts, which are extinct.

100. (B): If the surface air temperature increases towards the north in the northern hemisphere, the direction of thermal wind will be Easterly. The thermal wind is a theoretical wind that would result from a difference in air pressure caused by a temperature gradient. In the northern hemisphere, an increase in temperature towards the north would create a pressure gradient force that, when combined with the Coriolis effect, results in winds blowing from high to low pressure, leading to an easterly thermal wind. This concept is fundamental in understanding atmospheric dynamics and how temperature gradients can influence wind patterns across different layers of the atmosphere.

101. (C): Turbidite deposits, which result from underwater landslides or turbidity currents, do cause discontinuous sedimentary records, and this is common in the eastern Bay of Bengal. The characteristics of the Bay of Bengal, including its narrow shelf, significant terrigenous material influx from rivers like the Ganges and Brahmaputra, and its steep continental slope, contribute to the frequent occurrence of turbidity flows. These flows transport sediment down the continental slope into the deep sea, where they form turbidite deposits. This process can interrupt the continuous deposition of marine sediments, creating gaps in the sedimentary record that can complicate the reconstruction of past environmental conditions.

102. (C): For the ocean to remain in a steady state, if the rate of input of a dissolved constituent increases, then the rate of removal of that constituent must also increase to maintain balance, making (A) correct. However, (B) is incorrect because if the rate of input increases and the ocean is to remain in steady state with an increased rate of removal, the residence time of that constituent (the average time a molecule spends in the ocean) will decrease. The residence time is determined by the total amount of the element in the ocean divided by the rate at which it is added or removed. An increase in the rate of input, coupled with a corresponding increase in the rate of removal to maintain steady state, will result in a change in the residence time of the constituent in the ocean.

103. (B): Clear Air Turbulence (CAT) is often associated with wind shear, which is a sudden change in wind speed and/or direction over a short distance. It can occur at high altitudes where there are no visual weather cues, such as clouds, to warn of its presence. The graph in option B shows a sharp increase in wind speed with height around the 10 km mark, which is typical of the jet stream level. This steep gradient in wind speed with respect to height is a classic setup for the development of CAT because it indicates significant wind shear. Such a profile can lead to the mixing of air at different speeds, resulting in turbulence. The other graphs show either a more gradual change in wind speed with height or lower speeds overall, which are less conducive to the formation of CAT. Therefore, the scenario depicted in option B is the most likely to cause Clear Air Turbulence.

104. (B): Slingram, VLF, AFMAG, and MT are electromagnetic (EM) survey methods that utilize different frequency ranges to investigate the subsurface.

(P) Slingram operates typically within the range of 10 Hz to 5000 Hz, making it effective for shallow to medium-depth investigations.

(Q) Very Low Frequency (VLF) methods utilize frequencies in the range of 5 kHz to 30 kHz, exploiting military navigation signals to map subsurface conductivity anomalies.

(R) Audio-Frequency Magnetic (AFMAG) surveys are not traditionally defined by a specific frequency range in the given options but are typically associated with natural or induced audio-frequency bands *i.e.* 1 Hz–1000 Hz.

(S) Magnetotellurics (MT), characterized by a wide frequency range, uses natural Earth field electromagnetic variations from 10^{-4} Hz to 1 Hz, allowing deep Earth exploration. This wide range of frequencies across these methods enables the detection of various geological features, from near-surface structures to deep-seated formations.

105. (B): Tropical cyclones do not attain maximum intensity during the Indian south-west monsoon period primarily due to strong vertical wind shear. Vertical wind shear disrupts the organization of cyclones by tilting the vortex and disrupting the heat engine that drives the cyclone. High wind shear can decouple the top of the cyclone from its base, preventing the cyclone from maintaining or increasing its strength. Despite the high moisture availability during the monsoon, which theoretically could fuel cyclone development, the shear associated with the monsoon circulation inhibits cyclone intensification.

108. (D): Statement I and Statement II have been misunderstood in their conventional interpretation within geophysical exploration. Bright spots on seismic sections actually represent amplitude highs, indicative of strong reflections that can signify gas accumulations. Dim spots, conversely, are amplitude lows and can suggest less porous or permeable layers, or the presence of fluids with different acoustic properties than gas, such as water or oil. Statement II's conventional understanding is incorrect because VS/VP (the ratio of shear wave velocity to primary wave velocity) typically increases in a gas-saturated zone relative to a water-saturated zone due to the lower density and bulk modulus of gas compared to water, affecting the seismic velocities differently. Thus, the correct understanding reverses the implications provided in both statements.

109. (B): Both the assertion that most sinuous rilles on the Moon were formed from lava tubes and the reason that roofs of lava tubes often collapse to reveal their interiors are true. However, the reason given does not serve as a direct explanation for the assertion in this context. Sinuous rilles are believed to form from a combination of volcanic and tectonic processes, including the collapse of lava tubes, but the formation mechanisms can also involve erosional processes by flowing lava. The collapse of lava tube roofs is just one factor in the broader geological processes that contribute to the formation of sinuous rilles.

110. (B): Upwelling regions in the ocean show the shortest food chain. These areas are characterized by the upward movement of nutrient-rich deep waters to the surface, stimulating the growth of primary producers like phytoplankton. This abundance of primary productivity supports a more direct and efficient transfer of energy up the food chain, typically leading to shorter food chains with fewer trophic levels. In upwelling zones, nutrients are readily available, allowing primary producers to flourish, which are then consumed directly by higher trophic levels such as fish, resulting in a rapid and efficient energy transfer.

111. (C): The magnitude of solar tides, generated by the gravitational pull of the Sun on the Earth's waters, is indeed about half that of the lunar tides, which are caused by the Moon. This difference in magnitude is explained by the tidal acceleration being inversely proportional to the cube of the distance between the Earth and the tide-generating body. Despite the Sun's larger mass, its significantly greater distance from the Earth compared to the Moon means that its tidal generating force is less, resulting in smaller solar tides. This relationship underscores the crucial role distance plays in the gravitational interactions governing tidal forces.

112. (C): The correct matches between the geological deposits and formations are:

(*a*) Glaciogenic deposit: Talchir Formation, indicating evidence of ancient glacial activity;

(*b*) Glossopteris flora: Raniganj Formation, known for its Late Carboniferous to Early Permian coal-bearing sediments containing Glossopteris leaves;

(*c*) Dicroidium flora: Panchet Formation, indicative of Permian age flora;

(*d*) Ptilophyllum flora, associated with the Mesozoic era, match with Jabalpur Formation.

113. (B): Weber's Line defines the line of supposed faunal balance between the Oriental and Australian faunal regions. It is one of several lines (including Wallace's Line and Lydekker's Line) proposed to demarcate the significant zoogeographical boundaries in the Indo-Pacific area, especially in and around the Indonesian archipelago. Weber's Line is an attempt to delineate the areas with predominantly Asian fauna from those with predominantly Australian fauna, reflecting the complex biogeographical history of this region where species from both continents intermingle and where unique species have evolved in isolation.

114. (B): The characteristics of the southwest monsoon over different regions of India vary significantly due to the complex interplay of topographical, geographical, and atmospheric factors. In Rajasthan, the characteristic of the southwest monsoon can be identified as the Monsoon Heat Zone (R), a region that experiences intense heating during the summer, contributing to the establishment and strength of the monsoon. The Head Bay of Bengal is known for Monsoon Depression (Q), where low-pressure systems frequently develop and move northwestward, bringing heavy rains to the eastern and central parts of India. The Southern Peninsular region is under the influence of the Subtropical Easterly Jet (P), which affects the rainfall patterns over this area, especially during the onset and progression of the monsoon season.

115. (C): In the Boussinesq approximation used in oceanography, it is assumed that density remains almost constant in all respects except when considering its effect on buoyancy (density multiplied by the acceleration due to gravity, g, in the calculation of pressure). This approximation simplifies the mathematics of fluid dynamics under certain conditions, making it suitable for studying buoyancy-driven flows. A critical assumption is that the vertical accelerations can be neglected, which contrasts with option C, making it the incorrect statement regarding the Boussinesq approximation. This approximation is particularly useful in studying ocean currents and temperature-induced density changes without dealing with the full complexity of compressible fluids.

116. (D): Tropical regions are characterized by high air temperatures and high moisture availability, leading to significant amounts of latent heat release during condensation processes. It's true that the air can hold more moisture as the temperature increases until saturation is reached. However, the change in saturation vapour pressure of air with temperature is not a linear function of air temperature; it is, in fact, an exponential relationship. The saturation vapour pressure increases exponentially with temperature, indicating that a small increase in air temperature can lead to a significantly higher capacity of the air to hold moisture, which is critical in understanding cloud formation and precipitation processes in the tropics.

117. (C): In ichnology, the study of trace fossils, Fugichnia refers to escape traces. These are structures left by organisms as they move upwards or change position within the sediment to escape adverse conditions, such as predation or environmental stress (e.g., burial by sediment or changes in sediment-water interface due to erosion). Escape traces provide valuable insights into the behaviour of ancient organisms and the environmental challenges they faced, contributing to our understanding of paleoecological dynamics.

118. (B): The correct statement about electromagnetic (EM) methods is that the TURAM (Towed Underwater and Marine) method measures the amplitude ratio and relative phase difference between two-receiver coils. This method is used in both ground and marine geophysical surveys to detect subsurface conductive anomalies. By comparing the amplitude and phase of the electromagnetic field at two different points, geophysicists can infer the presence and characteristics of subsurface features, such as mineral deposits or archaeological remains. This technique is valuable in exploration geophysics for providing detailed subsurface conductivity profiles.

120. (A): The peak absorption wavelengths of atmospheric species are key to understanding the Earth's radiation balance and greenhouse effect. Carbon dioxide (CO_2) has a significant absorption band at 15 μm (R), which plays a crucial role in trapping infrared radiation and contributing to the greenhouse effect. Water vapor, another potent greenhouse gas, shows strong absorption in various parts of the infrared spectrum, with a notable peak around 6.7 μm (Q). Ozone (O_3) absorbs ultraviolet radiation from the sun, but in terms of infrared radiation, its most notable absorption peak occurs at 9.6 μm (P), contributing to the greenhouse effect and playing a critical role in the thermal structure of the Earth's atmosphere.

121. (C): The P wave velocity (Vp) of a material can be calculated using the formula

$$Vp = \frac{\left(K+\frac{4}{3}G\right)}{e},$$

where K is the bulk modulus, G is the shear modulus (for a Poisson's solid, G can be derived from K and the Poisson's ratio ν), and ρ is the density. Given a bulk modulus (K) of 120 GPa and a density (ρ) of 3 gm/cc, and knowing that for a Poisson's solid, the relation between K and G is defined by ν, we can calculate the P wave velocity. Assuming a standard Poisson's ratio for Earth materials, the P wave velocity calculated falls around 8.5 km/s, demonstrating how material properties dictate the speed of seismic waves through the Earth's crust and mantle.

122. (A): In the Indian Ocean during winter (December-February), surface currents follow specific patterns due to the seasonal shift in monsoon winds. The Winter Monsoon Current (WMC) predominantly moves westward (Q), influenced by the northeast monsoon winds. The East India Coastal Current, due to the same monsoonal dynamics, flows southward (S) along India's eastern coast. The Somalia Current (SC), affected by the seasonal reversal, flows southward (S) along the coast of Somalia. The West India Coastal Current, running along India's western coast, moves northward (R) during this season. These patterns illustrate the dynamic nature of ocean currents, driven by atmospheric circulation changes with the seasons.

123. (D): Global sea surface temperature (SST) is used as boundary forcing in long-range (4 months & beyond) predictions by global atmospheric Numerical Weather Prediction (NWP) models. SST influences atmospheric circulation patterns and can provide a predictive signal for climate phenomena such as the El Niño-Southern Oscillation (ENSO), which significantly impacts weather patterns worldwide. The inclusion of SST in NWP models is crucial for improving the accuracy of long-term weather forecasts, as it represents a critical component of the Earth's climate system, affecting moisture availability, heat content, and atmospheric circulation.

124. (B): The 2015 Gorkha earthquake in Kathmandu originated on the Main Himalayan Thrust (MHT), a major fault system where the Indian Plate is underthrusting the Eurasian Plate. This megathrust earthquake is characteristic of the tectonic activity in the Himalayan region, which results from the ongoing continental collision between the Indian and Eurasian plates. The MHT is responsible for many significant historical earthquakes in the region, and understanding its behaviour is crucial for assessing seismic hazards in the Himalayas. The earthquake was not an in-sequence event, nor was it associated with a strike-slip fault or deep focus mechanisms, but rather resulted from thrust faulting related to the compressional forces driving the uplift of the Himalayas.

125. (B): Light-absorbing aerosols in the atmosphere cause surface cooling and atmospheric warming. These aerosols, including black carbon and dust, absorb sunlight, reducing the amount of solar radiation reaching the Earth's surface, thereby cooling it. However, the energy absorbed by these aerosols heats the atmosphere itself. This dual effect can alter thermal gradients and potentially affect weather patterns and cloud formation. The atmospheric warming can also contribute to the melting of glaciers and ice caps when these aerosols deposit on snow, absorbing more solar radiation than the surrounding white ice and snow.

126. (C): The separation distance between the maximum and minimum anomaly values along a total field magnetic anomaly profile over a single pole can provide information about the depth of the pole. Given that the horizontal component of the Earth's magnetic field is thrice its vertical component in the survey area, this ratio influences the shape of the magnetic anomaly. Based on the given separation and the characteristics of the Earth's magnetic field, the pole is located at a depth of 80 meters. This depth can be estimated by analyzing the geometry of the magnetic anomaly and applying principles from magnetic field theory that relate the anomaly's features to the source depth.

127. (A): Among the given options, chloride ions (Cl^-) form the most stable complex with copper (Cu) in acidic hydrothermal fluids. Copper readily complexes with chloride in these environments, significantly affecting its mobility and concentration. The stability of copper-chloride complexes is especially notable in hydrothermal systems, where high temperatures and acidic conditions prevail. These complexes play a crucial role in the transportation and deposition of copper, leading to the formation of copper-rich mineral deposits. The interaction between copper and chloride is a key factor in the geochemistry of hydrothermal ore-forming processes.

128. (B): Matching the column-I terms with their correct associations in column-II results in: Density-based spatial clustering is a technique used for identifying clusters of points in space based on their density, making it related to unsupervised learning methods (S). Random forest, a versatile machine learning algorithm used for classification and regression tasks, plays a significant role in supervised image classification (R), effectively managing high-dimensional data like satellite images. The Receiver Operating Characteristic (ROC) curve is a tool used to assess the performance of a classification algorithm (P), by plotting the true positive rate against the false positive rate at various threshold settings. Dark object subtraction is a method used in the atmospheric correction of satellite images (Q), aiming to remove atmospheric haze by subtracting the reflectance values of the darkest pixels.

129. (B): In a VLF electromagnetic survey, the real anomaly is calculated based on the ratio of the secondary field to the primary field. Given a primary magnetic field of 20 units and a secondary field making an angle of 120° with a magnitude of 5 units, the real component of the secondary field that is in phase with the primary field can be determined using trigonometric relationships. The real anomaly, in this case, represents the percentage increase or decrease in the field strength due to subsurface conductive structures. With the given values and angle, the real anomaly percentage can be calculated to be approximately 25%, indicating a significant influence of subsurface features on the observed electromagnetic fields.

130. (C): The Köppen climate classification system uses letters to represent various climate types based on temperature and precipitation patterns. For the given climate types and symbols: (*a*) Tropical wet climate with no dry season is represented by Af, indicating constant, year-round precipitation and high temperatures typical of tropical rainforests. (*b*) Mediterranean climate is designated as Cs, characterized by hot, dry summers and cool, wet winters, typical of the regions bordering the Mediterranean Sea. (*c*) Marine west coast type climate is represented by Cfb, which is common in areas with mild winters, cool summers, and precipitation year-round, often found on the western coasts of continents. (*d*) Mid-latitude desert climate is marked by BWk, indicating a dry climate with significant temperature variation, found in continental interiors away from the moderating effects of large water bodies.

131. (A): For clouds with a fixed liquid water path, cloud optical depth is inversely proportional to the cloud droplet effective radius. This relationship implies that, for a given amount of water content in a cloud, a larger number of smaller droplets will result in a higher optical depth compared to fewer larger droplets. This is because smaller droplets scatter light more efficiently than larger ones, making the cloud appear thicker or more "optically dense" to incoming solar radiation. The optical depth of a cloud is a crucial parameter in determining the cloud's radiative properties and its effect on climate by influencing both solar reflectance and terrestrial emissivity.

133. (A): The statement that the time scale of large-scale motion in the atmosphere is much smaller than the time scale of the rotating Earth is not true. In fact, large-scale atmospheric motions, such as planetary waves and jet streams, have time scales that are significant compared to the rotation period of the Earth. These motions are influenced by the Earth's rotation, which is a fundamental aspect of geophysical fluid dynamics. The Coriolis effect, a result of Earth's rotation, significantly affects the path of these large-scale motions. Therefore, their dynamics cannot be properly understood without considering the time scale of Earth's rotation, making the time scale of these motions not "much smaller" but rather comparable or responsive to the rotational period.

134. (B): Shear failure in rocks with pre-existing fractures under confining pressures greater than 300 MPa is governed by Byerlee's Law. Byerlee's Law provides an empirical relationship that describes the stress conditions under which rocks will fracture or slip along pre-existing fractures. It states that the shear stress on a fault increases with confining pressure until a critical point, beyond which even high confining pressures cannot prevent slip or shear failure along the fault. This law is particularly useful in understanding the mechanics of faulting and earthquake generation deep within the Earth's crust and upper mantle, where high-pressure conditions prevail.

135. (D): The magnetic anomaly profiles of two anomalous bodies A and B, positioned vertically and extending infinitely close to the magnetic equator in the N-S and E-W directions, respectively, without remanence, would be dissimilar, with A producing little or no anomaly. This is because the Earth's magnetic field at the magnetic equator is horizontal, and the magnetization of a body aligned in the N-S direction (parallel to the Earth's field) would produce a very weak or negligible magnetic anomaly. In contrast, a body oriented in the E-W direction would cut across the Earth's magnetic field lines, creating a stronger and more noticeable magnetic anomaly.

136. (B): When a landmass undergoes subsidence to achieve a thickness of 1.1 km, from an original thickness of 2.0 km, with a previously associated Bouguer anomaly of −113 mgals and free-air anomaly of +113 mgals, the free-air anomaly would adjust to 0 mgals. The free-air anomaly corrects for the elevation of the landmass above sea level, and if the landmass subsides, reducing its elevation, the gravitational effect of the reduced elevation would lead to a decrease in the free-air anomaly. Since the landmass's thickness and, consequently, its elevation has decreased significantly due to subsidence, the gravitational attraction at the surface decreases, balancing out the effect and resulting in a free-air anomaly closer to zero.

137. (C): Assertion (A) is correct in stating that Cheniers are linear beach ridges separated by low-lying swamps and developed parallel to the coast. These features are typically composed of shell fragments and coarse sands, formed above the high tide level by wave and wind action. They represent episodes of marine deposition separated by periods of non-deposition or erosion, often influenced by changes in relative sea level or sediment supply. Reason (R), however, is false regarding the specific process leading to chenier development. While sequential transgression and regression of a coastal area do lead to changes in the coastal environment, they are not the direct cause of chenier formation. Instead, cheniers are more closely associated with the dynamic interaction between sediment supply, wave action, and sea-level changes, rather than changes in littoral drifts alone.

138. (B): The mineral assemblages listed in Group-I correspond to specific metamorphic facies, which are indicative of the pressure-temperature conditions under which the minerals formed. Garnet-muscovite-biotite-sillimanite-quartz assemblage is characteristic of the Amphibolite facies (3), which represents medium to high-temperature and pressure conditions. Orthopyroxene-clinopyroxene-plagioclase-garnet assemblage is typical of the Granulite facies (1), indicative of high-temperature and medium to high-pressure conditions. Glaucophane-lawsonite-albite-jadeite assemblage is found in the Blueschist facies (4), which forms under high-pressure and relatively low-temperature conditions, typical of subduction zones. Lastly, Chlorite-albite-epidote-actinolite assemblage is indicative of the Greenschist facies (2), representing low to medium-temperature and pressure conditions.

139. **(C):** The normal log response for a high resistivity formation that is thinner than the spacing AM and is sandwiched between two thick low resistivity formations will indicate a larger thickness than the actual H1 but with lower resistivity than R1. This effect is due to the averaging nature of the logging tool's response over its measuring volume. The tool's inability to fully resolve the thin high-resistivity layer results in a reading that blends the resistivities of the high and low-resistivity formations, leading to an apparent resistivity that is lower than the true resistivity of the high-resistivity layer and an apparent thickness that is greater than the true thickness.

140. **(B):** Statement (A) is incorrect because sea breeze circulation is an example of a thermally driven circulation and is fundamentally baroclinic, not barotropic. Baroclinic circulation involves density variations with depth, primarily caused by temperature differences, such as those between land and sea surfaces that drive the sea breeze. Statement (B) is correct; sea breeze circulation can indeed be explained using Bjerknes circulation theorem, which describes the generation of circulation from thermal contrasts. The theorem applies to various scales of atmospheric motions, including sea breezes, where the temperature difference between the warmer land and cooler sea surfaces in the afternoon generates a circulation pattern.

141. **(B):** The given schematic topographic profile is showing different geomorphic settings that can be identified as they occur from the foothills of the Himalayas towards the Ganga River. Region A is labeled as Bhabhar, which is the narrow zone of coarse alluvial deposits where the streams coming down from the mountains disappear into permeable sediments. Region B is labeled as Terai, which follows Bhabhar; it is a marshy and swampy region where the streams re-emerge. This area is characterized by thick forests and a variety of wildlife. Region C is labeled as Bhangar, which represents the older alluvium forming terraces higher than the floodplains. Lastly, region D is labeled as Khadar, which is the newer, younger deposits of the floodplains that are renewed almost every year. Thus, these regions collectively show the transition from mountainous to riverine environments.

142. **(B):** Denitrification is not responsible for the formation of Oxygen Minimum Zones (OMZ) in the ocean; rather, it is a process that occurs within OMZs. OMZs form primarily due to high primary production at the surface, which results in a large supply of organic matter sinking to depth. This organic matter is then respired by bacteria, consuming oxygen and leading to low oxygen concentrations. Slow vertical mixing limits the replenishment of oxygen from the surface or surrounding waters. Denitrification, the conversion of nitrate to nitrogen gas by bacteria in the absence of oxygen, is a consequence of the low-oxygen conditions within OMZs but does not cause the oxygen depletion itself.

143. (C): In a hydrostatic model, vertical velocity is computed using the continuity equation. The continuity equation in atmospheric and oceanic dynamics represents the principle of mass conservation. It relates the divergence of horizontal winds or currents to the vertical velocity. Specifically, in a hydrostatic model, where vertical acceleration is assumed to be negligible due to the hydrostatic balance, the vertical velocity is derived to ensure mass conservation given the horizontal divergence. This approach accounts for the upward or downward movement of air or water necessary to maintain the balance of mass as air or water moves horizontally in the system.

144. (C): To determine the contribution of magmatic fluid in the formation of a Volcanogenic Massive Sulphide (VMS) deposit with a $\delta^{34}S$ value of +12‰, given the magmatic hydrothermal fluid has a $\delta^{34}S$ of 0‰ and seawater has a $\delta^{34}S$ of +20‰, we use isotopic mixing calculations. The $\delta^{34}S$ value of +12‰ suggests that the sulphur isotopic composition is a result of mixing between magmatic fluid and seawater. Using a simple two-end-member mixing model, the fraction of sulphur derived from the magmatic fluid can be calculated. The calculated contribution of magmatic fluid to the deposit's sulphur isotopic composition is approximately 40%, indicating that 40% of the sulphur in the deposit originated from magmatic hydrothermal fluid and the remaining 60% from seawater.

145. (C): Mass wasting is the movement of soil and rock downslope under the influence of gravity. The types of mass wasting are often categorized by their moisture content and the speed of movement. In the diagram, 'X' is placed in the 'fast' and 'dry' category, which corresponds to Rockfall. Rockfalls occur very quickly and involve the detachment and free fall of rocks from a steep slope or cliff.

'Y' is in the 'wet' and 'fast' category, which is indicative of Solifluction. Solifluction is a slow mass wasting process that occurs in periglacial environments, where the ground thaws on the surface and becomes saturated with water from melting permafrost, causing the soil to flow slowly downhill.

'Z' is in the 'wet' and 'slow' category, representing Creep. Soil creep is a very slow movement of soil down a slope, typically aided by the expansion and contraction of materials due to freeze-thaw cycles, the hydration and dehydration of clays, and the activities of organisms. It can take years for creep to noticeably affect structures and landscapes.

146. (B): Dish and pillar structures are sedimentary features observed on the vertical section of a bed. They result from the dewatering of sediments, where water escapes upwards through the sediment column, leading to the formation of dish-shaped depressions and vertical conduits or pillars. These features are indicative of rapid sediment deposition and subsequent compaction, often seen in turbidite sequences or other rapidly deposited sedimentary environments. Dish structures help in interpreting paleoenvironments and understanding the depositional processes, particularly in recognizing events of high-energy deposition followed by rapid burial.

147. (A): Sun-synchronous polar orbiting satellites are designed to pass over any given point on the Earth's surface at the same local solar time on each pass. This is achieved by placing the satellite in an orbit with a tilt of approximately 98 degrees to the equator. The orbit's orientation relative to the Earth-sun system slowly rotates with the same period as the Earth's orbit around the sun, ensuring that the satellite's overpass time at any given point remains constant throughout the year. This characteristic is particularly useful for Earth observation satellites, allowing for consistent lighting conditions for imagery and data collection.

148. **(B):** Embayments are observed in δ-type porphyroclasts in a mylonite. Mylonites are strongly deformed rocks formed in the deeper parts of the Earth's crust along zones of intense shearing. δ-type porphyroclasts are specific types of mineral inclusions within the mylonite matrix that exhibit embayment structures, which are indicative of deformation processes where the surrounding matrix engulfs the harder porphyroclasts. These structures are key in understanding the kinematics of shear zones, indicating the sense of movement and providing insights into the dynamics of crustal deformation.

149. **(B):** The statement that "Four categories of ecosystem services were first documented in Global Environmental outlook 6" is false. The four categories of ecosystem services—provisioning, regulating, cultural, and supporting—were actually conceptualized and widely disseminated before the Global Environmental Outlook 6. They were prominently featured in the Millennium Ecosystem Assessment report published in 2005. This comprehensive assessment brought widespread attention to the concept of ecosystem services, outlining the immense value ecosystems provide to human well-being and survival. The categorization of these services has since become a foundational concept in environmental science and policy, guiding conservation efforts and the sustainable management of natural resources.

Previous Years' Paper

Joint CSIR-UGC NET/JRF

Earth, Atmospheric, Ocean & Planetary Sciences

JUNE-2023

(Exam held on 08-06-2023)

PART-A

1. Three fair cubical dice are thrown, independently. What is the probability that all the dice read the same?

A. 1/6 B. 1/36

C. 1/216 D. 13/216

2. Price of an item is increased by 20% of its cost price and is then sold at 10% discount for ₹ 2160. What is its cost price?

A. 1680 B. 1700

C. 1980 D. 2000

3. Sum of all the internal angles of a regular octagon is _______ degrees.

A. 360 B. 1080

C. 1260 D. 900

4. Consider two datasets A and B, each with 3 observations, such that both the datasets have the same median. Which of the following MUST be true?

A. Sum of the observations in A = Sum of the observations in B.

B. Median of the squares of the observations in A = Median of the squares of the observations in B.

C. The median of the combined dataset = median of A + median of B.

D. The median of the combined dataset = median of A.

5. If the sound of its thunder is heard 1 s after a lightning was observed, how far away (in m) was the source of thunder/lightning from the observer (given, speed of sound = x m s^{-1}, speed of light = y m s^{-1})?

A. x^2/y B. $xy/(y - x)$

C. $xy/(x - y)$ D. y^2/x

6. Three friends having a ball each stand at the three corners of a triangle. Each of them throws her ball independently at random to one of the others, once. The probability of no two friends throwing balls at each other is:

A. 1/4 B. 1/8

C. 1/3 D. 1/2

7. Two semicircles of same radii centred at A and C, touching each other, are placed between two parallel lines, as shown in the figure. The angle BAC is:

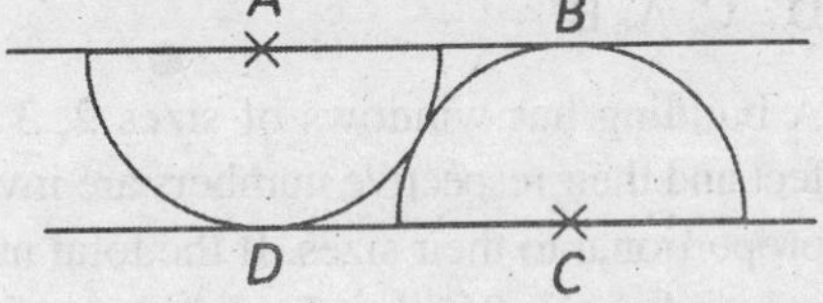

A. 30° B. 35°

C. 45° D. 60°

1. B	2. D	3. B	4. D	5. B	6. A	7. A

8. What is the largest number of father-son pairs that can exist in a group of four men?

A. 3 B. 2
C. 4 D. 6

9. The populations and gross domestic products (GDP) in billion USD of three countries A, B and C in the years 2000, 2010 and 2020 are shown in the two figures below.

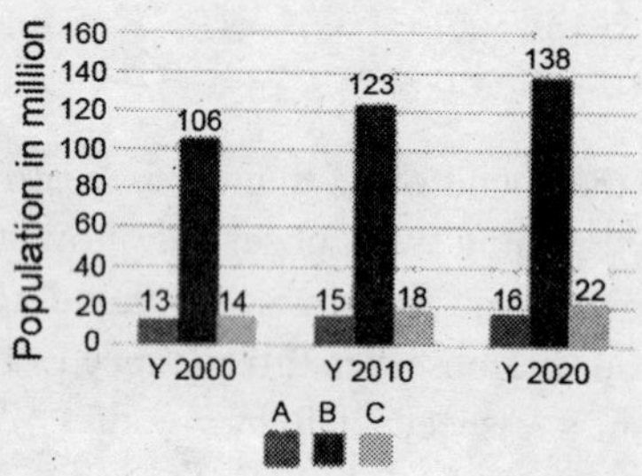

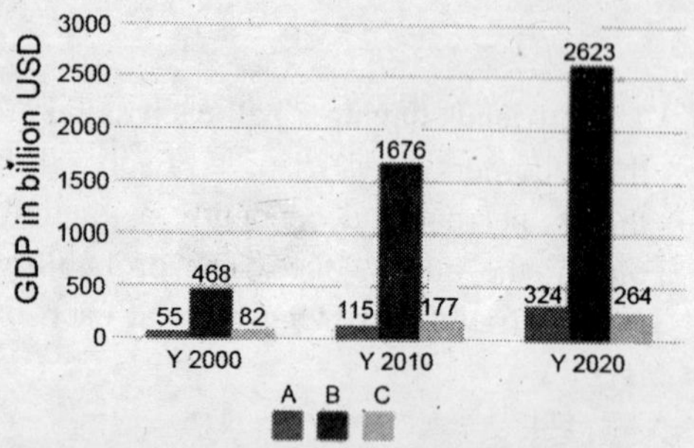

The decreasing order of per capita GDP of these countries in the year 2020 is:

A. A, B, C
B. A, C, B
C. B, C, A
D. C, A, B

10. A building has windows of sizes 2, 3 and 4 feet and their respective numbers are inversely proportional to their sizes. If the total number of windows is 26, then how many windows are there of the largest size?

A. 4 B. 6
C. 12 D. 9

11. In a buffet, 4 curries A, B, C and D were served. A guest was to eat any one or more than one curry, but not the combinations having C and D together. The number of options available for the guest were:

A. 3 B. 7
C. 11 D. 15

12. At a spot S en-route, the speed of a bus was reduced by 20% resulting in a delay of 45 minutes. Instead, if the speed were reduced at 60 km after S, it would have been delayed by 30 minutes. The original speed, in km/h, was:

A. 90 B. 80
C. 70 D. 60

13. A 50 litre mixture of paint is made of green, blue, and red colours in the ratio 5 : 3 : 2. If another 10 litre of red colour is added to the mixture, what will be the new ratio?

A. 5 : 2 : 4 B. 4 : 3 : 2
C. 2 : 3 : 5 D. 5 : 3 : 4

14. Which of the numbers $A = 162^3 + 327^3$ and $B = 612^3 - 123^3$ is divisible by 489?

A. Both A and B
B. A but not B
C. B but not A
D. Neither A nor B

15. Three consecutive integers a, b, c, add to 15. Then the value of $(a - 2)^2 + (b - 2)^2 + (c - 2)^2$ would be:

A. 25 B. 27
C. 29 D. 31

16. Given only one full 3 litre bottle and two empty ones of capacities 1 litre and 4 litres, all ungraduated, the minimum number of pourings required to ensure 1 litre in each bottle is:

A. 2 B. 3
C. 4 D. 5

8. A **9.** A **10.** B **11.** C **12.** D **13.** D **14.** A **15.** C **16.** B

17. Persons A and B have 73 secrets each. On some day, exactly one of them discloses his secret to the other. For each secret A discloses to B in a given day, B discloses two secrets to A on the next day. For each secret B discloses to A in a given day, A discloses four secrets to B on the next day. The one who starts, starts by disclosing exactly one secret. What is the smallest possible number of days it takes for B to disclose all his secrets?

A. 5 B. 6
C. 7 D. 8

18. If two trapeziums of the same height, as shown below, can be joined to form a parallelogram of area $2(a + b)$, then the height of the parallelogram will be:

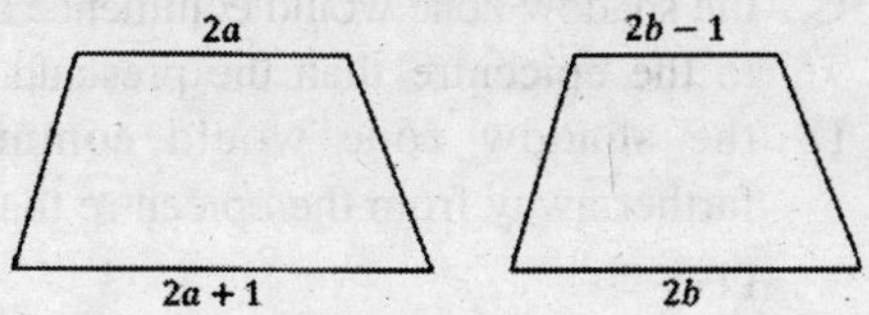

A. 4 B. 1
C. 1/2 D. 2

19. Twenty litres of rainwater having a 2.0 µmol/L concentration of sulphate ions is mixed with forty litres water having 4.0 µmol/L sulphate ions. If 50% of the total water evaporated, what would be sulphate concentration in the remaining water:

A. 3 µmol/L B. 3.3 µmol/L
C. 4 µmol/L D. 6.7 µmol/L

20. When a student in Section A who scored 100 marks in a subject is exchanged for a student in Section B who scored 0 marks, the average marks of the Section A falls by 4, while that of Section B increases by 5. Which of the following statements is true?

A. A has the same strength as B
B. A has 5 more students than B
C. B has 5 more students than A
D. The relative strengths of the classes cannot be assessed from the data

PART-B

21. The Moon has a stronger influence on tides than the Sun because:

A. the gradient of the gravitational pull by the Moon at the Earth is larger than that by the Sun.
B. gravitational pull exerted by the Moon on the Earth is larger than that by the Sun
C. the gradient of the gravitational pull by the Sun at the Earth is larger than that by the Moon
D. the moon has higher surface density than the Sun

22. If the positions of Earth and Mars were to be interchanged in the solar system, then compared to their present velocities:

A. both will orbit around the Sun without any change in their velocities
B. both will orbit around the Sun with lower velocities
C. Earth orbits around the Sun with a higher velocity, while Mars orbits with a lower velocity
D. Earth orbits around the Sun with a lower velocity, while Mars orbits with, a higher velocity

23. Which one of the following is the predominant mechanism of heat transfer through the Earth's lithosphere?

A. Convection B. Radiation
C. Conduction D. Advection

17. A	**18.** B	**19.** D	**20.** B	**21.** A	**22.** D	**23.** C

24. Which one of the following is the CORRECT statement for Geoid and Spheroid?
A. Both are equipotential surfaces.
B. Geoid is equipotential surface but Spheroid is not equipotential surface.
C. Geoid is not equipotential surface but Spheroid is equipotential surface.
D. Neither Geoid nor Spheroid is an equipotential surface.

25. The inclination of the Earths magnetic field is the least at which one of the following locations?
A. Trivandrum B. Visakhapatnam
C. Shillong D. Mumbai

26. Which one of the following is an elliptical streamline ice-moulded landform with an elongated down-glacier tail?
A. Cuesta B. Drumlin
C. Esker D. Till

27. The longest lived volatile organic compound in the atmosphere is:
A. Isoprene B. Methane
C. Ethane D. Benzene

28. The thickness of which of the following atmospheric layers is the greatest?
A. 10 hPa to 1 hPa
B. 110 hPa to 101 hPa
C. 510 hPa to 501 hPa
D. 1010 hPa to 1001 hPa

29. An example of supergeostrophic flow is:
A. Anticyclonic flow
B. Tornado
C. Extra tropical cyclone
D. Gale wind

30. Which one of the following ocean currents has the largest volumetric flow rate?
A. Antarctic Circumpolar Current
B. Kuroshio Current
C. Agulhas Current
D. Gulf Stream

31. 'Osmosis' in aquatic organisms is a process that involves exchange of:
A. salt from high to low concentration through a semi-permeable membrane
B. dissolved oxygen and carbon dioxide through gills of an organism.
C. water from low to high salt concentration through a semipermeable membrane.
D. nutrients from high to low concentration regime.

32. If the seismic wave velocities do not vary with depth inside the Earth's mantle, then:
A. there would not be any shadow zone.
B. the shadow zone would not change.
C. the shadow zone would commence closer to the epicentre than the present.
D. the shadow zone would commence farther away from the epicentre than the present.

33. Which phytoplankton group is commonly associated with the following terms: Corals, Red tides, paralytic shellfish poisoning, and zooxanthellae?
A. Coccolithophores
B. Blue-green algae
C. Silicoflagellates
D. Dinoflagellates

34. Which radioactive parent-daughter pair has half-life approximately equal to the age of the Earth?
A. ^{87}Rb – ^{87}Sr B. ^{238}U – ^{206}Pb
C. ^{40}K – ^{40}Ar D. ^{235}U – ^{207}Pb

35. Which one of the following types of mass wasting is typically associated with unstable fresh tephra on hillslopes?
A. Earth flow B. Mud flow
C. Debris flow D. Lahar

24. B	**25.** A	**26.** B	**27.** B	**28.** A	**29.** A	**30.** A	**31.** C	**32.** D	**33.** D
34. B	**35.** D								

36. Which among the following is primarily a cyclostrophic flow?
A. Tropical cyclone
B. Monsoon depression
C. Tornado
D. Anticyclone

37. The lowering of temperature from 4°C to 0°C causes the density of seawater (salinity 35) to:
A. increase non-linearly
B. decrease linearly
C. decrease non-linearly
D. remain unchanged

38. Which one of the following is CORRECT with respect to the residence time of water at the global level?
A. Atmosphere > Rivers
B. Oceans < Atmosphere
C. Rivers > Groundwater
D. Oceans > Groundwater

39. Which one of the following is NOT a local or temporary base level of erosion for the trunk or parent stream?
A. Dyke or sill B. Lake
C. Dam D. Tributary

40. Which one of the following minerals contains potassium?
A. Kaolinite B. Chamosite
C. Illite D. Berthierine

41. Select the CORRECT statement:
A. The oligotrophic regions have high nutrient concentration but low productivity due to less sunlight.
B. The oligotrophic regions have low nutrient concentration and low productivity.
C. The eutrophic regions have low nutrient concentration but high productivity due to plenty of sunlight.
D. The eutrophic regions have low nutrient concentration and low productivity.

42. Negative geothermal gradients are observed over:
A. hot spots B. mid-oceanic ridges
C. volcanoes D. subduction zones

43. The Sun is directly overhead at Chennai (13°N):
A. once a year B. twice a year
C. four times a year D. everyday

44. Red animals at 300 m depth in the ocean will appear:
A. Red B. Blue
C. White D. Black

45. Which soil is deficient in nitrogen and humus but rich in calcium and phosphate?
A. Black soil B. Red soil
C. Desert soil D. Laterite soil

46. Which one of the following gases has net flux from air to sea?
A. N_2O B. SO_2
C. CH_4 D. CO

47. In seas, the 'rule of constant proportions' relates to:
A. Salinity
B. Water mass identification
C. T-S diagram
D. Pressure-Density relationship

48. The most abundant gas in the stratosphere is:
A. N_2 B. O_2
C. O_3 D. CFCs

49. Under invariant moisture conditions, the maximum relative humidity in India is:
A. at the noon
B. at midnight
C. just before sunrise
D. just after sunset

36. C	**37.** A	**38.** D	**39.** D	**40.** C	**41.** B	**42.** D	**43.** B	**44.** D	**45.** C
46. B	**47.** A	**48.** A	**49.** C						

50. The Instantaneous Field of View (IFOV) is a measure of which of the following resolution aspects of a remote sensing image?
A. Spatial B. Spectral
C. Radiometric D. Temporal

51. Diurnal tide, in each tidal day, refers to:
A. two highs and two lows
B. one high and one low of almost similar magnitude
C. a large high and a small low
D. a small high and a large low

52. Ratio of Cl^- and Na^+ is constant everywhere in the open ocean because:
A. the residence time of both is more than mixing time of the ocean.
B. both are removed in equal proportion when NaCl is formed
C. as compared to Na^+, Cl^- is more abundant and has larger residence time.
D. as compared to Na^+, Cl^- is more abundant and has smaller residence time.

53. The angle between the orbital plane of the Earth around the sun and the plane of the Earth's equator is known as:
A. Solar zenith angle
B. Solar declination angle
C. Solar elevation angle
D. Solar inclination angle

54. Energy condition is the least in which of the following depositional environments?
A. Beach B. Barrier bar
C. Lagoon D. Tidal channel

55. What is the best described in the given equation?

$$Mg_2SiO_4 + 4CO_2 + 4H_2O \rightarrow 2Mg^{2+} + 4HCO_3^- + H_4SiO_4$$

A. Carbonate formation
B. Weathering
C. Primary production
D. Dolomitization

56. Low pressure systems that form over the northern Indian Ocean during the Indian southwest monsoon season do not grow to a tropical cyclone category since:
A. the Inter-Tropical Convergent Zone (ITCZ) is found in its northernmost location over India
B. there exists strong vertical shear of the horizontal winds.
C. India experiences abundant and widespread rainfall.
D. Indian subcontinent is rich with abundant moisture.

57. Which among the following is a product of volcanic eruption?
A. Ladang B. Laccolith
C. Lapilli D. Lapies

58. Arranging from older to younger geological age, which one is the correct sequence of these continental breakup episodes:

A Columbia
B Ur
C Rodinia
D Pangaea

A. BADC B. BDAC
C. ABDC D. BACD

59. The movement of particles obliquely up the slope of a beach by the swash and directly down this slope by the backwash is referred to as:
A. Beach Drift B. Beach Accretion
C. Saltation D. Illuviation

60. The water table is the top surface of:
A. zone of aeration B. vadose zone
C. phreatic zone D. unsaturated zone

61. The maximum radiation of the Sun occurs in which one of the following wavelengths?
A. 0.3 μm B. 0.4 μm
C. 0.5 μm D. 0.6 μm

50. A **51.** B **52.** A **53.** B **54.** C **55.** B **56.** B **57.** C **58.** D **59.** A **60.** C **61.** C

62. The island arcs and the back-arc basins are located on:

A. the overriding plate.
B. the subducting plate.
C. the overriding and subducting plates, respectively
D. the subducting and overriding plates, respectively.

63. In which of the following atmospheric layers, temperature decreases with altitude?

A. Tropopause B. Stratosphere
C. Mesosphere D. Thermosphere

64. If the temperature in the atmosphere decreases at a rate of 11°C/km with height, a saturated air parcel would be:

A. stable B. conditionally stable
C. neutral D. unstable

65. Foreland basin is associated with:

A. Himalaya B. African Rift Valley
C. Hawaii D. Mid-Atlantic Ridge

66. Which one of the following atmospheric oscillations DOES NOT influence the Indian Monsoon significantly?

A. Semiannual Oscillation (SAO)
B. North Atlantic Oscillation (NAO)
C. El Niño-Southern Oscillation (ENSO)
D. Pacific Decadal Oscillation (PDO)

67. Meghalayan stage is associated with:

A. Late Pleistocene B. Early Holocene
C. Mid Holocene D. Late Holocene

68. The M-Plane of a fault plane is the one that includes; the slickenline on the plane as well as its:

A. strike B. dip
C. pole D. rake

69. For which one of the following pairs of stations the difference in their normal gravity fields is the least?

A. New Delhi and Chennai
B. Ahmedabad and Kolkata
C. Hyderabad and Nagpur
D. Panaji and Mumbai

70. Which of the following layers of the Earth contributes the maximum to its gravity?

A. Crust B. Mantle
C. Outer core D. Inner core

PART-C

71. Baroclinic instability can be viewed as a shear instability that draws energy from:

A. horizontal shear of mean flow
B. kinetic energy from vertical shear of mean flow
C. potential energy of background state
D. vertical temperature gradient of background state

72. Match the following ecosystems with the feature associated with them.

Biome	**Feature**
(*a*) Lentic	(*i*) softer bed helps in colonization of invertebrate
(*b*) Seashores	(*ii*) occurs in running water
(*c*) Estuaries	(*iii*) highly productive due to huge inflow of nutrients from land
(*d*) Lotic	(*iv*) occurs in lake or pond

Choose the CORRECT option:

	(*a*)	(*b*)	(*c*)	(*d*)
A.	(*ii*)	(*i*)	(*iii*)	(*iv*)
B.	(*iii*)	(*iv*)	(*i*)	(*ii*)
C.	(*iv*)	(*i*)	(*iii*)	(*ii*)
D.	(*ii*)	(*iii*)	(*i*)	(*iv*)

62. A **63.** C **64.** D **65.** A **66.** A **67.** D **68.** C **69.** B **70.** B **71.** C **72.** C

73. The following diagram shows phase relations in Orthoclase-Albite system at 1 bar pressure. If 'P' is the initial composition of liquid, which one of the following statements is INCORRECT regarding cooling and crystallization of liquid?

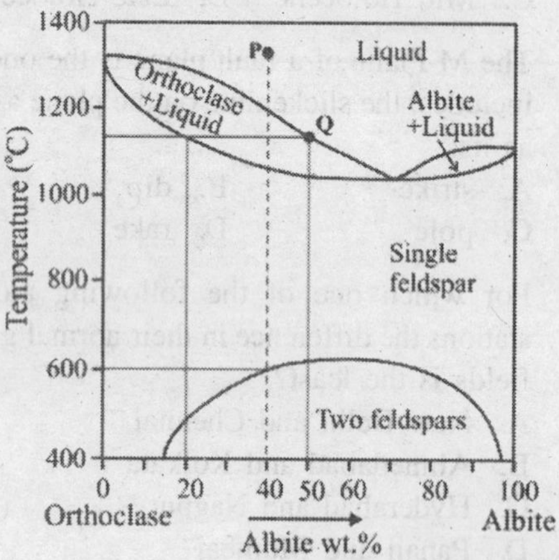

A. The initial composition of liquid contains 40 wt% albite and 60 wt% orthoclase

B. At point 'Q', the proportions (wt%) of crystal and liquid are 33.33 and 66.67, respectively

C. On complete crystallization of liquid, the final composition of rock contains 60 wt% perthite and 40 wt% antiperthite

D. On cooling of liquid, the first appearance of albite exsolution in orthoclase occurs at 600 °C

74. Match the zooplankton types with their respective foods.

Zooplankton type	**Food**
(*a*) Herbivores	(*i*) Live animal
(*b*) Carnivores	(*ii*) Live plant material/ algae
(*c*) Omnivores	(*iii*) Both plant and animal
(*d*) Detrivores	(*iv*) Dead organic matter

Choose the CORRECT option:

	(*a*)	(*b*)	(*c*)	(*d*)
A.	(*ii*)	(*i*)	(*iii*)	(*iv*)
B.	(*i*)	(*ii*)	(*iii*)	(*iv*)
C.	(*ii*)	(*i*)	(*iv*)	(*iii*)
D.	(*ii*)	(*iv*)	(*iii*)	(*i*)

75. Consider the following statements regarding trace of fault scarps.

(*a*) The steeper the dip of the fault surface, the more linear the resulting fault scarp.

(*b*) In the case of low-angle or nearly horizontal thrust fault, even without erosional dissection, the scarp will follow the topography.

(*c*) If the landscape is irregular, the scarp will be as sinuous or crenulated as a contour line.

Choose the CORRECT option:

A. (*a*) and (*b*) are correct, but (*c*) is incorrect

B. (*a*) and (*c*) are correct, but (*b*) is incorrect

C. (*b*) is correct and (*a*) and (*c*) are incorrect

D. (*a*), (*b*) and (*c*) are correct

76. The distribution of the pelagic sediments shown in dark shade in the figure above indicate:

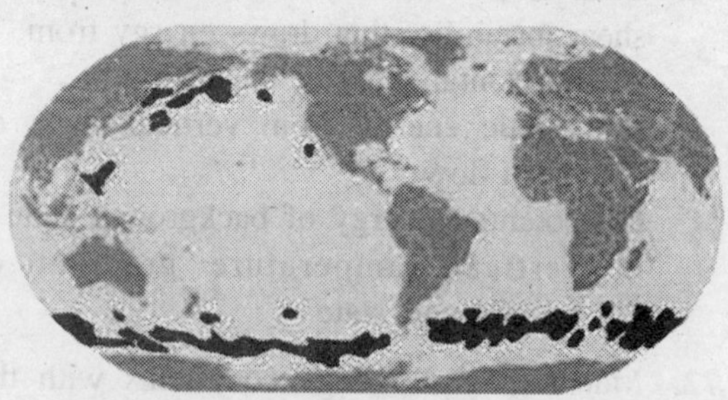

A. Siliceous ooze of diatoms

B. Siliceous ooze of radiolarians

C. Abyssal clay

D. Calcareous ooze

73. C	**74.** A	**75.** D	**76.** A

77. Match the geophysical inversion methods in Column-I with the corresponding associated terms in Column-II.

	Column-I	Column-II
(*a*)	Marquardt-Levenberg Least Squares inversion	(*i*) Quenching
(*b*)	Minimum norm Least Square inversion	(*ii*) Overdetermined problem
(*c*)	Simulated Annealing	(*iii*) Lagrange multiplier
(*d*)	Genetic Algorithm	(*iv*) L-∞ norm
		(*v*) Fitness function

Choose the CORRECT option:

	(*a*)	(*b*)	(*c*)	(*d*)
A.	(*i*)	(*iii*)	(*ii*)	(*iv*)
B.	(*ii*)	(*iii*)	(*i*)	(*v*)
C.	(*iii*)	(*v*)	(*iv*)	(*i*)
D.	(*iii*)	(*iv*)	(*i*)	(*ii*)

78. Analysis of time series data of kinetic energy shows a spectral peak at a periodicity of 24 hours. If this periodicity corresponds to an inertial oscillation, what is the latitude at which the velocity observations are taken?

A. 10 °N B. 24 °N
C. 30 °N D. 45 °N

79. Rainfall of intensity of 20 mm/h occurred over a watershed of area 10^6 m^2 for a duration of 6 h. Measured direct runoff volume in the stream draining the watershed was 30,000 m^3. The precipitation not available to runoff in this case is:

A. 9 cm B. 3 cm
C. 17.5 mm D. 5 mm

80. Viviparous germination is a characteristic feature of:

A. Marine algae B. Sandy beach flora
C. Mangroves D. Periphyton

81. Match the following:

	List-I	List-II
(*a*)	Beheaded stream	(*i*) A valley or col in a ridge or range through which no stream passes
(*b*)	Water gap	(*ii*) Sharp change in the direction of a stream
(*c*)	Wind gap	(*iii*) A valley or pass through a ridge or range through which a stream runs
(*d*)	Elbow of capture	(*iv*) Stream that is deprived of part or all of its former watershed by stream capture
		(*v*) Stream that has gained more area by stream capture

Choose the CORRECT option:

	(*a*)	(*b*)	(*c*)	(*d*)
A.	(*i*)	(*iii*)	(*v*)	(*ii*)
B.	(*iv*)	(*iii*)	(*i*)	(*ii*)
C.	(*v*)	(*ii*)	(*i*)	(*iii*)
D.	(*iv*)	(*iii*)	(*i*)	(*v*)

82. The figure shows seasonal variations in three biogeochemical parameters in the North Atlantic Ocean. Identify the parameters shown in curves A, B and C.

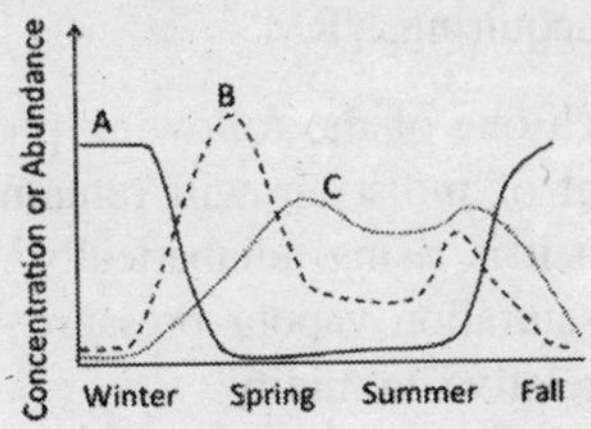

A. A–Phytoplankton, B–Nitrate, C–Zooplankton
B. A–Nitrate, B–Phytoplankton, C–Zooplankton
C. A–Zooplankton, B–Nitrate, C–Phytoplankton
D. A–Zooplankton, B–Phytoplankton, C–Nitrate

77. B **78.** C **79.** A **80.** C **81.** B **82.** B

83. Consider the following statements and choose the CORRECT option:

Statement (A): Impoundment of a river decreases its downstream entrainment capacity.

Statement (B): River flow velocity drops in a reservoir.

A. Both (A) and (B) are true
B. Both (A) and (B) are false
C. (A) is true, but (B) is false
D. (A) is false, but (B) is true

84. Which of the following group is the food source for the large Antarctic whales?

A. Ostracodes B. Amphipods
C. Euphausiids D. Copepods

85. Consider a hypothetical rock unit at 10° N with little or no north (X) and vertical (Z) components of NRM, but a strong east (Y) component. Which one of the following inferences is NOT VALID?

A. The rock unit acquired its NRM when it was at the magnetic equator.
B. Earth's magnetic field was under transition to a reversal, when the rock unit acquired its NRM.
C. The rock unit moved northward by 10° since acquiring NRM.
D. The rock unit rotated through 90° since acquiring NRM.

86. Which one of the following properties of a parcel of moist air will remain unchanged when it is rising adiabatically?

A. saturation vapour pressure
B. relative humidity
C. mixing ratio
D. air temperature

87. Consider the following statements:

Statement (A): In the tri-cell hypothesis proposed to explain the general circulation of the atmosphere, the Ferrel cell is thermally direct cell.

Statement (B): Monsoon depressions that form during the southwest Indian monsoon season weaken considerably like tropical cyclones as they experience landfall on the east coast of India.

Choose the CORRECT option:

A. Statement (A) is true; Statement (B) is false
B. Statement (A) is false; Statement (B) is true
C. Both Statements (A) and (B) are true
D. Both statements (A) and (B) are false

88. For an un-limited nutrient supply scenario, which of the following schematic diagrams would depict the correct Chlorophyll profile in the euphotic zone?

A. 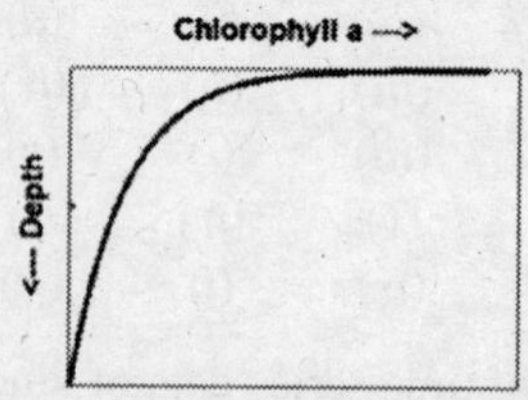

B. 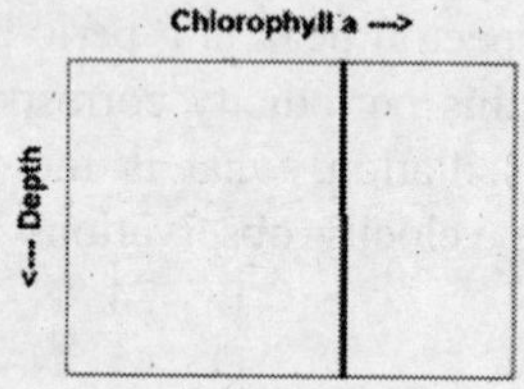

C. 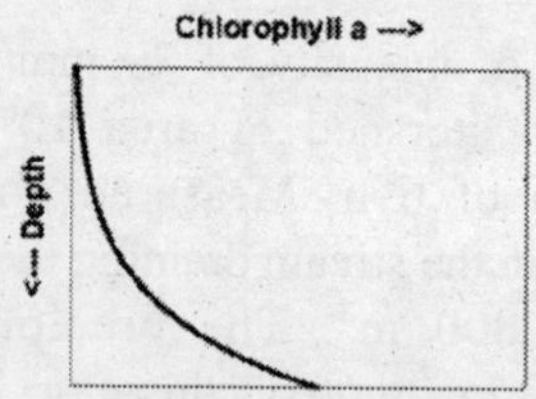

D. 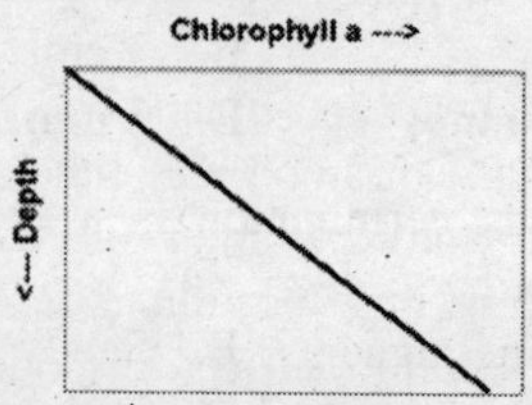

83. D	84. C	85. B	86. C	87. D	88. A

89. Imbrication is a good indication to identify which type of deposit?

A. Glacial B. Fluvial
C. Aeolian D. Landslide

90. The following AFM diagram shows the stability of minerals in garnet zone where P, Q, R and S represent four pelitic assemblages. Identify garnet absent assemblage.

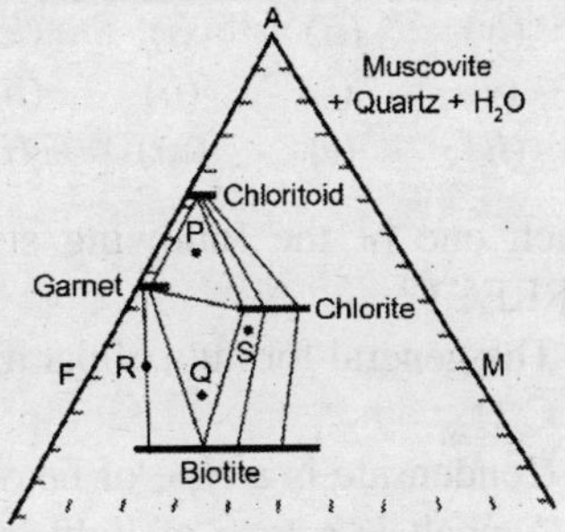

A. R B. Q
C. P D. S

91. Match the following:

Column-I	Column-II
(*a*) Tropical cyclone	(*i*) Balance between Coriolis force and centrifugal force
(*b*) Thermal wind	(*ii*) Statically stable atmosphere
(*c*) Inertial motion	(*iii*) Warm core
(*d*) Buoyancy oscillation	(*iv*) Jet stream

Choose the CORRECT option:

	(*a*)	(*b*)	(*c*)	(*d*)
A.	(*iv*)	(*ii*)	(*i*)	(*iii*)
B.	(*iii*)	(*iv*)	(*i*)	(*ii*)
C.	(*iv*)	(*iii*)	(*ii*)	(*i*)
D.	(*iii*)	(*i*)	(*iv*)	(*ii*)

92. The surface heat flux (q_s) and bathymetry (b) at a location A of an oceanic lithosphere are 70 mW/m^2 and 2.5 km, respectively. The lithosphere at this location is 25 My old. Using the cooling half-space model for the oceanic lithosphere and assuming all physical properties remain constant, the q_s (in mW/m^2) and b (in km) pair at the location B at 50 My will be:

A. 35.0, 5.0 B. 49.5, 3.54
C. 44.2, 3.82 D. 51.5, 2.96

93. Approximately how much water vapour needs to be added to dry air (molecular weight = 29) to raise the moist air's temperature by 1%?

A. 1% B. 3%
C. 7% D. 10%

94. **Assertion (A):** Velocities necessary to erode a consolidated clay bank are comparable to those that move pebbles and cobbles.

Reason (R): This is because of the strong cohesiveness of clay-size particles and their relative smoothness.

Choose the CORRECT option:

A. (A) is correct, but (R) is incorrect
B. (A) is incorrect, but (R) is correct
C. Both (A) and (R) are correct and (R) is the correct explanation of (A)
D. Both (A) and (R) are correct and (R) is not the correct explanation of (A)

95. In the given schematic plot (from surface to 1000 m) showing the subsurface euxinic condition for tropical ocean, what parameters are represented by blue, green and red curves?

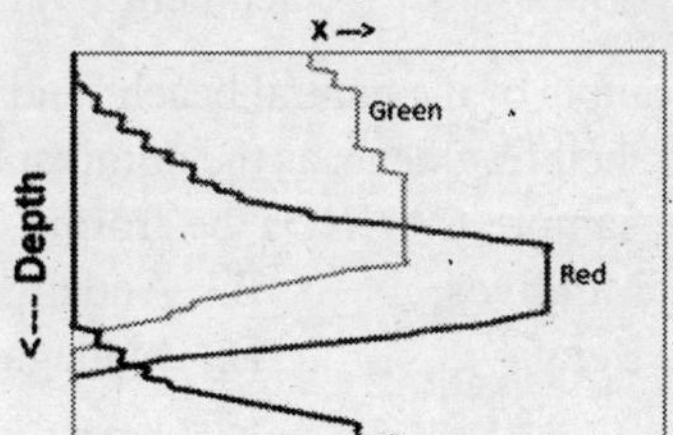

A. Blue - [O_2], Green - [NO_3^-], Red - [SO_4^{2-}]
B. Blue - [NO_3^-], Green - [Chlorophyll a], Red - [SO_4^{2-}]
C. Blue - [NO_2^-], Green - [O_2], Red - [H_2S]
D. Blue - [H_2S], Green - [O_2], Red - [NO_3^-]

89. B **90.** D **91.** B **92.** B **93.** B **94.** C **95.** D

96. The narrowest bound within which all eigen values (λ) of the matrix

$$A = \begin{bmatrix} 2 & 1 & 1 \\ 1 & 3 & 1 \\ 1 & 1 & 3 \end{bmatrix} \text{ fall is:}$$

A. $0 \le \lambda \le 5$ B. $-1 \le \lambda \le 4$
C. $-1 \le \lambda \le 6$ D. $1 \le \lambda \le 4$

97. Consider the following statements:

Statement (A): While nitrogen is the most abundant element in the Earth's atmosphere, concentration of carbon is much lower.

Statement (B): CO_2 reacts with seawater and forms bicarbonate and carbonate, making the concentration of carbon more than nitrogen in the ocean.

Choose the CORRECT option:
A. Both the statements are TRUE.
B. Both the statements are FALSE
C. Statement (A) is TRUE and (B) is FALSE
D. Statement (A) is FALSE and (B) is TRUE

98. In the Himalaya, great earthquakes are associated with slip along which one of the following major thrusts?
A. Main Himalayan Thrust (MHT)
B. Main Boundary Thrust (MBT)
C. Main Central Thrust (MCT)
D. South Tibet Detachment (STD)

99. A sample of the natural beach sand has quartz and shell fragments as the dominant minerals. The sample CANNOT be from:
A. Maldives B. Andaman
C. Kerala D. Madagascar

100. Match the geomorphic concepts with the earth scientists who proposed them.

Geomorphic concept	Proponent
(*a*) Systems	(*i*) B. Willis and E.J. Wayland
(*b*) Etchplanation	(*ii*) G.K. Gilbert
(*c*) Landscape equilibrium	(*iii*) M.F Thomas
(*d*) Bornhardt formation	(*iv*) J. Tricart
	(*v*) J. T. Hack

Choose the CORRECT option:

	(*a*)	(*b*)	(*c*)	(*d*)
A.	(*iv*)	(*iii*)	(*i*)	(*v*)
B.	(*iv*)	(*ii*)	(*i*)	(*iii*)
C.	(*v*)	(*i*)	(*ii*)	(*iii*)
D.	(*iv*)	(*v*)	(*iii*)	(*i*)

101. Which one of the following statements is CORRECT?
A. The general formula of paraffin series is C_nH_{2n}
B. Condensate is a type of heavy crude oil
C. Asphalt is a type of light crude oil
D. The formula of Toluene is C_7H_8

102. Match the following:

Event	Main Effect
(*a*) Opening of the Drake passage	(*i*) Intensification of the Kuroshio current
(*b*) Panama seaway closure	(*ii*) Saltier North Atlantic surface waters
(*c*) Closing of the Indonesian-Australian passage	(*iii*) Formation of Antarctic Circumpolar Current
(*d*) Closure of the Bering Strait	(*iv*) Strengthening of the Atlantic thermohaline circulation

Choose the CORRECT option:

	(*a*)	(*b*)	(*c*)	(*d*)
A.	(*iii*)	(*iv*)	(*i*)	(*ii*)
B.	(*iii*)	(*i*)	(*iv*)	(*ii*)
C.	(*i*)	(*iv*)	(*ii*)	(*iii*)
D.	(*ii*)	(*iii*)	(*i*)	(*iv*)

96. A	**97.** A	**98.** A	**99.** A	**100.** C	**101.** D	**102.** A

103. If the tilt of the Earth is increased from 23.5° to 40°, we would expect the climate at 40° N to have:

A. hotter summers and colder winters than at present.
B. cooler summers and milder winters than at present.
C. hotter summers and milder winters than at present.
D. cooler summers and colder winters than at present.

104. At an altitude equivalent to 50% of the Scale Height of the atmosphere (8 km), the air density will be approximately ______ % of the surface air density.

A. 40 B. 50
C. 60 D. 70

105. Ten electrodes are arranged at equal intervals of 10 m along a profile. Wenner-Schlumberger configuration is used for data recording with highest lateral resolution, What will be the apparent resistivity (in Ω m) corresponding to the deepest level measurement when 1 Ampere current flow between current electrodes yields 200 mV potential difference between potential electrodes?

A. 40.6 B. 81.2
C. 125.6 D. 251.2

106. In a Horizontal Coplanar loop system (Slingram method), 4% error was made while measuring the T-R separation. The % error in the measured anomaly is:

A. 2% B. 4%
C. 8% D. 12%

107. Match the geomorphic features with the geomorphic processes:

Geomorphic feature	Geomorphic process
(*a*) Demoiselle	(*i*) Fluvioglacial process
(*b*) Ridge and swell	(*ii*) Coastal process
(*c*) Varve	(*iii*) Fluvial process
(*d*) Pingo	(*iv*) Arid process
	(*v*) Periglacial process

Choose the CORRECT option:

	(*a*)	(*b*)	(*c*)	(*d*)
A.	(*iv*)	(*iii*)	(*i*)	(*v*)
B.	(*v*)	(*i*)	(*ii*)	(*iv*)
C.	(*iv*)	(*ii*)	(*i*)	(*iii*)
D.	(*iv*)	(*v*)	(*iii*)	(*i*)

108. Match the pelitic mineral assemblages in Group-I with the corresponding metamorphic facies in Group-II.

Group-I	Group-II
(*a*) Muscovite + chlorite + chloritoid + quartz	(*i*) Amphibolite
(*b*) Biotite + muscovite + garnet + sillimanite + quartz	(*ii*) Eclogite
(*c*) Biotite + garnet + cordierite + sillimanite + quartz	(*iii*) Green schist
(*d*) Muscovite + kyanite + garnet + biotite + quartz	(*iv*) Granulite

Choose the CORRECT option:

	(*a*)	(*b*)	(*c*)	(*d*)
A.	(*iv*)	(*iii*)	(*i*)	(*ii*)
B.	(*ii*)	(*i*)	(*iv*)	(*iii*)
C.	(*iii*)	(*i*)	(*iv*)	(*ii*)
D.	(*iii*)	(*iv*)	(*ii*)	(*i*)

109. The following figure shows locations of a few volcanic islands on an active tectonic plate. The numbers on them indicate their ages in Ma. The plate is:

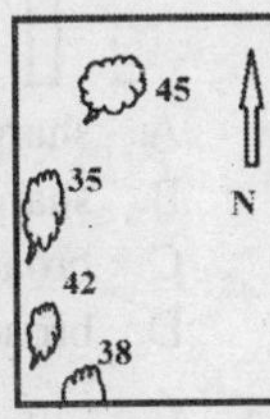

A. oceanic and subducting towards west, under a continental plate
B. oceanic and overriding, over a subducting oceanic plate on the west
C. continental and overriding, over a subducting oceanic plate on the east
D. continental and moving northwards over a hotspot

103. A **104.** C **105.** C **106.** D **107.** A **108.** C **109.** B

110. Consider the following statement and conclusions and decide which of the conclusions logically follows the statement.

Statement: Normalized Difference Vegetation Index (NDVI) is computed from difference between visible and near-infrared (NIR) reflectance.

Conclusions:

I. Vegetation strongly reflects in visible band and absorbs NIR radiation.

II. In standard false colour composite, red colour is assigned to NIR band and other colours to visible bands.

A. Only I is true
B. Only II is true
C. Both I and II are true
D. Both I and II are false

111. Consider the two-dimensional geophysical models, A, a vertical sheet and B, a horizontal sheet of equal dimensions as shown in the following figure. Compared to A, the gravity anomaly profile across B is:

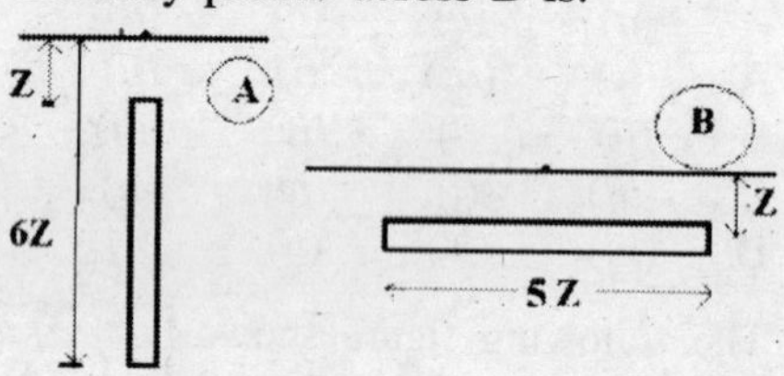

A. sharper and has a larger magnitude
B. sharper but has a smaller magnitude
C. broader but has a smaller magnitude
D. broader and has a larger magnitude

112. If S is the solar constant and α is the planetary albedo, which of the following is the correct expression for the effective temperature (Te) of the Earth? ($\in$ is emissivity and σ is Stefan-Boltzmann constant).

A. $T_e = \sqrt{\frac{s(1-\alpha)}{\in\sigma}}$ B. $T_e = \sqrt[4]{\frac{s(1-\alpha)}{4\in\sigma}}$

C. $T_e = \sqrt[4]{\frac{s(1-\alpha)}{\in\sigma}}$ D. $T_e = \sqrt[4]{\frac{s(\alpha-1)}{\in\sigma}}$

113. Which of the following lithostratigraphic units are CORRECTLY paired?

A. Ambaji Basin - South Delhi Terrane
B. Berach Granite - Singhbhum Craton
C. Ongole Domain - Southern Granulite Terrain
D. Mahadek Formation - Cuddapah Basin

114. If a vertical photograph was taken at a flying height of 5000 m above sea level using a camera with a 152-mm-focal-length lens, then what would be the photo scale at points A and B, which lie at elevations of 1200 m and 1960 m, respectively?

A. 1 : 25,000 & 1 : 20,000
B. 1 : 50,000 & 1 : 40,000
C. 1 : 12,500 & 1 : 10,000
D. 1 : 20,000 & 1 : 25,000

115. If the tropical upper troposphere is warming and the mid-latitude upper troposphere is cooling, and the mid-latitude lower troposphere is warming at a higher rate than the tropical lower troposphere, then:

A. the subtropical jet stream weakens
B. the intensity of the subtropical jet stream remains the same
C. the wind shear will increase at upper levels and decrease at lower levels
D. the wind shear weakens at upper levels and strengthens at lower levels

116. According to the 2011 census, the correct decreasing order of the Indian states in terms of urban population to total population ratio is:

A. Tamil Nadu, Kerala, Maharashtra, Gujarat
B. Maharashtra, Tamil Nadu, Kerala, Gujarat
C. Kerala, Maharashtra, Gujarat, Tamil Nadu
D. Kerala, Maharashtra, Tamil Nadu, Gujarat

110. D **111.** D **112.** B **113.** A **114.** A **115.** C **116.** A

117. A vector field $\vec{F}$ is given by

$$\vec{F} = (x + c_1 z)\vec{i} + (c_2 x - 3z)\vec{j} + (x + c_3 y + c_4 z)\vec{k}.$$

If $\vec{F}$ is irrotational, then:

A. $c_1 = 2, c_2 = 0, c_3 = -1$
B. $c_1 = 0, c_2 = 1, c_3 = 2$
C. $c_1 = 1, c_2 = 0, c_3 = -3$
D. $c_1 = 3, c_2 = 1, c_3 = 0$

118. If the angular velocity of the Earth is reduced by half, which of the following can happen?

A. The size of the extratropical cyclones will increase.
B. The size of the extratropical cyclones will reduce.
C. The size of the extratropical cyclones will remain the same.
D. The extratropical cyclones will not form.

119. Consider the following statements in connection with water particles' motion under a propagating ocean wave:

Statement P: Water particles move in circular orbits with a decrease in the diameter with increasing depth when ocean depth is more than half of the wavelength of a propagating surface wave.

Statement Q: If the depth is between 1/2 and 1/20 of the wavelength of propagating surface wave, the particle's trajectory becomes elliptical without any change in the diameter with increasing depth.

Statement R: If the depth is less than 1/20 of the wavelength of propagating surface wave, the particle's trajectory becomes elliptical with a reduction in diameter with increasing depth.

Choose the CORRECT option.

A. Statements P and Q are True, Statement R is False
B. Statement P is True, Statements Q and R are False
C. Statements P and Q are False, Statement R is True
D. All the Statements are True

120. Consider the following statements about streams that formerly flowed across a now faulted landscape. The stream will be:

(*a*) impounded against the scarp if they flow from the downthrown block to the upthrown block.
(*b*) impounded against the scarp if they flow from the upthrown block to the downthrown block.
(*c*) rejuvenated if they flow from the upthrown to the downthrown block.
(*d*) rejuvenated if they flow from the downthrown block to the upthrowm block.

Choose the CORRECT option:

A. (*a*) and (*d*) are true
B. (*b*) and (*c*) are true
C. (*a*) and (*c*) are true
D. (*b*) and (*d*) are true

121. A cyclone with a central low of 950 hPa is embedded in a region with surface pressure of 1020 hPa. The height of the 250 hPa level is the same within and outside the cyclone. If the mean virtual temperature of the surface to 250 hPa layer is 10 °C within the cyclone, the same outside the cyclone will be _____ by approximately _____ °C.

A. lower, 15
B. lower, 10
C. higher, 10
D. higher, 15

122. S-tectonite foliations typically trace the ________ plane of the finite strain ellipsoid.

A. XZ
B. XY
C. YZ
D. XYZ

117. C	118. A	119. B	120. C	121. A	122. B

123. Match the following S.P. logging responses in column-I with the corresponding causes in column-II.

Column-I	Column-II
(*a*) Negative S.P.	(*i*) Rmf > Rw
(*b*) SSP	(*ii*) Rw > Rmf
(*c*) Positive S.P.	(*iii*) Shaly sandstone bed
(*d*) PSP	(*iv*) Sand bed with 100% Sw

Choose the CORRECT option:

	(*a*)	(*b*)	(*c*)	(*d*)
A.	(*i*)	(*iv*)	(*iii*)	(*ii*)
B.	(*ii*)	(*iii*)	(*iv*)	(*i*)
C.	(*i*)	(*iv*)	(*ii*)	(*iii*)
D.	(*ii*)	(*iv*)	(*iii*)	(*i*)

124. Which one of the following statements is FALSE?

A. Photosynthesis increases seawater pH.
B. Rise in atmospheric CO_2 has decreased ocean pH.
C. Rise in atmospheric CO_2 has affected ocean alkalinity.
D. Rise in atmospheric CO_2 has decreased ocean carbonate concentrations.

125. Which one of the following is NOT a characteristic of sheath folds?

A. Develop in Shear zones
B. Folded hinge line
C. Folded stretching lineation
D. Strongly non-cylindrical

126. The following table mentions some of the Global Navigation Satellite Systems (GNSS) along with their country and status of operation.

GNSS		Country of operation		Operational status	
A1	GPS	B1	India	C1	Fully Operational
A2	Galileo	B2	European Union (EU)	C2	Not fully operational
A3	NavIC	B3	USA		

Which of the following sets describes a correct combination?

A. A1 - B2 - C1, A2 - B2 - C2, A3 - B1 - C1
B. A1 - B3 - C1, A2 - B2 - C2, A3 - B1 - C2
C. A1 - B1 - C1, A2 - B2 - C2, A3 - B3 - C1
D. A1 - B1 - C2, A2 - B3 - C1, A3 - B2 - C1

127. Given profiles are the second derivative of zonal wind with the meridional distance.

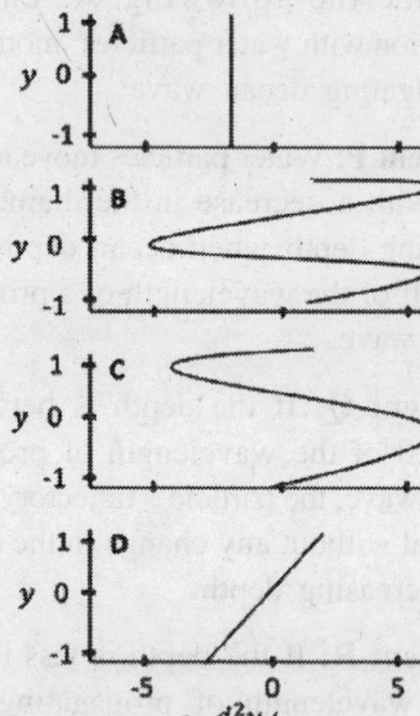

Choose the profiles corresponding to barotropic instability.

A. A and D B. B, C and D
C. B and C D. D

123. C	124. C	125. C	126. B	127. B

128. Which of the following phytoplankton biomass distribution pattern (Chlorophyll a fluorescence) can be expected in oligotrophic seas under prolonged summer days?

Choose the correct option:

A. 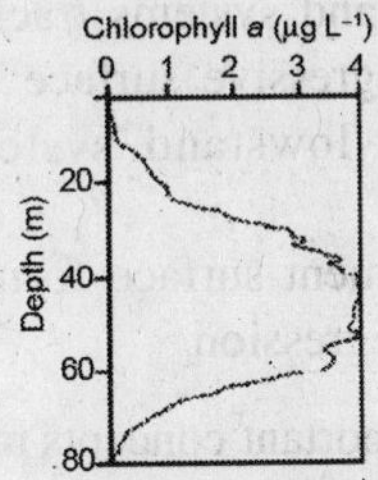

B. 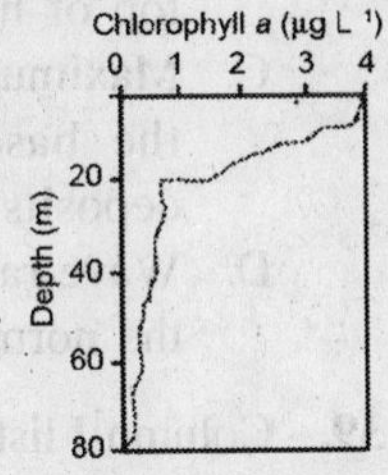

C. 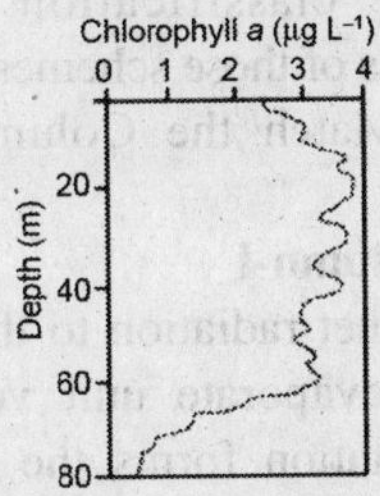

D. 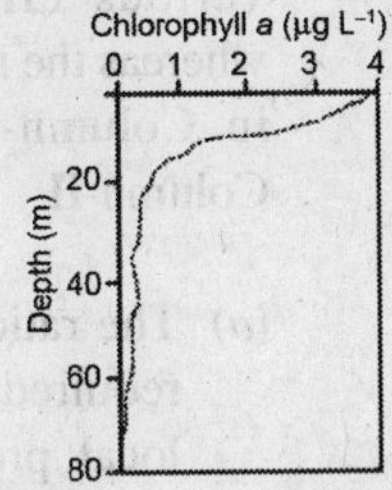

129. Match the following morphological features with the invertebrate fossils.

Morphology	**Fossil**
(*a*) Hypostome	(*i*) Brachiopod
(*b*) Cameral deposits	(*ii*) Trilobite
(*c*) Deltidium	(*iii*) Echinoid
(*d*) Perignathic girdle	(*iv*) Cephalopod

Choose the CORRECT option:

	(*a*)	(*b*)	(*c*)	(*d*)
A.	(*iv*)	(*ii*)	(*i*)	(*iii*)
B.	(*i*)	(*iv*)	(*ii*)	(*iii*)
C.	(*ii*)	(*i*)	(*iii*)	(*iv*)
D.	(*ii*)	(*iv*)	(*i*)	(*iii*)

130. Match the following aspects of spatial data with the statistical techniques used to measure them.

Aspect of spatial data	**Measurement Technique**
(*a*) Spatial randomness	(*i*) Mean centre
(*b*) Centre of gravity of a point pattern	(*ii*) Standard distance
(*c*) Absolute dispersion of points over space	(*iii*) Krigging
(*d*) Spatial autocorrelation	(*iv*) Average Nearest Neighbour ratio

Choose the CORRECT option:

	(*a*)	(*b*)	(*c*)	(*d*)
A.	(*iii*)	(*iv*)	(*i*)	(*ii*)
B.	(*iii*)	(*iv*)	(*ii*)	(*i*)
C.	(*iv*)	(*iii*)	(*ii*)	(*i*)
D.	(*iv*)	(*i*)	(*ii*)	(*iii*)

131. The principal stresses (in GPa) for the 2D stress matrix (A) in which the normal stresses are 20 GPa and 10 GPa and the shear stresses are 5 GPa and 5 GPa, are:

A. 5 and 10
B. 15 and 15
C. 20 and 10
D. 22 and 8

132. At which latitude the Earth's magnetic field (F), its vertical (V) and horizontal (H) components are connected by the relation $F = 2V + \sqrt{3}H$?

A. 15°
B. 30°
C. 45°
D. 60°

133. An earthquake of Mw 6.6 occurs on a 100 km long fault having a width of 10 km. Assuming the modulus of rigidity to be 10 GPa, the slip on the fault is:

A. 0.1 m
B. 1 m
C. 10 m
D. 100 m

134. Consider the following statements:

(*a*) The crescentic form of Barchan dunes consists of a steep windward slope and a gently inclined lee side.

(*b*) The horns or cusps of the Barchan dune project downwind, making the slip face concave to the downward B direction

Choose the CORRECT option:

A. (*a*) is False and (*b*) is True
B. Both (*a*) and (*b*) are True
C. (*a*) is True and (*b*) is False
D. Both (*a*) and (*b*) are False

128. A **129.** D **130.** D **131.** D **132.** B **133.** B **134.** A

135. Match the following cross-stratification type with their process of formation:

Cross-stratification	Process
(*a*) Epsilon	(*i*) Migration of 3-D dune
(*b*) Trough	(*ii*) Lateral accretion
(*c*) Tabular	(*iii*) Storm actions
(*d*) Swaley	(*iv*) Migration of 2-D dune

Choose the CORRECT option:

	(*a*)	(*b*)	(*c*)	(*d*)
A.	(*iii*)	(*i*)	(*iv*)	(*ii*)
B.	(*ii*)	(*i*)	(*iv*)	(*iii*)
C.	(*iii*)	(*ii*)	(*iv*)	(*i*)
D.	(*ii*)	(*iii*)	(*i*)	(*iv*)

136. Match the following stratigraphic units with their basin:

Stratigraphic unit	Basin
(*a*) Pali	(*i*) Pranhita-Godavari
(*b*) Dharmaram	(*ii*) Narmada
(*c*) Lathi	(*iii*) South Rewa
(*d*) Nimar	(*iv*) Jaisalmer

Choose the CORRECT option:

	(*a*)	(*b*)	(*c*)	(*d*)
A.	(*i*)	(*iii*)	(*iv*)	(*ii*)
B.	(*iii*)	(*i*)	(*iv*)	(*ii*)
C.	(*iii*)	(*ii*)	(*iv*)	(*i*)
D.	(*ii*)	(*iii*)	(*i*)	(*iv*)

137. The criteria for declaring the onset date of the Indian Southwest Monsoon over India is NOT based on:

A. the observed rainfall over Kerala in early June in terms of both the magnitude and the spread of rainfall.

B. the observed latitudinal location of the sub-tropical westerly jet stream over Kerala in early June.

C. the observed strength and vertical extent of the westerly winds in early June in and around Kerala.

D. the observed moisture content up to mid-troposphere in early June in and around Kerala.

138. Which one of the following statements is CORRECT?

A. Regressive surface of marine erosion forms during the forced regression

B. Maximum flooding surface occurs at the top of highstand systems tract

C. Maximum regressive surface occurs at the base of lowstand systems tract deposits

D. Wave-ravinement surface forms during the normal regression

139. Column-I lists important concepts underlying various climate classification schemes whereas the names of those schemes are listed in Column-II. Match the Column-I with Column-II.

Column-I

(*a*) The ratio of net radiation to the energy required to evaporate unit volume of local precipitation forms the basis for classifying climates

(*b*) Five of the six first order climate types are based on monthly mean temperature values

(*c*) In delineation of climate classes temperature is not an adequate indicator of ecological productivity

(*d*) 0°C isotherm of the coldest month separates the cold dry climate from the hot dry climate

Column-II

(*i*) Koppen's classification

(*ii*) Trewartha's classification

(*iii*) Budyko's classification

(*iv*) Thornthwaite's classification

Choose the CORRECT option:

	(*a*)	(*b*)	(*c*)	(*d*)
A.	(*iii*)	(*iv*)	(*i*)	(*ii*)
B.	(*iv*)	(*i*)	(*ii*)	(*iii*)
C.	(*ii*)	(*i*)	(*iv*)	(*iii*)
D.	(*iii*)	(*i*)	(*iv*)	(*ii*)

135. B **136.** B **137.** B **138.** A **139.** D

140. Which of the following minerals would replace hypersthene in the normative composition of silica undersaturated igneous rock?

A. Leucite B. Wollastonite
C. Diopside D. Olivine

141. Interaxial angle between two 3-fold axes in point group 233 is:

A. 54°44′ B. 70°32′
C. 35°16′ D. 45°

142. Consider the following statements about the Walker circulation.

(*a*) It is associated with atmospheric subsidence over Indonesia.
(*b*) It is a meridional circulation between equator to 30°N
(*c*) It is associated with atmospheric subsidence over eastern Pacific
(*d*) Sea surface temperature over west Pacific is higher than east Pacific.

Choose the CORRECT option.

A. (*a*) and (*b*) are true
B. (*a*) and (*c*) are true
C. (*c*) and (*d*) are true
D. (*b*) and (*d*) are true

143. If H and L in circles denote the positive and negative sea surface height anomalies, respectively, and the arrows are the flow fields. Identify the flow field associated with $n = 1$ equatorial Rossby waves:

1. 

2. 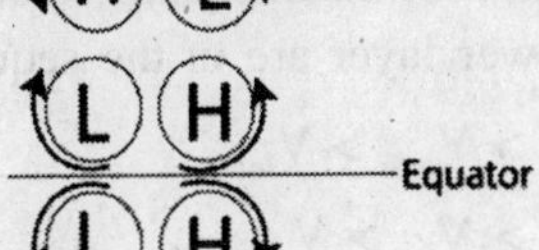

3. 

4. 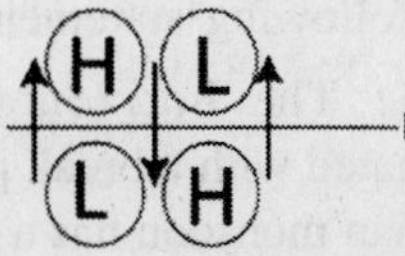

Choose the CORRECT options:

A. 1 B. 2
C. 3 D. 4

144. Consider the following statements regarding the angular momentum budget for northern hemisphere:

Statement A: There is an equatorward atmospheric flux of westerly angular momentum.

Statement B: The atmosphere gains westerly angular momentum from the Earth surface in low latitudes.

Statement C: The atmosphere loses westerly angular momentum to the Earth surface in middle latitudes.

Choose the correct option

A. Statements A and B are True, Statement C is False
B. Statement A is True, Statements B and C are False
C. Statement A is False, Statements B and C are True
D. Statements A and B are False, Statement C is True

145. The correct match in the following figure associated with an image interpolation method is:

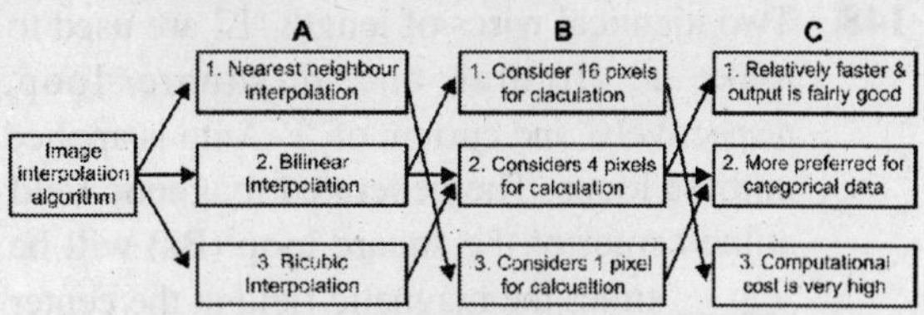

Choose the CORRECT option:

A. A1 - B3 - C2 B. A2 - B1 - C3
C. A3 - B2 - C1 D. A2 - B2 - C2

140. D	141. B	142. C	143. A	144. C	145. A

146. Consider the following statements.

Statement A: The horizontal pressure gradient associated with a break phase of the Southwest Indian monsoon has a lower value as compared to the horizontal pressure gradient associated with an active phase of the Southwest Indian monsoon.

Statement B: As compared to other regions, the latitudinal position of the Intertropical Convergence Zone (ITCZ) over the Indian region during Southwest Indian Monsoon is the farthest from equator.

Choose the CORRECT option:

A. A is true and B is false
B. A is false and B is true
C. A and B are true
D. A and B are false

147. A is a gravity station at latitude 15 °N. B is 10 km south and C is 10 km north of A. The observed gravity values at B and C are 4.06 mgals smaller and 2.10 mgals larger than at A, respectively. Which one of the following statements is true?

A. B and C are at the same elevation as at A.
B. B is at the same elevation as A, but C is at a higher elevation.
C. B is at the same elevation as A, but C is at a lower elevation.
D. B is at lower elevation than A, but C is at the same elevation.

148. Two identical wires of length 'L' are used to make a circular and a square loop, respectively, and current of 'I' Amp is applied in these loops. The generated magnetic field at the center of the square loop (Bs) will be ______ times the magnetic field at the center of the circular loop (Bc).

A. 2.0 B. 1.15
C. 0.87 D. 0.5

149. Match the equations with their corresponding processes.

Equations

(a) $Ca^{2+} + 2HCO_3^- \rightarrow CaCO_3 + CO_2 + H_2O$

(b) $CaSiO_3 + 2CO_2 + 3H_2O \rightarrow Ca^{2+} + 2HCO_3^- + H_4SiO_4$

(c) $106CO_2 + 16HNO_3 + H_3PO_4 + 122H_2O + (Fe, Zn ...) + h\nu \rightarrow C_{106}H_{263}O_{110}N_{16}P + 138O_2$

(d) $(CH_2O)_{106}(NH_3)_{16}H_3PO_4 + 94.4HNO_3 \rightarrow 106CO_2 + 55.2N_2 + 177.2H_2O + H_3PO_4$

Processes

(i) Weathering
(ii) Photosynthesis
(iii) Anaerobic respiration
(iv) Carbonate precipitation

Choose the CORRECT option:

	(a)	*(b)*	*(c)*	*(d)*
A.	*(i)*	*(ii)*	*(iii)*	*(iv)*
B.	*(iv)*	*(i)*	*(ii)*	*(iii)*
C.	*(iv)*	*(ii)*	*(i)*	*(iii)*
D.	*(i)*	*(iv)*	*(iii)*	*(ii)*

150. A seismic survey was done over a two-layer Earth model. The two layers are of equal thicknesses, and the P velocity of the lower layer is double that of the upper layer. The interval velocity (V_{int}), the average velocity (V_{avg}) and root mean square velocity (V_{rms}) of the lower layer are in the sequence:

A. $V_{rms} > V_{avg} > V_{int}$
B. $V_{rms} > V_{int} > V_{avg}$
C. $V_{int} > V_{avg} > V_{rms}$
D. $V_{int} > V_{rms} > V_{avg}$

146. C	**147.** B	**148.** B	**149.** B	**150.** D

Explanatory Answers

1. (B): $\because$ 3 fair cubical dice are thrown

$\therefore \quad n(S) = 6 \times 6 \times 6 = 216$

Let E = event of getting all the dice read the same.

Then, E = {(1, 1, 1), (2, 2, 2), (3, 3, 3), (4, 4, 4), (5, 5, 5), (6, 6, 6)}

$\therefore \quad n(E) = 6$

$$\therefore \quad P(E) = \frac{n(E)}{n(S)} = \frac{6}{216} = \frac{1}{36}.$$

2. (D): Let the cost price of an item = ₹ x

Then, increased cost price

$$= ₹\ x \times \frac{120}{100} = ₹\ \frac{6}{5}x$$

$$\text{and selling price} = \frac{6}{5}x \times \frac{90}{100}$$

$$\Rightarrow \quad ₹\ 2160 = \frac{54x}{50}$$

$\Rightarrow \quad x = 40 \times 50$

$\Rightarrow \quad x =$ ₹ 2000

Hence, its cost price = ₹ 2000.

3. (B): In a regular octagon,

$n = 8$

$\therefore$ Sum of all the internal angles of a regular octagon $= (n - 2)\pi$

$= (8 - 2) \times 180°$

$= 6 \times 180 = 1080°.$

4. (D): A has 8, 10, 20 then, median of A = 10

B has 9, 10, 15, then median of B = 10

Combined observations of A and B are 8, 9, 10, 10, 15, 20

$$\text{Median} = \frac{10+10}{2} = \frac{20}{2}$$

= 10 = median of A

Hence, the median of the combined dataset = median of A.

5. (B): $\because$ Speed of light is faster than speed of sound.

$\therefore$ Required distance = $(xy/y - x)$ m

[Speed of light = y m/s and speed of sound = x m/s].

7. (A): In ΔBAC,

$$\sin A = \frac{r}{2r} = \frac{1}{2}$$

$\Rightarrow \quad \sin A = \sin 30°$

$\Rightarrow \quad A = 30°$

Hence, $\angle BAC = 30°$.

8. (A): Let A, B, C and D are 4 men in a group

Then,

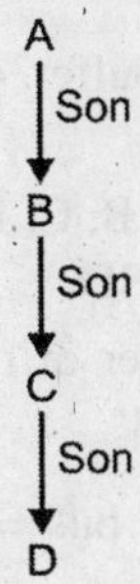

Here, Father-son pairs are AB, BC and CD

Hence, the largest number of father-son pair is 3.

9. (A): From the given figures,

Per capita GDP of these countries in year 2020

$$A = \frac{324}{16} = \frac{81}{4} = 20.25$$

$$B = \frac{2623}{138} = 19$$

$$C = \frac{264}{22} = \frac{132}{11} = 12$$

Now, the decreasing order of per capita GDP of these countries in the year 2020 is A > B > C (A, B, C).

10. (B): Given, respective number of windows are inversely proportional of their sizes

Let the number of windows are $\frac{k}{2}$, $\frac{k}{3}$ and $\frac{k}{4}$

Then, the total number of windows

$$= \frac{k}{2}+\frac{k}{3}+\frac{k}{4}$$

$$\Rightarrow \quad 26 = \frac{k}{2}+\frac{k}{3}+\frac{k}{4}$$

$$\Rightarrow \quad 26 = \frac{6k+4k+3k}{12}$$

$$\Rightarrow \quad 13k = 26 \times 12$$

$$\Rightarrow \quad k = 24$$

Hence, the number of the largest size windows

$$= \frac{k}{4} = \frac{24}{4} = 6.$$

11. (C): Given, In a buffet, 4 curries A, B, C and D were served

∴ Options are A, B, C, D, AB, AC, AD, BC, BD, ABC and ABD

Hence, the number of options available for the guest were 11.

12. (D): speed of the bus = 60 km/hr

$$\text{speed decrease} = 60 - \frac{20}{100}\times 60$$

$$= (60 - 12) = 48 \text{ km/hr}$$

Let distance = x km

$$\frac{x}{48}-\frac{x}{60} = \frac{45}{60}$$

$$\Rightarrow \quad \frac{5x-4x}{240} = \frac{3}{4}$$

$$\Rightarrow \quad x = \frac{240\times 3}{4}$$

$$= 60 \times 3 = 180 \text{ km}$$

Again, let original speed = y km/hr

$$\text{Now,} \quad \frac{180}{y} - \frac{120}{y-\frac{y}{5}} = \frac{30}{60}$$

$$\Rightarrow \quad \frac{180}{y}-\frac{120\times 5}{4y} = \frac{1}{2}$$

$$\Rightarrow \quad \frac{180\times 4-120\times 5}{4y} = \frac{1}{2}$$

$$\Rightarrow \quad \frac{720-600}{2y} = 1$$

$$\Rightarrow \quad 120 = 2y$$

$$\Rightarrow \quad y = \frac{120}{2} = 60 \text{ km/hr}$$

Hence, original speed = 60 km/hr.

13. (D): Here, Mixture of a paint = 50 litre, Green : Blue : Red = 5 : 3 : 2

$$\text{quantity of green paint} = 50\times\frac{5}{5+3+2}$$

$$= 50\times\frac{5}{10} = 25 \text{ litre}$$

$$\text{quantity of blue paint} = 50\times\frac{3}{10} = 15 \text{ litre}$$

$$\text{quantity of red paint} = 50\times\frac{2}{10} = 10 \text{ litre}$$

Given, another 10 litre of red colour is added to the mixture

∴ Quantity of red colour paint

$$= 10 + 10$$

$$= 20 \text{ litre}$$

Hence, the new ratio = 25 : 15 : 20

= 5 : 3 : 4.

14. (A): Given,

$A = 162^3 + 327^3$-

$= (162 + 327)\,(162^2 - 162 \times 327 + 327^2)$

$= (489)\,(162^2 - 162 \times 327 + 327^2)$

and $B = 612^3 - 123^3$

$= (612 - 123)\,(612^2 - 612 \times 123 + 123^2)$

$= 489(612^2 - 612 \times 123 + 123^2)$

Here, A and B is divisible by 489.

15. **(C):** Let 3 consecutive integers a, b, c are x, $x + 1$, $x + 2$

Then, $a + b + c = 15$

$\Rightarrow x + x + 1 + x + 2 = 15$

$\Rightarrow 3x + 3 = 15$

$\Rightarrow 3x = 12$

$\Rightarrow x = 4$

$\therefore a = x = 4$

$b = x + 1 = 5$

$c = x + 2 = 6$

Hence, $(a - 2)^2 + (b - 2)^2 + (c - 2)^2$

$= (4 - 2)^2 + (5 - 2)^2 + (6 - 2)^2$

$= 4 + 9 + 16 = 29.$

18. **(B):** $\because$ Area of trapezium

$= \frac{1}{2}$ (Sum of parallel sides) $\times h$

$\therefore$ Sum of area of two trapezium

= Area of a parallelogram

$\Rightarrow \frac{1}{2}(2a+2a+1)\times h+\frac{1}{2}(2b-1+2b)\times h$

$= 2(a + b)$

$\Rightarrow \frac{1}{2}h[4a+1+4b-1] = 2(a + b)$

$\Rightarrow 2h[a + b] = 2(a + b)$

$\Rightarrow h = 1$

Hence, the height of the parallelogram will be 1.

21. **(A):** The Moon's stronger influence on Earth's tides, despite the Sun's larger overall gravitational pull, is due to the gradient of the Moon's gravitational field. Tidal forces are not determined by the total strength of gravity but by its differential effect across the Earth's diameter. The Moon, being much closer to Earth than the Sun, exerts a more varied gravitational force from one side of Earth to the other. This variation, or gradient, in gravitational pull is what leads to the stretching effect that causes tides. Essentially, the side of Earth nearest to the Moon experiences a stronger pull than the side farthest from it, resulting in the bulging of Earth's oceans towards and away from the Moon, creating high and low tides. Despite the Sun's greater gravitational strength overall, its far greater distance from Earth means that the difference in gravitational pull from one side of Earth to the other is less significant, thus making its tidal effect weaker compared to that of the Moon.

22. **(D):** If Earth and Mars were to switch places, their orbital velocities around the Sun would change due to their new positions in the solar system. Orbital velocity is determined by the balance between the gravitational pull of the Sun and the inertia of a planet. This balance is influenced by the distance from the Sun; planets further away need to move at slower speeds to maintain their orbits. Therefore, if Earth were in Mars' current orbit, it would move slower than it does now, because it would be further from the Sun. Conversely, if Mars were in Earth's current orbit, closer to the Sun, it would need to move faster to maintain its orbit due to the stronger gravitational pull at this closer distance. This scenario illustrates Kepler's Third Law, which states that the square of the orbital period of a planet is directly proportional to the cube of the semi-major axis of its orbit, implying that planets further from the Sun orbit at slower speeds.

23. **(C):** The predominant mechanism of heat transfer through Earth's lithosphere is conduction. The lithosphere, comprising the crust and the uppermost part of the mantle, is a solid layer where heat transfer occurs primarily through the process of conduction. In conduction, heat moves through a material without the material itself moving. It involves the transfer of energy from more energetic to less energetic molecules when neighbouring molecules collide. This is in contrast to convection, which is the dominant heat transfer mechanism in the asthenosphere below the lithosphere, where heat is transferred by the movement of fluid. Radiation, the transfer of energy through electromagnetic waves, is not a significant mode of heat transfer in the lithosphere due to the solid state of the material. Advection, which involves the bulk movement of material, is also not applicable to the solid lithosphere.

24. **(B):** The Geoid and the Spheroid are two different concepts used in geodesy to represent the shape of the Earth. The Geoid is an equipotential surface that represents the mean sea level extended continuously through the continents. It is an irregular shape that approximates the mean ocean surface of the Earth if the oceans and atmosphere were in equilibrium, at rest relative to the rotating Earth, and extended through the continents. This surface is important for determining the actual shape and gravity field of the Earth. On the other hand, a Spheroid (or ellipsoid) is a mathematical model of the Earth which is a slightly flattened sphere. It is used as a reference surface in geodetic calculations and map projections. Unlike the Geoid, the Spheroid is not an equipotential surface because it does not accurately represent Earth's gravitational field or sea level.

25. **(A):** The inclination of the Earth's magnetic field, or magnetic inclination, is the angle made with the horizontal by the Earth's magnetic field. It varies depending on one's geographic location. At the magnetic equator, the inclination is zero, and it increases towards the magnetic poles. Among the given locations, Trivandrum, being closest to the magnetic equator, would have the least inclination. The magnetic field lines are more horizontal near the magnetic equator and become more vertical as one moves towards the magnetic poles. Therefore, locations like Visakhapatnam, Shillong, and Mumbai, being further from the magnetic equator compared to Trivandrum, will have a greater inclination of the Earth's magnetic field.

26. **(B):** A Drumlin is an elliptical, streamlined, ice-molded landform typically found in groups in areas that were covered by glaciers in the past. It is characterized by a long axis parallel to the direction of ice movement, with a tapered end pointing in the down-glacier direction, resembling an inverted spoon or half-buried egg. Drumlins are formed under the ice by the movement and reshaping of pre-existing unconsolidated sediments and are part of glacial drift. They provide clues about the direction and nature of past glacial movements. Other options like Cuesta, Esker, and Till represent different glacial or geographical features: Cuesta is a ridge with a gentle slope on one side and a steep slope on the other, Esker is a long, winding ridge of stratified sand and gravel, and Till is unsorted glacial sediment deposited directly by a glacier.

27. **(B):** Among the listed volatile organic compounds (VOCs), methane is the longest-lived in the atmosphere. Methane (CH_4) is a significant greenhouse gas, known for its ability to trap heat in the atmosphere. Its atmospheric lifetime is much longer than other VOCs like isoprene, ethane, or benzene. Isoprene and ethane have relatively short atmospheric lifetimes, and benzene, while more stable than isoprene and ethane, does not persist as long as methane. Methane's longer lifetime, combined with its effectiveness in trapping heat, makes it a particularly important focus in discussions about climate change and atmospheric chemistry.

28. (A): The thickness of atmospheric layers varies significantly, and it is related to the pressure range of each layer. Atmospheric pressure decreases with altitude. The layer from 10 hPa to 1 hPa represents a higher altitude range in the stratosphere, nearing the stratopause. Due to the exponential nature of the decrease in air pressure with altitude, the physical thickness of this layer is much greater than those closer to the Earth's surface. For layers at lower altitudes (such as 110 hPa to 101 hPa, 510 hPa to 501 hPa, and 1010 hPa to 1001 hPa), the pressure change represents a much smaller vertical distance because the air is denser and the pressure decreases more rapidly with altitude in these lower layers.

29. (A): Supergeostrophic flow refers to a situation where the wind speed is higher than would be expected from the geostrophic wind alone. Geostrophic wind is a theoretical wind that results from a balance between pressure gradient force and Coriolis force. Supergeostrophic flow typically occurs around high-pressure systems, or anticyclones, especially in the upper atmosphere. In these systems, the centrifugal force adds to the pressure gradient and Coriolis forces, leading to stronger winds than would be predicted by geostrophic balance alone. Tornadoes, extra tropical cyclones, and gale winds, while significant meteorological phenomena with strong winds, do not specifically represent supergeostrophic flow as defined in meteorology. Anticyclonic flow, characterized by winds moving around a high-pressure area, is a classic example of supergeostrophic flow.

30. (A): The Antarctic Circumpolar Current (ACC) is known for having the largest volumetric flow rate of any ocean current. It encircles Antarctica and connects the Atlantic, Pacific, and Indian Oceans. The ACC is unique because it is unimpeded by any significant landmass, which allows it to transport a larger volume of water than any other current. In contrast, currents like the Gulf Stream, Kuroshio Current, and Agulhas Current, while also strong and significant in their respective areas, do not match the Antarctic Circumpolar Current in terms of the sheer volume of water they move.

31. (C): Osmosis in aquatic organisms primarily involves the movement of water across a semipermeable membrane from an area of low salt concentration (or high water concentration) to an area of high salt concentration (or low water concentration). This process is critical for maintaining fluid balance within cells and across tissues. Osmosis does not involve the direct exchange of salts, oxygen, carbon dioxide, or nutrients, but rather the passive movement of water molecules. While these other substances do move in and out of cells and organisms, their transport mechanisms are different and not typically referred to as osmosis.

32. (D): If seismic wave velocities did not vary with depth inside the Earth's mantle, the seismic shadow zone would commence farther away from the epicenter than it currently does. The shadow zone is an area of the Earth's surface where seismic waves from a given earthquake are not detected. It exists primarily because of the refraction (bending) of seismic waves as they pass through different layers of the Earth, particularly the core-mantle boundary. If seismic wave velocities were uniform throughout the mantle, the waves would not refract as sharply at the core-mantle boundary. This would result in the shadow zone starting at a greater distance from the epicenter, as the waves would travel deeper into the Earth before being refracted or absorbed by the core. Currently, the shadow zone exists because the seismic waves are refracted by the core, creating an area where these waves are not detected.

33. **(D):** Dinoflagellates are the phytoplankton group commonly associated with corals, red tides, paralytic shellfish poisoning, and zooxanthellae. Dinoflagellates are a diverse group of flagellate eukaryotes. Some species of dinoflagellates live in symbiosis with corals, known as zooxanthellae, and play a crucial role in coral nutrition and health. Red tides, which are harmful algal blooms, are often caused by the overgrowth of certain dinoflagellates, leading to the discoloration of seawater. These blooms can produce toxins that cause paralytic shellfish poisoning, a serious health hazard for humans who consume contaminated shellfish. Coccolithophores, blue-green algae, and silicoflagellates are other groups of phytoplankton but are not primarily associated with these phenomena.

34. **(B):** The radioactive parent-daughter pair of Uranium-238 (^{238}U) decaying to Lead-206 (^{206}Pb) has a half-life that is approximately equal to the age of the Earth. The half-life of ^{238}U is about 4.5 billion years, which is close to the current scientific estimate of Earth's age. This makes the ^{238}U-^{206}Pb system extremely useful in dating rocks and minerals that formed during the early history of the Earth. The other pairs listed, such as Rubidium-87 to Strontium-87, Potassium-40 to Argon-40, and Uranium-235 to Lead-207, also have significant half-lives but are used for different ranges or types of radiometric dating.

35. **(D):** Lahar is the type of mass wasting typically associated with unstable fresh tephra on hillslopes. Lahars are volcanic mudflows or debris flows that occur when water mobilizes the loose volcanic material on the slopes of a volcano. They can be triggered by heavy rainfall, melting snow, or the sudden release of water from a crater lake. Lahars can flow rapidly down valleys and river channels, causing widespread destruction. They are particularly associated with volcanic areas where fresh volcanic ash and tephra are deposited on the slopes. Earth flows, mudflows, and debris flows are other types of mass wasting, but they are not specifically linked to volcanic activity like lahars.

36. **(C):** Cyclostrophic flow is a meteorological term referring to the balance of forces in a small-scale, rapidly rotating weather system, such as a tornado. In cyclostrophic flow, the centripetal force (due to the circular motion of the flow) is balanced by the pressure gradient force. This kind of balance is typically observed in small-scale, intense weather systems with strong rotational motion. Tornadoes are the prime example of cyclostrophic flow, as they are characterized by extremely tight and intense rotation. In contrast, larger systems like tropical cyclones, monsoon depressions, and anticyclones are governed more by a balance between the pressure gradient force and the Coriolis force, known as geostrophic balance, rather than cyclostrophic balance.

37. **(A):** The density of seawater with a salinity of 35 increases non-linearly when its temperature is lowered from 4°C to 0°C. Pure water reaches its maximum density at 4°C; however, the presence of salt in seawater affects this relationship. As the temperature decreases from 4°C to 0°C, the density of seawater continues to increase, but not in a linear fashion. The freezing point of seawater is also lower than that of pure water due to the salt content, allowing the density increase to continue below 0°C. This behaviour is significant in ocean circulation, as it influences the sinking of cold, saline water in polar regions, a key component of thermohaline circulation.

38. **(D):** In terms of the global hydrological cycle, the residence time of water in oceans is significantly longer than that in groundwater.

The residence time of a substance in a reservoir is a measure of the average time a molecule spends in that reservoir. Oceans, containing the vast majority of Earth's water, have a residence time of water measured in thousands of years. Groundwater, although it represents a significant portion of Earth's freshwater, has a shorter residence time compared to oceans but still longer than other components of the hydrological cycle such as rivers or the atmosphere. The residence time of water in rivers and the atmosphere is much shorter, often measured in days to weeks for rivers and about a week for the atmosphere.

39. **(D):** A tributary is not considered a local or temporary base level of erosion for the trunk or parent stream. The base level of a stream or river is the lowest point to which it can flow and erode. Local or temporary base levels can include physical barriers or changes in topography that affect the stream's ability to erode further. Examples include a dyke or sill, which can impede the flow and cause deposition upstream, and a lake or dam, where sediment is deposited as the river enters a larger, still body of water. However, a tributary, being a smaller stream or river that flows into a larger one, does not act as a base level; instead, it contributes to the flow and sediment load of the parent stream.

40. **(C):** Illite is a mineral that contains potassium. Illite is a group of clay minerals that are typically formed by the weathering of muscovite and feldspar. It is a significant component of argillaceous rocks and is known for its potassium content. In contrast, kaolinite, chamosite, and berthierine are clay minerals that do not have significant potassium content. Kaolinite is a common clay mineral that is part of the group of industrial minerals, while chamosite and berthierine belong to the chlorite group of minerals and are iron-rich.

41. **(B):** The correct statement is that oligotrophic regions have low nutrient concentration and low productivity. Oligotrophic waters are characterized by low levels of nutrients such as nitrogen and phosphorus, which limits the growth of aquatic plants and algae, resulting in low productivity. These regions are often found in deep lakes with clear water and minimal algal growth. In contrast, eutrophic regions have high nutrient concentrations, leading to high productivity and often excessive algal blooms. The availability of nutrients is a key factor driving productivity in aquatic ecosystems, with sunlight also playing an important role, particularly in shallower waters.

42. **(D):** Negative geothermal gradients are observed over subduction zones. A geothermal gradient is the rate of temperature increase with respect to increasing depth in the Earth's interior. In most places on Earth, this gradient is positive, meaning that temperatures increase with depth. However, in subduction zones, where one tectonic plate is forced under another and descends into the mantle, the influx of cold oceanic crust can temporarily reverse this gradient, creating a negative geothermal gradient. This means that in these areas, temperatures initially decrease with depth, contrasting with the usual increase in temperature. This phenomenon is part of the complex thermal dynamics associated with subduction processes. Hot spots, mid-oceanic ridges, and volcanoes typically exhibit positive geothermal gradients, where temperature increases with depth.

43. **(B):** The Sun is directly overhead at Chennai (13°N) twice a year. This occurs because Chennai is located near the Tropic of Cancer (23.5°N latitude). The Sun is directly overhead at any given latitude between the Tropic of Cancer and the Tropic of Capricorn (23.5°S latitude) twice each year: once as it moves northward to the Tropic of Cancer during the March equinox to the June solstice, and again as it moves southward towards the Tropic of Capricorn during the September equinox to the December solstice. These overhead sun events are known as solar culminations.

44. **(D):** Red animals at 300 m depth in the ocean will appear black. This is because red light is absorbed at shallower depths in the ocean, typically within the first 10-30 meters. By the time you reach 300 meters, almost no red light from the sun penetrates the water. As a result, red animals or objects will not reflect any red light at this depth because there is no red light to reflect. They will therefore appear black or very dark, as black is the colour perceived when an object absorbs all the wavelengths of light that hit it, or when no light reaches it. This phenomenon is a result of the absorption and scattering of light as it passes through water.

45. **(C):** Desert soil is typically deficient in nitrogen and humus but rich in calcium and phosphate. These soils, found in arid and semi-arid regions, often have limited organic material due to the scarcity of vegetation, which results in low levels of humus and nitrogen. However, they can be rich in minerals like calcium and phosphate, as there is less leaching due to the low rainfall. In contrast, black soil is known for its high fertility and is rich in calcium carbonate, magnesium, potash, and lime. Red soil, typical in regions with a warm, moist climate, is rich in iron and poor in nitrogen, phosphorus, and organic matter. Laterite soil, formed in wet tropical areas, is rich in iron and aluminum oxides but poor in nitrogen, potassium, lime, and organic matter.

46. **(B):** SO_2 (Sulphur dioxide) has a net flux from air to sea. In the atmosphere, SO_2 is primarily produced from human activities such as the burning of fossil fuels and from volcanic emissions. It is a soluble gas and can be readily absorbed by seawater, where it can undergo various chemical reactions, including forming sulphates. This absorption process contributes to the ocean's role as a sink for sulphur compounds, helping to mitigate some impacts of atmospheric pollution. In contrast, gases like N_2O (Nitrous oxide), CH_4 (Methane), and CO (Carbon monoxide) primarily have fluxes from other sources to the atmosphere, although they can also be absorbed by the oceans to varying degrees.

47. **(A):** The 'rule of constant proportions' in marine science relates to salinity. This rule, also known as Forchhammer's principle, states that the relative proportions of major salts in seawater are constant, regardless of variations in total salinity. Essentially, while the salinity of seawater can vary, the ratio of major ions like sodium, chloride, magnesium, sulphate, and calcium remains nearly constant. This principle is fundamental in oceanography and helps in determining the salinity of seawater from a limited set of measurements. It does not directly relate to water mass identification, T-S (Temperature-Salinity) diagrams, or the pressure-density relationship, although these aspects are also crucial in the study of oceanography.

48. **(A):** The most abundant gas in the stratosphere is N_2 (Nitrogen). Nitrogen and Oxygen (O_2) are the two most abundant gases in the Earth's atmosphere as a whole, including the stratosphere. Even though the stratosphere is often associated with Ozone (O_3) because it contains the ozone layer, which absorbs and scatters the solar ultraviolet radiation, ozone is not the most abundant gas there. Its concentration is much lower compared to nitrogen and oxygen. CFCs (chlorofluorocarbons) are present in the stratosphere but in much smaller concentrations compared to nitrogen, oxygen, and even ozone.

49. **(C):** Under invariant moisture conditions, the maximum relative humidity in India is typically just before sunrise. Relative humidity is a measure of the amount of moisture in the air relative to what the air can hold at that temperature. As the temperature drops during the night, the air can hold less moisture, and thus the relative humidity increases. Just before sunrise, typically the coolest part of the day, the relative humidity reaches its maximum. After sunrise, as the temperature begins to rise, the air can hold more moisture, and the relative humidity decreases. This pattern is generally observed under stable moisture conditions.

50. **(A):** The Instantaneous Field of View (IFOV) is a measure of the spatial resolution aspect of a remote sensing image. IFOV describes the angular cone of visibility of a sensor (its field of view) and determines the area on the Earth's surface that is "seen" from a given altitude at any instant in time. This measurement is critical in determining the spatial resolution of the sensor: the smaller the IFOV, the finer the spatial resolution of the image, and the smaller the surface detail that can be resolved. Spectral resolution refers to the ability of a sensor to distinguish wavelength intervals, radiometric resolution to the ability to distinguish levels of intensity, and temporal resolution to the frequency at which the sensor can revisit and acquire data for the same area.

51. **(B):** Diurnal tide, in each tidal day, refers to one high and one low of almost similar magnitude. This type of tidal pattern is characterized by a single high tide and a single low tide each day. Diurnal tides are less common than the semidiurnal tides (which have two highs and two lows of approximately equal magnitude each day) and mixed tides (which have two high tides and two low tides of different heights each day). The diurnal tidal pattern is typically observed in certain coastal areas and is influenced by the alignment of the Earth, Moon, and Sun, as well as local geographical features.

52. **(A):** The ratio of Cl^- (chloride) to Na^+ (sodium) is constant everywhere in the open ocean because the residence time of both is more than the mixing time of the ocean. The residence time of an ion in the ocean is the average time an ion spends in the ocean before being removed. Both chloride and sodium ions have long residence times (millions of years), much longer than the time it takes to mix the ocean (thousands of years). This long residence time in comparison to the mixing time ensures that their ratio remains remarkably constant throughout the open ocean, despite various processes that add or remove salts from seawater. The formation of NaCl (salt) and the relative abundance of these ions do not directly influence this constant ratio.

53. **(B):** The angle between the orbital plane of the Earth around the sun and the plane of the Earth's equator is known as the solar declination angle. The solar declination angle varies over the course of the year as the Earth orbits the Sun due to the tilt of Earth's axis. This tilt is responsible for the changing seasons and the variation in the length of day and night at different times of the year. The solar zenith angle refers to the angle between the sun's rays and the vertical direction, solar elevation angle is the angle of the sun above the horizon, and solar inclination angle is not a commonly used term in this context.

54. **(C):** In the context of depositional environments, the energy condition is typically the least in a lagoon. A lagoon is a shallow body of water separated from a larger body of water (usually the sea) by barrier islands, reefs, or a barrier peninsula.

The conditions in lagoons are generally more protected and calmer compared to open ocean environments like beaches and barrier bars, where wave action is a significant shaping force. Tidal channels, which are pathways through which tides move in and out of estuaries, coastal lagoons, or between islands, also tend to have higher energy conditions due to the flow of water. In a lagoon, the limited circulation and reduced wave action result in lower energy conditions, making it a more tranquil depositional environment.

55. (B): The given equation describes a process of weathering, specifically the chemical weathering of the mineral forsterite (Mg_2SiO_4), a type of olivine. In this reaction, forsterite reacts with carbon dioxide (CO_2) and water (H_2O) to form dissolved magnesium ions (Mg^{2+}), bicarbonate ions (HCO_3^-), and silicic acid (H_4SiO_4). This type of chemical weathering process is important in the breakdown of silicate minerals and contributes to the overall weathering of rocks on Earth's surface. It also plays a role in the global carbon cycle by consuming atmospheric CO_2. The other options - carbonate formation, primary production, and dolomitization - do not accurately describe this chemical process.

56. (B): Low-pressure systems that form over the northern Indian Ocean during the Indian southwest monsoon season often do not grow into tropical cyclones primarily due to the existence of strong vertical shear of the horizontal winds. Wind shear refers to the change in wind speed or direction with height in the atmosphere. Strong vertical wind shear disrupts the organization of convection within a tropical disturbance, which is essential for the development of a tropical cyclone. This wind shear can tilt the cyclone's circulation and prevent the temperature and pressure structure necessary for intensification. The other factors mentioned, such as the position of the Inter-Tropical Convergence Zone (ITCZ), widespread rainfall, and moisture availability, can influence weather patterns, but the key inhibiting factor for cyclone development in this context is the strong vertical wind shear.

57. (C): Lapilli are a product of volcanic eruptions. Lapilli are small volcanic fragments, typically between 2 and 64 millimeters in diameter, that are ejected into the air during a volcanic eruption. They can consist of various materials, including rock, glass, and crystal fragments, and are formed when magma or lava is torn apart by explosive gases during the eruption process. Other options like ladang (a term related to agriculture), laccolith (a type of igneous intrusion), and lapies (karstic limestone formations) are not directly associated with volcanic eruptions.

58. (D): The correct sequence from older to younger geological age for these continental breakup episodes is B (Ur), A (Columbia), C (Rodinia), D (Pangaea). Ur is one of the earliest known continents or supercontinents and is believed to have formed about 3 billion years ago. Columbia (or Nuna) is thought to have existed approximately 1.8 to 1.5 billion years ago. Rodinia is believed to have assembled 1.3 billion to 900 million years ago. Finally, Pangaea is the most recent of these supercontinents, forming about 335 million years ago and beginning to break apart around 175 million years ago.

59. (A): Beach Drift refers to the movement of particles obliquely up the slope of a beach by the swash and directly down this slope by the backwash. This process occurs due to the action of breaking waves, which approach the beach at an angle and carry sediment up and along the beach face in a zigzag pattern. The swash (uprush of water from a breaking wave) moves sediment up the beach at an angle, while the backwash (water flowing back to the ocean) carries it straight down the slope. Over time, this process results in the gradual lateral movement of beach material along the shore, a phenomenon known as littoral drift or longshore drift. Beach accretion, saltation, and illuviation are different geological processes not specifically related to this pattern of sediment movement on beaches.

60. (C): The water table is the top surface of the phreatic zone. The phreatic zone, also known as the saturated zone, is the area in an aquifer where all the pores and fractures in the rock are filled with water. The water table represents the boundary between the phreatic zone and the vadose zone (zone of aeration or unsaturated zone) above it. In the vadose zone, the pores and fractures are not completely filled with water; instead, they contain a mixture of air and water.

61. (C): The maximum radiation of the Sun occurs at a wavelength of approximately 0.5 μm (micrometers), which is in the visible light spectrum, specifically towards the green part of the spectrum. This is due to the Sun's surface temperature, which determines the peak wavelength of its emission spectrum according to Wien's Displacement Law. This law states that the wavelength at which a black body (like the Sun) radiates most strongly is inversely proportional to its temperature.

62. (A): Island arcs and the back-arc basins are located on the overriding plate in a subduction zone. In a typical subduction zone, one tectonic plate (the subducting plate) is forced under another (the overriding plate). Island arcs form as a result of volcanic activity on the overriding plate due to the melting of the subducted plate and the subsequent rise of magma. Back-arc basins, which are areas of seafloor spreading and crustal extension, typically develop behind (landward of) the volcanic island arc on the overriding plate. This geological setting is common in the Pacific Ocean's "Ring of Fire."

63. (C): In the mesosphere, temperature decreases with altitude. The mesosphere is the third layer of the Earth's atmosphere, located above the stratosphere and below the thermosphere. In this layer, temperature decreases with increasing altitude, reaching some of the coldest temperatures in Earth's atmosphere. This cooling trend is due to the decrease in solar heating and the very low density of the air. In contrast, in the stratosphere, temperature increases with altitude due to the absorption of ultraviolet radiation by the ozone layer, and in the thermosphere, temperature also increases with altitude. The tropopause is not an atmospheric layer but rather the boundary between the troposphere and the stratosphere.

64. (D): If the temperature in the atmosphere decreases at a rate of 11°C/km with height, a saturated air parcel would be unstable. Atmospheric stability is determined by comparing the environmental lapse rate (the rate at which air temperature decreases with altitude) with the adiabatic lapse rates of rising air parcels. The dry adiabatic lapse rate (DALR) is 10°C/km, and the saturated adiabatic lapse rate (SALR) is less than 10°C/km, varying with temperature and moisture content but typically around 6°C/km. If the environmental lapse rate is greater than the SALR (as in this case, with 11°C/km), it indicates that the environment is unstable, meaning that a lifted air parcel will be warmer and less dense than its surroundings and will continue to rise.

65. (A): A foreland basin is associated with the Himalayas. Foreland basins are geological depressions that form adjacent to mountain ranges and are filled with sediments eroded from the mountains. They are typically created by the flexural bending of the lithosphere due to the weight of the mountain range. The Himalayan mountain range, formed by the collision of the Indian and Eurasian plates, is a classic example of a region where a foreland basin has developed. In contrast, the African Rift Valley is associated with continental rifting, Hawaii with volcanic hotspot activity, and the Mid-Atlantic Ridge with a mid-ocean ridge and seafloor spreading.

70. (B): The mantle contributes the maximum to Earth's gravity. While the Earth's core, both inner and outer, is denser than the mantle, the mantle accounts for a much larger volume of the Earth. About 84% of Earth's volume is mantle, and its mass, combined with its proximity to the Earth's surface (compared to the core), makes it the largest contributor to Earth's overall gravity. The crust, even though it's the outermost layer, is much less dense and significantly thinner compared to the mantle, and therefore contributes less to the overall gravity of Earth.

71. (C): Baroclinic instability can be viewed as a shear instability that draws energy from the potential energy of the background state. This kind of instability is a key mechanism in the development of mid-latitude weather systems. It occurs in the atmosphere when there is a horizontal temperature gradient, which leads to a situation where surfaces of constant pressure (isobars) intersect surfaces of constant density (isopycnals) at an angle. The potential energy associated with this temperature (and density) gradient can be converted into kinetic energy, leading to the development of large-scale weather systems like cyclones. This process is different from drawing energy directly from the kinetic energy of mean flow or vertical temperature gradient.

72. (C): The correct matching of the ecosystems with their associated features is as follows:

- Lentic: occurs in lake or pond.
- Seashores: softer bed helps in colonization of invertebrate.
- Estuaries: highly productive due to huge inflow of nutrients from land.
- Lotic: occurs in running water.

73. (C): To understand why this statement is incorrect, we need to delve into the basics of phase diagrams and the specific characteristics of the Orthoclase-Albite system. A phase diagram shows the stability of phases in terms of temperature and composition. In this binary system, the crystallization path of a melt (liquid) is determined by its initial composition and the cooling process.

1. **Initial Composition:** The diagram would typically show the crystallization behaviour of a melt starting with an initial composition 'P'. The composition of 'P' dictates the initial proportions of Orthoclase and Albite in the melt.
2. **Cooling Path:** As the melt cools, it follows a path dictated by the phase diagram. The first crystals to form will alter the composition of the remaining melt, typically moving its composition towards the other component in the system.
3. **Final Solid Composition:** On complete crystallization, the final solidified rock is a mixture of two solid phases whose compositions are determined by the intersection of the cooling path with the solidus line at the crystallization temperature. The specific phases and their compositions depend on the eutectic point and the solid solution behaviour of the system.
4. **Incorrect Assumption in Statement C:** The statement incorrectly assumes a specific final composition without considering the actual crystallization path and the phase equilibrium rules. Perthite and antiperthite are specific textures/ types of rocks formed due to exsolution

processes, not directly due to the primary crystallization of a melt of composition 'P'. The actual final composition would depend on the exact cooling path and the phase relations at lower temperatures, particularly considering any solid solution or exsolution phenomena that might occur.

Thus, the final composition of the rock cannot be accurately stated as "60 wt% perthite and 40 wt% antiperthite" without more specific information about the cooling history and phase relations at lower temperatures, making statement C incorrect.

74. **(A):** The matching of zooplankton types with their respective foods is correctly done in option A. Zooplankton, small drifting organisms in water bodies, are classified based on their dietary habits. Herbivorous zooplankton primarily consume live plant material or algae, making them important primary consumers in aquatic food webs. This category includes species that feed on phytoplankton and other microscopic plant material, which is abundant in aquatic environments. Carnivorous zooplankton, on the other hand, prey on live animals, including other smaller zooplankton. These organisms are secondary or even tertiary consumers, depending on their position in the food web. Omnivores are versatile in their diet and can consume both plant and animal matter. They play a dynamic role in the ecosystem by linking the trophic levels and contributing to the cycling of nutrients. Detritivores are specialized in feeding on dead organic matter, which includes decaying plant and animal material, as well as fecal matter. This group plays a crucial role in breaking down and recycling organic matter, thus maintaining the ecological balance in aquatic systems.

75. **(D):** The statements regarding the trace of fault scarps are all correct, as indicated in option D. Fault scarps are steep slopes or cliffs formed by the displacement of the Earth's crust along a fault line, and their appearance is influenced by several factors. Statement (*a*) notes that the steeper the dip of the fault surface, the more linear the resulting fault scarp. This is because steeper faults create a more pronounced displacement at the surface, leading to a sharper and more linear scarp. In contrast, faults with a gentler dip produce less distinct and more diffused scarps. Statement (*b*) refers to low-angle or nearly horizontal thrust faults. In these cases, the fault scarp may closely follow the existing topography due to the shallow angle of the fault plane, resulting in a scarp that may be less noticeable and more integrated with the surrounding landscape features. Statement (*c*) addresses the influence of the pre-existing landscape on the scarp's appearance. If the landscape is irregular, the resulting scarp will tend to mimic these irregularities, leading to a sinuous or crenulated appearance. This occurs because the displacement along the fault interacts with the existing topographical features, creating a scarp that reflects the underlying terrain's complexity.

76. **(A):** The distribution of the pelagic sediments shown in dark shade in the figure indicates Siliceous ooze of diatoms. Pelagic sediments, deposited in the open ocean, vary in composition based on several factors, including water depth, temperature, and productivity of the overlying waters. Siliceous oozes are composed primarily of the silica-based skeletons of microscopic marine organisms such as diatoms and radiolarians.

The key to identifying diatomaceous siliceous ooze in the provided figure lies in understanding the ecological and geographical conditions favourable for diatom proliferation. Diatoms are predominant in nutrient-rich, cooler waters, often found at higher latitudes and in areas with upwelling currents. These conditions support high biological productivity, leading to a significant accumulation of diatom remains on the ocean floor. Diatoms, being photosynthetic, are also largely found in the photic zone where sunlight penetrates, supporting their growth.

In contrast, radiolarian oozes are more commonly found in deeper, warmer waters, typically at lower latitudes. Abyssal clay, another type of pelagic sediment, is usually found in areas of very low productivity and consists of very fine particles, including clay minerals and tiny fragments of silica and other minerals. Calcareous ooze, composed primarily of calcium carbonate from organisms such as foraminifera and cocco-lithophores, predominantly accumu-lates in warmer, shallower waters where the depth is less than the carbonate compensation depth.

Given these characteristics, the dark-shaded areas in the figure likely represent regions of high diatom productivity and accumulation, indicative of cooler, nutrient-rich waters, possibly at higher latitudes or in upwelling zones, thereby supporting the identification of siliceous ooze of diatoms.

77. (B): The correct match for geophysical inversion methods and associated terms in this case is option B:

- The Marquardt-Levenberg algorithm is a modification of the classic least squares method. It is particularly useful in solving overdetermined problems, where the number of observations exceeds the number of unknowns. This algorithm combines the gradient descent and Gauss-Newton methods to find a solution that minimizes the sum of squares of nonlinear functions.
- The minimum norm least squares method is often used in inverse problems where the solution is underdetermined (fewer equations than unknowns). The Lagrange multiplier technique is employed here to minimize the norm of the solution while still fitting the data, ensuring that the solution is the smallest in length or norm.
- Simulated annealing is a probabilistic technique for approximating the global optimum of a given function. The term "quenching" in this context refers to the process of cooling in simulated annealing, which is a metaphor for reducing the probability of accepting worse solutions as the algorithm progresses. This helps in escaping local optima and moving towards a global optimum.
- Genetic algorithms are a family of computational models inspired by evolution. These algorithms use bio-inspired operators such as mutation, crossover, and selection. The fitness function in genetic algorithms is used to evaluate how close a given solution is to achieving the set objectives. It plays a crucial role in guiding the evolutionary process.

78. (C): Inertial oscillations are a type of fluid dynamic phenomenon observed in rotating systems like the Earth's atmosphere and oceans. The spectral peak at a periodicity of 24 hours representing an inertial oscillation can be related to the Coriolis effect, which is latitude-dependent.

The formula to determine the latitude based on the period of inertial oscillation T is given by $T = \frac{2\pi}{f}$, where f is the Coriolis parameter, $f - 2\Omega \sin(\phi)$.

Here, Ω is the Earth's angular velocity, and ϕ is the latitude. Given T – 24 hours, we can solve for ϕ to find the latitude. The result is approximately 30°N, considering the Earth's angular velocity $\Omega \approx 7.2921 \times 10^{-5}$ radians per second.

79. (A): To calculate the precipitation not available for runoff, we need to determine the total precipitation volume and subtract the measured runoff volume. The total precipitation volume over the watershed is calculated by multiplying the rainfall intensity by the area and duration. The rainfall intensity is 20 mm/h over an area of 10^6 m^2 for a duration of 6 hours. The direct runoff volume is 30,000 m^3. The difference between the total precipitation volume and the runoff volume gives the amount of precipitation not available for runoff. The units should be converted appropriately to match and provide a comparison. After calcu-lation, this results in a value close to 9 cm.

80. (C): Viviparous germination is a characteristic feature of mangroves. Viviparous germination refers to a process where seeds germinate while still attached to the parent plant, rather than falling to the ground and germinating there. This adaptation is particularly notable in mangroves, a group of trees and shrubs that grow in coastal intertidal zones. The harsh and variable environment of these zones, with fluctuating salinity and water levels, makes it difficult for seeds to germinate and establish after dispersal. Therefore, in many mangrove species, the seedling develops while still attached to the parent tree, gaining nutrients and establishing a root system. Once it is sufficiently developed, the seedling drops off and can rapidly establish itself in the muddy substrate. This adaptation gives mangroves a significant advantage in the challenging environments they inhabit. Marine algae, sandy beach flora, and periphyton do not exhibit viviparous germination.

81. (B): The correct matching of geographical features with their descriptions is given in option B:

- **Beheaded stream:** Stream that is deprived of part or all of its former watershed by stream capture. A beheaded stream is a stream whose upper course has been captured by another stream, leaving it with a reduced flow or no flow at all.
- **Water gap:** A valley or pass through a ridge or range through which a stream runs. A water gap is a feature where a river cuts through a ridge or mountain range, creating a narrow passageway.
- **Wind gap:** A valley or col in a ridge or range through which no stream passes. Wind gaps are like water gaps but without the water; they are dry valleys or cols that were once used by streams or rivers which have since been diverted or disappeared.
- **Elbow of capture:** Sharp change in the direction of a stream. An elbow of capture is created when a river or stream is captured by a neighbouring river or stream, leading to a sharp change in its course. This is a form of stream piracy where one stream or river diverts the flow of another.

82. (B): The answer, based on the typical seasonal variations in biogeochemical parameters in the North Atlantic Ocean, is that Curve A represents Nitrate, Curve B represents Phytoplankton, and Curve C represents Zooplankton.

The reasoning behind this identification is grounded in the understanding of oceanic biogeochemical cycles, particularly how phytoplankton, zooplankton, and nutrients like nitrate interact in marine ecosystems.

1. **Nitrate (Curve A)**: Nitrate levels in the ocean typically increase during the winter months when phytoplankton growth is low due to reduced sunlight and potentially cooler temperatures. During this time, nitrate is not heavily utilized and can accumulate in the water. As spring approaches, with increased sunlight and warmer temperatures,

phytoplankton begin to bloom, utilizing the available nitrate, which leads to a decrease in nitrate concentration in the water. This pattern is often seen in temperate regions like the North Atlantic.

2. **Phytoplankton (Curve B)**: Phytoplankton populations typically peak during the spring and early summer, corresponding to the period of high nutrient availability (following the winter accumulation) and favourable light conditions. This results in a significant bloom, often visible from space as large green patches in the oceans. The curve representing phytoplankton would show a peak during this period, followed by a decline as nutrients become depleted and as zooplankton grazing increases.
3. **Zooplankton (Curve C)**: Zooplankton populations often lag slightly behind phytoplankton blooms. As primary consumers, they feed on phytoplankton, and their numbers increase following the increase in available food (phytoplankton). Thus, a peak in zooplankton abundance typically occurs after the peak in phytoplankton biomass, reflecting this predator-prey relationship.

The cyclic pattern represented in the figure, showing a peak in nitrate during the colder months, followed by a peak in phytoplankton, and then a peak in zooplankton, is characteristic of seasonal phytoplankton blooms and subsequent zooplankton growth in response to the availability of food, consistent with option B.

83. **(D):** The statement that impoundment of a river decreases its downstream entrainment capacity (Statement A) is false, while the statement that river flow velocity drops in a reservoir (Statement B) is true.

- Impoundment, typically through the construction of a dam, does not necessarily decrease a river's downstream entrainment capacity. Entrainment capacity refers to a river's ability to pick up and carry sediment. While impoundment can alter sediment transport, leading to sediment accumulation in the reservoir, the effect on downstream entrainment capacity can vary. In some cases, the release of clearer water from a reservoir can increase the river's capacity to erode downstream areas, potentially leading to increased entrainment capacity. Therefore, the impact of impoundment on downstream entrainment is complex and not uniformly a decrease.
- River flow velocity does indeed drop in a reservoir. When a river is dammed, the water upstream is stored in a reservoir, where the flow velocity is significantly reduced compared to the flowing river. This reduction in flow velocity causes sediments carried by the river to settle out, leading to sediment deposition in the reservoir. The reduction in flow velocity is a fundamental aspect of reservoirs, transforming the riverine environment into a more lacustrine (lake-like) environment.

84. **(C):** The food source for large Antarctic whales is primarily Euphausiids, commonly known as krill. Krill are small, shrimp-like crustaceans that form a significant part of the diet of many marine animals, including whales. In Antarctic waters, krill are abundant and form large swarms, making them an efficient and nutritious food source for large whales. These whales, including the baleen whales like the blue whale and humpback whale, feed by filtering large volumes of water to extract the krill. Other options like ostracodes, amphipods, and copepods are also part of the marine food web but are not the primary food source for large Antarctic whales.

85. **(B):** The inference that is not valid for a hypothetical rock unit at 10° N with little or no north (X) and vertical (Z) components of Natural Remanent Magnetization (NRM), but a strong east (Y) component is that Earth's magnetic field was under transition to a reversal when the rock unit acquired its NRM (Statement B).

- Natural Remanent Magnetization (NRM) is the permanent magnetization acquired by rocks, recording the Earth's magnetic field at the time of their formation. The characteristics of NRM (direction and intensity) depend on the Earth's magnetic field at the location and time of the rock's formation.
- The lack of north and vertical components with a strong east component does not necessarily imply a magnetic field reversal. Reversals involve a significant change in the direction of the magnetic field, typically from north to south or vice versa. The described NRM could be due to various factors, such as the rock's formation near the magnetic equator, where the magnetic field would be primarily horizontal, or post-formation processes like tilting or rotation of the rock unit.
- The absence of north and vertical components and the presence of a strong east component could suggest the rock was formed near the magnetic equator, where the magnetic field lines are horizontal. However, it's important to consider other geological evidence and comprehensive magnetic studies to draw definitive conclusions about the rock's magnetic history and formation conditions.

86. (C): When a parcel of moist air is rising adiabatically (without heat exchange with its surroundings), the property that remains unchanged is the mixing ratio. The mixing ratio is defined as the mass of water vapor in a unit mass of dry air. This value remains constant in an adiabatic process as long as condensation does not occur. During the adiabatic ascent, the air parcel expands and cools, but the total amount of water vapor in the parcel does not change unless water vapor begins to condense into liquid water. In contrast, other properties like saturation vapor pressure, relative humidity, and air temperature do change. Saturation vapor pressure decreases with decreasing temperature, relative humidity varies as the air parcel cools and may reach saturation, and the air temperature decreases due to the expansion of the air parcel as it rises.

88. (A): The correct chlorophyll profile in the euphotic zone under an unlimited nutrient supply scenario, as depicted in Diagram A, follows a distinctive pattern that reflects the interplay between light availability and nutrient abundance in marine ecosystems.

In the euphotic zone, where sunlight penetrates the ocean and photosynthesis is possible, the availability of light is a key factor influencing the distribution of phytoplankton, which contain chlorophyll. Near the surface, light is plentiful, but nutrients can be quickly depleted due to the rapid growth and consumption by phytoplankton. However, in a scenario with unlimited nutrients, this typical limitation is removed.

Diagram A likely shows an increase in chlorophyll concentration starting from the surface and peaking at a certain depth. This pattern can be explained as follows: At the surface, despite abundant light, the rapid consumption of nutrients in a typical environment limits phytoplankton growth. But with unlimited nutrients, phytoplankton can proliferate extensively, leading to an increased concentration of chlorophyll.

As depth increases, light intensity decreases, leading to a reduction in photosynthetic activity. However, the presence of ample nutrients supports a higher concentration of phytoplankton until a certain depth.

This results in the formation of a deep chlorophyll maximum (DCM), where chlorophyll concentration peaks. This peak represents an optimal balance between light availability and nutrient abundance.

Beyond this depth, the decrease in light becomes the limiting factor, and despite the abundance of nutrients, the concentration of chlorophyll and phytoplankton decreases due to reduced photosynthetic activity.

In summary, Diagram A correctly represents the expected chlorophyll profile in the euphotic zone under unlimited nutrient conditions, highlighting the importance of both light and nutrients in determining phytoplankton distribution and, consequently, chlorophyll concentration in marine environments.

89. (B): Imbrication is a good indication to identify fluvial deposits. Imbrication refers to the arrangement of sedimentary particles, particularly pebbles and stones, in a way that they are tilted or stacked in a consistent direction. This feature is commonly observed in stream and river environments.

In fluvial settings, the current or flow of water arranges these particles with their long axes oriented roughly parallel to the direction of flow and with a tilt upstream. This happens because the current tends to lift the upstream side of a stone or pebble and then deposit it in such a manner that the stone tilts into the current, leading to a shingled arrangement. This characteristic arrangement can help geologists and sedimentologists determine the direction of past water flow in an area, which is crucial in understanding the paleoenvironment and reconstructing ancient river systems.

Imbrication is less common or not typically associated with glacial, aeolian (wind-driven), or landslide deposits. Glacial deposits are usually more mixed and unsorted, aeolian deposits are more likely to show features like cross-bedding related to wind direction, and landslide deposits are generally chaotic and lack any consistent orientation of particles.

90. (D): In an AFM diagram used for understanding metamorphic rock assemblages, the point 'S'—corresponding to Option D in question—represents a garnet-absent assemblage. The AFM diagram is a triangular graph displaying the relationships between the components Al_2O_3 (A), FeO (F), and MgO (M) in metamorphic rocks, particularly in pelitic (clay-rich) rocks.

The positioning of 'S' on this diagram indicates a specific combination of these three components under which garnet is not stable. Garnet, a common and significant mineral in metamorphic rocks, forms under certain conditions of temperature, pressure, and chemical composition. Its stability field in the AFM diagram is defined by the appropriate ratios of Al_2O_3, FeO, and MgO. When the composition veers away from this field, garnet no longer forms or is not retained in the rock.

The absence of garnet at point 'S' can be due to several factors:

1. **Chemical Composition**: The specific ratios of Al_2O_3, FeO, and MgO at 'S' might not be conducive to garnet formation. Garnet requires a certain amount of these components, particularly Al_2O_3, to stabilize. If the chemical environment is skewed away from this requirement, garnet won't form.
2. **Metamorphic Conditions**: Even if the chemical composition is marginally suitable, the temperature and pressure conditions represented at 'S' may not favor garnet formation. Garnet typically forms under specific metamorphic grades, and if the conditions are too low or too high, other minerals may form instead.
3. **Other Mineral Competitions**: In a metamorphic environment, different

minerals vie for available components. The presence of other minerals that consume the components necessary for garnet formation could inhibit its development.

Understanding where garnet is absent in a metamorphic setting is crucial for reconstructing the metamorphic history and conditions of rock formation. It provides insights into the metamorphic pathways and the original composition of the parent rock. The AFM diagram, thus, is a valuable tool in metamorphic petrology for interpreting the history and processes that have shaped a rock.

91. **(B):** The correct match for each phenomenon in Column-I with its associated term in Column-II is option B:

- Tropical cyclones are characterized by a warm core, which is a region of relatively warmer air at the center of the cyclone. This warm core is crucial for the cyclone's energy, as it is formed by the release of latent heat during the condensation of water vapor in the air. The warm core contributes to the low pressure at the center of the cyclone and drives its powerful winds and rain.
- The thermal wind relationship describes the change in wind speed with height in the atmosphere, related to horizontal temperature gradients. It is a key concept in understanding the formation and behavior of jet streams, which are fast-flowing, narrow air currents found in the atmospheres of some planets, including Earth. Jet streams form along the boundaries of adjacent air masses with significant differences in temperature, such as the polar regions and the warmer air to the south.
- Inertial motion refers to the movement of air or water masses in the absence of other forces except for the Coriolis force and centrifugal force. This type of motion typically occurs in the ocean as inertial currents or in the atmosphere in certain balanced wind patterns.
- Buoyancy oscillation, or buoyancy frequency, is a measure of the stability of the atmosphere or ocean. In a statically stable atmosphere, a displaced parcel of air tends to return to its original position, leading to oscillations. These oscillations are a response to the restoring force provided by the static stability of the atmosphere.

92. **(B):** To calculate the surface heat flux (qs) and bathymetry (b) at location B for an oceanic lithosphere that is 50 My old, we use the cooling half-space model for the oceanic lithosphere. According to this model, the heat flow decreases with the square root of the age, and the depth of the lithosphere increases with the square root of its age. Given the initial values at location A (70 mW/m^2 and 2.5 km for 25 My), we can calculate the expected values at 50 My. The heat flow would decrease, and the depth would increase proportionally to the square root of the age increase from 25 My to 50 My.

93. **(B):** The amount of water vapor needed to raise the moist air's temperature by 1% can be estimated based on the specific heat capacities of dry air and water vapor and their respective molecular weights. Water vapor has a higher specific heat capacity than dry air, meaning it can absorb more heat before its temperature rises. To achieve a 1% increase in temperature, a certain percentage of water vapor needs to be added to the dry air. This percentage can be estimated by considering the relative heat capacities and the molecular weight differences between dry air and water vapor. The calculation involves balancing the heat capacities and the mass contributions of both dry air and water vapor to achieve the desired temperature increase.

94. **(C):** Both Assertion (A) and Reason (R) are correct, and (R) is the correct explanation of (A).

Assertion (A) states that the velocities necessary to erode a consolidated clay bank are comparable to those that move pebbles and cobbles. This statement is correct. Although clay particles are much smaller than pebbles and cobbles, when they are consolidated into a bank, their cohesive nature makes them quite resistant to erosion. The cohesive forces between the clay particles, along with any additional compaction and cementation that may have occurred, can make a clay bank surprisingly resilient to erosive forces.

Reason (R) provides the explanation that this resistance to erosion is because of the strong cohesiveness of clay-size particles and their relative smoothness. This is a correct explanation. The cohesiveness of clay is due to the electrostatic forces between the fine particles, which are much stronger compared to the forces between larger particles like sand, pebbles, or cobbles. The smoothness of clay particles also contributes to this effect, as it allows the particles to pack closely together, increasing the cohesion.

In summary, the high erosion resistance of consolidated clay banks, similar to that required to move larger sediment like pebbles and cobbles, is indeed due to the strong cohesive nature and smoothness of clay particles.

95. **(D):** Option D suggests that the blue curve represents $[H_2S]$ (hydrogen sulphide concentration), the green curve represents $[O_2]$ (oxygen concentration), and the red curve represents $[NO_3^-]$ (nitrate concentration) in the schematic plot of the subsurface euxinic condition for a tropical ocean.

In a marine environment, especially under euxinic conditions where oxygen is depleted, the chemistry of the water column is characterized by distinct layers of chemical gradients, known as chemoclines. Euxinic conditions imply anoxic (oxygen-depleted) conditions, often coupled with the presence of hydrogen sulphide (H_2S), which is a product of sulphate reduction under anoxic conditions.

- **Blue $[H_2S]$:** The presence of H_2S in significant concentrations typically occurs in deeper water layers where oxygen is absent or very low. This is because H_2S is produced by the anaerobic breakdown of organic matter, often involving sulphate-reducing bacteria that thrive in oxygen-depleted environments. The increase in H_2S concentration with depth is a characteristic feature of anoxic or euxinic conditions.
- **Green $[O_2]$:** The concentration of dissolved oxygen ($[O_2]$) is expected to decrease with depth, especially in stratified water columns where deeper waters are isolated from atmospheric oxygen exchange. In the upper layers, oxygen is more prevalent due to diffusion from the atmosphere and photosynthetic activity, but it decreases with depth as it gets consumed by respiration and other biological and chemical processes.
- **Red $[NO_3^-]$:** Nitrate ($[NO_3^-]$) is a key nutrient in marine ecosystems and is typically consumed in the upper layers of the ocean where phytoplankton are active. However, in anoxic conditions, nitrate can also be reduced to nitrogen gas (denitrification) or even used as an electron acceptor for the oxidation of organic matter, which can alter its concentration profile with depth.

The schematic plot thus represents the typical chemical stratification observed in tropical oceans under euxinic conditions, with distinct zones characterized by the presence or absence of oxygen, nitrate, and hydrogen sulphide.

96. (A): The eigenvalues are the values for which the matrix equation $(A - \lambda I)x = 0$ has a non-trivial solution, where A is the matrix, λ is the eigenvalue, I is the identity matrix, and x is a non-zero vector. The eigenvalues give important insights into the properties of the matrix, such as its stability and behavior under various transformations.

97. (A): Both statements are true regarding the abundance of nitrogen and carbon in the Earth's atmosphere and oceans.

Statement (A): Nitrogen is indeed the most abundant element in the Earth's atmosphere, comprising about 78% by volume. In contrast, the concentration of carbon, primarily in the form of carbon dioxide (CO_2), is much lower. The current concentration of CO_2 in the atmosphere is around 0.04% by volume, significantly less than that of nitrogen. This vast difference in concentration is a fundamental characteristic of Earth's atmosphere.

Statement (B): When CO_2 reacts with seawater, it indeed forms bicarbonate (HCO_3^-) and carbonate (CO_3^{2-}) ions. This process is a part of the ocean's carbon cycle, where CO_2 is absorbed from the atmosphere and converted into these ions in seawater. This chemical transformation helps regulate the Earth's climate by controlling the amount of CO_2 in the atmosphere. In the ocean, the concentration of carbon, in the form of dissolved inorganic carbon (which includes CO_2, bicarbonate, and carbonate), is higher than that of nitrogen, which is primarily present as dissolved nitrogen gas (N_2).

98. (A): The Main Himalayan Thrust (MHT) is the primary geological fault responsible for great earthquakes in the Himalayas. This thrust fault marks the boundary where the Indian Plate is being subducted under the Eurasian Plate. The movement along this fault is a major source of seismic activity in the region, leading to significant earthquakes. Other thrusts, such as the Main Boundary Thrust (MBT), Main Central Thrust (MCT), and South Tibet Detachment (STD), also contribute to the tectonic activity in the Himalayas but are not the primary sites for the largest earthquakes.

99. (A): Beach sand composed predominantly of quartz and shell fragments suggests a marine origin with significant biological activity. This type of sand is characteristic of tropical and subtropical environments where coral and shell-bearing organisms are abundant. Maldives, known for its coral atolls, is the least likely source of such sand, as its beaches are primarily composed of biogenic material, like coral sands, which are distinctly different from quartz-rich sands. Beaches in Andaman, Kerala, and Madagascar can have a mix of quartz and shell fragments due to their diverse geological and biological environments.

101. (D): The correct statement is that the formula of Toluene is C_7H_8. Toluene is an aromatic hydrocarbon and part of the benzene series, with a chemical formula of C_7H_8. It consists of a benzene ring with a single methyl group (CH_3) attached. The other options are incorrect: (A) The general formula for the paraffin series (alkanes) is C_nH_{2n+2}, not C_nH_{2n}. (B) Condensate is not a heavy crude oil; it is actually a light, low-density mixture of hydrocarbon liquids present in the gaseous phase in natural gas deposits. (C) Asphalt is not a type of light crude oil; it is a heavy, thick substance that is a residue from the distillation process of certain crude oils.

102. (A): The correct matches are:

- Opening of the Drake Passage: Formation of the Antarctic Circumpolar Current. This event led to the creation of a continuous eastward current around Antarctica, impacting global ocean circulation.
- Panama Seaway Closure: Strengthening of the Atlantic Thermohaline Circulation. The closure of this seaway increased the salinity of the North Atlantic, affecting the thermohaline circulation.

- Closing of the Indonesian-Australian Passage: Intensification of the Kuroshio Current. This closure altered ocean currents in the Pacific, including the Kuroshio.
- Closure of the Bering Strait: Saltier North Atlantic Surface Waters. This event influenced the salinity and circulation patterns in the North Atlantic.

103. **(A):** If the Earth's tilt increased to 40°, we would expect hotter summers and colder winters at 40° N. An increased tilt amplifies the seasonal temperature differences because the sun's rays would strike the Earth more directly during summer and more obliquely during winter. This would lead to more extreme temperatures in both seasons, with hotter summers due to increased solar radiation and colder winters due to less solar radiation.

104. **(C):** At an altitude equivalent to 50% of the scale height of the atmosphere, which is approximately 8 km for Earth's atmosphere, the air density will be about 60% of the surface air density. The scale height is defined as the height at which the atmospheric pressure decreases by a factor of e (approximately 2.71828). Since air density and pressure are directly related through the ideal gas law, a decrease in pressure by a factor of e results in a similar decrease in density. At half the scale height, the pressure and thus the density would decrease to about 60% of its surface value, following an exponential decline.

105. **(C):** In the Wenner-Schlumberger configuration for resistivity measurement, the apparent resistivity (ρ_a) is calculated using the formula:

$$\rho_a = \pi . a . \frac{\Delta V}{I}$$

where a is the electrode spacing, ΔV is the potential difference, and I is the current. The deepest level measurement in a Wenner-Schlumberger array is achieved when the electrode spacing is at its maximum.

Given that the total length of the profile is 90 m (10 electrodes with 9 intervals of 10 m each), the maximum spacing (a) is 22.5 m (quarter of the total profile length). Substituting the given values (a = 22.5 m, ΔV = 200 mV = 0.2 V, I = 1 A), we calculate the apparent resistivity.

107. **(A):** Matching the geomorphic features with the geomorphic processes:

- Demoiselle is a result of arid processes: It's a feature often found in desert landscapes.
- Ridge and swell formation is related to fluvial processes, occurring in river and stream systems.
- Verve is a product of fluvioglacial processes, formed by the action of glacial meltwater.
- Pingo is a feature associated with periglacial processes, typically formed in areas subject to freezing and thawing.

108. **(C):** Matching the pelitic mineral assemblages with the corresponding metamorphic facies:

- Muscovite + chlorite + chloritoid + quartz are typically found in the green schist facies, which is characterized by low to moderate temperature and pressure conditions.
- Biotite + muscovite + garnet + sillimanite is an assemblage indicative of the amphibolite facies, representing intermediate to high-temperature and pressure conditions.
- Biotite + garnet + cordierite + sillimanite + quartz is characteristic of the granulite facies, which forms under high temperatures and pressures.
- Muscovite + kyanite + garnet + biotite + quartz is typical of the eclogite facies, which forms under very high pressures and moderate to high temperatures.

109. (B): A key observation in such tectonic settings is the age progression of volcanic islands. If the ages of the islands increase in a certain direction, it indicates the movement of the tectonic plate over a stationary hotspot or a subduction zone where magma is rising. This conclusion can be explained through the following geological concepts:

1. **Oceanic Plate Dynamics**: The scenario described in option B involves two interacting oceanic plates. One plate is subducting beneath the other, which is a common occurrence at convergent plate boundaries in oceanic settings. The overriding plate is typically less dense or younger than the subducting plate.
2. **Volcanic Island Formation**: As the oceanic plate subducts, it descends into the mantle where it begins to melt due to the high temperatures and pressures. This melting generates magma, which is less dense than the surrounding rock and thus rises towards the surface. When this magma reaches the ocean floor of the overriding plate, it can form volcanic islands.
3. **Direction of Plate Movement**: The presence of volcanic islands with varying ages suggests that the overriding plate is moving over a region where magma generation is occurring, likely due to the subducting plate. If the islands increase in age in a certain direction, it indicates the direction of plate movement. In this case, the plate is moving in such a way that it passes over the subduction zone, creating a trail of islands that are older further away from the subduction zone.
4. **Tectonic Setting**: The described setting fits the typical scenario of an island arc, which is a chain of volcanic islands that commonly form along the concave edge of a subducting oceanic plate. The nature and arrangement of these islands provide insights into the direction of plate movement and the dynamics of the subduction process.

In summary, the formation of volcanic islands in an oceanic setting, with an age progression that aligns with the direction of plate movement, is indicative of an active tectonic environment where one oceanic plate is overriding another that is subducting beneath it. This process leads to the formation of a series of volcanic islands, each marking a point where the magma from the subducting plate reached the surface at different times as the overriding plate moved.

110. (D): Both conclusions I and II are false in the context of the Normalized Difference Vegetation Index (NDVI) and its relation to vegetation reflectance and standard false colour composites.

1. **Conclusion I: Vegetation Reflectance Characteristics**: This conclusion is false. Vegetation typically absorbs most of the visible light (especially in the blue and red wavelengths) for use in photosynthesis and strongly reflects near-infrared (NIR) radiation. This characteristic contrast in reflectance between the visible and NIR bands is what makes NDVI a useful tool for assessing vegetation health and density. The NDVI is calculated using the difference in reflectance between the NIR and red bands, taking advantage of the fact that healthy vegetation strongly reflects NIR and absorbs red light.
2. **Conclusion II: Standard False Colour Composites**: This conclusion is also false. In standard false colour composites, which are commonly used in remote sensing to represent vegetation, the NIR band is indeed often assigned to the red colour. However, this doesn't mean that "other colours are assigned to visible bands" in a general sense. Usually, the green band in these composites represents the NIR reflectance (which is high for vegetation), while the red and blue bands are assigned to different wavelengths, often green and

red reflectance, respectively. This assignment enhances the contrast between vegetation and other land covers, making vegetation appear in shades of red.

In summary, neither of the provided conclusions accurately describes the reflectance properties of vegetation or the standard assignment of colours in false colour composites used in remote sensing.

111. **(D):** The gravity anomaly profile across a horizontal sheet is broader and has a larger magnitude compared to a vertical sheet – this conclusion can be explained through the principles of gravitational field anomalies and their relation to subsurface structures.

1. **Gravity Anomaly Characteristics**: The gravity anomaly caused by a subsurface structure depends on the distribution of mass within that structure. Gravity anomalies are a measure of variations in the Earth's gravitational field resulting from density variations in the subsurface.
2. **Vertical Sheet (Model A)**: In a vertical sheet, the mass is distributed in a narrow, vertical plane. This configuration produces a gravity anomaly that is typically sharp and narrow because the influence of the mass is concentrated over a smaller area at the surface. The magnitude of the anomaly is directly related to the mass of the sheet but is spread over a limited area, leading to a sharper but not necessarily larger magnitude profile.
3. **Horizontal Sheet (Model B)**: A horizontal sheet, on the other hand, spreads its mass over a larger horizontal area. This distribution leads to a broader gravity anomaly because the influence of the mass is spread over a wider area at the surface. The magnitude of the anomaly is influenced both by the mass of the sheet and its orientation. In this case, the broader distribution can lead to a larger magnitude anomaly because the mass affects a larger area of the gravitational field at the surface.
4. **Geophysical Implications**: The broader anomaly of a horizontal sheet indicates a wider influence zone on the gravitational field, which can result in a larger magnitude change in the gravitational reading. This is due to the larger area over which the gravitational effect of the sheet is felt.

In summary, the orientation of a geophysical body significantly influences the characteristics of the gravity anomaly it produces. A horizontal sheet, with its mass distributed over a larger area, generates a broader and larger magnitude anomaly compared to a vertical sheet, where the mass is concentrated in a narrower zone.

112. **(B):** To understand why option B is correct, let's break down the components of the formula:

1. **Solar Constant (S):** This is the amount of solar energy received per unit area at the top of the Earth's atmosphere. It's a measure of the solar radiation's intensity.
2. **Planetary Albedo (α):** Albedo refers to the reflectivity of a surface. The Earth's planetary albedo is the fraction of solar energy reflected back into space by the Earth's atmosphere and surface. A higher albedo means more energy is reflected and less is absorbed.
3. **Emissivity (∈) and Stefan-Boltzmann Constant (σ):** Emissivity is a measure of how efficiently a surface emits thermal radiation. The Stefan-Boltzmann constant is a physical constant that describes the power radiated from a black body in terms of its temperature.

The formula in option B represents the balance between the energy received by the Earth from the Sun and the energy emitted by the Earth as thermal radiation. It takes into account the solar constant, the fraction of energy not reflected ($1 - \alpha$), and the principles of black body radiation represented by $\in$ and σ. This balance is crucial in determining the Earth's climate and temperature. Understanding this formula is essential in the study of Earth's climate system, as it helps in quantifying the energy inputs and outputs of the planet, which in turn influences global temperature and climate patterns.

114. **(A):** To calculate the photo scale, the formula used is Scale = Focal Length / (Flying Height-Terrain Elevation). In this scenario, the focal length of the camera lens is 152 mm, and the flying height above sea level is 5000 m.

For point A, which is at an elevation of 1200 m, the scale would be 152/(5000 – 1200) = 152/3800 = 1 : 25,000.

For point B, at an elevation of 1960 m, the scale would be 152/(5000 – 1960) = 152/3040 = 1 : 20,000.

These scales indicate the ratio of distance on the photograph to the corresponding distance on the ground. Therefore, the correct answer is that the photo scale at points A and B would be 1 : 25,000 and 1 : 20,000, respectively.

115. **(C):** The warming of the tropical upper troposphere and the cooling of the mid-latitude upper troposphere would lead to an increase in wind shear at upper levels. Wind shear refers to the variation of wind speed or direction over a relatively short distance in the atmosphere. A warming upper troposphere in the tropics implies a steeper temperature gradient between the tropics and mid-latitudes at these levels, which would enhance the wind shear. Conversely, the warming of the midlatitude lower troposphere at a higher rate than the tropical lower troposphere suggests a reduction in temperature gradient and consequently a decrease in wind shear at lower levels. Wind shear is a critical factor in the formation and behavior of weather systems, and its variation can significantly impact atmospheric circulation patterns, including the intensity and path of jet streams.

116. **(A):** According to the 2011 Indian Census, the correct order in decreasing terms of urban population to total population ratio among the given states is Tamil Nadu, Kerala, Maharashtra, and Gujarat. Tamil Nadu has historically been one of the most urbanized states in India, with a significant portion of its population residing in urban areas. Kerala, known for its high human development index and quality of life, also has a substantial urban population, although slightly less than Tamil Nadu. Maharashtra, with major urban centers like Mumbai and Pune, follows closely, and Gujarat, while having significant urban centers like Ahmedabad and Surat, has a lower urban-to-total population ratio compared to the other three states. This ordering reflects the varying levels of urbanization in these states, influenced by factors such as industrial development, migration patterns, and historical urban growth.

117. **(C):** To determine if the vector field is irrotational, we need to check if the curl of the vector field is zero. The curl of a vector field $\vec{F}$ is given by $\Delta \times \vec{F}$. For a vector field defined as $\vec{F} = (c_1x^2, c_2y^2, c_3z^2)$, the curl is calculated using the partial derivatives of its components. If the field is irrotational, all components of the curl should equal zero. In this case, setting $c_1 = 1$, $c_2 = 0$ and $c_3 = -3$ would satisfy the condition that the curl of the vector field is zero, indicating that the field is irrotational. This is a fundamental property in vector calculus used in fields such as fluid dynamics and electromagnetism.

118. **(A):** If the angular velocity of the Earth is reduced by half, it would have several significant effects on atmospheric phenomena, including the size of extratropical cyclones. Extratropical cyclones are largely driven by the temperature gradient between the equator and the poles. A reduced angular velocity would mean a slower rotation of the Earth, which could lead to a decrease in the Coriolis effect. The Coriolis effect is crucial in the formation and movement of these cyclones. With a reduced Coriolis effect, the wind patterns would change, potentially leading to larger, more slowly-moving extratropical cyclones. This change could result in cyclones covering a larger area, as the dynamics of the cyclones' formation and progression would be altered by the change in the Earth's rotation speed.

119. **(B):** Statement P is true. In deep water (depth greater than half the wavelength of the wave), water particles move in circular orbits, with the diameter of these orbits decreasing with depth. This is a characteristic of deep-water waves, where the motion of the water particles diminishes rapidly with depth. Statement Q is false because when the depth is between 1/2 and 1/20 of the wavelength, the water particles' motion does become elliptical, but the size of these ellipses decreases with depth, not remains constant. Statement R is also false because in shallow water (depth less than 1/20 of the wavelength), the particles' motion is indeed elliptical, but the diameter of these ellipses reduces significantly with depth, reflecting the decreasing energy of the wave as it interacts with the seabed.

120. **(C):** Option (*a*) is true as streams flowing from the downthrown block to the upthrown block would impound against the scarp, forming a barrier due to the relative elevation difference. Option (*c*) is also true as streams flowing from the upthrown block to the downthrown block would experience a relative increase in gradient, leading to rejuvenation. Rejuvenation refers to the reactivation of the erosional capabilities of the stream due to an increase in the energy gradient. Options (*b*) and (*d*) are incorrect because streams flowing from the upthrown to downthrown block would not impound against the scarp, and streams flowing from the downthrown to upthrown block would not be rejuvenated but rather impounded.

121. **(A):** In this scenario, the cyclone with a central low pressure of 950 hPa is surrounded by a region with higher pressure (1020 hPa). The height of the 250 hPa level being the same inside and outside the cyclone implies that the atmospheric column within the cyclone must be warmer than outside, as warm air expands and occupies more vertical space. The difference in virtual temperature is a result of the hydrostatic balance, which relates the vertical distribution of pressure to the density (and therefore temperature) of the air column. Since the pressure at the surface is lower within the cyclone (950 hPa) compared to outside (1020 hPa) but the height of a significant pressure level (250 hPa) is the same, the mean virtual temperature of the air column from the surface to 250 hPa must be higher within the cyclone. Therefore, the temperature outside the cyclone will be lower, and given the significant difference in surface pressures, the temperature difference can be quite substantial, approximately 15 °C.

122. **(B):** S-tectonite foliations typically trace the XY plane of the finite strain ellipsoid. In the context of structural geology, an S-tectonite is a type of metamorphic rock that has been deformed and recrystallized under differential stress, leading to the development of a planar fabric known as foliation. The finite strain ellipsoid is a geometric representation of the deformation a rock has undergone. It has three principal axes: X (longest), Y (intermediate), and Z (shortest). The XY plane of this ellipsoid typically corresponds to the plane of maximum flattening, which is where the foliation in S-tectonites is usually developed. This is because the XY plane represents the orientation in which the rock has been stretched the most (X-axis) and squeezed the least (Y-axis), thus forming a prominent planar structure.

124. **(C):** The false statement among the given options is C: "Rise in atmospheric CO_2 has affected ocean alkalinity." This statement is misleading because the rise in atmospheric CO_2 actually increases the acidity of ocean waters, which is referred to as ocean acidification. While it is true that the addition of CO_2 to seawater forms carbonic acid, leading to a decrease in pH, this process does not directly affect the overall alkalinity of the ocean. Alkalinity in ocean chemistry primarily refers to the capacity of seawater to neutralize acids, which is largely determined by the concentration of bicarbonate and carbonate ions. The rise in atmospheric CO_2 affects the concentration of these ions, but the overall alkalinity of the ocean remains relatively stable. The other statements are correct: Photosynthesis increases seawater pH (A), the rise in atmospheric CO_2 has decreased ocean pH (B), and this rise has decreased ocean carbonate concentrations (D), which is a part of the process of ocean acidification.

125. **(C):** The characteristic that is NOT associated with sheath folds is "Folded stretching lineation". Sheath folds are a type of geological structure commonly found in high-strain zones, such as shear zones. They are characterized by:

- **Development in shear zones:** Sheath folds are typically formed in regions of intense deformation, such as shear zones, where the material undergoes significant stretching and shearing.
- **Folded hinge line:** The hinge line of a sheath fold is often folded or curved, which is a distinctive feature of this type of fold. This results from the intense deformation and rotation of material within the shear zone.
- **Strongly non-cylindrical:** Sheath folds are known for their non-cylindrical shape. Unlike classic cylindrical folds, where the hinge line is straight and parallel to the axis of the fold, sheath folds have a more complex, often sigmoidal shape due to the intense shear deformation they undergo.

In contrast, "Folded stretching lineation" is not a typical characteristic of sheath folds. Stretching lineations are linear features that indicate the direction of maximum stretching during deformation. In the context of sheath folds, the stretching lineation is typically parallel to the elongation of the fold and may not necessarily be folded. The presence of a folded stretching lineation would suggest a more complex deformation history than is typical for sheath folds.

126. **(B):** The Question deals with the identification of correct combinations of Global Navigation Satellite Systems (GNSS), their country of operation, and their operational status. The correct answer is B, which corresponds to:

- A1 – GPS (B3 - USA, C1 - Fully Operational)
- A2 - Galileo (B2 - European Union, C2 - Not fully operational)
- A3 - NavIC (B1 - India, C2 - Not fully operational)

1. **GPS (Global Positioning System)**: Operated by the United States (USA), GPS is fully operational and is the most widely used GNSS system globally. It provides accurate location and time information under all weather conditions, anywhere on or near the Earth.
2. **Galileo**: This is a global navigation satellite system created by the European Union (EU). As of the question's context, it is not fully operational. Galileo aims to provide high-precision positioning services and is interoperable with GPS and GLONASS.

3. **NavIC (Navigation with Indian Constellation)**: Developed by India, NavIC is designed to provide accurate position information to users in India and the surrounding region. It is not fully operational in the context of this question, indicating ongoing development or limited operational capacity at the time.

The combination in answer B correctly matches each GNSS with its country and operational status, reflecting the current state of these satellite navigation systems.

127. (B): The Question is about identifying profiles that correspond to barotropic instability, based on the second derivative of zonal wind with meridional distance. The correct answer is B, which includes profiles B, C, and D.

Barotropic Instability:

1. **Concept**: Barotropic instability occurs in a fluid flow where the flow is uniform in the vertical direction (barotropic) and becomes unstable under certain conditions. This instability is a key mechanism in the atmosphere and oceans, leading to the formation of large-scale structures like cyclones.
2. **Second Derivative of Zonal Wind**: The second derivative of zonal wind with respect to meridional distance is a measure of the curvature of the wind profile. In the context of barotropic instability, this curvature can indicate the presence of shear and the potential for instability.
3. **Profiles B, C, and D**: These profiles likely exhibit characteristics indicative of barotropic instability, such as significant curvature or shear in the zonal wind profile. This could manifest as rapid changes in wind speed or direction over a short meridional distance.
4. **Instability Criteria**: For barotropic instability to occur, certain criteria must be met, such as the presence of a critical layer where the wind speed equals the phase speed of waves, or the violation of the Rayleigh's stability criterion. Profiles B, C, and D presumably meet these criteria, making them representative of barotropic instability.

In summary, the selection of profiles B, C, and D as corresponding to barotropic instability suggests that these profiles exhibit the necessary characteristics and meet the criteria for such instability in the atmospheric or oceanic context.

128. (A): The Question asks about the expected pattern of phytoplankton biomass distribution, indicated by Chlorophyll *a* fluorescence, in oligotrophic seas under prolonged summer days. The correct answer is A.

Phytoplankton Biomass in Oligotrophic Seas:

1. **Oligotrophic Seas**: These are areas of the ocean with low nutrient levels, particularly low nitrogen and phosphorus, which are essential for phytoplankton growth. As a result, phytoplankton biomass is generally low in these regions.
2. **Chlorophyll *a* Fluorescence**: Chlorophyll *a* is a pigment found in phytoplankton that is crucial for photosynthesis. Fluorescence of this pigment is often used as an indicator of phytoplankton biomass and productivity.
3. **Prolonged Summer Days**: Longer daylight hours during summer increase the duration of sunlight available for photosynthesis. In oligotrophic seas, this can lead to a slight increase in phytoplankton biomass due to enhanced photosynthetic activity.
4. **Expected Pattern (Answer A)**: Given the conditions of oligotrophic seas and prolonged summer days, the expected pattern of phytoplankton biomass would likely show a modest increase in Chlorophyll *a* fluorescence. This increase, however, would be limited due to the inherently low nutrient availability in

these waters. The pattern would not show a significant bloom or high biomass, as oligotrophic conditions restrict extensive phytoplankton growth.

In summary, the answer A represents a pattern showing a slight increase in phytoplankton biomass during prolonged summer days in oligotrophic seas, reflecting the limited but enhanced photosynthetic activity under extended daylight conditions.

129. (D): The correct matching of the morphological features with the invertebrate fossils is as follows:

- Hypostome is associated with Trilobites. The hypostome is the hard mouthpart found in the ventral side of trilobites, a group of extinct marine arthropods.
- Cameral deposits are found in Cephalopods. These deposits are found within the shell chambers of some cephalopods, indicating the presence of fluids or soft tissue during the organism's life.
- Deltidium is a feature of Brachiopods. It is a small plate or structure located at the hinge line of brachiopod shells.
- Perignathic girdle is characteristic of Echinoids. It is part of the skeletal structure in echinoids (sea urchins) that supports the jaw apparatus.

130. (D): The correct matching of aspects of spatial data with the statistical techniques used to measure them is as follows:

- Spatial randomness is best measured by the Average Nearest Neighbour ratio. This ratio helps determine the degree of clustering or dispersion of points in a given space.
- The centre of gravity of a point pattern is identified using the Mean centre. This technique calculates the geographic center based on the spatial distribution of points.
- Absolute dispersion of points over space is measured by Standard distance. This technique provides a measure of how spread out points are in a spatial pattern.
- Spatial autocorrelation, which measures the degree to which one object is similar to other nearby objects, is best analyzed through Kriging. Kriging is a geostatistical technique used for interpolating the value of a random field (like elevation or rainfall) at a certain point based on the values at nearby points.

131. (D): To find the principal stresses for a 2D stress matrix, we need to solve the characteristic equation of the stress matrix.

The stress matrix is given by $\sigma = \begin{pmatrix} 20 & 5 \\ 5 & 10 \end{pmatrix}$ GPa. The principal stresses are the eigenvalues of this matrix, which are found by solving the characteristic equation det $(\sigma - \lambda I) = 0$, where λ are the principal stresses and I is the identity matrix. Solving this equation will give us the principal stresses for the matrix. The correct principal stresses are most likely to be 22 GPa and 8 GPa.

133. (B): To calculate the slip on a fault during an earthquake, we can use the seismic moment formula: $M_0 = \mu AD$, where M_0 is the seismic moment, μ is the modulus of rigidity, A is the area of the fault slip, and D is the average slip on the fault. Rearranging this for slip, we get $D = \frac{M_0}{\mu}$. Given an earthquake of magnitude M*w* 6.6 (which can be converted to seismic moment), a fault length of 100 km, a width of 10 km, and a modulus of rigidity of 10 GPa, we can calculate the average slip on the fault. Using typical conversion factors from moment magnitude to seismic moment, we can estimate the slip to be approximately 1 meter.

134. **(A)**

(*a*) The statement about the crescentic form of Barchan dunes is false. In Barchan dunes, the steep slope is on the leeward side, not the windward side. The windward slope is gently inclined, where the sand is gradually pushed up the dune, and the steep slope is on the leeward side where the sand cascades down.

(*b*) The statement about the horns or cusps of the Barchan dune is true. The horns of a Barchan dune do project downwind, and the slip face is concave in the downward direction. This shape is a characteristic feature of Barchan dunes, which are formed by winds consistently coming from one direction.

135. **(B):** The correct matching of the cross-stratification type with their process of formation is as follows:

- Epsilon cross-stratification is associated with lateral accretion. It is typically formed in point bar deposits in meandering streams and rivers.
- Trough cross-stratification is formed by the migration of 3-D dunes. This type of cross-bedding is characterized by sets of cross-strata that are concave-up.
- Tabular cross-stratification results from the migration of 2-D dunes. These are planar, tabular sets of cross-bedding, often formed in environments with unidirectional flow.
- Swaley cross-stratification is linked to storm actions. This type is typically formed in shallow marine environments affected by storm waves.

137. **(B):** The criteria for declaring the onset date of the Indian Southwest Monsoon over India do not include the observed latitudinal location of the sub-tropical westerly jet stream over Kerala in early June. The criteria for the onset of the monsoon are primarily based on meteorological factors such as rainfall, wind patterns, and humidity. The key factors include:

- Observed rainfall over Kerala in early June in terms of both the magnitude and the spread of rainfall.
- Observed strength and vertical extent of the westerly winds in early June in and around Kerala.
- Observed moisture content up to mid-troposphere in early June in and around Kerala.

The position of the sub-tropical westerly jet stream is an important factor in the overall monsoon dynamics but is not a direct criterion for declaring the monsoon's onset over Kerala.

140. **(D):** In the normative composition of silica-undersaturated igneous rocks, olivine (D) would replace hypersthene. Hypersthene is a pyroxene mineral that is typically found in silica-saturated to oversaturated rocks. In contrast, olivine is a common mineral in silica-undersaturated rocks, often associated with lower silica content. In the normative mineral calculation (a theoretical calculation of mineral composition), when silica is undersaturated, olivine is one of the minerals that is used to balance the chemical composition, effectively replacing minerals like hypersthene that require more silica. The other options, leucite (A), wollastonite (B), and diopside (C), have different chemical compositions and form under different conditions compared to hypersthene and olivine.

141. (B): The interaxial angle between two 3-fold axes in the point group 233 is 70°32'. In crystallography, point group 233 belongs to the cubic crystal system, which is characterized by its high symmetry. In this system, the 3-fold axes are arranged in such a way that they intersect at specific angles that are characteristic of the cubic symmetry. The angle of 70°32' is a result of the geometric constraints imposed by the cubic symmetry, where the 3-fold axes are oriented towards the corners of a cube.

142. (C): The correct statements about the Walker circulation are:

- It is associated with atmospheric subsidence over the eastern Pacific. The Walker circulation is a large-scale air flow pattern in the equatorial region, characterized by rising air over the western Pacific and subsiding air over the eastern Pacific.
- Sea surface temperature over the west Pacific is higher than over the east Pacific. This temperature gradient is a driving factor for the Walker circulation, as the warmer waters in the western Pacific contribute to rising air and low pressure, while the cooler waters in the eastern Pacific lead to subsidence and high pressure.

The other statements are incorrect:

- (*a*) is false because atmospheric subsidence actually occurs over the eastern Pacific, not Indonesia.
- (*b*) is false because the Walker circulation is a zonal (east-west) circulation, not meridional (north-south).

143. (A): Equatorial Rossby waves are characterized by a specific pattern in the sea surface height anomalies and associated flow fields. The positive (H) and negative (L) anomalies represent the highs and lows in sea surface height. In the context of equatorial Rossby waves, these anomalies are aligned in a way that reflects the wave's propagation and structure. The flow field in option A most accurately represents the typical flow associated with $n = 1$ equatorial Rossby waves, which generally show a specific pattern of movement and distribution of these anomalies.

144. (C): Statement A is false, and Statements B and C are true. The angular momentum budget for the northern hemisphere involves the distribution and transfer of westerly angular momentum.

In low latitudes, the atmosphere tends to gain westerly angular momentum from the Earth's surface due to the Earth's rotation and wind patterns. In contrast, in middle latitudes, the atmosphere often loses westerly angular momentum to the Earth's surface. The equatorward atmospheric flux of westerly angular momentum is not a universally accurate statement, hence Statement A being false.

145. (A): Image interpolation involves estimating pixel values in an image to either increase its size (upsampling) or decrease its size (downsampling). Different methods of interpolation, such as nearest-neighbor, bilinear, or bicubic, have unique characteristics in how they handle the interpolation process. In the context of the question, the correct match of the figures to their respective interpolation methods suggests a specific understanding of how these methods manipulate pixel values and the resulting visual output in images.

146. (C): Both statements A and B are true.

Statement A: The horizontal pressure gradient associated with a break phase of the

Southwest Indian monsoon is indeed lower compared to an active phase. During the active phase, the monsoon system is characterized by a stronger pressure gradient, which leads to more intense winds and heavier rainfall. In contrast, during the break phase, this gradient weakens, resulting in reduced wind strength and less rainfall.

Statement B: The Intertropical Convergence Zone (ITCZ) does indeed move farther from the equator over the Indian region during the Southwest Indian Monsoon than in other regions. This northward shift of the ITCZ is a characteristic feature of the monsoon system and is crucial for bringing the seasonal rains to the Indian subcontinent.

147. **(B):** Based on the gravity readings, we can infer the following:

Since the gravity value at B is 4.06 mgals smaller than at A, and gravity decreases with an increase in elevation, this suggests that B is at the same elevation as A or very close in elevation. The latitude difference alone (being only 10 km south) would not result in such a significant gravity change.

The gravity value at C is 2.10 mgals larger than at A. Since gravity increases with a decrease in elevation, this indicates that C is at a higher elevation than A.

Therefore, the correct statement is that B is at the same elevation as A, but C is at a higher elevation.

148. **(B):** When two identical wires are shaped into a circular and a square loop and the same current is passed through them, the magnetic field at the center of the square loop (Bs) will be approximately 1.15 times the magnetic field at the center of the circular loop (Bc). This is due to the geometry of the loops and how the magnetic field contributions from different segments of the wire add up at the center of each loop. The square loop, with its straight segments, contributes differently to the magnetic field at its center compared to the uniform circular loop. Calculating the exact ratio involves integrating the magnetic field contributions from each segment of the loops based on the Biot-Savart law, and the result is that Bs is slightly greater than Bc.

149. **(B):**

- **Equation** ***(a)*** represents carbonate precipitation ($Ca^{2+} + 2HCO_3^- \rightarrow CaCO_3 + CO_2 + H_2O$), where calcium ions combine with bicarbonate ions to form calcium carbonate, carbon dioxide, and water. This is a fundamental process in geological formations like limestone and plays a significant role in the carbon cycle.
- **Equation** ***(b)*** depicts the weathering process $CaSiO_3 + 2CO_2 + 3H_2O \rightarrow Ca^{2+} + 2HCO_3^- + H_4SiO_4$, showing the breakdown of calcium silicate in the presence of carbon dioxide and water. This reaction forms calcium ions, bicarbonate, and silicic acid, illustrating the chemical weathering of silicate minerals.
- **Equation** ***(c)*** corresponds to photosynthesis $106CO_2 + 16HNO_3 + H_3PO_4 + 122H_2O + (Fe, Zn ...) + h\nu \rightarrow C_{106}H_{263}O_{110}N_{16}P + 138O_2$. This complex chemical equation represents the synthesis of organic compounds from carbon dioxide and water, using sunlight as an energy source, crucial for plant life and the global carbon cycle.
- **Equation** ***(d)*** is anaerobic respiration ($(CH_2O)_{106}(NH_3)_{16}H_3PO_4 + 94.4HNO_3 \rightarrow 106CO_2 + 55.2N_2 + 177.2H_2O + H_3PO_4$) illustrating the breakdown of organic

matter in the absence of oxygen, producing carbon dioxide, nitrogen, water, and phosphoric acid.

150. (D) Context: This question involves a seismic survey over a two-layer Earth model, where the P-wave velocity of the lower layer is double that of the upper layer.

Interval Velocity (V_{int}) is the velocity of seismic waves within a specific layer.

Average Velocity (V_{avg}) is the cumulative average velocity of seismic waves across both layers.

Root Mean Square Velocity (V_{rms}) is a statistical measure used in seismology to quantify the average seismic wave velocity, considering variations in different layers.

The correct sequence is $V_{int} > V_{rms} > V_{avg}$. This indicates that the interval velocity in the lower layer, being significantly higher, surpasses the root mean square velocity.

The average velocity, which accounts for the slower upper layer and the faster lower layer, is the lowest among the three. This ordering aligns with the physics of seismic wave propagation, where the interval velocity of a faster layer can exceed the RMS velocity, which is an average measure influenced by the slower upper layer.

Previous Years' Paper

Joint CSIR-UGC NET/JRF

Earth, Atmospheric, Ocean & Planetary Sciences

SEPTEMBER-2022

(Exam held on 16/09/2022)

PART-A

1. The squares in the following sketch are filled with digits 1 to 9, without any repetition, such that the numbers in the two horizontal rows add up to 20 each. What number appears in the square labelled A in the vertical column?

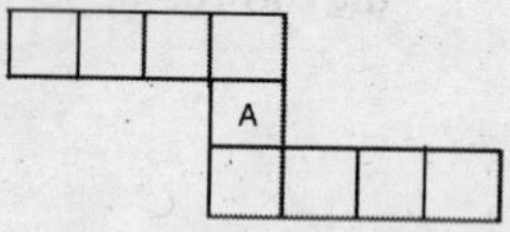

A. It cannot be ascertained in the absence of the sum of the numbers in the column
B. 3
C. 5
D. 7

2. Sections A, B, C and D of a class have 24, 27, 30 and 36 students, respectively. One section has boys and girls who are seated alternately in three rows, such that the first and the last positions in each row are occupied by boys. Which section could this be?

A. A B. B
C. C D. D

3. In a round-robin tournament, after each team has played exactly four matches, the number of wins/losses of 6 participating teams are as follows:

Team	Win	Loss
A	4	0
B	0	4
C	3	1
D	2	2
E	0	4
F	3	1

Which of the two teams have certainly NOT played with each other?

A. A and B B. C and F
C. E and D D. B and E

4. Given plot describes the motion of an object with time.

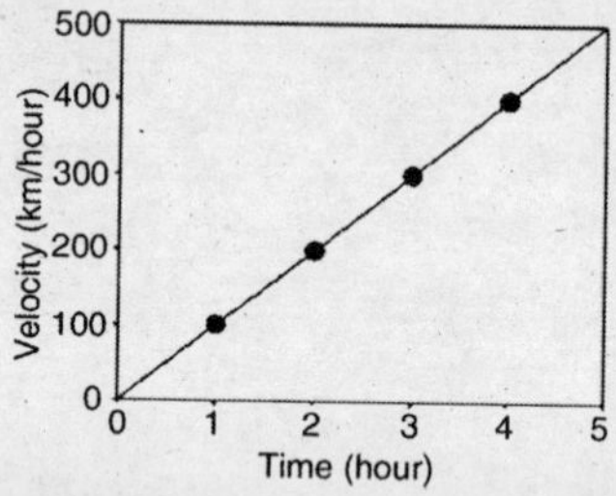

Which one of the following statements is CORRECT?

A. The object is moving with a constant velocity.
B. The object covers equal distance every hour.
C. The object is accelerating.
D. Velocity of the object doubles every hour.

5. If one letter each is drawn at random from the words CAUSE and EFFECT, the chance that they are the same is:

A. 1/30 B. 1/11
C. 1/10 D. 2/11

6. A vehicle has tyres of diameter 1 m connected by a shaft directly to gearwheel A which meshes with gearwheel B as shown in the diagram. A has 12 teeth and B has 8. If points

x on A and y on B are initially in contact, they will again be in contact after the vehicle has travelled a distance (in meters)

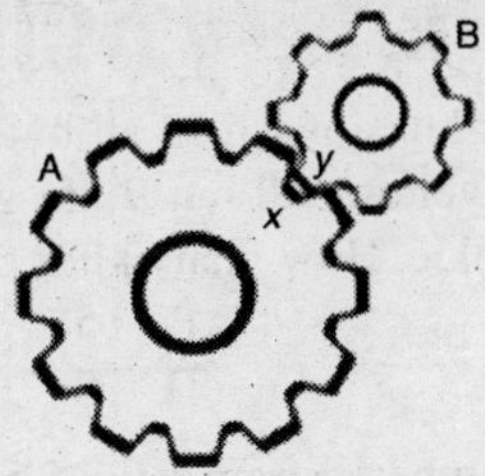

A. 2 π B. 3 π
C. 4 π D. 12 π

7. A liar always lies and a non-liar, never. If in a group of n persons seated around a round-table everyone calls his/her left neighbour a liar, then:
A. all are liars.
B. n must be even and every alternate person is a liar
C. n must be odd and every alternate person is a liar
D. n must be a prime

8. The correct pictorial representation of the relations among the categories PLAYERS, FEMALE CRICKETERS, MALE FOOTBALLERS and GRADUATES is:

(*a*) 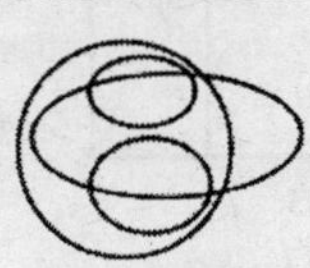 (*b*) 

(*c*)  (*d*) 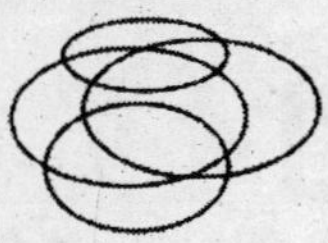

A. (*a*) B. (*b*)
C. (*c*) D. (*d*)

9. What is the product of the number of capital letters and the number of small letters of the English alphabet in the following text?
A4;={c8%$56((+B/;,.H&r]]](u];#~K@>83<??/
STvx%^(d)L:/<-N347)))2;:$+}E$###[w}'"..;/89
A. 17 B. 37
C. 53 D. 63

10. On a track of 200 m length, S runs from the starting point and R starts 20 m ahead of S at the same time. Both reach the end of the track at the same time. S runs at a uniform speed of 10 m/s. If R also runs at a uniform speed, what is R's speed (in m/s)?
A. 9 B. 10
C. 12 D. 8

11. A plant grows by 10% of its height every three months. If the plant's height today is 1 m, its height after one year is the closest to:
A. 1.10 m B. 1.21 m
C. 1.33 m D. 1.46 m

12. Starting from the top of a page and pointing downward, an ant moves according to the following commands:

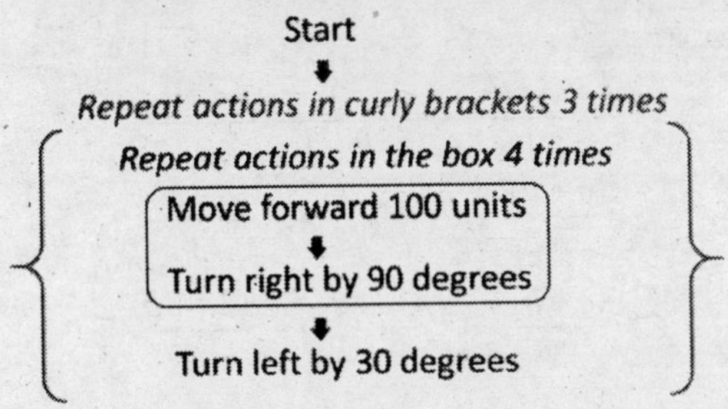

Of the following paths:

(*a*) 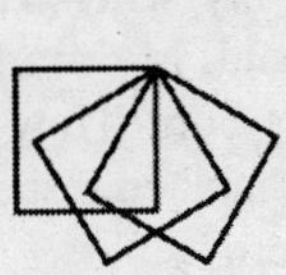 (*b*) 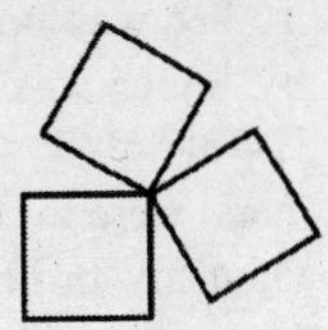

(*c*) 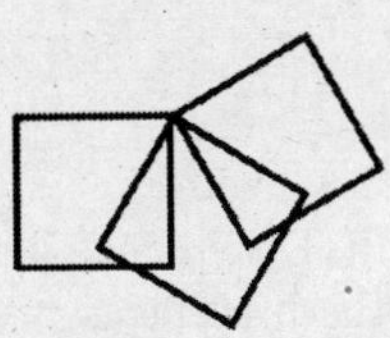 (*d*) 

Which is the correct path of the ant?
A. (*a*) B. (*b*)
C. (*c*) D. (*d*)

13. In a four-digit PIN, the third digit is the product of the first two digits and the fourth digit is zero. The number of such PINs is:

A. 42 B. 41
C. 40 D. 39

14. After 12 : 00 : 00 the hour hand and minute hand of a clock will be perpendicular to each other for the first time at:

A. 12 : 16 : 21 B. 12 : 15 : 00
C. 13 : 22 : 21 D. 12 : 48 : 08

15. At what horizontal distance from A should a vertical line be drawn so as to divide the area of the trapezium shown in the figure into two equal parts? (*a* and *b* are lengths of the parallel sides.)

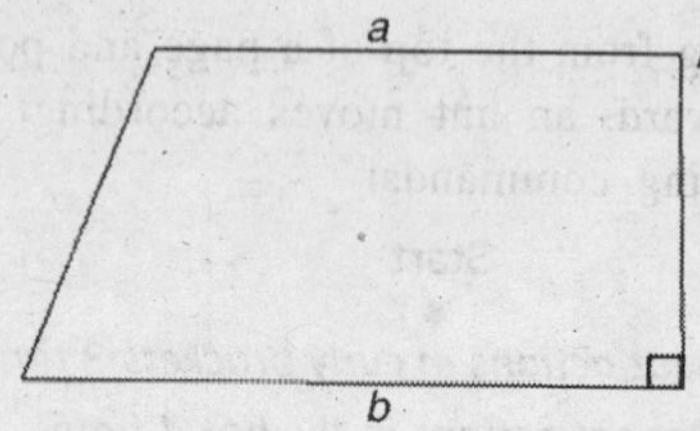

A. $\frac{(a+b)}{4}$ B. $\frac{(a+b)}{3}$
C. $\frac{(a+b)}{2}$ D. $\frac{(2a+b)}{2}$

16. I have a brother who is 4 years elder to me, and a sister who was 5 years old when my brother was born. When my sister was born, my father was 24 years old. My mother was 27 years old when I was born. How old (in years) were my father and mother, respectively, when my brother was born?

A. 29 and 23
B. 27 and 25
C. 27 and 23
D. 29 and 25

17. A boy has kites of which all but 9 are red, all but 9 are yellow, all but 9 are green, and all but 9 are blue. How many kites does he have?

A. 12 B. 15
C. 9 D. 18

18. Tokens numbered from 1 to 25 are mixed and one token is drawn randomly. What is the probability that the number on the token drawn is divisible either by 4 or by 6?

A. 8/25 B. 10/25
C. 9/25 D. 12/25

19. A beam of square cross-section is to be cut out of a wooden log. Assuming that the log is cylindrical, what approximately is the largest fraction of the wood by volume that can be fruitfully utilised as the beam?

A. 49% B. 64%
C. 71% D. 81%

20. How many rectangles are there in the given figure?

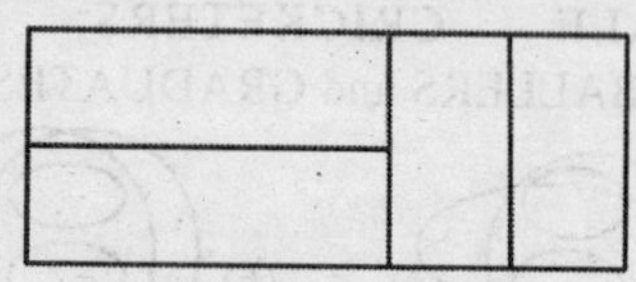

A. 6 B. 7
C. 8 D. 9

PART-B

21. Choose the CORRECT sequence based on albedo of different Earth surfaces.

A. Snow > Vegetation > Desert sands > Calm water
B. Snow > Desert sands > Vegetation > Calm water
C. Calm water > Vegetation > Desert sands > Snow
D. Calm water > Desert sands > Vegetation > Snow

22. Choose the CORRECT statement

A. Low frequency Rossby waves propagate westward in the northern hemisphere.
B. Low frequency Rossby waves propagate eastward in the northern hemisphere.
C. Low frequency Rossby waves propagate eastward in the southern hemisphere.
D. Low frequency Rossby waves propagate eastward along the equator.

23. Which one of the following is true for a large intraplate earthquake recorded worldwide?
A. Both magnitude and intensity decrease with increase in epicentral distance
B. Magnitude is constant but intensity varies
C. Both magnitude and intensity are constant
D. Magnitude varies but intensity is constant

24. Thunderstorms occur more often in the late afternoon and early evening over land because
A. the atmosphere is mostly stable.
B. radiational heating and instability are high.
C. winds are mostly weak.
D. the atmosphere is mostly dry.

25. Which one of the following is ultimate limiting nutrient (on geological time scales) for ocean productivity?
A. Nitrate B. Phosphate
C. Silicate D. Iron

26. If sea ice constitutes 2% of the ocean water with an average oxygen isotopic composition ($\delta^{18}O$) of –55‰, then what would be the $\delta^{18}O$ (in ‰) of an ice free ocean?
A. 0 B. –5.5
C. –11 D. –1.1

27. [HCO_3^-] and [CO_3^{2-}] of a seawater sample are 1.8 and 0.25 mM, respectively. What is the carbonate alkalinity (roughly in eq kg^{-1}) of this sample?
A. 0.45 B. 2.05
C. 2.3 D. 2.55

28. How is the concentration of dissolved organic matter [DOC] comparable to particulate organic matter [POC] in the open surface ocean?
A. [DOC] $\geq$ [POC]
B. [DOC] $\leq$ [POC]
C. [DOC] $\approx$ 10 [POC]
D. [POC] $\approx$ 10 [DOC]

29. Identify the INCORRECT pair
A. Solute load – Dissolved load
B. Bed load – Traction load
C. Suspended load – Wash Load
D. Traction load – Solute load

30. Mercury has no known natural satellite because of its
A. proximity to the sun.
B. slower orbital velocity.
C. retrograde motion.
D. higher temperature.

31. If the mantle were richer in iron than the present, then its
A. gravity and magnetic fields would be the same as the present.
B. gravity field would be the same, but the magnetic field would increase.
C. gravity field would increase, but the magnetic field would be the same.
D. both the gravity and magnetic fields would increase.

32. The epicentre of a deep focus earthquake is normally located at a depth (in km) of
A. $\geq$ 700 B. 300 to 700
C. 70 to 300 D. 0

33. The mean sea level on the Earth is best approximated by which one of the following?
A. WGS 84 Ellipsoid
B. Geoid
C. Oblate Spheroid
D. Everest Spheroid

34. Rayleigh waves
A. propagate as spherical wavefronts
B. propagate as cylindrical wavefronts
C. travel faster than Love waves
D. are generated at the hypocenter by an earthquake

35. Which of the following meteorites are compositionally and texturally similar to terrestrial basalts?
A. Iron meteorites
B. Carbonaceous chondrites
C. Enstatite chondrites
D. Achondrites

36. The decrease in P-wave velocity from ~13.6 km/s to ~8.1 km/s is known to be represented by which of the following discontinuity?

A. Repetti B. Lehmann
C. Gutenberg D. Conrad

37. Which of the following is NOT an example of isomorphic mineral pairs?
A. Pyrite and Marcasite
B. Rutile and Pyrolusite
C. Calcite and Siderite
D. Barite and Anhydrite

38. Which ONE of the following equations relates horizontal-convergence with vertical motion?
A. Navier Stokes equation
B. Vorticity equation
C. Geostrophic balance equation
D. Continuity equation

39. If z and ρ are depth and density of seawater, respectively then, the amplitude of internal wave will
A. increase with decreasing $\frac{\partial \rho}{\partial z}$
B. decrease with decreasing $\frac{\partial \rho}{\partial z}$
C. increase with increasing $\frac{\partial \rho}{\partial z}$
D. remain independent of changes in $\frac{\partial \rho}{\partial z}$

40. Which one of the following places exposes 'flysch' type of sedimentary sequence?
A. Hyderabad B. Mumbai
C. Port Blair D. Kolkata

41. Which one of the following periods is known as the "Age of fishes"?
A. Cambrian B. Ordovician
C. Devonian D. Silurian

42. The strengthening of westerlies with height above the Earth's surface is attributable to the
A. weakening of easterlies with height
B. increasing north-south temperature gradient with height
C. decreasing atmospheric pressure with height
D. increasing height of the tropopause towards the equator

43. In the context of ecosystem biodiversity evaluation, the species of organisms that are particularly sensitive to pollutants, human interferences, ecosystem instability or other such disturbances are referred to as
A. vulnerable species
B. indicator species
C. sensitive species
D. keystone species

44. A freely suspended magnetic needle will be vertical at
A. Geographic Equator
B. Geomagnetic Equator
C. Geographic poles
D. Geomagnetic poles

45. The stability of the boundary layer can be considered neutral when the vertical gradient of the potential temperature is _____.
A. Equal to the Dry Adiabatic Lapse Rate
B. Equal to the Moist Adiabatic Lapse Rate
C. Zero
D. Negative

46. Which planet has the highest orbital angular momentum?
A. Jupiter B. Saturn
C. Mars D. Earth

47. In areas modified by glaciers, kames represent:
A. A detached block of glacial ice.
B. Remnants of disjointed lateral moraines.
C. Mounds of stratified sands and gravels.
D. Terraces formed in valley sidewalls due to change in glacial mass balance.

48. Which one of the following is NOT a zonal soil?
A. Podsol
B. Chernozem
C. Saline and alkaline
D. Pedalfer

49. In standard FCCs, red stands for vegetation because:
A. For strategic purpose, true colours are not disclosed.
B. Green band of the sensor is in shown red.

C. NIR band of the sensor is represented in red.
D. Reflectance of chlorophylls is processed as red by the satellite sensor

50. Development of the Earth's tidal bulge on the opposite direction of the moon is best explained by:
A. Centripetal Force
B. Gravitational force
C. Centrifugal force
D. Coriolis force

51. Water flows in the river channel transporting fine sediment and dissolved material, but its gradient, form and elevation above sea level remain essentially the same. This type of equilibrium is defined as
A. Static B. Dynamic
C. Decay D. Cyclic

52. Identify the type of mass movement

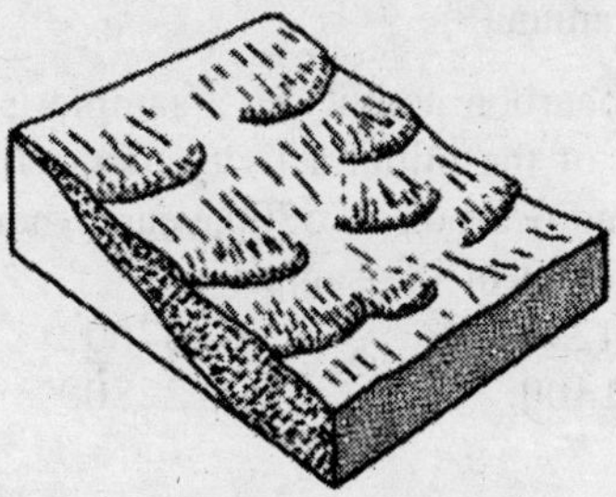

A. Rotational slide B. Rotational slump
C. Rock fall D. Solifluction

53. Which one of the following is an example of impeded sand dune?
A. Barchan B. Transverse
C. Star D. Parabolic

54. If the density of a compact rock of sandstone is 2.5 gm/cc, then what will be its density (in gm/cc), if it is 10% porous and water saturated?
A. 2.25 B. 2.3
C. 2.35 D. 2.4

55. Kepler's third law of planetary motion is represented by which one of the following expressions? (here P = orbital period; a = semi-major axis of the planetary orbit)
A. $P^3 \alpha\, a^2$ B. $P^2 \alpha\, a^3$
C. $P^3 \alpha\, a^3$ D. $P^2 \alpha\, a^2$

56. Which one of the following is the fastest moving plate?
A. Nazca B. Eurasia
C. Africa D. North America

57. Downward bending of isotherms is commonly observed in which of the tectonic settings?
A. Subduction zone
B. Volcanic arc environment
C. Craton interior
D. Divergent plate boundary

58. Which one of the following ore deposits is typically formed by magmatic segregation process?
A. Porphyry copper B. Bauxite
C. Chromite D. Phosphorite

59. A seismic phase which has undergone a single reflection is
A. PKIKP B. pPcP
C. PP D. PKP

60. Which one of the following basins form in collision zones?
A. Fore Arc B. Foreland
C. Back Arc D. Pull apart

61. An air mass is characterized by similar properties of ____ and ____ in any horizontal direction.
A. pressure, temperature
B. wind speed, pressure
C. wind speed, temperature
D. temperature, moisture

62. In which of the following weather systems the contribution of the Coriolis force can be neglected in the balance of forces?
A. Tornado
B. Tropical Cyclone
C. Monsoon Depression
D. Polar Vortex

63. Which one of the following options is the best way to protect yourself from lightning if you get caught in an open field during a thunderstorm?

A. Lie flat on the ground with your face down
B. Take shelter under the nearest tree
C. Crouch on your toes
D. Stand straight up

64. Choose the correct combination of the processes that contribute to the global sea level rise.
A. Arctic sea ice melt, sea surface warming
B. Warming of the ocean, land ice melt
C. Antarctic and Arctic sea ice melt
D. Underwater volcanic eruption, earthquakes

65. How does the depth of the ocean relate to the age of the ocean floor?
A. It increases with age
B. It decreases with age
C. It is independent of age
D. It decreases until 55 Ma

66. In a cloud formation mechanism, cloud base and cloud top, respectively, are represented by
A. Planetary boundary layer and Level of free convection
B. Planetary boundary layer and Lifting condensation level
C. Lifting condensation level and Level of free convection
D. Planetary boundary layer and Level of saturation

67. Which one of the following indicates that the mantle is solid?
A. Mantle convection
B. Phase transformation
C. Propagation of S waves
D. Subduction of a slab to a depth of 600 km

68. The longest mountain chain on the Earth is
A. Himalaya
B. Mid-Atlantic ridge
C. Andes
D. Alps

69. Which one of the following rivers of the Ganga system is a perennial, dominantly groundwater-fed river?
A. Son
B. Gomti
C. Pindar
D. Yamuna

70. Radiocarbon activity in a sample is found to be ¼ of the initial activity. If the half-life of the radiocarbon is 5700 years, then the age (in years) of the sample is
A. 1425 B. 5700
C. 11400 D. 22800

PART-C

71. Choose the CORRECT option based on the following two statements (I) and (II):

Statement I: Transient geotherms typically describe the temperature-depth relationship at a given time for a specific geographic location.

Statement II: Collision of lithospheric plates lead to crustal thickening and disturbs the pre-tectonic steady-state geotherms.
A. Both the statements are correct
B. Both the statements are incorrect
C. Statement I is correct but II is incorrect
D. Statement I is incorrect but II is correct

72. Choose the correct sequence of porphyroblast growth (from the oldest to the youngest) based on the figure showing relationships between porphyroblast growth and matrix foliations.

A. X → Y → Z B. Y → Z → X
C. Y → X → Z D. X → Z → Y

73. The following diagram shows phase relations for the orthoclase ($KAlSi_3O_8$)–albite ($NaAlSi_3O_8$) system at constant pressure. If 'S' is the initial composition of magma, what is the proportion (%) of perthite and antiperthite crystallized from this magma at 550°C?

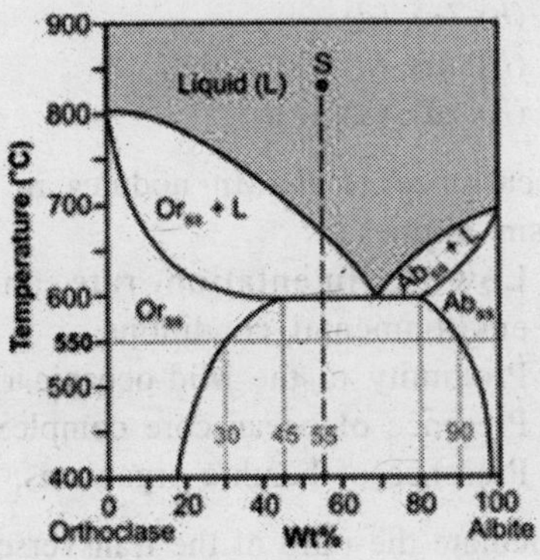

A. 42% perthite; 58% antiperthite
B. 58% perthite; 42% antiperthite
C. 70% perthite; 30% antiperthite
D. 10% perthite; 90% antiperthite

74. The pitch of a slickenline on a fault slickenside (230°, 48° SW) is measured to be 90°. Which one of the following is the correct plunge amount of the slickenline?

A. 90° B. 81°
C. 48° D. 42°

75. In the Himalaya, which one of the following is the correct sequence of in-sequence thrusts from north to south? (STD-South Tibetan Detachment; MBT-Main Boundary Thrust; MCT-Main Central Thrust; MFT-Main Frontal Thrust; ITSZ-Indus-Tsangpo Suture Zone)

A. ITSZ, STD, MCT, MBT, MFT
B. MFT, MBT, MCT, STD, ITSZ
C. ITSZ, MCT, MBT, STD, MFT
D. MBT, MFT, STD, ITSZ, MCT

76. Three fossils (Ec, Mc and Vt) are present in two continents and the following are true:

(*a*) Ec, Mc and Vt have a short temporal range.
(*b*) Vt and Mc have hard skeleton.
(*c*) Ec, Mc and Vt live in lakes, grassland, and in shallow marine environments, respectively.
(*d*) Ec is a microfossil; Mc and Vt are megascopic fossils.

Which fossil would you choose for correlation?

A. Ec
B. Mc
C. Vt
D. Ec and Mc are equally good

77. Absence of which one of the following played a role in preserving soft-bodied organisms of Ediacaran fauna?

A. oxygen in the atmosphere
B. stromatolites
C. acidifying conditions
D. mobile/bioturbating organism

78. Choose the correct statement:

A. Ichnofacies indicates paleobathymetry.
B. *Ophiomorpha* is a horizontal burrow along the bed boundary.
C. Laminae truncate against burrow.
D. *Thalassinoides* is only produced by crabs.

79. Which one is the correct statement out of the following?

A. Maximum flooding surface occurs above the highstand systems tract deposits.
B. Regressive surface of marine erosion forms during forced regression.
C. Shelf edge delta forms during highstand normal regression.
D. Rate of sea level rise is lower than the rate of sedimentation during transgression.

80. The following shear zones occur in the Southern Granulite Terrain

SASZ – Salem Attur shear zone
AKSZ – Achankovil shear zone
PCSZ – Palghat-Cauvery shear zone;
KKPT – Karur-Kambam-Palnavu-Trichur shear zone

The correct sequence of shear zones along a south to north traverse is

A. AKSZ – KKPT – PCSZ – SASZ
B. AKSZ – SASZ – PCSZ – KKPT
C. KKPT – PCSZ – AKSZ – SASZ
D. SASZ – PCSZ – KKPT – AKSZ

81. Critical entrainment velocity for grains
(*a*) larger than 0.5 mm increases gradually with increasing mean grain size
(*b*) smaller than 0.5 mm increases gradually with decreasing mean grain size
(*c*) larger than 0.5 mm decreases gradually with increasing mean grain size
(*d*) smaller than 0.5 mm decreases gradually with decreasing mean grain size

Based on the above statements, which one of the following options is TRUE?
A. (*a*) and (*b*)
B. (*c*) and (*d*)
C. (*b*) and (*c*)
D. (*a*) and (*c*)

82. Using the following garnet-melt trace element partition coefficients, the correct sequence of trace elements accommodated in garnet mineral structure during its crystallization from a basaltic magma is

Element	Partition coefficient
Y – Yttrium	8.500
Sm – Samarium	0.870
Gd – Gadolinium	2.550
Lu – Lutetium	13.700

A. Sm → Gd → Y → Lu
B. Lu → Y → Gd → Sm
C. Y → Sm → Gd → Lu
D. Y → Lu → Gd → Sm

83. Where would you expect the highest $CaCO_{-3}$ production within an ocean basin?
A. Continental shelves
B. Continental slopes
C. Pelagic Ocean
D. Oceanic rift valley

84. Antarctic and Greenland ice sheets store today about 2% of the ocean water mass with an average $\delta^{18}O$ value of –45‰ w.r.t. SMOW. What would be the $\delta^{18}O$ of value (in ‰) of the ocean water in an ice free world?
A. 0
B. –45
C. –0.9
D. 9

85. Arrange the following events in the order of increasing age:
(*a*) Younger Dryas
(*b*) Meghalayan Stage
(*c*) Last Glacial Maximum
(*d*) H1 Heinrich event

Choose the correct option
A. (*a*), (*b*), (*c*), (*d*)
B. (*b*), (*c*), (*d*), (*a*)
C. (*b*), (*a*), (*d*), (*c*)
D. (*b*), (*d*), (*a*), (*c*)

86. Occurrence of Fe-Mn nodules in an ocean basin implies
A. Low sedimentation rate and stable environmental conditions.
B. Proximity to the Mid-oceanic ridge.
C. Presence of ocean core complex.
D. Presence of benthic organisms.

87. Calculate the ratio of the transverse strain to longitudinal strain in a granite sample which has a P wave velocity of 6 km/s and the value of the Lamé parameter λ is twice that of the shear modulus of the rock sample.
A. 0.23
B. 0.25
C. 0.33
D. 0.38

88. A near surface local earthquake is recorded by a station at the surface at an epicentral distance of 120 km. Assuming a homogeneous, isotropic medium with a Poisson ratio of 0.25 and P wave velocity of 6 km/s, calculate the difference in the arrival times of the S and P waves at the station. Choose the correct option.
A. 12.6 s
B. 13.6 s
C. 14.6 s
D. 15.6 s

89. In a two way-travel time seismic section with 101 traces and a trace interval of 100 m, the depth to 1.0 s is 1000 m and the interval velocity between 1.0 s to 1.5 s is 3000 m/s. The dip of the reflector that is observed at 1.080 s and 1.050 s on the first and last trace, respectively, corresponds to a gradient of
A. 3 m/km
B. 3.5 m/km
C. 4 m/km
D. 4.5 m/km

90. Match the logging tools in column-I with their corresponding characteristics in column-II

Column-I	Column-II
1. Lateral Log	(*a*) Depth of investigation is twice spacing
2. Deep Laterolog	(*b*) Measures resistivity of flushed zone
3. Long Normal log	(*c*) Asymmetrical response
4. Proximity log	(*d*) Power is held constant

	1	2	3	4
A.	(*a*)	(*b*)	(*c*)	(*d*)
B.	(*b*)	(*d*)	(*c*)	(*a*)
C.	(*c*)	(*d*)	(*a*)	(*b*)
D.	(*c*)	(*d*)	(*b*)	(*a*)

91. The rate of increase of the Earth's gravity field at latitudes 30° and 60° are in the ratio

A. 1 : 1　　B. $1:\sqrt{2}$

C. $\sqrt{2}:\sqrt{3}$　　D. $\sqrt{3}:2$

92. An anomalous body, in the form of a horizontal circular disc at a depth of 173 m, produces a maximum gravity anomaly, which is half that of a Bouguer slab of same thickness and density contrast. The radius (in m) of the disc is

A. 192　　B. 260

C. 300　　D. 346

93. Consider a situation wherein the magnetic anomaly in the horizontal component, at some station, over an ore deposit is zero and the anomaly in the total field is twice that in the vertical component. Such an ore body can occur

A. nowhere on the earth

B. at many latitudes

C. at only the magnetic latitude 30°N

D. at only the magnetic latitude 60°N.

94. An ore body that can be equated to a single pole occurs at a place where the vertical (V) and horizontal (H) components of the Earth's magnetic field are in the ratio 1 : 3. The positions of the maximum and minimum anomaly values along a NS profile across this model are separated by a distance of 150m. What would be the distance between this point pair, if the body were located at a place where V : H = $2\sqrt{2}$: 3?

A. 150 m, same as that where V : H = 1 : 3

B. 200 m

C. $200\sqrt{2}$ m

D. $200\sqrt{3}$ m

95. A sinusoidal wave $x(t) = A_0 \cos(100\pi t)$ is digitized at a sampling frequency f_s. However, the output signal obtained is $y(t) = B_0 \cos(60\pi t)$. The sampling frequency f_s (in Hz) is:

A. 50　　B. 30

C. 20　　D. 100

96. For a symmetric matrix

$$A = \begin{bmatrix} 6 & 3 & 2 \\ 3 & 5 & 1 \\ 2 & 1 & 4 \end{bmatrix},$$

the narrowest bound within which all eigenvalues (λ_i, i =1, 2, 3) of A should lie is:

A. [2,15]　　B. [0, 9]

C. [–1, 9]　　D. [1, 11]

97. A discrete signal $x(n)$ = {2,1,0, –1,1} passes through a linear system, shown in the figure below. The energy of the output signal $y(n)$ will be approximately _______ times the energy of the input signal.

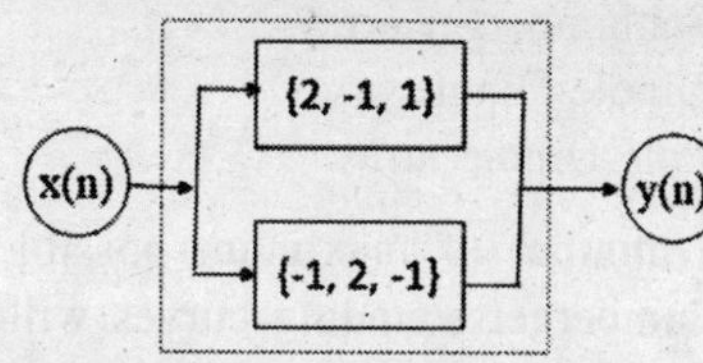

A. 2.285　　B. 4.571

C. 1.0　　D. 3.478

98. An oceanic lithosphere, being created at a mid-oceanic ridge (MOR), is moving away from the MOR at a speed of 5 cm/yr.

The spreading rate was double the present rate during the Cretaceous period (145.5 Ma to 65.5 Ma). Assuming the Cartesian geometry for the plate motion, the Cretaceous Superchron (121 Ma to 83 Ma) should be located between ________from the MOR.

A. 5025 km and 8825 km
B. 4150 km and 6050 km
C. 3275 km and 5025 km
D. 3275 km and 6050 km

99. The Primary magnetic field (Hp) varies inversely proportional to cube of the distance (r) between transmitter and observation point $\left(Hp \propto \frac{1}{r^3}\right)$ due to which type of transmitter?

A. a long horizontal grounded wire (Two Frame method)
B. a large horizontal rectangular loop (Bieler-Watson Method)
C. a small circular loop (Slingram method)
D. a long vertical wire (VLF method)

100. Which combination of electromagnetic methods measure Real and Imaginary components of Secondary field?

A. Compensator and TURAM methods
B. Compensator and Sundberg methods
C. Two-Frame and VLF methods
D. AFMAG and INPUT method

101. For a fixed number of electrodes in ERT survey, which electrode array gives the maximum depth of investigation

A. Wenner array
B. Schlumberger array
C. Dipole-Dipole array
D. Pole-Dipole array

102. The number of maximum possible 6-layer Schlumberger sounding curves will be

A. 16 B. 24
C. 32 D. 40

103. **Statement (A):** The equilibrium solubility of a mineral represents the extent to which it will dissolve in water.

Statement (B): Equilibrium solubility is unaffected by the temperature and pH of the environment.

Choose the correct option

A. Both statements are incorrect.
B. Statement (A) is incorrect but statement (B) is correct
C. Statement (A) is correct but statement (B) is incorrect
D. Both statements are correct

104. **Assertion (A):** In the great majority of river systems discharge increases downstream.

Reason (R): The tributaries progressively add more runoff to the trunk stream.

Choose the correct option

A. (A) is correct but (R) is incorrect
B. (A) is incorrect but (R) is correct
C. Both (A) and (R) are correct and (R) is the correct explanation of (A)
D. Both (A) and (R) are correct but (R) is not the correct explanation of (A)

105. Match the following columns:

Column-I	Column-II
(*a*) Changes in discharge through time	1. Ephemeral streams
(*b*) Elevation of the water surface in a river channel	2. Bankfull discharge
(*c*) Channels carry only occasional flow after storms	3. Overbank flow
(*d*) Discharge at which the channel is filled to capacity	4. Hydrograph
	5. Stage

Choose the correct option

	(*a*)	(*b*)	(*c*)	(*d*)
A.	4	5	1	2
B.	4	2	1	5
C.	1	5	3	2
D.	3	5	4	1

106. Statement (A): The Manning roughness coefficient increases as flow depth increases up to bankfull discharge.

Statement (B): Once the channel capacity is exceeded the flow spreads over a much larger area and the Manning roughness coefficient decreases.

Choose the correct option

A. Both statements are incorrect.

B. Statement (A) is incorrect but statement (B) is correct.

C. Statement (A) is correct but statement (B) is incorrect.

D. Both statements are correct.

107. Read the following statements that are used to describe Till.

(*a*) These are unconsolidated sediments deposited by glacier ice.

(*b*) These are consolidated sediments deposited only by glacial meltwater and exhibit stratification.

(*c*) These are typically unsorted and non stratified.

(*d*) These are typically well-sorted and are dominated by well-rounded clasts.

Choose the CORRECT option:

A. Only (*a*) and (*c*) are True

B. Only (*b*) and (*d*) are True

C. Only (*d*) is True

D. Only (*c*) is False

108. The following diagram shows two offshore islands (IS). The zone of diffraction will be approximately located at:

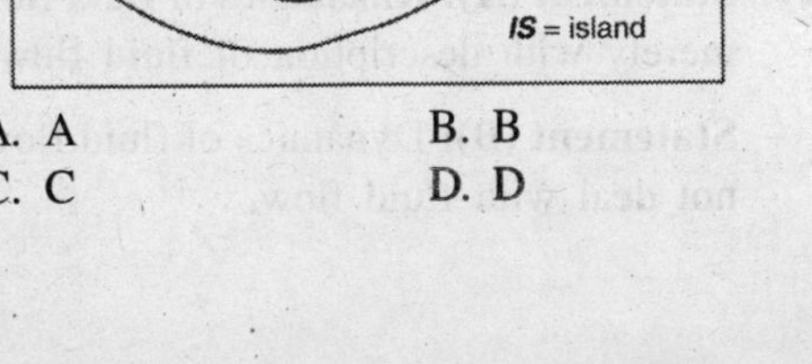

A. A B. B

C. C D. D

109. In general, which one of the following types of breakers DOES NOT produce net shoreward movement of sediment

A. Plunging B. Surging

C. Spilling D. Collapsing

110. Stranded or raised beach deposits, marine shell beds and wave-cut platforms backed by steep cliff-like slopes indicate a

(*a*) Fall in sea level

(*b*) Rise in sea level

(*c*) Uplift of land

(*d*) Subsidence of land

Choose the correct option:

A. (*b*)

B. (*d*)

C. (*a*) and/or (*c*)

D. (*b*) and/or (*d*)

111. Identify the correct set of karst features or landforms

A. Poljes, Tors, Cockpit, Doline

B. Uvalas, Karren, Ponor, Poljes

C. Karren, Bajada, Poljes, Sinkholes

D. Uvalas, Ponor, Tarn, Cockpit

112. Which one of the following is a bank-attached arcuate-shaped feature developed along the convex banks of meander bends?

A. Ramp B. Riffle

C. Point Bar D. Braid

113. Match the Earth scientists with the hypotheses on pediment formation proposed by them:

Proponent	**Principal cause of pediment formation**
(*a*) A.C. Lawson	1. Erosion by sheetflood and rillwash
(*b*) W.M. Davis	2. Lateral planation by streams
(*c*) G.K. Gilbert	3. Structurally controlled irregular landscape lowering
(*d*) C.R. Twidale	4. Deep weathering and stripping
	5. Parallel retreat of hill front

Choose the correct option

	(a)	(b)	(c)	(d)
A.	4	3	1	5
B.	5	1	2	3
C.	4	2	1	3
D.	4	5	3	1

114. Velocity of water flowing over sands is higher than the speed of waves propagated in the flow. The following type of bedforms are likely to form:

A. Antidunes
B. Dunes or megaripples
C. Ripples
D. Lower plane beds

115. In the given figure, identify the clay minerals that usually appear in soil due to weathering of plagioclase feldspar with increasing rainfall:

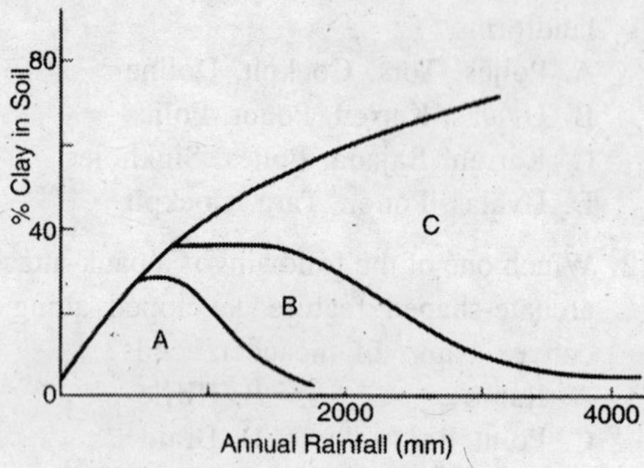

A. (A) Gibbsite (B) Montmorillonite (C) Kaolinite
B. (A) Smectite (B) Gibbsite (C) Kaolinite
C. (A) Montmorillonite (B) Kaolinite (C) gibbsite
D. (A) Kaolinite (B) Gibbsite(C) Smectite

116. Which one among the following is most ideal site for achieving steady state in an open system?

A. Leeward slope of a frontal dune
B. A glacier at the upper limit of ablation zone
C. A beach characterised by rhythmic topography (cusps and horns)
D. A stretch of a river between two bridges

117. Which one of the following is the correct sequence of Koppen's climate types according to their positions on the globe starting from the equator?

A. Af - BWh - BSh - Dfc - Dfd
B. Af - BSh - BWh - Dfd - Dfc
C. Af - BSh - BWh - Dfc - Dfd
D. Dfc - Dfd - BSh - BWh - Af

118. Match the ecological adaptive strategies with the plant types:

Plant Type	Adaptive strategies
(a) Hydrophytes	1. germination of seeds before they shed; adventitious roots that develop from the base of the stem; negatively geotropic roots for supply of oxygen
(b) Mesophytes	2. root systems are very deep; stems are dwarf and branched; stomata are less in number and generally confined to the lower surface of leaves
(c) Xerophytes	3. leaves are thin, narrow, and linear; extensive aerenchyma in all organs; stomata are generally absent
(d) Halophytes	4. leaves are large; stem is rigid and stout; normal physiological processes

Choose the correct option

	(a)	(b)	(c)	(d)
A.	3	4	1	2
B.	3	4	2	1
C.	4	3	1	2
D.	3	1	4	2

119. Statement (A): Kinematics of fluid flow deals merely with description of fluid flow.

Statement (B): Dynamics of fluid flows does not deal with fluid flow.

Which of the following options is CORRECT?
A. Both Statements (A) and (B) are true.
B. Both Statements (A) and (B) are false.
C. Statement (A) is false; Statement (B) is true.
D. Statement (A) is true; Statement (B) is false.

120. Statement (A): Dynamic viscosity coefficient of a liquid increases with increase in temperature.

Statement (B): Dynamic viscosity coefficient of a gas increases with increase in temperature.

Which of the following options is CORRECT?
A. Both Statements (A) and (B) are false.
B. Both Statements (A) and (B) are true.
C. Statement (A) is true; Statement (B) is false.
D. Statement (A) is false; Statement (B) is true.

121. Identify the INCORRECT statement: Atmospheric boundary layer ______.
A. is characterized by turbulent motion
B. is associated with small Reynolds Number
C. is a layer where viscous forces cannot be ignored
D. experiences a diurnal (daily) cycle of temperature, humidity, wind, and pollution variations

122. The stationary Rossby waves from the mid latitudes often decay in the tropics because
A. the waves have travelled a long distance and lost energy.
B. frequent convection and the diabatic heating in the tropics.
C. mean zonal winds are easterly.
D. Hadley Cell subsidence acts as a barrier between subtropics and tropics

123. The anticyclones do not intensify as cyclones because
A. of the absence of latent heating in anticyclones
B. of the radius of anticyclones is large
C. they form over colder waters
D. the relative vorticity and planetary vorticity have opposite signs

124. The given figure shows a vertical cross-section of an Occluded Front. Which of the following is true about the temperatures of the 3 air masses A, B, C associated with the front?

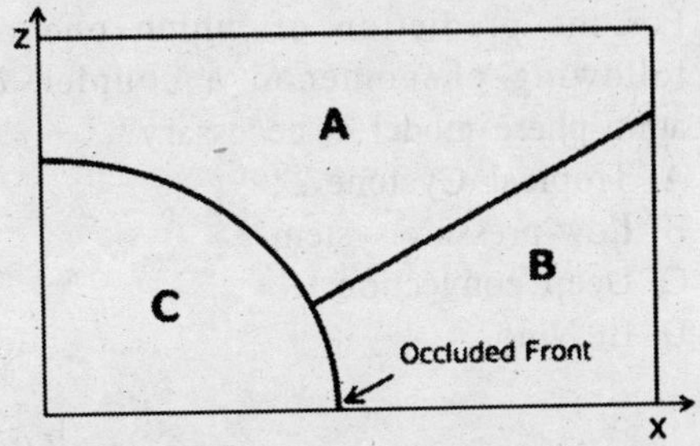

A. $T_A < T_B < T_C$ B. $T_A > T_B < T_C$
C. $T_A > T_B > T_C$ D. $T_A = T_B = T_C$

125. If the absolute vorticity of the flow is conserved, air moving northeastward in the northern hemisphere will turn ____ to compensate for the ____ in the planetary vorticity.
A. anticyclonically, decrease
B. anticyclonically, increase
C. cyclonically, increase
D. cyclonically, decrease

126. If an initially motionless airmass centered over the equator is moved adiabatically to the north pole, then it will
A. attain a cyclonic relative vorticity.
B. attain an anticyclonic relative vorticity.
C. disintegrate.
D. remain motionless.

127. Statement (A): Thick clouds reflect more solar radiation than thin clouds.

Statement (B): Absorption of solar radiation in extensive cloud systems is about 20%.

Choose the correct option.
A. Statement (A) is true; Statement (B) is false
B. Statement (A) is false; Statement (B) is true
C. Both Statements (A) and (B) are false
D. Both Statements (A) and (B) are true

128. Which part of a thunderstorm cloud dissipates first?
A. Top
B. Bottom
C. Sides
D. All parts dissipate together

129. For the prediction of which one of the following phenomenon a coupled ocean atmosphere model is necessary?
A. Tropical Cyclone
B. Low-pressure system
C. Deep convection
D. El Nino

130. Courant-Friedrich-Levy (CFL) $\left|\frac{c\Delta t}{\Delta x}\right| \le 1$, condition is known for
A. Unstability
B. Conditional instability
C. Computational stability
D. Inconsistency

131. Thermal wind is the change of ________ in vertical troposphere.
A. Inertial wind
B. Geostrophic wind
C. Cyclostrophic wind
D. Gradient wind

132. If isobaric surfaces are also the surfaces of constant density, then atmosphere is
A. Conditional unstable
B. Baroclinic
C. Barotropic
D. Unstable

133. Larger values of Rossby number are likely to be seen
A. when the horizontal length scale is large.
B. when the vertical extent of the system is large.
C. closer to the equator.
D. closer to the poles.

134. In a tropical cyclone, the conservation of mass requires
A. upper-level divergent flow.
B. weakening of the low-level winds.
C. thunderstorms in the eyewall.
D. calm and clear eye.

135. Statement (A): The Earth's atmosphere became oxygen rich around 2.4 billion years ago – called the great oxidation event (GOE).

Statement (B): Photosynthetic bacteria produced first oxygen on the Earth.

Choose the correct answer?
A. Both statements are correct and (B) explains (A).
B. Both statements are incorrect.
C. (A) is correct but (B) is incorrect.
D. (A) is incorrect but (B) is correct.

136. Match the wave types in Column-I with their properties in Column-II:

Column-I	Column-II
(*a*) Capillary waves	1. Free waves in open ocean with gravity as a restoring force
(*b*) Standing waves	2. Free waves with surface tension as a restoring force
(*c*) Tidal waves	3. Forced waves in open ocean with gravity as a restoring force
(*d*) Wind waves	4. Formation of Nodes and Antinodes
	5. Forced waves with surface tension as a restoring force

Select the CORRECT option

	(*a*)	(*b*)	(*c*)	(*d*)
A.	2	4	5	3
B.	5	3	1	2
C.	5	1	4	2
D.	2	4	3	1

137. Consider the following statements

Statement (A): Diffusional mixing rate of salinity is higher than that of temperature in ocean.

Statement (B): Larger density gradient in the vertical leads to shorter wavelength waves.

Choose the correct option

A. Statement (A) and (B) are True.

B. Statement (A) is False, Statement (B) is True.

C. Statement (A) is True, Statement (B) is False.

D. Statement (A) and (B) are False.

138. The given figure shows the continents (shaded) surrounded by ocean (unshaded) and vectors represent surface wind directions. Identify the processes in the coastal regions marked with A, B, C, and D.

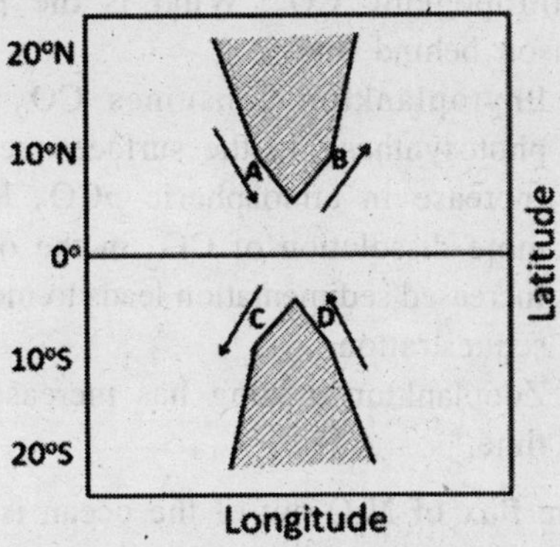

A. Upwelling at B and D, Downwelling at A and C

B. Upwelling at A and D, Downwelling at B and C

C. Upwelling at A and C, Downwelling at B and D

D. Upwelling at A and B, Downwelling at C and D

139. Identify the CORRECT combinations of ocean circulation theories in Column-I with their mechanism in Column-II.

Column-I	Column-II
(*a*) Sverdrup theory	1. Friction between the currents and the side walls added to the potential vorticity conservation.
(*b*) Stommel theory	2. Ocean interior meridional flow directions described through a potential vorticity argument
(*c*) Munk's theory	3. Inclusion of dissipation of potential vorticity to explain westward intensification of western boundary currents

Select the CORRECT option

	(*a*)	(*b*)	(*c*)
A.	2	1	3
B.	3	1	2
C.	2	3	1
D.	3	2	1

140. Which one of the following shows a CORRECT relationship of Tide generating force (F) on the Earth's surface due to the Moon? (R: The Earth's radius, D: Earth to Moon distance, M: mass of Moon)

A. $F \propto MRD^{-3}$

B. $F \propto MR^2D^{-2}$

C. $F \propto MR^{-2}D^{-3}$

D. $F \propto MRD^{-2}$

141. A wave having a wavelength 624 m, frequency 0.05 s^{-1} is propagating in deep water. The wave passes a fixed point P, 30 seconds after crossing a crest. If the amplitude of the wave is α then, what is displacement at point P?

A. α B. 0

C. $-\alpha$ D. $\frac{\alpha}{2}$

142. Given figures represent nutrient profiles at a site in the tropical Pacific Ocean. Which one of the following options correctly represents these nutrients?

(*a*)

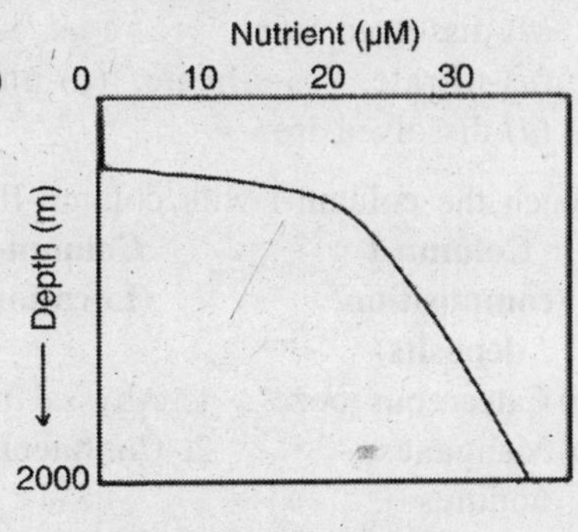

(*b*)

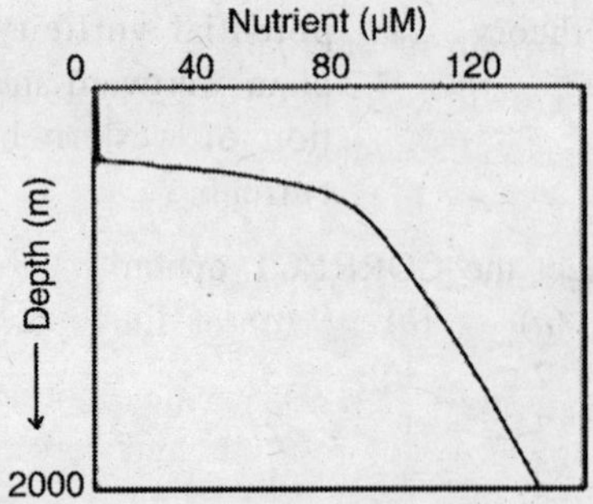

(*c*)

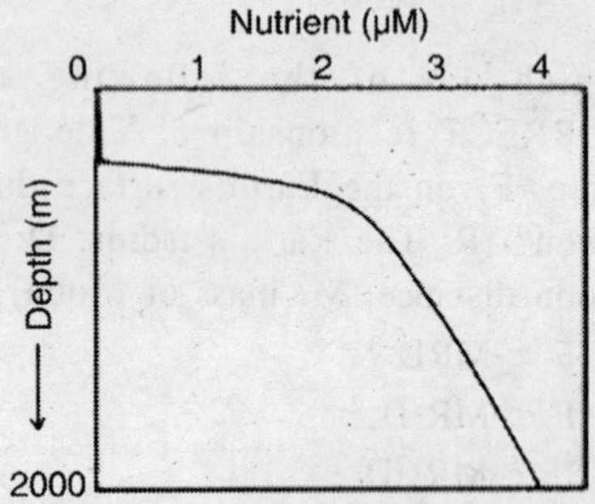

(*d*)

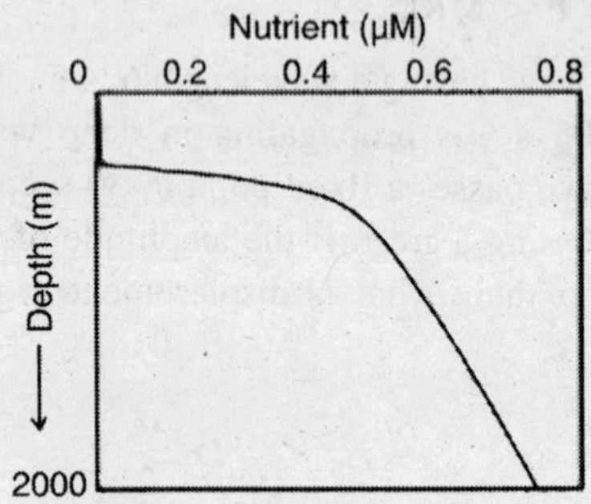

A. (*a*)-nitrate, (*b*)-phosphate, (*c*)-dissolved iron, (*d*)-silicate
B. (*a*)-silicate, (*b*)-phosphate, (*c*)-nitrate, (*d*)-dissolved iron
C. (*a*)-silicate, (*b*)-nitrate, (*c*)-nitrite, (*d*)-dissolved iron
D. (*a*)-nitrate, (*b*)-silicate, (*c*)-phosphate, (*d*)-dissolved iron

143. Match the column-I with column-II:

Column-I (composition/ deposits)	**Column-II (Locations)**
(*a*) Calcareous ooze	1. Abyssal plain
(*b*) Manganese nodules	2. Continental shelf
(*c*) Metal sulphides	3. Seafloor above CCD
(*d*) Phosphorites	4. Hydrothermal vents

Choose the correct option

	(*a*)	(*b*)	(*c*)	(*d*)
A.	2	4	1	3
B.	3	1	4	2
C.	4	1	2	3
D.	4	3	2	1

144. Ocean takes up significant amount of anthropogenic CO_2. What is the primary reason behind this?
A. Phytoplankton consumes CO_2 during photosynthesis in the surface ocean.
B. Increase in atmospheric pCO_2 leads to more dissolution of CO_2 in the ocean.
C. Increased sedimentation leads to more CO_2 sequestration.
D. Zooplankton grazing has increased over time.

145. The flux of N_2O out of the ocean is mostly concentrated in the upwelling areas and high latitudes because
A. there is more N_2 available in these regions.
B. the solubility of N_2O is less in these regions so it escapes to the atmosphere.
C. the processes that produce N_2O are inhibited by light.
D. the winds are stronger in these regions and help the gas to go out.

146. There are two particles, X and Y, on the sea surface. The density of particle X is twice the density of seawater, while Y has the same density as the seawater. If X's radius is thrice the radius of Y, which of the following statements is correct.
A. Sinking velocity of X is 9 times that of Y.
B. Sinking velocity of X is 3 times that of Y.
C. Sinking velocity of X is 18 times that of Y.
D. X might get deposited in the sediments but Y will not sink.

147. What is the preferred sequence of oxidants utilized by bacteria during the decomposition of organic matter?

A. $O_2 > NO_3^- > SO_4^{2-} > CO_3^{2-}$

B. $O_2 > NO_3^- > CO_3^{2-} > SO_4^{2-}$

C. $O_2 > SO_4^{2-} > CO_3^{2-} > NO_3^-$

D. $NO_3^- > SO_4^{2-} > CO_3^{2-} > O_2$

148. Ongoing climate change would likely result in:

A. frequent hypoxia in coastal waters.
B. decrease in nutrient loading in coastal waters.
C. inhibition of stratification in coastal waters.
D. increase in ocean pH.

149. Secondary production in ocean typically refers to

A. growth of microalgae
B. growth of heterotrophic biomass
C. overall biomass
D. growth of haptophytes

150. Statement (A): Benthic infauna plays important functional role in bioturbation.

Statement (B): Oxygenic photoautotrophs synthesize chlorophylls and carotenoids.

Choose the correct answer

A. Both the statements are correct
B. Both the statements are incorrect
C. Statement (A) is correct but (B) is incorrect
D. Statement (A) is incorrect and (B) is correct

ANSWERS

1. (C): Numbers from 1 to 9

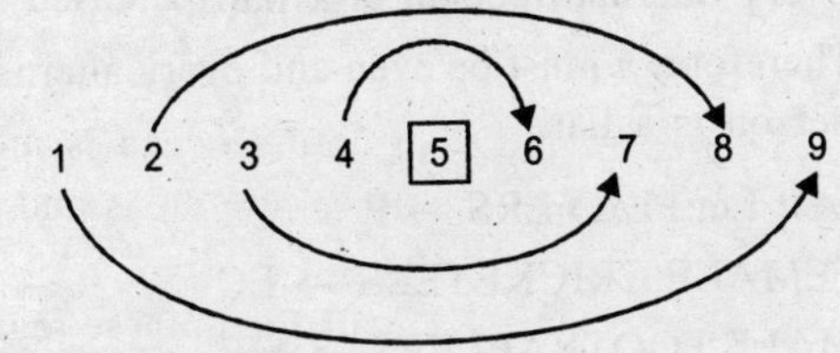

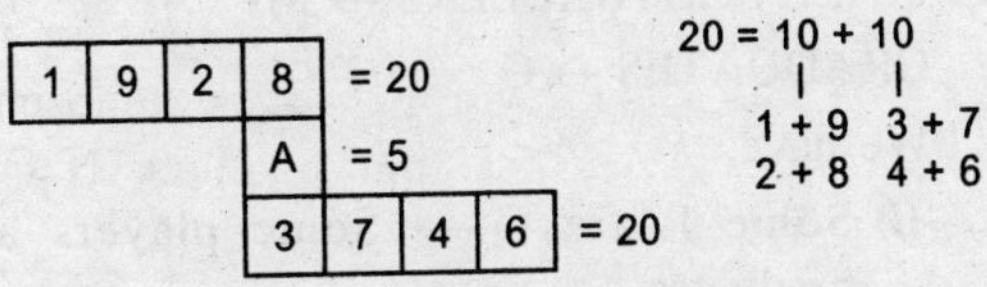

Thus, number appears in the square labelled A in the vertical column is A = 5.

Hence, correct answer is (C).

2. (B): Given data:

Sections	Students	In 3 Rows
A	24	3 × 8
B	27	3 × 9
C	30	3 × 10
D	36	3 × 12

	1	2	3	4	5	6	7	8	9
Row I.	B	G	B	G	B	G	B	G	B
Row II.	B	G	B	G	B	G	B	G	B
Row III.	B	G	B	G	B	G	B	G	B

Boys represent → B

Girls represent → G

Therefore, first and last positions are occupied by boys. Only option (B) satisfies this conditions. Thus, correct answer is (B).

3. (D): Let teams are I, II, III, IV, V and VI.

We take given options for solving the questions.

Option (A): I and II, Let I played one match with II, then from the given data in question, clearly I win and II lost the match.

Hence, option (A) is false.

Option (B): III and IV, from the given data, III and VI had played the match in which either III or VI win/loss the match.

Hence, Option (B) is false.

Option (C): V and IV, Again, same reason as the given data, then option (C) is false.

Option (D): II and V, Now we observed that II-played 4-matches and loss all 4 matches and same with also V loss all four matches. If they were played with each other, since one can win and other can loss.

Then, II and V are correct.

Hence, correct option is (D).

4. (C): From the given options,

Clearly, from the plot, the velocity is not constant. Then from

Option (A): The object moving with constant velocity. It is false.

Option (D): Velocity of object doubles every hour. It is also false.

Option (B): The object covers equal distance every hour. It is false.

Therefore, the given plot has slope. That's why we can find the acceleration.

Thus, the object is accelerating.

Hence, option (C) is correct.

5. (C): Given, words : CAUSE and EFFECT

Total letters: CAUSE = 5

and EFFECT = 6

Required the chance, if one letter each is drawn at random from these words, that they are same, then

CC and EE, EF

$\therefore$ Probabiltiy (CC) = $\frac{1}{5} \times \frac{1}{6} = \frac{1}{30}$

and probability (EE) = $\frac{1}{5} \times \frac{2}{6} = \frac{2}{30}$

$\therefore$ Required chance is given as

$$= \frac{1}{30} + \frac{2}{30} = \frac{1+2}{30} = \frac{3}{30} = \frac{1}{10}$$

Hence, $\quad P(\text{Same}) = \frac{1}{10}$

Thus, correct answer is (C).

6. (A): According to question,

For A, Multiples of 12 $\rightarrow$ 12, 24, 36

For B, Multiples of 8 $\rightarrow$ 8, 16, 24

To go to 24 teeth $\rightarrow$ Wheel A rotates two times

To go to 24 teeth $\rightarrow$ Wheel B rotates three times

$\because$ Diameter of vehicle tyre = 1 m = $2r$

$\therefore$ Circumference of tyre = $\pi \times 2r = \pi \times 1$

$= \pi$ m

$\therefore$ Tyre travelled two times

$= 2 \times \pi \text{ m} = 2\pi \text{ m}$

Hence, correct answer is (A).

7. (B): According to question,

Let Liar-represented by L and no-liar represented by T

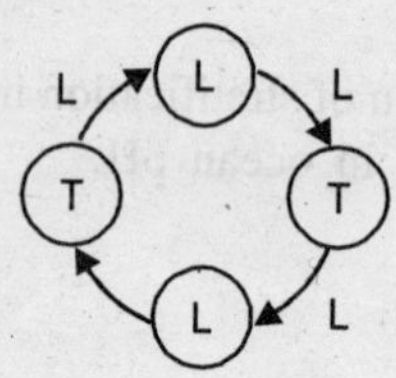

From the diagram, $n \rightarrow$ even

Every alternate person is a liar

Therefore, n must be even and every alternate person is a liar.

8. (A): Let PLAYERS $\rightarrow$ P

FEMALE CRICKETERS $\rightarrow$ FC

MALE FOOTBALLERS $\rightarrow$ MF

GRADUATES $\rightarrow$ G

We have,

(*i*) Some P are G $\rightarrow$ Some players are graduates

(*ii*) All FC are P $\rightarrow$ All female cricketers are players

(*iii*) All MF are P $\rightarrow$ All male footballers are players

(*iv*) Some FC are G $\rightarrow$ Some female cricketers are graduates

(*v*) Some MF are G $\rightarrow$ Some male footballers are graduates

(*vi*) No FC can MF $\rightarrow$ No female cricketers can be footballers.

So, We can represent these given statements by diagram:

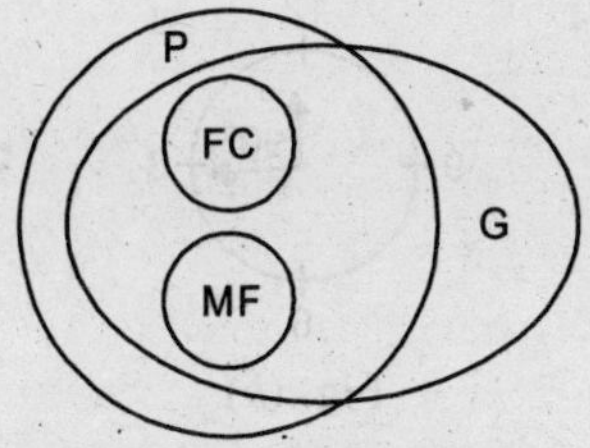

Here, Correct answer is (A).

9. (D): The result is simply obtained by the counting number of capital letter and smaller letters of english alphabet from the given question are

Capital letters →

(A, B, H, K, S, T, L, N, E) = 9

Small letters →

(c, r, u, v, x, d, w) → 7

Hence, the product of the number of capital and small letters = 9 × 7 = 63

Hence, correct answer is (D).

10. (A): Given, length of the track = 200 m

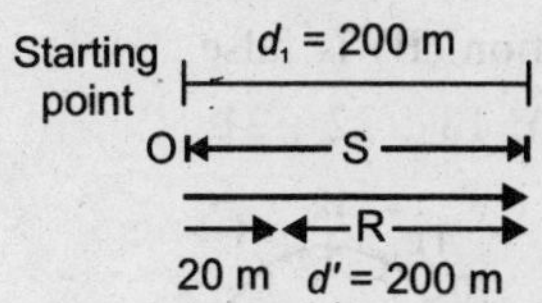

According to question, S runs from point O with speed of 10 m/s (uniform speed)

R starts 20 m ahead from S.

$$\text{Speed} = \frac{\text{Distance}}{\text{Time}}$$

Let speed of S be v_1 and speed of R be v_2

$\therefore \quad v_1 = 10$ m/s and $v_2 = ?$

Time is same to reach the final point S covers distance, $d_1 = 200$ m

But R covers distance, $d_2 = 180$ m

Therefore, $$\frac{d_1}{v_1} = \frac{d_2}{v_2}$$

$$\Rightarrow \quad v_2 = \frac{v_1 \times d_2}{d_1}$$

$$= \frac{10 \times 180}{200}$$

$$= 9 \text{ m/s}$$

Hence, speed of R is 9 m/s.

11. (D): Let height of plant = h m

After three months, the height of plant

$$= h + \frac{10}{100}h = 1.1\,h$$

Today height of plant be 1 m = 100 cm

After 3 months, height of plant

$$= 100 + \frac{10}{100} \times 100$$

$$= 110 + 10$$

$$= 110 \text{ cm}$$

After 6 months height will be

$$= 110 + \frac{110 \times 10}{100}$$

$$= 110 + 11$$

$$= 121 \text{ cm}$$

After 9 months, height will be

$$= 121 + \frac{10}{100} \times 121$$

$$= 121 + 12.1$$

$$= 133.1 \text{ cm}$$

Now, after 12 months or 1 year, height will be

$$= 133.1 + \frac{133.1 \times 10}{100}$$

$$= 133.1 + 13.31$$

$$= 146.41 \text{ cm}$$

$$= 1.46 \text{ m}$$

Hence, height of plant after one year will be 1.46 m.

Therefore, correct answer is (D).

12. (A)

13. (A): Let first digit number be = x

Second digit number = y

According to question,

Third digit number = xy

and last digit = 0

$\therefore$ Number of four-digit PIN

x		y	xy	0
0	$\rightarrow$	0	0	0
0		1	0	
1		2	= 2	
2		3	= 6	
⋮				
⋮				
⋮	...	⋮		
9	...	9		

If $x = 0$, there are 10 possibilities

$x = 1$, there are 10 possibilities

$x = 2$, there are 5 possibilities

$x = 3$, there are 4 possibilities

$x = 4$, there are 3 possibilities

$x = 5$, there are 2 possibilities

$x = 6$, there are 2 possibilities

$x = 7$, there are 2 possibilities

$x = 8$, there are 2 possibilities

$x = 9$, there are 2 possibilities

Total possibilities

$= 10 + 10 + 5 + 4 + 3 + 2 + 2 + 2 + 2 + 2$

$= 42.$

Hence, correct answer is (A).

14. (A): We have some observations,

Given, initial Fig. (*a*) 12 : 00

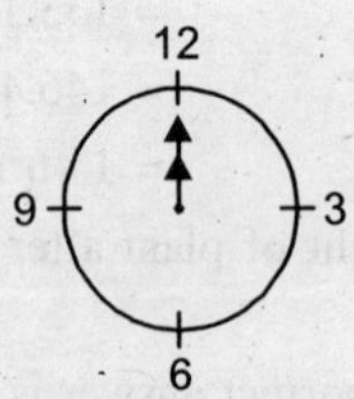

Fig. (*a*)

From the given options,

Option (A): 12 : 16 : 21

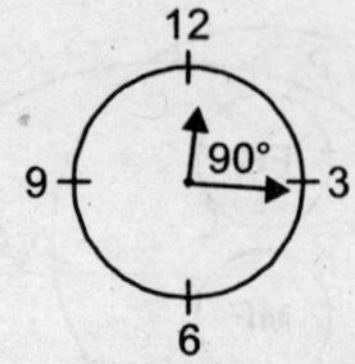

Fig. (*b*)

The hour hand and minute hands perpendicular to each other. From the Fig. (*b*) of watch the time is 12 : 16 : 21.

Hence, correct option is (A).

and Fig. (*b*) 12 : 15

Option (B): 12 : 15 : 00.

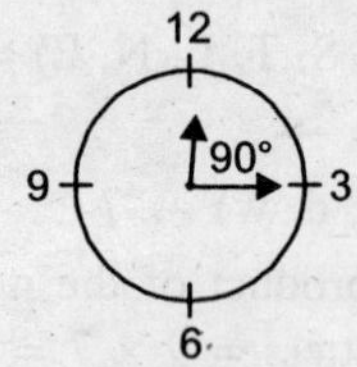

Fig. (*c*)

It is not possible, but clock's hand also perpendicular to each other.

Hence, option (B) is false.

Option (C): 13 : 22 : 21

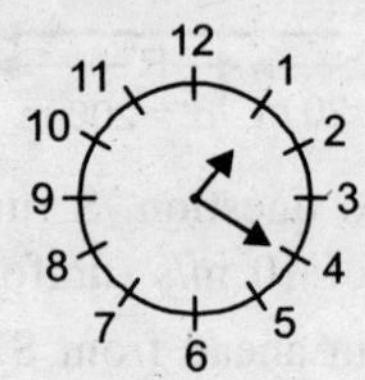

Fig. (*d*)

Fig. (*d*) is not possible.

Hence, option (C) is incorrect.

Option (D): 12 : 48 : 08

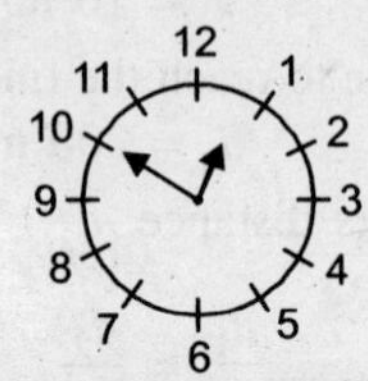

Fig. (*e*)

It is impossible. Hence, option (D) is incorrect.

So, correct option is (A).

15. (A): Given, opposite sides of trapezium are a and b

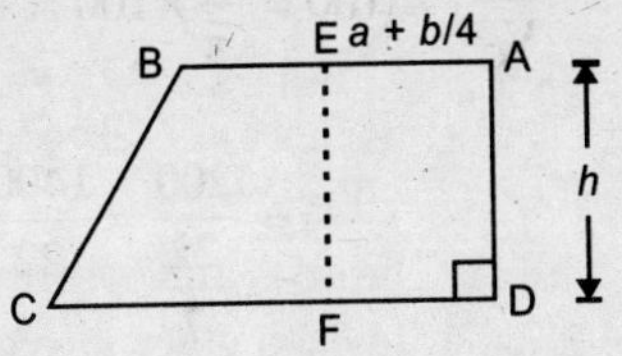

Fig. (*i*)

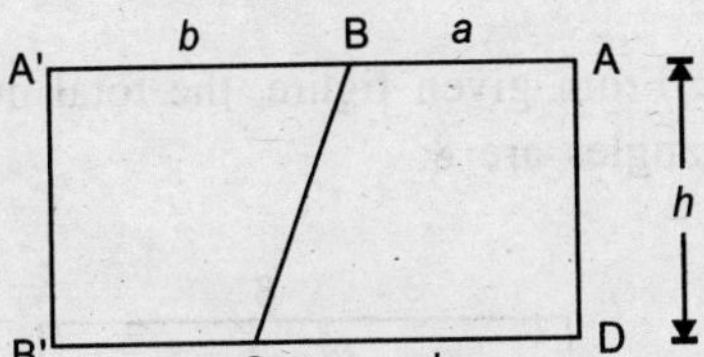

Fig. (*ii*)

From fig. (*ii*), length of rectangle AA′B′B

$$= a + b$$

$$\text{height} = h$$

$$\text{Area of rectangle} = (a + b) \times h$$

$$\text{Half area of rectangle} = \frac{1}{2}(a+b)\times h$$

$$\text{Area of trapezium} = \frac{1}{2}(a+b)\times h$$

From fig. (*i*), area of each part

$$= \frac{1}{2}\left(\frac{1}{2}(a+b)\times h\right)$$

$$= \frac{1}{4}(a+b)\times h$$

$$\text{Now, length of EA} = \frac{\text{Area}}{\text{Height}} \text{ (from fig. } i\text{)}$$

$$= \frac{\frac{1}{4}(a+b)\times h}{h} = \frac{1}{4}(a+b)$$

Hence, correct answer is (A).

16. (A): Let brother is represented by B. Sister is represented by S.

Father is represented by F.

Mother is represented by M

and myself is represented by I

Now, we can represent year as x years.

According to question,

$$\frac{\text{S}}{x-5} \qquad \frac{\text{B}}{x} \qquad \frac{\text{I}}{x+4}$$

When S was born, F's age = 24 years

When I was born, M's age = 27 years

Therefore,

F's age is x year = 24 + 5 = 29 years

and

M's age in x year = 27 − 4 = 23 years

Hence, correct answer is (A).

17. (A): Let the number of kites are x

(*i*) All boys has kites, but 9 are red = $x - 9$

(*ii*) All boys has kites, but 9 are yellow = $x - 9$

(*iii*) All boys has kites, but 9 are green = $x - 9$

(*iv*) All boys has kites, but 9 are blue = $x - 9$

$\therefore$ Total = $x - 9 + x - 9 + x - 9 + x - 9 = x$

$\Rightarrow x + x + x + x - (9 + 9 + 9 + 9) = x$

$\Rightarrow \quad 4x - 36 = x$

$\Rightarrow \quad 3x = 36$

$\therefore \quad x = 12$

$\therefore$ The boy has number of kites = 12

Hence, correct answer is (A).

18. (A): Given, tokens numbered from 1 to 25

Multiples of 4 or 6 were

4 → 8, 12, 16, 20, 24 → Total numbers = 5

and 6 → 12, 18, 24 → Total numbers = 3

Probability of A ∪ B *i.e.*,

$$P(A \cup B) = P(A) + P(B) - P(A \cap B)$$

$$P(4 \text{ or } 6) = \frac{6}{25} + \frac{4}{25} - \frac{2}{25}$$

$$= \frac{6+4-2}{25} = \frac{8}{25}$$

So, probability *i.e.*, P(divisible 4 or 6)

$$= \frac{5}{25} + \frac{3}{25} = \frac{5+3}{25} = \frac{8}{25}$$

Hence, probability that the number on the token drawn is divisible either by 4 or by 6

i.e., $P(4 \text{ or } 6) = \frac{8}{25}$

Hence, correct answer is (A).

19. (B): Let radius of circular log = R

Length of wooden log = L

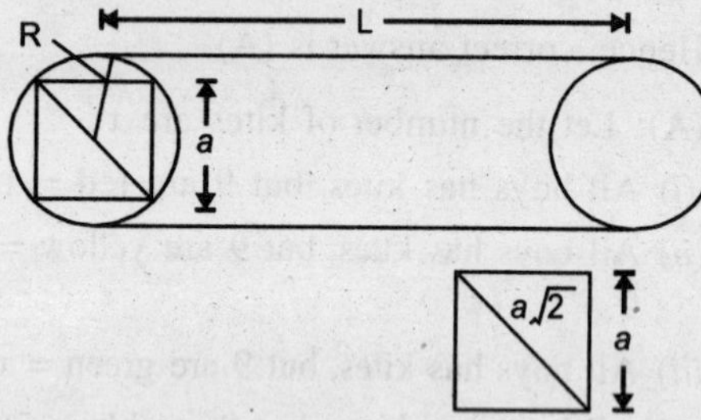

Side of Square = a

Diagonal of square = $a\sqrt{2}$

Diameter of circular log = 2R

Now, volume of the cylindrical log

$$V_C = \pi R^2 L \quad ...(i)$$

and volume of beam,

$$V_B = a^2 \times L = a^2 L \quad ...(ii)$$

From equation (*i*) and (*ii*), we get,

$$\frac{V_B}{V_C} = \frac{a^2 L}{\pi R^2 L} = \frac{a^2}{\pi R^2} \quad ...(iii)$$

Since, $2R = a\sqrt{2}$

$$\therefore \quad a = \frac{2R}{\sqrt{2}} = \sqrt{2}R$$

$$\therefore \quad \frac{V_B}{V_C} = \frac{(\sqrt{2}R)^2}{\pi R^2} = \frac{2R^2}{\pi R^2} = \frac{2}{\pi}$$

∴ Percentage,

$$\frac{V_B}{V_C} \times 100 = \frac{2}{\pi} \times 100 = \frac{200}{\pi}$$

$$= \frac{200}{\frac{22}{7}} = \frac{1400}{22}$$

$$= \frac{700}{11} \simeq 64\%.$$

20. (C): From given figure, the total number of rectangles are 8.

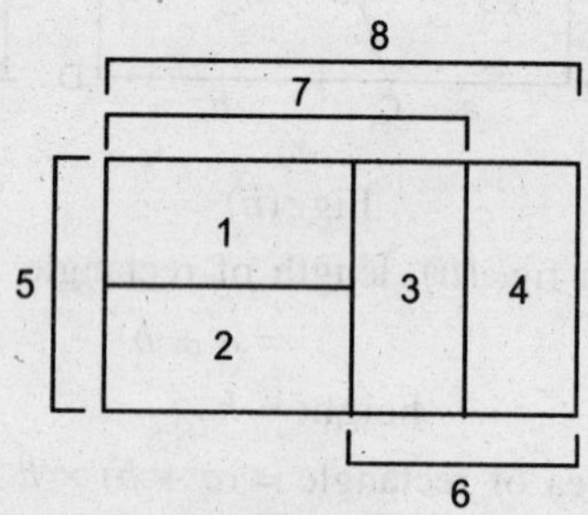

Hence, correct answer is (C).

21. (B)	**22. (A)**	**23. (B)**
24. (B)	**25. (B)**	**26. (D)**
27. (C)	**28. (C)**	**29. (D)**
30. (A)	**31. (C)**	**32. (D)**
33. (B)	**34. (B)**	**35. (D)**
36. (C)	**37. (A)**	**38. (D)**
39. (A)	**40. (C)**	**41. (C)**
42. (B)	**43. (B)**	**44. (D)**
45. (C)	**46. (A)**	**47. (C)**
48. (C)	**49. (C)**	**50. (C)**
51. (A)	**52. (D)**	**53. (D)**
54. (C)	**55. (B)**	**56. (A)**
57. (A)	**58. (C)**	**59. (C)**
60. (B)	**61. (D)**	**62. (A)**

63. (C)	**64. (B)**	**65. (A)**	**108. (C)**	**109. (A)**	**110. (C)**
66. (C)	**67. (C)**	**68. (B)**	**111. (B)**	**112. (C)**	**113. (B)**
69. (B)	**70. (C)**	**71. (A)**	**114. (A)**	**115. (C)**	**116. (D)**
72. (C)	**73. (B)**	**74. (C)**	**117. (C)**	**118. (B)**	**119. (D)**
75. (A)	**76. (C)**	**77. (D)**	**120. (D)**	**121. (B)**	**122. (C)**
78. (C)	**79. (B)**	**80. (A)**	**123. (D)**	**124. (C)**	**125. (B)**
81. (A)	**82. (B)**	**83. (C)**	**126. (B)**	**127. (D)**	**128. (B)**
84. (C)	**85. (C)**	**86. (A)**	**129. (D)**	**130. (C)**	**131. (B)**
87. (C)	**88. (C)**	**89. (D)**	**132. (C)**	**133. (C)**	**134. (A)**
90. (C)	**91. (A)**	**92. (C)**	**135. (C)**	**136. (D)**	**137. (B)**
93. (A)	**94. (B)**	**95. (C)**	**138. (D)**	**139. (C)**	**140. (A)**
96. (D)	**97. (A)**	**98. (A)**	**141. (C)**	**142. (D)**	**143. (B)**
99. (C)	**100. (B)**	**101. (D)**	**144. (B)**	**145. (C)**	**146. (D)**
102. (C)	**103. (C)**	**104. (C)**	**147. (A)**	**148. (A)**	**149. (B)**
105. (A)	**106. (A)**	**107. (A)**	**150. (A)**		

Previous Years' Paper

Joint CSIR-UGC NET/JRF

Earth, Atmospheric, Ocean & Planetary Sciences

JUNE-2021

(Exam held on 29-01-2022)

PART-A

1. A 10 km long and 1 m wide sheet of thickness 0.1 mm is rolled along the length parallel to its width forming a perfectly compact solid cylinder. The diameter of the cylinder in meter is approximately:

A. $\frac{1000}{\pi}$ B. $\frac{1}{\pi^{1/2}}$

C. $(2\pi)^{1/2}$ D. $\frac{2}{\pi^{1/2}}$

2. The digit at the unit's place of $(489^{86} - 351^{63})$ is:

A. 8   B. 5

C. 2   D. 0

3. The variation of w against x is shown in the figure for selected values of parameter y.

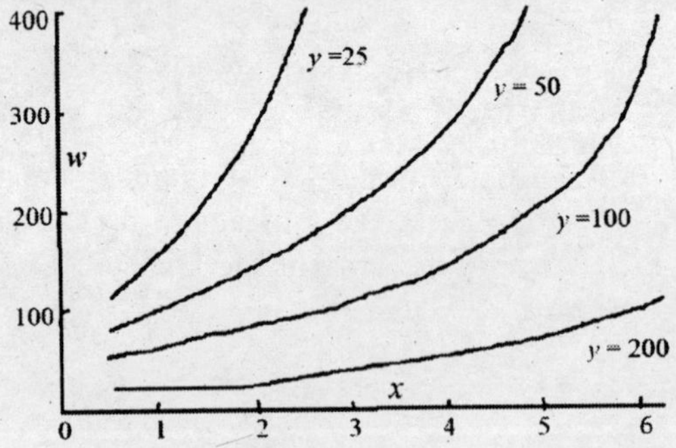

The graph indicates that w

A. increases linearly with x and y.

B. increases non-linearly with x, but linearly with y.

C. increases non-linearly with x, but decreases linearly with y.

D. increases non-linearly with x, but decreases non-linearly with y.

4. Area of a circle which circumscribes a regular hexagon with side a is

A. $\frac{3\sqrt{3}}{2}a^2$ B. $6a^2$

C. πa^2 D. $\frac{3\pi}{4}a^2$

5. There are three fathers and six sons in a room. If every father's son(s) and every son's father are present, then the minimum number of individuals in the room are:

A. 5   B. 7

C. 8   D. 9

6. The linear correlation coefficient between the variable X and Y in the given figure is closest to:

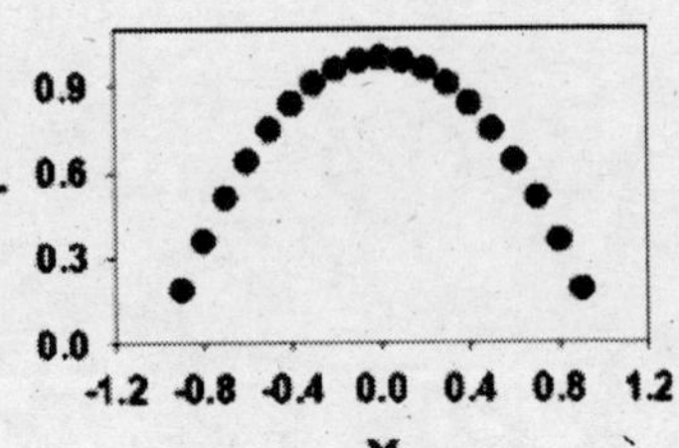

A. 0   B. 1

C. −1   D. $\frac{1}{2}$

7. Which one of the following plots does NOT show cumulative runs scored in a T-20 cricket match?

A.

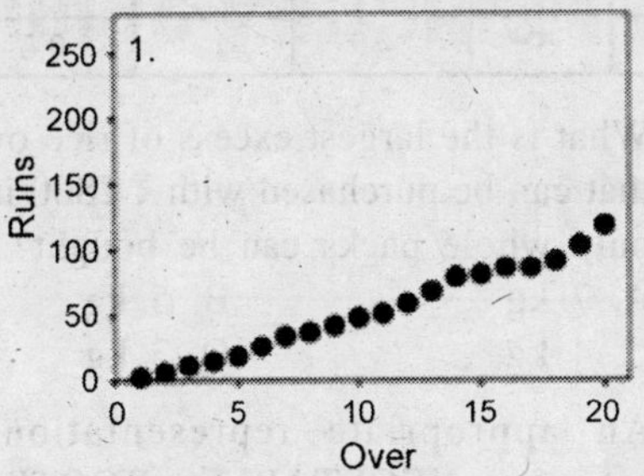

B.

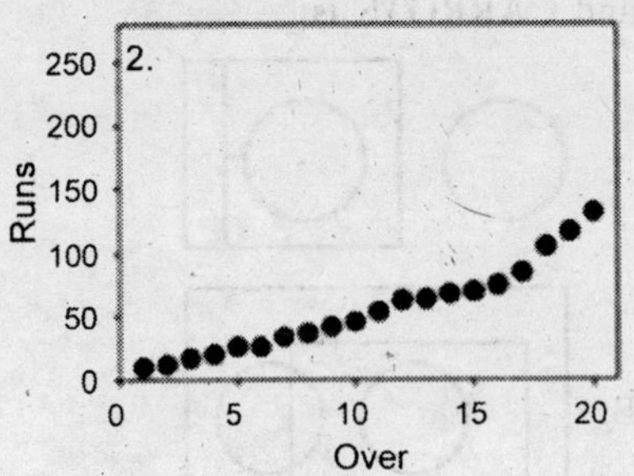

C.

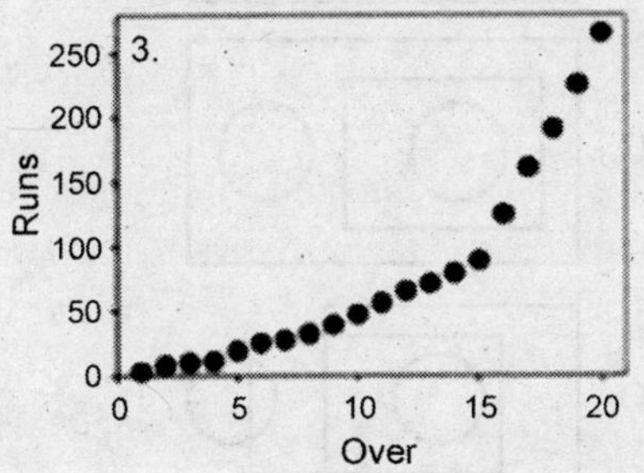

D.

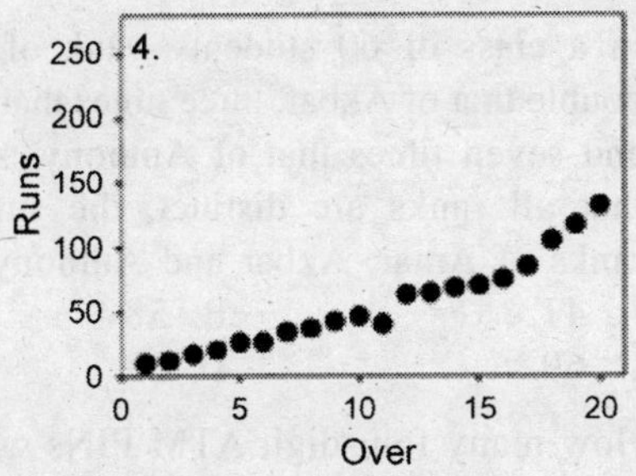

8. The Sun is at an elevation of 45° on one side of a vertical wall. The wall casts a rectangular shadow on the ground. Which of the following dimensions of the wall does the area of the shadow not depend on?

A. Length
B. Height
C. Neither length nor height
D. Thickness

9. The probability that a student will attempt a certain question in an exam is 1/2. The probability that none of the 5 students writing the exam independently will attempt that question is:

A. $\frac{1}{2}$

B. The same as that of all the 5 students attempting this question.

C. $\frac{1}{4}$

D. $\frac{1}{16}$

10. Out of 2000 people, 300 play volleyball, 500 play cricket whereas 200 play both volleyball and cricket. How many people do NOT play either of the games?

A. 1000 B. 1100
C. 1200 D. 1400

11. How many integers in the set {1,2, 3,……, 100} have an odd number of divisors?

A. 27 B. 10
C. 36 D. 12

12. Three identical balls of radius r are to be tightly packed in a triangular box as shown. What is the area of the triangular base of box?

A. $2\sqrt{3}r^2$ B. $2\sqrt{3}\left(1+\sqrt{3}\right)r^2$
C. $2\sqrt{3}\left(2+\sqrt{3}\right)r^2$ D. $3\pi r^2$

13. The average yield of four different crops, A, B, C and D is shown in the bar chart along with 2σ (standard deviation) variation shown as error bars.

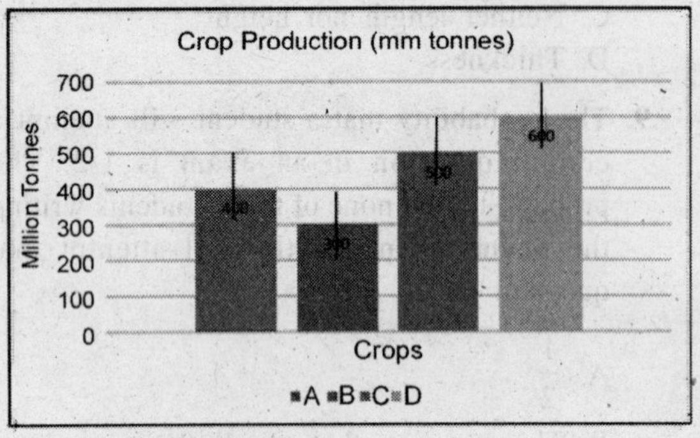

The crop with the highest per cent variation in the yield is:

A. A B. B

C. C D. D

14. The average heights of boys and girls in a class are 165 cm and 150 cm, respectively. If the average height of the entire class is 160 cm then the ratio of the number of girls to the number of boys in the class is:

A. 1 : 3

B. 1 : 2

C. 1.65 : 1.6

D. 2 : 3

15. Choose the option that makes the following statement correct:

"This sentence contains the letter e .... times".

A. Seven B. Eight

C. Nine D. Ten

16. If A calls both B and C liars and B calls C a liar, then which of the following is FALSE?

A. A is a liar

B. Exactly one of B and C is a liar

C. Exactly one among A, B and C is a liar

D. Exactly two among A, B and C are liars

17. A store sells three packs of groceries as follows:

Pack	Rice (kg)	Wheat (kg)	Pulses (kg)	Sugar (kg)	Prices (Rs.)
A	3	4	0.5	0.5	400
B	4	3	1	1	500
C	5	4	1	0.5	600

What is the largest excess of rice over wheat that can be purchased with ₹ 2800 in hand, if only whole packs can be bought?

A. 7 kg B. 5 kg

C. 4 kg D. 3 kg

18. An appropriate representation of the categories VEGETABLES, ROOTS, FRUITS and CARROTS is:

A. 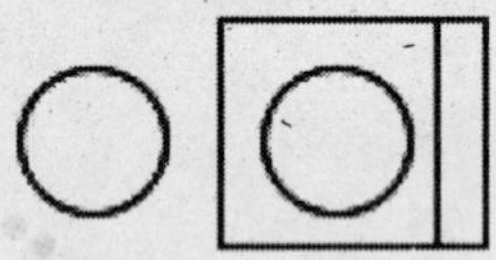

B. 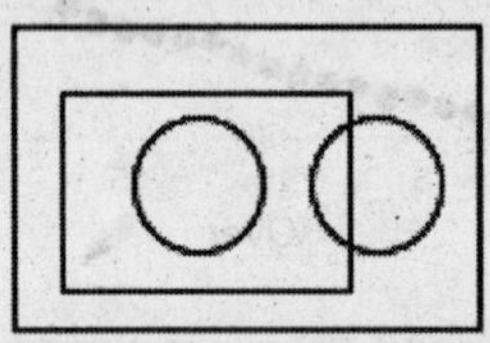

C. 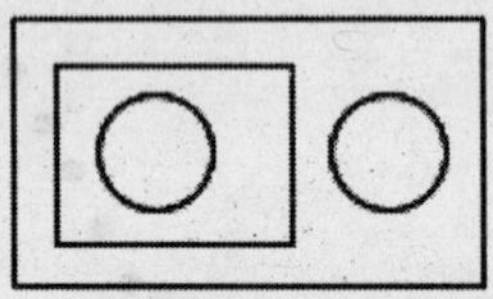

D. 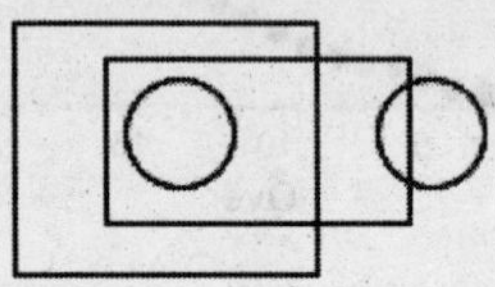

19. In a class of 60 students, rank of Amar is double that of Akbar, three times that of Amita and seven times that of Anthony. Assuming that all ranks are distinct, the sum of the ranks of Amar, Akbar and Anthony is:

A. 41 B. 58

C. 69 D. 83

20. How many four-digit ATM PINs which read the same from left to right and right to left are possible?

A. 20 B. 72

C. 82 D. 100

PART-B

21. If the Moon were farther away from the Earth, the number of full-moon days in a year would be:
A. fewer with a darker Moon
B. larger with a brighter Moon
C. the same as the present, but with a brighter Moon
D. the same as the present, but with a darker Moon

22. Which planet has the fastest rotation about its axis?
A. Earth B. Mars
C. Jupiter D. Saturn

23. A large geoid low is seen in the:
A. Indian Ocean B. Pacific Ocean
C. Arctic Ocean D. Atlantic Ocean

24. Which one of the following radioactive isotopes is produced in the Earth's atmosphere by cosmic ray interaction (spallation)?
A. ^{222}Rn B. ^{87}Rb
C. ^{10}Be D. ^{147}Sm

25. The lowest geothermal gradient in the oceanic crust is observed at:
A. Subduction zones
B. Mid oceanic ridges
C. Ocean islands
D. Transform faults

26. Foliations are generally .... plane of the strain ellipsoid?
A. Parallel to the XZ
B. Parallel to the YZ
C. Parallel to the XY
D. Oblique to the XY

27. The Slab Graveyard, a zone where cold subducted oceanic lithosphere ends up, is located in the:
A. Lower crust B. D″ layer
C. Upper mantle D. Outer core

28. Which one of the following minerals has a metallic lustre, a greenish black streak and is an ore of copper?
A. Cuprite B. Chalcopyrite
C. Malachite D. Covellite

29. The Earth's near-dipole magnetic field today can be compared to a short magnet at the center of the Earth with its north magnetic 'pole' directed towards the Earth's geographic:
A. North B. South
C. East D. West

30. Which one of the following is NOT a cryptocrystalline form of quartz?
A. Jasper B. Agate
C. Chalcedony D. Amethyst

31. Which one of the following coal deposits is from the Palaeozoic age?
A. Singareni B. Akli
C. Vastan D. Gurha

32. Which one of the following pore types in carbonate rocks is primary?
A. Vug B. Intraparticle
C. Intercrystalline D. Moldic

33. Which one of the following represents the CORRECT sequence of phase transformations with increasing depth in the mantle?
A. Pyroxene → Garnet → Ilmenite → Perovskite
B. Garnet → Perovskite → Pyroxene → Ilmenite
C. Olivine → Ringwoodite → Perovskite → Wadsleyite
D. Olivine → Pyroxene → Periclase → Ilmenite

34. Which one of the following events is caused by liquefaction?
A. Lahar B. Avalanche
C. Rockslide D. Quicksand

35. Bauxite deposits are formed by
A. Mechanical concentration
B. Supergene enrichment

C. Residual concentration
D. Magmatic concentration

36. The P wave velocity inside the Earth's solid inner core is:
A. Larger than that in the mantle and outer core
B. Larger than that in the mantle, but smaller than that in the outer core
C. Less than that in the mantle, but larger than that in the outer core
D. Less than that in the mantle and outer core

37. Which of the following statements is correct for Magnetic Equator?
A. It is imaginary line parallel to Geographic Equator
B. It meanders north and south of Geographic Equator
C. It is always north of the Geographic Equator
D. It is always south of the Geographic Equator

38. Poisson's ratio is the ratio of:
A. Axial strain to lateral strain
B. Lateral strain to axial strain
C. Axial stress to axial strain
D. Transverse stress to lateral strain

39. Which one of the following discontinuities represents a mineral phase transition boundary?
A. Conrad B. Mohorovicic
C. 410-km D. Gutenberg

40. A seismic gap is:
A. Any aseismic zone
B. A gap between two active faults
C. A segment of an active fault which is aseismic for a long time
D. A time gap between two seismic zones

41. Which planet has the strongest magnetic field?
A. Earth B. Mars
C. Jupiter D. Saturn

42. From the epicentre of an earthquake, its magnitude:
A. decreases linearly with distance
B. decreases sharply with distance near the epicentre and gently thereafter
C. decreases gently with distance near the epicentre and sharply thereafter
D. remains the same at any distance

43. Poorest sorting will be exhibited by .... sandstone.
A. Fluvial B. Glacial
C. Shoreface D. Foreshore

44. Lines of zero magnetic declination on a map of the Earth are known as .... lines.
A. Isoclinic B. Agonic
C. Isogonic D. Aclinic

45. According to the PREM model, which of the following statements correctly represents the change in the average density (ρ_c) and the bulk sound velocity (v_c) across the Core-Mantle Boundary (CMB)?
A. Both ρ_c and v_c increases from outer core to the D″ layer
B. Both ρ_c and v_c decrease from outer core to the D″ layer
C. ρ_c decreases but v_c increases from outer core to the D″ layer
D. ρ_c increases but v_c decreases from the outer core to the D″ layer.

46. Streamlined wind-erosion forms with their long axes parallel to the wind are known as:
A. Nebkha B. Yardang
C. Drumlin D. Seif

47. The upper part of the soil profile that shows strong evidence of alteration by pedogenic processes is known as:
A. Catena B. Talus
C. Grus D. Solum

48. Which one of the following landforms is NOT formed by the groundwater action?
A. Blind valley
B. Dry valley
C. Hanging valley
D. Allogenic valley

49. The correct arrangement of the earth movement types in order of increasing wetness of materials is:
A. Solifluction, rockslide, mudflow, creep
B. Rockslide, solifluction, creep, mudflow
C. Creep, rockslide, mudflow, solifluction
D. Rockslide, creep, solifluction, mudflow

50. Which of the following process in the coastal area is responsible for focused erosion of headlands?
A. Formation of longshore current
B. High tides
C. Formation of Rip current
D. Wave refraction

51. Areas like Marianas Trench, constituting the deepest part of the oceans, belong to a zone named:
A. Bathypelagic B. Epipelagic
C. Hadopelagic D. Abyssopelagic

52. Which one of the following is a secondary attribute computed from Digital Elevation Models (DEMs)?
A. Aspect
B. Topographic Wetness Index
C. Slope
D. Plan curvature

53. Which of the following would you NOT expect to observe when the eye of a hurricane passes directly over your location?
A. Increase in surface temperature
B. Very low surface pressure reading
C. Very strong winds
D. Little or no precipitation

54. The upper part of a thunderstorm cloud is normally .... charged, and the middle and lower parts are .... charged.

Choose the right combination from the list below to fill in the blanks in the right order.
A. negatively, negatively
B. negatively, positively
C. positively, positively
D. positively, negatively

55. Choose the INCORRECT statement

Western disturbance is a weather system that:
A. is observed during the winter months over India
B. moves in the direction towards West
C. is an extratropical system originating in the Mediterranean region
D. brings rain to the northern and north-western part of India

56. El-Nino over central pacific region leads to dampening of the:
A. Hadley circulation
B. Ferrell circulation
C. Walker circulation
D. Polar circulation

57. Which air mass has abundant moisture and warm air?
A. Maritime Tropical
B. Maritime Polar
C. Continental Tropical
D. Continental Polar

58. Choose the INCORRECT option.

Incoming solar radiation is absorbed in the atmosphere by:
A. Carbon dioxide (CO_2)
B. Ozone (O_3)
C. Oxygen (O_2)
D. Water vapour (H_2O)

59. A stationary front does not move because:
A. Winds on both sides of the front are calm
B. Winds blow parallel to the front
C. The front is between high and low pressure
D. Winds blow against each other and are of equal strength

60. Halo is the optical phenomenon formed due to:
A. reflection of sunlight/moonlight
B. refraction of sunlight/moonlight
C. reflection and refraction of sunlight/moonlight
D. diffraction of sunlight/moonlight.

61. Rossby Number is a measure of:
A. magnitude of the acceleration compared to the Coriolis force

B. magnitude of the inertial force compared to viscous force
C. magnitude of the inertial force compared to the Coriolis force
D. magnitude of the viscous force compared to acceleration

62. Choose the INCORRECT statement:
A. Water particles at surface move in a vertically orbital track when a wind wave propagates
B. Tsunami and Tides are shallow water waves.
C. Ocean surface current and surface wave can travel in opposite directions
D. The wave refraction at sea surface occurs when waves approach parallel to the coast.

63. Phycocyanin and Phycoerythrin pigments are abundant in:
A. *Prochlorococcus* B. *Synecococcus*
C. *Trichodesmium* D. *Diatom*

64. Which one of the following oceanic regions removes CO_2 through solubility pump most efficiently?
A. Equatorial B. Tropical
C. Sub-tropical D. Polar

65. If the oxygen and carbon compensation depths are approximately 120 m and 3800 m, respectively; which of the following species will be found in sediments deposited at 4500 m water depth?
A. Noctiluca B. Foraminifera
C. Radiolarians D. Pteropods

66. High N : P ratio (≥ 40) signifies which one of the following biogeochemical processes?
A. Nitrification
B. Denitrification
C. Sulphate reduction
D. Nitrogen Fixation

67. The faster rate of subduction is likely to:
A. result in deeper and narrower trench
B. result in shallower and wider trench
C. result in semi-circular trench
D. not have any effect on a trench shape

68. Choose the correct statement.
Coastal Kelvin wave propagation
A. is always opposite to the associated current direction
B. is always in the direction of associated current
C. can be opposite to the associated current direction
D. is never associated with currents

69. Choose the correct answer for the subsurface water column.
Potential temperature
A. is equal to *in-situ* temperature
B. is always higher than *in-situ* temperature
C. is always lower than *in-situ* temperature
D. can be higher or lower than *in-situ* temperature

70. Which one of the following can produce Neap tide in the ocean?
A. Full Moon B. First quarter Moon
C. New Moon D. Crescent Moon

PART-C

71. On a given fault plane, the magnitude of the netslip vector is .... the magnitude of the separation vector.
A. greater than or equal to
B. greater than
C. equal to
D. less than or equal to

72. Match the terms describing the stress states applied to laboratory specimens during rock strength tests, in Column-A with the principal (normal) stress conditions in Column-B.

Column-A	Column-B
(*a*) Uniaxial Stress	(*i*) $\sigma_1 = k; \sigma_2 = -k; \sigma_3 = 0$; where $k > 0$

(*b*) Biaxial Stress (*ii*) $\sigma_1 \neq 0; \sigma_2 \neq 0; \sigma_3 = 0$

(*c*) Triaxial Stress (*iii*) $\sigma_1 \neq 0; \sigma_2 \neq 0; \sigma_3 \neq 0$

(*d*) Polyaxial Stress (*iv*) $\sigma_1 \neq 0; \sigma_2 = \sigma_3 = 0$

(*e*) Pure Shear Stress (*v*) $\sigma_1 \neq 0; \sigma_2 = \sigma_3 \neq 0$

Choose the correct answer:

	(*a*)	(*b*)	(*c*)	(*d*)	(*e*)
A.	(*i*)	(*ii*)	(*iii*)	(*iv*)	(*v*)
B.	(*iv*)	(*ii*)	(*v*)	(*iii*)	(*i*)
C.	(*v*)	(*iii*)	(*ii*)	(*iv*)	(*i*)
D.	(*ii*)	(*v*)	(*iii*)	(*i*)	(*iv*)

73. Glide plane in crystal symmetry operations is defined by:

A. translation and rotation
B. translation and reflection
C. reflection
D. inversion

74. Match following bivalves with their mode of living.

Bivalves	**Mode of Living**
(*a*) Lima	(*i*) Shallow burrower
(*b*) Lucina	(*ii*) Borer
(*c*) Mya	(*iii*) Swimmer
(*d*) Pholas	(*iv*) Deep burrower

Choose the correct answer:

	(*a*)	(*b*)	(*c*)	(*d*)
A.	(*iii*)	(*ii*)	(*iv*)	(*i*)
B.	(*i*)	(*iii*)	(*iv*)	(*ii*)
C.	(*iii*)	(*i*)	(*iv*)	(*ii*)
D.	(*iv*)	(*i*)	(*ii*)	(*iii*)

75. Match the microfossils with their affinity.

Microfossils	**Affinity**
(*a*) Ostracoda	(*i*) Protista
(*b*) Calcareous nanoplankton	(*ii*) Gasteropod
(*c*) Pteropod	(*iii*) Crustaceans
(*d*) Foraminifera	(*iv*) Marine algae

Choose the correct answer:

	(*a*)	(*b*)	(*c*)	(*d*)
A.	(*ii*)	(*iv*)	(*i*)	(*iii*)
B.	(*iv*)	(*iii*)	(*ii*)	(*i*)
C.	(*iii*)	(*iv*)	(*ii*)	(*i*)
D.	(*iii*)	(*i*)	(*ii*)	(*iv*)

76. In which of the following environments does double mud drape form?

A. Eolian B. Fluvial
C. Subtidal D. Intertidal

77. The following reaction can be used as a geobarometer:

$$\underset{\text{(Plagioclase)}}{3CaAl_2Si_2O_8} = \underset{\text{(Grossular)}}{Ca_3Al_2Si_3O_{12}} + \underset{\text{(Kyanite)}}{2Al_2SiO_5} + \underset{\text{(Quartz)}}{SiO_2}$$

Assuming kyanite and quartz as pure phases, and X as activity in ideal conditions, the appropriate expression of equilibrium constant (K) for this reaction is:

A. $K = \dfrac{(X_{Ca}^{Garnet})}{(X_{Ca}^{Plagioclase})^{3'}}$

B. $K = \dfrac{(X_{Ca}^{Garnet})^3}{(X_{Ca}^{Plagioclase})'}$

C. $K = \dfrac{X_{Ca}^{Garnet}}{X_{Ca}^{Plagioclase'}}$

D. $K = \dfrac{(X_{Ca}^{Garnet})^3}{(X_{Ca}^{Plagioclase})^{3'}}$

78. The correct mineral sequence that describes prograde metamorphism in a calc-silicate rock is:

A. Phlogopite → Tremolite → Diopside → Scapolite → Forsterite
B. Talc → Grossular → Diopside → Scapolite → Epidote
C. Phlogopite → Grossular → Scapolite → Tremolite → Diopside
D. Talc → Tremolite → Scapolite → Forsterite → Diopside

79. Given below is an isobaric binary temperature (T)-composition (X) diagram in the X-Y system. 'e' is eutectic point and 'd' is end-point of crystallization.

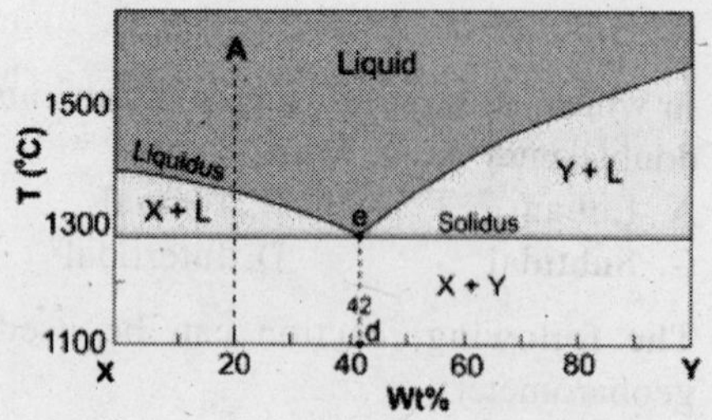

If 'A' is the initial magma composition, what is the proportion of mineral 'X' that crystallizes as magma cools from 1300°C to 1100°C?

A. 58% B. 42%
C. 28% D. 22%

80. Identify the INCORRECT pair from the following minerals and corresponding crystal systems.

A. Spinel – Cubic system
B. Biotite – Triclinic system
C. Augite – Monoclinic system
D. Olivine – Orthorhombic system

81. For a mantle nodule composed of garnet and olivine, and another nodule comprising orthopyroxene, clinopyroxene and spinel which of the following statements is NOT true?

A. Both these types can occur in kimberlites
B. Nodule containing garnet and olivine represents deeper mantle than the one composed of orthopyroxene, clinopyroxene and spinel
C. The two nodules represent mantles of different bulk compositions
D. They have been brought up to the surface in a rapidly ascending magma

82. What would be the average drawdown over an area where 25 million m^3 of water has been pumped through a number of uniformly distributed wells? The area is 100 km^2 and the specific yield of the unconfined aquifer is 25 per cent.

A. 1 m B. 10 m
C. 25 m D. 100 m

83. Which one of the following is useful for estimating the thermal maturity of hydrocarbon source rocks?

A. Total organic carbon content
B. Type of kerogen
C. Colour of spore
D. Amount of clay minerals

84. What would be the residence time of water in the ocean if the volume of the ocean is considered to be 1.4×10^{21} litres and the annual flux of freshwater into the ocean is 3.5×10^{17} litres/year, assuming that the volume of the ocean remains unchanged?

A. 40000 years B. 4000 years
C. 2500 years D. 25 years

85. Match the type of analysis or proxy record in Column-Y with the paleoclimate parameter derived from ice cores, in Column-X?

Column-X	Column-Y
(*a*) Temperature	(*i*) CO_2; NO_2
(*b*) Humidity	(*ii*) ^{10}Be
(*c*) Volcanic Activity	(*iii*) d-excess
(*d*) Atmospheric Circulation	(*iv*) $\delta^{18}O$
(*e*) Solar Activity	(*v*) Conductivity
(*f*) Atmospheric Composition (natural vs manmade)	(*vi*) Major Ion Content

Choose the correct answer:

	(*a*)	(*b*)	(*c*)	(*d*)	(*e*)	(*f*)
A.	(*iv*)	(*iii*)	(*v*)	(*vi*)	(*ii*)	(*i*)
B.	(*i*)	(*iii*)	(*ii*)	(*v*)	(*iv*)	(*vi*)
C.	(*iv*)	(*ii*)	(*iii*)	(*vi*)	(*v*)	(*i*)
D.	(*iv*)	(*iii*)	(*vi*)	(*v*)	(*ii*)	(*i*)

86. The carbon isotope fractionation factor α at a given temperature between CO_2 and diamond is 1.0115 and that between diamond and graphite is 1.0029. The value of the isotope fractionation factor of carbon between CO_2 and graphite at this temperature will be:

A. 1.0144 B. 1.0086
C. 0.9915 D. 2.0144

87. Given two functions $f_1(x, y) \equiv 2x + 5y - 1 = 0$ and $f_2(x, y) \equiv \left(\frac{x}{2}\right)^2 + \left(\frac{y}{3}\right)^2 - 1 = 0$, the determinant of the Jacobian matrix at $x = 1$, $y = 6$ will be:

A. $\frac{11}{6}$ B. $\frac{1}{2}$

C. $\frac{1}{6}$ D. 3

88. The rectangular (R) and triangular (T) signals, shown in the diagram below, have the same area and have energies E_R and E_T, respectively.

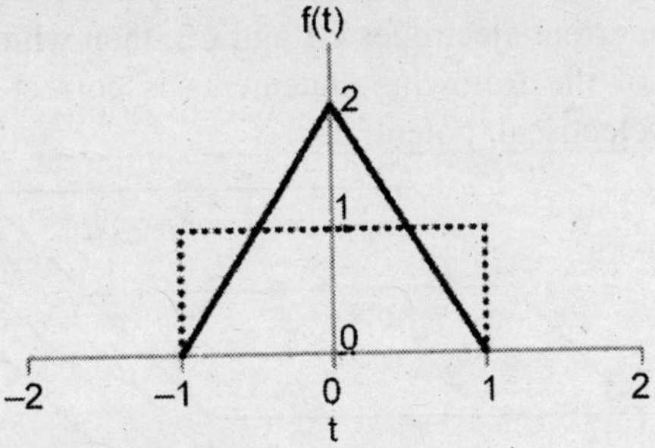

The ratio E_T/E_R is:

A. 1 B. $\frac{1}{2}$

C. $\frac{4}{3}$ D. 2

89. g_A and g_B are gravity values measured at the foot (A) and the top (B) of a vertical cliff like structure (see figure) extending for a few km on the earth in a locality. A is at the sea level. If g_A and g_B are less than the normal gravity at that location by 8.8 mgals and 40.6 mgals respectively, then the thickness (in m) of the cliff will be around.

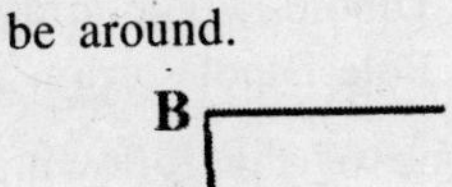

A. 103 B. 148

C. 160 D. 192

90. A 1.0 km thick elevated landmass of density 2.7 gm/cc, associated with an 8.0 km thicker crust below it, undergoes subsidence at a uniform rate of 5.0 cm per century. In how many years will it stop subsiding completely? Assume that the mantle is denser than its overlying crust by 0.3 gm/cc.

A. 0.2 my B. 0.4 my

C. 1.2 my D. 2.0 my

91. The following figure shows the inclination of the Natural Remanent Magnetization (NRM) measured in deep sea sediments at two locations A and B up to a depth of 12 m. Which one of the following statements is INCORRECT?

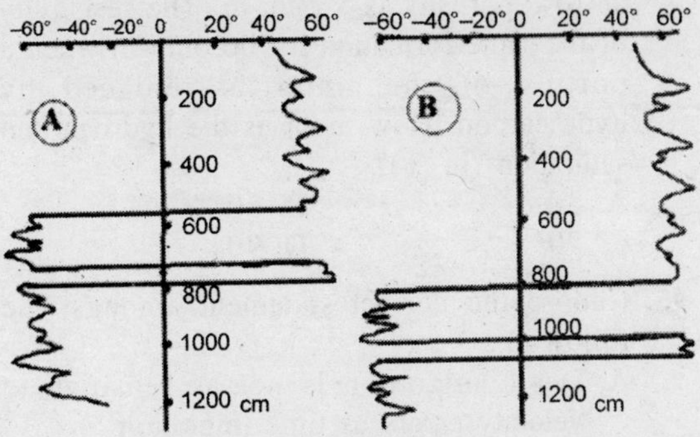

A. The magnetic reversal occurs at an age corresponding to the 800 cm position in B following a short event at position 1000 cm.

B. The rate of deposition at A is larger than at B

C. Both the locations are on the same magnetic longitude

D. The Earth's magnetic field at position 800 cm in B is substantially smaller than that at 600 cm.

92. What is the frequency (in Hz) of the Larmor signal induced in a proton precession magnetometer at a location on the Earth where the horizontal and vertical components of its magnetic field are equal? Assume that the Earth's magnetic field at the Earth's magnetic equator is $\sqrt{(0.1)}$ Oe.

A. 1150 B. 1380
C. 1700 D. 2480

93. A near surface earthquake is recorded by a station at an epicentral distance of 200 km. Assume a two layered crust having equal thicknesses of 15 km each and velocities V_1 = 6.0 km/s and V_2 = 6.5 km/s overlying a mantle with velocity 8 km/s. The correct sequence of primary phase arrivals in the recorded seismogram with increasing arrival time is

A. Pg, P* and Pn B. P*, Pg and Pn
C. Pn, Pg and P* D. Pn, P* and Pg

94. The resistivity of a consolidated sandstone formation which is 100% saturated with water at 10% porosity is 5 ohm-m. The resistivity of the same formation is 500 ohm-m when a portion of the water is replaced by hydrocarbon. How much is the hydrocarbon saturation (in %)?

A. 30 B. 50
C. 70 D. 90

95. Choose the correct statement amongst the following.

A. Depth migration is not as sensitive to velocity errors as time migration
B. The impulse response of pre-stack time migration is an ellipse.
C. A causal non-minimum phase wavelet can be shaped into a minimum phase spike using causal filter
D. Dix's method of estimating interval velocity is valid for any subsurface model, as long as all layers are isotropic.

96. A very shallow and a deep earthquake occur simultaneously at equal distances of 40 km from a station. Which one of the following statements is correct for the crustal model given in Fig. A?

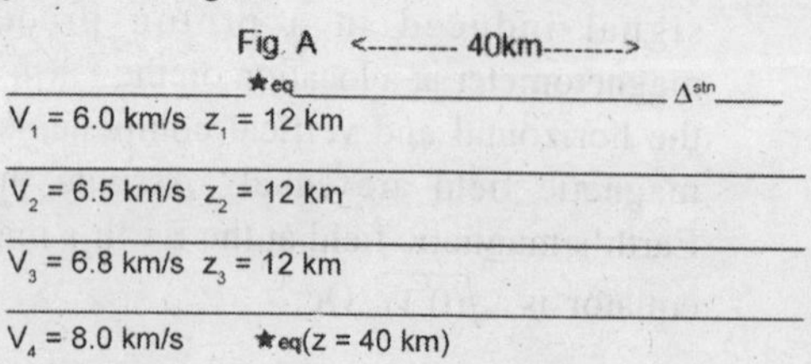

A. The first arrivals (P phases) from both earthquakes reach at the same time.
B. Ts-Tp is larger for the deeper earthquake than the shallower earthquake.
C. Ts-Tp is smaller for the deeper earthquake than the shallower earthquake.
D. Ts-Tp is the same for both earthquakes.

97. A pair of current electrodes C1(+I) and C2(−I) is placed on *x-y* plane over a horizontally stratified multilayered earth as shown in figure below. P, Q, R and S are four points placed on earth surface and at equal distances from mid-point (O) between C1 and C2 (line RS is perpendicular to line PQ in *x-y* plane). If a current, I is passed between current electrodes C1 and C2, then which one of the following statements is correct about electrical potential?

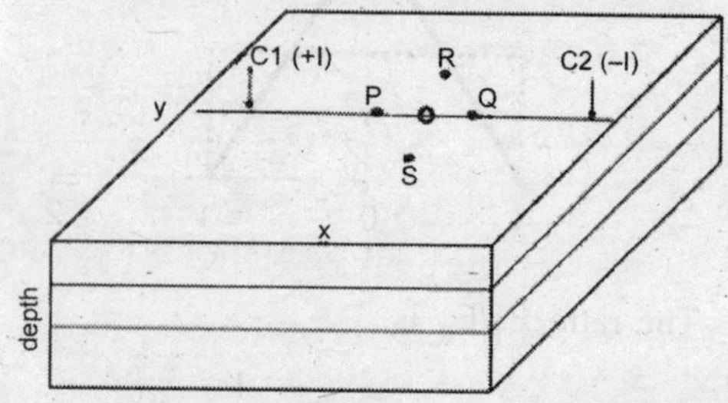

A. Potentials at all four points P, Q, R and S will be the same
B. Potentials at P and Q will be the same
C. Potentials at R and S will be the same
D. Potentials at P and R will be the same

98. In an Electrical Resistivity Tomography (ERT) survey using 100 equi-spaced electrodes, which array among the following yields the maximum depth of investigation?

A. Wenner array
B. Schlumberger array
C. Axial Dipole-Dipole array
D. Axial Pole-Dipole array

99. Which one of the following statements is correct about electromagnetic induction in the earth?

A. The frequency of Primary and Secondary magnetic fields will not be the same

B. The resultant field is nearly circularly polarized over a perfectly conducting body

C. The resultant field is nearly polarized in a straight line over a perfectly resistive body

D. The Phase difference between the Primary and Secondary magnetic fields will be 180 degrees for a perfectly conducting body.

100. Match the Electromagnetic methods given in Column I with the appropriate frequency range given in Column II.

Column-I	**Column-II**
(*a*) VLF method	(*i*) 1 Hz-10^{-4} Hz
(*b*) Magnetotelluric method	(*ii*) 100-5000 Hz
(*c*) Slingram Method	(*iii*) 5 kHz-30 kHz
(*d*) AFMAG method	(*iv*) 1 Hz-1000 Hz

Choose the correct answer:

	(*a*)	(*b*)	(*c*)	(*d*)
A.	(*iii*)	(*i*)	(*ii*)	(*iv*)
B.	(*iii*)	(*iv*)	(*i*)	(*ii*)
C.	(*i*)	(*iii*)	(*ii*)	(*iv*)
D.	(*i*)	(*iv*)	(*iii*)	(*ii*)

101. A swarm of microearthquakes is recorded in the vicinity of a volcano. The number of microearthquakes recorded of magnitude 2 and 1 are 100 and 10000 respectively. What will be the estimate of the *b* value?

A. 1.0 B. 1.5

C. 2.0 D. 2.5

102. A linear system is described by the differential equation $\frac{d^2y}{dt^2} + 5\frac{dy}{dt} + 6y = 2\frac{du}{dt} + 1$. Which one of the following statements is correct about the Poles and Zeros of the system?

A. It has 2 real zeros at –1/2 and +1/2

B. It has only one real zero at +1/2

C. It has two real poles at 3 and –2

D. It has two real poles at –3 and –2

103. Among the following values of hypsometric integral, which one denotes minimum erosion of a drainage basin area down to its base level?

A. 0.92 B. 0.48

C. 0.51 D. 0.02

104. Match the geomorphic features with the dominant geomorphic processes.

Geomorphic feature	**Primary geomorphic process**
(*a*) Estevelle	(*i*) Coastal
(*b*) Kettle Hole	(*ii*) Periglacial
(*c*) Gloup	(*iii*) Glacial
(*d*) Sandur	(*iv*) Karstic
	(*v*) Glaciofluvial

Choose the correct answer:

	(*a*)	(*b*)	(*c*)	(*d*)
A.	(*iv*)	(*iii*)	(*i*)	(*v*)
B.	(*v*)	(*i*)	(*ii*)	(*iii*)
C.	(*iv*)	(*ii*)	(*i*)	(*iii*)
D.	(*iv*)	(*v*)	(*iii*)	(*ii*)

105. **Statement A:** Most hydrographs tend to be positively skewed.

Statement B: During the rain event, flow tends to increase rapidly above baseflow as various forms of runoff become concentrated on the valley floor, and once the rain stops it takes considerable time for the flow to return to baseflow conditions.

Choose the correct option.

A. Both the statements are incorrect

B. Statement A is incorrect but Statement B is correct.

C. Statement A is correct but Statement B is incorrect.

D. Both the statements are correct.

106. Which one of the following does NOT represent a flat or gently sloping relatively smooth rock surface formed in the zone between high and low tide levels?

A. Abrasion platform

B. Spit platform

C. Shore platform

D. Wave-cut platform

107. Match the river and its coastline configuration at the mouth.

River	Coastline configuration
(*a*) Mississippi	(*i*) Tide-dominated coastline with elongated peninsulas separated by tidal creeks oriented roughly perpendicular to the shore
(*b*) Nile	(*ii*) Estuary with a complex of large and small islands
(*c*) Ganga–Brahmaputra	(*iii*) Gently arcuate, smooth shoreline with two slightly protruding distributary mouths
(*d*) Amazon	(*iv*) Highly indented coastline, with multiple extended digitate distributaries
	(*v*) Smooth, straight shoreline with a single protruding river channel

Choose the correct answer:

	(*a*)	(*b*)	(*c*)	(*d*)
A.	(*i*)	(*iii*)	(*v*)	(*ii*)
B.	(*iv*)	(*iii*)	(*i*)	(*ii*)
C.	(*v*)	(*ii*)	(*iv*)	(*iii*)
D.	(*i*)	(*iii*)	(*ii*)	(*v*)

108. Which one of the following terrestrial biomes is found in regions dominantly characterized by oxisols?

A. Evergreen tropical rain forest
B. Shrubs or sparse grasses
C. Coniferous forest
D. Boreal forest

109. Assertion (A): Sediment transport-limited systems are characterized by sediment deposition and storage.

Reason (R): Sediment transport-limited conditions occur when sediment volume or size exceeds the capacity of the flow to transport it.

A. A is correct but R is incorrect
B. A is incorrect but R is correct
C. Both A and R are correct and R is the correct explanation of A
D. Both A and R are correct and R is not the correct explanation of A

110. Darwin's paradox refers to:

A. evolutionary appearance of hominids in the East African grasslands
B. infliction of disease by microscopic bacteria on much larger life forms
C. the role of mutations in altering the course of natural selection
D. high productivity of coral reefs in apparently nutrient poor conditions

111. Match the deltas represented in the figure with the dominant process(es) shaping them.

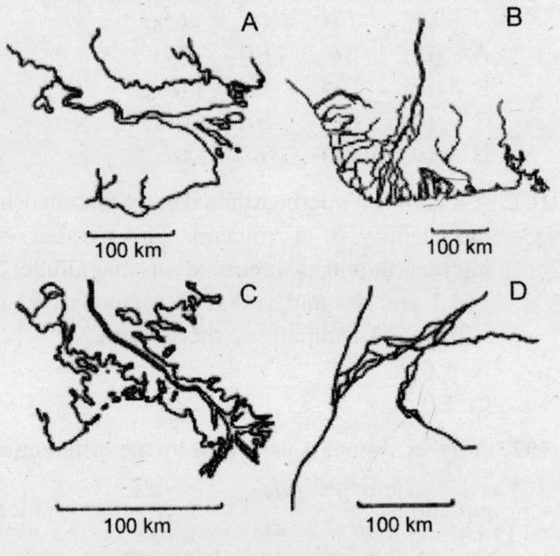

Choose the correct option:

A. A – Wave & Tide, B – River, C – Wave, D – Tide
B. A – Tide, B – Wave & Tide, C – River, D – Wave
C. A – Wave, B – River, C – Wave & Tide, D – Tide
D. A – Tide, B – Wave & Tide, C – River, D – Wave

112. In India, an area is categorised as 'dark' when its groundwater development rate is estimated to be:

A. more than 75%.
B. between 75% and 90%
C. between 85% and 100%
D. more than 100%.

113. Identify the cloud types. Choose the correct option.

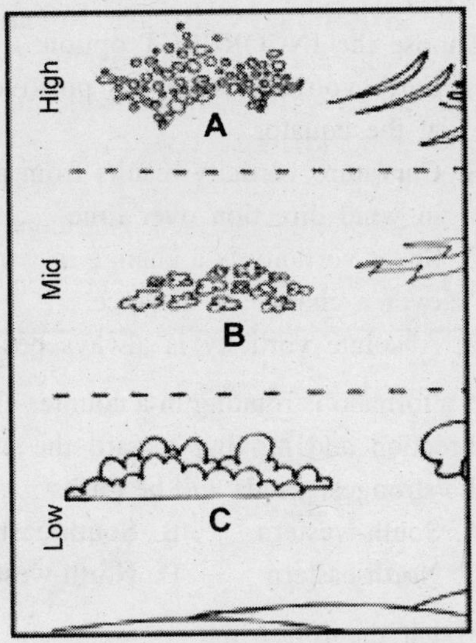

A. A = Cirrocumulus, B = Altostratus, C = Stratocumulus
B. A = Cirrocumulus, B = Altocumulus, C = Stratocumulus
C. A = Cumulus, B =Altostratus, C = Stratocumulus
D. A = Cirrus, B = Altostratus, C = Cumulonimbus

114. Flooding is more common in the eastern Ganga Plains (Bihar plains) in comparison to the western Ganga Plains (UP plains) because

I. River channels in the eastern Ganga plains are shallow in nature.
II. Rivers in the eastern Ganga plains are characterised by high sediment load.
III. Average rainfall is higher in the catchment area of eastern Ganga plains.
IV. Rivers in the western Ganga plains are characterised by higher stream power.

Choose the correct option

A. Only I
B. Only I and II
C. Only I, II and III
D. I, II, III and IV

115. Plunging sea cliffs, affected largely by swell waves, suffer relatively minimal erosion by wave action due to wave:

A. refraction
B. reflection
C. diffraction
D. attenuation

116. Match Columns I and II.

Column-I (Climates)	Column-II (Köppen's categories)
(*a*) Hot and rainy throughout the year	(*i*) Cwa
(*b*) Hot deserts	(*ii*) Am
(*c*) Mild in winter, hot in summer, and dry winters	(*iii*) BWh
(*d*) Hot and excessively rainy in one season	(*iv*) Af
	(*v*) As

Choose the correct answer:

	(*a*)	(*b*)	(*c*)	(*d*)
A.	(*i*)	(*iii*)	(*v*)	(*ii*)
B.	(*iv*)	(*iii*)	(*i*)	(*ii*)
C.	(*v*)	(*ii*)	(*i*)	(*iii*)
D.	(*i*)	(*iii*)	(*ii*)	(*iv*)

117. Identify the glacial features and find the correct match.

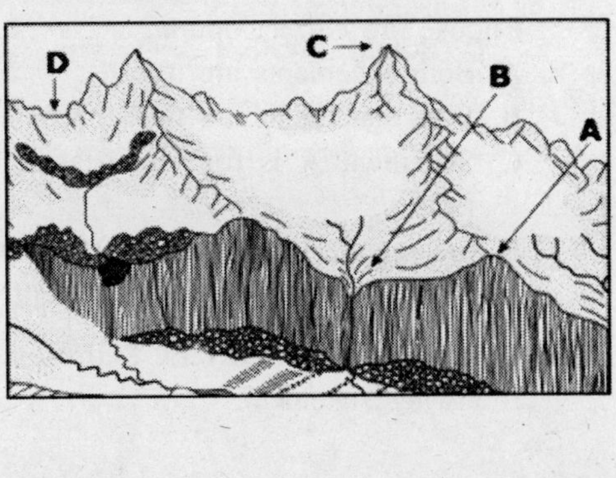

A. A – Arête, B – Hanging Valley, C – Horn, D – Tarn
B. A – Nunatak, B – Tarn, C – Matterhorn, D – Truncated spur
C. A – Truncated spur, B – Hanging Valley, C – Horn, D – Arête
D. A – Roche moutonnée; B – Hanging Valley, C – Arête, D – Truncated spur

118. Moving downstream a concave-upward longitudinal river profile:
A. channel slope decreases, while catchment area and sediment storage increase
B. mean sediment size decreases, while catchment area and channel slope increase
C. sediment storage increases, while mean sediment size and discharge decrease
D. discharge increases, while channel area and sediment storage decrease

119. In conditional instability, within a range of temperature profiles:
A. a wet air parcel is unstable and a dry air parcel is stable
B. a wet air parcel is stable and a dry air parcel is unstable
C. both wet and dry air parcels are stable
D. both wet and dry air parcels are unstable

120. **Statement A:** For a given value of mixing ratio, the virtual temperature is linearly related to air temperature.

Statement B: Clausius Clapeyron equation provides saturation vapour pressure as a linear function of air temperature.

Choose the correct option.
A. Both statements are true
B. Both statements are false
C. Statement A is true and statement B is false
D. Statement A is false and statement B is true

121. Choose the INCORRECT option in the following statement.

The collision – coalescence mechanism for growth of cloud drop in warm clouds depend on:
A. liquid water content
B. relative difference between the velocity of the large drop and velocity of the smaller droplet
C. collision – coalescence efficiency
D. applicability of Raoult's law

122. Choose the INCORRECT option:
A. Earth vorticity is always positive except at the equator
B. Curvature vorticity results from a change in wind direction over time
C. Shear vorticity is a change in wind speed over a change in distance
D. Absolute vorticity is always positive

123. If a tornado is rotating in a counter clockwise direction and moving toward the northeast, the strongest winds will be on its .... side.
A. South-western B. South-eastern
C. North-eastern D. North-western

124. Match the following:

(Instrument)	**(Parameter Measured)**
(*a*) Pyranometer	(*i*) Temperature
(*b*) Pyrheliometer	(*ii*) Diffused solar radiation
(*c*) Thermometer	(*iii*) Wind speed
(*d*) Anemometer	(*iv*) Direct solar radiation

Choose the correct answer:

	(*a*)	(*b*)	(*c*)	(*d*)
A.	(*ii*)	(*iv*)	(*i*)	(*iii*)
B.	(*i*)	(*iii*)	(*ii*)	(*iv*)
C.	(*iv*)	(*ii*)	(*i*)	(*iii*)
D.	(*iii*)	(*ii*)	(*i*)	(*iv*)

125. **Statement A:** Backing of wind with increase of height in northern hemisphere contributes to cold air advection.

Statement B: Veering of wind with increase of height in southern hemisphere contributes to warm air advection.

Choose the correct option.

A. Statement A is true and statement B is false

B. Statement A is false and statement B is true

C. Both statements are true

D. Both statements are false

126. Which one of the following occurs when the downstream wind speeds are faster than the upstream wind speeds?

A. Rising air

B. Sinking air

C. Convergence

D. Divergence

127. Towering and Stooping occurs when:

(*a*) there is a linear variation of temperature with height.

(*b*) there is a strong temperature inversion.

(*c*) there is a non-linear variation of temperature with height.

(*d*) the temperature distribution shows a density increases with height.

Choose the correct option.

A. (*a*) is true

B. (*a*) and (*b*) are true

C. (*a*), (*b*) and (*c*) are true

D. (*a*), (*b*), (*c*) and (*d*) are true

128. Statement A: In the equivalent barotropic model, direction of thermal wind is different from the directions of geostrophic winds at all heights.

Statement B: Primitive equations are based on hydrostatic balance but not on geostrophic balance.

Choose the correct option:

A. Statement A is true and statement B is false

B. Statement A is false and statement B is true

C. Both statements are true

D. Both statements are false

129. Choose the INCORRECT option in the following statement.

Sea surface temperature measurements from satellite infrared radiometers require

A. correction for cloud effects

B. correction for clear sky atmospheric effects

C. correction for surface emissivity

D. measurements in atmospheric window channels

130. What is the virtual temperature of an unsaturated tropical environment with temperature of 40°C and mixing ratio of 35g/kg?

A. 26.7°C

B. 36.7°C

C. 46.7°C

D. 56.7°C

131. Horizontal wind's clockwise turning with ascent in the northern hemisphere determines the:

A. Gaussian distribution

B. Vertical trajectory

C. Ekman spiral

D. Thermal wind

132. Thunderstorms that produce tornadoes:

A. have very little cloud-to-ground lightning

B. have updraft velocities that exceed 150 kmph

C. have rotating updrafts

D. will not produce hail

133. "Acceleration of the circulation of a moving closed physical curve is equal to the instantaneous circulation acceleration" is given by:

A. Bjerkenes circulation theorem

B. Bjerkenes Homboe theory

C. Kelvin circulation theorem
D. Poincaré–Bjerknes circulation theorem

134. The Rossby radius of deformation is considerably larger near equator because the size of the radius depends on the:
A. distribution of the humidity
B. presence of clouds
C. density or potential temperature changes with height and Coriolis parameter
D. incoming solar radiation

135. Choose the correct velocity profile where the flow is likely to become unstable due to shear instability. [Use Rayleigh's inflexion point theorem and Fjørtoft's instability criterion]

A.
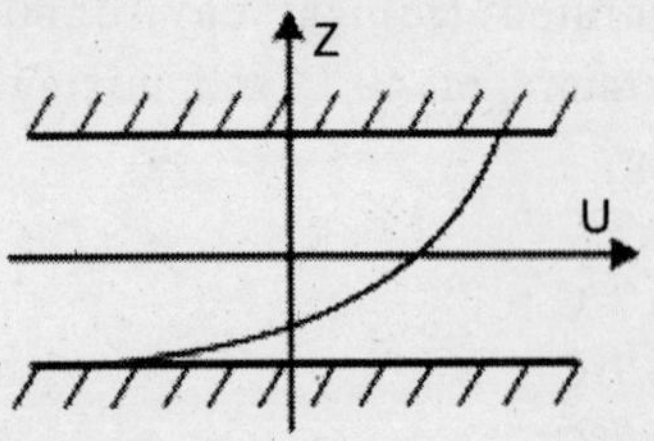

B.
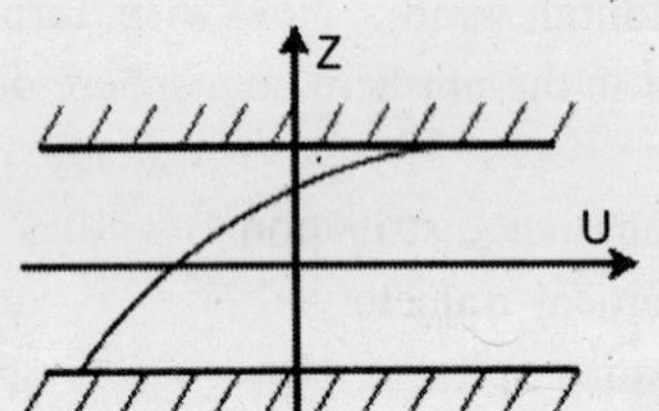

C.
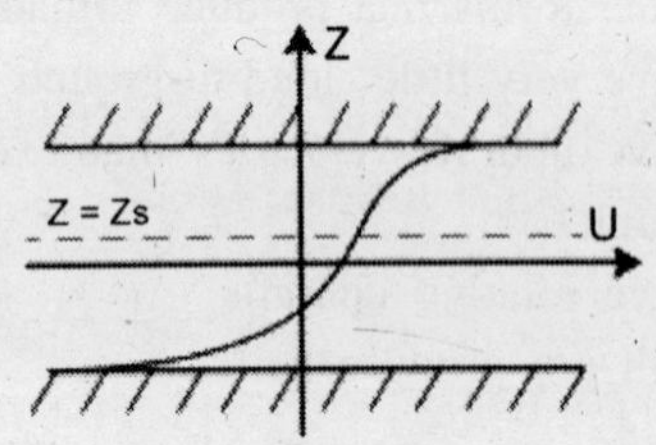

D.
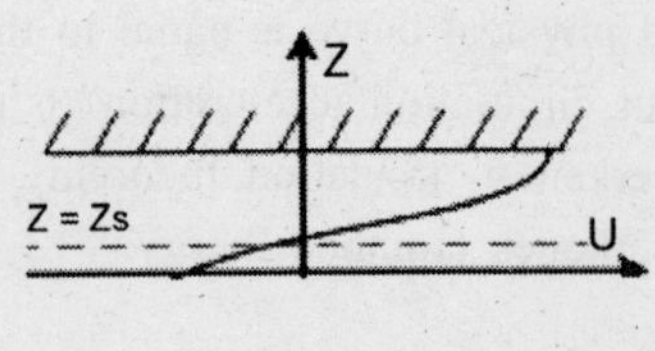

136. Assertion (A): Some part of carbon transfer by zooplankton is not measured in the sediment traps.

Reason (R): Zooplankton graze in the euphotic zone and respire/defecate in the deep ocean.

Choose the correct option:
A. Both A and R are true and R is the correct explanation of A
B. Both A and R are true but R is not the correct explanation of A
C. A is true but R is false
D. A is false but R is true

137. Statement A: The northern Arabian Sea is highly productive during winter.

Statement B: Intense upwelling occurs due to the winter monsoonal winds in the northern Arabian Sea.

Choose the CORRECT option from below:
A. Both A and B are true and B is the correct explanation of A
B. Both A and B are true but B is not the correct explanation of A
C. A is true but B is false
D. A is false but B is true

138. Match the Micro-organisms (Column-I) with their environment/ properties (Column-II)

Column-I	Column-II
(*a*) Diatoms	(*i*) Tropical and sub-tropical waters
(*b*) Dinoflagellates	(*ii*) Temperate and polar waters, silica shell
(*c*) Coccolithophores	(*iii*) Warm water gyres, blue green algae
(*d*) Cyanobacteria	(*iv*) Tropical waters, calcium carbonate shells

Choose the correct answer:

	(*a*)	(*b*)	(*c*)	(*d*)
A.	(*iii*)	(*iv*)	(*i*)	(*ii*)
B.	(*ii*)	(*i*)	(*iv*)	(*iii*)
C.	(*ii*)	(*i*)	(*iii*)	(*iv*)
D.	(*iii*)	(*ii*)	(*iv*)	(*i*)

139. Choose the correct statement for Kelvin waves.

[Here, N is Brunt-Viäsälä frequency and f is Coriolis parameter]

A. Group speed is more than phase speed for sigma > N
B. Group speed is less than phase speed for sigma < f
C. Group speed is equal to phase speed for all sigma
D. Group speed is more than phase speed for all sigma

140. Statement A: Stronger coastal upwelling occurs off Peru during El-Niño.

Statement B: Warmer than normal sea surface temperature in eastern equatorial Pacific Ocean during El-Niño.

Statement C: Stronger trade winds in the Pacific Ocean during La-Niña.

Choose the correct option.

A. Statements A and B are true; statement C is false
B. Statements B and C are true; statement A is false
C. Statement B is true, statements A and C are false
D. Statements A, B, and C are true

141. Choose the correct statement:

A. Chlorophyll-b absorption is maximum in 500-550 nm wavelength range
B. Increase in bloom intensity results in decrease of Dimethyl Sulphide (DMS) emission into the atmosphere
C. High concentration of Dissolved Organic Matter results in increase of the photic depth
D. Dimethyl Sulphide (DMS) does not absorb solar radiation in the sea water

142. Find the correct match of elements and their generic profiles in the ocean.

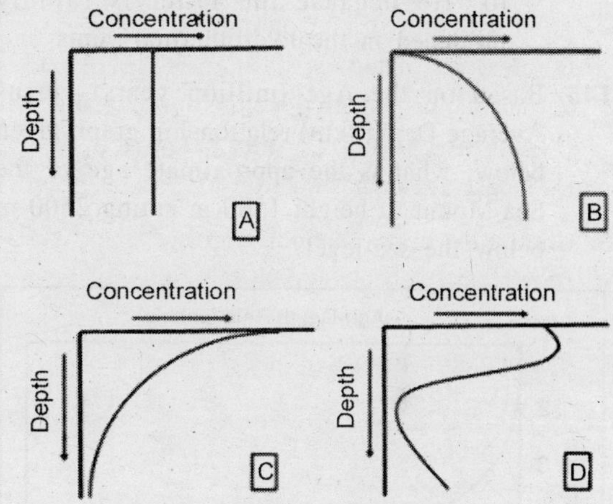

A. A-Cu, Zn; B-Al, Mn; C-O, N; D-Cl, Br
B. A-Cl, Br; B-O, N; C-Al, Mn; D-Cu, Zn
C. A-Cl, Br; B-Cu, Zn; C-Al, Mn; D-O, N
D. A-Al, Mn; B-O, N; C-Cu, Zn; D-Cl, Br

143. Reynolds number is a ratio between:

A. inertial force and viscous force
B. coriolis force and pressure gradient force
C. viscous force and coriolis force
D. inertial force and coriolis force

144. High Nutrient Low Chlorophyll (HNLC) regions are:

A. formed as iron is consumed by high primary producers
B. formed due to the non-availability of sunlight for a longer period
C. the regions of high dust inputs
D. the regions of low micronutrient concentrations

145. Which one of the following statements is INCORRECT about ^3He?

A. At any given time, $^3He/^4He$ ratio in seawater will be greater than that in the Earth's atmosphere

B. ^3He is released by mantle outgassing in the volcanic activity

C. ^3He is produced by cosmic ray bombardment in the atmosphere

D. Abundance of ^3He is much less compared to ^4He because the latter is rapidly produced in the hydrothermal vents

146. Based on the Age (million years) versus Average Depth (km) relationship graph given below, what is the approximate age of the Sea-Mount of height 1500 m sitting 2500 m below the sea-level?

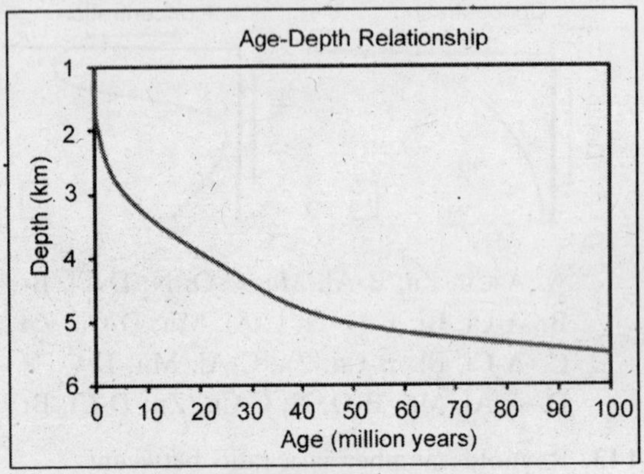

A. 80 million years
B. 20 million years
C. 0.1 million years
D. 40 million years

147. Which one of the following biogeochemial processes indicates anoxic condition?

A. Nitrification
B. Nitrogen Fixation
C. Ammonium Oxidation
D. Annamox reaction

148. Match the items in Column-I and Column-II:

Column-I	Column-II
(*a*) Mid Atlantic ridge	(*i*) is in the central Indian Ocean
(*b*) Rodriguez triple Junction	(*ii*) is the junction of Indo-Australian, Pacific, and Antarctic Plates
(*c*) 90°E ridge in the Indian Ocean	(*iii*) extends from the Ice land in north to Bouvet triple junction in the south.
(*d*) Macquarie triple junction	(*iv*) is an aseismic ridge

Choose the correct answer:

	(*a*)	(*b*)	(*c*)	(*d*)
A.	(*iii*)	(*i*)	(*iv*)	(*ii*)
B.	(*iii*)	(*ii*)	(*i*)	(*iv*)
C.	(*ii*)	(*iv*)	(*iii*)	(*i*)
D.	(*ii*)	(*iii*)	(*i*)	(*iv*)

149. Match the ocean currents in Column-I to their properties in Column-II:

Column-I	Column-II
(*a*) Agulhas current	(*i*) Cold current in north Pacific Ocean
(*b*) Gulf stream	(*ii*) Western boundary current in Indian Ocean
(*c*) Kuroshio current	(*iii*) Warm current in north Pacific Ocean
(*d*) California current	(*iv*) Warm current in north Atlantic Ocean

Choose the correct answer:

	(*a*)	(*b*)	(*c*)	(*d*)
A.	(*iv*)	(*iii*)	(*ii*)	(*i*)
B.	(*iii*)	(*ii*)	(*i*)	(*iv*)
C.	(*ii*)	(*iv*)	(*iii*)	(*i*)
D.	(*ii*)	(*iii*)	(*i*)	(*iv*)

150. Match the isotopes in Column-I to the ocean-atmospheric processes in Column-II that they are used to study.

Column-I	Column-II
(*a*) ^2H	(*i*) Palaeotemperature
(*b*) ^{13}C	(*ii*) Hydrological cycle
(*c*) ^{15}N	(*iii*) Primary production
(*d*) ^{18}O	(*iv*) Denitrification

Choose the correct answer:

	(*a*)	(*b*)	(*c*)	(*d*)
A.	(*i*)	(*ii*)	(*iii*)	(*iv*)
B.	(*ii*)	(*i*)	(*iv*)	(*iii*)
C.	(*ii*)	(*iii*)	(*iv*)	(*i*)
D.	(*i*)	(*iv*)	(*iii*)	(*ii*)

ANSWERS

1	2	3	4	5	6	7	8	9	10
D	D	D	C	B	A	D	D	B	D
11	**12**	**13**	**14**	**15**	**16**	**17**	**18**	**19**	**20**
B	C	B	B	C	C	B	D	C	D
21	**22**	**23**	**24**	**25**	**26**	**27**	**28**	**29**	**30**
A	C	A	C	A	C	B	B	B	D
31	**32**	**33**	**34**	**35**	**36**	**37**	**38**	**39**	**40**
A	B	A	D	C	C	B	B	C	C
41	**42**	**43**	**44**	**45**	**46**	**47**	**48**	**49**	**50**
C	D	B	B	C	B	D	C	D	D
51	**52**	**53**	**54**	**55**	**56**	**57**	**58**	**59**	**60**
C	B	C	D	B	C	A	A	B	B
61	**62**	**63**	**64**	**65**	**66**	**67**	**68**	**69**	**70**
C	D	B	D	C	D	A	C	C	B
71	**72**	**73**	**74**	**75**	**76**	**77**	**78**	**79**	**80**
A, D	B	B	C	C	C	D	A	A	B
81	**82**	**83**	**84**	**85**	**86**	**87**	**88**	**89**	**90**
C	A	C	B	A	A	C	C	C	A
91	**92**	**93**	**94**	**95**	**96**	**97**	**98**	**99**	**100**
B	C	D	D	B	C	C	D	D	A
101	**102**	**103**	**104**	**105**	**106**	**107**	**108**	**109**	**110**
C	D	A	A	D	B	B	A	C	D
111	**112**	**113**	**114**	**115**	**116**	**117**	**118**	**119**	**120**
B, D	C	B	D	B	B	C	A	A	C
121	**122**	**123**	**124**	**125**	**126**	**127**	**128**	**129**	**130**
D	D	B	A	A	D	B	B	C	C
131	**132**	**133**	**134**	**135**	**136**	**137**	**138**	**139**	**140**
C	C	C	C	D	A	C	B	C	B
141	**142**	**143**	**144**	**145**	**146**	**147**	**148**	**149**	**150**
D	C	A	D	D	B	D	A	C	C

Previous Years' Paper

Joint CSIR-UGC NET/JRF

Earth, Atmospheric, Ocean & Planetary Sciences

NOVEMBER-2020

(Exam held on 19-11-2020)

PART-A

1. Which of the following numbers is a perfect square?

A. 48841 B. 58287
C. 68763 D. 38262

2. The surface area of water in a circular well with vertical wall is 30 m^2. When an idol made of a material of density 2 g/cm^3 is fully immersed, the water level rises by 10 cm. What is the mass of the idol?

A. 300 kg B. 600 kg
C. 3000 kg D. 6000 kg

3. The hour and minute hands of a clock are along the same line at a certain time. They will be collinear next after a lapse of time which is closest to:

A. 30 minutes B. 60 minutes
C. 63 minutes D. 33 minutes

4.

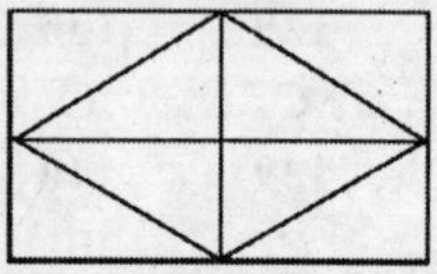

Which of the following is true for the given figure?

A. Number of rectangles > Number of triangles.
B. Number of rectangles = Number of triangles.
C. Number of rectangles + 1 = Number of triangles.
D. Number of rectangles + 1 < Number of triangles.

5. Marks of five students Brijesh, Paresh, Ramesh, Naresh and Suresh in an examination are distinct. Marks of Brijesh is the average of the marks of all these students. Marks of Naresh is the average of the marks of Paresh and Ramesh. Marks of Paresh is the least and marks of Naresh is more than the marks of Suresh. Who got the highest marks?

A. Brijesh B. Naresh
C. Ramesh D. Suresh

6. In a test attempting all given questions is compulsory. A candidate is given 3 questions to start with. On every correct answer the candidate is given 2 additional questions. If the candidate attempted a total of 11 questions, how many were correctly answered?

A. 3 B. 5
C. 6 D. 4

7. Which one of the following pairs of statements represents negative feedback in a stimulus-response pair?

A. Praise increases performance. Higher performance leads to praise.
B. Criticism reduces performance.
C. Increase in body temperature results in sweating. Sweating reduces the body temperature.
D. Reduction in air temperature increases polar ice. Increase in the polar ice reduces air temperature.

8. Maximum retail price (MRP) of each of 3 different brands of biscuits A, B and C is ₹ 20 per 100g packet. During a festive offer, A is available at 25% off on MRP, B is available with 25% extra biscuits for the same MRP, and one packet of C is free on purchase of three packets of C. If a person wants to buy biscuits for ₹ 60, which brand should the person choose to get the maximum amount of biscuits by weight?

A. B only
B. Either A or B, not C
C. Either B or C, not A
D. Either A or C, not B

9. The figure shows a circle inscribed in a square.

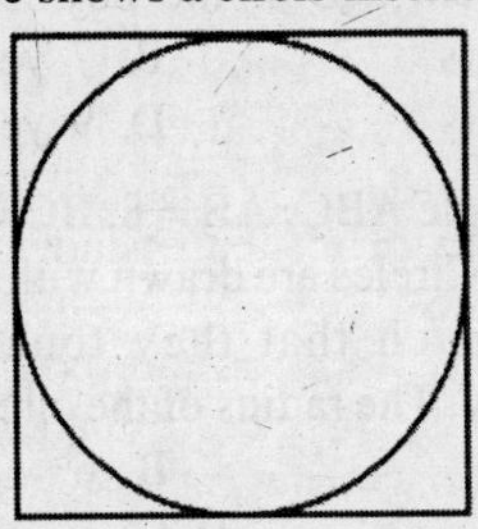

If a large number of points are randomly marked within the square, the expected percentage of points inside the circle is closest to:

A. 52 B. 79
C. 75 D. 70

10.

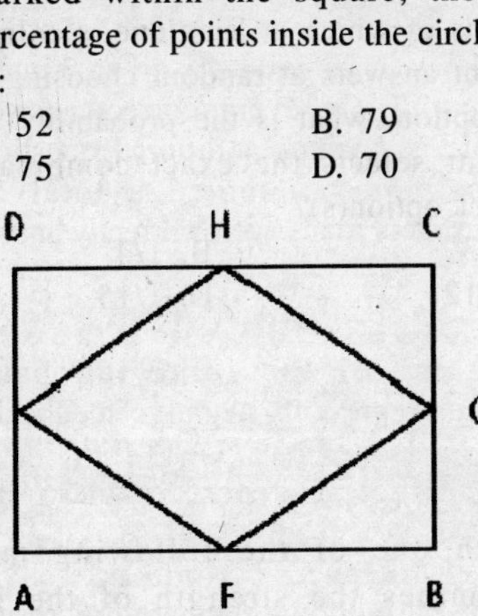

If points E,F,G, and H bisect the sides of rectangle ABCD as shown in the figure, what is the ratio of the areas of quadrilateral EFGH and rectangle ABCD?

A. 1 : 4 B. 1 : 3
C. 1 : 2 D. 2 : 1

11. A cube of side 3 cm is made by assembling cubes of side 1 cm. How many small cubes can be counted on the surface?

A. 24 B. 25
C. 26 D. 27

12. Diamonds of a particular quality are available in 4 different sizes, whose prices are given below.

Size (carats)	Price (rupees/carat)
0.25	50,000
0.5	100,000
1	200,000
2	400,000

What are the minimum and maximum numbers of diamonds that can be purchased for ₹ 400,000?

A. 1 and 8 B. 1 and 32
C. 2 and 8 D. 2 and 32

13. The pointer of a spring balance is offset from zero. This balance showed a weight of 8 kg for an object A and 6 kg for another object B. When A and B are weighed together, the balance showed 16 kg. The true weights, in kg, of A and B, respectively are

A. 4 and 6 B. 10 and 6
C. 10 and 8 D. 8 and 8

14. Consider a moving object whose velocity v varies with its position x as shown in the given plot.

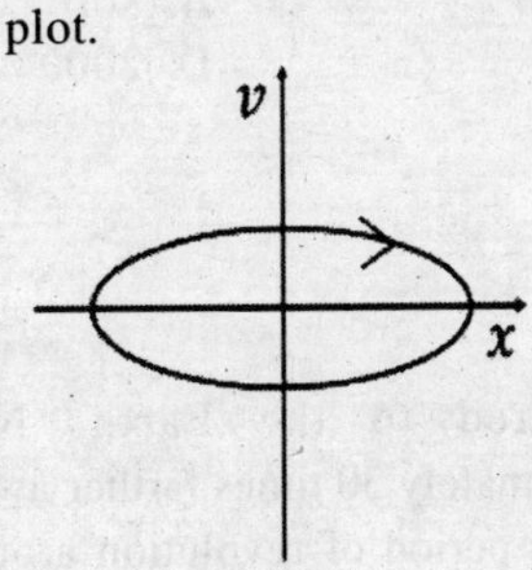

Which of the following plots showing the change in position with time is admissible for the above object?

A.

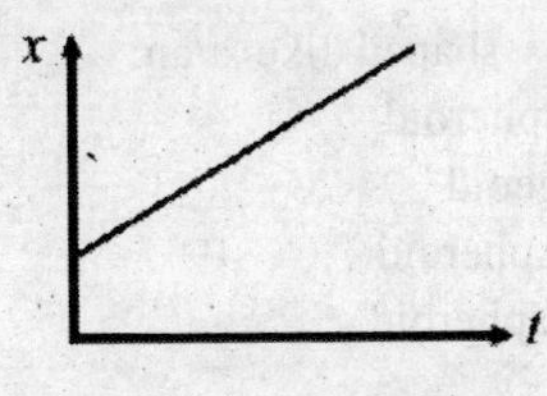

B. 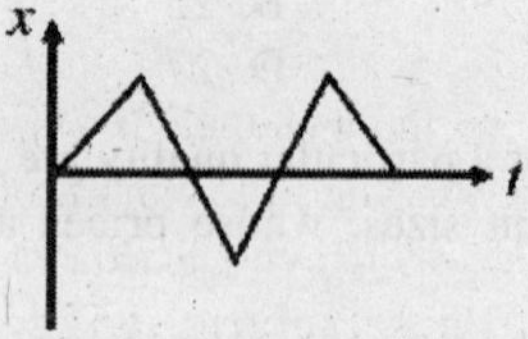

C. 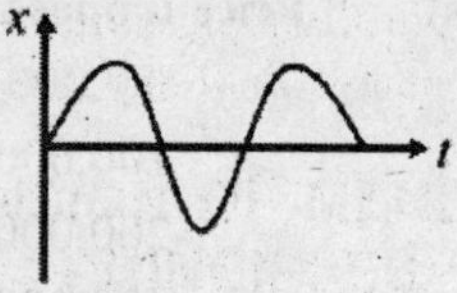

D. 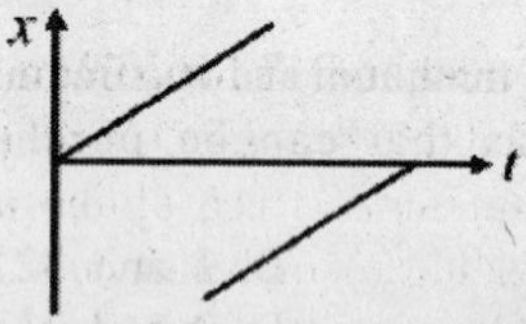

15. In a ten-digit mobile number 999ABCDEEE, A, B, C and D are distinct prime numbers. The mobile number is never divisible by

A. 3　　B. 4
C. 5　　D. 8

16. A person invests a certain amount of money. Whenever the amount gets exactly doubled, he donates ₹ 200. After four such donations he is left with ₹ 200. The initial amount of money he invested was rupees:

A. 1000　　B. 800
C. 400　　D. 200

17. I bought some bananas for ₹ 120. The vendor gave me two extra bananas and in the process incurred a loss of ₹ 10 per dozen on the earlier price. How many bananas did I ultimately get for ₹ 120?

A. 18　　B. 16
C. 14　　D. 12

18. The difference between the ages of a boy and his father is same as that between the father and grandfather. Five years earlier, the grandfather was twice as old as the father. The present age of the boy is:

A. 5 years　　B. 7 years
C. 8 years　　D. 9 years

19. In a triangle ABC, AB = 8, BC = 14, and CA = 12 units. Circles are drawn with centres at A, B and C, such that they touch each other externally. The radius of the circle around A is:

A. 4　　B. 6
C. 2　　D. 3

20. A certain multiple choice question has four options of which at least one is correct. If a student answers at random choosing at least one option, what is the probability that the student selects the exact combination of correct option(s)?

A. 1/3　　B. 1/4
C. 1/12　　D. 1/15

PART-B

21. Compared to the Earth, Neptune is approximately 30 times farther away from the Sun. Its period of revolution around the Sun (in Neptune years) would be

A. 1　　B. 30
C. 165　　D. 423

22. The Earth is shaped like a/an:

A. Oblate spheroid
B. Oblate geoid
C. Prolate spheroid
D. Everest spheroid

23. Which one of the following minerals determines the strength of the Earth's continental crust?

A. Feldspar　　B. Mica
C. Quartz　　D. Amphibole

24. If the attitude of the two limbs of a fold was measured as 263°/29°N and 351°/40°E, the fold axis will plunge in which one of the following quadrants?

A. North East　　B. South West
C. North West　　D. South East

25. Which one of the following is the fastest spreading ridge on Earth?
A. Mid-Atlantic ridge
B. Southwest Indian ridge
C. East Pacific ridge
D. Carlsbad ridge

26. Which of the following is TRUE for a disconformity?
A. A gap in the geological record bounded below by igneous rocks and bounded above by sedimentary rocks.
B. A sequence of rocks that does not contain any gap in the geological record.
C. A gap in the geological record where the strata below and above an erosional surface are horizontal.
D. A gap in the geological record bounded below by tilted sedimentary strata and bounded above by horizontal sedimentary strata.

27. In the Earth's interior, the increase of P-wave velocity at 670 km discontinuity is caused by phase transition from:
A. olivine to spinel
B. garnet to perovskite
C. olivine to perovskite
D. β-spinel to γ-spinel

28. Which of the following minerals exhibit maximum number of cleavage planes?
A. Calcite B. Galena
C. Fluorite D. Sphalerite

29. Which one of the following boundaries approximately represents the Great Oxidation Event (GOE) in the Earth's history?
A. Proterozoic-Paleozoic
B. Archean-Proterozoic
C. Mesozoic-Cenozoic
D. Paleozoic-Mesozoic

30. Which one of the following clay minerals is devoid of iron?
A. Chlorite B. Glauconite
C. Chamosite D. Kaolinite

31. Precambrian rocks are exposed in which of the following cities?
A. Mumbai B. Delhi
C. Lucknow D. Bhuj

32. Extensive living coral reefs occur in which of the following places?
A. Silvassa B. Kovalam
C. Kavaratti D. Diu

33. Which one of the following forces inhibits plate motion?
A. Slab pull B. Ridge push
C. Trench suction D. Basal drag

34. Which of the following symmetry operations would give a result similar to an operation of a bar 6 symmetry axis?
A. A 6-fold symmetry axis with a mirror plane perpendicular to it.
B. A 6-fold symmetry axis with a mirror plane parallel to it.
C. A 3-fold symmetry axis with a mirror plane perpendicular to it.
D. A 3-fold symmetry axis with a mirror plane parallel to it.

35. The texture in a graphic granite can represent which of the following stages of crystallization in the Albite-Silica binary system?
A. At liquidus in the albite rich composition
B. At liquidus in the silica rich composition
C. At the eutectic point
D. At the temperature below the eutectic point

36. The masses of the Earth's crust, its mantle and core are in the ratio 7 : 690 : 303. Then their contributions to the Earth's gravity field will be in the ratio:
A. 7 : 690 : 303
B. 303 : 690 : 7
C. $\sqrt{303} : \sqrt{690} : \sqrt{7}$
D. $\sqrt{7} : \sqrt{690} : \sqrt{303}$

37. The Earth's magnetic field in the mantle:
A. is zero everywhere, due to high temperatures
B. increases sharply with depth
C. decreases sharply with depth
D. attains a finite constant value

38. If σ_1, σ_2 and σ_3, are the principal stresses, then which one of the following stress states is uniaxial?
A. $\sigma_1 \geq \sigma_2 \geq \sigma_3 > 0$
B. $\sigma_1 \neq 0, \sigma_2 = 0, \sigma_3 = 0$
C. $\sigma_1 \neq 0, \sigma_2 = 0, \sigma_3 = 0$
D. $\sigma_1 = \sigma_2 = \sigma_3 \neq 0$

39. The 27-day periodicity of magnetic storms observed on the Earth is attributed to:
A. rotation of the Sun around its axis.
B. rotation of the Earth around its axis.
C. revolution of the Moon around the Earth.
D. rotation of the Moon around its axis.

40. The magnitudes of two earthquakes A and B are measured on Richter scale as 6 and 5 respectively. Which of the following inferences is valid?
A. The energy released in A is 10 times that of B.
B. The amount of destruction in case of A is 30 times that of B.
C. The ground motion in case of A is 10 times that of B.
D. Earthquake A is 1.2 times deeper than B.

41. According to the NUVEL-I model of global plate motion, the correct sequence of the plates in increasing order of their angular velocity with respect to the Pacific Plate is:
A. South America - Antarctica - India - Nazca
B. Antarctica - South America - India - Nazca
C. South America - Antarctica - Nazca - India
D. Antarctica - South America - Nazca - India

42. The duration of the Cretaceous Normal Superchron (CNS) is about:
A. 25 Ma B. 30 Ma
C. 40 Ma D. 50 Ma

43. The S shadow zone on the Earth is nearly:
A. same as the P shadow zone.
B. two times the P shadow zone.
C. three times the P shadow zone.
D. four times the P shadow zone.

44. For seismic wave propagation, the Earth acts as:
A. high cut filter. B. low cut filter.
C. all pass filter. D. high pass filter.

45. The ray path of a body wave propagating through an isotropic, radially symmetric layered Earth model is:
A. a curved path due to the spherical shape of the Earth.
B. a straight line.
C. a curved path due to linear increase in velocity with depth.
D. a curved path due to dispersion.

46. Which one of the following is NOT an autotrophic organism?
A. *Noctiluca* B. *Diatom*
C. *Copepod* D. *Nodularia*

47. Which one of the following is true for ocean?
A. $[HCO_3^-] > [CO_3^{2-}] > [H_2CO_3]$
B. $[HCO_3^-] < [CO_3^{2-}] < [H_2CO_3]$
C. $[H_2CO_3] > [HCO_3^-] > [CO_3^{2-}]$
D. $[CO_3^{2-}] > [H_2CO_3] > [HCO_3^-]$

48. Redfield ratio refers to the:
A. ratio among the different conservative tracers in the ocean.
B. ratio of calcium to magnesium in foraminifera.
C. mean molar ratio of carbon, nitrogen and phosphorus in the organic matter.
D. ratio of carbon, nitrogen and phosphorus in the surface waters.

49. Which one of the following fishes is a mesopelagic fish?
A. *Argyropelecus affinis*
B. *Eurypharynx pelecanoides*
C. *Ceratias holboelli*
D. *Deep-sea angler-fish*

50. What type of a marine environment would have slowest rate of recovery from a large oil spill?
A. cyclonic gyres
B. anticyclonic gyres
C. highly productive waters
D. cold environment with little wave action

51. Which of the following satellite does NOT provide information on oceanic bathymetry?
A. GEOSAT
B. ERS-I & II

C. Coastal Zone Colour Scanner (CZCS)
D. TOPEX/Poseidon

52. The magnetic North Pole is currently migrating from Canada towards which of the regions given below?
A. Greenland B. Siberia
C. Iceland D. America

53. Which one of the following DOES NOT influence the Latent heat flux at the air-sea interface?
A. atmospheric pressure
B. wind speed
C. relative humidity
D. evaporation

54. Which one of the following processes can be related to the 'continuity equation'?
A. Divergence or convergence at a given horizontal level leads to vertical velocity.
B. Ocean currents tend to flow parallel to isobars due to the Coriolis force.
C. The upward pressure gradient force is almost in balance with downward gravitational force.
D. Wind-driven turbulent mixing generates a mix layer in the upper ocean.

55. Select the CORRECT group of forces which are primarily considered in the derivation of Ekman spiral in the upper-ocean.
A. wind stress, pressure gradient, friction
B. wind stress, Coriolis force, friction
C. pressure gradient, Coriolis force, gravitational force
D. wind stress, Coriolis force, gravitational force.

56. For which one of the following ocean waves, surface tension is the principal restoring force?
A. Internal waves
B. Tsunami
C. Standing waves (Seiche)
D. Capillary waves

57. River discharge is estimated on the basis of:
A. Unit hydrograph B. Hyetograph
C. Rating curve D. Current meter

58. The highest variability of annual rainfall in India is observed over the:
A. Thar desert region
B. Assam valley region
C. Central India
D. East coast of India

59. Littoral drift is the volume or mass of sediment transported by:
A. longshore current and wind-drift
B. beach drift and rip currents
C. swash and wind-drift
D. longshore current and swash

60. A drainage system, which has maintained its general direction across an area of localized or regional uplift is known as:
A. annular drainage.
B. antecedent drainage.
C. truncated drainage.
D. offset drainage.

61. In an isobaric/adiabatic process the temperature that is attained in an isobaric process when water vapour, present in a sample of air is condensed, is called:
A. wet bulb temperature.
B. virtual temperature.
C. equivalent temperature.
D. dew point temperature.

62. The concentration of the trace gases by volume in the lower troposphere in decreasing order is:
A. Nitrous oxide; Carbon dioxide; Methane; Nitric oxide
B. Methane; Nitrous oxide; Nitric oxide; Carbon dioxide
C. Nitric oxide; Methane; Carbon dioxide; Nitrous oxide
D. Carbon dioxide; Methane; Nitrous oxide; Nitrogen dioxide

63. Which one of the statements about satellites in the geo-stationary orbit is INCORRECT?
A. They orbit at a height which is about 5.6 times the radius of the Earth.
B. They move in the opposite direction of the Earth's rotation.
C. They complete a single orbit in one sidereal day.

D. GSAT and INSAT satellites are placed in geostationary orbits.

64. In the ICAO Standard Atmosphere (ISA) the lapse rate (°C/km) in the 11-20 km layer is:

A. 6.5 B. 9.8
C. –0.001 D. 0

65. The seasons on the Earth occur primarily because of:

A. the variability of the earth's distance from the sun.
B. shifting of ocean currents.
C. the tilt of the Earth's axis of rotation.
D. the jet stream.

66. Which of the following is a diabatic process?

A. Convection
B. Orographic lifting
C. Radiational heating or cooling
D. Rising air due to convergence in the Planetary Boundary Layer (PBL).

67. Rossby number is a ratio of:

A. inertial force to Coriolis force.
B. mechanical production to buoyance.
C. inertial force to viscous force.
D. inertial and gravitational force.

68. The rate of change of relative circulation following the motion for a barotropic atmosphere can NOT change due to changes in:

A. meridional location.
B. area of domain.
C. zonal location.
D. inclination of domain.

69. The time interval between consecutive 'Spring Tide' and 'Neap Tide' is:

A. 14 days B. 1 day
C. 28 days D. 7 days

70. The cone of depression in groundwater forms:

A. around a dry well
B. in the freshwater of a fast-pumped flow well.
C. in the salt water intruding from the sea to the well.
D. in a sink hole.

PART-C

71. Sense of Shear (SoS) plane is defined by which one of the following combinations?

A. The SoS plane is parallel to foliation and perpendicular to stretching lineation.
B. The SoS plane is perpendicular to foliation and parallel to stretching lineation.
C. Both foliation and stretching lineation are parallel to SoS plane.
D. Both foliation and stretching lineation are perpendicular to SoS plane.

72. Match the following:

Deformation setting	**Structure**
(*a*) Convergent	1. Tulip structure
(*b*) Divergent	2. Ramp Anticline
(*c*) Strike-Slip Transpression	3. Metamorphic Core Complex
(*d*) Strike-Slip Transtension	4. Palm tree structure

Choose the correct option:

	(*a*)	(*b*)	(*c*)	(*d*)
A.	2	4	1	3
B.	2	3	4	1
C.	3	4	1	2
D.	4	3	2	1

73. Coulomb's law of failure differs from Byerlee's law of failure in which one of the listed characteristics?

A. Defines a failure envelope.
B. Applicable for intact homogenous rocks.
C. Law for shear failure.
D. Includes a coefficient of friction.

74. The following assemblage of foraminifera are recorded from bottom to top of a stratigraphic section:

Uvigerina, Bulimina, Globorotalia Eponides, Lenticulina, Textularia

Quinqueloculina, Ammonia, Cibicides Trochammina, Ammobaculites, Miliammina

The stratigraphic section represents

A. Lowstand System Tract.
B. Highstand System Tract.
C. Transgressive System Tract.
D. Falling Stage System Tract.

75. Which one of the following statements is correct?

A. Load cast forms by erosional processes.
B. Groove mark represents deformational feature.
C. The bounce mark occurs at the top of a sandstone bed.
D. Current crescent forms against an obstacle.

76. A grain-supported limestone containing around 10% lime mud is known as:

A. packstone B. grainstone
C. wackestone D. floatstone

77. Consider the following thermobarometric equations:

Reaction A: $KAlSi_3O_8 + NaAl_2(Si_3Al)O_{10}(OH)_2 = NaAlSi_3O_8 + KAl_2(Si_3Al)O_{10}(OH)_2$

Reaction B: $Mg_3Al_2Si_3O_{12} + KAl_2(Si_3Al)O_{10}(OH)_2 = KMg_3(Si_3Al)O_{10}(OH)_2 + 2Al_2SiO_5 + SiO_2$.

Which of the following is TRUE for reactions 'A' and 'B'?

A. 'A' is an example of barometer; 'B' is an example of thermometer
B. 'A' is an example of thermometer; 'B' is an example of barometer
C. Both 'A' and 'B' are examples of thermometers
D. Both 'A' and 'B' are examples of barometers

78. Which one of the following textures explicitly form during decompression stage of a metamorphic P-T path?

A. Corona texture
B. Granoblastic texture
C. Normal growth zoning in garnet
D. Spherulitic texture

79. Choose the correct sequence of minerals that are usually crystallized from the cooling of magma (High-T to Low-T).

A. $Mg_2SiO_4 \rightarrow Ca_2Mg_5Si_8O_{22}(OH)_2 \rightarrow Mg_2Si_2O_6 \rightarrow KAlSi_3O_8 \rightarrow KMg_3(Si_3Al)O_{10}(OH)_2$
B. $NaAlSi_3O_8 \rightarrow Ca_2Mg_5Si_8O_{22}(OH)_2 \rightarrow KAl_2(Si_3Al)O_{10}(OH)_2 \rightarrow SiO_2 \rightarrow KAlSi_3O_8$
C. $Mg_2SiO_4 \rightarrow Mg_2Si_2O_6 \rightarrow Ca_2Mg_5Si_8O_{22}(OH)_2 \rightarrow KMg_3(Si_3Al)O_{10}(OH)_2 \rightarrow KAlSi_3O_8$
D. $KAlSi_3O_8 \rightarrow NaAlSi_3O_8 \rightarrow Mg_2Si_2O_6 \rightarrow SiO_2 \rightarrow KAl_2(Si_3Al)O_{10}(OH)_2$

80. Which one of the following mineral pairs are NOT polymorphs?

A. Quartz - moganite
B. Chrysotile - Lizardite
C. Anatase - Brookite
D. Marcasite - Chalcopyrite

81. A homogeneous liquid with binary components FeO - SiO_2 cools, at a constant pressure, to a temperature at which it unmixes to form two liquids of different compositions. On further cooling to the complete equilibrium crystallization:

A. there would be four minerals, two crystallizing from silica rich liquid and two from FeO rich liquid.
B. the silica rich liquid would crystallize a silica mineral, while the FeO rich liquid would form a glass.
C. there would be fayalite and a silica mineral in eutectic proportion.
D. there would be a fayalite within a glass separating it from silica mineral.

82. In an unconfined coastal aquifer, the depth to groundwater table in a well is 1 m. The well is situated at an elevation of 2 m above mean sea level. What should be the depth of freshwater-saline water interface below the ground surface?

A. 40 m B. 42 m
C. 80 m D. 38 m

83. The 'depleted mantle' model age of a rock, as calculated using Sm-Nd systematics is 2.5 Ga. It means that

A. the isotope ratios $^{143}Nd/^{144}Nd$ in source of this rock at 2.5 Ga were the same as in the depleted mantle at that time.
B. this rock crystalized at 2.5 Ga.
C. the $^{147}Sm/^{144}Nd$ and the $^{143}Nd/^{144}Nd$ ratios in the rock were same as that in the depleted mantle at 2.5 Ga.
D. The terrane that it is found in, formed at 2.5 Ga.

84. Paired metamorphic belts, which juxtapose HP/LT and LP/HT metamorphic belts, are typically associated with:

A. greenstone terrains
B. convergent plate margins
C. mid-oceanic ridges
D. transform plate boundaries

85. Which one of the matches is correct for the stratigraphic unit and their ages?

Stratigraphic Unit	**Period**
A Dhosa Oolite	E Palaeogene
B Karai Shale	F Cretaceous
C Maleri Formation	G Jurassic
D Lakadong Limestone	H Triassic

Choose the correct option:

A. A-E, B-F, C-H, D-G
B. A-G, B-F, C-H, D-E
C. A-G, B-E, C-H, D-F
D. A-G, B-H, C-E, D-F

86. Porphyry type Cu-deposits are formed in which of the following tectonic setting?

A. Spreading centre
B. Oceanic island arc
C. Continent-continent collision
D. Continental arc

87. The Fourier transform of a function $f(t)$ is $\sin \omega$. Then, the Fourier transform of $t^2 f(t)$ is:

A. $\sin \omega$
B. $\sin \omega^2$
C. $\omega^2 \sin \omega^2$
D. $\omega^2 \sin \omega$

88. An input signal $x(n) = \{2, 1, -1\}$ is passed through two serially connected linear time-invariant systems $h1(n) = \{1, -1\}$ and $h2(n) = \{-1, 1\}$. The output signal $y(n)$ will be:

A. {0, 0, 0, 0}
B. {–2, –3, 0, 1}
C. {–2, 3, 1, –3, 1}
D. {1, –2, 3, –1, –3}

89. A spherical ore body with a density of 3.0 gm/cc is surrounded by country rock of density 2.7 gm/cc. A gravity profile across the body recorded an anomaly of 0.1 mgal at a distance of 100 m from the position of the maximum gravity anomaly, which is 0.3 mgal. The ore body weighs (in units of 10^6 tons):

A. 0.45 B. 1.50
C. 2.25 D. 4.50

90. The following figure shows a sketch of an E-W gravity profile across a sulphide vein. The maximum anomaly occurs at point O. Then, the vein dips due:

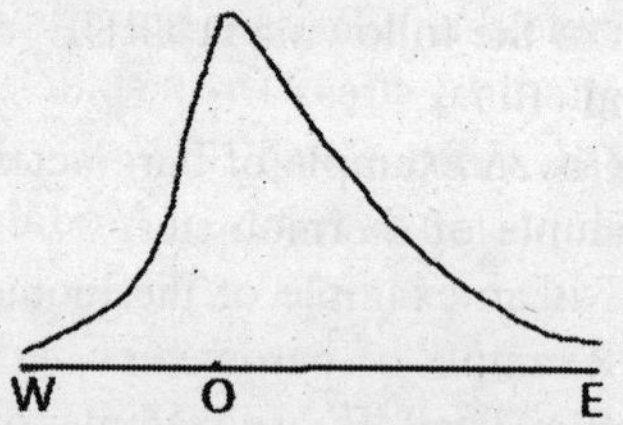

A. east and its top lies towards east of O.
B. west and its top lies towards west of O.
C. east and its top lies towards west of O.
D. west and its top lies towards east of O.

91. X, Y and V are the components of the Earth's magnetic field F, X being along the geographical north. H is its horizontal component and i and δ are its dip and declination respectively. Then, at a place on the Earth's surface where F is minimum, the value of $\dfrac{X\cos\delta + Y\sin\delta}{V\sin i + H\cos i}$ is:

A. 1 B. $\dfrac{\sqrt{3}}{2}$

C. $\dfrac{1}{2}$ D. $\dfrac{1}{\sqrt{2}}$

92. The distance between the points of the maximum and minimum anomaly values along a total field anomaly profile across an anomalous body resembling a single pole is 224 m. If the magnetic latitude of the place of survey is 30°, then the depth to the pole is:

A. 112 m B. 100 m

C. 86 m D. 72 m

93. In the time-distance plot for a seismic survey over a two-layered medium, the travel time at which the direct P-wave intersects the refracted wave is 3s. Estimate the depth to the velocity interface, assuming the slope of the direct wave to be 0.5 s/km and the velocity of the lower medium to be twice the velocity of the upper medium.

A. 1.73 km B. 2.73 km

C. 3.73 km D. 4.73 km

94. Assume that a Poisson solid is subjected to a longitudinal stress (σ_{xx}) while the transverse stresses are zero. Then, the Young's Modulus (E) in terms of Modulus of Rigidity (μ) will be:

A. $E = \mu$ B. $E = 1.5\mu$

C. $E = 2.5\mu$ D. $E = 3\mu$

95. Which one of the following statements is correct?

A. Zero-offset rays are always perpendicular to the data acquisition surface.

B. Receiver arrays are used to suppress ground roll.

C. Time migration honours ray bending across an interface.

D. Dix's method of estimating interval velocity is valid for any surface model as long as all layers are isotropic.

96. A country rock at temperature T_c is intruded by a thick dyke at temperature T_m ($T_m > T_c$). Assuming that the temperature of the dyke remains constant with time, the temperature in the country rock away from the dyke contact will decrease as:

A. an exponential function

B. a linear function

C. a hyperbolic function

D. an error function

97. An oceanic plate is moving away from the spreading center at a speed of 6 cm/yr. Assuming that the plate motion is constant with geological time, the location of the Gauss –Gilbert paleomagnetic epoch boundary from the spreading center will be at approximate distance of:

A. 155 km B. 185 km

C. 215 km D. 255 km

98. Two current electrodes C_1 (+I) and C_2(–I) are placed 1000 m apart on the Earth surface and 5 Ampere current flows through the subsurface. Two potential electrodes P_1 and P_2 with electrode separation 10 m are placed between C_1 and C_2 such that midpoint of P_1 and P_2 is located at 400 m from the midpoint of C_1 and C_2. If 500 mV potential difference is measured between P_1 and P_2, then the apparent resistivity (in Ωm) will be (do not use approximate formulation)

A. 418 B. 518

C. 618 D. 718

99. If in an electromagnetic survey, dip angle is measured over widely spaced vertical conductors along a profile, the number of 'false crossover' in the dip angle anomaly will be:

A. 1 B. 2

C. 3 D. 4

100. An over pressured zone encountered in borehole logging is characterized by:
A. high porosity and high density
B. low resistivity and low density
C. low resistivity and low porosity
D. low porosity and low density

101. As per Gutenberg-Richter relationship for global seismicity, how many earthquakes of magnitude 2 will occur given the number of earthquakes of magnitude 6 to be 100 and *b* value to be 1.5?
A. 10^4 B. 10^6
C. 10^8 D. 10^{10}

102. In case of resistivity sounding over multi-layered earth if $A_1(\lambda)$ is the kernel function then the correct relationship between resistivity transform function 'T(λ)' and $A_1(\lambda)$ is (ρ_1 is the resistivity of the first layer)
A. $T(\lambda) = \rho_1\{1 + 2A_1(\lambda)\}$
B. $T(\lambda) = \rho_1\{1 + A_1(\lambda)\}$
C. $T(\lambda) = \rho_1 + \{1 + 2A_1(\lambda)\}$
D. $T(\lambda) = \rho_1 + \{1 + A_1(\lambda)\}$

103. Sediment rating curve represents the relation between:
A. sediment yield and catchment area.
B. sediment transport rate and water discharge.
C. sediment concentration and total dissolved load.
D. sediment delivery rate and relief-length ratio.

104. Match Köppen's climate symbols with climate types.

Köppen's symbols	Climate types
A EF	L Continental Dry Summer
B Ds	M Ice Cap
C BS	N Savanna
D Aw/As	O Steppe
	P Tropical Rainforest

Choose the correct option:
A. A-O, B-N, C-L, D-P
B. A-L, B-P, C-M, D-N,
C. A-M, B-L, C-N, D-P
D. A-M, B-L, C-O, D-N

105. Statement A: The tropics experience large annual temperature variations.

Statement B: Highest values of annual temperature range occur in the middle of large landmasses in the subpolar latitudes.

Choose the correct option.
A. Both are true
B. Both are false
C. A is true but B is false
D. A is false but B is true

106. Which one of the following values of hypsometric integral denotes maximum erosion of a drainage basin area down to its base level?
A. 0.18 B. 0.44
C. 0.51 D. 0.91

107. Match the geomorphic features with the geomorphic processes.

Geomorphic feature	Geomorphic processes
A Cockpit	L Coastal
B Moulin	M Fluvial
C Runnel	N Glacial
D Talik	O Karstic
	P Periglacial

Choose the correct option.
A. A-O, B-N, C-L, D-P
B. A-P, B-L, C-M, D-N
C. A-O, B-M, C-L, D-N
D. A-O, B-P, C-N, D-L

108. Match the earth scientists who were the first to propose the geomorphic concepts.

First proponent	Geomorphic concept
A A. Linton	L Etchplanation
B B. Willis and E.J. Wayland	M Morphogenetic region

C	J. Büdel	N	Slope replacement
D	W. Penck	O	Slope retreat
		P	Theory of tor formation

Choose the correct option.
A. A-O, B-N C-L, D-P
B. A-P, B-L, C-M, D-N
C. A-O, B-M, C-L, D-N
D. A-O, B-P, C-N, D-P

109. Assertion (A): Coasts tend to become sandy to muddy as tidal range changes from meso to macro.

Reason (R): In tropical coasts, mangrove vegetation is conducive to deposition of fine sediments.

A. Both (A) and (R) are true and (R) is the correct explanation
B. Both (A) and (R) are true but (R) is not a correct explanation
C. (A) is true but (R) is false
D. (A) is false but (R) is true

110. Identify the correct sequence considering cause and effect relationship in the Indian context.
A. Malnutrition → High morbidity → Low per capita income → High mortality
B. High morbidity → Malnutrition → Low per capita income → High mortality
C. Low per capita income → Malnutrition → High morbidity → High mortality
D. Malnutrition → Low per capita income → High morbidity → High mortality

111. Match the columns I and II.

	Column-I (Regions)		Column-II (Process)
A	Warmer forest	X	Alkaline compounds accumulate near the surface
B	Deciduous and mixed forest	Y	Bacterial actions and rapid chemical actions
C	Steppe grassland	Z	Soils are less acidic
D	Humid tropics	K	Leaching is less significant

Choose the correct option.
A. A-X; B-Z; C-Y; D-K
B. A-K; B-Z; C-Y; D-X
C. A-K; B-Z; C-X; D-Y
D. A-X; B-Y; C-Z; D-K

112. One of the following set of features correctly represents former higher sea levels or lake levels:
A. Estuaries, Abandoned cliffs, Mangrove swamps
B. Storm beaches, Foredunes, Submarine platforms
C. Strand lines, Raised beaches, Marine terraces
D. Plunging cliffs, Shingle beaches, Spits

113. The diagram shows the vertical variation in the texture and grading of river bank deposits. It is:

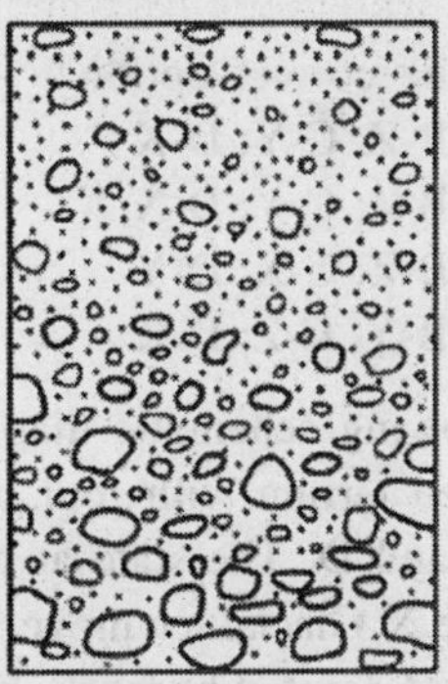

A. Fining upwards and well sorted
B. Coarsening upwards and well sorted.
C. Fining upwards and poorly sorted.
D. Coarsening upwards and poorly sorted.

114. Plateaus, mesas, buttes and pinnacles are:
A. evaporated landforms containing sediment and salt.
B. landforms of flat-lying rocks in arid regions.

C. formed when mountain streams carrying large amounts of rock waste drain into an adjacent lowland.
D. flood plain features.

115. Acid rain is NOT associated with:
A. aluminium toxicity in lakes.
B. removal of nutrients from soil.
C. blackening of Taj Mahal.
D. increase in biological oxygen demand in lake.

116. Match the columns I and II.

Column-I		Column-II
A Bolson	X	Low-angle foot slope with veneer of wash material
B Bajada	Y	Unconsolidated, highly dissected materials in semiarid regions
C Pediment	Z	Coalesced alluvial fans
D Badland	K	A slope-and-basin area between two adjacent ridges in a dry region with internal drainage

Choose the correct option.
A. A-X; B-Z; C-Y; D-K
B. A-K; B-Z; C-Y; D-X
C. A-K; B-Z; C-X; D-Y
D. A-X; B-Y; C-Z; D-K

117. The following schematic diagram represents a glaciated terrain with four different points A, B, C and D. The state at different points shown are X-Glacial Ice movement, Y-Glacial plucking, Z-Jointed bedrock, K-Abrasion and polishing. Find the correct match.

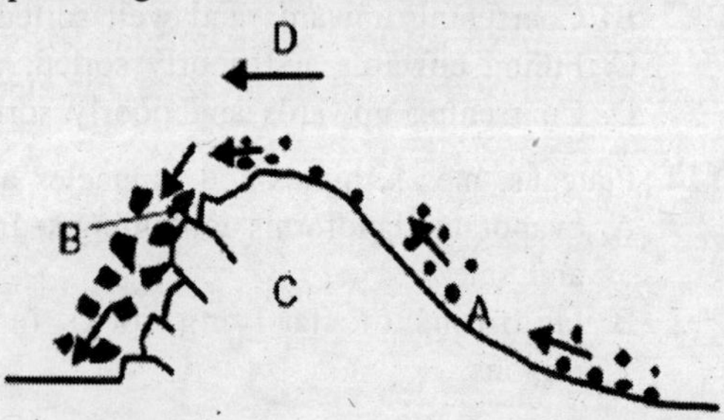

A. A-X; B-Z; C-Y; D-K
B. A-K; B-Y; C-Z; D-X
C. A-K; B-Z; C-X; D-Y
D. A-X; B-Y; C-Z; D-K

118. Highest cation exchange capacity is most likely to be in a soil that is:
A. very sandy
B. low in organic matter
C. high in clay and organic matter
D. silty and low in organic matter.

119. The difference between the barotropic and baroclinic atmosphere is that:
A. density is a function of pressure in the former while it is a function of temperature in the latter.
B. density is a function of pressure in the former while it is a function of pressure and temperature in the latter.
C. density is a function of temperature in both.
D. density is a function of temperature and pressure in both.

120. The following schematic diagram shows velocities observed by a ground Doppler radar for two atmospheric phenomena. The solid lines indicate wind component towards the radar, the dashed lines indicate wind components away from the radar, and the dotted line indicates the zero isodop. Which of the following options correctly identifies the two phenomena?

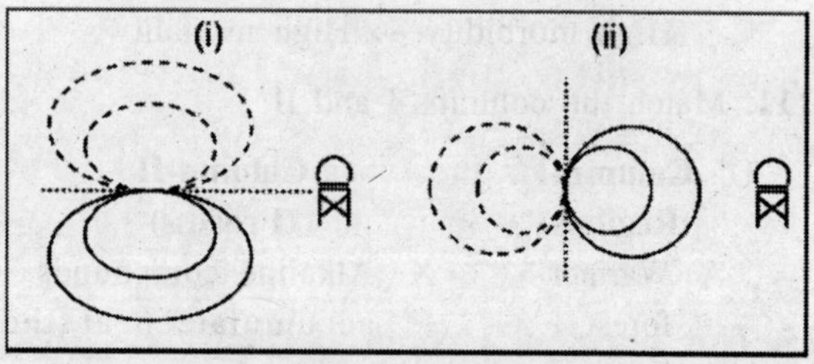

A. (i) Tornadic mesocyclone and (ii) Cold air downburst from a thunderstorm.
B. (i) Sea-breeze and (ii) Mountain-valley winds.

C. (i) Occluded front and (ii) Extra-tropical cyclone.
D. (i) Butterfly effect and (ii) Coriolis effect.

121. Choose the INCORRECT option in the following statement. Assumption of hydrostatic balance in the atmosphere leads to the following inference:
A. Coriolis force is not important in vertical motion.
B. Vertical acceleration is absent.
C. Vertical motion is absent.
D. There is a perfect balance between upward directed vertical pressure gradient force and downward directed gravity force.

122. Choose the INCORRECT option. In the geostrophic approximation:
A. pressure gradient force is in balance with Coriolis force.
B. it fails at equator.
C. it holds good in mid-latitudes.
D. Coriolis force varies linearly with latitude.

123. Occluded front occurs when:
A. cold front overtakes warm front.
B. warm front overtakes cold front.
C. cold air mass overtakes warm air mass.
D. warm air mass overtakes cold air mass.

124. Choose the correct option from the following statements. Relaxation methods are:
A. used to solve parabolic partial differential equations.
B. used to solve hyperbolic partial differential equations.
C. examples of iterative methods that are used to solve elliptic partial differential equations.
D. examples of direct methods that are used to solve elliptic partial differential equations.

125. The horizontal wind in the planetary boundary layer is the resultant of:
A. gravity, Coriolis and centrifugal forces.
B. pressure gradient, gravity and Coriolis forces.
C. Coriolis, pressure gradient and friction forces.
D. centrifugal, Coriolis and friction forces.

126. Which one of these moisture variables will increase in a rising parcel of air?
A. Mixing ratio
B. Relative humidity
C. Vapour pressure
D. Specific humidity

127. Diabatic thermodynamic processes can heat or cool the air at different rates. These processes include:
(*a*) Radiative heating/cooling.
(*b*) Conduction from the surface.
(*c*) Turbulent mixing.
(*d*) Latent heat released/absorbed due to phase change.

Choose the correct option
A. (*a*) is true.
B. (*a*) and (*b*) are true.
C. (*a*), (*b*) and (*c*) are true.
D. (*a*), (*b*), (*c*) and (*d*) are true.

128. Statement A: The duration of Indian summer monsoon increases from south to north.

Statement B: The amount of Indian summer monsoon rainfall in the northern plains decreases from east to west.

A. Both A and B are true
B. Both A and B are false
C. A is true, but B is false
D. A is false, but B is true

129. In numerical weather prediction models with hydrostatic approximation, vertical velocity can be:
A. calculated from the Navier-Stokes' equation
B. calculated from continuity equation
C. assumed to be zero
D. assumed to be constant

130. Cyclogenesis in Northern hemisphere is associated with
(*a*) sea level pressure decrease
(*b*) upward motion increase
(*c*) relative vorticity increase

Choose the correct option
A. (*a*) is true, (*b*) and (*c*) are false.
B. (*a*), (*b*) and (*c*) are true.
C. (*a*) and (*b*) are true and (*c*) is false
D. (*a*), (*b*) and (*c*) are false.

131. .... refers to the horizontal transport of air while .... is the vertical transport of air.
A. Advection, convection
B. Convection, advection
C. Propagation, transportation
D. Velocity, updraft

132. The chemical cycles that correspond to the catalytic destruction of the stratospheric ozone are
(*a*) Cl/ClO cycle. (*b*) NO/NO_2 cycle.
(*c*) SO_2/SO_3 cycle. (*d*) OH/H_2O cycle

Choose the correct option
A. (*a*) and (*b*) B. (*a*), (*b*) and (*d*)
C. (*c*) and (*d*) D. (*a*) and (*c*)

133. What will be the virtual temperature of an unsaturated air with temperature of 35°C and mixing ratio of $30g_{water}/kg_{dry\ air}$?
A. 40.0°C B. 40.2°C
C. 40.4°C D. 40.6°C

134. Which of the following statements related to the tropical easterly jet over Indian subcontinent is INCORRECT?
A. It is formed due to the reversed meridional temperature gradient
B. It is located over Peninsular India.
C. The northeast monsoon rainfall increases with the intensification of the jet stream.
D. It is found at an altitude of 14-16 km.

135. If a column of seawater moves from high latitude to low latitude (equatorward movement) then the relative vorticity of the water column will:
A. increase
B. decrease
C. remain unchanged
D. increase up to 30° latitude and then decrease

136. Which direction of meridional wind stress would cause coastal upwelling at the West Coast of India (WCI) and West Coast of Australia (WCA)?
A. Northward at WCI and Southward at WCA
B. Southward at WCI and Southward at WCA
C. Northward at WCI and Northward at WCA
D. Southward at WCI and Northward at WCA

137. Statement A: Ekman pumping velocity in the ocean is proportional to the curl of the wind stress.

Statement B: Low salinity water from river runoff and precipitation reduces mixed layer depth.

Choose the CORRECT option from below.
A. Both the statements are true but B is not a correct explanation of A
B. Statement A is false, statement B is true
C. Statement A is true, statement B is false
D. Both the statements are true and B is a correct explanation of A

138. Match the 'Type of flow/circulation' in Column I to their most relevant Oceanic process/condition in Column II.

Column-I	Column-II
P Barotropic flow	T Pressure gradient and Coriolis forces are in balance
Q Baroclinic flow	U Surfaces of constant density and constant pressure intersect at some angle
R Geostrophic flow	V Sinking motion of water at selected high latitude locations
S Thermohaline circulation	W Independent of depth in the ocean
	X Pressure gradient and gravitational forces are in balance

Choose the correct option.
A. P-U, Q-T, R-X, S-V
B. P-W, Q-U, R-T, S-V
C. P-U, Q-W, R-T, S-X
D. P-W, Q-U, R-X, S-V

139. Which one of the following options correctly represents the relationship between oceanic surface Ekman layer depth (D_E), surface wind speed (U), and latitude (ϕ)?
A. $D_E \propto U$, $D_E \propto 1/\phi$
B. $D_E \propto U$, D_E independent of ϕ
C. $D_E \propto 1/U$, $D_E \propto 1/\phi$
D. $D_E \propto U$, $D_E \propto \phi$

140. Statement A: Siliceous sediments are abundant on the deep ocean floor at high latitudes.

Statement B: Radiolarian are more abundant in high latitude waters.
A. Statement A is true and statement B is untrue.
B. Statement B is true and statement A is untrue.
C. Both the statements are true but B doesn't explain A.
D. Both the statements are true and B explains A.

141. Which one of the following is NOT true?
A. Primary production occurs up to 125 m in open ocean waters, while in turbid coastal waters a few meters to tens of meters.
B. Light absorption depends upon water, suspended material, dissolved organisms, phytoplankton.
C. Primary productivity in the Arabian Sea is primarily limited by phosphate.
D. Upwelling makes the Arabian Sea one of the highly productive regions.

142. Identify parameters A, B and C in the schematic depth profile of a tropical oceanic basin.

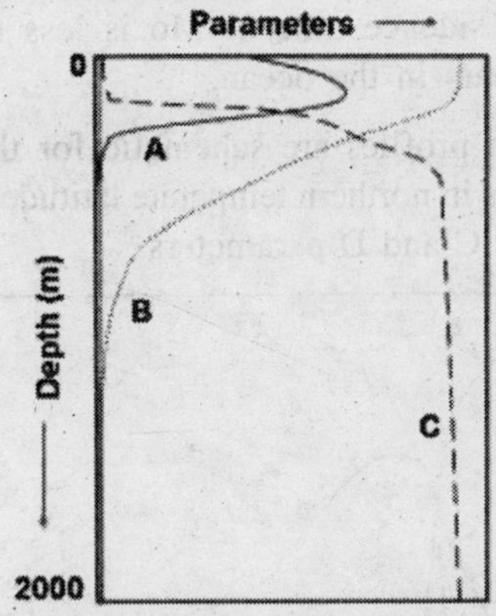

A. A–[Cl^-], B–[Oxygen], C–[nutrients]
B. A–[Chlorophyll], B–[nutrients], C–[Na^+]
C. A–Primary productivity, B–[Pb], C–[Fe]
D. A–Primary productivity, B–[Fe], C–[Pb]

143. Match the following marine organisms with their sizes:

Marine organisms	Size range (m)
A Zooplankton	E 10^{-6} – 10^{-4}
B Virus	F 10^{-5} – 10^{-2}
C Bacteria	G 10^{-8} – 10^{-6}
D Phytoplankton	H 10^{-7} – 10^{-5}

A. A–F, B–G, C–H, D–E
B. A–F, B–E, C–H, D–G
C. A–H, B–G, C–F, D–E
D. A–G, B–H, C–E, D–F

144. What is the correct preference order (first one first) of oxidizing agent for marine heterotrophs?
A. oxygen, sulphate, nitrate
B. oxygen, phosphate nitrate
C. phosphate, sulphate, nitrate
D. oxygen, nitrate, sulphate

145. Which one of the following statements is INCORRECT for molybdenum (Mo) in the ocean?
A. [Mo] ≈ 100 nM
B. Mo exists mainly in the dissolved form and has a conservative distribution (though it is a micronutrient) in the ocean.
C. Dissolved molybdenum exists as the molybdate (MoO_4^{2-}) anion in seawater.

D. Residence time of Mo is less than 1000 years in the ocean.

146. Given profiles are schematic for the surface waters in northern temperate latitudes. Identify A, B, C and D parameters.

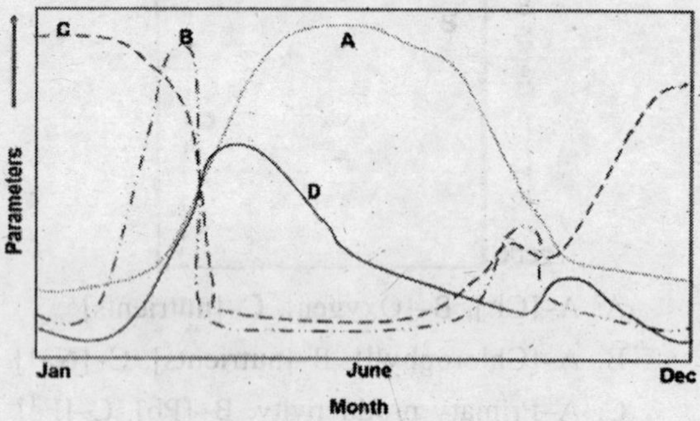

A. A–Nutrients, B–Phytoplankton, C–Zooplankton, D–Sunlight
B. A–Sunlight, B–Phytoplankton, C–Nutrients, D–Zooplankton
C. A–Zooplankton, B–Phytoplankton, C–Chlorophyll, D–Sunlight
D. A–Sunlight, B–Phytoplankton, C–Nutrients, D–Chlorophyll

147. The chaetognath *Sagittci elegans* consumes 10 mg of copepods per day and produces 2 mg of faecal material per day. What is the assimilation efficiency of this carnivore?

A. 20% B. 40%
C. 60% D. 80%

148. Which of the following statements is INCORRECT?

A. Hydrothermal event plumes represent continuous venting of material, gases and magma.
B. Hydrothermal event plumes are larger but transient plumes.
C. Hydrothermal event plumes often travel thousands and more meters above its source.
D. Hydrothermal event plumes are often associated with formation of new volcanic mounds.

149. Choose the correct match between the columns I and II:

Column I	Column II
(*a*) Littoral Zone	1. A flat topped ridge on the beach face formed by the deposition of beach material by wave action.
(*b*) Foreshore	2. A group of linear depressions that run parallel to the shoreline.
(*c*) Runnel	3. Zone between seaward boundary of land vegetation and to a point in the sea where sediments are not disturbed.
(*d*) Berm	4. Part of beach that is exposed during low tide and submerged during high tide.

Choose the correct option:

	(*a*)	(*b*)	(*c*)	(*d*)
A.	3	4	2	1
B.	4	3	1	2
C.	4	3	2	1
D.	1	2	3	4

150. Choose the correct match between the columns I and II:

Column I	Column II
(*a*) Active Margin	1. It is formed when separated continental tracts move perpendicular to the coastline.
(*b*) Rifted Margin	2. It develops when rifting is oblique to the coastline.
(*c*) Sheared Margin	3. It is formed when continental breakup is associated with strike-slip faulting.
(*d*) Transtensional Margin	4. It is found on the edge of continents where subduction occurs.

Choose the correct option:

	(*a*)	(*b*)	(*c*)	(*d*)
A.	1	4	2	3
B.	4	1	3	2
C.	1	3	2	4
D.	4	3	1	2

ANSWERS

1	**2**	**3**	**4**	**5**	**6**	**7**	**8**	**9**	**10**
A	D	D	D	C	D	C	D	B	C
11	**12**	**13**	**14**	**15**	**16**	**17**	**18**	**19**	**20**
C	D	C	C	A	D	A	A	D	D
21	**22**	**23**	**24**	**25**	**26**	**27**	**28**	**29**	**30**
A	A	C	A	C	C	B	D	B	D
31	**32**	**33**	**34**	**35**	**36**	**37**	**38**	**39**	**40**
B	C	D	C	C	A	B	C	A	C
41	**42**	**43**	**44**	**45**	**46**	**47**	**48**	**49**	**50**
A	C	D	A	C	C	A	C	A	D
51	**52**	**53**	**54**	**55**	**56**	**57**	**58**	**59**	**60**
C	B	A	A	B	D	C	A	D	B
61	**62**	**63**	**64**	**65**	**66**	**67**	**68**	**69**	**70**
C	D	B	D	C	C	A	C	D	B
71	**72**	**73**	**74**	**75**	**76**	**77**	**78**	**79**	**80**
B	B	B	C	D	A	B	A	C	D
81	**82**	**83**	**84**	**85**	**86**	**87**	**88**	**89**	**90**
C	B	A	B	B	B, D	A	C	D	C
91	**92**	**93**	**94**	**95**	**96**	**97**	**98**	**99**	**100**
A	B	A	C	B	D	C	C	C	B
101	**102**	**103**	**104**	**105**	**106**	**107**	**108**	**109**	**110**
C	A	B	D	D	A	A	B	B	C
111	**112**	**113**	**114**	**115**	**116**	**117**	**118**	**119**	**120**
C	C	C	B	D	C	B	C	B	A
121	**122**	**123**	**124**	**125**	**126**	**127**	**128**	**129**	**130**
C	D	A	C	C	B	D	D	B	B
131	**132**	**133**	**134**	**135**	**136**	**137**	**138**	**139**	**140**
A	B	D	C	A	D	A	B	A	A
141	**142**	**143**	**144**	**145**	**146**	**147**	**148**	**149**	**150**
C	C	A	D	D	B	D	A	A	B

Previous Years' Paper

Joint CSIR-UGC NET/JRF

Earth, Atmospheric, Ocean & Planetary Sciences

DECEMBER-2019

(Exam held on 15-12-2019)

PART-A

1. A four-wheeled cart is going around a circular track. Which of the following statements is correct, if the four wheels are free to rotate independent of each other, and the cart negotiates the track stably?

A. All wheels rotate at the same speed.
B. The four wheels have different speeds each.
C. The wheels closer to the inside of the track move slower than the outer-side wheels.
D. The wheels closer to the inside of the track move faster than the outer-side wheels.

2. What day of the week will it be 61 days from a Friday?

A. Saturday B. Sunday
C. Friday D. Wednesday

3. Karan's house is 20 m to the east of Rahul's house. Mehul's house is 25 m to the North-East of Rahul's house. With respect to Mehul's house in which direction is Karan's house?

A. East B. South
C. North-East D. West

4. Which of the following 7-digit numbers CANNOT be perfect squares?

A = 45*xyz*26, B = 2*xyz*175, C = *xyz*3310

A. Only A B. Only B
C. Only C D. All three

5. A cyclist covers a certain distance at a constant speed. If a jogger covers half the distance in double the time as the cyclist, the ratio of the speed of the jogger to that of the cyclists is

A. 1 : 4 B. 4 : 1
C. 1 : 2 D. 2 : 1

6. What is the ratio of the surface area of a cube with side 1 cm to the total surface area of the cubes formed by breaking the original cube into identical cubes of side 1 mm?

A. $\frac{1}{6}$ B. $\frac{1}{10}$
C. $\frac{1}{100}$ D. $\frac{1}{36}$

7. Based on the bar chart shown here, which of the following inferences is correct?

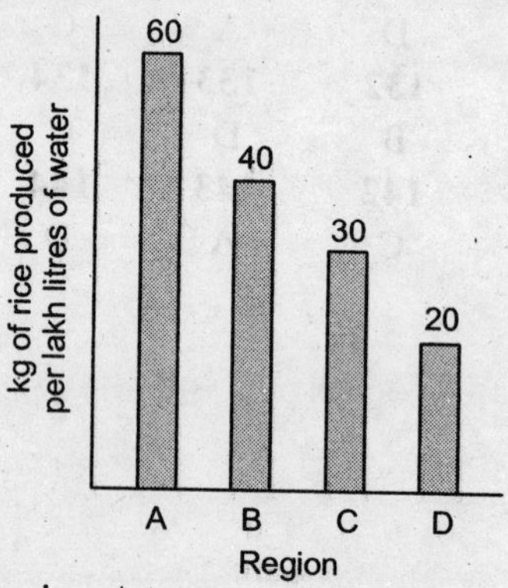

A. Region A uses maximum water per kg of rice.
B. Average water consumption of the four regions is 37.5 lakh litres.

C. Region D uses thrice the amount of water used by region A per kg of rice.

D. Region B uses 20 lakh litres of less water than region A.

8. How many non-square rectangles are there in the following figure, consisting of 7 squares?

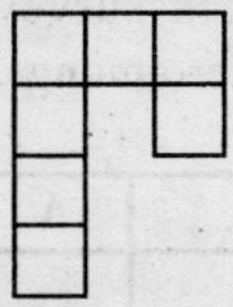

A. 8 B. 9

C. 10 D. 11

9. Of three children, Uma plays all three of cricket, football and hockey. Iqbal plays cricket but not football, and Tarun plays hockey but neither football nor cricket. The number of games played by at least two of the children is

A. one B. two

C. three D. zero

10. Given that K! = 1 × 2 × 3 × . . . × K, which is the largest among the following numbers?

A. $(2!)^{1/2}$ B. $(3!)^{1/2}$

C. $(4!)^{1/4}$ D. $\left(\frac{3!}{2}\right)$

11. In a college admission where applicants have to choose only one subject. $\frac{1}{4}$th of the applicants opted for Biology, $\frac{1}{6}$th for Chemistry, $\frac{1}{8}$th for Physics and $\frac{1}{12}$th for Maths. 18 applicants did not opt for any of the above four subjects. How many applicants were there?

A. 22 B. 24

C. 36 D. 48

12. In a race five drivers were in the following situation. M was following V, R was just ahead of T, and K was the only one between T and V. Who was in the second place at that instant?

A. V B. R

C. T D. K

13. An ice cube of volume 10 cm^3 is floating over a glass of water of 10 cm^2 cross-section area and 10 cm height. The level of the water is exactly at the brim of the glass. Given that the density of ice is 10% less than that of water, what will be the situation when ice melts completely?

A. The level falls by 10% of the side of the cube.

B. The level falls by 10% of the original height of the water column.

C. The level increases by 10% of the side of the cube and water spills out.

D. There is no change in the level of the water.

14. The mean of a set of 10 numbers is M. By combining with it a second set of M numbers, the mean of the combined set becomes 10. What is the sum of the second set of numbers?

A. 10M – 1 B. 10M + 1

C. 20 D. 100

15. Which is the curve in the figure whose points satisfy the equation y = const × e^x?

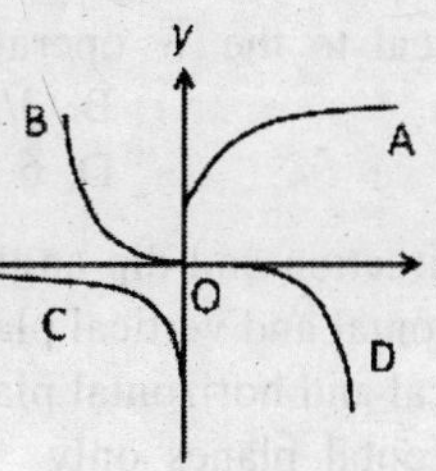

A. A B. B

C. C D. D

16. A multiple choice exam has 4 questions, each with 4 answer choices. Every question has only one correct answer. The probability of getting all answers correct by independent random guesses for each one is:

A. $\frac{1}{4}$ B. $\left(\frac{1}{4}\right)^4$

C. $\left(\frac{3}{4}\right)$ D. $\left(\frac{3}{4}\right)^4$

17. A two-digit number is such that if the digit 4 is placed to its right, its value would increase by 490. Find the original number.

A. 48 B. 54

C. 64 D. 56

18. In a very old, stable forest, a particular species of plants grows to a maximum height of 3 m. In a large survey, it is found that 30% of the plants have heights less than 1 m, and 50% have heights more than 2 m. From these observations we can say that the height of the plants increases:

A. at the slowest rate when they are less than 1 m tall.

B. at the fastest rate when they are between 1 m and 2 m tall.

C. at the fastest rate when they are more than 2 m tall.

D. at the same rate at all stages.

19. A bag contains 8 red balls, 10 blue balls, 17 green balls. What is the minimum number of balls that needs to be taken out from the bag to ensure getting at least one ball of each colour?

A. 19 B. 18

C. 28 D. 27

20. The result of a survey to find the most preferred leader among A, B, C is shown in the table.

Votes	A	B	C
Ist preference	13	54	33
IInd preference	24	37	39
IIIrd preference	63	9	28

First, second and third preferences are given weights 3, 2, 1, respectively. Statistically, which of the following can be said to represent the preferences of the voters?

A. A and C are within 10% of each other.

B. B is the most preferred.

C. B and C are within 10% of each other.

D. C is the most preferred.

PART-B

21. Which of the following symmetry operations is identical to the $\overline{6}$ operations?

A. $3 + i$ B. 3/m

C. 6/m D. $6 + i$

22. Strike direction and dip angle are measure in

A. horizontal and vertical planes, respectively

B. vertical and horizontal planes, respectively

C. horizontal planes only

D. vertical planes only

23. Which one of the following is NOT a major ingredient of photochemical smog?

A. NO_x B. Hydrocarbons

C. SO_x D. Carbon monoxide

24. Which one of the following does NOT belong to Volcanic Massive Sulphide (VMS) deposit?

A. Cyprus type B. Besshi type

C. Kuroko type D. SEDEX type

25. Which one of the following is the cause of magmatism in the collision zone?

A. decompression

B. accumulation of radioactive heat

C. seismicity

D. increased erosion

26. Which one of the following astronomical objects is more massive than the Earth?

A. Neptune B. Pluto

C. Venus D. Mars

27. Conditional instability in the atmosphere is observed when:

A. the environmental lapse rate is lower than the saturated adiabatic lapse rate
B. the environmental lapse rate is greater than the dry adiabatic lapse rate
C. the environmental lapse rate is greater than the saturated adiabatic lapse rate but lower than the dry adiabatic lapse rate
D. the environmental lapse rate is greater than the dry adiabatic lapse rate but lower than the saturated adiabatic lapse rate

28. Stratified circulation in peninsular Indian estuaries occurs during
A. tropical cyclones
B. higher river discharge
C. peak summer
D. peak winter

29. On transport-limited slopes, the rate of:
A. erosion is higher
B. weathering is higher
C. denudation higher
D. mass movement is higher

30. The microwave region of the electromagnetic spectrum is mostly absorbed by which of the following components of the atmosphere?
A. CO_2 only B. O_2 only
C. O_2 and H_2O D. O_2 and CO_2

31. Stream competence denotes the transport of sediment of:
A. average size B. smallest size
C. largest size D. all sizes

32. Which one of the following statements is NOT true for Chondrites?
A. contain olivine, pyroxene and metallic iron
B. composed of three main components Chondrules, CAIs, Metric
C. subdivided into carbonaceous (C), Ordinary (O), and Enstatite (E)
D. come from a parent body which has been fractionated since its aggregation early in the history of the solar system

33. The coldest part of the Earth's atmosphere is:
A. tropopause
B. stratopause
C. mesopause
D. upper thermosphere

34. Flux Richardson number is ratio of:
A. transport and pressure force
B. buoyant production and mechanical production
C. buoyant production and pressure force
D. mechanical production and transport force

35. How old are the oldest fossils recorded on the Earth?
A. < 1 Ga B. 1 – 2 Ga
C. 2 – 3 Ga D. > 3 Ga

36. Which one of the following DOES NOT apply to a baroclinic atmosphere?
A. density depends only on pressure
B. density depends on both temperature and pressure
C. geostrophic wind has vertical shear
D. vertical shear depends on horizontal thermal gradient

37. Mid oceanic ridges are characterised by
A. shallow and small magnitude earthquakes
B. shallow and intermediate depth, small magnitude earthquakes
C. deep and small magnitude earthquakes
D. intermediate depth, large magnitude earthquakes

38. The solubility of a gas in sea water increases with
A. increase of temperature, pressure and salinity
B. decrease of temperature, pressure and salinity
C. increase of temperature, and decrease of pressure and salinity
D. decrease of temperature and salinity, and increase of pressure

39. Geostrophic approximation is the balance between
A. viscous and inertial forces
B. pressure gradient and Coriolis forces
C. pressure gradient and inertial forces
D. inertial and Coriolis forces

40. Which one of the following minerals is characterised by a lack of cleavage?

A. Calcite B. Fluorite
C. Quartz D. Feldspar

41. Mantle plumes are
A. linked to plate-tectonics
B. not able to explain ocean island chains
C. able to explain volcanic arc magmatism
D. used to calculate absolute plate motion

42. Electrical discharge suddenly heats the conducting air channel in the Earth's atmosphere, which expands and generates shock waves. These waves spread as:
A. Inertia-gravity wave
B. Seismic wave
C. Rossby wave
D. Sound wave

43. Over geological time scale, the Earth's global average heatflow
A. remained constant
B. decreased
C. increased
D. varied randomly

44. Ozone in stratosphere protects us from UV radiation by
A. reflecting it back to space
B. absorbing it and decomposing
C. refracting it to lower altitude
D. scattering it back to space

45. Equatorial Current systems in the global ocean are produced by
A. rotation of the Earth
B. surface wind forcing over the equatorial region of the global ocean
C. changes in temperature and salinity in the polar regions
D. high solar radiation and heavy precipitation over the equatorial region

46. Rocks in the upper crust and lower mantle are
A. both ferromagnetic
B. both paramagnetic
C. ferromagnetic and paramagnetic, respectively
D. paramagnetic and ferromagnetic, respectively

47. Oxygenation of the Earth's atmosphere was caused by
A. mantle degassing
B. the initial planetary accretion
C. photosynthetic life
D. weathering processes

48. Which ions are the most abundant in rain water, river water and sea water, respectively?
A. Na^+, Cl^-, Na^+ B. Cl^-, HCO_2^-, Cl^-
C. Cl^-, Na^+, Cl^- D. Na^+, Ca^{2+}, Na^+

49. Western boundary ocean currents are stronger in both hemispheres compared to eastern boundary ocean currents due to:
A. centrifugal force
B. pressure gradient force
C. Coriolis force
D. variation of Coriolis force with latitude

50. Which one of the following statements is NOT true given that the salinity distribution with depth over mid-latitude ocean shows a decrease with depth?
A. Evaporation exceeds precipitation
B. Density increases with depth
C. Temperature decreases with depth
D. Precipitation exceeds evaporation

51. Which one of the following seismic phases is the earliest to reach a station at an epicentral distance of 120°?
A. P_{diff} B. P_cP
C. PKP D. PPP

52. Which one of the following geomorphological features is a proven crater created by meteorite impact?
A. Ramgarh Lake, Rajasthan
B. Lonar Lake, Maharashtra
C. Chilka Lake, Odisha
D. Tso Moriri Lake, Laddakh

53. Sr isotope ratios in two cogenetic basalts are found to be significantly different. This implies that:
A. these basalts had different initial Sr isotope ratios
B. these basalts formed in Recent time

C. $\frac{Rb}{Sr}$ ratios in these basalts were different at the time of their formation long back in time

D. $\frac{Rb}{Sr}$ ratios in these basalts were same but formed at different times

54. Which one of the following is the correct sequence of organisms benefitting from upwelling of nutrient rich deep water towards the surface?

A. Mangroves → Urchins → Seaweeds
B. Gastropods → Crabs → Seagrasses
C. Dinoflagellates → Kelps → Otters
D. Diatoms → Copepods → Anchovies

55. The mixing ratio of water vapour in the Earth's atmosphere is approximately

A. 0.21 B. 0.78
C. 0.04 D. 0.0093

56. Which one of the following is the correct sequence of mass wasting in decreasing order of speed?

A. Rockfall – Creep – Earth flow
B. Earth flow – Creep – Rockfall
C. Rockfall – Earth flow – Creep
D. Earth flow – Rockfall – Creep

57. Which of the following is a semi-conservative element in seawater?

A. Ca B. Cl
C. Fe D. CO_2

58. Which one of the followings evolved earliest on the Earth?

A. Amphibians B. Birds
C. Mammals D. Prokaryotes

59. A geological cross-section, drawn through strike line of uniformly dipping beds, shows the bedding traces as a set of lines that are

A. horizontal
B. inclined at true dip angle
C. inclined at apparent dip angle > 0°
D. vertical

60. Which one of the following sets of processes best exemplifies the key functions of heterotrophic bacteria in the marine environment?

A. Autotrophic production, organic matter production
B. New production, secondary production, chemolithotrophy
C. Remineralisation, respiration, organic matter oxidation
D. Chemoheterotrophy, chemolithotrophy, chemosynthesis

61. In the atmospheric boundary layer

A. viscous force cannot be neglected
B. pressure gradient force can be neglected
C. inertial force can be neglected
D. gravitational force can be neglected

62. Which one of the following parts of the Himalaya contains complete succession of marine rocks ranging in age from the Cambrian to the Cretaceous?

A. Sub Himalaya B. Lesser Himalaya
C. Higher Himalaya D. Tethys Himalaya

63. Where rainfall is higher, the grassland biome steppe grades into:

A. Savanna B. Tundra
C. Prairie D. Alpine Tundra

64. A depositional feature attached at one end to the mainland and backed by a lagoon or marshland is known as:

A. Beach ridge B. Beach cusp
C. Spit D. Tidal flat

65. Relative vorticity is defined as the curl of:

A. absolute velocity
B. relative velocity
C. difference of absolute and relative vorticity
D. sum of absolute and relative vorticity

66. Which one of the following is a high nutrient and low chlorophyll (HNLC) region?

A. Bay of Bengal
B. Equatorial Indian Ocean
C. Subarctic North Pacific Ocean
D. Mediterranean Sea

67. If surface heatflows of oceanic and continental lithospheres are same, which one of the following is true?

A. Both oceanic and continental lithospheres have same mantle heatflow
B. Continental lithosphere has lower mantle heatflow than oceanic lithosphere
C. Oceanic lithosphere has lower mantle heatflow than continental lithosphere
D. Oceanic lithosphere has more radiogenic heat source concentration than continental lithosphere

68. Extension joints develop perpendicular to the

A. minimum principal stress
B. intermediate principal stress
C. maximum principal stress
D. plane of maximum shear stress

69. The travel time taken by a P wave for a surface focus earthquake to travel along a straight line path through the earth and be recorded at the antipodal point is approximately

A. 100 s B. 1200 s
C. 2400 s D. 3600 s

70. For planet Earth, the

A. ocean formed after the plants
B. ocean formed after the atmosphere
C. atmosphere formed after the ocean
D. atmosphere formed after the plants

PART-C

71. Analyse the following statements:

(*a*) Isotherms in the Southern Hemisphere are much more regular than in the Northern Hemisphere
(*b*) In the Northern Hemisphere the isotherms bend sharply southward in July and northward in January over the continents
(*c*) The warmest temperatures are always found over land but the coldest temperatures are found over ocean

Choose the correct option:

A. (*a*) is true, (*b*) and (*c*) are false
B. (*a*) is false, (*b*) and (*c*) are true
C. (*a*) and (*b*) are true, (*c*) is false
D. (*a*) and (*c*) are true, (*b*) is false

72. The most general relationship between atmospheric circulation and vorticity is given by:

A. Gauss-Divergence theorem
B. Helmboltz theorem
C. Stokes theorem
D. Kelvin circulation theorem

73. An MT survey was conducted over a fault. If one of the axis of measurement coincides with the fault extension, then the impedance elements Zxx, Zyy, Zxy and Zyx are:

A. $Zxx = Zyy \neq 0$, $Zxy = Zyx$
B. $Zxx = Zyy = 0$, $Zxy = Zyx$
C. $Zxx = Zyy = 0$, $Zxy = -Zyx$
D. $Zxx = -Zyy \neq 0$, $Zxy = Zyx$

74. Precambrian-Cambrian boundary in India is marked at the contact of:

A. Blaini and Krol Groups
B. Krol and Tal Groups
C. Cuddapah and Kurnool Groups
D. Lower and Middle Vindhyan Groups

75. Secondary aerosols are products of:

A. emission of dust
B. particulates emitted from sea
C. particles formed in air from gaseous substances
D. black carbon

76. Fair weather electrical field near the Earth's surface is typically about:

A. 100 V/m and upward directed
B. 100 V/m and downward directed
C. 1000 V/m and upward directed
D. 1000 V/m and downward directed

77. If U and W are the gravity and magnetic potentials, respectively, due to a mass distribution magnetized uniformly in the direction ϕ, then:

A. $U \propto \frac{\partial W}{\partial \phi}$ B. $W \propto \frac{\partial U}{\partial \phi}$

C. $\frac{\partial U}{\partial z} \propto \frac{\partial W}{\partial \phi}$ D. $\frac{\partial W}{\partial z} \propto \frac{\partial U}{\partial \phi}$

78.

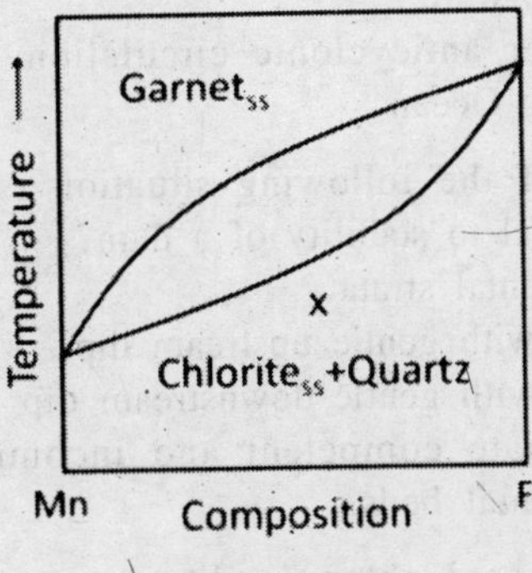

Above is a schematic plot of the reaction of chlorite solid solution with quartz to form garnet solid solution. In case of Rayleigh fractionation during the growth of successive zones in a garnet, which one of the following diagrams correctly depicts the concentration profile of Mn in garnet given the initial composition *x*?

A.

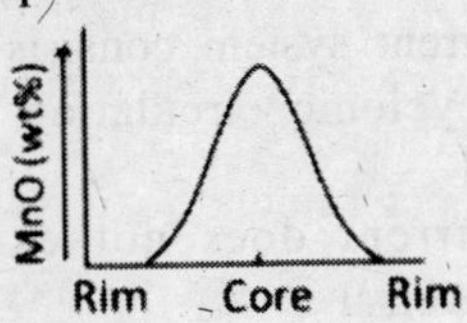

B.

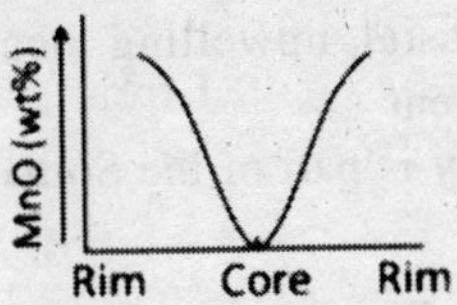

C.

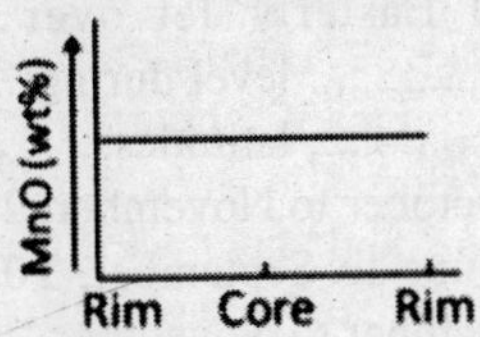

D.

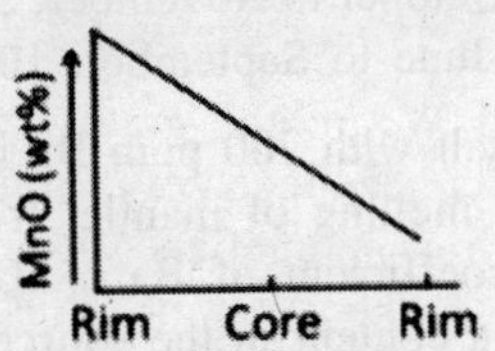

79. Rise in atmospheric CO_2 will NOT lead to

A. ocean acidification

B. ocean warming

C. decrease in $[CO_3^{2-}]$ in ocean

D. decrease in efficiency of biological pump

80. What is the correct order of occurrence (older to younger) of the fossils listed below in the Phanerozoic stratigraphic succession of India?

(*a*) *Fenestella*

(*b*) *Numumulites*

(*c*) *Redhichia*

(*d*) *Macrocephalites*

A. (*c*) – (*b*) – (*a*) – (*d*)

B. (*a*) – (*d*) – (*c*) – (*b*)

C. (*b*) – (*c*) – (*a*) – (*d*)

D. (*c*) – (*a*) – (*d*) – (*b*)

81. A long columnar stromatolite is generally indicative of ______ environment.

A. subtidal   B. intertidal

C. supratidal   D. tidal channel

82. Which form of dissolved inorganic carbon is most abundant in sea water?

A. Carbonate ion   B. Carbon dioxide

C. Bicarbonate   D. Carbonic acid

83. In a homogeneous isotropic elastic medium, the P-wave travels 1.5 times faster than the S-wave. The ratio (λ/μ) of the Lame's constant λ and μ will be

A. 0.5   B. 0.25

C. 0.75   D. 1.0

84. Study the diagram and identify the type of mass movement from the choice given below:

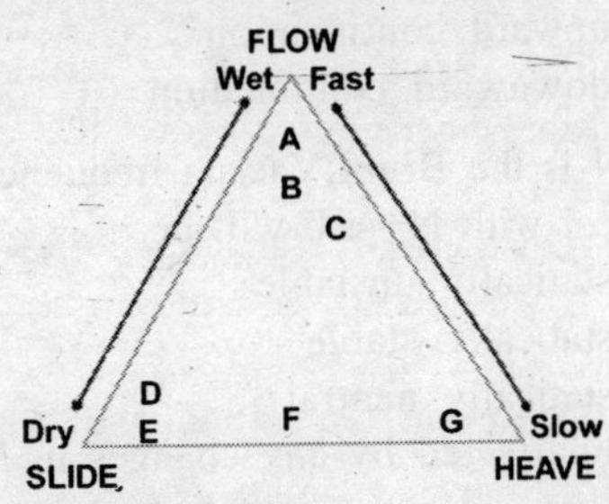

A. A is earthflow and G is talus creep

B. C is solifluction and F is talus creep

C. D is landslide and B is mudflow

D. E is rock slide and B is creep

85. Match column I and II

Column-I	Column-II
(*a*) Oxygen isotopes	1. Dietary information
(*b*) Phosphorus fractions	2. Climatic conditions in river catchment
(*c*) Carbon isotopes	3. Palaeotemperature in ocean
(*d*) Chemical Index of alteration	4. Palaeoproductivity in oligotropic lake

	(*a*)	(*b*)	(*c*)	(*d*)
A.	1	2	3	4
B.	2	3	4	1
C.	3	4	1	2
D.	4	1	2	3

86. Match the ichnofossil assemblage (column-I) with its marine environment (column-II).

Column-I	Column-II
(*a*) *Cruziana*	1. Abyssal
(*b*) *Nereites*	2. Bathyal
(*c*) *Skolithos*	3. Littoral
(*d*) *Zoophycos*	4. Sublittoral

	(*a*)	(*b*)	(*c*)	(*d*)
A.	4	1	3	2
B.	4	2	3	1
C.	1	2	4	3
D.	2	3	1	4

87. A strong magnetic anomalous body occurs below a country rock which also exhibits randomly distributed magnetization of moderate magnitude. Which of the following technique is useful for anomaly interpretation?

A. reduction to pole
B. derivative calculations
C. upward continuation
D. downward continuation

88. If N is the Brunt-Vaisala frequency, any air parcel with $N^2 < 0$ will be

A. statically unstable
B. statically stable
C. statically neutral
D. unaffected by any changes in N

89. The mean latitudinal position of TTCZ over the Indian region in July is:

A. 8 – 10° N B. 18 – 20° N
C. 25 – 28° N D. 38 – 40° N

90. Sverdrup's theory of large scale wind driven circulation in the oceans explained the existence of:

A. California current
B. equatorial counter current
C. weaker eastern boundary currents that flow equatorward
D. weaker anticyclonic circulation in the Pacific Ocean

91. Which of the following situation is most detrimental to stability of a dam?

A. Horizontal strata
B. Beds with gentle upstream dip
C. Beds with gentle downstream dip
D. Alternate competent and incompetent horizontal beds

92. Marine zooplankton facilitates downward carbon flux by:

A. continuous and copious reproduction.
B. regular seasonal hibernation.
C. diel vertical migration.
D. excessive rapid photosynthesis.

93. Which one of the following is INCORRECT with regard to Somali current system?

A. Somali current system consists of large scale anticyclonic circulation cell, the Great whirl
B. Somali current does not experience seasonal reversal
C. Intense coastal upwelling occurs with Somali current
D. Sacotra eddy is part of the Somali current system

94. The Tropical Easterly Jet over India is observed at .... level during............... period over .... latitudes.

A. 200 hPa; October to November, 25 – 30°N
B. 200 hPa; June to September, 10 – 15°N
C. 100 hPa; October to November, 25 – 30°N
D. 100 hPa; June to September, 10 – 15°N

95. An alkali basalt with 700 ppm Ba is formed by 1% batch melting of mantle. If the bulk distribution coefficient of Ba is 0.01, what will be the Ba content in the source mantle?

A. 1.4 ppm B. 14 ppm
C. 700 ppm D. 140 ppm

96. Which one of the following gas has the highest solubility in water?
A. Nitrous oxide B. Oxygen
C. Nitrogen D. Carbon dioxide

97. Match the Koeppen's climate types with regions in India.

Climate type	Region
(*a*) Dfc	1. Coromandal coast of Tamil Nadu
(*b*) As	2. Ganga plain
(*c*) Amw	3. Arunachal Pradesh
(*d*) Cwg	4. West coast of India south of Goa

	(*a*)	(*b*)	(*c*)	(*d*)
A.	2	1	3	4
B.	3	1	4	2
C.	1	4	3	2
D.	4	3	2	1

98. Name the pair of master variables in natural waters:
A. O_2 and redox potential
B. pH and redox potential
C. O_2 and temperature
D. Temperature and salinity

99. The Fourier transforms of two functions $f(x)$ and $g(x)$ are in the ratio $1 : \omega^4$ then $g(x) =$
A. $f(4x)$ B. $f(x^4)$
C. $\dfrac{\partial^4 f(x)}{\partial x^4}$ D. $\dfrac{x^4 \partial f(x)}{\partial x}$

100. An earthquake is recorded at 4 stations which are equidistant from double-couple source in the 4 cardinal directions. Which one of the following remains constant at all the stations?
A. Seismic moment
B. Amplitude of displacement pulse
C. Duration of displacement pulse
D. Seismic energy of signal

101. Match the weather/climate phenomena in column-I with their typical spatial scales (size/wavelength) in column-II.

Column-I	Column-II
(*a*) Cyclone	1. 1 km
(*b*) Madden-Juhan Oscillation	2. 10 km
(*c*) Tornado	3. 1000 km
(*d*) Sea-breeze	4. 10000 km

	(*a*)	(*b*)	(*c*)	(*d*)
A.	4	3	1	2
B.	3	4	1	2
C.	3	4	2	1
D.	2	1	4	3

102. An antisymmetric heat source about the equator creates a warm region in the northern hemisphere and a corresponding cool region in the southern hemisphere. As a result, a long planetary wave develops to the .... of the heating source, with .... air motion and .... circulation associated with surplus heating.
A. west, subsiding, anticyclonic
B. east, subsiding cyclonic
C. east, rising, anticyclonic
D. west, rising, cyclonic

103. Forming agent, landform and processes are given in columns (*a*), (*b*) and (*c*), respectively

	(*a*)	(*b*)	(*c*)
P	Glacial	Moraine	Erosional
Q	Peri-glacial	Horn	Frost Heave
R	Glacio-fluvial	Pingo	Depositional
S	Glacial	Kame	Erosional

Identify the correct match

	(*a*)	(*b*)	(*c*)
A.	P	Q	S
B.	Q	R	Q
C.	Q	S	P
D.	S	R	Q

104. Which one of the following formations shows the maximum negative deflection (assuming $R_w < R_{ef}$) in a SP long response?
A. Thick limestone
B. Gas-bearing thick sandstone
C. Thin shaly sandstone
D. Oil-bearing thick shaly sandstone

105. Match columns I and II

Column-I	Column-II
(*a*) The peeling away of layers or sheets of rock	1. Exhumation
(*b*) The interface between weathered material and unweathered bed rock	2. Exfoliation
(*c*) The uncovering of surfaces beneath regolith or younger geological material	3. Pseudokarst
(*d*) Dark staining of rock surface in and regions	4. Rock varnish
	5. Weathering front

	(*a*)	(*b*)	(*c*)	(*d*)
A.	2	5	4	1
B.	3	1	2	4
C.	3	5	1	2
D.	2	5	1	4

106. Which of the following mineral deposits are associated with Archaean greenstones?

A. Diamond (kimberlitic) deposits
B. Porphyry deposits
C. Stratiform Pb-Zn deposits
D. Cu-Zn massive sulphides, Ni-Cu sulphides, Au-bearing quartz veins

107. Seawater having salinity of 35 psu was subjected to icing in steps as shown below:

Seawater

(*a*)	⟶	(*b*)	⟶	(*c*)
1 litre		900 ml		750 ml
(liquid)		(liquid)		(liquid)

Which is the correct sequence of salinity of (*a*), (*b*) and (*c*)?

A. (*a*) > (*b*) > (*c*)
B. (*a*) < (*b*) < (*c*)
C. (*a*) > (*c*) > (*b*)
D. (*a*) < (*b*) > (*c*)

108. As per the Stokes' law, the terminal velocity of a rain drop

A. increases with size
B. decreases with size
C. is independent of size
D. is zero

109. Which one of the following statements is INCORRECT?

A. Water vapour has more global warming potential than CO_2
B. Volatile organic compounds are not responsible for ozone production in troposphere
C. N_2O has more global warming potential than CO_2
D. NO_2 and N_2O are potential source of nitrogenous species in troposphere and stratosphere, respectively

110. A sandstone formation has porosities varying from 10 to 30%. The 100% water saturated sand with 10% porosity has a formation resistivity of 0.5 Ωm. What is the hydrocarbon saturation (%) in the sand formation with 20% porosity and formation resistivity of 50 Ωm (assume $a = 1$ and $n = 2$)?

A. 65 B. 75
C. 85 D. 95

111. As wind in the lower atmosphere moves over the Earth's surface three forces X, Y and Z shown in the diagram operate on the air mass. If these forces are Pressure gradient force (P), Frictional force (F) and Coriolis force (C), find the correct match:

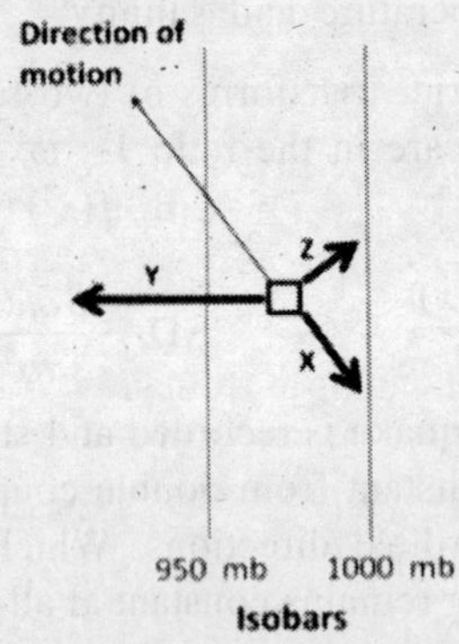

A. X – P, Y – C, Z – F
B. X – F, Y – C, Z – P
C. X – F, Y – P, Z – C
D. X – C, Y – P, Z – F

112. Coastal currents in the Bay of Bengal:

A. are weak throughout the year
B. are not at all generated

C. reverse their flow direction with season and are intense during non-monsoon seasons and eddies are embedded in these currents

D. do not change with season

113. g_1 and g_2 are the gravity values measured at depths z_1 and z_2, respectively, in a borehole $(z_2 > z_1)$. Consider the following statements:

Statement I: $g_2 < g_1$

Statement II: Gravity decreases with depth in the Earth's crust

A. I and II are true, II explains I
B. I and II are true, but II does not explain I
C. I is true, II is false
D. Both I and II are false

114. A reversed refraction profile is carried out over a gently dipping interface separating two media with velocities V_1 and V_2.

Statement I : The intercept time for the up dip shot is greater than the intercept time for a down dip shot.

Statement II: The apparent up dip velocity is lower than apparent down dip velocity.

Choose the correct option.
A. Both statements I and II are true
B. Statement I is true and statement II is false
C. Both statements are false
D. Statement I is false and statement II is true

115. Satellite observed outgoing longwave radiation is lower over equatorial latitudes due to
A. reduced emission from the Earth's surface.
B. absorption due to atmospheric gases.
C. persistent cloudiness.
D. high insolation.

116. In which of the following class of folds, the curvature of inner and outer arcs is equal?

A. Class 1A	B. Class 1B
C. Class 2	D. Class 3

117. Consider a one component S_1O_2-system with geologically relevant seven phases. The maximum number of invariant points for this system is:

A. 35	B. 21
C. 15	D. 20

118. Match the following

Sandstone	**Tectonic setup**
(*a*) Mature quartz arenite	1. Continental rift valleys
(*b*) Immature wacke	2. Passive continental margins
(*c*) Feldspathic arenite	3. Fore arc basins at convergent plate boundaries

	(*a*)	(*b*)	(*c*)
A.	1	2	3
B.	3	2	1
C.	2	1	3
D.	2	3	1

119. The total amount of an element dissolved in the ocean is 10^7 kg and its removal rate from seawater is 10^5 g/y. Under steady-state condition, the residence time of the element is

A. 10^{15} years	B. 10^5 years
C. 10^2 years	D. $10^{0.5}$ years

120. Statement A: The Radar pulse width (the length of the time that a radar pulse is transmitted) is of the order of microseconds.

Statement B: The Doppler Weather Radar detects the "shift in the phase" of the pulse of energy.

A. Both Statements A and B are false
B. Statement A is true and Statement B is false
C. Both Statements A and B are true
D. Statement A is false and Statement B is true

121. At what time of the day the near-surface air temperature will be the highest?
A. Immediately after sunrise
B. When the sun is directly overhead
C. When the incoming solar and outgoing longwave radiation balance each other
D. Immediately before sunset

122. A sandstone comprises 70% Quartz, 5% feldspar, 20% matrix and 5% mica. This sandstone is most likely a
A. Quartzarenite
B. Feldspathic arenite
C. Quartzwacke
D. Arkose

123. **Statement I:** Electrical current lines bend towards the normal to the interface if the resistivity of the underlying medum is more than the resistivity of the overlying medum.

Statement II: For a homogeneous, isotropic, topographically undulating earth of constant resistivity, the apparent resistivity over a hill will be anomalously low compared to that over a flat surface.
A. Both Statements I and II are false
B. Statement I is true, but Statement II is false
C. Statement I is false, but Statement II is true
D. Both Statements I and II are true

124. In a transient electromagnetic (TEM) survey, the maximum transient pulse of a step signal is recorded at 10 m depth at 10 μs time. The time (in μs) needed for the pulse to reach 20 m depth is:
A. 40 B. 20
C. 16 D. 24

125. Which one of the following types of folds defines the geometry of a sheath fold?
A. Plane – Noncylindrical
B. Nonplane – Noncylindrical
C. Plane – Cylindrical
D. Nonplane – Cylindrical

126. The 1.4 and 1.9 μm water absorption features are obliterated in soils with
A. high organic content and moderately fine texture
B. high iron content and fine texture
C. low organic and low iron content
D. high organic content and moderately coarse texture

127. Near beach wave breaking occurs when
A. wave height (h) doubles as the wave approaches the coast.
B. wave length (L) decreases as the wave approaches the coast.
C. wave height (h) approaches one-seventh (1/7th) of wave length
D. wave lenght (L) doubles as the wave approaches the coast

128. The travel time in a reflection survey over a reflector of velocity 4.0 km/s underlain by a medium of velocity 2.40 km/s is 1.0 s. What will be the travel time if the underlying medium has a velocity of 6.0 km/s?
A. 400 ms B. 650 ms
C. 875 ms D. 1.0 s

129. Identify relative contribution of autotrophs to net primary production in marine ecosystems:
A. Coral reef algae > sea grasses > mangroves > marsh plant
B. Mangroves > coral reef algae > sea grasses > marsh plant
C. Marsh plant > sea grasses > coral reef algae > mangroves
D. Sea grasses > coral reef algae > mangroves > marsh plant

130. Which one of the following occurs during El Nino?
A. Stronger Trade Winds
B. Warmer than normal sea surface temperature in the western Pacific Ocean
C. Reduced upwelling along Peru coast
D. More monsoon rainfall in India

131. Which one of the following is NOT required for the formation of tropical cyclone?
A. Weak winds
B. Coriolis force
C. Convective instability
D. High precipitation

132. Microbial loop is often understood as a temporary, surrogate food chain with heterotropic bacteria at its base. Identify the more efficient, linear, energy transfer pathway from the following.
A. Heterotrophic bacteria → primary omnivore → Heterotrophic nanoflagellate → primary carnivore

B. Heterotrophic bacteria → Heterotrophic nanoflagellate → primary omnivore → primary carnivore
C. Heterotrophic bacteria → primary carnivore → Heterotrophic nanoflagellate → primary omnivore
D. Heterotrophic bacteria → primary omnivore → primary carnivore → Heterotrophic nanoflagellate

133. In a continental lithosphere with a 20 km thick crustal layer containing radiogenic heat source concentrate of 1 μW/m^2 and surface heat flow of 40 mW/m^2 is uniformaly stretched by a factor β = 2. The surface heat flow (in W/m^2) of the stretched lithosphere will be:

A. 40 B. 50
C. 60 D. 80

134.

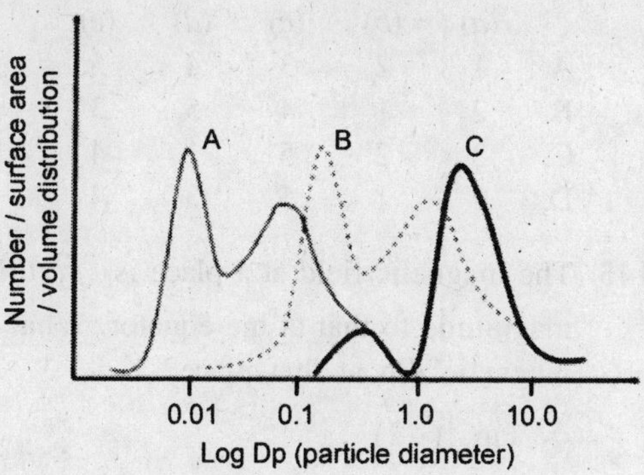

In the above figure, the curves A, B and C denote ...., ... and .... distributions, respectively.

A. surface area, number and volume
B. number, volume and surface area
C. number, surface area and volume
D. surface area, volume and number

135. Identify the correct decreasing order of the periodicity of Earth's orbital parameters (E = Eccentricity, P = Precession, O = Obliquity)

A. E > P > O B. P > E > O
C. O > P > E D. E > O > P

136. Marine phosphorite deposits occur in

A. deep-sea sediments
B. estuarine sediments
C. manganese nodules
D. near-shore sediments

137. In a semi-isolated barred basin as shown below, which rock types would form because of evaporative mechanism in regions marked by A, B and C?

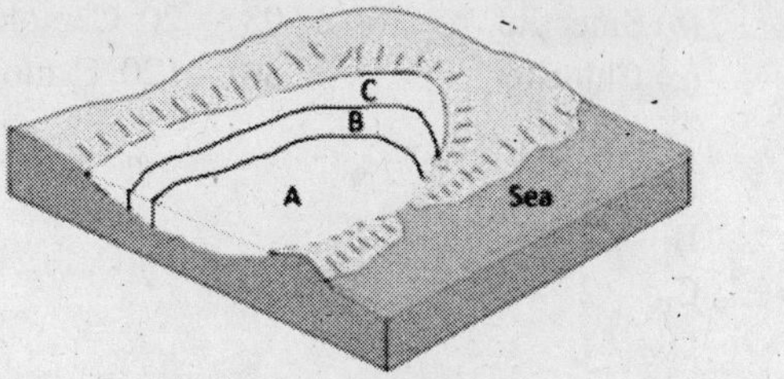

A. A – Halite, B – Gypsum, C – Carbonates
B. A – Gypsum, B – Carbonates, C – Halite
C. A – Gypsum, B – Halite, C – Carbonates
D. A – Carbonates, B – Gypsum, C – Halite

138. What is the approximate change in pressure due to a height increase of 200 m in the atmosphere? (Assume air density = 1.0 kg/m^3, g = 9.8 m/s^2)

A. –0.019 KPa B. –0.19 KPa
C. –1.9 KPa D. –19.0 KPa

139.

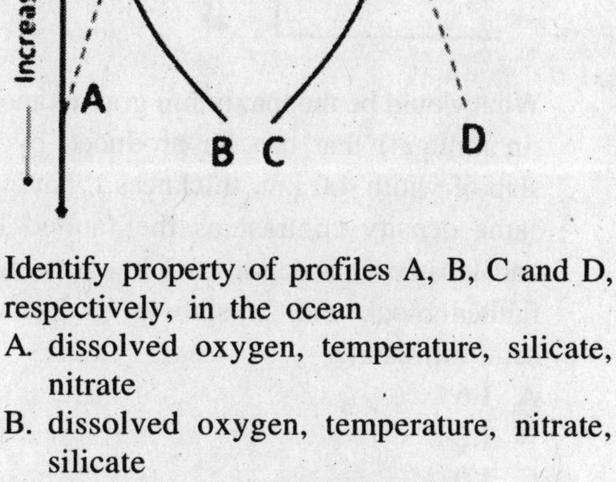

Identify property of profiles A, B, C and D, respectively, in the ocean

A. dissolved oxygen, temperature, silicate, nitrate
B. dissolved oxygen, temperature, nitrate, silicate
C. temperature, dissolved oxygen, nitrate, silicate
D. temperature, dissolved oxygen, silicate, nitrate

140. Match the following:

Clay mineral	Cation exchange capacity
(*a*) Kaolinite	1. 10 – 40 C mole/kg
(*b*) Smectite	2. 03 – 20 C mole/kg
(*c*) Chlorite	3. 80 – 120 C mole/kg

	(*a*)	(*b*)	(*c*)
A.	1	2	3
B.	2	3	1
C.	2	1	3
D.	1	3	2

141. In the marine food chain, consumer cannot digest and assimilate everything it eats. In this scenario, the paradigm of gross growth efficiency can be understood as proportions of prey carbon converted to

A. refractory carbon
B. predator carbon
C. dissolved carbon
D. respired carbon

142. The gravity anomaly recorded at a point A on the edge of a faulted block of material of limited throw *t* (see figure) is 2.0 milligal.

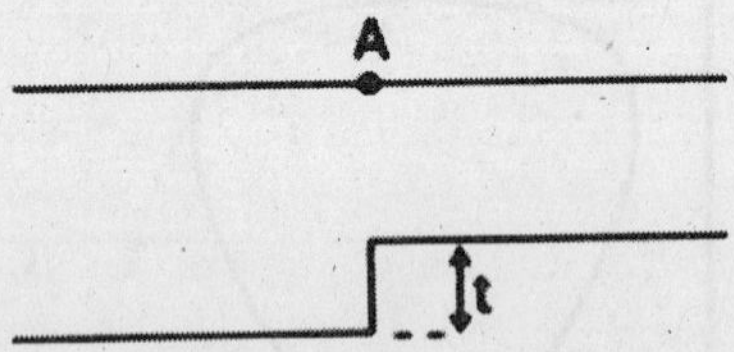

What would be the maximum gravity anomaly (in milligal) that can be produced by a 2*d* slab of width 4.0 km, thickness *t*, having the same density contrast as the faulted block and located at a depth of 2 km (assume the faulted block and 2*d* slab to be horizontal semi-infiniste)?

A. 1.6
B. 1.2
C. 1.0
D. 0.8

143. A relative sea level rise CANNOT result from the

A. sea level rising while the land surface subsiding at a slower rate.
B. sea level remaining stationary while the land surface subsiding.
C. sea level rising while the land surface rising at a faster rate.
D. sea level falling while the land surface subsiding at a faster rate.

144. Match the stratigraphic units in column-I with their corresponding ages in column-II.

Column-I	Column-II
(*a*) Uttatur Formation	1. Jurassic
(*b*) Chars Formation	2. Cretaceous
(*c*) Ophioceras Beds	3. Eocene
(*d*) Subathu Formation	4. Devoman
(*e*) Muth Quartzite	5. Triassic

	(*a*)	(*b*)	(*c*)	(*d*)	(*e*)
A.	1	2	3	4	5
B.	2	1	4	5	3
C.	3	2	5	1	4
D.	2	1	5	3	4

145. The magnetic field at a place is $\sqrt{3}$ times in magnitude to that at the equator. What is the magnetic dip at that place?

A. $\tan^{-1}(\sqrt{2})$
B. $\tan^{-1}(\sqrt{3})$
C. $\tan^{-1}(2\sqrt{2})$
D. $\tan^{-1}(2\sqrt{3})$

146. Statement A: Clean Air Turbulence is associated with standing mountain wave and Jet stream.

Statement B: To be identified as a Jet stream, the speed of wind should be greater than 60 Knots.

A. Statement A is false and Statement B is true
B. Both Statements A and B are true
C. Both Statements A and B are false
D. Statement A is true and Statement B is false

147. The $^{87}Sr/^{86}Sr$ of global seawater has been increasing since –40 Ma. This increase is attributed to:

A. the increase in submarine volcanism
B. the higher weathering and erosion in the Himalaya
C. the higher weathering and erosion in the Andes
D. the increase in subduction magmatism

148. The threshold temperature for all cloud droplets to freeze spontaneously into ice crystals is

A. 0°C
B. –33°C
C. –40°C
D. –50°C

149. Assertion (A): The monsoon enters West Bengal and Bangladesh from south and southeast direction.

Reason (R): Arakan Hills along the coast of Myanmar deflect the monsoon winds of the Bay of Bengal towards the Indian subcontinent

A. A is true and R is false
B. A is false and R is true
C. A and R are true and R is the correct explanation of A
D. A and R are true and R is not the correct explanation of A

150. The radiation emitted by the sea surface in the atmospheric window region may experience alteration and the resulting atmospheric transmission DOES NOT depend on

A. vertical distribution of water vapour.
B. vertical distribution of oxygen.
C. total water vapour content.
D. presence of clouds.

ANSWERS

1	2	3	4	5	6	7	8	9	10
C	D	B	D	A	B	C	C	B	D
11	**12**	**13**	**14**	**15**	**16**	**17**	**18**	**19**	**20**
D	C	D	*	C	B	B	B	C	B
21	**22**	**23**	**24**	**25**	**26**	**27**	**28**	**29**	**30**
B	A	C	D	A, B	A	C	B	B	C
31	**32**	**33**	**34**	**35**	**36**	**37**	**38**	**39**	**40**
C	D	C	B	D	A	A	D	B	C
41	**42**	**43**	**44**	**45**	**46**	**47**	**48**	**49**	**50**
D	D	B	B	B	C	C	B	D	D
51	**52**	**53**	**54**	**55**	**56**	**57**	**58**	**59**	**60**
A	B	C	D	C	C	A	D	A	C
61	**62**	**63**	**64**	**65**	**66**	**67**	**68**	**69**	**70**
A	D	C	C	B	C	B	A	B	B
71	**72**	**73**	**74**	**75**	**76**	**77**	**78**	**79**	**80**
A	C	C	B	C	B	B	A	D	D

81	82	83	84	85	86	87	88	89	90
B	C	B	B	C	A	C	A	C	B
91	92	93	94	95	96	97	98	99	100
C	C	B	D	B	D	B	B	C	A
101	102	103	104	105	106	107	108	109	110
B	D	A, B	B	D	D	B	A	B	D
111	112	113	114	115	116	117	118	119	120
C	C	D	B	C	C	A	D	B	C
121	122	123	124	125	126	127	128	129	130
C	C	D	A	A	B	C	D	B	C
131	132	133	134	135	136	137	138	139	140
D	B	B	C	D	D	D	C	C	B
141	142	143	144	145	146	147	148	149	150
B	C	C	D	C	B	B	C	C	B

CSIR-UGC (NET)

EARTH, ATMOSPHERIC, OCEAN AND PLANETARY SCIENCES

PAPER (PART B & C)

PAPER I (PART B & C)

1. The Earth and the Solar System
2. Earth Materials, Surface Features & Process
3. Interior of the Earth, Deformation and Tectonics
4. Oceans and Atmosphere
5. Environmental Earth Sciences

1. The Earth and the Solar System

MILKY WAY AND THE SOLAR SYSTEM

THE SOLAR SYSTEM

The solar system comprises the sun and its eight planets which are belived to have been originated from the condensation of gases and other lesser bodies. All planet of solar system revolve round the sun in Elliptical orbits. The sun form center of soalr system having surface temperature of 6,000 degree centigrade. The temperature of sun increasing in interior up to 20 million degree centigrade.

THE EARLY SOLAR SYSTEM

No one can go back in time to view the formation of the Solar System and the Earth. Therefore, scientists will never be able to describe the sequence of events with certainty.

The hypothesis given here is based on calculations about the behavior of dust and gas in space and on observations of stars and dust clouds in our galaxy.

The hypothesis states that about 5 billion years ago the matter that became our Solar System was an immense, diffuse, frozen cloud of dust and gas rotating slowly in space. This cloud formed from matter ejected from an exploding star. More than 99 per cent of the cloud consisted of hydrogen and helium, the most abundant elements in the Universe. The temperature of this cloud was about 270ºC. Small gravitational attractions among the dust and gas particles caused the cloud to condense into a sphere (Figs. 1(a) and 1(b). As condensation continued, the cloud rotated more rapidly, and the sphere spread into a disk, as shown in Figure 1(c). Some scientists have suggested that a nearby star ex ploded and the shock wave triggered the condensation.

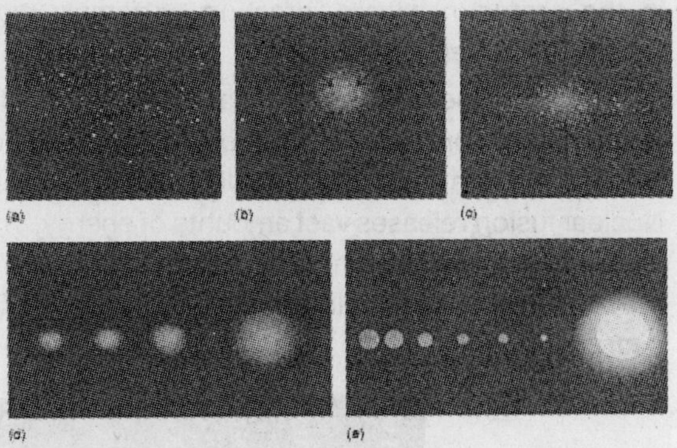

Figure-1 Formation of the Solar System. (a) The Solar System was originally a diffuse cloud of dust and gas. (b) This dust and gas began to coalesce due to gravity. (c) The shrinking mass began to rotate and formed a disk. (d) The mass broke up into a discrete protosun orbited by large protoplanets. (e) The Sun heated until fusion temperatures were reached. The heat from the Sun drove most of the hydrogen and helium away from the closest planets, leaving small, solid cores behind.

More than 90 per cent of the matter in the cloud collapsed toward the center of the disk under the influence of gravity, forming the protosun. Collisions among high speed particles released heat within this early version of the Sun, but it was not a true star because it did not yet generate energy by nuclear fusion. Heat from the protosun warmed the inner region of the disk. Then, after the gravitational collapse was nearly complete, the disk cooled. Gases in the outer part of the disk condensed to form small aggregates, much as snowflakes form when moist air cools in the Earth's atmosphere. Over time, the aggregates stuck together as snowflakes sometimes do. As they increased in size and developed stronger gravitational forces, they attracted additional particles. This growth continued until a number of small rocky spheres, called planetesimals, formed, ranging from a few kilometers to about 100 km in diameter. The entire process, from the disk to the planetesimals, occurred quickly in geologic terms, over a period of 10,000 to 100,000 years. The planetesimals then coalesced to form a few large planets, including Earth. At the same time that planets were forming, gravitational attraction pulled the gases in the protosun inward, creating extremely high pressure and temperature.

The core became so hot that hydrogen nuclei combined to form the nucleus of the next heavier element, helium, in a process called nuclear fusion. Nuclear fusion releases vast amounts of energy. The onset of nuclear fusion marked the birth of the modern Sun, which still generates its energy by hydrogen fusion.

THE MODERN SOLAR SYSTEM

Heat from the Sun boiled most of the hydrogen, helium, and other light elements away from the inner Solar System. As a result, the four planets closest to the Sun Mercury, Venus, Earth, and Mars–are now mainly rocky with metallic centers. These four are called the terrestrial planets because they are "Earthlike." In contrast, the four outer planets– Jupiter, Saturn, Uranus, and Neptune–are called the Jovian planets and are composed primarily of liquids and gases with small rocky and metallic cores (Fig. 1.1). Pluto, the outermost known planet, is anomalous. It is the smallest planet in the Solar System and is composed of rock mixed with froze water and methane. Figure 1.2 is a schematic representation of the modern Solar System.

Figure 1.1 (a) Mercury is a small planet close to the Sun. Consequently, most of the lighter elements have long since been boiled off into space, and today the surface is solid and rocky. (b) Jupiter, on the other hand, is composed mainly of gases and liquids, with a small solid core. This photograph shows its turbulent atmosphere. The scales in these two photographs are different. Jupiter is much larger than Mercury. (NASA)

Figure 1.2 The Solar System. Now, Pluto is considered as dwarf planet.

Among the eight planets, Mercury is the smallest and closet to the sun 36 million miles away. It completes its orbit in only 88 days. Venus, is next closest planet. It is similar to earth in terms of size, mass and density and therefore considered as 'Earth Twin'. Earth is unique planet in terms of existence of life and presence of water. Like many other planet of solar system, the earth has a natural satellite, the moon, 382,480 km away, that revolves eastward around the earth once in every 27 days.

The fourth planet from the sun is Mars which has dark patches on its surface. Scientist is giving much attention on mars to explore the possibility of life. Next to this is Jupiter, the largest planet in the solar system. Its surface is made up of gases such as hydrogen, helium, and methane. It has twelve satellites that circle around it. Its surface is very cold.

Next to it is a unique planet called Saturn having three rings and nine satellites around it. In terms of size it is next to Jupiter. It is quite far from sun and therefore it takes 29.5 years to complete its orbit.

The next planet of solar system after Saturn is Uranus. It is another giant planet, around fifty times larger than earth. Uranus is unique as it moves in a clockwise direction from east to west with five satellites revolving around it.

Neptune closely resemble with Uranus. It has only two satellites and colder surface. Pluto is now considered as dwarf planet and removed from the list of Planet by Astronomical Union.

Modern theories on the origin of the Earth and other planetary bodies.

The most popular argument regarding the origin of the universe is the Big Bang Theory. It is also called expanding universe hypothesis. Edwin Hubble, in 1920, provided evidence that the universe is expanding. As time passes, galaxies move further and further apart. Yexperiment and find what does the expanding universe mean. the distance between the galaxies is found to be increasing and thereby, the universe is considered to be expanding. Scientists believe that though the space between the galaxies is increasing, observations do not support the expansion of galaxies.

The Big Bang Theory considers the following stages in the development of the universe.

(i) In the beginning, all matter forming the universe existed in one place in the form of a "tiny ball" (singular atom) with an unimaginably small volume, infinite temperature and infinite density.

(ii) At the Big Bang the "tiny ball" exploded violently. This led to a huge expansion. It is now generally accepted that the event of big bang took place 13.7 billion years before the present. The expansion continues even to the present day. As it grew, some energy was converted into matter. There was particularly rapid expansion within fractions of a second after the bang. Thereafter, the expansion has slowed down. Within first three minutes from the Big Bang event, the first atom began to form.

(iii) Within 300,000 years from the Big Bang, temperature dropped to 4,500 K and gave rise to atomic matter. The universe became transparent. The expansion of universe means increase in space between the galaxies. An alternative to this was Hoyle's concept of steady state. It considered the universe to be roughly the same at any point of time. However, with greater evidence becoming available about the expanding universe, scientific community at present favours argument of expanding universe.

Formation of Planets

The following are considered to be the stages in the development of planets :

(i) The stars are localised lumps of gas within a nebula. The gravitational force within the lumps leads to the formation of a core to the gas cloud and a huge rotating disc of gas and dust develops around the gas core.

(ii) In the next stage, the gas cloud starts getting condensed and the matter around the core develops into small- rounded objects. These small-rounded objects by the process of cohesion develop into what is called planetesimals. Larger bodies start forming by collision, and gravitational attraction causes the material to stick together. Planetesimals are a large number of smaller bodies.

(iii) In the final stage, these large number of small planetesimals accrete to form a fewer large bodies in the form of planets.

KEPLER'S LAW OF PLANETARY MOTION

In astronomy, Kepler's laws give an approximate description of the motion of planets around the Sun.

Kepler's laws are:

1. The orbit of every planet is an ellipse with the Sun at a focus.
2. A line joining a planet and the Sun sweeps out equal areas during equal intervals of time.
3. The square of the orbital period of a planet is directly proportional to the cube of the semi-major axis of its orbit.

Kepler's laws were discovered empirically, around 1605, by Johannes Kepler who found them by analyzing the astronomical observations of Tycho Brahe. Almost a century later, Isaac Newton proved that relationships like Kepler's would apply exactly under certain ideal conditions approximately fulfilled in the solar system, as consequences of Newton's own laws of motion and law of universal gravitation, using classical Euclidean geometry.

Because of the nonzero planetary masses and resulting perturbations, Kepler's laws apply only approximately and not exactly to the motions in the solar system.

Kepler's laws and his analysis of the observations on which they were based, the assertion that the Earth orbited the Sun, proof that the planets' speeds varied, and use of elliptical orbits rather than circular orbits with epicycles–challenged the long-accepted geocentric models of Aristotle and Ptolemy, and generally supported the heliocentric theory of Nicolaus Copernicus (although Kepler's ellipses likewise did away with Copernicus's circular orbits and epicycles). Together with Newton's mathematical theories, they are part of the foundation of modern astronomy and physics. after Isaac Newton showed that relationships of similar form would apply exactly as consequences of the laws of motion and gravitation under certain ideal conditions (not exactly fulfilled in the the solar system).

Kepler's laws are concerned with the motion of the planets around the Sun. Newton's laws of motion in general are concerned with the motion of objects subject to impressed forces. Newton's law of universal gravitation describes how masses attract each other through the force of gravity. Using the law of gravitation to determine the impressed forces in Newton's laws of motion enables the calculation of planetary orbits, as discussed below.

While Kepler's laws are expressed either in geometrical language, or as equations connecting the coordinates of the planet and the time variable with the orbital elements, Newton's second law is a differential equation. So the derivations below involve the art of solving differential equations. Kepler's second law is derived first, as the derivation of the first law depends on the derivation of the second law. The derivations that follow use heliocentric polar coordinates, that is, polar coordinates with the Sun as the origin.

Equations of motion

Assume that the planet is so much lighter than the Sun that the acceleration of the Sun can be neglected. In other words, the barycenter is approximated as the center of the Sun. Introduce the polar coordinate system in the plane of the orbit, with radial coordinate from the Sun's center, r and angle from some arbitrary starting direction è.

Newton's law of gravitation says that "every object in the universe attracts every other object along a line of the centers of the objects, proportional to each object's mass, and inversely proportional to the square of the distance between the objects," and his second law of motion says that "the mass times the acceleration is equal to the force." So the mass of the planet times the acceleration vector of the planet equals the mass of the Sun times the mass of the planet, divided by the square of the distance, times minus the radial unit vector $\hat{\mathbf{r}}$ times a constant of proportionality. This is written:

$$m\ddot{r} = -\frac{GMm}{r^2}\hat{\mathbf{r}}$$

where a dot on top of the variable signifies differentiation with respect to time, the second dot indicates the second derivative, and the position vector $\mathbf{r} = r\hat{\mathbf{r}}$

In polar coordinates, as discussed in Vector calculus and Polar coordinates in an inertial frame of reference

$$\dot{\hat{r}} = \dot{\theta}\hat{\theta}$$

where $\hat{\theta}$ is the tangential (azimuthal) unit vector orthogonal to $\hat{r}$ pointing in the direction of rotation, and θ is the polar angle.

So differentiating the position vector $r = r\hat{r}$ twice to obtain the velocity and the acceleration vectors:

$$\dot{r} = \dot{r}\hat{r} + r\dot{\hat{r}} = \dot{r}\hat{r} + r\dot{\theta}\hat{\theta}$$

$$\ddot{r} = \left(\ddot{r}\hat{r} + \dot{r}\dot{\hat{r}}\right) + \left(\dot{r}\dot{\theta}\hat{\theta} + r\ddot{\theta}\hat{\theta} + r\dot{\theta}\dot{\hat{\theta}}\right) = \left(\ddot{r} - r\dot{\theta}^2\right)\hat{r} + \left(r\ddot{\theta} + 2\dot{r}\dot{\theta}\right)\hat{\theta}.$$

Note that for constant distance r, the planet is subject to the centripetal acceleration, $r\dot{\theta}^2$, and for constant angular speed, θ, the planet is subject to the Coriolis acceleraton, $2\dot{r}\dot{\theta}$.

Inserting the acceleraton vector into Newton's laws, and dividing by m, gives the vector equation of motion

$$\left(\ddot{r} - r\dot{\theta}^2\right)\hat{r} + \left(r\ddot{\theta} + 2\dot{r}\dot{\theta}\right)\hat{\theta} = -GMr^{-2}\hat{r}$$

Equation components, we get the two ordinary differential equations of motion, one for the acceleration in the $\hat{r}$ direction, the radial acceleration

$$\ddot{r} - r\dot{\theta}^2 = -GMr^{-2},$$

and one for the acceleration in the $\hat{\theta}$ direction, the tangential or azimuthal acceleration:

$$r\ddot{\theta} + 2\dot{r}\dot{\theta} = 0$$

Deriving Kepler's first law

To derive Kepler's first law, define:

$$u = pr^{-1}$$

where the constant

$$p = l^2 G^{-1} M^{-1}$$

has the dimension of length. Then

$$GMr^{-2} = l^3 p^{-3} u^2 \text{ and } \dot{\theta} = lr^{-2} = lp^{-2}u^2.$$

Differentiation with respect to time is transformed into differentiation with respect to angle:

$$\dot{X} = \frac{dX}{dt} = \frac{dX}{d\theta}.\frac{d\theta}{dt} = \frac{dX}{d\theta}.\dot{\theta} = \frac{dX}{d\theta}.lp^{-2}u^2.$$

Differentiate

$$r = pu\text{-}1$$

twice:

$$\dot{r} = \frac{d\left(pu^{-1}\right)}{d\theta}\cdot lp^{-2}u^2 = -pu^{-2}\frac{du}{d\theta}.lp^{-2}u^2 = -lp^{-1}\frac{du}{d\theta}$$

$$\ddot{r} = \frac{d\dot{r}}{d\theta}\cdot lp^{-2}u^2 = \frac{d}{d\theta}\left(-lp^{-1}\frac{du}{d\theta}\right).lp^{-2}u^2 = -l^2p^{-3}u^2\frac{d^2u}{d\theta^2}$$

Substitute into the radial equation of motion

$$\ddot{r} - r\dot{\theta}^2 = -GMr^{-2}$$

and get

$$\left(-l^2p^{-3}u^2\frac{d^2u}{d\theta^2}\right) - \left(pu^{-1}\right)\left(lp^{-2}u^2\right)^2 = -l^2p^{-3}u^2$$

Divide by $-l^2p^{-3}u^2$ to get a simple non-homogeneous linear differential equation for the orbit of the planet:

$$\frac{d^2u}{d\theta^2} + u = 1$$

An obvious solution to this equation is the circular orbit $u = 1$.

Other solutions are obtained by adding solutions to the homogeneous linear differential equation with constant coefficients.

$$\frac{d^2u}{d\theta^2} + u = 0$$

These solutions are $u = \varepsilon.\cos(\theta - \theta_0)$

where ε and θ_0 are arbitary constants of integration.

So the result is $u = 1 + \varepsilon.\cos(\theta - \theta_0)$

Choosing the axis of the coordinate system such that $\theta = 0$, and inserting $u = pr^{-1}$, gives:

$$pr^{-1} = 1 + \varepsilon.\cos\theta$$

If $|\varepsilon| < 1$, this is Kepler's first law.

Deriving Kepler's second law

Only the tangential acceleration equation is needed to derive Kepler's second law.

The magnitude of the specific angular momentum $l = r^2\dot{\theta}$ is a constant of motion, even if both the distance r, and the angular speed $\dot{\theta}$, and the tangential velocity $r\dot{\theta}$, vary, because

$$\frac{dl}{dt} = \frac{d\left(r^2\dot{\theta}\right)}{dt} = r^2\ddot{\theta} + 2r\dot{r}\dot{\theta} = r\left(r\ddot{\theta} + 2\dot{r}\dot{\theta}\right) = 0$$

Where the expression in the last parentheses vanishes due to the tangential acceleration equation. The area swept out from time t_1 to t_2,

$$\int_{t_1}^{t_2} \frac{1}{2}\cdot base\cdot d(\text{heght}) = \int_{t_1}^{t_2} \frac{1}{2}\cdot r\cdot r\dot{\theta}dt = \frac{1}{2}\cdot l\cdot(t_2 - t_1)$$

depends only on the duration $t_2 - t_1$. This is Kepler's second law.

Deriving Kepler's third law

In the special case of circular obrits, which are ellipes with zero eccentricity, the relation between the radius a of the orbit and its period P can be derived relatively easily. The centripetal force of circular motion is proportional to a/P^2, and it is provided by the gravitational force, whihc is proporational to $1/a^2$. Hence,

$$P^2 \propto a^3$$

which is Kepler's third law for the special case. In the general case of elliptical orbits, the derivation is more complicated.

The area of the planetary orbit ellipse is

$$A = \pi ab = \pi a\left(a\sqrt{1-\varepsilon^2}\right) = \pi a^2\sqrt{1-\varepsilon^2}$$

The area speed of the radius vector sweeping the orbit area is

$$\dot{A} = l/2$$

where

$$l^2 = pGM = a\left(1-\varepsilon^2\right)GM$$

The period of the orbit is

$$P = \frac{A}{\dot{A}} = \frac{\pi a^2\sqrt{1-\varepsilon^2}}{l/2} = 2\pi\frac{a^2\sqrt{1-\varepsilon^2}}{l}$$

satisfying

$$\left(\frac{P}{2\pi}\right)^2 = \left(\frac{a^2\left(\sqrt{1-\varepsilon^2}\right)}{l}\right)^2$$

$$= \frac{a^4\left(1-\varepsilon^2\right)}{l^2} = \frac{a^4\left(1-\varepsilon^2\right)}{a\left(1-\varepsilon^2\right)GM} = \frac{a^3}{GM}$$

implying Kepler's third law

$$P^2 \propto a^3.$$

GEOLOGICAL TIME SCALE

Geologists have divided Earth history into units displayed in the geologic time scale (Table 1.1). The units are called eons, eras, periods, and epochs and are identified primarily by the types of life that existed at the various times. The two earliest eons, the Hadean and Archean, cover the first 2.5 billion years of Earth history. Life originated during Archean time. Living organisms then evolved and proliferated during the Proterozoic Eon (protero is from a Greek root meaning "earlier" or"before" and zoon is from the Greek word meaning "life"). However, most Proterozoic organisms had no hard parts such as shells and bones. Most were single celled, although some multicellular organisms existed. The Proterozoic Eon ended about 538 million years ago.

Then, within an astonishingly short time–perhaps as little as 5 million years–many new species evolved. These organisms were biologically more complex than their Proterozoic ancestors, and many had shells and skeletons. The most recent 13 percent of geologic time, from 538 million years ago to the present, is called the Phanerozoic Eon (phaneros is Greek for "evident"). The Phanerozoic Eon is subdivided into the Paleozoic Era ("ancient life"), the Mesozoic Era ("middle life"), and the Cenozoic Era ("recent life") .

Table 1.1: THE GEOLOGIC TIME SCALE

TIME UNITS OF THE GEOLOGIC TIME SCALE

Eon	Era	Period		Epoch	Boundary	Distinctive plants and animals	
Phanerozoic Eon (*Phaneros* = "evident"; *Zoon* = "life")	Cenozoic Era	Quaternary		Recent or Holocene		"Age of Mammals"	Humans
				Pleistocene	2		Mammals develop and become dominant
		Tertiary	Neogene	Pliocene	5		
				Miocene	24		
			Paleogene	Oligocene	37		
				Eocene	58		
				Paleocene	66		Extinction of dinosaurs and many other species
	Mesozoic Era	Cretaceous			144	"Age of Reptiles"	First flowering plants, greatest development of dinosaurs
		Jurassic			208		First birds and mammals, abundant dinosaurs
		Triassic			245		First dinosaurs
	Paleozoic Era	Permian			286	"Age of Amphibians"	Extinction of trilobites and many other marine animals
		Carboniferous	Pennsylvanian		320		Great coal forests; abundant insects, first reptiles
			Mississippian		360		Large primitive trees
		Devonian			408	"Age of Fishes"	First amphibians
		Silurian			438		First land plant fossils
		Ordovician			505	"Age of Marine Invertebrates"	First fish
		Cambrian			538		First organisms with shells, trilobites dominant
Proterozoic		Sometimes collectively called Precambrian			2500		First multicelled organisms
Archean					3800		First one-celled organisms
							Approximate age of oldest rocks
Hadean					4600±		Origin of the Earth

Figure: Representation of Geological Time Scale in tabular form. Here, time is given in millions of years.

AGE OF THE EARTH

The age of the Earth is around 4.54 billion years (4.54×10^9 years ± 1%). This age has been determined by radiometric age dating of meteorite material and is consistent with the ages of the oldest-known terrestrial and lunar samples.

Following the scientific revolution and the development of radiometric age dating, measurements of lead in uranium-rich minerals showed that some were in excess of a billion years old. The oldest such minerals analyzed to date – small crystals of zircon from the Jack Hills of Western Australia – are at least 4.404 billion years old. Comparing the mass and luminosity of the Sun to the multitudes of other stars, it appears that the solar system cannot be much older than those rocks. Ca-Al-rich inclusions (inclusions rich in calcium and aluminium) – the oldest known solid constituents within meteorites that are formed within the solar system – are 4.567 billion years old, giving an age for the solar system and an upper limit for the age of Earth. It is hypothesised that the accretion of Earth began soon after the formation of the Ca-Al-rich inclusions and the meteorites.Because the exact accretion time of Earth is not yet known, and the predictions from different accretion models range from a few millions up to about 100 million years, the exact age of Earth is difficult to determine

Studies of strata, the layering of rock and earth, gave naturalists an appreciation that Earth may have been through many changes during its existence. These layers often contained fossilized remains of unknown creatures, leading some to interpret a progression of organisms from layer to layer.

Radiometric dating & Age of the earth

Rock minerals naturally contain certain elements and not others. By the process of radioactive decay of radioactive isotopes occurring in a rock, exotic elements can be introduced over time. By measuring the concentration of the stable end product of the decay, coupled with knowledge of the half life and initial concentration of the decaying element, the age of the rock can be calculated. Typical radioactive end products are argon from potassium-40 and lead from uranium and thorium decay. If the rock becomes molten, as happens in Earth's mantle, such nonradioactive end products typically escape or are redistributed. Thus the age of the oldest terrestrial rock gives a minimum for the age of Earth assuming that a rock cannot have been in existence for longer than Earth itself.

Theories about the origin of life and the nature of fossil record.

ORIGIN OF LIFE & FOSSIL RECORD

The sun and its planets formed between 5 and 4.6 billion years ago as matter in our solar system began to coalesce because of gravity. By about 3.9 billion years ago, the Earth had an atmosphere that contained the right mix of hydrogen, oxygen, carbon, and nitrogen to allow for the creation of life. Scientists believe that the energy from heat, lightning, or radioactive elements caused the formation of complex proteins and nucleic acids into strands of replicating genetic code. These molecules then organized and evolved to form the first simple forms of life. At 3.8 billion years ago, conditions became right for the fossilization of the Earth's early cellular life forms.

These fossilized cells resemble present day cyanobacteria. Such cells are known as prokaryotes. Prokaryote cells are very simple, containing few specialized cellular structures and their DNA is not surrounded by a membranous envelope. The more complex cells of animals and plants, known as eukaryotes, first showed up about 2.1 billion year ago. Eukaryotes have a membrane-bound nucleus and many specialized structures located within their cell boundary. By 680 million years ago, eukaryotic cells were beginning to organize themselves into multicellular organisms. Starting at about 570 million years ago a n enormous diversification of multicellular life occurred

known as the Cambrian explosion. During this period all but one modern phylum of animal life made its first appearance on the Earth. Table 1.2 describes the approximate time of origin of the Earth' s major groups of plants and animals.

Organism Group	*Time of Origin*
Marine Invertebrates	570 Million Years Ago
Fish	505 Million Years Ago
Land Plants	438 Million Years Ago
Amphibians	408 Million Years Ago
Reptiles	320 Million Years Ago
Mammals	208 Million Years Ago
Flowering Plants (Angiosperms)	140 Million Years Ago
Hominid Line Begins Its Evolution	20-15 Million Years Ago

Table 1.2: Time of origin of some major plant and animal groups.

All cultures have developed stories to explain the origin of life. During medieval ages, for example, European scholars argued that small creatures such as insects, amphibians, and mice appeared by "spontaneous generation"–natural self-assembly of nonliving ingredients–in old clothes or piles of garbage. Italian physician Francesco Redi (1626–1698) challenged this belief in 1668, when he showed that maggots come from eggs laid by flies, rather than forming spontaneously from the decaying matter in which they are found.

A series of experiments conducted in the 1860s by the French microbiologist Louis Pasteur (1822–1895) also helped to disprove the idea that life originated by spontaneous generation. Pasteur sterilized two containers, both of which contained a broth rich in nutrients. He exposed both containers to the air, but one had a trap in the form of a loop in a connecting tube, which prevented dust and other particles from reaching the broth. Bacteria and mold quickly grew in the open container and made its broth cloudy and rank, but the container with the trap remained sterile. Pasteur interpreted this experiment as indicating that microorganisms did not arise spontaneously in the open container, but were introduced by dust and other airborne contaminants.

Although Redi, Pasteur, and other scientists thoroughly disproved the theory of spontaneous generation as an explanation for the origin of present-day life on whatever scale, they raised a new question: If organisms can arise only from other organisms, how then did the first organism arise?

Charles Darwin (1809–1882), the famous English naturalist, suggested that life might have first occurred in "some warm little pond" rich in minerals and chemicals, and exposed to electricity and light. Darwin argued that once the first living beings appeared, all other creatures that have ever lived could have evolved from them. In other words, spontaneous generation did occur–but only a long time ago, when the first, minimally complex forms of life would have faced no competition from more-competent cells. Many of the laboratory experiments that would eventually be conducted to shed light on the origin of life have been variations on Darwin's "warm little pond." First, however, another influential suggestion regarding the origin of life was provided by Russian scientist Aleksandr Oparin (1894–1980) and English scientist J. B. S. Haldane (1892–1964). Oparin and Haldane suggested in the 1920s that the atmosphere of billions of years ago would have been very different from today's. The modern atmosphere is about 79% nitrogen (N_2) and 20.9% free oxygen (O_2), with only trace quantities of other gases. Because of the presence of oxygen, which combines readily with many other substances, such an atmosphere is termed oxidizing. Oparin noted that oxygen interferes with the formation of organic compounds necessary for life by combining with their hydrogen atoms and reasoned that the atmosphere present when life began must have been a reducing atmosphere, which contained little or no oxygen but had high concentrations of gases that can react to provide hydrogen atoms to synthesize the compounds needed to create life. Oparin and Haldane suggested that this primordial, reducing atmosphere consisted of hydrogen (H_2), ammonia (NH_3), methane (CH_4), and additional simple hydrocarbons (molecules consisting only of carbon and hydrogen atoms). Oxygen could not have been present in large quantities because it is chemically unstable, and is only maintained as a major ingredient of the atmosphere by the action of green plants and algae–that is, by life itself. Before life, the Earth's atmosphere could not have been strongly oxidizing.

According to this theory, energy for rearranging atoms and molecules into organic forms that promoted the genesis of life came from sunlight, lightning, or geothermal heat. This model of the early environment became especially popular among scientists after a U.S. graduate student of physics named Stanley Miller (1930), then studying at the University of Chicago, designed an experiment to test it. In 1953 Miller filled a closed glass container with a mixture of the gases that Oparin and Haldane suggested were in the ancient atmosphere. In the bottom of the container was a reservoir of boiling water, and above it an apparatus that caused electrical sparks to pass through the gas mixture. After one week of reaction, Miller found that amino acids and other organic chemicals had formed from the gases and water. In the years since Miller reported his results, other researchers have performed more sophisticated "warm little pond" experiments, and have been to synthesize additional amino acids and even nucleic acids, the molecules that organize into RNA and DNA, which in turn encode the genetic information of organisms.

Subsequent research influenced by these experiments led many scientists to believe that the concentration of organic molecules in the primordial, nutrient-laden, warm "ponds" (which may have been tidal pools, puddles, shallow lakes, or deep-sea hot springs) increased progressively over time. Eventually more complex molecules formed, such as carbohydrates, lipids, proteins, and nucleic acids. The complexity gap between simple nucleic acids and self-replicating RNA or DNA is, however, large; therefore, some scientists have theorized that assembly of more complex compounds from simpler ones may have occurred on the surface of oily drops floating on the water surface, or on the surfaces of minerals–inanimate objects whose atomic structure might have provided a template for stringing together nucleic acids and giving them a place to "live" until free-floating cells protected by lipid membranes could evolve.

However, some scientists believe that the young Earth was too inhospitable a place for life to have developed on its surface at all; lacking O_2, the atmosphere would also have lacked its present-day stratospheric layer of ozone (O_3), which screens large quantities of harmful ultraviolet radiation from the surface. They believe that a more likely environment for abiogenesis (life from prelife) was in the vicinity of deep-sea vents, holes in the crust under the ocean from which hot, mineral-laden water flows.

Furthermore, many scientists today believe that the prelife atmosphere may not have been as strongly reducing as the one proposed by Oparin and Haldane and used in Miller's experiment. They assert that volcanoes added carbon monoxide (CO), carbon dioxide (CO_2), and nitrogen to the early atmosphere, which may even have contained traces of oxygen. Nevertheless, more recent experiments of the Miller type, run using a less reducing atmosphere, have also resulted in the synthesis of organic compounds. In fact, all 20 of the amino acids found in organisms have been created in the laboratory under experimental conditions designed to mimic what scientists believe the prelife Earth was like billions of years ago–whether using Miller's model or its less-reducing competitors.

But in the absence of life, how did these amino acids link together into more complex compounds? Living cellular chemistry links amino acids together using specific enzymes to form particular proteins. An amino acid is any compound which contains at least one amino group (NH_2) and one carboxyl group (-COOH). When amino acids are linked, a hydrogen molecule and a hydroxyl group (OH) are removed from each amino acids, which then link up into a protein chain, while the hydrogen and hydroxyl link up as a water molecule ($H + OH = H_2O$). Without enzymes, amino acids do not link up in this way–or, as a biochemist might describe it, polymerization does not proceed. How, then, could amino acids have joined to form proteins without the proteins termed enzymes to help them? One possibility is that amino acids may have joined together on hot sand, clay, or other minerals. Laboratory experiments have shown that amino acids and other organic building blocks of larger molecules, called polymers, will join together if dilute solutions of them are dripped onto warm sand, clay, or other minerals. The larger molecules formed in this way have been named proteinoids. It is easy to imagine some version of Darwin's "warm little pond"–a soup of spontaneously-formed amino acids–splashing onto hot volcanic rocks. Clay and iron pyrite have particularly favorable properties making them good "platforms" for the formation of larger molecules from smaller building blocks. One recently proposed theory of the origin of life suggests that tiny (0 .01 mm diameter) hollows in iron sulfide minerals, such as are deposited in the vicinity of deep-sea hot springs, might have incubated the earliest life chemistry. Iron sulfide catalyzes the formation of organic molecules, and is used by some modern bacteria for this purpose. Sheltered in tiny iron-sulfide caverns, prebiotic chemistry might have developed at leisure, leaving this protected environment only after evolving a protective lipid membrane. This theory, however, like all theories of the origin of life, has its scientific opponents, and awaits the production of confirming or disconfirming laboratory evidence.

Proteinoids produced in laboratories can cluster together into droplets that separate, and that may protect their components from degrading influences of the surrounding environment. These droplets are like extremely simple cells, although they can not reproduce. Such droplets are called microspheres. When fats (i.e., lipids) are present, the microspheres that form are even more cell-like. If a mixture of linked amino acids called polypeptides, sugars called polysaccharides, and nucleic acids is shaken, droplets called coacervates will form. All of these kinds of droplets are called protobionts, and they may represent a stage in the genesis of cellular life.

The formation of amino acids and other organic compounds is presumed to have been a necessary step in the genesis of life; it is certain, at least, that somewhere along the line all life became dependent on DNA and RNA for reproduction. Scientists thus presume that the first self-replicating molecules were similar to the nucleic acids of modern organisms. (These early molecular systems need not have been as complex as the self-replicating systems that comprise modern cells. Researchers have recently shown, by deleting genes, that even the genetically simplest bacteria alive today can reproduce with much less than their full natural complement of DNA.) Once molecules that could self-replicate were formed, the process of evolution would account for the subsequent development of life. The particular molecules best adapted to the local environmental conditions would have duplicated themselves more efficiently than competing molecules. Eventually, primitive cells appeared; perhaps coacervates or other protobionts played a role at this stage in the genesis of life. Once cells became established, evolution by natural selection could have resulted in the development of all of the life-forms that have ever existed on Earth.

EARTH'S GRAVITY AND MAGNETIC FIELDS AND ITS THERMAL STRUCTURE

EARTH'S GRAVITY

Earth's gravity, denoted g, refers to the acceleration that the Earth imparts to objects on or near its surface. In SI units this acceleration is measured in m/s^2 (metres per second per second, equivalently written as $m \cdot s^{-2}$ or N/kg). It has an approximate value of 9.81 m/s^2, which means that, ignoring air resistance, the speed of an object falling freely near the Earth's surface increases by about 9.81 metres per second every second.

There is a direct relationship between gravitational acceleration and the downwards weight force experienced by objects on Earth.

The precise strength of the Earth's gravity varies depending on location. The nominal "average" value at the Earth's surface, known as **standard gravity** is, by definition, 9.80665 m/s^2 (32.1740 ft/s^2). This quantity is denoted variously as g_n, g_e (though this sometimes means the normal equatorial value on Earth, 9.78033 m/s^2), g_0, gee, or simply g (which is also used for the variable local value). The symbol g should not be confused with g, the abbreviation for gram (which is not italicized)

VARIATION IN GRAVITY

Earth's gravitational force is often modeled as though the Earth were an inert sphere of uniform density. Such a body would produce a field of uniform magnitude and direction at all points on its surface. In reality there are slight deviations in both the magnitude and direction of gravity across the surface of the Earth because none of those qualities are exactly true of Earth.

The strength of Earth's apparent gravity varies with latitude, altitude, local topography and geology:

LATITUDE

The differences of Earth's gravity around the Antarctic continent.

Apparent gravity is weaker nearer the equator because the Earth's rotation produces an apparent centrifugal force.

The second major cause for the difference in gravity at different latitudes is that the Earth's equatorial bulge (itself also caused by centrifugal force) causes objects at the equator to be farther from the planet's centre than objects at the poles. Because the force due to gravitational attraction between two bodies (the Earth and the object being weighed) varies inversely with the square of the distance between them, objects at the equator experience a weaker gravitational pull than objects at the poles.

ALTITUDE

Gravity decreases with altitude, since greater altitude means greater distance from the Earth's centre. All other things being equal, an increase in altitude from sea level to the top of Mount Everest (8,850 metres) causes a weight decrease of about 0.28%.

The following formula approximates the Earth's gravity variation with altitude:

$$g_h = g_o\left(\frac{r_e}{r_e + n}\right)^2$$

Where

- g_h is the gravity measure at height above sea level.
- g_o is the Earth's mean radius.
- r_e is the standard gravity.

Local topography and geology

Local variations in topography (such as the presence of mountains) and geology (such as the density of rocks in the vicinity) cause fluctuations in the Earth's gravitational field, known as gravitational anomalies. Some of these anomalies can be very extensive, resulting in bulges in sea level, and throwing pendulum clocks out of synchronisation.

The study of these anomalies forms the basis of gravitational geophysics. The fluctuations are measured with highly sensitive gravimeters, the effect of topography and other known factors is subtracted, and from the resulting data conclusions are drawn. Such techniques are now used by prospectors to find oil and mineral deposits. Denser rocks (often containing mineral ores) cause higher than normal local gravitational fields on the Earth's surface. Less dense sedimentary rocks cause the opposite.

Magnetic field

The Earth's magnetic field is shaped roughly as a magnetic dipole, with the poles currently located proximate to the planet's geographic poles. According to dynamo theory, the field is generated within the molten outer core region where heat creates convection motions of conducting materials, generating electric currents. These in turn produce the Earth's magnetic field. The convection movements in the core are chaotic, and periodically change alignment. This results in field reversals at irregular intervals averaging a few times every million years. The most recent reversal occurred approximately 700,000 years ago.

The field forms the magnetosphere, which deflects particles in the solar wind. The sunward edge of the bow shock is located at about 13 times the radius of the Earth. The collision between the magnetic field and the solar wind forms the Van Allen radiation belts, a pair of concentric, torus-shaped regions of energetic charged particles. When the plasma enters the Earth's atmosphere at the magnetic poles, it forms the aurora

Thermal structure

Earth's internal heat comes from a combination of residual heat from planetary accretion (about 20%) and heat produced through radioactive decay (80%). The major heat-producing isotopes in the Earth are potassium-40, uranium-238, uranium-235, and thorium-232. At the center of the planet, the temperature may be up to 7,000 K and the pressure could reach 360 GPa. Because much of the heat is provided by radioactive decay, scientists believe that early in Earth history, before isotopes with short half-lives had been depleted, Earth's heat production would have been much higher. This extra heat production, twice present-day at approximately 3 billion years ago, would have increased temperature gradients within the Earth, increasing the rates of mantle convection and plate tectonics, and allowing the production of igneous rocks such as komatiites that are not formed today.

Present-day major heat-producing isotopes

Isotope	Heat release W/kg isotope	Half-life years	Mean mantle concentration kg isotope/kg mantle	Heat release W/kg mantle
^{238}U	9.46×10^{-5}	4.47×10^{9}	30.8×10^{-9}	2.91×10^{-12}
^{235}U	5.69×10^{-4}	7.04×10^{8}	0.22×10^{-9}	1.25×10^{-13}
^{232}Th	2.64×10^{-5}	1.40×10^{10}	124×10^{-9}	3.27×10^{-12}
^{40}K	2.92×10^{-5}	1.25×10^{9}	36.9×10^{-9}	1.08×10^{-12}

Total heat loss from the earth is 4.2×10^{13} Watts. A portion of the core's thermal energy is transported toward the crust by Mantle plumes; a form of convection consisting of upwellings of higher-temperature rock. These plumes can produce hotspots and flood basalts. More of the heat in the Earth is lost through plate tectonics, by mantle upwelling associated with mid-ocean ridges. The final major mode of heat loss is through conduction through the lithosphere, majority of which occurs in the oceans because the crust there is much thinner than that of the continents.

GEOID

The **geoid** is that equipotential surface which would coincide exactly with the mean ocean surface of the Earth, if the oceans were in equilibrium, at rest, and extended through the continents.

The geoid surface is irregular, unlike the reference ellipsoid which is a mathematical idealized representation of the physical Earth, but considerably smoother than Earth's physical surface.

Although the physical Earth has excursions of +8,000 m (Mount Everest) and −11,000 m (Mariana Trench), the geoid's total variation is less than 200 m (−106 to +85 m) compared to a perfect mathematical ellipsoid.

Sea level, if undisturbed by currents and weather, would assume a surface equal to the geoid. If the continental land masses were criss-crossed by a series of tunnels or narrow canals, the sea level in these canals would also coincide with the geoid. In reality the geoid does not have a physical meaning under the continents, but geodesists are able to derive the heights of continental points above this imaginary, yet physically defined, surface by a technique called spirit leveling.

Being an equipotential surface, the geoid is by definition a surface to which the force of gravity is everywhere perpendicular. This means that when travelling by ship, one does not notice the undulations of the geoid; the local vertical is always perpendicular to the geoid and the local horizon tangential component to it. Likewise, spirit levels will always be parallel to the geoid.

SPHEROID

The shape and size of a geographic coordinate system's surface is defined by a sphere or spheroid. Although the earth is best represented by a spheroid, the earth is sometimes treated as a sphere to make mathematical calculations easier. The assumption that the earth is a sphere is possible for small-scale maps (smaller than 1:5 000 000) At this scale, the difference between a sphere and a spheroid is not detectable on a map. However, to maintain accuracy for larger-scale maps (scales of 1:1,000,000 or larger), a spheroid is necessary to represent the shape of the earth. Between those scales, choosing to use a sphere or spheroid will depend on the map's purpose and the accuracy of the data.

Definition of a Spheroid

A sphere is based on a circle, while a spheroid (or ellipsoid) is based on an ellipse.

The shape of an ellipse is defined by two radii. The longer radius is called the semimajor axis, and the shorter radius is called the semiminor axis.

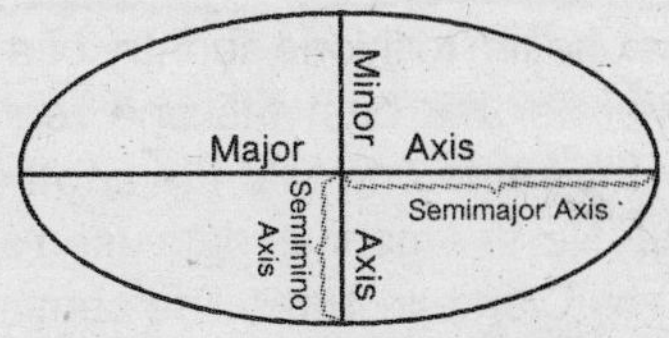

Rotating the ellipse around the semiminor axis creates a spheroid. A spheroid is also known as an oblate ellipsoid of revolution. The following graphic shows the semimajor and semiminor axes of a spheroid.

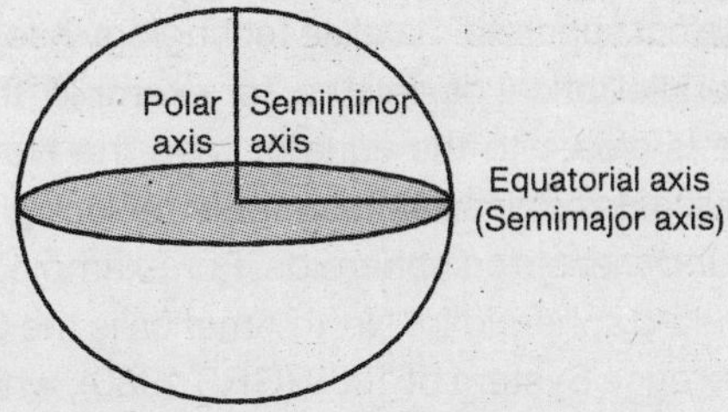

A spheroid is defined by either the semimajor axis, a, and the semiminor axis, b, or by a and the flattening. The flattening is the difference in length between the two axes expressed as a fraction or a decimal. The flattening, f, is:

$$f = (a - b) / a$$

The flattening is a small value, so usually the quantity 1/f is used instead. The spheroid parameters for the World Geodetic System of 1984 (WGS 1984 or WGS84) are:

a = 6378137.0 meters

b = 6356752.31424 meters

1/f = 298.257223563

The flattening ranges from zero to one. A flattening value of zero means the two axes are equal, resulting in a sphere. The flattening of the earth is approximately 0.003353. Another quantity that, like the flattening, describes the shape of a spheroid is the square of the eccentricity, e^2. It is represented by:

$$e^2 = \frac{a^2 - b^2}{a^2}$$

The earth has been surveyed many times to better understand its surface features and their peculiar irregularities. The surveys have resulted in many spheroids that represent the earth. Generally, a spheroid is chosen to fit one country or a particular area. A spheroid that best fits one region is not necessarily the same one that fits another region. Until recently, North American data used a spheroid determined by Clarke in 1866. The semimajor axis of the Clarke 1866 spheroid is 6,378,206.4 meters, and the semiminor axis is 6,356,583.8 meters.

Because of gravitational and surface feature variations, the earth is neither a perfect sphere nor a perfect spheroid. Satellite technology has revealed several elliptical deviations; for example, the South Pole is closer to the equator than the North Pole. Satellite-determined spheroids are replacing the older ground-measured spheroids. For example, the new standard spheroid for North America is the Geodetic Reference System of 1980 (GRS 1980), whose radii are 6,378,137.0 and 6,356,752.31414 meters. The GRS 1980 spheroid parameters were set by the International Union for Geodesy and Geophysics in 1979.

Because changing a coordinate system's spheroid will change all feature coordinate values, many organizations haven't switched to newer (and more accurate) spheroids.

ISOSTASY

The concept that the lithosphere is in floating equilibrium on the asthenosphere is called isostasy. When weight such as a glacier is added to or removed from the Earth's surface, the lithosphere sinks or rises. This vertical movement in response to changing burdens is called isostatic adjustment. In a simple term isostasy means a mechanical stability between the upstanding parts and low-lying basin on a rotating earth.

This theory was developed in 1950 during a gravity surveys in the mountains of India. This doctrine states that wherever equilibrium exists in the earth surface, equal mass must underlie equal surface area; that is; a great continental mass must be formed of lighter materials than that supposed to constitutes the oceanic basin and further, in order to compensate for its greater height theses lighter continental material must extend downward to some distance under the continent and below the ocean floor level in order that unit areas beneath oceans and continents may remain in stable equilibrium. Accordingly, a level of of uniform pressure is thought to exist where the pressure due to elevated masses and depresses area would be same. This is known as Isopiestic level.

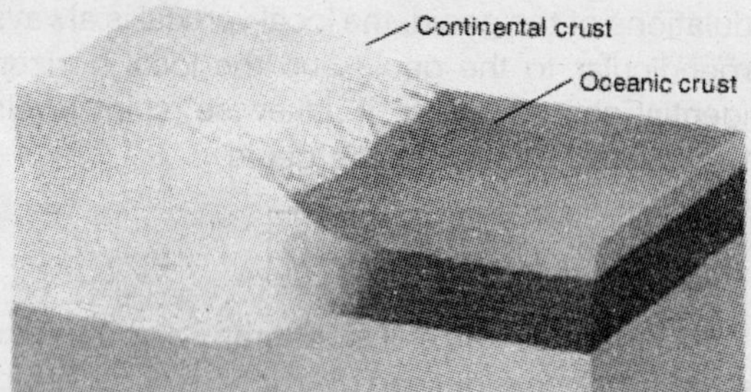

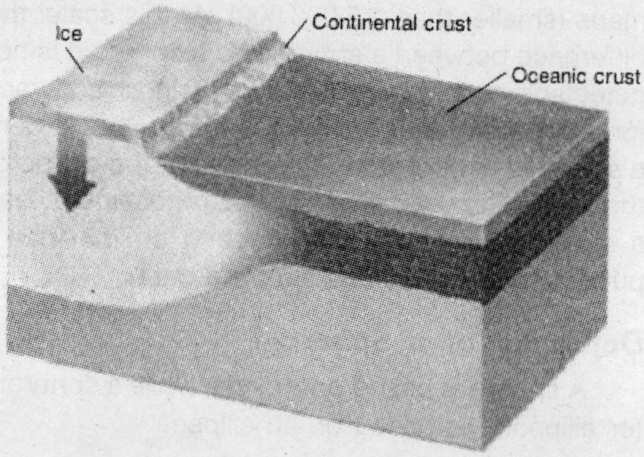

Figure: The weight of an ice sheet causes continental crust to sink isostatically.

THEORY OF ISOSTASY

1. Airy's theory of Isostacy
2. Pratt's theory of Isostacy
3. Heiskanen's theory of Isostacy

Airy's theory of Isostacy

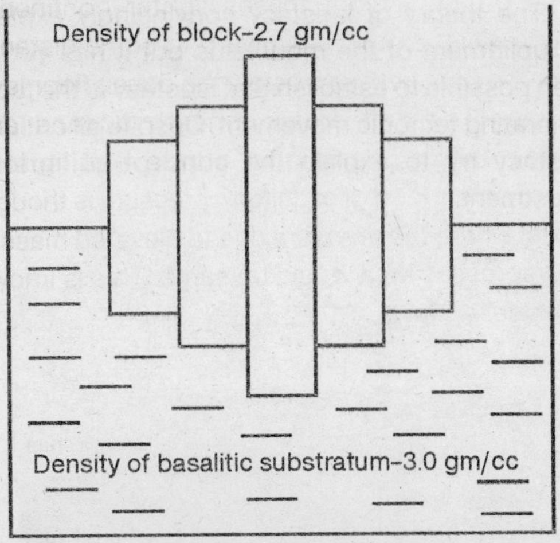

Figure: Airy's theory of Isostacy

According to Airy's theory of Isostacy, the crustal rocks of the earth are of equal density and unequal thickness. In general, the rocks constituting the mountains are thicker than those on which the plains lie and as a result they stand higher up similarly a mass of ice floating in water similarly, the root of the mountains are supported by their roots which penetrate deep down into the denser substratum and keep the mountain floating due to its buoyancy. This is supported by geophysical data. For example: Mount Everest in the Himalaya rises about nine kilometer, right beneath it the crust is about 80 Kilometer thick; whereas the crust is only 32 kilometer thick in the Deccan plateau and only 13 to 20 kilometer near sea cost of India.

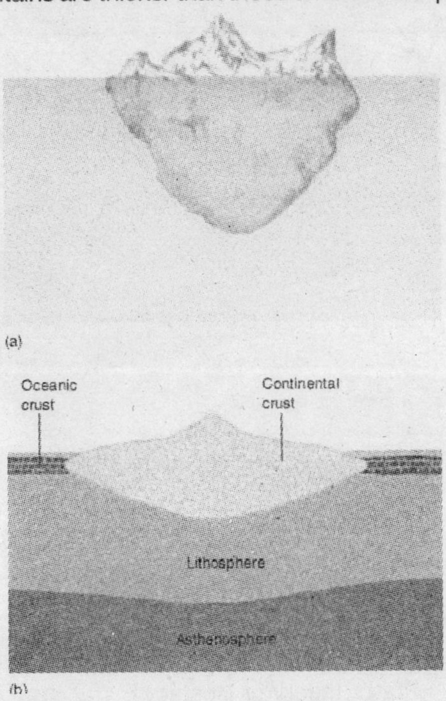

Figure (a) Icebergs illustrate the effects of Isostasy. The large iceberg has a deep root and also a high Peak. (b) Lithosphere covered by continental crust extends more deeply into the asthenosphere than lithosphere covered by oceanic crust.

Pratt's theory of Isostacy

According to Pratt's theory of Isostacy, there is a difference in the density of earth's rocks in the crust and that the heights of crustal rock blocks are determined by their respective density. In general, block made up of lighter material are at higher elevation than those of denser one. Therefore, the mountains mainly consist of lighter material whereas oceanic features consist of heavier materials. But, the underlying principle of Pratt's theory of Isostacy is that, there is a level of compensation above which there is variation in the density of different columns of land but there is no change in density below this level. Thus, the central theme of the concept of Pratt's theory of Isostacy can be expressed as 'Uniform Depth with varying Density'. Therefore the Pratt's theory of Isostacy was related to the 'law of compensation'. Thus, the different physical relief features of earth exert equal pressure at the level of compensation.

Heiskanen's theory of Isostacy

Heiskanen's theory of Isostacy proposed a new concept of isostasy in which Heiskanen combines the concept of Pratt (Varying density with varying thickness) and Airy (Uniform density of varying thickness). According to Heiskanen density varies both between crustal blocks and within each block. For example, rocks of a column at the sea level have higher density than at higher elevation of the same rock column which means as we go downward the center of earth the rock of a section of the earth's crust become denser. It simply means that density increases with depth of the earth. Thus, the density of the earth varies both vertically and horizontally.

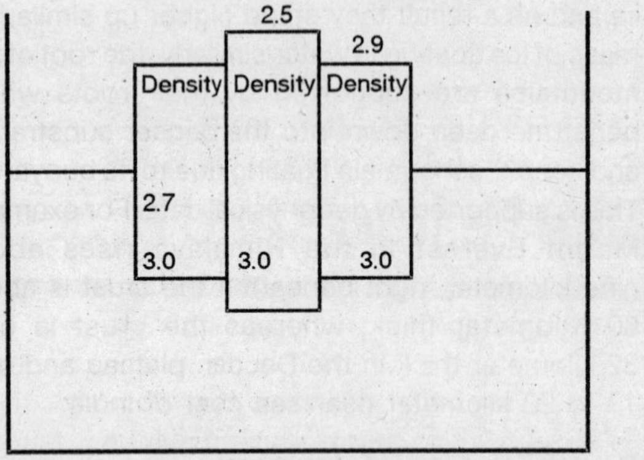

Heiskanen's theory of Isostacy

OUTCOME

The theory of Isostacy convincingly explains the upliftment of the mountains but it has yet not been possible to establish that isostasy is the factor generating tectonic movement. Despite all criticism Isostacy try to explain the concept of isostatic adjustment.

2. Earth Materials, Surface Features and Process

MINERALS

A mineral is a naturally occurring inorganic solid with a characteristic chemical composition and a crystalline structure. Chemical composition and crystalline structure are the two most important properties of a mineral: They distinguish any mineral from all others. Before discussing them, however, let us briefly consider the other properties of minerals described by this definition.

OCCURRENCE OF MINERAL IN NATURE

A synthetic diamond can be identical to a natural one, but it is not a true mineral because a mineral must form by natural processes. Like diamond, most gems that occur naturally can also be manufactured by industrial processes. Natural gems are valued more highly than manufactured ones. For this reason, jewelers should always tell their customers whether a gem is natural or artificial, and they usually preface the name of a manufactured gem with the term synthetic.

ELEMENTS, ATOMS, & THE CHEMICAL COMPOSITION OF MINERALS

To consider the chemical composition and crystalline structure of minerals, we must understand the nature of chemical elements–the fundamental components of matter. An element cannot be broken into simpler particles by ordinary chemical processes. Most common minerals consist of a small number–usually two to five–of different chemical elements. A total of 88 elements occur naturally in the Earth's crust. However, eight elements–oxygen, silicon, aluminum, iron, calcium, magnesium, potassium, and sodium–make up more than 98 per cent of the crust. A complete list of all eight major elements is given in Table 2.1.

Each element is represented by a one- or two-letter symbol, such as O for oxygen and Si for silicon. The table shows a total of 108 elements, not 88, because 20 elements are produced in nuclear reactors but do not occur naturally.

An atom is the basic unit of an element. An atom is tiny; the diameter of the average atom is about 1/10,000,000,000 meters. A single copper penny contains about 1.56 1022 (1.56 followed by 22 zeros) copper atoms. An atom consists of a small, dense, positively charged center called a nucleus surrounded by negatively charged electrons

An electron is a fundamental particle; it is not made up of smaller components. An electron orbits the nucleus, but not in a clearly defined path like that of the Earth around the Sun.

Element	Weight by %	Atom %	Volume %
O	46.60	62.55	93.8
Si	27.72	21.22	0.9
Al	8.13	6.47	0.5
Fe	5.00	1.92	0.4
Ca	3.62	1.94	1.0
Na	2.83	2.64	1.3
K	2.59	1.42	1.8
Mg	2.09	1.84	0.3
Total	98.58	100.00	100.00

Table 2.1: The eight most abundant chemical element in the earth crust.

Most minerals are compounds. When ions bond together to form a mineral, they do so in proportions so that the total number of negative charges exactly balances the total number of positive charges. Thus, minerals are always electrically neutral. For example, the mineral quartz proportionally consists of one (4+) silicon cation and two (2–) oxygen anions.

The 88 elements that occur naturally in the Earth's crust can combine in many ways to form many different minerals. In fact, about 3500 minerals are known.

However, the eight abundant elements commonly combine in only a few ways. As a result, only nine rock-forming minerals (or mineral "groups") make up most rocks of the Earth's crust. They are olivine, pyroxene, amphibole, mica, the clay minerals, quartz, feldspar, calcite, and dolomite.

Element	Chemical Symbol	Common ion (s)
Oxygen	O	O^{2-}
Silicon	Si	Si^{4+}
Aluminum	Al	Al^{3+}
Iron	Fe	Fe^{2+} and Fe^{3+}
Calcium	Ca	Ca^{2+}
Magnesium	Mg	Mg^{2+}
Potassium	K	K^{+}
Sodium	Na	Na^{+}

Table 2.2: THE MOST COMMON IONS OF THE EIGHT MOST ABUNDANT CHEMICAL ELEMENTS IN THE EARTH'S CRUST

PHYSICAL PROPERTIES OF MINERALS

Minerals can be identified by their hardness, color, the way they reflect light, the way they break (cleavage and fracture), and their density.

Geologists commonly identify minerals by visual recognition, and they confirm the identification with simple tests.

Most minerals have distinctive appearances. Once you become familiar with common minerals, you will recognize them just as you recognize any familiar object. For example, an apple just looks like an guava, even though guava come in many colors and shapes. In the same way, quartz looks like quartz to a geologist. The color and shape of quartz may vary from sample to sample, but it still looks like quartz. Some minerals, however, look enough alike that their physical properties must be examined further to make a correct identification. Geologists commonly use physical properties such as crystal habit, cleavage, and hardness to identify minerals.

CRYSTAL HABIT

Crystal habit is the characteristic shape of a mineral and the manner in which aggregates of crystals grow. If a crystal grows freely, it develops a characteristic shape controlled by the arrangement of its atoms

Cleavage

Cleavage is the tendency of some minerals to break along flat surfaces. The surfaces are planes of weak bonds in the crystal. Some minerals, such as mica and graphite, have one set of parallel cleavage planes. Some minerals, like the micas, have excellent cleavage. Many minerals have no cleavage at all because they have no planes of weak bonds.

Fracture

Fracture is the pattern in which a mineral breaks other than along planes of cleavage. Many minerals fracture into characteristic shapes. Conchoidal fracture create smooth, curved surfaces. It is characteris of quartz and olivine. Glass, although not a mineral because it has no crystalline structure, also typically fratures in a conchoidal pattern. Some minerals break in splintery or fibrous fragments. Most fracture into irregular shapes.

Hardness

Hardness is the resistance of a mineral to scratching. It is easily measured and is a fundamental property of each mineral because it is controlled by bond strength between the atoms in the mineral. Geologists commonly gauge hardness by attempting to scratch a mineral with a knife or other object of known hardness. If the blade scratches the mineral, the mineral is softer than the knife. If the knife cannot scratch the mineral, the mineral is harder. To measure hardness more accurately, geologists use a scale based on ten minerals, numbered 1 through 10. Each mineral is harder than those with lower numbers on the scale, so 10 (diamond) is the hardest and 1talc) is the softest. The scale is known as the Mohs hardness scale after F. Mohs, the Austrian mineralogist who developed it in the early nineteenth century.

When testing hardness, it is important to determine whether the mineral has actually been scratched by the object, or whether the object has simply left a trail of its own powder on the surface of the mineral. To check, simply rub away the powder trail and feel the surface of the mineral with your fingernail for the groove of the scratch. Fresh, unweathered mineral surfaces must be used in hardness measurements because weathering of ten produces a soft rind on minerals.

Mohs Scale No.	Minerals
1.	Talc
2.	Gypsum
3.	Calcite
4.	Fluorite
5.	Apatite
6.	Orthoclase
7.	Quartz
8.	Topaz
9	Corundum
10	Diamond

Table 2.3: Mohr's scale of hardness

Specific Gravity

Specific gravity is the weight of a substance relative to that of an equal volume of water. If a mineral weighs 2.5 times as much as an equal volume of water, its specific gravity is 2.5. You can estimate a mineral's specific gravity simply by hefting a sample in your hand. If you practice with known minerals, you can develop a feel for specific gravity. Most common minerals have specific gravities of about 2.7. Metals have much greater specific gravities; for example, gold has the highest specific gravity of all minerals, 19. Lead is 11.3, silver is 10.5, and copper is 8.9.

Colour

Color is the most obvious property of a mineral, but it is commonly unreliable for identification. Color would be a reliable identification tool if all minerals were pure and had perfect crystal structures. However, both small amounts of chemical impurities and imperfections in crystal structure can dramatically alter color. For example, corundum (Al_2O_3) is normally a cloudy, translucent, brown or blue mineral. Addition of a small amount of chromium can convert corundum to the beautiful, clear, red gem known as ruby. A small quantity of iron or titanium turns corundum into the striking blue gem called sapphire.

Streak

When a mineral is rubbed across the white porceline plate, known as streak plate, it may leave a streak of mineral powder of distinctive colour. The colour of powder of mineral may sometimes be different than the color of the mineral.

Streak is the color of a fine powder of a mineral. Many minerals leave a streak of powder with a diagnostic color on the plate. Streak is commonly more reliable than the color of the mineral itself for identification.

Luster

The appearance of a mineral surface under reflected light is referred to as its mineral luster. It is described by several descriptive adjectives, such as metallic (metal like), adamantine (diamond like), vitreous (glass like), resinous (oil like), pearly or silky (pearl or silk like). The luster of nonmetallic minerals is usually described by self-explanatory words such as glassy, pearly, earthy, and resinous.

Although about 3500 minerals are known to exist in the Earth's crust, only a small number– between 50 and 100 are important because they are common or valuable.

Rock-Forming Minerals

The rock-forming minerals make up the bulk of most rocks in the Earth's crust. They are important to geologists simply because they are the most common minerals. They are olivine, pyroxene, amphibole, mica, the clay minerals, feldspar, quartz, calcite, and dolomite.

The first six minerals in this list are actually mineral "groups," in which each group contains several varieties with very similar chemical compositions, crystalline structures, and appearances.

Ore Minerals

Ore minerals are minerals from which metals or other elements can be profitably recovered. A few, such as native gold and native silver, are composed of a single element. However, most metals are chemically bonded to anions. Copper, lead, and zinc are commonly bonded to sulfur to form the important ore minerals chalcopyrite, galena , and sphalerite.

Industrial Minerals

Several minerals are industrially important, although they are not considered ore because they are mined for purposes other than the extraction of metals. Halite is mined for table salt, and gypsum is mined as the raw material for plaster and sheetrock. Apatite and other phosphorus minerals are sources of the phosphate fertilizers crucial to modern agriculture. Many limestones are made up of nearly pure calcite and are mined as the raw material of cement.

Geologists classify minerals according to their anions (negatively charged ions). Anions can be either simple or complex. A simple anion is a single negatively charged ion, such as O_2. Alternatively, two or more atoms can bond firmly together and acquire a negative charge to form a complex anion. Two common examples are the silicate, $(SiO_4)_4$, and carbonate, $(CO_3)_2$, complex anions. Each mineral group (except the native elements) is named for its anion. For example, the oxides all contain O_2, the silicates contain $(SiO_4)_4$, and the carbonates contain $(CO_3)_2$.

Native Elements

About 20 elements occur naturally in their native states as minerals. Fewer than ten, however, are common enough to be of economic importance. Gold, silver, platinum, and copper are all mined in their pure forms. Iron is rarely found in its native state in the Earth's crust, but metallic iron is common in certain types of meteorites. Native iron and nickel are thought to comprise most of the Earth's core. Native sulfur, used to manufacture sulfuric acid, insecticides, fertilizer, and rubber, is mined from volcanic craters, where it is deposited from gases emanating from the vents

Oxides

The oxides are a large group of minerals in which oxygen is combined with one or more metals. Oxide minerals are the most important ores of iron, manganese, tin, chromium, uranium, titanium, and several other industrial metals. Hematite (iron oxide, Fe_2O_3) occurs widely in many types of rocks and is the most abundant ore of iron. Although typically red in color, it occasionally occurs as black crystals used as semiprecious gems. Magnetite (Fe_3O_4), a naturally magnetic iron oxide, is another ore of iron. Spinel ($MgAl_2O_4$) often occurs as attractive red or blue crystals that are used as inexpensive, semiprecious gems. Synthetic spinels are also commonly used in jewelry. Ice, the oxide of hydrogen (H_2O), is a common mineral at the Earth's surface.

Sulfides

Sulfide minerals consist of sulfur combined with one or more metals. Many sulfides are extremely important ore minerals. They are the world's major sources of copper, lead, zinc, molybdenum, silver, cobalt, mercury, nickel, and several other metals. The most common sulfides are pyrite (FeS_2), chalcopyrite ($CuFeS_2$), galena (PbS), and sphalerite (ZnS).

Sulfates

The sulfate minerals contain the sulfate complex anion $(SO_4)_2$. Gypsum ($CaSO_4$ $2H_2O$) and anhydrite ($CaSO_4$) are two important industrial sulfates used to manufacture plaster and sheetrock. Both form by evaporation of seawater or salty lake water.

Phosphates

Phosphate minerals contain the complex anion $(PO_4)_3$. Apatite, $Ca_5(F,Cl,OH)(PO_4)_3$, is the substance that makes up both teeth and bones. Phosphate is an essential fertilizer in modern agriculture. It is mined from fossil bone beds near Tampa, Florida, and from great sedimentary apatite deposits in the northern Rocky Mountains.

Corbonates

The complex carbonate anion $(CO_3)_2$ is the basis of two common rock-forming minerals, calcite ($CaCO_3$) and dolomite [$CaMg(CO_3)_2$]. Most limestone is composed of calcite, and dolomite makes up the similar rock that is also called dolomite or sometimes dolostone. Limestone is mined as a raw in- gredient of cement. Aragonite is a polymorph of calcite that makes up the shells of many marine animals.

Silicates

The silicate minerals contain the $(SiO_4)_4$ complex anion. Silicates make up about 95 per cent of the Earth's crust. They are so abundant for two reasons. First, silicon and oxygen are the two most plentiful elements in the crust. Second, silicon and oxygen combine readily.

To understand the silicate minerals, remember four principles:

1. Every silicon atom surrounds itself with four oxygens. The bonds between each silicon and its four oxygens are very strong.
2. The silicon atom and its four oxygens form a pyramid-shaped structure called the silicate tetrahedron with silicon in the center and oxygens at the four corners. The silicate tetrahedron has a 4^- charge and forms the $(SiO_4)^{4-}$ complex anion. The silicate tetrahedron is the fundamental building block of all silicate minerals.
3. To make silicate minerals electrically neutral, other cations must combine with the silicate tetrahedra to balance their negative charges. (The lone exception is quartz, in which the positive charges on the silicon's exactly balance the negative ones on the oxy-gens.
4. Silicate tetrahedra commonly link together by sharing oxygens. Thus, two tetrahedra may share single oxygen, bonding the tetrahedral together.

SURFACE FEATURES AND PROCESSES

PHYSIOGRAPHIC OF THE EARTH

The Earth's continental crust consists of three discernible units, each with their own characteristics. These units are cratons, mountain belts, and continental margins.

Cratons

All of the continental masses on the Earth have a central foundation of very old basement rock. Basement rock is composed of mixtures of ancient granite, gneiss, schist, volcanic, plutonic, and sedimentary rocks. Some of the Earth's oldest rocks are found in this geologic formation. Basement rock that is exposed at the Earth's surface is called shield. The shields extend for thousands of kilometers and dip ever so slightly from a slightly elevated center. Layers of younger sedimentary strata up to 2000 meters deep cover most of the basement rock. These sedimentary deposits are sometimes called the platform of the continents. The deposits making up the platform were laid down in shallow seas in repeated episodes over the last 600 million years.

The platform and the basement rock together form a craton. The continents of Australia, North America, South America, and Africa each have a single continuous craton forming their nucleus. Eurasia is composed several distinct cratons that are separated from each other by the Alps, Ural, and Himalaya mountain belts.

The craton of North America has been relatively stable for about 600 million years. Prior to this period, the North American continent saw several periods of very active growth with the amalgamation of once distinct cratons and the addition of rock along it's margins. Geologic evidence suggests that North America is made up of several once independent minicontinents. Scientists believe that the amalgamation of these minicontinents into the core of the North America continent was complete by about 2.5 billion years ago.

On a global scale, about 70 per cent of the Earth's continental crust was formed by 2.5 billion years ago. Over the next 2 billion years, the planet's continents would continue to growth through the accretion of sedimentary rock and the addition of igneous rocks along the continental margins. This growth was also driven by tectonic processes. The accretion of sedimentary rock occurred with the collision of tectonic plates which pushed ocean sediments onto the continents. Plate subduction created enough heat to melt rock into magma beneath the margins of the continents. This magma then migrated upward through the crust to form intrusive and extrusive igneous features and deposits. This process also added significant mass to the continents.

Mountain Belts

Numerous mountain belts are also found on the continents. These features are often located on the edge of cratons. Mountain belts are the result of tectonic processes that cause to crustal plates to collide. This collision results in the folding and faulting of rock, igneous intrusive and extrusive activity, and metamorphism. The elevated relief common to mountain belts is generally caused by the compression of rock into a smaller area. Uplift may also be caused by the upward migration of magma through the crust to produce granitic batholiths. Some mountains occur in isolation like Mount Rainier in the state of Washington, USA. These features are volcanic and are produced by localized extrusive igneous activity.

Continental Margin

Located between the terrestrial continents and the ocean basins is the continental margin. Two basic types of continental margin are recognized: active and passive. Active continental margins occur in the Pacific ocean. Active margins are generally narrow tectonically active areas. They are also associated with earthquakes, oceanic trenches, and volcanoes. Passive continental margins are relatively wide and have a lack of volcanic activity and few earthquakes. The continental margin is actually made up of three structures: the continental shelf, the continental slope and the continental rise. Both the continental shelf and slope are structurally part of the continents, even though they are below the sea surface.

The continental shelf is a shallow (average depth 130 meters) gently sloping part of the continental crust that borders the continents. The extent of this feature varies from tens of meters to a maximum width of about 1300 kilometers.

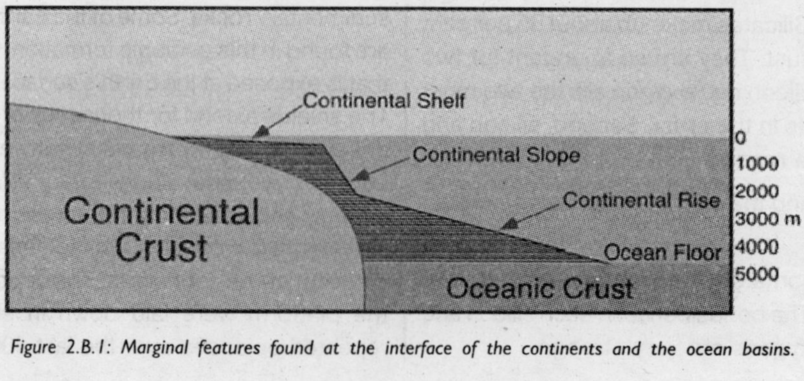

Figure 2.B.1: Marginal features found at the interface of the continents and the ocean basins.

The continental slope extends from the continental shelf at an average depth of about 135 meters. The base of this steeply sloping (from 1 to 25°, average about 4°) topographic feature occurs at a depth of approximately 2000 meters, marking the edge of the continents. The width of the slope varies from 20 to 100 kilometers. The boundary between the continental slope and shelf is called the continental shelf break.

At the base of the continental slope an accumulation of sediments may develop. This accumulation of sediments is properly known as the continental rise. The continental rise is composed of a number abyssal fans that run side-by-side along the edge of the continental slope. Abyssal fans are usually associated with a deep submarine canyon cut into the continental slope. Under water abyssal fans can be compared to terrestrial landforms known as alluvial fans. The sediments that make up this feature are transported down the continental slope by turbidity currents, underwater landslides, and several different processes that move clay, silt, and sand. Most of this sediment is terrestrial in origin. The depth of the continental rise ranges from 2000 to 5000 meters deep. The continental rise can be as much as 300 kilometers wide.

TOPOGRAPHY OF THE TERRESTRIAL SURFACE

The Earth's terrestrial surface in to six different categories based on topography. Most of the Earth's terrestrial surface is dominated by reltively flat low and high plains. The low plains tend to be areas of sediment deposition because of their low elevation. The high plains can have elevations as high as 600 meters and are more strongly influenced by erosion. Both of these topographic features are often associated with craton's and their exposed shield and platform surfaces. Local relief on both types of plains is less than 100 meters. The three types of mountains shown in have local relief in excess of 500 meters and slope angles greater than 5°. Many of the "low" mountains are very old structures that have been reduced in height by erosion. Plateaus have altitudes that are greater than the high plains but less than mountains. Local relief of this topographic feature varies between 100 and 500 meters. Some plateaus are the remnants of eroded mountains. Others have formed because of large-scale block faulting.

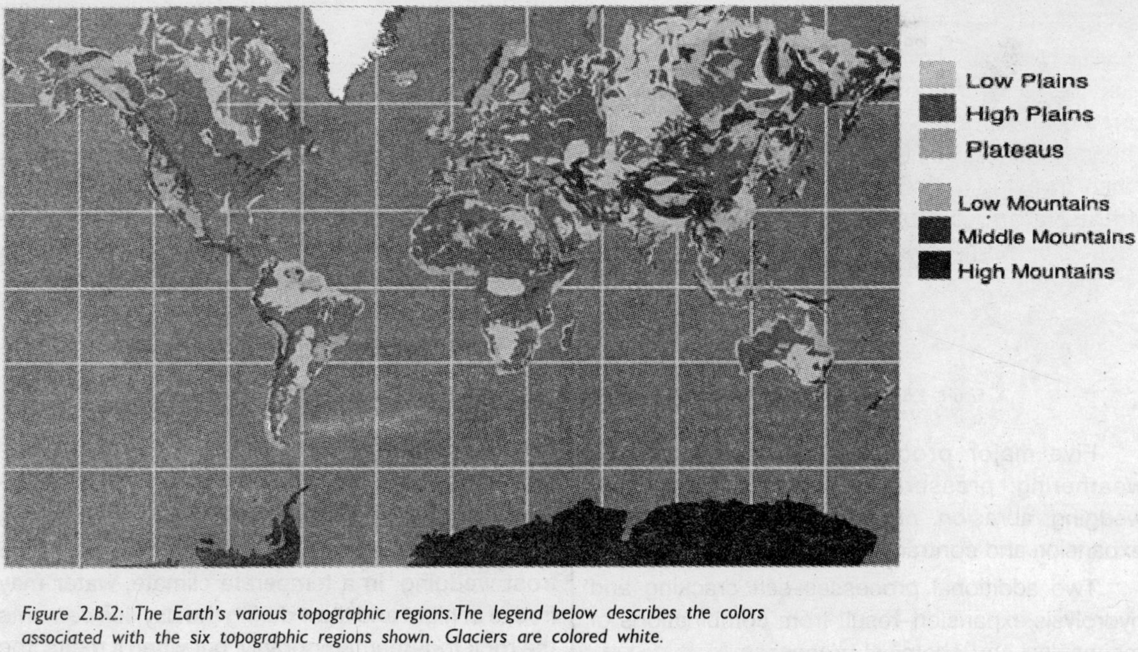

Figure 2.B.2: The Earth's various topographic regions. The legend below describes the colors associated with the six topographic regions shown. Glaciers are colored white.

WEATHERING, EROSION, TRANSPORTATION AND DEPOSITION OF EARTH'S MATERIAL.

WEATHERING

Weathering is the decomposition and disintegration of rocks and minerals at the Earth's surface. Weathering itself involves little or no movement of the decomposed rocks and minerals. This material accumulates where it forms and overlies unweathered bedrock.

Erosion is the removal of weathered rocks and minerals by moving water, wind, glaciers, and gravity. After a rock fragment has been eroded from its place of origin, it may be transported large distances by those same agents: flowing water, wind, ice, and gravity. When the wind or water slows down and loses energy or, in the case of glaciers, when the ice melts, transport stops and sediment is deposited. These four processes–weathering, erosion, transportation, and deposition–work together to modify the Earth's surface.

The environment at the Earth's surface is corrosive to most materials. An iron tool left outside will rust. Even stone is vulnerable to corrosion. As a result, ancient stone cities have fallen to ruin. Over longer periods of time, rock outcrops and entire mountain ranges wear away.

Weathering occurs by both mechanical and chemical processes. Mechanical weathering reduces solid rock to rubble but does not alter the chemical composition of rocks and minerals. In contrast, chemical weathering occurs when air and water chemically react with rock to alter its composition and mineral content. These chemical changes are analogous to rusting in that the final products differ both physically and chemically from the starting material.

Mechanical Weathering

Mechanical weathering breaks large rocks into smaller ones but does not alter the rock's chemical nature or its minerals. Think of grinding a rock in a crusher; the fragments are no different from the parent rock, except that they are smaller.

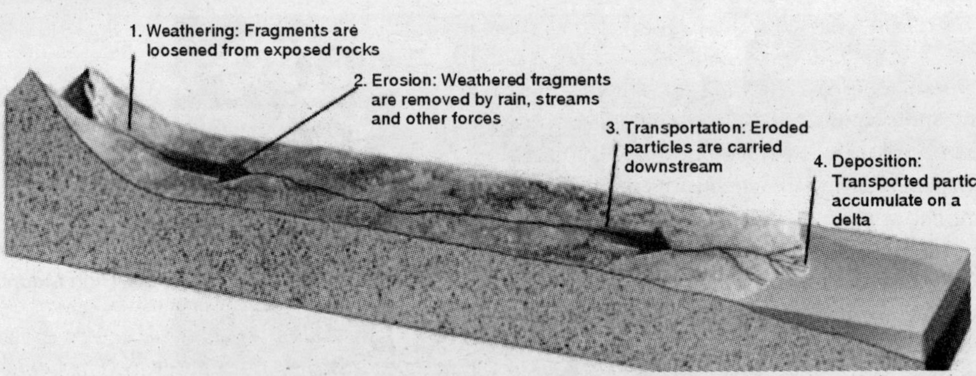

Figure 2.B. 3 : A schematic view shows weathering, erosion, transport, and deposition of sediment.

Five major processes cause mechanical weathering: pressure-release fracturing, frost wedging, abrasion, organic activity, and thermal expansion and contraction.

Two additional processes–salt cracking and hydrolysis expansion–result from combinations of mechanical and chemical processes.

Frost Wedging

Water expands when it freezes. If water accumulates in a crack and then freezes, its expansion pushes the rock apart in a process called frost wedging. In a temperate climate, water may freeze at night and thaw during the day. Ice cements the rock together temporarily, but when it melts, the rock fragments may tumble from a steep cliff. If you hike or climb in mountains when the daily freeze–thaw cycle occurs, be careful; rockfall due to frost wedging is common. Experienced climbers travel in the early morning when the water is still frozen and ice holds the rock together.

Abrasion

Many rocks along a stream or beach are rounded and smooth. They have been shaped by collisions with other rocks as they tumbled downstream and with silt and sand carried by moving water. As particles collide, their sharp edges and corners wear away. The mechanical wearing and grinding of rock surfaces by friction and impact is called abrasion.

Thermal Weathering

Rocks at the Earth's surface are exposed to daily and yearly cycles of heating and cooling. They expand when they are heated and contract when they cool. When temperature changes rapidly, the surface of a rock heats or cools faster than its interior and, as a result, the surface expands or contracts faster than the interior. The resulting forces may fracture the rock.

Chemical Weathering

The most important processes of chemical weathering are dissolution, hydrolysis, and oxidation. W1ater, carbon dioxide, acids and bases, and oxygen are common substances that cause these processes to decompose rocks.

Dissolution

If you put a crystal of halite (rock salt) in water, it dissolves and the ions disperse to form a solution. Halite dissolves so rapidly and completely that this mineral is rare in moist environments.

A small proportion of water molecules spontaneously dissociate (break apart) to form an equal number of hydrogen ions (H^+) and hydroxyl ions (OH^-)

Many common chemicals dissociate in water to increase either the hydrogen or the hydroxyl ion concentration. For example, HCl (hydrochloric acid) dissociates to release H^+ and Cl^- ions. The H^+ ions increase the hydrogen ion concentration and the solution becomes acid. In a similar manner, NaOH dissociates to increase the hydroxyl ion concentration and the solution becomes a base. Hydrogen and hydroxyl ions are chemically reactive and therefore acids and bases are much more corrosive than pure water.

Hydrolysis

During dissolution, a mineral dissolves but does not otherwise react chemically with the solution. However, during hydrolysis, water reacts with a mineral to form a new mineral with the water incorporated into its crystal structure. Many common minerals weather by hydrolysis. For example, feldspar, the most abundant mineral in the Earth's crust, weathers by hydrolysis to form clay. As feldspar converts to clay, flowing water carries off soluble cations such as potassium. The water combines with the less soluble ions to form clay minerals.

Oxidation

Many elements react with atmospheric oxygen, O_2. Iron rusts when it reacts with water and oxygen. Rusting is one example of a more general process called oxidation.

Oxidation reactions are so common in nature that pure metals are rare in the Earth's crust, and most metallic elements exist in nature as compounds. Only a few metals, such as gold, silver, copper, and platinum commonly occur in their pure states.

Chemical and Mechanical Weathering Operating Together

Chemical and mechanical weathering work together, often on the same rock at the same time. Chemical processes generally act only on the surface of a solid object, so the reaction speeds up if the surface area increases. Think of a burning log; the fire starts on the outside and works its way toward the interior. A split log burns faster because the surface area is greater. Mechanical processes crack rocks, thereby exposing more surface area for chemical agents to work on.

EXFOLIATION

Granite commonly fractures by exfoliation, a process in which large plates or shells split away like the layers of an onion. The plates may be only 10 or 20 centimeters thick near the surface, but they thicken with depth. Because exfoliation fractures are usually absent below a depth of 50 to 100 meters, they seem to be a result of exposure of the granite at the Earth's surface.

Exfoliation is frequently explained as a form of pressure-release fracturing. However, many geologists suggest that hydrolysis may contribute to exfoliation. During hydrolysis, feldspars and other silicate minerals react to form clay. As a result of the addition of water, clays have a greater volume than that of the original minerals. Thus a chemical reaction (hydrolysis) forms clay, and the mechanical expansion of the clay contributes to the ex foliation fractures.

Formation of soil, sediments and sedimentary rocks

Mechanical weathering produces both large rock fragments and small particles such as sand and silt. Chemical weathering forms clay and dissolved ions. Some of these weathering products accumulate on the Earth over bed rock. This material is called regolith. Soil scientists define soil as upper layers of regolith that support plant growth.

Soil commonly consists of sand, silt, clay, and organic material. Clay particles are so small and pack so tightly that water does not flow through them readily. In fact, even gases have trouble passing through clay-rich soils, so plants growing in clay soils suffer from lack of oxygen. In contrast, water and oxygen travel easily through loosely packed sandy soils. The most fertile soils contain a mixture of sand, clay, and silt as well as generous amounts of organic matter. Such a mixture is called loam.

When litter decomposes sufficiently that you can no longer determine the origin of individual pieces, it becomes humus. Humus is an essential component of most fertile soils. If you pour a small amount of water into soil rich in humus, the soil absorbs most of the water. Humus retains so much moisture that humus-rich soil swells after a rain and shrinks during dry spells. This alternate shrinking and swelling loosens the soil, allowing roots to grow into it easily. A rich layer of humus also insulates the soil from excessive heat and cold and reduces water loss by evaporation. Humus also retains nutrients in soil and makes them available to plants.

SOIL-FORMING FACTORS

Six factors control soil characteristics: parent rock, climate, rates of plant growth and decay, slope angle and aspect, time, and transport.

PARENT ROCK

The texture and composition of a soil depends partly on its parent rock. For example, when granite decomposes, the feldspar converts to clay and the rock releases quartz as sand grains. If the clay leaches into the B horizon, a sandy soil forms. In contrast, because basalt contains no quartz, soil formed from basalt is likely to be rich in clay and contain only small amounts of sand. Nutrient abundance also depends in part on the parent rock. For example, a pure quartz sandstone contains no nutrients, and soil formed on it must get its nutrients from outside sources.

CLIMATE

Temperature and rainfall affect soil formation. Rain seeps downward through soil, but several other factors pull the water back upward. Roots suck soil water toward the surface, and water near the surface evaporates. In addition, water is electrically attracted to soil particles. If the pore size between particles is small enough, capillary action draws water upward.

During a rainstorm, water seeps through the A horizon, dissolving soluble ions such as calcium, magnesium, potassium, and sodium. In arid and semiarid regions, when the water reaches the B horizon, capillary action and plant roots then draw it back up toward the surface, where it evaporates or is incorporated into plant tissue. After the water escapes, many of its dissolved ions precipitate in the B horizon, encrusting the soil with salts. A soil of this type is a pedocal. This process often deposits enough calcium carbonate to form a hard cement called caliche in the soil. In the Imperial

Valley in California, for example, irrigation water contains high concentrations of calcium carbonate. A thick continuous layer of caliche forms in the soil as the water evaporates. To continue growing crops, farmers must then rip this layer apart with heavy machinery.

Because nutrients concentrate when water evaporates, many pedocals are fertile if irrigation water is available. However, salts often concentrate so much that they become toxic to plants. All streams contain small concentrations of dissolved salts. If arid or semiarid soils are intensively irrigated, salts can accumulate until plants cannot grow.

In a wet climate, water seeping down through the soil leaches soluble ions from both the A and B horizons. The less soluble elements, such as aluminum, iron, and some silicon, remain behind, accumulating in the B horizon to form a soil type called a pedalfer.The subsoil in a pedalfer is commonly rich in clay, which is mostly aluminum and silicon, and has the reddish color of iron oxide. In regions of very high rainfall, such as a tropical rainforest, so much water seeps through the soil that it leaches away nearly all the soluble cations. Only very insoluble aluminum and iron minerals remain. Soil of this type is called a laterite. Laterites are often colored rust-red by iron oxide. A highly aluminous laterite, called bauxite, is the world's main type of aluminum ore.

The second important component of climate, average annual temperature, affects soil formation in two ways. First, chemical reactions proceed more rapidly in warm temperatures than in cooler conditions, so chemical weathering is faster in warmer climates than in cold ones. Second, plant growth and decay are temperature dependent as discussed below.

RATES OF GROWTH AND DECAY OF ORGANIC MATERIAL

In the tropics, plants grow and decay rapidly all year long. When leaves and stems decay, the nutrients are quickly absorbed by the growing plants. As a result, little humus accumulates and few nutrients are stored in the soil. The Arctic, on the other hand, is so cold that plant growth and decay are slow. Therefore, litter and humus form slowly and Arctic soils contain little organic matter.

SLOPE ASPECT AND STEEPNESS

Aspect is the orientation of a slope with respect to the Sun. In the semiarid American West, thick soils and dense forests cover the cool, shady north slopes of hills, but thin soils and grass dominate hot, dry southern exposures. The reason for this difference is that in the Northern Hemisphere more water evaporates from the hot, sunny southern slopes. Therefore, fewer plants grow, weathering occurs slowly, and soil development is retarded. The moister northern slopes weather more deeply to form thicker soils. In general, hillsides have thin soils and valleys are covered by thicker soil, because soil erodes from hills and accumulates in valleys. When hilly regions were first settled and farmed, people naturally planted their crops in the valley bottoms, where the soil was rich and water was abundant. Recently, as population has expanded, farmers have moved to the thinner, less stable hillside soils.

TIME

Most chemical weathering occurs at the relatively low temperatures of the Earth's surface. Consequently, chemical weathering goes on slowly in most places, and time becomes an important factor in determining the extent of weathering. Feldspars weather to form clay, whereas quartz does not decompose easily. In geologically young soils, the decomposition of feldspars may be incomplete and the soils are likely to be sandy. As soils mature, more feldspars decompose, and the clay content increases.

Formation of sediments and sedimentary rocks

Sediments are particles that settle to the bottom of a basin of deposition such as a lake, river, sea, etc. Although many sedimentary rocks form as the result of the erosion (picking up), transportation (carrying away), deposition (laying down), and lithification (compaction and/or cementation) of sediments (mechanical processes), some are the result of chemical processes, and some are the result of the accumulation and lithification of organic material (plants or shells).

Weathering decomposes bedrock. Flowing water, wind, gravity, and glaciers then erode the decomposed rock, transport it downslope, and finally deposit it on the sea coast or in lakes and river valleys. Finally, the loose sediment is cemented to form hard sedimentary rock.

The sedimentary rocks form an outer skin on the Earth's crust, covering three-quarters of the continental areas and most of the sea floor. They vary in thickness up to 10 km. Nevertheless, they only comprise about 5% of the crust.

Most sedimentary rocks are of secondary origin, in that they consist of detrital material derived by the breakdown of pre-existing rocks. Indeed, it has been variously estimated that shales and sandstones, both of mechanical derivation, account for between 75 and 95% of all sedimentary rocks. However, certain sedimentary rocks are the products of chemical or biochemical precipitation whereas others are of organic origin. Thus, the sedimentary rocks can be divided into two principal groups, namely, the clastic (detrital) or exogenetic, and the

non-clastic or endogenetic types. Nevertheless, one factor that all sedimentary rocks have in common is that they are deposited, and this gives rise to their most noteworthy characteristic, that is, they are bedded or stratified.

most sedimentary rocks are formed from the breakdown products of pre-existing rocks. Accordingly, the rate at which denudation takes place acts as a control on the rate of sedimentation, which in turn affects the character of a sediment.

The particles of which most sedimentary rocks are composed have undergone varying amounts of transportation. The amount of transport together with the agent responsible, be it water, wind or ice, play an important role in determining the character of a sediment. For instance, transport over short distances usually means that the sediment is unsorted (the exception being beach sands), as does transportation by ice. With lengthier transport by water or wind, not only does the material become better sorted but it is further reduced in size.

The composition of a sedimentary rock depends partly on the composition of the parent material and the stability of its component minerals, and partly on the type of action to which the parent rock was subjected and the length of time it had to suffer such action. The least stable minerals tend to be those that are developed in environments very different from those experienced at the

Earth's surface. In fact, quartz, and, to a much lesser extent, mica, are the only common detrital constituents of igneous and metamorphic rocks that are found in abundance in sediments. Most of the other minerals are ultimately broken down chemically to give rise to clay minerals. The more mature a sedimentary rock is, the more it approaches a stable end product, and very mature sediments are likely to have experienced more than one cycle of sedimentation.

The type of climatic regime in which a deposit accumulates and the rate at which this takes place also affect the stability and maturity of the resultant sedimentary product. For example, chemical decay is inhibited in arid regions so that less stable minerals are more likely to survive than in humid regions.

In order to turn unconsolidated sediment into solid rock, it must be lithified. Lithification involves two processes, consolidation and cementation. The amount of consolidation that takes place within a sediment depends, first, on its composition and texture and, second, on the pressures acting on it, notably that due to the weight of overburden. Consolidation of sediments deposited in water also involves dewatering, that is, the expulsion of connate water from the sediments. The porosity of a sediment is reduced as consolidation takes place, and, as the individual particles become more closely packed, they may even be deformed. Pressures developed during consolidation may lead to the differential solution of minerals and the authigenic growth of new ones.

Cementation involves the bonding together of sedimentary particles by the precipitation of material in the pore spaces. This reduces the porosity. The cementing material may be derived by partial intrastratal solution of grains or may be introduced into the pore spaces from an extraneous source by circulating waters. Conversely, cement may be removed from a sedimentary rock by leaching. The type of cement and, more importantly, the amount, affect the strength of a sedimentary rock. The type also influences its colour. For example, sand-stones with siliceous or calcium carbonate cement are usually whitish grey, those with sideritic (iron carbonate) cement are buff coloured, whereas a red colour is indicative of hematitic (iron oxide) cement and brown of limonite (hydrated iron oxide). However, sedimentary rocks are frequently cemented by more than one material.

Physiographic Features and River Basins in India

The land of India displays great physical variation. Geologically, the Peninsular Plateau constitutes one of the ancient landmasses on the earth's surface. It was supposed to be one of the most stable land blocks. The Himalayas and the Northern Plains are the most recent landforms. From the view point of geology, Himalayan mountains form an unstable zone. The whole mountain system of Himalaya represents a very youthful topography with high peaks, deep valleys and fast flowing rivers. The northern plains are formed of alluvial deposits. The peninsular plateau is composed of igneous and metamorphic rocks with gently rising hills and wide valleys.

MAJOR PHYSIOGRAPHIC DIVISIONS

The physical features of India can be grouped under the following physiographic divisions:

(i) The Himalayan Mountains

(ii) The Northern Plains

(iii) The Peninsular Plateau

(iv) The Indian Desert

(v) The Coastal Plains

(vi) The Islands

THE HIMALAYAN MOUNTAINS

The Himalayas, geologically young and structurally fold mountains stretch over the northern borders of India. These mountain ranges run in a west-east direction from the Indus to the Brahmaputra. The Himalayas represent the loftiest and one of the most rugged mountain barriers of the world. They form an arc, which covers a distance of about 2,400 Km. Their width varies from 400 Km in Kashmir to 150 Km in Arunachal Pradesh. The altitudinal variations are greater in the eastern half than those in the western half. The Himalaya consists of three parallel ranges in its longitudinal extent. A number of valleys lie between these ranges. The northern most range is known as the Great or Inner Himalayas or the 'Himadri'. It is the most continuous range consisting of the loftiest peaks with an average height of 6,000 metres. It contains all the prominent Himalayan peaks.

The folds of Great Himalayas are asymmetrical in nature. The core of this part of Himalayas is composed of granite. It is perennially snow bound, and a number of glaciers descend from this range.

The range lying to the south of the Himadri forms the most rugged mountain system and is known as Himachal or lesser Himalaya. The ranges are mainly composed of highly compressed and altered rocks. The altitude varies between 3,700 and 4,500 metres and the average width is of 50 Km. While the Pir Panjal range forms the longest and the most important range, the Dhaula Dhar and the Mahabharat ranges are also prominent ones. This range consists of the famous valley of Kashmir, the Kangra and Kullu Valley in Himachal Pradesh. This region is well known for its hill stations.

The outer most range of the Himalayas is called the Shiwaliks. They extend over a width of 10-50 Km and have an altitude varying between 900 and 1100 metres. These ranges are composed of unconsolidated sediments brought down by rivers from the main Himalayan ranges located farther north. These valleys are covered with thick gravel and alluvium. The longitudinal valley lying between lesser Himalaya and the Shiwaliks are known as Duns. Dehra Dun, Kotli Dun and Patli Dun are some of the well-known Duns. Besides the longitudinal divisions, the Himalayas have been divided on the basis of regions from west to east. These divisions have been demarcated by river valleys. For example, the part of Himalayas lying between Indus and Satluj has been traditionally known as Punjab Himalaya but it is also known regionally as Kashmir and Himachal Himalaya from west to east respectively. The part of the Himalayas lying between Satluj and Kali rivers is known as Kumaon Himalayas. The Kali and Tista rivers demarcate the Nepal Himalayas and the part lying between Tista and Dihang rivers is known as Assam Himalayas. There are regional names also in these broad categories. Find out some regional names of the Himalayas

The Brahmaputra marks the eastern most boundary of the Himalayas. Beyond the Dihang gorge, the Himalayas bend sharply to the south and spread along the eastern boundary of India. They are known as the Purvanchal or the Eastern hills and mountains. These hills running through the north-eastern states are mostly composed of strong sandstones which are sedimentary rocks. Covered with dense forests, they mostly run as parallel ranges and valleys. The Purvanchal comprises the Patkai hills, the Naga hills, Manipur hills and the Mizo hills.

The Northern Plain

The northern plain has been formed by the interplay of the three major river systems, namely-the Indus, the Ganga and the Brahmaputra along with their tributaries. This plain is formed of alluvial soil. The deposition of alluvium in a vast basin lying at the foothills of the Himalaya over millions of years, formed this fertile plain. It spreads over an area of 7 lakh sq. km. The plain being about 2400 Km long and 240 to 320 Km broad, is a densely populated physiographic division. With a rich soil cover combined with adequate water supply and favourable climate it is agriculturally a very productive part of India.

The Northern Plain is broadly divided into three sections. The Western part of the Northern Plain is referred to as the Punjab Plains. Formed by the Indus and its tributaries, the larger part of this plain lies in Pakistan. The Indus and its tributaries–the Jhelum, the Chenab, the Ravi, the Beas and the Satluj originate in the Himalaya. This section of the plain is dominated by the doabs.

The Ganga plain extends between Ghaggar and Teesta rivers. It is spread over the states of North India, Haryana, Delhi, U.P., Bihar, partly Jharkhand and West Bengal to its East, particularly in Assam lies the Brahmaputra plain. The northern plains are generally desribed as flat land with no variations in its relief. It is not true. These vast plains also have diverse relief features. According to the variations in relief features, the Northern plains can be divided into four regions. The rivers, after descending from the mountains deposit pebbles in a narrow belt of about 8 to 16 km in width lying parallel to the slopes of the Shiwaliks. It is known as bhabar. All the streams disappear in this bhabar belt. South of this belt, the streams and rivers re-emerge and create a wet, swampy and marshy region known as terai. This was a thickly forested region full of wildlife. The forests have been cleared to create agricultural land and to settle migrants from Pakistan after partition. Locate Dudhwa National Park in this region. The largest part of the northern plain is formed of older alluvium. They lie above the flood plains of the rivers and present a terrace like feature. This part is known as bhangar.

The soil in this region contains calcareous deposites locally known as kankar. The newer, younger deposits of the flood plains are called khadar. They are renewed almost every year and so are fertile, thus, ideal for intensive agriculture.

The Peninsular Plateau

The Peninsular plateau is a tableland composed of the old crystalline, igneous and metamorphic rocks. It was formed due to the breaking and drifting of the Gondwana land and thus, making it a part of the oldest landmass. The plateau has broad and shallow valleys and rounded hills. This plateau consists of two broad divisions, namely, the Central Highlands and the Deccan Plateau.

The part of the Peninsular plateau lying to the north of the Narmada river covering a major area of the Malwa plateau is known as the Central Highlands. The Vindhyan range is bounded by the Central

Highlands on the south and the Aravalis on the northwest. The further westward extension gradually merges with the sandy and rocky desert of Rajasthan. The flow of the rivers draining this region, namely the Chambal, the Sind, the Betwa and Ken is from southwest to northeast, thus indicating the slope. The Central Highlands are wider in the west but narrower in the east.

The eastward extensions of this plateau are locally known as the Bundelkhand and Baghelkhand. The Chotanagpur plateau marks the further eastward extension, drained by the Damodar river.

The Deccan Plateau is a triangular landmass that lies to the south of the river Narmada. The Satpura range flanks its broad base in the north while the Mahadev, the Kaimur hills and the Maikal range form its eastern extensions. Locate these hills and ranges in the physical map of India. The Deccan Plateau is higher in the west and slopes gently eastwards. An extension of the Plateau is also visible in the northeast- locally known as the Meghalaya and Karbi-Anglong Plateau. It is separated by a fault from the Chotanagpur Plateau. Three Prominent hill ranges from the west to east are the Garo, the Khasi and the Jaintia Hills. The Western Ghats and the Eastern Ghats mark the western and the eastern edges of the Deccan Plateau respectively. Western ghats lie parallel to the western coast. They are continuous and can be crossed through passes only. Locate the Thal, Bhor and the Pal Ghats in the Physical map of India.

One of the distinct features of the peninsular plateau is the black soil area known as Decean Trap. This is of volcanic origin hence the rocks are igneous. Actually these rocks have denuded over time and are responsible for the formation of black soil. The Aravali Hills lie on the western and northwestern margins of the peninsular plateau. These are highly eroded hills and are found as broken hills. They extend from Gujarat to Delhi in a southwest-northeast direction.

The Indian Desert

The Indian desest lies towards the western margins of the Aravali Hills. It is an undulating sandy plain covered with sand dunes. This region receives very low rainfall below 150 mm per year. It has arid climate with low vegetation cover. Streams appear during the rainy season. Soon after they disappear into the sand as they do not have enough water to reach the sea. Luni is the only lárge river in this region.

The Coastal Plains

The Peninsular plateau is flanked by stretch of narrow coastal strips, running along the Arabian Sea on the west and the Bay of Bengal on the east. The western coast, sandwiched between the Western Ghats and the Arabian Sea, is a narrow plain. It consists of three sections. The northern part of the coast is called the Konkan (Mumbai - Goa), the central stretch is called the Kannad Plain while the southern stretch is referred to as the Malabar coast.

The Islands

Lakshadweep Islands group lying close to the Malabar coast of Kerala. This group of islands is composed of small coral isalnds. Earlier they were known as Laccadive, Minicoy and Amindive. In 1973 these were named as Lakshadweep. It covers small area of 32 sq km. Kavaratti island is the administrative headquarters of Lakshadweep. This island group has great diversity of flora and fauna. The Pitli island, which is uninhabited, has a bird sanctuary.

ENERGY BALANCE OF THE EARTH'S SURFACE PROCESSES

Energy Balance

Available net radiation is used to do work in the Earth system. The principal use of this energy is in the phase change of water (latent heat, LE), changing the temperature of the air (sensible heat, H), and subsurface (ground heat, G) or,

$$Q^* = H + LE + G$$

Though there are other uses for net radiation like photosynthesis and the weathering of rocks, it is the three previously stated uses that are most important. LE, H, and G involve non-radiative transfers of heat. That is, conduction or convection/advection are responsible for the transfer of heat, not electromagnetic radiation.

When work is done, like heating the air above the surface, there is a transfer of energy (heat) from one place to the next. To illustrate the transfer of energy we'll use arrows either pointing away from or toward the surface of the Earth to indicate the direction of heat transfer. We will also use positive and negative signs to indicate that heat is being added to, or taken away from a body. Following the conventions of Sellers (1965) and Oke (1987), non-radiative fluxes directed away from a surface are positive. Thus positive values indicates a loss of heat from the surface while negative values indicate a gain.

SENSIBLE HEAT TRANSFER (H)

Figure 2.B. 4 : Sensible heat transfer

Sensible heat is heat energy transferred between the surface and air when there is a difference in temperature between them. A change in temperature over distance is called a "temperature gradient". In this case, it is a vertical temperature gradient, i.e., between the surface and the air above. We feel the transfer of sensible heat as a rise or fall in the temperature of the air. Heat is initially transferred into the air by conduction as air molecules collide with those of the surface. As the air warms it circulates upwards via convection. Thus the transfer of sensible heat is accomplished in a two-step process. Because air is such a poor conductor of heat, it is convection that is the most efficient way of transferring sensible heat into the air.

When the surface is warmer than the air above, heat will be transferred upwards into the air as a **positive sensible heat transfer**. The transfer of heat raises the air's temperature but cools the surface. If the air is warmer than the surface, heat is transferred from the air to the surface creating a **negative sensible heat transfer**. If heat is transferred out of the air, the air cools and the surface warms. This situation may take place at night when the sun goes down and there is no input of solar radiation. At this time, the ground cools due to longwave emission and the air directly above the surface is warmer.

LATENT HEAT TRANSFER (LE)

When energy is added to water it will change states or phase. The phase change of a liquid to a gas is called **evaporation**. If we could see down to the molecular level we would find water being comprised of cluster of water molecules (H_2O). The clusters are bound together by bonding between the hydrogen atoms of water molecules. The heat added during evaporation breaks the bonds between the clusters creating individual molecules that escape the surface as a gas. The heat used in the phase change from a liquid to a gas is called the **latent heat of vaporization**. We say it is "latent" because it is being stored in the water molecules to later be released during the condensation process. We can't sense or feel latent heat as it does not raise the temperature of the water molecules.

When evaporation is taking place we say there is a **positive latent heat flux** (transfer). A positive latent heat flux (Figure 2.B. 5) is illustrated with an arrow pointing up away from the surface of the earth. This indicates that the surface is losing energy to the air above. Evaporation is a cooling process for a surface because energy is removed from the water as molecules escape the surface. This causes the surface temperature to decrease. You've probably experienced this cooling when water or sweat evaporates from your skin.

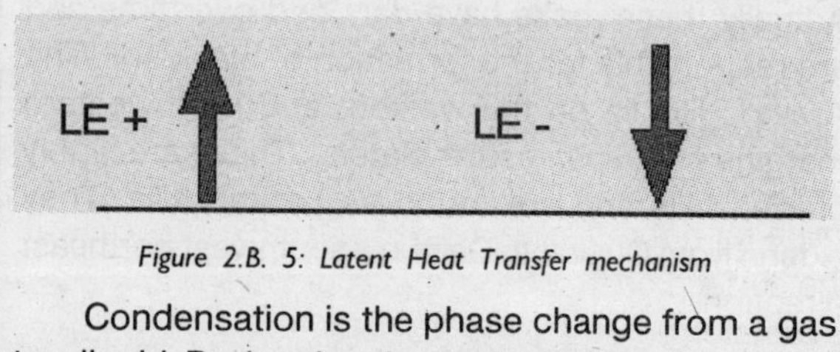

Figure 2.B. 5: Latent Heat Transfer mechanism

Condensation is the phase change from a gas to a liquid. During the phase change, the latent heat that was taken up during evaporation is released from the water molecule and passed into the surrounding air. During this process latent heat is converted to sensible heat causing an increase in the temperature of the air.

When radiation is absorbed by the Earth it will raise the temperature of the surface. But if the surface is water, some of that energy is used in evaporation rather than heating the water. As a result, with equal inputs of energy to land and water surfaces, land will heat up more than water. This is one of the reasons why it is cooler near large bodies of water.

GROUND HEAT TRANSFER (G)

The third major use of radiant energy is to warm the subsurface of the Earth. Heat is transferred from the surface downwards via conduction. Like in the case of sensible heat transfer, a temperature gradient must exist between the surface and the subsurface for heat transfer to occur. Heat is transferred downwards when the surface is warmer than the subsurface (positive ground heat flux). If the subsurface is warmer than the surface then heat is transferred upwards (negative ground heat flux). The transfer of energy to and from the surface varies over the course of a day. Figure 2.B. 6 shows the relative amounts and direction of energy flow during the day and night for a moist surface. During the day net radiation is a positive value as incoming radiation exceeds outgoing radiation allowing the surface to gain energy. The energy is distributed over the three major categories of energy use, LE, H, and G. During the day, the available radiant energy is used to evaporate water into the air, raising the air's humidity. Sensible heat is transferred upwards to warm the air above the surface. Heat is also conducted down into the subsurface. At night the processes reverse. At night with no incoming solar radiation there is more outgoing radiation than incoming creating a negative value for net radiation. Under these circumstances the surface cools due to a loss of energy and heat is transferred from the air toward the surface. As air cools through the evening the loss of energy allow condensation to occur, so long as the air's humidity is at or near saturation. Notice that the arrow for the ground heat flux G is pointing upward toward the surface. This indicates that the energy that had been stored in the subsurface during the day is now conducted toward the surface. This occurs as the surface is cooler than the subsurface.

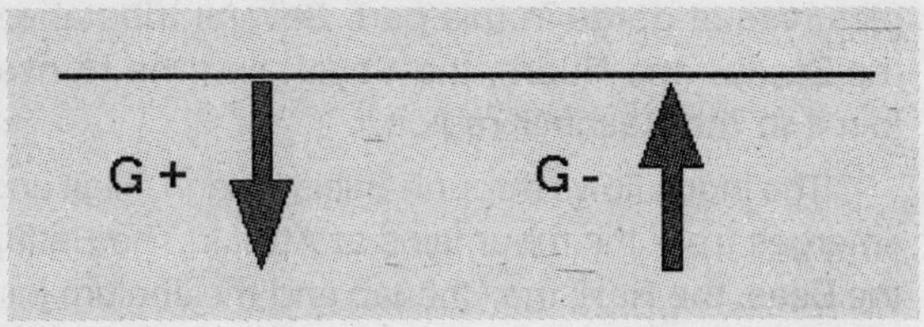

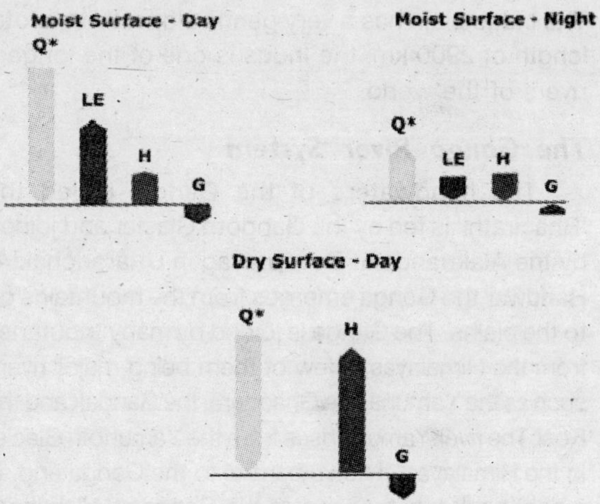

Figure 2.B. 6: Types of energy balances.

RIVER BASIN IN INDIA

The drainage systems of India are mainly controlled by the broad relief features of the subcontinent. Accordingly, the Indian rivers are divided into two major groups:

- the Himalayan rivers; and
- the Peninsular rivers.

The Himalayan Rivers

The major Himalayan rivers are the Indus, the Ganga and the Brahmaputra. These rivers are long, and are joined by many large and important tributaries. A river alongwith its tributaries may be called a river system.

The Indus River System

The river Indus rises in Tibet, near Lake Mansarowar. Flowing west, it enters India in the Ladakh district of Jammu and Kashmir. It forms a picturesque gorge in this part. Several tributaries, the Zaskar, the Nubra, the Shyok and the Hunza, join it in the Kashmir region.

The Indus flows through Baltistan and Gilgit and emerges from the mountains at Attock. The Satluj, the Beas, the Ravi, the Chenab and the Jhelum join together to enter the Indus near Mithankot in Pakistan. Beyond this, the Indus flows southwards eventually reaching the Arabian Sea, east of Karachi. The Indus plain has a very gentle slope. With a total length of 2900 km, the Indus is one of the longest rivers of the world.

The Ganga River System

The headwaters of the Ganga, called the 'Bhagirathi' is fed by the Gangotri Glacier and joined by the Alaknanda at Devaprayag in Uttaranchal. At Haridwar the Ganga emerges from the mountains on to the plains. The Ganga is joined by many tributaries from the Himalayas, a few of them being major rivers such as the Yamuna, the Ghaghara, the Gandak and the Kosi. The river Yamuna rises from the Yamunotri Glacier in the Himalayas. It flows parallel to the Ganga and as a right bank tributary, meets the Ganga at Allahabad.

The Ghaghara, the Gandak and the Kosi rise in the Nepal Himalaya. They are the rivers, which flood parts of the northern plains every year, causing widespread damage to life and property but enriching the soil for the extensive agricultural lands.

The Brahmaputra River System

The Brahmaputra rises in Tibet east of Mansarowar lake very close to the sources of the Indus and the Satluj. It is slightly longer than the Indus, and most of its course lies outside India. It flows eastwards parallel to the Himalayas. On reaching the Namcha Barwa (7757 m), it takes a 'U' turn and enters India in Arunachal Pradesh through a gorge. Here, it is called the Dihang and it is joined by the Dibang, the Lohit, the Kenula and many other tributaries to form the Brahmaputra in Assam.

The Peninsular Rivers

The main water divide in Peninsular India is formed by the Western Ghats, which runs from north to south close to the western coast. Most of the major rivers of the Peninsula such as the Mahanadi, the Godavari, the Krishna and the Kaveri flow eastwards and drain into the Bay of Bengal.

The Narmada Basin

The Narmada rises in the Amarkantak hills in Madhya Pradesh. It flows towards the west in a rift valley formed due to faulting. On its way to the sea, the Narmada creates many picturesque locations. The 'Marble rocks', near Jabalpur where the Narmada flows through a deep gorge, and the 'Dhuadhar falls' where the river plunges over steep rocks, are some of the notable ones.

The Tapi Basin

The Tapi rises in the Satpura ranges, in the Betul district of Madhya Pradesh. It also flows in a rift valley parallel to the Narmada but it is much shorter in length. Its basin covers parts of Madhya Pradesh, Gujarat and Maharashtra.

The Godavari Basin

The Godavari is the largest Peninsular river. It rises from the slopes of the Western Ghats in the Nasik district of Maharashtra. Its length is about 1500 km. It drains into the Bay of Bengal. Its drainage basin is also the largest among the peninsular rivers. The basin covers parts of Maharashtra (about 50 per cent of the basin area lies in Maharashtra), Madhya Pradesh, Orissa and Andhra Pradesh. The Godavari is joined by a number of tributaries such as the Purna, the Wardha, the Pranhita, the Manjra, the Wainganga and the Penganga. The last three tributaries are very large. Because of its length and the area it covers, it is also known as the 'Dakshin Ganga'.

The Mahanadi Basin

The Mahanadi rises in the highlands of Chhattisgarh. It flows through Orissa to reach the Bay of Bengal. The length of the river is about 860 km. Its drainage basin is shared by Maharashtra, Chhattisgarh, Jharkhand, and Orissa.

The Krishna Basin

Rising from a spring near Mahabaleshwar, the Krishna flows for about 1400 km and reaches the Bay of Bengal. The Tungabhadra, the Koyana, the Ghatprabha, the Musi and the Bhima are some of its tributaries. Its drainage basin is shared by Maharasthra, Karnataka and Andhra Pradesh.

The Kaveri Basin

The Kaveri rises in the Brahmagri range of the Western Ghats and it reaches the Bay of Bengal in south of Cuddalore, in Tamil Nadu. Total length of the river is about 760 km. Its main tributaries are Amravati, Bhavani, Hemavati and Kabini. Its basin drains parts of Karnataka, Kerala and Tamil Nadu.

3. Interior of the Earth, Deformation and Tectonics

BASIC CONCEPTS OF SEISMOLOGY AND INTERNAL STRUCTURE OF THE EARTH

Waves that travel through rock are called seismic waves. Earthquakes and explosions produce seismic waves. Seismology is the study of earthquakes and the nature of the Earth's interior based on evidence from seismic waves

An earthquake produces several different types of seismic waves - body waves and surface waves. Body waves are generated due to the release of energy at the focus and move in all directions travelling through the body of the earth. Hence, the name body waves. The body waves interact with the surface rocks and generate new set of waves called surface waves. These waves move along the surface. The velocity of waves changes as they travel through materials with different densities. The denser the material, the higher is the velocity. Their direction also changes as they reflect or refract when coming across materials with different densities.

BODY WAVES

Two main types of body waves travel through the Earth's interior. They are called P and S-waves. P-waves move faster and are the first to arrive at the surface. These are also called 'primary waves'. The P-waves are similar to sound waves. They travel through gaseous, liquid and solid materials. S-waves arrive at the surface with some time lag. These are called secondary waves. An important fact about S-waves is that they can travel only through solid materials. This characteristic of the S-waves is quite important. It has helped scientists to understand the structure of the interior of the earth. Reflection causes waves to rebound whereas refraction makes waves move in different directions. The variations in the direction of waves are inferred with the help of their record on seismograph. The surface waves are the last to report on seismograph.

These waves are more destructive. They cause displacement of rocks, and hence, the collapse of structures occurs.

SURFACE WAVES

Surface waves travel more slowly than body waves. Two types of surface waves occur simultaneously in the Earth. A Rayleigh wave moves with an up-and- down rolling motion like an ocean wave. Love waves produce a side-to-side vibration. Thus, during an earthquake, the Earth's surface rolls like ocean waves and writhes from side to side like a snake.

Propagation of seismic Waves in earths interior

There are Different types of seismic waves travel with different velocity in different manners. As they move or propagate, they cause vibration in the body of the rocks through which they pass. P-waves vibrate parallel to the direction of the wave. This exerts pressure on the material in the direction of the propagation. As a result, it creates density differences in the material leading to stretching and squeezing of the material. Other three waves vibrate perpendicular to the direction of propagation. The direction of vibrations of S-waves is perpendicular to the wave direction in the vertical plane. Hence, they create troughs and crests in the material through which they pass. Surface waves are considered to be the most damaging waves.

The earth's radius is 6,370 km. No one can reach the centre of the earth and make observations or collect samples of the material. The study of seismic waves provides a complete picture of the layered interior. An earthquake in simple words is shaking of the earth. It is a natural event. It is caused due to release of energy, which generates waves that travel in all directions.

THE EARTH'S INTERIOR

The Earth is composed of a thin crust, a thick mantle, and a core. The three layers are distinguished by different chemical compositions. In turn, both the mantle and core contain finer layers based on changing physical properties. Scientists have learned a remarkable amount about the Earth's structure even though the deepest well is only a 12-kilometer hole in northern Russia. Scientists deduce the composition and properties of the Earth's interior by studying the behavior of seismic waves. Some of the principles necessary for understanding the behavior of seismic waves are as follows:

1. In a uniform, homogeneous medium, a wave radiates outward in concentric spheres and at constant velocity.
2. The velocity of a seismic wave depends on the nature of the material that it travels through. Thus, seismic waves travel at different velocities in different types of rock. In addition, wave velocity varies with changing rigidity and density of a rock.
3. When a wave passes from one material to another, it refracts (bends) and sometimes reflects (bounces back). Both refraction and reflection are easily seen in light waves. If you place a pencil in [illegible] half filled with water, the pencil appears bent. Of course the pencil does not bend; the light rays do. Light rays slow down when they pass from air to water, and as the velocity changes, the waves refract. If you look in a mirror, the mirror reflects your image. In a similar manner, boundaries between the Earth's layers refract and reflect seismic waves.
4. P waves are compressional waves and travel through all gases, liquids, and solids, whereas S-waves travel only through solids.

DISCOVERY OF THE CRUST–MANTLE BOUNDARY

Some waves like P waves travel directly through the crust to a nearby seismograph. Others travel downward into the mantle and then refract back upward to the same seismograph. The route through the mantle is longer than that through the crust. However, seismic waves travel faster in the mantle than they do in the crust. Over a short distance (less than 300 kilometers), waves traveling through the crust arrive at a seismograph before those following the longer route through the mantle. However, for longer distances, the longer route through the mantle is faster because waves travel more quickly in the mantle.

The situation is analogous to the two different routes you may use to travel from your house to a friend's. The shorter route is a city street where traffic moves slowly. The longer route is an interstate highway, but you have to drive several kilometers out of your way to get to the highway and then another few kilometers from the highway to your friend's house. If your friend lives nearby, it is faster to take the city street. But if your friend lives far away, it is faster to take the longer route and make up time on the highway.

In 1909, Andrija Mohorovicic discovered that seismic waves from a distant earthquake traveled more rapidly than those from a nearby earthquake. By analyzing the arrival times of earthquake waves to many different seismographs, Mohorovicic identified the boundary between the crust and the mantle. Today, this boundary is called the MohoroviЎ cir' c discontinuity, or the Moho in honor of its discoverer.

The Moho lies at a depth ranging from 5 to 70 kilometers. Oceanic crust is thinner than continental crust, and continental crust is thicker under mountain ranges than it is under plains.

THE STRUCTURE OF THE MANTLE

The mantle is almost 2900 kilometers thick and comprises about 80 per cent of the Earth's volume. Much of our knowledge of the composition and structure of the mantle comes from seismic data. As explained earlier, seismic waves speed up abruptly at the crust-mantle boundary Between 75 and 125 kilometers, at the base of the lithosphere, seismic waves slow down again because the high temperature at this depth causes solid rock to become plastic. Recall that the plastic layer is called the asthenosphere. The plasticity and partially melted character of the asthenosphere slow down the seismic waves. At the base of the asthenosphere 350 kilometers below the surface, seismic waves speed up again because increasing pressure overwhelms the temperature effect, and the mantle becomes less plastic. At a depth of about 660 kilometers, seismic wave velocities increase again because pressure is great enough that the minerals in the mantle recrystallize to form denser minerals. The zone where the change occurs is called the 660 kilometer discontinuity. The base of the mantle lies at a depth of 2900 kilometers.

DISCOVERY OF THE CORE

Using a global array of seismographs, seismologists detect direct P and S-waves up to 105° from the focus of an earthquake. Between 105° and 140° is a "shadow zone" where no direct P-waves arrive at the Earth's surface. This shadow zone is caused by a discontinuity, which is the mantle-core boundary. When P waves pass from the mantle into the core, they are refracted, or bent. The refraction deflects the P-waves away from the shadow zone.

No S-waves arrive beyond 105°. Their absence in this region shows that they do not travel through the outer core. Recall that S-waves are not transmitted through liquids. The failure of S-waves to pass through the outer core indicates that the outer core is liquid.

Refraction patterns of P-waves, shows that another boundary exists within the core. It is the boundary between the liquid outer core and the solid inner core. Although seismic waves tell us that the outer core is liquid and the inner core is solid, other evidence tells us that the core is composed of iron and nickel.

Behaviour of rocks under stress

Rocks, be they igneous, metamorphic or sedimentary, do not behave in the same manner when placed in different environments when they are deformed. Deeply buried rocks exposed to large confining pressures become more ductile than when they are deformed at shallow depths in low confining pressures. Regardless of the environment some rocks are inherently weak and others very strong. The nature and direction of the applied forces also affects the way various rocks behave. For example, a metamorphic schist will be much stronger when compressed at ninety degrees- normal- to its foliation than if it was pulled apart - placed in tension-in the same direction.

Mechanical characteristics of rocks are usually determined in the laboratory using hydraulic devices which can compress or extend (place in tension) the rock samples. Because it is difficult to attach testing devices to rock samples for extension most of this type of work compresses samples. The associated animation (this is a large file- don't download it unless you have a very fast connection) provides some idea about what the apparatus looks like and what happens as a typical sample is compressed. The example shows simple uniaxial compression. Some laboratories utilize triaxial devices where it is possible not only to compress the sample parallel to its long axis but also perpendicular to the axis thus imitating conditions where the sample might lie at great depth within the earth. This is carried out by changing the configuration of the sample chamber by placing the sample, now in a soft, copper jacket, between th[illegible] pistons, as usual, but [illegible] chamber so the sa[illegible] can be confined laterally by the introduction of high-pressure hydraulic fluid around it. Note that in the animation as the sample is compressed it not only shortens but also increases in width or bulges. The small diagram - a stress-strain diagram- which appears after the sample begins to undergo strain (deformation is usually designated with the shorthand lower case Greek symbol ε – epsilon and stress is designated with lower case σ –sigma) plots the amount of stress applied to the sample (this can be in pounds per square inch (psi), tons/square inch, kilobars, where one bar is about one atmosphere or in mega Pascals (MPa) where one bar = 100,000 Pascals (100 KPa) and 1bar is 100 KPa- one might put 700 KPa in a high-pressure bike tire) versus the amount of shortening in per cent. The stress applied can be read directly off the instrument and the strain is measured by a precise caliper-like device attached, but not shown, to the main instrument. Each rock type, when deformed, displays a different response to stress. These difference can be represented by variously defined modulii. Each modulus describes various types of physical responses of the sample. As the sample deforms it passes through three different types of behaviors: elastic- recoverable strain- , ductile/plastic- non-recoverable- strain and finally failure where cohesion is lost between the components of the rock.

To show these responses graphically stress-strain curves (see below) are plotted from data derived from the compression tests. The horizontal axis is commonly reserved for strain and the vertical axis for stress values.

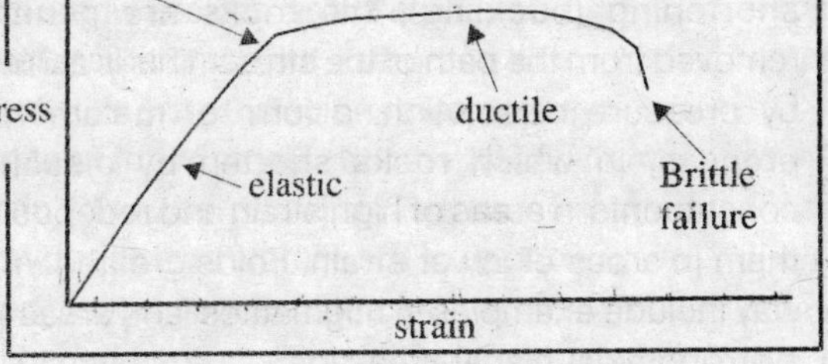

The response of a particular type of rock to applied stress can be described by various quantitative values or modulii. Among the most widely used are Young's modulus, Poisson's ratio, rigidity modulus and bulk modulus.

Young's modulus 'E' is applied to so-called Hookean solids where strain is proportional to applied stress. This value can be extracted from the first portion of the stress-strain curve where the relationship is linear. One simply divides stress in whatever units is desired by the amount of strain (0.1% = .001). Thus if on the linear part of the curve the sample shortened 0.1% when 0.5 kbar stress was applied E = 0.5 kbar/0.001 = 500 kbar.

Poisson's ratio 'ν' is a measure of how much the sample increases in its lateral dimension as it is compressed axially. This is determined by measuring the lateral shortening and dividing it by the axial shortening. Only axial strain can be extracted from our stress-strain curves so a little extra data must be provided to derive Poisson's ratio. If a sample were an ideal incompressible sample where no volume change occurs under strain the Poisson's ratio is 0.5. In reality the Poisson's ratio of rocks is less than 0.5.

FOLDS

The term fold is used in geology when one or a stack of originally flat and planar surfaces, such as sedimentary strata, are bent or curved as a result of plastic (that is, permanent) deformation.

Causes of folding

Folds appear on all scales, in all rock types, at all levels in the crust and arise from a variety of causes.

Layer-parallel shortening

When a sequence of layered rocks is shortened parallel to its layering, this deformation may be accommodated in a number of ways, homogeneous shortening, reverse faulting or folding. The response depends on the thickness of the mechanical layering and the contrast in properties between the layers.

If the layering does begin to fold, the fold style is also dependent on these properties. Isolated thick competent layers in a less competent matrix will control the folding and typically generate classic rounded buckle folds accommodated by deformation in the matrix. In the case of regular alternations of layers of contrasting properties, such as sandstone-shale sequences, kink-bands, box-folds and chevron folds are normally produced

Fault-related folding

Many folds are directly related to faults, associate with their propagation, displacement and the accommodation of strains between neighbouring faults.

Fault propagation folding

Fault propagation folds or tip-line folds are caused when displacement occurs on an existing fault without further propagation. In both reverse and normal faults this leads to folding of the overlying sequence, often in the form of a monocline

Detachment folding

When a thrust fault continues to displace above a planar detachment without further fault propagation, detachment folds may form, typically of box-fold style. These generally occur above a good detachment such as in the Jura mountains, where the detachment occurs on middle Triassic evaporites

Compaction

Folds can be generated in a younger sequence by differential compaction over older structures such as fault blocks and reefs

Folding in shear zones

Shear zones that approximate to simple shear typically contain minor asymmetric folds, with the direction of overturning consistent with the overall shear sense. Some of these folds have highly curved hinge lines and are referred to as sheath folds. Folds in shear zones can be inherited, formed due to the orientation of pre-shearing layering or formed due to instability within the shear flow.

Sedimentary folding

Recently deposited sediments are normally mechanically weak and prone to remobilisation.

Igneous intrusion

The emplacement of igneous intrusions tends to deform the surrounding country rock. In the case of high-level intrusions, near the Earth's surface, this deformation is concentrated above the intrusion and often takes the form of folding, as with the upper surface of a laccolith.

Folding mechanisms

Folding of rocks must balance the deformation of layers with the conservation of volume in a rock mass. This occurs by several mechanisms.

Flexural slip

Flexural slip allows folding by creating layer-parallel slip between the layers of the folded strata which, altogether, result in deformation. The best analogy is bending a phone book, where volume preservation is accommodated by slip between the pages of the book.

BUCKLING

Typically, folding is thought to occur by simple buckling of a planar surface and its confining volume. The volume change is accommodated by layer parallel shortening the volume, which grows in thickness. Folding under this mechanism is typically of the similar fold style, as thinned limbs are shortened horizontally and thickened hinges do so vertically.

Mass displacement

If the folding deformation cannot be accommodated by flexural slip or volume-change shortening (buckling), the rocks are generally removed from the path of the stress. This is achieved by pressure dissolution, a form of metamorphic process, in which rocks shorten by dissolving constituents in areas of high strain and redepositing them in areas of lower strain. Folds created in this way include examples in migmatites, and areas with a strong axial planar cleavage.

FAULT

In geology, a fault is a planar fracture in rock in which the rock on one side of the fracture has moved with respect to the rock on the other side. Large faults within the Earth's crust are the result of differential or shear motion and active fault zones are the causal locations of most earthquakes. Earthquakes are caused by energy release during rapid slippage along a fault.

A fault line is the surface trace of a fault, the line of intersection between the fault plane and the Earth's surface.

Mechanics

The creation and behavior of faults, in both an individual small fault and within the greater fault zones which define the tectonic plates, is controlled by the relative motion of rocks on either side of the fault surface.

Because of friction and the rigidity of the rock, the rocks cannot simply glide or flow past each other. Rather, stress builds up in rocks and when it reaches a level that exceeds the strain threshold, the accumulated potential energy is released as strain, which is focused into a plane along which relative motion is accommodated – the fault.

Strain is both accumulative and instantaneous depending on the rheology of the rock; the ductile lower crust and mantle accumulates deformation gradually via shearing, whereas the brittle upper crust reacts by fracture, or instantaneous stress release to cause motion along the fault. A fault in ductile rocks can also release instantaneously when the strain rate is too great. The energy released by instantaneous strain release is the cause of earthquakes, a common phenomenon along transform boundaries.

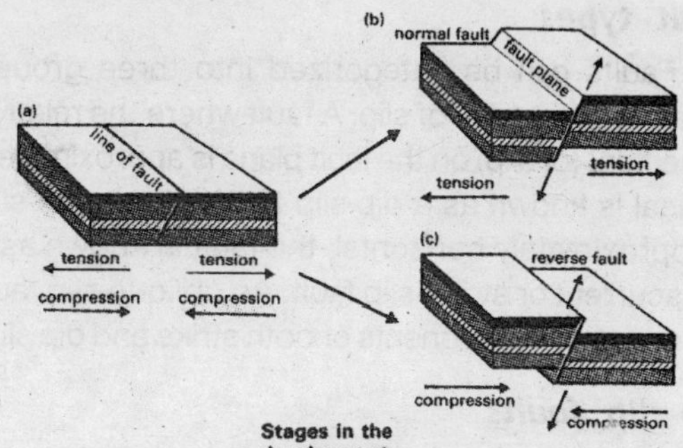

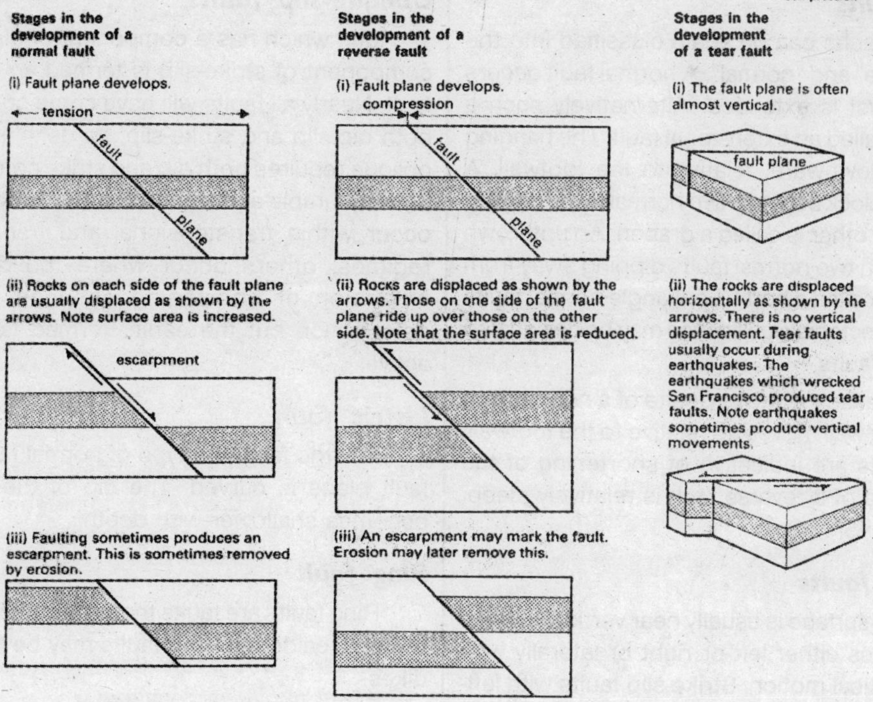

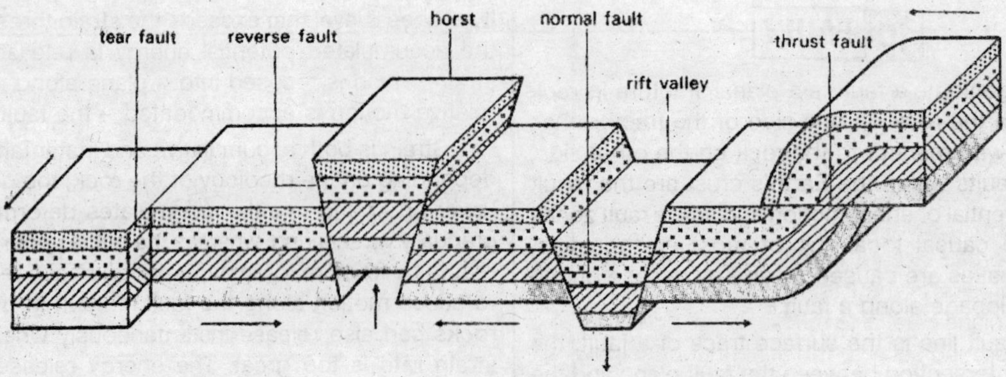

fig. 2.4: Some faults and associated features.

Fault types

Faults can be categorized into three groups based on the sense of slip. A fault where the relative movement (or slip) on the fault plane is approximately vertical is known as a dip-slip fault. Where the slip is approximately horizontal, the fault is known as a transcurrent or strike-slip fault. An oblique-slip fault has non-zero components of both strike and dip slip.

Dip-slip faults

Dip-slip faults can be again classified into the types "reverse" and "normal". A normal fault occurs when the crust is extended. Alternatively such a fault can be called an extensional fault. The hanging wall moves downward, relative to the footwall. A downthrown block between two normal faults dipping towards each other is called a graben. An upthrown block between two normal faults dipping away from each other is called a horst. Low-angle normal faults with regional tectonic significance may be designated detachment faults.

A reverse fault is the opposite of a normal fault – the hanging wall moves up relative to the footwall. Reverse faults are indicative of shortening of the crust. The dip of a reverse fault is relatively steep, greater than 45°.

Strike-slip faults

The fault surface is usually near vertical and the footwall moves either left or right or laterally with very little vertical motion. Strike-slip faults with left-lateral motion are also known as sinistral faults. Those with right-lateral motion are also known as dextral faults.

A special class of strike-slip faults is the transform fault, which is a plate tectonics feature related to spreading centers such as mid-ocean ridges. Transform faults are often referred to as transform plate boundaries.

Oblique-slip faults

fault which has a component of dip-slip and a component of strike-slip is termed an oblique-slip fault. Nearly all faults will have some component of both dip-slip and strike-slip, so defining a fault as oblique requires both dip and strike components to be measurable and significant. Some oblique faults occur within transtensional and transpressional regimes, others occur where the direction of extension or shortening changes during the deformation but the earlier formed faults remain active.

Listric fault

A listric fault is a type of normal fault in which fault plane is curved. The dip of the fault plane becomes shallower with depth.

Ring fault

Ring faults are faults that occur within collapsed volcanic calderas. Ring faults may be filled by ring dikes.

JOINT

In geology the term joint refers to a fracture in rock where there has been no lateral movement in the plane of the fracture (up, down or sideways) of one side relative to the other.

Joints form in solid, hard rock that is stretched such that its brittle strength is exceeded (the point at which it breaks). When this happens the rock fractures in a plane parallel to the maximum principal stress and perpendicular to the minimum principal stress (the direction in which the rock is being stretched). This leads to the development of a single sub-parallel joint set. Continued deformation may lead to development of one or more additional joint sets. The presence of the first set strongly affects the stress orientation in the rock layer, often causing subsequent sets to form at a high angle to the first set.

Joint sets are commonly observed to have relatively constant spacing, which is roughly proportional to the thickness of the layer

TYPES OF JOINTS

Tectonic joints

Tectonic joints are formed during deformation episodes whenever the differential stress is high enough to induce tensile failure of the rock, irrespective of the tectonic regime. They will often form at the same time as faults. Measurement of tectonic joint patterns can be useful in analyzing the tectonic history of an area because they give information on stress orientations at the time of formation.

Unloading joints

Joints are most commonly formed when uplift and erosion removes the overlying rocks thereby reducing the compressive load and allowing the rock to expand laterally. Joints related to uplift and erosional unloading have orientations reflecting the principal stresses during the uplift. Care needs to be taken when attempting to understand past tectonic stresses to discriminate, if possible, between tectonic and unloading joints.

Cooling Joints

Joints can also form via cooling of hot rock masses, particularly lava, forming cooling joints, most commonly expressed as vertical columnar jointing. The joint systems associated with cooling typically are polygonal because the cooling introducing stresses that are isotropic in the plane of the layer.

EARTHQUAKES – THEIR CAUSES AND MEASUREMENT

Although earthquakes have been reported from all parts of the world, they are primarily associated with the margins of the crustal plates that move with respect to each other. Differential displacements give rise to elastic strains that eventually exceed the strength of the rocks involved and fault movement then occurs. The strained rocks rebound along the fault under the elastic stresses until the strain is partly or wholly dissipated. Initially, movement may occur over a small area of a fault plane, to be followed later by slippage over a much larger surface. Such initial movements account for the foreshocks that precede an earthquake.

These are followed by the main movement, but complete stability is not restored immediately. The shift of rock masses involved in faulting relieves the main stress but develops new stresses in adjacent areas. Because stress is not relieved evenly everywhere, minor adjustments may arise along a fault plane and thereby generate aftershocks.

The decrease in strength of the aftershocks is irregular, and occasionally, they may continue for a year or more.

The epicentre of an earthquake is located on the surface of the Earth immediately above the focus (i.e. the location of the origin of the earthquake), and shock waves radiate from the focus in all directions. Earthquake foci are confined to within a limited zone of the upper Earth, the lower boundary occurring at around 700 km depth from the surface.

No earthquakes are known to have originated below this level. Moreover, earthquakes rarely originate at the Earth's surface. In fact, most earthquakes originate within the upper 25 km of the

Earth. Because of its significance, the depth of foci has been used as the basis of a threefold classification of earthquakes; those occurring within the upper 70 km are referred to as shallow, those located between 70 and 300 km as intermediate, and those between 300 and 700 km as deep. Seventy per cent of all earthquakes are of shallow type.

An earthquake propagates three types of shock waves. The first pulses that are recorded on a seismograph are the P or compression waves. The next pulses recorded are the S or

shear waves. S waves usually have larger amplitude than the P waves but the latter travel almost three times as fast as the former. Both P and S waves travel directly from their source to the surface. The third type of shocks are known as the L waves. These waves travel from the focus of the earthquake to the epicentre above, and from there they radiate over the Earth's surface. P waves are not as destructive as S or L waves. This is because they have smaller amplitude, and the force their customary vertical motion creates rarely exceeds the force of gravity. On the other hand, S waves may develop violent tangential vibrations strong enough to cause great destruction. The intensity of an earthquake depends on the amplitude and frequency of wave motion. S waves commonly have a higher frequency than L waves, nevertheless the latter may be more powerful because of their larger amplitude.

MEASUREMENT OF EARTHQUAKE

A seismograph is a device that records seismic waves. To understand how a seismograph works, consider the act of writing a letter while riding in an airplane. If the plane hits turbulence, inertia keeps your hand relatively stationary as the plane moves back and forth beneath it, and your handwriting becomes erratic. Early seismographs worked on the same principle. A weight was suspended from a spring. A pen attached to the weight was aimed at the zero mark on a piece of graph paper. The graph paper was mounted on a rotary drum that was attached firmly to bedrock.

During an earthquake, the graph paper jiggled up and down, but inertia kept the pen stationary. As a result, the paper moved up and down beneath the pen. The rotating drum recorded earthquake motion over time. This record of Earth vibration is called a seismogram.

Modern seismographs use electronic motion detectors which transmit the signal to a computer.

In 1935 Charles Richter devised the Richter scale to express earthquake magnitude. Richter magnitude is calculated from the height of the largest earthquake body wave recorded on a specific type of seismograph. The Richter scale is more quantitative than earlier intensity scales, but it is not a precise measure of earthquake energy. A sharp, quick jolt would register as a high peak on a Richter seismograph, but a very large earthquake can shake the ground for a long time without generating extremely high peaks. In this way, a great earthquake can release a huge amount of energy that is not reflected in the height of a single peak, and thus is not adequately expressed by Richter magnitude.

INTERPLATE AND INTRAPLATE SEISMICITY

INTERPLATE SEISMICITY

An interplate seismicity is an earthquake that occurs at the boundary between two tectonic plates. If one plate is trying to move past the other, they will be locked until sufficient stress builds up to cause the plates to slip relative to each other. The slipping process creates an earthquake with land deformations and resulting seismic waves which travel through the Earth and along the Earth's surface. Relative plate motion can be lateral as along a transform fault boundary or vertical if along a convergent subduction boundary or a rift at a divergent boundary. At a subduction boundary the motion is due to one plate slipping beneath the other plate resulting in an interplate thrust or megathrust earthquake.

Some areas of the world that are particularly prone to such events include the west coast of North America (especially California and Alaska), the northeastern Mediterranean region (Greece, Italy, and Turkey in particular), Iran, New Zealand, Indonesia, Japan, and parts of China.

Intraplate Seismicity

An intraplate earthquake is an earthquake that occurs in the interior of a tectonic plate, whereas an interplate earthquake is one that occurs at a plate boundary.

Intraplate earthquakes are rare compared to earthquakes at plate boundaries.

Causes

Many cities live with the seismic risk of a rare, large intraplate earthquake. The cause of these earthquakes is often uncertain. In many cases, the causative fault is deeply buried, and sometimes cannot even be found. Under these circumstances it is difficult to calculate the exact seismic hazard for a given city, especially if there was only one earthquake in historical times. Some progress is being made in understanding the fault mechanics driving these earthquakes.

According to the theory of plate tectonics, the surface of the Earth is modeled as being made up of about a dozen large tectonic plates. These plates move very slowly (about the rate that human fingernails grow), owing to convection currents within the mantle below the crust. Because they do not all move in the same direction, plates often directly collide or move laterally along each other, a tectonic environment that makes earthquakes frequent. Relatively few earthquakes occur in intraplate environments; most occur on faults near plate margins. By definition, intraplate earthquakes do not occur near plate boundaries, but along faults in the normally stable interior of plates. These earthquakes often occur at the location of ancient failed rifts, because such old structures may present a weakness in the crust that can easily slip and shorten to accommodate regional tectonic strain.

Compared to earthquakes near plate boundaries, intraplate earthquakes are not well understood, and the hazards associated with them may be difficult to quantify.

PALEOMAGNETISM

Paleomagnetism is the study of the record of the Earth's magnetic field preserved in various magnetic minerals through time. The study of paleomagnetism has demonstrated that the Earth's magnetic field varies substantially in both orientation and intensity through time.

The study of paleomagnetism is possible because iron-bearing minerals such as magnetite may record past directions of the Earth's magnetic field. Paleomagnetic signatures in rocks can be recorded by three different mechanisms.

Thermal remanent magnetization

Paleomagnetism occurs at plate boundaries. First, iron-titanium oxide minerals in basalt and other igneous rocks may preserve the direction of the Earth's magnetic field when the rocks cool through the Curie temperatures of those minerals. The Curie temperature of magnetite, a spinel-group iron oxide, is about 580°C, whereas most basalt and gabbro are completely crystallized at temperatures above 900°C. Hence, the mineral grains are not rotated physically to align with the Earth's field, but rather they may record the orientation of that field. The record so preserved is called a thermal remanent magnetization (TRM). Because complex oxidation reactions may occur as igneous rocks cool after crystallization, the orientations of the Earth's magnetic field are not always accurately recorded, nor is the record necessarily maintained. Nonetheless, the record has been preserved well enough in basalts of the ocean crust to have been critical in the development of theories of sea floor spreading related to plate tectonics.

Detrital remanent magnetization

In a completely different process, magnetic grains in sediments may align with the magnetic field during or soon after deposition; this is known as detrital remnant magnetization (DRM). If the magnetization is acquired as the grains are deposited, the result is a depositional detrital remanent magnetization; if it is acquired soon after deposition, it is a post-depositional detrital remanent magnetization.

Chemical remanent magnetization

In a third process, magnetic grains may be deposited from a circulating solution, or be formed during chemical reactions, and may record the direction of the magnetic field at the time of mineral formation. The field is said to be recorded by chemical remanent magnetization (CRM). The mineral recording the field commonly is hematite, another iron oxide. Redbeds, clastic sedimentary rocks (such as sandstones) that are red primarily because of hematite formation during or after sedimentary diagenesis, may have useful CRM signatures, and magnetostratigraphy can be based on such signatures.

Examples

Paleomagnetic evidence, both reversals and polar wandering data, was instrumental in verifying the theories of continental drift and plate tectonics in the 1960s and 70s. Some applications of paleomagnetic evidence to reconstructing histories of terranes have continued to arouse controversies. Paleomagnetic evidence also is used in constraining possible ages for rocks and processes and in reconstructions of the deformational histories of parts of the crust.

Reversal magnetostratigraphy is often used to estimate the age of fossil and hominin bearing sites.

Paleomagnetic studies are combined with geochronological methods to determine absolute ages for rocks in which the magnetic record is preserved. For igneous rocks such as basalt, commonly used methods include potassium-argon and argon-argon geochronology.

4. Oceans and Atmosphere

HYPSOGRAPHY OF THE CONTINENTS AND OCEAN FLOOR –CONTINENTAL SHELF, SLOPE, RISE AND ABYSSAL PLAINS

INTRODUCTION

Oceans cover approximately 71% or 360 million square kilometers of the Earth's surface. On average, the depth of the world's oceans is about 3.9 kilometers. Maximum depths, however, can exceed 11 kilometers! The oceans contain 97% of our planet's free water. The other 3% is found in atmosphere, on the Earth's terrestrial surface, or in the Earth's lithosphere in various forms and stores. The distribution of ocean basins and continents is unevenly arranged over the Earth's surface. In the Northern Hemisphere, the ratio of land to ocean is about 1 to 1.5. The ratio of land to ocean in the Southern Hemisphere is 1 to 4. The greater abundance of water in the Southern Hemisphere has some interesting effects on the environment of this area. For example, climate tends to be more moderate in the Southern Hemisphere because of the ocean's ability to release large amounts of stored heat energy.

THE RELIEF OF THE OCEAN

The ocean basins are in many ways similar to the land surface. There are submarine ridges, plateaus, canyon, plains and trenches. A typical submarine relief feature includes continental shelf, the continental slope, the deep-sea plain, the ocean deeps, and abyssal plains.

THE CONTINENTAL SHELF

The sediment forms a shallow, gently sloping submarine surface called a continental shelf on the edge of the continent. Continental shelf is in fact the seaward extension of the continent from the shoreline to the continental edge marked, approximately, by the 100 fathom isobaths (isobaths are contours marking depths below sea level). As sediment accumulates on a continental shelf, the edge of the continent sinks isostatically because of the added weight.

The depth of the shelf increases gradually from the shore to about 200 meters at the outer shelf edge. The average inclination of the continental shelf is about 0.1°. A continental shelf on a passive margin can be a large feature.

Some of the world's richest petroleum reserves occur on the continental shelves of the North Sea between England and Scandinavia, in the Gulf of Mexico, and in the Beaufort Sea on the northern coast of Alaska and western Canada.

THE CONTINENTAL SLOPE AND RISE

At the outer edge of a shelf, the sea floor suddenly steepens to about 4° to 5° as it falls away from 200 meters to about 5 kilometers in depth. This steep region of the sea floor averages about 50 kilometers wide and is called the continental slope. It is a surface formed by sediment accumulation, much like the shelf. Its steeper angle is due primarily to gradual thinning of continental crust in a transitional zone where it nears the junction with oceanic crust. Seismic profiler exploration shows that the sedimentary layering is commonly disrupted where sediment has slumped and slid down the steep incline.

A continental slope becomes less steep as it gradually merges with the deep ocean floor. This region, called the continental rise, consists of an apron of terrigenous sediment that was transported across the continental shelf and deposited on the deep ocean floor at the foot of the slope. The continental rise averages a few hundred kilometers wide. Typically, it joins the deep sea floor at a depth of about 5 kilometers.

ABYSSAL PLAIN

This is the undulating plain lying three to five kilometer below sea level, and covering two-thirds of the ocean floor, generally referred as Abyssal Plain. This plain has extensive submarine plateaux, ridges, trenchs, basins, and oceanic islands that rises above sea level in the midst of oceans.

Physical and chemical properties of sea water and their spatial variations

Seawater is a mixture of various salts and water. Most of the water in the ocean basins is believed to originate from the condensation of water found in the early atmosphere as the Earth cooled after its formation. This water was released from the lithosphere as the Earth's crust solidified. Additional water has also been added to the oceans over geologic time from periodic volcanic action. Some scientists have recently speculated that comets entering the Earth's atmosphere may be another important source of water for the oceans.

Most of the dissolved chemical constituents or salts found in seawater have a continental origin. It seems that these chemicals were released from continental rocks through weathering and then carried to the oceans by stream runoff. Over time, the concentration of these chemicals increased until equilibrium was met. This equilibrium occurred when the ocean's water could not dissolve any more material in solution. Similarities between fossilized sea life and organisms living today indicate that the composition of seawater stopped changing drastically about 600 million years ago.

Only six elements comprise about 99 % of sea salts: chlorine (Cl^-), sodium (Na^+), sulfur, magnesium (Mg^{+2}), calcium (Ca^{+2}), and potassium (K^+). The relative abundance of the major salts in seawater are constant regardless of the ocean. Only the amount of water in the mixture varies because of differences between ocean basins because of regional differences in freshwater loss (evaporation) and gain (runoff and precipitation).

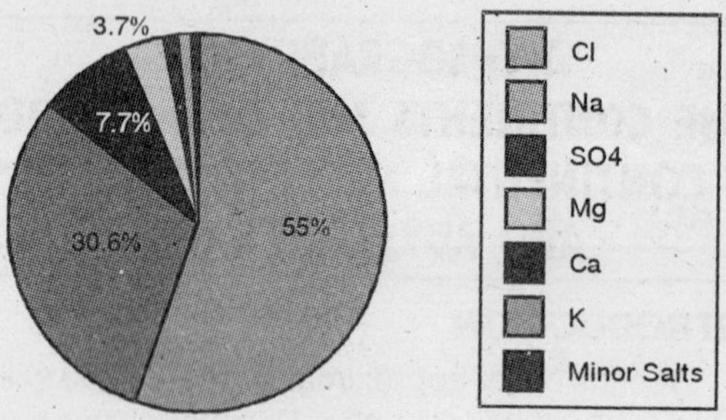

Figure 4.1: Relative proportions of dissolved salts in seawater.

Seawater freezes at a temperature that is slightly colder than fresh water (0.0 degrees Celsius). The freezing temperature of seawater also varies with the concentration of salts. More salt the lower the initial freezing temperature. At a salinity of 35 parts per thousand, seawater freezes at a temperature of -1.9 degrees Celsius.

Sea ice normally contains considerably less salt than seawater. Most of the salts found in liquid seawater are forced out it when freezing occurs. The reason for the exclusion is because the molecules of the various salts do not fit well in the highly orderly molecular structure of frozen water. Because of the density difference between ice and seawater, ice floats on the surface of the ocean.

Seawater also contains small amounts of dissolved gases. Many of these gases are added to seawater from the atmosphere through the constant stirring of the sea surface by wind and waves. The concentration of gases that can be dissolved into seawater from the atmosphere is determined by temperature and salinity of the water.

Increasing the temperature or salinity reduces the amount of gas that ocean water can dissolve.

Some of the important atmospheric gases found in seawater include: nitrogen, oxygen, carbon dioxide (in the form of bicarbonate HCO_3), argon, helium, and neon. Compared to the other atmospheric gases, the amount of carbon dioxide dissolved in saturated seawater is unusually large.

Some gases found within seawater are also involved in oceanic organic and inorganic processes that are indirectly related to the atmosphere. For example, oxygen and carbon dioxide may be temporally generated or depleted by such processes to varying concentrations at specific locations within the ocean.

RESIDENCE TIME OF A CONSTITUENT (ELEMENT) IN SEA WATER.

The residence time of an element in sea water is the average time that the element spends in the oceans before it is removed. The concept of residence time applies to a steady-state ocean (where input = output). Under these conditions, the residence time of an element is defined as the mass of the element in sea water divided by either the element input rate or the element removal rate.

residence time = mass ÷ input rate = mass ÷ output rate

The mass of an element in the oceans is easy to calculate. It is simply the concentration (in g/kg) times the mass of sea water (in kg). Most residence times are calculated using the input rate by rivers.

river input rate of element (g/time) = conc. in river water (g/kg) X river runoff rate (kg of water/time)

Residence times for element in the oceans vary widely. Here are some representative values:

Residence time, years

Cl 80 million
Na 60 million
Mg 10 million
SO4 9 million
Ca 1 million
P 0.7 million
Mn 7,000
Fe, Al 100

residence time is a measure of an element's "reactivity" in sea water.

* A long residence time (e.g., Cl, Na) indicates that an element is relatively unreactive in sea water; it is removed at a slow rate.

* A short residence time (e.g., Mn, Al, Fe) indicates that an element is removed rapidly from sea water.

The **relationship between residence time and reactivity in seawater** can be illustrated by contrasting the behavior of two major cations, Na^+ and Ca^{2+}.

* In river water, the concentration of Ca^{2+} is higher than that of Na^+ (i.e., $[Ca^{2+}] > [Na^+]$).

* But in sea water, just the opposite is the case (i.e., $[Ca^{2+}] < [Na^+]$).

* This apparent "reversal" occurs because Ca^{2+} is removed rapidly and efficiently as $CaCO_3$. The relatively high reactivity of Ca^{2+} is reflected in its comparatively short residence time (1 m.y.). In contrast, Na^+ is unreactive in sea water; it tends to accumulate until removal by a major evaporite event.

OCEAN CURRENTS, WAVES AND TIDES, IMPORTANT CURRENT SYSTEMS, THERMOHALINE CIRCULATION AND THE OCEANIC CONVEYOR BELT

OCEAN CURRENTS

Ocean currents represent a regular volume of water in a definite path and direction. Ocean currents are influenced by two types of forces, they are:

- primary forces that initiate the movement of water;
- secondary forces that influence the currents to flow.

The primary forces that influence the currents are:

- heating by solar energy;
- wind;
- gravity;
- coriolis force.

Heating by solar energy causes the water to expand. That is why, near the equator the ocean water is about 8 cm higher in level than in the middle latitudes. This causes a very slight gradient and water tends to flow down the slope. Wind blowing on the surface of the ocean pushes the water to move. Friction between the wind and the water surface affects the movement of the water body in its course. Gravity tends to pull the water down to pile and create gradient variation. The Coriolis force intervenes and causes the water to move to the right in the northern hemisphere and to the left in the southern hemisphere. These large accumulations of water and the flow around them are called Gyres. These produce large circular currents in all the ocean basins.

WAVES

Waves are ac energy, which moves across the ocean surface. Water particles only travel in a small circle as a wave passes. Wind provides energy to the waves. Wind causes waves to travel in the ocean and the energy is released on shorelines. The motion of the surface water seldom affects the stagnant deep bottom water of the oceans. As a wave approaches the beach, it slows down. This is due to the friction occurring between the dynamic water and the sea floor. The largest waves are found in the open oceans. Waves continue to grow larger as they move and absorb energy from the wind.

Most of the waves are caused by the wind driving against water. When a breeze of two knots or less blows over calm water, small ripples form and grow as the wind speed increases until white caps appear in the breaking waves. Waves may travel thousands of km before rolling ashore, breaking and dissolving as surf.

Movement of Waves

Waves travel because wind pushes the water body in its course while gravity pulls the crests of the waves downward. The falling water pushes the former troughs upward, and the wave moves to a new position the actual motion of the water beneath the waves is circular. It indicates that things are carried up and forward as the wave approaches, and down and back as it passes.

TIDES

Tides are the rising of Earth's ocean surface caused by the tidal forces of the Moon and the Sun acting on the oceans. Tides cause changes in the depth of the marine and estuarine water bodies and produce oscillating currents known as tidal streams, making prediction of tides important for coastal navigation.

The changing tide produced at a given location is the result of the changing positions of the Moon and Sun relative to the Earth coupled with the effects of Earth rotation and the bathymetry of oceans, seas and estuaries.

Characteristics of Tide

Tide is a repeated cycle of sea level changes in the following stages:

- Over several hours the water rises or advances up a beach in the flood
- The water reaches its highest level, called high water.
- The sea level lowers or falls over several hours during the ebb tide.
- The level stops falling at low water.

Types of Tides

Tides vary in their frequency, direction and movement from place to place and also from time to time. Tides may be grouped into various types based on their frequency of occurrence in one day or 24 hours or based on their height.

Tides based on Frequency

Semi-diurnal tide: The most common tidal pattern, featuring two high tides and two low tides each day. The successive high or low tides are approximately of the same height.

Diurnal tide: There is only one high tide and one low tide during each day. The successive high and low tides are approximately of the same height.

Mixed tide: Tides having variations in height are known as mixed tides. These tides generally occur along the west coast of North America and on many islands of the Pacific Ocean.

Tides based on the Sun, Moon and the Earth Positions

Around new and full moon when the Sun, Moon and Earth form a line (a condition known as syzygy), the tidal forces due to the Sun reinforce those of the Moon. The tide's range is then maximum: this is called the spring tide.

When the Moon is at first quarter or third quarter, the Sun and Moon are separated by 90° when viewed from the Earth, and the forces induced by the Sun partially cancel those of the Moon. At these points in the lunar cycle, the tide's range is minimum: this is called the neap tide, or neaps.

Spring tides result in high waters that are higher than average, low waters that are lower than average, slack water time that is shorter than average and stronger tidal currents than average. Neaps result in less extreme tidal conditions. There is about a seven day interval between springs and neaps.

Power generation by Tide

Power can be extracted by two means: inserting a water turbine into a tidal current, or building impoundment ponds so as to release or admit water through a turbine. In the first case, the generation is entirely determined by the timing and magnitude of the tidal currents, and the best currents may be unavailable because the turbines would obstruct navigation. In the second, the impoundment dams are expensive to construct, the natural water cycles are completely disrupted, as is navigation, but with multiple impoundment ponds power can be generated at chosen times. So far, there are few systems for tidal power generation (most famously, La Rance by Saint Malo, France) and many difficulties. Aside from environmental issues, simply withstanding sea-water corrosion and fouling by biological growths poses engineering challenges.

THERMOHALINE CIRCULATION

The term thermohaline circulation (THC) refers to the part of the large-scale ocean circulation that is driven by global density gradients created by surface heat and freshwater fluxes. The adjective thermohaline derives from thermo- referring to temperature and -haline referring to salt content, factors which together determine the density of sea water. Wind-driven surface currents (such as the Gulf Stream) head polewards from the equatorial Atlantic Ocean, cooling all the while and eventually sinking at high latitudes (forming North Atlantic Deep Water). This dense water then flows into the ocean basins. While the bulk of it upwells in the Southern Ocean, the oldest waters (with a transit time of around 1600 years) upwell in the North Pacific (Primeau, 2005). Extensive mixing therefore takes place between the ocean basins, reducing differences between them and making the Earth's ocean a global system. On their journey, the water masses transport both energy (in the form of heat) and matter (solids, dissolved substances and gases) around the globe. As such, the state of the circulation has a large impact on the climate of the Earth.

The thermohaline circulation is sometimes called the ocean conveyor belt, the great ocean conveyor, or the global conveyor belt. On occasion, it is used to refer to the meridional overturning circulation (often abbreviated as MOC). The term MOC, however, is more accurate and well defined, as it is difficult to separate the part of the circulation which is actually driven by temperature and salinity alone as opposed to other factors such as the wind.

The movement of surface currents pushed by the wind is fairly intuitive. For example, the wind easily produces ripples on the surface of a pond. Thus the deep ocean – devoid of wind – was assumed to be perfectly static by early oceanographers. However, modern instrumentation shows that current velocities in deep water masses can be significant (although much less than surface speeds).

In the deep ocean, the predominant driving force is differences in density, caused by salinity and temperature (the more saline the denser, and the colder the denser). There is often confusion over the components of the circulation that are wind and density driven. Note that ocean currents due to tides are also significant in many places; most prominent in relatively shallow coastal areas, tidal currents can also be significant in the deep ocean.

The density of ocean water is not globally homogeneous, but varies significantly and discretely. Sharply defined boundaries exist between water masses which form at the surface, and subsequently maintain their own identity within the ocean. They position themselves one above or below each other according to their density, which depends on both temperature and salinity.

Warm seawater expands and is thus less dense than cooler seawater. Saltier water is denser than fresher water because the dissolved salts fill interstices between water molecules, resulting in more mass per unit volume. Lighter water masses float over denser ones (just as a piece of wood or ice will float on water. This is known as "stable stratification". When dense water masses are first formed, they are not stably stratified. In order to take up their most stable positions, water masses of different densities must flow, providing a driving force for deep currents.

The thermohaline circulation is mainly triggered by the formation of deep water masses in the North Atlantic and the Southern Ocean and Haline forcing caused by differences in temperature and salinity of the water.

Movement of thermohaline circulation

Formation and movement of the deep water masses at the North Atlantic Ocean, creates sinking water masses that fill the basin and flows very slowly into the deep abyssal plains of the Atlantic. This high latitude cooling and the low latitude heating drives the movement of the deep water in a polar southward flow. The deep water flows through the Antarctic Ocean Basin around South Africa where it is split into two routes: one into the Indian Ocean and one past Australia into the Pacific.

At the Indian Ocean, some of the cold and salty water from Atlantic – drawn by the flow of warmer and fresher upper ocean water from the tropical Pacific – causes a vertical exchange of dense, sinking water with lighter water above. It is known as overturning. In the Pacific Ocean, the rest of the cold and salty water from the Atlantic undergoes Haline forcing and slowly becomes warmer and fresher.

The out-flowing undersea of cold and salty water makes the sea level of the Atlantic slightly lower than the Pacific and salinity or halinity of water at the Atlantic higher than the Pacific. This generates a large but slow flow of warmer and fresher upper ocean water from the tropical Pacific to the Indian Ocean through the Indonesian Archipelago to replace the cold and salty Antarctic Bottom Water. This is also known as Haline forcing (net high latitude freshwater gain and low latitude evaporation). This warmer, fresher water from the Pacific flows up through the South Atlantic to Greenland, where it cools off and undergoes evaporative cooling and sinks to the ocean floor, providing a continuous thermohaline circulation.

Hence, a recent and popular name for the thermohaline circulation, emphasizing the vertical nature and pole-to-pole character of this kind of ocean circulation, is the meridional overturning circulation.

BIOLOGICAL PRODUCTIVITY IN THE OCEAN

Primary production is the total amount of carbon (C) in grams converted into organic material per square meter of sea surface per year (gm $C/m^2/yr$). Factors that limit plant growth and reduce primary production include solar radiation and nutrients as major factors and upwelling, turbulence, grazing intensity and turbidity as secondary factors. Only 0.1 to 0.2% of the solar radiation is employed for photosynthesis and its energy stored in organic compounds.Macronutrients and Micronutrients are chemicals needed for survival, growth and reproduction.

Upwelling and turbulence can return nutrients to the surface. Over-grazing of autotrophs can deplete the population and lead to a decline in productivity.Turbidity reduces the depth of light penetration and restricts productivity even if nutrients are abundant.

Productivity varies greatly in different parts of the ocean in response to the availability of nutrients and sunlight. In the tropics and subtropics sunlight is abundant, but it generates a strong thermocline that restricts upwelling of nutrients and results in lower productivity. High productivity locally can occur in areas of coastal upwelling, in the tropical waters between the gyres and at coral reefs. In temperate regions productivity is distinctly seasonal. Polar waters are nutrient-rich all year but productivity is only high in the summer when light is abundant. Primary productivity varies from 25 to 1250 gm C/m^2/yr in the marine environment and is highest in estuaries and lowest in the open ocean. In the open ocean productivity distribution resembles a "bull's eye " pattern with lowest productivity in the center and highest at the edge of the basin. Water in the center of the ocean is a clear blue because it is an area of downwelling, above a strong thermocline and is almost devoid of biological activity.

Continental shelves display moderate productivity between 50 and 200 gm C/m^2/yr because nutrients wash in from the land and tide- and wave- generated turbulence recycle nutrients from the bottom water.Polar areas have high productivity because there is no pycnocline to inhibit mixing.Equatorial waters have high productivity because of upwelling.

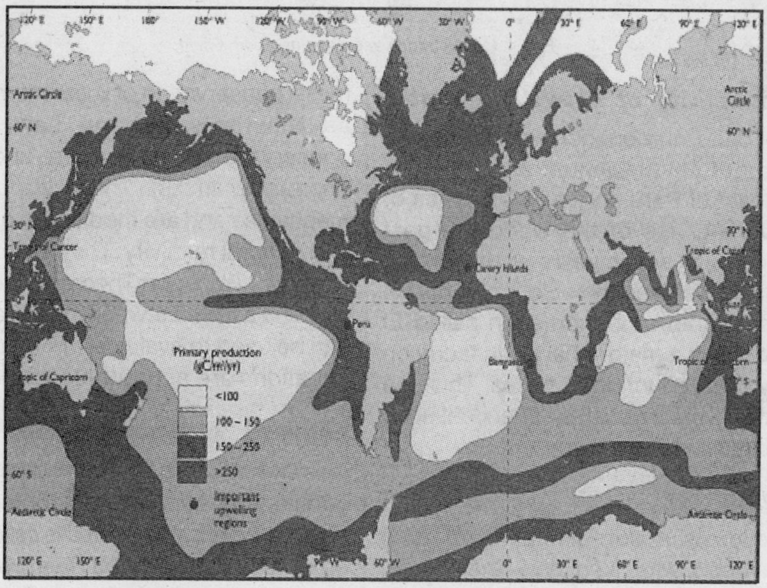

4.2: Primary Productivity

Global Patterns of Productivity

It is possible to estimate plant and fish productivity in the ocean. The size of the plankton biomass is a good indicator of the biomass of the remainder of the food web. Annual primary production (APP) is equal to primary production rate (PPR) times the area for which the rate is applicable.

– APP = PPR x Area (to which applicable)

Transfer efficiency (TE) is a measure of the amount of carbon that is passed between trophic levels and is used for growth. Transfer efficiency varies from 10 to 20% in most food chains. Potential production (PP) at any trophic level is equal to the annual primary production (APP) times the transfer efficiency (TE) for each step in the food chain to the trophic level of the organism under consideration.

– PP = APP x TE (for each step)

Although rate of productivity is very low for the open ocean compared to areas of upwelling, the open ocean has the greatest biomass productivity because of its enormous size. In the open ocean the food chains are longer and energy transfer is low, so fish populations are small.

Most fish production is equally divided between area of upwelling and coastal waters. Calculations suggest that the annual fish production is about 240 million tons/yr. Over-fishing is removing fish from the ocean faster than they are replaced by reproduction and this can eventually lead to the collapse of the fish population.

FISH PRODUCTION

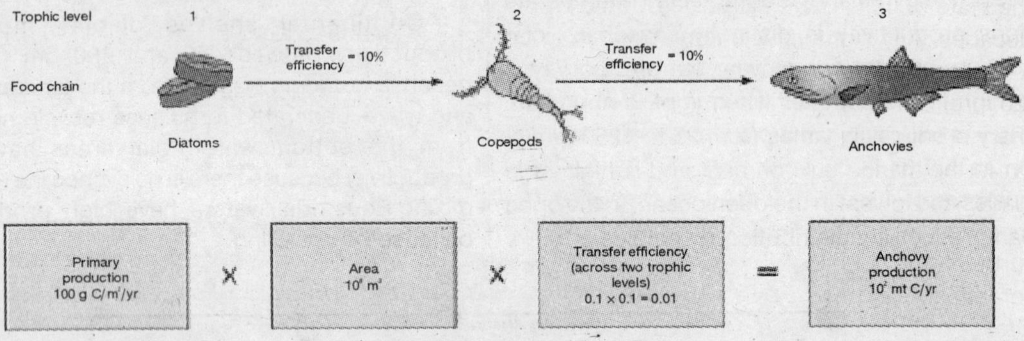

Fig. 4.3: Illustration representing Food Chain

Biological Productivity of Upwelling Water

Upwelling of deep, nutrient-rich water supports large populations of phytoplankton and fish. The waters off the coast of Peru normally is an area of upwelling, supporting one of the world's largest fisheries. Every three to seven years warm surface waters in the Pacific displace the cold, nutrient-rich water on Peru's shelf in a phenomenon called El Nino. El Nino results in a major change in fauna on the shelf and a great reduction in fishes. This can lead to mass starvation of organisms dependent upon the fish as their major food source.

Motion of fluids

fluid dynamics is a sub-discipline of fluid mechanics that deals with fluid flow–the natural science of fluids (liquids and gases) in motion. It has several subdisciplines itself, including aerodynamics (the study of air and other gases in motion) and hydrodynamics (the study of liquids in motion). Fluid dynamics has a wide range of applications, including calculating forces and moments on aircraft, determining the mass flow rate of petroleum through pipelines, predicting weather patterns, understanding nebulae in interstellar space and reportedly modeling fission weapon detonation.

Equations of fluid dynamics

The foundational axioms of fluid dynamics are the conservation laws, specifically, conservation of mass, conservation of linear momentum (also known as Newton's Second Law of Motion), and conservation of energy (also known as First Law of Thermodynamics). These are based on classical mechanics and are modified in quantum mechanics and general relativity. They are expressed using the Reynolds Transport Theorem. The Reynolds number, which is a ratio between inertial and viscous forces, can be used to evaluate whether viscous or inviscid equations are appropriate to the problem.

Laminar vs turbulent flow

Turbulence is flow characterized by recirculation, eddies, and apparent randomness. Flow in which turbulence is not exhibited is called laminar. It should be noted, however, that the presence of eddies or recirculation alone does not necessarily indicate turbulent flow–these phenomena may be present in laminar flow as well. Mathematically, turbulent flow is often represented via a Reynolds decomposition, in which the flow is broken down into the sum of an average component and a perturbation component.

It is believed that turbulent flows can be described well through the use of the Navier–Stokes equations. Direct numerical simulation (DNS), based on the Navier–Stokes equations, makes it possible to simulate turbulent flows at moderate Reynolds numbers. Restrictions depend on the power of the computer used and the efficiency of the solution algorithm. The results of DNS agree with the experimental data.

Most flows of interest have Reynolds numbers much too high for DNS to be a viable option[3], given the state of computational power for the next few decades. Any flight vehicle large enough to carry a human (L > 3 m), moving faster than 72 km/h (20 m/s) is well beyond the limit of DNS simulation (Re = 4 million). Transport aircraft wings (such as on an Airbus A300 or Boeing 747) have Reynolds numbers of 40 million (based on the wing chord). In order to solve these real-life flow problems, turbulence models will be a necessity for the foreseeable future. Reynolds-averaged Navier–Stokes equations (RANS) combined with turbulence modeling provides a model of the effects of the turbulent flow. Such a modeling mainly provides the additional momentum transfer by the Reynolds stresses, although the turbulence also enhances the heat and mass transfer. Another promising methodology is large eddy simulation (LES), especially in the guise of detached eddy simulation (DES)–which is a combination of RANS turbulence modeling and large eddy simulation.

Newtonian vs non-Newtonian fluids

Sir Isaac Newton showed how stress and the rate of strain are very close to linearly related for many familiar fluids, such as water and air. These Newtonian fluids are modeled by a coefficient called viscosity, which depends on the specific fluid.

However, some of the other materials, such as emulsions and slurries and some visco-elastic materials (e.g. blood, some polymers), have more complicated non-Newtonian stress-strain behaviours. These materials include sticky liquids such as latex, honey, and lubricants which are studied in the sub-discipline of rheology.

STRUCTURE AND CHEMICAL COMPOSITION OF THE ATMOSPHERE

STRUCTURE OF THE ATMOSPHERE

The atmosphere consists of different layers with varying density and temperature. Density is highest near the surface of the earth and decreases with increasing altitude. The column of atmosphere is divided into five different layers depending upon the temperature condition. They are:

- troposphere,
- stratosphere,
- mesosphere,
- ionosphere and
- exosphere.

Troposphere

The troposphere is the lowermost layer of the atmosphere. Its average height is 13 km and extends roughly to a height of 8 km near the poles and about 18 km at the equator. Thickness of the troposphere is greatest at the equator because heat is transported to great heights by strong convectional currents. This layer contains dust particles and water vapour. All changes in climate and weather take place in this layer. The temperature in this layer decreases at the rate of 1°C for every 165m of height. This is the most important layer for all biological activity.

Tropopause

The zone separating the tropsophere from stratosphere is known as the tropopause. The air temperature at the tropopause is about minus 800C over the equator and about minus 45C over the poles. The temperature here is nearly constant, and hence, it is called the tropopause.

Stratosphere

The stratosphere is found above the tropopause and extends up to a height of 50 km. One important feature of the stratosphere is that it contains the ozone layer. This layer absorbs ultra-violet radiation and shields life on the earth from intense, harmful form of energy.

Mesosphere

The mesosphere lies above the stratosphere, which extends up to a height of 80 km. In this layer, once again, temperature starts decreasing with the increase in altitude and reaches up to minus 100°C at the height of 80 km. The upper limit of mesosphere is known as the mesopause. The ionosphere is located between 80 and 400 km above the mesopause. It contains electrically charged particles known as ions, and hence, it is known as ionosphere. Radio waves transmitted from the earth are reflected back to the earth by this layer. Temperature here starts increasing with height.

Exosphere

The uppermost layer of the atmosphere above the ionosphere is known as the exosphere. This is the highest layer but very little is known about it. Whatever contents aré there, these are extremely rarefied in this layer, and it gradually merges with the outer space.

The atmosphere is composed of gases, water vapour and dust particles. Nitrogen constitute largest percentage by volume among all the gases present in the atmosphere. Nitrogen has 78.08% of atmospheric gases, followed by Oxygen, Argon and Carbon Dioxide.

Constituent	*Percentage by Volume*
Nitrogen	78.08
Oxygen	20.95
Argon	0.93
Carbon dioxide	0.036
Neon	0.002
Helium	0.0005
Krypton	0.001
Xenon	0.00009
Hydrogen	0.00005

Table 4.1 : Permanent Gases of the Atmosphere

CHEMICAL COMPOSITION OF THE ATMOSPHERE

Earth's atmosphere is composed primarily of nitrogen (at 78%), 21% oxygen and much smaller amounts of argon, carbon dioxide and water. The biological processes constantly replenish oxygen into the atmosphere as others consume it. When the Earth was first formed, there was probably a lot of carbon dioxide, but most of went into carbonate rocks and oceans. Now the small amount of carbon dioxide contributes to the regulation of temperature on Earth. The relatively large amount of oxygen on Earth is remarkable due to the fact that other planets have little or almost no free oxygen. The ecological cycle between plants and animals, living things in general is what makes this possible.

Water Vapour

Water vapour is also a variable gas in the atmosphere, which decreases with altitude. In the warm and wet tropics, it may account for our per cent of the air by volume, while in the dry and cold areas of desert and polar regions, it may be less than one per cent of the air. Water vapour also decreases from the equator towards the poles. It also absorbs parts of the insolation from the sun and preserves the earth's radiated heat. It thus, acts like a blanket allowing the earth neither to become too cold nor too hot. Water vapour also contributes to the stability and instability in the air.

LAPSE RATE

INTRODUCTION

The Lapse rate is defined as the decrease of an atmospheric variable with height, the variable being temperature unless otherwise specified. The term applies ambiguously to the environmental lapse rate and the process lapse rate, and the meaning must often be ascertained from the context.

MATHEMATICAL DEFINITION

In general, a lapse rate is the negative of the rate of temperature change with altitude change, thus:

$$\gamma = -\frac{dT}{dz}$$

where γ is the lapse rate given in units of temperature divided by units of altitude, T = temperature, and z = altitude.

Note: In some cases, Γ or α can be used to represent the adiabatic lapse rate in order to avoid confusion with other terms symbolized by γ, such as the specific heat ratio or the psychrometric constant.

TYPES OF LAPSE RATES

There are two types of lapse rate:

- Environmental lapse rate – which refers to the actual change of temperature with altitude for the stationary atmosphere (i.e. the temperature gradient)
- The adiabatic lapse rates – which refer to the change in temperature of a mass of air as it moves upwards. There are two adiabatic rates:
  - Dry adiabatic lapse rate
  - Moist (or saturated) adiabatic lapse rate

Environmental Lapse Rate

The environmental lapse rate (ELR), is the rate of decrease of temperature with altitude in the stationary atmosphere at a given time and location. As an average, the International Civil Aviation Organization (ICAO) defines an international standard atmosphere (ISA) with a temperature lapse rate of 6.49 K(°C)/1,000 m (3.56°F or 1.98 K(°C)/1,000 Ft) from sea level to 11 km (36,090 ft). From 11 km (36,090 ft or 6.8 mi) up to 20 km (65,620 ft or 12.4 mi), the constant temperature is –56.5°C (-69.7°F), which is the lowest assumed temperature in the ISA. The standard atmosphere contains no moisture. Unlike the idealized ISA, the temperature of the actual atmosphere does not always fall at a uniform rate with height. For example, there can be an inversion layer in which the temperature increases with height.

Dry Adiabatic Lapse Rate

The dry adiabatic lapse rate (DALR) is the rate of temperature decrease with height for a parcel of dry or unsaturated air rising under adiabatic conditions. Unsaturated air has less than 100% relative humidity; i.e. its actual temperature is higher than its dew point. The term adiabatic means that no heat transfer occurs into or out of the parcel. Air has low thermal conductivity, and the bodies of air involved are very large, so transfer of heat by conduction is negligibly small.

Under these conditions when the air rises (for instance, by convection) it expands, because the pressure is lower at higher altitudes. As the air parcel expands, it pushes on the air around it, doing work. Since the parcel does work but gains no heat, it loses internal energy so that its temperature decreases. The rate of temperature decrease is 9.8°C per 1,000 m. (The reverse occurs for a sinking parcel of air.)

For an adiabatic process, first law of thermodynamics can be written as

$$c_p dT - \alpha dP = 0$$

where c_p is the specific heat at constant pressure and α is the specific volume.

Assuming an atmosphere in hydrostatic equilibrium:

$$dP = -\rho g dz$$

where g is the standard gravity and c is the density. Combining these two equations to eliminate the pressure, one arrives at the result for the DALR,

$$\Gamma_d = -\frac{dT}{dz} = \frac{g}{c_p} = 9.8\,^\circ\mathrm{C/km}$$

Saturated Adiabatic Lapse Rate

When the air is saturated with water vapor (at its dew point), the moist adiabatic lapse rate (MALR) or saturated adiabatic lapse rate (SALR) applies. This lapse rate varies strongly with temperature. A typical value is around 5°C/km (2.7°F/1,000 ft).

The reason for the difference between the dry and moist adiabatic lapse rate values is that latent heat is released when water condenses, thus decreasing the rate of temperature drop as altitude increases. This heat release process is an important source of energy in the development of thunderstorms. An unsaturated parcel of air of given temperature, altitude and moisture content below that of the corresponding dewpoint cools at the dry adiabatic lapse rate as altitude increases until the dewpoint line for the given moisture content is intersected. As the water vapor then starts condensing the air parcel subsequently cools at the slower moist adiabatic lapse rate if the altitude increases further.

The saturated adiabatic lapse rate is given approximately by this equation from the glossary of the American Meteorology Society.

$$\Gamma = g\frac{1+\dfrac{H_v r}{R_{sd}T}}{C_{pd}+\dfrac{H_v^2 r\,\varepsilon}{R_{sd}T^2}}$$

where:

Γ_w = Wet adiabatic lapse rate, K/m

g = Earth's gravitational acceleration = 9.8076 m/s^2

H_v = Heat of vaporization of water, J/kg

r = The ratio of the mass of water vapor to the mass of dry air, kg/kg

R = The universal gas constant = 8,314 J kmol^{-1} K^{-1}

M = The molecular weight of any specific gas, kg/kmol = 28.964 for dry air and 18.015 for water vapor R/M = The specific gas constant of a gas, denoted as R_s

R_{sd} = Specific gas constant of dry air = 287 J kg^{-1} K^{-1}

R_{sw} = Specific gas constant of water vapor = 462 J kg^{-1} K^{-1}

ε = The dimensionless ratio of the specific gas constant of dry air to the specific gas constant for water vapor = 0.6220

T = Temperature of the saturated air, K

c_{pd} = The specific heat of dry air at constant pressure, J kg^{-1} K^{-1}

Application of Lapse rate in meteorology

The varying environmental lapse rates throughout the Earth's atmosphere are of critical importance in meteorology, particularly within the troposphere. They are used to determine if the parcel of rising air will rise high enough for its water to condense to form clouds, and, having formed clouds, whether the air will continue to rise and form bigger shower clouds, and whether these clouds will get even bigger and form cumulonimbus clouds (thunder clouds).

As unsaturated air rises, its temperature drops at the dry adiabatic rate. The dew point also drops (as a result of decreasing air pressure) but much more slowly, typically about –2°C per 1,000 m. If unsaturated air rises far enough, eventually its temperature will reach its dew point, and condensation will begin to form. This altitude is known as the lifting condensation level (LCL) when mechanical lift is present and the convective condensation level (CCL) absent mechanical lift, in which case, the parcel must be heated from below to its convective temperature. The cloud base will be somewhere within the layer bounded by these parameters.

The difference between the dry adiabatic lapse rate and the rate at which the dew point drops is around 8°C per 1,000 m. Given a difference in temperature and dew point readings on the ground, one can easily find the LCL by multiplying the difference by 125 m/°C.

If the environmental lapse rate is less than the moist adiabatic lapse rate, the air is absolutely stable – rising air will cool faster than the surrounding air and lose buoyancy. This often happens in the early morning, when the air near the ground has cooled overnight. Cloud formation in stable air is unlikely.

If the environmental lapse rate is between the moist and dry adiabatic lapse rates, the air is conditionally unstable – an unsaturated parcel of air does not have sufficient buoyancy to rise to the LCL or CCL, and it is stable to weak vertical displacements in either direction. If the parcel is saturated it is unstable and will rise to the LCL or CCL, and either be halted due to an inversion layer of convective inhibition, or if lifting continues, deep, moist convection (DMC) may ensue, as a parcel rises to the level of free convection (LFC), after which it enters the free convective layer (FCL) and usually rises to the equilibrium level (EL).

If the environmental lapse rate is larger than the dry adiabatic lapse rate, it has a superadiabatic lapse rate, the air is absolutely unstable – a parcel of air will gain buoyancy as it rises both below and above the lifting condensation level or convective condensation level. This often happens in the afternoon over many land masses. In these conditions, the likelihood of cumulus clouds, showers or even thunderstorms is increased.

SCALE HEIGHT

Scale height is a term often used in scientific contexts for a distance over which a quantity decreases by a factor of e (the base of natural logarithms). It is usually denoted by the capital letter H.

For planetary atmospheres, it is the vertical distance upwards, over which the pressure of the atmosphere decreases by a factor of 1/e. The scale height remains constant for a particular temperature. It can be calculated by

$$H = \frac{kT}{Mg}$$

where:

- k = Boltzmann constant = 1.38 x 10^{-23} J·K^{-1}
- T = mean planetary surface temperature in kelvins
- M= mean molecular mass of dry air (units kg/mol)
- g = acceleration due to gravity on planetary surface (m/sl)

The pressure in the atmosphere is caused by the weight on the atmosphere of the overlying atmosphere [force per unit area]. If at a height of z the atmosphere has density ñ and pressure P, then moving upwards at an infinitesimally small height dz will decrease the pressure by amount dP, equal to the weight of a layer of atmosphere of thickness dz.

Thus: $$\frac{dP}{dz} = -g\rho$$

where g is used to denote the acceleration due to gravity. For small dz it is possible to assume g to be constant; the minus sign indicates that as the height increases the pressure decreases. Therefore using the equation of state for an ideal gas of mean molecular mass M at temperature T, the density can be expressed as such:

$$\rho = \frac{MP}{kT}$$

Therefore combining the equations gives

$$\frac{dP}{P} = \frac{-dz}{\frac{kT}{Mg}}$$

which can then be incorporated with the equation for H given above to give:

$$\frac{dP}{P} = -\frac{dz}{H}$$

which will not change unless the temperature does. Integrating the above and assuming where P_0 is the pressure at height z = 0 (pressure at sea level) the pressure at height z can be written as:

$$P = P_0 \exp\left(-\frac{z}{H}\right)$$

This translates as the pressure decreasing exponentially with height.

In the Earth's atmosphere, the pressure at sea level P_0 averages about 1.01 × 10^5 Pa, the mean molecular mass of dry air is 28.964 u and hence 28.964 × 1.660×10^{-27} = 4.808 × 10^{-26} kg, and g = 9.81 m/sl. As a function of temperature the scale height of the Earth's atmosphere is therefore 1.38/(4.808 × 9.81) × 10^3 = 29.26 m/deg. This yields the following scale heights for representative air temperatures.

T = 290 K, H = 8500 m

T = 273 K, H = 8000 m

T = 260 K, H = 7610 m

T = 210 K, H = 6000 m

These figures should be compared with the temperature and density of the Earth's atmosphere plotted at NRLMSISE-00, which shows the air density dropping from 1200 g/m^3 at sea level to 0.5^3 = 0.125 g/m^3 at 70 km, a factor of 9600, indicating an average scale height of 70/ln(9600) = 7.64 km, consistent with the indicated average air temperature over that range of close to 260 K.

GEOPOTENTIAL

Geopotential is the potential of the Earth's gravity field. For convenience it is often defined as minus the potential energy per unit mass, so that the gravity vector is obtained as the gradient of this potential, without the minus.

For geophysical applications, gravity is distinguished from gravitation. Gravity is defined as the resultant of gravitation and the centrifugal force caused by the Earth's rotation. The global mean sea surface is close to one of the equipotential surfaces of the geopotential of gravity. This equipotential surface, or surface of constant geopotential, is called the geoid.

For the purpose of satellite orbital mechanics, the geopotential is typically described by a series expansion into spherical harmonics (spectral representation). In this context the geopotential is taken as the potential of the gravitational field of the Earth, that is, leaving out the centrifugal potential.

GREENHOUSE GASES AND GLOBAL WARMING

Carbon dioxide, Methane, Choloro Flouro Carbons (CFCS), Nitrogen oxide and Ozone are considered as greenhouse gases, since they initiate the process of Green house effect i.e. warming of earth.

The greenhouse effect is a naturally occurring process that aids in heating the Earth's surface and atmosphere. It results from the fact that certain atmospheric gases, such as carbon dioxide, water vapor, and methane, are able to change the energy balance of the planet by absorbing longwave radiation emitted from the Earth's surface. Without the greenhouse effect life on this planet would probably not exist as the average temperature of the Earth would be a chilly −18° Celsius, rather than the present 15° Celsius.

As energy from the sun passes through the atmosphere a number of things take place. A portion of the energy (26 % globally) is reflected or scattered back to space by clouds and other atmospheric particles. About 19% of the energy available is absorbed by clouds, gases (like ozone), and particles in the atmosphere. Of the remaining 55 % of the solar energy passing through the Earth's atmosphere, 4% is reflected from the surface back to space. On average, about 51% of the sun's radiation reaches the surface. This energy is then used in a number of processes, including the heating of the ground surface; the melting of ice and snow and the evaporation of water; and plant photosynthesis. The heating of the ground by sunlight causes the Earth's surface to become a radiator of energy in the longwave band (sometimes called infrared radiation). This emission of energy is generally directed to space. However, only a small portion of this energy actually makes it back to space. The majority of the outgoing infrared radiation is absorbed by the greenhouse gases.

Absorption of longwave radiation by the atmosphere causes additional heat energy to be added to the Earth's atmospheric system. The now warmer atmospheric greenhouse gas molecules begin radiating longwave energy in all directions. Over 90% of this emission of longwave energy is directed back to the Earth's surface where it once again is absorbed by the surface. The heating of the ground by the longwave radiation causes the ground surface to once again radiate, repeating the cycle described above, again and again, until no more longwave is available for absorption.

The amount of heat energy added to the atmosphere by the greenhouse effect is controlled by the concentration of greenhouse gases in the Earth's atmosphere. All of the major greenhouse gases have increased in concentration since the beginning of the Industrial Revolution (about 1700 AD). As a result of these higher concentrations, scientists predict that the greenhouse effect will be enhanced and the Earth's climate will become warmer. Predicting the amount of warming is accomplished by computer modeling. Computer models suggest that a doubling of the concentration of the main greenhouse gas, carbon dioxide, may raise the average global temperature between 1 and 3° Celsius. However, the numeric equations of computer models do not accurately simulate the effects of a number of possible negative feedbacks. For example, many of the models cannot properly simulate the negative effects that increased cloud cover would have on the radiation balance of a warmer Earth. Increasing the Earth's temperature would cause the oceans to evaporate greater amounts of water, causing the atmosphere to become cloudier. These extra clouds would then reflect a greater proportion of the sun's energy back to space reducing the amount of solar radiation absorbed by the atmosphere and the Earth's surface. With less solar energy being absorbed at the surface, the effects of an enhanced greenhouse effect may be counteracted.

A number of gases are involved in the human caused enhancement of the greenhouse effect. These gases include: carbon dioxide (CO_2); methane (CH_4); nitrous oxide (N_2O); chlorofluorocarbons (CFxClx); and tropospheric ozone (O_3). Of these gases, the single most important gas is carbon dioxide which accounts for about 55% of the change in the intensity of the Earth's greenhouse effect. The contributions of the other gases are 25% for chlorofluorocarbons, 15% for methane, and 5% for nitrous oxide. Ozone's contribution to the enhancement of greenhouse effect is still yet to be quantified.

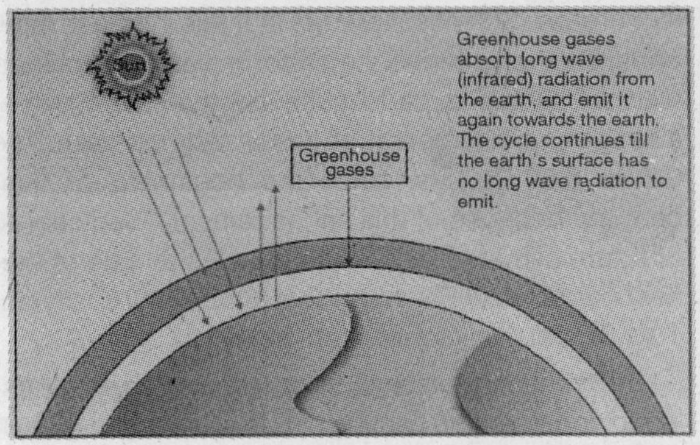

Figure 4.4 : Solar Isolation at the outermost atmosphere.

Average concentrations of atmospheric carbon dioxide in the year 2005 were about 380 parts per million. Prior to 1700, levels of carbon dioxide were about 280 parts per million. This increase in carbon dioxide in the atmosphere is primarily due to the activities of humans. Beginning in 1700, societal changes brought about by the Industrial Revolution increased the amount of carbon dioxide entering the atmosphere. The major sources of this gas include fossil fuel combustion for industry, transportation, space heating, electricity generation and cooking; and vegetation changes in natural prairie, woodland, and forested ecosystems. Emissions from fossil fuel combustion account for about 65% of the extra carbon dioxide now found in our atmosphere. The remaining 35% is derived from deforestation and the conversion of prairie, woodland, and forested ecosystems primarily into agricultural systems. Natural ecosystems can hold 20 to 100 times more carbon dioxide per unit area than agricultural systems.

Artificially created chlorofluorocarbons are the strongest greenhouse gas per molecule. However, low concentrations in the atmosphere reduce their overall importance in the enhancement of the greenhouse effect. Current measurements in the atmosphere indicate that the concentration of these chemicals may soon begin declining because of reduced emissions. Reports of the development of ozone holes over the North and South Poles and a general decline in global stratospheric ozone levels over the last two decades has caused many nations to cutback on their production and use of these chemicals. In 1987, the signing of the Montreal Protocol agreement by forty-six nations established an immediate timetable for the global reduction of chlorofluorocarbons production and use.

Since 1750, methane concentrations in the atmosphere have increased by more than 150%. The primary sources for the additional methane added to the atmosphere (in order of importance) are rice cultivation, domestic grazing animals, termites, landfills, coal mining, and oil and gas extraction. Anaerobic conditions associated with rice paddy flooding results in the formation of methane gas. However, an accurate estimate of how much methane is being produced from rice paddies has been difficult to obtain. More than 60% of all rice paddies are found in India and China where scientific data concerning emission rates are unavailable. Nevertheless, scientists believe that the contribution of rice paddies is large because this form of crop production has more than doubled since 1950. Grazing animals release methane to the environment as a result of herbaceous digestion. Some researchers believe the addition of methane from this source has more than quadrupled over the last century. Termites also release methane through similar processes. Land-use change in the tropics, due to deforestation, ranching, and farming, may be causing termite numbers to expand. If this assumption is correct, the contribution from these insects may be important. Methane is also released from landfills, coal mines, and gas and oil drilling. Landfills produce methane as organic wastes decompose over time. Coal, oil, and natural gas deposits release methane to the atmosphere when these deposits are excavated or drilled.

The average concentration of nitrous oxide in the atmosphere is now increasing at a rate of 0.2 to 0.3% per year. Sources for this increase include land-use conversion; fossil fuel combustion; biomass burning; and soil fertilization. Most of the nitrous oxide added to the atmosphere each year comes from deforestation and the conversion of forest, savanna and grassland ecosystems into agricultural fields and rangeland. Both of these processes reduce the amount of nitrogen stored in living vegetation and soil through the decomposition of organic matter. Nitrous oxide is also released into the atmosphere when fossil fuels and biomass are burned. However, the combined contribution of these sources to the increase of this gas in the atmosphere is thought to be minor. The use of nitrate and ammonium fertilizers to enhance plant growth is another source of nitrous oxide. Accurate measurements of how much nitrous oxide is being released from fertilization have been difficult to obtain. Estimates suggest that the contribution from this source may represent from 50% to 0.2% of nitrous oxide added to the atmosphere annually.

Ozone's role in the enhancement of the greenhouse effect has been difficult to determine scientifically. Accurate measurements of past long-term (more than 25 years in the past) levels of this gas in the atmosphere are currently unavailable. Concentrations of ozone gas are found in two different regions of the Earth's atmosphere. The majority of the ozone (about 97%) found in the atmosphere is localized in the stratosphere at an altitude of 15 to 55 kilometers above the Earth's surface. In recent years, the concentration of the stratospheric ozone has been decreasing because of the buildup of chlorofluorocarbons in the atmosphere. Since the late 1970s, scientists have discovered that total column ozone amounts over Antarctica in the springtime have decreased by as much as 70%. Satellite measurements have indicated that the zone from 65° North to 65° South latitude has had a 3% decrease in stratospheric ozone since 1978. Ozone is also highly concentrated at the Earth's surface. Most of this ozone is created as an artificial by product of photochemical smog.

In summary, the greenhouse effect causes the atmosphere to trap more heat energy at the Earth's surface and within the atmosphere by absorbing and re-emitting longwave energy. Of the longwave energy emitted back to space, 90% is intercepted and absorbed by greenhouse gases. Without the greenhouse effect the Earth's average global temperature would be –18° Celsius, rather than the present 15° Celsius. In the last few centuries, the activities of humans have directly or indirectly caused the concentration of the major greenhouse gases to increase. Scientists predict that this increase may enhance the greenhouse effect making the planet warmer. Some experts estimate that the Earth's average global temperature has already increased by 0.3 to 0.6° Celsius, since the beginning of this century, because of this enhancement. Predictions of future climates indicate that by the middle of the next century the Earth's global temperature may be 1 to 3° Celsius higher than today.

Increase in the level of greenhouse gases has led to considerable heating of Earth leading to global warming. During the past century, the emperature of Earth has increased by 0.6 three decades. Scientists believe that this rise in temperature is leading to deleterious changes in the environment and resulting in odd climatic changes (e.g. El Nino effect) , thus leading to increased melting of polar ice caps as well as of other places like the Himalayan snow caps. Over many years, this will result in a rise in sea level that can submerge many coastal areas. The total spectrum of changes that global warming can bring about is a subject that is still under active research.

CLOUD FORMATION AND PRECIPITATION PROCESSES

Condensation or deposition of water above the Earth's surface creates clouds. In general, clouds develop in any air mass that becomes saturated (relative humidity becomes 100%). Saturation can occur by way of atmospheric mechanisms that cause the temperature of an air mass to be cooled to its dew point or frost point. The following mechanisms or processes can achieve this outcome causing clouds to develop:

(1) **Orographic uplift** occurs when air is forced to rise because of the physical presence of elevated land. As the parcel rises it cools as a result of adiabatic expansion at a rate of approximately 10° Celsius per 1000 meters until saturation. The development of clouds and resulting heavy quantities of precipitation along the west coast of Canada are mainly due to this process.

(2) **Convectional lifting** is associated with surface heating of the air at the ground surface. If enough heating occurs, the mass of air becomes warmer and lighter than the air in the surrounding environment, and just like a hot air balloon it begins to rise, expand, and cool. When sufficient cooling has taken place saturation occurs forming clouds. This process is active in the interior of continents and near the equator forming cumulus clouds and or cumulonimbus clouds (thunderstorms). The rain that is associated with the development of thunderstorm clouds is delivered in large amounts over short periods of time in extremely localized areas.

(3) **Convergence or frontal lifting** takes place when two masses of air come together. In most cases, the two air masses have different temperature and moisture characteristics. Oneof the air masses is usually warm and moist, while the other is cold and dry. The leading edge of the latter air mass acts as an inclined wall or front causing the moist warm air to be lifted. Of course the lifting causes the warm moist air mass to cool due to expansion resulting in saturation. This cloud formation mechanism is common at the mid-latitudes where cyclones form along the polar front and near the equator where the trade winds meet at the intertropical convergence zone.

(4) **Radiative cooling** occurs when the sun is no longer supplying the ground and overlying air with energy derived from solar insolation (e.g., night). Instead, the surface of the Earth now begins to lose energy in the form of longwave radiation which causes the ground and air above it to cool. The clouds that result from this type of cooling take the form of surface fog.

Of course these causes of cloud development do not always act in a singular fashion. It is possible to get combinations of all four types, such as when convection and orographic uplift cause summer afternoon cloud development and showers in the mountains.

PRECIPITATION

The word precipitation is derived from a latin word 'precipitatio' meaning a headlong falling down. In the meterological language it means condensed or frozen water vapour that falls on the ground. It not only includes rain or snow but also hail, sleet and fog. These forms depend upon the following conditions:

- The temperature at which condensation takes place.
- The condition encountered as the particles pass through the air.
- The type of clouds and their height from the ground.
- The process generating phenomena.

Forms of Precipitation

Precipitation results from the continued condensation and growth of the moisture particles until they become too large to remain suspended in the air. If condensation takes place at a temperature above 00 C, the resulting precipitation is in the form of rain. If rain passes through a layer of colder air on the way down it may freeze and fall as sleet. In a strong turbulent currents of thunderstorms, water drops may be carried upward into freezing temperatures and eventually fall as hail. In fact, violent air currents may keep hailstones shuttling up and down until they grow to enormous sizes. Snow is not frozen rain, but forms when moisture crystallises directly from vapour at a temperature below freezing. If snowflakes grow without interference they form beautiful symmetrical, six-sided crystals. Ice storms result when rain, already near the freezing point, falls on the colder ground and vegetation and freezes upon contact.

Insolation and heat budget, radiation balance, general circulation of the atmosphere and ocean.

INSOLATION

The word insolation connotes incoming solar radiation. It is absorbed in the lower layer of the atmosphere as bright light. Light is the visible portion of the spectrum lying between infra-red and ultra-violet. The ultra-violet has dimension of shortest wavelength. It forms only 6 per cent of insolation and is consumed in photochemical reaction. While the infra- red rays, though invisible, form 43 per cent of insolation. They are largely absorbed by water vapour that is concentrated in the lower atmosphere.

Insolation is greatest at the equator. It decreases polewards. The total amount of insolation received at the equator is roughly about 4 times of that received at the poles. In tropical regions, the amount of insolation is not only large but there is also little seasonal variation. It is because all places between Tropics of Cancer and Capricorn experience overhead sun twice during the course of a year. In the temperate region, the amount of insolation is less than the tropical region and the seasonal variation is high.

Effects of Atmosphere on Insolation

The energy from the sun passes through different layers of the atmosphere before it reaches the ground. Atmospheric gases are essentially transparent to visible light, but suspended particles of liquid or solid material can absorb or reflect light. A thick cloud may allow less than 10 per cent of sunlight passing through it to reach the earth's surface. Clouds generally behave like mirrors; they reflect sunlight in different directions rather than absorbing it. Reflected sunlight is permanently lost to the earth. The blue colour of daytime sky is due to scattering of sunlight. But for scattering effect, the sky would be black starry even when the sun is high up in the sky.

HEAT BUDGET

Shortwave radiation from the sun enters the surface-atmosphere system of the Earth and is ultimately returned to space as longwave radiation (because the Earth is cooler than the sun). A basic necessity of this energy interchange is that incoming solar insolation and outgoing radiation be equal in quantity.

Insolation is subjected to several processes of absorption, reflection and scattering. They decide the heat budget of the earth and the atmosphere. The amount of solar energy passing through the atmosphere depends upon the angle of the sunrays and transparency of the atmosphere. It varies according to time and place. The solar energy absorbed by the earth gets translated into heat day after day, year after year. All of our weather records reveal, certainly in general fashion, a strong continuity of temperature characteris- tics with little to indicate the warming trend that would be mandatory if energy receipt exceeded loss, so the counter flow must exist. The gains and losses in heat by incoming and outgoing radiation is known as heat budget. The term 'budget' implies balance in the gains and losses of the solar energy on the earth.

The sun emits the short wave radiation to space, while the earth radiates long-wave or infra-red radiation to space. The solar energy strikes the upper limits of the atmosphere and it gradually reaches the earth's surface directly and indirectly (scattered) and is absorbed. It is estimated that out of 100 units of incoming solar energy, only 22 units travel directly to the earth's surface. This energy flow is called direct radiation. The 35 units received at the upper limit of the troposphere is reflected and scattered back into space by clouds (24 units), dust particles (7 units) and by surface of the earth (4 units) in its original short-wave. Some of the scattered rays (25 units in all) eventually, find their way down to the earth's surface and are absorbed by it. They are collectively called diffuse radiation. Another 18 units of incoming solar radiation is absorbed by ozone (3 units), water, dust and other components of the atmosphere (13 units) and by clouds (2 units).

In all, 47 units of solar energy reach the earth's surfae as direct or diffuse radiation, while 18 units are absorbed by the atmosphere.

As such 65 units in all (47 units of the earth's surface +18 units of the atmosphere) take part in heating the earth and its atmosphere. To balance the budget, 65 units are lost to space in the form of long waves by the earth's surface directly (5 units) and reradiated from the earth to the atmosphere (60 units).

EL NINO AND THE SOUTHERN OSCILLATION (ENSO)

El Nino is the name given to the occasional development of warm ocean surface waters along the coast of Ecuador and Peru. When this warming occurs the usual upwelling of cold, nutrient rich deep ocean water is significantly reduced. El Nino normally occurs around Christmas and lasts usually for a few weeks to a few months. Sometimes an extremely warm event can develop that lasts for much longer time periods. In the 1990s, strong El Ninos developed in 1991 and lasted until 1995, and from fall 1997 to spring 1998.

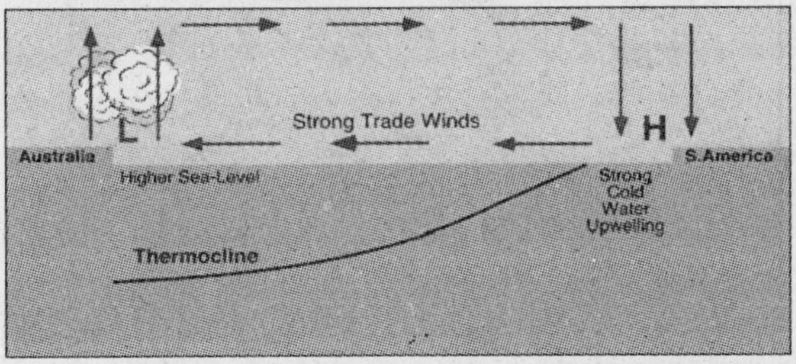

Figure 4.5: This cross-section of the Pacific ocean, along the equator, illustrates the pattern of atmospheric circulation typically found at the equatorial Pacific.

The formation of an El Nino is linked with the cycling of a Pacific Ocean circulation pattern known as the southern oscillation. In a normal year, a surface low pressure develops in the region of northern Australia and Indonesia and a high pressure system over the coast of Peru. As a result, the trade winds over the Pacific Ocean move strongly from east to west. The easterly flow of the trade winds carries warm surface waters westward, bringing convective storms to Indonesia and coastal Australia. Along the coast of Peru, cold bottom water wells up to the surface to replace the warm water that is pulled to the west.

In an El Nino year, air pressure drops over large areas of the central Pacific and along the coast of South America. The normal low pressure system is replaced by a weak high in the western Pacific (the southern oscillation). This change in pressure pattern causes the trade winds to be reduced. This reduction allows the equatorial counter current to accumulate warm ocean water along the coastlines of Peru and Ecuador. This accumulation of warm water causes the thermocline to drop in the eastern part of Pacific Ocean which cuts off the upwelling of cold deep ocean water along the coast of Peru. Climatically, the development of an El Nino brings drought to the western Pacific, rains to the equatorial coast of South America, and convective storms and hurricanes to the central Pacific.

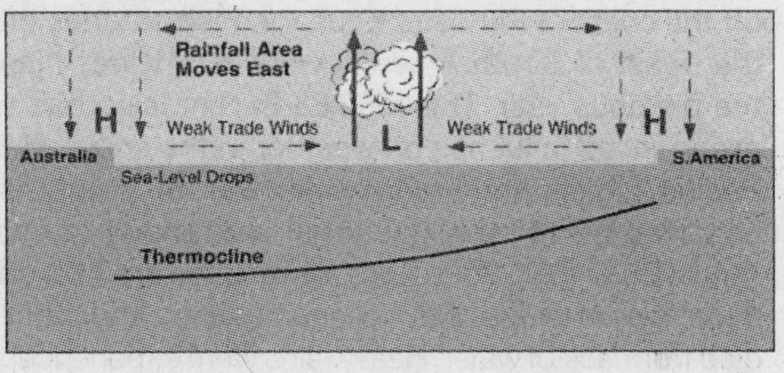

Figure 4-6: This cross-section of the Pacific ocean, along the equator, illustrates the pattern of atmospheric circulation that causes the formation of the El Nino. Here position of the thermocline has changed from Figure 4-5.

After an El Nino event weather conditions usually return back to normal. However, in some years the trade winds can become extremely strong and an abnormal accumulation of cold water can occur in the central and eastern Pacific. This event is called a La Nina. A strong La Nina occurred in 1988 and scientists believe that it may have been responsible for the summer drought over central North America. The most recent La Nina began developing in the middle of 1998 and have been persistent into the winter of 2000. During this period, the Atlantic ocean has seen very active hurricane seasons in 1998 and 1999. In 1998, ten tropical storm developed of which six become full-blown hurricanes. One of the hurricanes that developed, named Mitch, was the strongest October hurricane ever to develop in about 100 years of record keeping. Some of the other weather effects of La Nina include abnormally heavy monsoons in India and Southeast Asia, cool and wet winter weather in southeastern Africa, wet weather in eastern Australia, cold winter in western Canada and northwestern United States, winter drought in the southern United States, warm and wet weather in northeastern United States, and an extremely wet winter in southwestern Canada and northwestern United States.

Prior to the 1980s and 1990s, strong El Nino events occurred on average every 10 to 20 years. In the early 1980s, the first of a series of strong events developed. The El Nino of 1982-83 brought extreme warming to the equatorial Pacific. Surface sea temperatures in some regions of the Pacific Ocean rose 6° Celsius above normal. The warmer waters had a devastating effect on marine life existing off the coast of Peru and Ecuador. Fish catches off the coast of South America were 50% lower than the previous year. The 1982-83 El Nino also had a pronounced influence on weather in the equatorial Pacific region and world wide. Severe droughts occurred in Australia, Indonesia, India and southern Africa. Dry conditions in Australia resulted in a 2 billion dollar loss in crops, and millions of sheep and cattle died from lack of water. Heavy rains were experienced in California, Ecuador, and the Gulf of Mexico.

Our understanding of the processes responsible for the development of El Nino is still incomplete. Scientists are able to predict the future development of an event by noting the occurrence of particular weather precursors. Researchers also now have a pretty complete understanding of the global weather effects caused by the formation of an El Nino

GENERAL WEATHER SYSTEMS OF INDIA

MONSOON SYSTEM, CYCLONE AND JET STREAM, WESTERN DISTURBANCES AND SEVERE LOCAL CONVECTIVE SYSTEMS, DISTRIBUTION OF PRECIPITATION OVER INDIA.

Climate refers to the sum total of weather conditions and variations over a large area for a long period of time (more than thirty years). Weather refers to the state of the atmosphere over an area at any point of time. The elements of weather and climate are the same, i.e. temperature, atmospheric pressure, wind, humidity and precipitation. On the basis of the generalised monthly atmospheric conditions, the year is divided into seasons such as winter, summer or rainy seasons.

The climate of India is described as the 'monsoon' type. This type of climate is found mainly in the south and the Southeast Asia. Despite an overall unity in the general pattern, there are perceptible regional variations in climatic conditions within the country.

MONSOON SYSTEM

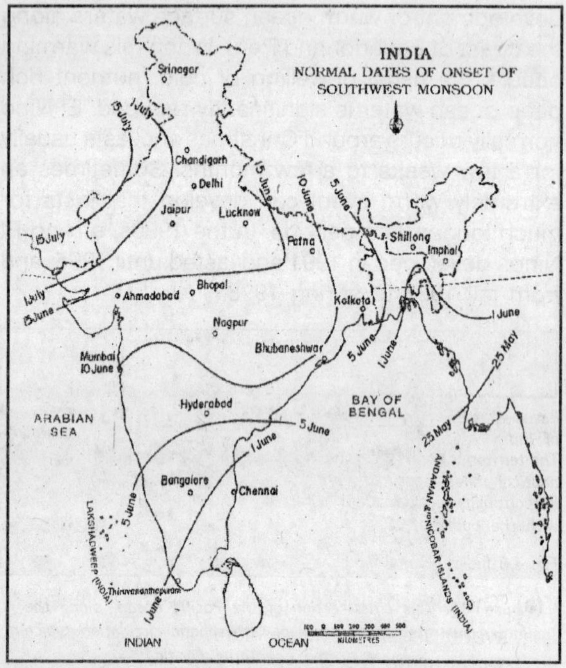

Based upon Survey of India map, with the permission of Surveyor General of India.
The territorial waters of India extend into the sea to a distance of twelve nautical miles measured from the appropriate base line.
Responsibility for correctness of internal details shown on the map rests with the publisher.

Fig. 4.7 India: Normal Dates of Onset of the Southwest Monsoon

The climate of India is strongly influenced by monsoon winds. The sailors who came to India in historic times were one of the first to have noticed the phenomenon of the monsoon. They benefited from the reversal of the wind system as they came by sailing ships at the mercy of winds. The Arabs, who had also come to India as traders named this seasonal reversal of the wind system 'monsoon'.

The monsoons are experienced in the tropical area roughly between 20°N and 20°S. To understand the mechanism of the monsoons, the following facts are important.

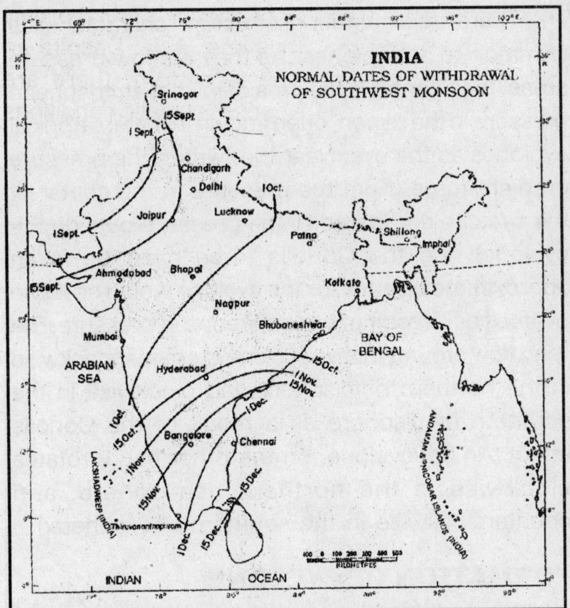

Based upon Survey of India map, with the permission of Surveyor General of India.
The territorial waters of India extend into the sea to a distance of twelve nautical miles measured from the appropriate base line.
Responsibility for correctness of internal details shown on the map rests with the publisher.

Fig. 4.8 India: Normal Dates of Withdrawal of the Southwest Monsoon

(a) The differential heating and cooling of land and water creates low pressure on the landmass of India while the seas around experience comparatively high pressure.

(b) The shift of the position of Inter Tropical Convergence Zone (ITCZ) in summer, over the Ganga plain (this is the equatorial trough normally positioned about 5°N of the equator – also known as the monsoon- trough during the monsoon season).

(c) The presence of the high-pressure area, east of Madagascar, approximately at 20°S over the Indian Ocean. The intensity and position of this high-pressure area affects the Indian Monsoon.

(d) The Tibetan plateau gets intensely heated during summer, which results in strong vertical air currents and the formation of high pressure over the plateau at about 9 km above sea level.

(e) The movement of the westerly jet stream to the north of the Himalayas and the presence of the tropical easterly jet stream over the Indian peninsula during summer.

Apart from this, it has also been noticed that changes in the pressure conditions over the southern oceans also affect the monsoons. Normally when the tropical eastern south Pacific Ocean experiences high pressure, the tropical eastern Indian Ocean experiences low pressure. But in certain years, there is a reversal in the pressure conditions and the eastern Pacific has lower pressure in comparison to the eastern Indian Ocean. This periodic change in pressure conditions is known as the Southern Oscillation. The difference in pressure over Tahiti (Pacific Ocean, 18°S/149°W) and Darwin in northern Australia (Indian Ocean, 12°30'S/131°E) is computed to predict the intensity of the monsoons. If the pressure differences were negative, it would mean below average and late monsoons. A feature connected with the SO is the El Nino, a warm ocean current that flows past the Peruvian Coast, in place of the cold Peruvian current, every 2 to 5 years. The changes in pressure conditions are connected to the El Nino. Hence, the phenomenon is referred to as ENSO (El Nino Southern Oscillations).

THE ONSET OF THE MONSOON AND WITHDRAWAL

The Monsoon, unlike the trades, are not steady winds but are pulsating in nature, affected by different atmospheric conditions encountered by it, on its way over the warm tropical seas. The duration of the monsoon is between 100-120 days from early June to mid-September. Around the time of its arrival, the normal rainfall increases suddenly and continues constantly for several days. This is known as the 'burst' of the monsoon, and can be distinguished from the pre-monsoon showers.

The monsoon arrives at the southern tip of the Indian peninsula generally by the first week of June. Subsequently, it divides into two – the Arabian Sea branch and the Bay of Bengal branch. The Arabian Sea branch reaches Mumbai about ten days later on approximately the 10th of June. This is a fairly rapid advance. The Bay of Bengal branch also advances rapidly and arrives in Assam in the first week of June. The lofty mountains causes the monsoon winds to deflect towards the west over the Ganga plains. By mid-June the Arabian Sea branch of the monsoon arrives over Saurashtra-Kuchchh and the central part of the country. The Arabian Sea and the Bay of Bengal branches of the monsoon merge over the northwestern part of the Ganga plains. Delhi generally receives the monsoon showers from the Bay of Bengal branch by the end of June (tentative date is 29th of June). By the first week of July, western Uttar Pradesh, Punjab, Haryana and eastern Rajasthan experience the monsoon. By mid-July, the monsoon reaches Himachal Pradesh and the rest of the country Withdrawal or the retreat of the monsoon is a more gradual process. The withdrawal of the monsoon begins in northwestern states of India by early September. By mid-October, it withdraws completely from the northern half of the peninsula. The withdrawal from the southern half of the peninsula is fairly rapid. By early December, the monsoon has withdrawn from the rest of the country.

The islands receive the very first monsoon showers, progressively from south to north, from the first week of April to the first week of May. The withdrawal, takes place progressively from north to south from the first week of December to the first week of January. By this time the rest of the country is already under the influence of the winter monsoon.

CYCLONE

In meteorology, a cyclone is an area of closed, circular fluid motion rotating in the same direction as the Earth. This is usually characterized by inward spiraling winds that rotate counter clockwise in the Northern Hemisphere and clockwise in the Southern Hemisphere of the Earth. Most large-scale cyclonic circulations are centered on areas of low atmospheric pressure. The largest low-pressure systems are cold-core polar cyclones and extratropical cyclones which lie on the synoptic scale. Warm-core cyclones such as tropical cyclones, mesocyclones, and polar lows lie within the smaller mesoscale. Subtropical cyclones are of intermediate size.

STRUCTURE OF CYCLONE

There are a number of structural characteristics common to all cyclones. As they are low pressure areas, their center is the area of lowest atmospheric pressure in the region, often known in mature tropical cyclones as the eye. Near the center, the pressure gradient force (from the pressure in the center of the cyclone compared to the pressure outside the cyclone) and the Coriolis force must be in an approximate balance, or the cyclone would collapse on itself as a result of the difference in pressure.The wind flow around a large cyclone is counterclockwise in the northern hemisphere and clockwise in the southern hemisphere as a result of the Coriolis effect.(An anticyclone, on the other hand, rotates clockwise in the northern hemisphere, and counterclockwise in the southern hemisphere.)

FORMATION OF CYCLONE

Cyclogenesis is the development or strengthening of cyclonic circulation in the atmosphere (a low pressure area). Cyclogenesis is an umbrella term for several different processes, all of which result in the development of some sort of cyclone. It can occur at various scales, from the microscale to the synoptic scale. Extratropical cyclones form as waves along weather fronts before occluding later in their life cycle as cold core cyclones. Tropical cyclones form due to latent heat driven by significant thunderstorm activity, and are warm core.Mesocyclones form as warm core cyclones over land, and can lead to tornado formation. Waterspouts can also form from mesocyclones, but more often develop from environments of high instability and low vertical wind shear. Cyclogenesis is the opposite of cyclolysis, and has an anticyclonic (high pressure system) equivalent which deals with the formation of high pressure areas–Anticyclogenesis.

The surface low has a variety of ways of forming. Topography can force a surface low when dense low-level high pressure system ridges in east of a north-south mountain barrier Mesoscale convective systems can spawn surface lows which are initially warm core. The disturbance can grow into a wave-like formation along the front and the low will be positioned at the crest. Around the low, flow will become cyclonic, by definition. This rotational flow will push polar air equatorward west of the low via its trailing cold front, and warmer air with push poleward low via the warm front. Usually the cold front will move at a quicker pace than the warm front and "catch up" with it due to the slow erosion of higher density airmass located out ahead of the cyclone and the higher density airmass sweeping in behind the cyclone, usually resulting in a narrowing warm sector. At this point an occluded front forms where the warm air mass is pushed upwards into a trough of warm air aloft, which is also known as a trowal.

Tropical cyclogenesis is the technical term describing the development and strengthening of a tropical cyclone in the atmosphere. The mechanisms through which tropical cyclogenesis occurs are distinctly different from those through which mid-latitude cyclogenesis occurs. Tropical cyclogenesis involves the development of a warm-core cyclone, due to significant convection in a favorable atmospheric environment. There are six main requirements for tropical cyclogenesis: sufficiently warm sea surface temperatures, atmospheric instability, high humidity in the lower to middle levels of the troposphere, enough Coriolis force to develop a low pressure center, a preexisting low level focus or disturbance, and low vertical wind shear. An average of 86 tropical cyclones of tropical storm intensity form annually worldwide, with 47 reaching hurricane/typhoon strength, and 20 becoming intense tropical cyclones (at least Category 3 intensity on the Saffir-Simpson Hurricane Scale).

Mesocyclones are believed to form when strong changes of wind speed and/or direction with height ("wind shear") sets parts of the lower part of the atmosphere spinning in invisible tube-like rolls. The convective updraft of a thunderstorm is then thought to draw up this spinning air, tilting the rolls' orientation upward (from parallel to the ground to perpendicular) and causing the entire updraft to rotate as a vertical column. Mesocyclones are normally relatively localized: they lie between the synoptic scale (hundreds of kilometers) and microscale (hundreds of meters). Radar imagery is used to identify these features.

TYPES OF CYCLONES

There are six main types of cyclones: Polar cyclones, Polar lows, Extratropical cyclones, Subtropical cyclones, Tropical cyclones, and Mesocyclones

Polar cyclone

A polar, sub-polar, or Arctic cyclone (also known as a polar vortex) is a vast area of low pressure which strengthens in the winter and weakens in the summer. A polar cyclone is a low pressure weather system, usually spanning 1,000 kilometres (620 mi) to 2,000 kilometres (1,200 mi), in which the air circulates in a counterclockwise direction in the northern hemisphere, and a clockwise direction in the southern hemisphere. In the Northern Hemisphere, the polar cyclone has two centers on average. One center lies near Baffin Island and the other over northeast Siberia. In the southern hemisphere, it tends to be located near the edge of the Ross ice shelf near 160 west longitude. When the polar vortex is strong, westerly flow descends to the Earth's surface. When the polar cyclone is weak, significant cold outbreaks occur.

Polar low Cyclone

A polar low is a small-scale, short-lived atmospheric low pressure system (depression) that is found over the ocean areas poleward of the main polar front in both the Northern and Southern Hemispheres. The systems usually have a horizontal length scale of less than 1,000 kilometres (620 mi) and exist for no more than a couple of days.

Extratropical Cyclone

An extratropical cyclone is a synoptic scale low pressure weather system that has neither tropical nor polar characteristics, being connected with fronts and horizontal gradients in temperature and dew point otherwise known as "baroclinic zones".

The descriptor "extratropical" refers to the fact that this type of cyclone generally occurs outside of the tropics, in the middle latitudes of the planet. These systems may also be described as "mid-latitude cyclones" due to their area of formation, or "post-tropical cyclones" where extratropical transition has occurred, and are often described as "depressions" or "lows" by weather forecasters and the general public. These are the everyday phenomena which along with anti-cyclones, drive the weather over much of the Earth.

Subtropical Cyclone

A subtropical cyclone is a weather system that has some characteristics of a tropical cyclone and some characteristics of an extratropical cyclone. They can form between the equator and the 50th parallel. As early as the 1950s, meteorologists were unclear whether they should be characterized as tropical cyclones or extratropical cyclones, and used terms such as quasi-tropical and semi-tropical to describe the cyclone hybrids. By 1972, the National Hurricane Center officially recognized this cyclone category. Subtropical cyclones began to receive names off the official tropical cyclone list in the Atlantic Basin in 2002. They have broad wind patterns with maximum sustained winds located farther from the center than typical tropical cyclones, and exist in areas of weak to moderate temperature gradient.

Tropical Cyclone

A tropical cyclone is a storm system characterized by a low pressure center and numerous thunderstorms that produce strong winds and flooding rain. A tropical cyclone feeds on heat released when moist air rises, resulting in condensation of water vapour contained in the moist air. They are fueled by a different heat mechanism than other cyclonic windstorms such as nor'easters, European windstorms, and polar lows, leading to their classification as "warm core" storm systems.

The term "tropical" refers to both the geographic origin of these systems, which form almost exclusively in tropical regions of the globe, and their formation in Maritime Tropical air masses. The term "cyclone" refers to such storms' cyclonic nature, with counterclockwise rotation in the Northern Hemisphere and clockwise rotation in the Southern Hemisphere. Depending on their location and strength, tropical cyclones are referred to by other names, such as hurricane, typhoon, tropical storm, cyclonic storm, tropical depression, or simply as a cyclone. Generally speaking, a tropical cyclone is referred to as a hurricane (from the name of the ancient Central American deity of wind, Huracan) in the Atlantic basin, and a Cyclone in the Pacific.

Many tropical cyclones develop when the atmospheric conditions around a weak disturbance in the atmosphere are favorable. Others form when other types of cyclones acquire tropical characteristics. Tropical systems are then moved by steering winds in the troposphere; if the conditions remain favorable, the tropical disturbance intensifies, and can even develop an eye. On the other end of the spectrum, if the conditions around the system deteriorate or the tropical cyclone makes landfall, the system weakens and eventually dissipates. A tropical cyclone can become extratropical as it moves toward higher latitudes if its energy source changes from heat released by condensation to differences in temperature between air masses; From an operational standpoint, a tropical cyclone is usually not considered to become subtropical during its extratropical transition.

JET STREAM

Jet streams are fast flowing, narrow air currents found in the atmospheres of some planets. The main jet streams are located near the tropopause, the transition between the troposphere (where temperature decreases with height) and the stratosphere (where temperature increases with height). The major jet streams on earth are westerly winds (flowing west to east). Their paths typically have a meandering shape; jet streams may start, stop, split into two or more parts, combine into one stream, or flow in various directions including the opposite direction of most of the jet. The strongest jet streams are the polar jets, at around 7-12 km (23,000-39,000 ft) above sea level, and the higher and somewhat weaker subtropical jets at around 10-16 km (33,000-52,000 ft).

Jet streams are caused by a combination of atmospheric heating (by solar radiation and, on some planets other than earth, internal heat) and the planet's rotation on its axis. They form near boundaries of adjacent air masses with significant differences in temperature, such as the polar region and the warmer air towards the equator.

Cause of Jet Stream

In general, winds are strongest under the tropopause (except during tornadoes, hurricanes or other anomalous situations). If two air masses of different temperatures or densities meet, the resulting pressure difference caused by the density difference (which causes wind) is highest within the transition zone. The wind does not flow directly from the hot to the cold area, but is deflected by the Coriolis effect and flows along the boundary of the two air masses.

All these facts are consequences of the thermal wind relation. The balance of forces on an atmospheric parcel in the vertical direction is primarily between the pressure gradient and the force of gravity, a balance referred to as hydrostatic. In the horizontal, the dominant balance outside of the tropics is between the Coriolis effect and the pressure gradient, a balance referred to as geostrophic. Given both hydrostatic and geostrophic balance, one can derive the thermal wind relation: the vertical derivative of the horizontal wind is proportional to the horizontal temperature gradient. The sense of the relation is such that temperatures decreasing polewards implies that winds develop a larger eastward component as one moves upwards. Therefore, the strong eastward moving jet streams are in part a simple consequence of the fact that the equator is warmer than the north and south poles.

The thermal wind relation does not immediately provide an explanation for why the winds are organized in tight jets, rather than distributed more broadly over the hemisphere. There are two factors that contribute to this sharpness of the jets. One is the tendency for developing cyclonic disturbances in midlatitudes to form fronts – sharp localized gradients in temperature.

Polar jet stream

The polar jet stream can be thought of as the result of this frontogenesis process in midlatitudes.

Subtropical jet

The subtropical jet forms at the poleward limit of the tropical Hadley cell and to first order this circulation is symmetric with respect to longitude. Tropical air rises to the tropopause, mainly because of thunderstorm systems in the intertropical convergence zone, and moves poleward before sinking; this is the Hadley circulation. As it does so it tends to conserve angular momentum, since friction is slight above the ground. In the northern hemisphere motions are deflected to the right by the Coriolis force, which for poleward (northward) moving air implies an increased eastward component of the winds.

APPLICATION OF JET STREAM

AVIATION

The location of the jet stream is extremely important for aviation. Commercial use of the jet stream began on November 18, 1952, when Pan Am flew from Tokyo to Honolulu at an altitude of 7,600 metres (24,900 ft). It cut the trip time by over one-third, from 18 to 11.5 hours. Not only does it cut time off the flight, it also nets fuel savings for the airline industry. Within North America, the time needed to fly east across the continent can be decreased by about 30 minutes if an airplane can fly with the jet stream, or increased by more than that amount if it must fly west against it.

FUTURE POWER GENERATION

Scientists are investigating ways to harness the wind energy within the jet stream. According to one estimate, of the potential wind energy in the jet stream, only 1 per cent would be needed to meet the world's current energy needs. The required technology would reportedly take 10–20 years to develop.

UNPOWERED AERIAL ATTACK

Towards the end of World War II the Japanese fire balloon was designed as a cheap weapon intended to make use of the jet stream over the Pacific Ocean to reach the west coast of Canada and the United States. They were relatively ineffective as weapons and were used in one of the few attacks on North America during World War II, causing six deaths and a small amount of damage

WESTERN DISTURBANCE

Western Disturbance is the term used in India, Pakistan and Nepal to describe an extratropical storm originating in the Mediterranean, that brings sudden winter rain and snow to the northwestern parts of the Indian subcontinent. This is a non-monsoonal precipitation pattern driven by the Westerlies. The moisture in these storms usually originates over the Mediterranean Sea and the Atlantic Ocean. Extratropical storms are a global, rather than a localized, phenomena with moisture usually carried in the upper atmosphere (unlike tropical storms where it is carried in the lower atmosphere). In the case of the subcontinent, moisture is sometimes shed as rain when the storm system encounters the Himalayas.

Western Disturbances are important to the development of the Rabi crop in the northern subcontinent, which includes the locally important staple wheat.

MARINE POLLUTION

Marine pollution occurs when harmful effects, or potentially harmful effects,can result from the entry into the ocean of chemicals, particles, industrial, agricultural and residential waste, noise, or the spread of invasive organisms. Most sources of marine pollution are land based. The pollution often comes from nonpoint sources such as agricultural runoff and wind blown debris.

Many potentially toxic chemicals adhere to tiny particles which are then taken up by plankton and benthos animals, most of which are either deposit or filter feeders. In this way, the toxins are concentrated upward within ocean food chains. Many particles combine chemically in a manner highly depletive of oxygen, causing estuaries to become anoxic.

When pesticides are incorporated into the marine ecosystem, they quickly become absorbed into marine food webs. Once in the food webs, these pesticides can cause mutations, as well as diseases, which can be harmful to humans as well as the entire food web.

Sources of Pollution

Pollution is often classed as point source or nonpoint source pollution. Point source pollution occurs when there is a single, identifiable, and localized source of the pollution. An example is directly discharging sewage and industrial waste into the ocean. Pollution such as this occurs particularly in developing nations. Nonpoint source pollution occurs when the pollution comes from ill-defined and diffuse sources. These can be difficult to regulate. Agricultural runoff and wind blown debris are prime examples.

One common path of entry by contaminants to the sea are rivers. The evaporation of water from oceans exceeds precipitation. The balance is restored by rain over the continents entering rivers and then being returned to the sea

Direct Discharge

Pollutants enter rivers and the sea directly from urban sewerage and industrial waste discharges, sometimes in the form of hazardous and toxic wastes.

Inland mining for copper, gold. etc., is another source of marine pollution. Most of the pollution is simply soil, which ends up in rivers flowing to the sea. However, some minerals discharged in the course of the mining can cause problems, such as copper, a common industrial pollutant, which can interfere with the life history and development of coral polyps.

Ship Pollution

Ships can pollute waterways and oceans in many ways. Oil spills can have devastating effects. While being toxic to marine life, polycyclic aromatic hydrocarbons (PAHs), the components in crude oil, are very difficult to clean up, and last for years in the sediment and marine environment.[5]

Discharge of cargo residues from bulk carriers can pollute ports, waterways and oceans. In many instances vessels intentionally discharge illegal wastes despite foreign and domestic regulation prohibiting such actions.

ATMOSPHERIC POLLUTION

Another pathway of pollution occurs through the atmosphere. Wind blown dust and debris, including plastic bags, are blown seaward from landfills and other areas. Dust from the Sahara moving around the southern periphery of the subtropical ridge moves into the Caribbean and Florida during the warm season as the ridge builds and moves northward through the subtropical Atlantic. Dust can also be attributed to a global transport from the Gobi and Taklamakan deserts across Korea, Japan, and the Northern Pacific to the Hawaiian Islands.

DEEP SEA MINING

Deep sea mining is a relatively new mineral retrieval process that takes place on the ocean floor. Ocean mining sites are usually around large areas of polymetallic nodules or active and extinct hydrothermal vents at about 1,400–3,700 meters below the ocean's surface. The vents create sulfide deposits, which contain precious metals such as silver, gold, copper, manganese, cobalt, and zinc. The deposits are mined using either hydraulic pumps or bucket systems that take ore to the surface to be processed. As with all mining operations, deep sea mining raises questions about environmental damages to the surrounding areas

ACIDIFICATION

The oceans are normally a natural carbon sink, absorbing carbon dioxide from the atmosphere. Because the levels of atmospheric carbon dioxide are increasing, the oceans are becoming more acidic. The potential consequences of ocean acidification are not fully understood, but there are concerns that structures made of calcium carbonate may become vulnerable to dissolution, affecting corals and the ability of shellfish to form shells.

EUTROPHICATION

Eutrophication is an increase in chemical nutrients, typically compounds containing nitrogen or phosphorus, in an ecosystem. It can result in an increase in the ecosystem's primary productivity (excessive plant growth and decay), and further effects including lack of oxygen and severe reductions in water quality, fish, and other animal populations.

The biggest culprit are rivers that empty into the ocean, and with it the many chemicals used as fertilizers in agriculture as well as waste from livestock and humans. An excess of oxygen depleting chemicals in the water can lead to hypoxia and the creation of a dead zone.

PLASTIC DEBRIS

Marine debris is mainly discarded human rubbish which floats on, or is suspended in the ocean. Eighty per cent of marine debris is plastic - a component that has been rapidly accumulating since the end of World War II. The mass of plastic in the oceans may be as high as one hundred million metric tons.

Discarded plastic bags, six pack rings and other forms of plastic waste which finish up in the ocean present dangers to wildlife and fisheries. Aquatic life can be threatened through entanglement, suffocation, and ingestion.

ADAPTATION AND MITIGATION MEASURE FOR MARINE POLLUTION

There are two ways the overall level of this pollution can be mitigated: either the human population is reduced, or a way is found to reduce the ecological footprint left behind by the average human. If the second way is not adopted, then the first way may be imposed as world ecosystems falter.

The second way is for humans, individually, to pollute less. That requires social and political will, together with a shift in awareness so more people respect the environment and are less disposed to abuse it. At an operational level, regulations, and international government participation is needed. It is often very difficult to regulate marine pollution because pollution spreads over international barriers, thus making regulations hard to create as well as enforce.

Perhaps the most important strategy for reducing marine pollution is education. Most are unaware of the sources, and harmful effects of marine pollution, and therefore little is done to address the situation. In order to inform the population of all the facts, in depth research must be done to provide the full scale of the situation. Then this information must be made public.

Air pollution is the introduction of chemicals, particulate matter, or biological materials that cause harm or discomfort to humans or other living organisms, or damages the natural environment into the atmosphere.

SOURCES OF AIR POLLUTION

Sources of air pollution refer to the various locations, activities or factors which are responsible for the releasing of pollutants in the atmosphere. These sources can be classified into two major categories which are:

Anthropogenic sources (human activity) mostly related to burning different kinds of fuel

- "Stationary Sources" include smoke stacks of power plants, manufacturing facilities (factories) and waste incinerators, as well as furnaces and other types of fuel-burning heating devices
- "Mobile Sources" include motor vehicles, marine vessels, aircraft and the effect of sound etc.
- Chemicals, dust and controlled burn practices in agriculture and forestry management. Controlled or prescribed burning is a technique sometimes used in forest management, farming, prairie restoration or greenhouse gas abatement. Fire is a natural part of both forest and grassland ecology and controlled fire can be a tool for foresters. Controlled burning stimulates the germination of some desirable forest trees, thus renewing the forest.
- Fumes from paint, hair spray, varnish, aerosol sprays and other solvents
- Waste deposition in landfills, which generate methane.Methane is not toxic; however, it is highly flammable and may form explosive mixtures with air. Methane is also an asphyxiant and may displace oxygen in an enclosed space. Asphyxia or suffocation may result if the oxygen concentration is reduced to below 19.5% by displacement
- Military, such as nuclear weapons, toxic gases, germ warfare and rocketry

Natural sources

- Dust from natural sources, usually large areas of land with little or no vegetation.
- Methane, emitted by the digestion of food by animals, for example cattle.
- Radon gas from radioactive decay within the Earth's crust. Radon is a colorless, odorless, naturally occurring, radioactive noble gas that is formed from the decay of radium. It is considered to be a health hazard. Radon gas from natural sources can accumulate in buildings, especially in confined areas such as the basement and it is the second most frequent cause of lung cancer, after cigarette smoking.
- Smoke and carbon monoxide from wildfires.
- Volcanic activity, which produce sulfur, chlorine, and ash particulates.

MITIGATION MEASURE

Control devices

The following items are commonly used as pollution control devices by industry or transportation devices. They can either destroy contaminants or remove them from an exhaust stream before it is emitted into the atmosphere.

- ***Particulate control***
  - — Mechanical collectors (dust cyclones, multicyclones)
  - — Electrostatic precipitators An electrostatic precipitator (ESP), or electrostatic air

cleaner is a particulate collection device that removes particles from a flowing gas (such as air) using the force of an induced electrostatic charge. Electrostatic precipitators are highly efficient filtration devices that minimally impede the flow of gases through the device, and can easily remove fine particulate matter such as dust and smoke from the air stream.

— Baghouses Designed to handle heavy dust loads, a dust collector consists of a blower, dust filter, a filter-cleaning system, and a dust receptacle or dust removal system (distinguished from air cleaners which utilize disposable filters to remove the dust).

— Particulate scrubbersWet scrubber is a form of pollution control technology. The term describes a variety of devices that use pollutants from a furnace flue gas or from other gas streams. In a wet scrubber, the polluted gas stream is brought into contact with the scrubbing liquid, by spraying it with the liquid, by forcing it through a pool of liquid, or by some other contact method, so as to remove the pollutants.

- ***Scrubbers***
  - — Baffle spray scrubber
  - — Cyclonic spray scrubber
  - — Ejector venturi scrubber
  - — Mechanically aided scrubber
  - — Spray tower
  - — Wet scrubber
- ***NOx control***
  - — Low NOx burners
  - — Selective catalytic reduction (SCR)
  - — Selective non-catalytic reduction (SNCR)
  - — NOx scrubbers
  - — Exhaust gas recirculation
  - — Catalytic converter (also for VOC control)
- ***VOC abatement***
  - — Adsorption systems, such as activated carbon
  - — Flares
  - — Thermal oxidizers
  - — Catalytic oxidizers
  - — Biofilters
  - — Absorption (scrubbing)
  - — Cryogenic condensers
  - — Vapor recovery systems
- ***Acid Gas/SO_2 control***
  - — Wet scrubbers
  - — Dry scrubbers
  - — Flue gas desulfurization
- ***Mercury Control***
  - — Sorbent Injection Technology
  - — Electro-Catalytic Oxidation (ECO)
  - — K-Fuel

OZONE DEPLETION

There are two type of Ozone – good ozone and bad ozone. Ozone in troposphere considered as bad ozone, since it causes green house effect. There is 'good' ozone also; this ozone is found in the upper part of the atmosphere called the stratosphere, and it acts as a shield absorbing ultraviolet radiation from the sun. UV rays are highly injurious to living organisms since DNA and proteins of living organisms preferentially absorb UV rays, and its high energy breaks the chemical bonds within these molecules. The thickness of the ozone in a column of air from the ground to the top of the atmosphere is measured in terms of Dobson units (DU).

Ozone gas is continuously formed by the action of UV rays on molecular oxygen, and also degraded into molecular oxygen in the stratosphere. There should be a balance between production and degradation of ozone in the stratosphere. Of late, the balance has been disrupted due to enhancement of ozone degradation by chlorofluorocarbons (CFCs). CFCs find wide use as refrigerants. CFCs discharged in the lower part of atmosphere move upward and reach stratosphere. In stratosphere, UV rays act on them releasing Cl atoms. Cl degrades ozone releasing molecular oxygen, with these atoms acting merely as catalysts; Cl atoms are not consumed in the reaction. Hence, whatever CFCs are added to the stratosphere, they have permanent and continuing affects on Ozone levels. Although ozone depletion is occurring widely in the stratosphere, the depletion is particularly marked over the Antarctic region. This has resulted in formation of a large area of thinned ozone layer, commonly called as the ozone hole.

UV radiation of wavelengths shorter than UV-B, are almost completely absorbed by Earth's atmosphere, given that the ozone layer is intact. But, UV-B damages DNA and mutation may occur. It causes aging of skin, damage to skin cells and various types of skin cancers. In human eye, cornea absorbs UV-B radiation, and a high dose of UV-B causes inflammation of cornea, called snow-blindness cataract, etc. Such exposure may permanently damage the cornea.

MITIGATION MEASURE TO CONTROL OZONE DEPLETION

Implementation of guideline of Montreal Protocol, was signed at Montreal (Canada) in 1987 (effective in 1989) to control the emission of ozone depleting substances. Subsequently many more efforts have been made and protocols have laid down definite roadmaps, separately for developed and developing countries, for reducing the emission of CFCs and other ozone depleting chemicals.

Apart from this change in human life style like optimum use of refrigeration, air conditioners, and other appliances that emits CFCs.

5. Environmental Earth Sciences

PROPERTIES OF WATER

Water is the most abundant molecule on Earth's surface, constituting about 70% of the planet's surface. In nature it exists in liquid, solid, and gaseous states. It is in dynamic equilibrium between the liquid and gas states at standard temperature and pressure. At room temperature, it is a nearly colorless with a hint of blue, tasteless, and odorless liquid. Many substances dissolve in water and it is commonly referred to as the universal solvent. Because of this, water in nature and in use is rarely pure and some of its properties may vary slightly from those of the pure substance. However, there are many compounds that are essentially, if not completely, insoluble in water. Water is the only common substance found naturally in all three common states of matter–for other substances, see chemical properties. Water is essential for life on Earth.

FORMS OF WATER

Like many substances, water can take numerous forms that are broadly categorized by phase of matter. The liquid phase is the most common among water's phases and is the form that's generally denoted by the word "water." The solid phase of water is known as ice and commonly takes the structure of hard, amalgamated crystals, such as ice cubes, or loosely accumulated granular crystals, like snow. For a list of the many different crystalline and amorphous forms of solid H_2O, see the article ice. The gaseous phase of water is known as water vapor (or steam), and is characterized by water assuming the configuration of a transparent cloud. The fourth state of water, that of a supercritical fluid, is much less common than the other three and only rarely occurs in nature.

PROPERTIES OF WATER

Heat capacity and heats of vaporization and fusion

Water has the second highest specific heat capacity of all known substances, after ammonia, as well as a high heat of vaporization (40.65 $kJ \cdot mol^{-1}$), both of which are a result of the extensive hydrogen bonding between its molecules. These two unusual properties allow water to moderate Earth's climate by buffering large fluctuations in temperature.

The specific enthalpy of fusion of water is 333.55 $kJ \cdot kg^{-1}$ at 0°C. Of common substances, only that of ammonia is higher. This property confers resistance to melting upon the ice of glaciers and drift ice. Before the advent of mechanical refrigeration, ice was in common use to retard food spoilage

Density of water and ice

The density of water is dependent on its temperature. When cooled from room temperature liquid water becomes increasingly dense, just like other substances. But at approximately 4°C, water reaches its maximum density. As it is cooled further under ambient conditions, it expands to become less dense.

The solid form of most substances is denser than the liquid phase; thus, a block of the solid will sink in the liquid. But, by contrast, a block of common ice floats in liquid water because ice is less dense than liquid water. The melting point of ice is 0°C (32°F, 273 K) at standard pressure, however, pure liquid water can be supercooled well below that temperature without freezing if the liquid is not mechanically disturbed.

Miscibility and Condensation of Water

Water is miscible with many liquids, for example ethanol in all proportions, forming a single homogeneous liquid. On the other hand water and most oils are immiscible usually forming layers according to increasing density from the top.

if the vapor partial pressure is 2% of atmospheric pressure and the air is cooled from 25°C, starting at about 22°C water will start to condense, defining the dew point, and creating fog or dew. The reverse process accounts for the fog burning off in the morning. If one raises the humidity at room temperature, say by running a hot shower or a bath, and the temperature stays about the same, the vapor soon reaches the pressure for phase change, and condenses out as steam. A gas in this context is referred to as saturated or 100% relative humidity, when the vapor pressure of water in the air is at the equilibrium with vapor pressure due to (liquid) water; water (or ice, if cool enough) will fail to lose mass through evaporation when exposed to saturated air. Because the amount of water vapor in air is small, relative humidity, the ratio of the partial pressure due to the water vapor to the saturated partial vapor pressure, is much more useful. Water vapor pressure above 100% relative humidity is called super-saturated and can occur if air is rapidly cooled, say by rising suddenly in an updraft.

Compressibility of Water

The compressibility of water is a function of pressure and temperature. At 0°C in the limit of zero pressure the compressibility is 5.1×10^{-10} Pa^{-1}. In the zero pressure limit the compressibility reaches a minimum of 4.4×10^{-10} Pa^{-1} around 45°C before increasing again with increasing temperature. The low compressibility of non-gases, and of water in particular, leads to their often being assumed as incompressible. The low compressibility of water means that even in the deep oceans at 4 km depth, where pressures are 40 MPa, there is only a 1.8% decrease in volume.

Triple Point of Water

The temperature and pressure at which solid, liquid, and gaseous water coexist in equilibrium is called the triple point of water. This point is used to define the units of temperature (the kelvin, the SI unit of thermodynamic temperature and, indirectly, the degree Celsius and even the degree Fahrenheit).

The triple point is at a temperature of 273.16 K (0.01°C) by convention, and at a pressure of 611.73 Pa. This pressure is quite low, about $^1/_{166}$ of the normal sea level barometric pressure of 101,325 Pa.

Electrical conductivity of water molecules

Pure water containing no ions is an excellent insulator, but not even "deionized" water is completely free of ions. Water undergoes auto-ionization in the liquid state. Further, because water is such a good solvent, it almost always has some solute dissolved in it, most frequently a salt. If water has even a tiny amount of such an impurity, then it can conduct electricity readily, as impurities such as salt separate into free ions in aqueous solution by which an electric current can flow.

Any electrical conductivity observable in water is the result of ions of mineral salts and carbon dioxide dissolved in it. Carbon dioxide forms carbonate ions in Water. Water self-ionizes in which two water molecules form one hydroxide anion and one hydronium cation, but not enough to carry enough electric current to do any work or harm for most operations. In pure water, sensitive equipment can detect a very slight electrical conductivity of 0.055 μS/cm at 25°C. Water can also be electrolyzed into oxygen and hydrogen gases but in the absence of dissolved ions this is a very slow process, as very little current is conducted.

Electrolysis of Water Molecules

Water can be split into its constituent elements, hydrogen and oxygen, by passing an electric current through it. This process is called electrolysis. Water molecules naturally dissociate into H^+ and OH^- ions, which are pulled toward the cathode and anode, respectively. At the cathode, two H^+ ions pick up electrons and form H_2 gas. At the anode, four OH^- ions combine and release O_2 gas, molecular water, and four electrons. The gases produced bubble to the surface, where they can be collected. The standard potential of the water electrolysis cell is 1.23 V at 25°C.

Dipolar Properties

An important feature of water is its polar nature. The water molecule forms an angle, with hydrogen atoms at the tips and oxygen at the vertex. Since oxygen has a higher electronegativity than hydrogen, the side of the molecule with the oxygen atom has a partial negative charge. An object with such a charge difference is called a dipole. The charge differences cause water molecules to be attracted to each other (the relatively positive areas being attracted to the relatively negative areas) and to other polar molecules. This attraction contributes to hydrogen bonding, and explains many of the properties of water, such as solvent action.

Capillary Action of Water

Due to an interplay of the forces of adhesion and surface tension, water exhibits capillary action whereby water rises into a narrow tube against the force of gravity. Water adheres to the inside wall of the tube and surface tension tends to straighten the surface causing a surface rise and more water is pulled up through cohesion. The process continues as the water flows up the tube until there is enough water such that gravity balances the adhesive force.

Surface tension and capillary action are important in biology. For example, when water is carried through xylem up stems in plants.

Solvent Properties of Water

Water is also a good solvent due to its polarity. Substances that will mix well and dissolve in water (e.g. salts) are known as hydrophilic ("water-loving") substances, while those that do not mix well with water (e.g. fats and oils), are known as hydrophobic ("water-fearing") substances. The ability of a substance to dissolve in water is determined by whether or not the substance can match or better the strong attractive forces that water molecules generate between other water molecules.

When an ionic or polar compound enters water, it is surrounded by water molecules (Hydration). The relatively small size of water molecules typically allows many water molecules to surround one molecule of solute. The partially negative dipole ends of the water are attracted to positively charged components of the solute, and vice versa for the positive dipole ends.

HYDROLOGICAL CYCLE

Water undergoes a cycle from the ocean to land and land to ocean. The hydrological cycle describes the movement of water on, in, and above the earth. The water cycle has been working for billions of years and all the life on earth depends on it. Next to air, water is the most important element required for the existence of life on earth. The distribution of water on earth is quite uneven. Many locations have plenty of water while others have very limited quantity. The hydrological cycle, is the circulation of water within the earth's hydrosphere in different forms i.e. the liquid, solid and the gaseous phases. It also refers to the continuous exchange of water between the oceans, atmosphere, landsurface and subsurface and the organisms.

Reservoir	*Percentage of the Total*
Oceans	97.25
Ice Caps and Glaciers	2.05
Groundwater	0.68
Lakes	0.01
Soil Moisture	0.005
Atmosphere	0.001
Streams and Rivers	0.0001
Biosphere	0.00004

Table 5.1 : Water on the Earth's surface

Table 5.1 shows distribution of water on the surface of the earth. About 71 per cent of the planetary water is found in the oceans. The remaining is held as freshwater in glaciers and icecaps, groundwater sources, lakes, soil moisture, atmosphere, streams and within life. Nearly 59 per cent of the water that falls on land returns to the atmosphere through evaporation from over the oceans as well as from other places. The remainder runs-off on the surface, infiltrates into the ground or a part of it becomes glacier.

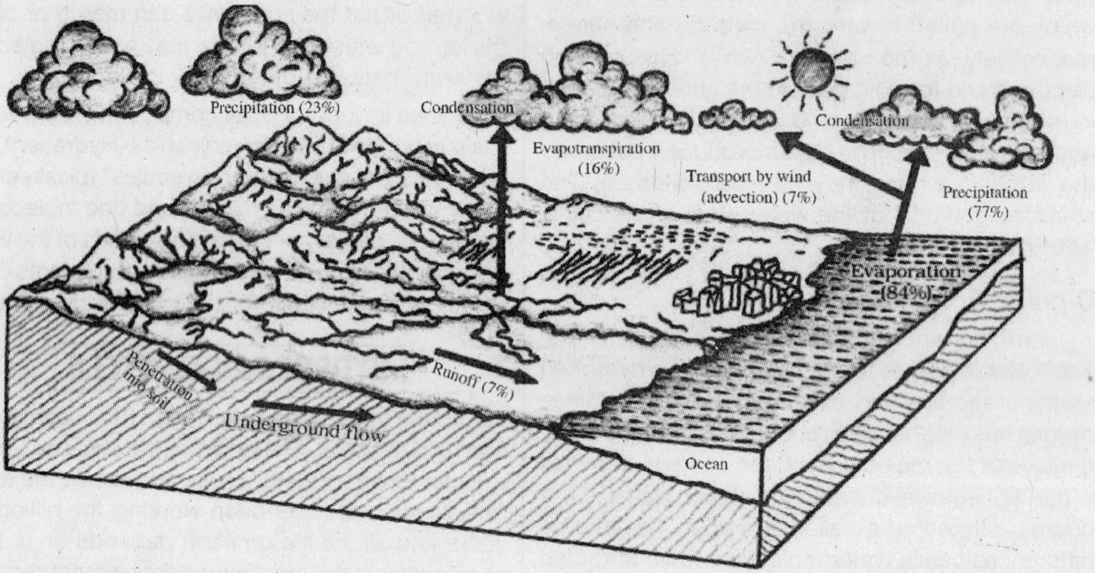

Figure 5.1: Hydrological Cycle

It is to be noted that the renewable water on the earth is constant while the demand is increasing tremendously. This leads to water crisis in different parts of the world – spatially and temporally. The pollution of river waters has further aggravated the crisis.

WATER RESOURCES AND MANAGEMENT

Water resources are sources of water that are useful or potentially useful to humans. Uses of water include agricultural, industrial, household, recreational and environmental activities.

96.5 per cent of the total volume of world's water is estimated to exist as oceans and only 2.5 per cent as freshwater. Nearly 70 per cent of this freshwater occurs as ice sheets and glaciers in Antarctica, Greenland and the mountainous regions of the world, while a little less than 30 per cent is stored as groundwater in the world's aquifers. The remaining unfrozen freshwater is mainly found as groundwater, with only a small fraction present above ground or in the air. Fresh water is a renewable resource, yet the world's supply of clean, fresh water is steadily decreasing. Water demand already exceeds supply in many parts of the world and as the world population continues to rise, so too does the water demand. Awareness of the global importance of preserving water for ecosystem services has only recently emerged as, during the 20th century, more than half the world's wetlands have been lost along with their valuable environmental services. Biodiversity-rich freshwater ecosystems are currently declining faster than marine or land ecosystems.

SOURCES OF WATER RESOURCES

Surface water

Surface water is water in a river, lake or fresh water wetland. Surface water is naturally replenished by precipitation and naturally lost through discharge to the oceans, evaporation, and sub-surface seepage.

Although the only natural input to any surface water system is precipitation within its watershed, the total quantity of water in that system at any given time is also dependent on many other factors. These factors include storage capacity in lakes, wetlands and artificial reservoirs, the permeability of the soil beneath these storage bodies, the runoff characteristics of the land in the watershed, the timing of the precipitation and local evaporation rates.

Ground water

Sub-surface water, or groundwater, is fresh water located in the pore space of soil and rocks. It is also water that is flowing within aquifers below the water table. Sometimes it is useful to make a distinction between sub-surface water that is closely associated with surface water and deep sub-surface water in an aquifer (sometimes called "fossil water").

Sub-surface water can be thought of in the same terms as surface water: inputs, outputs and storage. The critical difference is that due to its slow rate of turnover, sub-surface water storage is generally much larger compared to inputs than it is for surface water. This difference makes it easy for humans to use sub-surface water unsustainably for a long time without severe consequences. Nevertheless, over the long term the average rate of seepage above a sub-surface water source is the upper bound for average consumption of water from that source.

The natural input to sub-surface water is seepage from surface water. The natural outputs from sub-surface water are springs and seepage to the oceans.

If the surface water source is also subject to substantial evaporation, a sub-surface water source may become saline. This situation can occur naturally under endorheic bodies of water, or artificially under irrigated farmland. In coastal areas, human use of a sub-surface water source may cause the direction of seepage to ocean to reverse which can also cause soil salinization. Humans can also cause sub-surface water to be "lost" (i.e. become unusable) through pollution. Humans can increase the input to a sub-surface water source by building reservoirs or detention ponds.

River flow

Throughout the course of the river, the total volume of water transported downstream will often be a combination of the visible free water flow together with a substantial contribution flowing through sub-surface rocks and gravels that underlie the river and its floodplain called the hyporheic zone. For many rivers in large valleys, this unseen component of flow may greatly exceed the visible flow. The hyporheic zone often forms a dynamic interface between surface water and true ground-water receiving water from the ground water when aquifers are fully charged and contributing water to ground-water when ground waters are depleted. This is especially significant in karst areas where pot-holes and underground rivers are common.

Frozen water

Several schemes have been proposed to make use of icebergs as a water source, however to date this has only been done for novelty purposes. Glacier runoff is considered to be surface water.

The Himalayas, which are often called "The Roof of the World", contain some of the most extensive and rough high altitude areas on Earth as well as the greatest area of glaciers and permafrost outside of the poles. Ten of Asia's largest rivers flow from there, and more than a billion people's livelihoods depend on them. To complicate matters, temperatures are rising more rapidly here than the global average.

APPLICATION OF WATER RESOURCES

Agricultural

It is estimated that 69% of worldwide water use is for irrigation, with 15-35% of irrigation withdrawals being unsustainable.

In some areas of the world irrigation is necessary to grow any crop at all, in other areas it permits more profitable crops to be grown or enhances crop yield. Various irrigation methods involve different trade-offs between crop yield, water consumption and capital cost of equipment and structures. Irrigation methods such as furrow and overhead sprinkler irrigation are usually less expensive but are also typically less efficient, because much of the water evaporates, runs off or drains below the root zone. Other irrigation methods considered to be more efficient include drip or trickle irrigation, surge irrigation, and some types of sprinkler systems where the sprinklers are operated near ground level. These types of systems, while more expensive, usually offer greater potential to minimize runoff, drainage and evaporation.

As global populations grow, and as demand for food increases in a world with a fixed water supply, there are efforts underway to learn how to produce more food with less water, through improvements in irrigation methods and technologies, agricultural water management, crop types, and water monitoring.

Industrial use

It is estimated that 22% of worldwide water use is industrial Major industrial users include power plants, which use water for cooling or as a power source (i.e. hydroelectric plants), ore and oil refineries, which use water in chemical processes, and manufacturing plants, which use water as a solvent.

Water is used in power generation. Hydroelectricity is electricity obtained from hydropower. Hydroelectric power comes from water driving a water turbine connected to a generator. Hydroelectricity is a low-cost, non-polluting, renewable energy source. The energy is supplied by the sun. Heat from the sun evaporates water, which condenses as rain in higher altitudes, from where it flows down.

Water is also used in many industrial processes and machines, such as the steam turbine and heat exchanger, in addition to its use as a chemical solvent. Discharge of untreated water from industrial uses is pollution. Pollution includes discharged solutes (chemical pollution) and discharged coolant water (thermal pollution). Industry requires pure water for many applications and utilizes a variety of purification techniques both in water supply and discharge.

Use of water in Household

Household use of water includes drinking water, bathing, cooking, sanitation, and gardening. Drinking water is water that is of sufficiently high quality so that it can be consumed or used without risk of immediate or long term harm. Such water is commonly called potable water. In most developed countries, the water supplied to households, commerce and industry is all of drinking water standard even though only a very small proportion is actually consumed or used in food preparation.

Water resources management addresses the connections between resource and service management. This means addressing:

- The institutional framework, including the definition and establishment of laws, rights and licenses; the responsibilities of different actors at levels ranging from local watershed management institutions to international basin agencies;
- The management instruments, including regulatory arrangements; financial instruments; standards and plans; mechanisms for effective participation of stakeholders; and knowledge and information systems;
- The development and management of infrastructure for annual and multi-year flow regulation, for floods and droughts, for multi-purpose storage, and for water quality and source protection; and
- The political economy of water management and reform, in which there is particular emphasis on the distribution of benefits and costs, and on the incentives that encourage or constrain more productive and sustainable resource use.

WATER SCARCITY AND THE NEED FOR WATER CONSERVATION AND MANAGEMENT

Given the abundance and renewability of water, it is difficult to imagine that we may suffer from water scarcity. The moment we speak of water shortages, we immediately associate it with regions having low rainfall or those that are drought prone. We instantaneously visualise the deserts of Rajasthan and women balancing many 'matkas' (earthen pots) used for collecting and storing water and travelling long distances to get water. True, the availability of water resources varies over space and time, mainly due to the variations in seasonal and annual precipitation, but water scarcity in most cases is caused by over- exploitation, excessive use and unequal access to water among different social groups.

MULTI -PURPOSE RIVER PROJECTS AND INTEGRATED WATER RESOURCES MANAGEMEN

Archaeological and historical records show that from ancient times we have been constructing sophisticated hydraulic structures like dams built of stone rubble, reservoirs or lakes, embankments and canals for irrigation. Not surprisingly, we have continued this tradition in modern India by building dams in most of our river basins.

Dams were traditionally built to impound rivers and rainwater that could be used later to irrigate agricultural fields. Today, dams are built not just for irrigation but for electricity generation, water supply for domestic and industrial uses, flood control, recreation, inland navigation and fish breeding. Hence, dams are now referred to as multi-purpose projects where the many uses of the impounded water are integrated with one another. For example, in the Sutluj-Beas river basin, the Bhakra –Nangal project water is being used both for hydel power production and irrigation. Similarly, the Hirakud project in the Mahanadi basin integrates conservation of water with flood control.

Multi-purpose projects, launched after Independence with their integrated water resources management approach, were thought of as the vehicle that would lead the nation to development and progress, overcoming the handicap of its colonial past. Jawaharlal Nehru proudly proclaimed the dams as the 'temples of modern India'; the reason being that it would integrate development of agriculture and the village economy with rapid industrialisation and growth of the urban economy.

In recent years, multi-purpose projects and large dams have come under great scrutiny and opposition for a variety of reasons. Regulating and damming of rivers affect their natural flow causing poor sediment flow and excessive sedimentation at the bottom of the reservoir, resulting in rockier stream beds and poorer habitats for the rivers' aquatic life. Dams also fragment rivers making it difficult for aquatic fauna to migrate, especially for spawning. The reservoirs that are created on the floodplains also submerge the existing vegetation and soil leading to its decomposition over a period of time.

RAINWATER HARVESTING

Many thought that given the disadvantages and rising resistance against the multi-purpose projects, water harvesting system was a viable alternative, both socio- economically and environmentally. In ancient India, along with the sophisticated hydraulic structures, there existed an extraordinary tradition of water-harvesting system. People had in-depth knowledge of rainfall regimes and soil types and developed wide ranging techniques to harvest rainwater, groundwater, river water and flood water in keeping with the local ecological conditions and their water needs. In hill and mountainous regions, people built diversion channels like the 'guls' or 'kuls' of the Western Himalayas for agriculture. 'Rooftop rain water harvesting' was commonly practised to store drinking water, particularly in Rajasthan. In the flood plains of Bengal, people developed inundation channels to irrigate their fields. In arid and semi-arid regions, agricultural fields were converted into rain fed storage structures that allowed the water to stand and moisten the soil like the 'khadins' in Jaisalmer and 'Johads' in other parts of Rajasthan.

In the semi-arid and arid regions of Rajasthan, particularly in Bikaner, Phalodi and Barmer, almost all the houses traditionally had underground tanks or tankas for storing drinking water. The tanks could be as large as a big room; one household in Phalodi had a tank that was 6.1 metres deep, 4.27 metres long and 2.44 metres wide. The tankas were part of the well-developed rooftop rainwater harvesting system and were built inside the main house or the courtyard. They were connected to the sloping roofs of the houses through a pipe. Rain falling on the rooftops would travel down the pipe and was stored in these underground 'tankas'. The first spell of rain was usually not collected as this would clean the roofs and the pipes. The rainwater from the subsequent showers was then collected.

The rainwater can be stored in the tankas till the next rainfall making it an extremely reliable source of drinking water when all other sources are dried up, particularly in the summers. Rainwater, or palar pani, as commonly referred to in these parts, is considered the purest form of natural water. Many houses constructed underground rooms adjoining the 'tanka' to beat the summer heat as it would keep the room cool.

ENERGY RESOURCES

Energy is required for all activities. It is needed to cook, to provide light and heat, to propel vehicles and to drive machinery in industries. Energy can be generated from fuel minerals like coal, petroleum, natural gas, uranium and from electricity. Energy resources can be classified as conventional and non- conventional sources. Conventional sources include: firewood, cattle dung cake, coal, petroleum, natural gas and electricity (both hydel and thermal). Non-conventional sources include solar, wind, tidal, geothermal, biogas and atomic energy. Firewood and cattle dung cake are most common in rural India. According to one estimate more than 70 per cent energy requirement in rural households is met by these two; continuation of these is increasingly becoming difficult due to decreasing forest area. Moreover, using dung cake too is being discouraged because it consumes most valuable manure which could be used in agriculture.

CONVENTIONAL SOURCES OF ENERGY

Coal: In India, coal is the most abundantly available fossil fuel. It provides a substantial part of the nation's energy needs. It is used for power generation, to supply energy to industry as well as for domestic needs. India is highly dependent on coal for meeting its commercial energy requirements. As you are already aware that coal is formed due the compression of plant material over millions of years. Coal, therefore, is found in a variety of forms depending on the degrees of compression and the depth and time of burial.

Decaying plants in swamps produce peat. Which has a low carbon and high moisture contents and low heating capacity.

Lignite is a low grade brown coal, which is soft with high moisture content. The principal lignite reserves are in Neyveli in Tamil Nadu and are used for generation of electricity.

Coal that has been buried deep and subjected to increased temperatures is bituminous coal. It is the most popular coal in commercial use. Metallurgical coal is high grade bituminous coal which has a special value for smelting iron in blast furnaces.

Anthracite is the highest quality hard coal.

In India coal occurs in rock series of two main geological ages, namely Gondwana, a little over 200 million years in age and in tertiary deposits which are only about 55 million years old. The major resources of Gondwana coal, which are metallurgical coal, are located in Damodar valley (West Bengal-Jharkhand). Jharia, Raniganj, Bokaro are important coalfields. The Godavari, Mahanadi, Son and Wardha valleys also contain coal deposits.

PETROLEUM

Petroleum or mineral oil is the next major energy source in India after coal. It provides fuel for heat and lighting, lubricants for machinery and raw materials for a number of manufacturing industries. Petroleum refineries act as a "nodal industry" for synthetic textile, fertiliser and numerous chemical industries. Most of the petroleum occurrences in India are associated with anticlines and fault traps in the rock formations of the tertiary age. In regions of folding, anticlines or domes, it occurs where oil is trapped in the crest of the upfold.

The oil bearing layer is a porous limestone or sandstone through which oil may flow. The oil is prevented from rising or sinking by intervening non-porous layers.

About 63 per cent of India's petroleum production is from Mumbai High, 18 per cent from Gujarat and 16 per cent from Assam. From the map locate the 3 major off shore fields of western India. Ankeleshwar is the most important field of Gujarat. Assam is the oldest oil producing state of India. Digboi, Naharkatiya and Moran-Hugrijan are the important oil fields in the state.

Natural Gas

Natural gas is an important clean energy resource found in association with or without petroleum. It is used as a source of energy as well as an industrial raw material in the petrochemical industry. Large reserves of natural gas have been discovered in the Krishna- Godavari basin. Along the west coast the reserves of the Mumbai High and allied fields are supplemented by finds in the Gulf of Cambay. Andaman and Nicobar islands are also important areas having large reserves of natural gas.

Nuclear or Atomic Energy

Nuclear Energy is obtained by altering the structure of atoms. When such an alteration is made, much energy is released in the form of heat and this is used to generate electric power. Uranium and thorium, which are available in Jharkhand and the Aravall ranges of Rajasthan are used for generating atomic or nuclear power. The Monazite sands of Kerala is also rich in thorium.

Non-Conventional Sources of Energy

The growing consumption of energy has resulted in the country becoming increasingly dependent on fossil fuels such as coal, oil and gas. Rising prices of oil and gas and their potential shortages have raised uncertainties about the security of energy supply in future, which in turn has serious repercussions on the growth of the national economy. Moreover, increasing use of fossil fuels also causes serious environmental problems. Hence, there is a pressing need to use renewable energy sources like solar energy, wind, tide, biomass and energy from waste material. These are called non-conventional energy sources.

Solar Energy

India is a tropical country. It has enormous possibilities of tapping solar energy. Photovoltaic technology converts sunlight directly into electricity. Solar energy is fast

becoming popular in rural and remote areas. The largest solar plant of India is located at Madhapur, near Bhuj, where solar energy is used to sterlise milk cans. It is expected that use of solar energy will be able to minimise the dependence of rural households on firewood and dung cakes, which in turn will contribute to environmental conservation and adequate supply of manure in agriculture.

Wind power

India now ranks as a "wind super power" in the world. The largest wind farm cluster is located in Tamil Nadu from Nagarcoil to Madurai. Apart from these, Andhra Pradesh, Karnataka, Gujarat, Kerala, Maharashtra and Lakshadweep have important wind farms. Nagarcoil and Jaisalmer are well known for effective use of wind energy in the country.

Biogas

Shrubs, farm waste, animal and human waste are used to produce biogas for domestic consumption in rural areas. Decomposition of organic matter yields gas, which has higher thermal efficiency in comparison to kerosene, dung cake and charcoal. Biogas plants are set up at municipal, cooperative and individual levels. The plants using cattle dung are know as 'Gobar gas plants' in rural India. These provide twin benefits to the farmer in the form of energy and improved quality of manure.

Tidal Energy

Oceanic tides can be used to generate electricity. Floodgate dams are built across inlets. During high tide water flows into the inlet and gets trapped when the gate is closed. After the tide falls outside the flood gate, the water retained by the floodgate flows back to the sea via a pipe that carries it through a power-generating turbine.

Geo Thermal Energy

Geothermal energy refers to the heat and electricity produced by using the heat from the interior of the Earth. Geothermal energy exists because, the Earth grows progressively hotter with increasing depth. Where the geothermal gradient is high, high temperatures are found at shallow depths. Groundwater in such areas absorbs heat from the rocks and becomes hot. It is so hot that when it rises to the earth's surface, it turns into steam. This steam is used to drive turbines and generate electricity.

Management of Energy Resources

Energy is a basic requirement for economic development. Every sector of the national economy – agriculture, industry, transport, commercial and domestic – needs inputs of energy. The economic development plans implemented since Independence necessarily required increasing amounts of energy to remain operational. As a result, consumption of energy in all forms has been steadily rising all over the country.

In this background, there is an urgent need to develop a sustainable path of energy development. Promotion of energy conservation and increased use of renewable energy sources are the twin planks of sustainable energy. India is presently one of the least energy efficient countries in the world. We have to adopt a cautious approach for the judicious use of our limited energy resources. For example, as concerned citizens we can do our bit by using public transport systems instead of individual vehicles; switching off electricity when not in use, using power-saving devices and using non-conventional sources of energy. After all, "energy saved is energy produced".

ECOLOGY AND BIODIVERSITY

Ecology is the interdisciplinary scientific study of the distributions, abundance and relations of organisms and their interactions with the environment. Ecology is also the study of ecosystems. Ecosystems describe the web or network of relations among organisms at different scales of organization.

Like many of the natural sciences, a conceptual understanding of ecology is found in the broader details of study, including:

- life processes explaining adaptations
- distribution and abundance of organisms
- the movement of materials and energy through living communities
- the successional development of ecosystems, and
- the abundance and distribution of biodiversity in context of the environment

There are many practical applications of ecology in conservation biology, wetland management, natural resource management (agriculture, forestry, fisheries), city planning (urban ecology), community health, economics, basic & applied science and it provides a conceptual framework for understanding and researching human social interaction (human ecology).

Population Ecology

The population is the unit of analysis in population ecology. A population consists of individuals of the same species that live, interact and migrate through the same niche and habitat. A primary law of population ecology is the Malthusian growth model. This law states that:

"...a population will grow (or decline) exponentially as long as the environment experienced by all individuals in the population remains constant

Community ecology

Community ecology is a subdiscipline of ecology which studies the distribution, abundance, demography, and interactions between coexisting populations. An example of a study in community ecology might measure primary production in a wetland in relation to decomposition and consumption rates. This requires an understanding of the community connections between plants (i.e., primary producers) and the decomposers (e.g., fungi and bacteria). or the analysis of predator-prey dynamics affecting amphibian biomass. Food webs and trophic levels are two widely employed conceptual models used to explain the linkages among species.

Food webs

Food webs are a type of concept map that illustrate ecological pathways, usually starting with solar energy being used by plants during photosynthesis. As plants grow, they accumulate carbohydrates and are eaten by grazing herbivores. Step by step lines or relations are drawn until a web of life is illustrated.

There are different ecological dimensions that can be mapped to create more complicated food webs, including: species composition (type of species), richness (number of species), biomass (the dry weight of plants and animals), productivity (rates of conversion of energy and nutrients into growth), and stability (food webs over time). A food web diagram illustrating species composition shows how change in a single species can directly and indirectly influence many others. Microcosm studies are used to simplify food web research into semi-isolated units such as small springs, decaying logs, and laboratory experiments using organisms that reproduce quickly, such as daphnia feeding on algae grown under controlled environments in jars of water.

BIODIVERSITY

In our biosphere immense diversity (or heterogeneity) exists not only at the species level but at all levels of biological organisation ranging from macromolecules within cells to biomes. Biodiversity is the term popularised by the sociobiologist Edward Wilson to describe the combined diversity at all the levels of biological organisation.

The most important of them are– .

(i) ***Genetic diversity:*** A single species might show high diversity at the genetic level over its distributional range. The genetic variation shown by the medicinal plant Rauwolfia vomitoria growing in different Himalayan ranges might be in terms of the potency and concentration of the active chemical (reserpine) that the plant produces. India has more than 50,000 genetically different strains of rice, and 1,000 varieties of mango.

(ii) ***Species diversity:*** The diversity at the species level. For example, the Western Ghats have a greater amphibian species diversity than the Eastern Ghats.

(iii) ***Ecological diversity:*** At the ecosystem level, India, for instance, with its deserts, rain forests, mangroves, coral reefs, wetlands, estuaries, and alpine meadows has a greater ecosystem diversity than a Scandinavian country like Norway.

PATTERNS OF BIODIVERSITY

(i) Latitudinal Gradients: The diversity of plants and animals is not uniform throughout the world but shows a rather uneven distribution. For many group of animals or plants, there are interesting patterns in diversity, the most well- known being the latitudinal gradient in diversity. In general, species diversity decreases as we move away from the equator towards the poles.

With very few exceptions, tropics (latitudinal range of 23.5° N to 23.5° S) harbour more species than temperate or polar areas. There is more solar energy available in the tropics, which contributes to higher productivity; this in turn might contribute indirectly to greater diversity. species-Area relationships: During his pioneering and extensive explorations in the wilderness of South American jungles, the great German naturalist and geographer Alexander von Humboldt observed that within a region species richness increased with increasing explored area, but only up to a limit. In fact, the relation between species richness and area for a wide variety of taxa (angiosperm plants, birds, bats, freshwater fishes) turns out to be a rectangular hyperbola. On a logarithmic scale, the relationship is a straight line described by the equation

$$\log S = \log C + Z \log A$$

where,

S= Species richness A= Area

Z = slope of the line (regression coefficient)

C = Y-intercept

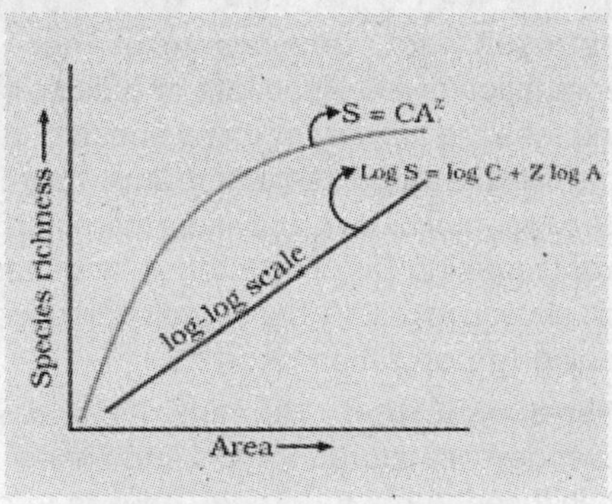

Figure 5.2 Showing species area relationship. On log scale the relationship becomes linear

Ecologists have discovered that the value of Z lies in the range of 0.1 to 0.2, regardless of the taxonomic group or the region (whether it is the plants in Britain, birds in California or molluscs in New York state, the slopes of the regression line are amazingly similar). But, if you analyse the species-area relationships among very large areas like the entire continents, one can find that the slope of the line to be much steeper (Z values in the range of 0.6 to 1.2).

BIODIVERSITY LOSS

In general, loss of biodiversity in a region may lead to

- decline in plant production,
- lowered resistance to environmental perturbations such as drought and
- increased variability in certain ecosystem processes such as plant productivity, water use, and pest and disease cycles.

Causes of biodiversity losses:

The accelerated rates of species extinctions that the world is facing now are largely due to human activities. There are four major causes:

(i) ***Habitat loss and fragmentation:*** This is the most important cause driving animals and plants to extinction. The most dramatic examples of habitat loss come from tropical rain forests. Once covering more than 14 per cent of the earth's land surface, these rain forests now cover no more than 6 per cent. They are being destroyed fast. Besides total loss, the degradation of many habitats by pollution also threatens the survival of many species. When large habitats are broken up into small fragments due to various human activities, mammals and birds requiring large territories and certain animals with migratory habits are badly affected, leading to population declines.

(ii) ***Over-exploitation:*** Humans have always depended on nature for food and shelter, but when 'need' turns to 'greed', it leads to over-exploitation of natural resources. Many species extinctions in the last 500 years (Steller's sea cow, passenger pigeon) were due to overexploitation by humans. Presently many marine fish populations around the world are over harvested, endangering the continued existence of some commercially important species.

(iii) ***Alien species invasions:*** When alien species are introduced unintentionally or deliberately for whatever purpose, some of them turn invasive, and cause decline or extinction of indigenous species.

(iv) ***Co-extinctions:*** When a species becomes extinct, the plant and animal species associated with it in an obligatory way also become extinct. When a host fish species becomes extinct, its unique assemblage of parasites also meets the same fate. Another example is the case of a coevolved plant-pollinator mutualism where extinction of one invariably leads to the extinction of the other.

BIODIVERSITY CONSERVATION

When we conserve and protect the whole ecosystem, its biodiversity at all levels is protected - we save the entire forest to save the tiger. This approach is called in situ (on site) conservation. However, when there are situations where an animal or plant is endangered or threatened and needs urgent measures to save it from extinction, ex situ (off site) conservation is the desirable approach.

In situ conservation—Faced with the conflict between development and conservation, many nations find it unrealistic and economically not feasible to conserve all their biological wealth. Invariably, the number of species waiting to be saved from extinction far exceeds the conservation resources available. On a global basis, this problem has been addressed by eminent conservationists. They identified for maximum protection certain 'biodiversity hotspots' regions with very high levels of species richness and high degree of endemism (that is, species confined to that region and not found anywhere else). Initially 25 biodiversity hotspots were identified but subsequently nine more have been added to the list, bringing the total number of biodiversity hotspots in the world to 34. These hotspots are also regions of accelerated habitat loss. Three of these hotspots - Western Ghats and Sri Lanka, Indo-Burma and Himalaya - cover our country's exceptionally high biodiversity regions.

Ex situ Conservation—In this approach, threatened animals and plants are taken out from their natural habitat and placed in special setting where they can be protected and given special care. Zoological parks, botanical gardens and wildlife safari parks serve this purpose. There are many animals that have become extinct in the wild but continue to be maintained in zoological parks. In recent years ex situ conservation has advanced beyond keeping threatened species in enclosures. Now gametes of threatened species can be preserved in viable and fertile condition for long periods using cryopreservation techniques, eggs can be fertilised in vitro, and plants can be propagated using tissue culture methods. Seeds of different genetic strains of commercially important plants can be kept for long periods in seed banks.

EXPLOITATION AND CONSERVATION OF MINERAL AND OTHER NATURAL RESOURCES

MINERAL

Geologists define mineral as a "homogenous, naturally occurring substance with a definable internal structure." Minerals are found in varied forms in nature, ranging from the hardest diamond to the softest talc. A particular mineral that will be formed from a certain combination of elements depends upon the physical and chemical conditions under which the material forms.

This, in turn, results in a wide range of colours, hardness, crystal forms, lustre and density that a particular mineral possesses. Geologists use these properties to classify the minerals.

EXPLOITATION OF MINERAL

Mineral exploration is the process undertaken by companies, partnerships or corporations in the endeavour of finding ore (commercially viable concentrations of minerals) to mine. Mineral exploration is a much more intensive, organised and professional form of mineral prospecting and, though it frequently uses the services of prospecting, the process of mineral exploration on the whole is much more involved.

STAGES OF MINERAL EXPLORATION

1. AREA SELECTION

Area selection is a crucial step in professional mineral exploration. Selection of the best, most prospective, area in a mineral field, geological region or terrain will assist in making it not only possible to find ore deposits, but to find them easily, cheaply and quickly.

Area selection is based on applying the theories behind ore genesis, the knowledge of known ore occurrences and the method of their formation, to known geological regions via the study of geological maps, to determine potential areas where the particular class of ore deposit being sought may exist. Oftentimes new styles of deposits may be found which reveal opportunities to find look-alike deposit styles in rocks and terranes previously though unprospective, which may result in a process of pegging of leases in similar geological settings based on this new model or methodology.

This process applies the disciplines of basin modeling, structural geology, geochronology, petrology and a host of geophysical and geochemical disciplines to make predictions and draw parallels between the known ore deposits and their physical form and the unknown potential of finding a 'lookalike' within the area selected.

Area selection is also influenced by the commodity being sought; exploring for gold occurs in a different manner and within different rocks and areas to exploration for oil or natural gas or iron ore. Areas which are prospective for gold may not be prospective for other metals and commodities.

The ultimate result of an area selection process is the pegging or notification of exploration licenses, known as tenements.

TARGET GENERATION

The target generation phase involves investigations of the geology via mapping, geophysics and conducting geochemical or intensive geophysical testing of the surface and subsurface geology. In some cases, for instance in areas covered by soil, alluvium and platform cover, drilling may be performed directly as a mechanism for generating targets.

MINERAL EXPLORATION - USING MODERN TECHNIQUES

GEOPHYSICAL METHODS

Geophysical instruments play a large role in gathering geological data which is used in mineral exploration. Instruments are used in geophysical surveys to check for variations in gravity, magnetism, electromagnetism (resistivity of rocks) and a number of different other variables in a certain area. The most effective and widespread method of gathering geophysical data is via flying airborne geophysics.

Geiger counters and scintillometers are used to determine the amount of radioactivity. This is particularly applicable to searching for uranium ore deposits but can also be of use in detecting radiometric anomalies associated with metasomatism.

Depending on the purpose of exploration there are a number of airborne techniques used for determining possible target zones and more often cutting exploration costs drastically by narrowing down the area to be covered by detailed ground geophysical studies.

The basic concept remaining the same, which collecting data from equipment aboard a low flying (80m above ground) aircraft at small line intervals. However in India the acceptance of this method of exploration planning has not been wide and the only state to boast of such a database is Orissa. The state now has an extremely marketable and valuable commodity in terms of a digital data base covering 75,000 sq. kms. and incorporating, High resolution Aeromagnetics, radiometrics, digital elevation, satellite imagery, topographical data all collected and collected at 1:50,000 scale.

The advantages of such a program are extensive, and to name a few:

- Reducecosts Lower field exploration and drilling costs, by identifying target sites for effective use of field resources.
- Find targets Increase target quality and confidence by integrating all types of data.
- Map geology Map and understand geological structures with interactive on-screen interpretation and creation of geology maps.
- Print maps Print professional maps by producing maps for field use, for management reporting and for investor relations.

Field exploration is expensive and the idea of using an airborne platform integrated with satellite imagery is to identify targets and anomalies from a regional to detailed view. By drilling only those areas showing a high potential, an effective exploration program can be carried out less expensively.

A well collated and structured data base can be sued to:

- Create large scale maps combining multiple airphotos
- Use airphotos to map subregional surface geology
- Show the geological interpretations over airphotos
- Create field exploration maps with detailed views of access roads
- Create 3D views of existing or proposed mines for planning

A well - structured data base for an effective exploration program will be of the type:

- Satellite Imagery
- Aeromagnetic Interpretations
- Radiometric Interpretations Combined with:
- Available, verified geology
- Topographical data watershed information

All integrated into a powerful GIS creates a valuable pool of data fo then planning an exploration program. A common mistake made in the Indian context is the line of thought that considers Satellite imagery and Aeromgnetic imagery as one and the same. It is important to point out that satellite imagery maps only the superficial ground cover whereas high resolution aeromagnetic maps the unseen or below surface lighology, actual depth depending on the terrain constituents.

GEOCHEMICAL METHODS

The primary role of geochemistry, here used to describe assaying or geological media, in mineral exploration is to find an area anomalous in the commodity sought, or in elements known to be associated with the type of mineralisation sought.

Regional geochemical exploration has traditionally involved use of stream sediments to target potentially mineralised catchments. Regional surveys may use low sampling densities such as one sample per 100 square kilometres. Follow-up geochemical surveys commonly use soils as the sampling media, possibly via the collection of a grid of samples over the tenement or areas which are amenable to soil geochemistry. Areas which are covered by transported soils, alluvium, colluvium or are disturbed too much by human activity (roads, rail, farmland), may need to be drilled to a shallow depth in order to sample undisturbed or unpolluted bedrock.

Once the geochemical analyses are returned, the data is investigated for anomalies (single or multiple elements) that may be related to the presence of mineralisation. The geochemical anomaly is often field checked against the outcropping geology and, in modern geochemistry, normalised against the regolith type and landform, to reduce the effects of weathering, transported materials and landforms.

Geochemical anomalies may be spurious or related to low-grade or sub-grade mineralisation. In order to determine if this is the case, geochemical anomalies must be drilled in order to test them for the existence of economic concentrations of mineralisation, or even to determine why they exist in the place they exist.

EXTRACTION

The ultimate goal of mineral exploration is the extraction, beneficiation and profitable and beneficial sale of mineral commodities.

Extraction methods may vary considerably and it is the discipline of engineers trained in mining engineering to determine the most safe, cost effective and efficient method of mining the ore body.

Mineral exploration and development does not cease upon a decision to mine. Exploration of a brownfields nature is conducted to find near-mine repetitions, extensions and continuity of the existing ore body. In-mine exploration and grade control drilling is a major concern of operating mines and can be an effective tool in adding value to existing mineral operations.

Often the lessons learned from studying an exposed ore body, both empirically and scientifically, are invaluable to the exploration geologist and geophysicist, for they get to see the proof of their concepts and the errors of the assumptions they used in the search for the ore body. It is always the case that the exact nature of the ore body does not exactly match the models used to find it.

CONSERVATION OF MINERALS

We all appreciate the strong dependence of industry and agriculture upon mineral deposits and the substances manufactured from them. The total volume of workable mineral deposits is an insignificant fraction i.e. one per cent of the earth's crust. We are rapidly consuming mineral resources that required millions of years to be created and concentrated. The geological processes of mineral formation are so slow that the rates of replenishment are infinitely small in comparison to the present rates of consumption. Mineral resources are, therefore, finite and non-renewable. Rich mineral deposits are our country's extremely valuable but short-lived possessions. Continued extraction of ores leads to increasing costs as mineral extraction comes from greater depths along with decrease in quality.

A concerted effort has to be made in order to use our mineral resources in a planned and sustainable manner. Improved technologies need to be constantly evolved to allow use of low grade ores at low costs. Recycling of metals, using scrap metals and other substitutes are steps in conserving our mineral resources for the future.

NATURAL HAZARDS

A natural hazard is a threat of a naturally occurring event that will have a negative effect on people or the environment. Many natural hazards are interrelated, e.g. earthquakes can cause tsunamis and drought can lead directly to famine.

GEOLOGICAL HAZARDS

Volcanic eruption

The volcanic eruption arises when Magma pushed upward through volcanic vent by pressure and effervesence of dissolved gases.

General characteristic of Volcanoes

Types of volcanoes are cindercones, shield volcanoes, composite volcanoes, and lava domes. Magma flowing out onto surface is lava and all solid particles ejected such as ash, pyroclastic flows, mud,debris, and lava flows.

Predictibility

Study of the geological history of volcanoes mainly located in a clearly defined volcanic belt, along with seismic activities and other observation may indicate an impeding volcano.

Factor contributing to vulnerability

Settlements on the flanks of volcanoes, Settlements in the historical paths of mud or lava lows. Strucyures with roof designs nor resistance to ash accumulation. Lack of evacuation plan or warning system.

Earthquake

An earthquake is a phenomenon that results from a sudden release of stored energy that radiates seismic waves. At the Earth's surface, earthquakes may manifest themselves by a shaking or displacement of the ground and sometimes tsunamis. Most of the world's earthquakes (90%, and 81% of the largest) take place in the 40,000-km-long, horseshoe-shaped zone called the circum-Pacific seismic belt, also known as the Pacific Ring of Fire, which for the most part bounds the Pacific Plate. Many earthquakes happen each day, few of which are large enough to cause significant damage.

Landslides and Mudflows

A landslide is a disaster closely related to an avalanche, but instead of occurring with snow, it occurs involving actual elements of the ground, including rocks , trees, parts of houses, and anything else which may happen to be swept up. Landslides can be caused by earthquakes, volcanic eruptions, or general instability in the surrounding land. Mudslides, or mudflows, are a special case of landslides, in which heavy rainfall causes loose soil on steep terrain to collapse and slide downwards.

Avalanche

An avalanche is a geophysical hazard a slide of a large snow (or rock) mass down a mountainside, caused when a buildup of snow is released down a slope, it is one of the major dangers faced in the mountains in winter. An avalanche is an example of a gravity current consisting of granular material. In an avalanche, lots of material or mixtures of different types of material fall or slide rapidly under the force of gravity. Avalanches are often classified by what they are made of.

HYDROLOGICAL HAZARDS

Tsunami

The tsunami caused by the December 26, 2004 earthquake strikes Ao Nang, Thailand.

A tsunami is a wave of water caused by the displacement of a body of water. The word comes from Japanese words "tsu" meaning harbor and "nami" meaning wave (tsu+nami=harbor wave). Tsunami can be caused by undersea earthquakes as in the 2004 Indian Ocean Earthquake, or by landslides such as the one which occurred at Lituya Bay, Alaska. Meteotsunamis are caused by meteorological phenomena. A megatsunami is an informal term used to describe very large tsunamis. The largest waves are caused by very large landslides, such as a collapsing island, into a body of water. The tsunami of 26th December 2005 in Indian Ocean causes havoc in south Asia region.

Flood

Floods are the result of prolonged rainfall from a storm, including thunderstorms, rapid melting of large amounts of snow, or rivers which swell from excess precipitation upstream and cause widespread damage to areas downstream, or less frequently the bursting of man-made dams or levees. Tropical cyclones can result in extensive flooding and storm surge.

Seiche

A seiche is a standing wave in an enclosed or partially enclosed body of water. Seiches and seiche-related phenomena have been observed on lakes, reservoirs, bays and seas. The key requirement for formation of a seiche is that the body of water be at least partially bounded.

ATMOSPHERIC HAZARDS

Blizzard

A blizzard is a severe winter storm icy and windy conditions characterized by low temperatures, strong winds, and heavy snow.

Cyclonic storms

Hurricane, tropical cyclone, and typhoon are different names for the same phenomenon: a cyclonic storm system that forms over the oceans. It is caused by evaporated water that comes off of the ocean and becomes a storm. The Coriolis Effect causes the storms to spin, and a hurricane is declared when this spinning mass of storms attains a wind speed greater than 74 mph (119 km/h). Hurricane is used for these phenomena in the Atlantic and eastern Pacific Oceans, tropical cyclone in the Indian, typhoon in the western Pacific.

Tornado

A tornado is a natural disaster resulting from a thunderstorm. Tornadoes are violent, rotating columns of air which can blow at speeds between 50 and 300 mph (480 km/h), and possibly higher. Tornadoes can occur one at a time, or can occur in large tornado outbreaks along squall lines or in other large areas of thunderstorm development. Waterspouts are tornadoes occurring over tropical waters in light rain conditions.

CLIMATIC HAZARDS

Drought

Drought is defined as an acute shortage of water and crop failure that results when the average rainfall is very less than the normal. A drought is an abnormally dry period when there is not enough water to support agricultural, urban or environmental water needs. Extended droughts can result in deaths by starvation or disease, and can result in wildfires. Scientists warn that global warming may result in more extensive droughts in coming years

Heat wave

A heat wave is a hazard characterized by heat which is considered extreme and unusual in the area in which it occurs. Heat waves are rare and require specific combinations of weather events to take place, and may include temperature inversions, katabatic winds, or other phenomena. There is potential for longer term events causing global warming, including stadial events (the opposite to glacial 'ice age' events), or through human induced climatic warming.

Ice storm

An ice storm is a particular weather event in which precipitation falls as ice, due to atmosphere conditions.

WILDFIRE HAZARD

A wildfire is an uncontrolled fire burning in wildland areas. Common causes include lightning and drought but wildfires may also be started by human negligence or arson. They can be a threat to those in rural areas and also wildlife. Wildfires can also produce ember attacks, where floating embers set fire to buildings at a distance from the fire itself.

Disease

Disease is a natural hazard that can be enhanced by human factors such as urbanization or poor sanitation. Disease affecting multiple people can be termed an outbreak or epidemic.

In some cases, a hazard exists in that a man-made defense against disease could fail, for example through antibiotic resistance.

ELEMENTS OF REMOTE SENSING

"Remote sensing is the science (and to some extent, art) of acquiring information about the Earth's surface without actually being in contact with it. This is done by sensing and recording reflected or emitted energy and processing, analyzing, and applying that information".

Remote sensing is the small or large-scale acquisition of information of an object or phenomenon, by the use of either recording or real-time sensing device(s) that are wireless, or not in physical or intimate contact with the object (such as by way of aircraft, spacecraft, satellite, buoy, or ship). In practice, remote sensing is the stand-off collection through the use of a variety of devices for gathering information on a given object or area. Thus, Earth observation or weather satellite collection platforms, ocean and atmospheric observing weather buoy platforms, the monitoring of a parolee via an ultrasound identification system, Magnetic Resonance Imaging (MRI), Positron Emission Tomography (PET), X-radiation (X-RAY) and space probes are all examples of remote sensing.

There are two kinds of remote sensing. Passive sensors detect natural radiation that is emitted or reflected by the object or surrounding area being observed. Reflected sunlight is the most common source of radiation measured by passive sensors. Examples of passive remote sensors include film photography, Infrared, charge-coupled devices, and radiometers. Active collection, on the other hand, emits energy in order to scan objects and areas whereupon a sensor then detects and measures the radiation that is reflected or backscattered from the target. RADAR is an example of active remote sensing where the time delay between emission and return is measured, establishing the location, height, speed and direction of an object.

In much of remote sensing, the process involves an interaction between incident radiation and the targets of interest. This is exemplified by the use of imaging systems where the following seven elements are involved. Note, however that remote sensing also involves the sensing of emitted energy and the use of non-imaging sensors.

1. ***Energy Source or Illumination (A)***- the first requirement for remote sensing is to have an energy source which illuminates or provides electromagnetic energy to the target of interest.
2. ***Radiation and the Atmosphere (B)***- as the energy travels from its source to the target, it will come in contact with and interact with the atmosphere it passes through. This interaction may take place a second time as the energy travels from the target to the sensor.
3. ***Interaction with the Target (C)***- once the energy makes its way to the target through the atmosphere, it interacts with the target depending on the properties of both the target and the radiation.
4. ***Recording of Energy by the Sensor (D)***- after the energy has been scattered by, or emitted from the target, we require a sensor (remote - not in contact with the target) to collect and record the electromagnetic radiation.
5. ***Transmission, Reception, and Processing (E)***- the energy recorded by the sensor has to be transmitted, often in electronic form, to a receiving and processing station where the data are processed into an image (hardcopy and/or digital).
6. ***Interpretation and Analysis (F)***- the processed image is interpreted, visually and/or digitally or electronically, to extract information about the target which was illuminated.
7. ***Application (G)***- the final element of the remote sensing process is achieved when we apply the information we have been able to extract from the imagery about the target in order to better understand it, reveal some new information, or assist in solving a particular problem.

These seven elements comprise the remote sensing process from beginning to end.

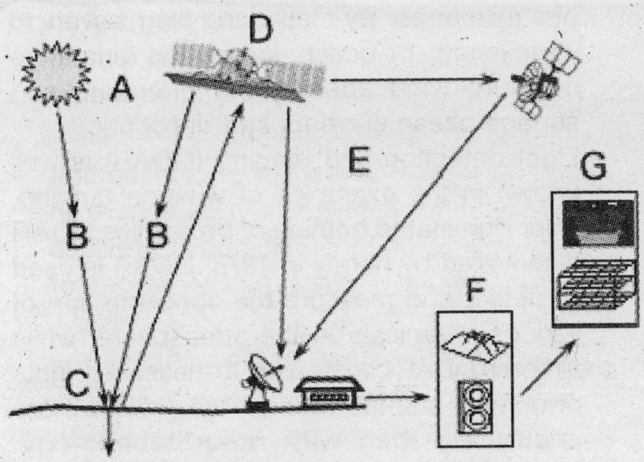

Fig. 5.3: Illustration showing remote sensing process

Electromagnetic Radiation

Electromagnetic radiation consists of an electrical field (E) which varies in magnitude in a direction perpendicular to the direction in which the radiation is traveling, and a magnetic field (M) oriented at right angles to the electrical field. Both these fields travel at the speed of light (c).

Two characteristics of electromagnetic radiation are particularly important for understanding remote sensing. These are the wavelength and frequency.

The wavelength is the length of one wave cycle, which can be measured as the distance between successive wave crests. Wavelength is usually represented by the Greek letter lambda (l). Wavelength is measured in metres (m) or some factor of metres such as nanometres (nm, 10^{-9} metres), micrometres (mm, 10^{-6} metres) or centimetres (cm, 10^{-2} metres). Frequency refers to the number of cycles of a wave passing a fixed point per unit of time. Frequency is normally measured in hertz (Hz), equivalent to one cycle per second, and various multiples of hertz.

Wavelength and frequency are related by the following formula:

$$c = \lambda v$$

where:

λ = wavelength (m)

v = frequency (cycles per second, Hz)

c = speed of light (3×10^8 m/s)

RADIATION - TARGET INTERACTIONS

There are three (3) forms of interaction that can take place when energy strikes, or is incident (I) upon the surface. These are: absorption (A); transmission (T); and reflection (R). The total incident energy will interact with the surface in one or more of these three ways. The proportions of each will depend on the wavelength of the energy and the material and condition of the feature.

Absorption (A) occurs when radiation (energy) is absorbed into the target while transmission (T) occurs when radiation passes through a target. Reflection (R) occurs when radiation "bounces" off the target and is redirected. In remote sensing, we are most interested in measuring the radiation reflected from targets. We refer to two types of reflection, which represent the two extreme ends of the way in which energy is reflected from a target: specular reflection and diffuse reflection.

When a surface is smooth we get specular or mirror-like reflection where all (or almost all) of the energy is directed away from the surface in a single direction. Diffuse reflection occurs when the surface is rough and the energy is reflected almost uniformly in all directions. Most earth surface features lie somewhere between perfectly specular or perfectly diffuse reflectors. Whether a particular target reflects specularly or diffusely, or somewhere in between, depends on the surface roughness of the feature in comparison to the wavelength of the incoming radiation. If the wavelengths are much smaller than the surface variations or the particle sizes that make up the surface, diffuse reflection will dominate. For example, fine-grained sand would appear fairly smooth to long wavelength microwaves but would appear quite rough to the visible wavelengths.

Leaves: A chemical compound in leaves called chlorophyll strongly absorbs radiation in the red and blue wavelengths but reflects green wavelengths. Leaves appear "greenest" to us in the summer, when chlorophyll content is at its maximum. In autumn, there is less chlorophyll in the leaves, so there is less absorption and proportionately more reflection of the red wavelengths, making the leaves appear red or yellow (yellow is a combination of red and green wavelengths). The internal structure of healthy leaves act as excellent diffuse reflectors of near-infrared wavelengths. If our eyes were sensitive to near-infrared, trees would appear extremely bright to us at these wavelengths. In fact, measuring and monitoring the near-IR reflectance is one way that scientists can determine how healthy (or unhealthy) vegetation may be.

Water: Longer wavelength visible and near infrared radiation is absorbed more by water than shorter visible wavelengths. Thus water typically looks blue or blue-green due to stronger reflectance at these shorter wavelengths, and darker if viewed at red or near infrared wavelengths. If there is suspended sediment present in the upper layers of the water body, then this will allow better reflectivity and a brighter appearance of the water. The apparent colour of the water will show a slight shift to longer wavelengths. Suspended sediment (S) can be easily confused with shallow (but clear) water, since these two phenomena appear very similar. Chlorophyll in algae absorbs more of the blue wavelengths and reflects the green, making the water appear more green in colour when algae is present. The topography of the water surface (rough, smooth, floating materials, etc.) can also lead to complications for water-related interpretation due to potential problems of specular reflection and other influences on colour and brightness.

Applications of Remote Sensing Data

- Conventional radar is mostly associated with aerial traffic control, early warning, and certain large scale meteorological data. Doppler radar is used by local law enforcements' monitoring of speed limits and in enhanced meteorological collection such as wind speed and direction within weather systems. Other types of active collection includes plasmas in the ionosphere). Interferometric synthetic aperture radar is used to produce precise digital elevation models of large scale terrain (See RADARSAT, TerraSAR-X, Magellan).
- Laser and radar altimeters on satellites have provided a wide range of data. By measuring the bulges of water caused by gravity, they map features on the seafloor to a resolution of a mile or so. By measuring the height and wave-length of ocean waves, the altimeters measure wind speeds and direction, and surface ocean currents and directions.
- Light detection and ranging (LIDAR) is well known in the examples of weapon ranging, laser illuminated homing of projectiles.LIDAR discovered by hendy in 1976. LIDAR is used to detect and measure the concentration of various chemicals in the atmosphere, while airborne LIDAR can be used to measure heights of objects and features on the ground more accurately than with radar technology. Vegetation remote sensing is a principle application of LIDAR.
- Radiometers and photometers are the most common instrument in use, collecting reflected and emitted radiation in a wide range of frequencies. The most common are visible and infrared sensors, followed by microwave, gamma ray and rarely, ultraviolet. They may also be used to detect the emission spectra of various chemicals, providing data on chemical concentrations in the atmosphere.
- Stereographic pairs of aerial photographs have often been used to make topographic maps by imagery and terrain analysts in trafficability and highway departments for potential routes.
- Simultaneous multi-spectral platforms such as Landsat have been in use since the 70's. These thematic mappers take images in multiple wavelengths of electro-magnetic radiation (multi-spectral) and are usually found on earth observation satellites, including (for example) the Landsat program or the IKONOS satellite. Maps of land cover and land use from thematic mapping can be used to prospect for minerals, detect or monitor land usage, deforestation, and examine the health of indigenous plants and crops, including entire farming regions or forests.

Within the scope of the combat against desertification, remote sensing allows to follow-up and monitor risk areas in the long term, to determine desertification factors, to support decision-makers in defining relevant measures of environmental management, and to assess their impacts.

MULTIPLE CHOICE QUESTIONS

1. The main layers of the Earth in correct order, from the surface moving down, are:
   (a) Upper mantle, lower mantle, inner core, crust
   (b) Crust, mantle, outer core, inner core
   (c) Upper crust, outer core, inner core, mantle
   (d) Outer core, inner core, upper mantle, lower crust
2. Which of the following is NOT one of the main families of rocks?
   (a) Meteorites (b) Sedimentary
   (c) Metamorphic (d) Igneous
3. What steps are involved in having a hypothesis become an established theory?
   (a) The hypothesis makes sense when explained by politicians
   (b) A United Nations scientific panel votes on whether the hypothesis is accepted
   (c) A U.S. government agency votes on whether the hypothesis is accepted
   (d) The hypothesis is consistent with new data and investigations used to test its predictions
4. The lithosphere can be described as a layer of the Earth that is located:
   (a) within the asthenosphere, and it consists of heat-softened, weak rock.
   (b) within the lower portion of the mantle and contains solid, relatively strong rock.
   (c) just below the asthenosphere, and it contains both the crust and some mantle material.
   (d) just above the asthenosphere and it consists of solid, relatively strong rock.
5. Little or no volcanic activity is associated with which of the following plate boundaries?
   (a) Subducting plate boundaries
   (b) Transform plate boundaries
   (c) Divergent plate boundaries
   (d) Converging plate boundaries
6. The mineral halite has cube-shaped crystals because:
   (a) Cubes are the most common way two tetrahedron can join
   (b) Of the arrangement of atoms in the crystal structure (a.k.a. the crystal 'lattice')
   (c) Halite is soluble in water
   (d) There are no planes along which the mineral can break (i.e. it has no cleavage).
7. Which of the following is NOT a main type of silicate structure?
   (a) Frameworks (b) Single chains
   (c) Triple chains (d) Double chains
8. The property that distinguishes an atom to be that of a particular element is:
   (a) the number of neutrons and protons together.
   (b) the number of electrons it has.
   (c) the number of neutrons it has.
   (d) the number of protons it has.
9. In the mineral olivine, iron and magnesium can substitute freely in the crystal for all of the following reasons EXCEPT:
   (a) they are both abundant in the Earth's crust
   (b) they are similar in size
   (c) they have the same charge
   (d) they have the same atomic mass
10. The primary difference between magma and lava is that:
    (a) magma becomes lava anytime it is in a cooling condition.
    (b) they are produced from different parent materials.
    (c) one is below the ground, the other is above the ground.
    (d) one occurs at divergent plate boundaries, the other at convergent plate boundaries.
11. Fluid magma rises for all of the following reasons EXCEPT:
    (a) The surrounding rock is more dense than the magma.
    (b) the Earth's magnetic field acts on the iron component of the magma.

(c) gases in the magma expand outward, driving the magma upward.
(d) it is less dense than the solid rock that surrounds it.

12. As the rate of cooling decreases, the sizes of the crystals in an igneous rock:
(a) decreases
(b) increases
(c) can not predict
(d) stays the same

13. A pyroclastic flow can best be described as a:
(a) a slow rain of cool ash particles.
(b) flow of air trapped underneath blocks of lava.
(c) flow of hot ash particles and hot volcanic gas.
(d) flow of hot lava.

14. Which of the following would be the best place to live if you wanted to avoid volcanic eruptions?
(a) In the middle of a tectonic plate, and far from a hot spot (a.k.a. site of a mantle plume)
(b) Near a divergent plate boundary
(c) Near a convergent plate boundary
(d) In the middle of a tectonic plate, and near a hot spot (a.k.a. mantle plume)

15. A volcanic dome (a.k.a. 'rhyolite dome') forms when:
(a) faulting causes uplift of a volcano.
(b) a large volcanic mountain is rounded off by erosion.
(c) a shield volcano takes on a relatively symmetrical dome shape.
(d) highly viscous lava can't flow far from the vent it's erupted from.

16. Which of the following is not one of the four stages in the development of a terrestrial planet?
(a) flooding
(b) cratering
(c) slow surface evolution
(d) sublimation
(e) differentiation

17. The central regions of Earth's core are a solid because
(a) the composition at the centre of the core is lower in iron.
(b) the pressure at the centre raises the melting point.
(c) the magnetic field cannot penetrate into the centre of the core.
(d) convection does not extend all the way to the centre of the core.
(e) Earth initially formed from solid particles in the solar nebula.

18. The youngest parts of Earth's crust are
(a) the bottom layer found in the walls of the Grand Canyon
(b) the continents
(c) the continental margins
(d) the Appalachian Mountains
(e) the midocean rifts

19. The oxygen in Earth's atmosphere
(a) was manufactured inside stars.
(b) was added to the atmosphere by plant life.
(c) has grown more abundant since the origin of Earth.
(d) all of these
(e) none of these

20. The gas that is most responsible for the greenhouse effect on Earth is
(a) oxygen (O_2)
(b) nitrogen (N_2)
(c) carbon dioxide (CO_2)
(d) ozone (O_3)
(e) ammonia (NH_3)

21. The Himalayan mountains are rugged, jagged peaks and the Appalachians are smooth and rolling. Why is there a difference?
(a) The Himalayas are much older and the rocks have begun breaking off.
(b) The Himalayas are volcanic mountains and the Appalachians are not.
(c) The Appalachians are much older and have been smoothed by erosion.
(d) The Appalachians are younger and just started to be thrust upward by plate tectonics.
(e) (a) and (d)

22. In the development of a planet, the stage of ____________ occurred when molten rock flowed through fissures and filled deep basins.
(a) differentiation (b) cratering
(c) glaciation (d) accretion
(e) flooding

23. The energy that moves the plates of Earth's crust comes from
(a) the solar wind.
(b) convection from the hot interior.
(c) tides in the oceans.
(d) friction between wind and the land surface.
(e) Earth's magnetic field.

24. Why would a decrease in the density of the ozone layer create a public health concern?
(a) The greenhouse effect would not be as efficient and the temperature of Earth would decrease.
(b) The greenhouse effect would be more efficient and the temperature of Earth would increase.
(c) Plant life would no longer have the ozone it needs for photosynthesis to create chlorophyll.
(d) Ultraviolet radiation from the sun would bombard Earth.
(e) None of the above

25. The lunar maria are
(a) the lava plains of the lunar lowlands.
(b) the smooth plateaus of the lunar highlands.
(c) less than one billion years old.
(d) moving plates of lunar crust.
(e) older than the lunar highlands.

26. The moon is no longer geologically active because
(a) it is rotating too slowly.
(b) its radioactive elements were never abundant.
(c) it is too small.
(d) its crust is too thin.
(e) it does not have water on its surface.

27. The fission theory of the moon's origin has been criticized because
(a) the Moon is more spherical than Earth.
(b) the Moon's composition is different from Earth's.
(c) the tidal forces are making the Moon approach Earth.
(d) it requires too many coincidences for it to occur.
(e) the Moon has a large iron-nickel core.

28. That Mercury has a large iron core is evidenced by
(a) the large lobate scarps.
(b) the large mean density of Mercury.
(c) the lava flows near Caloris Basin.
(d) all of the above
(e) none of the above

29. The condensation hypothesis for the formation of the Moon suggests that the Moon and Earth formed as a double planet from the same cloud within the solar nebula. This hypothesis predicts that
(a) the Moon and Earth should have nearly the same mass and radius.
(b) the surfaces of the Moon and Earth should be very similar and show evidence of plate tectonics.
(c) the Moon and Earth should have identical compositions and densities.
(d) all of the above
(e) (a) and (c)

30. That the Moon has no magnetic field implies that
(a) the Moon is spinning to slowly to produce a magnetic field.
(b) the interior of the Moon is too hot to produce a magnetic field.
(c) the crust of the Moon is so thick that the magnetic field can not get out of the interior
(d) the Moon's core contains little if any molten iron.
(e) the Moon is moving further from Earth.

31. The geology of Venus appears to be dominated by
(a) volcanism
(b) plate tectonics
(c) erosion by flowing water
(d) impact cratering
(e) strip mining

32. The greenhouse effect keeps Venus hot because
(a) the atmosphere contains free oxygen.
(b) the atmosphere is rich in carbon dioxide.
(c) the surface converts infrared into visible radiation.
(d) the surface is free of sulphur compounds.
(e) the magnetic field traps a large number of particles from the solar wind.

33. The flow patterns found on the surface of Mars suggest
(a) that Mars is a water-rich world.
(b) that the climate on Mars was different in the past.
(c) that volcanism is occurring on Mars.
(d) that the polar caps are made of water.
(e) all of the above

34. Coronae on Venus are believed to be
(a) impact craters.
(b) caused by rising convection currents in the interior of Venus.
(c) the result of plate tectonics.
(d) located only in the polar regions of Venus.
(e) much older than the highlands such as Ishtar Terra.

35. The density of mantle is
(a) 2.7 g/cm^3 (b) 3.0 g/cm^3
(c) 5.4 g/cm^3 (d) 4.4 g/cm^3

36. The crust of Mars is believed to ________ than Earth's.
(a) be much thinner
(b) be younger
(c) contain more water
(d) be more geologically active
(e) be much stronger

37. Mars has a sufficient mass and a low enough temperature that water molecules could exist in its atmosphere. Why doesn't Mars' atmosphere contain a significant amount of water?
(a) Mars formed in a part of the solar nebula that lacked oxygen.
(b) Mars formed in a part of the solar nebula that lacked hydrogen.
(c) All of the water vapour was released in the impact that formed Deimos.
(d) Ultraviolet radiation breaks the water molecule into less massive particles that can escape.
(e) The water molecule combines readily with chlorine to form hydrochloric acid.

38. The continental crust is thicker in the areas of major mountain systems. It is as much as ________ km thick in the Himalayan region.
(a) 5 (b) 30
(c) 70 (d) 10

39. Besides Earth, which of the terrestrial planets and/or satellites of terrestrial planets show(s) evidence for the possible existence of liquid water flowing on its surface in the past?
(a) Venus (b) The Moon
(c) Phobos (d) Mars
(e) both (b) and (d)

40. One hypothesis suggested to explain the uniform age of the surface of Venus is that
(a) Venus' surface is 4 billion years old and has not been affected by flooding or slow evolution.
(b) Venus' surface is made of rocks that are much harder than Earth's and thus last longer.
(c) Venus periodically goes through a catastrophic melting of the entire surface.
(d) Venus' clouds protect it from meteorites so that very few impacts occur to change its surface.
(e) Dust storms deposit large amount of dust on the surface making it appear of uniform age.

41. Which is the slowest moving type of mass wasting?
(a) Avalanche (b) Debris flow
(c) Creep (d) Earth flow

43. What major disaster occurred in the U.S. in the 1930's:
(a) The dust bowl
(b) Long Beach oil field subsidence

(c) First man on the moon.
(d) Tsunami in Hawaii
(e) Eruption of Mt. St. Helens volcano.

43. What mineral is the major source of phosphate for humans and animals?
(a) Granite (b) Basalt
(c) Quartz (d) Mercury
(e) Apatite

44. The type of weathering reaction whereby salt and calcite are turned from solid materials in to ions carried away by water is called
(a) Oxidation (b) Dissolution
(c) Hydration (d) Hydrolysis
(e) Fettucine

45. Diorite is an example of
(a) Chemically formed sedimentary rock
(b) Extrusive igneous rock
(c) Plutonic igneous rock
(d) Metamorphic rock

46. Among the following regions of India, which one receives comparatively least amount of annual rainfall ?
(a) An 80 km wide coastal belt from Nellore to Point Calimere
(b) The middle and lower Assam valley
(c) North-eastern Rajasthan
(d) The coastal plains of Gujarat south of Narmada

47. The plain formed due to coalescence of series of alluvial fans in the piedmont zone is known as
(a) Pediment (b) Bajada
(c) Pediplain (d) Hamada

48. Aretes are sharp ridges which develop between the adjacent
(a) Cirques
(b) Roche moutonnee
(c) Medial moraines
(d) U-shaped valleys

49. Calcium carbonate deposited by precipitation from carbonate-saturated waters around a hot spring is called
(a) Stalactite (b) Stalagmite
(c) Travertine (d) Lapies

50. The Mississippi River is __________ kilometres long
(a) 40 (b) 400
(c) 4,000 (d) 40,000

51. On average, flooding on a given stream or river occurs every __________ years.
(a) 2.5 (b) 5
(c) 10 (d) 20
(e) 40

52. Of all the water on the planet, what percentage is in the oceans?
(a) 10 (b) 31
(c) 63 (d) 85
(e) 97

53. Water that has a pH of 4 is :
(a) Acidic
(b) Basic (Alkaline)
(c) Neutral
(d) None of the above

54. When a solid such as ice goes directly to a gaseous (vapour) state, the transformation is called:
(a) Plate tectonics (b) Evaporation
(c) Sublimation (d) Freezing
(e) None of the above

55. On the rainiest day in Cilaos, La reunion, about this amount of rain fell
(a) 6 feet (b) 12 feet
(c) 18 .feet (d) 24 feet
(e) None of the above

56. A region where evapotranspiration exceeds rainfall is probably
(a) In a foreign country
(b) A desert
(c) A swamp
(d) Heavily forested
(e) A rain forest

57. Maximum known depth to which permafrost extends is about:
(a) 15 feet (b) 35 feet
(c) 100 feet (d) 500 feet
(e) 5000 feet

58. Polje is a land form formed in
(a) Arid region (b) Gleciated region
(c) Limestone region (d) Flucial region

59. The water bearing rock is called
(a) Aquifer
(b) Aquaclude
(c) Unconfired aquifer
(d) Confired aquifer

60. The instrumed used for measuring seismicity is known as
(a) Isobar (b) Seismograph
(c) Seismogram (d) Seismology

61. Which of the below is an instream use of water?
(a) Hydroelectric (b) Showering
(c) Irrigation (d) Hog farming
(e) Car washing

62. When stream stage exceeds the river banks it is called a
(a) Precipitation event
(b) Flood
(c) Earthquake
(d) Ventricular fibrillation
(e) Weathering event

63. The aid rain occus when pH of rain water becomes
(a) 5.5 or less (b) 6.5 or more
(c) 7.4 (d) 9.0

64. The most important (major) original source of groundwater is
(a) Rivers (b) Rain
(c) Floods (d) Tsunami
(e) Snow

65. Sand is quite porous, and would usually be considered to be a(n)
(a) Aquiplast
(b) Aquifer
(c) Aquiclude
(d) Transform boundary
(e) Important source of water

66. The range of intensity of an earthquake in Mercalli scale varies between
(a) 1-10 (b) 1-11
(c) 0-10 (d) 1-12

67. What are "gabions"?
(a) Baskets of rock
(b) Lakes that form next to meandering streams
(c) Creatures from outer space that will conquer the earth.
(d) Breaks in the surface of the earth.
(e) Speleothems found in Lechuguilla Cave.

68. Potable water is ...
(a) only drinkable if boiled in a pot first.
(b) fine for drinking as is.
(c) both (a) & (b)
(d) none of the above

69. What portion of rainwater ends up (almost immediately) in rivers?
(a) 1/8 (b) 1/4
(c) 1/2 (d) 3/4
(e) All of it

70. The volume of water per unit time that is moving past a measurement point on a stream is called
(a) Traction (b) Stage
(c) Palimsest (d) Saltation
(e) Discharge

71. Which of the following is not a transport mechanism for material in a stream:
(a) Bed-load (b) Saltation
(c) Solution (d) Suspension
(e) None; all of the above are transport mechanisms.

72. In what type rock do most caves form?
(a) Limestone (b) Basalt
(c) Granite (d) Shale
(e) Sandstone

73. Where does most beach sand come from?
(a) Tsunami (b) Human activities
(c) Rivers (d) Gypsum
(e) Wind

74. Match List I with List II and select the correct answer using the code given below the lists:

List I (Genetic Phases)	List II (Resultant Tides)
A. The Sun and the Moon are at right angles with the Earth	1. Spring tide
B. The Sun, the Moon and the Earth are in a straight line	2. Neap tide
C. The Moon is nearest to the Earth	3. Apogean tide
D. The Moon is farthest from the Earth	4. Perigean tide

Code :	A	B	C	D
(a)	2	1	4	3
(b)	2	4	1	3
(c)	3	4	1	2
(d)	3	1	4	2

75. Consider the following :
1. Gulf of California
2. Mediterranean Sea
3. Baltic Sea

In terms of decreasing salinity, which one of the following is the correct sequence?

(a) 1-2-3 (b) 2-1-3
(c) 3-1-2 (d) 2-3-1

76. Consider the following statements:
1. Globigerina ooze is a calcareous pelagic deposit.
2. Globigerina ooze is found mostly in the tropical and temperate zones of the Atlantic Ocean.

Which of the statements given above is/are correct ?

(a) 1 only (b) 2 only
(c) Both 1 and 2 (d) Neither 1 nor 2

77. Regular oscillations in the water surface of large water bodies are formed because of
(a) Gravitational effect of Moon
(b) Difference in temperature of sea water and the air above
(c) Rotation of Earth
(d) Friction of wind on the water surface

78. Which sphere provides the platform for most life forms on Earth?
(a) atmosphere (b) hydrosphere
(c) lithosphere (d) biosphere

79. The second abundant gas in the atmosphere is:
(a) oxygen (b) carbon dioxide
(c) nitrogen (d) ozone

80. The Sun emits ____________, and the Earth emits __________.
(a) longwave radiation ; Electromagnetic waves
(b) shortwave radiation ; Electromagnetic waves
(c) longwave radiation ; shortwave radiation
(d) shortwave radiation ; longwave radiation

81. The planet closest to the Earth is:
(a) Neptune (b) Saturn
(c) Mercury (d) Venus

82. The cause of seasonality is:
(a) parallelism (b) axis tilt
(c) revolution (d) all of the above

83. The main driving force for winds is the:
(a) Coriolis force
(b) frictional force
(c) pressure-gradient force
(d) centrifugal force

84. A wind coming from the east to the west is called a/an:
(a) westerly wind
(b) easterly wind
(c) northeasterly wind
(d) northwesterly wind

85. The grid of the Earth is made up of:
(a) east-west latitudes and north-south longitudes
(b) east-west meridians and north south parallels
(c) east-west longitudes and north-south latitudes
(d) east-north latitudes and west-south longitudes

86. L wave is a type of
(a) P wave (b) S wave
(c) Body wave (d) Surface waves

87. Which of the following remote sensing techniques is a passive system?
(a) thermal infrared
(b) colour infrared
(c) aerial photos
(d) all of the above

88. Starting from the surface, the temperature decreases in the __________, then increases in the ____________, then decreases in the ____________ till it finally increases in the ______________.
(a) stratosphere; thermosphere; troposphere; mesosphere
(b) troposphere; stratosphere; mesosphere; thermosphere
(c) thermosphere; stratosphere; troposphere; mesosphere
(d) troposphere; thermosphere; mesosphere; stratosphere

89. Continental drift theory is given by
(a) Alfred Wegner (b) Tuzo Wilson
(c) Newton (d) Henry Hess

90. Sea floor spreading hypothesis is given by
(a) Alfred Wegner (b) Tuzo Wilson
(c) Newton (d) Henry Hess

91. According to the idealized model of surface atmospheric circulation,_________ broad pressure areas (features) exist the Northern hemisphere and a _________ set exists in the Southern hemisphere of which one feature is in common.
(a) 2 ; similar (b) 4 ; different
(c) 2 ; different (d) 4 ; similar

92. Wind change its direction due to ....
(a) Coriolis force
(b) density differences
(c) frictional drag of winds
(d) all of the above

93. The amount of solar insolation falling on the surface of the Earth depends mainly on the:
(a) angle of incidence
(b) solar radiation output of the Sun
(c) amount of glacial coverage in a particular area
(d) amount of ocean surface in a particular region

94. The circulation systems of surface ocean currents are known as ___________, and they move ___________ in the Southern hemisphere.
(a) highs ; clockwise
(b) highs ; counterclockwise
(c) gyres ; clockwise
(d) gyres ; counterclockwise

95. The greatest amount of insolation reaching the Earth is at:
(a) the poles
(b) the equatorial region
(c) the midlatitudes
(d) the subtropics

96. Consider the following statements:
1. Pyramidal peak is a gentle-sided mountain summit.
2. Tarn is formed often in the cirques
3. The long axis of drumlins are parallel to the direction of glacial movement

Which of the statements given above are correct?
(a) 1 and 2 only (b) 2 and 3 only
(c) 1 and 3 only (d) 1, 2 and 3

97. A landform developed by the process of deposition occurring towards the centre of intermontane basins in arid or semi-arid regions is known as
(a) Pediment (b) Bajada
(c) Playa (d) Peneplain

98. Eskers are of glacio-fluvial origin. Which one of the following statements characterize them?
(a) They are long, narrow and sinuous ridges of sands.
(b) They are small, irregular mounds of bedded sands.
(c) They are small alluvial cones.
(d) They are flat-topped terraces.

99. Match List I with List II and select the correct answer using the code given below the lists:

List I (Author)	List II (Concept)
A. Davis	1. Pediplanation
B. Hack	2. Peneplanation
C. Hutton	3. Dynamic Equilibrium
D. King L.C	4. Uniformitarianism

Code :	A	B	C	D
(a)	1	4	3	2
(b)	1	3	4	2
(c)	2	4	3	1
(d)	2	3	4	1

100. The air pressure surface zone located between about 10ºN & 10ºS is called the ________, and it is caused by ____________ factors.
(a) subtropical high ; dynamic
(b) subtropical high ; thermal
(c) equatorial low ; thermal
(d) equatorial low ; dynamic

101. The Coriolis effect is:
(a) curve to the right in the Northern Hemisphere
(b) on from the west to the east and causes objects to curve to the right in the Northern Hemisphere
(c) to curve to the left in the Northern Hemisphere
(d) none

102. There are three kinds of jet streams, two are __________ and strong, and the third is _________ but weak.
(a) easterly ; westerly
(b) easterly ; northerly
(c) westerly ; southerly
(d) westerly ; easterly

103. A cyclone is a __________ pressure zone rotating ____________ in the Northern hemisphere, whereas an anticyclone is a _________ pressure zone rotating in the opposite direction.
(a) high ; counterclockwise ; low
(b) high ; clockwise ; low
(c) low ; clockwise ; high
(d) low ; counterclockwise ; high

104. When a descending air contracts and its volume decreases, what happens to its temperature?
(a) Its temperature decreases
(b) Its temperature increases
(c) Its temperature remains constant
(d) Its temperature first increases, then decreases

105. What are Chinooks?
(a) Cold local winds which blow from north-west to south-east direction in Spain
(b) Extremely dry winds blowing from north-east and east to west in eastern parts of Sahara desert
(c) Warm and dry winds which blow down the eastern slopes of Rocky Mountains of North America
(d) Warm and dry winds along the northern slopes of Alps Mountains

106. Condensation is a process which occurs when
(a) Temperature falls below 0ºC
(b) Absolute humidity becomes equal to relative humidity
(c) Temperature in the air parcel remains static
(d) Relative humidity becomes 100% and more

107. Which of the following sequences of clouds in ascending order would one meet 500 metres and above the mean sea level?
(a) Stratus, Nimbus, Cirrostratus, Cirrus
(b) Nimbus, Cirrostratus, Cirrocumulus, Stratus
(c) Cirrostratus, Stratus, Nimbus, Cumulonimbus
(d) Stratus, Cirrostratus, Cumulo-nimbus, Cirrocumulus

108. Consider the following statements regarding the distribution and pattern of isotherms :
1. In the northern hemisphere, isotherms bend sharply equator-ward over the continents during winter.

2. Temperature gradients are greater in summer than in winter in the northern hemisphere:

Which of the statements given above is/are correct ?

(a) 1 only (b) 2 only
(c) Both 1 and 2. (d) Neither 1 nor 2

109. Match List I with List II and select the correct answer using the code given below the lists:

List I (Local Wind)	List II (Country /Region)
A. Harmattan	1. Argentina
B. Haboob	2. Adriatic coast
C. Bora	3. West Africa
D. Zonda	4. Sudan

Code :	A	B	C	D
(a)	1	2	4	3
(b)	1	4	2	3
(c)	3	4	2	1
(d)	3	2	4	1

110. With reference to convectional type of rainfall, consider the following statements:

1. It is a warm weather phenomenon
2. This rainfall is associated with cumulonimbus clouds.

Which of the statements given above is/are correct ?

(a) 1 only (b) 2 only
(c) Both 1 and 2 (d) Neither 1 nor 2

111. With reference to the sub-tropical high pressure belt, consider the following statements:

1. It is affected by Earth's rotation and descent of winds from higher altitudes.
2. It is dynamically induced and characterised with anti-cyclonic conditions.

Which of the statements given above is/are correct ?

(a) 1 only (b) 2 only
(c) Both 1 and 2 (d) Neither 1 nor 2

112. In Koppen's classification of world climate, Aw climates refer to

(a) Humid tropical wet monsoon climate with a short dry season
(b) Tropical wet and dry climate with dry season in winter
(c) Tropical desert climate
(d) Humid meso-thermal climates

113. With reference to equatorial climate, consider the following statements:

1. Thermally induced low pressure belt develops around the equator but the pressure gradient is very low.
2. Temporal variability in the amount of rainfall is not found.

Which of the statements given above is/are correct?

(a) 1 only (b) 2 only
(c) Both 1 and 2 (d) Neither 1 nor 2

114. Ice caps and glaciers constitute percent of earth surface

(a) 2.8% (b) 35%
(c) 76% (d) 97%

115. In the phase change of 1 gram of ice at 0ºC to 1 gram of water at 0ºC, ______ is/are required:

(a) 1 calorie (b) 80 calories
(c) 597 calories (d) 677 calories

116. Caledonian orogenic movements are related to the geological history of

(a) Late Jurassic and early Cretaceous period
(b) Late Silurian and early Devonian period
(c) Middle Triassic period
(d) Late Devonian and early Carboniferous period

117. Match List I with List II and select the correct answer using the code given below the lists:

List I (Discontinuities)	List II (Layers of Earth's interior associated with discontinuity)
A. Weichert Gutenberg discontinuity	1. Outer core and inner core
B. Mohorovicic (Moho) discontinuity	2. Lower mantle and outer core
C. Lehman discontinuity	3. Upper mantle and lower mantle
D. Conrad discontinuity	4. Lower crust and upper mantle
	5. Division of Sial and Sima within the crust

Code :	A	B	C	D
(a)	5	1	3	2
(b)	2	1	3	5
(c)	2	4	1	5
(d)	5	4	1	2

118. A lens-shaped igneous intrusion situated beneath an anticlinal fold or in the base of a syncline is called
(a) Lapolith (b) Lacolith
(c) Phacolith (d) Batholith

119. Open folds are those in which the angle between the two limbs of the fold is
(a) more than 90° but less than 180°
(b) more than 75° but less than 150°
(c) more than 45° but less than 90°
(d) more than 120° but less than 210°

120. Consider the following statements :
1. Kaolinite is the weathered silicate clay.
2. Kaolinization process occurs due to hydrothermal alteration of feldspar.

Which of the statements given above is/are correct ?
(a) 1 only (b) 2 only
(c) Both 1 and 2 (d) Neither 1 nor 2

121. The __________ you are to the equator, the __________ the precipitation you expect.
(a) closer; higher
(b) closer ; lower
(c) farther ; higher
(d) none of the above

122. Evaporation of water from plants is called:
(a) radiation
(b) transpiration
(c) evapotranspiration
(d) evaporation

123. A parcel of air whose relative humidity is 10% cools following the:
(a) dry adiabatic lapse rate (DALR)
(b) saturated adiabatic lapse rate (SALR)
(c) environmental lapse rate (ELR)
(d) none

124. The temperature at which air achieves saturation is called the:
(a) sublimation temperature
(b) condensation temperature
(c) coalescence point
(d) dew point

125. Air at 100 m altitude has a temperature of 20°C. It rises over a 2000 m mountain before it descends into a basin with an elevation of 100 m. What is the lifting condensation level? (given: dew point is 5°C)
(a) 100 m (b) 500 m
(c) 1500 m (d) 1600 m

126. Using the saturation curve, what is the relative humidity at 1100 m.
(a) 0% (b) 43%
(c) 71% (d) 100%

127. What is the relative humidity at 1650 m?
(a) 0% (b) 43%
(c) 71% (d) 100%

128. Who introduced the term anticyclone for the first time?
(a) Fitzroy (b) J. Bjerknes
(c) F. Galton (d) V. Bjerknes

129. Consider the following statements regarding general characteristics associated with tropical cyclones :
1. Tropical cyclones, move with very low velocity over the oceans but become strong while moving over the land areas.
2. They are confined to a particular period of the year (mainly summer) and normally move from east to west.

Which of the statements given above is/are correct?
(a) 1 only (b) 2 only
(c) Both 1 and 2 (d) Neither 1 nor 2

130. Consider the following statements:
1. Temperature of surface water is comparatively higher in the northern hemisphere than in the Southern hemisphere.
2. The isotherms in the southern hemisphere are not regular and do not follow the latitudes while they (isotherms) are regular and follow the latitudes in the northern hemisphere.

Which of the statements given above is/are correct?

(a) 1 only (b) 2 only
(c) Both 1 and 2 (d) Neither 1 nor 2

131. Two main cold currents in the North Pacific Ocean are known as
(a) Oyashio and California currents
(b) Alaska and Kuroshio currents
(c) North Equatorial and Counter Equatorial currents
(d) North Pacific and Kuroshio currents

132. What is the temperature in the basin on the leeward side of the mountain?
(given: SALR = 0.60 C/100m)
(a) 20°C (b) 21°C
(c) 21.6°C (d) 22.4°C

133. Clouds are visible masses made up of:
(a) water vapour
(b) water liquid droplets
(c) water ice crystals
(d) (b) or (c)

134. The heat involved in the change of water from the solid state to the liquid state is called:
(a) latent heat of fusion
(b) latent heat of vapourization
(c) latent heat of condensation
(d) latent heat of melting

135. Most form of cloud found is which part of atmosphere
(a) Stratosphere (b) Trophosphere
(c) Thermosphere (d) Ionosphere

136. Mixing ratio:
(a) is the total amount of water vapour present in the air
(b) is the amount of water vapour in the air to the total mass of air
(c) is the amount of water vapour in the air to the capacity
(d) it is the amount of water vapour present in the air to the mass of dry air

137. Clouds are usually classified on the basis of ________ and ________.
(a) altitude ; process of formation
(b) colour ; shape
(c) altitude ; shape
(d) altitude ; temperature

138. When a cold air mass moves in a warmer surrounding, it results in a/an:
(a) warm front (b) cold front
(c) stationary front (d) occluded front

139. Line joining equal precipitation is world map is referred as
(a) Isobar (b) Isohyet
(c) Isotherm (d) Countour

140. A ridge, 64,000 km long and 1000 to 4000 km wide, runs down the middle of the North and the South Atlantic Ocean basins, into the Indian Ocean basins, then passes between Australia and Antarctica to enter the South Pacific basin. What is this ridge?
(a) Socotra-Lakshadweep-Chagos ridge
(b) Pacific-Antarctic ridge
(c) Dolphin-Challenger ridge
(d) Mid-Oceanic ridge

141. Match List I with List II and select the correct answer using the code given below the lists:

List I (Sediment Types)	List II (Examples)
A. Terrigenous	1. Calcareous oozes
B. Biogenous	2. Quartz and clay
C. Hydrogenous	3. Tektite spheres
D. Comogenous	4. Manganese nodules

Code :	A	B	C	D
(a)	2	4	1	3
(b)	2	1	4	3
(c)	3	1	4	2
(d)	3	4	1	2

142. In vertical distribution of ocean deposits, what is the correct sequence (from oceanic surface towards bottom) of the following deposits?
1. Calcareous oozes
2. Siliceous oozes
3. Terrigenous deposits
4. Red clay

Select the correct answer using the code given below:
(a) 1, 2, 3, 4 (b) 3, 1, 2, 4
(c) 3, 2, 1, 4 (d) 4, 3, 2, 1

143. The Silicon percentage by weight on the earth's crust is
(a) 46.6% (b) 27.72%
(c) 8.14% (d) 6.14%

144. On Moon, the percentage of silicon is
(a) 42 (b) 20
(c) 18 (d) 9.3

145. Wandering stac Hypothesis regarding origin of earth is given by
(a) Kant (b) Laplace
(c) Chamberlin (d) Harold Jeffrey

146. 2003 UB_{313} is a
(a) dwarf planet (b) giant planet
(c) normal planet (d) not a planet at all

147. A mesothermal climate that is dry in winter and wet in summer is a/an:
(a) Bs climate (b) Am climate
(c) Cw climate (d) Dw climate

148. Bs climate is:
(a) dry and semiarid
(b) dry and arid
(c) tropical and always moist
(d) microthermal and dry in summer

149. The stage in a thunderstorm characterized by rapid updrafts with the absence of downdraft is the:
(a) mature stage
(b) precipitation stage
(c) developing stage
(d) dissipating stage

150. Black soil reflects:
(a) high amount of iron oxides
(b) low amount of iron oxides
(c) high amount of decomposed organic matter
(d) low amount of decomposed organic matter

151. The process by which precipitation initially falls from the cloud as liquid is the:
(a) ice-crystal process
(b) cyclonic process
(c) convectional process
(d) coalescence process

152. A soil made up of columnar peds has a/an:
(a) platy structure
(b) prismatic structure
(c) spheroidal structure
(d) angular structure

153. The precipitation producing mechanism where hot humid air rises due to thermal differences is called:
(a) cyclonic precipitation
(b) convectional precipitation
(c) frontal precipitation
(d) orographic precipitation

154. Hard pan and clay pan in soil are found in
(a) A-horizon (b) B-horizon
(c) C-horizon (d) A-C horizon

155. Very thick A-horizon is often found in
(a) Chernozem soil (b) Chestnut soil
(c) Brown forest soil (d) Podzolic soil

156. Match List I with List II and select the correct answer using the code given below the lists:

List I (Soil group)	List II (Climatic Regimes)
A. Chernozem	1. Temperate grasslands
B. Terra Rossa	2. Mediterranean
C. Podsol	3. Cool temperate
D. Sierozem	4. Hot deserts

Code :	A	B	C	D
(a)	4	3	2	1
(b)	1	2	3	4
(c)	4	2	3	1
(d)	1	3	2	4

157. The high altitude tropical forest which has dwarfed trees is known as
(a) Alpine forest
(b) Elfin forest
(c) Montane forest
(d) Sclerophyll forest

158. Consider the following statements :
1. Laterite consists essentially of oxides of iron and aluminium.
2. Ferrallitic soils occur widely in the humid tropics where chemical weathering and leaching are intense.

Which of the statements given above is/are correct ?

(a) 1 only (b) 2 only
(c) Both 1 and 2 (d) Neither 1 nor 2

159. Consider the following pairs :
1. Podzolization : Eluviation of clays, organic matter, calcium, sodium, iron, and aluminium out of the A horizon
2. Gleization : Accumulation of organic matter in a swampy environment

Which of the pairs given above is/are correctly matched?
(a) 1 only
(b) 2 only
(c) Both 1 and 2
(d) Neither 1 nor 2

160. Chernozems are
(a) Silica rich temperate grassland soils
(b) Iron rich humid upland soils
(c) Humus rich dark brown colour soils in semi-arid region
(d) Humus rich tropical grassland soils

161. Folds in which one limb inclines moderately with regular slope while other inclines steeply at right angle and the slope is almost vertical are known as
(a) Isoclinal (b) Monoclinal
(c) Recumbent (d) Asymmetrical

162. The Value of hardness for Diamond on Moh's Scale of hardness is
(a) 2 (b) 5
(c) 10 (d) 15

163. The Value of normal lapse rate in troposphere is
(a) 0.65°C per 100 metres
(b) 0.5°C per 100 metre
(c) 0.72°C per 100 metres
(d) None of these

164. The gas most abundant in tropospheric atmosphere is
(a) Nitrogen (b) Oxygen
(c) Argon (d) Neon

165. Nebular Hypothesis of origin of the planets is given by which of the following geologist
(a) Newton (b) Imanuel Kant
(c) Aristotle (d) Aryabhatt

166. Shadow zone in earth interior occurs between
(a) 0° to 90° from focus
(b) 103° to 143° from focus
(c) 95° to 105° from focus
(d) None of the above

167. The radius of earth is around
(a) 6370 km (b) 1240 km
(c) 5650 km (d) 3470 km

168. The outer core of the earth is in
(a) Solid State (b) Liquid State
(c) Plasma State (d) Gaseous State

169. The velocity of P wave near earth surface is
(a) 15 km/second (b) 6 km/second
(c) 2 km/second (d) 4 km/second

170. The M discontinuity separate crust from
(a) Mantle (b) Lower crust
(c) Core (d) All

171. P wave can travel through
(a) Solid (b) Gas
(c) Liquid (d) All

172. S wave can travel through
(a) Solid (b) Gas
(c) Liquid (d) All

173. S wave can't pass through which part of the earth?
(a) Crust (b) Mantle
(c) Outer core (d) Inner core

174. Earthquake prediction can performed on the basis of
(a) Emission of radon gas
(b) Shifting of some burrowing animals like ants, termites etc.
(c) Both (a) and (b)
(d) None of the above

175. The steep sided crater is known as
(a) Volcanic ash (b) Caldera
(c) Crater (d) Volcanic vent

176. The 'ring of fire' is located in
(a) Indian Ocean (b) Atlantic Ocean
(c) Pacific Ocean (d) Antarctica

177. Identify the dwarf planet among the given choice
(a) Mercury (b) Venus
(c) Earth (d) Pluto

178. USA has how many time zones ?
(a) 1 (b) 2
(c) 3 (d) 5

179. The average density of Continental crust in gm/cc is
(a) 2.7 (b) 3.0
(c) 5.5 (d) 11.0

180. The average density of Oceanic crust in gm/cc is
(a) 2.7 (b) 3.0
(c) 5.5 (d) 11.0

181. The average density of whole earth in gm/cc is
(a) 2.7 (b) 3.0
(c) 5.5 (d) 11.0

182. Granite is an example of
(a) Acid igneous rock
(b) Basic igneous rock
(c) Sedimentary rock
(d) Metamorphic rock

183. Gabbro is an example of
(a) Plutonic rock
(b) Sedimentary rock
(c) Metamorphic rock
(d) None of the above

184. Fossil is found in which of the following rocks
(a) Igneous (b) Metamorphic
(c) Both (a) & (b) (d) Sedimentary

185. Quartzite is an example of
(a) Igneous rock
(b) Metamorphic rock
(c) Sedimentary rock
(d) Plutonic rock

186. Identify Chemically formed sedimentary rock from the choices given below
(a) Gabbro (b) Rock Salts
(c) Schist (d) Graphite

187. The highest peak in west Malaysia is
(a) Gunong Tahan (b) Harz
(c) Ural (d) Pennines

188. The Caledonian folds formed around
(a) 320 million years ago
(b) 240 million years ago
(c) 30 million years ago
(d) 570 million years ago

189. The Hercynian folds formed during
(a) Tertiary period (b) Paleozoic era
(c) Proterozoic era (d) Jurassic period

190. Mt. Manodnock in USA is an example of
(a) Volcanic Mountain
(b) Residual Mountain
(c) Block Mountain
(d) Fold Mountain

191. Which one of the following periods is largely associated with extinction of Dinosaurs and the increase in flowering plants and reptiles?
(a) Permian (b) Cretaceous
(c) Trissic (d) Jurassic

192. Consider the following statements:
The Circum Pacific belt is highly prone to the occurrence of earthquakes because it is a zone of
1. Young fold mountain
2. Active Volcanoes
3. Divergent plate boundaries
4. Convergent plate boundaries
Which of the statements given above are correct?
(a) 1, 2 & 3 (b) 1, 2 & 4
(c) 2, 3 & 4 (d) 1, 3 & 4

193. Laterite is produced by
(a) high temperature & high precipitation condition
(b) low temperature & high precipitation condition
(c) high temperature & low precipitation condition
(d) None of the above

194. Which one of the following statements is correct? Plateaus are the product of
(a) Rejuvenation of the old mountain
(b) Old stage of cycle of erosion
(c) Youth stage of cycle of erosion
(d) Mature stage of cycle of erosion

195. Corndon Hill in Shropshire, England is an example of
(a) lopolith (b) laccolith
(c) phacolith (d) batholith

196. The Henry Mountains, in Utah USA is an example of
(a) lopolith (b) laccolith
(c) phacolith (d) batholith

197. Wicklow Mountains of Ireland is an example of
(a) lopolith (b) laccolith
(c) phacolith (d) batholith

198. The Magma contains which of the following gases
(a) CO_2 (b) Nitrogen
(c) Chlorine (d) All

199. The temperature of basic Lavas is about
(a) 1,000°C (b) 1200°C
(c) 1,500°C (d) 2000°C

200. The concept of Pangaea is given by
(a) Alfred Wegner (b) Henry Hess
(c) Tuzo Wilson (d) Newton

201. The super-continent Pangaea evolved some .... million years ago
(a) 200 (b) 280
(c) 300 (d) 320

202. Coral reef thrive in warm water between the latitudes
(a) 30°N and 30°S (b) 45°N and 45°S
(c) 50°N and 50°S (d) 60°N and 60°S

203. The changing position of poles in geological time scale is known as
(a) Sea floor spreading
(b) Polar wandering
(c) Continental drift
(d) Plate tectonic

204. The Hypothesis of Hot spot is proposed by
(a) Wegner (b) Wilson
(c) Morgan (d) Newton

205. The earth's magnetic poles reverse in about every
(a) 10,000 – 200,000 years
(b) 20,000 – 200,000 years
(c) 20,000 – 500,000 years
(d) 40,000 – 500,000 years

206. The spreading rate of mid Indian Ocean ridge is about
(a) 14–20 cm/years
(b) 14–20 m/years
(c) 14–20 km/years
(d) None of the above

207. All processes of physical and chemical change affecting sediments during its conversion into solid rock are called
(a) Lithification (b) Oiagenesis
(c) Foliation (d) Disintegration

208. A system of grading of mineral grains has been established by geologists, which is known as
(a) Moh's Scale
(b) Wentworth Scale
(c) Linear Scale
(d) None of the above

209. Halite mineral is an example of
(a) Isometric system
(b) Tetragonal system
(c) Hexagonal system
(d) Orthorhombic system

210. Three axes of crystal are of equal length and lie at right angle to each other. This kind of crystal system is known as
(a) Orthorhombic system
(b) Hexagonal system
(c) Tetragonal system
(d) Isometric system

211. A crystal system in which three axes make right angles with each other. The two horizontal axes, a and b, are of equal length but the third c axis, is of different length comes under the categories of
(a) Hexagonal system
(b) Isometric system
(c) Tetragonal system
(d) Orthorhombic system

212. In a crystal system, where, four axes are present. Three of the axes are horizontal and of equal length, intersecting at angle of 60є and 120є. The fourth axis is perpendicular to other axes and is of different length. This type of crystal system is known as
(a) Isometric system
(b) Tetragonal system

(c) Hexagonal system
(d) Orthorhombic system

213. Bery mineral is an example of
(a) Isometric system
(b) Hexagonal system
(c) Orthorhombic system
(d) Tetragonal system

214. In a crystal system in which three axes intersect at right angle to each other, but they are of unequal lengths. They are
(a) Orthorhombic system
(b) Hexagonal system
(c) Tetragonal system
(d) Isometric system

215. Staurolite mineral is an example of
(a) Tetragonal system
(b) Isometric system
(c) Hexagonal system
(d) Orthorhombic system

216. Zircon mineral is an example of
(a) Isometric system
(b) Tetragonal system
(c) Hexagonal system
(d) Orthorhombic system

217. In a crystal system in which the three axes are of unequal length. Two axes intersect at right angles whereas the third axis intersects obliquely forming an acute angle comes under
(a) Triclinic system
(b) Isometric system
(c) Monoclinic system
(d) Orthorhombic system

218. Gypsum mineral is a perfect example of
(a) Monoclinic system
(b) Triclinic system
(c) Isometric system
(d) Hexagonal system

219. In a crystal system where, the three axes are of unequal length and intersect at oblique angles comes under
(a) Monoclinic system
(b) Triclinic system
(c) Tetragonal system
(d) Hexagonal system

220. Albite mineral is an example of
(a) Monoclinic system
(b) Tetragonal system
(c) Triclinic system
(d) None of the above

221. Identify the crystal system

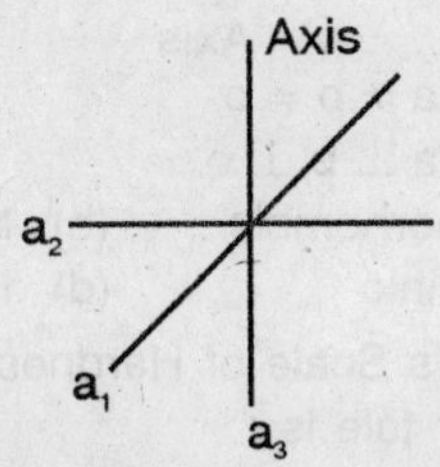

where, $a_1 = a_2 = a_3$
$a_1 \perp a_2 \perp a_3$

(a) Isometric (b) Hexagonal
(c) Monoclinic (d) Triclinic

222. Identify the crystal system

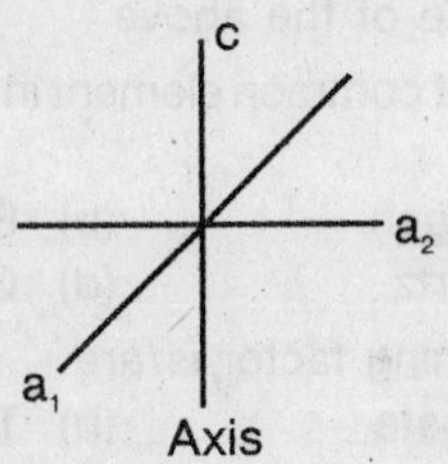

where, $a_1 = a_2 \neq c$
& $a_1 \perp a_2 \perp c$

(a) Isometric system (b) Hexagonal
(c) Tetragonal (d) Orthorhombic

223. Identify the crystal system

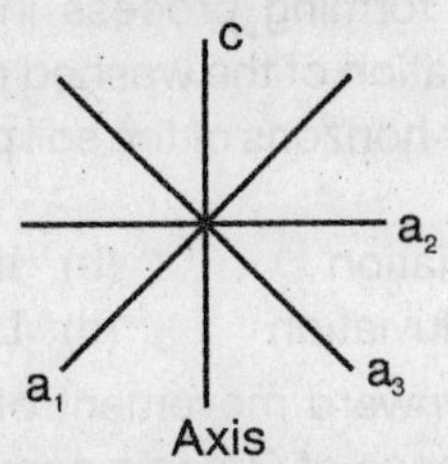

where, $a_1 = a_2 = a_3 \neq c$

(a) Isometric (b) Tetragonal
(c) Hexagonal (d) Orthorhombic

224. Identify the crystal system

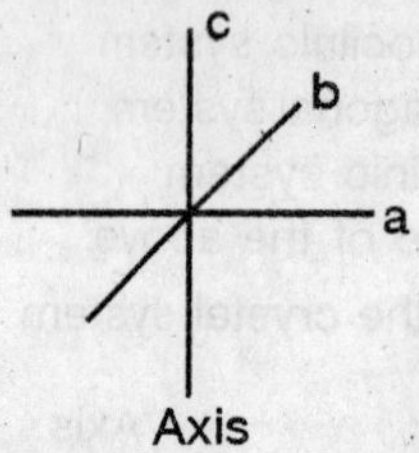

where, $a \neq b \neq c$
& $a \perp b \perp c$
(a) Orthorhombic (b) Monoclinic
(c) Triclinic (d) Isometric

225. On Moh's Scale of Hardness, the hardness value for talc is
(a) 1 (b) 2
(c) 3 (d) 4

226. The shades of colour to a mineral is due to
(a) Impurities
(b) Oil
(c) fracture
(d) None of the above

227. The most common element in the earth's crust is
(a) Oxygen (b) Silicon
(c) Quartz (d) Cullinar diamond

228. Soil forming factor is/are
(a) Climate (b) Topography
(c) Age/Time (d) All

229. The process through which there is mechanical translocation of clay or other five particles down the soil profile is known as
(a) Leaching (b) Cheluviation
(c) Illuviation (d) Eluviation

230. The soil forming process in which there is accumulation of the washed down material in the lower horizons of the soil profile is referred as
(a) Eluviation (b) Illuviation
(c) Cheluviation (d) Leaching

231. The downward movement of material under the influence of Organic complex compound is known as
(a) Cheluviation (b) Eluviation
(c) Illuviation (d) Leaching

232. The capital letters, A, B, C, D, E, O and R are used in soil horizon to designate
(a) Soil fertility (b) Plant nutrition
(c) Master horizons (d) Time

233. Chernozem soil is an example of
(a) Zonal Soil (b) Intrazonal Soil
(c) Azonal Soil (d) Alluvial Soil

234. The soil that reflects climate and vegetation to a large degree is referred as
(a) Azonal Soil (b) Zonal Soil
(c) Intrazonal Soil (d) Black Soil

235. The poorly developed soil profile is found in
(a) Zonal Soil
(b) Intrazonal Soil
(c) Azonal Soil
(d) None of the above

236. The Indian Council of Agricultural Research (ICAR) classified Indian soils into
(a) Four groups (b) Eight groups
(c) Twelve groups (d) Sixteen groups

237. The basis of classification of Indian soil into eight group by the Indian Council of Agricultural Research is/are
(a) Genesis of soil (b) Colour
(c) Composition (d) All of the above

238. The Great Indian Plains contain which of the following major soil type
(a) Alluvial soil
(b) Black soil
(c) Red and Yellow soil
(d) Arid soil

239. The soil which swells when wetted and shrinks when dried is
(a) Alluvial soil
(b) Black soil
(c) Red and Yellow soil
(d) Arid soil

240. Black soil is good for cotton cultivation because
(a) it has moisture retention capacity
(b) it has good porosity of soil
(c) it has good permeability of soil
(d) None of the above

241. Black soil are well developed in
(a) Maharashtra
(b) Western Madhya Pradesh
(c) Gujarat
(d) All of the above

242. Red soil is derived from the
(a) Old crystalline and metamorphic rocks
(b) Sedimentary rocks
(c) Igneous rocks
(d) Plutonic rocks

243. Red colour in Red and Yellow soil is due to
(a) the presence of iron oxides
(b) the presence of Aluminium
(c) the presence of chromium
(d) the presence of gold

244. The laterite soil is/are
(a) acidic and rich in aluminium and iron oxide
(b) basic and rich in aluminium and iron oxide
(c) Neutral and rich in aluminium and iron oxide
(d) None of the above

245. The soil type used in bricks formation
(a) Alluvial soil (b) Black soil
(c) Red soil (d) Laterite soil

246. The colour of Arid soil in western Rajasthan is
(a) Black (b) Red to brown
(c) Yellow (d) Green

247. The arid soil can be fertile by
(a) Using fertiliser
(b) Increasing Irrigation facility
(c) Drainage
(d) None of the above

248. The soil type of Rann of Kuchch in Gujarat is predominantly of
(a) Black (b) Saline
(c) Yellow (d) Red

249. The Saline soil can be fertile by application of
(a) Irrigation
(b) Fertilizer
(c) Gypsum
(d) None of the above

250. The branch of science that deals with the study of soil is called
(a) Ornithology (b) Pedology
(c) Paleology (d) Paleogeography

251. The book 'Theory of the Earth with Proof and Illustration' is written by
(a) J. Hutton (b) Henry Hess
(c) Wegner (d) Morgan

252. The first order land forms include
(a) Continents (b) Ocean basin
(c) Both (a) & (b) (d) Plateaus

253. Plateau is an example of
(a) first order landform
(b) second order landform
(c) third order landform
(d) none of the above

254. Hills and Valleys are example of
(a) first order landform
(b) second order landform
(c) third order landform
(d) fourth order landform

255. Frost action of weathering belongs to categories of
(a) Mechanical weathering
(b) Chemical weathering
(c) Biological weathering
(d) Both (b) & (c)

256. Some rocks disintegrate like skin of onions, which are called
(a) granular disintegration
(b) exfoliation
(c) spheroidal weathering
(d) both (b) & (c)

257. Mechanical weathering is most prominent in
(a) Dry climate of low and middle latitude
(b) Wet climate of low and middle latitude
(c) Wet climate of high latitude
(d) None of the above

258. Hydrolysis is an example of
(a) Mechanical weathering
(b) Chemical weathering
(c) Biological weathering
(d) All of the above

259. Match list I with list II and choose the correct answer

List I (Land form)	List II (Agent of erosion)
A. Natural levee	1. Wind
B. Drumlin	2. Glacier
C. Polje	3. Running water
D. Seif	4. Underground water

Code :	A	B	C	D
(a)	1	2	3	4
(b)	2	3	4	1
(c)	3	2	4	1
(d)	1	4	2	3

260. The molten igneous material is called
(a) Mantle (b) Magma
(c) Sial (d) Sima

261. Which among the following represents the correct sequence in increasing height, of different types of cloud formation?
(a) Cirrus, Cumulonimbus, Stratus, Cumulus
(b) Cumulonimbus, Cumulus, Stratus, Cirrus
(c) Stratus, Cumulus, Cumulonimbus, Cirrus
(d) Cirrus, Stratus, Cumulus, Cumulonimbus

262. Which one of the following is the characteristic feature of karst topography?
(a) Casitice (b) Caverns
(c) Caves (d) Polje

263. Identify the Oceanic current associated with the 'El Nino' phenomena?
(a) Humboldt (b) Labrador
(c) Canaries (d) Benguela

264. The line joining places of same height is known as
(a) Isobar (b) Isotherm
(c) Contour (d) Isochrones

265. The line joining places of same barometric pressure is known as
(a) Isobar (b) Isotherm
(c) Contour (d) Isogonic lines

266. The proportion of the area of the surface of various elevation above or depths below a given datum is properly represented by the
(a) Lorenz curve
(b) Hypsometric curve
(c) Altimetric curve
(d) Clinographic curve

267. Which of the following features is common to the Deccan Plateau and the Columbian Plateau?
(a) Inland drainage (b) Lava composition
(c) Uranium deposit (d) Regged plains

268. The "cinque" is a French word which is known in Scotland as
(a) Corrie (b) Cwn
(c) Com (d) Corriw

269. Consider the following factors
1. Convergence of cold and warm Oceanic currents
2. Shallow depth of ocean waters
3. Nearness of fishing ports
4. Abundance of driffing plankton

Those responsible for the location of the great fishing ground would include
(a) 1 alone (b) 2, 3 and 4
(c) 1 & 2 (d) 1, 2 and 4

270. Iron is obtained mostly from
(a) Haematite Ores (b) Magnetite Ores
(c) Siderite Ores (d) Iron Pyrites

271. Match List I with List II and choose the correct answer.

List I	List II
A. Basic in exhaustible	1. Hydel power
B. Conventional renewable source of energy	2. Tidal energy
C. Non-conventional renewable source of energy	3. Solar power
D. Non-conventional nonrenewable source of energy	4. Natural gas

Code :	A	B	C	D
(a)	3	2	1	4
(b)	2	3	4	1
(c)	2	1	3	4
(d)	3	1	2	4

272. The coal type with highest percentage of carbon is

(a) Anthracite (b) Bituminous
(c) Peat (d) Lignite

273. The value of coriolis force is zero at
(a) Equator (b) Pole
(c) At 30º N latitude (d) At 30ºS latitude

274. Match List I with List II and select the correct answer

	List I (Composition)	List II (Rock Type)
A.	Quartz & feldspar	1. Basalt
B.	Quartz, feldspar & mica	2. Tuff
C.	Compacted volcanic ash	3. Granite
D.	Feldspar, mice, pyloxenes and limes	4. Sandstone

Code :	A	B	C	D
(a)	4	1	2	3
(b)	1	2	3	4
(c)	3	2	1	4
(d)	4	3	2	1

275. Relative humidity refers to
(a) absolute amount of water vapour in the atmosphere
(b) the amount of hygroscopic nuclei in the atmosphere
(c) saturated vapour pressure
(d) ratio of actual amount of water vapour in the air to the amount it could hold at that temperature

276. The cyclones of temperate latitudes differ from those of the tropics in a number of ways. Which one of the following is the most prominent of them all?
(a) Their size is far greater
(b) They are caused by frontal systems whereas the tropical cyclones are not
(c) They occur more frequently
(d) The precipitation is more evenly distributed in a temperate cyclone

277. Match List I with List II and select the correct answer:

	List I	List II
A.	Ozone Hole	1. Difference in the outgoing and incoming long wave radiation of the atmosphere
B.	Greenhouse Effect	2. Acceleration of ozone destruction
C.	Global Warming	3. Increase in the carbon dioxide level
D.	Albedo	4. Ratio of reflected radiation to radiation received

Code :	A	B	C	D
(a)	1	2	3	4
(b)	1	2	4	3
(c)	1	3	4	2
(d)	2	3	1	4

278. Which of the following depositional landforms are produced by glaciers?
1. Roche moutonnes 2. Outwash plains
3. Eskers 4. U-shaped Valleys
Select the correct answer using the codes given below
(a) 1 & 2 (b) 2 & 3
(c) 3 & 4 (d) 1 & 4

279. Playas are depressions formed due to
(a) Defloting action of winds
(b) Glacial erosion
(c) River erosion
(d) Marine erosion

280. Which of the following pairs are correctly matched?
1. Karst topography : Blind Vally
2. Humid topography : Stone lattice
3. Aeolian topography : Ventifacts
4. Periglacial topography : Pingo
Select the correct answer using the codes given below:
(a) 1, 2 & 3 (b) 1, 3 & 4
(c) 1, 2 & 4 (d) 2, 3 & 4

281. The following relief zones are the characteristics of ocean basins:
1. Continental slope
2. Continental shelf
3. Deep sea plain
4. Oceanic trench
The correct sequence of their seaward appearance from the coast is
(a) 2, 1, 4, 3 (b) 1, 2, 4, 3
(c) 2, 1, 3, 4 (d) 1, 2, 3, 4

282. The normal lapse rate of temperature in the troposphere is 1єC for every
(a) 150 m (b) 153 m
(c) 160 m (d) 176 m

283. Which one of the following is the correct sequence in terms of descending values of Albedo?
(a) Forest, Snow, Water
(b) Water, Snow, Forest
(c) Snow, Water, Forest
(d) Forest, Water, Snow

284. Match List I with List II and select the correct answer:

List I (Geological Era)	List II (Geological Period)
A. Mesozoic	1. Tertiary
B. Proterozoic	2. Triassic
C. Cainozoic	3. Pre-Cambrian
D. Palaeozoic	4. Permian

Code :	A	B	C	D
(a)	3	2	1	4
(b)	2	3	1	4
(c)	2	4	1	3
(d)	2	4	3	1

285. The doctrine of uniformitarianism was advocated by
(a) Davis (b) Penek
(c) Hutton (d) Gilbert

286. Match List I with List II and choose the correct answer:

List I (Theory)	List II (Related Aspect)
A. Geosynclinal Theory	1. Origin of Tides
B. Tetrahedral hypothesis	2. Origin of coral reefs & atolls
C. Stationary wave theory	3. Mountains building
D. Subsidence theory	4. Origin of Continents and Ocean basins

Code :	A	B	C	D
(a)	3	4	2	1
(b)	3	4	1	2
(c)	1	2	3	4
(d)	1	2	4	3

287. Which one of the following is the correct sequence of landforms developed under fluvial cycle of erosion?
(a) Gorge, Piedmont plain, Flood plain, Delta
(b) Gorge, Flood plain, Delta, Piedmont plain
(c) Gorge, Delta, Flood plain, Piedmont plain
(d) Piedmont plain, Gorge, Delta, Flood plain

288. Alluvial Cone is prominent in
(a) Coastal belt (b) Delta region
(c) Piedmont zone (d) Mountain region

289. Physical weathering is most prominent in
(a) Arid region
(b) Semi-arid region
(c) Humid region
(d) Mediterranean region

290. Two places situated on the same contour line in a world map will have the same
(a) ground pollution (b) Cloud cover
(c) Height (d) None of these

291. Two places situated on the same isogonic line in a world map will have the same
(a) Pressure
(b) Temperature
(c) Height
(d) Magnetic declination

292. Moho-discontinuity is found between the
(a) Crust & mantle
(b) Mantle & core
(c) Outer & inner core
(d) Upper & lower crust

293. Conard discontinuity is found between the
(a) Crust & mantle
(b) Outer & inner crust
(c) Outer & inner core
(d) None of the above

294. Lehman discontinuity is found between the
(a) Outer & inner core
(b) Crust & mantle
(c) Upper & lower crust
(d) Mantle and core

295. Weichest-Gutenberg discontinuity is found between
(a) Outer & inner core
(b) Mantle and core

(c) Outer & inner crust
(d) Crust & mantle

296. Consider the following statements:
1. Ozone is found mostly in the stratosphere
2. Ozone layer lies 55-75 km above the surface of the earth
3. Ozone absorbs ultraviolet radiation from Sun
4. Ozone layer has no significance for life on the earth

Which of the above statements are correct?
(a) 1 and 3 (b) 2 and 4
(c) 2 and 3 (d) 1 and 4

297. Oceanic waves caused by a earthquake are known as
(a) P wave (b) S wave
(c) L wave (d) Tsunami

298. The average salinity of Seawater in parts per thousand is
(a) 20 (b) 25
(c) 30 (d) 35

299. Which of the following is not a greenhouse gas?
(a) Methane
(b) Carbon dioxide
(c) Ozone
(d) Carbon monoxide

300. The most abundant gas emitted from volcanoes is
(a) Water vapour
(b) Carbon dioxide
(c) Hydrogen sulphide
(d) Nitrogen

301. Match List I with List II and select the correct answer:

List I (Deposits)	List II (Locations)
A. Salt	1. Continental shelves
B. Red clay	2. Ocean plains
C. Ooze	3. Continental slopes
D. Gravel	4. Oceanic deeps

Code :	A	B	C	D
(a)	2	1	3	4
(b)	3	4	2	1
(c)	2	4	3	1
(d)	3	1	4	2

302. Identify the phenomena associated with El Nino:
(a) Heavy rains in South America and drought in Australia
(b) Drought in South America and heavy rains in Australia
(c) Heavy rains in both South America and Australia
(d) Drought in both South America and Australia.

303. Spring tide means
(a) Higher high tide, higher low tide
(b) Higher high tide, lower low tide
(c) Lower high tide, lower low tide
(d) Lower high tide, higher low tide

304. Which of the following is/are the correct characteristics of primary seismic wave?
(a) It is a longitudinal wave
(b) It is similar to sound waves
(c) It travels with faster speed in solid than in liquid
(d) All of the above

305. Identify the mountain system formed due to collision of continental plates?
1. The Himalayas
2. The Alps
3. The Rockies
4. The Caucasus mountains

Select the correct answer using the codes given below:
(a) 1, 2 & 3 (b) 2, 3 and 4
(c) 1, 2 & 4 (d) 1, 3 & 4

306. Match List I with List II and select the correct answer:

List I (Rock type)	List II (Example)
A. Plutonic	1. Conglomerate
B. Sedimentary	2. Granite
C. Metamorphic	3. Tuff
D. Volcanic	4. Gneiss

Code :	A	B	C	D
(a)	2	1	3	4
(b)	2	1	4	3
(c)	1	4	3	2
(d)	1	3	2	4

307. Consider the following statements:
1. P-wave are the first seismic waves to reach a place
2. S-waves travel only through liquids
3. Arrival time of P and S-waves is used to locate the epicentre
4. Richter Scale is a logarithmic scale

Which of the statements given above are correct?
(a) 1, 2 & 3 (b) 1, 3 & 4
(c) 1 & 4 (d) 3 & 4

308. A physical weathering process in which layers of rock peel off as expansion on alternates with contraction is known as
(a) Exfoliation (b) Hydration
(c) Hydrolysis (d) Oxidation

309. Residual hill in the desert region is known as
(a) Inselberg (b) Peneplain
(c) Valley (d) Playa

310. The drainage pattern developed like tree shape is
(a) Rectangular (b) Radial
(c) Dendritic (d) Trellis

311. The correct sequence of the following zonal pressure belts is–
1. Subpolar low 2. Equatorial low
3. Polar high 4. Subtropical high

Select the correct answer using the code given below:
(a) 2-3-1-4 (b) 1-4-2-3
(c) 2-4-1-3 (d) 1-3-2-4

312. The clouds extending from one side of horizon to other as a dark grey sheet having uniform base are called
(a) Stratus clouds (b) Cumulus clouds
(c) Cirrus clouds (d) Nimbus clouds

313. In the Hadly cell, rising air is found in the
(a) Subtropical high pressure zone
(b) Trade winds
(c) Westerlies
(d) ITCZ

314. Coral reefs are formed by
(a) Volcanic rock
(b) Marine sediments
(c) Earthquake product
(d) Tiny colonial marine animals which construct limestone skeleton material

315. The 'Syzygy' is refers to when the
(a) Earth is at perihelion and Moon at perigee
(b) Earth is at aphelion and Moon at apogee
(c) Moon and Sun are at right angles with reference to the Earth
(d) Moon, Earth and Sun lie along a straight line

316. Identify the true statement about the kepler's law:
(a) The orbit of every planet is an ellipse with the sun at a focus
(b) A line joining a planet and the sun sweeps out equal area during equal intervals of time
(c) The square of the orbital period of a planet is directly proportional to the cube of the semi-major axis of its orbit
(d) All of the above

317. The age of Mammals is
(a) Cenozoic Era (b) Mesozoic Era
(c) Paleozoic Era (d) Proterozoic Era

318. Mesozoic Era is famous for
(a) Mammals (b) Amphibians
(c) Reptiles (d) Fishes

319. The first flowering plant is originated during
(a) Devonian period
(b) Cretaceous period
(c) Silurian period
(d) Cambrian period

320. The first dinosaurs appears during
(a) Triassic (b) Jurassic
(c) Cretaceous (d) Paleogene

321. The Extinction of Trilobites occurs during
(a) Permian (b) Jurassic
(c) Cretaceous (d) Triassic

322. Coal formation takes place during
(a) Carboniferous Period
(b) Permian Period
(c) Devonian Period
(d) Silurian Period

323. The first amphibians appears at the time of
(a) Devonian period (b) Silurian period
(c) Ordovician period (d) Cambrian period

324. Origin of earth takes place at
(a) Hadean Eon
(b) Archean Eon
(c) Proterozoic Eon
(d) None of the above

325. The first multicellular organism originate during
(a) Paleozoic Era (b) Proterozoic Eon
(c) Mesozoic Era (d) Cenozoic Era

326. Ordovician Period is known for origin of
(a) first amphibians
(b) first land plant fossil
(c) first fish
(d) first mammals

327. The unique shape of the earth is called
(a) Geoid (b) Spheroid
(c) Cuboid (d) Trapaloid

328. The Moh's scale No. 4 is for which of the following minerals:
(a) Tale (b) Gypsum
(c) Calcite (d) Fluorite

329. Frost wedging is a type of weathering where .... play a crucial role
(a) air (b) water
(c) gas (d) plasma

330. The most abundant element in sea salt is
(a) Calcium (b) Sodium
(c) Sulphur (d) Chlorine

331. Mathematically, residence time can be represented by

(a) Residence time = $\frac{\text{Mass}}{\text{Input rate}}$

(b) Residence time = $\frac{\text{Volume}}{\text{Inputrate}}$

(c) Residence time = $\frac{\text{Mass}}{\text{Volume}}$

(d) None of the above

332. The residence time for chlorine is about
(a) 9 million years (b) 10 million years
(c) 60 million years (d) 80 million years

333. Mesosphere extends upto a height of
(a) 10 km (b) 40 km.
(c) 80 km (d) 160 km

334. The most abundant gas in troposphere is
(a) Nitrogen (b) Oxygen
(c) Carbon (d) Argon

335. The Environmental lapse rate value is
(a) 6.5ºC/1000 m (b) 9.8ºC/1000 m
(c) 2.6ºC/1000 m (d) 11.6ºC/1000 m

336. The value of Dry Adiabatic lapse rate is
(a) 6.5ºC/1000 m (b) 9.8ºC/1000 m
(c) 5ºC/1000 m (d) 12.5ºC/1000 m

337. El Nino is the name given to the occasional development of warm ocean surface waters along the coast of
(a) Chennai and Hongkong
(b) Ecuador and Peru
(c) Both (a) & (b)
(d) None of the above

338. Identify the El Nino year
(a) 1990 (b) 1995
(c) 1997 (d) All

339. Indian monsoon is affected by
(a) Labrador current
(b) El Nino
(c) Benguela current
(d) Ohio current

340. The concept of Geosyncline was given by
(a) James Hall and Dana
(b) E. Hang
(c) Both (a) & (b)
(d) None of the above

341. The intermediate layer of earth is composed of
(a) Granite rock (b) Basalt rock
(c) Periodotite (d) Durite

342. The major rock in upper crust of earth is
(a) Granite (b) Basalt rock
(c) Durite (d) Periodotite

343. The inner or lower layer of earth is composed of:
(a) Periodotite or Durite
(b) Granite
(c) Basaltic rock
(d) None of the above

344. The S wave is absent in which of the following parts of the earth
(a) Crust (b) Mantle
(c) Outer core (d) Inner core

345. Aleutian trench is found in
(a) Indian Ocean (b) Atlantic Ocean
(c) Pacific Ocean (d) Antarctic Ocean

346. Puerto Rico trench is found in
(a) Indian Ocean (b) Atlantic Ocean
(c) Pacific Ocean (d) Arctic Ocean

347. The concept of mega ocean called Panthelassa was given by
(a) Alfred Wegner (b) Tuzo Wilson
(c) Aristotle (d) Newton

348. The North East of India, comes under which of the following Earthquake zone type:
(a) Zone II (b) Zone III
(c) Zone IV (d) Zone V

349. Identify the geologist associated with concept of Isostacy
(a) Airy theory (b) Pratt theory
(c) Heiskenen theory (d) All of the above

350. The concept of Sea floor spreading is proposed by
(a) Henry Hess & Robert Dietz
(b) Alfred Wegner
(c) Tuzo Wilson
(d) Hutton

351. Which of the following geologist proposed a model for Denudation System
(a) Davis
(b) Strahler
(c) Both (a) & (b)
(d) None of the above

352. The slope with elevation 5є to 10є is referred as
(a) Gentle slope
(b) Moderate slope
(c) Moderately steep slope
(d) Level to gentle slope

353. The Hillslope cycle theory for slope development is proposed by
(a) Davis (b) Strahler
(c) L.C. King (d) A. Wood

354. Under Trewartha system of climatic classification, Tundra region is depicted by letters
(a) Ar (b) Aw
(c) Ft (d) Fi

355. In geology, an isograde is a plane of constant __________ grade is a field.
(a) Metamorphic
(b) Igneous
(c) Sedimentary
(d) Extrusive Igneous

356. The biotic component of an ecosystem is/are
(a) Primary producer (b) Herbivores
(c) Carnivores (d) All

357. Identify the modes of fossil preservation types:
(a) Unaltered (b) Molds and casts
(c) Carbonization (d) All of the above

358. Match List-I with List-II and select the correct answer

List-I (Sediment)	*List-II (Diameter in mm)*
A. Boulders	(i) 256-64
B. Cobbles	(ii) 2-64
C. Sand	(iii) 0.0625-2
D. Silt	(iv) 0.00390-0.0625

	A	B	C	D
(a)	(i)	(ii)	(iii)	(iv)
(b)	(i)	(iii)	(ii)	(iv)
(c)	(i)	(iv)	(iii).	(ii)
(d)	(iv)	(ii)	(i)	(iii)

359. Milankovitch theory is used to explain climate change. The theory includes
(a) the eccentricity of the earths orbit
(b) the tilt of the earths axis relative to the orbital plane
(c) seasonal changes in the time when the earth is most proximal to the sun (precession)
(d) All of the above

360. When the earth is closet to the sun is known as
(a) Aphelion (b) Perihelion
(c) Solariholion (d) None of the above

361. The Greenhouse gases absorb mostly
(a) Ultraviolet ray (b) Infrared (IR)
(c) Visible (d) Microwave

362. The species **Homo Sapiens sapiens** evolved around
(a) 200 thousand years ago to present
(b) 200 to 300 thousand years ago
(c) 400 million year ago
(d) 4 million year ago

363. Identify the correct sequence of human evolution:
(a) Homo habitis - Homo sapiens archaic - Homo erectus - Homo sapiens sapiens
(b) Homo habitis - Homo erectus - Homo sapiens neandertalensis - Homo sapiens sapiens
(c) Ardipithicus ramidus - Australopithecus robustus - Australopithecus anamensis - Homo sapiens sapiens
(d) Homo erectus - Homo habilus - Homo sapiens neandertalensis - Homo sapiens sapiens

364. Identify the correct sequence of ages of Holocene epoch (modern climate)
(a) Mesolithic or Epipaleolithic age - Neolithic age - Copper age - Bronze age - Iron age
(b) Neolithic age - Copper age - Mesolithic or Epipaleolithic age - Bronze age - Iron age
(c) Mesolithic age - Bronze age - Copper age - Neolithic age - Iron age
(d) Iron age - Bronze age - Copper age - Neolithic age- Mesolithic or Epipaleolithic age

365. The file format of Roster data is/are:
(a) Tif (b) Jpeg
(c) BLoB (d) All

366. Metadata is defined as data of data. It often includes:
(a) elevation data, either in raster or vector form
(b) shape layers
(c) coordinate system descriptions
(d) all of the above

367. Which of the following is a Vector format?
(a) Geo TIFF (b) MVSID
(c) ESRI Gird (d) TIGER

368. The space segment of Global positioning system consist of __________ operating satellites that transmit one-way signals that give the current GPS satellite position and time
(a) 20 (b) 24
(c) 30 (d) 1

369. To find location of a moving object how many satellites required?
(a) 2 (b) 3
(c) 4 (d) 5

370. The Raster date represent digital image is a
(a) point (b) line
(c) polygon (d) grid

371. The Darcy's law is used to describe the flow of a fluid through a porous medium. Darcy's law can be described by the equation:

(a) $Q = \dfrac{-KA(P_b - P_a)}{\mu L}$

(b) $Q = \dfrac{-KAL(P_b - P_a)}{L}$

(c) $Q = \dfrac{-AL(P_b - P_a)}{\mu K}$

(d) $Q = \dfrac{-KL(P_b - P_a)}{\mu A}$

Where,
Q = The total discharge
K = Permeability
A = Area
L = Length through which water flows
$P_b - P_a$ = Pressure difference from point b to a.

372. The BOD (Biological Oxygen Demand) of a polluted water bodies will be
(a) High
(b) Low
(c) Extremely low
(d) None of the above

373. Sunspots are temporary phenomena on the surface of the sun (the photosphere) that appear visibly as dark spots compared to surrounding regions. They are caused by intense __________ which inhibits convection, forming areas of reduced temperature.
(a) Electric field
(b) Magnetic activities
(c) Heating activities
(d) None of the above

374. The Sun synchronous satellites moving at a distance of ________ from the earth surface
(a) 700 - 900 km (b) 36,000 km
(c) 10,000 km (d) 12,000 km

375. The coverage of Sun synchronous satellites lies between
(a) 81°N to 72°S (b) 81°N to 81°S
(c) 1°N to 90°N (d) 1°S to 90°S

376. The Sun synchronous satellites used for the
(a) Telecommunication
(b) Weather monitoring
(c) Earth Resources Applications
(d) All of the above

377. The orbital period for Sun synchronous satellite is
(a) 14 orbits per day
(b) 24 Hours
(c) 2 Hours
(d) None of the above

378. The Geostationary satellites place at a distance of _________ from the earth surface
(a) 700 - 900 km (b) 36,000 km
(c) 10,000 km (d) 12,000 km

379. The coverage of Geostationary satellites lies between
(a) 81°N to 81°S (b) 1/3rd of the Globe
(c) 1°N to 90°S (d) 1°S to 90°S

380. The Geostationary satellite looks static because
(a) the time period of earth is equal to that of satellite
(b) it remains static in sky
(c) it moves at constant speed
(d) All of the above

381. The Geostationary satellites used for the purpose of
(a) Telecommunicatoin
(b) Weather monitoring
(c) Earths resources applications
(d) Both (a) & (b)

382. The condition in which earth, moon and sun lies is a straight line is known as
(a) Syzygy
(b) Synchronization
(c) Neap tide
(d) None of the above

383. A reef separated from a mainland or island shore by a deep lagoon is referred as
(a) Barrier reef (b) Fringing reef
(c) Atoll reef (d) None of the above

384. A reef that is directly attached to a shore or borders it with an intervening shallow channel or lagoon is known as
(a) Fringing reef (b) Barrier reef
(c) Platform reef (d) Atoll reef

385. A more or less circular or continuous barrier reef extending all the way around a lagoon without a central island is known as
(a) Fringing reef (b) Barrier reef
(c) Atoll reef (d) Platform reef

386. The Great Barrier reef is found in
(a) Queensland, Australia
(b) Coast of Belize
(c) Maldives
(d) Gulf of Kuchchh

387. The Himalayan rivers in the Gangetic Basin form a special type of drainage pattern known as
(a) Trellis pattern (b) Circular pattern
(c) Radial pattern (d) Dendritic pattern

388. Exfoliation is removal of outer skin of a rock mass. It is observed is arid region and the process involved in this feature is referred as
(a) Mechanical weathering
(b) Chemical weathering
(c) Biological weathering
(d) Hydrolysis

389. The centrifugal pattern of drainage is / are observed in
(a) Hazaribagh plateau
(b) Dalma lava upland
(c) Parasnath hill
(d) Amarkantak plateau

390. The weathering residue of the well-exposed limestone left at the surface are called
(a) Lapie (b) Terra Rossa
(c) Sinkholes (d) Ovala

391. Lappies is a French name of a Karst land form, it is known as Karren in
(a) Germany (b) Yogoslavia
(c) India (d) China

392. The wind erosional feature, formed by the excavation of loose soil by blowing wind is known as
(a) Desert pavement (b) Driekanter
(c) Ventifacts (d) Deflation hollows

393. The term Pediment was first used by
(a) F. Galton (b) G.K. Gilbert
(c) Wilson (d) Wegner

394. Match List-I with List-II and select the correct Answer

List-I (Landforms)	List-II (Features)
A. Arid	(i) Polje
B. Fluvial	(ii) Moraine
C. Glacial	(iii) Zeugen
D. Karst	(iv) Waterfall

	A	B	C	D
(a)	(i)	(ii)	(iii)	(iv)
(b)	(i)	(ii)	(iv)	(iii)
(c)	(iii)	(iv)	(ii)	(i)
(d)	(iv)	(iii)	(i)	(ii)

395. A glacial landform produced as the result of the presence of an obstructive mass of rock that lies in the path of oncoming ice is known as
(a) Crag and Tail (b) Nunatek
(c) Ruches moutonees (d) Moraines

396. The last glaciation takes place in
(a) Cretaceous (b) Carboniferous
(c) Pleistocene (d) Pre-Cambrian

397. Noctilucent cloud is observed in
(a) Troposphere (b) Stratosphere
(c) Mesosphere (d) Ionosphere

398. The earths average albedo is about
(a) 0.32 (b) 0.80
(c) 0.03 (d) 0.40

399. Ox-bow lake is formed in
(a) Young stage of river
(b) Mature stage of river
(c) Old stage of river
(d) None of the above

400. A ________ pattern develops in a region which is made up of alternating beds of resistant and less resistant rocks which all dip in the same direction
(a) Dendritic (b) Trellis
(c) Radial (d) Braided

401. Which of the following is an example of Bird's foot delta
(a) The Mississipi delta
(b) The Omorine delta
(c) Both (a) & (b)
(d) None of the above

402. A tarnado is differ from a tropical cyclone in that it forms over
(a) River (b) Ocean
(c) Land (d) Sky

403. An anticyclone develops in a region of descending air in an area of
(a) High pressure (b) Low pressure
(c) Low temperature (d) High temperature

404. A cloud formed within a height of 2100 metres is
(a) altocumulus (b) altostratus
(c) cumulus (d) cirrus

405. The maximum difference in elevation on the earth's surface is about 20 kilometres between Mount Everest, 8,848 metres above sea level and the Mariana Trench in the Pacific Ocean, 11,022 metres below sea level.
(a) Tonga deep
(b) Eleizabeth deep
(c) Challenger deep
(d) None of the above

406. During Ice age, when the Sea-level was lower, North America and Asia were connected by dry land today exist the
(a) Tasmania strait (b) Bering strait
(c) Sunda strait (d) Palk strait

407. According to German Geologist, Alfred Wegner nearly 150 million years ago, there was a single continent on the earth known as
(a) Pangaea (b) Lauresia
(c) Panthelessia (d) Gondwanaland

408. The Super continent Pangea broke into several pieces, which began to drift apart. North and South Americas pulled away from Africa and Eurasia, and driffed to the west. As a result, western edge was wrikled and the _______ and the _______ were formed
(a) Himalaya, Sulaman (b) Rockies, Andes
(c) Both (a) & (b) (d) None of these

409. The continental crust is mainly made up of
(a) Felsic (b) Mafic
(c) Olivine (d) Pyrozine

410. The Oceanic crust is mainly made up of
(a) Felsic (b) Mafic
(c) Olivine (d) Pyrozine

411. The mantle layer of earth is mainly made up of
(a) Felsic
(b) Mafic
(c) Olivine and Pyrozine
(d) Nickel and Iron

412. The discontinuity between mantle and core is referred as
(a) Mohorovic discontinuity
(b) Gutenberg discontinuity
(c) Repetiti discontinuity
(d) Conard discontinuity

413. The intrusive igneous rock is formed by solidification of magma at moderate depths beneath the earth's surface. Choose the rock type having intrusive igneous type:
(a) Granite (b) Dolerite
(c) Both (a) & (b) (d) Basalt

414. The batholiths are the large intrusive igneous rock bodies. They may be 50 to 80 kilometre across and hundreds of kilometres in length. The batholiths covering smaller areas are known as
(a) Laccoliths (b) Dykes
(c) Sills (d). Stocks

415. Sometimes, magma trying to reach the surface squeezes between two rock layers and solidifies into a thin sheet in horizontal position parallel to the layers of already existing rocks. Such an intrusion is known as:
(a) Sill (b) Dykes
(c) Stocks (d) Batholiths

416. The percentage of sedimentary rock in earth's crust is
(a) 5% (b) 15%
(c) 50% (d) 75%

417. Among the sedimentary rock, the most numerous is
(a) Limestone (b) Sandstone
(c) Shales (d) None of the above

418. An unsorted mixture of clay and boulders known as _________ is an example of ice-deposited sedimentary rock.
(a) boulder clay (b) till
(c) both (a) & (b) (d) moraine

419. The coal type with 60-70% carbon content is
(a) 45% (b) 60-70%
(c) 10-20% (d) 90%

420. In Dynamic metamorphism, the metamorphism process initiated by the action of
(a) Temperature (b) Pressure
(c) Water (d) Minerals

421. In Contact metamorphism, metamorphism process initiated by the action of
(a) Temperature (b) Pressure
(c) Water (d) Impurities

422. Clay and shale is changed into slate and slate into Phyllite at 150°-200°C. This process of metamorphism is referred as
(a) Dynamic metamorphism
(b) Contract metamorphism
(c) Both (a) & (b)
(d) None of the above

423. In our country, a mountain is differentiated from a hill, when its summit or top rises to more than _____ metres above the base.
(a) 100 (b) 500
(c) 450 (d) 900

424. Identify the structural fold mountains among the choices given below:
(a) the Alps in Europe
(b) the Rockies in North America
(c) the Andes of South America
(d) all of the above

425. The Granitic cone of structural fold mountains is surrounded by _____ merging with sedimentary layers along the margins.
(a) Metamorphic rocks
(b) Igneous rocks
(c) Plutonic rocks
(d) Extrusive Igneous rocks

426. The rock-strata of structural fold mountains was originally laid down as sediments in narrow elongated sea basin called as
(a) Geosynclines
(b) The earth's depressions
(c) Both (a) & (b)
(d) None of the above

427. The mountain type, formed when great blocks of the earth's crust may be raised or lowered during the late stages of mountain-building is
(a) Structural fold mountains
(b) Block mountains
(c) Volcanic mountains
(d) Residual mountains

428. The Vosges is France, Black Forest mountains in Germany and Salt Range in Pakistan are typical examples of
(a) Structural mountains
(b) Block mountains
(c) Volcanic mountains
(d) Dissected mountains

429. The Nilgiris Hill is an example of
(a) Fold mountains
(b) Block mountains
(c) Volcanic mountains
(d) Residual mountains

430. The plateaus which are partly or fully enclosed by mountains are known as
(a) Continental plateau
(b) Intermontane plateau
(c) Piedmont plateaus
(d) Titled plateau

431. The plateau of Tibet, Bolivia and Mexico are example of
(a) Intermontane plateau
(b) Continental plateau
(c) Piedmont plateau
(d) None of the above

432. The plateaus which are situated at the foot of a mountain, bounded on the opposite side by a plain or an ocean is known as
(a) Intermontane plateaus
(b) Continental plateau
(c) Piedmont plateaus
(d) Titled plateau

433. The plateau of Malwa in India, the Patagonia in Argentina and the Appalachian in United States are examples of
(a) Intermontane plateaus
(b) Continental plateau
(c) Piedmont plateaus
(d) None of the above

434. The great plains of Russian platform, the great plains of U.S.A and the Central lowlands of Australia are example of
(a) Structural plains
(b) Erosional plains
(c) Depositional plains
(d) None of the above

435. The plains formed by the uplift of a part of the Sea floor usually bordering a continent, *i.e.*, the continental shelf is known as
(a) Depositional plains (b) Erosional plains
(c) Structural plains (d) Deltaic plains

436. The soil found in humid climatic condition is known as
(a) Pedalfers (b) Pedocals
(c) Usar (d) Reh

437. The chernozems or black earths soil is / are rich in

(a) Humus (b) Calcium
(c) Potassium (d) Both (a) & (b)

438. The desert soils are ________ in colour in temperate region and _______ in hot deserts of the tropics.
(a) grey, red (b) grey, black
(c) red, grey (d) black, grey

439. The rocks that have large connected pores through which water can flow freely are known as
(a) Water fable (b) Aquaclude
(c) Aquifers (d) None of the above

440. A special type of well in which water rises automatically under the influence of the pressure of a column of water to the ground surface, either through a natural or man-made hole, is known as
(a) Aquifer (b) Confined Aquifer
(c) Unconfined Aquifer (d) Artesian Well

441. Artesian Well is / are found in which of the following state of India?
(a) Gujarat
(b) Puducherry
(c) South Arcot district of Tamil Nadu
(d) All of the above

442. Hot spring is found in
(a) Tatapani (H.P.) (b) Barabar
(c) Sindri (Jharkhand) (d) Sohna (Haryana)

443. Manikaran Hot spring is found in
(a) Himachal Pradesh
(b) Jammu and Kashmir
(c) Punjab
(d) Uttar Pradesh

444. In India, Sink hole (a Karst topography) is observed in
(a) Himachal Pradesh (b) Uttar Pradesh
(c) Meghalaya (d) Orissa

445. The Gorges formation is / are observed in
(a) Satluj (b) Indus
(c) Brahmaputra (d) All of the above

446. The formation of rapids and waterfalls is a characteristic feature of
(a) Upper course of a river
(b) Middle course of a river
(c) Old stage of river
(d) None of the above

447. The Jog or Gersoppa fall is located on the river
(a) Ganga (b) Yamuna
(c) Krishna (d) Kavari

448. The Matterhorn Peak of Sriss Alps is example of
(a) U-shaped Valley
(b) Cirque or Corrie Basin
(c) Roche Moutonnes
(d) Glaciated Lakes

449. The Coast of South-west Ireland is a typical example of a
(a) Ria coast
(b) Dalmatian coast
(c) Drowned lowland coast
(d) Fiord coast

450. Kerala Coast is an example of
(a) An emergent coast
(b) Submergent coast
(c) Both emergent and submergent coast
(d) Ria coast

451. The maximum salinity occurs between
(a) 0° to 20°N latitudes
(b) 20° to 40°N latitudes
(c) 10°S to 30°S latitudes
(d) 40°N to 60°N latitudes

452. In India, tidal bores are common in the river
(a) Ganga (b) Yamuna
(c) Godavari (d) Hooghly

453. Red clay is the most widely spread pelagic deposit. It covers more than _______ of the Pacific ocean
(a) One-fourth (b) Half
(c) Three fourth (d) Twenty percent

454. Nearly 150 million years ago, there was a single continent on the earth known as Pangea. This super-continent broke into several pieces, which began to drift apart. North and South Americas pulled away from Africa and Eurasia, and drifted to the west. As a result, western edge was wrinked and the _______ and the ___________ were formed.

(a) Himalaya and Sulaman
(b) Rockies and Andes
(c) Alps, Jogras
(d) Aravali, Parasnath

455. Cow is an example of
(a) Primary producer
(b) Secondary producer
(c) Primary consumer
(d) Secondary consumer

456. At present the geothermal source of energy has already been developed in the
(a) USA (b) Mexico
(c) New Zealand (d) All

457. Petroleum is found mainly in:
(a) Continental Shelves
(b) Continental Slopes
(c) Both (a) & (b)
(d) None of the above

458. The depth of ocean can be measured by
(a) Ultrasound (b) Echo-sounders
(c) Altimeter (d) Thermometer

459. Which of the following belongs to the calcareous ooze
(a) Pteropod Ooze (b) Globegerina Ooze
(c) Both (a) & (b) (d) Diatom Ooze

460. Which of the following belongs to the siliceous ooze
(a) Radiolarian Ooze (b) Diatom Ooze
(c) Pteropod Ooze (d) Both (a) & (b)

461. Atolls are far more common in the
(a) Atlantic ocean (b) Indian ocean
(c) Pacific ocean (d) Arctic ocean

462. Coral polyps need for their growth temperature of about ________.
(a) 10°C (b) 20°C
(c) 35°C (d) 40°C

463. The main processes of cooling the ocean water include:
(a) back radiation of heat from the sea surface
(b) convection
(c) evaporation
(d) all of the above

464. During Summer, the marginal ice-field break away and begin to drift towards the equator. The drifting ice-fields are called
(a) ice floes (b) ice berg
(c) ice cap (d) ice sheet

465. The average salinity of the sea water, as estimated by scientists is about
(a) 30‰ (b) 35‰
(c) 40‰ (d) 45‰

466. In the Atlantic ocean the salinity near the tropics is about
(a) 30‰ (b) 35‰
(c) 37‰ (d) 39‰

467. Arrange the following lakes in order of increasing salinity.
Great salt lake - Lake Van - Dead sea
(a) Great salt lake - Dead sea - Lake Van
(b) Dead sea - Great salt lake - Lake Van
(c) Salt lake - Lake Van - Dead sea
(d) Lake Van - Salt lake - Dead sea

468. The factors affecting the movements of oceanic water is/are
(a) Density (b) Temperature
(c) Salinity (d) All

469. Identify the types of wind generated waves:
(a) Sea (b) Snell
(c) Surf (d) All

470. Several trains of differing wave lengths and directional movements of sea waves occur simultaneously in the oceans. It results into an overall irregular and chaotic wave pattern called the
(a) Sea (b) Snell
(c) Surf (d) None of the above

471. As the waves were away from the winds that disturb the smoothness of sea surface they begin to move in an uniform pattern of equivalent period and height. These trains of waves are called
(a) Sea (b) Snell
(c) Surf (d) Current

472. The broken mass of water dashes up the shore as swash. It then descends seaward as the back wash. Those breaking waves in coastal regions are called

(a) Sea (b) Surf
(c) Snell (d) Currents

473. Catastrophic waves are sudden, violent and temporary and are cause by
(a) Earthquakes (b) Volcanoes
(c) Land slides (d) All of the above

474. Identify the cold current among the choices given below
(a) Oye siwo (b) Okhotsk current
(c) Labrador current (d) All of the above

475. The abyssal plains or abyssal floors are uniquely flat with a gradient of less than
(a) 1 : 10 (b) 1 : 100
(c) 1 : 5 (d) 1 : 20

476. Flat topped seamount are known as
(a) Guyots (b) Trench
(c) Shelas (d) Plains

477. The Atlantic Ocean resembles the letter ____ in shape.
(a) A (b) V
(c) U (d) S

478. Aleutian trench is found in
(a) Atlantic Ocean (b) Pacific Ocean
(c) Indian Ocean (d) Antarctica

479. The weight of actual amount of water-vapour present in a unit volumn of air is called the
(a) Absolute humidity
(b) Specific humidity
(c) Relative humidity
(d) Gravity humidity

480. The ratio of air's actual water vapour content to its water-vapour capacity at a given temperature is known as
(a) Absolute humidity (b) Relative humidity
(c) Specific humidity (d) None of the above

481. In doldrum only
(a) Vertical currents are found
(b) Horizontal currents are found
(c) Both (a) & (b)
(d) None of the above

482. Due to coriolis effect, winds in the Northern Hemisphere get deflected to the ________ of their path.
(a) right
(b) left
(c) first left then right
(d) first right then left

483. The westerlies are winds blowing from the sub-tropical high pressure belts towards the sub-polar low pressure belts. The westerlies are best developed between
(a) 40° and 65°S latitudes
(b) 20° and 40°N latitudes
(c) at equator
(d) 15° and 25°N latitudes

484. The rain water contains carbon dioxide in solution. It has an acidic effect and it reacts with rocks to form new chemical compounds. This is the process of
(a) Hydrolysis (b) Hydration
(c) Carbonation (d) Solution

485. Carbonation process is noticed in the
(a) Higher humid latitudes
(b) Lower humid latitudes
(c) Every where on earth
(d) Desert region

486. The transporting power of running water increases by 64 times if the speed of water is
(a) tripled
(b) doubled
(c) remains constant
(d) increased by four folds

487. Which of the following is an example of piedmont plateau?
(a) Tibet plateau
(b) Columbian plateau
(c) Patagonian plateau
(d) Ozark Massif plateau

488. Potwar Plateau is an example of
(a) Glacial plateau (b) Fluvial plateau
(c) Aeolian plateau (d) Piedmont plateau

489. Karoo series of South Africa is an example of
(a) Concordant lopoliths
(b) Laccoliths
(c) Dykes
(d) Concordant Sills

490. Henry Mountain, Utah is an example of
(a) Volcanic Neck (b) Laccolith
(c) Dyke (d) Sill

491. Flood basalts are formed by fissure eruption with no explosive activity due to the less viscous basaltic lava. The example of flood basalts is
(a) Parana plateau (b) Deccan plateau
(c) Etheopian plateau (d) All of the above

492. The Volcano of Lipari island near Sicily is an example of:
(a) The Hawaiian type
(b) The Strombolian type
(c) The Volcanian type
(d) The Vesuvian type

493. Peninsular rivers form
(a) Dendritic pattern of drainage
(b) Trellis pattern
(c) Annular pattern
(d) Centrifugal pattern

494. Terra rossa is a physical features produced by erosion in
(a) Limestone area (b) Desert area
(c) Mountainous region(d) Plateau region

495. Cumulus cloud is formed in
(a) Troposphere (b) Stratosphere
(c) Mesosphere (d) Ionosphere

496. The beaufort scale is used to measure the wind strength. The Beaufort number 8 is for
(a) Storm (b) Hurricane
(c) Gale (d) Calm air

497. Taifer is name of tropical cyclone of
(a) Carribbean sea (b) Australia
(c) Philippines (d) Japan

498. The tropical cyclone of Australia is called
(a) Hurricanes (b) Typhoons
(c) Willy-wilies (d) Taifer

499. Baguio is the name given for tropical cyclone of
(a) Philippines (b) Australia
(c) Japan (d) America

500. Hyplomnior layer of Ocean is characterized by
(a) Uniform temperature
(b) Uniform salinity
(c) Uniform pressure
(d) Uniform biodiversity

501. Red mud is an example of
(a) Terrigeneous deposits
(b) Organic deposits
(c) Pelagic deposits
(d) Volcanic materials

502. Globigerina Ooze is an example of
(a) Pteropod Ooze (b) Calcareous Ooze
(c) Silicious Ooze (d) None of the above

503. The percentage of Argon is atmosphere is
(a) 0.036% (b) 0.002%
(c) 0.93% (d) 0.001%

504. Syerite is an example of
(a) Igneous rock
(b) Metamorphic rock
(c) Sedimentary rock
(d) None of the above

505. The Hardness of Quartz and Topaz in Mohr's Scale
(a) 1 & 2 respectively
(b) 3 & 4 respectively
(c) 5 & 6 respectively
(d) 7 & 8 respectively

506. The Hardness of finger nail in Mohr's scale is
(a) 1.5 (b) 2.5
(c) 3.5 (d) 4.5

507. Mica comprises of potassium, aluminium, magnesium, iron, silica etc. It forms ______ percent of the earth's crust.
(a) 4 (b) 5
(c) 6 (d) 7

508. Olivine is usually a greenish crustal often found in ________ rocks.
(a) Acidic rocks (b) Basaltic rocks
(c) Granitic rocks (d) Plutonic rocks

509. Pyroxene consist of calcium, aluminium, magnesium, iron and silica. It forms ______ percent of the earth's crust.
(a) 6 (b) 7
(c) 9 (d) 10

510. Hornblende is a form of
(a) Feldspar (b) Pyroxene
(c) Amphibole (d) Mica

ANSWERS

1	2	3	4	5	6	7	8	9	10
(b)	(a)	(d)	(d)	(b)	(b)	(c)	(d)	(d)	(c)
11	12	13	14	15	16	17	18	19	20
(b)	(b)	(c)	(a)	(d)	(b)	(b)	(e)	(b)	(c)
21	22	23	24	25	26	27	28	29	30
(c)	(e)	(b)	(d)	(b)	(e)	(d)	(d)	(c)	(d)
31	32	33	34	35	36	37	38	39	40
(a)	(b)	(d)	(a)	(c)	(a)	(c)	(c)	(e)	(a)
41	42	43	44	45	46	47	48	49	50
(d)	(b)	(e)	(d)	(c)	(c)	(b)	(a)	(c)	(c)
51	52	53	54	55	56	57	58	59	60
(a)	(e)	(a)	(c)	(c)	(b)	(e)	(c)	(a)	(e)
61	62	63	64	65	66	67	68	69	70
(c)	(b)	(a)	(b)	(c)	(d)	(c)	(b)	(d)	(e)
71	72	73	74	75	76	77	78	79	80
(a)	(a)	(c)	(a)	(b)	(c)	(d)	(d)	(a)	(d)
81	82	83	84	85	86	87	88	89	90
(c)	(d)	(c)	(a)	(c)	(d)	(a)	(b)	(a)	(d)
91	92	93	94	95	96	97	98	99	100
(c)	(a)	(a)	(c)	(b)	(b)	(b)	(a)	(b)	(c)
101	102	103	104	105	106	107	108	109	110
(a)	(d)	(d)	(b)	(c)	(d)	(a)	(b)	(c)	(c)
111	112	113	114	115	116	117	118	119	120
(a)	(a)	(d)	(a)	(b)	(d)	(c)	(b)	(a)	(a)
121	122	123	124	125	126	127	128	129	130
(a)	(b)	(d)	(d)	(b)	(c)	(b)	(b)	(b)	(a)
131	132	133	134	135	136	137	138	139	140
(a)	(c)	(d)	(d)	(b)	(b)	(c)	(d)	(b)	(d)
141	142	143	144	145	146	147	148	149	150
(b)	(c)	(b)	(b)	(c)	(a)	(a)	(a)	(c)	(c)
151	152	153	154	155	156	157	158	159	160
(d)	(a)	(c)	(b)	(a)	(b)	(a)	(c)	(c)	(c)
161	162	163	164	165	166	167	168	169	170
(a)	(c)	(a)	(a)	(b)	(b)	(a)	(b)	(b)	(a)
171	172	173	174	175	176	177	178	179	180
(d)	(a)	(c)	(c)	(b)	(c)	(d)	(d)	(a)	(b)
181	182	183	184	185	186	187	188	189	190
(c)	(a)	(a)	(d)	(b)	(b)	(a)	(a)	(b)	(b)
191	192	193	194	195	196	197	198	199	200
(d)	(c)	(a)	(d)	(c)	(b)	(d)	(d)	(a)	(a)

201	202	203	204	205	206	207	208	209	210
(b)	(a)	(b)	(c)	(d)	(a)	(b)	(b)	(a)	(d)
211	212	213	214	215	216	217	218	219	220
(c)	(c)	(b)	(a)	(d)	(b)	(c)	(a)	(b)	(c)
221	222	223	224	225	226	227	228	229	230
(a)	(c)	(c)	(a)	(a)	(a)	(a)	(d)	(c)	(b)
231	232	233	234	235	236	237	238	239	240
(a)	(c)	(a)	(b)	(c)	(b)	(d)	(a)	(b)	(a)
241	242	243	244	245	246	247	248	249	250
(d)	(a)	(a)	(a)	(d)	(b)	(b)	(b)	(c)	(b)
251	252	253	254	255	256	257	258	259	260
(a)	(c)	(b)	(c)	(a)	(d)	(a)	(b)	(c)	(b)
261	262	263	264	265	266	267	268	269	270
(b)	(c)	(d)	(c)	(a)	(b)	(b)	(a)	(d)	(a)
271	272	273	274	275	276	277	278	279	280
(d)	(a)	(a)	(c)	(d)	(b)	(d)	(b)	(a)	(b)
281	282	283	284	285	286	287	288	289	290
(c)	(b)	(b)	(b)	(c)	(b)	(a)	(c)	(a)	(c)
291	292	293	294	295	296	297	298	299	300
(d)	(a)	(b)	(a)	(b)	(a)	(d)	(d)	(d)	(a)
301	302	303	304	305	306	307	308	309	310
(b)	(a)	(a)	(d)	(c)	(b)	(b)	(a)	(a)	(c)
311	312	313	314	315	316	317	318	319	320
(c)	(a)	(d)	(d)	(d)	(d)	(a)	(c)	(a)	(a)
321	322	323	324	325	326	327	328	329	330
(a)	(a)	(a)	(a)	(b)	(c)	(a)	(d)	(b)	(d)
331	332	333	334	335	336	337	338	339	340
(a)	(d)	(c)	(a)	(a)	(b)	(b)	(d)	(b)	(c)
341	342	343	344	345	346	347	348	349	350
(b)	(a)	(a)	(c)	(c)	(b)	(a)	(d)	(d)	(a)
351	352	353	354	355	356	357	358	359	360
(c)	(b)	(c)	(c)	(a)	(d)	(d)	(a)	(d)	(b)
361	362	363	364	365	366	367	368	369	370
(b)	(a)	(b)	(a)	(d)	(d)	(d)	(b)	(c)	(d)
371	372	373	374	375	376	377	378	379	380
(a)	(a)	(b)	(a)	(b)	(c)	(a)	(b)	(b)	(a)
381	382	383	384	385	386	387	388	389	390
(d)	(a)	(a)	(a)	(c)	(a)	(d)	(a)	(b)	(b)
391	392	393	394	395	396	397	398	399	400
(a)	(d)	(b)	(c)	(a)	(c)	(c)	(a)	(c)	(b)
401	402	403	404	405	406	407	408	409	410
(a)	(c)	(a)	(c)	(c)	(b)	(a)	(b)	(a)	(b)

411	412	413	414	415	416	417	418	419	420
(b)	(b)	(c)	(d)	(a)	(a)	(c)	(c)	(b)	(b)
421	422	423	424	425	426	427	428	429	430
(a)	(b)	(d)	(d)	(a)	(c)	(b)	(b)	(d)	(b)
431	432	433	434	435	436	437	438	439	440
(a)	(c)	(c)	(a)	(c)	(a)	(d)	(a)	(c)	(d)
441	442	443	444	445	446	447	448	449	450
(d)	(a)	(a)	(c)	(d)	(b)	(d)	(b)	(a)	(a)
451	452	453	454	455	456	457	458	459	460
(b)	(d)	(b)	(b)	(c)	(d)	(c)	(b)	(c)	(d)
461	462	463	464	465	466	467	468	469	470
(c)	(b)	(d)	(a)	(b)	(c)	(a)	(d)	(d)	(a)
471	472	473	474	475	476	477	478	479	480
(b)	(b)	(d)	(d)	(b)	(a)	(d)	(b)	(a)	(b)
481	482	483	484	485	486	487	488	489	490
(a)	(a)	(a)	(c)	(b)	(b)	(c)	(c)	(d)	(b)
491	492	493	494	495	496	497	498	499	500
(d)	(b)	(d)	(a)	(a)	(c)	(d)	(c)	(a)	(a)
501	502	503	504	505	506	507	508	509	510
(a)	(b)	(c)	(b)	(d)	(b)	(a)	(b)	(d)	(c)

6. GEOLOGY

1. Mineralogy And Petrology
2. Structural Geology and Geotectonics
3. Paleontology and Its Applications
4. Sedimentology and Stratigraphy
5. Marine Geology and Paleoceanography
6. Geochemistry
7. Economic Geology
8. Precambrian Geology and Crustal Evolution
9. Quaternary Geology
10. Applied Geology
    - *(i)* Remote Sensing and GIS
    - *(ii)* Engineering Geology
    - *(iii)* Mineral Exploration
    - *(iv)* Hydrogeology

1. Mineralogy and Petrology

CONCEPT OF POINT GROUP, SPACE GROUP, RECIPROCAL LATTICE, DIFFRACTION AND IMAGING

POINT GROUP

The concept of point group is introduced, first for the Bravais lattice. In crystallography, a crystallographic point group is a set of symmetry operations, like rotations or reflections, that leave a point fixed while moving each atom of the crystal to the position of an atom of the same kind. That is, an infinite crystal would look exactly the same before and after any of the operations in its point group. In the classification of crystals, each point group corresponds to a crystal class.

There are infinitely many 3D point groups; in crystallography, however, they are restricted to be compatible with the discrete translation symmetries of a crystal lattice. This crystallographic restriction of the infinite families of general point groups results in 32 crystallographic point groups.

The point group of a crystal, among other things, determines some of the crystal's optical properties, such as whether it is birefringent, or whether it shows the Pockels effect.

NOTATION

The point groups are denoted by their component symmetries. There are a few standard notations used by crystallographers, mineralogists, and physicists.

SCHÖNFLIES NOTATION

In Schunflies notation, point groups are denoted by a letter symbol with a subscript. The symbols used in crystallography mean the following:

- The letter O (for octahedron) indicates that the group has the symmetry of an octahedron (or cube), with (O_h) or without (O) improper operations (those that change handedness).
- The letter T (for tetrahedron) indicates that the group has the symmetry of a tetrahedron. T_d includes improper operations, T excludes improper operations, and T_h is T with the addition of an inversion.
- C_n (for cyclic) indicates that the group has an n-fold rotation axis. C_{nh} is C_n with the addition of a mirror (reflection) plane perpendicular to the axis of rotation. C_{nv} is C_n with the addition of a mirror plane parallel to the axis of rotation.
- S_n (for Spiegel, German for mirror) denotes a group that contains only an n-fold rotation-reflection axis.
- D_n (for dihedral, or two-sided) indicates that the group has an n-fold rotation axis plus a twofold axis perpendicular to that axis. D_{nh} has, in addition, a mirror plane perpendicular to the n-fold axis. D_{nv} has, in addition to the elements of D_n, mirror planes parallel to the n-fold axis.

Due to the crystallographic restriction theorem, n = 1, 2, 3, 4, or 6 in 2 or 3 dimension space.

n	1	2	3	4	6
C_n	C_1	C_2	C_3	C_4	C_6
C_{nv}	$C_{1v}=C_{1h}$	C_{2v}	C_{3v}	C_{4v}	C_{6v}
C_{nh}	C_{1h}	C_{2h}	C_{3h}	C_{4h}	C_{6h}
D_n	$D_1=C_2$	D_2	D_3	D_4	D_6
D_{nh}	$D_{1h}=C_{2v}$	D_{2h}	D_{3h}	D_{4h}	D_{6h}
D_{nd}	$D_{1d}=C_{2h}$	D_{2d}	D_{3d}	D_{4d}	D_{6d}
S_n	$S_1=C_{1h}$	S_2	$S_3=C_{3h}$	S_4	S_6

D_{4d} and D_{6d} are actually forbidden because they contain improper rotations with n=8 and 12 respectively. The 27 point groups in the table plus T, T_d, T_h, O and O_h constitute 32 crystallographic point groups

HERMANN-MAUGUIN NOTATION

An abbreviated form of the Hermann-Mauguin notation commonly used for space groups also serves to describe crystallographic point groups. Group names are

- 1, 1
- 2, m, $^2/_m$
- 222, mm2, mmm
- 4,4, $^4/_m$, 422, 4mm, 42m, $^4/_m$mm
- 3, 3, 32, 3m, 3m
- 6, 6, $^6/_m$, 622, 6mm, 62m, $^6/_m$mm
- 23, m3, 432, 43m, m3m

The correspondence between the three notations is:

Hermann-Mauguin	*Schoenflies*	*Orbifold*
1	C_1	11
2	C_2	22
222	D_2	222
4	C_4	44
3	C_3	33
6	C_6	66
23	T	332
1	S_2	1x
m	C_{1h}	1*
mm2	C_{2v}	*22
4	S_4	2x
3	S_6	3x
6	C_{3h}	3*
m3	T_h	3*2
2/m	C_{2h}	2*
mmm	D_{2h}	*222
4/m	C_{4h}	4*
32	D_3	223
6/m	C_{6h}	6*
432	O	432
422	D_4	224
3m	C_{3v}	*33
622	D_6	226
43m	T_d	*332
4mm	C_{4v}	*44
3m	D_{3d}	2*3
6mm	C_{6v}	*66
m3m	O_h	*432
42m	D_{2d}	2*2
62m	D_{3h}	*223
4/m mm	D_{4h}	*224
6/m mm	D_{6h}	*226

SPACE GROUP

In crystallography, the space group (or crystallographic group, or Fedorov group) of a crystal is a description of the symmetry of the crystal, and can have one of 230 types. In mathematics space groups are also studied in dimensions other than 3 where they are sometimes called Bieberbach groups, and are discrete cocompact groups of isometries of an oriented Euclidean space.

ELEMENTS OF A SPACE GROUP

The space groups in three dimensions are made from combinations of the 32 crystallographic point groups with the 14 Bravais lattices which belong to one of 7 lattice systems. This results in a space group being some combination of the translational symmetry of a unit cell including lattice centering, the point group symmetry operations of reflection, rotation and improper rotation (also called rotoinversion), and the screw axis and glide plane symmetry operations. The combination of all these symmetry operations results in a total of 230 unique space groups describing all possible crystal symmetries.

ELEMENTS FIXING A POINT

The elements of the space group fixing a point of space are rotations, reflections, the identity element, and improper rotations.

TRANSLATIONS

The translations form a normal abelian subgroup of rank 3, called the Bravais lattice. There are 14 possible types of Bravais lattice. The quotient of the space group by the Bravais lattice is a finite group which is one of the 32 possible point groups.

GLIDE PLANES

A glide plane is a reflection in a plane, followed by a translation parallel with that plane. This is noted by a, b or c, depending on which axis the glide is along. There is also the n glide, which is a glide along the half of a diagonal of a face, and the d glide, which is a fourth of the way along either a face or space diagonal of the unit cell. The latter is called the diamond glide plane as it features in the diamond structure.

CLASSIFICATION SYSTEMS FOR SPACE GROUPS

There are (at least) 10 different ways to classify space groups into classes. The relations between some of these are described in the following table. Each classification system is a refinement of the ones below it.

(Crystallographic) space group types (230 in three dimensions). Two space groups, considered as subgroups of the group of affine transformations of space, have the same space group type if they are conjugate by an orientation-preserving affine transformation. In three dimensions, for 11 of the affine space groups, there is no orientation-preserving map from the group to its mirror image, so if one distinguishes groups from their mirror images these each split into two cases. So there are 54+11=65 space group types that preserve orientation.

Affine space group types (219 in three dimensions). Two space groups, considered as subgroups of the group of affine transformations of space, have the same affine space group type if they are conjugate under an affine transformation. The affine space group type is determined by the underlying abstract group of the space group. In three dimensions there are 54 affine space group types that preserve orientation.

Arithmetic crystal classes (73 in three dimensions). These are determined by the point group together with the action of the point group on the subgroup of translations. In other words the arithmetic crystal classes correspond to conjugacy classes of finite subgroup of the general linear group $GL_n(Z)$ over the integers. A space group is called symmorphic (or split) if there is a point such that all symmetries are the product of asymmetry fixing this point and a translation. Equivalently, a space group is symmorphic if it is a semidirect product of its point group with its translation subgroup. There are 73 symmorphic space groups, with exactly one in each arithmetic crystal class. There are also 157 nonsymmorphic space group types with varying numbers in the arithmetic crystal classes.

(geometric) Crystal classes (32 in three dimensions). The crystal class of a space group is determined by its point group: the quotient by the subgroup of translations, acting on the lattice. Two space groups are in the same crystal class if and only if their point groups, which are subgroups of $GL_2(Z)$, are conjugate in the larger group $GL_2(Q)$.

Crystal systems. (7 in three dimensions) Crystal systems are an ad hoc modification of the lattice systems to make them compatible with the classification according to point groups. They differ from crystal families in that the hexagonal crystal family is split into two subsets, called the trigonal and hexagonal crystal systems. The trigonal crystal system is larger than the rhombohedral lattice system, the hexagonal crystal system is smaller than the hexagonal lattice system, and the remaining crystal systems and lattice systems are the same.

Crystal families (6 in three dimensions). The point group of a space group does not quite determine its lattice system, because occasionally two space groups with the same point group may be in different lattice systems. Crystal families are formed from lattice systems by merging the two lattice systems whenever this happens, so that the crystal family of a space group is determined by either its lattice system or its point group. In 3 dimensions the only two lattice families that get merged in this way are the hexagonal and rhombohedral lattice systems, which are combined into the hexagonal crystal family. The 6 crystal families in 3 dimensions are called triclinic, monoclinic, orthorhombal,. tetragonal, hexagonal, and cubic. Crystal families are commonly used in popular books on crystals, where they are sometimes called crystal systems.

Bravais flocks (14 in three dimensions). These are determined by the underlying Bravais lattice type.

These correspond to conjugacy classes of lattice point groups in $GL_2(Z)$, where the lattice point group is the group of symmetries of the underlying lattice that fix a point of the lattice, and contains the point group.

Lattice systems (7 in three dimensions). The lattice system of a space group is determined by the conjugacy class of the lattice point group (a subgroup of $GL_2(Z)$) in the larger group $GL_2(Q)$. In three dimensions the lattice point group can have one of the 7 different orders 2, 4, 8, 12, 16, 24, or 48. The hexagonal crystal family is split into two subsets, called the rhombohedral and hexagonal lattice systems.

RECIPROCAL LATTICE

In crystallography, the reciprocal lattice of a Bravais lattice is the set of all vectors K such that

$$C^{iK.R} = 1$$

for all lattice point position vectors R. This reciprocal lattice is itself a Bravais lattice, and the reciprocal of the reciprocal lattice is the original lattice.

For an infinite three dimensional lattice, defined by its primitive vectors (a_1, a_2, a_3) its reciprocal lattice can be determined by generating its three reciprocal primitive vectors, through the formulae

$$b_1 = 2\pi \frac{a_2 \times a_3}{a_1 \cdot (a_2 \times a_3)}$$

$$b_2 = 2\pi \frac{a_3 \times a_1}{a_2 \cdot (a_3 \times a_1)}$$

$$b_3 = 2\pi \frac{a_1 \times a_2}{a_3 \cdot (a_1 \times a_2)}.$$

Using column vector representation of (reciprocal) primitive vectors, the formulae above can be rewritten using matrix inversion:

$$[b_1 b_2 b_3]^T = 2\pi [a_1 a_2 a_3]^{-1}$$

This method appeals to the definition, and allows generalization to arbitrary dimensions. Curiously, the cross product formula dominates introductory materials on crystallography.

The above definition is called the "physics" definition, as the factor of 2π comes naturally from the study of periodic structures. An equivalent definition, the "crystallographer's" definition, comes from defining the reciprocal lattice to be $c^{2\pi iK.R} - 1$ which changes the definitions of the reciprocal lattice vectors to be $b_1 = \frac{a_2 \times a_3}{a_1.(a_2 \times a_3)}$ and so on for the other vectors. The crystallographer's definition has the advantage that the definition of is just the reciprocal magnitude of in the direction of dropping the factor of 2π. This can simplify certain mathematical manipulations, and expresses reciprocal lattice dimensions in units of spatial frequency. It is a matter of taste which definition of the lattice is used, as long as the two are not mixed.

Each point (hkl) in the reciprocal lattice corresponds to a set of lattice planes (hkl) in the real space lattice. The direction of the reciprocal lattice vector corresponds to the normal to the real space planes, and the magnitude of the reciprocal lattice vector is equal to the reciprocal of the interplanar spacing of the real space planes.

The reciprocal lattice plays a fundamental role in most analytic studies of periodic structures, particularly in the theory of diffraction. For Bragg reflections in neutron and X-ray diffraction, the momentum difference between incoming and diffracted X-rays of a crystal is a reciprocal lattice vector. The diffraction pattern of a crystal can be used to determine the reciprocal vectors of the lattice. Using this process, one can infer the atomic arrangement of a crystal.

RECIPROCAL LATTICES OF VARIOUS CRYSTALS

Reciprocal lattices for the cubic crystal system are as follows.

Simple cubic lattice

The simple cubic Bravais lattice, with cubic primitive cell of side a, has for its reciprocal a simple cubic lattice with a cubic primitive cell of side side in the crystallographer's definition). The cubic lattice is therefore said to be self-dual, having the same symmetry in reciprocal space as in real space.

Face-centered cubic (FCC) lattice

The reciprocal lattice to an FCC lattice is the body-centered cubic (BCC) lattice.

Finding the reciprocal lattice of a face-centered cubic lattice

Consider an FCC compound unit cell. Locate a primitive unit cell of the FCC, i.e., a unit cell with one lattice point. Now take one of the vertices of the primitive unit cell as the origin. Give the basis vectors of the real lattice. Then from the known formulae you can calculate the basis vectors of the reciprocal lattice. These reciprocal lattice vectors of the FCC represent the basis vectors of a BCC real lattice. Note that the basis vectors of a real BCC lattice and the reciprocal lattice of an FCC resemble each other in direction but not in magnitude.

Body-centered cubic (BCC) lattice

The reciprocal lattice to a BCC lattice is the FCC lattice.

It can be easily proven that only the Bravais lattices which have 90 degrees between (a_1, a_2, a_3) (cubic, tetragonal, orthorhombic) have (b_1, b_2, b_3) parallel to their real-space vectors.

Simple hexagonal lattice

The reciprocal to a simple hexagonal Bravais lattice with lattice constants c and a is another simple hexagonal lattice with lattice constants d hrough 30° about the c axis with respect to the direct lattice.

DIFFRACTION

Diffraction refers to various phenomena which occur when a wave encounters an obstacle. It is described as the apparent bending of waves around small obstacles and the spreading out of waves past small openings. Similar effects are observed when light waves travel through a medium with a varying refractive index or a sound wave through one with varying acoustic impedance. Diffraction occurs with all waves, including sound waves, water waves, and electromagnetic waves such as visible light, x-rays and radio waves. As physical objects have wave-like properties (at the atomic level), diffraction also occurs with matter and can be studied according to the principles of quantum mechanics.

While diffraction occurs whenever propagating waves encounter such changes, its effects are generally most pronounced for waves where the wavelength is on the order of the size of the diffracting objects. If the obstructing object provides multiple, closely-spaced openings, a complex pattern of varying intensity can result. This is due to the superposition, or interference, of different parts of a wave that traveled to the observer by different paths (see diffraction grating).

The formalism of diffraction can also describe the way in which waves of finite extent propagate in free space. For example, the expanding profile of a laser beam, the beam shape of a radar antenna and the field of view of an ultrasonic transducer are all explained by diffraction theory.

Diffraction refers to various phenomena which occur when a wave encounters an obstacle. It is described as the apparent bending of waves around small obstacles and the spreading out of waves past small openings. Similar effects are observed when light waves travel through a medium with a varying refractive index or a sound wave through one with varying acoustic impedance. Diffraction occurs with all waves, including sound waves, water waves, and electromagnetic waves such as visible light, x-rays and radio waves. As physical objects have wave-like properties (at the atomic level), diffraction also occurs with matter and can be studied according to the principles of quantum mechanics.

While diffraction occurs whenever propagating waves encounter such changes, its effects are generally most pronounced for waves where the wavelength is on the order of the size of the diffracting objects. If the obstructing object provides multiple, closely-spaced openings, a complex pattern of varying intensity can result. This is due to the superposition, or interference, of different parts of a wave that traveled to the observer by different paths (see diffraction grating).

The formalism of diffraction can also describe the way in which waves of finite extent propagate in free space. For example, the expanding profile of a laser beam, the beam shape of a radar antenna and the field of view of an ultrasonic transducer are all explained by diffraction theory.

THE MECHANISM OF DIFFRACTION

Diffraction arises because of the way in which waves propagate; this is described by the Huygens–Fresnel principle. The propagation of a wave can be visualized by considering every point on a wavefront as a point source for a secondary radial wave. The subsequent propagation and addition of all these radial waves form the new wavefront. When waves are added together, their sum is determined by the relative phases as well as the amplitudes of the individual waves, an effect which is often known as wave interference. The summed amplitude of the waves can have any value between zero and the sum of the individual amplitudes. Hence, diffraction patterns usually have a series of maxima and minima.

The form of a diffraction pattern can be determined from the sum of the phases and amplitudes of the Huygens wavelets at each point in space. There are various analytical models which can be used to do this including the Fraunhofer diffraction equation for the far field and the Fresnel Diffraction equation for the near field. Most configurations cannot be solved analytically, but can yield numerical solutions through finite element and boundary element methods.

BRAGG DIFFRACTION

Diffraction from a three dimensional periodic structure such as atoms in a crystal is called Bragg diffraction. It is similar to what occurs when waves are scattered from a diffraction grating. Bragg diffraction is a consequence of interference between waves reflecting from different crystal planes. The condition of constructive interference is given by Bragg's law:

$$n\lambda = 2d\sin\theta$$

where

λ is the wavelength,

d is the distance between crystal planes,

θ is the angle of the diffracted wave.

and m is an integer known as the order of the diffracted beam.

Bragg diffraction may be carried out using either light of very short wavelength like x-rays or matter waves like neutrons (and electrons) whose wavelength is on the order of (or much smaller than) the atomic spacing. The pattern produced gives information of the separations of crystallographic planes d, allowing one to deduce the crystal structure. Diffraction contrast, in electron microscopes and x-topography devices in particular, is also a powerful tool for examining individual defects and local strain fields in crystals.

Imaging is the representation or reproduction of an object's outward form; especially a visual representation (i.e., the formation of an image).

CONCEPTS OF CRYSTAL FIELD THEORY AND MINERALOGICAL SPECTROSCOPY

CRYSTAL FIELD THEORY

Crystal field theory (CFT) is a model that describes the electronic structure of transition metal compounds, all of which can be considered coordination complexes. CFT successfully accounts for some magnetic properties, colours, hydration enthalpies, and spinel structures of transition metal complexes, but it does not attempt to describe bonding.

According to CFT, the interaction between a transition metal and ligands arises from the attraction between the positively charged metal cation and negative charge on the non-bonding electrons of the ligand. The theory is developed by considering energy changes of the five degenerate d-orbitals upon being surrounded by an array of point charges consisting of the ligands. As a ligand approaches the metal ion, the electrons from the ligand will be closer to some of the d-orbitals and farther away from others causing a loss of degeneracy. The electrons in the d-orbitals and those in the ligand repel each other due to repulsion between like charges. Thus the d-electrons closer to the ligands will have a higher energy than those further away which results in the d-orbitals splitting in energy. This splitting is affected by the following factors:

- the nature of the metal ion.
- the metal's oxidation state. A higher oxidation state leads to a larger splitting.
- the arrangement of the ligands around the metal ion.
- the nature of the ligands surrounding the metal ion. The stronger the effect of the ligands then the greater the difference between the high and low energy 3d groups.
- The most common type of complex is octahedral; here six ligands form an octahedron around the metal ion. In octahedral symmetry the d-orbitals split into two sets with an energy difference, Δ_{oct} (the crystal-field splitting parameter) where the d_{xy}, d_{xz} and d_{yz} orbitals will be lower in energy than the d_{z^2} and $d_{x^2-y^2}$, which will have higher energy, because the former group are farther from the ligands than the latter and therefore experience less repulsion. The three lower-energy orbitals are collectively referred to as t_{2g}, and the two higher-energy orbitals as e.g. (These labels are based on the theory of molecular symmetry). Typical orbital

energy diagrams are given below in the section High-spin and low-spin.

- Tetrahedral complexes are the second most common type; here four ligands form a tetrahedron around the metal ion. In a tetrahedral crystal field splitting the d-orbitals again split into two groups, with an energy difference of Δ_{tet} where the lower energy orbitals will be d_{z^2} and $d_{x^2-y^2}$, and the higher energy orbitals will be d_{xy}, d_{xz} and d_{yz} - opposite to the octahedral case. Furthermore, since the ligand electrons in tetrahedral symmetry are not oriented directly towards the d-orbitals, the energy splitting will be lower than in the octahedral case. Square planar and other complex geometries can also be described by CFT.

CRYSTAL FIELD STABILIZATION ENERGY

The crystal field stabilization energy (CFSE) is the stability that results from placing a transition metal ion in the crystal field generated by a set of ligands. It arises due to the fact that when the d-orbitals are split in a ligand field (as described above), some of them become lower in energy than before with respect to a spherical field known as the barycenter in which all five d-orbitals are degenerate. For example, in an octahedral case, the t_{2g} set becomes lower in energy than the orbitals in the barycenter. As a result of this, if there are any electrons occupying these orbitals, the metal ion is more stable in the ligand field relative to the barycenter by an amount known as the CFSE. Conversely, the e_g orbitals (in the octahedral case) are higher in energy than in the barycenter, so putting electrons in these reduces the amount of CFSE.

LATTICE DEFECTS (POINT, LINE AND PLANAR)

Crystalline solids have a very regular atomic structure: that is, the local positions of atoms with respect to each other are repeated at the atomic scale. These arrangements are called crystal structures, and their study is called crystallography. However, most crystalline materials are not perfect: the regular pattern of atomic arrangement is interrupted by crystallographic defects.

POINT DEFECTS

Point defects are defects which are not extended in space in any dimension. There is no strict limit for how small a "point" defect should be, but typically the term is used to describe defects which involve at most a few extra or missing atoms without an ordered structure of the defective positions. Larger defects in an ordered structure are usually considered dislocation loops. For historical reasons, many point defects especially in ionic crystals are called 'centers': for example the vacancy in many ionic solids is called an F-center. These dislocations allow for ionic transport through crystals leading to electrochemical reactions which are frequently specified using Kröger–Vink Notation.

- Vacancies are sites which are usually occupied by an atom but which are unoccupied. If a neighboring atom moves to occupy the vacant site, the vacancy moves in the opposite direction to the site which used to be occupied by the moving atom. The stability of the surrounding crystal structure guarantees that the neighboring atoms will not simply collapse around the vacancy. In some materials, neighboring atoms actually move away from a vacancy, because they can form better bonds with atoms in the other directions. A vacancy (or pair of vacancies in an ionic solid) is sometimes called a Schottky defect.
- Interstitials are atoms which occupy a site in the crystal structure at which there is usually not an atom. They are generally high energy configurations. Small atoms in some crystals can occupy interstices without high energy, such as hydrogen in palladium.
- A nearby pair of a vacancy and an interstitial is often called a Frenkel defect or Frenkel pair. This is caused when an ion moves into an interstitial site and creates a vacancy.
- Impurities occur because materials are never 100% pure. In the case of an impurity, the atom is often incorporated at a regular atomic site in

the crystal structure. This is neither a vacant site nor is the atom on an interstitial site and it is called a substitutional defect. The atom is not supposed to be anywhere in the crystal, and is thus an impurity. There are two different types of substitutional defects. Isovalent substitution and aliovalent substitution. Isovalent substitution is where the ion that is substituting the original ion is of the same oxidation state as the ion it is replacing. Aliovalent substitution is where the ion that is substituting the original ion is of a different oxidation state as the ion it is replacing. Aliovalent substitutions change the overall charge within the ionic compound, but the ionic compound must be neutral. Therefore a charge compensation mechanism is required. Hence either one of the metals is partially or fully oxidised or reduced, or ion vacancies are created.

- Antisite defects occur in an ordered alloy or compound. For example, some alloys have a regular structure in which every other atom is a different species; for illustration assume that type A atoms sit on the corners of a cubic lattice, and type B atoms sit in the center of the cubes. If one cube has an A atom at its center, the atom is on a site usually occupied by an atom, but it is not the correct type. This is neither a vacancy nor an interstitial, nor an impurity.
- Topological defects are regions in a crystal where the normal chemical bonding environment is topologically different from the surroundings. For instance, in a perfect sheet of graphite (graphene) all atoms are in rings containing six atoms. If the sheet contains regions where the number of atoms in a ring is different from six, while the total number of atoms remains the same, a topological defect has formed. An example is the Stone Wales defect in nanotubes, which consists of two adjacent 5-membered and two 7-membered atom rings.
- Also amorphous solids may contain defects. These are naturally somewhat hard to define, but sometimes their nature can be quite easily understood. For instance, in ideally bonded amorphous silica all Si atoms have 4 bonds to O atoms and all O atoms have 2 bonds to Si atom. Thus e.g. an O atom with only one Si bond (a dangling bond) can be considered a defect in silica.
- Complexes can form between different kinds of point defects. For example, if a vacancy encounters an impurity, the two may bind together if the impurity is too large for the lattice. Interstitials can form 'split interstitial' or 'dumbbell' structures where two atoms effectively share an atomic site, resulting in neither atom actually occupying the site.

LINE DEFECTS

Line defects can be described by gauge theories.

- Dislocations are linear defects around which some of the atoms of the crystal lattice are misaligned.

There are two basic types of dislocations, the edge dislocation and the screw dislocation. "Mixed" dislocations, combining aspects of both types, are also common.

Edge dislocations are caused by the termination of a plane of atoms in the middle of a crystal. In such a case, the adjacent planes are not straight, but instead bend around the edge of the terminating plane so that the crystal structure is perfectly ordered on either side. The analogy with a stack of paper is apt: if a half a piece of paper is inserted in a stack of paper, the defect in the stack is only noticeable at the edge of the half sheet.

The screw dislocation is more difficult to visualise, but basically comprises a structure in which a helical path is traced around the linear defect (dislocation line) by the atomic planes of atoms in the crystal lattice.

The presence of dislocation results in lattice strain (distortion). The direction and magnitude of such distortion is expressed in terms of a Burgers vector. For an edge type, Burgers Vector is perpendicular to the dislocation line, whereas in the cases of the screw type it is parallel. In metallic materials, b is aligned with close-packed crytallographic directions and its magnitude is equivalent to one interatomic spacing.

Dislocations can move if the atoms from one of the surrounding planes break their bonds and rebond with the atoms at the terminating edge.

It is the presence of dislocations and their ability to readily move (and interact) under the influence of stresses induced by external loads that leads to the characteristic malleability of metallic materials.

Dislocations can be observed using transmission electron microscopy, field ion microscopy and atom probe techniques. Deep level transient spectroscopy has been used for studying the electrical activity of dislocations in semiconductors, mainly silicon.

Disclinations are line defects corresponding to "adding" or "subtracting" an angle around a line. Basically, this means that if you track the crystal orientation around the line defect, you get a rotation. Usually they play a role only in liquid crystals.

PLANAR DEFECTS

- Grain boundaries occur where the crystallographic direction of the lattice abruptly changes. This usually occurs when two crystals begin growing separately and then meet.
- Anti-phase boundaries occur in ordered alloys: in this case, the crystallographic direction remains the same, but each side of the boundary has an opposite phase: For example if the ordering is usually ABABABAB, an anti phase boundary takes the form of ABABBABA.
- Stacking faults occur in a number of crystal structures, but the common example is in close-packed structures. Face-centered cubic (fcc) structures differ from hexagonal close packed (hcp) structures only in stacking order: both structures have close packed atomic planes with sixfold symmetry–the atoms form equilateral triangles. When stacking one of these layers on top of another, the atoms are not directly on top of one another–the first two layers are identical for hcp and fcc, and labelled AB. If the third layer is placed so that its atoms are directly above those of the first layer, the stacking will be ABA–this is the hcp structure, and it continues ABABABAB. However there is another location for the third layer, such that its atoms are not above the first layer. Instead, the fourth layer is placed so that its atoms are directly above the first layer. This produces the stacking ABCABCABC, and is actually a cubic arrangement of the atoms. A stacking fault is a one or two layer interruption in the stacking sequence, for example if the sequence ABCABABCAB were found in an fcc structure.

ELECTRICAL, MAGNETIC AND OPTICAL PROPERTIES OF MINERALS

A mineral is a naturally occurring inorganic substance, having an orderly atomic structure and a definite chemical composition and physical properties. A mineral is composed of two or more elements. But, sometimes single element minerals like sulphur, copper, silver, gold, graphite etc. are found.

METALLIC MINERALS

These minerals contain metal content and can be sub-divided into three types:

(i) Precious metals: gold, silver, platinum etc.
(ii) Ferrous metals: iron and other metals often mixed with iron to form various kinds of steel.
(iii) Non-ferrous metals: include metals like copper, lead, zinc, tin, aluminium etc.

NON-METALLIC MINERALS

These minerals do not contain metal content. Sulphur, phosphates and nitrates are examples of non-metallic minerals. Cement is a mixture of non-metallic minerals.

ELECTRICAL PROPERTIES OF MINERAL

Conduction

Conduction in mineral terms is the ability of a mineral to conduct electricity. Only a very small number of minerals are good conductors; they are the metallic elements and the mineral graphite. These conductors can be placed between a wire carrying electricity, and the electricity will pass through it. Conduction is an important property that can distinguish true metals from metallic looking sulfides and oxides.

Pyroelectricity

Pyroelectricity is where a mineral develops electrical charges when exposed to temperature changes. Some minerals develop an electrical charge when heated, others when cooled.

Piezoelectricity

Piezoelectricity is where a mineral develops electrical charges when put under stress. Piezoelectric minerals will develop charges when rubbed or struck repeatedly.

Conduction is very useful in distinguishing true metals, but pyroelectricity and piezoelectricity are not practical testing methods for normal mineral collectors.

MAGNETIC PROPERTIES OF MINERAL

Several minerals react when placed within a magnetic field. Some minerals are strongly attracted to the magnet, others are weakly attracted, and one mineral is repelled. There are also several minerals that are attracted to magnetic fields only when heated. A magnetic field is an area encompassing a magnet or electrical current that has the ability to attract or repel certain objects placed in the field. The closer the object is to the magnet or electrical current, the more powerful the magnetic effect. The presence of iron in a mineral is responsible for the magnetic properties of minerals in virtually all cases.

Magnetic properties of minerals are defined as follows:

- Ferromagnetism, or strong attraction to magnetic fields is exhibited in only few minerals, notably magnetite and pyrrhotite.
- Paramagnetism is weak attraction to magnetic fields. The attraction is usually discernible, but it may be so weak that it is undetectable. Most paramagnetic minerals become strongly magnetic when heated. A small number of paramagnetic minerals, such as platinum, are not essentially paramagnetic, but contain iron impurities which are responsible for the paramagnetism. However, some specimens lacking iron also exist, and these are not paramagnetic. Some examples of paramagnetic minerals are hematite and franklinite.
- Diamagnetism. Only one mineral, bismuth, is diamagnetic, meaning it is repelled from magnetic fields.
- Another property, which is unnamed, is attraction to magnetic fields when heated. Some iron sulfides and oxides become ferromagnetic after heating, as a result of combined sulfur or oxygen ions freeing themselves from the iron. Some minerals may even act as magnets when heated.
- Magnetism. Only a variety of one mineral acts as a magnet, generating magnetic fields. This is the lodestone variety of magnetite, found in only a few deposits throughout the world. Although it is only weakly magnetic, its magnetism is definitely discernible.

Magnetic properties are useful for identifying a mineral, for if observed it can pinpoint a mineral. The most effective testing results are obtained with the use of a powerful magnet. The only minerals that possibly respond to magnets without heating are opaque, metallic-looking minerals.

OPTICAL PROPERTIES OF MINERALS

The light has a dual nature. Firstly, light behaves like a particle. In this behavior light particle known as photon act as a compact entity and can knock out loosely metalic bonded electrons from large atoms like Cs and Rb. This effect is known as photoelectric effect.

Secondly, light behaves like a wave and bends around corners and passing through small holes produces interference and diffraction patterns. In optical mineralogy most phenomena can be explained by the wave nature of light.

In the wave theory of light, the light waves are defined by oscillating electric $E^{\rightarrow}$ and magnetic $H^{\rightarrow}$ vectors perpendicular to each other and are also oriented perpendicular to the propagation direction of light-ray. So to simplify, we can consider an oscillating light vector; $L^{\rightarrow}$ which is a resultant of the $E^{\rightarrow}$ and $H^{\rightarrow}$ vectors. In this way a light wave forms a sine wave. The light wave vibration has a characteristic wavelenght (λ). In fact considering the whole electromagnetic spectrum including cosmic rays-X-rays at the short λ's region to radio waves and microwave radiation at long λ's region; visible light is only a small part of this spectrum. The λ range of visible light is from approximately 390-710 nm (nanometer=10^{-9} m). This range of light corresponds to 390-440 nm Violet; 440-500 nm Blue; 500-570 nm Green; 570-590 nm Yellow; 590-650 nm Orange; 650-710 nm Red.

OTHER WAVE PROPERTIES OF LIGHT WAVES

When light rays move away from a source in a medium, at a given moment these rays will have traveled and define a 3-D surface known as Ray Velocity Surface (RVS). In isotropic minerals these rays will have travelled same distance, independent of the direction they travel hence spherical RVS forms. However, in anisotropic minerals, because the minerals have different atoms along different directions, light will travel at different velocities along different crystallographic direction, hence RVS surface is not spherical, but will form complex double surfaces.

Tangent to the RVS along any light ray is known as the wave front. Followed from above discussion in isotropic minerals wave front is perpendicular to the ray (or propagation direction) and its wave normal will be along the propagation direction. However, in anisotropic minerals wave front is perpendicular to the propagation direction only at special directions, but will be at an angle in other directions. Similarly, wave normal will be along the propagation direction only at special crystallographic direction, but will be at an angle in other directions.

REFLECTION-TOTAL REFLECTION-REFRACTION-INDEX OF REFRACTION

When light ray travels from one isotropic medium into another isotropic medium certain changes occur to the direction of propagation at the interface. If light travels from a less dense isotropic medium to higher density isotropic medium some of the rays will be reflected at the interface while others will enter into the denser isotropic medium. According to law of reflection, the angle of the incident ray with the normal will be reflected with the same angle back to the former isotropic medium-with the same velocity. However, light entering into denser isotropic medium bends closer to the normal at the interface and the velocity of light will drop. This is known as refraction. According to the Snell's Law sini/sinr=RI of the latter isotropic medium. This can also be expressed as RI_{medium}=velocity of light in vacuum/ velocity of light in the isotropic medium, $RI_{medium}=c/V_{nedium}$ ie., RI of a medium is inversely proportional to the speed of light in that medium. Higher RI means lower speed of light in that medium.

Hence, RI is Refractive Index, C is velocity of light and V is velocity in medium.

If light travels from a higher RI isotropic medium to lower RI isotropic medium same laws apply, but in this case refracted ray moves away from the normal to the interface. At a certain critical angle of incidence, no light will pass through the interface into low RI isotropic medium.This is known as total reflection which is used to determine RI's of isotropic media. Measured RI of minerals has a fundamental importance. This parameter, especially in solid solution series is very important, as it may be used to determine the composition of the solid solution species. RI's of diffrent polymorphs also show linear relationship when compared with density of the polymorphs.

There is a direct relationship between the optic properties of minerals and their symmetry, where light is affected similarly in the same crystal system. The specific parameter that seems to control the interaction of light with solid matter is the number of unique crystallographic axes within a crystal system.

DISPERSION

When natural white light consisting of different wavelenghts is refracted at the interface of two isotropic media or minerals, refracted rays with different λ's are seperated from red to violet with different refraction angles. Blue rays refracted more appears closer to the normal whereas red rays is slightly away from the normal.

This is known as dispersion.

Dispersion in anisotropic media resolves two different sets of red and blue refracted rays, since anisotropic minerals have more than one RI.

POLARIZATION AND POLARIZED LIGHT

Light vector of natural light vibrates perpendicular to the direction of propagation, along all direction. If light is forced to vibrate along certain direction than the light is said to be polarized, and the phenomenon is called polarization.

The simplest polarization is produced when light is forced to vibrate in a single plane containing the direction of propagation. This is called plane polarization, or linear polarization. Here, light vector again vibrates perpendicular to the propagation direction but confined to the polarization plane.

When two plane polarized lights vibrating along their plane of polarizations meet along the same direction of propagation, where the planes of vibrations are perpendicular to each other two different kinds of polarized light is obtained, depending on the phase differences between them. If the phase difference is equal to $\frac{1}{4}\lambda$ circular polarized light is obtained. If the phase difference is not equal to $\neq \frac{1}{4}\lambda$, and $\neq$ even multiples of $\frac{1}{2}\lambda$'s, then elliptically polarized light is obtained. Both circularly-and elliptically-polarized light can move clock-wise or anti clock-wise direction.

There are three important methods of producing plane polarized light:

1. By reflection and refraction: When natural light strikes the interface between two media, it is split into plane polarized reflected light where the direction of vibration is perpendicular to the plane that is defined by the normal to the interface and the incident ray. Best polarization is obtained when i+r=90° which is called the Brewster Law.
2. By absorbtion: Certain dichroic anisotropic minerals absorb light strongly in one direction, and let it pass with minimum absorbtion in a direction perpendicular to this direction.Hence plane polarized light is obtained. Synthetic substances like herapatite (iodocinchonidine-sulphate) also shows this property.
3. By double refraction: When natural light enters into anisotropic uniaxial mineral like Cal, it splits into two rays which are plane polarized and their vibration planes are perpendicular to each other. Since they travel at different velocities, ε-fast (vibrating //[l] to c-axis) & ω-slow (vibrating ⊥[r] to c-axis), they also have different propagation directions. A Cal crystal suitably cut and glued together with CB (nicol prism) is used to separate ε and ω completely, where ω is totally reflected at crystal-CB interface whereas ε is refracted into the upper crystal.

In a polarizing microscope there are two polarizers, one below the stage converting natural light into E-W vibration plane called polarizer and an upper polarizer above the objective known as analyser with N-S vibration plane.

EXTINCTION-INTERFERENCE COLOURS-BIREFRINGENCE-RETARDATION

When natural light entering to the microscope passes through polarizer it becomes polarized E-W direction. If there is a colourless isotropic substance on the stage, ie, air, liquid, glass, or a mineral with only one RI, and if analyser is out, the E-W vibrating plane polarized white light from the polarizer passes through the ocular unchanged as a plane polarized white light. On the other hand, if the analyser is in position, there will no light observed at the ocular since there is no light available vibrating N-S direction to pass through the analyser. This phenomenon is known as extinction, and as the microscope stage is turned extinction is continuous and the mineral is said to be at continuous extinction.

Anisotropic minerals however behave differently since they have more than one RI. In fact, anisotropic crystals split incident E-W polarized light into two light waves that are constrained to vibrate perpendicular to one another. The orientations of the vibration directions of the two light rays being fixed relative to the crystal axes. If the analyser is out, these two rays passes through the ocular as two plane polarized white light. But if the analyser is in position and and if the vibration direction of the mineral is at an angle to E-W & N-S directions., a colourful disposition occurs on the mineral surfaces. These colours are interference colours which are completely different from normal colour of the mineral. Here the complementary phases of λ's are allowed to pass through the N-S vibration plane and interact to produce the interference colours. The components of the two differently vibrating white polarized lights are resolved along the N-S and E-W vibration directions. Components perpendicular to N-S is absorbed while those components vibrating parallel to the N-S analyser vibration direction is allowed to pass through the analyser. In the analyser, the components vibrating parallel to the vibration plane of the analyser interfere to produce interference colours. The strength of interference, also known as retardation is proportional directly to the differnce of RI's indices of the relative crystallographic orientation of the section of the crystal or inversely proportional to the different ray velocities of corresponding ray velocities. Retardation is also directly proportional to the thickness of the mineral section; therefore, $\Delta = t(|RI_1 - RI_2|)$. Here retardation (Δ) is equal to the product of the thickness of the mineral section and the absolute difference in the RI's related to that particular section. The difference RI_1-RI_2 is called the birefringence of the mineral and has maximum value when $|\varepsilon-\omega|$ or $|\alpha-\gamma|$, or for intermediate values of ε' and β the minerals will have smaller value of birefringence.

When unique vibration directions of the mineral is parallel to the E-W and N-S vibration direction of polarizer and analyser one of the plane polarized light rays emerging from the anisotropic crystal is absored completely at the N-S vibrating plane of analyser. Therefore, there will no interference at analyser, a single N-S vibrating light passes through, hence extinction occurs. At every 90° of revolution of the microscope stage alternately extinction and illumination are encountered, after the first extinction.

Sometimes high RI minerals and at other times minerals with perfect cleavage cause reflection of light from below which appear as tiny specks of illumination during extinction. This is called mottled extinction, a characteristic feature of micas.

The colour of maximum retardation is presented in charts ranging from first order to seventh order interference colour. Retardation orders are separated by the appearance of red (550 nm) colours. The colours become pale beige as the order of retardation increases. There is no true blue or green colour in the first order. When birefringence is very low anamolous interference colours of navy blue and olive green or purple is observed in first order.

If the composition or thickness of the crystal varies in the thin section, different interference colors may occur on the same crystal surface resulting a patchy birefringence, a characteristic feature of epidote.

COLOUR AND PLEOCHROISM

Colour of a transparent minerals in thin section is observed with analyser out position which then depends on the absorbtion of certain λ's of E-W vibrating plane polarized white light emerging from the mineral. The λ's that pass through the mineral interfere and produce characteristic colour of the mineral. The colour due to transmission of light through the mineral may be different from the colour of the mineral due to reflected light from the surface of the mineral, in hand specimen.

If the colourful mineral is isotropic, there is no change of colours when the stage of microscope is rotate, because the isotropic mineral has only one characteristic RI. However, if the colourful mineral is anisotropic, absorption of different λ's of E-W vibrating white plane polarized light is direction dependent, hence different colours appear as the stage rotated, because of anisotropic mineral's principle vibration direction is aligned alternatively parallel to the E-W direction. This phenomenon is known as pleochroism. Hence uniaxial crystals with two principle RI's will have maximum two different colours, on the other hand biaxial crystals with three principle RI's will have maximum three different colours, depending on the orientation of the section that is cut from the crystal.

If the composition of the crystal changes from centre to its edge roughly concentric colouring may occur which is called compositional zonning.

Colour of opaque minerals cannot be viewed with transmission polarizing microscopes. Since opaque minerals do not transmit light, whatever thin the section is. Therefore they appear black and collectively referred to as the opaque minerals, ie., Mat, Pyt, Ilm, etc. Opaque minerals are studied by reflection polarizing microscopes, or ore microscopes.

BONDING AND CRYSTAL STRUCTURES OF SILICATES

The chemical compound silicon dioxide, also known as silica (from the Latin silex), is an oxide of silicon with a chemical formula of SiO_2 and has been known for its hardness since antiquity. Silica is most commonly found in nature as sand or quartz, as well as in the cell walls of diatoms. Silica is the most abundant mineral in the Earth's crust.

CRYSTAL STRUCTURE OF SILICATES

In the vast majority of silicates, the Si atom shows tetrahedral coordination, with 4 oxygen atoms surrounding a central Si atom. The most common example is seen in the quartz crystalline form of silica SiO_2. In each of the most thermodynamically stable crystalline forms of silica, on average, only 2 out of 4 of each the vertices (or oxygen atoms) of the SiO_4 tetrahedra are shared with others, yielding the net chemical formula: SiO_2.

SiO_2 has a number of distinct crystalline forms in addition to amorphous forms. With the exception of stishovite and fibrous silica, all of the crystalline forms involve tetrahedral SiO_4 units linked together by shared vertices in different arrangements. Silicon-oxygen bond lengths vary between the different crystal forms, for example in α-quartz the bond length is 161 pm, whereas in α-tridymite it is in the range 154–171 pm. The Si-O-Si angle also varies between a low value of 140° in α-tridymite, up to 180° in β-tridymite. In α-quartz the Si-O-Si angle is 144°.

Fibrous silica has a structure similar to that of SiS_2 with chains of edge-sharing SiO_4 tetrahedra. Stishovite, the highest pressure form, in contrast has a rutile like structure where silicon is 6 coordinate. The density of stishovite is 4.287 g/cm^3, which compares to α-quartz, the densest of the low pressure forms, which has a density of 2.648 g/cm^3. The difference in density can be ascribed to the increase in coordination as the six shortest Si-O bond lengths in stishovite (four Si-O bond lengths of 176 pm and two others of 181 pm) are greater than the Si-O bond length (161 pm) in α-quartz. The change in the coordination increases the ionicity of the Si-O bond. But more important is the observation that any deviations from these standard parameters constitute microstructural differences or variations which represent an approach to an amorphous, vitreous or glassy solid.

The high pressure minerals, stishovite and coesite, on the other hand, have a higher density and index of refraction when compared to quartz. This is probably due to the intense compression of the atoms that must occur during their formation, resulting in a more condensed structure.

Faujasite silica is another form of crystalline silica. It is obtained by dealumination of a low-sodium, ultra-stable Y zeolite with a combined acid and thermal treatment. The resulting product contains over 99% silica, has high crystallinity and high surface area (over 800 m^2/g). Faujasite-silica has very high thermal and acid stability. For example, it maintains a high degree of long-range molecular order (or crystallinity) even after boiling in concentrated hydrochloric acid.

Crystalline forms of SiO_2		
Form	Crystal symmetry Pearson symbol, group, No rhombohedral (trigonal)	Notes
α-quartz	hP9, $P3_121$, No.152	Helical chains making individual single crystals optically active; α-quartz converts to β-quartz at 573°C
β-quartz	hexagonal hP18, $P6_222$, No.180	closely related to α-quartz (with an Si-O-Si angle of 155°) and optically active; β-quartz converts to β-tridymite at 870°C
α-tridymite	orthorhombic oS24, $C222_1$, No.20	metastable form under normal pressure
β-tridymite	hexagonal hP12, $P6_3/mmc$, No. 194	closely related to α-tridymite; β-tridymite converts to в-cristobalite at 1470°C
α-cristobalite	tetragonal tP12, $P4_12_12$, No. 92	metastable form under normal pressure
β-cristobalite	cubic cF104, Fd3m, No.227	closely related to α-cristobalite; melts at 1705°C
keatite	tetragonal tP36, $P4_12_12$, No. 92	Si_5O_{10}, Si_4O_{14}, Si_8O_{16} rings; synthesised from amorphous silica and alkali at high pressure
coesite	monoclinic mS48, C2/c, No.15	Si_4O_8 and Si_8O_{16} rings; high pressure form (higher than keatite)
stishovite	tetragonal tP6, $P4_2/mnm$, No.136	rutile like with 6-fold coordinated Si; high pressure form (higher than coesite) and the densest of the polymorphs

melanophlogite	cubic cP*, $P4_232$, No.208	Si_5O_{10}, Si_6O_{12} rings; mineral always found with hydrocarbons in interstitial spaces-a clathrasil
fibrous	orthorhombic oI12, Ibam, No.72	like SiS_2 consisting of edge sharing chains
faujasite	cubic cF576, Fd3m, No.227	sodalite cages connected by hexagonal prisms; 12-membered ring pore opening; faujasite structure.

Molten silica exhibits several peculiar physical characteristics that are similar to the ones observed in liquid water: negative temperature expansion, density maximum and a heat capacity minimum. When molecular silicon monoxide, SiO, is condensed in an argon matrix cooled with helium along with oxygen atoms generated by microwave discharge, molecular SiO_2 is produced which has a linear structure. Dimeric silicon dioxide, $(SiO_2)_2$ has been prepared by reacting O_2 with matrix isolated dimeric silicon monoxide, (Si_2O_2). In dimeric silicon dioxide there are two oxygen atoms bridging between the silicon atoms with an Si-O-Si angle of 94° and bond length of 164.6 pm and the terminal Si-O bond length is 150.2 pm. The Si-O bond length is 148.3 pm which compares with the length of 161 pm in α-quartz.

CHEMISTRY OF SILICON DIOXIDE

Silicon dioxide is formed when silicon is exposed to oxygen (or air). A very thin layer (approximately 1 nm or 10 E) of so-called 'native oxide' is formed on the surface when silicon is exposed to air under ambient conditions. Higher temperatures and alternative environments are used to grow well-controlled layers of silicon dioxide on silicon, for example at temperatures between 600° and 1200°C, using the so-called "dry" or "wet" oxidation with O_2 or H_2O, respectively. The thickness of the layer of silicon replaced by the dioxide is 44% of the thickness of the silicon dioxide layer produced.

Alternative methods used to deposit a layer of SiO_2 include

- Low temperature oxidation (400–450°C) of silane
  $SiH_4 + 2O_2 \rightarrow SiO_2 + 2H_2O$
- Decomposition of tetraethyl orthosilicate (TEOS) at 680–730°C
  $Si(OC_2H_5)_4 \rightarrow SiO_2 + 2\,H_2O + 4C_2H_4$
- Plasma enhanced chemical vapor deposition using TEOS at about 400°C
  $Si(OC_2H_5)_4 + 12\,O_2 \rightarrow SiO_2 + 10\,H_2O + 8\,CO_2$
- Polymerization of tetraethyl orthosilicate (TEOS) at below 100°C using amino acid as catalyst.

Pyrogenic silica (sometimes called fumed silica or silica fume), which is a very fine particulate form of silicon dioxide, is prepared by burning $SiCl_4$ in an oxygen rich hydrocarbon flame to produce a "smoke" of SiO_2:

$$SiCl_4 + 2\,H_2 + O_2 \rightarrow SiO_2 + 4\,HCl$$

Amorphous silica, silica gel, is produced by the acidification of solutions of sodium silicate to produce a gelatinous precipitate that is then washed and then dehydrated to produce colorless microporous silica.

Quartz exhibits a maximum solubility in water at temperatures about 340°C. This property is used to grow single crystals of quartz in a hydrothermal process where natural quartz is dissolved in superheated water in a pressure vessel which is cooler at the top. Crystals of 0.5–1 kg can be grown over a period of 1–2 months. These crystals are a source of very pure quartz for use in electronic applications.

Fluorine reacts with silicon dioxide to form SiF_4 and O_2 whereas the other halogen gases (Cl_2, Br_2, I_2) react much less readily.

Silicon dioxide is attacked by hydrofluoric acid (HF) to produce "hexafluorosilicic acid":

$$SiO_2 + 6\ HF \rightarrow H_2SiF_6 + 2\ H_2O$$

HF is used to remove or pattern silicon dioxide in the semiconductor industry.

Silicon dioxide dissolves in hot concentrated alkali or fused hydroxide:

$$SiO_2 + 2\ NaOH \rightarrow Na_2SiO_3 + H_2O$$

Silicon dioxide reacts with basic metal oxides (e.g. sodium oxide, potassium oxide, lead(II) oxide, zinc oxide or mixtures of oxides forming silicates and glasses as the Si-O-Si bonds in silica are broken successively). As an example the reaction of sodium oxide and SiO_2 can produce sodium orthosilicate, sodium silicate and glasses, depending on the proportions of reactants:

$$2\ Na_2O + SiO_2 \rightarrow Na_4SiO_4$$

$$Na_2O + SiO_2 \rightarrow Na_2SiO_3$$

$$(0.25\text{–}0.8)Na_2O + SiO_2 \rightarrow \text{glass}$$

Examples of such glasses have commercial significance e.g. soda lime glass, borosilicate glass, lead glass. In these glasses, silica is termed the network former or lattice former.

With silicon at high temperatures gaseous SiO is produced:

$$SiO_2 + Si \rightarrow 2\ SiO\ (gas)$$

TRANSFORMATION OF MINERALS – POLYMORPHISM & POLYTYPISM

POLYMORPHISM

Polymorphism is existence of several different morphologic kinds occurring species or mineral. Polymorphism is the ability of a specific chemical composition to crystallize in more than one form. This generally occurs as a response to changes in temperature or pressure or both. The different structures of such a chemical substance are called polymorphic forms, or polymorphs. For example, the element carbon (C) occurs in nature in two different polymorphic forms, depending on the external (pressure and temperature) conditions. These forms are graphite, with a hexagonal structure, and diamond, with an isometric structure.

The characteristic of a chemical compound to crystallize in more than one crystal class; e.g.: (1) kyanite, andalusite, and sillimanite; (2) quartz, tridymite, cristobalite, coesite, and stishovite. Allotropy refers specif. to chemical elements crystallizing in more than one class; e.g., graphite, diamond, chaoite, and lonsdaleite. Polymorphism limited to two or three crystal classes is dimorphism or trimorphism, respectively. Individual species are polymorphs (dimorphs, trimorphs). Polytypism refers to variable stacking of identical layer structures in different crystal classes.

POLYTYPISM

Polytypism of crystals is the existence of multiple forms differing in only one of the dimensions of the unit cell. An element or compound is polytypic if it occurs in several structural modifications, each of which can be regarded as built up by stacking layers of (nearly) identical structure and composition, and if the modifications differ only in their stacking sequence. Polytypism is a special case of polymorphism: the two-dimensional translations within the layers are essentially preserved.

The complete definition is given in the Report of the International Union of Crystallography Ad-Hoc Committee on the Nomenclature of Disordered, Modulated and Polytype Structures: Acta Cryst. A40, 399-404(1984), "Nomenclature of Polytype Structures".

SOLID SOLUTION AND EXSOLUTION

SOLID SOLUTION

A solid solution is a solid-state solution of one or more solutes in a solvent. Such a mixture is considered a solution rather than a compound when the crystal structure of the solvent remains unchanged by addition of the solutes, and when the mixture remains in a single homogeneous phase.This often happens when the two elements (generally metals) involved are close together on the periodic table; conversely, a chemical compound is generally a result of the non proximity of the two metals involved on the periodic table.

The solute may incorporate into the solvent crystal lattice substitutionally, by replacing a solvent particle in the lattice, or interstitially, by fitting into the space between solvent particles. Both of these types of solid solution affect the properties of the material by distorting the crystal lattice and disrupting the physical and electrical homogeneity of the solvent material.

Some mixtures will readily form solid solutions over a range of concentrations, while other mixtures will not form solid solutions at all. The propensity for any two substances to form a solid solution is a complicated matter involving the chemical, crystallographic, and quantum properties of the substances in question. Solid solutions, in accordance with the Hume-Rothery rules, may form if the solute and solvent have:

- Similar atomic radii (15% or less difference)
- Same crystal structure
- Similar electronegativities
- Similar valency

The phase diagram displays an alloy of two metals which forms a solid solution at all relative concentrations of the two species. In this case, the pure phase of each element is of the same crystal structure, and the similar properties of the two elements allow for unbiased substitution through the full range of relative concentrations.

Solid solutions have important commercial and industrial applications, as such mixtures often have superior properties to pure materials. Many metal alloys are solid solutions. Even small amounts of solute can affect the electrical and physical properties of the solvent.

The binary phase diagram at right shows the phases of a mixture of two substances in varying concentrations, α and β. The region labeled "α" is a solid solution, with β acting as the solute in a matrix of α. On the other end of the concentration scale, the region labeled "β" is also a solid solution, with α acting as the solute in a matrix of β. The large solid region in between the α and β solid solutions, labeled "α and β", is not a solid solution. Instead, an examination of the microstructure of a mixture in this range would reveal two phases – solid solution α-in-β and solid solution β-in-α would form separate phases, perhaps lamella or grains.

EXSOLUTION

Sometimes, mineral compositions that are stable at high temperature become unstable when temperature decreases. They may exsolve ("unmix") so that a grain that was once uniform contains blebs, patches or stringers of two minerals.

When a solid solution becomes unstable – due to a lower temperature, for example – exsolution occurs and the two phases separate into distinct microscopic to megascopic lamellae. An example of this is the alkali feldspar mineral variety perthite in which thin white albite layers alternate between typically pink microcline.

STEADY-STATE GEOTHERM

Geotherm is heat inside the earth system. Temperature within the Earth increases with greater depth. Highly viscous or partially molten rock at temperatures between 650 to 1,200°C (1,202 to 2,192°F) is postulated to exist everywhere beneath the Earth's surface at depths of 50 to 60 miles (80 to 100 kilometers), and the temperature at the Earth's center, nearly 4,000 miles (6,400 km) deep, is estimated to be 5650 ± 600 kelvins. The heat content of the earth is 10^{31} Joules.

- Much of the heat is believed to be created by decay of naturally radioactive elements. An estimated 45 to 90 per cent of the heat escaping from the Earth originates from radioactive decay of elements within the mantle.
- Heat of impact and compression released during the original formation of the Earth by accretion of in-falling meteorites.

- Heat released as abundant heavy metals (iron, nickel, copper) descended to the Earth's core.
- Some heat may be created by electromagnetic effects of the magnetic fields involved in Earth's magnetic field.
- 10 to 25% of the heat flowing to the surface may be produced by a sustained nuclear fission reaction in Earth's inner core, the "georeactor" hypothesis.
- Heat may be generated by tidal force on the Earth as it rotates; since land cannot flow like water it compresses and distorts, generating heat.

The geothermal gradient is the rate at which the Earth's temperature increases with depth, indicating outward heat flows from a hot interior. Away from tectonic plate boundaries, it is 25-30°C per km of depth in most of the world.

Calculate the setady-state geotherm:

Calculate the setady-state geotherm for a 30 km thick crust with a uniform distribution of heat producing elements. Assume that the average heat production (A) is 2.0 x 10^{-6} W/m^3, that the steady mantle heat flux into the base of the crust is 1.0 x 10^{-2} W/m^2, that the thermal conductivity (k) of the crust is 2.5 W/mK, that the volumetric heat capacity (cCP) of the crust is 2.5 x 10^6 J/m^{3}K, and that the temperature (T) at the surface is 0°C. Let the depth z=0 at the surface and z= –3.0 x 10^4 m at the base of the crust. The required heat conduction equations are heat flux

$$= -k\left(\frac{\partial T}{\partial z}\right)_1 \text{ and } \left(\frac{\partial T}{\partial t}\right)_z = \frac{k}{\rho C_p}\left(\frac{\partial^2 T}{\partial z^2}\right)_t - \frac{A}{\rho C_p}$$

where t (s) is the time, ρ (Kg/m^3) is the density of the crust, and CP (J/KgK) is the specific heat capacity of the crust. The second equation assumes

(1) that the thermal parameters for the crust are uniform throughout the crust and

(2) that the symmetry of the problem permits a one dimensional solution.

In the steady-state, $\partial T/\partial t = 0$. Therefore, the heat conduction equation reduces to

$$\left(\frac{d^2T}{dz^2}\right) = -\frac{A}{k},$$

which is a comparatively simple differential equation. The solution is of the form

$$T = \left(-\frac{A}{2k}\right)z^2 + \alpha z + \beta \text{ with } \left(\frac{dT}{dz}\right) = \left(-\frac{A}{k}\right)z + \alpha$$

where α and β are constants. At the surface, z = 0 and T = 0; therefore, β=0. At z = –30,000 m,

$$\text{heat flux} = -k\left(\frac{dT}{dz}\right) = -k\left(-\frac{A}{k}\right)z - k\alpha = 0.01\,\text{Wm}^2,$$

which may be solved for α to yield

$$\alpha = \frac{Az}{k} - \frac{0.01}{k} = \frac{(2.0\times10^{-6})(-3.0\times10^{4})}{2.5} - \frac{0.01}{2.5}$$

$$= 0.028 \text{ K/m}.$$

The solution is then

$T = -(4.0 \times 10^{-7})z^2 - (0.028)z.$

The heat flow at the surface for this model is given by heat flux

$$= -k\left(\frac{dT}{dz}\right)_{z=0} = -k\alpha = (2.5)(0.028) = 0.07\,\text{W/m}^2$$

where Z is depth (meters) and T is temperature (in kelvin or centrigrade).

GENESIS, PROPERTIES, EMPLACEMENT AND CRYSTALLIZATION OF MAGMAS

Magmas are developed when melting occurs either within or beneath the Earth's crust, that is, in the upper mantle. They comprise hot solutions of several liquid phases, the most conspicuous of which is a complex silicate phase.

GENESIS OF MAGMA

Three different processes melt the asthenosphere: rising temperature, decreasing pressure, and addition of water. We will consider these processes and then look at the tectonic environments in which they generate magma.

RISING TEMPERATURE

An increase in temperature will melt a hot rock. Oddly, however, increasing temperature is the least important cause of magma formation in the asthenosphere.

DECREASING PRESSURE

A mineral is composed of an ordered array of atoms bonded together. When a mineral melts, the atoms become disordered and move freely, taking up more space than when they were in the solid mineral. Consequently, magma occupies about 10 per cent more volume than the rock that melted to form it. a rock is heated to its melting point on the Earth's surface, it melts readily because there is little pressure to keep it from expanding. The temperature in the asthenosphere is more than hot enough to melt rock, but there, the high pressure prevents the rock from expanding, and it cannot melt. However, if the pressure were to decrease, large volumes of the asthenosphere would melt. Melting caused by decreasing pressure is called pressure-release melting.

ADDITION OF WATER

A wet rock generally melts at a lower temperature than an otherwise identical dry rock. Thus, addition of water to rock that is near its melting temperature can melt the rock. Certain tectonic processes add water to the hot rock of the asthenosphere to form magma.

PROPERTIES OF MAGMA

Temperature

The temperature of magma varies from about 600° to 1400°C, depending on its chemical composition and the depth at which it forms. Generally, basaltic magma forms at great depth and has a temperature near the high end of this scale. Granitic magmas, which form at shallower depths, tend to lie near the cooler end of the scale. As a comparison, an iron bar turns red hot at about 600°C and melts at slightly over 1500°C.

Chemical Composition

Because oxygen and silicon are the two most abundant elements in the crust and mantle, nearly all magmas are silicate magmas. In addition to oxygen and silicon, they also contain lesser amounts of the six other common elements of the Earth's crust: aluminum, iron, magnesium, calcium, potassium, and sodium. The main variations among different types of magmas are differences in the relative proportions of these eight elements. For example, basaltic magma contains more iron and magnesium than granitic magma, but granitic magma is richer in silicon, potassium, and sodium. A few rare magmas are of carbonate composition. The rocks that form from these are called carbonatites and contain carbonate minerals such as calcite and dolomite.

Behavior

When a silicate rock melts, the resulting magma expands by about 10 per cent. It is then of lower density than the rock around it, so magma rises as it forms–much as a hot air balloon ascends in the atmosphere. When magma rises, it enters the cooler, lower-pressure environment near the Earth's surface. When temperature and pressure drop sufficiently, it solidifies to form solid igneous rock.

PHASE EQUILIBRIUM

In the physical sciences, a phase is a region of space (a thermodynamic system), throughout which all physical properties of a material are essentially uniform. Examples of physical properties include density, index of refraction, and chemical composition. A simple description is that a phase is a region of material that is chemically uniform, physically distinct, and (often) mechanically separable. In a system consisting of ice and water in a glass jar, the ice cubes are one phase, the water is a second phase, and the humid air over the water is a third phase. The glass of the jar is another separate phase.

The term phase is sometimes used as a synonym for state of matter. Also, the term phase is sometimes used to refer to a set of equilibrium states demarcated in terms of state variables such as pressure and temperature by a phase boundary on a phase diagram. Because phase boundaries relate to changes in the organization of matter, such as a change from liquid to solid or a more subtle change from one crystal structure to another, this latter usage is similar to the use of "phase" as a synonym for state of matter. However, the state of matter and phase diagram usages are not commensurate with the formal definition given above and the intended meaning must be determined in part from the context in which the term is used.

TYPES OF PHASES

Distinct phases may be described as different states of matter such as gas, liquid, solid, plasma or Bose–Einstein condensate. Phases may also be differentiated based on solubility as in polar (hydrophilic) or non-polar (hydrophobic). A mixture of water (a polar liquid) and oil (a non-polar liquid) will spontaneously separate into two phases. Water has a very low solubility (is insoluble) in oil, and oil has a low solubility in water. Solubility is the maximum amount of a solute that can dissolve in a solvent before the solute ceases to dissolve and remains in a separate phase. A mixture can separate into more than two liquid phases and the concept of phase separation extends to solids, i.e. solids can form solid solutions or crystallize into distinct crystal phases. Metal pairs that are mutually soluble can form alloys, whereas metal pair that are mutually insoluble cannot.

As many as eight immiscible liquid phases have been observed. Mutually immiscible liquid phases are formed from water (aqueous phase), hydrophobic organic solvents, perfluorocarbons (fluorous phase), silicones, several different metals, and also from molten phosphorus. Not all organic solvents are completely miscible, e.g. a mixture of ethylene glycol and toluene may separate into two distinct organic phases. Emulsions and colloids are examples of immiscible phase pair combinations that do not physically separate.

PHASE EQUILIBRIUM

Left to equilibrate, many compositions will form a uniform single phase, but depending on the temperature and pressure even a single substance may separate into two or more distinct phases. Within each phase, the properties are uniform but between the two phase properties differ.

Water in a closed jar with an air space over it forms a two phase system. Most of the water is in the liquid phase, where it is held by the mutual attraction of water molecules. Even at equilibrium molecules are constantly in motion and, once in a while, a molecule in the liquid phase gains enough kinetic energy to break away from the liquid phase and enter the gas phase. Likewise, every once in a while a vapor molecule collides with the liquid surface and condenses into the liquid. At equilibrium, evaporation and condensation processes exactly balance and there is no net change in the volume of either phase.

At room temperature and pressure, the water jar reaches equilibrium when the air over the water has a humidity of about 3%. This percentage increases as the temperature goes up. At 100°C and atmospheric pressure, equilibrium is not reached until the air is 100% water. If the liquid is heated a little over 100°C, the transition from liquid to gas will occur not only at the surface, but throughout the liquid volume the water boils.

NUMBER OF PHASES

For a given composition, only certain phases are possible at a given temperature and pressure. The number and type of phases that will form is hard to predict and is usually determined by experiment. The results of such experiments can be plotted in phase diagrams.

In this simple system, which phases that are possible depends only on pressure and temperature. The markings show points where two or more phases can co-exist in equilibrium. At temperatures and pressures away from the markings, there will be only one phase at equilibrium.

In the diagram, the blue line marking the boundary between liquid and gas does not continue indefinitely, but terminates at a point called the critical point. As the temperature and pressure approach the critical point, the properties of the liquid and gas become progressively more similar. At the critical point, the liquid and gas become indistinguishable. Above the critical point, there are no longer separate liquid and gas phases: there is only a generic fluid phase referred to as a supercritical fluid. In water, the critical point occurs at around 647 K (374°C or 705°F) and 22.064 MPa.

An unusual feature of the water phase diagram that the solid-liquid phase line (illustrated by the dotted green line) has a negative slope. For most substances, the slope is positive as exemplified by the dark green line. This unusual feature of water is related to ice having a lower density than liquid water. Increasing the pressure drives the water into the higher density phase, which causes melting.

Another interesting though not unusual feature of the phase diagram is the point where the solid-liquid phase line meets the liquid-gas phase line. The intersection is referred to as the triple point. At the triple point, all three phases can coexist.

Experimentally, the phase lines are relatively easy to map due to the interdependence of temperature and pressure that develops when multiple phases forms. Consider a test apparatus consisting of a closed and well insulated cylinder equipped with a piston. By charging the right amount of water and applying heat, the system can be brought to any point in the gas region of the phase diagram. If the piston is slowly lowered, the system will trace a curve of increasing temperature and pressure within the gas region of the phase diagram. At the point where liquid begins to condense, the direction of the temperature and pressure curve will abruptly change to trace along the phase line until all of the water has condensed.

PHASE TRANSITIONS

When a substance undergoes a phase transition i.e changes from one state of matter to another, it usually either takes up or releases energy. For example, when water evaporates, the kinetic energy expended as the evaporating molecules escape the attractive forces of the liquid is reflected in a decrease in temperature. The amount of energy required to induce the transition is more than the amount required to heat the water from room temperature to just short of boiling temperature, which is why evaporation is useful for cooling. The reverse process, condensation, releases heat. The heat energy, or enthalpy, associated with a solid to liquid transition is the enthalpy of fusion and that associated with a solid to gas transition is the enthalpy of sublimation.

MAGMA-MIXING, MINGLING AND IMMISCIBILITY

Magma mixing is the mixing of two or more magmas or magma batches to form a hybrid magma. The resulting magma commonly inherits intermediate properties of the two parent magmas.

While this definition makes the process of magma mixing sound straight forward, the occurrence of mixed rocks, where for example both rhyolite and basalt are found within the same rock mass, suggest a more complex process.

Magma mixing can occur by two end-member processes: blending, and mingling.

Blending involves the homogeneous mixing of two or more unlike magmas, forming a chemically and physically homogeneous mixture with an intermediate composition. In contrast, many features recorded in "mixed rocks" indicate that blending is less important than mingling.

Mingling of dissimilar magmas produces a heterogeneous mixture containing discrete portions of the end-member magmas, (eg: rhyolite and basalt), due to the incomplete mixing of the different magmas. The resulting igneous rock is chemically intermediate between the two original magmas. However, the rock comprises spatially discrete portions of each rock type and is very heterogeneous.

CONTROLLING FACTORS

Mixing depends to a large extent on physical properties of magma, especially, viscosity and density.

VISCOSITY

Viscosity is a measure of the internal resistance of a liquid body to flow. It is the inverse of mobility or fluidity. Water is highly fluid and has a very low viscosity, whereas honey, or heavy machine oil is much more viscous. Viscosity varies with temperature and composition of liquid.

Viscosity increases with an increase in SiO_2 in a magma.

DENSITY

Density is the mass per unit volume of a substance. We are used to thinking of density (specific gravity, really) as it applies to a single mineral, but magmas are mixtures of substances. The only information we have is from whole rock chemistry. So, we calculate the density of a rock as the sum of the masses for all components of a substance divided by the sum of all their volumes.

$$p = \frac{\Sigma M_i * X_i}{\Sigma V_i * X_i}$$

where:

p = density

Σ = sum of all components

M_i = molecular weight of component i

X_i = mole fraction of component i

V_i = partial molar volume of component i

More importantly, density varies with composition. Mafic melts such as basalts have a higher density relative to felsic melts. Increasing water content, regardless of composition, will lower the density of the melt.

Example

The photograph below is of a scoriaceous basalt with bands of rhyolite pumice. The sample is the result of two magmas of different composition coming into contact at or before the time of eruption. Cooling after eruption was rapid enough to "freeze" the mingling-action in place. What we see is incomplete mixing of the two magmas due to the density and viscosity contrasts that exist between them.

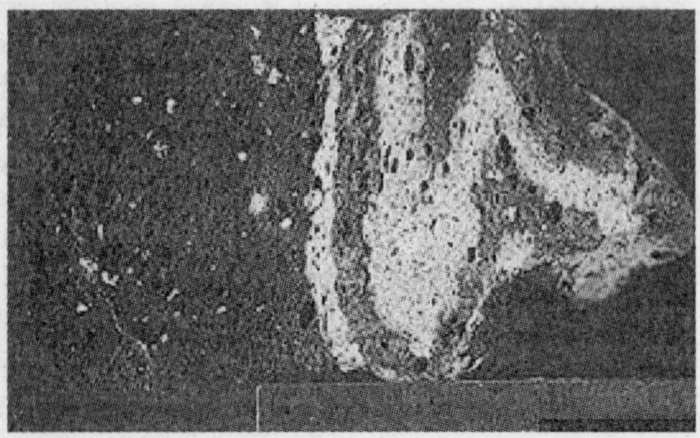

The two magmas (rhyolite and basalt) that formed the rock shown above may have come into contact via the eruption process or they may have occupied the same chamber prior to the eruption. In other words the pre-eruption situation may have involved two separate, but physically connected chambers, or a single, compositionally stratified magma chamber (shown below).

Single, Compositionally Stratified Chamber

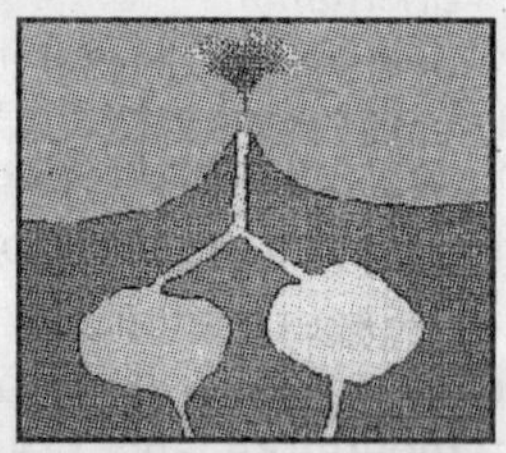

Separate Physically Connected Chamber

METAMORPHIC STRUCTURES AND TEXTURES

Metamorphic rocks have been changed, usually by heat and pressure, from their original condition into rock with new minerals and/or structures. Texture, structure, and mineral content of metamorphic rock depend both on its protolith (parent material) and metamorphic conditions. Presence of some specific minerals in a metamorphic rock can indicate the degree of heat and pressure it endured. Some metamorphic processes (e.g. tectonic collisions) distort large regions of the earth's crust.

Metamorphism (from the Greek words for "changing form") is the process by which rising temperature–and changes in other environmental conditions–transforms rocks and minerals. Metamorphism occurs in solid rock–like the transformations in the vase as the potter fires it in her kiln. Metamorphism can change any type of parent rock: sedimentary, igneous, or even another metamorphic rock. Metamorphism occurs because each mineral is stable only within a certain range of temperature, pressure, and chemical environment. If temperature or pressure rises above that range, or if chemicals are added to or removed from the rock, the rock's original minerals may decompose and their components recombine to form new minerals that are stable under the new conditions.

METAMORPHIC TEXTURES AND STRUCTURES

Most deformed metamorphic rocks possess some kind of preferred orientation. Preferred orientations may be exhibited as mesoscopic linear or planar structures that allow the rocks to split more easily in one direction than in others. One of the most familiar examples is cleavage in slate; a similar type of structure in metamorphic rocks of higher grade is schistosity. Foliation comprises a segregation of particular minerals into inconstant bands or contiguous lenticles that exhibit a common parallel orientation.

Slaty cleavage is probably the most familiar type of preferred orientation and occurs in rocks of low metamorphic grade. It is characteristic of slates and phyllites. It is independent of bedding, which it commonly intersects at high angles; and it reflects a highly developed preferred orientation of minerals, particularly of those belonging to the mica family.

Strain-slip cleavage occurs in fine-grained metamorphic rocks, where it may maintain a regular, though not necessarily constant, orientation. This regularity suggests some simple relationship between the cleavage and movement under regionally homogeneous stress in the final phase of deformation.

Foliation in a metamorphic rock is a very conspicuous feature, consisting of parallel bands or tabular lenticles formed of contrasting mineral assemblages such as quartz–feldspar and biotite–hornblende. It is characteristic of gneisses. This parallel orientation agrees with the direction of schistosity, if any is present in nearby rocks. Foliation, therefore, would seem to be related to the same system of stress and strain responsible for the development of schistosity. However, the influence of stress becomes less at higher temperatures and so schistosity tends to disappear in rocks of high-grade metamorphism. By contrast, foliation becomes a more significant feature. What is more, minerals of flaky habit are replaced in the higher grades of metamorphism by minerals such as garnet [$Fe_3Al_2(SiO_4)_3$], kyanite (Al_2SiO_5), sillimanite (Al_2SiO_5), diopside [$Ca,Mg(Si_2O_6)$] and orthoclase.

ISOGRAD

In geology, an isograd is a plane of constant metamorphic grade in the field; it separates metamorphic zones of different metamorphic index minerals. On geologic maps focusing on metamorphic terranes (or landscapes underlain by metamorphic rocks), the boundaries between rocks of different metamorphic grade are commonly demarcated by isograd lines. The garnet isograd, for example, would mark the first occurrence of garnet in the rocks.

The minerals present in a metamorphic rock are important because laboratory experiments at high pressures and temperatures have provided a lot of information on the pressure and temperature conditions under which certain metamorphic minerals form. For example, with increasing temperature and pressure the first minerals to form from a shale are micas, particularly chlorite and biotite. With increasing temperature and pressure garnet appears, and then kyanite (at relatively high pressure) or sillimanite (at relatively high temperature). The metamorphic zone with chlorite can be referred to as the chlorite zone, the zone with garnet as garnet zone, and so forth. To communicate this easily, the dominant metamorphic minerals in schists are usually included in the name, as, for example, garnet schist, or garnet-staurolite schist, and so forth.

FACIES

In geology, facies are a body of rock with specified characteristics. [Reading (1996)] Ideally, a facies is a distinctive rock unit that forms under certain conditions of sedimentation, reflecting a particular process or environment.

The term facies was introduced by the Swiss geologist Amanz Gressly in 1838 and was part of his significant contribution to the foundations of modern stratigraphy, [Cross and Homewood (1997)] which replaced the earlier notions of Neptunism.

WALTHER'S LAW OF FACIES

Walther's Law of Facies, named after the geologist Johannes Walther, states that the vertical succession of facies reflects lateral changes in environment. Conversely, it states that when a depositional environment "migrates" laterally, sediments of one depositional environment come to lie on top of another. A classic example of this law is the vertical stratigraphic succession that typifies marine trangressions and regressions. However, the law is not applicable where the contact between different lithologies is non-conformable (i.e. sedimentation was not continuous), or in instances of rapid environmental change where non-adjacent environments may replace one another.

FACIES TYPES

Sedimentary facies

Bodies of sediment recognizably different from adjacent sediment deposited in a different depositional environment. Generally, facies are distinguished by what aspect of the rock or sediment is being studied. Thus, facies based on petrological characters such as grain size and mineralogy are called lithofacies, whereas facies based on fossil content are called biofacies.

These facies types are usually further subdivided, for examples, you might refer to a "tan, cross-bedded oolitic limestone facies" or a "shale facies". The characteristics of the rock unit come from the depositional environment and original composition. Sedimentary facies reflect depositional environment, each facies being a distinct kind of sediment for that area or environment.

Since its inception, the facies concept has been extended to related geological concepts. For example, characteristic associations of organic microfossils, and particulate organic material, in rocks or sediments, are called palynofacies. Discrete seismic units are similarly referred to as seismic facies.

Metamorphic facies

The sequence of minerals that develop during progressive metamorphism (that is, metamorphism at progressively higher temperatures and/or pressures) define a facies series.

THERMOBAROMETRY

Thermobarometry is the quantitative determination of the temperature and pressure at which a metamorphic or igneous rock reached chemical equilibrium. The term "classical" thermobarometry refers to methods for calculating the P-T conditions of a specific chemical reaction.

If one knows the pressure (P) and temperature (T) at which an igneous or metamorphic rock equilibrated, one can determine a lot about where in the Earth the rock formed and how the rock formed. For example, some tectonic processes are associated with characteristic pressures and temperatures: e.g., low temperatures at high pressure occur only in subduction zones.

Mineral assemblages and textures may provide information about the conditions at which a rock equilibrated. In metamorphic rocks, we use qualitative terms such as low-grade, medium-grade, and high-grade (and even 'medium-low' or 'very high grade') to describe the approximate temperature conditions of metamorphism. These designations do not provide information about pressure, and are therefore not useful for describing subduction zone rocks.

Other methods for characterizing metamorphic conditions include:

1. **index minerals** : characteristic minerals that provide an indication of the temperature (and, in some cases, pressure) conditions at which a rock formed (e.g., kyanite in metamorphosed shale; magmatic epidote in plutons and volcanic rocks). Not all rocks have a suitable bulk composition to produce index minerals.
2. **metamorphic facies** : assemblages of minerals, each characteristic for a particular bulk composition and indicating the range of pressure-temperature conditions at which the rock equilibrated. For example, high-pressure - low-temperature conditions characterize the blueschist facies.

Some igneous assemblages are also characteristic of crystallization within particular ranges of temperature/pressure conditions. But the question is qualitative methods for determining P-T conditions 'good enough'?

Qualitative methods don't necessarily provide information about both pressure and temperature. In addition, qualitative techniques in some cases give only a minimum pressure or temperature: e.g., the presence of a high-T index mineral may not tell you whether the rock formed at 700°C or 1000°C, and the occurrence of eclogite facies minerals may not tell you whether the rock formed at a depth of 40 km or 75 km. This degree of uncertainty makes the interpretation of metamorphic and tectonic processes difficult.

Conceptual basis of Thermobarometry : The compositions of coexisting minerals in equilibrium are related by the thermodynamic properties of the minerals to the pressure and temperature conditions of equilibration. Thermometers are assemblages that form by reactions that are sensitive to temperature but not (much) to pressure. Barometers are assemblages that are sensitive to pressure but not (much) to temperatures. Not all rocks contain assemblages that make suitable thermometers or barometers.

UNCERTAINTIES

Uncertainties in thermobarometric calculations can be determined by propagating errors from all stages of the P-T determinations: the mineral composition analyses, the thermodynamic data, and the calibration method. Typical uncertainties are ± 50°C, ± 1 kbar.

Sources of error in thermobarometry

Common sources of error in thermobarometric calculations include:

- The assumption that the minerals record equilibrium conditions may not be valid.
- The choice of mineral compositions to use in thermobarometric calculations is easy if all phases are homogeneous, but if minerals are zoned, the selection of compositions to use can be more uncertain.
- The stability of minerals may be affected by the presence of elements that are difficult to analyze with standard techniques. For example, electron microprobe analyses do not distinguish between Fe^{2+} and Fe^{3+}, but the difference is important. A thermobarometric calculation may be substantially in error if all Fe is assumed to be Fe^{2+} for minerals that contain substantial Fe^{3+}.
- Thermobarometric calculations rely on thermodynamic data and a 'calibration' that allows mineral composition to be related to temperature or pressure. The mineral compositions and crystal structures in the rock being analyzed should not be too different from the compositions and structures on which the calibrations are based.
- Temperature calculations require an estimation of pressure, and pressure calculations require an estimation of pressure. You therefore either need to know one variable, or use a thermometer or barometer that is very insensitive to the other variable. Hence, the best thermometers have nearly vertical slopes on a P-T diagram and the best barometers have nearly horizontal slopes.

METAMORPHISM OF PELITES, MAFIC-ULTRA MAFIC ROCKS AND SILICEOUS DOLOMITES

PELITE

Pelite (Greek Pelos, Clay) is a descriptive name for a clastic rock with a grain size of less than 1/16mm (originally sand or silt) Examples include slate and mudstone. The equivalent Latin-derived term is Lutite. Pelite is more commonly used for a metamorphosed sediment.

The term pelite is not to be confused with pilite, a rarely used name for an altered olivine that has partially pseudomorphically replaced by an assemblage of carbonate–chlorite–actinolite and can be identified only in a thin section.

Example of Pelites in Southern Africa

- Barberton Granite-Greenstone Belt, Mpumalanga
- Damara Orogen, Namibia
- Contact metamorphism associated with Bushveld Complex, Limpopo Province

ULTRAMAFIC ROCK

Ultramafic (also referred to as ultrabasic) rocks are igneous and meta-igneous rocks with very low silica content (less than 45%), generally more than 18% MgO, high FeO, low potassium, and are composed of usually greater than 90% mafic minerals (dark colored, high magnesium and iron content). The Earth's mantle is composed of ultramafic rocks.

METAMORPHIC ULTRAMAFIC ROCKS

Metamorphism of ultramafic rocks in the presence of water and/or carbon dioxide results in two main classes of metamorphic ultramafic rock; talc carbonate and serpentinite.

Talc carbonation reactions occur in ultramafic rocks at lower greenschist through to granulite facies metamorphism when the rock in question is subjected to metamorphism and the metamorphic fluid has more than 10% molar proportion of carbon dioxide.

When the metamorphic fluids in contact with the ultramafic rock have less than 10% CO_2 the metamorphic reactions favor serpentinisation reactions, resulting in chlorite-serpentine-amphibole type assemblages.

MAFIC

Mafic is an adjective describing a silicate mineral or rock that is rich in magnesium and iron; the term was derived by contracting "magnesium" and "ferric". Most mafic minerals are dark in color and the relative density is greater than 3gm/cc. Common rock-forming mafic minerals include olivine, pyroxene, amphibole, and biotite. Common mafic rocks include basalt and gabbro.

In terms of chemistry, mafic rocks are on the other side of the rock spectrum from the felsic rocks. The term roughly corresponds to the older basic rock class.

Mafic lava, before cooling, has a low viscosity, in comparison to felsic lava, due to the lower silica content in mafic magma. Water and other volatiles can more easily and gradually escape from mafic lava, so eruptions of volcanoes made of mafic lavas are less explosively violent than felsic lava eruptions. Most mafic lava volcanoes are oceanic volcanoes, like Hawaii.

PLATE TECTONICS AND METAMORPHISM

In general, metamorphic rocks do not drastically change chemical composition during metamorphism, except in the special case where metasomatism is involved (such as in the production of skarns). The changes in mineral assemblages are due to changes in the temperature and pressure conditions of metamorphism. Thus, the mineral assemblages that are observed must be an indication of the temperature and pressure environment that the rock was subjected to. This pressure and temperature environment is referred to as Metamorphic Facies. (This is similar to the concept of sedimentary facies, in that a sedimentary facies is also a set of environmental conditions present during deposition). The sequence of metamorphic facies observed in any metamorphic terrain, depends on the geothermal gradient that was present during metamorphism.

METAMORPHISM AND PLATE TECTONICS

At present, the geothermal gradients observed are strongly affected by plate tectonics.

- Along zones where subduction is occurring, magmas are generated near the subduction zone and intrude into shallow levels of the crust. Because high temperature is brought near the surface, the geothermal gradient in these regions becomes high (geothermal gradient "A" in the figure above) and may be in the range of 50° to 70°C/km, and contact metamorphism (hornfels facies) results.
- Because compression occurs along a subduction margin (the oceanic crust moves toward the volcanic arc) rocks may be pushed down to depths along either a normal or slightly higher than normal geothermal gradient 25°C/km ("B" in the figure above). Actually the geothermal gradient is likely to be slightly higher than B (30°C/km), because the passage of magma through the crust will tend to heat the crust somewhat. In these regions we expect to see greenschist, amphibolite, and granulite facies metamorphic rocks.

Along a subduction zone, relatively cool oceanic lithosphere is pushed down to great depths. This results in producing a low geothermal gradient (temperature increases slowly with depth) of 10-15°C/km. This low geothermal gradient ("C") in the diagram above, results in metamorphism into the blueschist and eclogite facies.

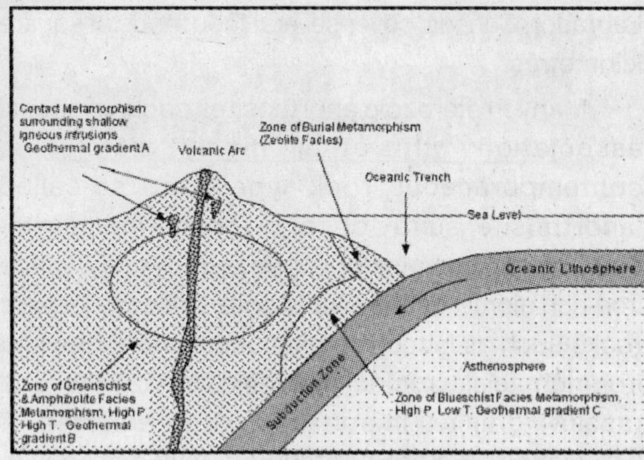

Fig.: Illustration showing relationship between Plate tectonics and metamorphism

ANORTHOSITES

Anorthosite is a phaneritic, intrusive igneous rock characterized by a predominance of plagioclase feldspar (90–100%), and a minimal mafic component (0–10%). Pyroxene, ilmenite, magnetite, and olivine are the mafic minerals most commonly present.

Anorthosite on Earth can be divided into two types: Proterozoic anorthosite (also known as massif or massif-type anorthosite) and Archean anorthosite. These two types of anorthosite have different modes of occurrence, appear to be restricted to different periods in Earth's history, and are thought to have had different origins.

PROTEROZOIC ANORTHOSITE

Although a few Proterozoic anorthosite bodies were emplaced either late in the Archean Eon, or early in the Phanerozoic Eon, the vast majority of Proterozoic anorthosites were emplaced, as their name suggests, during the Proterozoic Eon (ca. 2,500 - 542 Ma).

MODE OF OCCURRENCE

Anorthosite plutons occur in a wide range of sizes. Some smaller plutons, exemplified by many anorthosite bodies in the U.S. and Harris in Scotland, cover only a few dozen square kilometres. Larger plutons, like the Mt. Lister Anorthosite, in northern

Labrador, Canada, cover several thousands of square kilometres.

Many Proterozoic anorthosites occur in spatial association with other highly distinctive, contemporaneous rock types (the so-called 'anorthosite suite' or 'anorthosite-mangerite-charnockite complex'). These rock types include iron-rich diorite, gabbro, and norite; leucocratic mafic rocks such as leucotroctolite and leuconorite; and iron-rich felsic rocks, including monzonite and rapakivi granite. Importantly, large volumes of ultramafic rocks are not found in association with Proterozoic anorthosites.

Occurrences of Proterozoic anorthosites are commonly referred to as 'massifs'. However, there is some question as to what name would best describe any occurrence of anorthosite together with the rock types mentioned above. Early works used the term 'complex' The term 'plutonic suite' has been applied to some large occurrences in northern Labrador, Canada; however, it has been suggested (in 2004-2005) that 'batholith' would be a better term.

The areal extent of anorthosite batholiths ranges from relatively small (dozens or hundreds of square kilometres) to nearly 20,000 km^2 (7,700 sq mi), in the instance of the Nain Plutonic Suite in northern Labrador, Canada.

Major occurrences of Proterozoic anorthosite are found in the southwest U.S., the Appalachian Mountains, eastern Canada, across southern Scandinavia and eastern Europe. Mapped onto the Pangaean continental configuration of that eon, these occurrences are all contained in a single straight belt, and must all have been emplaced intracratonally. The conditions and constraints of this pattern of origin and distribution are not clear.

Anorthosites are also common in layered intrusions. Anorthosite in these layered intrusions can form as cumulate layers in the upper parts of the intrusive complex or as later-stage intrusions into the layered intrusion complex.

PHYSICAL CHARACTERISTICS OF ANORTHOSITES

Since they are primarily composed of plagioclase feldspar, most of Proterozoic anorthosites appear, in outcrop, to be grey or bluish. Individual plagioclase crystals may be black, white, blue, or grey, and may exhibit an iridescence known as labradorescence on fresh surfaces. The feldspar variety labradorite is commonly present in anorthosites. Mineralogically, labradorite is a compositional term for any calcium-rich plagioclase feldspar containing between 50–70 molecular per cent anorthite (An 50–70), regardless of whether it shows labradorescence. The mafic mineral in Proterozoic anorthosite may be clinopyroxene, orthopyroxene, olivine, or, more rarely, amphibole. Oxides, such as magnetite or ilmenite, are also common.

Most anorthosite plutons are very coarse grained; that is, the individual plagioclase crystals and the accompanying mafic mineral are more than a few centimetres long. Less commonly, plagioclase crystals are megacrystic, or larger than one metre long. However, most Proterozoic anorthosites are deformed, and such large plagioclase crystals have recrystallized to form smaller crystals, leaving only the outline of the larger crystals behind.

While many Proterozoic anorthosite plutons appear to have no large-scale relict igneous structures (having instead post-emplacement deformational structures), some do have igneous layering, which may be defined by crystal size, mafic content, or chemical characteristics. Such layering clearly has origins with a rheologically liquid-state magma.

CHEMICAL AND ISOTOPIC CHARACTERISTICS OF ANORTHOSITES

The composition of plagioclase feldspar in Proterozoic anorthosites is most commonly between An_{40} and An_{60} (40-60% anorthite). This compositional range is intermediate, and is one of the characteristics which distinguish Proterozoic anorthosites from Archean anorthosites. Mafic minerals in Proterozoic anorthosites have a wide range of composition, but are not generally highly magnesian.

The trace-element chemistry of Proterozoic anorthosites, and the associated rock types, has been examined in some detail by researchers with the aim of arriving at a plausible genetic theory. However, there is still little agreement on just what the results mean for anorthosite genesis; see the 'Origins' section below. A very short list of results, including results for rocks thought to be related to Proterozoic anorthosites.

Some research has focused on neodymium (Nd) and strontium (Sr) isotopic determinations for anorthosites, particularly for anorthosites of the Nain Plutonic Suite (NPS). Such isotopic determinations are of use in gauging the viability of prospective sources for magmas that gave rise to anorthosites. Some results are detailed below in the 'Origins' section.

ORIGINS OF PROTEROZOIC ANORTHOSITES

The origins of Proterozoic anorthosites have been a subject of theoretical debate for many decades. A brief synopsis of this problem is as follows. The problem begins with the generation of magma, the necessary precursor of any igneous rock.

Magma generated by small amounts of partial melting of the mantle is generally of basaltic composition. Under normal conditions, the composition of basaltic magma requires it to crystallize between 50 and 70% plagioclase, with the bulk of the remainder of the magma crystallizing as mafic minerals. However, anorthosites are defined by a high plagioclase content (90–100% plagioclase), and are not found in association with contemporaneous ultramafic rocks. This is now known as 'the anorthosite problem'. Proposed solutions to the anorthosite problem have been diverse, with many of the proposals drawing on different geological subdisciplines.

It was suggested early in the history of anorthosite debate that a special type of magma, anorthositic magma, had been generated at depth, and emplaced into the crust. However, the solidus of an anorthositic magma is too high for it to exist as a liquid for very long at normal ambient crustal temperatures, so this appears to be unlikely. The presence of water vapour has been shown to lower the solidus temperature of anorthositic magma to more reasonable values, but most anorthosites are relatively dry. It may be postulated, then, that water vapour be driven off by subsequent metamorphism of the anorthosite, but some anorthosites are undeformed, thereby invalidating the suggestion.

The discovery, in the late 1970s, of anorthositic dykes in the Nain Plutonic Suite, suggested that the possibility of anorthositic magmas existing at crustal temperatures needed to be reexamined. However, the dykes were later shown to be more complex than was originally thought. In summary, though liquid-state processes clearly operate in some anorthosite plutons, the plutons are probably not derived from anorthositic magmas.

Many researchers have argued that anorthosites are the products of basaltic magma, and that mechanical removal of mafic minerals has occurred. Since the mafic minerals are not found with the anorthosites, these minerals must have been left at either a deeper level or the base of the crust. A typical theory is as follows: partial melting of the mantle generates a basaltic magma, which does not immediately ascend into the crust. Instead, the basaltic magma forms a large magma chamber at the base of the crust and fractionates large amounts of mafic minerals, which sink to the bottom of the chamber. The cocrystallizing plagioclase crystals float, and eventually are emplaced into the crust as anorthosite plutons. Most of the sinking mafic minerals form ultramafic cumulates which stay at the base of the crust.

HIGH-ALUMINA ORTHOPYROXENE MEGACRYSTS

The high-alumina orthopyroxene megacrysts (HAOM) have, like Proterozoic anorthosites, been the subject of great debate, although a tentative consensus about their origin appears to have emerged. The peculiar characteristic worthy of such debate is reflected in their name. Normal orthopyroxene has chemical composition $(Fe,Mg)_2Si_2O_6$, whereas the HAOM have anomalously large amounts of aluminium (up to about 9%) in their atomic structure.

Because the solubility of aluminium in orthopyroxene increases with increasing pressure, many researchers,have suggested that the HAOM crystallized at depth, near the base of the Earth's crust. The maximum amounts of aluminium correspond to a 30–35 km (19–22 mi) depth.

Other researchers consider the chemical compositions of the HAOM to be the product of rapid crystallization at moderate or low pressures.

ARCHAEAN ANORTHOSITE

Smaller amounts of anorthosite were emplaced during the Archaean eon (ca 3,800-2,400 Ma), although most have been dated between 3,200 and 2,800 Ma. They are distinct texturally and mineralogically from Proterozoic anorthosite bodies. Their most characteristic feature is the presence of equant megacrysts of plagioclase surrounded by a fine-grained mafic groundmass.

ECONOMIC VALUE OF ANORTHOSITE

The primary economic value of anorthosite bodies is the titanium-bearing oxide ilmenite. However, some Proterozoic anorthosite bodies have large amounts of labradorite, which is quarried for its value as both a gemstone and a building material. Archean anorthosites, because they are calcium-rich, have large amounts of aluminium substituting for silicon; a few of these bodies are mined as ores of aluminium.

Anorthosite was prominently represented in rock samples brought back from the Moon, and is important in investigations of Mars, Venus, and meteorites.

CARBONATITE

Carbonatites are intrusive or extrusive igneous rocks defined by mineralogic composition consisting of greater than 50 per cent carbonate minerals. Carbonatites may be confused with marble, and may require geochemical verification.

Carbonatites usually occur as small plugs within zoned alkalic intrusive complexes, or as dikes, sills, breccias, and veins. They are, almost exclusively, associated with continental rift-related tectonic settings. The majority of carbonatites are Proterozoic or Phanerozoic in age. It seems that there has been a steady increase in the carbonatitic igneous activity through the Earth's history, from Archean to present.

Nearly all carbonatite occurrences are intrusives or subvolcanic intrusives. This is because carbonatite lava flows are unstable and react quickly in the atmosphere. Carbonatite lavas may not be as uncommon as thought, but have been poorly preserved throughout Earth's history.

Only one carbonatite volcano is known to have erupted in historical time, Ol Doinyo Lengai in Tanzania. It erupted the lowest temperature lava in the world, at 500-600°C. The lava is natrocarbonatite dominated by nyerereite and gregoryite.

GENESIS OF CARBONATITES

Carbonatites are rare, peculiar igneous rocks formed by unusual processes and from unusual source rocks. Three models of their formation exist:

- direct generation by very low degree partial melts in the mantle and melt differentiation
- liquid immiscibility between a carbonate melt and a silicate melt
- peculiar, extreme crystal fractionation

Evidence for each process exists, but the key is that these are unusual phenomena. Historically, carbonatites were thought to form by melting of limestone or marble by intrusion of magma, however geochemical and mineralogical data discount this.

MINERALOGY

Primary mineralogy is highly variable, but may include natrolite, sodalite, apatite, magnetite, barite, fluorite, ancylite group minerals, and other rare minerals not found in more common igneous rocks. Recognition of carbonatites may be difficult, especially as their mineralogy and texture may not differ much from marble save for the presence of igneous minerals. They may also be sources of mica or vermiculite.

Carbonatites are classed as calcitic sovite (coarse textured) and alvikite (finer textured) varieties or facies. The two are also distinguished by minor and trace element composition. The terms rauhaugite and beforsite refer to dolomite and ankerite rich occurrences respectively. The alkali-carbonatites are termed lengaite. Examples with 50 - 70% carbonate minerals are termed silico-carbonatites. Additionally carbonatites may be either enriched in magnetite and apatite or rare earth elements, fluorine and barium.

GEOCHEMISTRY

Carbonatite is composed predominatly of carbonate minerals and extremely unusual in its major element composition as compared to silicate igneous rocks, obviously because it is composed primarily of Na_2O and CaO plus CO_2.

Most carbonatites tend to include some silicate mineral fraction; by definition an igneous rock containing >50% carbonate minerals is classified as a carbonatite. Silicate minerals associated with such compositions are pyroxene, olivine, and silica-undersaturated minerals such as nepheline and other feldspathoids.

Geochemically, carbonatites are dominated by incompatible elements (Ba, Cs, Rb) and depletions in compatible elements (Hf, Zr, Ti). This together with their silica-undersaturated composition supports inferences that carbonatites are formed by low degrees of partial melting.

OCCURRENCE

Associated igneous rocks typically include ijolite, melteigite, teschenite, lamprophyres, phonolite, foyaite, shonkinite, silica undersaturated foid-bearing pyroxenite (essexite), and nepheline syenite.

Carbonatites are typically associated with undersaturated (low silica) igneous rocks that are either alkali (Na_2O and K_2O), ferric iron (Fe_2O_3) and zirconium-rich agpaitic rocks or alkali-poor, FeO-CaO-MgO-rich and zirconium-poor miaskitic rocks.

The Mount Weld carbonatite is unassociated with a belt or suite of alkaline igneous rocks, although calc-alkaline magmas are known in the region. The genesis of this Archaean carbonatite remains contentious as it is the sole example of an Archaean carbonatite in Australia.

INTRUSIVE MORPHOLOGY

Carbonatite is known to form in association with concentrically zoned complexes of alkaline-igneous rocks, the typical example of this being Phalaborwa, South Africa.

Chilean carbonatites take the form of sills, lopoliths and rare dikes are reported in the Guyana Shield.

The Mud Tank and Mount Weld carbonatites take the form of multi-stage cylindrical intrusive bodies with several distinct phases of carbonatite intrusion. Smaller carbonatite sills and dikes are present in other Proterozoic mobile belts in Australia, typically as dikes and discontinuous pods.

KNOWN EXAMPLES

Dozens of carbonatites are known including Oka and St. Honore, Quebec; Gem Park and Iron Hill, Colorado; Magnet Cove igneous complex, Arkansas; Mountain Pass, California; the Palabora Complex near Phalaborwa, South Africa; Jacupiranga, Brazil; Ayopaya, Bolivia; Kovdor, Russia, from India; the Mud Tank and Mount Weld, Australia; the Fen Complex, Norway.

The Ol Doinyo Lengai volcano, in the Great Rift Valley, Africa, is the world's only active carbonatite volcano. Other older carbonatite volcanoes are located in the same region, including Homa Mountain.

ECONOMIC IMPORTANCE

Carbonatites may contain economic or anomalous concentrations of rare earth elements, phosphorus, niobium - tantalum, uranium, thorium, copper, iron, titanium, vanadium, barium, fluorine, zirconium, and other rare or incompatible elements. Apatite, barite and vermiculite are among the industrially important minerals associated with some carbonatites.

Vein deposits of thorium, fluorite, or rare earth elements may be associated with carbonatites, and may be hosted internal to or within the metasomatized aureole of a carbonatite.

As an example the Palabora complex of South Africa has produced significant copper (as chalcopyrite, bornite and chalcocite), apatite, vermiculte along with lesser magnetite, linnaeite (cobalt), baddeleyite (zirconium-hafnium), and by-product gold, silver, nickel and platinum.

CHARNOCKITE

Charnockite is applied to any orthopyroxene-bearing granite, composed mainly of quartz, perthite or antiperthite and orthopyroxene (usually hypersthene), as an end-member of the charnockite series.

CHARNOCKITE SERIES

The Charnockite suite or series is a group of igneous rocks, variably metamorphosed of wide distribution and great importance in India, Ceylon, Madagascar and Africa. The name was given by Dr. T. H. Holland from the fact that the tombstone of Job Charnock, the founder of Kolkata, is made of a block of this rock.

COMPOSITION

The charnockite series includes rocks of many different types, some being acid and rich in quartz and microcline, others basic and full of pyroxene and olivine, while there are also intermediate varieties corresponding mineralogically to norites, quartz-norites and diorites. A special feature, recurring in many members of the group, is the presence of strongly pleochroic, reddish or green hypersthene. They may be named by adding orthopyroxene or specifally hypersthene to the normal igneous nomenclature (e.g. hypersthene-granite), but specific names are in widespread use such as norite, mangerite, enderbite, jotunite, farsundite, opdalite and charnockite (in the strict sense); equivalents of gabbro, monzonite, tonalite, monzodiorite, monzogranite, granodiorite and granite.

GEOLOGY

Many of the minerals of these rocks are schillerized, as they contain minute platy or rod-shaped inclusions, disposed parallel to certain crystallographic planes or axes. The reflection of light from the surfaces of these inclusions gives the minerals often a peculiar appearance, e.g. the quartz is blue and opalescent, the feldspar has a milky shimmer like moonshine, the hypersthene has a bronzy metalloidal gleam. Very often the different rock types occur in close association as one set forms bands alternating with another set,or veins traversing it, and where one facies appears the others also usually are found.

The term charnockite in this sense is consequently not the name of a rock, but of an assemblage of rock types. The assemblage is connected by origin, the differentiation of the same parent magma. The banded structure which these rocks commonly present in the field is only in a small measure due to plastic deformation, but is to a large extent original, and has been produced by flow in a viscous crystallizing intrusive magma, together with differentiation or segregation of the mass into bands of different chemical and mineralogical composition. There have also been, of course, earth movements acting on the solid rock at a later time and injection of dikes both parallel to and across the primary foliation.

DISTRIBUTION

A striking fact is the very wide distribution of rocks of this group in the southern hemisphere; but they, or rocks very similar to them, occur in Norway, France, Germany, Scotland and North America, though in these countries they have been mostly described as pyroxene granulites, pyroxene gneisses & anorthosites. They are usually of Proterozoic age (late Precambrian).

In India they form the Nilgiri Hills, the Shevaroys, the Biligirirangan Hills and part of the Western Ghats, extending southward to Cape Comorin and reappearing in Ceylon.

KHONDALITE

Khondalite is a regional rock name rooted in the history of petrological research in the Indian subcontinent. The use of the term remains overwhelmingly linked to this region, although it has been transported beyond its original use in India to Burma (Iyer, 1949), Sri Lanka (e.g., Vitanage, 1959), Vietnam, China, Antarctica and even the Grenville-age metamorphic terrane of the Adirondack Mountains in New York state, in North America. More than 95% (176 out of 182) of the records on khondalites in the MINLIB database are from India and Sri Lanka. Within India, most references to khondalite follow an arc of southern and eastern states: Kerala, Tamil Nadu, Andhra Pradesh and Orissa. The usage of the name khondalite dates to Walker (1902). Walker originated the term to refer to the suite of rocks including quartz- garnet-sillimanite- graphite gneisses, together with garnet gneiss, quartzofeldspathic gneiss and quartzite, which host manganese deposits in the state of Orissa.

Figure : A khondalite rock from Kerela, south India

The khondalite suite are a distinctive group of rocks, but the minimal "export" of the term beyond India and Sri Lanka led P.G. Cooray (J. Geol. Soc. India 51 no.5, p.7 10, May 1998) to suggest that it be dropped in favour of garnet-sillimanite granulite/ gneiss. In comparison, the charnockite suite, first described in Tamil Nadu, and often found in geographic proximity to the khondalites, were readily adopted by petrologists. Varietal names were added, principally in Scandinavia, the term is in use worldwide, and MINLIB now lists 770 records on charnockites, 1900 onwards.

THE KERALA KHONDALITE BELT

The Kerala khondalite belt contains three sets of interlayered rocks: (1) garnet- biotite ± orthopyroxene ± graphite gneisses; (2) khondalites (graphite- garnet- biotite- sillimanite ± cordierite gneisses); and (3) cordierite gneisses (garnet, biotite, cordierite ± orthopyroxene). The pre-metamorphic protoliths of these rocks were probably a spectrum of quartzitic, arkosic and argillaceous sediments, perhaps with interbedded felsic volcanic units (Chacko et al., 1992).

The name persists to this day - it appears useful within the subcontinent, a well-understood term, the physical conditions of metamorphism which generated these striking rocks now well-constrained by pressure-temperature estimates from numerous areas of India and beyond (Lal, 2003). Metamorphic terranes with khondalites may contain a range of metallic and industrial mineral deposits. Indian examples include iron and manganese oxides, bauxite, graphite and gemstones.

2. Structural Geology and Geotectonics

Theory of stress and strain. Behaviour of rocks under stress. Mohr circle. Various states of stress and their representation by Mohr circles. Different types of failure and sliding criteria. Geometry and mechanics of fracturing and conditions for reactivation of pre-existing discontinuities. Paleostress analyses. Common types of finite strain ellipsoids. L-, L-S-, and S-tectonic fabrics. Techniques of strain analysis. Particle paths and flow patterns. Progressiv strain history and methods for its determination. Deformation mechanisms. Role of fluids in deformation processes. Geometry and analyses of brittle-ductile and ductile shear zones. Sheath folds. Geometry and mechanics of development of folds, boudins, foliations and lineations. Interference patterns and structural analyses in areas of superposed folding. Fault-related folding. Gravity induced structures. Major tectonic features and associated structures in extensional, compressional-, and strike-slip terranes. Geological and geophysical characteristics of plate boundaries. Geodynamic evolution of Himalaya.

THEORY OF STRESS AND STRAIN

Within the Earth rocks are continually being subjected to forces that tend to bend them, twist them, or fracture them. When rocks bend, twist or fracture we say that they deform such as change in shape or size etc. The forces that cause deformations of rock are referred to as stresses empirically calculated as Force/unit area. To understand rock deformation we must first explore these forces or stresses.

STRESS AND STRAIN

Stress is a force applied over an area. One type of stress that we are all used to is a uniform stress, called pressure. A uniform stress is a stress wherein the forces act equally from all directions. In the Earth the pressure due to the weight of overlying rocks is a uniform stress, and is sometimes referred to as confining stress.

If stress is not equal from all directions then we say that the stress is a differential stress. Three kinds of differential stress occur.

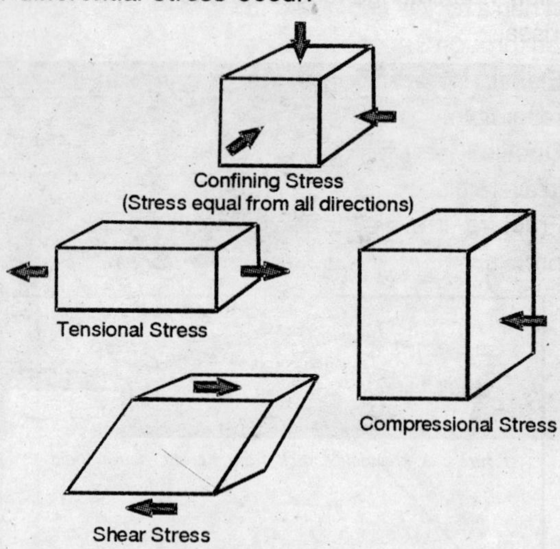

1. Tensional stress (or extensional stress), which stretches rock;
2. Compression stress, which squeezes rock; and
3. Shear stress, which result in slippage and translation.

STRAIN

When rocks deform they are said to strain. A strain is a change in size, shape, or volume of a material.

STRESS–STRAIN CURVE

During testing of a material sample, the stress-strain curve is a graphical representation of the relationship between stress, derived from measuring the load applied on the sample, and strain, derived from measuring the deformation of the sample, i.e. elongation, compression, or distortion. The nature of the curve varies from material to material. The following diagrams illustrate the stress-strain behaviour of typical materials in terms of the engineering stress and engineering strain where the stress and strain are calculated based on the original dimensions of the sample and not the instantaneous values.

STAGES OF DEFORMATION

When a rock is subjected to increasing stress it passes through 3 successive stages of deformation.

1. Elastic Deformation – wherein the strain is reversible.
2. Ductile Deformation – wherein the strain is irreversible.
3. Fracture - irreversible strain wherein the material breaks.

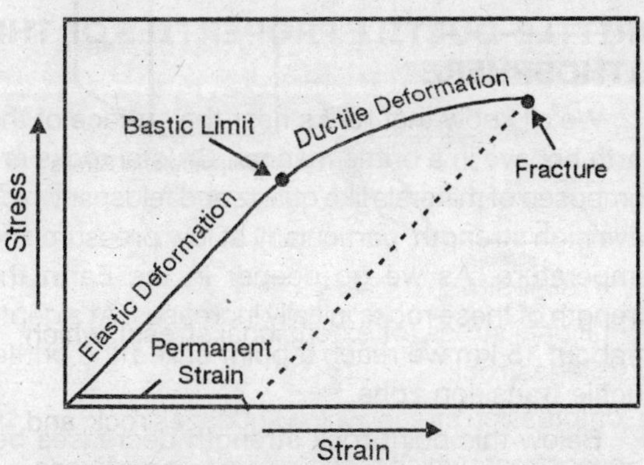

We can divide materials into two classes that depend on their relative behavior under stress.

1. Brittle materials have a small or large region of elastic behavior but only a small region of ductile behavior before they fracture.
2. Ductile materials have a small region of elastic behavior and a large region of ductile behavior before they fracture.

BRITTLE MATERIALS

Brittle materials such as concrete and carbon fiber do not have a yield point, and do not strain-harden. Therefore the ultimate strength and breaking strength are the same. A most unusual stress-strain curve is shown in the figure. Typical brittle materials like glass do not show any plastic deformation but fail while the deformation is elastic. One of the characteristics of a brittle failure is that the two broken parts can be reassembled to produce the same shape as the original component as there will not be a neck formation like in the case of ductile materials. A typical stress strain curve for a brittle material will be linear. Testing of several identical specimen, cast iron, or soil, tensile strength is negligible compared to the compressive strength and it is assumed zero for many engineering applications. Glass fibers have a tensile strength stronger than steel, but bulk glass usually does not. This is because of the Stress Intensity Factor associated with defects in the material. As the size of the sample gets larger, the size of defects also grows. In general, the tensile strength of a rope is always less than sum of the tensile strength of its individual fibers.

Brittle Material

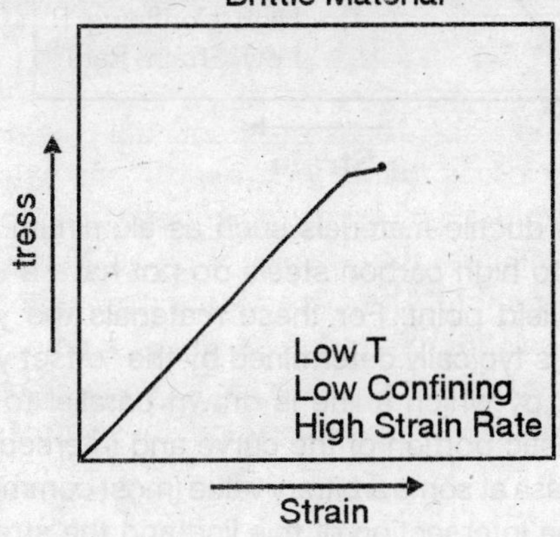

DUCTILE MATERIALS

Steel generally exhibits a very linear stress-strain relationship up to a well defined yield point. The linear portion of the curve is the elastic region and the slope is the modulus of elasticity or Young's Modulus. After the yield point, the curve typically decreases slightly because of dislocations escaping from Cottrell atmospheres. As deformation continues, the stress increases on account of strain hardening until it reaches the ultimate strength. Until this point, the cross-sectional area decreases uniformly because of Poisson contractions. The actual rupture point is in the same vertical line as the visual rupture point.

However, beyond this point a neck forms where the local cross-sectional area decreases more quickly than the rest of the sample resulting in an increase in the true stress. On an engineering stress–strain curve this is seen as a decrease in the stress. Conversely, if the curve is plotted in terms of true stress and true strain the stress will continue to rise until failure. Eventually the neck becomes unstable and the specimen ruptures (fractures).

Ductile Material

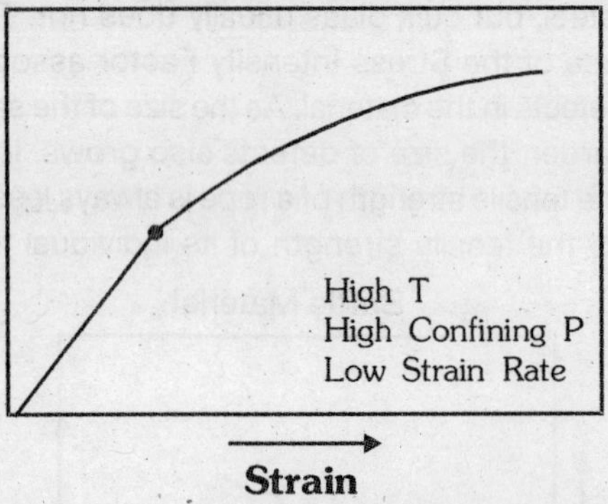

Less ductile materials such as aluminum and medium to high carbon steels do not have a well-defined yield point. For these materials the yield strength is typically determined by the "offset yield method", by which a line is drawn parallel to the linear elastic portion of the curve and intersecting the abscissa at some arbitrary value (most commonly 0.2%). The intersection of this line and the stress-strain curve is reported as the yield point.

There are factors that affect the behavior of material, they are

1. Temperature - At high temperature molecules and their bonds can stretch and move, thus materials will behave in more ductile manner. At low Temperature, materials are brittle.
2. Confining Pressure - At high confining pressure materials are less likely to fracture because the pressure of the surroundings tends to hinder the formation of fractures. At low confining stress, material will be brittle and tend to fracture sooner.
3. Strain rate – At high strain rates material tends to fracture. At low strain rates more time is available for individual atoms to move and therefore ductile behavior is favored.
4. Composition – Some minerals, like quartz, olivine, and feldspars are very brittle. Others, like clay minerals, micas, and calcite are more ductile This is due to the chemical bond types that hold them together. Thus, the mineralogical composition of the rock will be a factor in determining the deformational behavior of the rock. Another aspect is presence or absence of water. Water appears to weaken the chemical bonds and forms films around mineral grains along which slippage can take place. Thus wet rock tends to behave in ductile manner, while dry rocks tend to behave in brittle manner.

BRITTLE-DUCTILE PROPERTIES OF THE LITHOSPHERE

We all know that rocks near the surface of the Earth behave in a brittle manner. Crustal rocks are composed of minerals like quartz and feldspar which have high strength, particularly at low pressure and temperature. As we go deeper in the Earth the strength of these rocks initially increases. At a depth of about 15 km we reach a point called the brittle-ductile transition zone.

Below this point rock strength decreases because fractures become closed and the temperature is higher, making the rocks behave in a ductile manner. At the base of the crust the rock type changes to peridotite which is rich in olivine. Olivine is stronger than the minerals that make up most crustal rocks, so the upper part of the mantle is again strong. But, just as in the crust, increasing temperature eventually predominates and at a depth of about 40 km the brittle-ductile transition zone in the mantle occurs. Below this point rocks behave in an increasingly ductile manner.

MOHR CIRCLE

MOHR'S CIRCLE

Introduced by Otto Mohr in 1882, Mohr's Circle illustrates principal stresses and stress transformations via a graphical format,

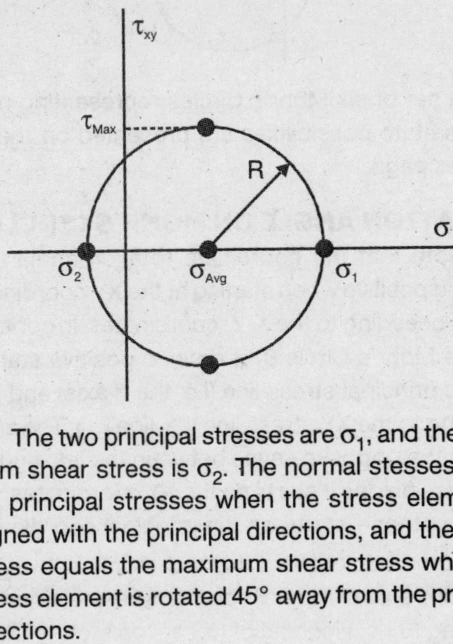

The two principal stresses are σ_1, and the maximum shear stress is σ_2. The normal stesses equal the principal stresses when the stress element is aligned with the principal directions, and the shear stress equals the maximum shear stress when the stress element is rotated 45° away from the principal directions.

As the stress element is rotated away from the principal (or maximum shear) directions, the normal and shear stress components will always lie on Mohr's Circle.

Mohr's Circle was the leading tool used to visualize relationships between normal and shear stresses, and to estimate the maximum stresses, before hand-held calculators became popular. Even today, Mohr's Circle is still widely used by engineers all over the world.

DERIVATION OF MOHR'S CIRCLE

To establish Mohr's Circle, we first recall the stress transformation formulas for plane stress at a given location,

$$\begin{cases} \sigma_{x'} - \dfrac{\sigma_x + \sigma_y}{2} = \dfrac{\sigma_x - \sigma_y}{2}\cos 2\theta + \tau_{xy}\sin 2\theta \\ \tau_{x'y'} = -\dfrac{\sigma_x - \sigma_y}{2}\sin 2\theta + \tau_{xy}\cos 2\theta \end{cases}$$

Using a basic trigonometric relation ($\cos^2 2\theta + \sin^2 2\theta = 1$) to combine the two above equations we have,

$$\left(\sigma_{x'} - \frac{\sigma_x + \sigma_y}{2}\right)^2 + \tau_{x'y'}2 = \left(\frac{\sigma_x - \sigma_y}{2}\right)^2 + \tau_{xy}2$$

This is the equation of a circle, plotted on a graph where the abscissa is the normal stress and the ordinate is the shear stress. This is easier to see if we interpret σ_x and σ_y as being the two principal stresses, and τ_{xy} as being the maximum shear stress. Then we can define the average stress, σ_{avg}, and a "radius" R (which is just equal to the maximum shear stress),

$$\sigma_{AVG} = \frac{\sigma_x + \sigma_y}{2} \qquad R = \sqrt{\left(\frac{\sigma_x - \sigma_y}{2}\right)^2 + \tau_{xy}2}$$

The circle equation above now takes on a more familiar form, $\left(\sigma_{x'} - \sigma_{AVG}\right)^2 + \tau_{x'y'}2 = R^2$

The circle is centered at the average stress value, and has a radius R equal to the maximum shear stress, as shown in the figure below,

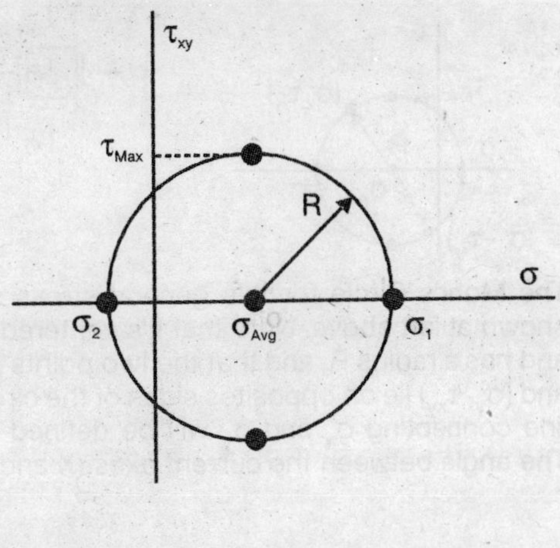

PRINCIPAL STRESSES FROM MOHR'S CIRCLE

A chief benefit of Mohr's circle is that the principal stresses σ_1 and σ_2 and the maximum shear stress max are obtained immediately after drawing the circle,

$$\begin{cases}\sigma_{1,2} = \sigma_{Avg} \pm R \\ \tau_{Max} = R\end{cases}$$

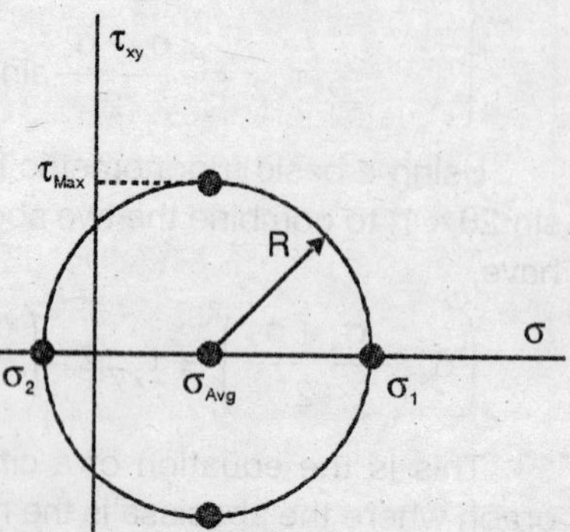

where,

$$\sigma_{Avg} = \frac{\sigma_x + \sigma_y}{2} \qquad R = \sqrt{\left(\frac{\sigma_x - \sigma_y}{2}\right)^2 + \tau_{xy} 2}$$

PRINCIPAL DIRECTIONS FROM MOHR'S CIRCLE

Mohr's Circle can be used to find the directions of the principal axes. To show this, first suppose that the normal and shear stresses, σ_x, σ_y, and τ_{xy}, are obtained at a given point O in the body. They are expressed relative to the coordinates XY, as shown in the stress element at right below.

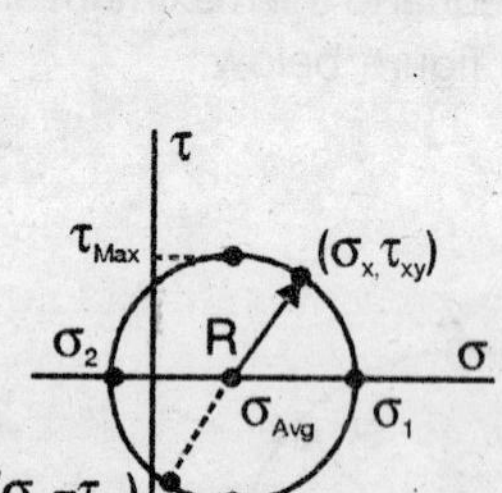

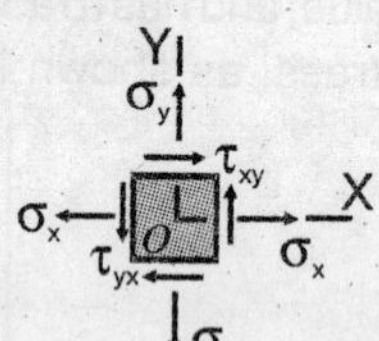

The Mohr's Circle for this general stress state is shown at left above. Note that it's centered at σ_{avg} and has a radius R, and that the two points $\{\sigma_x, \tau_{xy}\}$ and $\{\sigma_y, \tau_{xy}\}$ lie on opposites sides of the circle. The line connecting σ_x and σ_y will be defined as L_{xy}. The angle between the current axes (X and Y) and the principal axes is defined as θ_p, and is equal to one half the angle between the line L_{xy} and the σ-axis as shown in the schematic below,

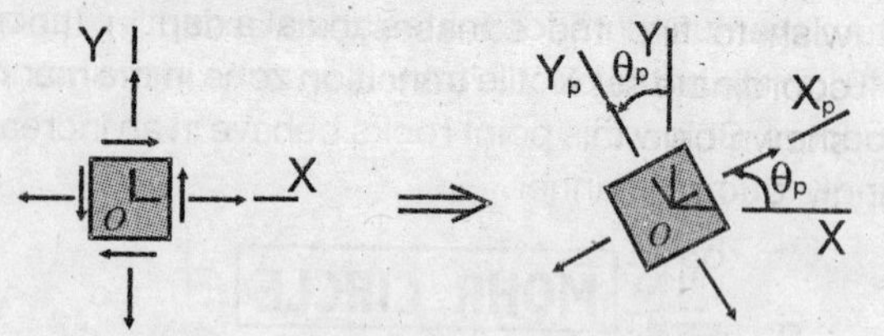

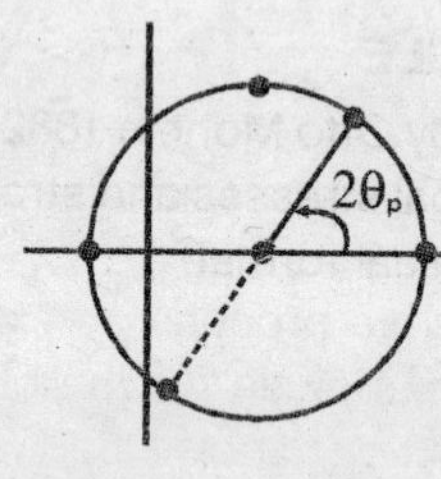

A set of six Mohr's Circles representing most stress state possibilities are presented on the examples page.

ROTATION ANGLE ON MOHR'S CIRCLE

Note that the coordinate rotation angle θ_p is defined positive when starting at the XY coordinates and proceeding to the X_pY_p coordinates. In contrast, on the Mohr's Circle θ_p is defined positive starting on the principal stress line (i.e. the σ-axis) and proceeding to the XY stress line (i.e. line L_{xy}). The angle θ_p has the opposite sense between the two figures, because on one it starts on the XY coordinates, and on the other it starts on the principal coordinates.

Some books avoid this dichotomy between θ_p on Mohr's Circle and θ_p on the stress element by locating (θ_x, τ_{xy}) instead of (σ_x, τ_{xy}) on Mohr's Circle. This will switch the polarity of θ_p on the circle. Whatever method you choose, the bottom line is that an opposite sign is needed either in the interpretation or in the plotting to make Mohr's Circle physically meaningful.

STRESS TRANSFORM BY MOHR'S CIRCLE

Mohr's Circle can be used to transform stresses from one coordinate set to another, similar that that described on the plane stress page.

Suppose that the normal and shear stresses, σ_x, σ_y, and τ_{xy}, are obtained at a point O in the body, expressed with respect to the coordinates XY. We wish to find the stresses expressed in the new coordinate set X'Y', rotated an angle θ from XY, as shown below:

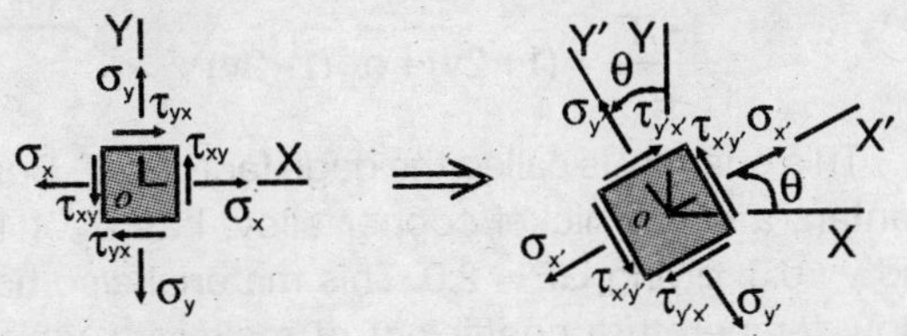

Stresses at given coordinate system *Stresses transformed to another coordinate*

To do this we proceed as follows:

- Draw Mohr's circle for the given stress state (σ_x, σ_y, and τ_{xy}; shown below).
- Draw the line L_{xy} across the circle from (σ_x, τ_{xy}) to (σ_y, τ_{xy}).
- Rotate the line L_{xy} by 2*θ (twice as much as the angle between XY and X'Y') and in the opposite direction of θ.
- The stresses in the new coordinates ($\sigma_{x'}$, $\sigma_{y'}$, and $\tau_{x'y'}$) are then read off the circle.

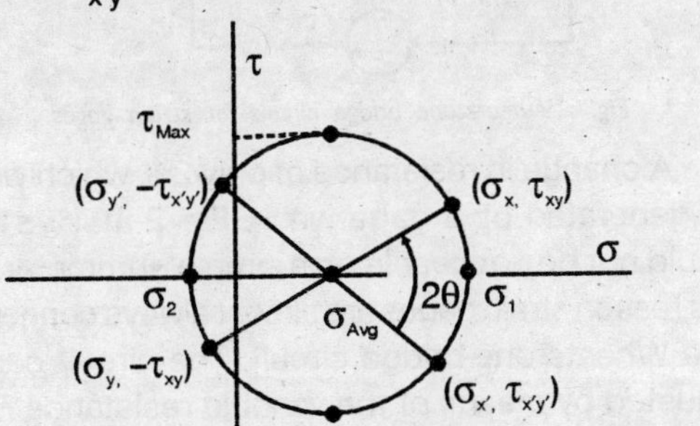

ROCK FABRICS

In geology, a rock's fabric describes the spatial and geometric configuration of all the elements that make it up.

TYPES OF FABRIC

- Primary fabric – a fabric created during the original formation of the rock e.g. a preferred orientation of clast long axes in a conglomerate, parallel to the flow direction, deposited by a fast waning current.
- Shape fabric – a fabric that is defined by the preferred orientation of inequant elements within the rock, such as platy or needle like mineral grains. It may also be formed by the deformation of originally equant elements such as mineral grains
- Crystallographic preferred orientation – In plastically deformed rocks the constituent minerals commonly display a preferred orientation of their crystal axes as a result of dislocation processes.
- S-fabric – a planar fabric such as cleavage or foliation, when it forms the dominant fabric in a rock, it may be called an S-tectonite
- L-fabric – a linear fabric such as mineral stretching lineation where aggregates of recrystallised grains are stretched out into the long axis of the finite strain ellipsoid, where it forms the dominant fabric in a rock, it may be called an L-tectonite.
- Penetrative fabric – a fabric that is present throughout the rock, down to the grain scale. Techniques of strain analysis

INTRODUCTION

It is the nature of forces and stresses that they cannot be measured directly. It is the effect of a force that is measurable: when we weigh an object on a spring scale, we are actually measuring the stretching of the spring, and then calculating the force from Hooke's law. Experimental stress analysis, then, is actually experimental strain analysis. The difficulty is that strains in the linear elastic regime are almost always small, on the order of 1% or less, and the art in this field is that of detecting and interpreting small displacements. We look for phenomena that exhibit large and measurable changes due to small and difficult-to-measure displacements. There a number of such techniques, and three of these will be outlined briefly in the sections to follow.

STRAIN GAGES

The term "strain gage" usually refers to a thin wire or foil, folded back and forth on itself and bonded to the specimen surface that is able to generate an electrical measure of strain in the specimen. As the wire is stretched along with the specimen, the wire's electrical resistance R changes both because its length L is increased and its cross-sectional area A is reduced. For many resistors, these variables are related by the simple expression discovered in 1856 by Lord Kelvin:

$$R = \frac{\rho L}{A}$$

where here ρ is the material's resistivity. To express the effect of a strain ε = dL=L in the wire's long direction on the electrical resistance, assume a circular wire with $A = \pi_{r2}$ and take logarithms:

$$\ln R = \ln \rho + \ln L - (\ln \pi + 2 \ln r)$$

Fig. : Wire resistance strain gage.

The total differential of this expression gives

$$\frac{dR}{R} = \frac{d\rho}{\rho} + \frac{dL}{L} - 2\frac{dr}{r}$$

Since

$$\in_r = \frac{dr}{r} = -v\frac{dL}{L}$$

Then

$$\frac{dR}{R} = \frac{d\rho}{\rho} + (1+2v)\frac{dL}{L}$$

P.W. Bridgeman (1882{1961) in 1929 studied the effect of volume change on electrical resistance and found these to vary proportionally:

$$\frac{d\rho}{\rho} = \alpha_R \frac{dV}{V}$$

Where α_R is the constant of proportionality between resistance change and volume change. Writing the volume change in terms of changes in length and area, this becomes

$$\frac{d\rho}{\rho} = \alpha_R\left(\frac{dL}{L} + \frac{dA}{A}\right) = \alpha_R(1-2v)\frac{dL}{L}$$

Hence

$$\frac{dR/R}{\in} = (1+2v) + \alpha_R(1-2v)$$

This quantity is called the gage factor, GF. Constantan, a 45/55 nickel/copper alloy, has α_R 1:13 and v =0:3, giving GF ≈ 2:0. This material also has a low temperature coefficient of resistivity, which reduces the temperature sensitivity of the strain gage.

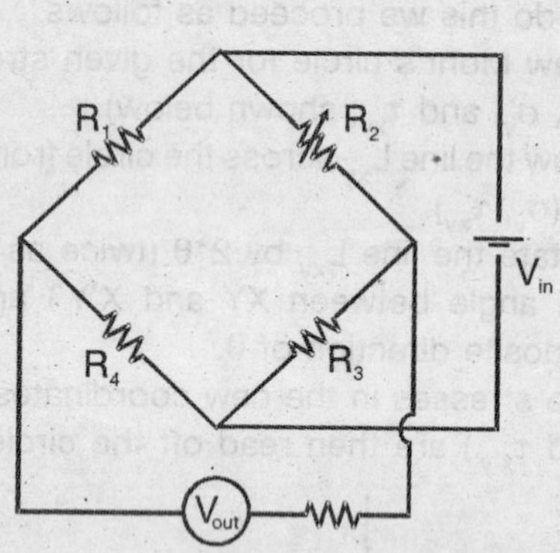

Fig. : Wheatstone bridge circuit for strain gages.

A change in resistance of only 2%, which would be generated by a gage with GF = 2 at 1% strain, would not be noticeable on a simple ohmmeter. For this reason strain gages are almost always connected to a Wheatstone-bridge circuit. The circuit can be adjusted by means of the variable resistance R_2 to produce a zero output voltage V_{out} before strain is applied to the gage. Typically the gage resistance is approximately 350Ω and the excitation voltage is near 10V. When the gage resistance is changed by strain, the bridge is unbalanced and a voltage appears on the output according to the relation

$$\frac{V_{out}}{V_{in}} = \frac{\Delta R}{2R_0}$$

Where R_0 is the nominal resistance of the four bridge elements. The output voltage is easily measured because it is a deviation from zero rather than being a relatively small change superimposed on a much larger quantity; it can thus be amplified to suit the needs of the data acquisition system.

Temperature compensation can be achieved by making a bridge element on the opposite side of the bridge from the active gage, say R_3, an inactive gage that is placed near the active gage but not bonded to the specimen. Resistance changes in the active gage due to temperature will then be offset be an equal resistance change in the other arm of the bridge.

It is often difficult to mount a tensile specimen in the testing machine without inadvertently applying bending in addition to tensile loads. If a single gage were applied to the convex-outward side of the specimen, its reading would be erroneously high. Similarly, a gage placed on the concave-inward or compressive-tending side would read low. These bending errors can be eliminated by using an active gage on each side of the specimen and wiring them on the same side of the Wheatstone bridge, e.g. R_1 and R_4. The tensile component of bending on one side of the specimen is accompanied by an equal but compressive component on the other side, and these will generate equal but opposite resistance changes in R_1 and R_4. The effect of bending will therefore cancel, and the gage combination will measure only the tensile strain (with doubled sensitivity, since both R_1 and R_4 are active).

The strain in the gage direction can be found directly from the gage factor Equation

$$\frac{dR/R}{\epsilon} = (1+2v)+\alpha_R(1-2v).$$

When the direction of principal stress is unknown, strain gage rosettes are useful; these employ multiple gages on the same lm backing, oriented in different directions. The rectangular three-gage rosette uses two gages oriented perpendicularly, and a third gage oriented at 45° to the first two.

For the specific case of a 0-45-90 rosette, the orientation of the principal strain axis can be given directly by

$$\tan 2\theta = \frac{2\epsilon_b - \epsilon_a - \epsilon_c}{\epsilon_a - \epsilon_c}$$

and the principal strains are

$$\epsilon_{1,2} = \frac{\epsilon_a + \epsilon_c}{2} \pm \sqrt{\frac{(\epsilon_a - \epsilon_b)^2 + (\epsilon_b - \epsilon_c)^2}{2}}$$

Graphical solutions based on Mohr's circles are also useful for reducing gage output data.

Strain gages are used very extensively, and critical structures such as aircraft may be instrumented with hundreds of gages during testing. Each gage must be bonded carefully to the structure, and connected by its two leads to the signal conditioning unit that includes the excitation voltage source and the Wheatstone bridge. This can obviously be a major instrumentation chore, with computer-aided data acquisition and reduction a practical necessity.

DEFORMATION MECHANISMS

In structural geology, metallurgy and materials science, deformation mechanisms refer to the various mechanisms at the grain scale that are responsible for accommodating large plastic strains in rocks, metals and other materials.

MECHANISMS OF DEFORMATION

The active deformation mechanism in a material depends on the homologous temperature, confining pressure, strain rate, stress, grain size, presence or absence of a pore fluid, presence or absence of impurities in the material. Note these variables are not fully independent e.g. for a pure material of a fixed grain size, at a given pressure, temperature and stress, the strain-rate is given by the flow-law associated with the particular mechanism(s). More than one mechanism may be active under a given set of conditions and some mechanisms cannot operate independently but must act in conjunction with another in order that significant permanent strain can develop. In a single deformation episode, the dominant mechanism may change with time e.g. recrystallization to a fine grain size at an early stage may allow diffusive mass transfer processes to become dominant.

The recognition of the active mechanism(s) in a material almost always requires the use of microscopic techniques, in most cases using a combination of optical microscopy, SEM and TEM.

Using a combination of experimental deformation to find the flow-laws under particular conditions and from microscopic examination of the samples afterwards it has been possible to represent the conditions under which individual deformation mechanisms dominate for some materials in the form of deformation mechanism maps.

Five main mechanisms are recognized; cataclastic flow, dislocation creep, recrystallization, diffusive mass transfer and grain-boundary sliding.

CATACLASTIC FLOW

This is a mechanism that operates under low to moderate homologous temperatures, low confining pressure and relatively high strain rates and involves fracturing, sliding and rolling of fragments.

DISLOCATION CREEP

Dislocation glide is the main process but cannot act on its own to produce large strains due to the effects of strain-hardening. Some form of recovery process, such as dislocation climb or grain-boundary migration must also be active.

DYNAMIC RECRYSTALLIZATION

Two main mechanisms of recrystallization are known, sub-grain rotation and grain boundary migration, and only the former involves actual deformation. Grain boundary migration involves no strain in itself, but is one of the recovery mechanisms that can allow dislocation processes to proceed to large strains.

DIFFUSIVE MASS TRANSFER

In this group of mechanisms, strain is accommodated by a change in shape involving the transfer of mass by diffusion; through the lattice (Nabarro-Herring creep), the grain boundaries and via a pore fluid

- Nabarro-herring creep acts at high homologous temperatures and is grain size dependent with the strain-rate inversely proportional to the square of the grain size.
- Coble-creep acts at high homologous temperatures and is strongly grain-size dependent, with a flow-law where strain-rate is inversely proportional to the cube of the grain size.
- Pressure solution operates at moderate homologous temperatures and relatively low strain-rates and requires the presence of a pore fluid.

GRAIN-BOUNDARY SLIDING

This mechanism must act with another to change the shapes of the grains so that they can slide past each other without creating significant voids. This mechanism, acting with diffusive mass transfer has been linked with the development of superplasticity.

3. Paleontology and its Applications

Theories on origin life. Organic evolution – Punctuated Equilibrium and Phyletic Gradualism models. Mass extinctions and their causes. Application of fossils in age determination and correlation. Paleoecology, Life habitats and various ecosystems, Paleobiogeography. Modes of preservation of fossils and taphonomic considerations.

Types of microfossils. Environmental significance of fossils and trace fossils. Use of microfossils in interpretation of sea floor tectonism. Application of micropaleontology in hydrocarbon exploration. Oxygen and Carbon isotope studies of microfossils and their use in paleoceanographic and paleoclimatic interpretation. Important invertebrate fossils, vertebrate fossils, plant fossils and microfossils in Indian stratigraphy.

ORGANIC EVOLUTION – PUNCTUATED EQUILIBRIUM AND PHYLETIC GRADUALISM MODELS

Evolutionary anthropologists, biologists, and palaeontologists interested in macroevolutionary questions examine and attempt to explain changes in the lineages of past and present organisms. These studies are ultimately interested in understanding how and why species change over time, how new life forms can appear in the fossil record, and how miniscule changes in trait frequencies build up to result in significant morphological changes.

CHARLES DARWIN'S EVOLUTION AND NATURAL SELECTION

Charles Darwin's contribution to evolution was the mechanism of natural selection. Natural selection is based on three main facts:

1. there is variation in the traits of any population of a species,
2. the variation in traits is hereditary,
3. there is differential success of the traits.

The result of these three facts is that the frequency of traits in a population change over time. Some traits become extremely rare or disappear, some traits become more common, and mutations introduce new traits. Over time, these changes accumulate so that the morphological traits of a population can change significantly. When a population is split up because of geographic isolation (e.g. islands), each group accumulates its own small changes over time so that eventually they can no longer breed with each other (i.e. they became a new species). This event is called speciation.

PHYLETIC GRADUALISM: EVOLUTIONARY CHANGE CAN OCCUR SLOWLY

Darwin saw speciation as a gradual process and his work ultimately led to what modern biologists call the phyletic gradualism hypothesis. In this view, macroevolution occurrs at a constant rate for all organisms, it is always occurring, and it is slow.

In the fossil record, the phyletic gradualism hypothesis should manifest itself with long sequences of transitional forms (also called 'missing links') in every lineage. This is true for some lineages at some scales, but there are gaps in the fossil record.

Phyletic gradualism is a speciation hypothesis rooted in uniformitarianism. The hypothesis states that species continue to adapt to new environmental and biological selection pressures over the course of their history, gradually becoming new species. Phyletic gradualism holds that a species population changes gradually; that is, there is no clear line of demarcation between an ancestral species and a descendant species unless a splitting (cladogenetic) event occurs or the gradually-changing lineage is divided arbitrarily. During this process, anagenetic evolution occurs at a smooth, steady, and incremental (but not necessarily constant or slow) rate on a geological timescale.

In contrast to punctuated equilibrium, phyletic gradualism states that new species arise by the gradual transformation and ultimate gradual splitting of ancestral species into descendant species lineages rather than by the abrupt splitting of relatively stable and unchanging ancestral species lineages. With phyletic gradualism, the rate of evolution during speciation is similar to anagenetic change at other times, not concentrated in a speciation event as is the case with the punctuated equilibrium hypothesis.

Phyletic gradualism was long considered to be the dominant pattern of speciation and evolution, but modern evolutionary biologists have deprecated it in favor of a variety of hypotheses such as punctuated equilibrium, quantum evolution, and punctuated gradualism.

Authors such as Richard Dawkins argue that such constant-rate gradualism is not present in academic literature, serving only as a straw-man for punctuated equilibrium advocates. He refutes the idea that Charles Darwin himself was a constant-rate gradualist, as suggested by Stephen Jay Gould. In the first edition of On the Origin of Species Darwin clearly stated that "Species of different genera and classes have not changed at the same rate, or in the same degree. In the oldest tertiary beds a few living shells may still be found in the midst of a multitude of extinct forms... The Silurian Lingula differs but little from the living species of this genus".Lingula is among the few brachiopods surviving today but also known from fossils over 500 million years old. In the fifth edition of On the Origin of Species Darwin wrote that "the periods during which species have undergone modification, though long as measured in years, have probably been short in comparison with the periods during which they retain the same form."

PUNCTUATED EQUILIBRIUM: EVOLUTIONARY CHANGE CAN OCCUR RAPIDLY

Punctuated equilibrium was proposed as an alternative hypothesis by Eldridge and Gould in 1972 to explain the gaps in the fossil record. The punctuated equilibrium hypothesis states that speciation events occur rapidly in geological time (i.e. over hundreds of thousands to millions of years) and that little change occurs in the time between speciation events. In other words, change only happens under certain conditions, and it happens rapidly.

Based on the punctuated equilibrium hypothesis, the apparent 'gaps' in the fossil record result because speciation events happen too quickly for the fossil record to appear continuous.

Punctuated equilibrium is a theory in evolutionary biology which proposes that some sexually reproducing species will experience little evolutionary change for most of their geological history, remaining in an extended state called stasis. When evolution occurs, it is localized in rare, rapid events of branching speciation, called cladogenesis. Cladogenesis is the process by which species split into two distinct species, rather than one species gradually transforming into another. Thus, "punctuated equilibria is a model for discontinuous tempos of change (in) the process of speciation and the deployment of species in geological time."

Punctuated equilibrium is commonly contrasted against the theory of phyletic gradualism, which states that evolution generally occurs uniformly and by the steady and gradual transformation of whole lineages (anagenesis). In this view, evolution is seen as generally smooth and continuous.

In 1972, paleontologists Niles Eldredge and Stephen Jay Gould published a landmark paper developing this theory and called it punctuated equilibria. Their paper built upon Ernst Mayr's theory of geographic speciation, I. Michael Lerner's theories of developmental and genetic homeostasis, as well as their own empirical research. Eldredge and Gould proposed that the degree of gradualism commonly attributed to Charles Darwin is virtually nonexistent in the fossil record, and that stasis dominates the history of most fossil species.

THEORETICAL MECHANISMS

When Eldredge and Gould published their 1972 paper, allopatric speciation was considered the "standard" theory of speciation. This theory was popularized by Ernst Mayr in his 1954 paper "Change of genetic environment and evolution," and his classic volume Animal Species and Evolution (1963).

Allopatric speciation suggests that species which are composed of large central populations are stabilized by their large volume and the genetic process of gene flow. New and even beneficial mutations are diluted by the population's size and are unable to reach fixation due to factors such as constantly changing environments. If this is the case, then the transformation of whole lineages should be rare, as the fossil record indicates. Smaller populations on the other hand, which are isolated from the parental stock, are decoupled from the homogenizing effects of gene flow. In addition, pressure from natural selection is especially intense, as peripheral isolated populations exist at the outer edges of ecological tolerance. If most evolution happens in these rare instances of allopatric speciation then evidence of gradual evolution should be rare. This stimulating hypothesis was alluded to by Mayr in the closing paragraph of his 1954 paper.

Ernst Mayr often emphasized the use of population thinking to describe species, rather than models which evoked a typological approach. In order to contrast the differences in population structures he coined the terms ecotypic and typostrophic variation. Ecotypic variation describes the genetics of large central populations which are stabilized by the homogenizing effects of gene flow. Small peripherally isolated populations, in contrast, possess typostrophic variation which "have the characteristic features of incipient species, but what is more important they often are species or incipient species of an entirely new type. That is, they may have morphological or ecological features that deviate quite strikingly and unexpectedly from the 'parental' pattern."

As time went on Gould moved away from wedding punctuated equilibrium to allopatric speciation, particularly as evidence accumulated in support of other modes of speciation. He also moved away from tying stasis to internal constraints. Gould was particularly attracted to Douglas Futuyma's work on the importance of reproductive isolating mechanisms.

The theory of punctuated equilibrium also contributed to the theory that species are Darwinian individuals, and not just classes, thereby providing a stronger framework for a hierarchical theory of evolution. Other biologists have applied punctuated equilibrium to non-sexual species, even the evolution of viruses.

RELATION TO DARWIN'S THEORIES

The sudden appearance of most species in the geologic record and the lack of evidence of substantial gradual change in most species–from their initial appearance until their extinction–has long been noted, including by Charles Darwin who appealed to the imperfection of the record as the favored explanation. When presenting his ideas against the prevailing influence of catastrophism put forward by Georges Cuvier which envisaged species being supernaturally created at intervals, Darwin needed to forcefully stress the gradual nature of evolution in accordance with the gradualism promoted by his friend Charles Lyell. He privately expressed concern, noting in the margin of his 1844 Essay "Better begin with this: If species really, after catastrophes, created in showers world over, my theory false."

It is often incorrectly assumed that he insisted that the rate of change must be constant, or nearly so, but even the first edition of On the Origin of Species states that "Species of different genera and classes have not changed at the same rate, or in the same degree. In the oldest tertiary beds a few living shells may still be found in the midst of a multitude of extinct forms... The Silurian Lingula differs but little from the living species of this genus". Lingula is among the few brachiopods surviving today but also known from fossils over 500 million years old. In the fifth edition of On the Origin of Species Darwin wrote that "the periods during which species have undergone modification, though long as measured in years, have probably been short in comparison with the periods during which they retain the same form." Thus punctuationism in general is consistent with Darwin's conception of evolution.

According to early versions of punctuated equilibrium, "peripheral isolates" are considered to be of critical importance for speciation. However, Darwin wrote, "I can by no means agree... that immigration and isolation are necessary elements.... Although isolation is of great importance in the production of new species, on the whole I am inclined to believe that largeness of area is still more important, especially for the production of species which shall prove capable of enduring for a long period, and of spreading widely."

The importance of isolation in forming species had played a significant part in Darwin's early thinking, as shown in his Essay of 1844. But by the time he wrote the Origin he had downplayed its importance.

Punctuated equilibrium contradicts some of Darwin's ideas regarding the specific mechanisms of evolution, but generally accords with Darwin's theory of evolution by natural selection.

PUNCTUATED EQUILIBRIUM IN SOCIAL THEORY

Punctuated equilibrium in social theory is a method of understanding change in complex social systems, particularly how policy change and the development of conflicts seem to progress in extended periods of stasis, punctuated by sudden shifts in radical change.

MASS EXTINCTIONS AND THEIR CAUSES

Mass extinction is a sharp decrease in the diversity and abundance of macroscopic life. They occur when the rate of extinction increases with respect to the rate of speciation. Because the majority of diversity and biomass on earth is microbial, and thus difficult to measure, mass extinctions have little effect on the total diversity and abundance of life, but rather affect the easily observed component of the biosphere.

Over 97% of species that ever lived are now extinct, but extinction occurs at an uneven rate. Based on the fossil record, the background rate of extinctions on Earth is about two to five taxonomic families of marine invertebrates and vertebrates every million years. Marine fossils are mostly used to measure extinction rates because of their superior fossil record and stratigraphic range compared to land organisms.

Since life began on Earth, several major mass extinctions have significantly exceeded the background extinction rate. The most recent, the Cretaceous–Tertiary extinction event, occurred 65 million years ago, and has attracted more attention than all others as it marks the extinction of nearly all dinosaur species, which were the dominant animal class of the period. In the past 540 million years there have been five major events when over 50% of animal species died. There probably were mass extinctions in the Archean and Proterozoic Eons, but before the Phanerozoic there were no animals with hard body parts to leave a significant fossil record.

Estimates of the number of major mass extinctions in the last 540 million years range from as few as five to more than twenty. These differences stem from the threshold chosen for describing an extinction event as "major", and the data chosen to measure past diversity.

MAJOR EXTINCTION EVENTS

The classical "Big Five" mass extinctions identified by Jack Sepkoski and David M. Raup in their 1982 paper are widely agreed upon as some of the most significant: End Ordovician, Late Devonian, End Permian, End Triassic, and End Cretaceous.

These and a selection of other extinction events are outlined below. The articles about individual mass extinctions describe their effects in more detail and discuss theories about their causes.

1. Cretaceous–Tertiary extinction event (K-T extinction) - 65 Ma ago at the Cretaceous-Paleogene transition. About 17% of all families, 50% of all genera and 75% of species went extinct. It ended the reign of dinosaurs and opened the way for mammals and birds to become the dominant land vertebrates. In the seas it reduced the percentage of sessile animals to about 33%. The K-T extinction was rather uneven – some groups of organisms became extinct, some suffered heavy losses and some appear to have been only minimally affected.
2. Triassic–Jurassic extinction event - 205 Ma at the Triassic-Jurassic transition. About 23% of all families and 48% of all genera (20% of marine families and 55% of marine genera) went extinct. Most non-dinosaurian archosaurs, most therapsids, and most of the large amphibians were eliminated, leaving dinosaurs with little terrestrial competition. Non-dinosaurian archosaurs continued to dominate aquatic environments, while non-archosaurian diapsids continued to dominate marine environments. The Temnospondyl lineage of large amphibians also survived until the Cretaceous in Australia (e.g., Koolasuchus).
3. Permian–Triassic extinction event - 251 Ma at the Permian-Triassic transition. Earth's largest extinction killed 57% of all families and 83% of all genera (53% of marine families, 84% of marine genera, about 96% of all marine species and an estimated 70% of land species) including vertebrates, insects and plants. The "Great Dying" had enormous evolutionary significance: on land, it ended the primacy of mammal-like reptiles. The recovery of vertebrates took 30 million years, but the vacant niches created the opportunity for archosaurs to become ascendant. In the seas, the percentage of animals that were sessile dropped from 67% to 50%. The whole late Permian was a difficult time for at least marine life, even before the "Great Dying".
4. Late Devonian extinction 360-375 Ma near the Devonian-Carboniferous transition. At the end of the Frasnian Age in the later part(s) of the Devonian Period, a prolonged series of extinctions eliminated about 19% of all families, 50% of all genera and 70% of all species. This extinction event lasted perhaps as long as 20 MY, and there is evidence for a series of extinction pulses within this period.
5. Ordovician–Silurian extinction event 440-450 Ma at the Ordovician-Silurian transition. Two events occurred that killed off 27% of all families and 57% of all genera. Together they are ranked by many scientists as the second largest of the five major extinctions in Earth's history in terms of percentage of genera that went extinct.

The older the fossil record gets, the more difficult it is to read it. This is because:

- Older fossils are harder to find because they are usually buried at a considerable depth in the rock.
- Dating older fossils is more difficult.
- Productive fossil beds are researched more than unproductive ones, therefore leaving certain periods unresearched.
- Prehistoric environmental disturbances can disturb the deposition process.
- The preservation of fossils varies on land, but marine fossils tend to be better preserved than their sought after land-based counterparts.

It has been suggested that the apparent variations in marine biodiversity may actually be an artifact, with abundance estimates directly related to quantity of rock available for sampling from different time periods. However, statistical analysis shows that this can only account for 50% of the observed pattern,and other evidence (such as fungal spikes) reassurance that most widely accepted extinction events are indeed real. A quantification of the rock exposure of Western Europe does indicate that many of the minor events for which a biological explanation has been sought are most readily explained by sampling bias.

CAUSES

There is still debate about the causes of all mass extinctions. In general, large extinctions may result when a biosphere under long-term stress undergoes a short-term shock.

Looking for the causes of particular mass extinctions

A good theory for a particular mass extinction should: (i) explain all of the losses, not just focus on a few groups (such as dinosaurs); (ii) explain why particular groups of organisms died out and why others survived; (iii) provide mechanisms which are strong enough to cause a mass extinction but not a total extinction; (iv) be based on events or processes that can be shown to have happened, not just inferred from the extinction.

It may be necessary to consider combinations of causes. For example the marine aspect of the end-Cretaceous extinction appears to have been caused by several processes which partially overlapped in time and may have had different levels of significance in different parts of the world.

Arens and West (2006) proposed a "press / pulse" model in which mass extinctions generally require two types of cause: long-term pressure on the eco-system ("press") and a sudden catastrophe ("pulse") towards the end of the period of pressure. Their statistical analysis of marine extinction rates throughout the Phanerozoic suggested that neither long-term pressure alone nor a catastrophe alone was sufficient to cause a significant increase in the extinction rate.

Most widely supported explanations

Macleod (2001) summarized the relationship between mass extinctions and events which are most often cited as causes of mass extinctions, using data from Courtillot et al. (1996), Hallam (1992) and Grieve et al. (1996):

- Flood basalt events: 11 occurrences, all associated with significant extinctionsBut Wignall (2001) concluded that only 5 of the major extinctions coincided with flood basalt eruptions and that the main phase of extinctions started before the eruptions.
- Sea-level falls: 12, of which 7 were associated with significant extinctions.
- Asteroid impacts producing craters over 100 km wide: one, associated with one mass extinction.
- Asteroid impacts producing craters less than 100 km wide: over 50, the great majority not associated with significant extinctions.

The most commonly suggested causes of mass extinctions are listed below.

FLOOD BASALT EVENTS

The formation of large igneous provinces by flood basalt events could have:

- produced dust and particulate aerosols which inhibited photosynthesis and thus caused food chains to collapse both on land and at sea
- emitted sulfur oxides which were precipitated as acid rain and poisoned many organisms, contributing further to the collapse of food chains
- emitted carbon dioxide and thus possibly causing sustained global warming once the dust and particulate aerosols dissipated.

Flood basalt events occur as pulses of activity punctuated by dormant periods. As a result they are likely to cause the climate to oscillate between cooling and warming, but with an overall trend towards warming as the carbon dioxide they emit can stay in the atmosphere for hundreds of years.

It is speculated that Massive volcanism caused or contributed to the End-Cretaceous, End-Permian, and End Triassic extinctions.

SEA-LEVEL FALLS

These are often clearly marked by worldwide sequences of contemporaneous sediments which show all or part of a transition from sea-bed to tidal zone to beach to dry land - and where there is no evidence that the rocks in the relevant areas were raised by geological processes such as orogeny. Sea-level falls could reduce the continental shelf area (the most productive part of the oceans) sufficiently to cause a marine mass extinction, and could disrupt weather patterns enough to cause extinctions on land. But sea-level falls are very probably the result of other events, such as sustained global cooling or the sinking of the mid-ocean ridges.

Sea-level falls are associated with most of the mass extinctions, including all of the "Big Five" – End-Ordovician, Late Devonian, End-Permian, End-Triassic, and End-Cretaceous.

A study, published in the journal Nature (online June 15, 2008) established a relationship between the speed of mass extinction events and changes in sea level and sediment. The study suggests changes in ocean environments related to sea level exert a driving influence on rates of extinction, and generally determine the composition of life in the oceans.

IMPACT EVENTS

The impact of a sufficiently large asteroid or comet could have caused food chains to collapse both on land and at sea by producing dust and particulate aerosols and thus inhibiting photosynthesis. Impacts on sulfur-rich rocks could have emitted sulfur oxides precipitating as poisonous acid rain, contributing further to the collapse of food chains. Such impacts could also have caused megatsunamis and / or global forest fires.

Most paleontologists now agree that an asteroid did hit the Earth about 65 Ma, but there is an ongoing dispute whether the impact was the sole cause of the extinctions. There is evidence that there was an interval of about 300 ka from the impact to the mass extinction. In 1997, paleontologist Sankar Chatterjee drew attention to the proposed and much larger 600 km (370 mi) Shiva crater and the possibility of a multiple-impact scenario.

In 2007, a hypothesis was put forth that argued the impactor that killed the dinosaurs 65 Ma years ago belonged to the Baptistina family of asteroids. Concerns have been raised regarding the reputed link, in part because very few solid observational constraints exist of the asteroid or family. Indeed, it was recently discovered that 298 Baptistina does not share the same chemical signature as the source of the K-T impact. Although this finding may make the link between the Baptistina family and K-T impactor more difficult to substantiate, it does not preclude the possibility.

In 2010, another hypothesis was offered which implicated the newly-discovered asteroid P/2010 A2, a member of the Flora family of asteroids, as a possible remnant cohort of the K/T impactor.

SUSTAINED AND SIGNIFICANT GLOBAL COOLING

Sustained global cooling could kill many polar and temperate species and force others to migrate towards the equator; reduce the area available for tropical species; often make the Earth's climate more arid on average, mainly by locking up more of the planet's water in ice and snow. The glaciation cycles of the current ice age are believed to have had only a very mild impact on biodiversity, so the mere existence of a significant cooling is not sufficient on its own to explain a mass extinction.

It has been suggested that global cooling caused or contributed to the End-Ordovician, Permian-Triassic, Late Devonian extinctions, and possibly others. Sustained global cooling is distinguished from the temporary climatic effects of flood basalt events or impacts.

SUSTAINED AND SIGNIFICANT GLOBAL WARMING

This would have the opposite effects: expand the area available for tropical species; kill temperate species or force them to migrate towards the poles; possibly cause severe extinctions of polar species; often make the Earth's climate wetter on average, mainly by melting ice and snow and thus increasing the volume of the water cycle. It might also cause anoxic events in the oceans.

Global warming as a cause of mass extinction is supported by several recent studies.

The most dramatic example of sustained warming is the Paleocene-Eocene Thermal Maximum, which was associated with one of the smaller mass extinctions. It has also been suggested to have caused the Triassic-Jurassic extinction event, during which 20% of all marine families went extinct. Furthermore, the Permian–Triassic extinction event has been suggested to have been caused by warming.

CLATHRATE GUN HYPOTHESIS

Clathrates are composites in which a lattice of one substance forms a cage round another. Methane clathrates (in which water molecules are the cage) form on continental shelves. These clathrates are likely to break up rapidly and release the methane if the temperature rises quickly or the pressure on them drops quickly – for example in response to sudden global warming or a sudden drop in sea level or even earthquakes. Methane is a much more powerful greenhouse gas than carbon dioxide, so a methane eruption ("clathrate gun") could cause rapid global warming or make it much more severe if the eruption was itself caused by global warming.

The most likely signature of such a methane eruption would be a sudden decrease in the ratio of carbon-13 to carbon-12 in sediments, since methane clathrates are low in carbon-13; but the change would have to be very large, as other events can also reduce the percentage of carbon-13.

It has been suggested that "clathrate gun" methane eruptions were involved in the end-Permian extinction ("the Great Dying") and in the Paleocene-Eocene Thermal Maximum, which was associated with one of the smaller mass extinctions.

ANOXIC EVENTS

Anoxic events are situations in which the middle and even the upper layers of the ocean become deficient or totally lacking in oxygen. Their causes are complex and controversial, but all known instances are associated with severe and sustained global warming, mostly caused by sustained massive volcanism.

It has been suggested that anoxic events caused or contributed to the Ordovician–Silurian, late Devonian, Permian-Triassic and Triassic-Jurassic extinctions, as well as a number of lesser extinctions (such as the Ireviken, Mulde, Lau, Toarcian and Cenomanian-Turonian events). On the other hand, there are widespread black shale beds from the mid-Cretaceous which indicate anoxic events but are not associated with mass extinctions.

HYDROGEN SULFIDE EMISSIONS FROM THE SEAS

Kump, Pavlov and Arthur (2005) have proposed that during the Permian-Triassic extinction event the warming also upset the oceanic balance between photosynthesising plankton and deep-water sulfate-reducing bacteria, causing massive emissions of hydrogen sulfide which poisoned life on both land and sea and severely weakened the ozone layer, exposing much of the life that still remained to fatal levels of UV radiation.

OCEANIC OVERTURN

Oceanic overturn is a disruption of thermo-haline circulation which lets surface water (which is more saline than deep water because of evaporation) sink straight down, bringing anoxic deep water to the surface and therefore killing most of the oxygen-breathing organisms which inhabit the surface and middle depths. It may occur either at the beginning or the end of a glaciation, although an overturn at the start of a glaciation is more dangerous because the preceding warm period will have created a larger volume of anoxic water.

Unlike other oceanic catastrophes such as regressions (sea-level falls) and anoxic events, overturns do not leave easily-identified "signatures" in rocks and are theoretical consequences of researchers' conclusions about other climatic and marine events.

It has been suggested that oceanic overturn caused or contributed to the late Devonian and Permian-Triassic extinctions.

A NEARBY NOVA, SUPERNOVA OR GAMMA RAY BURST

A nearby gamma ray burst (less than 6000 light years away) could sufficiently irradiate the surface of Earth to kill organisms living there and destroy the ozone layer in the process. From statistical arguments, approximately 1 gamma ray burst would be expected to occur close to Earth in the last 540 million years. A proposal that a supernova or gamma ray burst had caused a mass extinction would also have to be backed up by astronomical evidence of such an explosion at the right place and time.

It has been suggested that a supernova or gamma ray burst caused the End-Ordovician extinction.

CONTINENTAL DRIFT

Movement of the continents into some configurations can cause or contribute to extinctions in several ways: by initiating or ending ice ages; by changing ocean and wind currents and thus altering climate; by opening seaways or land bridges which expose previously isolated species to competition for which they are poorly-adapted (for example, the extinction of most of South America's native ungulates and all of its large metatherians after the creation of a land bridge between North and South America). Occasionally continental drift creates a super-continent which includes the vast majority of Earth's land area, which in addition to the effects listed above is likely to reduce the total area of continental shelf (the most species-rich part of the ocean) and produce a vast, arid continental interior which may have extreme seasonal variations.

It is widely thought that the creation of the super-continent Pangaea contributed to the End-Permian mass extinction. Pangaea was almost fully formed at the transition from mid-Permian to late-Permian, and the "Marine genus diversity" diagram at the top of this article shows a level of extinction starting at that time which might have qualified for inclusion in the "Big Five" if it were not overshadowed by the "Great Dying" at the end of the Permian.

PLATE TECTONICS

Plate tectonics is the mechanism which drives many of the possible causes of mass extinctions, especially volcanism and continental drift. So it is implicated in many extinctions, but in each case it is necessary to specify which manifestations of plate tectonics were involved.

OTHER HYPOTHESES

Many other hypotheses have been proposed, such as the spread of a new disease, the Shiva hypothesis, or simple out-competition following an especially successful biological innovation. But all have been rejected, usually for one of the following reasons: they require events or processes for which there is no evidence; they assume mechanisms which are contrary to the available evidence; they are based on other theories which have been rejected or superseded.

APPLICATION OF FOSSILS IN AGE DETERMINATION AND CORRELATION

There are several different methods scientists use to determine age of fossils. Sometimes, it is possible to determine age directly from the fossil. Many times however, fossils are to old to have their age directly measured. Instead, age can be determined from radioactive elements occuring within rock found in association with the fossils.

RADIOMETRIC (OR RADIOACTIVE) DATING

This method is based upon radioactive decay. The spontaneous release of energy and/or particles from the nucleus of an unstable atom (referred to as the parent) into a stable atom (referred to as the daughter) is radioactive decay. This rate of decays occurs at a specific and constant rate. The age of a rock can be determined by measuring the amount of the daughter product and adding that to the amount of the remaining parent material.

There are four standards necessary for elements to be useful in radometric dating.

1. The numbers of parent atoms and daughter atoms must be measurable.
2. The parent element must decay rapidly enough to produce measurable amounts of the daughter element, but measurable amounts of the parent element must also be present in the sample.
3. Little or no daughter element must have been present in the sample when it was formed.

4. The sample used must have been chemically isolated from outside chemical changes.

These systems meet the standards listed above. Half-life refers to the length of time required for 50% of the parent material to decay into the daughter product.

- Uranium 235 to Lead 207 (half-life = 710,000,000 years)
- Uranium 238 to Lead 206 (half-life = 4,500,000,000 years)
- Thorium 232 to Lead 208 (half-life = 14,000,000,000 years)
- Rubidium 87 to Strontium 87 (half-life = 47,000,000,000 years) - this is the most common system used for dating rocks older than 100 million years.
- Potassium 40 to Argon 40 (half-life = 1,300,000,000 years) - this method is very often used to date rock less than 60 million years old.
- Carbon 14 to Nitrogen 14 (half-life = 5,570 years)– There are 3 forms (isotopes) of carbon occuring in nature: Carbon 12 (accounts for 99%), Carbon 13 (accounts for 1%), and Carbon 14 (accounts for less than 1%). While alive, plants and animals incorporate these isotopes of carbon into their tissues at the ratio found in the atmosphere. Upon death, the Carbon 14 in their tissues begins to decay. By measuring the remaining amount of Carbon 14, the age of the fossil can be determined. This method can be used to date material ranging in age from a few hundred years to about 50,000 years. The use of Carbon 14 permits the determination of age directly a fossil. For fossils greater than 50,000 years old, the age of the fossil is found indirectly by determing the age of the rock associated with the fossil. Carbon 14 dating has a dating range of several hundred years before present to 50,000 years before present.

FISSION-TRACK DATING

Fission-track dating is based on the presence of Uranium 238 and Uranium 235 in the sample to be tested. These two uranium isotopes always occur in the same ratio in nature. Uranium 238 will undergone spontaneous decay or fission. Each time this happens, a tiny damage track is created in the surrounding material. Etching with acid enlarges the tracks allowing them to be seen under a microscope and counted. However, Uranium 235 does not undergo spontaneous fission. Uranium 235 can be induced to undergo fission by irradiating the sample with high energy neutrons in a nuclear reactor. By counting the number of induced tracks and knowing the neutron dose, the uranium content can be determined. From the ratio of natural fission tracks to induced fission tracks and knowing the half-life of Uranium 238 (half-life = 4,500,000,000 years), the sample's age can be determined.

PALEOMAGNETISM

At the time of their formation, iron-bearing rocks and sediments may acquire a natural remnant magnetism. This primary magnetism aligns parallel to the existing magnetic field of the Earth. In a sense, a rock becomes a compass capturing its orientation to the Earth's magnetic field in its structure.

The orientation of the magnetic field of the Earth at any point on Earth is specified by two measurements: declination (direction) and inclination (plunge). The inclination varies from horizontal at the equator to vertical at the poles. Today, the magnetic field is directed downward in the northern hemisphere and upward in the southern hemisphere. Earth's magnetic field periodically reverses its polarity. During the time of reversed polarity, a compass needle would point south. These reversals make excellent markers in the geologic record because they global in extend. The age of these reversals can be determined by radiometric dating. The age of a fossil can be determined by correlating the position of the strata of rock where it was found and where a reversal occurs.

AMINO-ACID DATING

Amino-acid dating is based upon the principle that amino acids which make up proteins change when an organism dies. The proteins produced by an orgamism when it is alive almost entirely consists of amino acids in a "left-handed" configuration. After death, amino acids begin to invert to their "right-handed" configuration. This process is called racemization. In fossils, an equilibrium ratio is eventually reached. The time needed to reach this equilibrium depends mainly upon temperature and secondarily on the species of the organism. Once the absolute date for a region is determined using radiometric dating and the temperature history of a region is established, amino-acid dating can be used to determine the age of a fossil. In the example of marine mollusks, the ratio for the amino acid isoleucine increases from nearly zero in modern shells to an equilibrium value of 1.30 +/- 0.05. At 10 degrees centigrade, it takes about 2 million years to reach equilibrium. At minus 10 degrees centigrade, it takes 20 million years to reach equilibrium.

PALEOECOLOGY

Paleoecology uses data from fossils and subfossils to reconstruct the ecosystems of the past. It includes the study of fossil organisms and their bromalites and other trace fossils in terms of their life cycle, their living interactions, their natural environment, their manner of death and burial. Paleoecology's aim is therefore to build the most detailed model possible of the life environment of those living organisms found today as fossils; such reconstruction work involves complex interactions among environmental factors (temperature, food supplies, degree of solar illumination, etc.). Of course, much of this complex data has been distorted or destroyed by the post-mortem fossilization processes, adding another layer of complexity.

The environmental complexity factor is normally tackled through statistical analysis of the available numerical data (quantitative paleontology or paleostatistics), while the study of post-mortem processes is known as the field of taphonomy.

Much paleoecological research focuses on the last two million years (the Quaternary period) because older environments are less well-represented in the fossil timeline of evolution. Indeed, many studies concentrate on the Holocene epoch (the last 11,000 years), or the last glacial stage of the Pleistocene epoch (the Wisconsin/Weichsel/Devensian/Würm glaciation of the ice age, from 50,000 to 10,000 years ago). Such studies are useful for understanding the dynamics of ecosystem change and for reconstructing pre-industrialization ecosystems. Many public policy decision-makers have pointed to the importance of using paleoecological studies as a basis for choices made in conservation ecology.

LIFE HABITATS AND VARIOUS ECOSYSTEMS

Ecosystems vary in size. They can be as small as a puddle or as large as the Earth itself. Any group of living and nonliving things interacting with each other can be considered as an ecosystem.

An ecosystem consists of the biological community that occurs in some locale, and the physical and chemical factors that make up its non-living or abiotic environment. There are many examples of ecosystems – a pond, a forest, an estuary, a grassland. The boundaries are not fixed in any objective way, although sometimes they seem obvious, as with the shoreline of a small pond. Usually the boundaries of an ecosystem are chosen for practical reasons having to do with the goals of the particular study.

Within each ecosystem, there are habitats which may also vary in size. A habitat is the place where a population lives. A population is a group of living organisms of the same kind living in the same place at the same time. All of the populations interact and form a community. The community of living things interacts with the non-living world around it to form the ecosystem. The habitat must supply the needs of organisms, such as food, water, temperature, oxygen, and minerals. If the population's needs are not met, it will move to a better habitat. Two different populations can not occupy the same niche at the same time, however. So the processes of competition, predation, cooperation, and symbiosis occur. Within each ecosystem, there are habitats which may also vary in size. A habitat is the place where a population lives. A population is a group of living organisms of the same kind living in the same place at the same time. All of the populations interact and form a community. The community of living things interacts with the non-living world around it to form the ecosystem. The habitat must supply the needs of organisms, such as food, water, temperature, oxygen, and minerals. If the population's needs are not met, it will move to a better habitat. Two different populations can not occupy the same niche at the same time, however. So the processes of competition, predation, cooperation, and symbiosis occur.

Habitats, then, are specific to a population. Each population has its own habitat. For example, a population of ants has its own habitat.

Several populations may share a habitat. For example, in a small pond several aquatic populations may co-exist in the same water at the same time. An aquarium is a good example of a shared habitat.

A terrarium is another place where several populations will peacefully co-exist in the same habitat. Vivaria are habitats where several plant and animal populations live together. Within any shared habitat, behavior influences the survival of a species. Behavior can be instinctual or learned.

Biomes are ecosystems where several habitats intersect. The Earth itself is one large biome. Smaller biomes include desert, tundra, grasslands, and rainforest.

The study of ecosystems mainly consists of the study of certain processes that link the living, or biotic, components to the non-living, or abiotic, components. Energy transformations and biogeochemical cycling are the main processes that comprise the field of ecosystem ecology. As we learned earlier, ecology generally is defined as the interactions of organisms with one another and with the environment in which they occur. We can study ecology at the level of the individual, the population, the community, and the ecosystem.

Studies of individuals are concerned mostly about physiology, reproduction, development or behavior, and studies of populations usually focus on the habitat and resource needs of individual species, their group behaviors, population growth, and what limits their abundance or causes extinction. Studies of communities examine how populations of many species interact with one another, such as predators and their prey, or competitors that share common needs or resources.

In ecosystem ecology we put all of this together and, insofar as we can, we try to understand how the system operates as a whole. This means that, rather than worrying mainly about particular species, we try to focus on major functional aspects of the system. These functional aspects include such things as the amount of energy that is produced by photosynthesis, how energy or materials flow along the many steps in a food chain, or what controls the rate of decomposition of materials or the rate at which nutrients are recycled in the system.

COMPONENTS OF AN ECOSYSTEM

You are already familiar with the parts of an ecosystem. We can clarify the parts of an ecosystem by listing them under the headings "abiotic" and "biotic".

ABIOTIC COMPONENTS	BIOTIC COMPONENTS
Sunlight	Primary producers
Temperature	Herbivores
Precipitation	Carnivores
Water or moisture	Omnivores
Soil or water chemistry (e.g., P, NH_4^+)	Detritivores
etc.	etc.

All of these vary over space/time

By and large, this set of environmental factors is important almost everywhere, in all ecosystems.

Usually, biological communities include the "functional groupings" shown above. A functional group is a biological category composed of organisms that perform mostly the same kind of function in the system; for example, all the photosynthetic plants or primary producers form a functional group. Membership in the functional group does not depend very much on who the actual players (species) happen to be, only on what function they perform in the ecosystem.

PROCESSES OF ECOSYSTEMS

This figure with the plants, zebra, lion, and so forth illustrates the two main ideas about how ecosystems function: ecosystems have energy flows and ecosystems cycle materials. These two processes are linked, but they are not quite the same

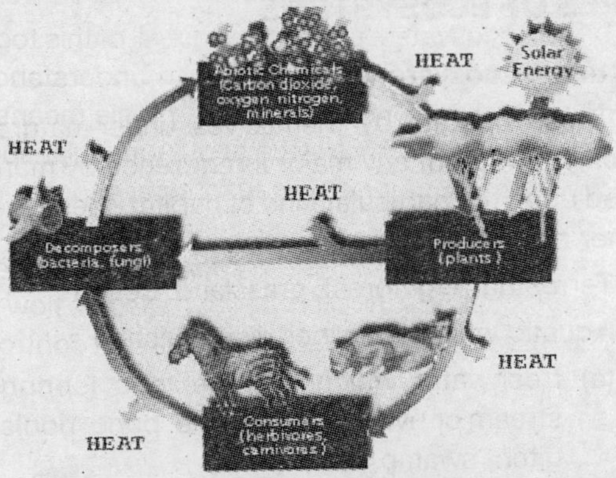

Fig. : Energy flows and material cycles.

Energy enters the biological system as light energy, or photons, is transformed into chemical energy in organic molecules by cellular processes including photosynthesis and respiration, and ultimately is converted to heat energy. This energy is dissipated, meaning it is lost to the system as heat; once it is lost it cannot be recycled. Without the continued input of solar energy, biological systems would quickly shut down. Thus the earth is an open system with respect to energy.

Elements such as carbon, nitrogen, or phosphorus enter living organisms in a variety of ways. Plants obtain elements from the surrounding atmosphere, water, or soils. Animals may also obtain elements directly from the physical environment, but usually they obtain these mainly as a consequence of consuming other organisms. These materials are transformed biochemically within the bodies of organisms, but sooner or later, due to excretion or decomposition, they are returned to an inorganic state. Often bacteria complete this process, through the process caiied decomposition or mineralization.

During decomposition these materials are not destroyed or lost, so the earth is a closed system with respect to elements (with the exception of a meteorite entering the system now and then). The elements are cycled endlessly between their biotic and abiotic states within ecosystems. Those elements whose supply tends to limit biological activity are called nutrients.

THE TRANSFORMATION OF ENERGY

The transformations of energy in an ecosystem begin first with the input of energy from the sun. Energy from the sun is captured by the process of photosynthesis. Carbon dioxide is combined with hydrogen (derived from the splitting of water molecules) to produce carbohydrates (CHO). Energy is stored in the high energy bonds of adenosine triphosphate, or ATP (see lecture on photosynthesis).

The prophet Isaah said "all flesh is grass", earning him the title of first ecologist, because virtually all energy available to organisms originates in plants. Because it is the first step in the production of energy for living things, it is called primary production. Herbivores obtain their energy by consuming plants or plant products, carnivores eat herbivores, and detritivores consume the droppings and carcasses of us all.

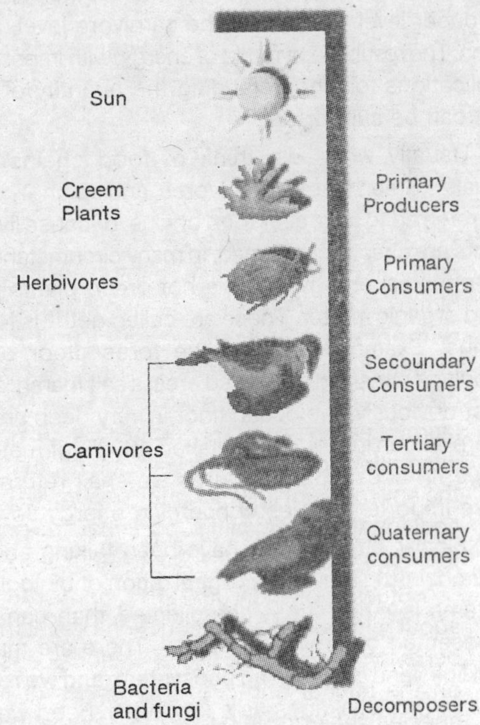

Fig.

Figure portrays a simple food chain, in which energy from the sun, captured by plant photosynthesis, flows from trophic level to trophic level via the food chain. A trophic level is composed of organisms that make a living in the same way, that is they are all primary producers (plants), primary consumers (herbivores) or secondary consumers (carnivores). Dead tissue and waste products are produced at all levels. Scavengers, detritivores, and decomposers collectively account for the use of all such "waste" – consumers of carcasses and fallen leaves may be other animals, such as crows and beetles, but ultimately it is the microbes that finish the job of decomposition. Not surprisingly, the amount of primary production varies a great deal from place to place, due to differences in the amount of solar radiation and the availability of nutrients and water.

For reasons that we will explore more fully in subsequent lectures, energy transfer through the food chain is inefficient. This means that less energy is available at the herbivore level than at the primary producer level, less yet at the carnivore level, and so on. The result is a pyramid of energy, with important implications for understanding the quantity of life that can be supported.

Usually when we think of food chains we visualize green plants, herbivores, and so on. These are referred to as grazer food chains, because living plants are directly consumed. In many circumstances the principal energy input is not green plants but dead organic matter. These are called detritus food chains. Examples include the forest floor or a woodland stream in a forested area, a salt marsh, and most obviously, the ocean floor in very deep areas where all sunlight is extinguished 1000's of meters above. In subsequent lectures we shall return to these important issues concerning energy flow.

Finally, although we have been talking about food chains, in reality the organization of biological systems is much more complicated than can be represented by a simple "chain". There are many food links and chains in an ecosystem, and we refer to all of these linkages as a food web. Food webs can be very complicated, where it appears that "everything is connected to everything else", and it is important to understand what are the most important linkages in any particular food web.

TYPES OF ECOSYSTEMS

Natural Ecosystems

These operate by themselves under natural conditions without any major interference by man. Based upon the particular kind of habitat, these are further divided as:

1. Terrestrial, e.g. forest, grassland, desert
2. Aquatic which is further distinguished as:
   (a) freshwater which may be lotic (spring, stream or river) or lentic (lake, pond, pools, ditch, swamp, etc.)
   (b) Marine, e.g. sea or ocean (deep bodies) and estuary (shallow bodies).

Artificial Ecosystems

They are also called man-made or man-engineered ecosystems. They are maintained artificially by man where, by addition of energy and planned manipulation, natural balance is distrurbed regularly, e.g. croplands such as sugarcane, maize, wheat, rice-fields; orchards, gardens, villages, cities, dams, aquarium and manned spaceship.

CONTROLS ON ECOSYSTEM FUNCTION

Now that we have learned something about how ecosystems are put together and how materials and energy flow through ecosystems, we can better address the question of "what controls ecosystem function"? There are two dominant theories of the control of ecosystems. The first, called bottom-up control, states that it is the nutrient supply to the primary producers that ultimately controls how ecosystems function. If the nutrient supply is increased, the resulting increase in production of autotrophs is propagated through the food web and all of the other trophic levels will respond to the increased availability of food (energy and materials will cycle faster).

The second theory, called top-down control, states that predation and grazing by higher trophic levels on lower trophic levels ultimately controls ecosystem function. For example, if you have an increase in predators, that increase will result in fewer grazers, and that decrease in grazers will result in turn in more primary producers because fewer of them are being eaten by the grazers. Thus the control of population numbers and overall productivity "cascades" from the top levels of the food chain down to the bottom trophic levels.

So, which theory is correct? Well, as is often the case when there is a clear dichotomy to choose from, the answer lies somewhere in the middle. There is evidence from many ecosystem studies that both controls are operating to some degree, but that neither control is complete. For example, the "top-down" effect is often very strong at trophic levels near to the top predators, but the control weakens as you move further down the food chain. Similarly, the "bottom-up" effect of adding nutrients usually stimulates primary production, but the stimulation of secondary production further up the food chain is less strong or is absent.

Thus we find that both of these controls are operating in any system at any time, and we must understand the relative importance of each control in order to help us to predict how an ecosystem will behave or change under different circumstances, such as in the face of a changing climate.

PALEOBIOGEOGRAPHY

Paleobiogeography goes one step further to include paleogeographic data and considerations of plate tectonics. Using molecular analyses and corroborated by fossils, it has been possible to demonstrate that perching birds evolved first in the region of Australia or the adjacent Antarctic (which at that time lay somewhat further north and had a temperate climate). From there, they spread to the other Gondwanan continents and Southeast Asia - the part of Laurasia then closest to their origin of dispersal - in the late Paleogene, before achieving a global distribution in the early Neogene. Not knowing the fact that at the time of dispersal, the Indian Ocean was much narrower than it is today, and that South America was closer to the Antarctic, one would be hard pressed to explain the presence of many "ancient" lineages of perching birds in Africa, as well as the mainly South American distribution of the suboscines.

MODES OF PRESERVATION OF FOSSILS AND TAPHONOMIC CONSIDERATIONS

Ordinarily, only the hard parts of organisms are preserved (for example, only the shells of invertebrates, and only the bones and teeth of vertebrates). In most instances we must make inferences about fossil organisms using only these hard parts. Despite this challenge, we must try to understand the soft-part anatomy of fossil organisms so that we can better appreciate them as organisms that were once alive, that consumed food, breathed oxygen, interacted with their physical and biological environments, etc. Taphonomy is the science that studies the information that is lost between the death of an individual and its final discovery.

What is a fossil and what processes are required for their preservation? A fossil is any evidence of a once-living organism. This includes body fossils, casts, molds, footprints, trackways and feeding traces. This evidence of previous living organisms can then be used to study changes in life forms through time. This includes their evolution, ecology, functional morphology, growth and form, as well as their geographic distribution. Fossils provide us with our best link to the history of life.

PROCESS OF FOSSIL FORMATION

One of the keys to preservation is resistance. Either the conditions are mild enough (calm water, little oxygen) not to destroy much of the organism, or those parts that do get preserved are the most resistant to chemical and physical damage. Good examples of this are the shells of clams and the teeth of mammals. Both of these examples demonstrate that there is a preservational bias for hard parts compared to soft parts.

The nature of preservation is dependent upon the interaction of several factors. The composition of the organism and its structure play vital roles in how the body will react to the physical and chemical activities that normally break down or damage dead organisms. Intimately related to this is the sedimentary environment in which the organism lived. It will determine the type and intensity of the physical and chemical processes. These all contribute to the post-depositional changes (such as replacement, recrystallization, carbonization, the formation of casts, etc.) that take place during fossilization. And finally, numerical abundance will affect the nature of preservation by increasing or decreasing the chances of something being preserved, simply because of the sheer numbers or lack of certain organisms (this does make sense, if you think about it for awhile).

As mentioned above, the bias of hard parts over soft parts can provide considerable problems for paleontologists. Often, as is the case with most molluscs for example, much of the diagnostic information is in the soft part morphology, making it difficult to say certain specific things about organisms whose only record is in the hard parts. It is then necessary to draw upon recent analogues and extrapolate that information back to the fossil record. This can be dangerous if the past was not entirely like the present in environmental or ecological conditions. We call this the "pull of the Recent analogue" and it can be a serious problem if not recognized at the outset.

One of the keys to preservation is resistance. Either the conditions are mild enough (calm water, little oxygen) not to destroy much of the organism, or those parts that do get preserved are the most resistant to chemical and physical damage. Good examples of this are the shells of clams and the teeth of mammals. Both of these examples demonstrate that there is a preservational bias for hard parts compared to soft parts.

The nature of preservation is dependent upon the interaction of several factors. The composition of the organism and its structure play vital roles in how the body will react to the physical and chemical activities that normally break down or damage dead organisms. Intimately related to this is the sedimentary environment in which the organism lived. It will determine the type and intensity of the physical and chemical processes. These all contribute to the post-depositional changes (such as replacement, recrystallization, carbonization, the formation of casts, etc.) that take place during fossilization. And finally, numerical abundance will affect the nature of preservation by increasing or decreasing the chances of something being preserved, simply because of the sheer numbers or lack of certain organisms (this does make sense, if you think about it for awhile).

As mentioned above, the bias of hard parts over soft parts can provide considerable problems for paleontologists. Often, as is the case with most molluscs for example, much of the diagnostic information is in the soft part morphology, making it difficult to say certain specific things about organisms whose only record is in the hard parts. It is then necessary to draw upon recent analogues and extrapolate that information back to the fossil record. This can be dangerous if the past was not entirely like the present in environmental or ecological conditions. We call this the "pull of the Recent analogue" and it can be a serious problem if not recognized at the outset.

MODES OF PRESERVATION

Unaltered

This form of preservation is rare in most of the geologic column, but becomes more frequent in younger sedimentary rocks. Types of unaltered preservation where even the soft body parts are preserved include: (i) mummification, (ii) encasement in tar, (iii) encasement in amber, (iv) encasement in sediment, and (v) freezing. More frequently, however, only the hard skeletal material is preserved after removal of soft body parts.

Examples of unaltered preservation include the skeleton of a horseshoe crab, whose shell is composed of interlocking plates and jointed appendages which quickly disarticulate after death; cockle bivalved molluscs, whose outer-most shell layer has been removed by abrasion, yet the original shell material of the inner layers remains; an ammonoid from the Cretaceous period in which you should note the pearly luster which is original aragonite shell material; and an insect encased in amber.

Molds & Casts

This general class of preservation entails making "replicas" of the skeletal hard parts of organisms. In general, a mold is an impression in the sediment of a skeleton or shell. Once encased in lithified sediment, the dissolution of skeletal material leaves behind the impression or mold of original skeletal form. Thus, a mold is a "mirror image" of the original skeleton. An internal mold (sometimes called a steinkern) is the impression of the inside surface of skeletal hard parts. An external mold is the impression of the outside surface of skeleton or bone. An example of both types of molds can be seen in this image of a trilobite.

A cast is formed by the filling-in of a mold. It is thus a true replica (not a "mirror image") of the original skeleton or shell. By this definition, the cast one gets for a broken limb is not really a cast at all but an external mold.

A graphical representation of the formation of casts and molds is provided in Figure given below.

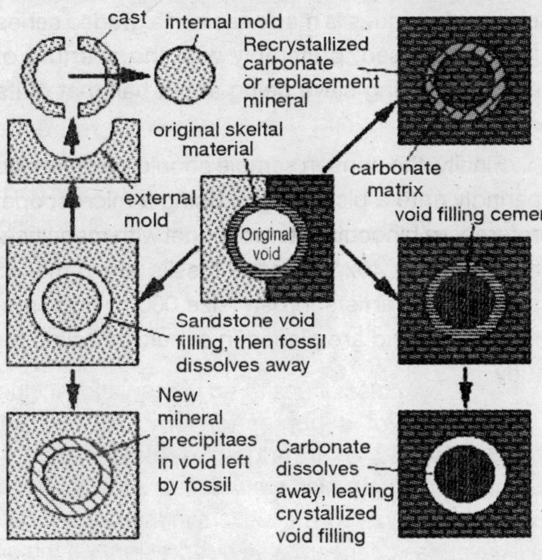

Figure - Different diagenetic processes leading to different preservational styles in skeletal materials.

Replacement & Recrystallization

This common form of preservation involves chemical and/or physical alteration or replacement of original skeletal material. To properly identify replacement and recrystallization, one must know what the original constituents of the organism's skeleton were. Replacement occurs often by the filling in (by various minerals) of the void space after dissolution of original skeletal material. Sometimes, the replacement occurs on a molecule by molecule basis. Common replacement minerals that you should be able to recognize include Silica (SiO_2) as shown in the coral, and Pyrite (FeS_2) shown in the ammonoid.

Recrystallization involves the physical re-arrangement of crystalline structure of skeletal material. This is a common phenomenon in shells which were originally aragonite and/or calcite (both forms of calcium carbonate- $CaCO_3$). Examples, both of which are now calcite, include a gastropod which was originally aragonite and a brachiopod which was originally calcite.

Carbonization

As organic remains decompose in sediments, volatile constituents such as oxygen, hydrogen, and nitrogen are slowly lost to the surrounding sediments frequently leaving behind a carbon film. This process is carbonization (or sometimes called distillation), and occurs most frequently in oxygen deficient, organic-rich environments such as basinal black shales, and coal swamps. The carbon films often show exquisite details of plants and soft-body parts of animals not readily preserved, and can often be recognized by a dark gray or black film with a metallic sheen such as these fern-like fossil plants.

Permineralization

Permineralization involves the filling-in of pore and/or void spaces in shell or bone by secondary mineral matter in solution. With permineralization, the tiny pore spaces in the fossil are filled and the original skeletal material is still retained. However, it is often common for other types of preservation (e.g. replacement) to occur during and/or after permineralization. Because of its porous nature, bone and wood is especially prone to permineralization.

TYPES OF MICROFOSSILS

Fossil specimens can be divided into one of two categories, macrofossils and microfossils. Macrofossils may be held in the hand and examined with nothing more than a good hand lens. Microfossils are very small and require a microscope to view them effectively. For practical reasons the members of the Kent Geologists' Group further restricts the definition of 'microfossil' to those fossils having a size in the range 1000 microns (1mm) to 50 microns.

'Microfossil' is a descriptive term applied to fossilized plants and animals whose size is just at or below the level at which the fossil can be analyzed by the naked eye. A commonly applied cut-off point between "micro" and "macro" fossils is 1 mm, although this is only an approximate guide. Microfossils may either be complete (or near-complete) organisms in themselves (such as the marine plankters foraminifera and coccolithophores) or component parts (such as small teeth or spores) of larger animals or plants. Microfossils are of critical importance as a reservoir of paleoclimate information, and are also commonly used by biostratigraphers to assist in the correlation of rock units.

Fossils smaller than 50 microns are called nanofossils; they include pollen, spores, dinoflagellates and coccoliths. They are excluded from the KGG definition of microfossil because their study requires the use of dangerous chemicals (not available to the amateur) and high power microscopes. These restrictions put the study of nanofossils very much into the realm of the professional palaeontologist.

EXTRACTION AND PREPARATION

Microfossils can be extracted from almost all fossiliferous sedimentary rocks - unconsolidated marine sediments being the most productive. The scientific value of the extracted fossils depends on the care taken in their extraction. It is essential to avoid contamination of the sample, which should be labelled clearly and securely in the field. The re-use of sample bags is not recommended and sieves should be thoroughly washed between processing sessions.

Unconsolidated clays, silts and fine sands are most easily processed and often yield rich and varied assemblages of well-preserved fossils. The sample should be dried thoroughly, then soaked in hot water to disaggregate the sediment. The resulting 'slurry' should be wet sieved. A dispersing agent such as 'Calgon', dissolved in the water at the soaking stage, can be helpful in breaking down the sediment. The 'dry/soak/sieve' cycle should be repeated two or three times to obtain a clean sample. It is worth taking trouble at this stage as it makes life so much easier later on.

Eight inch diameter brass test sieves are recommended for sorting the residue though these are very expensive. As an alternative, one can make sieves or buy cheaper sieves, though these are unlikely to last as long as the better quality product. Sorting of residues is made easier if a graded series of sieves is used; preferably with the aperture of each succeeding sieve being about half that of its predecessor.

Finally, the chosen sample should be sprinkled sparingly onto a picking tray. Using a microscope, preferably a binocular stereo model with magnification of 10x to 40x, selected fossils are removed using a damp artists' brush (size 000 or 0000 recommended) and are placed in a multi-cell slide for study.

4. Sedimentology and stratigraphy

Clastic sediments- gravel, sand and mud; biogenic, chemical and volcanogenic sediments. Classification of conglomerates, sandstones and mudstones, and carbonate rocks. Flow regimes and processes of sediment transport. Sedimentary textures and structures. Sedimentary facies and environments, reconstruction of paleoenvironments. Formation and evolution of sedimentary basins. Diagenesis of siliciclastic and carbonate rocks.

Recent developments in stratigraphic classification. Code of stratigraphic nomenclature - Stratotypes, Global Boundary Stratotype Sections and Points (GSSP). Lithostratigraphic, chronostratigraphic and biostratigraphic-subdivisions. Methods of startigraphic correlation including Shaw's Graphic correlation. Concept of sequence stratigraphy. Rates of sediment accumulation, unconformities. Facies concept in Stratigraphy - Walther's law.

Methods for paleogeographic reconstruction. Earth's Climatic History. Phanerozoic stratigraphy of India with reference to the type areas- their correlation with equivalent formations in other regions. Boundary problems in Indian Phanerozoic stratigraphy.

CLASTIC SEDIMENTS

Clastic sediment consists of grains and particles that were eroded from weathered rocks and then were transported and deposited in loose, unconsolidated layers at the Earth's surface. The sand on a beach, boulders in a river bed, and mud in a puddle are all clastic sediments. Clastic sediment is named according to particle size. Gravel includes all rounded particles larger than 2 millimeters in diameter. Angular particles in the same size range are called rubble. Sand ranges from 1/16 to 2 millimeters in diameter. Silt varies from 1/256 to 1/16 millimeter. Clay is less than 1/256 millimeter in diameterMud is wet silt and clay.

DIAMETER (mm)	SEDIMENT		CLASTIC SEDIMENTARY ROCK
256-64	Boulders Cobbles Pebbles	Gravel (rubble)	Conglomerate (rounded particles) or breccias (angular particles)
2- 0.0625	Sand		Sandstone
0.0625-0.00390625	Silt	Mud	Siltstone
	Clay		Claystone or shale

Table: Sizes and Names of Sedimentary Particles and Clastic Rocks

GRAVEL

Gravel deposits usually represent local accumulations, for example, channel fillings. In such instances, they are restricted in width and thickness but may have considerable length. Fan-shaped deposits of gravels or aprons may accumulate at the snouts of ice masses, or blanket deposits may develop on transgressive beaches. The latter type of deposits are usually thin and patchy, whereas the former are frequently wedge shaped.

A gravel deposit consists of a framework of pebbles between which are voids. The voids are rarely empty, being occupied by sand, silt or clay material. River and fluvio-glacial gravels are otably bimodal, the principal mode being in the gravel grade, the secondary in the sand grade. Marine gravels, however, are often unimodal and tend to be more uniformly sorted than fluvial types of similar grade size.

The shape and surface texture of the pebbles in a gravel deposit are influenced by the agent responsible for its transportation and the length of time taken in transport, although shape is also dependent on the initial shape of the fragment, which in turn is controlled by the fracture pattern within the parental rock. Gravel particles can be classified as rounded, irregular, angular, flaky and elongated in shape. Anon defines a flakiness index, an elongation index and an angularity number. The flakiness index of an aggregate is the percentage of particles, by weight, whose least dimension (thickness) is less than 0.6 times their mean dimension. The elongation index of an aggregate is the percentage, by weight, of particles whose greatest dimension (length) is greater than 1.8 times their mean dimension. The angularity number is a measure of relative angularity based on the percentage of voids in the aggregate. The least angular aggregates are found to have about 33% voids, and the angularity number is defined as the amount by which the percentage of voids exceeds 33. The angularity number ranges from 0 to about 12. Anon also recognized the following types of surface texture, glassy, smooth, granular, rough, crystalline and honeycombed.

The composition of a gravel deposit reflects not only the type of rocks in the source area, but is also influenced by the agents responsible for its formation and the climatic regime in which it was or is being deposited. Furthermore, relief influences the character of a gravel deposit, for example, under low relief, gravel production is small and the pebbles tend to be chemically inert residues such as vein quartz, quartzite, chert and flint. By contrast, high relief and rapid erosion yield coarse, immature gravels. All the same, gravel achieves maturity much more rapidly than does sand under the same conditions. Gravels that consist of only one type of rock fragment are referred to as oligomictic. Such deposits are usually thin and well sorted. Polymictic gravels usually consist of a varied assortment of rock fragments and occur as thick, poorly sorted deposits.

Gravel particles generally possess surface coatings that may be the result of weathering or may represent mineral precipitates derived from circulating groundwater. The latter type of coating may be calcareous, ferruginous, siliceous or, occasionally, gypsiferous. Clay also may form a coating about pebbles. Surface coatings generally reduce the value of gravels for use as concrete aggregate, thick and/or soft and loosely adhering surface coatings are particularly suspect. Clay and gypsum coatings, however, can often be removed by screening and washing. Siliceous coatings tend to react with the alkalies in high-alkali cements and are, therefore, detrimental to concrete.

In a typical gravel pit, the material is dug from the face by a mechanical excavator. This loads the material into trucks or onto a conveyor that transports it to the primary screening and crushing plant. After crushing, the material is further screened and washed. This sorts the gravel into various grades and separates it from the sand fraction. The latter is usually sorted into coarser and finer grades, the coarser is used for concrete and the finer is preferred for mortar. Because gravel deposits are highly permeable, if the water table is high, then the gravel pit will flood. The gravels then have to be worked by dredging. Sea-dredged aggregates are becoming increasingly important.

PROCESSES OF SEDIMENT TRANSPORT

After weathering creates clastic sediment, flowing water, wind, glaciers, and gravity erode it and carry it down slope. Streams carry the greatest proportion of clastic sediment. Because most streams empty into the oceans, most sediment accumulates near continental coastlines. However, some streams deposit their sediment in lakes or in inland basins. Streams and wind modify sediment as they carry it downslope. Water and wind round clastic particles as fine as silt by tumbling them against each other during transport. Finer particles do not round as effectively because they are so small and light that water and even wind, to some extent, cushion them as they bounce along,minimizing abrasion. Glaciers do not round clastic particles because the ice prevents the particles from abrading each other. Weathering breaks bedrock into particles of all sizes, ranging from clay to boulders. Yet most clastic sediment and sedimentary rocks are well sorted–that is, the grains are of uniform size. Some sandstone formations extend for hundreds of square kilometers and are more than a kilometer thick, but they consist completely of uniformly sized sand grains.

Sorting depends on three factors: the viscosity and velocity of the transporting medium and the durability of the particles. Viscosity is resistance to flow; ice has high viscosity, air has low viscosity, and water is intermediate. Ice does not sort effectively because it transports particles of all sizes, from house-sized boulders to clay. In contrast, wind transports only sand, silt, and clay and leaves the larger particles behind. Thus, wind sorts particles according to size.

A stream transports only small particles when it flows slowly, but larger particles when it picks up speed. For example, a stream transports large and small particles when it is flooding, but only small particles during normal flows. As a flood recedes and the water gradually slows down, the stream deposits the largest particles first and the smallest ones last, creating layers of different sized particles.

Finally, durability of the particles affects sorting. Sediment becomes abraded as it travels downstream. Thus a stream may transport cobbles from the mountains toward a delta, but the cobbles may never complete the journey because they wear down to smaller grains along the way. This is one reason why mountain streams are frequently boulder choked but deltas are composed of mud and sand.

SAND

SAND

The textural maturity of sand varies appreciably. A high degree of sorting, coupled with a high degree of rounding, characterizes mature sand. The shape of sand grains, however, is not greatly influenced by the length of transport. Maturity is reflected in the particle composition of sand, and it has been argued that the ultimate sand is a concentration of pure quartz. This is because the less-stable minerals disappear due to mechanical or chemical breakdown during erosion and transportation or even after sand has been deposited.

Sands are used for building purposes to give bulk to concrete, mortars, plasters and renderings. For example, sand is used in concrete to lessen the void space created by the coarse aggregate. Sand consisting of a range of grade sizes gives a lower proportion of voids than one in which the grains are of uniform size. Indeed, grading is probably the most important property as far as the suitability of sand for concrete is concerned.

Anon (1992) recognizes four grades of sand that can produce good-quality concrete. In any concrete mix, consideration should be given to the total specific surface of the coarse and fine aggregates, since this represents the surface that has to be lubricated by the cement paste to produce a workable mix. Poorly graded sands can be improved by adding the missing grade sizes to them, so that high-quality material can be produced with correct blending.

It is generally alleged that sand with rounded particles produces slightly more workable concrete than one consisting of irregularly shaped particles. Sands used for building purposes are usually siliceous in composition and should be as free from impurities as possible. Ideally, they should contain less than 3%, by weight, of silt or clay, since they need a high water content to produce a workable concrete mix. A high water content leads to shrinkage and cracking in concrete on drying. Furthermore, clay and shaley material tend to retard setting and hardening, or they may spoil the appearance of concrete. If sand particles are coated with clay, they form a poor bond with cement and produce a weaker and less durable concrete.

The presence of feldspars in sands used in concrete has sometimes given rise to hair cracking, and mica and particles of shale adversely affect the strength of concrete. Organic impurities may affect the setting and hardening properties of cement adversely by retarding hydration and, thereby, reduce its strength and durability. Organic and coaly material also cause popping, pitting and blowing. If iron pyrite occurs in sand, then it gives rise to unsightly rust stains when used in concrete. The salt content of marine sands is unlikely to produce any serious adverse effects in good-quality concrete, although it probably will give rise to efflorescence. Salt can be removed by washing sand.

MUDSTONE

Mudstone is a nonfissile rock composed of clay and silt. In some mudstone and claystone, layering is absent because burrowing animals such as worms, clams, and crabs disrupted it by churning the sediment.

BIOGENIC, CHEMICAL AND VOLCANOGENIC SEDIMENTS

Sedimentary rocks are broadly divided into four categories:

1. Clastic sedimentary rocks are composed of fragments of weathered rocks, called clasts, that have been transported, deposited, and cemented together. Clastic rocks make up more than 85 per cent of all sedimentary rocks. This category includes sandstone, silt-stone, and shale.

Classification - Clastic sedimentary particles are classified in terms of size

Name of Particle	Size Range	Loose Sediment	Consolidated Rock
Boulder	>256 mm	Gravel	Conglomerate or Breccia (depends on rounding)
Cobble	64 - 256 mm	Gravel	
Pebble	2 - 64 mm	Gravel	
Sand	1/16 - 2mm	Sand	Sandstone
Silt	1/256 - 1/16 mm	Silt	Siltstone
Clay	<1/256 mm	Clay	Claystone, mudstone, and shale

The formation of a clastic sedimentary rock involves three processes:

1. Transportation - Sediment can be transported by sliding down slopes, being picked up by the wind, or by being carried by running water in streams, rivers, or ocean currents. The distance the sediment is transported and the energy of the transporting medium all leave clues in the final sediment that tell us something about the mode of transportation.
2. Deposition - Sediment is deposited when the energy of the transporting medium becomes too low to continue the transport

process. In other words, if the velocity of the transporting medium becomes too low to transport sediment, the sediment will fall out and become deposited. The final sediment thus reflects the energy of the transporting medium.

3. Diagenesis - Diagenesis is the process that turns sediment into rock. The first stage of the process is compaction. Compaction occurs as the weight of the overlying material increases. Compaction forces the grains closer together, reducing pore space and eliminating some of the contained water. Some of this water may carry mineral components in solution, and these constituents may later precipitate as new minerals in the pore spaces. This causes cementation, which will then start to bind the individual particles together. Further compaction and burial may cause recrystallization of the minerals to make the rock even harder.

   Other conditions present during diagenesis, such as the presence of absence of free oxygen may cause other alterations to the original sediment. In an environment where there is excess oxygen (Oxidizing Environment) organic remains will be converted to carbon dioxide and water. Iron will change from Fe^{2+} to Fe^{3+}, and will change the color of the sediment to a deep red (rust) color. In an environment where there is a depletion of oxygen (Reducing Environment), organic material may be transformed to solid carbon in the form of coal, or may be converted to hydrocarbons, the source of petroleum.

2. Organic sedimentary rocks consist of the remains of plants or animals. Coal is an organic sedimentary rock made up of decomposed and compacted plant remains.

3. Chemical sedimentary rocks form by direct precipitation of minerals from solution. Rock salt, for example, forms when salt precipitates from evaporating sea-water or saline lake water.

CHERTS - CHEMICALLY PRECIPITATED SiO_2

Evaporites - formed by evaporation of sea water or lake water. Produces halite (salt) and gypsum deposits by chemical precipitation as concentration of solids increases due to water loss by evaporation.

Bioclastic sedimentary rocks. Most limestone is composed of broken shell fragments. The fragments are clastic, but they form from organic material. As a result, limestone formed in this way is called a bioclastic rock.

Limestone - calcite ($CaCO_3$) is precipitated by organisms usually to form a shell or other skeletal structure. Accumulation of these skeletal remains results in a limestone.

Diatomite - Siliceous ooze consisting of the remains of radiolarian or diatoms can form a light colored soft rock called diatomite.

Coal - accumulation of dead plant matter in large abundance in a reducing environment (lack of oxygen).

Oil Shale - actually a clastic sedimentary rock that contains a high abundance of organic material that is converted to petroleum during diagenesis.

CLASSIFICATION OF CONGLOMERATES, SANDSTONES AND MUDSTONES, AND CARBONATE ROCKS

A conglomerate is a rock consisting of individual clasts within a finer-grained matrix that have become cemented together. Conglomerates are sedimentary rocks consisting of rounded fragments and are thus differentiated from breccias, which consist of angular clasts.

CLASSIFICATION OF CONGLOMERATES

Conglomerates are classified in terms of both their rounding and sorting.

TEXTURE

Paraconglomerates consist of a matrix-supported rock that contains at least 15% sand-sized or smaller grains (<2 mm), the rest being larger grains of varying sizes.

Orthoconglomerates consist of a clast-supported rock with less than 15% matrix of sand and finer particles.

Metamorphic alteration transforms conglomerate into metaconglomerate.

CLAST COMPOSITION

Conglomerates are classified for the lithologies of the clasts

- Monomict - clasts with only a single lithology
- Oligomict - clasts of only a few different lithologies
- Polymict - clasts of many different lithologies
- Intraformational - clasts derived from the same formation in which they are found
- Extraformational - clasts derived older rocks than the formation in which they are found

CLAST SIZE

Conglomerates are also classified by the dominant clast size.

- Granule conglomerate 2–4 mm
- Pebble conglomerate 4–64 mm
- Cobble conglomerate 64–256 mm
- Boulder conglomerate >256 mm

CLASSIFICATION OF SANDSTONES

Sandstone is a sedimentary rock composed mainly of sand-sized minerals or rock grains. Most sandstone is composed of quartz and/or feidspar because these are the most common minerals in the Earth's crust. Like sand, sandstone may be any color, but the most common colors are tan, brown, yellow, red, gray and white. Since sandstone beds often form highly visible cliffs and other topographic features, certain colors of sandstone have been strongly identified with certain regions.

Some sandstones are resistant to weathering, yet are easy to work. This makes sandstone a common building and paving material. However, some that have been used in the past, such as the Collyhurst sandstone used in North West England, have been found less resistant, necessitating repair and replacement in older buildings. Because of the hardness of the individual grains, uniformity of grain size and friability of their structure, some types of sandstone are excellent materials from which to make grindstones, for sharpening blades and other implements. Non-friable sandstone can be used to make grindstones for grinding grain, e.g., gritstone.

Rock formations that are primarily composed of sandstone usually allow percolation of water and other fluids and are porous enough to store large quantities, making them valuable aquifers and petroleum reservoirs. Fine-grained aquifers, such as sandstones, are more apt to filter out pollutants from the surface than are rocks with cracks and crevices, such as limestone or other rocks fractured by seismic activity.

Sandstones fall into several major groups based on their mineralogy and texture. Below is a partial list of common sandstone types.

- quartz arenites are made up almost entirely of quartz grains, usually well sorted and rounded. These pure quartz sands result from extensive weathering that occurred before and during transport and removed everything but quartz, the most stable mineral. They are common in beach environments.
- arkoses are more than 25 per cent feldspar. The grains tend to be poorly rounded and less well sorted than those of pure quartz sandstones. These feldspar-rich sandstones come from rapidly eroding granitic and metamorphic terrains where chemical weathering is subordinate to physical weathering.
- lithic sandstones contain many lithic fragments derived from fine-grained rocks, mostly shales, volcanic rocks, and fine-grained metamorphic rocks.
- graywacke is a heterogeneous mixture of lithic fragments and angular grains of quartz and feldspar, and/or grains surrounded by a fine-grained clay matrix. Much of this matrix is formed by relatively soft fragments, such as shale and some volcanic rocks, that are chemically altered and physically compacted after deep burial of the sandstone formation.

- Eolianite is a term used for a rock which is composed of sand grains that show signs of significant transportation by wind. These have usually been deposited in desert environments. They are commonly extremely well sorted and rich in quartz.
- Oolite is more a limestone than a sandstone, but is made of sand-sized carbonate ooids, and is common in saline beaches with gentle wave action.

CLASSIFICATION OF MUDSTONE

Mudstone (also called mudrock) is a fine grained sedimentary rock whose original constituents were clays or muds. Grain size is up to 0.0625 mm (0.0025 in) with individual grains too small to be distinguished without a microscope. With increased pressure over time the platey clay minerals may become aligned, with the appearance of fissility or parallel layering. This finely bedded material that splits readily into thin layers is called shale, as distinct from mudstone. The lack of fissility or layering in mudstone may be due either to original texture or to the disruption of layering by burrowing organisms in the sediment prior to lithification. Mud rocks, such as mudstone and shale comprise some 65% of all sedimentary rocks. Mudstone looks like hardened clay and, depending upon circumstances under which it was formed, it may show cracks or fissures, like a sun-baked clay deposit. They can be separated into these categories:

- Siltstone - greater than half of the composition is silt-sized particles.
- Claystone - greater than half of the composition is clay-sized particles.
- Mudstone - hardened mud; a mix of silt and clay sized particles. Mudstone can include:
  - o Shale - exhibits lamination or fissility.
  - o Argillite - has undergone low grade metamorphism.

Shale is a fine-grained, clastic sedimentary rock composed of mud that is a mix of flakes of clay minerals and tiny fragments (silt-sized particles) of other minerals, especially quartz and calcite. The ratio of clay to other minerals is variable. Shale is characterized by breaks along thin laminae or parallel layering or bedding less than one centimeter in thickness, called fissility. Mudstones, on the other hand, are similar in composition but do not show the fissility.

Shale is a fine-grained, clastic sedimentary rock composed of mud that is a mix of flakes of clay minerals and tiny fragments (silt-sized particles) of other minerals, especially quartz and calcite. The ratio of clay to other minerals is variable. Shale is characterized by breaks along thin laminae or parallel layering or bedding less than one centimeter in thickness, called fissility. Mudstones, on the other hand, are similar in composition but do not show the fissility.

ARGILLITE

An argillite is a fine-grained sedimentary rock composed predominantly of indurated clay particles. Argillites are basically lithified muds and oozes. They contain variable amounts of silt-sized particles. The argillites grade into shale when the fissile layering typical of shale is developed. Another name for poorly lithified argillites is mudstone. These rocks, although variable in composition, are typically high in aluminium and silica with variable alkali and alkaline earth cations. The term pelitic or pelite is often applied to these sediments and rocks. Metamorphism of argillites produces slate, phyllite, and pelitic schist.

SEDIMENTARY TEXTURES AND STRUCTURES

TEXTURES OF SEDIMENTARY ROCKS

When sediment is transported and deposited, it leaves clues to the mode of transport and deposition. For example, if the mode of transport is by sliding down a slope, the deposits that result are generally chaotic in nature, and show a wide variety of particle sizes. Grain size and the interrelationship between grains gives the resulting sediment texture. Thus, we can use the texture of the resulting deposits to give us clues to the mode of transport and deposition.

Sorting - The degree of uniformity of grain size. Particles become sorted on the basis of density, because of the energy of the transporting medium. High energy currents can carry larger fragments. As the energy decreases, heavier particles are deposited and lighter fragments continue to be transported.

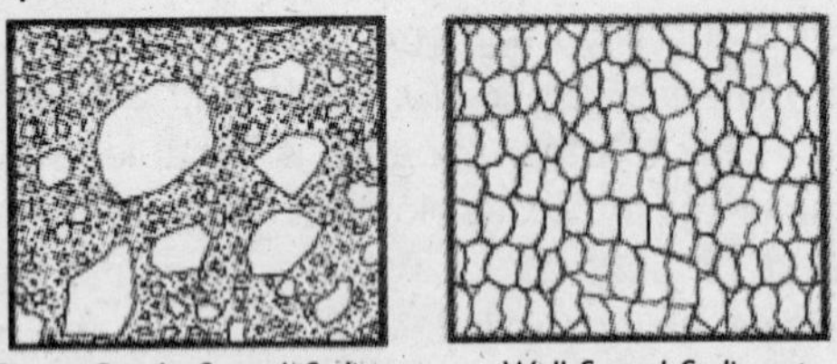

Fig. 1: Poorly Sorted Sodiment   Well Sorted Sediment

If the particles have the same density, then the heavier particles will also be larger, so the sorting will take place on the basis of size. We can classify this size sorting on a relative basis - well sorted to poorly sorted. Sorting gives clues to the energy conditions of the transporting medium from which the sediment was deposited.

Examples

- Beach deposits and wind blown deposits generally show good sorting because the energy of the transporting medium is usually constant.
- Stream deposits are usually poorly sorted because the energy (velocity) in a stream varies with position in the stream.

Rounding - During the transportation process, grains may be reduced in size due to abrasion. Random abrasion results in the eventual rounding off of the sharp corners and edges of grains. Thus, rounding of grains gives us clues to the amount of time a sediment has been in the transportation cycle. Rounding is classified on relative terms as well.

Sedimentary structures

Almost all sedimentary rocks contain sedimentary structures, features that developed during or shortly after deposition of the sediment. These structures help us understand how the sediment was transported and deposited.

The most obvious and common sedimentary structure is bedding, or stratification–layering that develops as sediment is deposited. Bedding forms because sediment accumulates layer by layer. Almost all sedimentary beds were originally horizontal because most sediment accumulates on nearly level surfaces.

Cross Bedding - Sets of beds that are inclined relative to one another. The beds are inclined in the direction that the wind or water was moving at the time of deposition. Boundaries between sets of cross beds usually represent an erosional surface. Very common in beach deposits, sand dunes, and river deposited sediment.

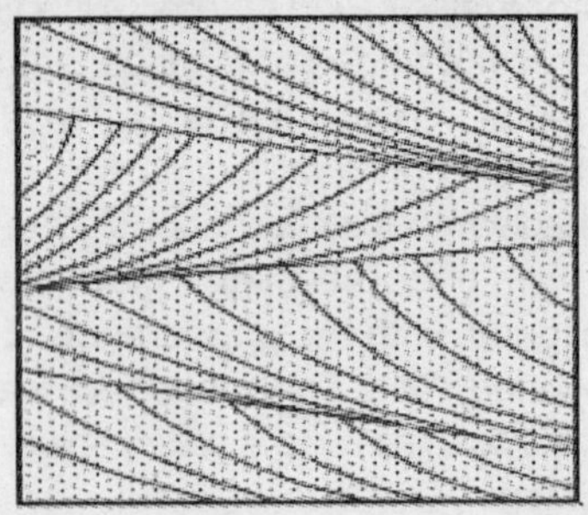

Fig. 2: Illustration showing cross bedding in sedimentary rock

Graded Bedding - As current velocity decreases, first the larger or more dense particles are deposited followed by smaller particles. This results in bedding showing a decrease in grain size from the bottom of the bed to the top of the bed. Graded beds commonly form when some violent activity, such as a major flood or submarine landslide, mixes a range of grain sizes together in water. The larger grains settle rapidly and concentrate at the base of the bed. Finer particles settle more slowly and accumulate in the upper parts of the bed.

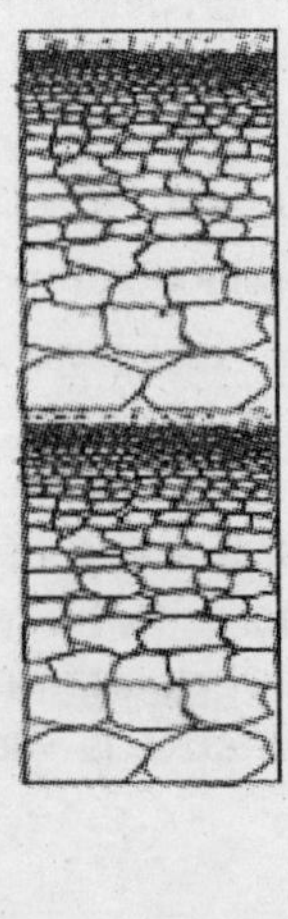

Fig. 3: Illustration representing Graded Bedding

Ripple Marks - Characteristic of shallow water deposition. Caused by waves or winds. They are like dunes and sand waves, but smaller. If the water or wind flows in a single direction, the ripple marks become asymmetrical, like miniature dunes. In other cases, waves move back and forth in shallow water, forming symmetrical ripple marks in bottom sand. Ripple marks are often preserved in sandy sedimentary rocks.

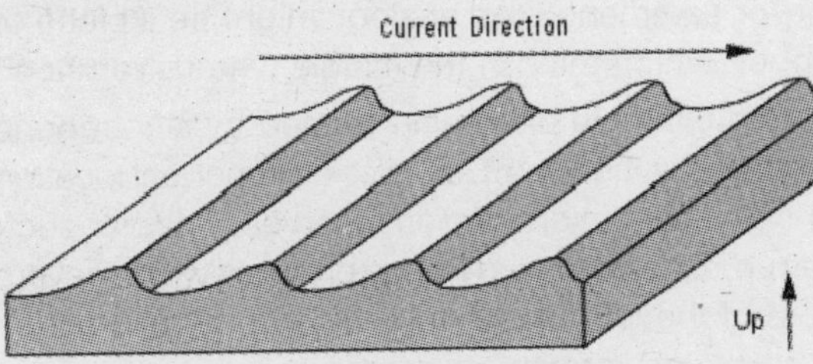

Fig. 4: Ripple Marks

Mud cracks - result from the drying out of wet sediment at the surface of the Earth. The cracks form due to shrinkage of the sediment as it dries. They indicate that the mud accumulated in shallow water that periodically dried up. For example, mud cracks are common on intertidal mud flats where sediment is flooded by water at high tide and exposed at low tide. The cracks often fill with sediment carried in by the next high tide and are commonly well preserved in rocks.

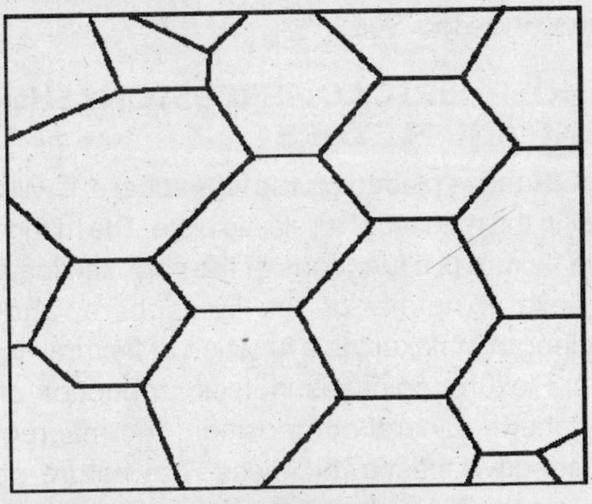

Fig. 5: Mud Cracks

Rhythmic Layering - Alternating parallel layers having different properties. Sometimes caused by seasonal changes in deposition (Varves). i.e. lake deposits wherein coarse sediment is deposited in summer months and fine sediment is deposited in the winter when the surface of the lake is frozen.

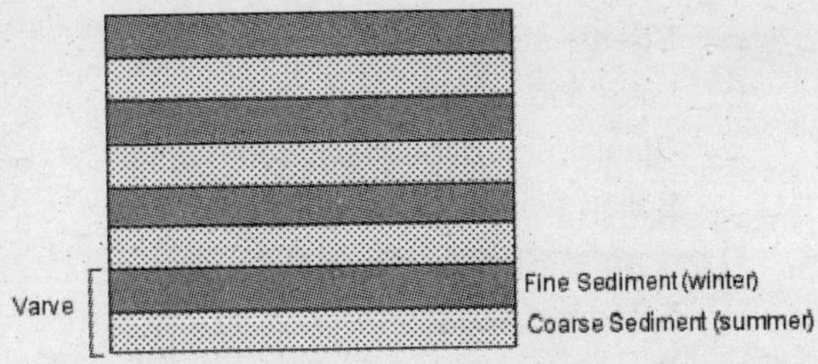

Fig. 6: Rhythmic Layering in sedimentary rock

Non-sorted Sediment - Sediment showing a mixture of grain sizes results from such things as rockfalls, debris flows, mudflows, and deposition from melting ice.

Raindrop Marks - pits (or tiny craters) created by falling rain. If present, this suggests that the sediment was exposed to the surface of the Earth.

Fossils - are any remains or traces of a plant or animal preserved in rock–any evidence of past life. Fossils include remains of shells, bones, or teeth; whole bodies preserved in amber or ice; and a variety of tracks, burrows, and chemical remains. Probably the most important indicator of the environment of deposition.

- Different species usually inhabit specific environments.
- Because life has evolved - fossils give clues to relative age of the sediment.
- Can also be important indicators of past climates.

SEDIMENTARY FACIES AND ENVIRONMENTS

A sedimentary facies is a group of characteristics which reflect a sedimentary environment different from those elsewhere in the same deposit. Thus, facies may change vertically through a sequence as a result of changing environments through time. Also, facies may change laterally through a deposit as a result of changing environments with distance at the same time.

Common Sedimentary Environments

- Non-marine environments
    - Stream sediments
    - Lake sediments
    - Glacial (ice deposited) sediments
    - Eolian (wind deposited) sediments
- Continental Shelf sediments
    - Estuarine sediments
    - Deltaic sediments
    - Beach sediments
    - Carbonate shelf sediments
    - Marine evaporite sediments
- Continental slope and rise sediments
    - Turbidites
    - Deep Sea Fans
    - Sediment drifts
- Deep Sea Sediments
    - Deep -Sea oozes
    - Land-derived sediments

FORMATION AND EVOLUTION OF SEDIMENTARY BASINS

SEDIMENTARY BASIN

The term sedimentary basin is used to refer to any geographical feature exhibiting subsidence and consequent infilling by sedimentation. As the sediments are buried, they are subjected to increasing pressure and begin the process of lithification.

METHODS OF FORMATION

It is common to categorise sedimentary basins according to the mechanism of formation: tectonic compression (e.g., foreland basins, caused by lithospheric flexure), tectonic extension (e.g., back-arc basins, caused by lithospheric stretching), and tectonic strike-slip (such as pull-apart basins).

LITHOSPHERIC STRETCHING

If the lithosphere is caused to stretch horizontally, by mechanisms such as ridge-push or trench-pull, the effect is believed to be twofold. The lower, hotter part of the lithosphere will "flow" slowly away from the main area being stretched, whilst the upper, cooler and more brittle crust will tend to fault (crack) and fracture. The combined effect of these two mechanisms is for the earth's surface in the area of extension to subside, creating a geographical depression which is then often infilled with water and/or sediments. (An analogy might be a piece of rubber, which thins in the middle when stretched.)

An example of a basin caused by lithospheric stretching is the North Sea - also an important location for significant hydrocarbon reserves. Another such feature is the Basin and Range province which covers most of the USA state of Nevada, forming a series of horst and graben structures.

Another expression of lithospheric stretching results in the formation of ocean basins with central ridges; The Red Sea is in fact an incipient ocean, in a plate tectonic context. The mouth of the Red Sea is also a tectonic triple junction where the Indian Ocean Ridge, Red Sea Rift and East African Great Rift Valley meet. This triple junction is also the only place on the planet where seafloor crust is subaerially exposed. The reason for this is twofold, due to a high thermal buoyancy of the junction, and a local crumpled zone of seafloor crust acting as a dam against the Red Sea.

LITHOSPHERIC COMPRESSION/SHORTENING AND FLEXURE

If a load is placed on the lithosphere, it will tend to flex in the manner of an elastic plate. The magnitude of the flexure is a functions of the imposed load and the flexural rigidity of the lithosphere, and the wavelength of flexure is a function of flexural rigidity alone. Flexural rigidity is in itself, a function of the lithospheric mineral composition, thermal regime, and effective elastic thickness. The nature of the load is varied. For instance, the Hawaiian Islands chain of volcanic edifices has sufficient mass to cause deflection in the lithosphere.

The obduction of one tectonic plate onto another also causes a load and often results in the creation of a foreland basin, such as the Po basin next to the Alps in Italy, the Molasse Basin next to the Alps in Germany, or the Ebro basin next to the Pyrenees in Spain.

STRIKE-SLIP DEFORMATION

Deformation of the lithosphere in the plane of the earth (i.e. such that faults are vertical) occurs as a result of near horizontal maximum and minimum principal stresses. The resulting zones of subsidence are known as strike-slip or pull apart basins. Basins formed through strike-slip action occur where a vertical fault plane curves. When the curve in the fault plane moves apart, a region of transtension results, creating a basin. Another term for a transtensional basin is a rhombochasm. A classic rhombochasm is illustrated by the Dead Sea rift, where northward movement of the Arabian Plate relative to the Anatolian Plate has caused a rhombochasm.

The opposite effect is that of transpression, where converging movement of a curved fault plane causes collision of the opposing sides of the fault. An example is the San Bernardino Mountains north of Los Angeles, which result from convergence along a curve in the San Andreas fault system. The Northridge earthquake was caused by vertical movement along local thrust and reverse faults bunching up against the bend in the otherwise strike-slip fault environment.

Code of stratigraphic nomenclature – Stratotypes, Global Boundary Stratotype Sections and Points (GSSP)

CODE OF STRATIGRAPHIC NOMENCLATURE

The American Commission on Stratigraphic Nomenclature, recognizing the desirability of uniform usage in stratigraphic classification and terminology throughout the continent of North America, has proposed a new code of stratigraphic nomenclature.

THE PRIME PURPOSE IS

1. to formulate a usefully comprehensive, yet explicit statement of principles and practices for classifying and naming stratigraphic units, and

2. to secure the greatest possible uniformity in applying these principles and practices. This code is applicable to all kinds of rocks, sedimentary, igneous, and metamorphic.

The Commission has been guided by the philosophy expressed in its reports on the nature, usage, and nomenclature of rock-stratigraphic, biostratigraphic, and time-stratigraphic units. The Articles of this code are recommendations that can not be generally mandatory, but geological organizations may adopt these articles as their rules of nomenclatorial procedure.

This code provides regulations and recommendations relating to

1) rock-stratigraphic units,
2) stratigraphic units,
3) biostratigraphic units, and
4) time-stratigraphic units.

The code also treats 2 categories of units that are not in themselves stratigraphic units but are closely related. These are

5) geologic-time units, which are fundamentally related in concept to time-stratigraphic units, and
6) geologic-climate units, which are based on Quaternary stratigraphic units.

GLOBAL BOUNDARY STRATOTYPE SECTIONS AND POINTS (GSSP)

A Global Boundary Stratotype Section and Point, abbreviated GSSP, is an internationally agreed upon stratigraphic section which serves as the reference section for a particular boundary on the geologic time scale. The effort to define GSSPs is conducted by the International Commission on Stratigraphy, a part of the International Union of Geological Sciences. Most, but not all, GSSPs are based on paleontological changes. Hence GSSPs are usually described in terms of transitions between different faunal stages, though far more faunal stages have been described than GSSPs. The GSSP definition effort commenced in 1977. As of 2004, 45 of the 96 GSSPs required have been approved.

AN IDEAL GSSP

An ideal GSSP would:

- be accessible to research
- be extensive enough to ensure future access
- be easily related to other exposures worldwide
- contain a radiometrically datable bed at the boundary, and
- include well defined markers at the stage boundary that can be applied worldwide.

AGREED-UPON GSSPS

The Precambrian-Cambrian boundary GSSP at Fortune Head, Newfoundland is a typical GSSP. It is accessible by paved road and is set aside as a nature preserve. A continuous section is available from beds that are clearly Precambrian into beds that are clearly Cambrian. The boundary is set at the first appearance of a complex trace fossil Treptichnus pedum that is found worldwide. The Fortune Head GSSP is unlikely to be washed away or built over. Nonetheless, Treptichnus pedum is less than ideal as a marker fossil as it is not found in every Cambrian sequence, and it is not assured that it is found at the same level in every exposure. In fact, further eroding its value as a boundary marker, it has since been identified in strata 4m below the GSSP! However, no other fossil is known that would be preferable. There is no radiometrically datable bed at the boundary at Fortune Head, but there is one slightly above the boundary in similar beds nearby. These factors have lead some geologists to suggest that this GSSP is in need of re-assigning.

Once a GSSP boundary has been agreed upon, a "golden spike" is driven into the geologic section to mark the precise boundary for future geologists (though in practice the "spike" need neither be golden nor an actual spike). The first stratigraphic boundary was defined in 1977 by identifying the Silurian-Devonian boundary with a bronze plaque at a locality called Klonk, northeast of the village of Suchomasty in the Czech Republic. GSSPs are also sometimes referred to as Golden Spikes.

LITHOSTRATIGRAPHIC, CHRONOSTRATIGRAPHIC AND BIOSTRATIGRAPHIC SUBDIVISIONS

LITHOSTRATIGRAPHIC SUBDIVISIONS

Lithostratigraphy is a sub-discipline of stratigraphy, the geological science associated with the study of strata or rock layers. Major focuses include geochronology, comparative geology, and petrology. In general a stratum will be primarily igneous or sedimentary relating to how the rock was formed.

Sedimentary layers are laid down by deposition of sediment associated with weathering processes, decaying organic matters (biogenic) or through chemical precipitation. These layers are distinguishable as having many fossils and are important for the study of biostratigraphy. Igneous layers are either plutonic or volcanic in character depending upon the cooling rate of the rock. These layers are generally devoid of fossils and represent intrusions and volcanic activity that occurred over the geologic history of the area.

There are a number of principles that are used to explain the appearance of stratum. When an igneous rock cuts across a formation of sedimentary rock, then we can say that the igneous intrusion is younger than the sedimentary rock. The principle of superposition states that a sedimentary rock layer in a tectonically undisturbed stratum is younger than the one beneath and older than the one above it. The principle of original horizontality states that the deposition of sediments occurs as essentially horizontal beds.

TYPES OF LITHOSTRATIGRAPHIC UNITS

A lithostratigraphic unit conforms to the law of superposition, which state that in any succession of strata, not disturbed or overturned since deposition, younger rocks lies above older rocks. The law of horizontal continuity states that a set of bed extends and can be traceable over a large area.

Lithostratigraphic units are recognized and defined on the basis of observable rock characteristics. The descriptions of strata based on physical appearance define facies. Lithostratigraphic units are only defined by lithic characteristics, and not by age.

Stratotype : A designated type of unit consisting of accessible rocks that contain clear-cut characteristics that are characteristic for a particular lithostratigraphic unit.

Lithosome: Masses of rock of essentially uniform character and having interchanging relationships with adjacent masses of different lithology. E.g.: Shale lithosome, limestone lithosome etc.

The fundamental Lithostratigraphic unit is the Formation. The formation is a lithologically distinctive stratigraphic unit that is large enough to be mappable and traceable.

Hierarchy of terms:

- Supergroup
- Group
- Formation
- Member
- Bed/Bed sets

STRATIGRAPHIC RELATIONSHIP

Two types of contact: Conformable and Unconformable.

Conformable: Unbroken deposition, no break or hiatus (break or interruption in the continuity of the geological record). The surface strata resulting is called a conformity.

Two types of contact between conformable strata: Abrupt contacts (Directly separate beds of distinctly different lithology, minor depositional break, called Diastems) Gradational contact (Gradual change in deposition, mixing zone).

Unconformable: Period of erosion/non-deposition. The surface stratum resulting is called an unconformity.

Four types of unconformity

Angular unconformity Younger sediment lies upon an eroded surface of tilted or folded older rocks. The older rock dips at a different angle than the younger.

Disconformity: The contact between younger and older beds is marked by visible, irregular erosional surfaces. Paleosol might develop right above the disconformity surface because of the non-deposition setting.

Paraconformity: The bedding plans below and above the unconformity are parallel. A time gap is present but there is no erosion, just a non-deposition period.

Nonconformity: Relatively young sediments are deposited right above older Igneous or metamorphic rocks.

LITHOSTRATIGRAPHIC CORRELATION

To correlate lithostratigraphic units, geologists define facies, and look for key beds or key sequences that can be used as a datum.

- Direct correlation: based on lithology, color, structure, thickness etc.
- Indirect correlation: electric log correlation (gamma-ray, density, resistivity etc.)

CHRONOSTRATIGRAPHIC SUBDIVISIONS

Chronostratigraphy is the branch of stratigraphy that studies the age of rock strata in relation to time.

The ultimate aim of chronostratigraphy is to arrange the sequence of deposition and the time of deposition of all rocks within a geological region, and eventually, the entire geologic record of the Earth.

The standard stratigraphic nomenclature is a chronostratigraphic system based on palaeontological intervals of time defined by recognised fossil assemblages (biostratigraphy). The aim of chronostratigraphy is to give a meaningful age date to these fossil assemblage intervals and interfaces.

METHODOLOGY OF CHRONOSTRATIGRAPHIC

Chronostratigraphy relies heavily upon isotope geology and geochronology to derive hard dating of known and well defined rock units which contain the specific fossil assemblages defined by the stratigraphic system. However it is practically very difficult to isotopically date most fossils and sedimentary rocks directly, and thus inferences must be made in order to arrive at an age date which reflecs the beginning of the interval.

The methodology used is derived from the law of superposition and the principles of cross-cutting relationships.

Because igneous rocks occur at specific intervals in time and are essentially instantaneous on a geologic time scale, and because they contain mineral assemblage which may be dated more accurately and precisely by isotopic methods, the construction of a chronostratigraphic column will rely heavily on intrusive and extrusive igneous rocks.

Metamorphism, often associated with faulting, may also be used to bracket depositional intervals in a chronostratigraphic column. Metamorphic rocks can, occasionally, be dated, and this may give some limits to the age at which a bed could be laid down. For example, if a bed containing graptolites overlies crystalline basement at some point, dating the crystalline basement will give a maximum age of that fossil assemblage.

However, this process requires a considerable degree of effort and checking of field relationships and age dates. For instance, there may be many millions of years between a bed being laid down and an intrusive rock cutting it; the estimate of age must necessarily be between the oldest cross-cutting intrusive rock in the fossil assemblage and the youngest rock upon which the fossil assemblage rests.

CHRONOSTRATIGRAPHIC UNITS

Chronostratigraphic units, with examples:

- eonothem - Phanerozoic
- erathem - Paleozoic
- system - Ordovician
- series - Upper Ordovician
- stage - Ashgill

BIOSTRATIGRAPHY SUBDIVISIONS

Biostratigraphy is the branch of stratigraphy which focuses on correlating and assigning relative ages of rock strata by using the fossil assemblages contained within them. Usually the aim is correlation, demonstrating that a particular horizon in one geological section represents the same period of time as another horizon at some other section. The fossils are useful because sediments of the same age can look completely different because of local variations in the sedimentary environment. For example, one section might have been made up of clays and marls while another has more chalky limestones, but if the fossil species recorded are similar, the two sediments are likely to have been laid down at the same time.

Ammonites, graptolites and trilobites are index fossils that are widely used in biostratigraphy. Microfossils such as acritarchs, chitinozoans, conodonts, dinoflagellate cysts, pollen, spores and foraminiferans are also frequently used. Different fossils work well for sediments of different ages; trilobites, for example, are particularly useful for sediments of Cambrian age. To work well, the fossils used must be widespread geographically, so that they can occur in many different places. They must also be short lived as a species, so that the period of time during which they could be incorporated in the sediment is relatively narrow. The longer lived the species, the poorer the stratigraphic precision, so fossils that evolve rapidly, such as ammonites, are favoured over forms that evolve much more slowly, like nautiloids. Often biostratigraphic correlations are based on a fauna, not an individual species, as this allows greater precision. Further, if only one species is present in a sample, it can mean that (1) the strata were formed in the known fossil range of that organism; (2) that the fossil range of the organism was incompletely known, and the strata extend the known fossil range. For instance, the presence of the fossil Treptichnus pedum was used to define the base of the Cambrian period, but it has since been found in older strata.

Fossil assemblages were traditionally used to designate the duration of periods. Since a large change in fauna was required to make early stragtigraphers create a new period, most of the periods we recognise today are terminated by a major extinction event or faunal turnover.

BASIS FOR STRATIGRAPHIC SUBDIVISION

Fossils forms basis for biostratigraphic subdivision.

CONCEPT OF STAGE

A stage is a major subdivision of strata, each systematically following the other each bearing a unique assemblage of fossils. Therefore, stages can be defined as a group of strata containing the same major fossil assemblages. French palaeontologist Alcide d'Orbigny is credited for the invention of this concept. He named stages after geographic localities with particularly good sections of rock strata that bear the characteristic fossils on which the stages are based.

CONCEPT OF ZONE

In 1856 German palaeontologist Albert Oppel introduced the concept of zone (also known as biozones or Oppel zone). A zone includes strata characterised by the overlapping range of fossils. They represent the time between the appearance of species chosen at the base of the zone and the appearance of other species chosen at the base of the next succeeding zone. Oppel's zones are named after a particular distinctive fossil species, called an index fossil. Index fossils are one of the species from the assemblage of species that characterise the zone.

The zone is the fundamental biostratigraphic unit. Its thickness range from a few to hundreds of metres, and its extant range from local to worldwide. Biostratigraphic units are divided into six principal kinds of biozones:

- Taxon range biozone represent the known stratigraphic and geographic range of occurrence of a single taxon.
- Concurrent range biozone include the concurrent, coincident, or overlapping part of the range of two specified taxa.
- Interval biozone include the stata between two specific biostratigraphic surfaces. It can be based on lowest or highest occurrences.
- Lineage biozone are strata containing species representing a specific segment of an evolutionary lineage.
- Assemblage biozones are strata that contain a unique association of three or more taxa.
- Abundance biozone are strata in which the abundance of a particular taxon or group of taxa is significantly greater than in the adjacent part of the section.

INDEX FOSSILS

To be useful in stratigraphic correlation index fossils should be:

- Independent of their environment
- Geographically widespread (provincialism/ isolation of species should be avoided as much as possible)
- Rapidly evolving
- Abundant (easy to find in the rock record)
- Easy to preserve (Easier in low-energy, non-oxidized environment)
- Easy to identify

METHODS OF STARTIGRAPHIC CORRELATION INCLUDING SHAW'S GRAPHIC CORRELATION

Graphic correlation was developed by Alan Shaw during the late 1950s with the aim to solve stratigraphic problems for which traditional stratigraphy could not provide a solution due to limited resolution. The methodology of graphic correlation is rather simple. However, utilization of its full potential requires a large archival database of stratigraphic ranges composited from hundreds to thousands of sections. Construction of such a Composite Standard Database involves a long-term, dedicated collection effort. Graphic correlation analysis begins by selecting the most complete available section called the standard reference section (Olin Mann and Lane, 1995). Data from a second best section is then composited via graphic correlation to the reference section. The resulting integration represents the incipient composite standard.

The extent of faunal ranges in the composite standard is expressed in units of rock thickness from the standard reference section. In practice, this section can be subdivided into smaller, arbitrary intervals called Composite Standard Units. Although, Composite Standard Units have a lineary distribution relative to the thickness of the standard reference section, they do not represent equal amounts of geologic time due to variation in the in rock accumulation rate that characterizes that section. However, a tie between the composite standard and geological time can be accomplished via integration of sections with absolute time datums such as radiometric dates, paleomagnetic units and orbital cyclicity.

Graphic correlation correlates two intervals via stratigraphic datums that the two sections have in common. Additional sections can then be composited to the resultant stratigraphic reference section by graphic comparison of datums that these sections have in common. This progressively growing composite data forms the Composite Standard Database. As more and more sections are integrated, the composited ranges in the database eventually approach the true range from the first to last stratigraphic appearance of the datums either locally or globally depending upon the geographic distribution of the chosen sections. A relatively mature database requires from 30 to 40 sections for a relatively small area to thousands of sections for a global system.

In general, datums used in graphic correlation consist of fossil first and last stratigraphic occurrences. However, any potentially isochronous stratigraphic event can be defined as a graphic datum, from absolute age events (e.g., radiometric date) to regional key beds such as bentonites or potential sequence boundaries defined by well log and/or seismic data.

When graphically correlating sections, the paleontologist can be presented with a large number of possible correlation datums. He/she must use their judgement to determine which of these datums represent true first or last stratigraphic occurrences and which do not, the latter indicating truncation of their ranges due to factors such as erosion or facies exclusion. A line of correlation between the sections is drawn by connecting the datums deemed to represent complete stratigraphic distributions. The successfully drawn line of correlation is a time/depth plot, a one-to-one correlation between the section being composited and the Composite Standard Database. The line can be used by the graphic correlation software to adjust stratigraphic datums that are deemed to be immature in the Composite Standard Database via comparison to the newly composited section; i.e., first stratigraphic appearance datums that occur to the left of the line and last stratigraphic appearance datums that occur to the right of line will be extended backwards and forwards in time to a point on the line of correlation.

As Carney and Pierce (1995) stressed, graphic correlation is not a "Black Box" to which one introduces data and automatically receives a stratigraphic correlation. Rather, graphic correlation is a tool that a paleontologists can use to make informed decisions for the biostratigraphic interpretation of a given section (outcrop or well) based upon a system designed for compiling, storing, organizing, and retrieving large volumes of data. All factors considered in traditional biostratigraphy must also be taken into account for graphic correlation. Thus, a full understanding of the local stratigraphy is important to have for a successful graphic correlation; e.g., factors such as faulting, unconformities, microfossil reworking, facies changes, diagenesis, and fossil taphonomy and preservation must be considered.

CONCEPT OF SEQUENCE STRATIGRAPHY

Sequence stratigraphy is a branch of geology that attempts to subdivide and link sedimentary deposits into unconformity bound units on a variety of scales and explain these stratigraphic units in terms of control by relative sea-level changes and variations in sediment supply. The essence of the method is mapping of strata based on identification of surfaces which are assumed to represent time lines (e.g. subaerial unconformities, maximum flooding surfaces), and therefore placing stratigraphy in chronostratigraphic framework. Sequence stratigraphy is sometimes a useful alternative to a lithostratigraphic approach, which emphasizes similarity of the lithology of rock units rather than time significance, but suffers from issues of testibility and the non-uniqueness of many of the predicted stratigraphic geometries.

The 'sequence' part of the name refers to cyclic sedimentary deposits. The term 'stratigraphy' refers to the geologic knowledge about the processes by which sedimentary deposits form and how those deposits change through time and space on the Earth's surface.

Sequence stratigraphy is a branch of geology that attempts to subdivide and link sedimentary deposits into unconformity bound units on a variety of scales and explain these stratigraphic units in terms of control by relative sea-level changes and variations in sediment supply. The essence of the method is mapping of strata based on identification of surfaces which are assumed to represent time lines (e.g. subaerial unconformities, maximum flooding surfaces), and therefore placing stratigraphy in chronostratigraphic framework. Sequence stratigraphy is sometimes a useful alternative to a lithostratigraphic approach, which emphasizes similarity of the lithology of rock units rather than time significance, but suffers from issues of testibility and the non-uniqueness of many of the predicted stratigraphic geometries.

The 'sequence' part of the name refers to cyclic sedimentary deposits. The term 'stratigraphy' refers to the geologic knowledge about the processes by which sedimentary deposits form and how those deposits change through time and space on the Earth's surface.

ECONOMIC SIGNIFICANCE

These events have economic significance because these changes in sea level cause large lateral shifts in the depositional patterns of seafloor sediments. These lateral shifts in deposition create alternating layers of good reservoir quality rock (porous and permeable sands) and poorer-quality mudstones (capable of providing a reservoir "seal" to prevent the leakage of any accumulated hydrocarbons that may have migrated into the sandstones). Hydrocarbon prospectors look for places in the world where porous and permeable sands are overlain by low permeability rocks, and where conditions are right for hydrocarbons to be generated and migrate into these "traps".

UNCONFORMITY

An unconformity is a buried erosion surface separating two roc k masses or strata of different ages, indicating that sediment deposition was not continuous. In general, the older layer was exposed to erosion for an interval of time before deposition of the younger, but the term is used to describe any break in the sedimentary geologic record.

The rocks above an unconformity are younger than the rocks beneath (unless the sequence has been overturned). An unconformity represents time during which no sediments were preserved in a region. The local record for that time interval is missing and geologists must use other clues to discover that part of the geologic history of that area.

TYPES OF UNCONFORMITIES

Disconformity

Disconformity is an unconformity between parallel layers of sedimentary rocks which represents a period of erosion or non-deposition. Paraconformity is a type of disconformity in which the separation is a simple bedding plane; i.e., there is no obvious buried erosional surface. Blended unconformity is a type of disconformity or nonconformity with no distinct separation plane or contact, sometimes consisting of soils, paleosols, or beds of pebbles derived from the underlying rock.

Nonconformity

A nonconformity exists between sedimentary rocks and metamorphic or igneous rocks when the sedimentary rock lies above and was deposited on the pre-existing and eroded metamorphic or igneous rock. Namely, if the rock below the break is igneous or has lost its bedding by metamorphism, the plane of juncture is a nonconformity.

Angular unconformity

Angular unconformity is an unconformity where horizontally parallel strata of sedimentary rock are deposited on tilted and eroded layers, producing an angular discordance with the overlying horizontal layers. The whole sequence may later be deformed and tilted by further orogenic activity.

Paraconformity

Paraconformity is a type of unconformity in which strata are parallel; there is little apparent erosion and the unconformity surface resembles a simple bedding plane. It is also known as nondepositional unconformity or pseudoconformity.

FACIES CONCEPT IN STRATIGRAPHY – WALTHER'S LAW

In geology, facies are a body of rock with specified characteristics. Ideally, a facies is a distinctive rock unit that forms under certain conditions of sedimentation, reflecting a particular process or environment.

FACIES TYPES

Sedimentary facies

Bodies of sediment recognizably different from adjacent sediment deposited in a different depositional environment. Generally, facies are distinguished by what aspect of the rock or sediment is being studied. Thus, facies based on petrological characters such as grain size and mineralogy are called lithofacies, whereas facies based on fossil content are called biofacies.

These facies types are usually further subdivided, for examples, you might refer to a "tan, cross-bedded oolitic limestone facies" or a "shale facies". The characteristics of the rock unit come from the depositional environment and original composition. Sedimentary facies reflect depositional environment, each facies being a distinct kind of sediment for that area or environment.

Since its inception, the facies concept has been extended to related geological concepts. For example, characteristic associations of organic microfossils, and particulate organic material, in rocks or sediments, are called palynofacies. Discrete seismic units are similarly referred to as seismic facies.

Metamorphic facies

The sequence of minerals that develop during progressive metamorphism (that is, metamorphism at progressively higher temperatures and/or pressures) define a facies series.

Walther's Law of Facies

Walther's Law of Facies, named after the geologist Johannes Walther, states that the vertical succession of facies reflects lateral changes in environment. Conversely, it states that when a depositional environment "migrates" laterally, sediments of one depositional environment come to lie on top of another. A classic example of this law is the vertical stratigraphic succession that typifies marine trangressions and regressions. However, the law is not applicable where the contact between different lithologies is non-conformable (i.e. sedimentation was not continuous), or in instances of rapid environmental change where non-adjacent environments may replace one another.

EARTH'S CLIMATIC HISTORY

Climatologists have used various techniques and evidence to reconstruct a history of the Earth's past climate. From this data, they have found that during most of the Earth's history global temperatures were probably 8 to 15 degrees Celsius warmer than today. In the last billion years of climatic history, warmer conditions were broken by glacial periods starting at 925, 800, 680, 450, 330, and 2 million years before present.

The period from 2,000,000 - 14,000 B.P. (before present) is known as the Pleistocene or Ice Age. During this period, large glacial ice sheets covered much of North America, Europe, and Asia for extended periods of time. The extent of the glacier ice during the Pleistocene was not static. The Pleistocene had periods when the glacier retreated (interglacial) because of warmer temperatures and advanced because of colder temperatures (glacial). During the coldest periods of the Ice Age, average global temperatures were probably 4 - 5 degrees Celsius colder than they are today.

The most recent glacial retreat is still going on. We call the temporal period of this retreat the Holocene epoch. This warming of the Earth and subsequent glacial retreat began about 14,000 years ago (12,000 BC). The warming was shortly interrupted by a sudden cooling, known as the Younger-Dryas, at about 10,000 - 8500 BC. Scientists speculate that this cooling may have been caused by the release of fresh water trapped behind ice on North America into the North Atlantic Ocean. The release altered vertical currents in the ocean which exchange heat energy with the atmosphere. The warming resumed by 8500 BC. By 5000 to 3000 BC average global temperatures reached their maximum level during the Holocene and were 1 to 2 degrees Celsius warmer than they are today. Climatologists call this period the Climatic Optimum. During the Climatic Optimum, many of the Earth's great ancient civilizations began and flourished. In Africa, the Nile River had three times its present volume, indicating a much larger tropical region.

From 3000 to 2000 BC a cooling trend occurred. This cooling caused large drops in sea level and the emergence of many islands (Bahamas) and coastal areas that are still above sea level today. A short warming trend took place from 2000 to 1500 BC, followed once again by colder conditions. Colder temperatures from 1500 - 750 BC caused renewed ice growth in continental glaciers and alpine glaciers, and a sea level drop of between 2 to 3 meters below present day levels.

The period from 750 BC - 800 AD saw warming up to 150 BC. Temperatures, however, did not get as warm as the Climatic Optimum. During the time of Roman Empire (150 BC - 300 AD) a cooling began that lasted until about 900 AD. At its height, the cooling caused the Nile River (829 AD) and the Black Sea (800-801 AD) to freeze.

The period 900 - 1200 AD has been called the Little Climatic Optimum. It represents the warmest climate since the Climatic Optimum. During this period, the Vikings established settlements on Greenland and Iceland. The snow line in the Rocky Mountains was about 370 meters above current levels. A period of cool and more extreme weather followed the Little Climatic Optimum. A great drought in the American southwest occurred between 1276 and 1299. There are records of floods, great droughts and extreme seasonal climate fluctuations up to the 1400s.

From 1550 to 1850 AD global temperatures were at their coldest since the beginning of the Holocene. Scientists call this period the Little Ice Age. During the Little Ice Age, the average annual temperature of the Northern Hemisphere was about 1.0 degree Celsius lower than today. During the period 1580 to 1600, the western United States experienced one of its longest and most severe droughts in the last 500 years. Cold weather in Iceland from 1753 and 1759 caused 25% of the population to die from crop failure and famine. Newspapers in New England were calling 1816 the year without a summer.

The period 1850 to present is one of general warming. Figure 7. describes the global temperature trends from 1880 to 2006. This graph shows the yearly temperature anomalies that have occurred from an average global temperature calculated for the period 1951-1980. The graph indicates that the anomolies for the first 60 years of the record were consistently negative. However, beginning in 1935 positive anomolies became more common, and from 1980 to 2006 most of the anomolies were between 0.20 to 0.63 degrees Celsius higher than the normal period (1951-1980) average.

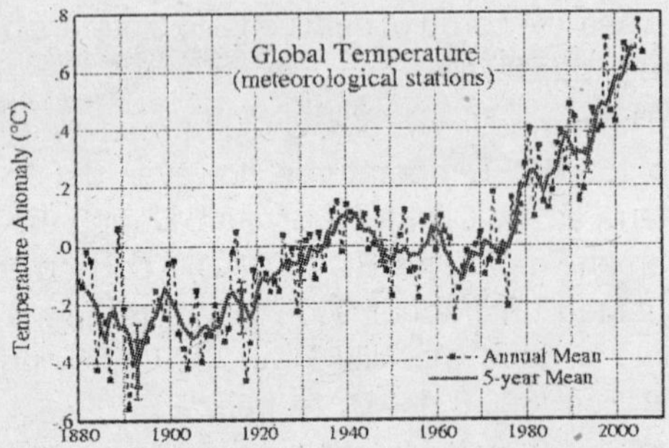

Fig. 7 : Near-global annual-mean temperature change for the period 1880 to 2006 (deviation from the normal period 1951-1980). (Source: NASA Goddard Institute for Space Studies - Global Temperature Trends).

In the 1930s and 1950s, the central United States experience two periods of extreme drought. In the seventeen year period from 1990 to 2006, ten of the warmest years in the last 100 years and possibly since the Little Climatic Optimum have occurred. Proxy and instrumental data indicate that 2005 was the warmest year globally in 1200 years of Earth history. Many scientists believe the warmer temperatures of the 20th and 21st centuries are being caused by the human enhancement of the Earth's greenhouse effect.

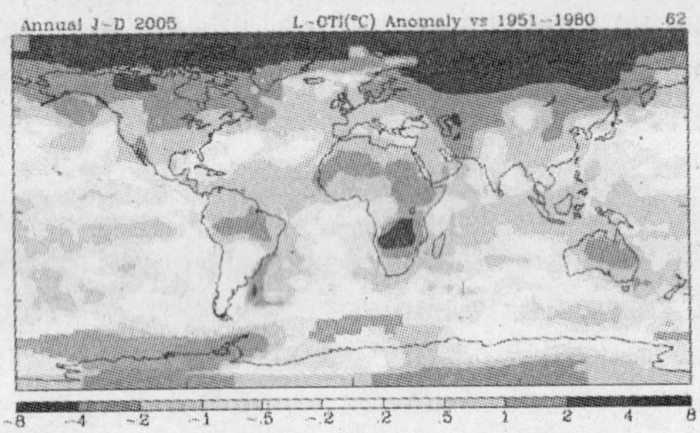

Fig. 8 : In 2005, most parts of the world were warmer than normal. The illustration above describes the annual temperature deviation (from the base normal period 1950-1980) in degrees Celsius for the Earth's surface. This illustration indicates that it was particularly warm across parts of Brazil, North America, northern and southern Africa, Australia, and most of Eurasia. (Source: NASA Goddard Institute for Space Studies - Global Temperature Trends).

PHANEROZOIC STRATIGRAPHY

PHANEROZOIC

Palaeozoic

- Lower Paleozoic–Rocks of the earliest Cambrian period are found in the Salt range in Punjab and the Spiti are in central Himalayas and consist of a thick sequence of fossiliferous sediments. In the Salt range, the stratigraphy starts with the Salt Pseudomorph zone, which has a thickness of 450 feet (137 m) and consists of dolomites and sandstones. It is overlain by magnesian sandstones with a thickness of 250 feet (76 m), similar to the underlying dolomites. These sandstones have very few fossils. Overlying the sandstones is the Neobolus Shale, which is composed of dark shales with a thickness of 100 feet (30 m). Finally there is a zone consisting of red or purple sandstones having a thickness of 250 feet (76 m) to 400 feet (122 m) called the Purple Sandstone. These are unfossiliferous and show sun-cracks and worm burrows which is typical of subaerial weathering. The deposits in Spiti are known as Haimanta system and they consist of Slates, micaceous quartzite and dolomitic limestones. The Ordovician rocks comprise flaggy shales, limestones, red quartzites, quartzites, sandstones and conglomerates. Siliceous limestones belonging to the Silurian overlie the Ordovician rocks. These limestones are in turn overlain by white quartzite and this is known as Muth quartzite. Silurian rocks which contain typical Silurian fauna are also found in the Vihi district of Kashmir.
- Upper Paleozoic–Devonian fossils and corals are found in grey limestone in the central Himalayas and in black limestone in the Chitral area. The Carboniferous is composed of two distinct sequences, the upper Carboniferous Po, and the lower Carboniferous Lipak. Fossils of Brachiopods and some Trilobites are found in the calcareous and sandy rocks of the Lipak series. The Syringothyris limestone in Kashmir also belongs to the Lipak. The Po series overlies the Lipak series, and the Fenestella shales are interbedded within a sequence of quartzites and dark shales. In many places Carboniferous strata are overlaid by grey agglomeratic slates, believed to be of volcanic origin. Many genera of productids are found in the limestones of the

Permo–Triassic, which has led to these rocks being referred to as "productus limestone". This limestone is of marine origin and is divided into three distinct litho-stratigraphic units based on the productus chronology: the Late Permian Chideru, which contains many ammonites, the Late - Middle Permain Virgal, and the Middle Permian Amb unit.

Mesozoic

In the Triassic the Ceratite beds, named after the ammonite ceratite, consist of arenaceous limestones, calcerous sandstones and marls. The Jurassic consists of two distinct units. The Kioto limestone, extends from the lower the middle Jurassic with a thickness 2,000 feet (610 m) to 3,000 feet (914 m). The upper Jurassic is represented by the Spiti black shales, and stretches from the Karakoram to Sikkim. Cretaceous rocks are cover an extensive area in India. In South India, the sedimentary rocks are divided into four stages; the Niniyur, the Ariyalur, the Trichinopoly, and the Utatur stages. In the Utatur stage the rocks host phosphatic nodules, which constitute an important source of phosphates in the country. In the central provinces, the well developed beds of Lameta contain fossil records which are helpful in estimating the age of the Deccan Traps. This sequence of basaltic rocks was formed near the end of the Cretaceous period due to volcanic activity. These lava flows occupy an area of 200,000 square miles. These rocks are a source of high quality building stone and also provide a very fertile clayey loam, particularly suited to cotton cultivation.

Cenozoic

- Tertiary period–In this period the Himalayan orogeny began, and the volcanism associated with the Deccan Traps continued. The rocks of this era have valuable deposits of petroleum and coal. Sandstones of Eocene age are found in Punjab, which grade into chalky limestones with oil seepages. Further north the rocks found in the Simla area are divided into three series, the Sabathu series consisting of grey and red shales, the Dagshai series comprising bright red clays and the Kasauli series comprising sandstones. Towards the east in Assam, Nummulitic limestone is found in the Khasi hills. Oil is associated with these rocks of the Oligo-Miocene age. Along the foothills of the Himilayas the Siwalik molasse is composed of sandstones, conglomerates and shales with thicknesses of 16,000 feet (4,877 m) to 20,000 feet (6,096 m) and ranging from Eocene to Pliocene. These rocks are famous for their rich fossil vertebrate fauna including many fossil hominoids.
- Quaternary period–The alluvium which is found in the Indo-Gangetic plain belongs to this era. It was eroded from the Himalayas by the rivers and the monsoons. These alluvial deposits consist of clay, loam, silt etc. and are divided into the older alluvium and the newer alluvium. The older alluvium is called Bhangar and is present in the ground above the flood level of the rivers. Khaddar or newer alluvium is confined to the river channels and their flood plains. This region has some of the most fertile soil found in the country as new silt is continually laid down by the rivers every year.

5. Marine Geology and Paleoceanography

Morphologic and tectonic domains of the ocean floor. Structure, composition and mechanism of the formation of oceanic crust. Seawater-basalt interactions, hydrothermal vents- chemical and biological significance of hydrothermal vents systems. Ocean margins and their significance. Ocean Circulation, Coriolis effect and Ekman spiral, convergence, divergence and upwelling, El Nino. Thermohaline circulation and oceanic conveyor belt. Formation of Bottom waters; major water masses of the world's oceans. Oceanic sediments: Factors controlling the deposition and distribution of oceanic sediments; geochronology of oceanic sediments, diagenetic changes in oxic and anoxic environments. Tectonic evolution of the ocean basins. Mineral resources. Paleoceanography – Approaches to paleoceanographic reconstructions; various proxy indicators for paleoceanographic interpretation.

Joint Global Ocean Flux Study (JGOFS) and its applications in Paleoceanography. Ocean Drilling Programme and its major accomplishments in paleoceanography. Opening and closing of ocean gateways and their effect on circulation and climate during the Cenozoic. Sea level processes and Sea level changes.

MORPHOLOGY OF THE OCEAN FLOOR

The seabed (also known as the seafloor, sea floor, or ocean floor) is the bottom of the ocean. At the bottom of the continental slope is the continental rise, which is caused by sediment cascading down the continental slope. The seabed has been explored by submersibles such as Alvin and, to some extent, scuba divers with special apparatuses. The process that continually adds new material to the ocean floor is seafloor spreading and the continental slope.

Ocean has Three Major Morphologic Provinces - Continental Margin that includes Continental Shelf, Slope & Rise; Ocean Basin which includes Abyssal Floor, Seamounts & Oceanic Rises and Mid-Ocean Ridge (MOR) such as Rift Valleys & Fracture Zones

CONTINENTAL MARGIN

1. Continental Shelf has gradient of <1:1000 (<0.057) [abrupt change to >1:40 at edge of shelf (shelf break)]. The relief of Continental margin is low generally less than 20 meter. The average width of continental shelf is 78 km. shelf break occurs at 130 m on average among all ocean.

   Continental Shelf is deepest at high latitudes –550 m max. (av. 350 m near Antarctica) and shallowest at low latitudes (av. 50 m).
2. Continental Slope has gradient of >1:40 (>1.432), av. 1:15 (4) [can be very steep (30-90)]. The relief of Continental Slope is great for oceans (a few 10's of m to several 100's of m). The average width of continental slope is 80 km. Continental Slope has Submarine Canyons - erosional features incised into slope, but which often cut into shelf edge & extend onto continental rise.

3. Continental Rise – found only on Atlantic-type margins. It has gradient of <1:40 (<1.432), generally between 1:100 & 1:700 (0.082-0.572). The relief feature of Continental Rise is low, generally less than 40 meter. The width of Continental rise varies from 100 to 1000 km. The submarine canyons may extend onto the continental rise as deep sea channels (generally <100 m deep). Deep sea fans are generally found on the continental rise at the base of canyons, &, in fact, the rise usually consists of coalesced fans.

C. OCEAN BASIN

1. *Abyssal Floor*

The abyssal plains dominate in the Atlantic & Indian ocean. It has gradient of <1:1000 & relief feature is less than 10 meter. The length of abyssal plains varies from less than 200 to 2000 km. it has a depth of 4000 to 6000 m (although some are perched on continental rises shallower than 4000 m & several occur in trenches deeper than 6000 m).

The sediment of oceanic basin has smoothed out rough morphology of underlying igneous oceanic crust.

Abyssal hills is a fabulous oceanic feature dominate the Pacific abyssal floor (80-85%).

It is small, sharply defined hills rising <1000 m above adjacent lows, and generally 1 to 10 km (some >50 km in diameter) in size and having slope of 1:4 to 1:60.

2. Seamounts are particularly abundant in the Pacific ocean. It is isolated features rising >1000 m above adjacent lows. It can occur in long chains (Hawaiian-Emperor seamount chain). The size of seamount is generally 10 to 50 km (the largest are >200 km in diameter) and slopes are 1:4 to 1:10.

   subsidence produces a flat-topped seamount called a GUYOT.

3. Oceanic Rises are large areas 100's to 1000's of km in size standing 2 to 3 km above adjacent seafloor. Some feature of are long, linear features; others are more equidimensional. Generally no earthquake activity now associated with them - hence aseismic.

   Oceanic Rises is of two types types

   (i) volcanic ridges & plataeaus - formed over voluminous hotspots so that volcanoes are discrete features (Atlantic - Iceland, Rio Grande Plateau, Walvis Ridge; Indian - Ninetyeast Ridge, Mascarene Plateau, Chagos-Laccadive Ridge, Kerguelen Plateau; Pacific - Magellan Plateau, Shatsky Rise)

   (ii) microcontinents - small fragments of continental crust stranded by rifting (Atlantic - Orphan Knoll, Rockall Plateau, Jan Mayen ridge, Lomonosov ridge, Agulhas Plateau; Indian - Seychelles, Madagascar Plateau; Pacific - Ontong Java plateau)

D. MID-OCEAN RIDGE

1. *General Characteristics of Mid-Ocean Ridge*

It is around 80,000 km long, a few 100 to 4000 km wide, crest averages 2500 m deep, 1000 to 3000 m above adjacent ocean basin and relief is 100 to 2000 m.

Mid-Ocean Ridge are greater in Atlantic & Indian, but lesser in Pacific ocean.

It form rift valley at crest.

2. *Rift Valleys*

The depth of rift valley is less than 500 m (4000 m max) in Atlantic & Indian, but more than 500 m in Pacific ocean. It has a width - 30 to 50 km in Atlantic & Indian, but 5 km in Pacific ocean. Rift valley is an indication of rate of spreading which is slow in Atlantic & Indian, fast in Pacific ocean.

OCEANIC CRUST

As the name already suggests, this crust is below the oceans. There, the crust is 4-7 miles (6-11 km) thick. The rocks of the oceanic crust are very young compared with the rocks of the continental crust.

The rocks of the oceanic crust are not older than 200 million years. The material of which the oceanic crust consists is for the greater part tholeiitic basalt (this is basalt without olivine). Basalt has a dark, fine and gritty volcanic structure. It is formed out of very liquid lava, which cools off quickly. The grains are so small that they are only visible under a microscope. The average density of the oceanic crust is 3g/cmi.

COMPOSITION

Although a complete section of oceanic crust has not yet been drilled, geologists have several pieces of evidence that help them understand the ocean floor. Estimations of composition are based on analyses of ophiolites (sections of oceanic crust that are preserved on the continents), comparisons of the seismic structure of the oceanic crust with laboratory determinations of seismic velocities in known rock types, and samples recovered from the ocean floor by submersibles, dredging (especially from ridge crests and fracture zones) and drilling. Oceanic crust is significantly simpler than continental crust and generally can be divided in *three layers.*

- Upper Layer consists of unconsolidated or semiconsolidated sediments, usually thin or even not present near the mid-ocean ridges but thickens farther away from the ridge. Near the continental margins sediment is terrigenous, meaning derived from the land, unlike deep sea sediments which are made of tiny shells of marine organisms, usually calcareous and siliceous, or it can be made of volcanic ash and terrigenous sediments transported by turbidity currents.
- Second Layer could be divided into two parts: layer (Upper part of second layer) – 0.5 km thick uppermost volcanic layer of glassy to finely crystalline basalt usually in the form of pillow basalt, and layer (Lower part of second layer) – 1.5 km thick layer composed of diabase dikes.
- Third Layer is formed by slow cooling of magma beneath the surface and consists of coarse grained gabbros and cumulate ultramafic rocks. It constitutes over two-thirds of oceanic crust volume with almost 5 km thickness.

OCEANIC CRUST FORMATION

Oceanic crust is continuously being created at mid-ocean ridges. At these ridges, magma rises into the upper mantle and crust, as the plates diverge. As it moves away from the ridge, the lithosphere becomes cooler and denser, and sediment gradually builds on top of it. The youngest oceanic lithosphere is at the oceanic ridges, and is progressively older away from the ridges.

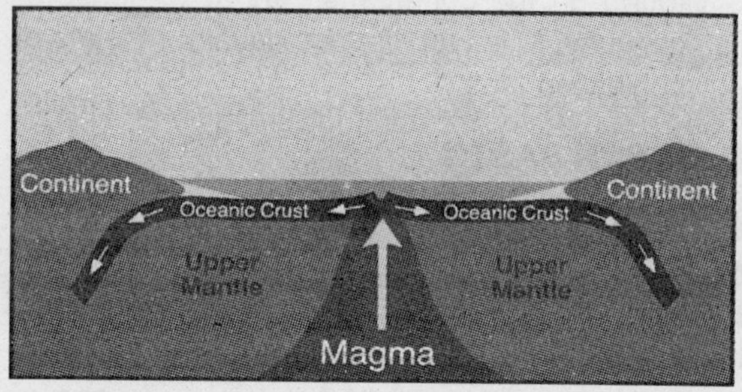

Figure: Formation of oceanic crust at rift zones located in the mid-oceanic ridges. Beneath the rift zone upwellings of magma occur in the mantle. These upwellings produce fissures and volcanoes on the ocean floor surface. The added rock, produced from the solidification of magma, pushes previously formed oceanic crust horizontally away from the rift zone like a conveyor belt. Ocean crust is returned to the mantle through subduction. This can occur when ocean crust meets continental crust or other ocean plates.

The oceanic lithosphere subducts at what are known as convergent boundaries. These boundaries can exist between oceanic lithosphere on one plate and oceanic lithosphere on another, or between oceanic lithosphere on one plate and continental lithosphere on another. In the second situation, the oceanic lithosphere always subducts because the continental lithosphere is less dense. The subduction process consumes older oceanic lithosphere, so oceanic crust is seldom more than 200 million years old. Plate tectonics is the study of these processes.

The overall process of repeated cycles of creation and destruction of oceanic crust is known as the Wilson cycle.

HYDROTHERMAL VENTS

A hydrothermal vent is a fissure in a planet's surface from which geothermally heated water issues. Hydrothermal vents are commonly found near volcanically active places, areas where tectonic plates are moving apart, ocean basins, and hotspots.

Hydrothermal vents are locally very common because the earth is both geologically active and has large amounts of water on its surface and within its crust. Common land types include hot springs, fumaroles and geysers. The most famous hydrothermal vent system on land is probably within Yellowstone National Park in the United States. Under the sea, hydrothermal vents may form features called black smokers.

Relative to the majority of the deep sea, the areas around submarine hydrothermal vents are biologically more productive, often hosting complex communities fueled by the chemicals dissolved in the vent fluids. Chemosynthetic archaea form the base of the food chain, supporting diverse organisms, including giant tube worms, clams, limpets and shrimp.

PHYSICAL PROPERTIES

Hydrothermal vents in the deep ocean typically form along the Mid-ocean ridges, such as the East Pacific Rise and the Mid-Atlantic Ridge. These are locations where two tectonic plates are diverging and new crust is being formed.

The water that issues from seafloor hydrothermal vents consists mostly of sea water drawn into the hydrothermal system close to the volcanic edifice through faults and porous sediments or volcanic strata, plus some magmatic water released by the upwelling magma.

In terrestrial hydrothermal systems the majority of water circulated within the fumarole and geyser systems is meteoric water plus ground water that has percolated down into the thermal system from the surface, but it also commonly contains some portion of metamorphic waters, sedimentary formational brines and magmatic water that is released by the magma. The proportion varies from location to location.

The water emerges from a hydrothermal vent at temperatures ranging up to 400°C, compared to a typical 2°C for the surrounding deep ocean water. The high pressure at these depths significantly expands the thermal range at which water remains liquid, and so the water doesn't boil. Water at a depth of 3,000 m and a temperature of 407°C becomes supercritical. However the increase in salinity pushes the water closer to its critical point.

Some hydrothermal vents form roughly cylindrical chimney structures. These form from minerals that are dissolved in the vent fluid. When the superheated water contacts the near-freezing sea water, the minerals precipitate out to form particles which add to the height of the stacks. Some of these chimney structures can reach heights of 60 m. An example of such a towering vent was "Godzilla", a structure in the Pacific Ocean near Oregon that rose to 40 m before it fell over.

The initial stages of a vent chimney begin with the deposition of the mineral anhydrite. Sulfides of copper, iron and zinc then precipitate in the chimney gaps, making it less porous over the course of time. Vent growths on the order of 30 cm per day have been recorded.

Chimney structures that emit a cloud of black material are called "black smokers", named for the dark hue of the particles they emit. The black smokers typically emit particles with high levels of sulfur-bearing minerals, or sulfides. "White smokers" refer to vents that emit lighter-hued minerals, such as those containing barium, calcium, and silicon. These vents also tend to have lower temperature plumes.

An April 2007 exploration of the deep-sea vents off the coast of Fiji found those vents to be a significant source of dissolved iron.

BIOLOGICAL SIGNIFICANCE OF HYDROTHERMAL VENTS SYSTEMS

Life has traditionally been seen as driven by energy from the sun, but deep sea organisms have no access to sunlight, so they must depend on nutrients found in the dusty chemical deposits and hydrothermal fluids in which they live. Previously marine biologists assumed that vent organisms were dependent on a "rain" of detritus from the upper levels of the ocean, like deep sea organisms are. This would leave them dependent on plant life and thus the sun. Some hydrothermal vent organisms do consume this "rain," but with only such a system, life forms would be very sparse. Compared to the surrounding sea floor, however, hydrothermal vent zones have a density of organisms 10,000 to 100,000 times greater.

Hydrothermal vent communities are able to sustain such vast amounts of life because vent organisms depend on chemosynthetic bacteria for food. The water that comes out of the hydrothermal vent is rich in dissolved minerals and supports a large population of chemo-autotrophic bacteria. These bacteria use sulfur compounds, particularly hydrogen sulfide, a chemical highly toxic to most known organisms, to produce organic material through the process of chemosynthesis.

The ecosystem so formed is reliant upon the continued existence of the hydrothermal vent field as the primary source of energy, which differs from most surface life on Earth which is based on solar energy. However, although it is often said that these communities exist independently of the sun, some of the organisms are actually dependent upon oxygen produced by photosynthetic organisms. Others are anaerobic as was the earliest life.

The chemosynthetic bacteria grow into a thick mat which attracts other organisms such as amphipods and copepods which graze upon the bacteria directly. Larger organisms such as snails, shrimp, crabs, tube worms, fish, and octopuses form a food chain of predator and prey relationships above the primary consumers. The main families of organisms found around seafloor vents are annelids, pogonophorans, gastropods, and crustaceans, with large bivalves, vestimentiferan worms, and "eyeless" shrimp making up the bulk of non-microbial organisms.

Life has traditionally been seen as driven by energy from the sun, but deep sea organisms have no access to sunlight, so they must depend on nutrients found in the dusty chemical deposits and hydrothermal fluids in which they live. Previously marine biologists assumed that vent organisms were dependent on a "rain" of detritus from the upper levels of the ocean, like deep sea organisms are. This would leave them dependent on plant life and

thus the sun. Some hydrothermal vent organisms do consume this "rain," but with only such a system, life forms would be very sparse. Compared to the surrounding sea floor, however, hydrothermal vent zones have a density of organisms 10,000 to 100,000 times greater.

Hydrothermal vent communities are able to sustain such vast amounts of life because vent organisms depend on chemosynthetic bacteria for food. The water that comes out of the hydrothermal vent is rich in dissolved minerals and supports a large population of chemo-autotrophic bacteria. These bacteria use sulfur compounds, particularly hydrogen sulfide, a chemical highly toxic to most known organisms, to produce organic material through the process of chemosynthesis.

The ecosystem so formed is reliant upon the continued existence of the hydrothermal vent field as the primary source of energy, which differs from most surface life on Earth which is based on solar energy. However, although it is often said that these communities exist independently of the sun, some of the organisms are actually dependent upon oxygen produced by photosynthetic organisms. Others are anaerobic as was the earliest life.

The chemosynthetic bacteria grow into a thick mat which attracts other organisms such as amphipods and copepods which graze upon the bacteria directly. Larger organisms such as snails, shrimp, crabs, tube worms, fish, and octopuses form a food chain of predator and prey relationships above the primary consumers. The main families of organisms found around seafloor vents are annelids, pogonophorans, gastropods, and crustaceans, with large bivalves, vestimentiferan worms, and "eyeless" shrimp making up the bulk of non-microbial organisms.

HYDROTHERMAL ORIGIN OF LIFE

Günter Wächtershäuser proposed the Iron-sulfur world theory and suggested that life might have originated at hydrothermal vents. Wächtershäuser proposed that an early form of metabolism predated genetics. By metabolism he meant a cycle of chemical reactions that produce energy in a form that can be harnessed by other processes.

It has been proposed that amino-acid synthesis could have occurred deep in the Earth's crust and that these amino-acids were subsequently shot up along with hydrothermal fluids into cooler waters, where lower temperatures and the presence of clay minerals would have fostered the formation of peptides and protocells. This is an attractive hypothesis because of the abundance of CH_4 and NH_3 present in hydrothermal vent regions, a condition that was not provided by the Earth's primitive atmosphere. A major limitation to this hypothesis is the lack of stability of organic molecules at high temperatures, but some have suggested that life would have originated outside of the zones of highest temperature. There are numerous species of extremophiles and other organisms currently living immediately around deep-sea vents, suggesting that this is indeed a possible scenario.

OCEAN CIRCULATION

An ocean current is a continuous, directed movement of ocean water generated by the forces acting upon this mean flow, such as breaking waves, wind, Coriolis force, temperature and salinity differences and tides caused by the gravitational pull of the Moon and the Sun. Depth contours, shoreline configurations and interaction with other currents influence a current's direction and strength.

Ocean currents can flow for great distances, and together they create the great flow of the global conveyor belt which plays a dominant part in determining the climate of many of the Earth's regions. Perhaps the most striking example is the Gulf Stream, which makes northwest Europe much more temperate than any other region at the same latitude. Another example is the Hawaiian Islands, where the climate is cooler (sub-tropical) than the tropical latitudes in which they are located, due to the effect of the California Current.

Seawater continuously moves around the globe as if it is on a huge conveyor belt, moving from the surface to the deep waters and back. Because the distance the water has to travel is so large, it takes about 1000 years for seawater to go all the way around the Earth.

The movement of water around the oceans has two parts which are strongly linked:

1. a density driven circulation which is driven by the differences in the density of seawater at different locations. The density of seawater depends on its temperature and how salty it is. As a result, this movement is known as the thermohaline circulation (Greek: thermo = heat, hàls = salt).
2. a wind driven circulation which results in huge surface currents like the Gulf Stream.

THERMOHALINE CIRCULATION

In the Northern Hemisphere

Ocean circulation transports surface seawater to the polar region where it cools. This cooling releases heat which warms the air and makes the water cold and, therefore, dense enough to sink to the bottom of the ocean. This results in the formation of new deep water which displaces existing deep water pushing it towards the equator. The major regions for this deep water formation are the Labrador and Greenland Seas in the northern North Atlantic Ocean. This North Atlantic Deep Water then flows south along the ocean floor allowing more warm surface water to flow into the region to replace it. Strong cooling also occurs in the Bering Sea in the North Pacific, but the structure of the ocean floor here prevents the deep water that forms from entering the ocean circulation.

Antarctica

Deep water formation also occurs around Antarctica during the production of sea ice. This ice contains very little salt and so, as the ice forms, the surrounding water becomes saltier and more dense. This very dense water slides down the edge of the Antarctic continent to form Antarctic Bottom Water. This water then spreads out and moves around most of the ocean floor.

For some time we thought that the deep waters that formed at the poles moved towards the equator, slowly warming and rising to the surface over the whole ocean, and that this water then returned to the poles in warm surface currents to complete the cycle. However, recent studies have shown that this gradual upwelling process is too slow to explain the age of seawater.

We now think that as deep water circulates around the bottom of the ocean, it meets the mid ocean ridges which are mountainous areas on the sea floor. The roughness of these causes strong mixing which forces the deep water to rise to the surface. The wind also causes strong mixing in the Southern Ocean and this also brings the deep water back to the surface. Once at the surface, the water returns to the poles in wind driven surface currents to complete its cycle.

WIND DRIVEN CIRCULATION

The Gulf Stream

The Gulf Stream is one of the most important wind driven currents. It transports very warm tropical water from the Caribbean Sea and the Gulf of Mexico across the North Atlantic to northern Europe. The warmth of the water heats the air above and the movement of this warm air is a very important way by which heat is transported northwards. As a result of this heat transport, northern Europe is very much warmer than corresponding latitudes in North America and countries around the Pacific Ocean.

For example, the yearly average temperature at Iqaluit (64°N, 068°W) in the Northwest Territories of Canada is -9.1°C. This compares with an average for Trondheim (63°N, 010°E) in Norway of +4.8°C. Long term records suggest that, as a result of the Gulf Stream, average temperatures in Northern Europe are 9°C higher than the average temperatures for the same latitude elsewhere.

The Gulf Stream is an example of a western boundary current, a current which flows along the western side of a major ocean basin. The corresponding current in the Pacific Ocean is the Kuroshio Current, and in the Indian Ocean, the Aghulas Current. They result from an interaction between the shape of the ocean basin, the general direction of the wind and the rotation of the earth. They all have a high velocity (the Gulf Stream has an average velocity of 1 m s^{-1}, thats 3.6 km h^{-1}) they are all quite narrow (between 100 and 200 km wide) and all have a very important influence on the climate of the region. Eastern boundary currents also occur; these transport cold surface waters from the poles to the equator. They tend to be weaker than their western counterparts.

IMPORTANCE

Knowledge of surface ocean currents is essential in reducing costs of shipping, since they reduce fuel costs. In the sail-ship era knowledge was even more essential. A good example of this is the Agulhas current, which long prevented Portuguese sailors from reaching India. Even today, the round-the-world sailing competitors employ surface currents to their benefit. Ocean currents are also very important in the dispersal of many life forms. An example is the life-cycle of the eel.

Ocean currents are important in the study of marine debris, and vice versa. These currents also affect temperatures throughout the world. For example, the current that brings warm water up the north Atlantic to northwest Europe stops ice from forming by the shores, which would block ships from entering and exiting ports.

CORIOLIS EFFECT

The Coriolis effect is an apparent deflection of moving objects when they are viewed from a rotating reference frame. For example, consider two children on opposite sides of a spinning roundabout (carousel), who are throwing a ball to each other. From the children's point of view, this ball's path is curved sideways by the Coriolis effect. From the thrower's perspective, the deflection is to the right with anticlockwise carousel rotation. Deflection is to the left with clockwise rotation.

The Earth's surface is rotating fastest (in km/h) at the equator, and rotates not at all at the poles. A bird flying away from the equator, carries this faster motion with it (or, equivalently, the surface under the bird is rotating more slowly than it was)–and the bird's flight curves eastward slightly. In general: objects moving away from the equator curve eastward; objects moving towards the equator curve westward. A particle travelling east, would tend to follow straight on, lifting off in a plane perpendicular to the axis. The projection of that on the ground, to which the particle is bound by gravity and pressure, veers off towards the equator. Conversely, a particle moving west is overtaken by the groundspeed and pursues its straight course bending down towards the axis, sliding off towards the pole.

Newton's laws of motion govern the motion of an object in an inertial frame of reference. When transforming Newton's laws to a rotating frame of reference, the Coriolis force appears, along with the centrifugal force. If the rotation speed of the frame is not constant, the Euler force will also appear. All three forces are proportional to the mass of the object. The Coriolis force is proportional to the speed of rotation and the centrifugal force is proportional to its square. The Coriolis force acts in a direction perpendicular to the rotation axis and to the velocity of the body in the rotating frame and is proportional to the object's speed in the rotating frame. The centrifugal force acts outwards in the radial direction and is proportional to the distance of the body from the axis of the rotating frame.

FORMULA

In non-vector terms: at a given rate of rotation of the observer, the magnitude of the Coriolis acceleration of the object is proportional to the velocity of the object and also to the sine of the angle between the direction of movement of the object and the axis of rotation.

The vector formula for the magnitude and direction of the Coriolis acceleration is

$$a_C = -2\Omega \times v$$

where v is the velocity of the particle in the rotating system, and Ω is the angular velocity vector which has magnitude equal to the rotation rate ω and is directed along the axis of rotation of the rotating reference frame, and the × symbol represents the cross product operator.

The equation may be multiplied by the mass of the relevant object to produce the Coriolis force:

$$F_C = -2m\Omega \times v$$

The Coriolis effect is the behavior added by the Coriolis acceleration. The formula implies that the Coriolis acceleration is perpendicular both to the direction of the velocity of the moving mass and to the frame's rotation axis. So in particular:

- if the velocity is parallel to the rotation axis, the Coriolis acceleration is zero.
- if the velocity is straight inward to the axis, the acceleration is in the direction of local rotation.
- if the velocity is straight outward from the axis, the acceleration is against the direction of local rotation.
- if the velocity is in the direction of local rotation, the acceleration is outward from the axis.
- if the velocity is against the direction of local rotation, the acceleration is inward to the axis.

The vector cross product can be evaluated as the determinant of a matrix:

$$\Omega \times v = \begin{vmatrix} i & j & k \\ \Omega_x & \Omega_y & \Omega_z \\ v_x & v_y & v_z \end{vmatrix} = \begin{pmatrix} \Omega_y v_z & - & \Omega_z v_y \\ \Omega_z v_x & - & \Omega_x v_z \\ \Omega_x v_y & - & \Omega_y v_x \end{pmatrix},$$

where the vectors i, j, k are unit vectors in the x, y and z directions.

CAUSES OF CORIOLIS FORCE

The Coriolis effect exists only when using a rotating reference frame. In the rotating frame it behaves exactly like a real force (that is to say, it causes acceleration and has real effects). However, Coriolis force is a consequence of inertia, and is not attributable to an identifiable originating body, as is the case for electromagnetic or nuclear forces, for example. From an analytical viewpoint, to use Newton's second law in a rotating system, Coriolis force is mathematically necessary, but it disappears in a non-accelerating, inertial frame of reference.

A denizen of a rotating frame, such as an astronaut in a rotating space station, very probably will find the interpretation of everyday life in terms of the Coriolis force accords more simply with intuition and experience than a cerebral reinterpretation of events from an inertial standpoint. For example, nausea due to an experienced push may be more instinctively explained by Coriolis force than by the law of inertia. In meteorology, a rotating frame (the Earth) with its Coriolis force proves a more natural framework for explanation of air movements than a hypothetical, non-rotating, inertial frame without Coriolis forces. In long-range gunnery, sight corrections for the Earth's rotation are based upon Coriolis force

The acceleration entering the Coriolis force arises from two sources of change in velocity that result from rotation: the first is the change of the velocity of an object in time. The same velocity (in an inertial frame of reference where the normal laws of physics apply) will be seen as different velocities at different times in a rotating frame of reference. The apparent acceleration is proportional to the angular velocity of the reference frame (the rate at which the coordinate axes change direction), and to the component of velocity of the object in a plane perpendicular to the axis of rotation. This gives a term $-\Omega \times v$.The minus sign arises from the traditional definition of the cross product (right hand rule), and from the sign convention for angular velocity vectors.

The second is the change of velocity in space. Different positions in a rotating frame of reference have different velocities (as seen from an inertial frame of reference). In order for an object to move in a straight line it must therefore be accelerated so that its velocity changes from point to point by the same amount as the velocities of the frame of reference. The effect is proportional to the angular velocity (which determines the relative speed of two different points in the rotating frame of reference), and to the component of the velocity of the object in a plane perpendicular to the axis of rotation (which determines how quickly it moves between those points). This also gives a term $-\Omega \times v$.

APPLICATION OF CORIOLIS FORCE

Meteorology

Perhaps the most important instance of the Coriolis effect is in the large-scale dynamics of the oceans and the atmosphere. In meteorology and ocean science, it is convenient to use a rotating frame of reference where the Earth is stationary. The fictitious centrifugal and Coriolis forces must then be introduced. Their relative importance is determined by the Rossby number. Tornadoes have a high Rossby number, so Coriolis forces are unimportant, and are not discussed here.

EKMAN SPIRAL

The Ekman spiral refers to a structure of currents or winds near a horizontal boundary in which the flow direction rotates as one moves away from the boundary. It derives its name from the Swedish oceanographer Vagn Ekman.

The effect is a consequence of the Coriolis effect which causes objects to move to the right of applied forces in the northern hemisphere and to the left in the Southern Hemisphere. Thus when the wind blows on the ocean surface in the northern hemisphere, the surface current moves to the right of the wind. As the water at the surface pushes on water below it, this water moves yet further to the right of the wind, and so on. As the current deflects, the velocity becomes progressively weaker. The depth to which the Ekman spiral penetrates is determined by how far turbulent mixing can penetrate over the course of a pendulum day.

The diagram on the right shows the forces associated with the Ekman spiral as applied to the Northern hemisphere. The force from above is in red (beginning with the wind blowing over the water surface), the Coriolis force (at right angles to the force from above) is in dark yellow, and the net resultant water movement is in pink, which then becomes the force from above for the layer below it, accounting for the gradual clockwise spiral motion as you move down.

The classic Ekman spiral has been observed under sea ice, but is not found in most open-ocean conditions. This is due both to the fact that the turbulent mixing in the surface layer of the ocean has a strong diurnal cycle and to the fact that surface waves can destabilize the Ekman spiral. Ekman spirals are, however, found in the atmosphere. Surface winds in the Northern Hemisphere tend to blow to the left of winds aloft.

The null point is the point in which the water does not spin. Beyond the null point the water spins back upward in the direction opposite of the downward moving water.

WATER MASSES & BOTTOM WATER

An oceanographic water mass is an identifiable body of water which has physical properties distinct from surrounding water. Properties include temperature, salinity, chemical - isotopic ratios, and other physical quantities.

The concept of water masses originates in meteorology. Vilhelm Bjerknes, a Norwegian meteorologist, first described the cold air masses that form in the polar regions. He showed how they move southward, where they collide with warm air masses at places he called fronts, just as masses of troops collide at fronts in war (Friedman, 1989). In a similar way, water masses are formed in different regions of the ocean, and the water masses are often separated by fronts. Note, however, that strong winds are associated with fronts in the atmosphere because of the large difference in density and temperature on either side of the front. Fronts in the ocean sometimes have little contrast in density, and these fronts have only weak currents.

Common water masses in the world ocean are: Antarctic Bottom Water (AABW), North Atlantic Deep Water (NADW), Circumpolar Deep Water (CDW), Antarctic Intermediate Water (AAIW), Subantarctic Mode Water (SAMW), Arctic Intermediate Water (AIW), the central waters of various oceanic basins, and various surface waters.

The production of bottom water is influenced by the salinity of surface waters in the north Atlantic. It is also influenced by the rate of upwelling due to mixing in other oceanic areas.

The production of bottom water is remarkably sensitive to small changes in salinity. Rahmstorf (1995), using a numerical model of the meridional overturning circulation, showed that a ±0.1 Sv variation of the flow of fresh water into the north Atlantic can switch on or of the deep circulation of 14 Sv. If the deep-water production is shut of during times of low salinity, the 1 petawatt of heat may also be shut of. Weaver and Hillaire-Marcel (2004) point out that the shutdown of the production of bottom water is unlikely, and if it did happen, it would lead to a colder Europe, not a new ice age, because of the higher concentrations of CO_2 now in the atmosphere.

The production of bottom water is also remarkably sensitive to small changes in mixing in the deep ocean. Munk and Wunsch (1998) calculate that 2.1 TW (terawatts = 1012 watts) are required to drive the deep circulation, and that this small source of mechanical mixing drives a poleward heat flux of 2000 TW. Most of the energy for mixing comes from winds which can produce turbulent mixing throughout the ocean. Some energy comes from the dissipation of tidal currents, which depend on the distribution of the continents. Thus during the last ice age, when sea level was much lower, tides, tidal currents, tidal dissipation, winds, and deep circulation all differed from present values.

OCEANIC SEDIMENTS

Sediment on the seafloor originates from a variety of sources, including biota from the overlying ocean water, eroded material from land transported to the ocean by rivers or wind, ash from volcanoes, and chemical precipitates derived directly from sea water. A very small amount of it even originates as interstellar dust. In short, the particles found in sediment on the seafloor vary considerably in composition and record a complex interplay of processes that have acted to form, transport, and preserve them.

Geological oceanographers have coined the terms "terrigenous" to describe those sediments derived from eroded material on land, "biogenic" for those derived from biological matter, "volcanogenic" for those that include significant amounts of ash, "hydrogenous" for those that precipitate directly from sea water, and "cosmogenic" for those that come from interstellar space.

The seafloor, however, is not a random arrangement of these different sediment types. Oceanographers have painstakingly mapped the distribution of sediment around the globe and have learned that at any given location the sediments provide important information regarding the history of the ocean as well as the overall state of climate on the Earth's surface. By studying how the heterogeneous composition of sediment varies as a function of geographic location and age, oceanographers are able to document the geologic and climatic conditions that are responsible for that sediment.

Oceanographers study sediment by taking long cylindrical cores, which individually can be as long as 18 to 30 meters (60 to 98 feet). Because the bottom of the ocean is extremely cold (only 1 to 3 degrees above freezing), the cores are stored in refrigerators onboard the research ship prior to being stored in large refrigerated repositories at shore-based laboratories. In their laboratories, scientists study the physical, chemical, and biological makeup of the sediment.

Regardless of which type of sediment, there are three processes that are responsible for its final composition: namely, the production of the sediment; its transport; and its preservation. It is important to differentiate between these three processes. For example, if a sedimentary particle is produced, but not preserved, there will be no resulting sedimentary record. Thus, only if material is produced and transported and preserved will marine sediment result.

The different combinations of each process' effectiveness result in a commensurate variety of sedimentation rates. Sediment can accumulate as slowly as 0.1 millimeter (0.04 inch) per 1,000 years (in the middle of the ocean where only wind-blown material is deposited) to as fast as 1 meter (3.25 feet) per year along continental margins. More typical deep-sea rates are on the order of several centimeters per 1,000 years.

PRODUCTION OF SEDIMENT

The production of marine sediment is more complex than it may seem. Terrigenous sediment is produced by an interplay of chemical and physical weathering processes, which collectively serve to create small grains of material ranging in size from thousandths of millimeters to 1 or 2 millimeters(0.04 or 0.08 inch). (The larger grains of coarse sand, gravel, and boulders are too large to be transported to the deep sea and therefore are not discussed here.)

Physical weathering is caused by mechanical fracturing of rocks, such as that due to the freezing of water in cracks, and results in finer grained, compositionally similar examples of the original rock. On the other hand, chemical weathering, caused by the weak acid produced by the interaction of rainwater and atmospheric carbon dioxide, degrades the rock slowly and often produces fine-grained minerals that are compositionally distinct from the original rock.

Biogenic (biologically derived) sediment is produced by marine plankton, which are small, often microscopic, unicellular plants and animals that float in the surface waters of the ocean. The shells of these organisms are made of either calcium carbonate ($CaCO_3$) or silica (SiO_2). Although ubiquitous, particularly elevated concentrations of such organisms are most commonly found in biologically productive waters such as the Equatorial Pacific, or the Southern Ocean ringing the continent of Antarctica.

Volcanic ash is produced during volcanic eruptions, as can be seen in the billowing ejected material from many volcanos. Cosmogenic material is the remains of primordial material left over from the creation of the solar system (and perhaps from beyond) and, although very low in abundance, is ubiquitously distributed.

The production of hydrogenous sediment is most difficult to visualize, but involves either the slow precipitation of dissolved chemicals from sea water or the leaching of chemical elements from rocks that have extremely hot sea water (greater than 300°C [572°F]) circulating through them along mid-ocean ridges. When these hot solutions are injected into the cold sea water the leached chemical elements precipitate from the cooling water, leading to hydrothermal sediments near the mid-ocean ridge that are enriched in iron, manganese, copper, zinc, and other metals.

TRANSPORT OF SEDIMENT

The transport of sediment depends on its grain size and the original location where it was produced. Terrigenous sediment can be transported to the deep sea via rivers or by wind. Material transported by rivers most commonly ends up deposited on the continental margin, the shallow portions of the ocean that are within several hundred kilometers of land. When continental margin deposits accumulate fast and get overly steep, or when an earthquake or storm causes the sediment to be resuspended, turbidity currents provide additional transport out to the deep sea. The resuspension of the sediment into the bottom water causes it to be more dense than the overlying water, and thus these turbidity currents flow downslope to the more distant ocean basin.

The transport of sediment by wind is also extremely significant, and is particularly relevant to studies of Earth's climate in the past. When the Earth's climate is relatively dry (arid), such as during glacial periods, the land surface tends to be more dusty, and thus during such periods there will be more windblown terrigenous material delivered to the deep ocean. Also, during such time periods the wind speed tends to be higher, and thus terrigenous grains that are slightly larger than usual are preferentially transported. Thus, by examining the amount of dust, as well as its grain size, in the different layers of a sediment core, oceanographers learn how arid the land surface was at a given time, as well as how fast the average wind speeds were.

Although such dust is essentially invisible to the human eye, its transport is still an important and long-ranging process. For example, dust derived from the Sahara in North Africa is easily observed in Miami, Florida and even in the eastern Pacific Ocean. Moreover, volcanic ash ejected tens of kilometers into the atmosphere during the largest eruptions can be transported by winds all around the globe.

The microscopic shells of the plankton do not just simply fall to the seafloor. In fact, because they are so small, the plankton may not be able to fall individually. Oceanographers learn how such sediment is delivered to the seafloor by suspending sediment traps in the ocean. These traps are essentially large funnels, up to 1 or 2 meters (3.3 to 6.6 feet) in diameter, that collect the material as it falls through sea water.

By examining the material trapped by these instruments, it was discovered that plankton shells are delivered to seafloor by "biopackaging" via fecal pellets. In other words, various microorganisms that eat other plankton excrete their shells in fecal pellets. These "biopackaged" fecal pellets are large enough (0.2-1.5 millimeters, or 0.008-0.059 inch) and dense enough to sink to the seafloor, where they become part of the sediment.

Hydrothermal sediment is largely localized to within less than 10 kilometers (6.2 miles) of the mid-ocean ridge. The concentration of metals in these sediments decreases with distance from a ridge, yet small amounts can be found up to 500 to 1000 kilometers (300-600 miles) away.

PRESERVATION OF SEDIMENT

Terrigenous sediment, whether it be delivered by rivers or wind, is not altered significantly on the seafloor and thus is well-preserved. During very deep burial (e.g., 5 kilometers, or 3 miles, below the seafloor), the terrigenous grains can be altered into different minerals, but this does not occur while the grains are lying on the seafloor and is generally a more important process for geologists rather than oceanographers.

Biogenic sediment, on the other hand, is very poorly preserved on the seafloor. The degradation of biogenic sediments is a complex, largely chemical suite of processes. The preservation of these sediments is a field of study that has captivated oceanographers for over 100 years, dating from when they were discovered in the mid-1800s during the first oceanographic research cruise by the ship HMS Challenger.

For example, significantly less than 1 per cent of the siliceous plankton that are biopackaged to the seafloor are preserved. This is because sea water is undersaturated with respect to silica. Therefore, the siliceous plankton are living in an environment that is corrosive to their shells.

While the plankon is alive, the shell is surrounded by organic protoplasm that protects it from the corrosive sea water. After death, however, even if biopackaged, this organic coating will degrade, exposing the shell of the siliceous plankton. When exposed to sea water, the shell will dissolve.

This process occurs over all depth and temperature ranges throughout the global ocean. Thus, the only regions of the seafloor where biogenic silica appreciably accumulates is where the production of biogenic silica is so enormous that it overwhelms the amount that is dissolved. In the modern oceans, this occurs at high latitudes in the North Pacific and Southern Ocean and the Equatorial Pacific Ocean.

Plankton with shells made of calcium carbonate also commonly dissolve, but not as commonly as siliceous plankton. The dissolution of carbonate plankton is controlled by water depth and water temperature. Water depth and hydrostatic pressure correlate with each other–at greater depths there is greater pressure. At greater pressures, the solubility of carbon dioxide gas increases. An excellent analogy of this process is observed in a bottled carbonated beverage that is under pressure until opened–when the pressure is released the carbon dioxide comes out of solution and bubbles form. Similarly, at the great depths of the deepest seafloor, the solubility of carbon dioxide increases so much that calcium carbonate sediment may dissolve. This dissolution is also facilitated at the lower temperatures of the deep sea.

The converse is also true. At shallow water depths (that is, lower pressure) the carbonate does not dissolve and the warmer water temperatures (along with the increased light for photosynthesis) each serve to enhance the construction and preservation of coral reefs and other carbonate-producing biota. Thus, there is both a depth and latitudinal effect on the distribution of carbonate sediments due to their influence on temperature and pressure.

MINERAL RESOURCES

MINERAL DEPOSITS CAN BE CLASSIFIED AS:

- Mineral occurrences or prospects of geological interest but not necessarily of economic interest
- Mineral resources that are potentially valuable, and for which reasonable prospects exist for eventual economic extraction.
- Mineral reserves or Ore reserves that are valuable and economically and technically feasible to extract

In common mining terminology, an "ore deposit" by definition must have an 'ore reserve', and may or may not have additional 'resources'.

Mineral occurrences, prospects

These classifications of mineral occurrences are generally the least important and least economic. They include all known occurrences of minerals of economic interest, including obviously uneconomic outcrops and manifestations. However, these are often mentioned in a company prospectus because of "proximity"; a concept that something valuable may be found near these occurrences because it has been in the past due to a similar geological environment. Often, such occurrences of mineralisation are the peripheral manifestations of nearby ore deposits. "Ore deposit" applies specifically to economic mineral occurrences that could be mined at a profit after consideration of all factors impacting a mining operation. Note that this distinction between amounts of raw material available as either a resource or reserve also applies to other materials considered to be minerals. This can include natural gas (legally defined as a mineral in some states of the United States) and hydrocarbons.

Mineral resources

Mineral resources are those economic mineral concentrations that have undergone enough scrutiny to quantify their contained metal to a certain degree. None of these resources are ore, because the economics of the mineral deposit may not have been fully evaluated.

Indicated resources are simply economic mineral occurrences that have been sampled (from locations such as outcrops, trenches, pits and drillholes) to a point where an estimate has been made, at a reasonable level of confidence, of their contained metal, grade, tonnage, shape, densities, physical characteristics

Measured resources are indicated resources that have undergone enough further sampling that a 'competent person' (defined by the norms of the relevant mining code; usually a geologist) has declared them to be an acceptable estimate, at a high degree of confidence, of the grade, tonnage, shape, densities, physical characteristics and mineral content of the mineral occurrence.

Resources may also make up portions of a mineral deposit classified as a mineral reserve, but:

- Have not been sufficiently drilled out to qualify for Reserve status; or
- Have yet to meet all criteria for Reserve status

Mineral reserves

Mineral reserves are resources known to be economically feasible for extraction. Reserves are either Probable Reserves or Proven Reserves. Generally the conversion of resources into reserves requires the application of various modifying factors, including:

- mining and geological factors, such as knowledge of the geology of the deposit sufficient that it is predictable and verifiable; extraction and mine plans based on ore models; quantification of geotechnical risk–basically, managing the geological faults, joints, and ground fractures so the mine does not collapse; and consideration of technical risk–essentially, statistical and variography to ensure the ore is sampled properly:
- metallurgical factors, including scrutiny of assay data to ensure accuracy of the information supplied by the laboratory–required because ore reserves are bankable. Essentially, once a deposit is elevated to reserve status, it is an economic entity and an asset upon which loans and equity can be drawn–generally to pay for its extraction at (hopefully) a profit;
- economic factors;
- environmental factors;
- marketing factors;
- legal factors;
- governmental factors;and
- social factors.

JOINT GLOBAL OCEAN FLUX STUDY (JGOFS)

GENERAL CONTEXT

The oceans contain some 50 times as much carbon dioxide as the atmosphere, and small changes in the ocean carbon cycle can therefore have large atmospheric consequences. Such changes are believed to have had important feedback effects on climate during the transitions to and from ice ages; they may also have important consequences for the global climate and environment, and for many human activities in the next 50-100 years, as a result of rapidly rising levels of atmospheric carbon dioxide and other greenhouse gases. Models indicate that the oceans are currently taking up at least a third of the anthropogenic carbon dioxide by dissolving it into water that then loses contact with the atmosphere because of sinking or vertical mixing. Biological processes complicate the oceanic carbon cycle although they probably do not affect much the present uptake of anthropogenic carbon dioxide. Nevertheless, they are important because they (1) are the determinant of the natural background distribution of carbon; (2) complicate our efforts to measure the background distribution due to the seasonal variation in biological processes; and (3) have the potential to amplify chemical and physical effects, via biological feedbacks in the system.

HISTORICAL BACKGROUND

The role of the ocean in controlling climate change through the storage and transport of heat (and liquid water) was recognised early on by the World Climate Research Programme (WCRP) and led to the planning of the Tropical Ocean-Global Atmosphere (TOGA) study and the World Ocean Circulation Experiment (WOCE). In parallel to these initiatives, the Joint SCOR (Scientific Committee on Oceanic Research) and IOC (International Oceanographic Commission) Committee on Climatic Change and the Ocean (CCCO) proposed a global survey of the oceanic carbon dioxide (CO_2) budget field, and WOCE agreed to accommodate a small CO_2 programme on the ships taking part in the WOCE Hydrographic Programme (WHP). At that time, marine geochemists and biologists were also concerned that a physical transport model with only an upper boundary condition would be inadequate to determine the role of the ocean in the atmospheric carbon dioxide budget and hence the prediction of climate change in response to the atmospheric build-up of greenhouse gases would not be possible. These concerns were articulated at a NATO meeting in 1982 on the chemistry of the upper ocean (Brewer, 1986) and at a workshop in the USA in 1984 (GOFS, 1984). The proceedings of these meetings provided the initial scientific focus and framework for ocean biogeochemistry and various national programmes.

As early as 1986, several European countries were nationally planning ocean studies with a focus on the carbon cycle and flux from the surface to the deep ocean and sediments. However, to determine global net fluxes and the processes controlling them was beyond the capability of any one nation. Shortly thereafter in February 1987, the formal organisation of JGOFS emerged under the Scientific Committee on Oceanic Research (SCOR). Sponsored by SCOR and the International Council of Scientific Unions (ICSU), leading experts in the ocean carbon cycle met in Paris and agreed upon the goals, scientific elements, topics of emphasis and organisational structure of JGOFS (SCOR, 1987), and in October 1987, the Executive Committee of SCOR approved an international planning committee for JGOFS that met for the first time in January 1988. Later the same year, JGOFS assumed responsibility for the carbon dioxide measurements programme and formed the Joint JGOFS-CCCO Advisory Panel on Carbon Dioxide.

At the turn of the decade, Germany was planning an extensive research cruise in the North Atlantic to commemorate the centennial of Hensenr's Plankton Expedition. JGOFS seized this opportunity to organise its first regional process study on the German R/V "Meteor", which led to the JGOFS North Atlantic Pilot Study in 1989. The participating countries were Germany, UK, Netherlands, USA and Canada. To further establish its position in the international communities, JGOFS also sought programme links with other global studies under ICSU and WCRP, such as the formal agreement between SCOR and the International Geosphere-Biosphere Programme (IGBP) in 1989. Under that agreement, JGOFS became a core project under IGBP, but responsible directly to SCOR.

Initially, the Scientific Steering Committee (SSC) for JGOFS created a number of Planning Groups and Task Teams to consider scientific and logistic questions and make recommendations to the SSC. These groups helped to identify and plan the most important processes and variables to study, the ocean regions that such studies should provide the greatest insight and most useful data, and the best experimental design for the studies. The SSC would then identify the sequence of events necessary to complete specific tasks, the resources required for the tasks and the level of international co-ordination that is required. During JGOFS field studies, more than twenty countries contributed to JGOFS SSC and helped to plan and coordinate the fieldwork. As task teams and planning groups completed their terms of reference, they would eventually disband after delivering their final reports, while others, such as the Data Management Task Team, would continue throughout JGOFS fieldwork and later synthesis.

The following scientific goals of JGOFS were published in its Science Plan:

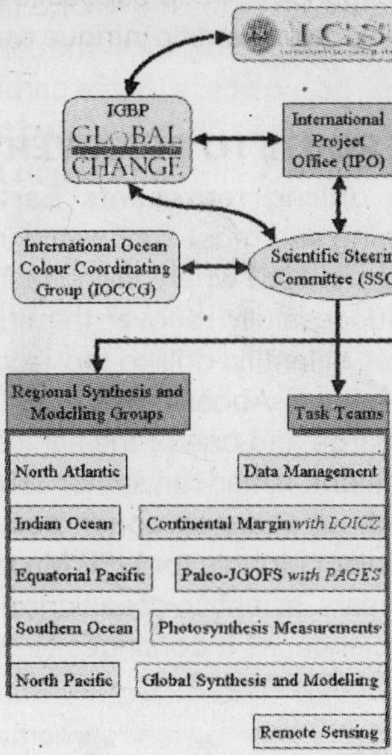

JGOFS Organizational Framework

SCIENTIFIC GOALS

- To determine and understand on a global scale the processes controlling the time-varying fluxes of carbon and associated biogenic elements in the ocean, and to evaluate the related exchanges with the atmosphere, sea floor and continental boundaries
- To develop a capacity to predict on a global scale the response to anthropogenic perturbations, in particular those related to climate change

To accomplish these scientific goals, JGOFS restricted itself to the most important tasks consistent with its lifetime and resources, i.e., carbon exchange between the atmosphere and ocean. However, for periods longer than a year, the main factors limiting this flux may be associated with the exchange of carbon between the upper ocean and the ocean interior. JGOFS had therefore adopted the following "operational goal" for evaluating components of the project.

OBJECTIVES

- An assessment of large-scale carbon fluxes, obtained from a greatly increased network of observations;
- a set of models that express our understanding of the processes controlling large-scale carbon fluxes; a procedure for observing the ocean in a routine, synoptic manner to detect possible changes in the ocean carbon cycle in response to climate change;
- a well-cared-for data set, comprising observations made according to standard protocols and a system for making subsets of these easily available to researchers;
- a better knowledge and understanding of fluxes across the continental margins, to provide reliable boundary conditions for global models;
- an increased number of countries with an interest and skill in planning JGOFS-type activities and making the appropriate measurements and global-scale inferences.

OCEAN DRILLING PROGRAMME

The Integrated Ocean Drilling Program (IODP) is an international marine research drilling program dedicated to advancing scientific understanding of the Earth by monitoring and sampling subseafloor environments. Through multiple platforms–a feature unique to IODP– the world's Earth and ocean scientists explore the deep subseafloor. Documenting environmental change, Earth processes and effects, the deep biosphere and solid earth cycles and geodynamics are principal program themes.

IODP: investigating Earth, oceans, and life

The Integrated Ocean Drilling Program (IODP) brings together hundreds of scientists from dozens of countries and scientific disciplines to conduct cutting-edge investigations of Earth deep below the seafloor. For each drilling project undertaken, IODP employs the best-suited drilling pla tform available along with complementary drilling tools and technologies. IODP affords scientists the opportunity to:

1. recover geological records and rock samples.
2. investigate and document ocean and climate change through time.
3. explore the presence of primitive life below the seafloor.
4. verify remote, near-seafloor observatories.
5. gain understanding of how tectonic plates move and recycle themselves into Earth's deep mantle.

FOCUS ON EARTH

IODP scientists are drawn from universities and institutes from all across the member countries and pursue new knowledge about Earth's past. Two previous scientific ocean drilling programs, Deep Sea Drilling Project and Ocean Drilling Program, generated abundant information about Earth's dynamic nature: tectonic processes, ocean circulation, climate change, continental rifting, and ocean basin formation. Today, scientific ocean drilling continues to provide a powerful tool to study the critical processes related to Earth's short-term change and long-term variability. IODP expands the scope of ocean drilling investigations, and pushes the limits of technology by providing diverse drilling platforms to meet specific requirements of each planned drilling project.

IODP focuses on ocean basins–rich archives and ideal natural laboratories–to study the interdependence of physical, chemical, and biological processes. IODP research also centers on those factors that control climate change, the vast circulation of fluids within Earth's crust,the nature of life on and within Earth, and the dynamics of lithospheric formation and recycling.

IODP was conceived as a 10-year Earth science and research program that started in 2003. Its prescribed drilling activities require weeks,sometimes months of drilling at a single location, a variety of drilling hardware, new engineering strategies to ensure pristine samples,and ventures into harsh and demanding environments. Despite the achievements made during the past 40+ years of ocean drilling activity, IODP continues to pioneer research in "inner space," investigating expansive, deep subseafloor environments that retain their scientific intrigue well into the 21st century.

NAVIGATING THE ROUTE TO DISCOVERY

Scientific ocean drilling represents Earth science's longest running and most successful international collaboration. In 1961 when drilling technology was used to successfully recover the first sample of oceanic crust, scientific drilling took root as a new scientific technique. Aboard the CUSS 1, a modified U.S. Navy barge and one of the earliest scientific drilling expeditions, American author John Steinbeck, also an amateur oceanographer, documented the historic Project Mohole for LIFE Magazine. Over the next 45 years, scientific ocean drilling revolutionized Earth science, as it continues to do today.

LEGACY PROGRAMS

The Deep Sea Drilling Project (DSDP), established in June 1966, operated the Glomar Challenger in drilling and coring operations in the Atlantic, Pacific, and Indian Oceans, as well as in the Mediterranean and Red Seas. The Challenger's success occurred nearly immediately: Its coring operations enabled DSDP to provide the next intellectual step in verifying the hypothesis of plate tectonics associated with seafloor spreading, by dating basal sediments on transects away from the Mid-Atlantic Ridge.

SCIENCE AND DRILLING OPERATORS

Drilling operations are conducted and managed by three IODP Implementing Organizations (IOs):

- USIO, the United States Implementing Organization, carries out expeditions on a riserless drilling vessel;
- ESO, the ECORD Science Operator, manages mission specific expeditions on various platforms;
- JPIO, the Japan Implementing Organization, manages operations aboard a riser-equipped drilling vessel.

Each drilling expedition is led by a team of co-chief scientists, with an international team of scientists supported by an IO staff scientist. Each IO provides a combination of services: technical, operational, and financial management; logging; laboratory; core repository; data management; and publication. Although each IO is responsible for its own platform operations and performance, its science operations are funded by the Lead Agencies.

OPENING AND CLOSING OF OCEAN GATEWAYS AND THEIR EFFECT ON CIRCULATION AND CLIMATE DURING THE CENOZOIC

With its low albedo and large capacity to store heat, the ocean represents one of the most important components of the global climatic system. With a specific heat per unit mass of 4 times that of air, water (i.e., the ocean) has a thermal capacity over 1000 times that of the atmosphere. The energy imbalance from incoming solar radiation between the summer and winter hemispheres and between high and low latitudes results in motions (i.e., transport) in the atmosphere and oceans. The result is a net transport of energy from summer to winter hemispheres and from low to high latitudes. There is little variation at low latitudes in temperature and energy transport. The ocean, with its high thermal capacity, acts as a buffer for such energy changes.

The ocean, at the same time, plays an important role in the meridional transport of energy. The question may then be asked: Has it always been so? The answer is unequivocally no. Present continent-ocean geometry is the result of a long [200 million year (m.y.)] history of changing spatial configurations. The role of gateways (and barriers) is fundamental for recreating the scenario of past circulation histories (and their concomitant effect on paleoclimate). We are only at an early stage in understanding this history, but we can outline the following tentative scenario.

The underlying assumption is the general view that the global climatic cooling characteristic of the Cenozoic is due to natural, earthbound causes, namely the poleward shift of continental masses and the gradual development of a meridional (Cenozoic) rather than latitudinal (Mesozoic) oceanic circulation pattern. Late Neogene (last 15 m.y.) climatic oscillations are, in turn, no doubt the result of the superposition on this global cooling trend of short-term periodic fluctuations in orbital parameters (i.e., the astronomical theory of glaciation, which is less a theory than a mechanism).

The discussion below is presented in two parts. The first deals with a brief summary of the role of the oceans (and their geometry) in heat transfer and thus, ultimately, as a source of climatic change. The second summarizes the main paleogeographic events that have had an influence on oceanic circulation and their effect, where discernible, on climatic evolution.

The oceans occupy nearly three quarters of the surface of the Earth and receive over 80 per cent of the total solar radiation absorbed at the surface. With a specific heat (0.93 cal $g^{-1}{}^{\circ}C^{-1}$) considerably larger than that of land (0.60–0.19 cal $g^{-1}{}^{\circ}C^{-1}$), seawater yields up its stored heat much more reluctantly than do land areas. With an overturn (i.e., mixing) rate of 500–1500 yr, the oceans may be viewed as vast heat reservoirs that act as a conservative element in maintaining climatic stability.

The Sun is the ultimate source of ocean currents. Uneven absorption of shortwave radiation over small areas on the ocean surface results in density differences that, in turn, set in motion, slow, lateral water-mass movements. Heat energy is transported and distributed accordingly. Deeper waters are warmed by the slower processes of convective mixing. In polar regions such mixing is ultimately complete, whereas elsewhere the thermocline denotes the level to which mixing is effective. In spite of the large amount of radiation that reaches the surface of the ocean, vertical heat transfer is limited to the surficial layers because nearly 90 per cent of the heat energy is used in evaporation.

The ocean accounts for nearly a third of the poleward transfer of heat energy [the remaining two thirds is accounted for by atmospheric transport in the form of sensible (50 per cent) and latent (15 per cent) heat]. This is accomplished primarily in the form of wind-driven surface currents. In a typical ocean basin, surface circulation assumes the form of an anticyclonic gyre centered on a semipermanent (seasonally shifting) area of stable high pressure within the basin. Equatorward the gyre is constrained by the seasonally migrating intertropical convergence zone, poleward by the high-latitude easterlies and longitudinally by landmasses. Gyres commonly consist of four components: a westerly equatorial current, a polar easterly current, a poleward ascending western boundary current, and an equatorial descending eastern boundary current. The intensity and volume of a given current gyre is dependent on wind stress and such geostrophic factors as the Coriolis force, the piling up of waters on the western margins of ocean basins, and the constrictions or deflections by continental geometry.

Heat energy is absorbed by surface waters as a function of latitude. The equatorial zone is the basic source of most of the heat energy in oceanic gyres, although additional radiation is added over the entire extent of a meridional current. In subequatorial belts, westward-moving gyre currents absorb heat at the rate of about 0.1°C for each degree of longitude. Because of this lengthy exposure to high insolation, the maximum surface temperatures are found in the western equatorial extremities of ocean basins. Eastwardly moving currents on the polar sides of gyres lose heat at about the same rate. Meridional currents moving poleward or equatorward cool and warm, respectively, at an average of 0.3°C for each degree of latitude.

At present, the most important oceanic currents from a climatic point of view are the poleward moving extremities of the western boundary currents (such as, North Atlantic Current, Kuroshio, and Brazil Current). These currents transport warm surface waters into regions of low temperatures and thus enhance high-latitude atmospheric heating and evaporation.

By way of contrast, the presence of the Antarctic Circumpolar Current in the southern hemisphere prevents penetration of westerly boundary current beyond 40° S and serves to isolate the Antarctic continent from major sources of precipitation.

This brief summary gives an idea of the role that the oceans play in transporting heat energy and their role as a stabilizing force in maintaining the climatic status quo.

At the same time, it will be apparent that the oceans contain the potential for playing a significant role in climatic change given the right set of conditions. The fact that the geologic record provides ample evidence of significantly different climates in the past (when compared with that of today) suggests significant changes in the ocean currents and atmospheric circulation patterns of the past.

Gateways (and barriers) represent the means for transporting (or blocking) heat energy from one area of the globe to another. Identifying these gateways (barriers) and their geometry and refining the time of their inception is of fundamental importance to delineating the scenario of the past climatic history of the Earth.

CENOZOIC

Paleogene

The continued fragmentation of the world ocean led to an increasingly inefficient latitudinal thermal energy exchange. Paleobiogeographic and oxygen isotopic studies yield a complementary picture of a long-term global temperature decline, development of a thermally stratified ocean, and enchanced zonal climatic differentiation during the Cenozoic (Berggren and Hollister, 1974, 1977; Frakes, 1979). This climatic decline followed a faunally and florally (Haq and Lohmann, 1976; Haq et al., 1977) and oxygen isotopically (Boersma and Shackleton, 1977; Vergnaud-Grazzini et al., 1978, 1979) recognizable "climatic optimum" in the early Eocene.

The opening of the northeast Atlantic (between Greenland and Norway) began in the early Eocene at about the same time as the separation of Australia and Antarctica (Berggren and Hollister, 1974, 1977). The widespread development of biogenic siliceous deposits in a circumequatorial belt during the Middle Eocene has been linked with the presence of persistent wind-driven (trade winds), diverging ocean-surface currents and associated upwelling, as well as temporally related volcanism in the northeast Atlantic associated with the early phase of rifting and seafloor spreading (Berggren and Hollister, 1974, 1977; Drewry et al., 1974). The high-latitude source of the intensification of oceanic surface and deep-water circulation has been the subject of considerable debate. Although vertebrate faunal evidence suggests elimination of a subaerial barrier in the Norwegian-Greenland Sea at 50 Ma (McKenna, 1972), recent geophysical data suggest a later, early Oligocene date (about 35 Ma) for the separation of Greenland-Spitsbergen (Talwani and Eldholm, 1977). The picture is complicated by the fact that the Greenland-Iceland-Faeroe Ridge may have prevented significant exchange of water from the polar regions to the North Atlantic until the Late Oligocene, about 23 Ma (Tucholke and Vogt, 1979).

An alternate source for the origin of cold, deep water formation–the "big flush"–may lie in the high southern latitude, probably from the Weddell region of the Antarctic (Schnitker, 1980). These cold bottom waters could have moved northward into the North Atlantic through the nascent fracture zones developing in the subsiding Rio Grande Rise.

In the southern hemisphere the northward transit of India diverted the westward flowing Pacific-equatorial current into the counterclockwise subtropical gyre, which penetrated southward, past eastern Australia into the nascent gateway that was opening up between Australia and Antarctica. Isolation of the warm Pacific gyres at these high southerly latitudes led, through adiabatic cooling and evaporation, to precipitation on the Antarctic continent, which eventually led to full continental glacial conditions. This was the beginning of the

gradual thermal isolation of the Antarctic continent, which was essentially completed by mid to late Oligocene time (about 25 Ma) with the subsidence of the Tasman Rise and the opening of the Drake Passage and which has continued to this day in the form of the circum-Antarctic current as the gateway has continued to widen during the Neogene.

Oxygen isotope studies indicate a progressive cooling from the Middle Eocene to Early Oligocene time in the sub-Antarctie (Shackleton and Kennett, 1975; Kennett and Shackleton, 1976; L.D. Keigwin, University of Rhode Island, personal communication), North Atlantic (Vergnaud-Grazzini et al., 1978, 1979), South Atlantic (Boersma and Shackleton, 1977), and mid-high latitude Pacific (Douglas and Savin, 1975; Savin et al., 1975). Superimposed on this trend is a pronounced cooling event seen near the Eocene-Oligocene boundary in the Pacific and sub-Antarctic regions, whereas in the Atlantic the cooling appears to be more gradual and of lesser magnitude (Kiegwin, 1980). The relationship of the opening of the Greenland-Norwegian Sea to the Arctic and the possible initial opening of the Drake Passage at about this time (about 38 Ma, J. Sclater, Massachussetts Institute of Technology, personal communication) to the climatic "event" at the Eocene-Oligocene boundary remains unclear because of the lack of precision in dating these various events, but they may be expected to have played a role in enhancing the latitudinal thermal gradients resulting from a greater latitudinal transport of cooler waters originating at high latitudes.

At about the same time, about 40 Ma, the significant generation of cold bottom waters in the Antarctic (and possibly the North Atlantic) resulted in the formation of the psychrospheric fauna, which today lives at temperatures less than 10°C. The appearance of this fauna in the Atlantic Ocean and Tethys Sea at about this time suggests that the Rio Grande Rise has been breached, allowing cold, dense waters to move along a north-south meridional corridor, enhancing the transition from a latitudinal thermospheric circulation to a meridional thermohaline circulation. This transition has been one of the major threshold events in the evolution of the present climate of the world. From this time on, thermally differentiated water masses have moved in a basically meridional pattern, transferring heat across latitudes and establishing a basically latitudinally controlled, zonal climatic gradient of significant proportions.

With the opening of the Drake Passage by mid- to late-Oligocene time the circumpolar current had been established, thermally isolating the Antarctic Continent from the influence of warmer waters to the north (Kennett et al., 1972, 1975). This event appears to be closely linked chronologically with the extension of glaciers on Antarctica to sea level, as shown by drilling in the Ross Sea (Hayes and Frakes, 1975).

Neogene

During the Late Cretaceous and Paleogene, northward movement and rotation of Africa continued to close the Tethys Sea in the east. In the west, right-lateral motion between Africa and Europe narrowed the western junction of the Tethys with the Atlantic between Spain and Morocco. The junction of Arabia and Asia, severing the marine gateway connection between the Indo-Pacific and Atlantic Oceans, occurred during the Early Miocene, about 18 Ma (Van Couvering and Miller, 1971; Berggren, 1972a; Berggren and Hollister, 1974). The transition from a thermospheric to two-layered psychrospheric structure in the Tethys Sea appears to have been effected by Late Eocene time, about 40 Ma (Benson and Sylvester-Bradley, 1971). The effect on climate of the closure of the east-west Tethyan gateway and the subsequent evolution of the Tethys into an eastern (Indo-Pacific Ocean) and western (Mediterranean Sea) part is not clear at this point.

A major decline in isotopic temperature occurs in the Middle Miocene, about 14 Ma (Savin, 1977; Woodruff et al., 1980), and it has been linked with the establishment of the East Antarctic Ice Sheet (Shackleton and Kennett, 1975; Savin, 1977). This cooling event is difficult to link with the development or termination of a structural barrier to flow of water masses because of the disparity in the data that exist on the timing of various events in the North Atlantic. However, the concomitant effects of the severance of the Tethys Seaway and the subsidence of the Iceland-Faeroe Ridge (linking the Arctic polar sea and the Atlantic Ocean) have been linked in a scenario that connects this thermal event with the development of Antarctic glaciation and the evolution of "modern" ocean circulation (Schnitker, 1980). The scenario is as follows:

1. Closure of Tethys in the east (18 Ma) created an evaporation basin that contributed increasing amounts of warm, saline waters to the North Atlantic.
2. Continued fragmentation of Tethys elsewhere (northward drift of Australia separated the equatorial Indian Ocean from the equatorial Pacific) closed off the deep-water connection and reduced the flow of the equatorial current system.
3. Restriction of the Central American Seaway by the gradual emergence of the Isthmus of Panama gradually reduced the flow of the equatorial current between the Atlantic and Pacific. Deflection of the North Equatorial Current northward increased the strength of the Gulf Stream.
4. The breakup of Tethys and its low-latitude circumglobal flow resulted in a temporary increase in surface-water temperatures in the late early Miocene.
5. The gradual subsidence of the Iceland-Faeroe Ridge allowed North Atlantic surface waters into the Norwegian during the early Miocene. By mid-Miocene time subsidence had progressed to the point where reflux of cold bottom water became significant. The Arctic Ocean was then linked with the world ocean as a heat sink.
6. Early North Atlantic deep water, resulting from Norwegian Sea overflow, traversed the length of the Atlantic and inserted itself as an intermediate water mass in the circumAntarctic current system.
7. Relatively "warm" and saline North Atlantic deep water would rise to the surface near the Antarctic rather than the cold, low-salinity local water. This warm, saline water contained heat that could be converted to latent heat by evaporation. The resulting high evaporation rates supplied moisture to Antarctica sufficient to push it across the threshold value needed to build up and maintain a stable continental ice cap.
8. During the latest Miocene (about 5.5–5.0 Ma) the west Tethys Sea was isolated from the

Atlantic Ocean. In the Pliocene, marine connections were established and the Mediterranean Sea gradually evolved from a thermohaline to its present thermospheric condition. The effect of the closure of the marine gateway linking the Tethys and Atlantic and the subsequent desiccation of the West Tethys Sea on climate is not clear. In general, the increased continentality would have resulted in enhanced climatic seasonality, although the formation of extensive evaporite deposits (i.e., sabkhas) indicate hot arid conditions as one component of the overall climate. The subsequent opening of the Gilbraltar gateway and the evolution of a thermospheric watermass in the Mediterranean has resulted in art "inland sea" in which there is an excess of surface evaporation over local inflow from rivers and precipitation. The Mediterranean would seem to have a buffering effect on climate, contributing (together with the circumMediterranean Alpine chain to the north and the broad, expansive desert areas to the south) to the "Mediterranean climate" to which it gives its name.

9. Perhaps one of the most significant late Neogene paleogeographic events was the elevation of the Isthmus of Panama, which resulted in the termination of the marine gateway linking the Atlantic and Pacific Oceans, at 3.5 Ma (Berggren and Hollister, 1974). This event had a dramatic effect on oceanic circulation patterns (interruption of the Atlantic to Pacific equatorial current system), paleobiogeography of marine (change from global to disjunct distribution patterns) and terrestrial (re-establishment of north-south migration route– "The Great American Faunal Interchange") organisms. The effect of this barrier on climate is not fully clear, but the proximity in time of its formation to the initiation of northern hemisphere polar glaciation (about 3 Ma; Berggren, 1972b) may indicate a significant role–pumping increased volumes of warm, high-salinity waters (Gulf Stream) into high latitudes where evaporation led to precipitation over the region of eastern Canada and Greenland, cooling, and eventually to the development of the polar ice cap (Luyendyk et al., 1972; Berggren and Hollister, 1974).

10. During the last 100,000 yr eustatic sea-level fluctuations have led to alternate opening and closing of the Straits of Bab el Mandab in the southern Red Sea and the temporal isolation (and partial evaporation) of the Red Sea (Berggren, 1969). This cyclic process may be expected to have occurred earlier in the Pleistocene as well, but stratigraphic evidence is lacking. What effect these events would have had on climate is not clear, but they may be expected to have been minor and of local extent.

SEA LEVEL PROCESSES AND SEA LEVEL CHANGES

sea level rise has occurred at a mean rate of 1.8 mm per year for the past century, and more recently, during the satellite era of sea level measurement, at rates estimated near 2.8 ± 0.4 to 3.1 ± 0.7 mm per year (1993-2003). Current sea level rise is due significantly to global warming, which will increase sea level over the coming century and longer periods. Increasing temperatures result in sea level rise by the thermal expansion of water and through the addition of water to the oceans from the melting of continental ice sheets. At the end of the 20th century, thermal expansion and melting of land ice contributed roughly equally to sea level rise, while thermal expansion is expected to contribute more than half of the rise in the upcoming century. Values for predicted sea level rise over the course of this century typically range from 90 to 880 mm, with a central value of 480 mm. Models of glacial flow give a theoretical maximum value for sea level rise in the current century of 2 metres (and a "more plausible" one of 0.8 metres), based on limitations on how quickly ice can flow.

LOCAL AND EUSTATIC SEA LEVEL

Local mean sea level (LMSL) is defined as the height of the sea with respect to a land benchmark, averaged over a period of time (such as a month or a year) long enough that fluctuations caused by waves and tides are smoothed out. One must adjust perceived changes in LMSL to account for vertical movements of the land, which can be of the same order (mm/yr) as sea level changes. Some land movements occur because of isostatic adjustment of the mantle to the melting of ice sheets at the end of the last ice age. The weight of the ice sheet depresses the underlying land, and when the ice melts away the land slowly rebounds. Atmospheric pressure, ocean currents and local ocean temperature changes also can affect LMSL.

"Eustatic" change (as opposed to local change) results in an alteration to the global sea levels, such as changes in the volume of water in the world oceans or changes in the volume of an ocean basin.

SHORT TERM AND PERIODIC CHANGES

There are many factors which can produce short-term (a few minutes to 18.6 years) changes in sea level.

Short-term (periodic) causes	Time scale (P = period)	Vertical effect
Periodic sea level changes		
Diurnal and semidiurnal astronomical tides	12–24 h P	0.2–10+ m
Long-period tides		
Rotational variations (Chandler wobble)	14 month P	
Lunar Node astronomical tides	18.613 year	
Meteorological and oceanographic fluctuations		
Atmospheric pressure	Hours to months	-0.7 to 1.3 m
Winds (storm surges)	1–5 days	Up to 5 m
Evaporation and precipitation (may also follow long-term pattern)	Days to weeks	
Ocean surface topography (changes in water density and currents)	Days to weeks	Up to 1 m
El Nico/southern oscillation	6 mo every 5–10 yr	Up to 0.6 m
Seasonal variations		
Seasonal water balance among oceans (Atlantic, Pacific, Indian)		
Seasonal variations in slope of water surface		
River runoff/floods	2 months	1 m
Seasonal water density changes (temperature and salinity)	6 months	0.2 m
Seiches		
Seiches (standing waves)	Minutes to hours	Up to 2 m
Earthquakes		
Tsunamis (generate catastrophic long-period waves)	Hours	Up to 10 m
Abrupt change in land level	Minutes	Up to 10 m

LONGER TERM CHANGES

Various factors affect the volume or mass of the ocean, leading to long-term changes in eustatic sea level. The two primary influences are temperature (because the density of water depends on temperature), and the mass of water locked up on land and sea as fresh water in rivers, lakes, glaciers, polar ice caps, and sea ice. Over much longer geological timescales, changes in the shape of the oceanic basins and in land/sea distribution will affect sea level.

Observational and modelling studies of mass loss from glaciers and ice caps indicate a contribution to sea-level rise of 0.2 to 0.4 mm/yr averaged over the 20th century.

6. Geochemistry

Structure and atomic properties of elements, the Periodic Table; ionic substitution in minerals; Phase rule and its applications in petrology, thermodynamics of reactions involving pure phases, ideal and non-ideal solutions, and fluids; equilibrium and distribution coefficients. Nucleation and diffusion processes in igneous, metamorphic and sedimentary environments, redox reactions and Eh-pH diagrams and their applications. Mineral/mineral assemblages as 'sensors' of ambient environments. Geochemical studies of aerosols, surface-, marine-, and ground waters.

Radioactive decay schemes and their application to geochronology and petrogenesis. Stable isotopes and their application to earth system processes.

STRUCTURE AND ATOMIC PROPERTIES OF ELEMENTS

ATOMS

Atoms make up the chemical elements. Each chemical element has nearly identical atoms. An atom is composed of three different particles:

- Protons – positively charged, reside in the center of the atom called the nucleus
- Electrons – negatively charged, orbit in a cloud around nucleus
- Neutrons – no charge, reside in the nucleus.

Each element has the same number of protons and the same number of electrons.

- Number of protons = Number of electrons.
- Number of protons = atomic number.
- Number of protons + Number of neutrons = atomic weight.

Isotopes are atoms of the same element with differing numbers of neutrons. i.e. the number of neutrons may vary within atoms of the same element. Some isotopes are unstable which results in radioactivity.

- **Example:**

(potassium) has 19 protons. Every atom of K has 19 protons. Atomic number of K = 19. Some atoms of K have 20 neutrons, others have 21, and others have 22. Thus atomic weight of K can be 39, 40, or 41. ^{40}K is radioactive and decays to ^{40}Ar and ^{40}Ca.

STRUCTURE OF ATOMS

Electrons orbit around the nucleus in different shells, labeled from the innermost shell as K, L, M, N, etc. Each shell can have a certain number of electrons. The K-shell can have 2 Electrons, the L-shell, 8, the M-shell 18, N-shell 32.

Number of electrons = $2N^2$, where N=1 for the K shell, N=2 for the L shell, N=3 for the M shell, etc.

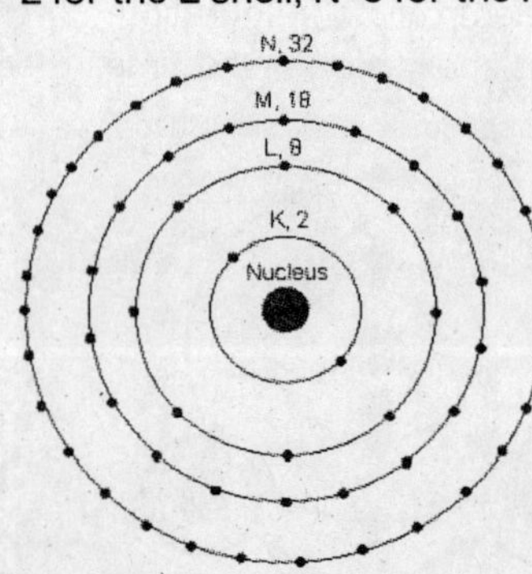

A Stable electronic configuratic . for an atom is one 8 electrons in outer shell (except in the K shell, which is completely filled with only 2 electrons). Thus, atoms often loose electrons or gain electrons to obtain stable configuration. Noble gases have completely filled outer shells, so they are stable. Examples He, Ne, Ar, Kr, Xe, Rn. Others like Na, K loose an electron. This causes the charge balance to become unequal. In fact to become + (positive) charged atoms called ions. Positively charged atoms = cations. Elements like F, Cl, O gain electrons to become (-) charged. (-) charged ions are called anions.

The drive to attain a stable electronic configuration in the outermost shell along with the fact that this sometimes produces oppositely charged ions, results in the binding of atoms together. When atoms become attached to one another, we say that they are bonded together.

Types of bonding:

Ionic bonding- caused by the force of attraction between ions of opposite charge.

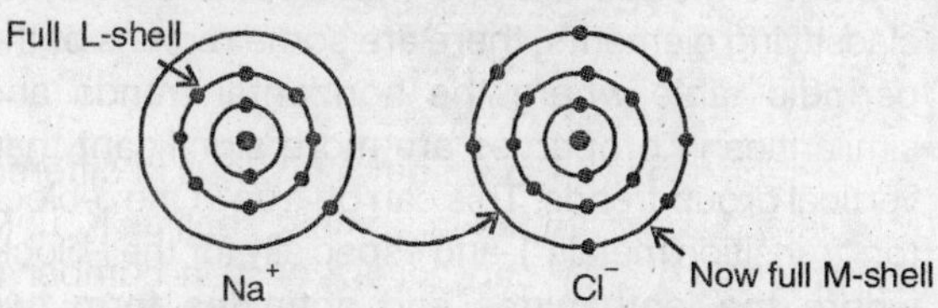

Example Na^{+1} and Cl^{-1}. Bond to form NaCl (halite or salt).

Covalent bonding - Electrons are shared between two or more atoms so that each atom has a stable electronic configuration (completely filled outermost shell) part of the time.

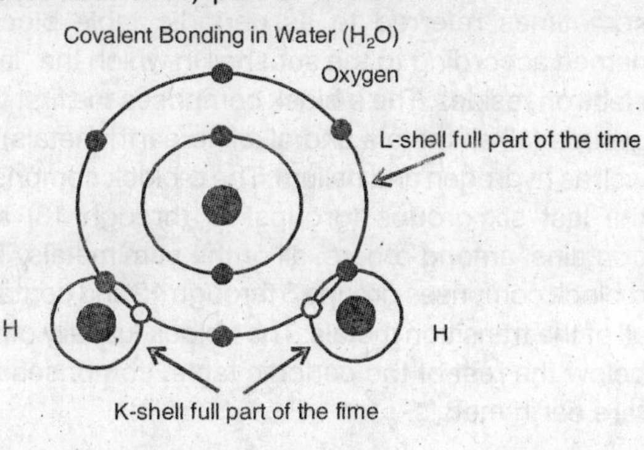

Example: H has one electron, needs to 2 to be stable. O has 6 electrons in its outer shell, needs 2 to be stable. So, 2 H atoms bond to 1 O to form H_2O, with all atoms sharing electrons, and each atom having a stable electronic configuration part of the time.

- Metallic bonding – Similar to covalent bonding, except innermost electrons are also shared. In materials that bond this way, electrons move freely from atom to atom and are constantly being shared. Materials bonded with metallic bonds are excellent conductors of electricity because the electrons can move freely through the material.
- Van der Waals bonding – a weak type of bond that does not share or transfer electrons. Usually results in a zone along which the material breaks easily (cleavage). A good example of Van der Waals bonding is graphite.

Several different bond types can be present in a mineral, and these determine the physical properties of the mineral.

THE PERIODIC TABLE

The first periodic table was devised by Dmitri Mendeleev and published in 1869.

Mendeleev found he could arrange the 65 elements that were then known in a grid or table so that each element had:

1. A higher atomic weight than the one on its left.
2. Similar chemical properties to other elements in the same column.

He realized that the table in front of him lay at the very heart of chemistry. In his table he noted gaps - spaces where elements should be but none had yet been discovered.

Although Mendeleev had made a crucial breakthrough, he made little further progress because the Rutherford-Bohr model of the atom had not yet been formulated.

In 1913, Henry Moseley, who worked with Rutherford, showed it is atomic number (charge) and not (as Mendeleev had proposed) atomic weight that is most fundamental to the chemical properties of any element. Like Mendeleev, Moseley was able to predict correctly the existence of new elements based on his work.

And today the elements are still arranged in order of increasing atomic number (Z) as you go from left to right across the table. We call the horizontal rows periods and the vertical rows groups.

We also know an element's chemistry is determined by the way its electrons are arranged - its electron configuration.

The noble gases are found in group 18, on the far right of each period. The reluctance of the noble gases to undergo chemical reactions indicates that the atoms of these gases strongly prefer their own electron configurations - featuring a full outer shell of electrons - to any other.

In contrast to the noble gases, the elements with the highest reactivity are those with the greatest need to gain or lose electrons in order to achieve a full outer shell of electrons.

Elements sitting in the same group (e.g. the alkali metals in Group 1) all have the same number of outer electrons, leading to similar chemical properties.

Likewise the halogens in Group 17 also have similar properties to one another. When halogens react, they gain an electron to form negatively charged ions. Each ion has the same electron configuration as the noble gas in the same period. The ions are therefore more chemically stable than the elements from which they formed.

There is a progression from metals to non-metals across each period.

The block of elements in groups 3 - 12 contains the transition metals. These are similar to one another in many ways; they produce colored compounds, have variable valency and are often used as catalysts. The rare earth elements can be divided into lanthanides (elements 58 - 71) and actinides (elements 90 - 103). The naturally occurring rare earths are found on earth in only very small amounts. The actinides include most of the well-known elements that take part in or are produced by nuclear reactions. No element with atomic number higher than 92 occurs naturally. These elements are produced artificially in nuclear reactors or particle accelerators.

CLASSIFICATION OF PERIODIC TABLE

Groups

A group or family is a vertical column in the periodic table. Groups are considered the most important method of classifying the elements. In some groups, the elements have very similar properties and exhibit a clear trend in properties down the group. These groups tend to be given trivial (unsystematic) names, e.g., the alkali metals, alkaline earth metals, halogens, pnictogens, chalcogens, and noble gases. Some other groups in the periodic table display fewer similarities and/ or vertical trends (for example Group 14), and these have no trivial names and are referred to simply by their group numbers.

Periods

A period is a horizontal row in the periodic table. Although groups are the most common way of classifying elements, there are some regions of the periodic table where the horizontal trends and similarities in properties are more significant than vertical group trends. This can be true in the d-block (or "transition metals"), and especially for the f-block, where the lanthanides and actinides form two substantial horizontal series of elements.

Blocks

Because of the importance of the outermost shell, the different regions of the periodic table are sometimes referred to as periodic table blocks, named according to the subshell in which the "last" electron resides. The s-block comprises the first two groups (alkali metals and alkaline earth metals) as well as hydrogen and helium. The p-block comprises the last six groups (groups 13 through 18) and contains, among others, all of the semimetals. The d-block comprises groups 3 through 12 and contains all of the transition metals. The f-block, usually offset below the rest of the periodic table, comprises the rare earth metals.

Other

The chemical elements are also grouped together in other ways. Some of these groupings are often illustrated on the periodic table, such as transition metals, poor metals, and metalloids. Other informal groupings exist, such as the platinum group and the noble metals.

Periodicity of chemical properties

The main value of the periodic table is the ability to predict the chemical properties of an element based on its location on the table. It should be noted that the properties vary differently when moving vertically along the columns of the table than when moving horizontally along the rows.

Trends of groups

Modern quantum mechanical theories of atomic structure explain group trends by proposing that elements within the same group have the same electron configurations in their valence shell, which is the most important factor in accounting for their similar properties. Elements in the same group also show patterns in their atomic radius, ionization energy, and electro negativity. From top to bottom in a group, the atomic radii of the elements increase. Since there are more filled energy levels, valence electrons are found farther from the nucleus. From the top, each successive element has a lower ionization energy because it is easier to remove an electron since the atoms are less tightly bound. Similarly, a group will also see a top to bottom decrease in electro negativity due to an increasing distance between valence electrons and the nucleus.

Trends of periods

Elements in the same period show trends in atomic radius, ionization energy, electron affinity, and electro negativity. Moving left to right across a period, atomic radius usually decreases. This occurs because each successive element has an added proton and electron which causes the electron to be drawn closer to the nucleus. This decrease in atomic radius also causes the ionization energy to increase when moving from left to right across a period. The more tightly bound an element is, the more energy is required to remove an electron. Similarly, electro negativity will increase in the same manner as ionization energy because of the amount of pull that is exerted on the electrons by the nucleus. Electron affinity also shows a slight trend across a period. Metals (left side of a period) generally have a lower electron affinity than nonmetals (right side of a period) with the exception of the noble gases.

IONIC SUBSTITUTION IN MINERALS

Ionic substitution - (also called solid solution), occurs because some elements (ions) have the same size and charge, and can thus substitute for one another in a crystal structure.

Examples:

- Olivines Fe_2SiO_4 and Mg_2SiO_4. Fe^{+2} and Mg^{+2} are about the same size, thus they can substitute for one another in the crystal structure and olivine thus can have a range of compositions expressed as the formula $(Mg,Fe)_2SiO_4$.
- Alkali Feldspars: $KAlSi_3O_8$ (orthoclase) and $NaAlSi_3O_8$, (albite) K^{+1} can substitute for Na^{+1}
- Plagioclase Feldspars: $NaAlSi_3O_8$ (albite) and $CaAl_2Si_2O_8$ (anorthite) $NaSi^{+5}$ can substitutes for $CaAl^{+5}$ (a complex solid solution).

PHASE RULE

phase rule, was proposed by Josiah Willard Gibbs in the 1870s as the equality $F = C - P + 2$ where P (alternatively p or Φ) is the number of phases in thermodynamic equilibrium with each other and C is the number of components. Typical phases are solids, liquids and gases. A system involving one pure chemical is an example of a one-component system. Two-component systems, such as mixtures of water and ethanol, have two chemically independent components. F is the number of degrees of freedom, which means the number of intensive properties such as temperature or pressure, which are independent of other intensive variables.

- A phase is a form of matter that is homogeneous in chemical composition and physical state. Typical phases are solid, liquid and gas. Two immiscible liquids (or liquid mixtures with different compositions) separated by a distinct boundary are counted as two different phases, as are two immiscible solids.
- The number of components (C) is the number of chemically independent constituents of the system.
- The number of degrees of freedom (F) in this context is the number of intensive variables which are independent of each other.

The basis for the rule is that equilibrium between phases places a constraint on the intensive variables. More rigorously, since the phases are in thermodynamic equilibrium with each other, the chemical potentials of the phases must be equal. The number of equality relationships determines the number of degrees of freedom. For example, if the chemical potentials of a liquid and of its vapour depend on temperature (T) and pressure (p), the equality of chemical potentials will mean that each of those variables will be dependent on the other. Mathematically, the equation $\mu_{liq}(T, p) = \mu_{vap}(T, p)$, where μ = chemical potential, defines temperature as a function of pressure or vice versa. (Caution: do not confuse p = pressure with P = number of phases.)

The rule is valid provided the equilibrium between phases is not influenced by gravitational, electrical or magnetic forces, or by surface area, and only by temperature, pressure, and concentration

IDEAL AND NON-IDEAL SOLUTIONS

IDEAL SOLUTIONS

Liquid-liquid solutions can be classified into ideal and non-ideal solutions on the basis of Raoult's law.

The solutions which obey Raoult's law over the entire range of concentration are known as ideal solutions. The ideal solutions have two other important properties. The enthalpy of mixing of the pure components to form the solution is zero and the volume of mixing is also zero, i.e.,

$$\Delta mixH = 0, \quad \Delta mixV = 0$$

It means that no heat is absorbed or evolved when the components are mixed. Also, the volume of solution would be equal to the sum of volumes of the two components. At molecular level, ideal behaviour of the solutions can be explained by considering two components A and B. In pure components, the intermolecular attractive interactions will be of types A-A and B-B, whereas in the binary solutions in addition to these two interactions, A-B type of interactions will also be present. If the intermolecular attractive forces between the A-A and B-B are nearly equal to those between A-B, this leads to the formation of ideal solution. A perfectly ideal solution is rare but some solutions are nearly ideal in behaviour. Solution of n-hexane and n-heptane, bromoethane and chloroethane, benzene and toluene, etc. fall into this category.

An ideal mixture is defined as a mixture that satisfies:

$$f_i = x_i f_i^*$$

where f_i is the fugacity of component i and f_i^* is the fugacity of i as a pure substance.

Since the definition of fugacity in a pure substance is:

$$g(T,P) = g^{gas}(T,P^u) + RT\ln\frac{f}{p^u}$$

Where $g^{gas}(T,p^u)$ is the molar free energy of an ideal gas at a temperature T and a reference pressure p^u which might be taken as P^0 or the pressure of the mix to ease operations.

If we differentiate this last equation with respect to P at T constant we get:

$$\left(\frac{\partial g(T,P)}{\partial P}\right)_T = RT\left(\frac{\partial \ln f}{\partial P}\right)_T$$

but we know from the Gibbs potential equation that:

$$\left(\frac{\partial g(T,P)}{\partial P}\right)_T = v$$

These last two equations put together give:

$$\left(\frac{\partial \ln f}{\partial P}\right)_T = \frac{v}{RT}$$

Since all this, done as a pure substance is valid in a mix just adding the subscript i to all the intensive variables and changing v to $\overline{v}_i$, standing for Partial molar volume.

$$\left(\frac{\partial \ln f}{\partial P}\right)_{T,x_i} = \frac{\overline{v}_i}{RT}$$

Applying the first equation of this section to this last equation we get

$$v_i^* = \overline{v}_i$$

which means that in an ideal mix the volume is the addition of the volumes of its components.

Proceeding in a similar way but derivative with respect of T we get to a similar result with enthalpies

$$\frac{g(T,P) - g^{gas}(T,p^u)}{RT} = \ln\frac{f}{p^u}$$

derivative with respect to T ang remembering that $\left(\frac{\partial \frac{g}{T}}{\partial T}\right)_P = -\frac{h}{T^2}$ we get:

$$-\frac{\overline{h}_i - h_i^{gas}}{R} = -\frac{h_i^* - h_i^{gas}}{R}$$

which in turn is $\overline{h}_i = h_i^*$.

Meaning that the enthalpy of the mix is equal to the sum of its components.

Since $\overline{u}_i = \overline{h}_i^* - p\overline{v}$ and $u_i^* = h_i^* - pv_i^*$:

$$u_i^* = \overline{u}_i$$

It is also easily verifiable that

$$C_{pi}^* = \overline{C}_{pi}$$

Finally since

$$\overline{g}_i = \mu_i = g_i^{gas} + RT\ln\frac{f_i}{p^u}$$

$$= g_i^{gas} + RT\ln\frac{f_j^*}{p^u} + RT\ln x_i = \mu_i^* + RT\ln x_i$$

Which means that

Δgi,mix = RTlnxi

and since

$$G = \sum_i x_i g_i$$

then

$$\Delta Gmix = RT\sum_i x_i \ln x_i$$

At last we can calculate the entropy of mixing since $g_i^* = h_i^* - Ts_i^*$ and

$$\Delta si,mix = -R\sum_i \ln x_i$$

$$\Delta Smix = -R\sum_i x_i \ln x_i$$

CONSEQUENCES

Since the enthalpy of mixing (solution) is zero, the change in Gibbs free energy on mixing is determined solely by the entropy of mixing. Hence the molar Gibbs free energy of mixing is

$$\Delta\ Gm,mix = RT\sum_i x_i \ln x_i$$

or for a two component solution

$$\Delta\ Gm,\ mix = RT(x_A \ln x_A + x_B \ln x_B)$$

where m denotes molar i.e. change in Gibbs free energy per mole of solution, and x_i is the mole fraction of component i.

Note that this free energy of mixing is always negative (since each x_i is positive and each $\ln x_i$ must be negative) i.e. ideal solutions are always completely miscible.

The equation above can be expressed in terms of chemical potentials of the individual

components

$$\Delta \text{ Gm,mix} = \sum_i x_i \Delta\mu_{i,mix}$$

where $\Delta\mu_{i,mix} = RT\ln x_i$ is the change in chemical potential of i on mixing.

If the chemical potential of pure liquid i is denoted μ_i^*, then the chemical potential of i in an ideal solution is

$$\mu_i = \mu_i^* + \Delta\mu_{i,mix} = \mu_i^* + RT \ln x_i$$

Any component i of an ideal solution obeys Raoult's Law over the entire composition range:

$P_i = (P_i)\ \text{pure}\, x_i$

where

(P_i)pure is the equilibrium vapor pressure of the pure component x_i is the mole fraction of the component in solution

It can also be shown that volumes are strictly additive for ideal solutions.

NON-IDEAL SOLUTIONS

When a solution does not obey Raoult's law over the entire range of concentration, then it is called non-ideal solution. The vapour pressure of such a solution is either higher or lower than that predicted by Raoult's law. If it is higher, the solution exhibits positive deviation and if it is lower, it exhibits negative deviation from Raoult's law. The cause for these deviations lie in the nature of interactions at the molecular level. In case of positive deviation from Raoult's law, A-B interactions are weaker than those between A-A or B-B, i.e., in this case the intermolecular attractive forces between the solute-solvent molecules are weaker than those between the solute-solute and solvent-solvent molecules. This means that in such solutions, molecules of A (or B) will find it easier to escape than in pure state. This will increase the vapour pressure and result in positive deviation. Mixtures of ethanol and acetone behave in this manner. In pure ethanol, molecules are hydrogen bonded.

On adding acetone, its molecules get in between the host molecules and break some of the hydrogen bonds between them. Due to weakening of interactions, the solution shows positive deviation from Raoult's law.

In a solution formed by adding carbon disulphide to acetone, the dipolar interactions between solute-solvent molecules are weaker than the respective interactions among the solute-solute and solvent-solvent molecules. This solution also shows positive deviation.

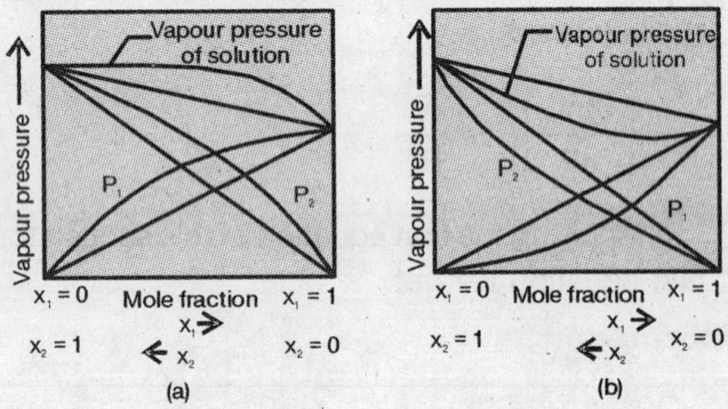

Fig. The vapour pressures of two component systems as a function of composition (a) a solution that shows positive deviation from Raoult's law and (b) a solution that shows negative deviation from Raoult's law.

In case of negative deviations from Raoult's law, the intermolecular attractive forces between A-A and B-B are weaker than those between A-B and leads to decrease in vapour pressure resulting in negative deviations. An example of this type is a mixture of phenol and aniline. In this case the intermolecular hydrogen bonding between phenolic proton and lone pair on nitrogen atom of aniline is stronger than the respective intermolecular hydrogen bonding between similar molecules. Similarly, a mixture of chloroform and acetone forms a solution with negative deviation from Raoult's law.

DISTRIBUTION COEFFICIENTS

Distribution coefficient (D) is the ratio of concentrations of a compound in the two phases of a mixture of two immiscible solvents at equilibrium.

The distribution coefficient is the ratio of the sum of the concentrations of all forms of the compound (ionized plus un-ionized) in each of the two phases. For measurements of distribution coefficient, the pH of the aqueous phase is buffered to a specific value such that the pH is not significantly perturbed by the introduction of the compound. The logarithm of the ratio of the sum of concentrations of the solute's various forms in one solvent, to the sum of the concentrations of its forms in the other solvent is called Log D:

$$\log D_{oct/wat} = \log\left(\frac{[solute]_{actanal}}{[solute]_{water}^{ionised} + [solute]_{water}^{neutral}}\right)$$

In addition, log D is pH dependent, hence the one must specify the pH at which the log D was measured. Of particular interest is the log D at pH = 7.4 (the physiological pH of blood serum). For un-ionizable compounds, log P = log D at any pH.

APPLICATIONS OF DISTRIBUTION COEFFICIENT

Pharmacology

A drug's distribution coefficient strongly effects how easily the drug can reach its intended target in the body, how strong an effect it will have once it reaches it target, and how long it will remain in the body in an active form.

Pharmacokinetics

In the context of pharmacokinetics (what the body does to a drug), the distribution coefficient has a strong influence on ADME properties (Absorption, Distribution, Metabolism, and Excretion) of the drug. Hence the hydrophobicity of a compound (as measured by its distribution coefficient) is a major determinant of how drug-like it is. More specifically, in order for a drug to be orally absorbed, it normally must first pass through lipid bilayers in the intestinal epithelium (a process known as transcellular transport). For efficient transport, the drug must be hydrophobic enough to partition into the lipid bilayer, but not so hydrophobic, that once it is in the bilayer, it will not partition out again. Likewise, hydrophobicity plays a major role in determining where drugs are distributed within the body after adsorption and as a consequence in how rapidly they are metabolized and excreted.

Pharmacodynamics

In the context of pharmacodynamics (what a drug does to the body), the hydrophobic effect is the major driving force for the binding of drugs to their receptor targets. On the other hand, hydrophobic drugs tend to be more toxic because they in general are retained longer, have a wider distribution within the body (e.g., intracellular), are somewhat less selective in their binding to proteins, and finally are often extensively metabolized. In some cases the metabolites may be chemically reactive. Hence it is advisable to make the drug as hydrophilic as possible while it still retains adequate binding affinity to the therapeutic protein target. Therefore the ideal distribution coefficient for a drug is usually intermediate (not too hydrophobic nor too hydrophilic).

Consumer Products

Many other industries take into account distribution coefficients for example in the formulation of make-up, topical ointments, dyes, hair colors and many other consumer products.

Agrochemicals

Hydrophobic insecticides and herbicides tend to be more active. On the other hand, hydrophobic agrochemicals in general have longer half lives and therefore display increased risk of adverse environmental impact.

Metallurgy

In metallurgy, the partition coefficient is an important factor in determining how different impurities are distributed between molten and solidified metal. It is a critical parameter for purification using zone melting, and determines how effective an impurity can be removed using directional solidification, described by the Scheil equation.

Environmental

The hydrophobicity of a compound can give scientists an indication of how easily a compound might be taken up in groundwater to pollute waterways, and its toxicity to animals and aquatic life. Distribution coefficients may be measured or predicted for compounds currently causing problems or with foresight to gauge the structural modifications necessary to make a compound environmentally more friendly in the research phase.

In the field of hydrogeology, the octanol water partition coefficient, or K_{ow}, is used to predict and model the migration of dissolved hydrophobic organic compounds in soil and groundwater.

REDOX REACTIONS AND EH-PH DIAGRAMS

Oxidation and reduction (Redox) reactions play an important role in the geochemical processes that occur in groundwater. Redox reactions are defined as reactions in which electrons are transferred. The species receiving electrons is reduced, that donating electrons is oxidized. Redox reactions determine the mobility of many inorganic compounds as well as biologically important materials such as nitrogen and sulfur. In addition, redox conditions govern the particulars for the biological degradation of complex hydrocarbon contaminants.

Redox potential is a an intensity parameter of overall redox reaction potential in the system (similar in concept to pH), not the capacity of the system for specific oxidation or reduction reactions. The redox value of standard half reactions (E°) and details of how to calculate redox capacity can be found in any elementary chemistry text.

In the literature redox potential is generally reported as Eh, which is the potential generated between a platinum electrode and a standard hydrogen electrode when placed into the groundwater being tested, where hydrogen is considered the reference electrode. Measurement of redox potential in groundwater can be a difficult task. The common platinum electrode is not responsive to many reactions involving solid phases, nor to the following soluble phase redox couples that are common in groundwater:

- O_2–H_2O
- SO_4^{2-}–H_2S
- CO_2–CH_4
- NO_3–N_2
- N_2–NH_4^+

Most work with redox reactions involves laboratory evaluation under static conditions, the focus is on solutions in closed systems that are in an equilibrium state. In groundwater with more than one redox couple the redox potential can not be accurately measured unless the redox reactants are at thermodynamic equilibrium. However, environmental processes are typically in disequilibrium, caused by:

- Flowing groundwater conditions.
- Biological activity.
- Redox reactions of light bioactive elements (C, H, O, and S) which most often involve the breaking of covalent bonds, a process that is normally slow.
- Electrochemical reactions of exposed active mineral surfaces.

Some redox reactions can take from 10 to 1000 years to reach equilibrium.

In oxidizing waters measurement of Eh with a platinum electrode can seldom be correlated to a single specific redox couple, and as such is usually of little value in quantifying the redox chemistry. Groundwater with reducing character can be more accurately tested with the platinum electrode, however, samples of strongly reduced water will have skewed redox values if exposed to air during sampling or testing. The latter places a particular burden on how to purge and sample wells in a manner to insure that the sample is truly indicative of the formation beyond the influence of the well bore.

Instead of measuring the redox potential from a field sample, the redox potential can be calculated using the relative concentrations and redox potential of major dissolved species. This is precisely the process used in fate and transport models utilized in support of risk assessments.

Groundwater typically contains both reduced and oxidized species, however what is termed the redox buffer capacity of an aquifer is normally dominated by the chemistry of the aquifer matrix.

- The oxidation capacity of the aquifer acts as a buffer to limit the transport of a plume in a reduced state that would be generated from hydrocarbon contamination or a landfill.
- The reduction capacity of an aquifer will buffer against attempts to increase the redox potential as part of the remediation program (such as air sparging or in-situ bioremediation) to address a contaminant plume.
- In most natural groundwater systems iron is the dominant (by 1 to 3 orders of magnitude) buffering species involved in redox reactions. In some organic rich aquifers TOC can equal ferrous iron as a reduction buffer.

The following inorganic oxidation reactions will consume dissolved oxygen in groundwater:

- Sulfide Oxidation
  $2O_2 + HS^- = SO_4^{2-} + H^+$
- Iron Oxidation
  $O_2 + 4Fe^{+2} + 4H+ = 4Fe^{3+} + 2H_2O$
- Nitrification
  $2O_2 + NH_4^+ = NO_3^- + 2H^+ + H_2O$
- Manganese (II) Oxidation
  $O_2 + 2Mn_2^+ + 2H_2O = 2MnO_2 + 4H^+$
- Iron Sulfide Oxidation
  $15O_2 + 4FeS_2 + 14H_2O = 4Fe(OH)_3 + 8SO_4^{2-} + 16H^+$

The following redox reactions will consume organic matter in groundwater:

- (1) Aerobic Degradation
  $CH_2O + O_2 = CO_2 + H_2O$
- (2) Denitrification
  $3CH_2O + 4NO^{3-} = 2N_2 + 3HCO^{3-} + H^+ + 2H_2O$
- (3) Manganese (IV) Reduction
  $CH_2O + 2MnO_2 + 3H^+ = 2Mn_2^+ + HCO^{3-} + 2H_2O$
- (4) Ferric Iron Reduction
  $CH_2O + 4Fe(OH)_3 + 7H^+ = 4Fe^{2+} + HCO^{3-} + 10H_2O$
- (5) Sulfate Reduction
  $2CH_2O + SO_4^{2-} = HS^- + HCO^{3-} + H^+$
- (6) Methane Fermentation
  $2CH_2O + H_2O = CH_4 + HCO^{3-} + H^+$

The above reactions are listed in order of decreasing Eh conditions as follows:

- (1) Aerobic Degradation
  - +250mv and higher
- (2) Oxygen - Nitrogen
  - +250mv to 100mv
- (3 & 4) Iron - Mn (IV)
  - +100mv to 0mv
- (5) Sulfate
  - 0mv to -200mv
- (6) Methane - Hydrogen
  - –200mv and lower

Water in contact with air will have an Eh in the range of 350mv to 500mv. Microbially mediated redox processes may decrease the redox potential to values as low as –300mv.

A method of handling Eh data that has proven of particular value to geochemist is the Eh-pH diagram, on which species oxidation state is plotted with variable Eh and pH conditions. The Eh- pH diagram works well in a qualitative fashion, but due to conditions previously discussed are usually unsuccessful when applied to quantitative applications. The figure given below illustrates the geologically important iron/water system. In addition to illustrating iron oxidation state, it shows how Eh in groundwater is governed at the upper range by the oxidation of water to O_2 and the lower range by the reduction of hydrogen ions to H_2.

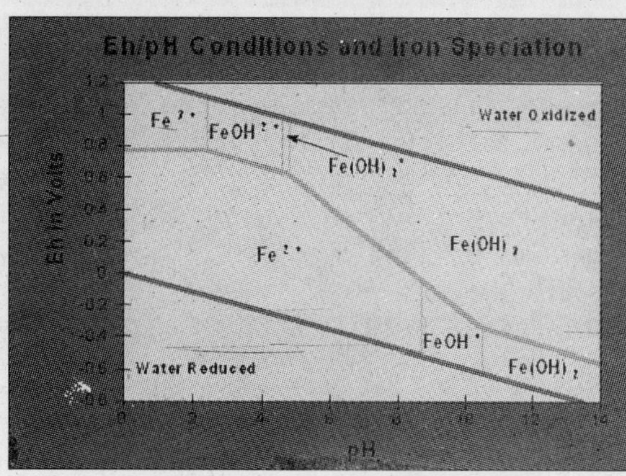

In conclusion, a cautionary note and suggestions for the obtaining the maximum value form the use of redox potential. The caution concerns the field measurement of Eh, it can be difficult to obtain representative samples and Eh measurements themselves may be unrepresentative of true Eh conditions due to the presence of multiple redox couples or general dis-equilibrium. The value of Eh resides primarily an indicator of contaminant transport and as a tool in support of intrinsic remediation activity within a contaminated aquifer. Evaluation for dissolved species generated from reactions 1 through 6 above provides direct evidence of Eh conditions as well as hydrocarbon degradation. Published Eh-pH diagrams can then be used in support of intrinsic remediation arguments, an important tool for those presenting those arguments to the regulatory community.

7. Economic Geology

Magmatic, hydrothermal and surface processes of ore formation. Metallogeny and its relation to crustal evolution; Active ore-forming systems, methods of mineral deposit studies including ore microscopy, fluid inclusions and isotopic systematics; ores and metamorphism- cause and effect relationships. Geological setting, characteristics, and genesis of ferrous, base and noble metals. Origin, migration and entrapment of petroleum; properties of source and reservoir rocks; structural, stratigraphic and combination traps. Methods of petroleum exploration. Petroliferous basins of India., lignite, bitumen and anthracite. Classification, rank and grading of coal; coal petrography, coal resources of India. Gas hydrates and coal bed methane. Nuclear and non-conventional energy resources.

MAGMATIC, HYDROTHERMAL AND SURFACE PROCESSES OF ORE FORMATION

An ore is a type of rock that contains minerals with important elements including metals. The ores are extracted through mining; these are then refined to extract the valuable element(s). Ore bodies are formed by a variety of geological processes. The process of ore formation is called ore genesis.

Current theories of the genesis of ore deposit can be divided into internal (endogene) and external (exogene) or surface processes. It must be understood that more than one mechanism may be responsible for the formation of an ore body. Example - stockwork porphyry copper deposit at depth (epigenetic) with a syngenetic massive sulfide deposit at the surface. The Table at the end of the document summarizes the principal theories of ore genesis, on page no. 123.

Depending upon whether an ore deposit formed at the time of and together with the enclosing rock, or was introduced into it by subsequent processes, they are classed as:

Syngenetic–A deposit formed at the same time as the rocks in which it occurs. Ex. Banded Iron Formation.

Epigenetic–A deposit introduced into the host rocks at some time after they were deposited. Ex. Mississippi Valley-type Deposits.

Magmatic Deposits: Those deposits, not including pegmatites that have formed by direct crystallization from a magma. Two types:

- *Fractional crystallization* - Any process whereby early formed crystals can not re-equilibrate with the melt. Includes 1) gravitative settling; 2) flowage differentiation; 3) filter pressing and 4) dilation. Number 1 is the most important and results from the settling of early formed crystals to the bottom of the magma chamber. Rocks formed in this manner are termed cumulates and are often characterized by rhythmic layering. In ore deposits the alternating layers are often magnetite and/or chromite between layers of silicate. Ex. Bushveld igneous complex.
- *Immiscible liquid* - Typical example is oil and water. In ore deposits we deal with silicate and

sulfide magmas. As a magma cools, sulfides coalesce as droplets and due to higher density settle out. Most common sulfides are iron sulfides, but nickel, copper and platinum also occur. Ex. Sudbury, Canada. The settling out of the heavier sulfides results in the peculiar net-textured ores often found in many of these deposits.

Pegmatitic Deposits: Pegmatites are very coarse grained igneous rocks. Commonly form dike-like masses a few meters to occasionally 1-2 km in length. Economic ore deposits are associated with granitic pegmatites since felsic magmas carry more water. Residual elements such as Li, Be Nb, Ta, Sn and U that are not readily accommodated in crystallizing silicate phases end up in the volatile fraction. When this fraction is injected into the country rock a pegmatite is formed. Temperatures of deposition vary from 250-750°C. Pegmatites are divided into simple and complex. Simple pegmatites consist of plagioclase, quartz and mica and are not zoned. Complex have a more varied mineralogy and are strongly zoned. Crystals in pegmatites can be large, exceeding several meters. Three hypotheses to explain their formation:

(a) fractional crystallization
(b) deposition along open channels from fluids of changing composition
(c) crystallization of a simple pegmatite and partial to complete hydrothermal replacement

Hydrothermal Deposits: Hot aqueous solutions are responsible for the formation of many ore deposits. Fluid inclusion research indicates most ore forming fluids range in temperature from 50°C to 650°C. Analysis of the fluid in inclusions has shown that water is the most important phase and salinities are often much greater than those of seawater. The chemistry of ore fluids and the mechanism of deposition of ore minerals remains a subject of hot debate. Arguments boil down to a) source and nature of the solutions b) means of transport of the metals and c) mechanism of deposition.

Metamorphic/Metasomatic Deposits: Pyrometasomatic deposits (skarns) developed at the contact of plutons and host rock. Generally, host rock is a carbonate and new minerals formed are the calc-silicates diopside, andradite and wollastonite. Temperatures involved are thought to be 300-500°C, but pressure is probably quite low. Three stage process:

1. Recrystallization
2. Introduction of Si, Al, Fe, Mg
3. Hydration and introduction of elements associated with volatile fraction

Other metamorphic processes are relatively unimportant, but hydration/dehydration during regional metamorphism may concentrate metals at the metamorphic front. Sodic metasomatism of K-spar is thought to have been important in the concentration of gold at Kalgoorlie. Conversion of feldspar from K-spar (1.33A) to Na plag (.97A) resulted in the expulsion of gold (1.37A) which could no longer be accommodated in the feldspar lattice. Skip over Mechanical-chemical sedimentary processes since they are covered in the other course.

Volcanic Exhalative Deposits: Some ore deposits often show spatial relationships to volcanic rocks. They are conformable with the host and frequently banded suggesting sedimentary processes. Principal constituent is pyrite with lesser chalcopyrite, aphalerite, galena, barite and Ag-Au. These were thought until the late 60's to be epigenetic, but it is now realized they are syngenetic. They show a progression of types with three distinct end members:

1. Cyprus type - Associated with mafic volcanics and ophiolite sequences. Found in spreading centers and back arc basins. Consist predominantly of pyrite with lesser chalcopyrite. Typified by the Cyprus pyrite-cu ores.
2. Besshi type - Associated with basaltic to dacitic volcanism. Thought to form during the initial stages of island arc formation. Many Besshi type deposits occur in Precambrian rocks and these may have been generated in entirely different tectonic settings. Pyrite dominant, but chalcopyrite and sphalerite very common.

Typified by many of the volcanogenic deposits of Canada.

3. Kuroko type - Associated with dacitic to rhyolitic volcanics. Form during the waning stages of island arc volcanism. Pyrite occurs, but is not dominant Usually galena or sphalerite are predominate with lesser chalcopyrite and tetrahedrite. Also significant silver in this type. Typified by the Kuroko deposits.

Although it is agreed ores are associated with volcanism the source of the ore bearing solutions continues to be debated. Many feel ore fluids are of magmatic origin, but others feel they are merely convecting seawater.

THEORIES OF ORE DEPOSIT GENESIS

Origin Due to Internal Processes		
Magmatic Segregation	Separation of ore minerals by fractional crystallization during magmatic differentiation.	Pt–Cr deposits Bushveld, S.A. Titanium deposit Tahawas, N.Y. (New York)
	Liquid immiscibility. Settling out from magmas of sulfide, sulfide-oxide or oxide melts which accumulate beneath the silicates or are injected into country rocks or extruded on the surface.	Cu-Ni ores of Sudbury, Canada and the nickel extrusives of Kambalda, West Australia.
Pegmatitic Deposition	Crystallization as disseminated grains or segregations in pegmatites.	Li-bearing pegmatites of Kings Mtn.
Hydrothermal	Deposition from hot aqueous solutions of various sources.	Porphyry Cu-Mo deposits of the W. Cordillera (USA).
Lateral Secretion	Diffusion of ore and gangue forming materials from the country rocks into faults and other structures.	Gold deposits of Yellowknife, B.C. and the Mother Lode, CA.
Metamorphic Processes	Pyrometasomatic (skarn) deposits formed by replacement of wall rocks adjacent to an intrusive.	W deposits at Bishop, CA. Fe deposits Iron Mtn UT.
	Initial or further concentration of ore elements by metamorphic processes.	Homestake Au Mine, Lead, South Dakota (USA).
Origin Due to Surface Processes		
Mechanical Accumulation	Concentration of heavy minerals into placer	Placer Au deposits of Alaska and California (USA)

Sedimentary Precipitation	Precipitation of certain elements in sedimentary environments.	Banded Iron Fm. of the Canadian Shield.
Residual Processes	Leaching of soluble elements leaving concentrations of insoluble elements.	Nickel laterites of New Caledonia and Arkansas bauxite.
Secondary or Supergene Enrichment	Leaching of certain elements from the upper part of a mineral deposit and their reprecipitation at depth to produce higher concentrations.	The upper portion of many porphyry copper deposits.
Volcanic Exhalative Process	Exhalations of sulfide-rich magmas at the surface, usually under marine conditions.	Mt. Isa, Aust., Sullivan and Kidd Creek,Canada, Kuroko, Japan.

FLUID INCLUSIONS

Fluid inclusions are microscopic bubbles of liquid and gas that are trapped within crystals. As minerals often form from a liquid or aqueous medium, tiny blebs of that liquid can become trapped within the crystal structure or in healed fractures within a crystal. These small inclusions range in size from 0.1 to 1 mm and are usually only visible in detail by microscopic study.

These inclusions occur in a wide variety of environments. For example they are found within cementing minerals of sedimentary rocks, in gangue minerals such as quartz or calcite in hydrothermal vein deposits, in fossil amber, and in deep ice cores from the Greenland and Antarctic ice caps. The inclusions can provide information about the conditions existing during the formation of the enclosing mineral.

Hydrothermal ore minerals typically form from high temperature aqueous solutions. The trapped fluid in an inclusion preserves a record of the composition, temperature and pressure of the mineralizing environment. An inclusion often contains two or more phases. If a vapor bubble is present in the inclusion along with a liquid phase, simple heating of the inclusion to the point of resorption of the vapor bubble gives a likely temperature of the original fluid. If minute crystals are present in the inclusion, such as halite, sylvite, hematite, or sulfides are present, they provide direct clues as to the composition of the original fluid.

PALEOCLIMATE APPLICATIONS

Trapped bubbles of air and water within fossil amber can be analyzed to provide direct evidence of the climate conditions existing when the resin or tree sap formed. The analysis of these trapped bubbles of air provides a record of atmosphere composition going back 140 million years. The data indicate that the oxygen content of the atmosphere reached a high of nearly 35% during the Cretaceous Period and then plummeted to near present levels during the early Tertiary. The abrupt decline corresponds to or closely follows the Cretaceous-Tertiary extinction event and may be the result of a major meteorite impact that created the Chicxulub Crater.

Air bubbles trapped within the deep ice caps can also be analyzed for clues to ancient climate conditions.

METHODS OF PETROLEUM EXPLORATION

Hydrocarbon exploration (or oil and gas exploration) is the search by petroleum geologists and geophysicists for hydrocarbon deposits beneath the Earth's surface, such as oil and natural gas. Oil and gas exploration are grouped under the science of petroleum geology.

EXPLORATION METHODS

Visible surface features such as oil seeps, natural gas seeps, pockmarks (underwater craters caused by escaping gas) provide basic evidence of hydrocarbon generation (be it shallow or deep in the Earth). However, most exploration depends on highly sophisticated technology to detect and determine the extent of these deposits using exploration geophysics. Areas thought to contain hydrocarbons are initially subjected to a gravity survey, magnetic survey, passive seismic or regional seismic reflection surveys to detect large scale features of the subsurface geology. Features of interest (known as leads) are subjected to more detailed seismic surveys which work on the principle of the time it takes for reflected sound waves to travel through matter (rock) of varying densities and using the process of depth conversion to create a profile of the substructure. Finally, when a prospect has been identified and evaluated and passes the oil company's selection criteria, an exploration well is drilled in an attempt to conclusively determine the presence or absence of oil or gas.

Oil exploration is an expensive, high-risk operation. Offshore and remote area exploration is generally only undertaken by very large corporations or national governments.

ELEMENTS OF A PETROLEUM PROSPECT

A prospect is a potential trap which geologists believe may contain hydrocarbons. A significant amount of geological, structural and seismic investigation must first be completed to redefine the potential hydrocarbon drill location from a lead to a prospect. Five elements have to be present for a prospect to work and if any of them fail neither oil nor gas will be present.

- A source rock - When organic-rich rock such as oil shale or coal is subjected to high pressure and temperature over an extended period of time, hydrocarbons form.
- Migration - The Hydrocarbons are expelled from source rock by three density-related mechanisms: the newly-matured hydrocarbons are less dense than their precursors, which causes overpressure; the hydrocarbons are lighter medium, and so migrate upwards due to buoyancy, and the fluids expand as further burial causes increased heating. Most hydrocarbons migrate to the surface as oil seeps, but some will get trapped.
- Trap - The hydrocarbons are buoyant and have to be trapped within a structural (e.g. Anticline, fault block) or stratigraphic trap
- Seal or cap Rock - The hydrocarbon trap has to be covered by an impermeable rock known as a seal or cap-rock in order to prevent hydrocarbons escaping to the surface

Reservoir - The hydrocarbons are contained in a reservoir rock. This is a porous sandstone or limestone. The oil collects in the pores within the rock. The reservoir must also be permeable so that the hydrocarbons will flow to surface during production.

8. Precambrian Geology and Crustal Evolution

Evolution of lithosphere, hydrosphere, atmosphere, biosphere, and cryosphere; lithological, geochemical and stratigraphic characteristics of granite - greenstone and granulite belts. Stratigraphy and geochronology of the cratonic nuclei, mobile belts and Proterozoic sedimentary basins of India. Life in Precambrian. Precambrian - Cambrian boundary with special reference to India.

EVOLUTION OF LITHOSPHERE

The lithosphere is the rigid outermost shell of a rocky planet. It comprises the crust and the portion of the upper mantle that behaves elastically on time scales of thousands of years or greater.

EARTH'S LITHOSPHERE

In the Earth, the lithosphere includes the crust and the uppermost mantle, which constitute the hard and rigid outer layer of the Earth. The lithosphere is underlain by the asthenosphere, the weaker, hotter, and deeper part of the upper mantle. The boundary between the lithosphere and the underlying asthenosphere is defined by a difference in response to stress: the lithosphere remains rigid for very long periods of geologic time in which it deforms elastically and through brittle failure, while the asthenosphere deforms viscously and accommodates strain through plastic deformation. The lithosphere is broken into tectonic plates.

The concept of the lithosphere as Earth's strong outer layer was developed by Barrell, who wrote a series of papers introducing the concept. The concept was based on the presence of significant gravity anomalies over continental crust, from which he inferred that there must exist a strong upper layer (which he called the lithosphere) above a weaker layer which could flow (which he called the asthenosphere). These ideas were expanded by Daly (1940), and have been broadly accepted by geologists and geophysicists. Although these ideas about lithosphere and asthenosphere were developed long before plate tectonic theory was articulated in the 1960s, the concepts that strong lithosphere exists and that this rests on weak asthenosphere are essential to that theory.

The lithosphere provides a conductive lid atop the convecting mantle; as such, it affects heat transport through the Earth.

There are two types of lithosphere:

- Oceanic lithosphere, which is associated with Oceanic crust and exists in the ocean basins
- Continental lithosphere, which is associated with Continental crust

The thickness of the lithosphere is considered to be the depth to the isotherm associated with the transition between brittle and viscous behavior. The temperature at which olivine begins to deform viscously (~1000°C) is often used to set this isotherm because olivine is generally the weakest mineral in the upper mantle. Oceanic lithosphere is typically about 50–100 km thick (but beneath the mid-ocean ridges is no thicker than the crust), while continental lithosphere has a range in thickness from about 40 km to perhaps 200 km; the upper ~30 to ~50 km of typical continental lithosphere is crust. The mantle part of the lithosphere consists largely of peridotite. The crust is distinguished from the upper mantle by the change in chemical composition that takes place at the Moho discontinuity.

OCEANIC LITHOSPHERE

Oceanic lithosphere consists mainly of mafic crust and ultramafic mantle (peridotite) and is denser than continental lithosphere, for which the mantle is associated with crust made of felsic rocks. Oceanic lithosphere thickens as it ages and moves away from the mid-ocean ridge. This thickening occurs by conductive cooling, which converts hot asthenosphere into lithospheric mantle, and causes the oceanic lithosphere to become increasingly thick and dense with age. The thickness of the mantle part of the oceanic lithosphere can be approximated as a thermal boundary layer that thickens as the square root of time.

$$h \sim 2\sqrt{kt}$$

Here, h is the thickness of the oceanic mantle lithosphere, κ is the thermal diffusivity (approximately 10^{-6} m^2/s), and t is time.

Oceanic lithosphere is less dense than asthenosphere for a few tens of millions of years, but after this becomes increasingly denser than asthenosphere. This is because the chemically-differentiated oceanic crust is lighter than asthenosphere, but due to thermal contraction, the mantle lithosphere is more dense than the asthenosphere. The gravitational instability of mature oceanic lithosphere has the effect that at subduction zones, oceanic lithosphere invariably sinks underneath the overriding lithosphere, which can be oceanic or continental. New oceanic lithosphere is constantly being produced at mid-ocean ridges and is recycled back to the mantle at subduction zones. As a result, oceanic lithosphere is much younger than continental lithosphere: the oldest oceanic lithosphere is about 170 million years old, while parts of the continental lithosphere are billions of years old. The oldest parts of continental lithosphere underlie cratons, and the mantle lithosphere there is thicker and less dense than typical; the relatively low density of such mantle "roots of cratons" helps to stabilize these regions.

EVOLUTION OF THE HYDROSPHERE AND THE ATMOSPHERE

The atmosphere and the oceans both arose from volcanic degassing very early in earth history. The lighter fraction made up the atmosphere while the heavier fraction made up the oceans. Also the presence of water served as transporter of soluble solids and gases between the land, sea and atmosphere.

EARLY DEGASSING : LOSS OF NOBLE GASES

Helium, argon and xenon in low concentration when compared to their cosmic abundance. It must have been lost from the earth at high rates, early on (i.e., the first 50 million years of earth history) in order to be so low now.

If degassing from volcanoes has always has the same composition, the major gasses would be water vapor and CO_2 while the minor gasses would be H_2S, CO, H_2, N_2, CH_4, NH_3, HF, HCl, and Ar. But no oxygen.

THE EVOLUTION OF OXYGEN

Oxygen is toxic to living systems. Oxygen-mediating enzymes had to evolve to handle the toxic properties of O_2

Different segments of the solar spectrum are capable of creating O_2.

1. Ultra-violet (1500 and 2100 angstroms causes the photodissociation of H_2O in the upper atmosphere. H_2 drifts into outer space, leaving O_2 behind. This this mechanism accounts for only 0.1% of the present atmospheric level i.e., PAL).
2. Visible light, used by photoautotrophs, creates far more O_2 from CO_2 and H_2O and photosynthetic enzymes (e.g., chlorophyll). The carbon released by photosynthesis was held by these organisms by the creation of organic chemicals used in growth.

Stages of Oxygen Development through Geologic Time

A. **Oceanic Oxygen**

1. 4.0-3.2 Billion Years Ago
   a. Oxygen held in mantle and oceanic crust. Little outgassed
   b. That which did was trapped in evaporite precipitation and the oxidation of CO to CO_2.
   c. Fe^{+2} and Mn^{+2} accumulated in the sea from hydrothermal vents and the leaching of volcanics and immature sediments. These two are soluble in their +2 state. The lack of O_2 kept them reduced and soluble.
2. 3.2-2.6 Billion Years Ago

   Early photoautotrophic organisms release small concentrations of O_2 that oxidized Fe^{+2} creating insoluble Fe^{+3} precipitates in Banded Iron Formations (i.e., BIF) in island arc (i.e., Algoma type BIF) and shallow shelf environments (i.e., Superior type BIF) as a result of oceanic upwellings.
3. 2.6-2.0 Billion Years Ago
   a. Development of extensive Superior-type BIF and manganese deposits capturing O_2 released by the photoautotrophs.
   b. Stromatolites in limestones expand rapidly both providing O_2 to the ocean while capturing carbon at the same time.
   c. The presence of oxygen cleared the sea of soluble iron and manganese so that little further oxygen was needed for BIF and manganese deposit formation.

B. **Atmospheric Oxygen**

Oxygen produced by photoautotrophs was used in BIF and manganese deposits. Once O_2 production increased beyond that needed by BIF and manganese deposit formations, could it accumulate in the ocean and in the atmosphere.

Free oxygen began to accumulate in the atmosphere between 2.4 and 1.9 billion years ago. Evidence for this includes the following.

1. BIF deposits iron-leaching from paleosols disappear after 1.9 billion years. The presence of oxygen rendered iron and manganese insoluble, hence they would not leach. Leaching could only occur if iron and manganese were in the +2 state and therefore soluble and mobile.
2. Presence of detrital uraninite and pyrite 2.3 billion years ago, then disappears. Grains of uraninite and pyrite indicate they are insoluble in the absense of oxygen. Once oxygen is present, they dissolve and won't occur as solid grains (i.e., detrital).
3. Development of hematite-rich paleosols by 2.2 and 2.0 billion years indicates that there is enough oxygen in the atmosphere to oxidize iron (i.e., rust). This indicates an increase in atmospheric oxygen of 15 fold 1.9 billion years ago.
4. Appearance of $CaSO_4$ in evaporites after 1.9 billion years ago indicates that there is enough atmospheric or oceanic oxygen to oxidize sulfides to sulfates.
5. First appearance of redbeds (red conglomerates, sandstones and shales) after 2.3 billion years ago
6. Accumulation of organic-rich limestones between 0.9 and 0.6 billion years ago indicates the retention of carbon compounds from photosynthesis which means an equal volume of oxygen had to be released into the atmosphere.

The atmospheric oxygen level fluctuated during the Phanerozoic. Oxygen increased during periods when plants evolved and expanded on the continents. Oxygen decreased during arid periods, when sea levels drops because newly exposed coals and organic-rich sediments would consume oxygen in their decomposition (i.e., the opposite process of photosynthesis).

CARBON DIOXIDE BALANCE

CO_2 concentration in the atmosphere was many hundred times greater in the Archean. This was due to (a) the oxidation of CO and CH_4 to form CO_2 by the ever-increasing concentrations of atmospheric and oceanic oxygen, (b) the release of CO_2 during the periods of massive volcanism in the Archean and (c) the much lower rates of subduction due to the lower thermal gradients in the mantle.

Higher CO_2 concentrations (i.e., 80 to 600 times PAL) led to the Greenhouse effect that kept temperatures above freezing and thereby prevented glaciations.

Higher CO_2 concentrations led to the photochemical production of major oxidants, hydrogen peroxide (H_2O_2) and formaldehyde (H_2CO), that enhanced ferrous iron solution in the Archean.

As the CO_2 concentration decreased through the Proterozoic, stromatolite production decreased.

In the Phanerozoic, CO_2 concentrations fluctuated for several reasons.

1. Uplift and mountain building due to plate tectonics induces the outgassing of CO_2, generated by metamorphism.
2. CO_2 concentrations drops almospheric concentrations due to loss of CO_2 in the creations of deep sea and shallow water limestones (i.e., $CaCO_3$).
3. Burial of coal and carbonates by silicate sediments reduces CO_2 concentration by burying it below the surface.

So uplift increases CO_2 concentration, while their erosion to low relief decreases CO_2 concentration.

ATMOSPHERIC EVOLUTION AND THE DEVELOPMENT OF LIFE

Reduced carbon and carbohydrate chemicals found in rocks 3.8 billion years old. First, prokarotic cell structures found around 3.5 billion years ago. Bacterial communities (stromatolites) found in rocks 3.2 billion years old.

First eukarotic cells found around 1.6 billion years ago. Atmospheric oxygen levels reached about 10% PAL. Respiration, a far more efficient metabolic set up is now possible. Eukarotes mark the beginning of sexual reproduction that, in turn, means greater possibilities of genetic development.

First metazoa found about 700 to 600 million years ago (0.6-0.7 billion years ago). Colligen produced and leads to the development of hardparts 570 million years ago (.57 billion years).

Camrian period marks the resting removal of atmospheric CO_2 from prokarotic tissue growth to metazoan eukarotic $CaCO_3$ shell formation.

CRYOSPHERE

The cryosphere, is the term which collectively describes the portions of the Earth's surface where water is in solid form, including sea ice, lake ice, river ice, snow cover, glaciers, ice caps and ice sheets, and frozen ground (which includes permafrost). Thus there is a wide overlap with the hydrosphere. The cryosphere is an integral part of the global climate system with important linkages and feedbacks generated through its influence on surface energy and moisture fluxes, clouds, precipitation, hydrology, atmospheric and oceanic circulation. Through these feedback processes, the cryosphere plays a significant role in global climate and in climate model response to global change.

STRUCTURE

Frozen water is found on the Earth's surface primarily as snow cover, freshwater ice in lakes and rivers, sea ice, glaciers, ice sheets, and frozen ground and permafrost (permanently-frozen ground). The residence time of water in each of these cryospheric sub-systems varies widely. Snow cover and freshwater ice are essentially seasonal, and most sea ice, except for ice in the central Arctic, lasts only a few years if it is not seasonal. A given water particle in glaciers, ice sheets, or ground ice, however, may remain frozen for 10-100,000 years or longer, and deep ice in parts of East Antarctica may have an age approaching 1 million years.

The thermal properties of cryospheric elements also have important climatic consequences. Snow and ice have much lower thermal diffusivities than air. Thermal diffusivity is a measure of the speed at which temperature waves can penetrate a substance. Snow and ice are many orders of magnitude less efficient at diffusing heat than air. Snow cover insulates the ground surface, and sea ice insulates the underlying ocean, decoupling the surface-atmosphere interface with respect to both heat and moisture fluxes. The flux of moisture from a water surface is eliminated by even a thin skin of ice, whereas the flux of heat through thin ice continues to be substantial until it attains a thickness in excess of 30 to 40 cm. However, even a small amount of snow on top of the ice will dramatically reduce the heat flux and slow down the rate of ice growth. The insulating effect of snow also has major implications for the hydrological cycle. In non-permafrost regions, the insulating effect of snow is such that only near-surface ground freezes and deep-water drainage is uninterrupted

GREENSTONE BELT

Greenstone belts are zones of variably metamorphosed mafic to ultramafic volcanic sequences with associated sedimentary rocks that occur within Archaean and Proterozoic cratons between granite and gneiss bodies.

The name comes from the green hue imparted by the colour of the metamorphic minerals within the mafic rocks. Chlorite, actinolite and other green amphiboles are the typical green minerals.

A greenstone belt is typically several dozens to several thousand kilometres long and although composed of a great variety of individual rock units, is considered a 'stratigraphic grouping' in its own right, at least on continental scales.

Typically, a greenstone belt within the greater volume of otherwise homogeneous granite-gneiss within a craton contains a significantly larger degree of heterogeneity and complications and forms a tectonic marker far more distinct than the much more voluminous and homogeneous granites. Additionally, a greenstone belt contains far more information on tectonic and metamorphic events, deformations and palaeogeologic conditions than the granite and gneiss events, because the vast majority of greenstones are interpreted as altered basalts and other volcanic or sedimentary rocks. As such, understanding the nature and origin of greenstone belts is the most fruitful way of studying Archaean geological history. Greenstone belts are basically metamorphosed volcanic belts.

NATURE AND FORMATION

Greenstone belts have been interpreted as having formed at ancient oceanic spreading centers and island arc terranes.

Greenstone belts are primarily formed of volcanic rocks, dominated by basalt, with minor sedimentary rocks inter-leaving the volcanic formations. Through time, the degree of sediment contained within greenstone belts has risen, and the amount of ultramafic rock (either as layered intrusions or as volcanic komatiite) has decreased.

There is also a change in the structure and relationship of greenstone belts to their basements between the Archaean where there is little clear relationship, if any, between basalt-peridotite sheets of a greenstone belt and the granites they abut, and the Proterozoic where greenstone belts sit upon granite-gneiss basements and/or other greenstone belts, and the Phanerozoic where clear examples of island arc volcanism, arc sedimentation and ophiolite sequences become more dominant.

This change in nature is interpreted as a response to the maturity of the plate tectonics processes throughout the Earth's geological history. Archaean plate tectonics did not take place on mature crust and as such the presence of thrust-in allochthonous greenstone belts is expected. By the Proterozoic, magmatism was occurring around cratons and with established sedimentary sources, with little recycling of the crust, allowing preservation of more sediments. By the Phanerozoic, extensive continental cover and lower heat flow from the mantle has seen greater preservation of sediments and greater influence of continental masses.

Greenstones, aside from containing basalts, also give rise to several types of metamorphic rocks which are used synonymously with 'metabasalt' et cetera; greenschist, whiteschist and blueschist are all terms spawned from the study of greenstone belts.

DISTRIBUTION

"Greenstone belts" are distributed throughout geological history from the Phanerozoic Franciscan Belts of California where blueschist, whiteschist and greenschist facies are recognised, through to the Palaeozoic greenstone belts of the Lachlan Fold Belt, Eastern Australia, and a multitude of Proterozoic and Archaean examples.

Archaean greenstones are found in the Slave craton, northern Canada, Pilbara craton and Yilgarn Craton, Western Australia, Gawler Craton in South Australia, and in the Wyoming Craton in the US. Examples are found in South and Eastern Africa, namely the Kaapvaal craton and also in the cratonic core of Madagascar, as well as West Africa and Brazil, northern Scandinavia and the Kola Peninsula (see Baltic Shield).

Proterozoic greenstones occur sandwiched between the Pilbara and Yilgarn cratons in Australia, and adjoining the Gawler Craton and within the extensive Proterozoic mobile belts of Australia, within West Africa, throughout the metamorphic complexes surrounding the Archaean core of Madagascar; the eastern United States, northern Canada and northern Scandinavia. The Abitibi greenstone belt in Ontario and Quebec is one of the largest Archean greenstone belts in the world.

Phanerozoic ophiolite belts and greenstone belts occur in the Franciscan Complex of south-western North America, within the Lachlan Fold Belt, the Gympie Terrane of Eastern Australia, the ophiolite belts of Oman and around the Guiana Shield.

The belts often contain ore deposits of gold, silver, copper, zinc and lead.

One of the best known greenstone belts in the world is the South African Barberton greenstone belt, where gold was first discovered in South Africa. The Barberton Greenstone belt was first uniquely identified by Prof Annhauser at the University of the Witwatersrand, Johannesburg. His work in mapping and detailing the characteristics of the Barberton Greenstone belt has been used a primer for other greenstone belts around the world.

Prof. Annhauser of University Witwatersrand, Johannesburg, noted the existence of pillow lavas, indicating a lava being rapidly cooled in water, as well as the spinifex textures created by crystals formed under rapidly cooling environments, namely water.

LIST OF GREENSTONE BELTS

Africa

- Barberton greenstone belt (South Africa)
- Pietersberg greenstone belt (South Africa)

Asia

- Taishan greenstone belt (Southeast Asia)

North America

- Abitibi greenstone belt (Quebec/Ontario, Canada)
- Bird River greenstone belt (Manitoba, Canada)
- Flin Flon greenstone belt (Manitoba/ Saskatchewan, Canada)
- Isua greenstone belt (Southwestern Greenland)
- Temagami greenstone belt (Ontario, Canada)
- South Pass greenstone belt (Wyoming, USA)
- Rattlesnake Hills greenstone belt (Wyoming, USA)
- Seminoe Mountains greenstone belt (Wyoming, USA)
- Elmers Rock greenstone belt (Wyoming, USA)

Oceania

- Norseman-Wiluna greenstone belt (Australia)
- Southern Cross greenstone belt (Australia)
- Yandal Greenstone Belt (Australia)
- Yalgoo-Singleton greenstone belt (Australia)
- Harris greenstone belt (Australia)
- Jack Hills greenstone belt (Australia)

PRECAMBRIAN LIFE

Following its origins, the record of life on earth is limited to stromatilites and bacterial microfossils until development of the metazoans in the late Precambrian. From 3.5 billion years to around 1.8 billion years the fossil record is dominated by prokaryotes. Between 2.5 and 1.8 billion years ago, major changes in the hydrosphere and atmosphere paved the way for the development of eukaryote cells.

The rise of free O_2 produced through bacterial photosynthesis is recorded in the changing nature of sedimentary rocks. Through Banded-Iron Formations, uraninite deposits, and terrestrial red-beds, we see oxidation of ocean waters and atmosphere. As the atmosphere and hydrosphere changed, so did the biosphere. Development of complex eukaryote cells allowed increasing differentiation of cell types and led to the development of multicellular plants and animals. By the late Precambrian (Proterozoic), soft-bodied metazoans begin to dominate the fossil record.

Very little is known about the Precambrian, despite it making up roughly seven-eighths of the Earth's history,and what little is known has largely been discovered in the past fifty years. The Precambrian fossil record is poor, and those fossils present (e.g. stromatolites) are of limited biostratigraphic use. Many Precambrian rocks are heavily metamorphosed, obscuring their origins, while others have either been destroyed by erosion, or remain deeply buried beneath Phanerozoic strata.

It is thought that the Earth itself coalesced from material in orbit around the Sun roughly 4500 Ma and may have been struck by a very large (Mars-sized) planetesimal shortly after it formed, splitting off material that came together to form the Moon (see Giant impact theory). A stable crust was apparently in place by 4400 Ma, since zircon crystals from Western Australia have been dated at 4404 Ma.

The term Precambrian is somewhat out-moded, but is still in common use among geologists and paleontologists. It was briefly also called the Cryptozoic eon. It seems likely that it will eventually be replaced by the preferred terms Proterozoic, Archaean, and Hadean, and become a deprecated term.

LIFE BEFORE THE CAMBRIAN

It is not known when life originated, but carbon in 3.8 billion year old rocks from islands off western Greenland may be of organic origin. Well-preserved bacteria older than 3.46 billion years have been found in Western Australia. Probable fossils 100 million years older have been found in the same area. There is a fairly solid record of bacterial life throughout the remainder of the Precambrian.

Excepting a few contested reports of much older forms from USA and India, the first complex multicelled life forms seem to have appeared roughly 600 Ma. A quite diverse collection of soft-bodied forms is known from a variety of locations worldwide between 542 and 600 Ma. These are referred to as Ediacaran or Vendian biota. Hard-shelled creatures appeared toward the end of that timespan.

A very diverse collection of forms appeared around 544 Ma, starting in the latest Precambrian with a poorly understood small shelly fauna and ending in the very early Cambrian with a very diverse, and quite modern Burgess fauna, the rapid radiation of forms called the Cambrian explosion of life.

9. Quaternary Geology

Definition of Quaternary. Quaternary Stratigraphy – Oxygen Isotope stratigraphy, biostratigraphy and magnetostratigraphy. Quaternary climates – glacial-interglacial cycles, eustatic changes, proxy indicators of paleoenvironmental/ paleoclimatic changes, - land, ocean and cryosphere (ice core studies). Responses of geomorphic systems to climate, sea level and tectonics on variable time scales in the Quaternary. Quaternary dating methods, –radiocarbon, Uranium series, Luminescence, Amino-acid, relative dating methods. Quaternary stratigraphy of India-continental records (fluvial, glacial, aeolian, palaeosols and duricrust); marine records; continental-marine correlation of Quaternary record.

Evolution of man and Stone Age cultures. Plant and animal life in relation to glacial and interglacial cycles during Quaternary. Tectonic geomorphology, neotectonics, active tectonics and their applications to natural hazard assessment.

DEFINITION OF QUATERNARY

THE QUATERNARY PERIOD

The Quaternary Period is the most recent of the three periods of the Cenozoic Era in the geologic time scale. The Quaternary is the most recent geological period of time in Earth's history, spanning the last two million years and extending up to the present day. The Quaternary period is subdivided into the Pleistocene ("Ice Age") and the Holocene (present warm interval) epochs, with the Pleistocene spanning most of the Quaternary and the Holocene covering the past 10000 years. The Quaternary period is characterized by a series of large-scale environmental changes that have profoundly affected and shaped both landscapes and life on Earth. One of the most distinctive features of the Quaternary has been the periodic build-up of major continental ice sheets and mountain ice caps in many parts of the world during long lasting glacial stages, divided by warm episodes (interglacials) of shorter duration, when temperatures were similar to or higher than today. During long periods of these climatic cycles, perhaps 8/10th of the time, temperatures were cool or cold.

HISTORICAL BACKGROUND

The term Quaternary ("fourth") was proposed by Giovanni Arduino in 1759 for alluvial deposits in the Po river valley in northern Italy. It was introduced by Jules Desnoyers in 1829 for sediments of France's Seine Basin that seemed clearly to be younger than Tertiary Period rocks. The Quaternary Period follows the Tertiary Period and extends to the present. The Quaternary covers the time span of glaciations classified as the Pleistocene, and includes the present interglacial period, the Holocene. This places the start of the Quaternary at the onset of Northern Hemisphere glaciation approximately 2.6 million years ago and includes portions of what has sometimes been classified as the upper Pliocene. This definition is favoured by the vast majority of Quaternary scientists.

Quaternary stratigraphers usually worked with regional subdivisions. From the 1960s, the International Commission on Stratigraphy (ICS) tried to make a single geologic time scale based on GSSP's, which could be used internationally. The Quaternary subdivisions were defined based on biostratigraphy instead of paleoclimate. This led to the problem that the proposed base of the Pleistocene was at 1.805 Ma, long after the start of the major glaciations of the northern hemisphere. The ICS then proposed to abolish use of the name Quaternary altogether, which appeared unacceptable to the International Union for Quaternary Research (INQUA). In 2009, it was decided to make the Quaternary the youngest period of the Cenozoic Era with its base at 2.588 Ma and including the Gelasian age, which was formerly considered part of the Neogene Period and Pliocene Epoch

The number of Quaternary interglacial-glacial cycles is probably in the order of 30-50. There have been shifts in the frequency of climate oscillations and amplitude of temperatures and glaciations through the Quaternary. At the onset of the Quaternary, many arctic areas were comparatively warm, with trees and bushes growing far north of the present treeline. Prior to about 800 000 years ago each interglacial-glacial cycle lasted for about 40 000 years, but after that the periodicity shifted to a prevailing rhythm of about 100 000 years. Prior to this shift in frequency there was a repeated build-up of relatively small-to-moderate sized ice sheets at high northern latitudes. After c. 800 000 years ago there occurred a major intensification of glaciations, with repeated growth of continental-scale ice sheets reaching mid-latitudes and with ice volumes much larger than during the earlier Quaternary glaciations. There have occurred 8-10 major glaciations during the past 800 000 years. Two of the largest Northern Hemisphere glaciations are the last one (called the Weichselian/Wisconsin glaciation, at its maximum about 20 000 years ago) and the one occurring prior to the last interglacial (called the Saalian/Illinoian glaciation, occurring prior to c. 130 000 years ago). During the peak of both glaciations, ice sheets covered extensive areas north of 40-50°N in both Eurasia and N America. The Saalian glaciation was particularly extensive in the high Eurasian north, covering vast areas of N Russia, coastal Arctic Ocean and Siberia.

The effects of the Quaternary climate oscillations were not only repeated expansion of glaciers at mid- and high latitudes, but mid-latitude areas were repeatedly subject to cold climate and permafrost, forcing plant and animal populations to migrate or adapt to changed environmental conditions – or become extinct. At lower latitudes, forested areas, deserts and savannahs shifted through several degrees of latitude as climate zones responded to higher latitude cooling. Global patterns of wind and energy transfer by ocean currents changed, causing large-scale shifts in the pattern of aridity and precipitation around the world. Rates of weathering and erosion changed globally in response to changes in temperature and precipitation, and river regimes fluctuated considerably. During peak glaciations in the Eurasian north, the large rivers of N Russia and Siberia entering the Arctic Ocean were dammed by the huge ice sheets and forced to flow southwards. When huge volumes of water were trapped in ice sheets during peak glaciations, global sea level fell up to 150 m. This caused vast continental shelf areas to become dry land, particularly the shallow shelf areas bordering the Arctic Ocean. Land bridges formed across sounds and between islands, in turn affecting ocean surface currents, shallow-sea life and productivity and opening and closing routes of migration for plants and animals. The Bering land bridge, existing due to lowering of sea level during the last glaciation, made possible the spread of humans from Asia to N America.

The frequent and rapid Quaternary environmental changes stimulated rapid evolution and the rise of large mammals, or megafauna. The Pleistocene megafauna included woolly rhinoceros, woolly mammoths and large wolves that were well adapted to cold climates. The major type of ecosystem covering the European, Asian and North American continents south of the ice sheets was a type of grass steppe that has been called the "mammoth steppe". It differed from the modern tundra environment in having higher biomass, much higher productivity and a reduced snow cover in winter. The changing precipitation patterns at the end of the last glaciation probably caused the collapse of the mammoth steppe. Since many animals were dependent on the grass steppe, they became highly vulnerable to extinction when the ecosystem collapsed. This, together with hunting by humans, has probably been the root cause of many of the megafaunal extinctions at the end of the Pleistocene. The last mammoths, lingering on the Siberian islands, became extinct 4000 years ago. Other mammals that evolved during the Pleistocene, like the caribou, the musk ox and the polar bear, continue to be an important part of the arctic fauna. It is also during the Pleistocene that humans evolve and develop the use of technology, language, art and religion. Earliest signs of human occupation in the Russian arctic are 30 000-40 000 years old. Much of the arctic flora and fauna, including native peoples of the arctic, have, however, during the past 10 000-15 000 years migrated from lower latitudes to the arctic latitudes.

The repeated Northern Hemisphere Quaternary glaciations have left a complex of landforms, sediments and landscapes that set the frame for mid-high latitude life and human activities. Human societies rely on natural resources that are products of the Pleistocene glaciations, like sands and gravels for construction activities, groundwater magazines in ancient fluvial deltas, fertile glacial till and outwash planes for forestry and agriculture. Large and rapid environmental changes define the Quaternary period – most Quaternary scientists adopt the view that the present (Holocene) interval of relatively warm and stable climate at mid- and high Northern Hemisphere latitudes is, like previous interglacial periods, an exception in the overall cool to cold Quaternary climate – and there is every reason to expect the future to hold major environmental shifts in store.

MAGNETOSTRATIGRAPHY

Magnetostratigraphy is a chronostratigraphic technique used to date sedimentary and volcanic sequences. The method works by collecting oriented samples at measured intervals throughout the section. The samples are analyzed to determine their detrital remanent magnetization (DRM), that is, the polarity of Earth's magnetic field at the time a stratum was deposited. This is possible because when very fine-grained magnetic minerals (< 17 micrometres) fall through the water column, they orient themselves with Earth's magnetic field. Upon burial, that orientation is preserved. The minerals, in effect, behave like tiny compasses.

TECHNIQUE OF MAGNETOSTRATIGRAPHY

When measurable magnetic properties of rocks vary stratigraphically they may be the basis for related but different kinds of stratigraphic units known collectively as "magnetostratigraphic units" ("magnetozones"). The magnetic property most useful in stratigraphic work is the change in the direction of the remanent magnetization of the rocks, caused by reversals in the polarity of the Earth's magnetic field. Such reversals of the polarity have taken place many times during geologic history. They are recorded in the rocks because the rocks may record the direction of the Earth's magnetic field at or near the time of rock formation (see paleomagnetism). The direction of the remnant magnetic polarity recorded in the stratigraphic sequence can be used as the basis for the subdivision of the sequence into units characterized by their magnetic polarity. Such units are called "magnetostratigraphic polarity units".

If the ancient magnetic field was oriented similar to today's field (North Magnetic Pole near the North Rotational Pole) the strata retain a Normal Polarity. If the data indicate that the North Magnetic Pole was near the South Rotational Pole, the strata exhibit Reversed Polarity.

SAMPLING PROCEDURES

Oriented paleomagnetic samples are collected in the field using a Pomeroy Drill, or as hand samples. A minimum of three samples is taken from each sample site for statistical purposes. Spacing of the sample sites within a stratigraphic section depends on: 1) the type of depositional environment: The farther away from the orogenic front, the closer the sample spacing due to generally lower rates of deposition; and 2) the suitability of the rocks for paleomagnetic analysis. Mudstones, siltstones, and very fine-grained sandstones are the preferred lithologies because the magnetic grains are finer and more likely to orient with the ambient field during deposition. It is more likely that these samples will deliver a reliable paleomagnetic signal.

ANALYTICAL PROCEDURES

Samples are first analyzed in their natural state to obtain their natural remnant magnetism (NRM). The NRM is then stripped away in a stepwise manner using thermal or alternating field demagnetization techniques to reveal the stable magnetic component. The stable component is usually interpreted to be the DRM (Depositional Remanent Magnetization).

DRM orientations of all samples from a site are then compared and their magnetic polarity is determined with Fisher statistics. Using Watson's criteria, the statistical significance of each sample site is evaluated. The latitudes of the Virtual Geomagnetic Poles from those sites determined to be statistically significant are plotted against the stratigraphic level at which they were collected. These data are then abstracted to the standard black and white magnetostratigraphic columns in which black indicates normal polarity and white is reversed polarity.

CORRELATION AND AGES

Because the polarity of a stratum can only be Normal or Reversed, variations in the rate at which the sediment accumulated can cause the thickness of a given polarity zone to vary from one area to another. This presents the problem of how to differentiate different zones of like polarities between different stratigraphic sections. To overcome the possibility of confusion at least one isotopic age (or at least an age based on paleontological data) needs to be collected from each section. These are usually obtained from intercalated airfall volcanic material. With the aid of the independent isotopic age or ages, the local magnetostratigraphic column is correlated with the Global Magnetic Polarity Time Scale (GMPTS).

Because the age of each reversal shown on the GMPTS is relatively well known, the correlation establishes numerous time lines through the stratigraphic section. These ages provide relatively precise dates for features in the rocks such as fossils, changes in sedimentary rock composition, changes in depositional environment, etc. They also constrain the ages of cross-cutting features such as faults, dikes, and unconformities.

SEDIMENT ACCUMULATION RATES

Perhaps the most powerful application of these data is to determine the rate at which the sediment accumulated. This is accomplished by plotting the age of each reversal (in millions of years ago) vs. the stratigraphic level at which the reversal is found (in meters). This provides the rate in meters per million years which is usually rewritten in terms of millimeters per year (which is the same as kilometers per million years).

These data are also used to model basin subsidence rates. Knowing the depth of a hydrocarbon source rock beneath the basin-filling strata allows calculation of the age at which the source rock passed through the generation window and hydrocarbon migration began. Because the ages of cross-cutting trapping structures can usually be determined from magnetostratigraphic data, a comparison of these ages will assist reservoir geologists in their determination of whether or not a play is likely in a given trap.

Another application of these results derives from the fact that they illustrate when sediment accumulation rates changed. Such changes require explanation. The answer is often related to either climatic factors or to tectonic developments in nearby or distant mountain ranges. Evidence to strengthen this interpretation can often be found by looking for subtle changes in the composition of the rocks in the section. Changes in sandstone composition are often used for this type of interpretation.

QUATERNARY CLIMATES – GLACIAL-INTERGLACIAL CYCLES

Within the ice ages (or at least within the last one), more temperate and more severe periods occur.

The colder periods are called glacial periods, the warmer periods interglacials. Glacials are characterized by cooler and drier climates over most of the Earth and large land and sea ice masses extending outward from the poles. Mountain glaciers in otherwise unglaciated areas extend to lower elevations due to a lower snow line. Sea levels drop due to the removal of large volumes of water above sea level in the icecaps. There is evidence that ocean circulation patterns are disrupted by glaciations. Since the Earth has significant continental glaciation in the Arctic and Antarctic, we are currently in a glacial minimum of a glaciation. Such a period between glacial maxima is known as an interglacial.

The Earth has been in an interglacial period known as the Holocene for more than 11,000 years. It was conventional wisdom that "the typical interglacial period lasts about 12,000 years," but this has been called into question recently. The current interglacial might be most analogous to a previous interglacial that lasted 28,000 years. Predicted changes in orbital forcing suggest that the next glacial period would begin at least 50,000 years from now, even in absence of human-made global warming. Moreover, anthropogenic forcing from increased greenhouse gases might outweigh orbital forcing for as long as intensive use of fossil fuels continues. At a meeting of the American Geophysical Union (December 17, 2008), scientists detailed evidence in support of the controversial idea that the introduction of large-scale rice agriculture in Asia, coupled with extensive deforestation in Europe began to alter world climate by pumping significant amounts of greenhouse gases into the atmosphere over the last 1,000 years. In turn, a warmer atmosphere heated the oceans making them much less efficient storehouses of carbon dioxide and reinforcing global warming, possibly forestalling the onset of a new glacial age.

EUSTATIC SEA LEVEL CHANGE

Eustatic sea-level changes occur on an oceanic to worldwide scale. They result from either a change in the volume of seawater, or a change in the size of the ocean basin that contains it. Even in these large-scale cases, however, mean sea level can vary from place to place due to local tectonic and hydrographic effects.

GLACIATION

For a number of reasons, the volume of glacial ice near the poles waxes and wanes over time. As a result, water is alternately taken from or added to the world oceans. This can result in sea-level oscillations of up to 200 meters. For example, modern continental glaciers are 1.5 to 2.5 km thick and have a total estimated volume of 33 million km^3. If we assume the maximum volume of Pleistocene glaciers to have been 71.3 million km^3. Using the assumption that glacial water volume is 91.7% of the volume of sea water from which it is derived, a sea-level drop of 106 m can be accounted for by Pleistocene glaciation. Melting of the present Greenland and Antarctic glaciers would produce a sea-level rise of approximately 60 meters.

Since 18,000 years ago, sea level has been rising in response to the melting of glacial ice, mainly from the Laurentian and the Scandinavian ice sheets of northern Canada. Rapid changes in the oxygen isotopic composition of skeletal foraminifera and corals (melt water has a low O^{18}/O^{16} ratio) indicate that this rise was not uniform; two major and several minor pulses of melt water were added to the ocean. Whatever the actual age or number of meltwater pulses, the main point is that sudden changes in glacial volume have resulted in significant and rapid transients in sea level.

In addition to sea-level changes caused by the transfer of seawater to and from glaciers, sea water volume can change due to thermal expansion and contraction – for every 1°C decrease in the mean temperature, world-wide sea level will drop by 2 m. Fauna from Pleistocene ocean sediments suggest a 5 degree lower surface temperature at that time, which would have resulted in a 10-meter lower sea level due solely to thermal contraction.

Despite a growing amount of data, we are still have basic questions about glacially driven sea-level change, including the amount of rise and fall and the cause of glacial cycles. The astronomic control of glaciation proposed by Milankovitch has been generally accepted to explain Pleistocene glacial cycles. The concept is that the nature of earth's orbit around the sun plays a primary role in patterns of glaciation and and, therefore, sea level change. The amount of solar radiation reaching the earth at any latitude or season is determined by three aspects of the position of the earth in its orbit around to the sun. These include:

- the eccentricity of the earth's orbit,
- the tilt of the earth's axis relative to the orbital plane, and
- seasonal changes in the time when the earth is most proximal to the sun (precession).

The earth follows an elliptical orbit around the sun. The shape of the elliptical orbit, which is measured by its eccentricity, varies from between one and five per cent through time. During times of minimum eccentricity, solar radiation is more uniformly distributed through the year, and seasonality is less pronounced than during times of high eccentricity. The period between successive eccentricity maxima and minima is about 96,000 years.

The season when the earth is closest to the sun (the perihelion) changes over time. Because of this precession, the vernal equinox occurs at perihelion every 22,000 years with the autumnal equinox occurring midway between (i.e., 11,000). If the earth is closest to the sun during the northern hemisphere summer and farthest during the northern winter, then the northern hemisphere climate will have hot summers and cold winters. These conditions are not conducive to glaciation because cold winters are usually drier than mild winters (i.e., less snowfall), and snow will likely melt during the hot summer. In contrast, when the earth is closest to the sun during the northern hemisphere winter and farthest during the summer, milder climates prevail year round. As a result, the wetter winters and cooler summers encourage glacial accumulation.

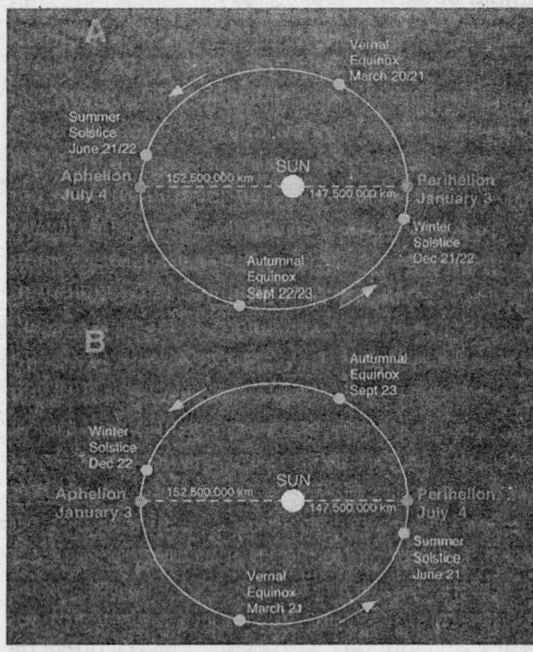

Figure : Modification of the timing of aphelion and perihelion over time (A = today; B = 13,000 years into the future).

Finally, the earth's axis of rotation can have a profound effect on global climate patterns. Presently the earth is tilted at 23.5° relative to the orbital plane of earth around the sun . As a result, latitudes north of 66.5°N are totally dark during the northern winter solstice while latitudes south of 66.5°S are in total daylight. This tilt varies by about three degrees, from 21.5° to 24.5°. This tilt or obliquity, influences the distribution of solar radiation throughout the year and over the 41,000-year cycle from one extreme to the other. During minimum obliquity, there is slightly less seasonal variability in solar radiation that during maxima.

All three elements (orbital eccentricity, its precession and the changing tilt of the earth) influence the distribution of solar radiation reaching the earth's atmosphere, acting to increase or diminish seasonal differences and, therefore, the tendency for glaciation. Milankovitch mathematically combined these variations to produce a northern hemisphere climate curve that predicted a clear periodicity to the amount of incident radiation and, therefore, glacial cycles. He claimed that astronomic factors could introduce significant cyclic variation into the earth's climate even with no changes in solar activity or the earth's albedo and no changes in composition of the earth's atmosphere. His proposal did not deny that other factors could be important, but suggested that variations in earth's orbital elements alone could trigger significant climatic change.

A "Greenhouse effect" is the behavior of solar radiation when it interacts with gases in the Earth's atmosphere like carbon dioxide, methane and water vapor. The radiation absorbed by atmospheric gasses is infrared (IR) radiation. These atmospheric gases are known as "greenhouse gases." Recent studies have highlighted carbon dioxide and other greenhouse gases as central to our understanding of global climate change. Ice cores tells us about the Earth's past climate by small bubbles of air that were trapped in glaciers, that are actual samples of ancient air.

Deep cores in Antarctic ice show that the amounts of carbon dioxide and methane in the earth's atmosphere have varied for at least the last 160,000 years. These changes correlate closely with changes in global temperature and the elevation of sea level. These variations may have been caused by natural changes in the biosphere, circulation of oceanic deep water or volcanic activity.

More recently, global warming has been tied to the dramatic increase in carbon dioxide and chloroflorocarbons associated with growing industrial pollution, increased automobile emissions and the destruction of large tracts of forest, especially in the tropical regions of the planet. According to the report of the Intergovernmental Panel on Climate Change (IPCC), 1990 levels of carbon dioxide and methane were 26 and 115 per cent, respectively above pre-industrial levels less than a century earlier. They continue to increase at rates of 0.5 to 0.9% annually. Because these "greenhouse gasses" tend to trap heat within the earth atmosphere, the expected result is an increase in the rate of sea-level rise. This is discussed in greater detail at the end of this chapter.

In contrast, the level of incident light and resulting global temperatures can be dramatically reduced by increased particulate material in the atmosphere during periods of unusually high volcanic eruptions or other large-scale events. For example, snowfall was recorded in the Bahamas as a result of the eruption of Pinatubo in the Philippines.

TECTONICS

Crustal movements may be local or global in scale. For example, tectonic activity along mid-ocean ridges will cause eustatic sea-level changes that are expressed worldwide. Locally the coast may be raised or lowered relative to regional sea level by subsidence or uplift. The 1964 Alaska earthquake raised the coast by more than 5 meters.

The most common tectonic mechanism to impact global sea-level change is the movement of the earth's lithospheric plates. This includes the opening and closing of major ocean basins, the addition of new crust along mid-ocean ridges, and changes in continental or plate margins with subduction and isostatic adjustments to loading by new crustal material. At the same time, volcanic activity along the mid-ocean ridges (as well as subaerial vulcanism) releases juvenal water that is released from the rock during extrusion.

As sea-floor spreading proceeds, basin shape and volume changes. Near the ridge, the new and more buoyant sea floor rises. Near the oceanic margins the older and increasingly dense crust sinks or is subducted beneath adjacent plates. Whether sea-floor spreading causes a sea-level rise or fall is related to the spreading rate. Under conditions of rapid spreading, the buoyant crust has less time to cool (and sink) and sea level rises in response to the shallowing basin. In ocean basins where spreading is slow, crustal sinking dominates and sea level will fall.

While the origin of the Atlantic provided a new ocean basin, ensuing events also affected the bathymetry of existing basins and further changed the volume of the world ocean. The early Atlantic Ocean was shallow until mid to late Cretaceous time, gradually replacing the deeper Pacific Ocean.

As the Atlantic Ocean continued to grow, changes in the rate of spreading and the volume of the mid-Atlantic ridge resulted in changes in the total volume of the ocean basins, thereby triggering changes in sea level. Similar tectonic processes have been present over the span of geologic time and probably account for most of the cyclicity of sea-level change in pre-Pleistocene marine sediments.

QUATERNARY DATING METHODS

RADIOCARBON DATING

Radiocarbon dating, or carbon dating, is a radiometric dating method that uses the naturally occurring radioisotope carbon-14 (^{14}C) to determine the age of carbonaceous materials up to about 58,000 to 62,000 years.

One of the most frequent uses of radiocarbon dating is to estimate the age of organic remains from archaeological sites. When plants fix atmospheric carbon dioxide (CO_2) into organic material during photosynthesis they incorporate a quantity of ^{14}C that approximately matches the level of this isotope in the atmosphere (a small difference occurs because of isotope fractionation, but this is corrected after laboratory analysis). After plants die or they are consumed by other organisms (for example, by humans or other animals) the ^{14}C fraction of this organic material declines at a fixed exponential rate due to the radioactive decay of ^{14}C. Comparing the remaining ^{14}C fraction of a sample to that expected from atmospheric ^{14}C allows the age of the sample to be estimated.

BASIC PHYSICS

Carbon has two stable, nonradioactive isotopes: carbon-12 (^{12}C), and carbon-13 (^{13}C). In addition, there are trace amounts of the unstable isotope carbon-14 (^{14}C) on Earth. Carbon-14 has a half-life of 5730 years, meaning that the amount of carbon-14 in a sample is halved over the course of 5730 years due to radioactive decay. Carbon-14 would have long ago vanished from Earth were it not for the unremitting cosmic ray impacts on nitrogen in the Earth's atmosphere, which create more of the isotope. The neutrons resulting from the cosmic ray interactions participate in the following nuclear reaction on the atoms of nitrogen molecules (N_2) in the atmosphere:

$$n + {}^{14}_{7}N^{1+} \rightarrow {}^{14}_{6}C + p$$

The highest rate of carbon-14 production takes place at altitudes of 9 to 15 km (30,000 to 50,000 ft), and at high geomagnetic latitudes, but the carbon-14 spreads evenly throughout the atmosphere and reacts with oxygen to form carbon dioxide. Carbon dioxide also permeates the oceans, dissolving in the water. For approximate analysis it is assumed that the cosmic ray flux is constant over long periods of time; thus carbon-14 is produced at a constant rate and the proportion of radioactive to non-radioactive carbon is constant: ca. 1 part per trillion (600 billion atoms/mole). In 1958 Hessel de Vries showed that the concentration of carbon-14 in the atmosphere varies with time and locality. For the most accurate work, these variations are compensated by means of calibration curves. When these curves are used, their accuracy and shape are the factors that determine the accuracy and age obtained for a given sample.

Plants take up atmospheric carbon dioxide by photosynthesis, and are ingested by animals, so every living thing is constantly exchanging carbon-14 with its environment as long as it lives. Once it dies, however, this exchange stops, and the amount of carbon-14 gradually decreases through radioactive beta decay with a half-life of 5,730±40 years.

$${}^{14}_{6}C \rightarrow {}^{14}_{7}N^{1+} + e^{-} + \bar{v}_e$$

COMPUTATION OF AGES AND DATES

The radioactive decay of carbon-14 follows an exponential decay. A quantity is said to be subject to exponential decay if it decreases at a rate proportional to its value. Symbolically, this can be expressed as the following differential equation, where N is the quantity and λ is a positive number called the decay constant:

$$\frac{dN}{dt} = -\lambda N.$$

The solution to this equation is:

$$N = N_0 e^{-\lambda t}$$

where, for a given sample of carbonaceous matter:

N_0 = number of radiocarbon atoms at t = 0, i.e. the origin of the disintegration time,

N = number of radiocarbon atoms remaining after radioactive decay during the time t,

λ = radiocarbon decay or disintegration constant.

Two related times can be defined:

- mean- or average-life: mean or average time each radiocarbon atom spends in a given sample until it decays.
- half-life: time lapsed for half the number of radiocarbon atoms in a given sample, to decay,

It can be shown that:

$$t_{avg} = \frac{1}{\lambda} = \text{radiocarbon mean- or average-life}$$

$$= 8033 \text{ years (Libby value)}$$

$$t_{\frac{1}{2}} = t_{avg}.\ln 2 = \text{radiocarbon half-life}$$

$$= 5568 \text{ years (Libby value)}$$

Notice that dates are customarily given in years BP which implies t(BP) = –t because the time arrow for dates runs in reverse direction from the time arrow for the corresponding ages. From these considerations and the above equation, it results:

For a raw radiocarbon date:

$$t(BP) = \frac{1}{\lambda} \ln \frac{N}{N_0}$$

and for a raw radiocarbon age:

$$t(BP) = -\frac{1}{\lambda} \ln \frac{N}{N_0}$$

After replacing values, the raw radiocarbon age becomes any of the following equivalent formulae:

using logs base e and the average life:

$$t(BP) = -t_{avg}.\ln \frac{N}{N_0}$$

and

using logs base 2 and the half-life:

$$t(BP) = -t_{\frac{1}{2}}.\log_2 \frac{N}{N_0}$$

Wiggle matching uses the non-linear relationship between the ^{14}C age and calendar age to match the shape of a series of closely sequentially spaced ^{14}C dates with the ^{14}C calibration curve.

MEASUREMENTS AND SCALES

Measurements are traditionally made by counting the radioactive decay of individual carbon atoms by gas proportional counting or by liquid scintillation counting. For samples of sufficient size (several grams of carbon) this method is still widely used in the 2000s. Among others, all the tree ring samples used for the calibration curves (see below) were determined by these counting techniques. Such decay counting, however, is relatively insensitive and subject to large statistical uncertainties for small samples. When there is little carbon-14 to begin with, the long radiocarbon half-life means that very few of the carbon-14 atoms will decay during the time allotted for their detection, resulting in few disintegrations per minute.

The sensitivity of the method has been greatly increased by the use of Accelerator Mass Spectrometry (AMS). With this technique ^{14}C atoms can be detected and counted directly vs only detecting those atoms that decay during the time interval allotted for an analysis. AMS allows dating samples containing only a few milligrams of carbon.

Raw radiocarbon ages (i.e., those not calibrated) are usually reported in "years Before Present" (BP). This is the number of radiocarbon years before 1950, based on a nominal (and assumed constant - see "calibration" below) level of carbon-14 in the atmosphere equal to the 1950 level. These raw dates are also based on a slightly-off historic value for the radiocarbon half-life. Such value is used for consistency with earlier published dates (see "Radiocarbon half-life" below). See the section on computation for the basis of the calculations.

Radiocarbon dating laboratories generally report an uncertainty for each date. For example, 3000±30BP indicates a standard deviation of 30 radiocarbon years. Traditionally this included only the statistical counting uncertainty. However, some laboratories supplied an "error multiplier" that could be multiplied by the uncertainty to account for other sources of error in the measuring process. More recently, the laboratories try to quote the overall uncertainty, which is determined from control samples of known age and verified by international intercomparison exercises. In 2008, a typical uncertainty better than ±40 radiocarbon years can be expected for samples younger than 10,000 years. This, however, is only a small part of the uncertainty of the final age determination (see section Calibration below).

As of 2007, the limiting age for a 1 milligram sample of graphite is about ten half-lives, approximately 60,000 years. This age is derived from that of the calibration blanks used in an analysis, whose ^{14}C content is assumed to be the result of contamination during processing (as a result of this, some facilities will not report an age greater than 60,000 years for any sample).

A variety of sample processing and instrument-based constraints have been postulated to explain the upper age-limit. To examine instrument-based background activities in the AMS instrument of the W. M. Keck Carbon Cycle Accelerator Mass Spectrometry Laboratory of the University of California, a set of natural diamonds were dated. Natural diamond samples from different sources within rock formations with standard geological ages in excess of 100 my yielded ^{14}C apparent ages 64,920±430 BP to 80,000±1100 BP as reported in 2007

CALIBRATION

The need for calibration

A raw BP date cannot be used directly as a calendar date, because the level of atmospheric ^{14}C has not been strictly constant during the span of time that can be radiocarbon dated. The level is affected by variations in the cosmic ray intensity which is in turn affected by variations in the Earth's magnetosphere. In addition, there are substantial reservoirs of carbon in organic matter, the ocean, ocean sediments (see methane hydrate), and sedimentary rocks. Changes in the Earth's climate can affect the carbon flows between these reservoirs and the atmosphere, leading to changes in the atmosphere's ^{14}C fraction.

Aside from these changes due to natural processes, the level has also been affected by human activities. From the beginning of the industrial revolution in the 18th century to the 1950s, the fractional level of ^{14}C decreased because of the admixture of large quantities of CO_2 into the atmosphere, due to the excavated oil reserves and combustion production of fossil fuel. This decline is known as the Suess effect, and also affects the ^{13}C isotope. However, atmospheric ^{14}C was almost doubled for a short period during the 1950s and 1960s due to atmospheric atomic bomb tests.

As a consequence, the radiocarbon method shows limitations on dating of materials that are younger than the industrial era. Due to these fluctuations, greater carbon-14 content cannot be taken to mean a lesser age. It is expected that in the future the radiocarbon method will become less effective. A calibration curve must sometimes be combined with contextual analysis, because there is not always a direct relationship between age and carbon-14 content

Calibration methods

The raw radiocarbon dates, in BP years, are calibrated to give calendar dates. Standard calibration curves are available, based on comparison of radiocarbon dates of samples that can be dated independently by other methods such as examination of tree growth rings (dendrochronology), deep ocean sediment cores, lake sediment varves, coral samples, and speleothems (cave deposits).

The calibration curves can vary significantly from a straight line, so comparison of uncalibrated radiocarbon dates (e.g., plotting them on a graph or subtracting dates to give elapsed time) is likely to give misleading results. There are also significant plateaus in the curves, such as the one from 11,000 to 10,000 radiocarbon years BP, which is believed to be associated with changing ocean circulation during the Younger Dryas period. Ove. the historical period from 0 to 10,000 years BP, the average width of the uncertainty of calibrated dates was found to be 335 years, although in well-behaved regions of the calibration curve the width decreased to about 113 years while in ill-behaved regions it increased to a maximum of 801 years. Significantly, in the ill-behaved regions of the calibration curve, increasing the precision of the measurements does not have a significant effect on increasing the accuracy of the dates.

The 2004 version of the calibration curve extends back quite accurately to 26,000 years BP. Any errors in the calibration curve do not contribute more than ±16 years to the measurement error during the historic and late prehistoric periods (0 - 6,000 yrs BP) and no more than ±163 years over the entire 26,000 years of the curve, although its shape can reduce the accuracy as mentioned above.

In late 2009, the journal Radiocarbon announced agreement on the INTCAL09 standard, which extends a more accurate calibration curve to 50,000 years.

Radiocarbon dating that is Research of Queen's University have helped produce a new archaeological tool which could answer key question about human evolution. The new caliberation curve called INTCAL09, which extends back 50,000 years, is a major landmark in radiocarbon dating.

URANIUM SERIES DATING

Uranium series dating techniques rely on the fact that radioactive uranium and thorium isotopes decay into a series of unstable, radioactive "daughter" isotopes; this process continues until a stable (non-radioactive) lead isotope is formed. The daughters have relatively short half-lives ranging from a few hundred thousand years down to only a few years. The "parent" isotopes have half-lives of several thousand million years. This provides a dating range for the different uranium series of a few thousand years to 500,000 years. Uranium series have been used to date uranium-rich rocks, deep-sea sediments, shells, bones, and teeth, and to calculate the ages of ancient lake beds. The two types of uranium series dating techniques are daughter deficiency methods and daughter excess methods.

In daughter deficiency situations, the parent radioisotope is initially deposited by itself, without its daughter (the isotope into which it decays) present. Through time, the parent decays to the daughter until the two are in equilibrium (equal amounts of each). The age of the deposit may be determined by measuring how much of the daughter has formed, providing that neither isotope has entered or exited the deposit after its initial formation. Carbonates may be dated this way using, for example, the daughter/parent isotope pair protactinium-231/ uranium-235 ($^{231}Pa/^{235}U$). Living mollusks and corals will only take up dissolved compounds such as isotopes of uranium, so they will contain no protactinium, which is insoluble. Protactinium-231 begins to accumulate via the decay of ^{235}U after the organism dies. Scientists can determine the age of the sample by measuring how much ^{231}Pa is present and calculating how long it would have taken that amount to form.

In the case of a daughter excess, a larger amount of the daughter is initially deposited than the parent. Non-uranium daughters such as protactinium and thorium are insoluble, and precipitate out on the bottoms of bodies of water, forming daughter excesses in these sediments. Over time, the excess daughter disappears as it is converted back into the parent, and by measuring the extent to which this has occurred, scientists can date the sample. If the radioactive daughter is an isotope of uranium, it will dissolve in water, but to a different extent than the parent; the two are said to have different solubilities. For example, ^{234}U dissolves more readily in water than its parent, ^{238}U, so lakes and oceans contain an excess of this daughter isotope. This excess is transferred to organisms such as mollusks or corals, and is the basis of $^{234}U/^{238}U$ dating.

LUMINESCENCE DATING METHODS

Luminescence dating is a relatively new method of dating archaeological sites and materials. Although the best known form of luminescence dating is thermoluminescence (or TL), there are several scientific methods which can specify the date of certain artifacts or soil sediments by measuring the amount of light energy they have trapped in the mineral's crystals.

To put it simply, certain minerals (quartz, feldspar, and calcite), store energy from the sun at a known rate. This energy is lodged in the imperfect lattices of the mineral's crystals. Heating these crystals (such as when a pottery vessel is fired or when rocks are heated) empties the stored energy, after which time the mineral begins absorbing energy again.

TL dating is a matter of comparing the energy stored in a crystal to what "ought" to be there, thereby coming up with a date-of-last-heated. In the same way, more or less, OSL (optically stimulated luminescence) dating measures the last time an object was exposed to sunlight. Luminescence dating is good for between a few hundred to several hundred thousand years, making it much more useful than carbon dating.

AMINO ACID DATING

Amino acid dating is a dating technique used to estimate the age of a specimen in paleobiology, archaeology, forensic science, and other fields. This technique relates changes in amino acid molecules to the time elapsed since they were formed.

PRINCIPLE

All biological tissues contain amino acids. All amino acids except glycine possess an asymmetric carbon atom, which means that the amino acid can have two different configurations, "D" or "L". With a few important exceptions, living organisms keep all their amino acids in the "L" configuration. When an organism dies, control over the configuration of the amino acids ceases, and the ratio of D/L moves slowly toward equilibrium, a process called racemization. Thus, measuring the ratio of D/L of a sample can allow calculations of how long ago the specimen died.

PROCEDURE

Amino acid racemization analysis consists of sample preparation, isolation of the amino acid wanted, and measure of its D:L ratio. Sample preparation entails the identification, raw extraction, and separation of proteins into their constituent amino acids, typically by grinding followed by acid hydrolysis. The amino acid hydrolysate can be combined with a chiral specific fluorescent, separated by chromatography or electrophoresis, and the particular amino acid D:L ratio determined by fluorescence. Or, the particular amino acid can be separated by chromatography or electrophoresis, combined with a metal cation, and the D:L ratio determined by mass spectrometry. Chromatographic and electrophoretic separation of proteins and amino acids is dependent upon molecular size, which generally corresponds to molecular weight, and to a lesser extent upon shape and charge.

APPLICATIONS

Data from the geochronological analysis of amino acid racemization has been building for thirty-five years. Stratigraphy, oceanography, paleogeography, and paleoclimatology have been particularly affected. Their applications include dating correlation, relative dating, sedimentation rate analysis, sediment transport studies, sea level determinations, and thermal history reconstructions.

Paleobiology and archaeology have also been strongly affected. Bone, shell, and sediment studies have contributed much to the paleontological record, including the hominoid. Verification of radiocarbon and other dating techniques by amino acid racemization and vice versa has occurred. The 'filling in' of large probability ranges, such as with radiocarbon reservoir effects, has sometimes been possible. Paleopathology and dietary selection, paleozoogeography and indigineity, taxonomy and taphonomy, and DNA viability studies abound. The differentiation of cooked from uncooked bone, shell, and residue is sometimes possible. Human cultural changes and their effects on local ecologies have been assessed using this technique.

The slight reduction in this repair capability during aging is important to studies of longevity and old age tissue breakdown disorders, and allows the determination of age of living animals.

Amino acid racemization also has a role in tissue and protein degradation studies, particularly useful to developing museum preservation methods. These have produced models of protein adhesive and other biopolymer deteriorations and the concurrent pore system development.

Forensic science can use this technique to estimate the age of a cadaver or an objet d'art to determine authenticity.

RELATIVE DATING

Relative dating is the science of determining the relative order of past events, without necessarily determining their absolute age.

In geology, rock or superficial deposits. Fossils and lithologies can be used to correlate one stratigraphic column with another, allowing relative dating to be used to show trends over long length-absolute dating in the 20th century, archaeologists and geologists were largely limited to the use of the relative dating techniques to determine the |geological]] events.

Principles of Relative Chronology

- Uniformitarianism (Hutton)
- Superposition (Steno)
- Original Horizontality (Steno)
- Lateral continuity (Steno)
- Faunal Succession(Smith)
- Cross cutting relationships (Hutton)
- Inclusions of Igneous rocks (Hutton)'

ARCHAEOLOGY

Relative dating methods in archaeology are similar to some of those applied in geology. Form a partially ordered set so that the true chronological sequence cannot be reconstructed by stratigraphic means. The principles of typology can be compared to the biostratigraphic approach described above.

PLANETOLOGY

Relative dating is used to determine the order of events on objects other than Earth; for decades, planetary scientists have used it to decipher the evolution of bodies in the Solar System, particularly in the vast majority of cases in which we have no surface samples. Many of the same principles are used; for instance, if a valley on Mars cuts across a crater, the valley must be younger than the crater.

Craters themselves are highly useful in relative dating; as a general rule, the younger a planetary surface is, the fewer craters it has. If long-term cratering rates are known to enough precision, crude absolute dates can be applied based on craters alone; however, cratering rates outside the Earth-Moon system are poorly known.(Hartmann, 258)

EVOLUTION OF MAN

Man has been a tribal animal since he first walked erect, more than four million years ago. With the impediment of being bipedal, he could not out-climb or outrun his predators. Only through tribal cooperation could he hold his predators at bay.

For two million years, the early hominid was a herd/tribal animal, primarily a herd herbivore. During the next two million years the human was a tribal hunter/warrior. He still is. All of the human's social drives developed long before he developed intellectually. They are, therefore, instinctive. Such instincts as mother-love, compassion, cooperation, curiosity, inventiveness and competitiveness are ancient and embedded in the human. They were all necessary for the survival of the human and pre-human. Since human social drives are instinctive (not intellectual), they can not be modified through education (presentation of knowledge for future assimilation and use). As with all other higher order animals, however, proper behavior may be obtained through training (edict and explanation followed by enforcement).

INTRODUCTION

The direct lineage from the ancestor of both man and the modern apes to modern man is not known. Evidence is increasing. Thousands of relics fit the general pattern.

The word hominidae is used to describe the total member species of the human family that have lived since the last common ancestor of both man and the apes. A hominid is an individual species within that family. The field of science which studies the human fossil record is known as paleoanthropology. It is the intersection of the disciplines of paleontology (the study of ancient life forms) and anthropology (the study of humans). Each hominid name consists of a genus name (e.g. Australopithecus, Homo) which is always capitalized, and a species name (e.g. africanus, erectus) which is always in lower case.

Some controversy exists on the time of this common ancestor to both ape and human, but it is believed to be about 5.5 million years ago. A key fossil record near that time is Ramapithecus, which was believed to be an early hominid for many years, but is now considered an ancient ape that lived near the fork in our common lineage. Ramapithecus is now thought to be an ancestor of the modern apes.

From a genome viewpoint, the difference between modern man and the modern apes is quite small, about 2 per cent. From a physical viewpoint, the greatest difference is in locomotion. The human walks upright. It is generally thought that this came about when the ancient hominid adopted the edge of the forest and plain and adapted to a life under the trees as opposed to in them. Fossil evidence shows that this bipedal adaptation was completed quite early, perhaps as early as four million years ago, long before we looked like or thought like we do today. Facial feature changes toward the modern appearance came much later. The facial characteristics of modern man are about 100,000 years old. The faces of earlier hominid were much more apelike

Controversy exists over whether brain size alone shows intellectual ability, but our only measure of intellectual growth in the hominid record is brain size. The fossil evidence, except for one notable blip, shows a steady growth in brain size. This can be misleading due to the different sizes of the people. Early man (with perhaps three exceptions) was quite small and the males were much larger than the females.

From a cultural viewpoint, modern man and the other apes are quite similar in some respects. Sexual practices of modern humans are quite similar to the chimpanzee (although stoutly denied by some), but with far more homosexual activity. Although homosexual play is common among the apes, a totally homosexual ape is rare. It is estimated that about 10% of the human population is so oriented.

The modern human's trend toward family dissolution places the human only a few percentage points from that of the chimp. In fact, unlike man, a gorilla male must be physically driven away and held at bay before he will leave his family. A great ape will rarely kill another member of the same species. On the other hand, music and art are peculiarities of the human and have no counterpart in any ape society.

History of Man

SPECIES	TIME PERIOD
Ardipithicus ramidus	5 to 4 million years ago
Australopithecus anamensis	4.2 to 3.9 million years ago
Australopithecus afarensis	4 to 2.7 million years ago
Australopithecus africanus	3 to 2 million years ago
Australopithecus robustus	2.2 to 1.6 million years ago
Homo habilis	2.2 to 1.6 million years ago
Homo erectus	2.0 to 0.4 million years ago
Homo sapiens archaic	400 to 200 thousand years ago
Homo sapiens neandertalensis	200 to 30 thousand years ago
Homo sapiens sapiens	200 thousand years ago to present

The times of existence of the various hominid shown in the chart above are based on dated fossil remains. Each species may have existed earlier and/ or later than shown, but fossil proof has not been discovered yet. There is also dispute concerning many overlapping species, for example, the overlap between Homo habilis and Homo erectus. It could well be that the two are continuing examples of the same species. The same dispute exists with Homo erectus, Homo sapiens archaic and homo sapiens sapiens. If all species have been discovered and the lineage of man lies within them, the most probable lineage would include all but the robust Australopithecines and the neandertal.

THE FOLLOWING CHRONOLOGY IS ABBREVIATED:

The earliest fossil hominid, Ardipithecus ramidus, is a recent discovery. It is dated at 4.4 million years ago. The remains are incomplete but enough is available to suggest it was bipedal and about 4 feet tall. Other fossils were found with the ramidus fossil which would suggest that ramidus was a forest dweller. A new skeleton was recently discovered which is about 45% complete. It is now being studied.

A new species, Australopithecus anamensis, was named in 1995. It was found in Allia Bay in Kenya. Anamensis lived between 4.2 and 3.9 million years ago. Its body showed advanced bipedal features, but the skull closely resembled the ancient apes.

Australopithecus afarensis lived between 3.9 and 3.0 million years ago. It retained the apelike face with a sloping forehead, a distinct ridge over the eyes, flat nose and a chinless lower jaw. It had a brain capacity of about 450 cc. It was between 3'6" and 5' tall. It was fully bipedal and the thickness of its bones showed that it was quite strong. Its build (ratio of weight to height) was about the same as the modern human but its head and face were proportionately much larger. This larger head with powerful jaws is a feature of all species prior to Homo sapiens sapiens.

Australopithecus africanus was quite similar to afarensis and lived between three and two million years ago. It was also bipedal, but was slightly larger in body size. Its brain size was also slightly larger, ranging up to 500 cc. The brain was not advanced enough for speech. The molars were a little larger than in afarensis and much larger than modern human. This hominid was a herbivore and ate tough, hard to chew, plants. The shape of the jaw was now like the human.

Australopithecus aethiopicus lived between 2.6 and 2.3 million years ago. This species is probably an ancestor of the robustus and boisei. This hominid ate a rough and hard to chew diet. He had huge molars and jaws and a large sagittal crest. A sagittal crest is a bony ridge on the skull extending from the forehead to the back of the head. Massive chewing muscles were anchored to this crest. See the opening picture of an early Homo habilis for an example. Brain sizes were still about 500cc, with no indication of speech functions.

Australopithecus robustus lived between two and 1.5 million years ago. It had a body similar to that of africanus, but a larger and more massive skull and teeth. Its huge face was flat and with no forehead. It had large brow ridges and a sagittal crest. Brain size was up to 525cc with no indication of speech capability.

Australopithecus boisei lived between 2.1 and 1.1 million years ago. It was quite similar to robustus, but with an even more massive face. It had huge molars, the larger measuring 0.9 inches across. The brain size was about the same as robustus. Some authorities believe that robustus and boisei are variants of the same species.

Homo habilis was called the handy man because tools were found with his fossil remains. This species existed between 2.4 and 1.5 million years ago. The brain size in earlier fossil specimens was about 500cc but rose to 800cc toward the end of the species life period. The species brain shape shows evidence that some speech had developed. Habilis was about 5' tall and weighed about 100 pounds. Some scientists believe that habilis is not a separate species and should be carried either as a later Australopithecine or an early Homo erectus. It is possible that early examples are in one species group and later examples in the other.

Homo erectus lived between 1.8 million and 300,000 years ago. It was a successful species for a million and a half years. Early examples had a 900cc brain size on the average. The brain grew steadily during its reign. Toward the end its brain was almost the same size as modern man, at about 1200cc. The species definitely had speech. Erectus developed tools, weapons and fire and learned to cook his food. He traveled out of Africa into China and Southeast Asia and developed clothing for northern climates. He turned to hunting for his food. Only his head and face differed from modern man. Like habilis, the face had massive jaws with huge molars, no chin, thick brow ridges, and a long low skull. Though proportioned the same, he was sturdier in build and much stronger than the modern human.

Homo sapiens (archaic) provides the bridge between erectus and Homo sapiens sapiens during the period 200,000 to 500,000 years ago. Many skulls have been found with features intermediate between the two. Brain averaged about 1200cc and speech was indicated. Skulls are more rounded and with smaller features. Molars and brow ridges are smaller. The skeleton shows a stronger build than modern human but was well proportioned.

Homo sapiens neandertalensis lived in Europe and the Mideast between 150,000 and 35,000 years ago. Neandertals coexisted with H.sapiens (archaic) and early H.sapiens sapiens. It is not known whether he was of the same species and disappeared into the H.sapiens sapiens gene pool or he may have been crowded out of existence (killed off) by the H.sapien sapien. Recent DNA studies have indicated that the neandertal was an entirely different species and did not merge into the H. sapiens sapiens gene pool. Brain sizes averaged larger than modern man at about 1450cc but the head was shaped differently, being longer and lower than modern man. His nose was large and was different from modern man in structure. He was a massive man at about 5'6" tall with an extremely heavy skeleton that showed attachments for massive muscles. He was far stronger than modern man. His jaw was massive and he had a receding forehead, like erectus.

Homo sapiens sapiens first appeared about 120,000 years ago. Modern humans have an average brain size of about 1350 cc (cranial capacity).

MODELS OF HUMAN EVOLUTION

Today, all humans belong to one, undivided by species barrier, population of Homo sapiens sapiens. However, according to the "Out of Africa" model this is not the first species of hominids: the first species of genus Homo, Homo habilis, evolved in East Africa at least 2 Ma, and members of this species populated different parts of Africa in a relatively short time. Homo erectus evolved more than 1.8 Ma, and by 1.5 Ma had spread throughout the Old World.

Anthropologists have been divided as to whether current human population evolved as one interconnected population (as postulated by the Multiregional Evolution hypothesis), or evolved only in East Africa, speciated, and then migrating out of Africa and replaced human populations in Eurasia (called the "Out of Africa" Model cr the "Complete Replacement" Model).

MULTIREGIONAL MODEL

Multiregional evolution, a model to account for the pattern of human evolution, was proposed by Milford H. Wolpoff in 1988. Multiregional evolution holds that human evolution from the beginning of the Pleistocene 2.5 million years BP to the present day has been within a single, continuous human species, evolving worldwide to modern Homo sapiens.

According to the multiregional hypothesis, fossil and genomic data are evidence for worldwide human evolution and contradict the recent speciation postulated by the Recent African origin hypothesis. The fossil evidence was insufficient for Richard Leakey to resolve this debate. Studies of haplogroups in Y-chromosomal DNA and mitochondrial DNA have largely supported a recent African origin. Evidence from autosomal DNA also supports the Recent African origin. However the presence of archaic admixture in modern humans remains a possibility and has been suggested by some studies.

OUT OF AFRICA

According to the Out of Africa model, developed by Chris Stringer and Peter Andrews, modern H. sapiens evolved in Africa 200,000 years ago. Homo sapiens began migrating from Africa between 70,000 – 50,000 years ago and eventually replaced existing hominid species in Europe and Asia. Out of Africa has gained support from research using mitochondrial DNA (mtDNA). After analysing genealogy trees constructed using 133 types of mtDNA, researchers concluded that all were descended from a woman from Africa, dubbed Mitochondrial Eve. Out of Africa is also supported by the fact that mitochondrial genetic diversity is highest among African populations.

There are differing theories on whether there was a single exodus or several. A multiple dispersal model involves the Southern Dispersal theory, which has gained support in recent years from genetic, linguistic and archaeological evidence. In this theory, there was a coastal dispersal of modern humans from the Horn of Africa around 70,000 years ago. This group helped to populate Southeast Asia and Oceania, explaining the discovery of early human sites in these areas much earlier than those in the Levant. A second wave of humans dispersed across the Sinai peninsula into Asia, resulting in the bulk of human population for Eurasia. This second group possessed a more sophisticated tool technology and was less dependent on coastal food sources than the original group. Much of the evidence for the first group's expansion would have been destroyed by the rising sea levels at the end of the Holocene era. The multiple dispersal model is contradicted by studies indicating that the populations of Eurasia and the populations of Southeast Asia and Oceania are all descended from the same mitochondrial DNA lineages, which support a single migration out of Africa that gave rise to all non-African populations.

The broad study of African genetic diversity headed by Dr.Sarah Tishkoff found the San people to express the greatest genetic diversity among the 113 distinct populations sampled, making them one of 14 "ancestral population clusters". The research also located the origin of modern human migration in south-western Africa, near the coastal border of Namibia and Angola.

STONE AGE CULTURES

The Stone Age is a broad prehistoric time period during which humans widely used stone for toolmaking. Stone tools were made from a variety of different sorts of stone. For example, flint and chert were shaped (or chipped) for use as cutting tools and weapons, while basalt and sandstone were used for ground stone tools, such as quern-stones. Wood, bone, shell, antler (deer) and other materials were widely used, as well. During the most recent part of the period, sediments (like clay) were used to make pottery. A series of metal technology innovations characterize the later Chalcolithic (Copper Age), Bronze Age and Iron Age.

The period from 2.7-2.58 Mya encompasses the first use of stone tools in Gona, Ethiopia and its spread and widespread use elsewhere soon thereafter. It ends with the development of agriculture, the domestication of certain animals, and the smelting of copper ore to produce metal. It is termed prehistoric since humanity had not yet started writing–the traditional start of history (i.e., recorded history).

CHRONOLOGY

The three-age system divides human technological prehistory into three periods:

- The Stone Age
- The Bronze Age
- The Iron Age

New ages and subages were added as new archaeological discoveries were made, and different schemes were developed to describe conditions in different places. A more modern periodization of the Stone Age stretches from the Paleolithic to the Neolithic in the following scheme (crossing an epoch boundary on the geologic time scale):

- Pleistocene epoch (highly glaciated climate)
    - Paleolithic age

- Holocene epoch (modern climate)
  - Mesolithic or Epipaleolithic age
  - Neolithic age
  - Copper Age
  - Bronze Age
  - Iron Age
- Historical period (written record begins)

PALEOLITHIC

The Paleolithic "old age of the stone"; was coined by archaeologist John Lubbock in 1865.) is a prehistoric era distinguished by the development of stone tools. It covers the greatest portion of humanity's time on Earth, extending from 2.5 or 2.6 million years ago, with the introduction of stone tools by hominids such as Homo habilis, to the introduction of agriculture and the end of the Pleistocene around 10,000 BC. The Paleolithic era ended with the Mesolithic, or in areas with an early neolithisation, the Epipaleolithic.

During the Paleolithic age, humans were grouped together in small scale societies such as bands and gained their subsistence from gathering plants and hunting wild animals. The Paleolithic is characterized by the use of knapped stone tools, although at the time, humans also used wood and bone tools. Other organic commodities were adapted for use as tools, including leather and vegetable fibers; however, given their nature, these have not been preserved to any great degree. Humankind gradually evolved from early members of the genus Homo such as Homo habilis, who used simple stone tools into fully behaviorally and anatomically modern humans (Homo sapiens sapiens) during the Paleolithic era. DNA and fossil evidence indicates that modern humans originated in east Africa about 200,000 years ago. During the end of the Paleolithic specifically the Middle and or Upper Paleolithic humans began to produce the earliest works of art and engage in religious and spiritual behavior such as burial and ritual. The climate during the Paleolithic consisted of a set of glacial and interglacial periods in which the climate periodically fluctuated between warm and cool temperatures.

LOWER PALAEOLITHIC

Near the end of the Pliocene epoch in Africa, an early ancestor of modern humans, called Homo habilis, developed the earliest stone tools. These were relatively simple tools known as choppers. Homo habilis is presumed to have mastered the Oldowan era tool case which utilized stone flakes and cores. This industry of stone tools is named after the site of Olduvai Gorge in Tanzania. These humans likely subsisted on scavenged meat and wild plants, rather than by hunting prey. Around 1.5 million years ago, a more evolved human species, Homo erectus, appeared. H. erectus learned to control fire and created more complex chopper tools, as well as expanding out of Africa to reach Asia, as shown by sites such as Zhoukoudian in China. By 1 million years ago, the earliest evidence of humans in Europe is known, as well use of the more advanced handaxe tool.

MIDDLE PALAEOLITHIC

This period is most well-known as being the era during which the Neanderthals lived (c. 120,000–24,000 years ago). The stone artefact technology of the Neanderthals is generally known as the Mousterian or more precisely Neandertal traits was found also in younger Chвtelperronian, Aurignacian and Gravettian archeological cultures. The Neanderthals traits eventually disappeared from the archaeological record, replaced by modern humans traits which first appeared in Ethiopia around 120,000 years ago although often identified as Archaic Homo sapiens. Neanderthals nursed their elderly and practised ritual burial indicating an organised society. The earliest evidence (Mungo Man) of settlement in Australia dates to around 40,000 years ago when modern humans likely crossed from Asia by hopping from island to island. Middle Palaeolithic peoples demonstrate the earliest undisputed evidence for art and other expressions of abstract thought such as intentional burial of the dead.

UPPER PALAEOLITHIC

From 35,000 to 10,000 years ago (the end of the last ice age) modern humans spread out further across the Earth during the period known as the

Upper Palaeolithic. In the time when Cro-Magnon and Neanderthal traits mixed in Europe (35–24.5 ky) a relatively rapid succession of often complex stone artefact technologies took place. During period between 35 and 10 kya evolved: from 35 to 29 kya Chвtelperronian, 32–26 Aurignacian, 28–22 Gravettian, 22–17 Solutrean, and 18–10 Magdalenian. The last two occurred after the disappearance of neanderthal traits from paleoantropological specimens.

The Americas were colonised via the Bering land bridge which was exposed during this period by lower sea levels. These people are called the Paleo-Indians, and the earliest accepted dates are those of the Clovis culture sites, some 13,500 years ago. Globally, societies were hunter-gatherers but evidence of regional identities begins to appear in the wide variety of stone tool types being developed to suit different environments.

EPIPALAEOLITHIC/MESOLITHIC

The period starting from the end of the last ice age, 10,000 years ago, to around 6,000 years ago was characterised by rising sea levels and a need to adapt to a changing environment and find new food sources. The development of microlith tools began in response to these changes. They were derived from the previous Palaeolithic tools, hence the term Epipalaeolithic. However, in Europe the term Mesolithic (Middle Stone Age) is used, as the tools (and way of life) were imported from the Near East. There, microlith tools permitted more efficient hunting, while more complex settlements, such as Lepenski Vir developed based on fishing. Domestication of the dog as a hunting companion probably dates to this period.

The earliest known battle occurred during the Mesolithic period at a site in Egypt known as Cemetery 117.

NEOLITHIC

The Neolithic, New Stone Age, was characterized by the adoption of agriculture, the so-called Neolithic Revolution, the development of pottery, polished stone tools and more complex, larger settlements such as Çatal Hüyük and Jericho. The first Neolithic cultures started around 7000 BC in the fertile crescent. Agriculture and the culture it led to spread to the Mediterranean, the Indus valley, China and Southeast Asia.

Due to the increased need to harvest and process plants, ground stone and polished stone artifacts became much more widespread, including tools for grinding, cutting, and chopping. The first large-scale constructions were built, including settlement towers and walls, e.g., Jericho and ceremonial sites, e.g.: Stonehenge. These show that there was sufficient resources and co-operation to enable large groups to work on these projects. To what extent this was a basis for the development of elites and social hierarchies is a matter of on-going debate. Although some late Neolithic societies formed complex stratified chiefdoms similar to Polynesian societies such as the Ancient Hawaiians, most Neolithic societies were relatively simple and egalitarian though Neolithic cultures were noticeably more hierarchical than the Paleolithic cultures that preceded them and Hunter-gatherer cultures in general. The earliest evidence for established trade exists in the Neolithic with newly settled people importing exotic goods over distances of many hundreds of miles. The Ggantija temples of Gozo in the Maltese archipelago are the oldest surviving free standing structures in the world, erected c. 3600-2500 BC. Skara Brae located on Orkney island off Scotland is one of Europe's best examples of a Neolithic village. The community contains stone beds, shelves and even an indoor toilet linked to a stream.

NEOTECTONICS

Neotectonics is a subdiscipline of tectonics. It is the study of the motions and deformations of the Earth's crust (geological and geomorphological processes) which are current or recent in geologic time. The term may also refer to the motions/deformations in question themselves. The corresponding time frame is referred to as the neotectonic period. Accordingly, the preceding time is referred to as palaeotectonic period.

Neotectonics is defined as "the study of geologically recent motions of the Earth's crust, particularly those produced by earthquakes, with the goals of understanding the physics of earthquake recurrence, the growth of mountains, and the seismic hazard embodied in these processes."

Some authors consider neotectonics to be basically synonymous with "active tectonics", while others start the neotectonic period from the middle miocene. A general agreement has been emerging that the actual time frame may be individual for each geological environment and it must be set back in time sufficiently far to fully understand the current tectonic activity.

10. Applied Geology

(i) **Remote Sensing and GIS:** Elements of photogrammetry, elements of photo-interpretation, electromagnetic spectrum, emission range, film and imagery, sensors, geological interpretations of air photos and imageries. Global positioning systems. GIS-data structure, attribute data, thematic layers and query analysis.

(ii) **Engineering Geology:** Engineering properties of rocks and physical characteristics of building stones, concretes and other aggregates. Geological investigations for construction of dams, bridges, highways and tunnels. Remedial measures. Mass movements with special emphasis on landslides and causes of hillslope instability. Seismic design of buildings.

(iii) **Mineral Exploration:** Geological, geophysical, geochemical and geobotanical methods of surface and sub-surface exploration on different scales. Sampling, assaying and evaluation of mineral deposits.

(iv) **Hydrogeology:** Groundwater, Darcy's law, hydrological characteristics of aquifers, hydrological cycle. Precipitation, evapotranspiration and infiltration processes. Hydrological classification of water-bearing formations. Fresh and salt-water relationships in coastal and inland areas. Groundwater exploration and water pollution. Groundwater regimes in India.

REMOTE SENSING

"Remote sensing is the science (and to some extent, art) of acquiring information about the Earth's surface without actually being in contact with it. This is done by sensing and recording reflected or emitted energy and processing, analyzing, and applying that information".

Remote sensing is the small or large-scale acquisition of information of an object or phenomenon, by the use of either recording or real-time sensing device(s) that are wireless, or not in physical or intimate contact with the object (such as by way of aircraft, spacecraft, satellite, buoy, or ship). In practice, remote sensing is the stand-off collection through the use of a variety of devices for gathering information on a given object or area. Thus, Earth observation or weather satellite collection platforms, ocean and atmospheric observing weather buoy platforms, the monitoring of a parolee via an ultrasound identification system, Magnetic Resonance Imaging (MRI), Positron Emission Tomography (PET), X-radiation (X-RAY) and space probes are all examples of remote sensing.

There are two kinds of remote sensing. Passive sensors detect natural radiation that is emitted or reflected by the object or surrounding area being observed. Reflected sunlight is the most common source of radiation measured by passive sensors. Examples of passive remote sensors include film photography, Infrared, charge-coupled devices, and radiometers. Active collection, on the other hand, emits energy in order to scan objects and areas whereupon a sensor then detects and measures the radiation that is reflected or backscattered from the target. RADAR is an example of active remote sensing where the time delay between emission and return is measured, establishing the location, height, speed and direction of an object.

In much of remote sensing, the process involves an interaction between incident radiation and the targets of interest. This is exemplified by the use of imaging systems where the following seven elements are involved. Note, however that remote sensing also involves the sensing of emitted energy and the use of non-imaging sensors.

1. Energy Source or Illumination (A) - the first requirement for remote sensing is to have an energy source which illuminates or provides electromagnetic energy to the target of interest.
2. Radiation and the Atmosphere (B) - as the energy travels from its source to the target, it will come in contact with and interact with the atmosphere it passes through. This interaction may take place a second time as the energy travels from the target to the sensor.
3. Interaction with the Target (C) - once the energy makes its way to the target through the atmosphere, it interacts with the target depending on the properties of both the target and the radiation.
4. Recording of Energy by the Sensor (D) - after the energy has been scattered by, or emitted from the target, we require a sensor (remote - not in contact with the target) to collect and record the electromagnetic radiation.
5. Transmission, Reception, and Processing (E) - the energy recorded by the sensor has to be transmitted, often in electronic form, to a receiving and processing station where the data are processed into an image (hardcopy and/or digital).
6. Interpretation and Analysis (F) - the processed image is interpreted, visually and/or digitally or electronically, to extract information about the target which was illuminated.
7. Application (G) - the final element of the remote sensing process is achieved when we apply the information we have been able to extract from the imagery about the target in order to better understand it, reveal some new information, or assist in solving a particular problem.

These seven elements comprise the remote sensing process from beginning to end.

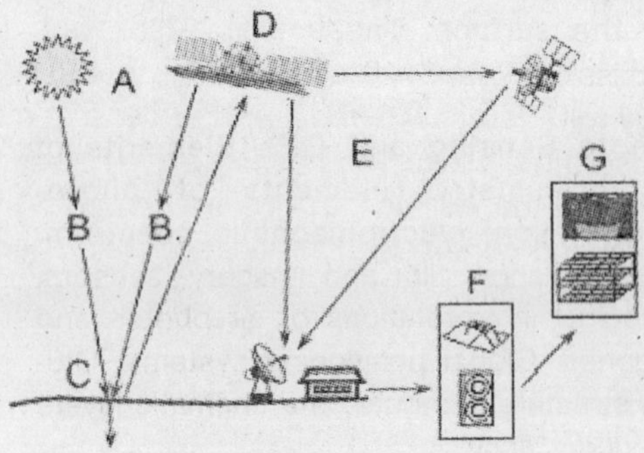

Illustration showing remote sensing process

ELECTROMAGNETIC RADIATION

Electromagnetic radiation consists of an electrical field (E) which varies in magnitude in a direction perpendicular to the direction in which the radiation is traveling, and a magnetic field (M) oriented at right angles to the electrical field. Both these fields travel at the speed of light (c).

Two characteristics of electromagnetic radiation are particularly important for understanding remote sensing. These are the wavelength and frequency.

The wavelength is the length of one wave cycle, which can be measured as the distance between successive wave crests. Wavelength is usually represented by the Greek letter lambda (l). Wavelength is measured in metres (m) or some factor of metres such as nanometres (nm, 10^{-9} metres), micrometres (mm, 10^{-6} metres) or centimetres (cm, 10^{-2} metres). Frequency refers to the number of cycles of a wave passing a fixed point per unit of time. Frequency is normally measured in hertz (Hz), equivalent to one cycle per second, and various multiples of hertz.

Wavelength and frequency are related by the following formula:

$$c = \lambda v$$

where:

λ = wavelength (m)

v = frequency (cycles per second, Hz)

c = speed of light (3×10^8 m/s)

RADIATION - TARGET INTERACTIONS

There are three (3) forms of interaction that can take place when energy strikes, or is incident (I) upon the surface. These are: absorption (A); transmission (T); and reflection (R). The total incident energy will interact with the surface in one or more of these three ways. The proportions of each will depend on the wavelength of the energy and the material and condition of the feature.

Absorption (A) occurs when radiation (energy) is absorbed into the target while transmission (T) occurs when radiation passes through a target. Reflection (R) occurs when radiation "bounces" off the target and is redirected. In remote sensing, we are most interested in measuring the radiation reflected from targets. We refer to two types of reflection, which represent the two extreme ends of the way in which energy is reflected from a target: specular reflection and diffuse reflection.

When a surface is smooth we get specular or mirror-like reflection where all (or almost all) of the energy is directed away from the surface in a single direction. Diffuse reflection occurs when the surface is rough and the energy is reflected almost uniformly in all directions. Most earth surface features lie somewhere between perfectly specular or perfectly diffuse reflectors. Whether a particular target reflects specularly or diffusely, or somewhere in between, depends on the surface roughness of the feature in comparison to the wavelength of the incoming radiation. If the wavelengths are much smaller than the surface variations or the particle sizes that make up the surface, diffuse reflection will dominate. For example, fine-grained sand would appear fairly smooth to long wavelength microwaves but would appear quite rough to the visible wavelengths.

Leaves: A chemical compound in leaves called chlorophyll strongly absorbs radiation in the red and blue wavelengths but reflects green wavelengths. Leaves appear "greenest" to us in the summer, when chlorophyll content is at its maximum. In autumn, there is less chlorophyll in the leaves, so there is less absorption and proportionately more reflection of the red wavelengths, making the leaves appear red or yellow (yellow is a combination of red and green wavelengths). The internal structure of healthy leaves act as excellent diffuse reflectors of near-infrared wavelengths. If our eyes were sensitive to near-infrared, trees would appear extremely bright to us at these wavelengths. In fact, measuring and monitoring the near-IR reflectance is one way that scientists can determine how healthy (or unhealthy) vegetation may be.

Water: Longer wavelength visible and near infrared radiation is absorbed more by water than shorter visible wavelengths. Thus water typically looks blue or blue-green due to stronger reflectance at these shorter wavelengths, and darker if viewed at red or near infrared wavelengths. If there is suspended sediment present in the upper layers of the water body, then this will allow better reflectivity and a brighter appearance of the water. The apparent colour of the water will show a slight shift to longer wavelengths. Suspended sediment (S) can be easily confused with shallow (but clear) water, since these two phenomena appear very similar. Chlorophyll in algae absorbs more of the blue wavelengths and reflects the green, making the water appear more green in colour when algae is present. The topography of the water surface (rough, smooth, floating materials, etc.) can also lead to complications for water-related interpretation due to potential problems of specular reflection and other influences on colour and brightness.

APPLICATIONS OF REMOTE SENSING DATA

- Conventional radar is mostly associated with aerial traffic control, early warning, and certain large scale meteorological data. Doppler radar is used by local law enforcements' monitoring of speed limits and in enhanced meteorological collection such as wind speed and direction within weather systems. Other types of active collection includes plasmas in the ionosphere). Interferometric synthetic aperture radar is used to produce precise digital elevation models of large scale terrain (See RADARSAT, TerraSAR-X, Magellan).

- Laser and radar altimeters on satellites have provided a wide range of data. By measuring the bulges of water caused by gravity, they map features on the seafloor to a resolution of a mile or so. By measuring the height and wave-length of ocean waves, the altimeters measure wind speeds and direction, and surface ocean currents and directions.
- Light detection and ranging (LIDAR) is well known in the examples of weapon ranging, laser illuminated homing of projectiles. LIDAR discovered by hendy in 1976. LIDAR is used to detect and measure the concentration of various chemicals in the atmosphere, while airborne LIDAR can be used to measure heights of objects and features on the ground more accurately than with radar technology. Vegetation remote sensing is a principle application of LIDAR.
- Radiometers and photometers are the most common instrument in use, collecting reflected and emitted radiation in a wide range of frequencies. The most common are visible and infrared sensors, followed by microwave, gamma ray and rarely, ultraviolet. They may also be used to detect the emission spectra of various chemicals, providing data on chemical concentrations in the atmosphere.
- Stereographic pairs of aerial photographs have often been used to make topographic maps by imagery and terrain analysts in trafficability and highway departments for potential routes.
- Simultaneous multi-spectral platforms such as Landsat have been in use since the 70's. These thematic mappers take images in multiple wavelengths of electro-magnetic radiation (multi-spectral) and are usually found on earth observation satellites, including (for example) the Landsat program or the IKONOS satellite. Maps of land cover and land use from thematic mapping can be used to prospect for minerals, detect or monitor land usage, deforestation, and examine the health of indigenous plants and crops, including entire farming regions or forests.
- Within the scope of the combat against desertification, remote sensing allows to follow-up and monitor risk areas in the long term, to determine desertification factors, to support decision-makers in defining relevant measures of environmental management, and to assess their impacts

GEOGRAPHIC INFORMATION SYSTEM

INTRODUCTION

A geographic information system (GIS), or geographical information system, is any system that captures, stores, analyzes, manages, and presents data that are linked to location. Technically, a GIS is a system that includes mapping software and its application to remote sensing, land surveying, aerial photography, mathematics, photogrammetry, geography, and tools that can be implemented with GIS software. Still, many refer to "Geographic Information System" as "GIS" even though it doesn't cover all tools connected to topology.

In the simplest terms, GIS is the merging of cartography and database technology. Consumer users would likely be familiar with applications for finding driving directions, like a GPS program on their hand-held device. GPS (Global Positioning System) is the, real-time location component that uses satellites to show your current position, "where am I now" on your device.

HISTORY OF DEVELOPMENT

The year 1962 saw the development of the world's first true operational GIS in Ottawa, Ontario, Canada by the federal Department of Forestry and Rural Development. Developed by Dr. Roger Tomlinson, it was called the "Canada Geographic

Information System" (CGIS) and was used to store, analyze, and manipulate data collected for the Canada Land Inventory (CLI)–an initiative to determine the land capability for rural Canada by mapping information about soils, agriculture, recreation, wildlife, waterfowl, forestry, and land use at a scale of 1:50,000. A rating classification factor was also added to permit analysis.

By the early 1980s, M&S Computing (later Intergraph), Environmental Systems Research Institute (ESRI) and CARIS (Computer Aided Resource Information System) emerged as commercial vendors of GIS software, successfully incorporating many of the CGIS features, combining the first generation approach to separation of spatial and attribute information with a second generation approach to organizing attribute data into database structures. In parallel, the development of two public domain systems began in the late 1970s and early 1980s. MOSS, the Map Overlay and Statistical System project started in 1977 in Fort Collins, Colorado under the auspices of the Western Energy and Land Use Team (WELUT) and the US Fish and Wildlife Service. GRASS GIS was begun in 1982 by the U.S. Army Corps of Engineering Research Laboratory (USA-CERL) in Champaign, Illinois, a branch of the U.S. Army Corps of Engineers to meet the need of the United States military for software for land management and environmental planning. The later 1980s and 1990s industry growth were spurred on by the growing use of GIS on Unix workstations and the personal computer. By the end of the 20th century, the rapid growth in various systems had been consolidated and standardized on relatively few platforms and users were beginning to export the concept of viewing GIS data over the Internet, requiring data format and transfer standards. More recently, there are a growing number of free, open source GIS packages which run on a range of operating systems and can be customized to perform specific tasks.

GIS TECHNIQUES AND TECHNOLOGY

Modern GIS technologies use digital information, for which various digitized data creation methods are used. The most common method of data creation is digitization, where a hard copy map or survey plan is transferred into a digital medium through the use of a computer-aided design (CAD) program, and geo-referencing capabilities. With the wide availability of ortho-rectified imagery (both from satellite and aerial sources), heads-up digitizing is becoming the main avenue through which geographic data is extracted. Heads-up digitizing involves the tracing of geographic data directly on top of the aerial imagery instead of by the traditional method of tracing the geographic form on a separate digitizing tablet (heads-down digitizing).

DATA REPRESENTATION

GIS data represents real world objects (roads, land use, elevation) with digital data. Real world objects can be divided into two abstractions: discrete objects (a house) and continuous fields (rain fall amount or elevation). Traditionally, there are two broad methods used to store data in a GIS for both abstractions: Raster and Vector. A new hybrid method of storing data is point clouds, which combine 3D points with RGB information at each point, returning a "3D color image".

RASTER

A raster data type is, in essence, any type of digital image represented in grids. Anyone who is familiar with digital photography will recognize the pixel as the smallest individual unit of an image. A combination of these pixels will create an image, distinct from the commonly used scalable vector graphics which are the basis of the vector model. While a digital image is concerned with the output as representation of reality, in a photograph or art transferred to computer, the raster data type will reflect an abstraction of reality. Aerial photos are one commonly used form of raster data, with only one purpose, to display a detailed image on a map or for the purposes of digitization. Other raster data sets will contain information regarding elevation, a DEM, or reflectance of a particular wavelength of light, LANDSAT.

Raster data type consists of rows and columns of cells, with each cell storing a single value. Raster data can be images (raster images) with each pixel (or cell) containing a color value. Additional values recorded for each cell may be a discrete value, such as land use, a continuous value, such as temperature, or a null value if no data is available. While a raster cell stores a single value, it can be extended by using raster bands to represent RGB (red, green, blue) colors, colormaps (a mapping between a thematic code and RGB value), or an extended attribute table with one row for each unique cell value. The resolution of the raster data set is its cell width in ground units.

Raster data is stored in various formats; from a standard file-based structure of TIF, JPEG, etc. to binary large object (BLOB) data stored directly in a relational database management system (RDBMS) similar to other vector-based feature classes. Database storage, when properly indexed, typically allows for quicker retrieval of the raster data but can require storage of millions of significantly-sized records.

VECTOR

In a GIS, geographical features are often expressed as vectors, by considering those features as geometrical shapes. Different geographical features are expressed by different types of geometry:

- **Points**

  A simple vector map, using each of the vector elements: points for wells, lines for rivers, and a polygon for the lake.

  Zero-dimensional points are used for geographical features that can best be expressed by a single point reference; in other words, simple location.

- **Lines or polylines**

  One-dimensional lines or polylines are used for linear features such as rivers, roads, railroads, trails, and topographic lines

- **Polygons**

  Two-dimensional polygons are used for geographical features that cover a particular area of the earth's surface. Such features may include lakes, park boundaries, buildings, city boundaries, or land uses

Advantages and disadvantages of Raster and Vector

There are some important advantages and disadvantages to using a raster or vector data model to represent reality:

– Raster datasets record a value for all points in the area covered which may require more storage space than representing data in a vector format that can store data only where needed.

– Raster data allows easy implementation of overlay operations, which are more difficult with vector data.

– Vector data can be displayed as vector graphics used on traditional maps, whereas raster data will appear as an image that may have a blocky appearance for object boundaries. (depending on the resolution of the raster file)

– Vector data can be easier to register, scale, and re-project, which can simplify combining vector layers from different sources.

– Vector data is more compatible with relational database environments, where they can be part of a relational table as a normal column and processed using a multitude of operators.

– Vector file sizes are usually smaller than raster data, which can be 10 to 100 times larger than vector data (depending on resolution).

– Vector data is simpler to update and maintain, whereas a raster image will have to be completely reproduced. (Example: a new road is added).

– Vector data allows much more analysis capability, especially for "networks" such as roads, power, rail, telecommunications, etc. (Examples: Best route, largest port, airfields connected to two-lane highways). Raster data will not have all the characteristics of the features it displays.

NON-SPATIAL DATA

Additional non-spatial data can also be stored along with the spatial data represented by the coordinates of a vector geometry or the position of a raster cell. In vector data, the additional data contains attributes of the feature. For example, a forest inventory polygon may also have an identifier value and information about tree species. In raster data the cell value can store attribute information, but it can also be used as an identifier that can relate to records in another table.

DATA CAPTURE

Data capture–entering information into the system–consumes much of the time of GIS practitioners. There are a variety of methods used to enter data into a GIS where it is stored in a digital format.

Existing data printed on paper or PET film maps can be digitized or scanned to produce digital data. A digitizer produces vector data as an operator traces points, lines, and polygon boundaries from a map. Scanning a map results in raster data that could be further processed to produce vector data.

Survey data can be directly entered into a GIS from digital data collection systems on survey instruments using a technique called Coordinate Geometry (COGO). Positions from a Global Navigation Satellite System (GNSS) like Global Positioning System (GPS), another survey tool, can also be directly entered into a GIS.

Remotely sensed data also plays an important role in data collection and consist of sensors attached to a platform. Sensors include cameras, digital scanners and LIDAR, while platforms usually consist of aircraft and satellites.

The majority of digital data currently comes from photo interpretation of aerial photographs. Soft copy workstations are used to digitize features directly from stereo pairs of digital photographs. These systems allow data to be captured in two and three dimensions, with elevations measured directly from a stereo pair using principles of photogrammetry. Currently, analog aerial photos are scanned before being entered into a soft copy system, but as high quality digital cameras become cheaper this step will be skipped.

Satellite remote sensing provides another important source of spatial data. Here satellites use different sensor packages to passively measure the reflectance from parts of the electromagnetic spectrum or radio waves that were sent out from an active sensor such as radar. Remote sensing collects raster data that can be further processed using different bands to identify objects and classes of interest, such as land cover.

When data is captured, the user should consider if the data should be captured with either a relative accuracy or absolute accuracy, since this could not only influence how information will be interpreted but also the cost of data capture.

In addition to collecting and entering spatial data, attribute data is also entered into a GIS. For vector data, this includes additional information about the objects represented in the system.

After entering data into a GIS, the data usually requires editing, to remove errors, or further processing. For vector data it must be made "topologically correct" before it can be used for some advanced analysis. For example, in a road network, lines must connect with nodes at an intersection. Errors such as undershoots and overshoots must also be removed. For scanned maps, blemishes on the source map may need to be removed from the resulting raster. For example, a fleck of dirt might connect two lines that should not be connected.

APPLICATIONS

GIS technology can be used for scientific investigations, resource management, asset management, archaeology, environmental impact assessment, urban planning, cartography, criminology, geographic history, marketing, logistics, prospectivity mapping, and other purposes. For example, GIS might allow emergency planners to easily calculate emergency response times (i.e. logistics) in the event of a natural disaster, GIS might be used to find wetlands that need protection from pollution, or GIS can be used by a company to site a new business location to take advantage of a previously under-served market.

A GIS file format is a standard of encoding geographical information into a file. They are created mainly by government mapping agencies (such as the USGS) or by GIS software developers.

Metadata often includes:

- Elevation data, either in raster or vector (e.g., contour lines) form
- Shape layers, usually expressed as line drawings, for streets, postal zone boundaries, etc.
- Coordinate system descriptions.
- One or more data describing the precise shape of the Earth assumed by the coordinates.

POPULAR GIS FILE FORMATS

Raster formats

- ADRG - National Geospatial-Intelligence Agency (NGA)'s ARC Digitized Raster Graphics
- BIL - Band Interleaved by Line (image format linked with satellite derived imagery)
- CADRG - National Geospatial-Intelligence Agency (NGA)'s Compressed ARC Digitised Raster Graphics (nominal compression of 55:1 over ADRG)
- CIB - National Geospatial-Intelligence Agency (NGA)'s Controlled Image Base (type of Raster Product Format)
- Digital raster graphic (DRG) - digital scan of a paper USGS topographic map
- ECW - Enhanced Compressed Wavelet (from ERMapper). A compressed wavelet format, often lossy.
- ESRI grid - proprietary binary and metadataless ASCII raster formats used by ESRI
- GeoTIFF - TIFF variant enriched with GIS relevant metadata
- IMG - ERDAS IMAGINE image file format
- JPEG2000 - Open-source raster format. A compressed format, allows both lossy and lossless compression.
- MrSID - Multi-Resolution Seamless Image Database (by Lizardtech). A compressed wavelet format, often lossy.
- netCDF-CF - netCDF file format with CF medata conventions for earth science data. Binary storage in open format with optional compression. Allows for direct web-access of subsets/aggregations of maps through OPeNDAP protocol.

Vector formats

- Geography Markup Language (GML) - XML based open standard (by OpenGIS) for GIS data exchange
- AutoCAD DXF - Contour elevation plots in AutoCAD DXF format
- Shapefile - ESRI's open, hybrid vector data format using SHP, SHX and DBF files
- Simple Features - Open Geospatial Consortium specification for vector data
- MapInfo TAB format - MapInfo's vector data format using TAB, DAT, ID and MAP files
- National Transfer Format (NTF) - National Transfer Format (mostly used by the UK Ordnance Survey)
- TIGER - Topologically Integrated Geographic Encoding and Referencing
- Cartesian coordinate system (XYZ) - Simple point cloud
- Vector Product Format - National Geospatial-Intelligence Agency (NGA)'s format of vectored data for large geographic databases.
- GeoMedia - Intergraph's Microsoft Access based format for spatial vector storage.
- ISFC - Intergraph's MicroStation based CAD solution attaching vector elements to a relational Microsoft Access database
- Personal Geodatabase - ESRI's closed, integrated vector data storage strategy using Microsoft's Access MDB format
- File Geodatabase - ESRI's file-based geodatabase format, stored as folders in a file system. ESRI also has an enterprise Geodatabase format for use in an RDBMS.

- Coverage - ESRI's closed, hybrid vector data storage strategy. Legacy ArcGIS Workstation / ArcInfo format with reduced support in ArcGIS Desktop lineup
- Spatial Data File - Autodesk's high-performance geodatabase format, native to MapGuide
- GeoJSON - a lightweight format based on JSON, used by many open source GIS packages

Grid formats (for elevation)

- USGS DEM - The USGS' Digital Elevation Model
- DTED - National Geospatial-Intelligence Agency (NGA)'s Digital Terrain Elevation Data
- GTOPO30 - Large complete Earth elevation model at 30 arc seconds
- SDTS - The USGS' successor to DEM

Other formats

- Binary Terrain - The Virtual Terrain Project's Binary Terrain format
- Dual Independent Map Encoding (DIME) – A historic GIS file format, developed in the 1960s
- Well-known text (WKT) – ASCII spatial projection description (ESRI uses a *.prj extension)
- Well-known binary (WKB) - Binary spatial projection description
- World file - Georeferencing a raster image file (e.g. JPEG, BMP)

THE BASICS PRINCIPLE OF PHOTOGRAMMETRY

Photogrammetry, as its name implies, is a 3-dimensional coordinate measuring technique that uses photographs as the fundamental medium for metrology (or measurement).

The fundamental principle used by photogrammetry is triangulation. By taking photographs from at least two different locations, so-called "lines of sight" can be developed from each camera to points on the object. These lines of sight (sometimes called rays owing to their optical nature) are mathematically intersected to produce the 3-dimensional coordinates of the points of interest. Triangulation is also the principle used by theodolites for coordinate measurement. If you are familiar with these instruments, you will find many similarities (and some differences) between photogrammetry and theodolites. Even closer to home, triangulation is also the way your two eyes work together to gauge distance (called depth perception).

This primer is separated into two parts. Photography describes the photographic principles involved in photogrammetry, while Metrology describes the techniques for producing 3-dimensional coordinates from two-dimensional photographs.

Photography - The First Part of Photogrammetry Taking photographs is, of course, essential for making a photogrammetric measurement. To obtain the high accuracy, reliability and automation the system is capable of, photographs must be of the highest quality. Fortunately, because of the design of the system, photography with V-STARS is actually simpler than film photography.

The three main considerations for good photography are:

1. Field of View
2. Focusing
3. Exposure

FIELD OF VIEW

The camera's field of view defines how much it sees and is a function of the focal length of the lens and the size (often called the format) of the digital sensor. For a given lens, a larger format sensor has a larger field of view. Similarly, for a given size sensor, a shorter focal length lens has a wider field of view.

FOCUSING

One consideration for normal photography is, of course, focusing the lens so the image is sharp. The range of acceptable sharpness is called the depth of focus. The depth of focus of a lens is a function of many factors, including: the focal length of the lens, the format size, the distance from the camera to the object, the size of the object, and the f-number of the lens. As you can appreciate from all the factors listed above, the depth of focus can be a complex function.

CAMERA EXPOSURE

For photogrammetry purposes, it is desirable to set the targets bright and the background dim. When retro-reflective targeting is used, the target and background exposures are almost completely independent of each other. The target exposure is completely determined by the flash power while the background exposure is determined by the ambient illumination. The amount of background exposure is controlled by the shutter time.

METROLOGY - THE SECOND PART OF PHOTOGRAMMETRY

Photography in its broadest sense is a process that converts the real 3-dimensional world into flat 2-dimensional images. The camera is the device that makes this transformation or mapping from 3 dimensions to 2-dimensions. Unfortunately, we cannot map the 3-dimensional world onto two dimensions completely so some information is lost (primarily the depth).

Photogrammetry in its broadest sense reverses the photographic process described above. It converts or maps the flat 2-dimensional images back into the real 3-dimensional world. However, since information is lost in the photographic process, we cannot reconstruct the 3-dimensional world completely with just one photograph. As a minimum, we require two different photographs to reconstruct the 3-dimensional world. If this process was perfect, the two photographs are more than enough information to perfectly reconstruct the 3-dimensional world they represent. Unfortunately, the photography and measuring process is not perfect so the reconstruction of the 3-dimensional world is also imperfect. However, we can take more photographs and use the extra information in them to improve the process. The 3-dimensional coordinates we produce from the measurements of multiple photographs are the end result of photogrammetry.

TRIANGULATION

Triangulation is the principle used by both photogrammetry and theodolites to produce 3-dimensional point measurements. By mathematically intersecting converging lines in space, the precise location of the point can be determined. However, unlike theodolites, photogrammetry can measure multiple points at a time with virtually no limit on the number of simultaneously triangulated points.

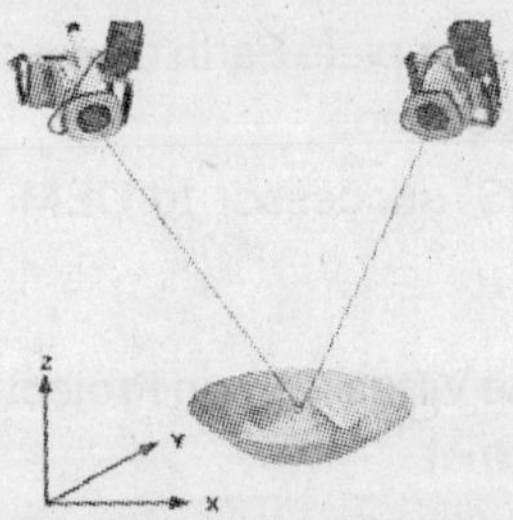

Single point triangulation

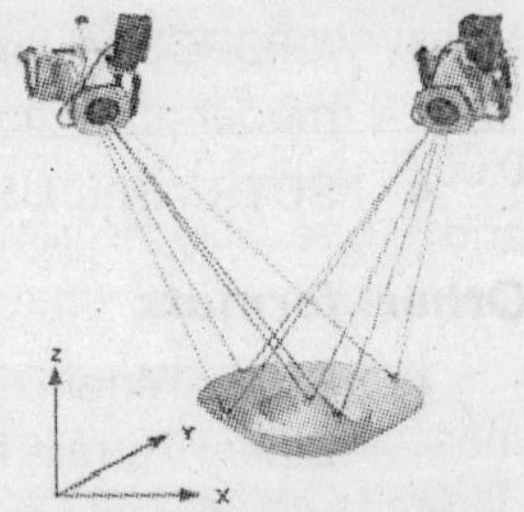

Multiple point triangulation

RESECTION

Resection is the procedure used to determine the final position and aiming (called the orientation) of the camera when a picture is taken. Typically all the points that are seen and known in XYZ in the image are used to determine this orientation.

SELF-CALIBRATION

Although the cameras and lenses used in the V-STARS system are of the highest quality, they must still be precisely calibrated to remove errors that are present in the system. Some of these error terms can be described in terms of their physical cause while others are more empirically derived. In any case, all of these error terms are automatically solved for by V-STARS along with the XYZ coordinates of the target points and the orientation (position and aiming angles) of each picture in a process called the Bundle Adjustment.

BUNDLE ADJUSTMENT

The Bundle Adjustment is the program that processes the photographic measurements to produce the final XYZ coordinates of all the measured points. In order to do this, it must Triangulate the target points, Resect the pictures and Self-calibrate the camera. The Bundle Adjustment program is called STAR, which stands for Self-Calibration, Triangulation and Resection.

MEASURING ACCURACY

V-STARS in the single camera mode provides accuracies comparable to those achieved by other large volume, high accuracy coordinate measurement systems such as Digital Theodolites, Co-ordinate Measuring Machines (CMMs), and Laser Trackers. Typical accuracies are 25 to 50 microns (0.001" to 0.002") on a 3-meter (ten foot) object for the INCA2 and 50 to 100 microns (0.002" to 0.004") on a 3-meter (ten foot) object for the E3 system.

However, the accuracy of a photogrammetric measurement can vary significantly since accuracy depends on several inter-related factors. The most important are:

1. The resolution (and quality) of the camera you are using,
2. The size of the object you're measuring,
3. The number of photographs you're taking, and
4. The geometric layout of the pictures relative to the object and to each other.

PROCEDURES FOR DIFFERENT TYPES OF MEASUREMENTS

We generally classify measurements as one of four types. Measurements can be initial or repeat and can be completely or partially overlapping. These two categories are not mutually exclusive so we can have four different types of measurements.

These are:

1. Repeat, Completely Overlapping (generally the easiest type of measurement)
2. Repeat, Partially Overlapping
3. Initial, Completely Overlapping
4. Initial, Partially Overlapping (generally the hardest type of measurement)

ELECTROMAGNETIC SPECTRUM

All matter with a certain temperature radiates electromagnetic waves of various wavelengths. The total range of wavelengths is commonly referred to as the electromagnetic spectrum. It extends from gamma rays to radio waves.

Remote sensing operates in several regions of the electromagnetic spectrum. The optical p art of the EM spectrum refers to that part of the EM spectrum in which optical laws can be applied. These relate to phenomena, such as re?ectance and refraction, that can be used to focus the radiation. The optical range extends from X-rays (0.02 μ m) through the visible part of the EM spectrum up to and including far-infrared (1000 μ m). The ultraviolet (UV) portion of the spectrum has the shortest wavelengths that are of practical use for remote sensing. This radiation is beyond the violet portion of the visible wavelengths. Some of the Earth's surface materials, primary rocks and minerals, emit or fluoresce visible light when illuminated with UV radiation. The microwave range covers wave- lengths from 1 mm to 1 m. The visible region of the spectrum is commonly called 'light'. It occupies a relatively small portion in the EM spectrum. It is important to note that this is the only portion of the spectrum that we can associate with the concept of colour. Blue, green and red are known as the primary colours or wavelengths of the visible spectrum. The longer wavelengths used for remote sensing are in the thermal infrared and microwave regions. Thermal infrared gives information about surface temperature. Surface temperature can be related, for example, to the mineral composition of rocks or the condition of vegetation. Microwaves can provide information on surface roughness and the properties of the surface such as water content.

SENSORS

A sensor is a device that measures and records electromagnetic energy. Sensors can be divided into two groups. Passive sensors depend on an external source of energy, usually the Sun (although sometimes the Earth itself). The group of passive sensors cover the electromagnetic spectrum in the range from less than 1 picometre (gamma rays) to over 1 metre (micro and radio waves). The oldest and most common type of passive sensor is the (photographic) camera.

Active sensors have their own source of energy. Measurements by active sensors are more controlled because they do not depend upon the (varying) illumination conditions. Active sensors include the laser altimeter (using infrared light) and radar.

GLOBAL POSITIONING SYSTEMS

The Global Positioning System (GPS) is a U.S.-owned utility that provides users with positioning, navigation, and timing (PNT) services. This system consists of three segments: the space segment, the control segment, and the user segment. The U.S. Air Force develops, maintains, and operates the space and control segments.

- The space segment consists of a nominal constellation of 24 operating satellites that transmit one-way signals that give the current GPS satellite position and time.
- The control segment consists of worldwide monitor and control stations that maintain the satellites in their proper orbits through occasional command maneuvers, and adjust the satellite clocks. It tracks the GPS satellites, uploads updated navigational data, and maintains health and status of the satellite constellation.
- The user segment consists of the GPS receiver equipment, which receives the signals from the GPS satellites and uses the transmitted information to calculate the user's three-dimensional position and time.

GPS Services

GPS satellites provide service to civilian and military users. The civilian service is freely available to all users on a continuous, worldwide basis. The military service is available to U.S. and allied armed forces as well as approved Government agencies.

A variety of GPS augmentation systems and techniques are available to enhance system performance to meet specific user requirements. These improve signal availability, accuracy, and integrity, allowing even better performance than is possible using the basic GPS civilian service.

The outstanding performance of GPS over many years has earned the confidence of millions of civil users worldwide. It has proven its dependability in the past and promises to be of benefit to users, throughout the world, far into the future.

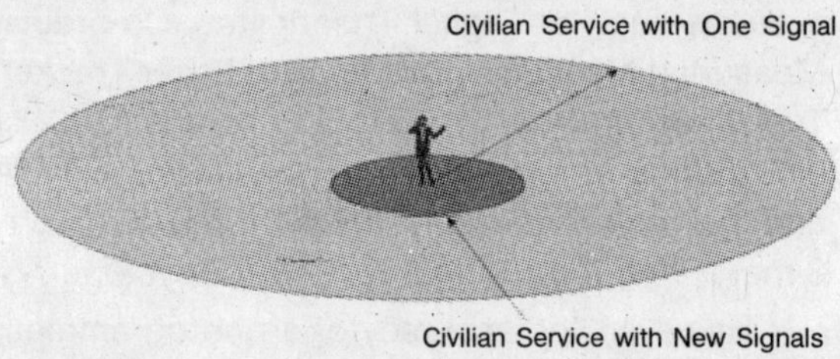

Fig. : Stand-Alone GPS Notional Horizontal Performance with New Signals

To meet the specific user requirements for positioning, navigation, and timing (PNT), a number of augmentations to the Global Positioning System (GPS) are available. An augmentation is any system that aids GPS by providing accuracy, integrity, reliability, availability, or any other improvement to positioning, navigation, and timing that is not inherently part of GPS itself. Such augmentations include, but are not limited to:

- **Nationwide Differential GPS System (NDGPS):** The NDGPS is a ground-based augmentation system operated and maintained by the Federal Railroad Administration, U.S. Coast Guard, and Federal Highway Administration, that provides increased accuracy and integrity of the GPS to users on land and water. Modernization efforts include the High Accuracy NDGPS (HA-NDGPS) system, currently under development, to enhance the performance and provide 10 to 15 centimeter accuracy throughout the coverage area. NDGPS is built to international standards, and over 50 countries around the world have implemented similar systems.

- **Wide Area Augmentation System (WAAS):** The WAAS, a satellite-based augmentation system operated by the U.S. Federal Aviation Administration (FAA), provides aircraft navigation for all phases of flight. Today, these capabilities are broadly used in other applications because their GPS-like signals can be processed by simple receivers without additional equipment. Using International Civil Aviation Organization (ICAO) standards, the FAA continues to work with other States to provide seamless services to all users in any region. Other ICAO standard space-based augmentation systems include: Europe's European Geostationary Navigation Overlay System (EGNOS), India's GPS and Geo-Augmented Navigation System (GAGAN), and Japan's Multifunction Transport Satellite (MTSAT) Satellite Augmentation System (MSAS). All of these international implementations are based on GPS. The FAA will improve the WAAS to take advantage of the future GPS safety-of-life signal and provide better performance and promote global adoption of these new capabilities.
- **Continuously Operating Reference Station (CORS):** The U.S. CORS network, which is managed by the National Oceanic & Atmospheric Administration, archives and distributes GPS data for precision positioning and atmospheric modeling applications mainly through post-processing. CORS is being modernized to support real-time users.
- **Global Differential GPS (GDGPS):** GDGPS is a high accuracy GPS augmentation system, developed by the Jet Propulsion Laboratory (JPL) to support the real-time positioning, timing, and orbit determination requirements of the U.S. National Aeronautics and Space Administration (NASA) science missions. Future NASA plans include using the Tracking and Data Relay Satellite System (TDRSS) to disseminate via satellite a real-time differential correction message. This system is referred to as the TDRSS Augmentation Service Satellites (TASS).
- **International GNSS Service (IGS):** IGS is a network of over 350 GPS monitoring stations from 200 contributing organizations in 80 countries. Its mission is to provide the highest quality data and products as the standard for Global Navigation Satellite Systems (GNSS) in support of Earth science research, multidisciplinary applications, and education, as well as to facilitate other applications benefiting society. Approximately 100 IGS stations transmit their tracking data within one hour of collection.

There are other augmentation systems available worldwide, both government and commercial. These systems use differential, static, or real-time techniques.

GIS - DATA STRUCTURE

The geographical data are available in analogue (map and aerial photographs) or digital form (scanned images). The data is of two types- spatial and non spatial.

SPATIAL DATA

The spatial data represent a geographical space. They are characterised by the points, lines and the polygons. The point data represent positional characteristics of the some of the geographical features such as schools, hospitals, wells, tube-wells, towns and villages, etc. on the map. In other words, if we want to present occurrence of the objects on a map in dimensionless scale but with reference to location, we use points. Similarly, lines are used to depict linear features like roads, railway lines, canals, rivers, power and communication lines, etc. Polygons are made up of a number of inter-connected lines bounding a certain area and are used to show area features such as administrative units (countries, districts, states, blocks); land use types (cultivated area, forest lands, degraded/waste lands, pastures, etc.) and features like ponds, lakes, etc.

Non-Spatial Data Non-Spatial Data Non-Spatial Data Non-Spatial Data Non-Spatial Data The data describing the information about spatial data are called as non-spatial or attribute data. For example, if you have a map showing positional location of your school you can attach the information such as the name of the school, subject stream it offers, number of students in each class, schedule of admissions, teaching and examinations, available facilities like library, labs, equipments, etc. In other words, you will be defining the attributes of the spatial data. Thus, non-spatial data are also known as attribute-data.

Spatial data and related tabular data are the backbone of GIS. The existing data may be acquired from a supplier or a new data may be created/collected in-house by the user. The digital map forms the basic data input for GIS. Tabular data related to the map objects can also be attached to the digital data. A GIS will integrate spatial data with other data resources and can even use a DBMS.

RASTER

A raster data type is, in essence, any type of digital image represented in grids. Anyone who is familiar with digital photography will recognize the pixel as the smallest individual unit of an image. A combination of these pixels will create an image, distinct from the commonly used scalable vector graphics which are the basis of the vector model. While a digital image is concerned with the output as representation of reality, in a photograph or art transferred to computer, the raster data type will reflect an abstraction of reality. Aerial photos are one commonly used form of raster data, with only one purpose, to display a detailed image on a map or for the purposes of digitization. Other raster data sets will contain information regarding elevation, a DEM, or reflectance of a particular wavelength of light, LANDSAT.

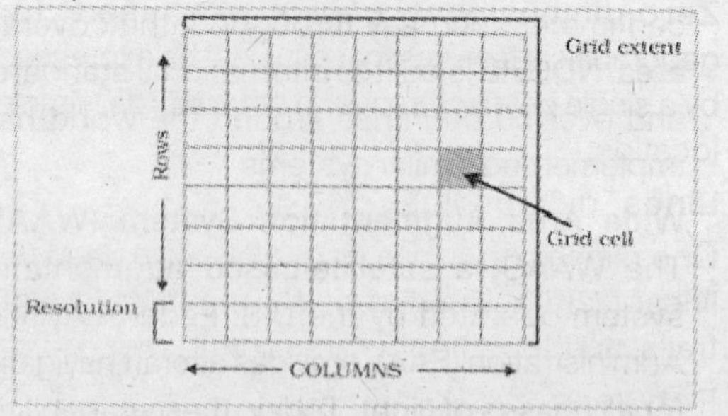

Fig. : Generic Structure for a Grid in Raster Data set

Raster data type consists of rows and columns of cells, with each cell storing a single value. Raster data can be images (raster images) with each pixel (or cell) containing a color value. Additional values recorded for each cell may be a discrete value, such as land use, a continuous value, such as temperature, or a null value if no data is available. While a raster cell stores a single value, it can be extended by using raster bands to represent RGB (red, green, blue) colors, colormaps (a mapping between a thematic code and RGB value), or an extended attribute table with one row for each unique cell value. The resolution of the raster data set is its cell width in ground units.

Raster data is stored in various formats; from a standard file-based structure of TIF, JPEG, etc. to binary large object (BLOB) data stored directly in a relational database management system (RDBMS) similar to other vector-based feature classes. Database storage, when properly indexed, typically allows for quicker retrieval of the raster data but can require storage of millions of significantly-sized records.

VECTOR

In a GIS, geographical features are often expressed as vectors, by considering those features as geometrical shapes. Different geographical features are expressed by different types of geometry:

- **Points**

  A simple vector map, using each of the vector elements: points for wells, lines for rivers, and a polygon for the lake.

Zero-dimensional points are used for geographical features that can best be expressed by a single point reference; in other words, simple location.

- **Lines or polylines**

  One-dimensional lines or polylines are used for linear features such as rivers, roads, railroads, trails, and topographic lines

- **Polygons**

  Two-dimensional polygons are used for geographical features that cover a particular area of the earth's surface. Such features may include lakes, park boundaries, buildings, city boundaries, or land uses

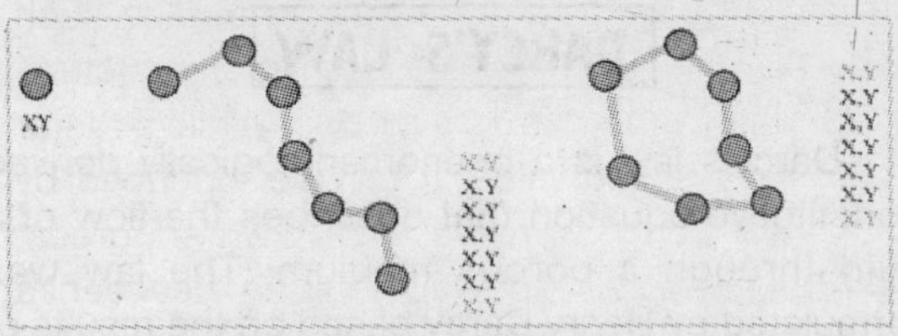

Fig. : Generic Structure of Vector Data set

GROUNDWATER

Groundwater is water located beneath the ground surface in soil pore spaces and in the fractures of lithologic formations. A unit of rock or an unconsolidated deposit is called an aquifer when it can yield a usable quantity of water. The depth at which soil pore spaces or fractures and voids in rock become completely saturated with water is called the water table. Groundwater is recharged from, and eventually flows to, the surface naturally; natural discharge often occurs at springs and seeps, and can form oases or wetlands. Groundwater is also often withdrawn for agricultural, municipal and industrial use by constructing and operating extraction wells. The study of the distribution and movement of groundwater is hydrogeology, also called groundwater hydrology.

Typically, groundwater is thought of as liquid water flowing through shallow aquifers, but technically it can also include soil moisture, permafrost (frozen soil), immobile water in very low permeability bedrock, and deep geothermal or oil formation water. Groundwater is hypothesized to provide lubrication that can possibly influence the movement of faults. It is likely that much of the Earth's subsurface contains some water, which may be mixed with other fluids in some instances.

An aquifer is a layer of porous substrate that contains and transmits groundwater. When water can flow directly between the surface and the saturated zone of an aquifer, the aquifer is unconfined. The deeper parts of unconfined aquifers are usually more saturated since gravity causes water to flow downward.

The upper level of this saturated layer of an unconfined aquifer is called the water table or phreatic surface. Below the water table, where generally all pore spaces are saturated with water is the phreatic zone.

Substrate with low porosity that permits limited transmission of groundwater is known as an aquitard. An aquiclude is a substrate with porosity that is so low it is virtually impermeable to groundwater.

A confined aquifer is an aquifer that is overlain by a relatively impermeable layer of rock or substrate such as an aquiclude or aquitard. If a confined aquifer follows a downward grade from its recharge zone, groundwater can become pressurized as it flows. This can create artesian wells that flow freely without the need of a pump and rise to a higher elevation than the static water table at the above, unconfined, aquifer.

The characteristics of aquifers vary with the geology and structure of the substrate and topography in which they occur. Generally, the more productive aquifers occur in sedimentary geologic formations. By comparison, weathered and fractured crystalline rocks yield smaller quantities of groundwater in many environments. Unconsolidated to poorly cemented alluvial materials that have accumulated as valley-filling sediments in major river valleys and geologically subsiding structural basins are included among the most productive sources of groundwater.

The high specific heat capacity of water and the insulating effect of soil and rock can mitigate the effects of climate and maintain groundwater at a relatively steady temperature. In some places where groundwater temperatures are maintained by this effect at about 50°F/10°C, groundwater can be used for controlling the temperature inside structures at the surface. For example, during hot weather relatively cool groundwater can be pumped through radiators in a home and then returned to the ground in another well. During cold seasons, because it is relatively warm, the water can be used in the same way as a source of heat for heat pumps that is much more efficient than using air. The relatively constant temperature of groundwater can also be used for heat pumps.

WATER CYCLE

Groundwater makes up about twenty per cent of the world's fresh water supply, which is about 0.61% of the entire world's water, including oceans and permanent ice. Global groundwater storage is roughly equal to the total amount of freshwater stored in the snow and ice pack, including the north and south poles. This makes it an important resource which can act as a natural storage that can buffer against shortages of surface water, as in during times of drought.

Groundwater is naturally replenished by surface water from precipitation, streams, and rivers when this recharge reaches the water table.

Groundwater can be a long-term 'reservoir' of the natural water cycle (with residence times from days to millennia), as opposed to short-term water reservoirs like the atmosphere and fresh surface water (which have residence times from minutes to years). The figure shows how deep groundwater (which is quite distant from the surface recharge) can take a very long time to complete its natural cycle.

The Great Artesian Basin in central and eastern Australia is one of the largest confined aquifer systems in the world, extending for almost 2 million km^2. By analysing the trace elements in water sourced from deep underground, hydrogeologists have been able to determine that water extracted from these aquifers can be more than 1 million years old.

By comparing the age of groundwater obtained from different parts of the Great Artesian Basin, hydrogeologists have found it increases in age across the basin. Where water recharges the aquifers along the Eastern Divide, ages are young. As groundwater flows westward across the continent, it increases in age, with the oldest groundwater occurring in the western parts. This means that in order to have travelled almost 1000 km from the source of recharge in 1 million years, the groundwater flowing through the Great Artesian Basin travels at an average rate of about 1 metre per year.

DARCY'S LAW

Darcy's law is a phenomenologically derived constitutive equation that describes the flow of a fluid through a porous medium. The law was formulated by Henry Darcy based on the results of experiments (published 1856) on the flow of water through beds of sand. It also forms the scientific basis of fluid permeability used in the earth sciences.

Darcy's law is a simple proportional relationship between the instantaneous discharge rate through a porous medium, the viscosity of the fluid and the pressure drop over a given distance.

$$Q = \frac{-kA}{\mu}\frac{(P_b - P_a)}{L}$$

The total discharge, Q (units of volume per time, e.g., fti/s or mi/s) is equal to the product of the permeability (k units of area, e.g. ml) of the medium, the cross-sectional area (A) to flow, and the pressure drop (P_b - P_a), all divided by the dynamic viscosity M (in SI units e.g. kg/(m·s) or Pa·s), and the length L the pressure drop is taking place over. The negative sign is needed because fluids flow from high pressure to low pressure. So if the change in pressure is negative (in the X-direction) then the flow will be positive (in the X-direction). Dividing both sides of the equation by the area and using more general notation leads to $q = \frac{-k}{\mu}\nabla P$

where q is the filtration velocity or Darcy flux (discharge per unit area, with units of length per time, m/s) and ∇P is the pressure gradient vector. This value of the filtration velocity (Darcy flux), is not the velocity which the water traveling through the pores is experiencing.

The pore (interstitial) velocity (v) is related to the Darcy flux (q) by the porosity (f). The flux is divided by porosity to account for the fact that only a fraction of the total formation volume is available for flow. The pore velocity would be the velocity a conservative tracer would experience if carried by the fluid through the formation.

$$v = \frac{q}{\phi}$$

ASSUMPTIONS

Darcy's law is a simple mathematical statement which neatly summarizes several familiar properties that groundwater flowing in aquifers exhibits, including:

- if there is no pressure gradient over a distance, no flow occurs (this of course, is the hydrostatic condition),
- if there is a pressure gradient, flow will occur from high pressure towards low pressure (opposite the direction of increasing gradient-hence the negative sign in Darcy's law),
- the greater the pressure gradient (through the same formation material), the greater the discharge rate, and
- the discharge rate of fluid will often be different - through different formation materials (or even through the same material, in a different direction) - even if the same pressure gradient exists in both cases.

A graphical illustration of the use of the steady-state groundwater flow equation (based on Darcy's law and the conservation of mass) is in the construction of flownets, to quantify the amount of groundwater flowing under a dam.

Darcy's law is only valid for slow, viscous flow; fortunately, most groundwater flow cases fall in this category. Typically any flow with a Reynolds number (based on a pore size length scale) less than one is clearly laminar, and it would be valid to apply Darcy's law. Experimental tests have shown that flow regimes with values of Reynolds number up to 10 may still be Darcian. Reynolds number (a dimensionless parameter) for porous media flow is typically expressed as

$$Re = \frac{\rho v d_{30}}{\mu}$$

where ρ is the density of the fluid (units of mass per volume), v is the specific discharge (not the pore velocity – with units of length per time), d_{30} is a representative grain diameter for the porous medium (often taken as the 30% passing size from a grain size analysis using sieves), and μ is the dynamic viscosity of the fluid.

DERIVATION

Assuming stationary, creeping, incompressible flow, the Navier-Stokes equation becomes

$$\mu \nabla^2 u_i + \rho g_i - \partial_{ip} = 0$$

where μ is the viscosity, u_1 is the velocity in the i direction, g_i is the gravity component in the i direction and p is the pressure. Assuming the viscous resisting force is proportional to the velocity, and opposite in direction, we may write

$$-\frac{\mu\phi}{k_i} u_i + \rho g_i - \partial_i p = 0,$$

where ϕ is the porosity.This gives the velocity

$$u_i = -\frac{k_i}{\phi\mu}(\partial_i p - \rho g_i),$$

which gives Darcy's law

$$q_i = -\frac{k_i}{\mu}(\partial_i p - \rho g_i).$$

One application of Darcy's law is to water flow through an aquifer. Darcy's law along with the equation of conservation of mass are equivalent to the groundwater flow equation, one of the basic relationships of hydrogeology. Darcy's law is also used to describe oil, water, and gas flows through petroleum reservoirs.

PRECIPITATION

Precipitation is any product of the condensation of atmospheric water vapor that is pulled down by gravity and deposited on the Earth's surface. The main forms of precipitation include rain, snow, ice pellets, and graupel. It occurs when the atmosphere, a large gaseous solution, becomes saturated with water vapour and the water condenses, falling out of solution (i.e., precipitates). Two processes, possibly acting together, can lead to air becoming saturated: cooling the air or adding water vapour to the air. Virga is precipitation that begins falling to the earth but evaporates before reaching the surface; it is one of the ways air can become saturated. Precipitation forms via collision with other rain drops or ice crystals within a cloud.

TYPES OF PRECIPITATION

Precipitation is a major component of the water cycle, and is responsible for depositing most of the fresh water on the planet. Approximately 505,000 km^3 (121,000 cu mi) of water falls as precipitation each year, 398,000 km^3 (95,000 cu mi) of it over the oceans. Given the Earth's surface area, that means the globally-averaged annual precipitation is 990 millimetres (39 inch).

Mechanisms of producing precipitation include convective, stratiform, and orographic rainfall. Convective processes involve strong vertical motions that can cause the overturning of the atmosphere in that location within an hour and cause heavy precipitation, while stratiform processes involve weaker upward motions and less intense precipitation. Precipitation can be divided into three categories, based on whether it falls as liquid water, liquid water that freezes on contact with the surface, or ice. Mixtures of different types of precipitation, including types in different categories, can fall simultaneously. Liquid forms of precipitation include rain and drizzle. Rain or drizzle that freezes on contact within a subfreezing air mass is called "freezing rain" or "freezing drizzle". Frozen forms of precipitation include snow, ice needles, ice pellets, hail, and graupel.

RAINDROPS

Coalescence occurs when water droplets fuse to create larger water droplets, or when water droplets freeze onto an ice crystal, which is known as the Bergeron process. Air resistance typically causes the water droplets in a cloud to remain stationary. When air turbulence occurs, water droplets collide, producing larger droplets. As these larger water droplets descend, coalescence continues, so that drops become heavy enough to overcome air resistance and fall as rain. Coalescence generally happens most often in clouds above freezing. In clouds below freezing, when ice crystals gain enough mass they begin to fall. This generally requires more mass than coalescence when occurring between the crystal and neighboring water droplets. This process is temperature dependent, as supercooled water droplets only exist in a cloud that is below freezing. In addition, because of the great temperature difference between cloud and ground level, these ice crystals may melt as they fall and become rain.

Raindrops have sizes ranging from 0.1 millimetres (0.0039 in) to 9 millimetres (0.35 in) mean diameter, above which they tend to break up. Smaller drops are called cloud droplets, and their shape is spherical. As a raindrop increases in size, its shape becomes more oblate, with its largest cross-section facing the oncoming airflow. Contrary to the cartoon pictures of raindrops, their shape does not resemble a teardrop. Intensity and duration of rainfall are usually inversely related, i.e., high intensity storms are likely to be of short duration and low intensity storms can have a long duration. Rain drops associated with melting hail tend to be larger than other rain drops.

ICE PELLETS

Ice pellets are a form of precipitation consisting of small, translucent balls of ice. This form of precipitation is also known as sleet. Ice pellets are usually (but not always) smaller than hailstones. They often bounce when they hit the ground, and generally do not freeze into a solid mass unless mixed with freezing rain.

Ice pellets form when a layer of above-freezing air is located between 1,500 metres (4,900 ft) and 3,000 metres (9,800 ft) above the ground, with sub-freezing air both above and below it. This causes the partial or complete melting of any snowflakes falling through the warm layer. As they fall back into the sub-freezing layer closer to the surface, they re-freeze into ice pellets. However, if the sub-freezing layer beneath the warm layer is too small, the precipitation will not have time to re-freeze, and freezing rain will be the result at the surface. A temperature profile showing a warm layer above the ground is most likely to be found in advance of a warm front during the cold season, but can occasionally be found behind a passing cold front.

HAIL

Like other precipitation, hail forms in storm clouds when supercooled water droplets freeze on contact with condensation nuclei, such as dust or dirt. The storm's updraft blows the hailstones to the upper part of the cloud. The updraft dissipates and the hailstones fall down, back into the updraft, and are lifted up again. Hail has a diameter of 5 millimetres (0.20 in) or more.

Hail forms in strong thunderstorm clouds, particularly those with intense updrafts, high liquid water content, great vertical extent, large water droplets, and where a good portion of the cloud layer is below freezing 0°C (32°F). Hail-producing clouds are often identifiable by their green coloration. The growth rate is maximized at about -13°C (9°F), and becomes vanishingly small much below –30°C (–22°F) as supercooled water droplets become rare. For this reason, hail is most common within continental interiors of the mid-latitudes, as hail formation is considerably

SNOWFLAKES

Snow crystals form when tiny supercooled cloud droplets (about 10 μm in diameter) freeze. These droplets are able to remain liquid at temperatures lower than -18°C (0°F), because to freeze, a few molecules in the droplet need to get together by chance to form an arrangement similar to that in an ice lattice; then the droplet freezes around this "nucleus." Experiments show that this "homogeneous" nucleation of cloud droplets only occurs at temperatures lower than -35°C (-31°F). In warmer clouds an aerosol particle or "ice nucleus" must be present in (or in contact with) the droplet to act as a nucleus. Our understanding of what particles make efficient ice nuclei is poor–what we do know is they are very rare compared to that cloud condensation nuclei on which liquid droplets form. Clays, desert dust and biological particles may be effective, although to what extent is unclear. Artificial nuclei include particles of silver iodide and dry ice, and these are used to stimulate precipitation in cloud seeding.

CAUSES OF PRECIPITATION

Frontal activity

Stratiform or dynamic precipitation occurs as a consequence of slow ascent of air in synoptic systems (on the order of cm/s), such as over surface cold fronts, and over and ahead of warm fronts. Similar ascent is seen around tropical cyclones outside of the eyewall, and in comma-head precipitation patterns around mid-latitude cyclones. A wide variety of weather can be found along an occluded front, with thunderstorms possible, but usually their passage is associated with a drying of the air mass. Occluded fronts usually form around mature low-pressure areas. Precipitation may occur on celestial bodies other than Earth. When it gets cold, Mars has precipitation that most likely takes the form of ice needles, rather than rain or snow.

Convection

Convective rain, or showery precipitation, occurs from convective clouds, e.g., cumulonimbus or cumulus congestus. It falls as showers with rapidly changing intensity. Convective precipitation falls over a certain area for a relatively short time, as convective clouds have limited horizontal extent. Most precipitation in the tropics appears to be convective;

however, it has been suggested that stratiform precipitation also occurs. Graupel and hail indicate convection. In mid-latitudes, convective precipitation is intermittent and often associated with baroclinic boundaries such as cold fronts, squall lines, and warm fronts.

Orographic effects

Orographic precipitation occurs on the windward side of mountains and is caused by the rising air motion of a large-scale flow of moist air across the mountain ridge, resulting in adiabatic cooling and condensation. In mountainous parts of the world subjected to relatively consistent winds (for example, the trade winds), a more moist climate usually prevails on the windward side of a mountain than on the leeward or downwind side. Moisture is removed by orographic lift, leaving drier air (see katabatic wind) on the descending and generally warming, leeward side where a rain shadow is observed.

EVAPOTRANSPIRATION

INTRODUCTION

Evapotranspiration (ET) is a term describing the transport of water into the atmosphere from surfaces, including soil (soil evaporation), and from vegetation (transpiration). The latter two are often the most important contributors to evapotranspiration. Other contributors to evapotranspiration may include evaporation from wet canopy surface (wet-canopy evaporation), and evaporation from vegetation-covered water surface in wetlands.

The process of evapotranspiration is one of the main consumers of solar energy at the Earth's surface. Energy used for evapotranspiration is generally referred to as latent heat flux; however, the term latent heat flux is broad, and includes other related processes unrelated to transpiration including condensation (e.g., fog, dew), and snow and ice sublimation. Apart from precipitation, evapotranspiration is one of the most significant components of the water cycle.

The evaporation component of ET is comprised of the return of water back to the atmosphere through direct evaporative loss from the soil surface, standing water (depression storage), and water on surfaces (intercepted water) such as leaves and/or roofs. Transpired water is that which is used by vegetation and subsequently lost to the atmosphere as vapor. The water generally enters the plant through the root zone, is used for various biophysiological functions including photosynthesis, and then passes back to the atmosphere through the leaf stomates. Transpiration will stop if the vegetation becomes stressed to the wilting point, which is the point in which there is insufficient water left in the soil for a plant to transpire, or if the plant to atmosphere vapor concentration gradient becomes prohibitive to plant physiological processes (e.g. photosynthesis).

FACTORS AFFECTING EVAPOTRANSPIRATION

The rate of evapotranspiration at any location on the Earth's surface is controlled by several factors:

- Energy availability. The more energy available, the greater the rate of evapotranspiration. It takes about 600 calories of heat energy to change 1 gram of liquid water into a gas.
- The humidity gradient away from the surface. The rate and quantity of water vapor entering into the atmosphere both become higher in drier air.
- The wind speed immediately above the surface. The process of evapotranspiration moves water vapor from ground or water surfaces to an adjacent shallow layer that is only a few centimeters thick. When this layer becomes saturated evapotranspiration stops. However, wind can remove this layer replacing it with drier air which increases the potential for evapotranspiration. Winds also affect evapotranspiration by bringing heat energy into an area. A 5-mile-per-hour wind will increase still-air evapotranspiration by 20 per cent; a 15-mile-per-hour wind will increase still-air evapotranspiration by 50 per cent

- Water availability. Evapotranspiration cannot occur if water is not available.
- Physical attributes of the vegetation. Such factors as vegetative cover,plant height, leaf area index and leaf shape and the reflectivity of plant surfaces can affect rates of evapotranspiration. For example coniferous forests and alfalfa fields reflect only about 25 per cent of solar energy, thus retaining substantial thermal energy to promote transpiration; in contrast, deserts reflect as much as 50 per cent of the solar energy, depending on the density of vegetation.
- Stomatal resistance. Plants regulate transpiration through adjustment of small openings in the leaves called stomata. As stomata close, the resistance of the leaf to loss of water vapor increases, decreasing to the diffusion of water vapor from plant to the atmosphere.
- Soil characteristics. Soil characteristics that can affect evapotranspiration include its heat capacity, and soil chemistry and albedo.

Seasonal trends of evapotranspiration within a given climatic region follow the seasonal declination of solar radiation and the resulting air temperatures. Minimum evapotranspiration rates generally occur during the coldest months of the year. Maximum rates generally coincide with the summer season. However since evapotranspiration depends on both solar energy and the availability of soil moisture and plant maturity the seasonal maximum evapotranspiration actually may precede or follow the seasonal maximum solar radiation and air temperature by several weeks.

GEOSPATIAL PATTERNS OF EVAPOTRANSPIRATION

Assuming that moisture is available, evapotranspiration is dependent primarily on the availability of solar energy to vaporize water. Evapotranspiration therefore varies with latitude, season of year, time of day, and cloud cover. Most of the evapotranspiration of water on the Earth's surface occurs in the subtropical oceans. In these areas, high quantities of solar radiation provide the energy required to convert liquid water into a gas. Evapotranspiration generally exceeds precipitation on middle and high latitude landmass areas during the summer season. Once again, the greater availability of solar radiation during this time enhances the evapotranspiration process.

Estimates of average nationwide evapotranspiration for the conterminous United States range from about 40 per cent of the average annual precipitation in the Northwest and Northeast to close to 100 per cent in the Southwest. During a drought, the significance of evapotranspiration is magnified, because evapotranspiration continues to deplete the limited remaining water supplies in lakes and streams and the soil.

The lower 5 miles of the atmosphere transports an average of about 40,000 billion gallons of water vapor over the conterminous United States each day. Slightly more than 10 per cent of this moisture, however, is precipitated as rain, sleet, hail, or snow. The greatest proportion, about 67 per cent, is returned to the atmosphere through evapotranspiration. About 29 per cent is discharged from the conterminous United States as surface-water flowing into the Pacific and Atlantic Oceans and across the borders into Canada and Mexico, about 2 per cent is discharged as groundwater outflow, and about 2 per cent is consumed by people, animals, plants, and used for industrial and commercial processes. For most of the United States, evaporation returns less moisture to the atmosphere than does transpiration. Globally, evaporation processes are resposible for an overwhelming majority of the water returned to the atmosphere.

INFILTRATION

Infiltration is the process by which water on the ground surface enters the soil. Infiltration rate in soil science is a measure of the rate at which soil is able to absorb rainfall or irrigation. It is measured in inches per hour or millimeters per hour. The rate decreases as the soil becomes saturated. If the precipitation rate exceeds the infiltration rate, runoff will usually occur unless there is some physical barrier. It is related to the saturated hydraulic conductivity of the near-surface soil.

Infiltration is governed by two forces: gravity and capillary action. While smaller pores offer greater resistance to gravity, very small pores pull water through capillary action in addition to and even against the force of gravity.

The rate of infiltration is affected by soil characteristics including ease of entry, storage capacity, and transmission rate through the soil. The soil texture and structure, vegetation types and cover, water content of the soil, soil temperature, and rainfall intensity all play a role in controlling infiltration rate and capacity. For example, coarse-grained sandy soils have large spaces between each grain and allow water to infiltrate quickly. Vegetation creates more porous soils by both protecting the soil from pounding rainfall, which can close natural gaps between soil particles, and loosening soil through root action. This is why forested areas have the highest infiltration rates of any vegetative types.

The top layer of leaf litter that is not decomposed protects the soil from the pounding action of rain, without this the soil can become far less permeable. In chapparal vegetated areas, the hydrophobic oils in the succulent leaves can be spread over the soil surface with fire, creating large areas of hydrophobic soil. Other conditions that can lower infiltration rates or block them include dry plant litter that resists re-wetting, or frost. If soil is saturated at the time of an intense freezing period, the soil can become a concrete frost on which almost no infiltration would occur. Over an entire watershed, there are likely to be gaps in the concrete frost or hydrophobic soil where water can infiltrate.

Once water has infiltrated the soil it remains in the soil, percolates down to the ground water table, or becomes part of the subsurface runoff process.

PROCESS

The process of infiltration can continue only if there is room available for additional water at the soil surface. The available volume for additional water in the soil depends on the porosity of the soil and the rate at which previously infiltrated water can move away from the surface through the soil. The maximum rate that water can enter a soil in a given condition is the infiltration capacity. If the arrival of the water at the soil surface is less than the infiltration capacity, all of the water will infiltrate. If rainfall intensity at the soil surface occurs at a rate that exceeds the infiltration capacity, ponding begins and is followed by runoff over the ground surface, once depression storage is filled. This runoff is called Horton overland flow. The entire hydrologic system of a watershed is sometimes analyzed using hydrology transport models, mathematical models that consider infiltration, runoff and channel flow to predict river flow rates and stream water quality.

INFILTRATION CALCULATION METHODS

Infiltration is a component of the general mass balance hydrologic budget. There are several ways to estimate the volume and/or the rate of infiltration of water into a soil. Three excellent estimation methods are the Green-Ampt method, SCS method, Horton's method, and Darcy's law.

DARCY'S LAW

This method used for infiltration is using a simplified version of Darcy's law. In this model the ponded water is assumed to be equal to h_0 and the head of dry soil that exists below the depth of the wetting front soil suction head is assumed to be equal to $-\psi - L$.

$$f = K\left[\frac{h_0 - (-\psi - L)}{L}\right]$$

where

h_0 is the depth of ponded water above the ground surface;

K is the hydraulic conductivity;

L is the total depth of subsurface ground in question.

In summary all of these equations should provide a relatively accurate assessment of the infiltration characteristics of the soil in question.

HORTON'S EQUATION

Named after the same Robert E. Horton mentioned above, Horton's equation is another viable option when measuring ground infiltration rates or volumes. It is an empirical formula that says that infiltration starts at a constant rate, f_0, and is decreasing exponentially with time, t. After some time when the soil saturation level reaches a certain value, the rate of infiltration will level off to the rate f_c.

$$f_t = f_c + (f_0 - f_c)e - kt$$

Where

f_t is the infiltration rate at time t;

f_0 is the initial infiltration rate or maximum infiltration rate;

f_c is the constant or equilibrium infiltration rate after the soil has been saturated or minimum infiltration rate;

k is the decay constant specific to the soil.

The other method of using Horton's equation is as below. It can be used to find the total volume of infiltration, F, after time t.

$$F_t = f_c t + \frac{(f_0 - f_c)}{k}(1 - e^{-kt})$$

GREEN-AMPT

Named for two men; Green and Ampt. The Green-Ampt method of infiltration estimation accounts for many variables that other methods, such as Darcy's law, do not. It is a function of the soil suction head, porosity, hydraulic conductivity and time.

$$\int_0^{F(t)} \frac{1-\psi\Delta\theta}{F+\psi\Delta\theta} dF = \int_0^t K\, dt$$

where

ψ is wetting front soil suction head;

θ is water content;

K is Hydraulic conductivity;

F is the total volume already infiltrated.

Once integrated, one can easily choose to solve for either volume of infiltration or instantaneous infiltration rate:

$$F(t) = Kt + \psi\Delta\theta \ln\left[1 + \frac{F(t)}{\psi\Delta\theta}\right].$$

Using this model one can find the volume easily by solving for F(t). However the variable being solved for is in the equation itself so when solving for this one must set the variable in question to converge on zero, or another appropriate constant. A good first guess for F is Kt. The only note on using this formula is that one must assume that h_0, the water head or the depth of ponded water above the surface, is negligible. Using the infiltration volume from this equation one may then substitute F into the corresponding infiltration rate equation below to find the instantaneous infiltration rate at the time, t, F was measured.

$$f(t) = K\left[\frac{\psi\Delta\theta}{F(t)} + 1\right]$$

GENERAL HYDROLOGIC BUDGET

The general hydrologic budget, with all the components, with respect to infiltration F. Given all the other variables and infiltration is the only unknown, simple algebra solves the infiltration question.

$$F = B_I + P - E - T - ET - S - R - I_A - B_O$$

where

F is infiltration, which can be measured as a volume or length;

B_I is the boundary input, which is essentially the output watershed from adjacent, directly connected impervious areas;

B_O is the boundary output, which is also related to surface runoff, R, depending on where one chooses to define the exit point or points for the boundary output;

P is precipitation;

E is evaporation;

ET is evapotranspiration;

S is the storage through either retention or detention areas;

I_A is the initial abstraction, which is the short term surface storage such as puddles or even possibly detention ponds depending on size;

R is surface runoff.

The only note on this method is one must be wise about which variables to use and which to omit, for doubles can easily be encountered. An easy example of double counting variables is when the evaporation, E, and the transpiration, T, are placed in the equation as well as the evapotranspiration, ET. ET has included in it T as well as a portion of E.

GROUND WATER EXPLORATION

Ground water exploration aided by drilling is one of the major activities of the Board with an objective to discover aquifers in different hydrogeological conditions and determination of hydraulic parameters. Large-scale sub-surface exploration programme for ground water was initiated during 1954. In the initial years, exploratory drilling activities were confined to alluvial tracts in major river basins and sub mountainous bouldary tracts of Himalayan foothills. In mid eighties, CGWB added 26 new DTH drilling rigs in its fleet with which the exploratory drilling in hard rock regions gained momentum. The major thrust of exploratory drilling programme in nineties was in areas underlain by hard rock. Another important development in first half of nineties was introduction of open hole drilling technology in India. CGWB acquired seven percussion drilling rigs for exploratory drilling in bouldary/ semi-consolidated formations in Himalyan foothills from Jammu & Kashmir in North West to Arunachal Pradesh in North East. These exploration programmes formed the background of scientific evaluation of the water bearing properties of various rock formations.

More than 26,700 wells have been drilled by Central Ground Water Board throughout the country. High yielding wells were drilled under ground water exploration programme in water deficient areas in the country, including the tribal and drought prone areas. Most of these high yielding wells have been handed over to the respective State Governments for public water supply. Board had also come forward in disaster mitigation activities during Latur earthquake during 1993, Bhuj earthquake during 2001, Super cyclone in Orissa during 2000 and Tsunami hit coastal belt of Tamil Nadu & Kerala and Andaman & Nicobar Islands during 2004 by way of construction of tube wells for water supply.

WATER POLLUTION

Water pollution is the contamination of water bodies (e.g. lakes, rivers, oceans, groundwater).

Water pollution affects plants and organisms living in these bodies of water; and, in almost all cases the effect is damaging either to individual species and populations, but also to the natural biological communities.

Water pollution occurs when pollutants are discharged directly or indirectly into water bodies without adequate treatment to remove harmful compounds.

WATER POLLUTION CATEGORIES

Surface water and groundwater have often been studied and managed as separate resources, although they are interrelated. Sources of surface water pollution are generally grouped into two categories based on their origin.

POINT SOURCE POLLUTION

Point source pollution refers to contaminants that enter a waterway through a discrete conveyance, such as a pipe or ditch. Examples of sources in this category include discharges from a sewage treatment plant, a factory, or a city storm drain.

NON-POINT SOURCE POLLUTION

Non-point source (NPS) pollution refers to diffuse contamination that does not originate from a single discrete source. NPS pollution is often accumulative effect of small amounts of contaminants gathered from a large area. The leaching out of nitrogen compounds from agricultural land which has been fertilized is a typical example. Nutrient runoff in stormwater from "sheet flow" over an agricultural field or a forest are also cited as examples of NPS pollution.

Contaminated storm water washed off of parking lots, roads and highways, called urban runoff, is sometimes included under the category of NPS pollution. However, this runoff is typically channeled into storm drain systems and discharged through pipes to local surface waters, and is a point source. However where such water is not channeled and drains directly to ground it is a non-point source.

CAUSES OF WATER POLLUTION

The specific contaminants leading to pollution in water include a wide spectrum of chemicals, pathogens, and physical or sensory changes such as elevated temperature and discoloration. While many of the chemicals and substances that are regulated may be naturally occurring (calcium, sodium, iron, manganese, etc.) the concentration is often the key in determining what is a natural component of water, and what is a contaminant.

Oxygen-depleting substances may be natural materials, such as plant matter (e.g. leaves and grass) as well as man-made chemicals. Other natural and anthropogenic substances may cause turbidity (cloudiness) which blocks light and disrupts plant growth, and clogs the gills of some fish species.

Many of the chemical substances are toxic. Pathogens can produce waterborne diseases in either human or animal hosts. Alteration of water's physical chemistry includes acidity (change in pH), electrical conductivity, temperature, and eutrophication. Eutrophication is an increase in the concentration of chemical nutrients in an ecosystem to an extent that increases in the primary productivity of the ecosystem. Depending on the degree of eutrophication, subsequent negative environmental effects such as anoxia (oxygen depletion) and severe reductions in water quality may occur, affecting fish and other animal populations.

MEASUREMENT OF WATER POLLUTION

Water pollution may be analyzed through several broad categories of methods: physical, chemical and biological. Most involve collection of samples, followed by specialized analytical tests. Some methods may be conducted in situ, without sampling, such as temperature. Government agencies and research organizations have published standardized, validated analytical test methods to facilitate the comparability of results from disparate testing events.

SAMPLING

Sampling of water for physical or chemical testing can be done by several methods, depending on the accuracy needed and the characteristics of the contaminant. Many contamination events are sharply restricted in time, most commonly in association with rain events. For this reason "grab" samples are often inadequate for fully quantifying contaminant levels. Scientists gathering this type of data often employ auto-sampler devices that pump increments of water at either time or discharge intervals.

Sampling for biological testing involves collection of plants and/or animals from the surface water body. Depending on the type of assessment, the organisms may be identified for biosurveys (population counts) and returned to the water body, or they may be dissected for bioassays to determine toxicity.

PHYSICAL TESTING

Common physical tests of water include temperature, solids concentration like total suspended solids (TSS) and turbidity.

CHEMICAL TESTING

Water samples may be examined using the principles of analytical chemistry. Many published test methods are available for both organic and inorganic compounds. Frequently-used methods include pH, biochemical oxygen demand (BOD), chemical oxygen demand (COD), nutrients (nitrate and phosphorus compounds), metals (including copper, zinc, cadmium, lead and mercury), oil and grease, total petroleum hydrocarbons (TPH), and pesticides.

BIOLOGICAL TESTING

Biological testing involves the use of plant, animal, and/or microbial indicators to monitor the health of an aquatic ecosystem.

7. PHYSICAL GEOGRAPHY

1. Geomorphology
2. Climatology
3. Bio-geography

1. Geomorphology

PEDOGENESIS

Pedogenesis or soil evolution (formation) is the process by which soil is created. It is the major topic of the science of pedology, whose other aspects include the soil morphology, classification (taxonomy) of soils, and their distribution in nature, present and past (soil geography and paleopedology).

CLIMATE

Climate regulates soil formation. Soils are more developed in areas with higher rainfall and more warmth. The rate of chemical weathering increases by 2-3 times when the temperature increases by 10 degrees Celsius (18°F). Climate also affects which organisms are present, affecting the soil chemically and physically (movement of roots).

ORGANISMS

The organisms living in and on the soil form distinct soil types. Coniferous forests have acidic leaf litter and form what are known as inceptisols. Mixed or deciduous forests leave a larger layer of humus, changing the elements leached and accumulated in the soil, forming alfisols. Prairies have very high humus accumulation, creating a dark, thick A horizon characteristic of mollisols.

PARENT MATERIAL

The rock from which soil is formed is called parent material. The main types are: aeolian, glacial till, glacial outwash, alluvium, lacustrine parent material and residual parent material, or bedrock.

Pedologists use the following generic functional relationship for understanding soil formation:

$$s = f(cl, o, r, p, t, ...)$$

where s - soil properties; cl - regional climate; o - potential biota; r - topography; p - parent material; t - time;... - additional variables.

EXAMPLES

A variety of mechanisms contribute to soil formation, including siltation, erosion, overpressure and lakebed succession. A specific example of the evolution of soils in prehistoric lake beds is in the Makgadikgadi Pans of the Kalahari Desert, where change in an ancient river course led to millennia of salinity buildup and formation of calcretes and silcretes.

WEATHERING

Weathering is the decomposition and disintegration of rocks and minerals at the Earth's surface. Weathering itself involves little or no movement of the decomposed rocks and minerals. This material accumulates where it forms and overlies unweathered bedrock. Erosion is the removal of weathered rocks and minerals by moving water, wind, glaciers, and gravity. After a rock fragment has been eroded from its place of origin, it may be transported large distances by those sameagents: flowing water, wind, ice, and gravity. When the wind or water slows down and loses energy or, in the case of glaciers, when the ice melts, transport stops and sediment is deposited.

These four processes-weathering, erosion, transportation, and deposition-work together to modify the Earth's surface.

MASS MOVEMENT

A variety of processes exist by which materials can be moved through the hillslope system. These processes are generically known as mass movement or mass wasting. The operation of mass movement processes relies upon the development of instability in the hillslope system. Under these conditions, failure of the slope material can occur on a range of time scales. Some types of mass movement involve rather rapid, spontaneous events. Sudden failures tend to occur when the stresses exerted on the slope materials greatly exceed their strength for short periods of time. In many cases, type of mass movement is produced by the operation of short term trigger mechanisms. Mass movement can also be a less continuous process that occurs over long periods of time. Slow failures often occur when the applied stresses only just exceed the internal strength of the hillslope system.

The magnitude of this force is related to the angle of the slope and the weight of hillslope sediments and rock. The following equation models this relationship:

$$F = W \sin \varnothing$$

where F is gravitational force, W is the weight of the material occurring at some point on the slope, and $\varnothing$ is the angle of the slope.

The internal strength of the hillslope system varies according to the nature of the materials making up the slope. Hillslopes composed of loose materials, like sand and gravel, derived their internal from frictional resistance which depends on the size, shape, and arrangement of the particles. Hillslopes consisting of silt and clay particles obtain their internal strength from particle cohesion which is controlled by the availability of moisture in the soil.

Too much moisture breaks the cohesive bonds and can turn a solid hillslope into a river of mud. Rock slopes generally have the greatest internal strength. Internal strength in these systems is derived from the effects of the solidification and crystallization of magma or the lithification of once loose particles.

The stability of a hillslope depends on the relationship between the stresses applied to the materials that make up the slope and their internal strength. Mass movement occurs when the stresses exceed the internal strength. This condition is not always caused by an increase in stress. In some cases, the internal strength of the materials can be reduced over relatively short periods of time resulting in mass movement.

Many factors can act as triggers for hillslope failure. One of the most common is prolonged or heavy rainfall.

Rainfall can lead to mass movement through three different mechanisms. Often these mechanisms do not act alone. The saturation of soil materials increases the weight of slope materials which then leads to greater gravitational force. Saturation of soil materials can reduce the cohesive bonds between individual soil particles resulting in the reduction of the internal strength of the hillslope. Lastly, the presence of bedding planes in the hillslope material can cause material above a particular plane below ground level to slide along a surface lubricated by percolating moisture.

Earthquakes are another common mechanism that can trigger mass movement. The seismic waves produced by earthquakes vibrate slope materials. This vibration can lead to failure by increasing the downward stress or by decreasing the internal strength of the hillslope sediments through particle movement.

MASS MOVEMENT IN NON-COHESIVE MATERIALS

Many slopes are composed of non-cohesive, coarse-grained sediments. This type of slope is common to landform features like alluvial fans, screes, talus cones, sand dunes, and glacial outwash deposits. On slopes of this type, mass movement often occurs through the sliding or rolling of a small number of particles as localized instabilities develop.

In some cases, these movements can organize themselves into larger avalanches through a domino effect. Mass movement on non-cohesive materials can also occur by way of shallow sliding. Shallow sliding occurs when planes of weakness develop just beneath the surface of the slope. Planes of weakness develop where horizontal layering occurs in the sediment. This layering can be caused by the nature of sediment deposition, percolation of water, or by the presence of subsurface soil, sediment or rock layers.

In many mountainous areas, shallow coarse soils develop over bedrock. Under the right consitions, large downslope movements of this material can occur. This type of mass movement is known as a debris flow.

MASS MOVEMENT IN COHESIVE MATERIALS

Slopes formed from clays and silts sediments display somewhat unique mass movement processes. Clay and silt particles have a degree of cohesion which gives them potentially more internal strength than non-cohesive sediments. This cohesion occurs because of electrochemical bonds which operate between particles and the surface tension effects of water films that forms around particles. Both of these sources of cohesion are dependent upon moisture content. Maximum cohesiveness takes place when mositure conditions are moderate. Too much or too little water reduces the strength of the cohesion.

Two common types of mass movements in cohesive materials are rotational slips and mudflows. Both of these processes occur over very short time periods. Rotational slips or slumps occur along clearly defined planes of weakness which generally have a concave form beneath the Earth's surface. Rotational slips can be caused by a variety of factors. The most common mechanism reason for them to occur is erosion at the base of the slope which reduces the suppcrt for overlying sediments. Erosion at the base of a slope can be caused by the presence of a stream channel or by wave action.

Some of the mass movement processes operating on cohesive materials occur over very long time spans. One of the most widespread of these processes is soil creep. Soil creep involves the movement of slope sediments in a series of numerous cyclical steps. The cyclical effects of temperature fluctuations, variations in moisture, and gravity on inclined soil sediments often cause this process.

MASS MOVEMENT ON HARD ROCK SLOPES

Mass movement on hard rock slopes is often dramatic and quick. Hard rocks derive their internal strength mainly from the strong inter-granular bonds that form when magma cools and crystallizes or when lithification occurs in sedimentary rocks. Because of their strong internal strength hard rock slopes can have relatively steep angles. Nevertheless, weaknesses do occur along bedding planes and joints naturally found in these materials. Most mass movement on hard rock slopes involves the downward movement of small rock fragments pried loose by gravitational stress and/or freeze-thaw processes. We call these types of mass wasting rockfalls.

Larger scale downslope movement of rock can also occur along well defined joints or bedding planes. This type of movement is called a rock slide. Most rock slides occur because the hillslope and rock layers dip in the same direction.

RIVER FORMS AND PROCESSES—STREAM FLOW

Streamflow, or channel runoff, is the flow of water in streams, rivers, and other channels, and is a major element of the water cycle. It is one component of the runoff of water from the land to waterbodies, the other component being surface runoff. Water flowing in channels comes from surface runoff from adjacent hillslopes, from groundwater flow out of the ground, and from water discharged from pipes. The discharge of water flowing in a channel is measured using stream gauges or can be estimated by the Manning equation. The record of flow over time is called a hydrograph. Flooding occurs when the volume of water exceeds the capacity of the channel.

Streamflow is the main mechanism by which water moves from the land to the oceans or to basins of interior drainage.

Geomorphologists often view streams as systems. The stream system, like almost all environmental systems, is open to both inputs and outputs of various types of materials. Water enters the stream system by direct precipitation in the channel, from runoff, throughflow, and by groundwater flow. The movement of water into a stream also carries with it dissolved and solid materials eroded from the surrounding landscape, stream banks, and the stream bed. Sediments carried by streams to lower elevations are occasionally deposited and stored at numerous locations for various periods of time within the stream system before they reach their final resting place.

Losses of material carried by the stream system occurs through a number of processes. Water is lost by evaporation, seepage, and flooding. Streamflow ends when the water carried by stream enters a receiving basin like a lake or an ocean. Sediment is lost by various types of deposition.

THE LONG PROFILE OF STREAMS

The topographic long profile or grade of an average stream is concave-upwards. At their headwaters, the grade of a stream is usually steep. As streams get closer to sea-level, the angle of the grade becomes more gently sloping. Near the mouth of the stream, the grade becomes almost flat.

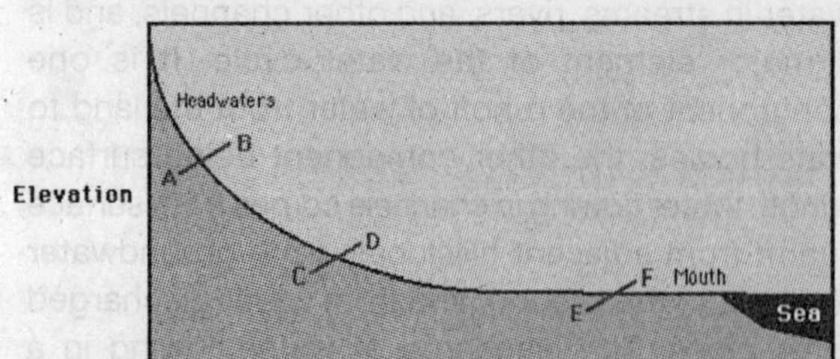

Figure : Long profile of a typical stream.

The grade of a stream develops over thousands and sometimes millions of years. It is an equilibrium process that attempts to reduce topographic bumps in the long profile through erosion and deposition. This process is without end as crustal uplift, due to plate tectonics, is always modifying the topographic nature of the Earth's landscape.

The following diagrams and photographs illustrate the nature of the stream channel at three different locations along the stream profile. This channel is located in the stream's headwaters. The stream gradient and surrounding topography is quite steep. Stream velocity is at a maximum and cuts a narrow deep channel. The floodplain is minimal as high velocities carry all sizes of load down stream. Stream load is high as the extreme relief provides the energy for extensive erosion producing a V-shaped river valley.

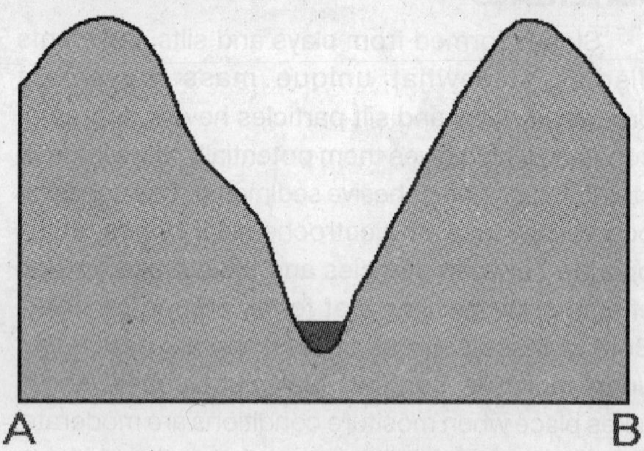

Figure : Stream channel near the headwaters.

Further down the profile, changes in relief causes the nature of the stream channel to modify. The channel is now leaving the mountainous terrain and entering a landscape that is more gently sloping. This change causes a sudden reduction in the stream's velocity. The stream adjusts to this change, by depositing most of its coarse stream load onto the floodplain. The stream also takes on a braided channel form. These channels are always changing in size, number, and location because of temporal variations in stream discharge. The amount of sediment in the floodplain also varies significantly over time because of temporal fluctuations in flow.

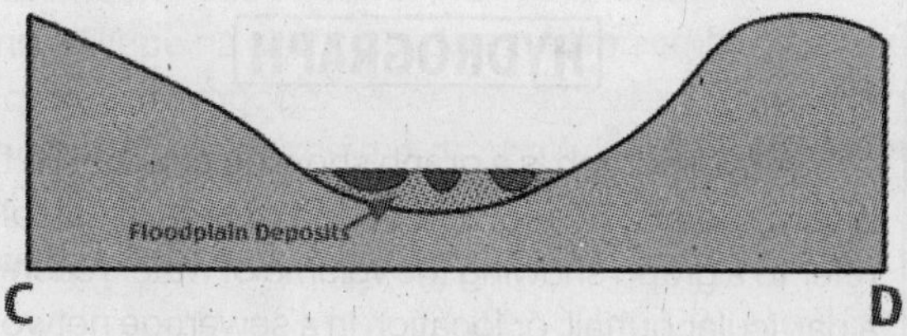

Figure : Stream channel near the middle of a typical stream profile.

The final image and illustration describes the channel near the mouth of the stream. The extensive flat floodplain is composed of flooding deposits or point bar deposits from channel meandering. The channel is quite large and U-shaped. Stream discharge is at a maximum and sediment load is generally composed of finer materials.

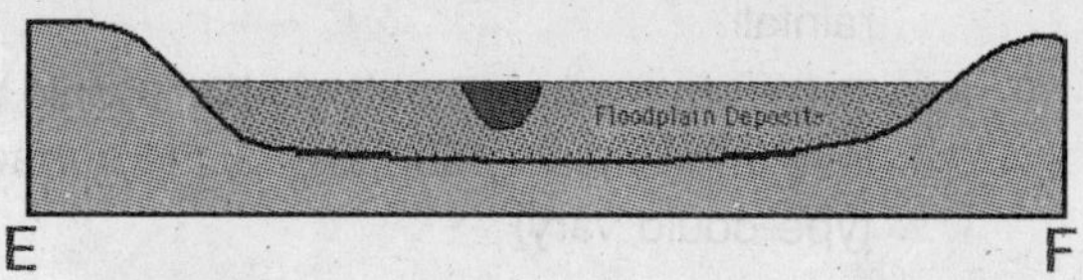

Figure : Stream channel near the mouth of a stream.

STREAM DISCHARGE

The flow of water through a stream channel is called stream discharge. In most countries, it is measured in cubic meters per second. The following equation defines stream discharge mathematically:

$$Q = V \times W \times D$$

where Q is the discharge, V is the velocity, W is the average width and D is the average depth of the flow. Stream discharge varies over both time and space. Discharge normally increases downstream as more water enters the stream channel from runoff and groundwater flow. Discharge varies temporally because of chaotic behavior of its inputs like precipitation and snow melt. As discharge increases corresponding changes in velocity, channel depth and width are made within the stream system. Of the three variables that change within the stream system with an increase in discharge, velocity is the least responsive.

VELOCITY AND TURBULENCE

Because of frictional drag, stream velocity is at a maximum at the center of the channel near the surface and a minimum near the bed and banks. If we examine stream velocity in three dimensions, a more complex pattern becomes apparent. The line of maximum velocity or thalweg moves from side to side within a channel.

The dynamics of stream flow is primarily influenced by friction, channel topography and channel shape. Within a stream channel, three types flow can be observed:

- Laminar flow - water flow in the stream is not altered in its direction. Water flows as parallel molecular streams.
- Turbulent flow - water flows as discrete eddies and vortices. Caused by channel topography and friction.
- Helical flow - spiral flow in a stream. Caused by channel shape. Meandering channels cause this type of flow. Helical flow has an important role in sediment transport and deposition, and in the creation of point bars.

Finally, flow is not always contained within the stream channel. During periods of high stream discharge overbank flow may occur. Overbank flow or flooding involves the spilling of water over the stream's banks and onto the floodplain.

SEDIMENT TRANSPORT

All streams carry sediment. Most of the sediment found in a stream has been washed into the channel from surface runoff. Sediment is also added from the erosion of the stream channel bed and banks. The quantity of sediment in a stream varies temporally due to changes in discharge. Normally, as discharge and velocity increase, the amount of sediment being carried by the stream rises correspondingly.

For many discharge stations, scientists have determined the quantitative relationship between stream discharge and concentration of sediment transported by the stream. This information is often displayed graphically as a sediment rating curve. The slope of such curves tend to vary with each stream as each stream system has its own unique environmental characteristics.

During periods of low discharge, very little sediment movement takes place, and material found in the beds and banks of river channels tend to be stable. When discharge increases, more and more sediment is eroded from the stream bed and stream banks. Loose sediment on the bed is picked up as the fluid drag of the flowing water increases. High levels of discharge also causes significant amounts of material to be added to the flow of the stream from the erosion of the stream bank. This process is called bank-caving by hydrologists.

MEASUREMENT

The are a variety of ways to measure the discharge of a stream or canal. A Stream gauge provides continuous flow over time at one location for water resource and environmental management or other purposes. For purposes that do not require a continuous measurement of stream flow over time, current meters or acoustic Doppler velocity profilers can be used. For small streams - a few meters wide or smaller - weirs may be installed. One informal method that provides an approximation of the stream flow termed the Orange Method or Float Method is:

1. Measure a length of stream, and mark the start and finish points. The longest length without changing stream conditions is desired to obtain the most accurate measurement.
2. Place an orange at the starting point and measure the time for it to reach the finish point with a stopwatch. Repeat this at least three times and average the measurement times.
3. Express velocity in meters per second. If the measurements were made at midstream (maximum velocity), the mean stream velocity is approximately 0.8 of the measured velocity for rough (rocky) bottom conditions and 0.9 of the measured velocity for smooth mud, sand, smooth bedrock) bottom conditions

Runoff of water in channels is responsible for transport of sediment, nutrients, and pollution downstream.

HYDROGRAPH

A hydrograph is a graph showing changes in the discharge of a river over a period of time. It can also refer to a graph showing the volume of water reaching a particular outfall, or location in a sewerage network, related to time. Hydrographs are commonly used in the design of sewerage, more specifically, the design of surface water sewerage systems and combined systems.

FACTORS AFFECTING THE HYDROGRAPH

- Soil Saturation is dependant on previous rainfall, or otherwise known as Antecedent rainfall.
- The surroundings; Rural or Urban (Could be less impermeable surface, or the surface type could vary)
- Vegetation type (Deforestation and amount of interception)
- Steepness of surrounding land, or 'relief' land
- Drainage density (Number of tributaries)
- Geology (Rock Type; Impermeable=flashier hydrographs. Or Permeable)
- Season dependant; Very dry weather creates a crust on the river bed. Wet winters create increase in dishcarge.
- Soil Type (Clay, sand etc.) Clay would create a flashy hydrograph, but there could be a continium between the two.
- Shape of drainage basin (circular or elongated).
- Precipitation (distribution of rainfall rates and locations)

SURFACE WATER HYDROGRAPHY

In surface water hydrology, a hydrograph is a time record of the discharge of a stream, river or watershed outlet. Rainfall is typically the main input to a watershed and the streamflow is often considered the output of the watershed; a hydrograph is a representation of how a watershed responds to rainfall. They are used in hydrology and water resources planning.

A watershed's response to rainfall depends on a variety of factors which affect the shape of a hydrograph:

- Watershed topography and geology (i.e. bedrock permeability)
- The area of a basin receiving rainfall
- Land-use (e.g. agriculture, urban development, forestry operations)
- Drainage density
- Duration of rainfall and precipitation intensity and type
- Evapotranspiration rates
- River geometrics
- The season
- Previous weather
- Vegetation type and cover
- River conditions (e.g. dams)
- Initial conditions (e.g. the degree of saturation of the soil and aquifers)
- Soil permeability and thickness

UNIT HYDROGRAPH

A unit hydrograph is used to more easily represent the effect of rainfall in a particular basin. It is a hypothetical unit response of the watershed to a unit input of rainfall. This allows easy calculation of the response to any arbitrary input (rainfall), by simply performing a convolution between the rain input and the unit hydrograph output.

FLOOD FREQUENCY ANALYSIS

Flood frequency analyses are used to predict design floods for sites along a river. The technique involves using observed annual peak flow discharge data to calculate statistical information such as mean values, standard deviations, skewness, and recurrence intervals. These statistical data are then used to construct frequency distributions, which are graphs and tables that tell the likelihood of various discharges as a function of recurrence interval or exceedence probability.

Flood frequency distributions can take on many forms according to the equations used to carry out the statistical analyses. Four of the common forms are:

- Normal Distribution
- Log-Normal Distribution
- Gumbel Distribution
- Log-Pearson Type III Distribution

Each distribution can be used to predict design floods; however, there are advantages and disadvantages of each technique. Click on the above links to learn more about each technique. According to the U.S. Water Advisory Committee on Water Data (1982), the Log-Pearson Type III Distribution is the recommended technique for flood frequency analysis

LOG-PEARSON TYPE III DISTRIBUTION

The Log-Pearson Type III distribution is a statistical technique for fitting frequency distribution data to predict the design flood for a river at some site. Once the statistical information is calculated for the river site, a frequency distribution can be constructed. The probabilities of floods of various sizes can be extracted from the curve. The advantage of this particular technique is that extrapolation can be made of the values for events with return periods well beyond the observed flood events. This technique is the standard technique used by Federal Agencies in the United States.

The Log-Pearson Type III distribution is calculated using the general equation:

$$\log x = \overline{\log x} + K\sigma_{bgx}$$

where x is the flood discharge value of some specified probability, $\overline{\log x}$ is the average of the log x discharge values, K is a frequency factor, and is the standard deviation of the log x values. The frequency factor K is a function of the skewness coefficient and return period and can be found using the frequency factor table. The flood magnitudes for the various return periods are found by solving the general equation. The mean, variance, and standard deviation of the data can be calculated using the two formulas below.

$$\overline{\log x} = \frac{\sum(\log x)}{n}$$

$$\frac{\sum_{i}^{n}(\log Q - avg(\log Q))^{\wedge}2}{n-1}$$

$$\text{and } \sigma_{bgx} = \sqrt{\frac{\sum\left(\log x - \overline{\log x}\right)^2}{n-1}}$$

$$\text{or } \quad \sigma \log Q = \sqrt{\text{variance}}$$

Next, the skewness coefficient C_s can be calculated as follows:

$$C_s = \frac{n\sum(\log x - \overline{\log x})^3}{(n-1)(n-2)(\sigma_{bgx})^3}$$

where n is the number of entries, x the flood of some specified probability and σ_{bgx} is the standard deviation. Excel functions can also be used to calculate the variance (=VAR( )), standard deviation (=STDEV( )), and skewness coefficient (=SKEW( )).

The skewness estimate (C_s) computed using the equation above is called the station estimate, meaning that the estimate incorporates data values only from the gaging station of interest.

Error and bias in the skewness estimate increase as the number of observations (n) decreases. The "Bulletin 17B method" recommended by the Interagency Advisory Committee on Water Data (IACWD) uses a generalized estimate of the coefficient of skewness, Cw (for instantaneous peak flow data only), based on the equation:

$$C_w = WC_s + (1-W)C_m$$

where W is a weighting factor, C_s is the coefficient of skewness computed using the sample data, and C_m is a regional skewness, which is determined from a map.

The weighting factor W is calculated to minimize the variance of C_w, where

$$W = \frac{V(C_m)}{V(C_s) + V(C_m)}$$

Determination of W requires knowledge of variance of C_m [$V(C_m)$] and variance of C_s[$V(C_s)$]. $V(C_m)$ has been estimated from the map of skew coefficients for the United States as 0.302 (IACWD, 1982). This simplifies the denominator of the above equation by substitution of 0.302 for $V(C_m)$.

The variance of the station skew C_s for log Pearson type 3 random variables can be obtained from the results of Monte Carlo experiments by Wallis et al. (1974). They showed that

$$V(C_s) = 10A - B \log_{10}(x/10)$$

where

$A = -0.33 + 0.08 \mid C_s \mid$ if $\mid C_s \mid \leq 0.90$ or

$A = -0.52 + 0.30 \mid C_s \mid$ if $\mid C_s \mid > 0.90$,

$B = 0.94 - 0.26 \mid C_s \mid$ if $\mid C_s \mid \leq 1.50$ or

$B = 0.55$ if $\mid C_s \mid > 1.50$

in which $\mid C_s \mid$ is the absolute value of the station skew (used as an estimate of population skew) and n is the record length in years.

The coefficient K is then found using tabulated values according to C_w and the return period for each discharge.

DIGITAL ELEVATION MODEL

A digital elevation model (DEM) is a digital representation of ground surface topography or terrain. It is also widely known as a digital terrain model (DTM). A DEM can be represented as a raster (a grid of squares) or as a triangular irregular network. DEMs are commonly built using remote sensing techniques, but they may also be built from land surveying. DEMs are used often in geographic information systems, and are the most common basis for digitally-produced relief maps.

Digital elevation models may be prepared in a number of ways, but they are frequently obtained by remote sensing rather than direct survey. One powerful technique for generating digital elevation models is interferometric synthetic aperture radar: two passes of a radar satellite (such as RADARSAT-1), or a single pass if the satellite is equipped with two antennas (like the SRTM instrumentation), suffice to generate a digital elevation map tens of kilometers on a side with a resolution of around ten meters.

Older methods of generating DEMs often involve interpolating digital contour maps that may have been produced by direct survey of the land surface; this method is still used in mountain areas, where interferometry is not always satisfactory. Note that the contour line data or any other sampled elevation datasets (by GPS or ground survey) are not DEMs, but may be considered digital terrain models. A DEM implies that elevation is available continuously at each location in the study area.

The quality of a DEM is a measure of how accurate elevation is at each pixel (absolute accuracy) and how accurately is the morphology presented (relative accuracy). Several factors play an important role for quality of DEM-derived products:

- terrain roughness;
- sampling density (elevation data collection method);
- grid resolution or pixel size;
- interpolation algorithm;
- vertical resolution;
- terrain analysis algorithm;

COMMON USES OF DEMS INCLUDE:

- Extracting terrain parameters
- Modeling water flow or mass movement (for example avalanches and landslides)
- Creation of relief maps
- Rendering of 3D visualizations.
- 3d flight planning
- Creation of physical models (including raised-relief maps)
- Rectification of aerial photography or satellite imagery.
- Reduction (terrain correction) of gravity measurements (gravimetry, physical geodesy).
- Terrain analyses in geomorphology and physical geography
- Geographic Information Systems (GIS)
- Engineering and infrastructure design
- Global positioning systems (GPS)
- Line-of-sight analysis
- Base mapping
- Flight simulation
- Precision farming and forestry
- Surface analysis
- Intelligent transportation systems (ITS)
- Auto safety / Advanced Driver Assistance Systems (ADAS)

2. Climatology

LATITUDINAL AND SEASONAL VARIATION OF INSOLATION

The figure shows that there is a surplus of net radiation balance between 40 degrees north and south and the regions near the poles have a deficit. The surplus heat energy from the tropics is redistributed pole wards and as a result the tropics do not get progressively heated up due to the accumulation of excess heat or the high latitudes get permanently frozen due to excess deficit.

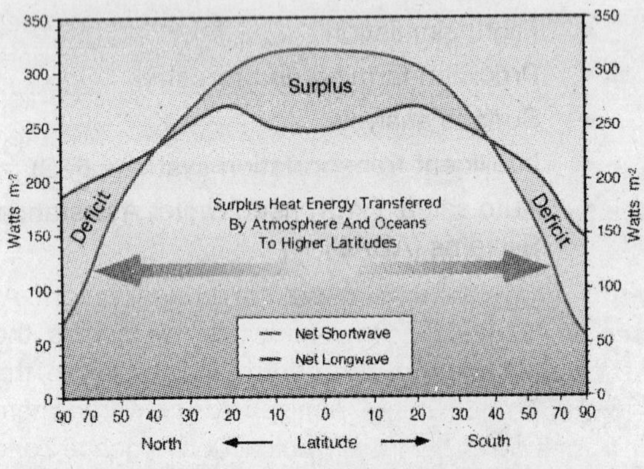

Figure : Balance between average net shortwave and longwave radiation from 90° North to 90° South.

TEMPERATURE

The interaction of insolation with the atmosphere and the earth's surface creates heat which is measured in terms of temperature. While heat represents the molecular movement of particles comprising a substance, the temperature is the measurement in degrees of how hot (or cold) a thing (or a place) is.

FACTORS CONTROLLING TEMPERATURE DISTRIBUTION

The temperature of air at any place is influenced by - the latitude of the place; the altitude of the place; distance from the sea, the air-mass circulation; the presence of warm and cold ocean currents; and the local aspects.

The latitude: The temperature of a place depends on the insolation received. It has been explained earlier that the insolation varies according to the latitude hence the temperature also varies accordingly.

The altitude: The atmosphere is indirectly heated by terrestrial radiation from below. Therefore, the places near the sea-level record higher temperature than the places situated at higher elevations. In other words, the temperature generally decreases with increasing height. The rate of decrease of temperature with height is termed as the normal lapse rate. It is 6.5°C per 1,000 m. Distance from the sea: Another factor that influences the temperature is the location of a place with respect to the sea. Compared to land, the sea gets heated slowly and loses heat slowly. Land heats up and cools down quickly.

Therefore, the variation in temperature over the sea is less compared to land. The places situated near the sea come under the moderating influence of the sea and land breezes whic ı moderate the temperature.

Air-mass and Ocean currents : Like the land and sea breezes, the passage of air masses also affects the temperature. The places, which come under the influence of warm air-masses experience higher temperature and the places that come under the influence of cold air-masses experience low temperature. Similarly, the places located on the coast where the warm ocean currents flow record higher temperature than the places located on the coast where the cold currents flow.

DISTRIBUTION OF TEMPERATURE

The global distribution of temperature can well be understood by studying the temperature distribution in January and July. The temperature distribution is generally shown on the map with the help of isotherms. The Isotherms are lines joining places having equal temperature.

In general the effect of the latitude on temperature is well pronounced on the map, as the isotherms are generally parallel to the latitude. The deviation from this general trend is more pronounced in January than in July, especially in the northern hemisphere. In the northern hemisphere the land surface area is much larger than in the southern hemisphere.

ATMOSPHERIC PRESSURE

The weight of a column of air contained in a unit area from the mean sea level to the top of the atmosphere is called the atmospheric pressure. The atmospheric pressure is expressed in units of mb and Pascals. The widely used unit is kilo Pascal written as hPa. At sea level the average atmospheric pressure is 1,013.2 mb or 1,013.2 hPa.

VERTICAL VARIATION OF PRESSURE

In the lower atmosphere the pressure decreases rapidly with height. The decrease amounts to about 1 mb for each 10 m increase in elevation. It does not always decrease at the same rate.

The vertical pressure gradient force is much larger than that of the horizontal pressure gradient. But, it is generally balanced by a nearly equal but opposite gravitational force. Hence, we do not experience strong upward winds.

WORLD DISTRIBUTION OF SEA LEVEL PRESSURE

Near the equator the sea level pressure is low and the area is known as equatorial low. Along 30° N and 30° S are found the high-pressure areas known as the subtropical highs. Further pole wards along 60° N and 60° S, the low-pressure belts are termed as the sub polar lows. Near the poles the pressure is high and it is known as the polar high. These pressure belts are not permanent n nature. They oscillate with the apparent movement of the sun. In the northern hemisphere in winter they move southwards and in the summer northwards.

WIND BELTS

The general circulation of winds arises from the global redistribution of heat from warm low latitudes to cold high latitudes, driven by the development of surface pressure gradients. Wind blows from high to low pressure regions, although airflow is deflected by the Coriolis force as a result of the Earth's rotation, and tends to follow more east-west trends rather than north-south trends.

Air movement at or near the equator is light. At sea the region became known to sailors as the Doldrums. Air from the subtropical zones in the Northern and Southern Hemispheres converges here in a zone called the Inter-Tropical Convergence Zone (ITCZ). These low latitude wind belts became known as the Northeast and Southeast Trades, which merchant ships used to cross the Atlantic Ocean from Europe to the New World. In the Indian Ocean, Northeast Trade winds blow throughout the winter months. During the Northern Hemisphere summer however, the ITCZ is shifted well to the north of the equator, when the midday Sun is overhead at the Tropic of Cancer at latitude 23.5° north. The Southeast Trade winds now cross the equator, and are deflected to the right by the Coriolis force, forming the Southwest Monsoons. This summertime airflow picks up considerable moisture crossing the Indian Ocean, and brings a heavy and prolonged wet season to India and Southeast Asia through April to September, known as the Monsoon.

The temperate mid-latitudes are influenced by a stream of westerly airflow. In the Northern Hemisphere the winds became known as the Southwest Antitrades, which prevail for much of the year. In the Atlantic, the Gulf Stream enhances the warmth of the southwesterly air masses, which influence the mild weather of the UK and Western Europe. This warm flow of air collides with the Polar Easterlies from the Arctic region, generating a zone of cyclonic low pressure, where frontal depressions frequently form. In the Southern Hemisphere, the westerlies are known as the Roaring Forties, which blow more or less continuously around the Earth due to the absence of significant landmasses.

HUMIDITY

Humidity is the amount of water vapor in the air. Relative humidity is defined as the ratio of the partial pressure of water vapor in a parcel of air to the saturated vapor pressure of water vapor at a prescribed temperature. The amount of humidity found in air varies because of a number of factors. Two important factors are evaporation and condensation. At the water/atmosphere interface over our planet's oceans large amounts of liquid water are evaporated into atmospheric water vapor. This process is mainly caused by absorption of solar radiation and the subsequent generation of heat at the ocean's surface. In our atmosphere, water vapor is converted back into liquid form when air masses lose heat energy and cool. This process is responsible for the development of most clouds and also produces the rain that falls to the Earth's surface.

TYPES OF HUMIDITY

Absolute humidity

Absolute humidity is the quantity of water in a particular volume of air. The most common units are grams per cubic meter, although any mass unit and any volume unit could be used. Pounds per cubic foot is common in the U.S., and occasionally even other units mixing the Imperial and metric systems are used.

If all the water in one cubic meter of air were condensed into a container, the container could be weighed to determine absolute humidity. The amount of vapor in that cube of air is the absolute humidity of that cubic meter of air. More technically, absolute humidity is the mass of water vapor, m_w, per cubic meter of air, V_a:

$$AH = \frac{m_w}{V_a}.$$

Absolute humidity ranges from 0 grams per cubic meter in dry air to 30 grams per cubic meter (0.03 ounce per cubic foot) when the vapour is saturated at 30°C. The absolute humidity changes as air pressure changes. This is very inconvenient for chemical engineering calculations, e.g. for dryers, where temperature can vary considerably.

MIXING RATIO OR HUMIDITY RATIO

Mixing or humidity ratio is expressed as a ratio of water vapor mass, m_w, per kilogram of dry air, m_d, at a given pressure. The colloquial term moisture content is also used instead of mixing/humidity ratio. Humidity ratio is a standard axis on psychrometric charts, and is a useful parameter in psychrometrics calculations because it does not change with temperature except when the air cools below dewpoint (at which time some water vapor condenses out of the air/vapor mixture).

That ratio can be given as:

$$MRi = \frac{m_w}{m_d}.$$

Mixing ratio can also be expressed with the partial pressure of water vapor:

$$MRi = \delta \frac{p_w}{p_a - p_w}$$

where

δ = 0.62197 is the ratio of molecular weights of water vapour and dry air

p_w = partial pressure of water vapor in moist air

p_a = atmospheric pressure of moist air.

Technically speaking, this is a dimensionless quantity as it is the mass of water vapor to the mass of dry air. So it is expressed as Kg/Kg. However, the mass of water vapor is much less than the value of the mass of dry air and most commonly meteorologists use g/Kg which is 10^{-3} Kg/Kg.

RELATIVE HUMIDITY

Relative humidity is defined as the ratio of the partial pressure of water vapor (in a gaseous mixture of air and water vapor) to the saturated vapor pressure of water at a given temperature. Relative humidity is expressed as a percentage and is calculated in the following manner:

$$RH = \frac{p(H_2O)}{p^*(H_2O)} \times 100\%$$

where

$p(H_2O)$is the partial pressure of water vapor in the gas mixture;

$p^*(H_2O)$ is the saturation vapor pressure of water at the temperature of the gas mixture; and

RH is the relative humidity of the gas mixture being considered.

Relative humidity is often mentioned in weather forecasts and reports, as it is an indicator of the likelihood of precipitation, dew, or fog. In hot summer weather, it also increases the apparent temperature to humans (and other animals) by hindering the evaporation of perspiration from the skin as the relative humidity rises. For example, if it was 27°C (80°F), with a relative humidity of approximately 75%, it would feel about 29°C (84°F).

SPECIFIC HUMIDITY

Specific humidity is the ratio of water vapor to air (including water vapor and dry air) in a particular mass. Specific humidity ratio is expressed as a ratio of kilograms of water vapor, mw, per kilogram of moist air mt.

That ratio can be shown as:

$$SH = \frac{m_w}{m_t}$$

Specific humidity is related to mixing ratio (and vice versa) by:

$$SH = \frac{MR}{m_t + MR}$$

$$MR = \frac{SH}{1 + SH}$$

MEASURING HUMIDITY

Humidity can be measured using a variety of instruments. Relative humidity is often determined using a sling psychrometer or a hair hygrometer. A sling psychrometer is a device that consists of two thermometers joined to a piece of plastic or metal. One of the thermometers, called the wet-bulb thermometer, has small cloth hood (wick) that is pulled over the reservoir bulb. The other thermometer has no hood and is called the dry-bulb thermometer. At one end of instrument is a rotating handle. To use the sling psychrometer, the wick is moistened with clean water and the device is twirled in the air using the handle. As the device is spun in the air, evaporation of the water from the wet-bulb thermometer occurs cooling it. The amount of evaporation and cooling taking place is controlled by the dryness of the air. If the air is saturated, the wet-bulb and dry-bulb thermometers would have the same temperature because no evaporation can occur. After a few minutes of twirling, the temperatures of the wet-bulb and dry-bulb thermometers are determined, a value called the wet-bulb depression is calculated (dry-bulb minus wet-bulb temperature), and a psychrometric table is used to find the corresponding relative humidity from the dry-bulb temperature and wet-bulb depression.

CLOUD FORMATION AND PRECIPITATION

Condensation or deposition of water above the Earth's surface creates clouds. In general, clouds develop in any air mass that becomes saturated (relative humidity becomes 100%). Saturation can occur by way of atmospheric mechanisms that cause the temperature of an air mass to be cooled to its dew point or frost point. The following mechanisms or processes can achieve this outcome causing clouds to develop:

1. Orographic uplift occurs when air is forced to rise because of the physical presence of elevated land. As the parcel rises it cools as a result of adiabatic expansion at a rate of approximately 10° Celsius per 1000 meters until saturation. The development of clouds and resulting heavy quantities of precipitation along the west coast of Canada are mainly due to this process.
2. Convectional lifting is associated with surface heating of the air at the ground surface. If enough heating occurs, the mass of air becomes warmer and lighter than the air in the surrounding environment, and just like a hot air balloon it begins to rise, expand, and cool. When sufficient cooling has taken place saturation occurs forming clouds. This process is active in the interior of continents and near the equator forming cumulus clouds and or cumulonimbus clouds (thunderstorms). The rain that is associated with the development of thunderstorm clouds is delivered in large amounts over short periods of time in extremely localized areas.
3. Convergence or frontal lifting takes place when two masses of air come together. In most cases, the two air masses have different temperature and moisture characteristics. Oneof the air masses is usually warm and moist, while the other is cold and dry. The leading edge of the latter air mass acts as an inclined wall or front causing the moist warm air to be lifted. Of course the lifting causes the warm moist air mass to cool due to expansion resulting in saturation. This cloud formation mechanism is common at the mid-latitudes where cyclones form along the polar front and near the equator where the trade winds meet at the intertropical convergence zone.
4. Radiative cooling occurs when the sun is no longer supplying the ground and overlying air with energy derived from solar insolation (e.g., night). Instead, the surface of the Earth now begins to lose energy in the form of longwave radiation which causes the ground and air above it to cool. The clouds that result from this type of cooling take the form of surface fog.

WATER BALANCE

In hydrology, a water balance equation can be used to describe the flow of water in and out of a system. A system can be one of several hydrological domains, such as a column of soil or a drainage basin. Water balance can also refer to the ways in which an organism maintains water in dry or hot conditions. It is often discussed in reference to plants or arthropods, which have a variety of water retention mechanisms, including a lipid waxy coating that has limited permeability.

EQUATION

A general water balance equation is:

$$P = Q + E + \Delta S$$

where

P is precipitation

Q is runoff

E is evapotranspiration

ΔS is the change in storage (in soil or the bedrock)

A water balance can be used to help manage water supply and predict where there may be water shortages. It is also used in irrigation, flood control and pollution control.

The water balance can be illustrated using a water balance graph which plots levels of precipitation and evapotranspiration often on a monthly scale.

Several monthly water balance models had been developed for several conditions and purposes. Monthly water balance models had been studied since the 1940s.

APPLICATIONS

- Evaluate the components of the hydrologic cycle
- Snowmelt simulation
- Climate change impact assessment
- Flow forecasting and project design
- Assess agricultural water management

3. Bio-geography

PRINCIPLES OF BIOGEOGRAPHY

INTRODUCTION

Vegetation appears to the casual observer as a rather haphazard and random element of the Earth's surface. Yet, on closer study, it is organized into well defined unities which operate at specific scales. Thus formations at the large scale subdivide into vegetation types, plant communities and populations of species at successively smaller scales. The vegetation-environment complex or ecosystem has come to be recognized as the fundamental unit of study in biogeography and ecology. At successively smaller scales the units of study are the biosphere or ecosphere, the biome, the regional ecosystem, the local ecosystem and the single organism-habitat system.

The ecosystem performs the role of harnessing the potential energy of the sun and converting it into chemical energy stored in the organic molecules of plants and animals. The distribution of ecosystems is explained by environmental controls, with all individual species in the ecosystems having a range of tolerance of each environmental factor. The niche of each species is defined by this range, and also by the function of each species in the ecosystem. Climate controls the distribution of the major vegetation regions of the Earth, and there has always been a close association between the subdivision of the Earth into climatic regions and vegetation regions.

Vegetation occupies a pivotal position in the natural landscapes of the world, owing to the variety of important functions it performs.

THE CONCEPT OF THE ECOSYSTEM

The Oxford botanist Tansley coined the term 'ecosystem' to emphasize that organisms cannot be separated from their environment, with which they form one physical system. The ecosystems are of various kinds and can exist at several scales. Tansley regarded the ecosystem as a self-regulating entity, maintaining specific internal conditions despite fluctuations in external environments. An ecosystem can be visualized in the form of a model like an electrical circuit, by which energy derived from the sun is transferred by means of chemical processes through soil and vegetation up the food chain, and then by decomposition through the cycle again. The ecosystem model adds a scientific dimension to ecology, giving access to the laws of thermodynamics and mathematics and incorporating biogeochemical cycles.

ENVIRONMENTAL FACTORS

Six factors are essential for successful plant growth - light, heat, moisture, air, nutrients and physical support. The environment of plants must always be beneficent enough to sustain the three major plant processes of photosynthesis, respiration and transpiration. Environmental factors are not themselves independent but act as a series of interdependent controls, with many mutual interactions. It is helpful to distinguish direct controls (e.g. water, nutrients) from indirect controls (e.g. aspect, slope, altitude), which influence a direct control and hence influence the plant only indirectly.

A synergistic effect is one which is greater than the sum of the individual effects from the controlling factors.

LIMITING FACTORS AND RANGE OF TOLERANCE

Autoecology is the study of a single species and its environment, whereas synecology studies whole communities and the links between the constituent organisms. According to Liebig's law of the minimum, plant growth is governed by the factor in shortest supply. Plants have a tolerance range for each environmental factor, consisting of a lower limit of tolerance, an ecological optimum and an upper limit of tolerance. The sum total of all environmental gradients is referred to as the ecological amplitude. Competition is a vital process governing plant distributions and occurs as interspecific competition between species, and as intraspecific competition between individuals of a species.

THE CONCEPT OF THE ECOLOGICAL NICHE

The ecological niche of a species is defined as the functional role of the species in its community and the position of the species along all environmental gradients (ecological amplitude). The fundamental niche is the full space which a species can occupy according to all its environmental gradients. The realized niche is a small space occupied by the species in the face of competition from all other species. The spatial distribution of a species is a good indicator of its realized niche, but the position of the species within the ecological pyramid must also be considered.

VEGETATION ZONES OF THE EARTH

The German biogeographer Walter produced a listing of nine climatic zones which in turn correlated with eleven vegetation zones (formations or biomes). Walter's classification of vegetation zones is a zonal one, and the units can be broadly correlated with zonal soils. Within each zone, it is recognized that regional variations will occur, owing to oceanity, exposure to winds and the presence of mountain ranges. Within these regions, local variations in the vegetation type will be related to topography, aspect and soil types. The English biogeographer Holdridge has produced a flexible model for classifying world vegetation based on mean annual temperature, mean annual precipitation and the ratio of potential to actual mean evapotranspiration. The Holdridge system can be modified for different locations and for different climatic scenarios, which explains its popularity among climate modellers.

SUCCESSION AND CLIMAX

The process whereby one plant community is succeeded by another through time is referred to as ecological succession. The final end point of the succession is the climax community or ecological climax. A succession which commences on a bare, previously unvegetated surface is a prisere or primary succession. A succession which commences on an area which was previously under human use, but which has now been abandoned, is a secondary succession. Successions modified by human actions are plagioseres, and their status is termed 'plagioclimax'.

CLASSIFICATION OF SUCCESSIONS

Successions are classified into four types - psammoseres, lithoseres, hydroseres and haloseres - depending on the nature of the original land - or water - surface. The principle of competitive replacement means that a plant community in a succession creates conditions more and more favourable for a competitor, which will replace it. Clements did much to establish the principles of succession, and he divided successional processes into five types: nudation, migration, ecesis, reaction and stablization. Concepts have developed since Clements's work, so that now it is recognized that there are three successional models: facilitation model, tolerance model and inhibition model. Allogenic successions are driven by external controls whereas autogenic successions proceed largely on the basis of internally caused changes.

LITHOSERES

A lithosere starts on a bare rock surface, e.g. cliff, quarry or scree. The dominant ecological problem for plants is aridity on the soilless surface. Soil formation proceeds very slowly beneath successive plant covers of lichen, mosses, grasses and shrubs. Hydrolysis and chelation are the main weathering processes which produce soil, liberate nutrients and allow a larger water-holding capacity. The invasion of the proto-soil by soil fauna and soil micro-organisms greatly speeds up the rates of soil formation. Psammoseres

A psammosere starts on bare loose sand on the sea- or lake-shore. Aridity is a severe ecological problem, owing to the inability of the sand to hold water. Secondary ecological problems are nutrient deficiency, unstable surfaces, abrasive quartz grains and soil alkalinity on seashores. The role of greater humus content and increasing thickness of humus surface horizons is vital in regulating the succession. Other soil changes during the succession involve leaching and a decline in pH and salt content, an increase in the organic population of the soil, and an increase in the thickness of the A, E and B soil horizons.

HYDROSERES

Hydroseres start in freshwater lakes and pools, which become progressively shallower by processes of siltation. Rushes, reeds and sedges dominate the early stages of hydroseres, owing to their hydrophytic nature and ability to use oxygen even in waterlogged conditions. Waterlogged soils also pose problems of nutrient unavailability and the possible toxicity of a range of organic and inorganic chemicals. Some plants in the hydrosere, e.g. alder and bog myrtle, are able to fix atmospheric nitrogen and thus play a pivotal role in the hydrosere. Only when the soil level builds up significantly above the water table are the wide range of terrestrial shrubs and trees able to become established.

HALOSERES

Haloseres commence in salt water on the salt marshes of estuaries, bays or inland drainage areas. The zonation of plant communities in the halosere is governed largely by height above sea level, which in turn controls the length of time of inundation by saline water. Halophytes are plants which have ecophysiological mechanisms which enable them to tolerate the high salt content of saline soils in haloseres. Height above sea level allows more salt to be leached from the soil, leading to a lowering of pH, greater rooting depth for non-halophytes, and a lessening of the problems of waterlogging and anaerobism. The invasion of European salt marshes by the cord grass, Spartina anglica, in the past two centuries has greatly speeded up the rates of succession in haloseres.

ECOSYSTEM CHANGES THROUGH SUCCESSION

General changes during a succession involve increasing height of plants, increasing biomass, increasing stratification, though not usually increasing species diversity. Soils usually deepen, contain more humus and show more horizons. E.P. Odum has recorded changes in the basic ecology of communities during succession which involve many fundamental properties such as nutrient conservation, increasing role of detrivores, narrower niches, complex interactions and greater stability. High rates of net primary production in the early stages of successions become lower in the later stages. In the early stages of succession, the communities are dominated by fast-growing r-species, whereas slow-growing k-species dominate in the later stages.

THEORIES OF CLIMAX VEGETATION

Clements introduced the monoclimax theory of succession, which emphasizes the dominance of climate in his so-called climatic climax. Tansley supported the polyclimax theory of succession, emphasizing that other factors, e.g. soil or topography, may be dominant and may thus permanently prevent the climatic climax. Whittaker put forward the mosaic theory, which emphasizes the patterning of vegetation communities. Aubrйville suggested the theory of cyclic climax, based on his observations in tropical forest vegetation and the processes of invasion and closure of gaps in the vegetation which he observed there. All these four theories of climax have points of relevance in understanding modern climax vegetation, though the work of Tansley would appear to be especially favoured.

ZOO-GEOGRAPHY OF INDIA

Organization Ecologically, and biologeographically, the Indian sub-continent is one of the most fascinating regions in the world. The subcontinent of India may be taken to extend from Baluchistan, and parts of Eastern Afghanisthan in the North west, through Gilgit, Ladakh, Kashmir, Nepal, Sikkim, Bhutan to the Burma border, including the entire Pakistan, India Bangladesh Ceylon. Defined this at the region stretches from 60°E to 100°E longitude and 6°N to 38°N latitude. Biogeographially the Indian sub-continent may be divide into two broad regions : 1) The cis gangetic region covering most of the Peninsula and 2) the trans gangetic region of Himalaya and Assam. The cis-gangetic region itself comprising of the following sub regions 1 the ganagetic plain 2 the Sahyaderis 3 the chota nagpur region and 4 the rest of peninsula, while the trans gangetic region divided into : 1 Himalayan region 2 Assam region Western Ghats Western Ghats from the river Tapi to Cape Comorin, along with the Western coastal strip is a hilly area with Peaks rising to over 8000 feet. The region receives over 100 inches of rain almost everywhere, with some areas such as Agumbe and Mahabaleshwar receiving as much as 200 to 300 inches. The Western Ghats tract has rich fauna, remarkable for the fact that some species occur only in the Ghats, and now where else in the peninsula. and for the fact that related groups occur only in the Himalayas and the Western Ghats. The rodent genus Platacanthomys is restricted to this region. Of the two species of Tahr in India, One the Nilgiri Tahr Hemitragus hylocrius occurs Nilgiri, Annamalai, Palni ranges while the Himalaynan Tahr H. jemlachius lives alone the Himalayas from Sir Panjal to Bhutan. Of the yellow throatened matens, one species, Martes gwatkinsi occurs in Coorg, Nilgiris and in Kerala while Martes flavigula and M. fiona occur in the Himalayas. The malabar Civet, Viverra megaspila occurs on the Western Ghats and in the Assam and Burma. The Western Ghats forests also rich in the other important forest mammals of the Peninsula such as Gaur, Samber and Elephant. Nilgiri Langur and Liontailed Macaque. The Western Ghats forests are also rich in birds with many not occurring anywhere else in the Peninsula, though found else where in Himalayan or Burmese regions. There are seven genera of reptiles, and five genera of amphibians that are peculiar to the Western Ghats Zoological survey of India reports.

BIOMES

Biomes are climatically and geographically defined as similar climatic conditions on the Earth, such as communities of plants, animals, and soil organisms, and are often referred to as ecosystems. Biomes are defined by factors such as plant structures (such as trees, shrubs, and grasses), leaf types (such as broadleaf and needleleaf), plant spacing (forest, woodland, savanna), and climate. Unlike ecozones, biomes are not defined by genetic, taxonomic, or historical similarities. Biomes are often identified with particular patterns of ecological succession and climax vegetation (quasi-equilibrium state of the local ecosystem). An ecosystem has many biotopes and a biome is a major habitat type. A major habitat type, however, is a compromise, as it has an intrinsic inhomogeneity.

A fundamental classification of biomes is:

1. Terrestrial (land) biomes
2. Freshwater biomes
3. Marine biomes

Climate is a minor factor determining the distribution of terrestrial biomes. Among the important climatic factors are:

- **latitude:** Arctic, boreal, temperate, subtropical, tropical.
- **humidity:** humid, semi-humid, semi-arid, and arid.

- o *seasonal variation:* Rainfall may be distributed evenly throughout the year or be marked by seasonal variations.
- o *dry summer, wet winter:* Most regions of the earth receive most of their rainfall during the summer months; Mediterranean climate regions receive their rainfall during the winter months.
- elevation: Increasing elevation causes a distribution of habitat types similar to that of increasing latitude.

The most widely used systems of classifying biomes correspond to latitude (or temperature zoning) and humidity. Biodiversity generally increases away from the poles towards the equator and increases with humidity.

DISTRIBUTION OF FORESTS AND MAJOR PLANT COMMUNITIES

The Forest Survey of India (FSI), set up on June,1, 1981 an attached office of the Ministry, is engaged in generating information and database on area under forest cover, tree cover and water resources of the country besides providing services of training, research and extension. The headquarters of FSI is located at Dehradun and its four zonal offices are situated at Shimla, Kolkata, Nagpur and Bangalore.

FSI assesses forest cover of the country every two years by digital interpretation of remote sensing satellite data and publishes the results in a biennial report called "State of Forest Report" (SFR). Beginning in 1987, nine SFRs have been brought out so far and the 10th SFR is under publication. In the current 10th cycle (i.e. for SFR 2005) FSI has used satellite data for IRS P6 Resource sat LISS III having 23.5 under resolution.

Exploration of plant resources of the country and identification of plant species with economic virtues is carried out by the Botanical Survey of India (BSI). The BSI undertakes exploration, inventorisation and documentation of phytodiversity in general and protected areas, hotspots, fragile ecosystems and sacred groves in particular and publication of National, State and District Flora to evaluate the qualitative changes in species in rich and sensitive areas; ex-situ conservation of critically threatened taxa in botanical gardens and identification of species with traditional economic uses and preparation of protocols for their conservation and sustainable utilization.

TROPICAL EVERGREEN FORESTS

These forests are also called tropical rainforests. These thick forests occur in the regions near the equator and close to the tropics. These regions are hot and receive heavy rainfall throughout the year. As there is no particular dry season, the trees do not shed their leaves altogether. This is the reason they are called evergreen. The thick canopies of the closely spaced trees do not allow the sunlight to penetrate inside the forest even in the day time. Hardwood trees like rosewood, ebony, mahogany are common here.

TROPICAL DECIDUOUS FORESTS

Tropical deciduous are the monsoon forests found in the large part of India,northern Australia and in central America.These regions experience seasonal changes. Trees shed their leaves in the dry season to conserve water. The hardwood trees found in these forests are sal, teak, neem and shisham. Hardwood trees are extremely useful for making furniture, transport and constructional materials. Tigers, lions, elephants, langoors and monkeys are the common animals of these regions.

TEMPERATE EVERGREEN FORESTS

The temperate evergreen forests are located in the mid-latitudinal coastal region . They are commonly found along the eastern margin of the continents, e.g., In south east USA, South China and in South East Brazil. They comprise both hard and soft wood trees like oak, pine, eucalyptus, etc.

TEMPERATE DECIDUOUS FORESTS

As we go towards higher latitudes, there are more temperate deciduous forests. These are found in the north eastern part of USA, China, New Zealand, Chile and also found in the coastal regions of

Western Europe. They shed their leaves in the dry season. The common trees are oak, ash, beech, etc. Deer, foxes, wolves are the animals commonly found. Birds like pheasants, monals are also found here.

CONIFEROUS FORESTS

In the higher latitudes (50°- 70°) of Northern hemisphere the spectacular Coniferous forests are found. These are also called as Taiga. These forests are also seen in the higher altitudes. These are the trees which Salima found in the Himalayas in abundance. They are tall, softwood evergreen trees. These woods are very useful for making pulp, which is used for manufacturing paper and newsprint. Match boxes and packing boxes are also made from softwood. Chir, pine, cedar are the important variety of trees in these forests. Silver fox, mink, polar bear are the common animals found here.

Forest conservation

Forests are a renewable source and contribute substantially to economic development. They play a major role in enhancing the quality of environment. The forest cover in the country is 6,78,333 sq km and constitutes 20.64 per cent of its geographical area. Of this, very dense forest constitutes 51,285 sq km (1.56 per cent) moderately dense forest constitutes 3,39,279 sq km (10.32 per cent) and open forest 2,87,669 sq km (8.76 per cent). A comparison of forest cover assessment of 2003 with that of 2001 reveals that there is an overall increase of 2,795 sq km.

The Ministry of Environment and Forests implements the Forest (Conservation) Act, 1980, which deals with grant of forestry clearances for diversion of forests land for non-forestry purposes in respect of development projects like power, roads, railways, irrigation, mining, schools, defence, drinking water, resettlement and rehabilitation of people etc. This act is regulatory in nature, and not prohibitory. For Forest conservation government of India implemented a law in 1894, then revised in 1952 and again in 1988. The main plank of the forest policy is protection, conservation and development of forests. Its aims are: (i) maintenance of environmental stability through preservation and restoration of ecological balance; (ii) conservation of natural heritage; (iii) check on soil erosion and denudation in catchment areas of rivers, lakes and reservoirs; (iv) check on extension of sand dunes in desert areas of Rajasthan and along coastal tracts; (v) substantial increase in forest tree cover through massive afforestation and social forestry programmes; (vi) steps to meet requirements of fuelwood, fodder, minor forest produce and soil timber for rural and tribal populations; (vii) increase in productivity of forests to meet the national need; (viii) encouragement to efficient utilization of forest produce and optimum substitution of wood; and (ix) steps to create massive people's movement with involvement of women to achieve the objectives and minimise pressure on existing forests.

WILDLIFE SANCTUARIES

India has over 500 animal sanctuaries, referred to as Wildlife Sanctuaries (IUCN Category IV Protected Area). Among these, the 28 Tiger Reserves are governed by Project Tiger, and are of special significance in the conservation of the tiger. Some wildlife sanctuaries are specifically named Bird Sanctuary, eg. Keoladeo National Park before attained National Park status. Many National Parks were initially Wildlife Sanctuaries. India has 99 National Park and 15 Biosphere reserve.

PHYSIOGRAPHIC OF INDIA

The land of India displays great physical variation. Geologically, the Peninsular Plateau constitutes one of the ancient landmasses on the earth's surface. It was supposed to be one of the most stable land blocks. The Himalayas and the Northern Plains are the most recent landforms. From the view point of geology, Himalayan mountains form an unstable zone.

The whole mountain system of Himalaya represents a very youthful topography with hign peaks, deep valleys and fast flowing rivers. The northern plains are formed of alluvial deposits. The peninsular plateau is composed of igneous and metamorphic rocks with gently rising hills and wide valleys.

MAJOR PHYSIOGRAPHIC DIVISIONS

The physical features of India can be grouped under the following physiographic divisions:

(i) The Himalayan Mountains
(ii) The Northern Plains
(iii) The Peninsular Plateau
(iv) The Indian Desert
(v) The Coastal Plains
(vi) The Islands

The Himalayan Mountains

The Himalayas, geologically young and structurally fold mountains stretch over the northern borders of India. These mountain ranges run in a west-east direction from the Indus to the Brahmaputra. The Himalayas represent the loftiest and one of the most rugged mountain barriers of the world. They form an arc, which covers a distance of about 2,400 Km. Their width varies from 400 Km in Kashmir to 150 Km in Arunachal Pradesh.

The altitudinal variations are greater in the eastern half than those in the western half. The Himalaya consists of three parallel ranges in its longitudinal extent. A number of valleys lie between these ranges. The northern most range is known as the Great or Inner Himalayas or the 'Himadri'. It is the most continuous range consisting of the loftiest peaks with an average height of 6,000 metres. It contains all the prominent Himalayan peaks.

The folds of Great Himalayas are asymmetrical in nature. The core of this part of Himalayas is composed of granite. It is perennially snow bound, and a number of glaciers descend from this range. The range lying to the south of the Himadri forms the most rugged mountain system and is known as Himachal or lesser Himalaya. The ranges are mainly composed of highly compressed and altered rocks. The altitude varies between 3,700 and 4,500 metres and the average width is of 50 Km. While the Pir Panjal range forms the longest and the most important range, the Dhaula Dhar and the Mahabharat ranges are also prominent ones.

This range consists of the famous valley of Kashmir, the Kangra and Kullu Valley in Himachal Pradesh.

The Northern Plain

The plains of the Ganga and the Indus, about 2,400 km long and 240 to 320 km broad, are formed by basins of three distinct river systems - the Indus, the Ganga and the Brahmaputra. They are one of the world's greatest stretches of flat alluvium and also one of the most densely populated areas on the earth. Between the Yamuna at Delhi and the Bay of Bengal, nearly 1,600 km away, there is a drop of only 200 metres in elevation.

This plain is formed of alluvial soil. The deposition of alluvium in a vast basin lying at the foothills of the Himalaya over millions of years, formed this fertile plain. It spreads over an area of 7 lakh sq. km. The plain being about 2400 Km long and 240 to 320 Km broad, is a densely populated physiographic division. With a rich soil cover combined with adequate water supply and favourable climate it is agriculturally a very productive part of India.

The Northern Plain is broadly divided into three sections. The Western part of the Northern Plain is referred to as the Punjab Plains. Formed by the Indus and its tributaries, the larger part of this plain lies in Pakistan. The Indus and its tributaries-the Jhelum, the Chenab, the Ravi, the Beas and the Satluj originate in the Himalaya. This section of the plain is dominated by the doabs.

The outer most range of the Himalayas is called the Shiwaliks. They extend over a width of 10-50 Km and have an altitude varying between 900 and 1100 metres. These ranges are composed of unconsolidated sediments brought down by rivers from the main Himalayan ranges located farther north. These valleys are covered with thick gravel and alluvium. The longitudinal valley lying between lesser Himalaya and the Shiwaliks are known as Duns. Dehra Dun, Kotli Dun and Patli Dun are some of the well-known Duns.

The Peninsular Plateau

The Peninsular Plateau is marked off from the plains of the Ganga and the Indus by a mass of mountain and hill ranges varying from 460 to 1,220 metres in height. Prominent among these are the Aravalli, Vindhya, Satpura, Maikala and Ajanta.

The Peninsular plateau is a tableland composed of the old crystalline, igneous and metamorphic rocks. It was formed due to the breaking and drifting of the Gondwana land and thus, making it a part of the oldest landmass. The plateau has broad and shallow valleys and rounded hills. This plateau consists of two broad divisions, namely, the Central Highlands and the Deccan Plateau. The part of the Peninsular plateau lying to the north of the Narmada river covering a major area of the Malwa plateau is known as the Central Highlands. The Vindhyan range is bounded by the Central Highlands on the south and the Aravalis on the northwest. The further westward extension gradually merges with the sandy and rocky desert of Rajasthan.

The flow of the rivers draining this region, namely the Chambal, the Sind, the Betwa and Ken is from southwest to northeast, thus indicating the slope. The Central Highlands are wider in the west but narrower in the east.

The eastward extensions of this plateau are locally known as the Bundelkhand and Baghelkhand. The Chotanagpur plateau marks the further eastward extension, drained by the Damodar river.

The Deccan Plateau is a triangular landmass that lies to the south of the river Narmada. The Satpura range flanks its broad base in the north while the Mahadev, the Kaimur hills and the Maikal range form its eastern extensions.

The Deccan Plateau is higher in the west and slopes gently eastwards. An extension of the Plateau is also visible in the northeast- locally known as the Meghalaya and Karbi-Anglong Plateau. It is separated by a fault from the Chotanagpur Plateau. Three Prominent hill ranges from the west to east are the Garo, the Khasi and the Jaintia Hills.

The Western Ghats and the Eastern Ghats mark the western and the eastern edges of the Deccan Plateau respectively. Western ghats lie parallel to the western coast. They are continuous and can be crossed through passes only. The Western Ghats are higher than the

Eastern Ghats. Their average elevation is 900-1600 metres as against 600 metres of the Eastern Ghats. The Eastern Ghats stretch from the Mahanadi Valley to the Nigiris in the south. The Eastern Ghats are discontinuous and irregular and dissected by rivers draining into the Bay of Bengal. The Western Ghats cause orographic rain by facing the rain bearing moist winds to rise along the western slopes of the Ghats. The Western Ghats are known by different local names. The height of the Western Ghats progressively increases from north to south. The highest peaks include the Anai Mudi (2,695 metres) and the Doda Betta (2,637 metres). Mahendragiri (1,501 metres) is the highest peak in the Eastern Ghats. ShevroyHills and the Javadi Hills are located to the southeast of the Eastern Ghats. Locate the famous hill stations of Udagamandalam, popularly known as Ooty and the Kodaikanal.

One of the distinct features of the peninsular plateau is the black soil area known as Decean Trap. This is of volcanic origin hence the rocks are igneous. Actually these rocks have denuded over time and are responsible for the formation of black soil. The Aravali Hills lie on the western and northwestern margins of the peninsular plateau. These are highly eroded hills and are found as broken hills. They extend from Gujarat to Delhi in a southwest-northeast direction.

The Indian Desert

The desert region can be divided into two parts - the great desert and the little desert. The great desert extends from the edge of the Rann of Kuchch beyond the Luni river northward. The whole of the Rajasthan-Sind frontier runs through this. The little desert extends from the Luni between Jaisalmer and Jodhpur up to the northern wastes. Between the great and the little deserts lies a zone of absolutely sterile country, consisting of rocky land cut up by limestone ridges.

This region receives very low rainfall below 150 mm per year. It has arid climate with low vegetatin cover. Streams appear during the rainy season. Soon after they disappear into the sand as they do not have enough water to reach the sea. Luni is the only large river in this region.

The Coastal Plains

The Peninsular plateau is flanked by stretch of narrow coastal strips, running along the Arabian Sea on the west and the Bay of Bengal on the east. The western coast, sandwiched between the Western Ghats and the Arabian Sea, is a narrow plain. It consists of three sections. The northern part of the coast is called the Konkan (Mumbai - Goa), the central stretch is called the Kannad Plain while the southern stretch is referred to as the Malabar coast.

The plain along the Bay of Bengal are wide and level. In the northern part, it is referred to as the Northern Circar, while the southern part is known as the Coromandal Coast. Large rivers such as the Mahanadi, the Godavari, the Krishna and the Kaveri have farmed extensive delta on this coast. Lake Chilika is an important feature along the eastern coast.

The Islands

Lakshadweep Islands group lying close to the Malabar coast of Kerala. This group of islands is composed of small coral isalnds. Earlier they were known as Laccadive, Minicoy and Amindive. It covers small area of 32 sq km. Kavaratti island is the administrative headquarters of Lakshadweep. This island group has great diversity of flora and fauna. the elongated chain of islands located in the Bay of Bengal extending from north to south. These are Andaman and Nicobar islands. They are bigger in size and are more numerous and scattered. The entire group of islands is divided into two broad categories–The Andaman in the north and the Nicobar in the south. It is believed that these islands are an elevated portion of submarine mountains. These island groups are of great strategic importance for the country. There is great diversity of flora and fauna in this group of islands too. These islands lie close to equator and experience equatorial climate.

DRAINAGE

The term drainage describes the river system of an area. small streams flowing from different directions come together to form the main river, which ultimately drains into a large water body such as a lake or a sea or an ocean. The area drained by a single river system is called a drainage basin. Any elevated area, such as a mountain or an upland, separates two drainage basins. Such an upland is known as a water divide.

DRAINAGE SYSTEMS IN INDIA

The drainage systems of India are mainly controlled by the broad relief features of the subcontinent. Accordingly, the Indian rivers are divided into two major groups:

- the Himalayan rivers; and
- the Peninsular rivers.

The Himalayan Rivers

The Himalayan rivers are formed by melting snow and glaciers and therefore, continuously flow throughout the year. During the monsoon months, Himalayas receive very heavy rainfall and rivers swell, causing frequent floods. The major Himalayan rivers are the Indus, the Ganga and the Brahmaputra. These rivers are long, and are joined by many large and important tributaries. A river alongwith its tributaries may be called a river system.

The Indus River System

The Indus, which is one of the great rivers of the world, rises near Mansarovar in Tibet and flows through India and thereafter through Pakistan and finally falls in the Arabian sea near Karachi. Its important tributaries flowing in Indian territory are the Sutlej (originating in Tibet), the Beas, the Ravi, the Chenab and the Jhelum. The Indus plain has a very gentle slope. With a total length of 2900 km, the Indus is one of the longest rivers of the world.

The Ganga River System

Ganga originate as a Bhagirathi river from Gangotri glacier of Himalaya. Bhagirathi and the Alaknanda, which join at Dev Prayag to form the Ganga. It traverses through Uttaranchal, Uttar Pradesh, Bihar and West Bengal States. Below Rajmahal hills, the Bhagirathi, which used to be the main course in the past, takes off, while the Padma continues eastward and enters Bangladesh. The Yamuna, the Ramganga, the Ghaghra, the Gandak, the Kosi, the Mahananda and the Sone are the important tributaries of the Ganga. Rivers Chambal and Betwa are the important sub-tributaries, which join Yamuna before it meets the Ganga. The Padma and the Brahmaputra join at Bangladesh and continue to flow as the Padma or Ganga. The Brahmaputra rises in Tibet, where it is known as Tsangpo and runs a long distance till it crosses over into India in Arunachal Pradesh under the name of Dihang. Near Passighat, the Debang and Lohit join the river Brahmaputra and the combined river runs all along the Assam in a narrow valley. It crosses into Bangladesh downstream of Dhubri.

The Brahmaputra River System

The Brahmaputra rises in Tibet east of Mansarowar lake very close to the sources of the Indus and the Satluj. It is slightly longer than the Indus, and most of its course lies outside India. It flows eastwards parallel to the Himalayas.

The principal tributaries of Brahmaputra in India are the Subansiri, Jia Bhareli, Dhansiri, Puthimari, Pagladiya and the Manas. The Brahmaputra in Bangladesh receives the flow of Tista, etc., and finally falls into Ganga. The Barak river, the Head stream of Meghna, rises in the hills in Manipur. The important tributaries of the river are Makku, Trang, Tuivai, Jiri, Sonai, Rukni, Katakhal, Dhaleswari, Langachini, Maduva and Jatinga. Barak continues in Bangladesh till the combined Ganga- Brahmaputra join it near Bhairab Bazar.

The Peninsular Rivers

Most of the major rivers of the Peninsula such as the Mahanadi, the Godavari, the Krishna and the Kaveri flow eastwards and drain into the Bay of Bengal. These rivers make deltas at their mouths. There are numerous small streams flowing west of the Western Ghats. The Narmada and the Tapi are the only long rivers, which flow west and make esturies. The drainage basins of the peninsular rivers are comparitevely small in size.

The Narmada Basin

The basin of the Narmada in the uplands of the Deccan, flowing to the Arabian Sea. Narmada rises in the Amarkantak hills in Madhya Pradesh. It flows towards the west in a rift valley formed due to faulting. Il the tributaries of the Narmada are very short and most of these join the main stream at right angles. The Narmada basin covers parts of Madhya Pradesh and Gujarat

The Tapi Basin

The Tapi rises in the Satpura ranges, in the Betul district of Madhya Pradesh. It also flows in a rift valley parallel to the Narmada but it is much shorter in length. Its basin covers parts of Madhya Pradesh, Gujarat and Maharashtra.

The Godavari Basin

It is also known as the 'Dakshin Ganga'. The Godavari in the southern Peninsula has the second largest river basin covering 10 per cent of the area of India. The Godavari is the largest Peninsular river. It rises from the slopes of the Western Ghats in the Nasik district of Maharashtra. Its length is about 1500 km. It drains into the Bay of Bengal. Its drainage basin is also the largest among the peninsular rivers. The basin covers parts of Maharashtra Madhya Pradesh, Orissa and Andhra Pradesh. The Godavari is joined by a number of tributaries such as the Purna, the Wardha, the Pranhita, the Manjra, the Wainganga and the Penganga.

The Mahanadi Basin

The Mahanadi rises in the highlands of Chhattisgarh. It flows through Orissa to reach the Bay of Bengal. The length of the river is about 860 km. Its drainage basin is shared by Maharashtra, Chhattisgarh, Jharkhand, and Orissa.

The Krishna Basin

Rising from a spring near Mahabaleshwar, the Krishna flows for about 1400 km and reaches the Bay of Bengal. The Tungabhadra, the Koyana, the Ghatprabha, the Musi and the Bhima are some of its tributaries. Its drainage basin is shared by Maharasthra, Karnataka and Andhra Pradesh.

The Kaveri Basin

The Kaveri rises in the Brahmagri range of the Western Ghats and it reaches the Bay of Bengal in south of Cuddalore, in Tamil Nadu. Total length of the river is about 760 km. Its main tributaries are Amravati, Bhavani, Hemavati and Kabini. Its basin drains parts of Karnataka, Kerala and Tamil Nadu.

CLIMATE

Climate refers to the sum total of weather conditions and variations over a large area for a long period of time (more than thirty years). Weather refers to the state of the atmosphere over an area at any point of time. The elements of weather and climate are the same, i.e. temperature, atmospheric pressure, wind, humidity and precipitation. On the basis of the generalised monthly atmospheric conditions, the year is divided into seasons such as winter, summer or rainy seasons. The climate of India may be broadly described as tropical monsoon type. There are four seasons:

(i) winter (January-February),
(ii) hot weather summer (March-May)
(iii) rainy south-western monsoon (June-September) and
(iv) post-monsoon, also known as north-east monsoon in the southern Peninsula (October-December).

FACTORS AFFECTING INDIA'S CLIMATE

Latitude

The Tropic of Cancer passes through the middle of the country from the Rann of Kuchchh in the west to Mizoram in the east. Almost half of the country, lying south of the Tropic of Cancer, belongs to the tropical area. All the remaining area, north of the Tropic, lies in the sub-tropics. Therefore, India's climate has characteristics of tropical as well as subtropical climates.

Altitude

The Himalayas prevent the cold winds from Central Asia from entering the subcontinent. It is because of these mountains that this subcontinent experiences comparatively milder winters as compared to central Asia.

Pressure and Winds

The climate and associated weather conditions in India are governed by the following atmospheric conditions:

- Pressure and surface winds;
- Upper air circulation; and
- Western cyclonic disturbances and tropical cyclones.

India lies in the region of north easterly winds. These winds originate from the subtropical high-pressure belt of the northern hemisphere. The pressure and wind conditions over India are unique. During winter, there is a high-pressure area north of the Himalayas. Cold dry winds blow from this region to the low-pressure areas over the oceans to the south. In summer, a low-pressure area develops over interior Asia as well as over northwestern India. This causes a complete reversal of the direction of winds during summer. Air moves from the high-pressure area over the southern Indian Ocean, in a south-easterly direction, crosses the equator, and turns right towards the low-pressure areas over the Indian subcontinent. These are known as the Southwest Monsoon winds. These winds blow over the warm oceans, gather moisture and bring widespread rainfall over the mainland of India.

The upper air circulation in this region is dominated by a westerly flow. An important component of this flow is the jet stream.

THE INDIAN MONSOON

The climate of India is strongly influenced by monsoon winds. The monsoons are experienced in the tropical area roughly between 20° N and 20° S. To understand the mechanism of the monsoons, the following facts are important.

(a) The differential heating and cooling of land and water creates low pressure on the landmass of India while the seas around experience comparatively high pressure.
(b) The shift of the position of Inter Tropical Convergence Zone (ITCZ) in summer, over the Ganga plain (this is the equatorial trough normally positioned about 5°N of the equator

also known as the monsoon- trough during the monsoon season).

(c) The presence of the high-pressure area, east of Madagascar, approximately at 20°S over the Indian Ocean. The intensity and position of this high-pressure area affects the Indian Monsoon.

(d) The Tibetan plateau gets intensely heated during summer, which results in strong vertical air currents and the formation of high pressure over the plateau at about 9 km above sea level.

(e) The movement of the westerly jet stream to the north of the Himalayas and the presence of the tropical easterly jet stream over the Indian peninsula during summer.

SOILS

Plant growth is directly affected by the type of soil the plants are grown in. The majority of plants depend on soil to provide nutrition, physical support (ie a place for roots to anchor), water and air. The exceptions to this are those plants known as epiphytes. These grow in such places as tree trunks, on rocks, or on fallen logs. The quality and quantity of plant growth will also affect how well other organisms (eg grazing animals, humans) will survive.

- Soil is composed of
  - o Particles, which consist of:
- Mineral particles of various sizes including clays, silts and sands
- Organic material in varying states of decomposition
- Living organisms - mostly microscopic, but also including insects, earthworms, nematodes, etc.
  - o Water, which contains varying amounts and types of nutrients (and other chemicals) in solution
  - o Air

These things affect the soil's ability to grow plants. It is possible to grow some plants in soils without living organisms, organic matter or mineral particles but plant roots must have air, water and nutrients. Generally however, you will require some amount of each of the above components to get the best growth from your plant.

The best types of soil for most agricultural production can be described as having the following attributes:

- o well drained
- o deep root zone
- o easily penetrated by air, water and roots
- o good water-holding capacity
- o maintains a balanced nutrient supply
- o erosion resistant.

Where these attributes do not exist or are in need of aid, then intervention from, for example, the farmer or land owner, is required to carry out management practices that will improve these characteristics, and ensure their sustainability.

PROBLEMS WITH SOILS

Soils are constantly affected by all that goes on around them, both by natural processes, and particularly in recent history, by human activity. Some of the more common human- induced changes include:

- Reduction in vegetation cover, opening up soils to increased rates of erosion
- Loss of soil structure due to poor cultivation techniques and the passage of heavy equipment, or regular traffic by hoofed animals (e.g. cows, horses)
- Reduction in soil fertility by not replacing nutrient losses from agricultural production
- An increase in saline-affected soils due to vegetation clearance or poor irrigation practices
- Waterlogging due to poor irrigation practices
- Soil acidification through the extensive use of acidifying fertilisers, or the extensive cropping of plants that remove large amounts of calcium from the soil (e.g. lucerne)
- Pollution of some soils through the use of persistent or toxic agricultural chemicals

When plants (trees and shrubs) are cleared from a site, soil is exposed to sunlight and the eroding effects of wind and water. Soil aeration is increased and the rate of weathering increases.

Apart from erosion, the proportion of organic matter in the soil gradually decreases through the action of microbes in the soil which use it as a source of energy - unless the new land use provides some replacement.

Major types of soil problems

Major soil problems include:

1. Loss of soil fertility
2. Erosion
3. Salinity
4. Soil sodicity
5. Soil structural decline
6. Soil acidification
7. Build up of chemical residues

POPULATION

India's population as on 1 March 2001 stood at 1,028 million (532.1 million males and 496.4 million females). India accounts for a meagre 2.4 per cent of the world surface area of 135.79 million sq km. Yet, it supports and sustains a whopping 16.7 per cent of the world population.

The population of India, which at the turn of the twentieth century was around 238.4 million, increased to reach 1,028 million at the dawn of the twenty-first century.The population of India as recorded at each decennial census from 1901 has grown steadily except for a decrease during 1911-21. The per cent decadal growth of population in the inter censal period 1991-2001 varies from a low of 9.43 in Kerala to a very high 64.53 in Nagaland. Delhi with 47.02 per cent, Chandigarh with 40.28 per cent and Sikkim with 33.06 per cent registered very high growth rates. In addition to Kerala, Tamil Nadu and Andhra Pradesh registered low growth rates during 1991-2001.

POPULATION DENSITY

One of the important indices of population concentration is the density of population. It is defined as the number of persons per sq km. The population density of India in 2001 was 324 per sq km. The density of population was increased in all States and Union Territories between 1991 and 2001. Among major states, West Bengal is still the most thickly populated state with a population density of 903 in 2001. Bihar is now the second highest densely populated state pushing Kerala to the third place.

SEX RATIO

Sex ratio, defined as the number of females per thousand males is an important social indicator to measure the extent of prevailing equality between males and females in a society at a given point of time. The sex ratio in the country had always remained unfavourable to females. It was 972 at the beginning of the 20th century and thereafter showed continuous decline until 1941.

LITERACY

For the purpose of census 2001, a person aged seven and above, who can both read and write with understanding in any language, is treated as literate. A person, who can only read but cannot write, is not literate. In the censuses prior to 1991, children below five years of age were necessarily treated as illiterates.

The results of 2001 census reveal that there has been an increase in literacy in the country. The literacy rate in the country is 64.84 per cent, 75.26 for males and 53.67 for females.

Kerala retained its position by being on top with a 90.86 per cent literacy rate, closely followed by Mizoram (88.80 per cent) and Lakshadweep (86.66 per cent). Bihar with a literacy rate of 47.00 per cent ranks last in the country preceded by Jharkhand (53.56 per cent) and Jammu and Kashmir (55.52 per cent).

POPULATION COMPOSITION

Population composition refers to the physical, socio-cultural and economic attributes of the population, such as age, sex, place of residence, language, religion, marital status, ethnicity, literacy, education and occupation.

Rural Population

Of the total 1027 million persons of the country (2001), 741.66 millions live in rural areas. It is slightly less than three-fourths (72.22 per cent) of the total population. The proportion of rural population to the total population varies from 50.23 per cent in Goa to 94.50 per cent in Arunachal Pradesh. All states of north India except Punjab andHaryana, all eastern and northeastern states except West Bengal, and all the states of central India have higher proportion of rural population than the national average.

Urban Population

About 285.35 million people live in urban areas (2001). They constitute 27.78 per cent of the total population of the country. Contrary to rural population, the proportion of urban population has been increasing since 1901. But the rate of addition was slow up to 1941 when it reached 13.86 per cent of total population from 10.85 per cent in 1901. It jumped to 17.29 per cent in 1951 and 27.78 per cent in 2001. Still India is one of the least urbanised countries in the world. Nearly 45 per cent of world population lives in urban centres.

URBANIZATION AND MIGRATION. ENVIRONMENTAL PROBLEMS AND ISSUES.

The process of society's transformation from a predominantly rural to a predominantly urban population is known as 'urbanisation'. It includes two things - an increase in the number of people living in urban settlements, and an increase in the percentage of the population engaged in non-agricultural activities, living in such places.

Degree of urbanisation varies widely among the states of the country. Goa, having 49.77 per cent of its population in urban areas, is the most urbanised state in the country. Among the larger ten states, Tamil Nadu with 43.86 per cent population being urban, tops the list. It is followed by Maharashtra (42.40 per cent). The degree of urbanisation is high in southern, western and northwestern states. All union territories are highly urbanised except Dadra and Nagar Haveli, and Andaman and Nicobar Islands. On the other hand, degree of urbanisation is low in all major states of north, central and northeastern India.

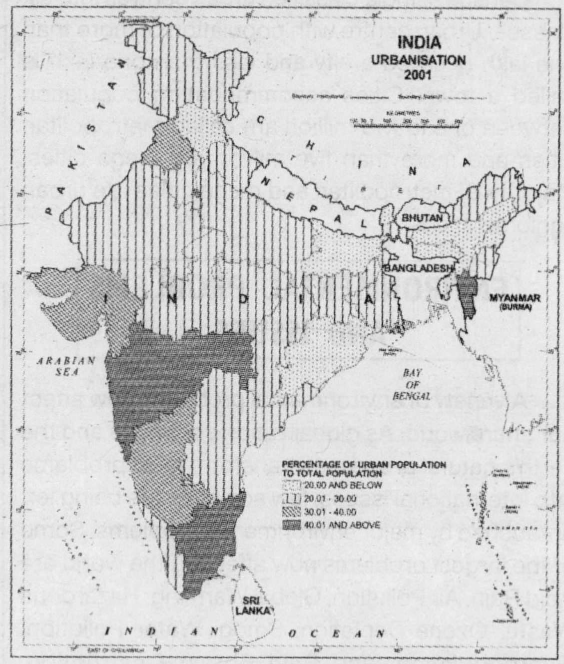

Town is defined in different ways in different countries. In India, the Census of India 2001 identifies two types of towns: Statutory and Census:

Statutory Towns: All places which have municipal, or corporation, or cantonment board, or a notified town area committee.

Census Towns: All other places which satisfy the following criteria:

(i) A minimum population of 5,000 persons;

(ii) At least 75 per cent of male working population engaged in non- agricultural pursuits; and

(iii) A density of population of at least 400 persons per sq. km.

More than one-fourth of the total population of India is urban. Total urban population increased eleven fold, from 25.85 million in 1901 to 285.35 million in 2001. Such a rapid growth has been possible by migration of opulation to urban places. Growth of cities involves two processes:

enlargement of urban centres and emergence of new towns. Both have played a significant role in growth of urban population and urbanization.

Census of India classifies urban centres into six classes. Urban centre with population of more than one lakh is called a city and less than one lakh is called a town. Cities accommodating population between one to five million are called metropolitan cities and more than five million are mega cities. Majority of metropolitan and mega cities are urban agglomerations.

ENVIRONMENTAL PROBLEMS AND ISSUES

A variety of environmental problems now affect our entire world. As globalization continues and the earth's natural processes transform local problems into international issues, few societies are being left untouched by major environmental problems. Some of the largest problems now affecting the world are Acid Rain, Air Pollution, Global Warming, Hazardous Waste, Ozone Depletion, Smog, Water Pollution, Overpopulation, and Rain Forest Destruction. Environmental problems emerge from the lowering of environmental quality in the process of development. Development involves greater use of natural resources. So long as the use is in consonance with ecological principles, no harm is done. But armed with modern technology, human becomes unmindful of ecology and gives rise to environmental pollution, which in turn affects his or her health and quality of life in general adversely.

Pollution results from 'the release of substances and energy from waste products of human activities, which result in changes, usually harmful, within the natural environment'. Pollution can thus be classified into three categories on the basis of medium of transportation of the pollutants. These are (i) air pollution, (ii) water pollution, and (iii) land pollution.

AIR POLLUTION

Air pollution is the introduction of chemicals, particulate matter, or biological materials that cause harm or discomfort to humans or other living organisms, or damages the natural environment into the atmosphere.

Sources of air pollution refer to the various locations, activities or factors which are responsible for the releasing of pollutants in the atmosphere. These sources can be classified into two major categories which are:

Anthropogenic sources (human activity) mostly related to burning different kinds of fuel

- "Stationary Sources" include smoke stacks of power plants, manufacturing facilities (factories) and waste incinerators, as well as furnaces and other types of fuel-burning heating devices
- "Mobile Sources" include motor vehicles, marine vessels, aircraft and the effect of sound etc.
- Chemicals, dust and controlled burn practices in agriculture and forestry management. Controlled or prescribed burning is a technique sometimes used in forest management, farming, prairie restoration or greenhouse gas abatement. Fire is a natural part of both forest and grassland ecology and controlled fire can be a tool for foresters. Controlled burning stimulates the germination of some desirable forest trees, thus renewing the forest.
- Fumes from paint, hair spray, varnish, aerosol sprays and other solvents
- Waste deposition in landfills, which generate methane.Methane is not toxic; however, it is highly flammable and may form explosive mixtures with air. Methane is also an asphyxiant and may displace oxygen in an enclosed space. Asphyxia or suffocation may result if the oxygen concentration is reduced to below 19.5% by displacement
- Military, such as nuclear weapons, toxic gases, germ warfare and rocketry

Natural sources

- Dust from natural sources, usually large areas of land with little or no vegetation.
- Methane, emitted by the digestion of food by animals, for example cattle.
- Radon gas from radioactive decay within the Earth's crust. Radon is a colorless, odorless, naturally occurring, radioactive noble gas that is formed from the decay of radium. It is considered to be a health hazard. Radon gas from natural sources can accumulate in buildings, especially in confined areas such as the basement and it is the second most frequent cause of lung cancer, after cigarette smoking.
- Smoke and carbon monoxide from wildfires.
- Volcanic activity, which produce sulfur, chlorine, and ash particulates.

Effects of air pollution

The air pollution modifies weather and climate, effects human health and biotic community. Chlorofluorocarbons (CFCs) cause depletion of ozone layer which enable ultraviolet rays of the sun to reach the earth and increase atmospheric temperature. Increased concentration of carbon dioxide and other gases in the atmosphere causes greenhouse effect raising the atmosphere temperature.

Smoky fog over cities called as urban smog is caused by these gases. It proves very harmful to human health. Air pollution can also cause acid rains. Air pollution causes diseases of the lungs, heart, nervous and circulatory systems.

A study conducted in the ambient air of

WATER POLLUTION

Water pollution is the contamination of water bodies. Water pollution occurs when pollutants are discharged directly or indirectly into water bodies without adequate treatment to remove harmful compounds.

Water pollution categories

Surface water and groundwater have often been studied and managed as separate resources, although they are interrelated. Sources of surface water pollution are generally grouped into two categories based on their origin.

Point source pollution refers to contaminants that enter a waterway through a discrete conveyance, such as a pipe or ditch. Examples of sources in this category include discharges from a sewage treatment plant, a factory, or a city storm drain. The U.S. Clean Water Act (CWA) defines point source for regulatory enforcement purposes. The CWA definition of point source was amended in 1987 to include municipal storm sewer systems, as well as industrial stormwater, such as from construction sites.

Non-point source pollution

Non-point source (NPS) pollution refers to diffuse contamination that does not originate from a single discrete source. NPS pollution is often accumulative effect of small amounts of contaminants gathered from a large area. The leaching out of nitrogen compounds from agricultural land which has been fertilized is a typical example. Nutrient runoff in stormwater from "sheet flow" over an agricultural field or a forest are also cited as examples of NPS pollution.

Causes of water pollution

The specific contaminants leading to pollution in water include a wide spectrum of chemicals, pathogens, and physical or sensory changes such as elevated temperature and discoloration. While many of the chemicals and substances that are regulated may be naturally occurring (calcium, sodium, iron, manganese, etc.) the concentration is often the key in determining what is a natural component of water, and what is a contaminant.

LAND POLLUTION

Land pollution is the degradation of Earth's land surfaces often caused by human activities and their misuse of land resources. It occurs when waste is not disposed properly. Haphazard disposal of urban and industrial wastes, exploitation of minerals, and improper use of soil by inadequate agricultural practices are a few factors. Urbanization and industrialization are major causes of land pollution. The Industrial Revolution set a series of events into motion which destroyed natural habitats and polluted the environment, causing diseases in both humans and other species of animals.

Causes of land pollution

- Increased mechanization.
- Herbicides
- Modern mining projects
- Burial practices
- Construction
- Increased waste disposal

8. GEOPHYSICS

1. Singal Processing
2. Field theory
3. Numerical analysis and inversion
4. Gravity and Magnetic fields of the earth
5. Plate Tectonics and Geodynamics
6. Seismology & Tomography
7. Gravity and Magnetic Methods
8. Seismic Methods
9. Well logging and other methods

1. Signal Processing

CONTINUOUS AND DISCRETE SIGNALS

In the fields of communications, signal processing, and in electrical engineering more generally, a signal is any time-varying or spatial-varying quantity. In the context of signal processing, arbitrary binary data streams are not considered as signals, but only analog and digital signals that are representations of analog physical quantities.

DISCRETE-TIME AND CONTINUOUS-TIME SIGNALS

If for a signal, the quantities are defined only on a discrete set of times, we call it a discrete-time signal. In other words, a discrete-time real (or complex) signal can be seen as a function from the set of integers to the set of real (or complex) numbers.

A continuous-time real (or complex) signal is any real-valued (or complex-valued) function which is defined for all time t in an interval, most commonly an infinite interval.

CONTINUOUS SIGNAL

A continuous signal or a continuous-time signal is a varying quantity (a signal) whose domain, which is often time, is a continuum (e.g., a connected interval of the reals). That is, the function's domain is an uncountable set. The function itself need not be continuous. To contrast, a discrete time signal has a countable domain, like the natural numbers.

The signal is defined over a domain, which may or may not be finite, and there is a functional mapping from the domain to the value of the signal. The continuity of the time variable, in connection with the law of density of real numbers, means that the signal value can be found at any arbitrary point in time.

A typical example of an infinite duration signal is:

$$f(t) = \sin(t), \quad t \in R$$

A finite duration counterpart of the above signal could be:

$$f(t) = \sin(t), \quad t \in [-\pi, \pi] \text{ and}$$

$$f(t) = 0 \text{ otherwise.}$$

The value of a finite (or infinite) duration signal may or may not be finite. For example,

$$f(t) = \frac{1}{t}, \; t \in [0, 1] \text{ and } f(t) = 0 \text{ otherwise,}$$

is a finite duration signal but it takes an infinite value for $t = 0$.

In many disciplines, the convention is that a continuous signal must always have a finite value, which makes more sense in the case of physical signals.

For some purposes, infinite singularities are acceptable as long as the signal is integrable over any finite interval (for example, the t^{-1} signal is not integrable, but t^{-2} is).

Any analogue signal is continuous by nature. Discrete signals, used in digital signal processing, can be obtained by sampling and quantization of continuous signals.

Continuous signal may also be defined over an independent variable other than time. Another very common independent variable is space and is particularly useful in image processing, where two space dimensions are used.

DISCRETE SIGNAL

Discrete signal or discrete-time signal is a time series consisting of a sequence of quantities. In other words, it is a time series that is a function over a domain of discrete integers. Each value in the sequence is called a sample.

Unlike a continuous-time signal, a discrete-time signal is not a function of a continuous argument; however, it may have been obtained by sampling from a continuous-time signal. When a discrete-time signal is a sequence corresponding to uniformly spaced times, it has an associated sampling rate; the sampling rate is not apparent in the data sequence, so may be associated as a separate data item.

ACQUISITION

Discrete signals may have several origins, but can usually be classified into one of two groups:

- By acquiring values of an analog signal at constant or variable rate. This process is called sampling.
- By accumulating a variable over time. For example, the number of people taking a certain elevator every day.

DIGITAL SIGNALS

A digital signal is a discrete-time signal that takes on only a discrete set of values.

The process of converting a continuous-valued discrete-time signal to a digital (discrete-valued discrete-time) signal is known as quantization. This process, also known as analog-to-digital conversion, loses information (by truncating or rounding the sample values). That is, discrete-valued signals are always an approximation to the original continuous-valued signal.

Common practical digital signals are represented as 8-bit (256 levels), 16-bit (65,536 levels), 32-bit (4.3 billion levels), and so on, though any number of quantization levels is possible, not just powers of two.

FOURIER SERIES

A Fourier series decomposes a periodic function or periodic signal into a sum of simple oscillating functions, namely sines and cosines (or complex exponentials). The study of Fourier series is a branch of Fourier analysis.

Fourier's formula for 2π-periodic functions using sines and cosines

For a periodic function $f(x)$ that is integrable on $[-\pi, \pi]$, the numbers

$$a_n = \frac{1}{\pi}\int_{-\pi}^{\pi} f(x)\cos(nx)dx, \quad n \geq 0$$

and

$$b_n = \frac{1}{\pi}\int_{-\pi}^{\pi} f(x)\sin(nx)dx, \quad n \geq 1$$

are called the Fourier coefficients of f. One introduces the partial sums of the Fourier series for f, often denoted by

$$(S_N f)(x) = \frac{a_0}{2} + \sum_{n=1}^{N}[a_n\cos(nx) + b_n\sin(nx)], \quad N \geq 0.$$

The partial sums for f are trigonometric polynomials. One expects that the functions $S_N f$ approximate the function f, and that the approximation improves as N tends to infinity. The infinite sum

$$\frac{a_0}{2} + \sum_{n=1}^{\infty}[a_n\cos(nx) + b_n\sin(nx)]$$

is called the Fourier series of f.

The Fourier series does not always converge, and even when it does converge for a specific value x_0 of x, the sum of the series at x_0 may differ from the value $f(x)_0$ of the function. It is one of the main questions in harmonic analysis to decide when Fourier series converge, and when the sum is equal to the original function. If a function is square-integrable on the interval $[-\pi, \pi]$, then the Fourier series converges to the function at almost every point. In engineering applications, the Fourier series is generally presumed to converge everywhere except at discontinuities, since the functions encountered in engineering are more well behaved than the ones that mathematicians can provide as counter-examples to this presumption. In particular, the Fourier series converges absolutely and uniformly to $f(x)$ whenever the derivative of $f(x)$ (which may not exist everywhere) is square integrable.

It is possible to define Fourier coefficients for more general functions or distributions, in such cases convergence in norm or weak convergence is usually of interest.

EXPONENTIAL FOURIER SERIES

We can use Euler's formula,

$$e^{inx} = \cos(nx) + i\sin(nx),$$

where i is the imaginary unit, to give a more concise formula:

$$f(x) = \sum_{n=-\infty}^{\infty} c_n e^{inx}.$$

The Fourier coefficients are then given by:

$$c_n = \frac{1}{2\pi}\int_{-\pi}^{\pi} f(x)e^{-inx}\,dx.$$

The Fourier coefficients a_n, b_n, c_n are related via

$$a_n = c_n + c_{-n} \quad \text{for } n = 0, 1, 2, \ldots$$

and

$$b_n = i(c_n - c_{-n}) \quad \text{for } n = 1, 2, \ldots$$

The notation cn is inadequate for discussing the Fourier coefficients of several different functions. Therefore it is customarily replaced by a modified form of f (in this case), such as F or $\hat{f}$ and functional notation often replaces subscripting. Thus:

$$f(x) = \sum_{n=-\infty}^{\infty} f(n)\cdot e^{inx}$$

$$= \sum_{n=-\infty}^{\infty} F(n)\cdot e^{inx} \quad \text{(engineering)}.$$

In engineering, particularly when the variable x represents time, the coefficient sequence is called a frequency domain representation. Square brackets are often used to emphasize that the domain of this function is a discrete set of frequencies.

FOURIER SERIES ON A SQUARE

We can also define the Fourier series for functions of two variables x and y in the square $[-\pi, \pi]\times[-\pi, \pi]$:

$$f(x,y) = \sum c_{j,k} e^{ijx} e^{iky},$$

$$c_{j,k} = \frac{1}{4\pi^2}\int_{-\pi}^{\pi}\int_{-\pi}^{\pi} f(x,y)e^{-ijx}e^{iky}\,dx\,dy,$$

Aside from being useful for solving partial differential equations such as the heat equation, one notable application of Fourier series on the square is in image compression.

BAND LIMITED SIGNAL

A bandlimited signal is a deterministic or stochastic signal whose Fourier transform or power spectral density is zero above a certain finite frequency. In other words, if the Fourier transform or power spectral density has finite support then the signal is said to be bandlimited.

A bandlimited signal can be fully reconstructed from its samples, provided that the sampling rate exceeds twice the maximum frequency in the bandlimited signal. This minimum sampling frequency is called the Nyquist rate. This result, usually attributed to Nyquist and Shannon, is known as the Nyquist-Shannon sampling theorem, or simply the sampling theorem.

An example of a simple deterministic bandlimited signal is a sinusoid of the form $x(t) = \sin(2\pi ft + \theta)$. If this signal is sampled at a rate $f_s = \frac{1}{T} > 2\text{B}$ so that we have the samples $x(nT)$, for all integers n, we can recover $x(t)$ completely from these samples. Similarly, sums of sinusoids with different frequencies and phases are also bandlimited.

The signal whose Fourier transform is shown in the figure is also bandlimited. Suppose $x(t)$ is a signal whose Fourier transform is $X(f)$, the magnitude of which is shown in the figure. The highest frequency component in $x(t)$ is B. As a result, the Nyquist rate is

$$R_N = 2B$$

or twice the highest frequency component in the signal, as shown in the figure. According to the sampling theorem, it is possible to reconstruct $x(t)$ completely and exactly using the samples

$x[n] \stackrel{\text{def}}{=} x(nT) = x\left(\dfrac{n}{f_s}\right)$ for integer n and

$T \stackrel{\text{def}}{=} \dfrac{1}{f_s}$ as long as $f_s > R_N$

The reconstruction of a signal from its samples can be accomplished using the Whittaker-Shannon interpolation formula.

DISCRETE TRANSFORM

The discrete Fourier transform (DFT) is a specific kind of Fourier transform, used in Fourier analysis. It transforms one function into another, which is called the frequency domain representation, or simply the DFT, of the original function (which is often a function in the time domain). But the DFT requires an input function that is discrete and whose non-zero values have a limited (finite) duration. Such inputs are often created by sampling a continuous function, like a person's voice. Unlike the discrete-time Fourier transform (DTFT), it only evaluates enough frequency components to reconstruct the finite segment that was analyzed. Using the DFT implies that the finite segment that is analyzed is one period of an infinitely extended periodic signal; if this is not actually true, a window function has to be used to reduce the artifacts in the spectrum. For the same reason, the inverse DFT cannot reproduce the entire time domain, unless the input happens to be periodic (forever). Therefore it is often said that the DFT is a transform for Fourier analysis of finite-domain discrete-time functions. The sinusoidal basis functions of the decomposition have the same properties.

The input to the DFT is a finite sequence of real or complex numbers (with more abstract generalizations discussed below), making the DFT ideal for processing information stored in computers. In particular, the DFT is widely employed in signal processing and related fields to analyze the frequencies contained in a sampled signal, to solve partial differential equations, and to perform other operations such as convolutions or multiplying large integers. A key enabling factor for these applications is the fact that the DFT can be computed efficiently in practice using a fast Fourier transform (FFT) algorithm.

The sequence of N complex numbers x_0, ..., is transformed into the sequence of N complex numbers $x_0, ..., x_{N-1}$ by the DFT according to the formula:

$$X_k = \sum_{n=0}^{N-1} x_n e^{-\frac{2\pi i}{N}kn} \qquad k = 0, ..., N-1$$

where i is the imaginary unit and $e^{\frac{2\pi i}{N}}$ is a primitive N'th root of unity. (This expression can also be written in terms of a DFT matrix; when scaled appropriately it becomes a unitary matrix and the X_k can thus be viewed as coefficients of x in an orthonormal basis.)

The transform is sometimes denoted by the symbol F, as in $X = F\{x\}$ or $F\{x\}$ or Fx.

The inverse discrete Fourier transform (IDFT) is given by

$$x_n = \frac{1}{N}\sum_{k=0}^{N-1} X_k e^{\frac{2\pi i}{N}kn} \qquad n = 0, ..., N-1.$$

A simple description of these equations is that the complex numbers X_k represent the amplitude and phase of the different sinusoidal components of the input "signal" x_n. The DFT computes the X_k from the x_n, while the IDFT shows how to compute the x_n as a sum of sinusoidal components $(1/N)X_k e^{\frac{2\pi i}{N}kn}$ with frequency k/N cycles per sample. By writing the equations in this form, we are making extensive use of Euler's formula to express sinusoids in terms of complex exponentials, which are much easier to manipulate. In the same way, by writing X_k in polar form, we immediately obtain the sinusoid amplitude A_k and phase φ_k from the complex modulus and argument of X_k, respectively:

$$A_k = |X_k| = \sqrt{\operatorname{Re}(X_k)^2 + \operatorname{Im}(X_k)^2},$$

$$\varphi_k = \arg(X_k) = \operatorname{atan}^2(\operatorname{Im}(X_k), \operatorname{Re}(X_k)).$$

Note that the normalization factor multiplying the DFT and IDFT (here 1 and 1/N) and the signs of the exponents are merely conventions, and differ in some treatments. The only requirements of these conventions are that the DFT and IDFT have opposite-sign exponents and that the product of their normalization factors be 1/N. A normalization of $1/\sqrt{N}$ for both the DFT and IDFT makes the transforms unitary, which has some theoretical advantages, but it is often more practical in numerical computation to perform the scaling all at once as above (and a unit scaling can be convenient in other ways .

(The convention of a negative sign in the exponent is often convenient because it means that X_k is the amplitude of a "positive frequency" $2\pi k/N$. Equivalently, the DFT is often thought of as a matched filter: when looking for a frequency of +1, one correlates the incoming signal with a frequency of −1.)

In the following discussion the terms "sequence" and "vector" will be considered interchangeable.

PROPERTIES OF DISCRETE TRANSFORM

Completeness

The discrete Fourier transform is an invertible, linear transformation

$$F : C^N \to C^N$$

with C denoting the set of complex numbers. In other words, for any N > 0, an N-dimensional complex vector has a DFT and an IDFT which are in turn N-dimensional complex vectors.

Orthogonality

The vectors $e^{\frac{2\pi i}{N}kn}$ form an orthogonal basis over the set of N-dimensional complex vectors:

$$\sum_{n=0}^{N-1}\left(e^{\frac{2\pi i}{N}kn}\right)\left(e^{-\frac{2\pi i}{N}k'n}\right) = N\,\delta_{kk'}$$

where is the Kronecker delta. This orthogonality condition can be used to derive the formula for the IDFT from the definition of the DFT, and is equivalent to the unitarity property below.

The Plancherel theorem and Parseval's theorem

If X_k and Y_k are the DFTs of x_n and y_n respectively then the Plancherel theorem states:

$$\sum_{n=0}^{N-1} x_n y_n^* = \frac{1}{N}\sum_{k=0}^{N-1} X_k Y_k^*$$

where the star denotes complex conjugation. Parseval's theorem is a special case of the Plancherel theorem and states:

$$\sum_{n=0}^{N-1} |x_n|^2 = \frac{1}{N}\sum_{k=0}^{N-1} |X_k|^2 .$$

Periodicity

If the expression that defines the DFT is evaluated for all integers k instead of just for $k = 0, ..., N-1$, then the resulting infinite sequence is a periodic extension of the DFT, periodic with period N.

The periodicity can be shown directly from the definition:

$$X_{k+N} \stackrel{def}{=} \sum_{n=0}^{N-1} x_n e^{-\frac{2\pi i}{N}(k+N)n} = \sum_{n=0}^{N-1} x_n e^{-\frac{2\pi i}{N}kn} \underbrace{e^{-2\pi i n}}_{1}$$

$$= \sum_{n=0}^{N-1} x_n e^{-\frac{2\pi i}{N}kn} = X_k.$$

Similarly, it can be shown that the IDFT formula leads to a periodic extension

The shift theorem

Multiplying x_n by a linear phase $e^{\frac{2\pi i}{N}nm}$ for some integer m corresponds to a circular shift of the output X_k : X_k is replaced by X_{k-m}, where the subscript is interpreted modulo N (i.e., periodically). Similarly, a circular shift of the input x_n corresponds to multiplying the output X_k by a linear phase. Mathematically, if $\{x\}_n$ represents the vector x then

if $F(\{x_n\})_k = X_k$

then $F\left(\left\{x_n \cdot e^{\frac{2\pi i}{N}nm}\right\}\right)_k = X_{k-m}$

and $F(\{x_{n-m}\})_k = X_k \cdot e^{-\frac{2\pi i}{N}km}$

Circular convolution theorem and cross-correlation theorem

The convolution theorem for the continuous and discrete time Fourier transforms indicates that a convolution of two infinite sequences can be obtained as the inverse transform of the product of the individual transforms. With sequences and transforms of length N, a circularity arises:

$$F^{-1}\{X \cdot Y\}_n \stackrel{\text{def}}{=} \frac{1}{N}\sum_{k=0}^{N-1} X_k \cdot Y_k \cdot e^{\frac{2\pi i}{N}kn}$$

$$= \frac{1}{N}\sum_{k=0}^{N-1}\left(\sum_{l=0}^{N-1} x_l e^{-\frac{2\pi i}{N}kl}\right)\cdot\left(\sum_{m=0}^{N-1} y_m e^{-\frac{2\pi i}{N}km}\right)\cdot e^{\frac{2\pi i}{N}kn}$$

$$= \sum_{l=0}^{N-1} x_l \sum_{m=0}^{N-1} y_m \left(\frac{1}{N}\sum_{k=0}^{N-1} e^{\frac{2\pi i}{N}k(n-l-m)}\right).$$

The quantity in parentheses is 0 for all values of m except those of the form n–1 –pN, where p is any integer. At those values, it is 1. It can therefore be replaced by an infinite sum of Kronecker delta functions, and we continue accordingly. Note that we can also extend the limits of m to infinity, with the understanding that the x and y sequences are defined as 0 outside [0, N–1]:

$$F^{-1}\{X \cdot Y\}_n = \sum_{l=0}^{N-1} x_l \sum_{m=-\infty}^{\infty} y_m \left(\sum_{p=-\infty}^{\infty} \delta_{m,(n-l-pN)}\right)$$

$$= \sum_{l=0}^{N-1} x_l \underbrace{\sum_{p=-\infty}^{\infty}\left(\sum_{m=-\infty}^{\infty} y_m \cdot \delta_{m,(n-l-pN)}\right)}_{y_{n-l-pN}}$$

$$= \sum_{l=0}^{N-1} x_l \left(\sum_{p=-\infty}^{\infty} y_{n-l-pN}\right) \stackrel{\text{def}}{=} (x * y_N)_n,$$

which is the convolution of the *x* sequence with a periodically extended *y* sequence defined by:

$$(y_N)_n \stackrel{\text{def}}{=} \sum_{p=-\infty}^{\infty} y_{(n-pN)}.$$

Similarly, it can be shown that:

$$F^{-1}\{X^* \cdot Y\}_n = \sum_{l=0}^{N-1} x_l^* \cdot (y_N)_{n+l} \stackrel{\text{def}}{=} (x * y_N)_n,$$

which is the cross-correlation of *x* and y_N.

A direct evaluation of the convolution or correlation summation (above) requires O(N[2]) operations for an output sequence of length N. An indirect method, using transforms, can take advantage of the O(NlogN) efficiency of the fast Fourier transform (FFT) to achieve much better performance. Furthermore, convolutions can be used to efficiently compute DFTs via Rader's FFT algorithm and Bluestein's FFT algorithm.

Methods have also been developed to use circular convolution as part of an efficient process that achieves normal (non-circular) convolution with an *x* or *y* sequence potentially much longer than the practical transform size (N). Two such methods are called overlap-save and overlap-add.

Applications of Discrete transform

The DFT has seen wide usage across a large number of fields; we only sketch a few examples below (see also the references at the end). All applications of the DFT depend crucially on the availability of a fast algorithm to compute discrete Fourier transforms and their inverses, a fast Fourier transform.

SPECTRAL ANALYSIS

When the DFT is used for spectral analysis, the $\{x_n\}$ sequence usually represents a finite set of uniformly-spaced time-samples of some signal $x(t)$, where t represents time. The conversion from continuous time to samples (discrete-time) changes the underlying Fourier transform of $x(t)$ into a discrete-time Fourier transform (DTFT), which generally entails a type of distortion called aliasing. Choice of an appropriate sample-rate (see Nyquist frequency) is the key to minimizing that distortion. Similarly, the conversion from a very long (or infinite) sequence to a manageable size entails a type of distortion called leakage, which is manifested as a loss of detail (aka resolution) in the DTFT. Choice of an appropriate sub-sequence length is the primary key to minimizing that effect. When the available data (and time to process it) is more than the amount needed to attain the desired frequency resolution, a standard technique is to perform multiple DFTs, for example to create a spectrogram. If the desired result is a power spectrum and noise or randomness is present in the data, averaging the magnitude components of the multiple DFTs is a useful procedure to reduce the variance of the spectrum (also called a periodogram in this context); two examples of such techniques are the Welch method and the Bartlett method; the general subject of estimating the power spectrum of a noisy signal is called spectral estimation.

A final source of distortion (or perhaps illusion) is the DFT itself, because it is just a discrete sampling of the DTFT, which is a function of a continuous frequency domain. That can be mitigated by increasing the resolution of the DFT. That procedure is illustrated in the discrete-time Fourier transform article.

- The procedure is sometimes referred to as zero-padding, which is a particular implementation used in conjunction with the fast Fourier transform (FFT) algorithm. The inefficiency of performing multiplications and additions with zero-valued "samples" is more than offset by the inherent efficiency of the FFT.
- As already noted, leakage imposes a limit on the inherent resolution of the DTFT. So there is a practical limit to the benefit that can be obtained from a fine-grained DFT.

DATA COMPRESSION

The field of digital signal processing relies heavily on operations in the frequency domain (i.e. on the Fourier transform). For example, several lossy image and sound compression methods employ the discrete Fourier transform: the signal is cut into short segments, each is transformed, and then the Fourier coefficients of high frequencies, which are assumed to be unnoticeable, are discarded. The decompressor computes the inverse transform based on this reduced number of Fourier coefficients. (Compression applications often use a specialized form of the DFT, the discrete cosine transform or sometimes the modified discrete cosine transform.)

PARTIAL DIFFERENTIAL EQUATIONS

Discrete Fourier transforms are often used to solve partial differential equations, where again the DFT is used as an approximation for the Fourier series (which is recovered in the limit of infinite N). The advantage of this approach is that it expands the signal in complex exponentials einx, which are eigenfunctions of differentiation: $d/dx\, e^{inx} = in\, e^{inx}$. Thus, in the Fourier representation, differentiation is simple-we just multiply by i n. (Note, however, that the choice of n is not unique due to aliasing; for the method to be convergent, a choice similar to that in the trigonometric interpolation section above should be used.) A linear differential equation with constant coefficients is transformed into an easily solvable algebraic equation. One then uses the inverse DFT to transform the result back into the ordinary spatial representation. Such an approach is called a spectral method.

POLYNOMIAL MULTIPLICATION

Suppose we wish to compute the polynomial product $c(x) = a(x) \cdot b(x)$. The ordinary product expression for the coefficients of c involves a linear (acyclic) convolution, where indices do not "wrap around." This can be rewritten as a cyclic convolution by taking the coefficient vectors for $a(x)$ and $b(x)$ with constant term first, then appending zeros so that the resultant coefficient vectors a and b have dimension $d > \deg(a(x)) + \deg(b(x))$. Then,

$$c = a * b$$

Where c is the vector of coefficients for $c(x)$, and the convolution operator $*$ is defined so

$$c_n = \sum_{m=0}^{d-1} a_m b_{n-m \bmod d} \qquad n = 0, 1 \ldots, d-1$$

But convolution becomes multiplication under the DFT:

$$f(c) = F(a)\, F(b)$$

Here the vector product is taken elementwise. Thus the coefficients of the product polynomial $c(x)$ are just the terms $0, ..., \deg(a(x)) + \deg(b(x))$ of the coefficient vector

$$c = F^{-1}\ (F(a)\ F(b)).$$

With a fast Fourier transform, the resulting algorithm takes O (N log N) arithmetic operations. Due to its simplicity and speed, the Cooley-Tukey FFT algorithm, which is limited to composite sizes, is often chosen for the transform operation. In this case, d should be chosen as the smallest integer greater than the sum of the input polynomial degrees that is factorizable into small prime factors.

MULTIPLICATION OF LARGE INTEGERS

The fastest known algorithms for the multiplication of very large integers use the polynomial multiplication method outlined above. Integers can be treated as the value of a polynomial evaluated specifically at the number base, with the coefficients of the polynomial corresponding to the digits in that base. After polynomial multiplication, a relatively low-complexity carry-propagation step completes the multiplication.

FAST FOURIER TRANSFORM

A fast Fourier transform (FFT) is an efficient algorithm to compute the discrete Fourier transform (DFT) and its inverse. There are many distinct FFT algorithms involving a wide range of mathematics, from simple complex-number arithmetic to group theory and number theory.

A DFT decomposes a sequence of values into components of different frequencies. This operation is useful in many fields (see discrete Fourier transform for properties and applications of the transform) but computing it directly from the definition is often too slow to be practical. An FFT is a way to compute the same result more quickly: computing a DFT of N points in the obvious way, using the definition, takes O(N^2) arithmetical operations, while an FFT can compute the same result in only O(N log N) operations. The difference in speed can be substantial, especially for long data sets where N may be in the thousands or millions-in practice, the computation time can be reduced by several orders of magnitude in such cases, and the improvement is roughly proportional to N/log(N). This huge improvement made many DFT-based algorithms practical; FFTs are of great importance to a wide variety of applications, from digital signal processing and solving partial differential equations to algorithms for quick multiplication of large integers.

The most well known FFT algorithms depend upon the factorization of N, but (contrary to popular misconception) there are FFTs with O(N log N) complexity for all N, even for prime N. Many FFT algorithms only depend on the fact that $e^{-\frac{2\pi i}{N}}$ is an Nth primitive root of unity, and thus can be applied to analogous transforms over any finite field, such as number-theoretic transforms.

Since the inverse DFT is the same as the DFT, but with the opposite sign in the exponent and a 1/N factor, any FFT algorithm can easily be adapted for it.

An FFT computes the DFT and produces exactly the same result as evaluating the DFT definition directly; the only difference is that an FFT is much faster. (In the presence of round-off error, many FFT algorithms are also much more accurate than evaluating the DFT definition directly, as discussed below.)

Let $x_0, ..., x_{N-1}$ be complex numbers. The DFT is defined by the formula

$$X_k = \sum_{n=0}^{N-1} x_n e^{-i2\pi k\frac{n}{N}} \qquad k = 0, ..., N-1.$$

Evaluating this definition directly requires O(N^2) operations: there are N outputs X_k, and each output requires a sum of N terms. An FFT is any method to compute the same results in O(N log N) operations. More precisely, all known FFT algorithms require (N log N) operations (technically, O only denotes an upper bound), although there is no proof that better complexity is impossible.

To illustrate the savings of an FFT, consider the count of complex multiplications and additions. Evaluating the DFT's sums directly involves N^2 complex multiplications and N(N–1) complex additions [of which O(N) operations can be saved by eliminating trivial operations such as multiplications by 1]. The well-known radix-2 Cooley-Tukey algorithm, for N a power of 2, can compute the same result with only (N/2) $\log_2 N$ complex multiplies (again, ignoring simplifications of multiplications by 1 and similar) and N $\log_2 N$ complex additions. In practice, actual performance on modern computers is usually dominated by factors other than arithmetic and is a complicated subject (see, e.g., Frigo & Johnson, 2005), but the overall improvement from $\Theta(N^2)$ to $\Theta(N \log N)$ remains.

ALGORITHMS OF FAST FOURIER TRANSFORM

Cooley-Tukey algorithm

By far the most common FFT is the Cooley-Tukey algorithm. This is a divide and conquer algorithm that recursively breaks down a DFT of any composite size $N = N_1N_2$ into many smaller DFTs of sizes N_1 and N_2, along with O(N) multiplications by complex roots of unity traditionally called twiddle factors (after Gentleman and Sande, 1966).

This method (and the general idea of an FFT) was popularized by a publication of J. W. Cooley and J. W. Tukey in 1965, but it was later discovered (Heideman & Burrus, 1984) that those two authors had independently re-invented an algorithm known to Carl Friedrich Gauss around 1805 (and subsequently rediscovered several times in limited forms).

The most well-known use of the Cooley-Tukey algorithm is to divide the transform into two pieces of size N / 2 at each step, and is therefore limited to power-of-two sizes, but any factorization can be used in general (as was known to both Gauss and Cooley/Tukey). These are called the radix-2 and mixed-radix cases, respectively (and other variants such as the split-radix FFT have their own names as well). Although the basic idea is recursive, most traditional implementations rearrange the algorithm to avoid explicit recursion. Also, because the Cooley-Tukey algorithm breaks the DFT into smaller DFTs, it can be combined arbitrarily with any other algorithm for the DFT.

Multidimensional Fast Fourier transform the multidimensional DFT

$$X_k = \sum_{n=0}^{N-1} e^{-2\pi i k\cdot(n/N)} x_n$$

transforms an array x_n with a d-dimensional vector of indices $n = (n_1, n_2, ..., n_d)$ by a set of d nested summations (over $n_j = 0 ... N_j - 1$ for each j), where the division n/N, defined as $n/N = (n_1/N_1 ..., n_d/N_d)$, is performed element-wise. Equivalently, it is simply the composition of a sequence of d sets of one-dimensional DFTs, performed along one dimension at a time (in any order).

This compositional viewpoint immediately provides the simplest and most common multidimensional DFT algorithm, known as the row-column algorithm (after the two-dimensional case, below). That is, one simply performs a sequence of d one-dimensional FFTs (by any of the above algorithms): first you transform along the n_1 dimension, then along the n_2 dimension, and so on (or actually, any ordering will work). This method is easily shown to have the usual O(NlogN) complexity, where $N = N_1N_2 ... N_d$ is the total number of data points transformed. In particular, there are N/N_1 transforms of size N_1, etcetera, so the complexity of the sequence of FFTs is:

$$\frac{N}{N_1} O(N_1 \log N_1) + ... + \frac{N}{N_d} O(N_d \log N_d)$$

In two dimensions, the x_k can be viewed as an $n_1 \times n_2$ matrix, and this algorithm corresponds to first performing the FFT of all the rows and then of all the columns (or vice versa), hence the name.

In more than two dimensions, it is often advantageous for cache locality to group the dimensions recursively. For example, a three-dimensional FFT might first perform two-dimensional

FFTs of each planar "slice" for each fixed n_1, and then perform the one-dimensional FFTs along the n1 direction. More generally, an asymptotically optimal cache-oblivious algorithm consists of recursively dividing the dimensions into two groups $(n_1, ..., n_{d/2})$ and $(n_{d/2+1}, ..., n_d)$ that are transformed recursively (rounding if d is not even) (see Frigo and Johnson, 2005). Still, this remains a straightforward variation of the row-column algorithm that ultimately requires only a one-dimensional FFT algorithm as the base case, and still has O(NlogN) complexity. Yet another variation is to perform matrix transpositions in between transforming subsequent dimensions, so that the transforms operate on contiguous data; this is especially important for out-of-core and distributed memory situations where accessing non-contiguous data is extremely time-consuming.

There are other multidimensional FFT algorithms that are distinct from the row-column algorithm, although all of them have O(NlogN) complexity. Perhaps the simplest non-row-column FFT is the vector-radix FFT algorithm, which is a generalization of the ordinary Cooley-Tukey algorithm where one divides the transform dimensions by a vector $r = (r_1, r_2 ..., r_d)$ of radices at each step. (This may also have cache benefits.) The simplest case of vector-radix is where all of the radices are equal (e.g. vector-radix-2 divides all of the dimensions by two), but this is not necessary. Vector radix with only a single non-unit radix at a time, i.e. $r = (1, ..., 1, r, 1, ..., 1)$, is essentially a row-column algorithm.

Z-TRANSFORM

The Z-transform converts a discrete time-domain signal, which is a sequence of real or complex numbers, into a complex frequency-domain representation.

It can be considered as a discrete equivalent of the Laplace transform. This similarity is explored in the theory of time scale calculus.

The Z-transform, like many integral transforms, can be defined as either a one-sided or two-sided transform.

BILATERAL Z-TRANSFORM

The bilateral or two-sided Z-transform of a discrete-time signal $x[n]$ is the function $X[z]$ defined as

$$X(z) = Z\{x[n]\} = \sum_{n=-\infty}^{\infty} x[n]z^{-n}$$

where n is an integer and z is, in general, a complex number:

$$z = Ae^{j\varphi} = A(\cos\varphi + j\sin\varphi)$$

where A is the magnitude of z, and φ is the complex argument (also referred to as angle or phase) in radians.

UNILATERAL Z-TRANSFORM

Alternatively, in cases where $x[n]$ is defined only for $n \geq 0$, the single-sided or unilateral Z-transform is defined as

$$X(z) = Z\{x[n]\} = \sum_{n=-\infty}^{\infty} x[n]z^{-n}$$

In signal processing, this definition is used when the signal is causal.

An important example of the unilateral Z-transform is the probability-generating function, where the component $x[n]$ is the probability that a discrete random variable takes the value n, and the function $X(z)$ is usually written as $X(s)$, in terms of $s = z^{-1}$. The properties of Z-transforms (below) have useful interpretations in the context of probability theory:

In geophysics, the usual definition for the Z-transform is a polynomial in z as opposed to z^{-1}. This convention is used by Robinson and Treitel and by Kanasewich. The geophysical definition is

$$X(z) = Z\{x[n]\} = \sum_{n} x[n]z^{n}.$$

The two definitions are equivalent; however, the difference results in a number of changes. For example, the location of zeros and poles move from inside the unit circle, using one definition, to outside the unit circle, using the other definition (and vice versa).

RELATIONSHIP TO FOURIER TRANSFORM

The Z-transform is a generalization of the discrete-time Fourier transform (DTFT). The DTFT can be found by evaluating the Z-transform $X(z)$ at $z = e^{jw}$ or, in other words, evaluated on the unit circle. In order to determine the frequency response of the system the Z-transform must be evaluated on the unit circle, meaning that the system's region of convergence must contain the unit circle. Otherwise, the DTFT of the system does not exist.

CONVOLUTION

Convolution is a mathematical operation on two functions f and g, producing a third function that is typically viewed as a modified version of one of the original functions. Convolution is similar to cross-correlation. It has applications that include statistics, computer vision, image and signal processing, electrical engineering, and differential equations.

The convolution can be defined for functions on groups other than Euclidean space In particular, the circular convolution can be defined for periodic functions (that is, functions on the circle), and the discrete convolution can be defined for functions on the set of integers. These generalizations of the convolution have applications in the field of numerical analysis and numerical linear algebra, and in the design and implementation of finite impulse response filters in signal processing.

Computing the inverse of the convolution operation is known as deconvolution.

The convolution of f and g is written $f{*}g$. It is defined as the integral of the product of the two functions after one is reversed and shifted. As such, it is a particular kind of integral transform:

$$(f*g)(t) \stackrel{\text{def}}{=} \int_{-\infty}^{\infty} f(r)\, g(t-r)\, dr$$

$$= \int_{-\infty}^{\infty} f(t-r)\, g(r)\, dr. \text{ (commutativity)}$$

While the symbol t is used above, it need not represent the time domain. But in that context, the convolution formula can be described as a weighted average of the function $f(\tau)$ at the moment t where the weighting is given by $g(-\tau)$ simply shifted by amount t. As t changes, the weighting function emphasizes different parts of the input function.

More generally, if f and g are complex-valued functions on R^d, then their convolution may be defined as the integral:

$$(f*g)(x) = \int_{R^d} f(y)g(x-y)dy = \int_{R^d} f(x-y)g(y)dy.$$

PROPERTIES OF CONVOLUTION

Algebraic properties

The convolution defines a product on the linear space of integrable functions. This product satisfies the following algebraic properties, which formally mean that the space of integrable functions with the product given by convolution is a commutative algebra without identity (Strichartz 1994, §3.3). Other linear spaces of functions, such as the space of continuous functions of compact support, are closed under the convolution, and so also form commutative algebras.

Commutativity

$$f*g = g*f$$

Associativity

$$f*(g*h) = (f*g)*h$$

Distributivity

$$f*(g+h) = (f*g)+(f*h)$$

Associativity with scalar multiplication

$$a(f*g) = (af)*g = f*(ag)$$

for any real (or complex) number a.

Multiplicative identity

No algebra of functions possesses an identity for the convolution. The lack of identity is typically not a major inconvenience, since most collections of functions on which the convolution is performed can be convolved with a delta distribution or, at the very least (as is the case of L^1) admit approximations to the identity. The linear space of compactly supported distributions does, however, admit an identity under the convolution. Specifically,

$$f*\delta = f$$

where δ is the delta distribution.

Inverse element

Some distributions have an inverse element for the convolution, $S^{(-1)}$, which is defined by

$$S^{(-1)} * S = \delta.$$

The set of invertible distributions forms an abelian group under the convolution.

Integration

If f and g are integrable functions, then the integral of their convolution on the whole space is simply obtained as the product of their integrals:

$$\int_{R^d} (f * g)(x)dx = \left(\int_{R^d} f(x)dx\right)\left(\int_{R^d} g(x)dx\right).$$

This follows from Fubini's theorem. The same result holds if f and g are only assumed to be nonnegative measurable functions, by Tonelli's theorem.

Differentiation

In the one-variable case,

$$\frac{d}{dx}(f * g) = \frac{df}{dx} * g = f * \frac{dg}{dx}$$

where d/dx is the derivative. More generally, in the case of functions of several variables, an analogous formula holds with the partial derivative:

$$\frac{\partial}{\partial x_i}(f * g)(x) = \frac{\partial f}{\partial x_i} * g = f * \frac{\partial g}{\partial x_i}.$$

A particular consequence of this is that the convolution can be viewed as a "smoothing" operation: the convolution of ŕ and g is differentiable as many times as f and g are together.

These identities hold under the precise condition that f and g are absolutely integrable and at least one of them has an absolutely integrable (L^1) weak derivative, as a consequence of Young's inequality. For instance, when f is continuously differentiable with compact support, and g is an arbitrary locally integrable function,

$$\frac{d}{dx}(f * g) = \frac{df}{dx} * g.$$

These identities also hold much more broadly in the sense of tempered distributions if one of f or g is a compactly supported distribution or a Schwartz function and the other is a tempered distribution. On the other hand, two positive integrable and infinitely differentiable functions may have a nowhere continuous convolution.

In the discrete case, the difference operator $D\,f(n) = f(n+1) - f(n)$ satisfies an analogous relationship:

$$d(f * g) = (Df) * g = f * (Dg).$$

The convolution theorem states that under suitable conditions the Fourier transform of a convolution is the pointwise product of Fourier transforms. In other words, convolution in one domain (e.g., time domain) equals point-wise multiplication in the other domain (e.g., frequency domain). Versions of the convolution theorem are true for various Fourier-related transforms. Let f and g be two functions with convolution $f * g$. (Note that the asterisk denotes convolution in this context, and not multiplication. The tensor product symbol ⊗ is sometimes used instead.) Let F denote the Fourier transform operator, so $F\{f\}$ and $F\{g\}$ are the Fourier transforms of f and g, respectively. Then

$$F\{f * g\} = F\{f\} \cdot F\{g\}$$

where denotes point-wise multiplication. It also works the other way around:

$$F\{f \cdot g\} = F\{f\} * F(g)$$

By applying the inverse Fourier transform F^{-1}, we can write:

$$f * g = F^{-1}\{F\{f\}.F(g)\}$$

The transform may be normalised in other ways, in which case constant scaling factors (typically 2π or $\sqrt{2\pi}$) will appear in the relationships above.

This theorem also holds for the Laplace transform, the two-sided Laplace transform and, when suitably modified, for the Mellin transform and Hartley transform It can be extended to the Fourier transform of abstract harmonic analysis defined over locally compact abelian groups.

This formulation is especially useful for implementing a numerical convolution on a computer: The standard convolution algorithm has quadratic computational complexity. With the help of the convolution theorem and the fast Fourier transform, the complexity of the convolution can be reduced to O(n log n). This can be exploited to construct fast multiplication algorithms.

Applications

Convolution and related operations are found in many applications of engineering and mathematics.

- In electrical engineering, the convolution of one function (the input) with a second function (the impulse response) gives the output of a linear time-invariant system (LTI). At any given moment, the output is an accumulated effect of all the prior values of the input function, with the most recent values typically having the most influence (expressed as a multiplicative factor). The impulse response function provides that factor as a function of the elapsed time since each input value occurred.
    - o In digital signal processing and image processing applications, the entire input function is often available for computing every sample of the output function. In that case, the constraint that each output is the effect of only prior inputs can be relaxed.
    - o Convolution amplifies or attenuates each frequency component of the input independently of the other components.
- In statistics, as noted above, a weighted moving average is a convolution.
- In probability theory, the probability distribution of the sum of two independent random variables is the convolution of their individual distributions.
- In optics, many kinds of "blur" are described by convolutions. A shadow (e.g. the shadow on the table when you hold your hand between the table and a light source) is the convolution of the shape of the light source that is casting the shadow and the object whose shadow is being cast. An out-of-focus photograph is the convolution of the sharp image with the shape of the iris diaphragm. The photographic term for this is bokeh.
- Similarly, in digital image processing, convolutional filtering plays an important role in many important algorithms in edge detection and related processes.
- In linear acoustics, an echo is the convolution of the original sound with a function representing the various objects that are reflecting it.
- In artificial reverberation (digital signal processing, pro audio), convolution is used to map the impulse response of a real room on a digital audio signal (see previous and next point for additional information).
- In time-resolved fluorescence spectroscopy, the excitation signal can be treated as a chain of delta pulses, and the measured fluorescence is a sum of exponential decays from each delta pulse.
- In radiotherapy treatment planning systems, most part of all modern codes of calculation applies a convolution-superpostion algorithm.
- In physics, wherever there is a linear system with a "superposition principle", a convolution operation makes an appearance.

FILTER

Filter design is the process of designing a filter (in the sense in which the term is used in signal processing, statistics, and applied mathematics), often a linear shift-invariant filter, which satisfies a set of requirements, some of which are contradictory. The problem is to find a realization of the filter which meets each of the requirements to a sufficient degree to make it useful.

The filter design process can be described as an optimization problem where each requirement contributes with a term to an error function which should be minimized. Certain parts of the design process can be automated, but normally an experienced electrical engineer is needed to get a good result.

A low-pass filter is a filter that passes low-frequency signals but attenuates (reduces the amplitude of) signals with frequencies higher than the cutoff frequency. The actual amount of attenuation for each frequency varies from filter to filter. It is sometimes called a high-cut filter, or treble cut filter when used in audio applications. A low-pass filter is the opposite of a high-pass filter, and a band-pass filter is a combination of a low-pass and a high-pass.

The concept of a low-pass filter exists in many different forms, including electronic circuits (like a hiss filter used in audio), digital algorithms for smoothing sets of data, acoustic barriers, blurring of images, and so on. Low-pass filters play the same role in signal processing that moving averages do in some other fields, such as finance; both tools provide a smoother form of a signal which removes the short-term oscillations, leaving only the long-term trend.

RECURSIVE FILTER

In signal processing, a recursive filter is a type of filter which re-uses one or more of its outputs as an input. This feedback typically results in an unending impulse response (commonly referred to as infinite impulse response (IIR)), characterised by either exponentially growing, decaying, or sinusoidal signal output components.

However, a recursive filter does not always have an infinite impulse response. Some implementations of moving average filter are recursive filters but with a Finite impulse response.

DECONVOLUTION

Deconvolution is an algorithm-based process used to reverse the effects of convolution on recorded data. The concept of deconvolution is widely used in the techniques of signal processing and image processing. Because these techniques are in turn widely used in many scientific and engineering disciplines, deconvolution finds many applications.

In general, the object of deconvolution is to find the solution of a convolution equation of the form:

$$f * g = h$$

Usually, h is some recorded signal, and f is some signal that we wish to recover, but has been convolved with some other signal g before we recorded it. The function g might represent the transfer function of an instrument or a driving force that was applied to a physical system. If we know g, or at least know the form of g, then we can perform deterministic deconvolution. However, if we do not know g in advance, then we need to estimate it.

APPLICATIONS OF DECONVOLUTION IN SEISMOLOGY

The concept of deconvolution had an early application in reflection seismology. In 1950, Enders Robinson was a graduate student at MIT. He worked with others at MIT, such as Norbert Wiener, Norman Levinson, and economist Paul Samuelson, to develop the "convolutional model" of a reflection seismogram. This model assumes that the recorded seismogram $s(t)$ is the convolution of an Earth-reflectivity function $e(t)$ and a seismic wavelet $w(t)$ from a point source, where t represents recording time. Thus, our convolution equation is

$$s(t) = (e * w)(t).$$

The seismologist is interested in e, which contains information about the Earth's structure. By the convolution theorem, this equation may be Fourier transformed to

$$S(w) = E(w)W(w)$$

in the frequency domain. By assuming that the reflectivity is white, we can assume that the power spectrum of the reflectivity is constant, and that the power spectrum of the seismogram is the spectrum of the wavelet multiplied by that constant. Thus,

$$|S(w)| \approx k|W(w)|.$$

If we assume that the wavelet is minimum phase, we can recover it by calculating the minimum phase equivalent of the power spectrum we just found. The reflectivity may be recovered by designing and applying a Wiener filter that shapes the estimated wavelet to a Dirac delta function (i.e., a spike). The result may be seen as a series of scaled, shifted delta functions (although this is not mathematically rigorous):

$$e(t) = \sum_{i=1}^{N} r_i \delta(t - \tau_i),$$

where N is the number of reflection events, $\tau_i \tau_i$ are the reflection times of each event, and r_i are the reflection coefficients.

In practice, since we are dealing with noisy, finite bandwidth, finite length, discretely sampled datasets, the above procedure only yields an approximation of the filter required to deconvolve the data. However, by formulating the problem as the solution of a Toeplitz matrix and using Levinson recursion, we can relatively quickly estimate a filter with the smallest mean squared error possible. We can also do deconvolution directly in the frequency domain and get similar results. The technique is closely related to linear prediction.

2. Field theory

NEWTONIAN POTENTIAL

the Newtonian potential or Newton potential is an operator in vector calculus that acts as the inverse to the negative Laplacian, on functions that are smooth and decay rapidly enough at infinity. As such, it is a fundamental object of study in potential theory. In its general nature, it is a singular integral operator, defined by convolution with a function having a mathematical singularity at the origin, the Newtonian kernel Γ which is the fundamental solution of the Laplace equation. It is named for Isaac Newton, who first discovered it and proved that it was a harmonic function in the special case of three variables, where it served as the fundamental gravitational potential in Newton's law of universal gravitation. In modern potential theory, the Newtonian potential is instead thought of as an electrostatic potential.

The Newtonian potential of a compactly supported integrable function f is defined as the convolution

$$u(x) = \Gamma * f(x) = \int_{R^d} \Gamma(x-y) f(y)\, dy$$

where the Newtonian kernel Γ in dimension d is defined by

$$\Gamma(x) = \begin{cases} \frac{1}{2}|x| & d = 1 \\ \frac{1}{2\pi}\log|x| & d = 2 \\ \frac{1}{d(2-)d\ \omega d}|x|^{2-d} & d > 2. \end{cases}$$

Here ω_d is the volume of the unit d-ball, and sometimes sign conventions may vary.

The Newtonian potential w of f is a solution of the Poisson equation

$$\Delta w = f,$$

which is to say that the operation of taking the Newtonian potential of a function is a partial inverse to the Laplace operator. The solution is not unique, since addition of any harmonic function to w will not affect the equation. This fact can be used to prove existence and uniqueness of solutions to the Dirichlet problem for the Poisson equation in suitably regular domains, and for suitably well-behaved functions f: one first applies a Newtonian potential to obtain a solution, and then adjusts by adding a harmonic function to get the correct boundary data.

The Newtonian potential is defined more broadly as the convolution

$$\Gamma * \mu(x) = \int_{R^d} \Gamma(x-y)\, d\mu(y)$$

when μ is a compactly supported Radon measure. It satisfies the Poisson equation

$$\Delta w = \mu$$

in the sense of distributions. Moreover, when the measure is positive, the Newtonian potential is subharmonic on R_d.

If f is a compactly supported continuous function (or, more generally, a finite measure) that is rotationally invariant, then the convolution of f with Γ satisfies for x outside the support of f

$$f * \Gamma(x) = \lambda\Gamma(x), \quad \lambda = \int_{\mathbb{R}^d} f(y)\,dy.$$

In dimension d = 3, this reduces to Newton's theorem that the potential energy of a small mass outside a much larger spherically symmetric mass distribution is the same as if all of the mass of the larger object were concentrated at its center.

When the measure μ is associated to a mass distribution on a sufficiently smooth hypersurface S (a Lyapunov surface of Hцlder class $C^{1,\alpha}$) that divides Rd into two regions D_+ and D_-, then the Newtonian potential of μ is referred to as a simple layer potential. Simple layer potentials are continuous and solve the Laplace equation except on S. They appear naturally in the study of electrostatics in the context of the electrostatic potential associated to a charge distribution on a closed surface. If $d\mu = f dH$ is the product of a continuous function on S with the (d –1)-dimensional Hausdorff measure, then at a point y of S, the normal derivative undergoes a jump discontinuity $f(y)$ when crossing the layer. Furthermore, the normal derivative is of w a well-defined continuous function on S. This makes simple layers particularly suited to the study of the Neumann problem for the Laplace equation.

LAPLACE EQUATIONS

Laplace's equation is a partial differential equation named after Pierre-Simon Laplace who first studied its properties. The solutions of Laplace's equation are important in many fields of science, notably the fields of electromagnetism, astronomy, and fluid dynamics, because they describe the behavior of electric, gravitational, and fluid potentials. The general theory of solutions to Laplace's equation is known as potential theory.

In three dimensions, the problem is to find twice-differentiable real-valued functions φ, of real variables x, y, and z, such that

$$\frac{\partial^2\varphi}{\partial x^2} + \frac{\partial^2\varphi}{\partial y^2} + \frac{\partial^2\varphi}{\partial z^2} = 0.$$

This is often written as $\nabla^2\varphi = 0$

or $\nabla\cdot\nabla\varphi = 0$,

where ∇ is the divergence, and is the gradient, or

where Δ is the Laplace operator.

Solutions of Laplace's equation are called harmonic functions.

If the right-hand side is specified as a given function, $f(x, y, z)$, i.e., if the whole equation is written as

$$\Delta\varphi = f$$

then it is called "Poisson's equation".

Laplace's equation and Poisson's equation are the simplest examples of elliptic partial differential equations. The partial differential operator, ∇^2 or Δ (which may be defined in any number of dimensions), is called the Laplace operator or just the Laplacian.

POISSON'S EQUATION

Poisson's equation is a partial differential equation with broad utility in electrostatics, mechanical engineering and theoretical physics. It is named after the French mathematician, geometer and physicist Simйon-Denis Poisson. The Poisson equation is

$$\Delta\varphi = f$$

where Δ is the Laplace operator, and f and φ are real or complex-valued functions on a manifold. When the manifold is Euclidean space, the Laplace operator is often denoted as ∇^2 and so Poisson's equation is frequently written as

$$\nabla^2\varphi = f.$$

In three-dimensional Cartesian coordinates, it takes the form

$$\left(\frac{\partial^2}{\partial x^2} + \frac{\partial^2}{\partial y^2} + \frac{\partial^2}{\partial z^2}\right)\varphi(x, y, z) = f(x, y, z).$$

For vanishing f, this equation becomes Laplace's equation

$$\Delta\varphi = 0.$$

The Poisson equation may be solved using a Green's function; a general exposition of the Green's function for the Poisson equation is given in the article on the screened Poisson equation.

GREEN'S THEOREM

Green's theorem gives the relationship between a line integral around a simple closed curve C and a double integral over the plane region D bounded by C. It is the two-dimensional special case of the more general Stokes' theorem, and is named after British mathematician George Green.

Let C be a positively oriented, piecewise smooth, simple closed curve in the plane R^2, and let D be the region bounded by C. If L and M are functions of (x, y) defined on an open region containing D and have continuous partial derivatives there, then

$$\oint_C (L\,dx + M\,dy) = \iint_D \left(\frac{\partial M}{\partial x} - \frac{\partial L}{\partial y} \right) dA.$$

For positive orientation, an arrow pointing in the counterclockwise direction may be drawn in the small circle in the integral symbol.

In physics, Green's theorem is mostly used to solve two-dimensional flow integrals, stating that the sum of fluid outflows at any point inside a volume is equal to the total outflow summed about an enclosing area.

GAUSS'S LAW

Gauss's law, also known as Gauss's flux theorem, is a law relating the distribution of electric charge to the resulting electric field. Gauss's law states that:

The electric flux through any closed surface is proportional to the enclosed electric charge.

The law was formulated by Carl Friedrich Gauss in 1835, but was not published until 1867. It is one of the four Maxwell's equations, which form the basis of classical electrodynamics. Gauss's law can be used to derive Coulomb's law, and vice versa.

Gauss's law may be expressed in its integral form:

$$\oint_S E \cdot dA = \frac{Q}{\varepsilon_0},$$

where the left-hand side of the equation is a surface integral denoting the electric flux through a closed surface S, and the right-hand side of the equation is the total charge enclosed by S divided by the electric constant.

Gauss's law also has a differential form:

$$\nabla \cdot E = \frac{\rho}{\varepsilon_0}$$

where is the divergence of the electric field, and ρ is the charge density.

The integral and differential forms are related by the divergence theorem, also called Gauss's theorem. Each of these forms can also be expressed two ways: In terms of a relation between the electric field E and the total electric charge, or in terms of the electric displacement field D and the free electric charge.

Gauss's law has a close mathematical similarity with a number of laws in other areas of physics, such as Gauss's law for magnetism and Gauss's law for gravity. In fact, any "inverse-square law" can be formulated in a way similar to Gauss's law: For example, Gauss's law itself is essentially equivalent to the inverse-square Coulomb's law, and Gauss's law for gravity is essentially equivalent to the inverse-square Newton's law of gravity.

Gauss's law can be used to demonstrate that there is no electric field inside a Faraday cage with no electric charges. Gauss's law is something of an electrical analogue of Ampиre's law, which deals with magnetism.

MAXWELL'S EQUATIONS AND ELECTROMAGNETIC THEORY

Maxwell's equations are a set of four partial differential equations that relate the electric and magnetic fields to their sources, charge density and current density. These equations can be combined to show that light is an electromagnetic wave. Individually, the equations are known as Gauss's law, Gauss's law for magnetism, Faraday's law of induction, and Ampиre's law with Maxwell's correction. The set of equations is named after James Clerk Maxwell.

These four equations, together with the Lorentz force law are the complete set of laws of classical electromagnetism. The Lorentz force law itself was actually derived by Maxwell under the name of Equation for Electromotive Force and was one of an earlier set of eight equations by Maxwell.

MAXWELL'S A DYNAMICAL THEORY OF THE ELECTROMAGNETIC FIELD

In 1864 Maxwell published A Dynamical Theory of the Electromagnetic Field in which he showed that light was an electromagnetic phenomenon. Confusion over the term "Maxwell's equations" is exacerbated because it is also sometimes used for a set of eight equations that appeared in Part III of Maxwell's 1864 paper A Dynamical Theory of the Electromagnetic Field, entitled "General Equations of the Electromagnetic Field,"a confusion compounded by the writing of six of those eight equations as three separate equations (one for each of the Cartesian axes), resulting in twenty equations and twenty unknowns. (As noted above, this terminology is not common: Modern references to the term "Maxwell's equations" refer to the Heaviside restatements.)

The eight original Maxwell's equations can be written in modern vector notation as follows:

(A) The law of total currents

$$J_{tot} = J + \frac{\partial D}{\partial t}$$

(B) The equation of magnetic force

$$\mu H = \nabla \times A$$

(C) Ampere's circuital law

$$\nabla \times H = J_{tot}$$

(D) Electromotive force created by convection, induction, and by static electricity. (This is in effect the Lorentz force)

$$E = \mu v \times H - \frac{\partial A}{\partial t} - \nabla \phi$$

(E) The electric elasticity equation

$$E = \frac{1}{\epsilon} D$$

(F) Ohm's law

$$E = \frac{1}{\sigma} J$$

(G) Gauss's law

$$\nabla \cdot D = \rho$$

(H) Equation of continuity

$$\nabla \cdot J = -\frac{\partial \rho}{\partial t}$$

or

$$\nabla \cdot J_{tot} = 0$$

Notation

H is the magnetizing field, which Maxwell called the magnetic intensity.

J is the electric current density (with J_{tot} being the total current including displacement current).

D is the displacement field (called the electric displacement by Maxwell).

ρ is the free charge density (called the quantity of free electricity by Maxwell).

A is the magnetic vector potential (called the angular impulse by Maxwell).

E is called the electromotive force by Maxwell. The term electromotive force is nowadays used for voltage, but it is clear from the context that Maxwell's meaning corresponded more to the modern term electric field.

ϕ is the electric potential (which Maxwell also called electric potential).

σ is the electrical conductivity (Maxwell called the inverse of conductivity the specific resistance, what is now called the resistivity).

When Maxwell derives the electromagnetic wave equation in his 1865 paper, he uses equation D to cater for electromagnetic induction rather than Faraday's law of induction which is used in modern textbooks. (Faraday's law itself does not appear among his equations.) However, Maxwell drops the $\mu v \times H$ term from equation D when he is deriving the electromagnetic wave equation, as he considers the situation only from the rest frame.

SEISMIC WAVE PROPAGATION

Seismic waves are waves of force that travel through the Earth or other elastic bodies, for example as a result of an earthquake, explosion, or some other process that imparts forces. Seismic waves are studied by seismologists, and measured by a seismograph, which records the output of a seismometer, or geophone.

The propagation velocity of the waves depends on density and elasticity of the medium which is penetrated. The velocities range from approximately 3-8 km/s in the Earth's crust up to 13 km/s in the deep mantle.

TYPES OF SEISMIC WAVES

There are two types of seismic waves, body waves and surface waves. Other modes of wave propagation exist than those described in this article, but they are of comparatively minor importance.

P-waves

P-waves (primary waves) are longitudinal or compressional waves. In solids, these waves generally travel almost twice as fast as S-waves and can travel through any type of material. In air, these pressure waves take the form of sound waves, hence they travel at the speed of sound. Typical speeds are 330 m/s in air, 1450 m/s in water and about 5000 m/s in granite.

S-waves

S waves (secondary waves) are transverse or shear waves, which means that the ground is displaced perpendicularly to the direction of propagation. In the case of horizontally polarized S waves, the ground moves alternately to one side and then the other. S waves can travel only through solids, as fluids (liquids and gases) do not support shear stresses. Their speed is about 60% of that of P waves in a given material. S waves arrive second in a seismic station because of their slower speed.

Body waves

Body waves travel through the interior of the Earth. They follow raypaths refracted by the varying density and modulus (stiffness) of the Earth's interior. The density and modulus, in turn, vary according to temperature, composition, and phase. This effect is similar to the refraction of light waves.

Surface waves

Surface waves are analogous to water waves and travel along the Earth's surface. They travel slower than body waves. Because of their low frequency, long duration, and large amplitude, they can be the most destructive type of seismic wave. There are two types of surface waves: Rayleigh waves and Love waves.

Rayleigh waves

Rayleigh waves, also called ground roll, are surface waves that travel as ripples with motions that are similar to those of waves on the surface of water (note, however, that the associated particle motion at shallow depths is retrograde, and that the restoring force in Rayleigh and in other seismic waves is elastic, not gravitational as for water waves). The existence of these waves was predicted by John William Strutt, Lord Rayleigh, in 1885. They are slower than body waves, roughly 90% of the velocity of S waves for typical homogeneous elastic media.

Love Waves

Love waves are surface waves that cause horizontal shearing of the ground. They are named after A.E.H. Love, a British mathematician who created a mathematical model of the waves in 1911. They usually travel slightly faster than Rayleigh waves, about 90% of the S wave velocity. They are the slowest and have the largest amplitude.

P and S waves in Earth's mantle and core

When an earthquake occurs, seismographs near the epicenter, out to about 90 km distance are able to record both P and S waves, but those at a greater distance no longer detect the high frequencies of the first S wave. Since shear waves cannot pass through liquids, this phenomenon was original evidence for the now well-established observation that the Earth has a liquid outer core, as demonstrated by Richard Dixon Oldham. This kind of observation has also been used to argue, by seismic testing, that the Moon has a solid core, although recent geodetic studies suggest the core is still molten.

3. Numerical analysis and inversion

NUMERICAL DIFFERENTIATION

Numerical differentiation is required when functions is given in data form as

x	x_o	x_1	x_2	x_3	...	x_n
$f(x)$	f_0	f_1	f_2	f_3	...	f_n

Simple formulas of first order and second order derivatives are also required for solving partial differential equation later in the course. Some of formulas can be derived easily Taylorl's series of a real function $f(x)$ of single variable x, is

$$f(x+h) = f(x) + h\ f'(x) + \frac{h^2}{2!} hf''(x) + ...$$

Where $f(x)$ and its all derivatives are continuous in the nbd of x.

Now suppose derivative is required at xi, when values of x are given with spacing h.

$$f(x_i+h) = f(x_i) + h\ f'(x_i) + \frac{h^2}{2} f''(x_i) + ...$$

$$\therefore f'(x_i) = \frac{f(x_i+h) - f(x_i)}{h}$$ by neglecting higher order terms of h.

$$f_i' = \frac{f_{i+1} - f_i}{h}$$

Similarly

$$f(x_i - h) = f(x_i) - hf'(x_i) + \frac{h^2}{2} f''(x_i)...$$

$$\therefore \quad f'(x_i) = \frac{f(x_i) - f(x_i - h)}{h},$$

be neglecting higher order terms.

$$f_i' = \frac{f_i - f_{i+1}}{h}$$

$$\therefore \quad f'(x_i) = \frac{f(x_i+h) - f(x_i - h)}{2h}$$

$$f_i' = \frac{f_{i+1} - f_{i-1}}{2h}$$

$$f(x_i + h) = f(x_i) + hf'(x_i) + \frac{h^2}{2} f''(x_i) + ...$$

Adding

$$f(x_i - h) = f(x_i) - hf'(x_i) + \frac{h^2}{2} f''(x_i)...$$

and we will get

$$f(x_i+h) + f(x_i - h) = 2f(x_i) + h^2 f''(x_i) + ...$$

$$\therefore \quad f''(x_i) = \frac{f(x_i+h) - 2f(x_i) + f(x_i - h)}{h^2}$$

$$f_i' = \frac{f_{i+1} - 2\ f_i + f_{i-1}}{h^2}$$

be neglecting h^3 and higher order terms.

If we want to use more data values to find the derivative of a function at a point, then we can use

$$f(x) \simeq p_n(x), \qquad x = x_0 + sh., \qquad \frac{ds}{dx} = \frac{1}{h}$$

$$p_n(x) = f_0 + \binom{s}{1}\Delta f_0 + \binom{s}{2} ?^2 f_0 + ... + \binom{s}{n} ?^n f_0$$

$$\frac{df}{dx} \simeq \frac{dp_n}{ds}\frac{ds}{dx} = \frac{1}{h}\left[\frac{dp_n}{ds}\right]$$

NUMERICAL INTEGRATION

Numerical integration is needed to evaluate the integral of a function given in data form as

x	x_0	x_1	x_2	...	x_n
Value of $f = f(x)$	f_0	f_1	f_2	...	f_n

or $\int_0^1 \frac{e^x \sin x}{1+x^2} dx$, which can not be evaluated by other methods.

Basis of numerical integration of $\int_0^1 f(x)dx$ is to replace the function $f(x)$ by a polynomial $p(x) = a_0 + a_1 x^2 + ... + a_n x^n$, which satisfies the conditions $f(x_i) = p(x_i), i = 0,1,2,...n$. This polynomial is known as interpolating polynomial.

Interpolation

A polynomial xp is said to interpolate $f(x)$ at $x_0, x_1 ... x_n, (n+1)$ distinct points if $p(x_i) = f(x_i)$ for $i = 0,1,2...n$. It is shown that for given such data, there exists unique polymenial of degree $\leq n$. The value of $f(x_i)$ is denoted by f_i.

Suppose the function is given in data form as

x	x_0	x_1	x_2	x_3	...	x_n
$f(x)$	f_0	f_1	f_2	f_3	...	f_n

Let $p(x) = a_0 + a_1 x + a_2 x^2 + ... + a_n x^n$ be such a polynomial. To satisfy the above data, we must have $a_0 + a_1 x_i + a_2 x_i^2 + ... + a_n x_i^n = p(x_i) = f_i \; i = 0,1,2...n. \; (n+1)$ conditions. These are $(n + 1)$ linear equations in $a_0, a_1 ... a_n, (n+1)$ unknowns. These equations can be solved. The solution of these equations exists and it is unique for $x_0, x_1 ... x_n$ distinct values.

Solving these equations enhance too much work, therefore there are some other techniques to get the same polynomial. Depending on the techniques used, forms of the interpolating polynomial are different and known accordingly as Langrangian, Newton's devided difference, Newtons forward difference form and so on.

Methods of numerical integration can be classified in two types. First type known as Newton cote's formulas are derived when abscissas are already fixed for interpolating polynomial. Second type of formulas is known as Gaussian Quadrature for deriving these formulas abscissas are not preassigned for the polynomial, but are chosen to increase accuracy by using lower degree polynomial, which is generally nearly half of degree as of that used in Newton Cotes.

NEWTON COTE'S FORMULAS

To evaluate the integral $\int f(x)\, d(x) f(x)$ is replaced by an interpolating polynomial, which interpolates $f(x)$ at some points $x_0 x_1 ... x_n$ spread over the interval $[a, b]$ In many case $x_0 = a$ and $x_n = b$.

The general principle of numerical integration of $\int f(x) d(x)$, is

$$= \int [f_0 l_0(x) + f_1 l_1(x) + ... + f_n l_n(x)] dx$$

$$= f_0 A_0 + f_1 A_1 + ... + f_n A_n.$$

Where $\{l_i(x)\}_{i=0}^n$ are Lagrangian polynomials, for the points $x_0, x_1 ... x_n$ and $A_i = \int l_i(x)dx, \; i = 0,1,2...n.$ are called weights.

Error in integration $E(I) = \int E(x)dx,$

Where $E(x) = f(x) - p_n(x)$, error in interpolation.

FINITE ELEMENT TECHNIQUES

The finite element method (FEM) (its practical application often known as finite element analysis (FEA)) is a numerical technique for finding approximate solutions of partial differential equations (PDE) as well as of integral equations.

In solving partial differential equations, the primary challenge is to create an equation that approximates the equation to be studied, but is numerically stable, meaning that errors in the input data and intermediate calculations do not accumulate and cause the resulting output to be meaningless. There are many ways of doing this, all with advantages and disadvantages. The Finite Element Method is a good choice for solving partial differential equations over complicated domains (like cars and oil pipelines), when the domain changes (as during a solid state reaction with a moving boundary), when the desired precision varies over the entire domain, or when the solution lacks smoothness. For instance, in a frontal crash simulation it is possible to increase prediction accuracy in "important" areas like the front of the car and reduce it in its rear (thus reducing cost of the simulation); Another example would be the simulation of the weather pattern on Earth, where it is more important to have accurate predictions over land than over the wide-open sea.

TYPES OF FINITE ELEMENT METHODS

Generalized finite element method

The Generalized Finite Element Method (FEM) uses local spaces consisting of functions, not necessarily polynomials, that reflect the available information on the unknown solution and thus ensure good local approximation. Then a partition of unity is used to "bond" these spaces together to form the approximating subspace. The effectiveness of GFEM has been shown when applied to problems with domains having complicated boundaries, problems with micro-scales, and problems with boundary layers.

hp-FEM

The hp-FEM combines adaptively elements with variable size h and polynomial degree p in order to achieve exceptionally fast, exponential convergence rates

Application

Variety of specializations under the umbrella of the mechanical engineering discipline (such as aeronautical, biomechanical, and automotive industries) commonly use integrated FEM in design and development of their products. Several modern FEM packages include specific components such as thermal, electromagnetic, fluid, and structural working environments. In a structural simulation, FEM helps tremendously in producing stiffness and strength visualizations and also in minimizing weight, materials, and costs.

FEM allows detailed visualization of where structures bend or twist, and indicates the distribution of stresses and displacements. FEM software provides a wide range of simulation options for controlling the complexity of both modeling and analysis of a system. Similarly, the desired level of accuracy required and associated computational time requirements can be managed simultaneously to address most engineering applications. FEM allows entire designs to be constructed, refined, and optimized before the design is manufactured.

This powerful design tool has significantly improved both the standard of engineering designs and the methodology of the design process in many industrial applications. The introduction of FEM has substantially decreased the time to take products from concept to the production line. It is primarily through improved initial prototype designs using FEM that testing and development have been accelerated. In summary, benefits of FEM include increased accuracy, enhanced design and better insight into critical design parameters, virtual prototyping, fewer hardware prototypes, a faster and less expensive design cycle, increased productivity, and increased revenue

FINITE DIFFERENCE TECHNIQUES

Finite-difference methods are numerical methods for approximating the solutions to differential equations using finite difference equations to approximate derivatives.

Finite-difference methods approximate the solutions to differential equations by replacing derivative expressions with approximately equivalent difference quotients. That is, because the first derivative of a function f is, by definition,

$$f'(a) = \lim_{h\to 0} \frac{f(a+h)-f(a)}{h},$$

then a reasonable approximation for that derivative would be to take

$$f'(a) \approx \frac{f(a+h)-f(a)}{h}$$

for some small value of h. In fact, this is the forward difference equation for the first derivative. Using this and similar formulae to replace derivative expressions in differential equations, one can approximate their solutions without the need for calculus.

SIMPSON'S RULE

In numerical analysis, Simpson's rule is a method for numerical integration, the numerical approximation of definite integrals. Specifically, it is the following approximation:

$$\int_a^b f(x)dx \approx \frac{b-a}{6}\left[f(a)+4f\left(\frac{a+b}{2}\right)+f(b)\right].$$

Simpson's rule can be derived in various ways.

QUADRATIC INTERPOLATION

One derivation replaces the integrand $f(x)$ by the quadratic polynomial $P(x)$ which takes the same values as $f(x)$ at the end points a and b and the midpoint m = (a+b)/2. One can use Lagrange polynomial interpolation to find an expression for this polynomial,

$$P(x)=f(a)\frac{(x-m)(x-b)}{(a-m)(a-b)}+f(m)\frac{(x-a)(x-b)}{(m-a)(m-b)}+f(b)\frac{(x-a)(x-m)}{(b-a)(b-m)}.$$

An easy (albeit tedious) calculation shows that

$$\int_a^b P(x)dx=\frac{b-a}{6}\left[f(a)+4f\left(\frac{a+b}{2}\right)+f(b)\right].$$

This calculation can be carried out more easily if one first observes that (by scaling) there is no loss of generality in assuming that a = –1 and b = 1.

Averaging the midpoint and the trapezoidal rules

Another derivation constructs Simpson's rule from two simpler approximations: the midpoint rule

$$M=(b-a)f\left(\frac{a+b}{2}\right)$$

and the trapezoidal rule

$$T=\frac{1}{2}(b-a)(f(a)+f(b)).$$

The errors in these approximations are

$\frac{1}{24}(b-a)^3 f''(a)+O((b-a)^4)$ and

$-\frac{1}{12}(b-a)^3 f''(a)+O((b-a)^4)$, respectively. It follows that the leading error term vanishes if we take the weighted average

$$\frac{2M+T}{3}.$$

This weighted average is exactly Simpson's rule.

Using another approximation (for example, the trapezoidal rule with twice as many points), it is possible to take a suitable weighted average and eliminate another error term. This is Romberg's method.

UNDETERMINED COEFFICIENTS

The third derivation starts from the ansatz

$$\frac{1}{b-a}\int_a^b f(x)dx \approx \alpha f(a)+\beta f\left(\frac{a+b}{2}\right)+\gamma f(b).$$

The coefficients α, β and γ can be fixed by requiring that this approximation be exact for all quadratic polynomials. This yields Simpson's rule.

GAUSSIAN QUADRATURE FORMULA

In numerical analysis, a quadrature rule is an approximation of the definite integral of a function, usually stated as a weighted sum of function values at specified points within the domain of integration. (See numerical integration for more on quadrature rules.) An n-point Gaussian quadrature rule, named after Carl Friedrich Gauss, is a quadrature rule constructed to yield an exact result for polynomials of degree 2n –1 or less by a suitable choice of the points xi and weights w_i for i = 1,...,n. The domain of integration for such a rule is conventionally taken as [–1, 1], so the rule is stated as

$$\int_{-1}^1 f(x)dx \approx \sum_{i=1}^n w_i f(x_i).$$

Gaussian quadrature as above will only produce accurate results if the function $f(x)$ is well approximated by a polynomial function within the range [-1,1]. The method is not, for example, suitable for functions with singularities.

Common weighting functions include $W(x)=(1-x^2)^{-1/2}$ (Gauss-Chebyshev) and $W(x)=e^{-x^2}$ (Gauss-Hermite).

FUNDAMENTAL THEOREM

Let p_n be a nontrivial polynomial of degree n such that

$$\int_a^b w(x)x^k p_n(x)\,dx = 0, \quad \text{for all } k=0,1,\dots,n-1.$$

If we pick the n nodes xi to be the zeros of pn, then there exist n weights wi which make the Gauss-quadrature computed integral exact for all polynomials h(x) of degree 2n -1 or less. Furthermore, all these nodes x_i will lie in the open interval (a, b).

The polynomial p_n is said to be an orthogonal polynomial of degree n associated to the weight function ω(x) It is unique up to a constant normalization factor. The idea underlying the proof is that, because of its sufficiently low degree, h(x) can be divided by $p_n(x)$ to produce quotient q(x) and remainder r(x), both latter polynomials which will have degree strictly lower than n, so that both will be orthogonal to $p_n(x)$, by the defining property of $p_n(x)$. Thus

$$\int_a^b \omega_i h(x_i) = \sum_{i=1}^{n} \omega_i r(x_i).$$

Because of the choice of nodes x_i, the corresponding relation

$$\sum_{i=1}^{n} \omega_i h(x_i) = \sum_{i=1}^{n} \omega_i r(x_i)$$

holds also. The exactness of the computed integral for h(x) then follows from corresponding exactness for polynomials of degree only n or less (as is r(x)). This (superficially less exacting) requirement can now be satisfied by choosing the weights w_i equal to the integrals (using same weight function $l_i(x)$ of the Lagrange basis polynomials of these particular n nodes x_i.

INITIAL VALUE PROBLEM

In the field of differential equations, an initial value problem is an ordinary differential equation together with specified value, called the initial condition, of the unknown function at a given point in the domain of the solution. In physics or other sciences, modeling a system frequently amounts to solving an initial value problem; in this context, the differential equation is an evolution equation specifying how, given initial conditions, the system will evolve with time.

An initial value problem is a differential equation

$y'(t)=f(t,y(t))$ with $f:\mathbb{R}\times\mathbb{R}\to\mathbb{R}$

together with a point in the domain of f

$(t_0, y_0)\in\mathbb{R}\times\mathbb{R}$, called the initial condition.

A solution to an initial value problem is a function y that is a solution to the differential equation and satisfies

$$y(t_0)=y_0.$$

This statement subsumes problems of higher order, by interpreting y as a vector. For derivatives of second or higher order, new variables (elements of the vector y) are introduced.

More generally, the unknown function y can take values on infinite dimensional spaces, such as Banach spaces or spaces of distributions.

A simple example is to solve $y'=0.85y$ and $y(0)=19$. We are trying to find a formula for y(t) that satisfies these two equations.

Start by noting that $y'=\frac{dy}{dt}$, so $\frac{dy}{dt}=0.85y$

Now rearrange the equation so that y is on the left and t on the right

$$\frac{dy}{y}=0.85dt$$

Now integrate both sides (this introduces an unknown constant B).

$$\ln|y|=0.85t+B$$

Eliminate the ln

$$|y|=e^{B}e^{0.85t}$$

Let C be a new unknown constant, $C = \pm e^{B}$, so $y = Ce^{0.85t}$

Now we need to find a value for C. Use $y(0) = 19$ as given at the start and substitute 0 for t and 19 for y

$19 = Ce^{0.85*0}$

C = 19

this gives the final solution of $y(t) = 19e^{0.85t}$.

WELL-POSED PROBLEM

The mathematical term well-posed problem stems from a definition given by Jacques Hadamard. He believed that mathematical models of physical phenomena should have the properties that

1. A solution exists
2. The solution is unique
3. The solution depends continuously on the data, in some reasonable topology.

Examples of archetypal well-posed problems include the Dirichlet problem for Laplace's equation, and the heat equation with specified initial conditions. These might be regarded as 'natural' problems in that there are physical processes that solve these problems. By contrast the inverse heat equation, deducing a previous distribution of temperature from final data is not well-posed in that the solution is highly sensitive to changes in the final data. Problems that are not well-posed in the sense of Hadamard are termed ill-posed. Inverse problems are often ill-posed.

Such continuum problems must often be discretized in order to obtain a numerical solution. While in terms of functional analysis such problems are typically continuous, they may suffer from numerical instability when solved with finite precision, or with errors in the data. Even if a problem is well-posed, it may still be ill-conditioned, meaning that a small error in the initial data can result in much larger errors in the answers. An ill-conditioned problem is indicated by a large condition number.

If the problem is well-posed, then it stands a good chance of solution on a computer using a stable algorithm. If it is not well-posed, it needs to be re-formulated for numerical treatment. Typically this involves including additional assumptions, such as smoothness of solution. This process is known as regularization and Tikhonov regularization is one of the most commonly used for regularization of linear ill-posed problems.

METHOD OF LEAST SQUARES

The method of least squares is a standard approach to the approximate solution of overdetermined systems, i.e. sets of equations in which there are more equations than unknowns. "Least squares" means that the overall solution minimizes the sum of the squares of the errors made in solving every single equation.

The most important application is in data fitting. The best fit in the least-squares sense minimizes the sum of squared residuals, a residual being the difference between an observed value and the value provided by a model.

Least squares problems fall into two categories, linear least squares and nonlinear least squares, depending on whether or not the residuals are linear in all unknowns. The linear least-squares problem occurs in statistical regression analysis; it has a closed form solution. The non-linear problem has no closed solution and is usually solved by iterative refinement; at each iteration the system is approximated by a linear one, thus the core calculation is similar in both cases.

The least-squares method was first described by Carl Friedrich Gauss around 1794. Least squares corresponds to the maximum likelihood criterion if the experimental errors have a normal distribution and can also be derived as a method of moments estimator.

The following discussion is mostly presented in terms of linear functions but the use of least-squares is valid and practical for more general families of functions. For example, the Fourier series approximation of degree n is optimal in the least-squares sense, amongst all approximations in terms of trigonometric polynomials of degree n. Also, by iteratively applying local quadratic approximation to the likelihood (through the Fisher information), the least-squares method may be used to fit a generalized linear model.

METHOD OF LEAST SQUARES

The method of least squares assumes that the best-fit curve of a given type is the curve that has the minimal sum of the deviations squared (least square error) from a given set of data.

Suppose that the data points are $(x_1, y_1), (x_2, y_2)$, ..., (x_n, y_n) where x is the independent variable and y is the dependent variable. The fitting curve $f(x)$ has the deviation (error) d from each data point, i.e., $d_1 = y_1 - f(x_1), d_2 = y_2 - f(x_2), ..., d_n = y_n - f(x_n)$. According to the method of least squares, the best fitting curve has the property that:

$$\Pi = d_1^2 + d_2^2 + ... + d_n^2 = \sum_{i=1}^{n} d_i^2 = \sum_{i=1}^{n} [y_i - f(x_i)]^2 = \text{a minimum}$$

Solving the least squares problem

The minimum of the sum of squares is found by setting the gradient to zero. Since the model contains m parameters there are m gradient equations.

$$\frac{\partial S}{\partial \beta_j} = 2\sum_i r_i \frac{\partial r_i}{\partial \beta_j} = 0, \; j = 1, ..., m$$

and since $r_i = y_i - f(x_i, \beta)$ the gradient equations become

$$-2\sum_i \frac{\partial f(x_i, \beta)}{\partial \beta_j} r_i = 0, \; j = 1, ..., m$$

The gradient equations apply to all least squares problems. Each particular problem requires particular expressions for the model and its partial derivatives.

Linear least squares

A regression model is a linear one when the model comprises a linear combination of the parameters, i.e.

$$f(x_i, \beta) = \sum_{j=1}^{m} \beta_j \phi_j(x_i)$$

where the coefficients, φ_j, are functions of x_i. Letting

$$X_{ij} = \frac{\partial f(x_i, \beta)}{\partial \beta_j} = \phi_j(x_i).$$

we can then see that in that case the least square estimate (or estimator, in the context of a random sample), β is given by

$$\hat{\beta} = (X^T X)^{-1} X^T y$$

SINGULAR VALUE DECOMPOSITION

In linear algebra, the singular value decomposition (SVD) is an important factorization of a rectangular real or complex matrix, with many applications in signal processing and statistics. Applications which employ the SVD include computing the pseudoinverse, least squares fitting of data, matrix approximation, and determining the rank, range and null space of a matrix.

APPLICATIONS OF THE SINGULAR VALUE DECOMPOSITION

Pseudoinverse

The singular value decomposition can be used for computing the pseudoinverse of a matrix. Indeed, the pseudoinverse of the matrix M with singular value decomposition $M = U \Sigma V^*$ is

$$M^+ = V \Sigma^+ U^*,$$

where Σ^+ is the pseudoinverse of Σ, which is formed by replacing every nonzero entry by its reciprocal and transposing the resulting matrix. The pseudoinverse is one way to solve linear least squares problems.

Solving homogeneous linear equations

A set of homogeneous linear equations can be written as Ax = 0 for a matrix A and vector x. A typical situation is that A is known and a non-zero x is to be determined which satisfies the equation. Such an x belongs to A's null space and is sometimes called a (right) null vector of A. x can be characterized as a right singular vector corresponding to a singular value of A that is zero. This observation means that if A is a square matrix and has no vanishing singular value the equation has no non-zero x as a solution. It also means that if there are several vanishing singular values, any linear combination of the corresponding right singular vectors is a valid solution. Analogously to the definition of a (right) null vector, a non-zero x satisfying x*A = 0, with x* denoting the conjugate transpose of x, is called a left null vector of A.

Total least squares minimization

A total least squares problem refers to determining the vector x which minimizes the 2-norm of a vector Ax under the constraint $\|x\| = 1$. The solution turns out to be the right singular vector of A corresponding to the smallest singular value.

Range, null space and rank

Another application of the SVD is that it provides an explicit representation of the range and null space of a matrix M. The right singular vectors corresponding to vanishing singular values of M span the null space of M. E.g., the null space is spanned by the last two columns of V in the above example. The left singular vectors corresponding to the non-zero singular values of M span the range of M. As a consequence, the rank of M equals the number of non-zero singular values which is the same as the number of non-zero elements in Σ.

In numerical linear algebra the singular values can be used to determine the effective rank of a matrix, as rounding error may lead to small but non-zero singular values in a rank deficient matrix.

Matrix approximation

Some practical applications need to solve the problem of approximating a matrix M with another matrix $\tilde{M}$ which has a specific rank r. In the case that the approximation is based on minimizing the Frobenius norm of the difference between M and $\tilde{M}$ under the constraint that $\text{rank}\,(\tilde{M}) = r$ it turns out that the solution is given by the SVD of M, namely

$$\tilde{M} = U\tilde{\Sigma}V^*$$

where $\tilde{\Sigma}$ is the same matrix as Σ except that it contains only the r largest singular values (the other singular values are replaced by zero). This is known as the Eckart-Young theorem, as it was proved by those two authors in 1936.

Quick proof: We hope to minimize $\|M - \tilde{M}\|_F$ subject to $\text{rank}\,(\tilde{M}) = r$.

Suppose the SVD of $M = U\Sigma V^*$. Since the Frobenius norm is unitarily invariant, we have an equivalent statement:

$$\min_{\tilde{M}} \left\| \Sigma - U^* M V \right\|_F.$$

Note that since Σ is diagonal, $U^*\tilde{M}V$ should be diagonal in order to minimize the Frobenius norm. Remember that the Frobenius norm is the square-root of the summation of the squared modulus of all entries. This implies that U and V are also singular matrices of $\tilde{M}$. Thus we can assume that $\tilde{M}$ to minimize the above statement has the form:

$$\tilde{M} = USV^*,$$

where S is diagonal. The diagonal entries s_i of S are not necessarily ordered as in SVD.

$$\min_{\tilde{M}} \|\Sigma - S\|_F \equiv \min_{s_i} \sqrt{\sum_{i=1}^{n} (\sigma_i - s_i)^2}.$$

From the rank constraint, i.e. S has r non-zero diagonal entries, the minimum of the above statement is obtained as follows:

$$\min_{s_i} \sqrt{\sum_{i=1}^{n} (\sigma_i - s_i)^2 + \sum_{i=r+1}^{n} \sigma_i^2} = \sqrt{\sum_{i=r+1}^{n} \sigma_i^2}.$$

Therefore, $\tilde{M}$ of rank r is the best approximation of M in the Frobenius norm sense when $\sigma_i = s_i \;\; (i = 1, ..., r)$ and the corresponding singular vectors are same as those of M.

In addition to being the best approximation of a given rank to the matrix under the Frobenius norm, $\tilde{M}$ as defined above is also the best approximation of that rank under the L_2 norm (see e.g. Trefethen and Bau, Numerical Linear Algebra).

Another example of matrix approximation by SVD is the solution to the orthogonal Procrustes problem of approximating any given matrix by an orthogonal matrix.

Separable models

The SVD can be thought of as decomposing a matrix into a weighted, ordered sum of separable matrices. By separable, we mean that a matrix A can be written as an outer product of two vectors $A = u \otimes v$, or, in coordinates, $A(i, j) = u(i)v(j)$. Specifically, the matrix M can be decomposed as:

$$M = \sum_i A_i = \sum_i \sigma_i U_i \otimes V_i^t .$$

Here U_i and V_i are the ith columns of the corresponding SVD matrices, A_i are the ordered singular values, and each is separable. The SVD can be used to find the decomposition of an image processing filter into separable horizontal and vertical filters. Note that the number of non-zero σ_i is exactly the rank of the matrix.

Separable models often arise in biological systems, and the SVD decomposition is useful to analyze such systems. For example, some visual area V1 simple cells receptive fields can be well described$\sigma$by a Gabor filter in the space domain multiplied by a modulation function in the time domain. Thus, given a linear filter evaluated through, for example, reverse correlation, one can rearrange the two spatial dimensions into one dimension, thus yielding a two dimensional filter (space, time) which can be decomposed through SVD. The first column of U in the SVD decomposition is then a Gabor while the first column of V represents the time modulation (or vice-versa). One may then define an index of separability, $\alpha = \sigma_1^2 / \sum_i \sigma_i^2$, which is the fraction of the power in the matrix M which is accounted for by the first separable matrix in the decomposition.

Nearest orthonormal matrix

The orthonormal matrix "nearest" A in the least squares sense is the product UV *. This intuitively makes sense because an orthonormal matrix would have the decomposition UIV * where I is the identity matrix, so that if $A = U\Sigma V^*$ then the product A = UV * amounts to replacing the singular values with ones.

GLOBAL OPTIMIZATION

Global optimization is a branch of applied mathematics and numerical analysis that deals with the optimization of a function or a set of functions to some criteria.

The most common form is the minimization of one real-valued function f in the parameter-space $\vec{x} \in P$. There may be several constraints on the solution vectors $\vec{x}_{\text{min.}}$.

In real-life problems, functions of many variables have a large number of local minima and maxima. Finding an arbitrary local optimum is relatively straightforward by using local optimisation methods. Finding the global maximum or minimum of a function is much more challenging and has been practically impossible for many problems so far.

The maximization of a real-valued function g(x) can be regarded as the minimization of the transformed function $f(x) := (-1).g(x)$.

APPLICATIONS OF GLOBAL OPTIMIZATION

Typical examples of global optimization applications include:

- Protein structure prediction (minimize the energy/free energy function)
- Computational phylogenetics (e.g., minimize the number of character transformations in the tree)
- Traveling salesman problem and circuit design (minimize the path length)
- Chemical engineering (e.g., analyzing the Gibbs free energy)
- Safety verification, safety engineering (e.g., of mechanical structures, buildings)
- Worst case analysis
- Mathematical problems (e.g., the Kepler conjecture)
- The starting point of several molecular dynamics simulations consists of an initial optimization of the energy of the system to be simulated.
- Spin glasses
- Calibration of radio propagation models

4 Gravity and Magnetic fields of the earth

CLAIRAUT'S THEOREM

Clairaut's theorem, published in 1743 by Alexis Claude de Clairaut in his Théorie de la figure de la terre, tirée des principes de l'hydrostatique, synthesized physical and geodetic evidence that the Earth is an oblate rotational ellipsoid. It is a general mathematical law applying to spheroids of revolution. It was initially used to relate the gravity at any point on the Earth's surface to the position of that point, allowing the ellipticity of the Earth to be calculated from measurements of gravity at different latitudes.

Clairaut's formula for the acceleration of gravity g on the surface of a spheroid at latitude φ, was:

$$g = G\left[1 + \left(\frac{5}{2}m - f\right)\sin^2\phi\right],$$

where G is the value of the acceleration of gravity at the equator, m the ratio of the centrifugal force to gravity at the equator, and f the flattening of a meridian section of the earth, defined as:

$$f = \frac{a-b}{a},$$

where

a = semimajor axis,

b = semiminor axis .

Clairaut derived the formula under the assumption that the body was composed of concentric coaxial spheroidal layers of constant density. This work was subsequently pursued by Laplace, who relaxed the initial assumption that surfaces of equal density were spheroids. Stokes showed in 1849 that the theorem applied to any law of density so long as the external surface is a spheroid of equilibrium. A history of the subject, and more detailed equations for g can be found in Khan.

The above expression for g has been supplanted by the Somigliana equation:

$$g = G\left[\frac{1 + k\sin^2\phi}{\sqrt{1 - e^2\sin^2\phi}}\right],$$

where, for the Earth, G = 9.7803267714 ms^{-2}; k = 0.00193185138639; e^2 = 0.00669437999013.

SHAPE OF THE EARTH

In 1672 another French astronomer, Jean Richer, was sent by Louis XIV to make astronomical observations on the equatorial island of Cayenne. He found that an accurate pendulum clock, which had been adjusted in Paris precisely to beat seconds, was losing about two and a half minutes per day, i.e., its period was now too long. The error was much too large to be explained by inaccuracy of the precise instrument. The observation aroused much interest and speculation, but was only explained some 15 years later by Sir Isaac Newton in terms of his laws of universal gravitation and motion. Newton argued that the shape of the rotating Earth should be that of an oblate ellipsoid; compared to a sphere, it should be somewhat flattened at the poles and should bulge outward around the equator. This inference was made on logical grounds. Assume that the Earth does not rotate and that holes could be drilled to its center along the rotation axis and along an equatorial radius. If these holes are filled with water, the hydrostatic pressure at the center of the Earth sustains equal water columns along each radius. However, the rotation of the Earth causes a centrifugal force at the equator but has no effect on the axis of rotation. At the equator the outward centrifugal force of the rotation opposes the inward gravitational attraction and pulls the water column upward. At the same time it reduces the hydrostatic pressure produced by the water column at the Earth's center. The reduced central pressure is unable to support the height of the water column along the polar radius, which subsides. If the Earth were a hydro- static sphere, the form of the rotating Earth should be an oblate ellipsoid of revolution. Newton assumed the Earth's density to be constant and calculated that the flattening should be about 1:230 (roughly 0.5%). This is somewhat larger than the actual flattening of the Earth, which is about 1:298 (roughly 0.3%).

To determine whether the Earth's shape was oblate or prolate, the Académie Royale des Sciences sponsored two scientific expeditions. In 1736-1737 a team of scientists measured the length of a degree of meridian arc in Lapland, near the Arctic Circle. They found a length appreciably longer than the meridian degree measured by Picard near Paris. From 1735 to 1743 a second party of scientists measured the length of more than 3 degrees of meridian arc in Peru, near the equator. Their results showed that the equatorial degree of latitude was shorter than the meridian degree in Paris. Both parties confirmed convincingly the prediction of Newton that the Earth's shape is that of an oblate ellipsoid. The ellipsoidal shape of the Earth resulting from its rotation has important consequences, not only for the variation with latitude of gravity on the Earth's surface, but also for the Earth's rate of rotation and the orientation of its rotational axis. These are modified by torques that arise from the gravitational attractions of the Sun, Moon and planets on the ellipsoidal shape.

THE EARTH'S MAGNETIC FIELD AND PALEOMAGNETISM

The Earth has a magnetic field that causes a compass needle to always point toward the North magnetic pole, currently located near the rotation pole. The Earth's magnetic field is what would be expected if there were a large bar magnet located at the center of the Earth (we now know that this is not what causes the magnetic field, but the analogy is still good). The magnetic field is composed of lines of force as shown in the diagram here.

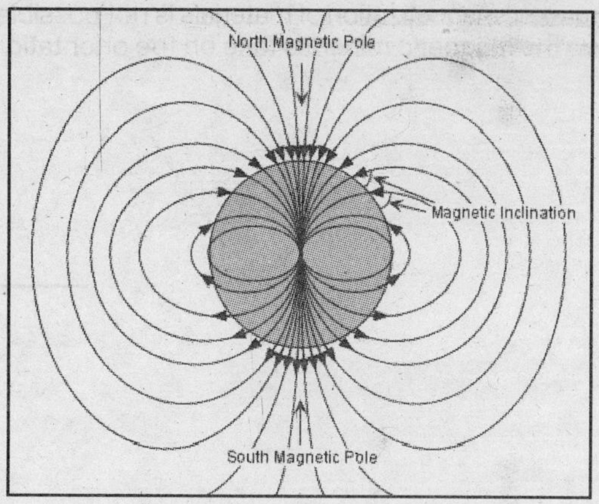

Diagram represnting Earth's magnetic lines of forces. The magnetic lines emerged from South magnetic pole and merge into North magnetic pole.

A compass needle or a magnetic weight suspended from a string, points along these lines of force. Note that the lines of force intersect the surface of the Earth at various angles that depend on position on the Earth's surface. This angle is called the magnetic inclination. The inclination is 0° at the magnetic equator and 90° at the magnetic poles. Thus, by measuring the inclination and the angle to the magnetic pole, one can tell position on the Earth relative to the magnetic poles.

In the 1950s it was discovered that when magnetic minerals cool below a temperature called the Curie Temperature, domains within the magnetic mineral take on an orientation parallel to any external magnetic field present at the time they cooled below this temperature.

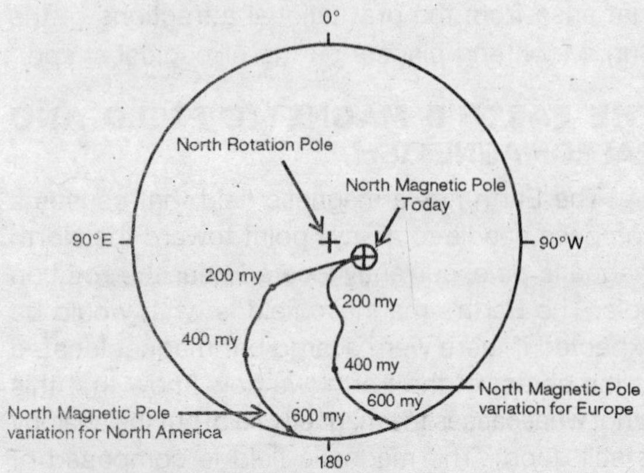

At temperatures above the Curie Temperature, permanent magnetization of materials is not possible. Since the magnetic minerals take on the orientation of the magnetic field present during cooling, we can determine the orientation of the magnetic field present at the time the rock containing the mineral cooled below the Curie Temperature, and thus, be able to determine the position of the magnetic pole at that time. This made possible the study of Paleomagnetism (the history of the Earth's magnetic field). Magnetite is the most common magnetic mineral in the Earth's crust and has a Curie Temperature of 580ºC.

Initial studies of the how the position of the Earth's magnetic pole varied with time were conducted in Europe. These studies showed that the magnetic pole had apparently moved through time. When similar measurements were made on rocks of various ages in North America, however, a different path of the magnetic pole was found.

5 Plate Tectonics and Geodynamics

VINE-MATHEWS HYPOTHESIS

The Morley-Vine-Matthews hypothesis, also known as the Vine-Matthews-Morley hypothesis was the first key scientific test of the seafloor spreading theory of continental drift.

Geophysicists Frederick John Vine and Lawrence W. Morley independently realized that if the seafloor spreading theory was correct, then the rocks surrounding the mid-oceanic ridges should show symmetric patterns of magnetization reversals, a record of the Earth's geomagnetic reversals, captured in the cooling volcanic rocks. Morley's letters to Nature and Journal of Geophysical Research were both rejected, so Vine and his adviser Drummond Hoyle Matthews were first to publish in 1963. Later geomagnetic surveys found the patterns are in fact present, providing strong confirmation of the theory.

Vine, Matthews, and Morely put this information together with the bands of magnetic stripes on the sea floor and postulated that the bands represents oppositely polarized rocks on either side of the oceanic ridges, and that new oceanic crust and lithosphere was created at the oceanic ridge by eruption and intrusion of magma. As this magma cooled it took on the magnetism of the magnetic field at the time. When the polarity of the field changed new crust and lithosphere created at the ridge would take on the different polarity. This hypothesis led to the theory of sea floor spreading.

MID-OCEANIC RIDGES

A mid-ocean ridge is an underwater mountain range, typically having a valley known as a rift running along its spine, formed by plate tectonics. This type of oceanic ridge is characteristic of what is known as an oceanic spreading center, which is responsible for seafloor spreading. The uplifted seafloor results from convection currents which rise in the mantle as magma at a linear weakness in the oceanic crust, and emerge as lava, creating new crust upon cooling. A mid-ocean ridge demarcates the boundary between two tectonic plates, and consequently is termed a divergent plate boundary.

The mid-ocean ridges of the world are connected and form a single global mid-oceanic ridge system that is part of every ocean, making the mid-oceanic ridge system the longest mountain range in the world.

Mid-ocean ridges are geologically active, with new magma constantly emerging onto the ocean floor and into the crust at and near rifts along the ridge axes. The crystallized magma forms new crust of basalt.

FORMATION PROCESSES OF MID-OCEAN RIDGES

There are two processes, ridge-push and slab-pull, thought to be responsible for the spreading seen at mid-ocean ridges, and there is some uncertainty as to which is dominant. Ridge-push occurs when the weight of the ridge pushes the rest of the tectonic plate away from the ridge, often towards a subduction zone. At the subduction zone, "slab-pull" comes into effect. This is simply the weight of the tectonic plate being subducted (pulled) below the overlying plate dragging the rest of the plate along behind it.

The other process proposed to contribute to the formation of new oceanic crust at mid-ocean ridges is the "mantle conveyor" (see image). However, there have been some studies which have shown that the upper mantle (asthenosphere) is too plastic (flexible) to generate enough friction to pull the tectonic plate along. Moreover, unlike in the image above, mantle upwelling that causes magma to form beneath the ocean ridges appears to involve only its upper 400 km (250 mi), as deduced from seismic tomography and from studies of the seismic discontinuity at about 400 kilometers. The relatively shallow depths from which the upwelling mantle rises below ridges are more consistent with the "slab-pull" process. On the other hand, some of the world's largest tectonic plates such as the North American Plate are in motion, yet are nowhere being subducted.

The rate at which the mid-ocean ridge creates new material is known as the spreading rate, and is generally measured in mm/yr. The common subdivisions of spreading rate are fast, medium and slow, whose values are generally >100 mm/yr, between 100 and 55 mm/yr and 55 to 20 mm/yr, respectively for full rates. The spreading rate of the north Atlantic Ocean is ~25 mm/yr, while in the Pacific region, it is 80-120 mm/yr. Ridges that spread at rates <20 mm/yr are referred to as ultraslow spreading ridges (e.g., the Gakkel ridge in the Arctic Ocean and the Southwest Indian Ridge) and they provide a much different perspective on crustal formation than their faster spreading brethren.

The mid-ocean ridge systems form new oceanic crust. As crystallized basalt extruded at a ridge axis cools below Curie points of appropriate iron-titanium oxides, magnetic field directions parallel to the Earth's magnetic field are recorded in those oxides. The orientations of the field in the oceanic crust record preserve a record of directions of the Earth's magnetic field with time. Because the field has reversed directions at irregular intervals throughout its history, the pattern of reversals in the ocean crust can be used as an indicator of age. Likewise, the pattern of reversals together with age measurements of the crust is used to help establish the history of the Earth's magnetic field.

Geodynamics is a subfield of geophysics dealing with dynamics of the Earth. Experts in geodynamics commonly use data from geodetic GPS, InSAR, and seismology, along with numerical models, to study the evolution of the Earth's lithosphere, mantle and core.

Work performed by geodynamicists may include:

- Modeling brittle and ductile deformation of geologic materials
- Predicting patterns of continental accretion and breakup of continents and supercontinents
- Observing surface deformation and relaxation due to ice sheets and post-glacial rebound, and making related conjectures about the viscosity of the mantle
- Finding and understanding the driving mechanisms behind plate tectonics.

PLATE TECTONICS

Plates are composed of lithosphere, about 100 km thick, that "float" on the ductile asthenosphere. While the continents do indeed appear to drift, they do so only because they are part of larger plates that float and move horizontally on the upper mantle asthenosphere. The plates behave as rigid bodies with some ability to flex, but deformation occurs mainly along the boundaries between plates.

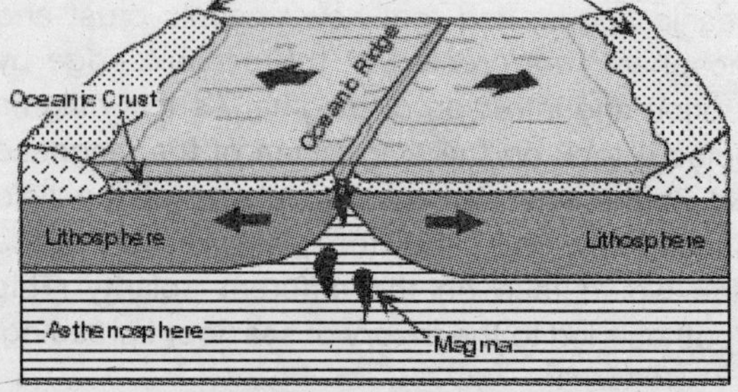

Diverging Plate Boundary
Oceanic Ridge - Spreading Center

TYPES OF PLATE BOUNDARIES

Divergent Plate Boundaries

These are oceanic ridges where new oceanic lithosphere is created by upwelling mantle that melts, resulting in basaltic magmas which intrude and erupt at the oceanic ridge to create new oceanic lithosphere and crust. As new oceanic lithosphere is created, it is pushed aside in opposite directions. Thus, the age of the oceanic crust becomes progressively older in both directions away from the ridge.

Because oceanic lithosphere may get subducted, the age of the ocean basins is relatively young. The oldest oceanic crust occurs farthest away from a ridge. In the Atlantic Ocean, the oldest oceanic crust occurs next to the North American and African continents and is about 180 million years old (Jurassic). In the Pacific Ocean, the oldest crust is also Jurassic in age, and occurs off the coast of Japan.

Because the oceanic ridges are areas of young crust, there is very little sediment accumulation on the ridges. Sediment thickness increases in both directions away of the ridge, and is thickest where the oceanic crust is the oldest.

Convergent Plate Boundaries

When a plate of dense oceanic lithosphere moving in one direction collides with a plate moving in the opposite direction, one of the plates subducts beneath the other. Where this occurs an oceanic trench forms on the sea floor and the sinking plate becomes a subduction zone. The Benioff zone identifies a subduction zone. The earthquakes may extend down to depths of 700 km before the subducting plate heats up and loses its ability to deform in a brittle fashion.

As the oceanic plate subducts, it begins to heat up and metamorphose. As it does so, dehydration reactions release water into the overlying mantle asthenosphere, causing a reduction in the melting temperature and the production of andesitic magmas. These magmas rise to the surface and create a volcanic arc parallel to the trench.

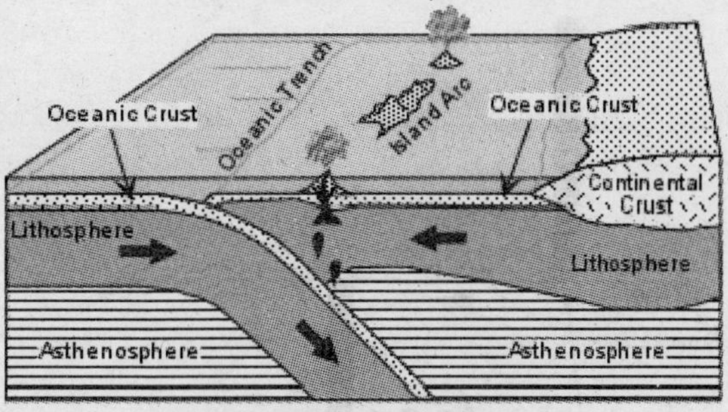

Ocean - Ocean Convergence

If the subduction occurs beneath oceanic lithosphere, an island arc is produced at the surface (such as the Japanese islands, the Aleutian Islands, the Philippine islands, or the Caribbean islands. If the subduction occurs beneath continental crust, a continental volcanic arc is produced (such as the Cascades of the western U.S., or the Andes mountains of the South America)

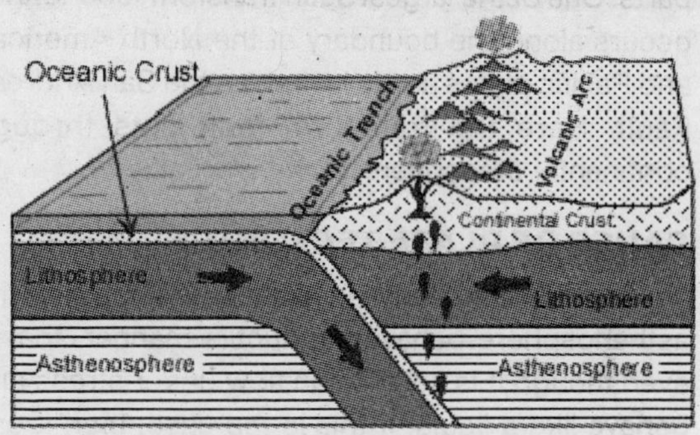

Ocean - Continent Convergence

If one of the plates has continental lithosphere on its margin, the oceanic plate will subduct because oceanic lithosphere has a higher density than continental lithosphere.

Sediment deposited along the convergent margin, and particularly that in the trench will be deformed by thrust faulting. This will break the rocks up into a chaotic mixture of broken, jumbled, and thrust faulted rock know as a mélange.

TRANSFORM PLATE BOUNDARIES

Where lithospheric plates slide past one another in a horizontal manner, a transform fault is created. Earthquakes along such transform faults are shallow focus earthquakes.

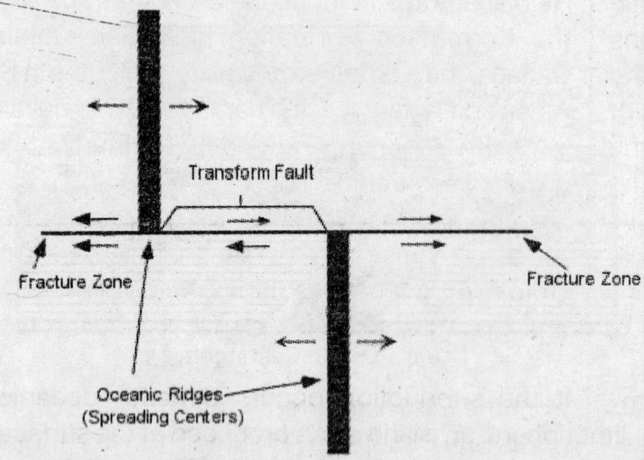

Most transform faults occur where oceanic ridges are offset on the sea floor. Such offset occurs because spreading takes place on the spherical surface of the Earth, and some parts of a plate must be moving at a higher relative velocity than other parts. One of the largest such transform boundaries occurs along the boundary of the North American and Pacific plates and is known as the San Andreas Fault. Here the transform fault cuts through continental lithosphere

CAUSE OF PLATE TECTONICS

From seismic wave velocities we know that the asthenosphere behaves in ductile manner, that is even though it is solid it can flow under stress and behave like a liquid. If this is the case, then it can also convect. Recall that convection is a mode of heat transfer wherein the heat moves with the material. Convection is caused when material that occurs at a deeper level is heated to the point where it expands and becomes less dense than the material above it. When this occurs, the hot less dense material rises. In a confined space, rising hot material will eventually cool and become denser than its surroundings. This cool dense material must then sink. This gives rise to convection cells, with hot rising currents and cool descending currents.

If the asthenosphere is in fact moving as a result of convection, then convection could be the mechanism responsible for plate tectonics. Hot rising currents would occur beneath oceanic ridges

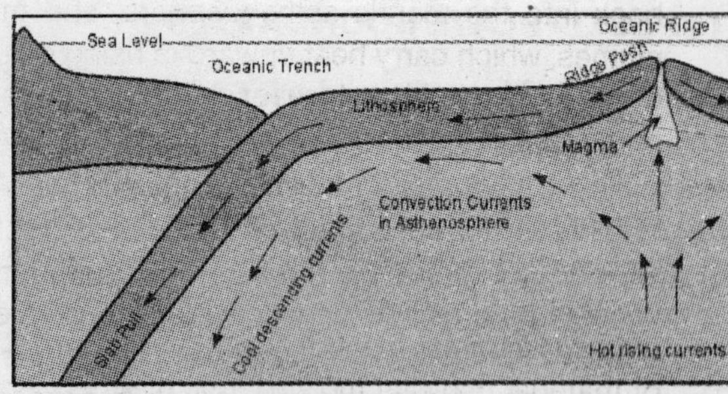

Magma intruding into the ridge would push lithosphere apart at the ridge. As the new lithosphere cools, it will slide off the topographic high that results from the upwelling of the mantle and will eventually become cold and dense. This dense lithosphere will tend to pull the rest of the lithosphere downward. A combination of dragging the lithosphere along the top of the convection cell, ridge push, sliding, and slab pull all appear to be contributing factors to the cause of plate tectonics.

MANTLE PLUMES

A mantle plume is an upwelling of abnormally hot rock within the Earth's mantle. As the heads of mantle plumes can partly melt when they reach shallow depths, they are thought to be the cause of volcanic centers known as hotspots and probably also to have caused flood basalts, often causing catastrophic effects on the Earth's surface once the magma spills out onto the crust. A hotspot (or hot spot) is a portion of the Earth's surface that may be far from tectonic plate boundaries and that experiences volcanism due to a rising mantle plume.

A mantle plume is a secondary way that Earth loses heat, much less important in this regard than is heat loss at plate margins (see Plate tectonics). Some scientists think that plate tectonics cools the mantle, and mantle plumes cool the core.

In 1971, geophysicist W. Jason Morgan proposed the theory of mantle plumes. In this theory, convection in the mantle slowly transports heat from the core to the Earth's surface. It is now understood that two convective processes drive heat exchange within the earth: plate tectonics, which is driven primarily by the sinking of cold plates of lithosphere back into the mantle asthenosphere, and mantle plumes, which carry heat upward in rising columns of hot material, driven by heat exchange across the core-mantle boundary. The sinking of vast sheets of oceanic lithosphere back into the mantle is the primary driving force of plate tectonics, where the sinking of these slabs is balanced by the passive upwelling of asthenosphere along mid-oceanic ridges. In contrast, mantle plumes are narrow columns of material that rise more-or-less independently of plate motions.

Fluid dynamics experiments in the early 1970s produced models of mantle plumes that consist of two parts: a long thin conduit that connects the top of the plume to its base, and a bulbous head that expands in size as the plume rises upward in the mantle; the result looks like a mushroom with a thin stalk and large top. The bulbous head forms because hot material moves upward through the plume conduit faster than the plume itself rises through the surrounding asthenosphere. In the late 1980s and early 1990s, experiments with thermal models shows that as the bulbous head expands it may entrain some of the adjacent asthenosphere into the rising head.

When the plume head encounters the base of the lithosphere, it flattens out against this surface barrier and undergoes widespread decompression melting to form enormous volumes of basalt magma. This basalt may erupt onto the surface over very short time scales (less than 1 million years) to form a continental flood basalt (if it erupts through continental crust) or an oceanic plateau (if it erupts through oceanic crust). Prominent continental flood basalt provinces include the Deccan traps and the Rajmahal traps in India, the Siberian traps of Asia, the Karmutsen Formation in British Columbia, Canada, the Karoo-Ferrar basalts/dolerites in South Africa and Antarctica, the Paraná and Etendeka traps in South America and Africa (formerly a single province separated by opening of the South Atlantic Ocean), and the Columbia River basalts of North America. Plume-related oceanic plateaux include the Ontong Java plateau of the southwest Pacific Ocean and the Maniheken plateau of the Indian Ocean.

The plume tail may continue to move material from the Earth's interior to the surface, providing a continuous supply of magma in a fixed location, often referred to as a hotspot. As the lithosphere moves over this fixed hotspot due to plate tectonics, the eruption of magma from the fixed hotspot onto the surface forms a chain of volcanoes that parallels plate motion. The classic example of this is the Hawaiian Islands chain in the Pacific Ocean.

The eruption of continental flood basalts is often associated with continental rifting and breakup, leading to the hypothesis that mantle plumes play an important role in continental rifting and the formation of ocean basins. Where this association of flood basalts with continental rifting is observed, it is not uncommon to find linear chains of volcanic islands that parallel the motion of plates on either side of the spreading center (South Atlantic Ocean).

EVIDENCE FOR THE THEORY

Mantle plumes provide an explanation for intra-plate tectonic volcanism called 'hotspots'. There are several lines of evidence used to support the theory: linear volcanic centers, hotspot fixity, geochemical, noble gas isotopes, and geophysical anomalies.

6 Seismology & Tomography

SEISMIC SOURCE

Seismology provides the only direct method for measuring the properties of the deep interior of our planet. eismology provides the only direct method for measuring the properties of the deep interior of our planet.

A seismic source generates controlled seismic energy that is used in both reflection and refraction seismic surveys. A seismic source can be simple, such as dynamite, or it can use more sophisticated technology, such as a specialized air gun. Seismic sources can provide single pulses or continuous pulses of energy that generates seismic waves, which travel through a medium such as water or layers of rocks. Some of the waves then reflect and refract to receivers, such as geophones or hydrophones.

Seismic exploration using sound sources may be used to investigate shallow subsoil structure, for engineering site work, or deeper structures, usually in the search for oil, or for scientific investigation. The returning signals from the sources are detected by geophones, laid in known locations relative to the position of the source. The recorded signals are then subjected to specialist analysis and processing to yield comprehensible data.

A seismic source signal has the following characteristics:

1. generated as an impulsive source
2. band-limited
3. the generated waves are time-varying

The generalized equation that shows all above properties is:

$$s(t) = \beta e^{-\alpha t^2} \sin(2\pi f_{\max} t)$$

where $f_{\max}$ is the maximum frequency component of the generated waveform.

TYPES OF SOURCES

Explosives

Explosives, such as dynamite, can be used as crude but effective sources of seismic energy. Generally the explosive charges are placed between 20 feet to 250 feet below ground. The charges are placed in a hole that is drilled with dedicated drilling equipment for this purpose. This type of seismic drilling is often referred to as "Shot Hole Drilling".

A common drill rig used for "Shot Hole Drilling" is the ARDCO C-1000 drill mounted on an ARDCO K 4X4 buggy. These drill rigs often use water or air in assisting the drilling.

Air gun

An air gun is used for marine reflection and refraction surveys. It consists of one or more pneumatic chambers that are pressurized with compressed air at pressures from 2,000 pounds per square inch to 3,000 pounds per square inch (14 to 21 MPa). The air gun array is submerged below the water surface, and is towed behind a ship. When the air gun is fired, a solenoid is triggered, which releases air into a fire chamber which in turn causes a piston to move and thereby allowing the air to escape the main chamber and to produce a pulse of acoustic energy. Air gun arrays are built up of up to 48 individual air guns with different size chambers, the aim being to create the optimum initial shock wave with minimum reverberation of the bubble after the first shot.

Gun arrays can be fired in flip-flop mode; typically this would be 48 guns per source, which would be selected and fired alternately. Large chambers (i.e., greater than 70 cubic inches or 1.15 L) tend to give low frequency signals, and the small chambers (less than 70 cubic inches) give higher frequency signals. The air gun is made from the highest grades of corrosion resistant stainless steel.

Plasma sound source

A plasma sound source (PSS), otherwise called a spark gap sound source, is a means of making very low frequency sonar pulse underwater.

For each firing, it stores electric charge in a large high-voltage bank of capacitors, and then releases all the stored energy in an arc across electrodes in the water. The underwater spark discharge produces a high-pressure plasma and vapor bubble, which expands and collapses, making a loud sound. Most of the sound produced is between 20 and 200 Hz.

The PSS has also been used for sonar. There are also plans to use PSS as a non-lethal weapon against submerged divers.

Thumper truck

A thumper truck (or weight-drop) truck is a vehicle mounted ground impact which can used to provide the seismic source. A heavy weight is raised by a hoist at the back of the truck and dropped, possibly about three metres, to impact (or "thump") the ground. To augment the signal, the weight may be dropped more than once at the same spot, the signal may also be increased by thumping at several nearby places in an array whose dimensions may be chosen to enhance the seismic signal by spatial filtering.

Thumping might be less damaging to the environment than firing explosives in shot-holes, though a heavily thumped seismic line with transverse ridges every few metres might create long-lasting disturbance of the soil. An advantage of the thumper (later shared with Vibroseis), especially in politically unstable areas, was that no explosives were required.

Seismic vibrator

Seismic vibrators, commonly known by their trademark name Vibroseis, propagate energy signals into the Earth over an extended period of time as opposed to the near instantaneous energy provided by impulsive sources. The data recorded in this way must be correlated to convert the extended source signal into an impulse. The source signal using this method was originally generated by a servo-controlled hydraulic vibrator or shaker unit mounted on a mobile base unit, but electro-mechanical versions have also been developed.

Vibroseis was developed by the Continental Oil Company (Conoco) during the 1950s and was a trademark until the company's patent lapsed.

Boomer sources

Boomer sound sources are used for shallow water seismic surveys, mostly for engineering survey applications. Boomers are towed in a floating sled behind a survey vessel. Similarly to the plasma source, it stores energy in capacitors, but it discharges through a flat spiral coil instead of generating a spark. A copper plate adjacent to the coil flexes away from the coil as the capacitors are discharged. This flexing is transmitted into the water as the seismic pulse.

Originally the storage capacitors were placed in a steel container (the bang box) on the survey vessel. The high voltages used, typically 3,000 V, required heavy cables and strong safety containers. Recently, low voltage boomers have become available. These use capacitors on the towed sled, allowing efficient energy recovery, lower voltage power supplies and lighter cables. The low voltage systems are generally easier to deploy and have fewer safety concerns.

Noise sources

Correlation-based processing techniques also enable seismologists to image the interior of the

Earth at multiple scales using natural (e.g., the oceanic microseism) or artificial (e.g., urban) background noise as a seismic source. For example, under ideal conditions of uniform seismic illumination, the correlation of the noise signals between two seismographs provides an estimate of the bidirectional seismic impulse response.

ELASTODYNAMICS

Elastodynamics is the study of linear elasticity which include variation in time. The most common case considered in elastodynamics is the wave equation. This section will discuss only the isotropic homogeneous case.

If the material is homogeneous (i.e. the elasticity tensor is constant throughout the material), the three basic equations can be combined to form the elastodynamic equation:

$$\mu u_{i,jj} + (\mu+\lambda) u_{j,ij} + F_i = \rho \partial_{tt} u_i \quad \text{or}$$

$$\mu \nabla^2 u + (\mu+\lambda)\nabla(\nabla . u) + F = \rho \frac{\partial^2 u}{\partial t^2}.$$

From the elastodynamic equation one gets the wave equation

$$(\delta_{kl}\partial_{tt} - A_{kl}[\nabla])u_l = \frac{1}{\rho} f_k$$

where

$$A_{kl}[\nabla] = \frac{1}{\rho}\partial_i C_{iklj}\partial_j$$

is the acoustic differential operator, and δ_{kl} is Kronecker delta.

In isotropic media, the elasticity tensor has the form

$$C_{ijkl} = K\,\delta_{ij}\delta_{kl} + \mu(\delta_{ik}\delta_{jk} + \delta_{il}\delta_{jk} - \frac{2}{3}\delta_{ij}\delta_{kl})$$

where K is the bulk modulus (or incompressibility), and μ is the shear modulus (or rigidity), two elastic moduli. If the material is homogeneous (i.e. the elasticity tensor is constant throughout the material), the acoustic operator becomes:

$$A_{ij}[\nabla] = \alpha^2 \partial_i \partial_j + \beta^2(\partial_m \partial_m \delta_{ij} - \partial_i \partial_j)$$

and the acoustic algebraic operator becomes

$$A_{ij}[k] = \alpha^2 k_i k_j + \beta^2(k_m k_m k_{ij} - k_i k_j)$$

where

$$\alpha^2 = \left(K + \frac{4}{3}\mu\right)/\rho \quad \beta^2 = \mu/\rho$$

are the eigenvalues of $A[\hat{k}]$ with eigenvectors $\hat{u}$ parallel and orthogonal to the propagation direction $\hat{k}$, respectively. In the seismological literature, the corresponding plane waves are called P-waves and S-waves

PLANE WAVES

A plane wave has the form

$$u[x,t] = U[k \cdot x - \omega t]\hat{u}$$

with $\hat{u}$ of unit length. It is a solution of the wave equation with zero forcing, if and only if ω^2 and $\hat{u}$ constitute an eigenvalue/eigenvector pair of the acoustic algebraic operator

$$A_{kl}[k] = \frac{1}{\rho} k_i C_{iklj} k_j.$$

This propagation condition may be written as

$$A[\hat{k}]\hat{u} = c^2 \hat{u}$$

where $\hat{k} = k/\sqrt{k \cdot k}$ denotes propagation direction and $c = \omega/\sqrt{k \cdot k}$ is phase velocity.

ELASTIC WAVE

An elastic wave is a type of mechanical wave that propagates in elastic or viscoelastic materials. The elasticity of the material provides the restoring force of the wave. When they occur in the Earth as the result of an earthquake or other disturbance, elastic waves are usually called seismic waves.

Solids are often assumed to exhibit linear elasticity. That is, Hooke's law is assumed to be valid. The restoring force is directly proportional to the displacement (or strain), but is oppositely directed.

FOCAL MECHANISM

The focal mechanism of an earthquake describes the inelastic deformation in the source region that generates the seismic waves. In the case of a fault-related event it refers to the orientation of the fault plane that slipped and the slip vector and is also known as a fault-plane solution. Focal mechanisms are derived from a solution of the moment tensor for the earthquake, which itself is estimated by an analysis of observed seismic waveforms. The focal mechanism can be derived from observing the pattern of "first motions", that is, whether the first arriving P waves break up or down. This method was used before waveforms were recorded and analysed digitally and this method is still used for earthquakes too small for easy moment tensor solution. Focal mechanisms are now mainly derived using semi-automatic analysis of the recorded waveforms.

SEISMIC GAP

seismic gap is a segment of an active fault that has not slipped in an unusually long time when compared with other segments along the same structure. Seismic gap hypothesis/theory states that, over long periods of time, the displacement on any segment must be equal to that experienced by all the other parts of the fault. Any large and longstanding gap is therefore considered to be the fault segment most likely to suffer future earthquakes. The applicability of this approach has been criticised by some seismologists, although it has been used successfully in some areas.

SEISMOTECTONICS AND STRUCTURE OF THE EARTH

Seismotectonics is the study of the relationship between the earthquakes, active tectonics and individual faults of a region. It seeks to understand which faults are responsible for seismic activity in an area by analysing a combination of regional tectonics, recent instrumentally recorded events, accounts of historical earthquakes and geomorphological evidence. This information can then be used to quantify the seismic hazard of an area.

METHODOLOGY

A seismotectonic analysis of an area requires the integration of a large number of disparate datasets.

REGIONAL TECTONICS

An understanding of the regional tectonics of an area is likely to be derived from published geological maps, research publications on the geological structure and seismic reflection profiles, where available, augmented by other geophysical data.

In order to understand the seismic hazard of an area it is necessary not only to know where potentially active faults are, but also the the orientation of the stress field. This is normally derived from a combination of earthquake data, borehole breakout analysis, direct stress measurement and the analysis of geologically young fault networks. The World Stress Map Project provides a useful online compilation of such data.

EARTHQUAKES

Instrumentally recorded events

Since the early 20th century, sufficient information has been available from seismometers to allow the location, depth and magnitude of earthquakes to be calculated. In terms of identifying the fault responsible for an earthquake where there is no clear surface trace, recording the locations of aftershocks generally gives a strong indication of the strike of the fault.

As focal mechanisms give two potential active fault plane orientations, other evidence is required to interpret the origin of an individual event. Although only available for a restricted time period, in areas of moderate to intense seismicity there is probably sufficient data to characterise the type of seismicity in an area, if not all the active structures.

Historical records

Attempts to understand the long-term seismicity of an area require information from earthquakes before the era of instrumental recording. This requires a careful assessment of historical data in terms of their reliability. In most cases, all that can be derived is an estimate of the location and magnitude of the event. However, such data is needed to fill the gaps in the instrumental record, particularly in areas with either relatively low seismicity or where the repeat periods for major earthquakes is more than a hundred years.

Field investigations

Information on the timing and magnitude of seismic events that occurred before instrumental recording can be obtained from excavations across faults that are thought to be seismically active and by studying recent sedimentary sequences for evidence of seismic activity such as seismites or tsunami deposits.

Geomorphology

Seismically active faults and related fault generated folds have a direct affect on the geomorphology of a region. This may allow the direct identification of active structures not previously known. In some cases such observations can be used quantitatively to constrain the repeat period of major earthquakes, such as the raised beaches of Turakirae Head recording the history of coseismic uplift of the Rimutaka Range due to displacement on the Wairarapa Fault in North Island, New Zealand.

RESERVOIR INDUCED SEISMICITY

In seismology induced seismicity refers to typically minor earthquakes and tremors that are caused by human activity that alters the stresses and strains on the Earth's crust. Most induced seismicity is of an extremely low magnitude.

The mass of water in a reservoir alters the pressure in the rock below, which can trigger earthquakes. Reservoir-induced seismic events can be relatively large compared to other forms of induced seismicity. The first case of reservoir induced seismicity occurred in 1932 in Algeria's Quedd Fodda Dam. Unfortunately, understanding of reservoir induced seismic activity is very limited. However, it has been noted that seismicity appears to occur on dams with heights larger than 100 meters. The extra water pressure created by vast reservoirs is the most accepted explanation for the seismic activity. Induced seismicity is usually overlooked due to cost cutting during the geological surveys of the locations for proposed dams. Once the reservoirs are filled, induced seismicity could occur immediately or with a small time lag.

In 1967 a 6.3 magnitude earthquake occurred in Maharashtra, India with its epicenter, fore and aftershocks all located near or under the Konya Dam reservoir. 180 people died and 1,500 were left injured. The effects of the earthquake were felt 230 Kilometers away in Bombay with tremors and power outages. During the beginnings of the Vajont Dam in Italy, there were seismic shocks recorded during its initial fill. With scares of landslide emerging, the dam was drained and consequently seismic activity was almost nonexistent. On August 1, 1975, a large magnitude earthquake at Oroville, California, was attributed to seismicity from a massive earth-fill dam and reservoir recently constructed and filled there.

The filling of the Katse Dam in Lesotho, and the Nurek Dam in Tajikistan is an example. In Zambia, Kariba Lake may have provoked similar effects.

Some experts worry that the Three Gorges Dam in China may cause an increase in the frequency and intensity of earthquakes.

Koyna dam in Maharashtra, India is afine example of reservoir induced seismicity.

SEISMIC HAZARD

Seismic hazard is an area prone to seimic activities of earth. The calculations for seismic hazard can be quite complex. First, the regional geology and seismology is examined for patterns (using seismometers and earthquake location). Zones of similar potential for seismicity are drawn. For example, the famous San Andreas Fault might be drawn as a long narrow zone. Zones in the continental interior (the site for intraplate earthquakes) would be drawn as broad areas, since causative faults are generally not identified.

Each zone is given properties associated with source potential: how many earthquakes per year, the maximum size of earthquakes (maximum magnitude), etc. Finally, the calculations require formulae that give the required hazard indicators for a given earthquake size and distance. For example, some districts prefer to use peak acceleration, others use peak velocity, and more sophisticated uses require response spectral ordinates.

The computer program then integrates over all the zones and produces probability curves for the key ground motion parameter. The final result gives you a 'chance' of exceeding a given value over a specified amount of time. Standard building codes for homeowners might be concerned with a 1 in 500 years chance, while nuclear plants look at the 10,000 year time frame. A longer-term seismic history can be obtained through paleoseismology. The results may in the form of a ground response spectrum for use in seismic analysis.

More elaborate variations on the theme also look at the soil conditions. If you build on a soft swamp, you are likely to experience many times the ground motions than your neighbour on solid rock. The standard seismic hazard calculations become adjusted upwards if you are postulating characteristic earthquakes.

In India, region is divided into different SESMIC Zonation categories like I, II,III, IV and V depends on vulnerability of area in terms of seismic activities. Category I is least prone to seismicity and V is most prone to seismicity.

EARTHQUAKE PREDICTION

The problem of earthquake prediction is extremely difficult and is associated with sundry other problems of a sociological nature. To predict an earthquake correctly means deciding, as far in advance as possible, exactly where and when it will occur. It is also necessary to judge how strong it will be, which means realistically that people want to know what the likely damage will be, a feature expressed in the earthquake intensity. In fact the geophysicist is almost helpless in this respect, because at best an estimate of the predicted magnitude can be made. even if it is possible to predict accurately the magnitude, the intensity depends on many factors (e.g., local geology, construction standards, secondary effects like fires and floods) which are largely outside the influence of the seismologist who is asked to presage the seriousness of the event. The problem of prediction rapidly assumes sociological and political proportions. Even if the approximate time and place of a major earthquake can be predicted with reasonable certainty, the question then remains of what to do about the situation.

Properly, the threatened area should be evacuated, but this would entail economic consequences of possibly enormous dimension. The di?culties are illustrated by the following possible scenario. Suppose that seismologists conclude that a very large earthquake, with probable magnitude 7 or greater, will take place sometime in a known month of a given year under a specific urban center. No more precise details are possible; in particular, the time of occurrence cannot be determined more exactly. Publication of this kind of prediction would cause great consternation, even panic, which for some of the population could be as disastrous as the earthquake itself. Should the warning be withheld? If the entire area, with its millions of inhabitants, were to be evacuated, the economic dislocation would be enormous.

How long should the evacuation last, when every day is economically ruinous? Clearly, earthquake prediction is only useful in a practical sense when it is accurate in both place and time. The problem then passes out of the domain of the scientist and into that of the politician, with the scientist retaining only a peripheral role as a consultant. But if the earthquake prediction is a failure, the consequences will rebound with certainty on the scientist.

PREDICTION OF THE LOCATION OF AN EARTHQUAKE

It is easier to predict where a major earthquake is likely to occur than when it will occur. The global seismicity patterns demonstrate that some regions are relatively aseismic. They are not completely free of earthquakes, many of which appear to occur randomly and without warning in these regions. Some intraplate earthquakes have a history of repeated occurrence at a known location, which can sensibly be expected to be the locus of a future shock. However, because most earthquakes occur in the seismically active zones at plate margins, these are the prime areas for trying to predict serious events. Predicting the location of a future earthquake in these zones combines a knowledge of the historical seismicity pattern with the elastic rebound model of what causes an earth-quake.

The seismic gap theory is based on the simple idea that global plates move under the influence of forces which affect the plates as entities. The interactions at a plate margin therefore act along the entire length of the inter-plate boundary. Models of plate tectonic reconstructions assume continuity of platemotions on a scale of millions of years.However, the global seismicity patterns show that on the scales of decades or centuries, the process is discontinuous both in time and place. This is because of the way individual earthquakes occur. According to the elastic rebound model, stress accumulates until it exceeds the local strength of the rocks, rupture produces motion on the fault, and an earthquake occurs.During the time of stress accumulation, the area experiences nomajor earthquake, and the regional pattern of seismicity. This is the potential location for an earthquake that is in the process of accumulating the strain energy necessary to cause rupture. For example, the magnitude 7.6 earthquake at Izmit, Turkey, in 1999 resulted in more than 11,000 deaths. It occurred in a 100-150 km seismic gap between events that occurred more than three decades earlier, in 1967 and 1964, and which subsequently had been tranquil.

7 Gravity and Magnetic Methods

GRAVIMETERS

A gravimeter or gravitometer is an instrument used in gravimetry for measuring the local gravitational field of the Earth. A gravimeter is a type of accelerometer, specialized for measuring the constant downward acceleration of gravity. Though the essential principle of design is the same as in other accelerometers, gravimeters are typically designed to be much more sensitive in order to measure very tiny fractional changes within the Earth's gravity of 1 g, caused by nearby geologic structures or the shape of the Earth. This sensitivity means that gravimeters are susceptible to extraneous vibrations including noise that tend to cause oscillatory accelerations. In practice this is counteracted by integral vibration isolation and signal processing. The constraints on temporal resolution are usually less for gravimeters, so that resolution can be increased by processing the output with a longer "time constant". Gravimeters display their measurements in units of gals, instead of ordinary units of acceleration.

Gravimeters are used for petroleum and mineral prospecting, seismology, geodesy, geophysical surveys and other geophysical research.

There are two types of gravimeters: relative and absolute. Absolute gravimeters measure the local gravity in absolute units, gals. Relative gravimeters compare the value of gravity at one point with another. They must be calibrated at a location where the gravity is known accurately, and then transported to the location where the gravity is to be measured. They measure the ratio of the gravity at the two points.

ABSOLUTE GRAVIMETERS

Absolute gravimeters, which nowadays are made compact so they too can be used in the field, work by directly measuring the acceleration of a mass during free fall in a vacuum, when the accelerometer is rigidly attached to the ground.

The mass includes a retroreflector and terminates one arm of a Micheison interferometer. By counting and timing the interference fringes, the velocity of the mass can be measured. A more recent development is a "rise and fall" version that tosses the mass upward and measures both upward and downward motion. This allows cancellation of some measurement errors. Absolute gravimeters are used to calibrate relative gravimeters, and for establishing the vertical control network.

RELATIVE GRAVIMETERS

Most common relative gravimeters are spring-based. They are used in gravity surveys over large areas for establishing the figure of the geoid over those areas. A spring-based relative gravimeter is basically a weight on a spring, and by measuring the amount by which the weight stretches the spring, local gravity can be measured. However, the strength of the spring must be calibrated by placing the instrument in a location with a known gravitational acceleration. A high-grade, calibrated spring gravimeter such as the portable LaCoste-Romberg gravimeter can measure the Earth's gravitational field to within 1 μGal (or 10 nm/sl).

The most accurate relative gravimeters are superconducting gravimeters, which operate by suspending a liquid helium cooled diamagetic superconducting niobium sphere in an extremely stable magnetic field; the current required to generate the magnetic field that suspends the niobium sphere is proportional to the strength of the Earth's gravitational field. The superconducting gravimeter achieves extraordinary sensitivities of one nanogal, one thousandth of one billionth (10-12) of the Earth surface gravity. In a dramatic demonstration of the sensitivity of the superconducting gravimeter, Virtanen (2006), describes how an instrument at Metsähovi, Finland, detected the gradual increase in surface gravity as workmen cleared snow from its laboratory roof. GWR Instruments, Inc. based out of San Diego, CA are the sole manufacturer of the superconducting gravity meter.

Transportable relative gravimeters also exist; they employ an extremely stable inertial platform to compensate for the masking effects of motion and vibration, a difficult engineering feat. The first transportable relative gravimeters were, reportedly, a secret military technology developed in the 1950-60s as a navigational aid for nuclear submarines. Subsequently in the 1980s, transportable relative gravimeters were reverse engineered by the civilian sector for use on ship, then in air and finally satellite borne gravity surveys.

MAGNETOMETER

Magnetometer is a scientific instrument used to measure the strength and/or direction of the magnetic field in the vicinity of the instrument. Magnetism varies from place to place and differences in Earth's magnetic field (the magnetosphere) can be caused by the differing nature of rocks and the interaction between charged particles from the Sun and the magnetosphere of a planet. Magnetometers are a frequent component instrument on spacecraft that explore planets.

TYPES

Magnetometers can be divided into two basic types:

- Scalar magnetometers measure the total strength of the magnetic field to which they are subjected, and
- Vector magnetometers have the capability to measure the component of the magnetic field in a particular direction, relative to the spatial orientation of the device.

The use of three orthogonal vector magnetometers allows the magnetic field strength, inclination and declination to be uniquely defined. Examples of vector magnetometers are fluxgates, superconducting quantum interference devices (SQUIDs), and the atomic SERF magnetometer. Some scalar magnetometers are discussed below.

A magnetograph is a special magnetometer that continuously records data.

ROTATING COIL MAGNETOMETER

The magnetic field induces a sine wave in a rotating coil. The amplitude of the signal is proportional to the strength of the field, provided it is uniform, and to the sine of the angle between the rotation axis of the coil and the field lines. This type of magnetometer is obsolete.

PROTON PRECESSION MAGNETOMETER

Proton precession magnetometers, also known as proton magnetometers, measure the resonance frequency of protons (hydrogen nuclei) in the magnetic field to be measured, due to nuclear magnetic resonance (NMR). Because the precession frequency depends only on atomic constants and the strength of the ambient magnetic field, the accuracy of this type of magnetometer is very good. They are widely used.

A direct current flowing in an inductor creates a strong magnetic field around a hydrogen-rich fluid, causing some of the protons to align themselves with that field. The current is then interrupted, and as protons realign themselves with ambient magnetic field, they precess at a frequency that is directly proportional to the magnetic field. This produces a weak alternating magnetic field that is picked up by a (sometimes separate) inductor, amplified electronically, and fed to a digital frequency counter whose output is typically scaled and displayed directly as field strength or output as digital data.

The relationship between the frequency of the induced current and the strength of the magnetic field is called the proton gyromagnetic ratio, and is equal to 0.042576 Hz/nT.

These magnetometers can be moderately sensitive if several tens of watts are available to power the aligning process. Measuring once per second, standard deviations in the readings in the 0.01 nT to 0.1 nT range can be obtained. Variations of about 0.1 nT can be detected.

The two main sources of measurement errors are magnetic impurities in the sensor and errors in the measurement of the frequency.

The Earth's magnetic field varies with time, geographical location, and local magnetic anomalies. The frequency of Earth's field NMR (EFNMR) for protons varies between approximately 1.5 kHz near the equator to 2.5 kHz near the geomagnetic poles. Typical short-term magnetic field variations at a particular location during Earth's daily rotation is about 25 nT (i.e., about 1 part in 2,000), with variations over a few seconds of typically around 1nT (i.e., about 1 part in 50,000).

Apart from the direct measurement of the magnetic field on Earth or in space, these magnetometers prove to be useful to detect variations of magnetic field in space or in time (often referred to as magnetic anomalies), caused by submarines, skiers buried under snow, archaeological remains, and mineral deposits.

USES

Magnetometers are used in ground-based electromagnetic geophysical surveys (such as magnetotellurics) to assist with detecting mineralization and corresponding geological structures. Airborne geophysical surveys use magnetometers that can detect magnetic field variations caused by mineralization, using airplanes like the Shrike Commander. Magnetometers are also used to detect archaeological sites, shipwrecks and other buried or submerged objects, and in metal detectors to detect metal objects, such as guns in security screening. Magnetic anomaly detectors detect submarines for military purposes.

They are used in directional drilling for oil or gas to detect the azimuth of the drilling tools near the drill bit. They are most often paired up with accelerometers in drilling tools so that both the inclination and azimuth of the drill bit can be found.

Magnetometers are very sensitive, and can give an indication of possible auroral activity before one can see the light from the aurora. A grid of magnetometers around the world constantly measures the effect of the solar wind on the Earth's magnetic field, which is published on the K-index.

A three-axis fluxgate magnetometer was part of the Mariner 2 and Mariner 10 missions. A dual technique magnetometer is part of the Cassini-Huygens mission to explore Saturn. This system is composed of a vector helium and fluxgate magnetometers.[5] Magnetometers are also a component instrument on the Mercury MESSENGER mission. A magnetometer can also be used by satellites like GOES to measure both the magnitude and direction of a planet's or moon's magnetic field.

SEPARATION OF REGIONAL AND RESIDUAL ANOMALIES

The separation of anomalies of regional and local origin is an important step in the interpretation of a gravity map. The analysis may be based on selected profiles across some structure, or it may involve the two- dimensional distribution of anomalies in a gravity map.

Numerous techniques have been applied to the decomposition of a gravity anomaly into its constituent parts. They range in sophistication from simple visual inspection of the anomaly pattern to advanced mathematical analysis.

VISUAL ANALYSIS

The simplestway of representing the regional anomaly on a gravity profile is by visually fitting the large-scale trendwith a smooth curve .The value of the regional gravity given by this trend is subtracted point by point from the Bouguer gravity anomaly. This method allows the interpreter to fit curves that leave residual anomalies with a sign appropriate tothe interpretationof thedensitydistribution.

This approach may be adapted to the analysis of a gravity map by visually smoothing the contour lines. The contour lines of equal Bouguer gravity curve sharply around a local abnormality. The more gently curved contours have been continued smoothly as dotted lines. They indicate how the interpreter thinks the regional gravity field would continue in the absence of the local abnormality. The values of the regional and original Bouguer gravity are interpolated from the corresponding maps at points spaced on a regular grid. The regional value is subtracted from the Bouguer anomaly at each point and the computed residuals are contoured to give a map of the local gravity anomaly. The experience and skill of the interpreter are important factors in the success of visual methods.

POLYNOMIAL REPRESENTATION

In an alternative method the regional trend is represented by a straight line or, more generally, by a smooth polynomial curve. If x denotes the horizontal position on a gravity profile, the regional gravity Δg_R may be written

$$\Delta g_R = \Delta g_0 + \Delta g_1 x + \Delta g_2 x^2 + \Delta g_3 x^3 + ... + \Delta g_n x^n$$

The polynomial is fitted by the method of least squares to the observed gravity profile. This gives optimum values for the coefficients Δg_n. The method also has drawbacks. The higher the order of the polynomial, the better it fits the observations. The ludicrous extreme is when the order of the polynomial is one less than the number of observations; the curve then passes perfectly through all the data points, but the regional gravity anomaly has no meaning geologically. The interpreter's judgement is important in selecting the order of the polynomial, which is usually chosen to be the lowest possible order that represents most of the regional trend.

Moreover, a curve fitted by least squares must pass through the mean of the gravity values, so that the residual anomalies are divided equally between positive and negative values. Each residual anomaly is flanked by anomalies of opposite sign., which are due to the same anomalous mass that caused the central anomaly and so have no significance of their own.

Polynomial fitting can also be applied to gravity maps. It is assumed that the regional anomaly can be represented by a smooth surface, g(x, y), which is a low order polynomial of the horizontal position coordinates x and y. In the simplest case the regional anomaly is expressed as a first-order polynomial, or plane. To express changes in the gradient of gravity a higher-order polynomial is needed. For example, the regional gravity given by a second-order polynomial is written

$$\Delta g(x, y) = \Delta g_0 + \Delta g_{x1} x + \Delta g_{y1} y$$
$$+ \Delta g_{x2} x^2 + \Delta g_{y2} y^2 + \Delta g_{xy} xy$$

As in the analysis of a profile, the optimum values of the coefficients Δg_{x1}, Δg_{y1}, etc., are determined by least-squares fitting. The residual anomaly is again computed point by point by subtracting the regional from the original data.

INDUCED POLARIZATION

Induced polarization (IP) is a geophysical imaging technique used to identify subsurface materials, such as ore. The method is similar to electrical resistivity tomography, in that an electric current is induced into the subsurface through two electrodes, and voltage is monitored through two other electrodes.

Time domain IP methods measure the voltage decay or chargeability over a specified time interval after the induced voltage is removed. The integrated voltage is used as the measurement.

Frequency domain IP methods (see Spectral Induced Polarisation) use alternating currents (AC) to induce electric charges in the subsurface, and the apparent resistivity is measured at different AC frequencies.

ELLIPTIC POLARIZATION

Elliptical polarization is the polarization of electromagnetic radiation such that the tip of the electric field vector describes an ellipse in any fixed plane intersecting, and normal to, the direction of propagation. An elliptically polarized wave may be resolved into two linearly polarized waves in phase quadrature, with their polarization planes at right angles to each other. Since the electric field can rotate clockwise or counterclockwise as it propagates, elliptically polarized waves exhibit chirality.

Other forms of polarization, such as circular and linear polarization, can be considered to be special cases of elliptical polarization.

The classical sinusoidal plane wave solution of the electromagnetic wave equation for the electric and magnetic fields is (cgs units)

$$E(r,t) = |E| \operatorname{Re}\{|\psi\rangle \exp[i(kz - \omega t)]\}$$

$$B(r,t) = \hat{z} \times E(r,t)$$

for the magnetic field, where k is the wavenumber,

$$\omega = ck$$

is the angular frequency of the wave, and c is the speed of light.

Here $|E|$ is the amplitude of the field and

$$|\psi\rangle \stackrel{\text{def}}{=} \begin{pmatrix} \psi_x \\ \psi_y \end{pmatrix} = \begin{pmatrix} \cos\theta \exp(i\alpha_x) \\ \sin\theta \exp(i\alpha_y) \end{pmatrix}$$

is the Jones vector in the x-y plane. The axes of the ellipse have lengths

$$\sqrt{\frac{1 - \sin(2\theta)\cos(\alpha_x - \alpha_y + \pi/2)}{2}} \text{ and}$$

$$\sqrt{\frac{1 + \sin(2\theta)\cos(\alpha_x - \alpha_y + \pi/2)}{2}} \text{.f}$$

α_x and α_y are equal the wave is linearly polarized. If they differ by $\pi/2$ the wave is circularly polarized.

VLF (VERY LOW FREQUENCY)

Very low frequency or VLF refers to radio frequencies (RF) in the range of 3 kHz to 30 kHz. Since there is not much bandwidth in this band of the radio spectrum, only the very simplest signals are used, such as for radio navigation. Also known as the myriametre band or myriametre wave as the wavelengths range from ten to one myriametres (an obsolete metric unit equal to 10 kilometres).

PC based VLF reception is a simple method whereby anyone can pick up VLF signals using the advantages of modern computer technology. An aerial in the form of a coil of insulated wire is connected to the input of the soundcard of the PC (via a jack plug) and placed a few metres away from it. Fast Fourier transform (FFT) software in combination with a sound card allows reception of all frequencies below the Nyquist frequency simultaneously in the form of spectrogrammes. Because CRT monitors are strong sources of noise in the VLF range, it is recommended to record the spectrograms on hard disk with any PC CRT monitors turned off. These spectrograms show many signals, which may include VLF transmitters, the horizontal electron beam deflection of TV sets and sometimes superpulses and twenty second pulses. The strength of the signal received can vary with a Sudden Ionospheric Disturbance. These cause the ionization level to drop in the atmosphere. The result of this is that the VLF signal will reflect down to Earth with greater strength.

APPLICATION OF VERY LOW FREQUENCY

VLF waves can penetrate water to a depth of roughly 10 to 40 metres (30 to 130 feet), depending on the frequency employed and the salinity of the water. VLF is used to communicate with submarines near the surface (for example using the transmitter DHO38), while ELF is used for deeply-submerged vessels. VLF is also used for radio navigation beacons (alpha) and time signals (beta).

VLF is also used in electromagnetic geophysical surveys.

Early in the history of radio engineering attempts were made to use radiotelephone using amplitude modulation and single-sideband modulation within the band starting from 20 kHz, but the result was unsatisfactory because of the small available bandwidth.

The frequency range below 9 kHz is not allocated by the International Telecommunication Union and may be used in some nations license-free. Many natural radio emissions, such as whistlers, can also be heard in this band.

In the USA, the time signal station WWVL began transmitting a 500 W signal on 20 kHz in August 1963. It used Frequency Shift Keying (FSK) to send data, shifting between 20 kHz and 26 kHz. The WWVL service was discontinued in July 1972.

The very long wave transmitter SAQ at Grimeton near Varberg in Sweden can be visited by the public at certain times, such as on Alexanderson Day.

AFMAG-AIRBORNE AND GROUND

Unlike other electromagnetic methods the AFMAG utilizes natural alternating magnetic fields in the audio-frequency range. This has advantages over active airborne EM systems using dipole artificial field sources. Such artificial fields decay inversely proportional to the cube of the distance from its source. Responses from deep conductive targets can be very low and masked by noise and anomalies of small but shallow geologic bodies.

The natural magnetic field used in the AFMAG technology is primarily homogeneous and its penetration depth depends on rock resistivity only. A deep conductor in highly resistive surroundings can be better detected by AFMAG. Another advantage of the AFMAG is good resolution for relatively resistive objects. It makes this method very useful not only for detecting conductors but also for general geological mapping and exploration of poorly conductive objects such as Kimberlite pipes. This new technology has now been proven over known test sites. These flights were conducted with a helicopter-borne AFMAG device and processed using advanced digital technologies and signal processing algorithms.

FEATURES

- Very deep investigation
- Multi-frequency geophysical information
- Resolution in wide-range of conductivity.
- Lower cost equipment and surveys.
- Surveys may be flown at 200 meters altitude.

MAGNETO-TELLURIC METHOD

Magnetotellurics (MT) is a natural-source electromagnetic geophysical method of imaging the earth's subsurface. Commercial uses include hydrocarbon (oil and gas) exploration, geothermal exploration, and mining exploration, as well as hydrocarbon and groundwater monitoring. Research applications include experimentation to further develop the MT technique, long-period deep crustal exploration, and earthquake precursor prediction research.

ELECTROMAGNETIC THEORY OF MAGNETO-TELLURIC

Energy Sources

Solar energy and lightning cause natural variations in the earth's magnetic field, inducing electric currents (known as telluric currents) under the Earth's surface. Simultaneous measurements of orthogonal components of the electric and magnetic fields are recorded, with the results calculated as the impedance tensor. A subsurface resistivity model is then created using this tensor.

Different rocks, sediments and subsurface geological structures display a wide range of different electrical conductivities. Measuring electrical resistivity is therefore a useful for distinguishing between different rock types and for understanding tectonic processes and geologic structures.

In magnetotellurics, the Earth's naturally varying electric and magnetic fields are measured over a wide range of frequencies from 10,000 Hz to 0.0001 Hz (10,000s). These fields are due to electric currents flowing in the Earth and the magnetic fields that induce these currents. The magnetic fields are produced mainly by the interaction between the solar wind and the magnetosphere. In addition, worldwide thunderstorm activity causes magnetic fields at frequencies above 1 Hz. These natural phenomena create strong Magneto-telluric source signals over the entire frequency spectrum.

The ratio of the electric field to magnetic field can give simple information about the subsurface conductivity. Because of the skin effect phenomenon that affects electromagnetic fields, the ratio at higher frequency ranges gives information on the shallow Earth, whereas deeper information is provided by the low-frequency range. The ratio is usually represented as MT-apparent resistivity and phase as a function of frequency. The technique was introduced by the French geophysicist Louis Cagniard and Russian geophysicist Tikhonov in the early 1950s. With advances in instrumentation, processing and modeling, MT has become one of the most important tools in deep Earth research.

Magneto-telluric Signal Strength and Recording Times

Magnetic fields in the frequency range of 1 Hz to approximately 20 kHz are part of the audio-magnetotelluric (AMT) range. These are parallel to the Earth surface and move towards the Earth's centre. This large frequency band allows for a range of depth penetration from several metres to several kilometres below the Earth's surface. Due to the nature of magnetotulluric source, the waves generally fluctuate in amplitude height. Long recording times are needed to ascertain usable reading due to the fluctuations and the low signal strength. Generally, the signal is weak between 1 to 5 kHz, which is a crucial range in detecting the top 100m of geology. The magnetotelluric method is also used in marine environments for hydrocarbon exploration and lithospheric studies. Due to the screening effect of the electrically conductive sea water, a usable upper limit of the spectrum is around 1 Hz.

2D and 3D Magnetotellurics

Two-dimensional surveys consist of a longitudinal profile of Magnetotellurics soundings over the area of interest, providing two-dimensional "slices" of subsurface resistivity.

Three-dimensional surveys consist of a loose grid pattern of Magnetotellurics soundings over the area of interest, providing a more sophisticated three-dimensional model of subsurface resistivity.

APPLICATIONS

Magnetotellurics Exploration for Mining

Magnetotellurics is used for various base metals (nickel and precious metals exploration, as well as for Kimberlite) mapping.

INCO's 1991 proof-of-concept study in Sudbury, Ontario, Canada sensed a 1750 meter-deep nickel deposit. Falconbridge followed with a feasibility study in 1996 that accurately located two Ni-Cu mineralized zones at ~800 m and ~1350 m. Since then, both major and junior mining companies are increasingly using MT and AMT for both brownfields and greenfields exploration. Significant Magnetotellurics mapping work has been done on areas of the Canadian Shield.

Diamond exploration, by detecting Kimberlites, is also a proven application.

Magnetotellurics Exploration for Geothermal

Magnetotellurics measurements allow detection of resistivity anomalies associated with productive geothermal structures, including faults and the presence of a cap rock, and allow for estimation of geothermal reservoir temperatures at various depths. Dozens of MT geothermal exploration surveys have been completed in Japan and the Philippines since the early 1980s, helping to identify several hundred megawatts of renewable power at places such as the Hatchobaru plant on Kyushu and the Togonang plant on Leyte Geothermal exploration with MT has also been done in the United States, Iceland, Hungary, China, Ethiopia, Indonesia, Peru, and India.

Magnetotellurics Exploration for Hydrocarbons

For hydrocarbon exploration, Magnetotellurics is mainly used as a complement to the primary technique of Reflection seismology exploration.

While seismic is able to image subsurface structure, it cannot detect changes in resistivity. MT does detect resistivity variations in subsurface structures, which can differentiate between structures bearing hydrocarbons and those that do not.

At a basic level of interpretation, resistivity is correlated with different rock types. High-velocity layers are typically highly resistive, whereas sediments - porous and permeable - are typically much less resistive. While high-velocity layers are an acoustic barrier and make seismic ineffective, their electrical resistivity means the magnetic signal passes through almost unimpeded. This allows Magnetotellurics to see deep beneath these acoustic barrier layers, complimenting the seismic data and assisting interpretation. 3-D Magnetotellurics survey results in Uzbekistan (32 x 32 stations, conducted by Uzkbekneftgaz, the state-owned oil and gas company) have been used to guide further seismic mapping of a large known gas-bearing formation with complex subsurface geology.

Earthquake Precursor Prediction Research

Fluctuations in the Magnetotellurics signal may be able to predict the onset of seismic events. Stationary Magnetotellurics monitoring systems have been installed in Japan since April 1996, providing a continuous recording of MT signals at the Wakuya Station (previously at the Mizusawa Geodetic Observatory) and the Esashi Station of the Geographical Survey Institute of Japan. These stations measure fluctuations in the Earth's electromagnetic field that correspond with seismic activity. The raw geophysical time-series data from these monitoring stations is freely available to the scientific community, enabling further study of the interaction between EM events and earthquake activity.

Additional MT earthquake precursor monitoring stations in Japan are located in Kagoshima, in Sawauchi, and on Shikoku. Similar stations are also deployed in Taiwan on Penghu Island, as well as in the Fushan Reserve on the island of Taiwan proper.

POLARIS is a Canadian research program investigating the structure and dynamics of the Earth's lithosphere and the prediction of earthquake ground motion

China National Petroleum Corporation (CNPC) uses onshore MT more than any other oil company in the world, conducting thousands of MT soundings for hydrocarbon exploration and mapping throughout all of China.

8 Seismic Methods

SNELL'S LAW

Snell's law used to describe the relationship between the angles of incidence and refraction, when referring to light or other waves passing through a boundary between two different isotropic media, such as water and glass. The law says that the ratio of the sines of the angles of incidence and of refraction is a constant that depends on the media.

In optics, the law is used in ray tracing to compute the angles of incidence or refraction, and in experimental optics and gemology to find the refractive index of a material.

Snell's law is also satisfied in the metamaterials which allow light to be bent "backward" at a negative index, with a negative angle of refraction.

Named after Dutch mathematician Willebrord Snellius, one of its discoverers, Snell's law states that the ratio of the sines of the angles of incidence and refraction is equivalent to the ratio of velocities in the two media, or equivalent to the opposite ratio of the indices of refraction:

$$\frac{\sin\theta_1}{\sin\theta_2} = \frac{v_1}{v_2} = \frac{n_2}{n_1}$$

Snell's law follows from Fermat's principle of least time, which in turn follows from the propagation of light as waves.

Snell's law is used to determine the direction of light rays through refractive media with varying indices of refraction. The indices of refraction of the media, labeled n_1,n_2 and so on, are used to represent the factor by which a light ray's speed decreases when traveling through a refractive medium, such as glass or water, as opposed to its velocity in a vacuum.

As light passes the border between media, depending upon the relative refractive indices of the two media, the light will either be refracted to a lesser angle, or a greater one. These angles are measured with respect to the normal line, represented perpendicular to the boundary. In the case of light traveling from air into water, light would be refracted towards the normal line, because the light is slowed down in water; light traveling from water to air would refract away from the normal line.

Refraction between two surfaces is also referred to as reversible because if all conditions were identical, the angles would be the same for light propagating in the opposite direction.

Snell's law is generally true only for isotropic or specular media (such as glass). In anisotropic media such as some crystals, birefringence may split the refracted ray into two rays, the ordinary or o-ray which follows Snell's law, and the other extraordinary or e-ray which may not be co-planar with the incident ray.

When the light or other wave involved is monochromatic, that is, of a single frequency, Snell's law can also be expressed in terms of a ratio of wavelengths in the two media, λ_1 and λ_2:

$$\frac{\sin\theta_1}{\sin\theta_2} = \frac{v_1}{v_2} = \frac{\lambda_1}{\lambda_2}$$

ZOEPPRITZ'S EQUATION

In seismology, the Zoeppritz equations describe how seismic waves are transmitted and reflected at media boundaries.

The Zoeppritz equations relate the amplitudes of P-waves and S-waves at each side of an interface. For practical purposes, various forms of approximations are usually used.

SEISMIC MIGRATION

Migration is a tool used in seismic processing to get an accurate picture of underground layers. It involves geometric repositioning of return signals to show an event (layer boundary or other structure) where it is being hit by the seismic wave rather than where it is picked up. Migration was first used in the 1920's, and today, it is has evolved into many variations. Two of the more important migration methods are: pre-stack and post-stack migration.

Pre-stack Migration

Pre-stack migration is essentially when seismic data is adjusted before the stacking sequence occurs. The popular form of pre-stack migration is depth migration (PDM). PDM requires the user to know more about velocites of the layers. Once the user inputs these into the data with velocity analysis methods, there will be some error in the image. This error is caused by dipping reflectors or diffractions.

Pre-stack migration is often applied only when the layers being observed have complicated velocity profiles, or when the structures are just too complex to see with post-stack migration. Pre-stack is an important tool in modeling salt diapirs because of their complexity and this has immediate benefits if the resolution can pick up any hydrocarbons trapped by the diapir. Overall, pre-stack migration, depth and time, is a valuable tool in better imaging seismic data, but it is limited by the amount of time and money required to conduct a pre-stack migration. Most of the pre-stack migration will be runwhen post-stacking has failed to resolve the layers or structures. However, with advances in computers, pre-stack migration will eventually become more economical.

Post-stack Migration

Post stack migration is the process of migration in which the data is stacked after it has been migrated. This process is for many reasons, mainly because of its reasonable cost compared to pre-stack migration. As in pre-stack migration, post stack migration is based on the idea that all data elements represent either primary reflections or diffractions. This is done by using an operation involving the rearrangement of seismic information so that reflections and diffractions are plotted at their true locations. The reason that migration is needed is due to the fact that variable velocities and dipping horizons cause the data to record surface positions different from their sub-surface positions. The stacking is accomplished by making a composite record by combining traces from different records. Filtering is involved with stacking because of timing errors or wave-shape difference among the data being stacked.

A disadvantage of using post stack migration compared to pre-stack migration is that it does not give as clear results as pre-stack.

SHEAR WAVES

Type of seismic wave, the S-wave, secondary wave, or shear wave (sometimes called an elastic S-wave) is one of the two main types of elastic body waves, so named because they move through the body of an object, unlike surface waves.

The S-wave move as a shear or transverse wave, so motion is perpendicular to the direction of wave propagation: S-waves, like waves in a rope, as opposed to waves moving through a slinky, the P-wave. The wave moves through elastic media, and the main restoring force comes from shear effects. These waves are divergenceless and obey the continuity equation for incompressible media:

$$\nabla \cdot u = 0.$$

As transverse waves, S-waves exhibit properties, such as polarization and birefringence, much like other transverse waves. S-waves polarized in the horizontal plane are classified as SH-waves. If polarized in the vertical plane, they are classified as

SV-waves. When an S- or P-wave strikes an interface at an angle other than 90 degrees, a phenomenon known as mode conversion occurs. As described above, if the interface is between a solid and liquid, S becomes P or vice versa. However, even if the interface is between two solid media, mode conversion results. If a P-wave strikes an interface, four propagation modes may result: reflected and transmitted P and reflected and transmitted SV. Similarly, if an SV-wave strikes an interface, the same four modes occur in different proportions. The exact amplitudes of all these waves are described by the Zoeppritz equations, which in turn are solutions to the wave equation. S-waves are slower than P-waves.

The prediction of S-waves came out of theory in the 1800s. Starting with the stress-strain relationship for an isotropic solid:

$$T_{ij} = \lambda\delta_{ij}e_{kk} + 2\mu e_{ij}$$

where τ is the stress, λ and μ are the Lamé parameters (with μ as the shear modulus), δ_{ij} is the Kronecker delta, and the strain tensor is defined

$$e_{ij} = \lambda\delta_{ij}\partial_k u_k + \mu(\partial_i u_j + \partial_j u_i).$$

for strain displacement u. Plugging the latter into the former yields:

$$\tau_{ij} = \lambda\delta_{ij}\partial_k u_k + \mu(\partial_i u_j + \partial_j u_i).$$

Newton's 2nd law in this situation gives the homogeneous equation of motion for seismic wave propagation:

$$\rho\frac{\partial^2 u_i}{\partial t^2} = \partial_j \tau_{ij}$$

where ρ is the mass density. Plugging in what the stress tensor is above gives:

$$\rho\frac{\partial^2 u_i}{\partial t^2} = \partial_j\lambda\partial_k u_k + \partial_j\mu(\partial_i u_j + \partial_j u_i) \times \lambda\partial_i\partial_k u_k$$
$$+\mu\partial_i\partial_j u_j + \mu\partial_j\partial_j u_i.$$

Applying vector identities and making certain approximations gives the seismic wave equation in homogeneous media:

$$\rho\ddot{u} = (\lambda + 2\mu)\nabla(\nabla\cdot u) - \mu\nabla\times(\nabla\times u)$$

where Newton's notation has been used for the time derivative. Taking the curl of this equation and applying vector identities eventually gives:

$$\nabla^2(\nabla\times u) - \frac{1}{\beta^2}\frac{\partial^2(\nabla\times u)}{\partial t^2} = 0$$

which is simply the wave equation applied to the curl of u with a velocity β satisfying

$$\beta^2 = \frac{\mu}{\rho}.$$

This describes S-wave propagation. Taking the divergence of seismic wave equation in homogeneous media instead of the curl, yields an equation describing P-wave propgation.

VERTICAL SEISMIC PROFILE

In geophysics, Vertical Seismic Profile (VSP) is a technique of seismic measurements used for correlation with surface seismic data. The defining characteristic of a VSP (of which there are many types) is that either the energy source, or the detectors (or sometimes both) are in a borehole. In the most common type of VSP, Hydrophones, or more often geophones or accelerometers, in the borehole record reflected seismic energy originating from a seismic source at the surface.

3D SEISMIC

3D seismic interpretation is a form of seismic interpretation which relies on the use of 3D surveys which provide visualizations of structures in three dimensions. People often use specialized software for this task, as 3D seismic interpretation requires a lot of math and the careful construction and interpretation of data. There are a number of applications for this process, including the examination of sites to determine whether or not they would make viable oilfields, exploration of the ocean floor, and general geological study.

In seismic surveys, controlled explosions are generated and the reflections of these explosions are read to generate data about what is going on underground. With 3D seismic interpretation, this data is mapped on a three dimensional representation which allows people to explore the data in a number of different ways. Rather than visualizing a site in the form of a flat elevation map or cross section, 3D seismic interpretation allows people to manipulate the angle of view and to visualize a site as a whole. It can also provide information about the surrounding area which may not be readily apparent with other mapping techniques.

Seismic interpretation can get very complex. Geologists are interested in the fundamental structure of the Earth, and they are also interested in the components of the sites they are studying. Different types of rock reflect explosions differently, and 3D seismic interpretation is designed to reveal not only the presence of underground formations, but what is in those formations, and where the transitions between different types of materials are occurring.

Using this information, a geologist can play with scenarios. Modeling scenarios on a map allows geologists to explore the possible results of various activities. For example, a geologist may be concerned that oilfield exploration could cause the collapse of a delicate formation, potentially putting people or the environment in danger. They may also believe that formations present on site hold a limited amount of useful resources, making investment in the site potentially unprofitable.

Seismic data from current and past surveys can both be loaded into seismic software which is used in 3D seismic interpretation. Many programs offer a range of options, some of which are tailored to specific applications such as oilfield geology.

9 Well logging and other methods

WELL LOGGING

Well logging, also known as borehole logging is the practice of making a detailed record (a well log) of the geologic formations penetrated by a borehole. The log may be based either on visual inspection of samples brought to the surface (geological logs) or on physical measurements made by instruments lowered into the hole (geophysical logs). Well logging is done when drilling boreholes for oil and gas, groundwater, minerals, and for environmental and geotechnical studies.

ELECTRIC OR GEOPHYSICAL WELL LOGS

The oil and gas industry records rock and fluid properties to find hydrocarbon zones in the geological formations intersected by a borehole. The logging procedure consists of lowering a 'logging tool' on the end of a wireline into an oil well (or hole) to measure the rock and fluid properties of the formation. An interpretation of these measurements is then made to locate and quantify potential depth zones containing oil and gas (hydrocarbons). Logging tools developed over the years measure the electrical, acoustic, radioactive, electromagnetic, nuclear magnetic resonance, and other properties of the rocks and their contained fluids. Logging is usually performed as the logging tools are pulled out of the hole. This data is recorded to a printed record called a "well log" and is normally transmitted digitally to office locations. Well logging is performed at various intervals during the drilling of the well and when the total depth is drilled, which could range in depths from 300 m to 8000 m (1000 ft to 25,000 ft) or more.

Electric line is the common term for the armored, insulated cable used to conduct current to downhole tools used for well logging. Electric line can be subdivided into open hole operations and cased hole operations.

Open hole operations, or reservoir evaluation, involves the deployment of tools into a freshly drilled well. As the toolstring traverses the wellbore, the individual tools gather information about the surrounding formations. A typical open hole log will have information about the density, porosity, permeability, lithology, presence of hydrocarbons, and oil and water saturation.

Cased hole operations, or production optimization, focuses of the optimization of the completed oil well through mechanical services and logging technologies. At this point in the well's life, the well is encased in steel pipe, cemented into the well bore and may or may not be producing. A typical cased hole log may show cement quality, production information, formation data. Mechanical services uses jet perforating guns, setting tools, and dump bailors to optimize the flow of hydrocarbons.

WIRELINE TOOL TYPES

Typically the wireline tools are cylindrical in shape, usually from 1.5 to 5 inches in diameter. There are three types of wireline tools:

1. With sensors without excitation

There are units to measure spontaneous potential (SP), which is a voltage difference between a surface electrode and another electrode located in the downhole instrument, other instruments that measure the natural radiation from natural isotopes of potassium, thorium, etc., to measure pressure and temperature, etc.

2. With sources of excitation and sensors

   There are sensor systems consistent of a source of excitation and a sensor. In this type we find acoustic (also called sonic), electric, inductive, magnetic resonance, sensing systems, just to name a few.

3. Instruments that produce some mechanical work, or retrieve a sample of fluid or rock to the surface.

   Devices to collect samples of rock, samples of fluid extracted from the rock, and some other mechanical devices.

TYPES OF ELECTRIC/ELECTRONIC LOGS

There are many types of electric/electronic logs and they can be categorized either by their function or by the technology that they use. "Open hole logs" are run before the oil or gas well is lined with pipe or cased. "Cased hole logs" are run after the well is lined with casing or production pipe.

Electric/electronic logs can also be divided into two general types based on what physical properties they measure. Resistivity logs measure some aspect of the specific resistance of the geologic formation. There are about 17 types of resistivity logs.

Porosity logs measure the fraction or percentage of pore volume in a volume of rock. Most porosity logs use either acoustic or nuclear technology. Acoustic logs measure characteristics of sound waves propagated through the well-bore environment. Nuclear logs utilize nuclear reactions that take place in the downhole logging instrument or in the formation. Nuclear logs include density logs and neutron logs, as well as gamma ray logs which are used for correlation. The basic principle behind the use of nuclear technology is that a neutron source placed near the formation of which the porosity is required to be measured will result in neutrons being scattered by the hydrogen atoms, largely those present in the formation fluid. Since there is little difference in the neutrons scattered by hydrocarbons or water, the porosity measured gives a figure close to the true physical porosity whereas the figure obtained from electrical resistivity measurements is that due to the conductive formation fluid. The difference between neutron porosity and electrical porosity measurements therefore indicates the presence of hydrocarbons in the formation fluid.

LOGGING WHILE DRILLING

In the 1980s, a new technique, logging while drilling (LWD), was introduced which provided similar information about the well. Instead of sensors being lowered into the well at the end of wireline cable, the sensors are integrated into the drill string and the measurements are made while the well is being drilled. While wireline well logging occurs after the drill string is removed from the well, LWD measures geological parameters while the well is being drilled. However, because there are no wires to the surface, data are recorded downhole and retrieved when the drill string is removed from the hole. A small subset of the measured data can also be transmitted to the surface in real time via pressure pulses in the well's mud fluid column. This mud telemetry method provides a bandwidth of much less than 100 bits per second, although, as drilling through rock is a fairly slow process, data compression techniques mean that this is an ample bandwidth for real-time delivery of information.

LOGGING MEASUREMENT TYPES

Logging measurements are quite sophisticated. The prime target is the measurement of various geophysical properties of the subsurface rock formations. Of particular interest are porosity, permeability, and fluid content. Porosity is the proportion of fluid-filled space found within the rock. It is this space that contains the oil and gas. Permeability is the ability of fluids to flow through the rock. The higher the porosity, the higher the possible oil and gas content of a rock reservoir. The higher the permeability, the easier for the oil and gas to flow toward the wellbore. Logging tools provide measurements that allow for the mathematical interpretation of these quantities.

Beyond just the porosity and permeability, various logging measurements allow the interpretation of what kinds of fluids are in the pores - oil, gas, brine. In addition, the logging measurements are used to determine mechanical properties of the formations. These mechanical properties determine what kind of enhanced recovery methods may be used (tertiary recovery) and what damage to the formation (such as erosion) is to be expected during oil and gas production.

The types of instruments used in well logging are quite broad. The first logging measurements consisted of basic electrical resistivity logs and spontaneous potential (SP) logs, introduced by the Schlumberger brothers in the 1920s. Tools later became available to estimate porosity via sonic velocity and nuclear measurements. Tools are now more specialized and better able to resolve fine details in the formation. Radiofrequency transmission and coupling techniques are used to determine electrical conductivity of fluid (brine is more conductive than oil or gas). Sonic transmission characteristics (pressure waves) determine mechanical integrity. Nuclear magnetic resonance (NMR) can determine the properties of the hydrogen atoms in the pores (surface tension, etc.). Nuclear scattering (radiation scattering), spectrometry and absorption measurements can determine density and elemental analysis or composition. High resolution electrical or acoustical imaging logs are used to visualize the formation, compute formation dip, and analyze thinly-bedded and fractured reservoirs.

In addition to sensor-based measurements above, robotic equipment can sample formation fluids which may then be brought to the surface for laboratory examination. Also, controlled flow measurements can be used to determine in situ viscosity, water and gas cut (percentage), and other fluid and production parameters.

GEOLOGICAL LOGS

Geological logs use data collected at the surface, rather than by downhole instruments. The geological logs include drilling time logs, core logs, sample logs, and mud logs. Mud logs have become the oil industry standard.

Drilling time logs record the time required to drill a given thickness of rock formation. A change in the drilling rate or penetration rate usually means a change in the type of rock penetrated by the bit. The drilling time is expressed as minutes per foot, while the rate of penetration is usually expressed as feet per hour. Therefore, drilling time is the inverse of penetration rate.

Sample logs are made by examining cuttings, which are bits of rock circulated to the surface by the drilling mud in rotary drilling. The cuttings have traveled up the wellbore suspended in the drilling fluid or mud which was pumped into the wellbore via the drill string/pipe and they return to the surface via the annulus, then to the shale shakers via the flow line. Cuttings are then separated from the drilling fluid as they move across the shale shakers and are sampled at regular depth intervals. These rock samples are analyzed and described by the wellsite geologist or mudlogger.

Mud logs are prepared by a mud logging company contracted by the operating company. One parameter a typical mud log displays is the formation gas (gas units or ppm). "The gas recorder usually is scaled in terms of arbitrary gas units, which are defined differently by the various gas-detector manufactures. In practice, significance is placed only on relative changes in the gas concentrations detected". The current industry standard mud log normally includes real-time drilling parameters such as rate of penetration (ROP), lithology, gas hydrocarbons, flow line temperature (temperature of the drilling fluid) and chlorides but may also include mud weight, estimated pore pressure and corrected d-exponent (corrected drilling exponent) for a pressure pack log. Other information that is normally notated on a mud log include lithology descriptions, directional data (deviation surveys), weight on bit, rotary speed, pump pressure, pump rate, viscosity, drill bit info, casing shoe depths, formation tops, mud pump info, to name just a few.

WIRELINE LOG

A continuous measurement of formation properties with electrically powered instruments to infer properties and make decisions about drilling and production operations. The record of the measurements, typically a long strip of paper, is also called a log. Measurements include electrical properties (resistivity at various frequencies), sonic properties, active and passive nuclear measurements, dimensional measurements of the wellbore, formation fluid sampling, formation pressure measurement, wireline-conveyed sidewall coring tools, and others. In wireline measurements, the logging tool (or probe) is lowered into the open wellbore on a multiple conductor, contra-helically armored wireline. Once lowered to the bottom of the interval of interest, the measurements are taken on the way out of the wellbore. This is done in an attempt to maintain tension on the cable (which stretches) as constant as possible for depth correlation purposes. (The exception to this practice is in certain hostile environments in which the tool electronics might not survive the temperatures on bottom for the amount of time it takes to lower the tool and then record measurements while pulling the tool up the hole. In this case, "down log" measurements might actually be conducted on the way into the well, and repeated on the way out if possible.) Most wireline measurements are recorded continuously even though the probe is moving. Certain fluid sampling and pressure-measuring tools require that the probe be stopped, increasing the chance that the probe or the cable might become stuck. LWD tools take measurements in much the same way as wireline-logging tools, except that the measurements are taken by a self-contained tool near the bottom of the bottomhole assembly and are recorded downward (as the well is deepened) rather than upward from the bottom of the hole (as wireline logs are recorded).

INFORMATION USE

In the oil industry, the well and mud logs are usually transferred in 'real time' to the operating company, which uses these logs to make operational decisions about the well, to correlate formation depths with surrounding wells, and to make interpretations about the quantity and quality of hydrocarbons present. Specialists involved in well log interpretation are called log analysts.

PERMEABILITY

Permeability in fluid mechanics and the earth sciences (commonly symbolized as κ, or k) is a measure of the ability of a porous material (often, a rock or unconsolidated material) to transmit fluids. The SI unit for permeability is m^2. A traditional unit for permeability is the darcy (D), or more commonly the millidarcy (mD) (1 darcy $\approx 10^{-12} m^2$). The unit of cm^2 is also sometimes used.

Permeability is part of the proportionality constant in Darcy's law which relates discharge (flow rate) and fluid physical properties (e.g. viscosity), to a pressure gradient applied to the porous media:

$$v = \frac{\kappa \Delta P}{\mu \Delta x}$$

Therefore:

$$\kappa = v \frac{\mu \Delta x}{\Delta P}$$

where:

v is the superficial (or bulk) fluid flow velocity through the medium (i.e., the average velocity calculated as if the fluid were the only phase present in the porous medium) (m/s)

κ is the permeability of a medium (m^2)

μ is the dynamic viscosity of the fluid (Pa s)

ΔP is the applied pressure difference (Pa)

Δx is the thickness of the bed of the porous medium (m)

The proportionality constant specifically for the flow of water through a porous media is the hydraulic conductivity; permeability is a portion of this, and is a property of the porous media only, not the fluid.

In naturally occurring materials, permeability values range over many orders of magnitude.

DETERMINATION OF PERMEABILITY

Permeability is typically determined in the lab by application of Darcy's law under steady state conditions or, more generally, by application of various solutions to the diffusion equation for unsteady flow conditions.

Permeability needs to be measured, either directly (using Darcy's law) or through estimation using empirically derived formulas. However, for some simple models of porous media, permeability can be calculated (e.g., random close packing of identical spheres).

The intrinsic permeability of any porous material is:

$$\kappa_I = C \cdot d^2$$

where

κ_I is the intrinsic permeability [L^2]

C is a dimensionless constant that is related to the configuration of the flow-paths

d is the average, or effective pore diameter [L]

APPLICATIONS

The concept of permeability is of importance in determining the flow characteristics of hydrocarbons in oil and gas reservoirs, and of groundwater in aquifers.

For a rock to be considered as an exploitable hydrocarbon reservoir without stimulation, its permeability must be greater than approximately 100 mD (depending on the nature of the hydrocarbon - gas reservoirs with lower permeabilities are still exploitable because of the lower viscosity of gas with respect to oil). Rocks with permeabilities significantly lower than 100 mD can form efficient seals (see petroleum geology). Unconsolidated sands may have permeabilities of over 5000 mD.

The concept has also many practical applications outside of geology, for example in chemical engineering (e.g., filtration).

POROSITY

Porosity is a measure of the void spaces in a material, and is a fraction of the volume of voids over the total volume, between 0-1, or as a percentage between 0-100%. The term is used in multiple fields including pharmaceutics, ceramics, metallurgy, materials, manufacturing, earth sciences and construction.

Used in geology, hydrogeology, soil science, and building science, the porosity of a porous medium (such as rock or sediment) describes the fraction of void space in the material, where the void may contain, for example, air or water. It is defined by the ratio:

$$\phi = \frac{V_V}{V_T}$$

where V_V is the v of void-space (such as fluids) and V_T is the total or bulk volume of material, including the solid and void components. Both the mathematical symbols φ and n are used to denote porosity.

Porosity is a fraction between 0 and 1, typically ranging from less than 0.01 for solid granite to more than 0.5 for peat and clay, although it may also be represented in percent terms by multiplying the fraction by 100.

The porosity of a rock, or sedimentary layer, is an important consideration when attempting to evaluate the potential volume of water or hydrocarbons it may contain. Sedimentary porosities are a complex function of many factors, including but not limited to: rate of burial, depth of burial, the nature of the connate fluids, the nature of overlying sediments (which may impede fluid expulsion). One commonly used relationship between porosity and depth is given by the Athy (1930) equation:

$$\phi(z) = \phi_0 e^{-kz}$$

where φ_0 is the surface porosity, k is the compaction coefficient (m^{-1}) and z is depth (m).

A value for porosity can alternatively be calculated from the bulk density ρ_{bulk} and particle density $\rho_{particle}$:

$$\phi = 1 - \frac{\rho_{bulk}}{\rho_{particle}}$$

Normal particle density is assumed to be approximately 2.65 g/cm^3, although a better estimation can be obtained by examining the lithology of the particles.

TYPES OF GEOLOGIC POROSITIES

Primary porosity

The main or original porosity system in a rock or unconfined alluvial deposit.

Secondary porosity

A subsequent or separate porosity system in a rock, often enhancing overall porosity of a rock. This can be a result of chemical leeching of minerals or the generation of a fracture system. This can replace the primary porosity or coexist with it.

Fracture porosity

This is porosity associated with a fracture system or faulting. This can create secondary porosity in rocks that otherwise would not be reservoirs for hydrocarbons due to their primary porosity being destroyed (for example due to depth of burial) or of a rock type not normally considered a reservoir (for example igneous intrusions or metasediments).

Vuggy porosity

This is secondary porosity generated by dissolution of large features (such as macrofossils) in carbonate rocks leaving large holes, vugs, or even caves.

Effective porosity (also called open porosity)

Refers to the fraction of the total volume in which fluid flow is effectively taking place (this excludes dead-end pores or non-connected cavities). This is very important for groundwater and petroleum flow, as well as for solute transport.

Dual porosity

Refers to the conceptual idea that there are two overlapping reservoirs which interact. In fractured rock aquifers, the rock mass and fractures are often simulated as being two overlapping but distinct bodies. Delayed yield, and leaky aquifer flow solutions are both mathematically similar solutions to that obtained for dual porosity; in all three cases water comes from two mathematically different reservoirs (whether or not they are physically different).

Macro porosity

Refers to pores greater than 50 nm in diameter. Flow through macropores is described by bulk diffusion.

Meso porosity

Refers to pores greater than 2 nm and less than 50 nm in diameter. Flow through mesopores is described by Knudsen diffusion.

Micro porosity

Refers to pores smaller than 2 nm in diameter. Movement in micropores is by activated diffusion.

Measuring porosity

Several methods can be employed to measure porosity:

- Direct methods (determining the bulk volume of the porous sample, and then determining the volume of the skeletal material with no pores (pore volume = total volume – material volume).
- Optical methods (e.g., determining the area of the material versus the area of the pores visible under the microscope). The "areal" and "volumetric" porosities are equal for porous media with random structure.
- Imbibition methods, i.e., immersion of the porous sample, under vacuum, in a fluid that preferentially wets the pores.
- Water saturation method (pore volume = total volume of water – volume of water left after soaking).
- Water evaporation method (pore volume in cubic centimeters = weight of saturated sample in grams – weight of dried sample in grams)

- Mercury intrusion porosimetry (several non-mercury intrusion techniques have been developed due to toxicological concerns, and the fact that mercury tends to form amalgams with several metals/alloys).
- Gas expansion method. A sample of known bulk volume is enclosed in a container of known volume. It is connected to another container with a known volume which is evacuated. When the valve connecting the two containers is opened, some of the gas passes from the first container to the second. Using ideal gas law:

$$V_V = V_T - V_a - V_b \frac{P_2}{P_2 - P_1}$$

where:

V_V is the effective volume of the pores,

V_T is the bulk volume of the sample,

V_a is the volume of the container containing the sample,

V_b is the volume of the evacuated container, and

P_1 and P_2 are the initial and final pressures, respectively.

9. METEOROLOGY

Physical Meteorology

Physical Meteorology

THERMAL STRUCTURE OF THE ATMOSPHERE AND ITS COMPOSITION

The atmosphere can be divided into four regions on the basis of temperature:

The bottom layer, where temperature decreases with altitude, is known as the troposphere (from the Greek for "turning layer"). The troposphere is approximately 12 kilometers thick, but there are slight variations. If the temperature increases with increasing altitude in the troposphere, then a temperature inversion exists. All the weather that we are primarily interested in, occurs in the troposphere. The top of the troposphere is marked by the tropopause.

Above the tropopause lies the stratosphere. It gets it's name from the Greek meaning "stratified layer." The layer is stratified with the denser, cooler air below the warmer, lighter air. This leads to an increase in temperature with height. Since the stratosphere isn't turbulent this is where most planes like to fly. The temperature increases with height until it reaches about 10°C at an altitude of 48 km. The primary reason that there is a temperature increase with altitude is that most of the ozone is contained in the stratosphere. Ultraviolet light interacting with the ozone causes the temperature increase. The boundary between the stratosphere and the next layer is called the stratopause.

Above the stratopause, the temperature again decreases with altitude. This layer is called the mesosphere, or "middle layer." The temperature drops to ~-90°C near the top of the mesosphere where the mesopausé is located.

Above the mesopause is the thermosphere, or "warm layer." In the thermosphere the temperature does increase with height (to >1000°C), but as we have already seen, the number of molecules present are so few that even thought they are very energetic, they have such a low density, that temperature as we call it means very little.

Above the thermosphere lies the exosphere ("outer layer"). The boundary between the two is very diffuse. Molecules in the exosphere have enough kinetic energy to escape the earth's gravity and thus fly off into space. This is where helium "disappears."

The outer part of the mesosphere and the thermosphere are sometimes called the ionosphere since most of the molecules and atoms are ionized by the ultraviolet light and other high energy particles at this height. The ionosphere is what radio signals bounce off.

RAYLEIGH SCATTERING

Rayleigh scattering (named after the English physicist Lord Rayleigh) is the elastic scattering of light or other electromagnetic radiation by particles much smaller than the wavelength of the light, which may be individual atoms or molecules. It can occur when light travels in transparent solids and liquids, but is most prominently seen in gases. Rayleigh scattering is a function of the electric polarizability of the particles.

Rayleigh scattering of sunlight in clear atmosphere is the main reason why the sky is blue: Rayleigh and cloud-mediated scattering contribute to diffuse light (direct light being sunrays).

The size of a scattering particle is parametrized by the ratio x of its characteristic dimension r and wavelength λ:

$$x = \frac{2\pi r}{\lambda}.$$

Rayleigh scattering can be defined as scattering in the small size parameter regime x << 1. Scattering from larger spherical particles is explained by the Mie theory for an arbitrary size parameter x. For small x the Mie theory reduces to the Rayleigh approximation.

The amount of Rayleigh scattering that occurs for a beam of light is dependent upon the size of the particles and the wavelength of the light. Specifically, the intensity of the scattered light varies as the sixth power of the particle size and varies inversely with the fourth power of the wavelength.

The intensity I of light scattered by a single small particle from a beam of unpolarized light of wavelength λ and intensity I_0 is given by:

$$I = I_0 \frac{1+\cos^2\theta}{2R^2}\left(\frac{2\pi}{\lambda}\right)^4\left(\frac{n^2-1}{n^2+2}\right)^2\left(\frac{d}{2}\right)^6$$

where R is the distance to the particle, θ is the scattering angle, n is the refractive index of the particle, and d is the diameter of the particle.

$$\sigma_s = \frac{2\pi^5}{3}\frac{d^6}{\lambda^4}\left(\frac{n^2-1}{n^2+2}\right)^2$$

The Rayleigh scattering coefficient for a group of scattering particles is the number of particles per unit volume N times the cross-section. As with all wave effects, for incoherent scattering the scattered powers add arithmetically, while for coherent scattering, such as if the particles are very near each other, the fields add arithmetically and the sum must be squared to obtain the total scattered power.

MIE SCATTERING

Mie scattering is an analytical solution of Maxwell's equations for the scattering of electromagnetic radiation by spherical particles.

In contrast to Rayleigh scattering, the Mie solution to the scattering problem is valid for all possible ratios of diameter to wavelength, although the technique results in numerical summation of infinite sums. In its original formulation it assumed an homogeneous, isotropic and optically linear material irradiated by an infinitely extending plane wave. However, solutions for layered spheres are also possible.

APPLICATIONS

Mie theory is very important in meteorological optics, where diameter-to-wavelength ratios of the order of unity and larger are characteristic of many problems regarding haze and cloud scattering. A further application is in the characterization of particles via optical scattering measurements. The Mie solution is also important for understanding the appearance of common materials like milk, biological tissue and latex paint.

ATMOSPHERIC SCIENCE

Mie scattering occurs when the particles in the atmosphere are the same size as the wavelengths being scattered. Dust, pollen, smoke and water vapour are common causes of Mie scattering which tends to affect longer wavelengths. Mie scattering occurs mostly in the lower portions of the atmosphere where larger particles are more abundant, and dominates when cloud conditions are overcast.

PARTICLE SIZING

Mie theory has been used in the detection of oil concentration in polluted waters.

SOLAR CONSTANT

the Solar Radiation that falls on an area above the atmosphere at a vertical angle: s = 1.37 kW/m^2.

In space, solar radiation is practically constant; on earth it varies with the time of day and year as well as with the latitude and weather. The maximum value on earth is between 0.8 and 1.0 kW / m^2. In Germany, the average annual amount of insolation varies between 950 and 1100 kWh / m^2, depending on the region.

The solar constant, a measure of flux, is the amount of incoming solar electromagnetic radiation per unit area that would be incident on a plane perpendicular to the rays, at a distance of one astronomical unit (AU) (roughly the mean distance from the Sun to the Earth). When solar irradiance is measured on the outer surface of Earth's atmosphere, the measurements can be adjusted using the inverse square law to infer the magnitude of solar irradiance at one AU and deduce the solar constant.

The solar constant includes all types of solar radiation, not just the visible light. It is measured by satellite to be roughly 1.366 kilowatts per square meter (kW/m^2).The actual direct solar irradiance at the top of the atmosphere fluctuates by about 6.9% during a year (from 1.412 kW/m^2 in early January to 1.321 kW/ml in early July) due to the Earth's varying distance from the Sun, and typically by much less than one part per thousand from day to day. Thus, for the whole Earth (which has a cross section of 127,400,000 km^2), the power is 1.740×10^{17} W, plus or minus 3.5%. The solar constant does not remain constant over long periods of time (see Solar variation), but over a year varies much less than the variation of direct solar irradiance at the top of the atmosphere arising from the ellipticity of the Earth's orbit. The approximate average value cited, 1.366 kW/m^2, is equivalent to 1.96 calories per minute per square centimeter, or 1.96 langleys (Ly) per minute.

The Earth receives a total amount of radiation determined by its cross section ($\pi \cdot R_E^2$), but as it rotates this energy is distributed across the entire surface area ($4 \cdot \pi \cdot R_E^2$). Hence the average incoming solar radiation, taking into account the angle at which the rays strike and that at any one moment half the planet does not receive any solar radiation, is one-fourth the solar constant (approximately 342 W/m^2).

At any given moment, the amount of solar radiation received at a location on the Earth's surface depends on the state of the atmosphere and the location's latitude.

The solar constant includes all wavelengths of solar electromagnetic radiation, not just the visible light (see Electromagnetic spectrum). It is linked to the apparent magnitude of the Sun, −26.8, in that the solar constant and the magnitude of the Sun are two methods of describing the apparent brightness of the Sun, though the magnitude is based on the Sun's visual output only.

In 1884, Samuel Pierpont Langley attempted to estimate the solar constant from Mount Whitney in California. By taking readings at different times of day, he attempted to remove effects due to atmospheric absorption. However, the value he obtained, 2.903 kW/m^2, was still too great. Between 1902 and 1957, measurements by Charles Greeley Abbot and others at various high-altitude sites found values between 1.322 and 1.465 kW/m^2. Abbott proved that one of Langley's corrections was erroneously applied. His results varied between 1.89 and 2.22 calories (1.318 to 1.548 kW/m^2), a variation that appeared to be due to the Sun and not the Earth's atmosphere.

The angular diameter of the Earth as seen from the Sun is approximately 1/11,000 radians, meaning the solid angle of the Earth as seen from the Sun is approximately 1/140,000,000 of a steradian. Thus the Sun emits about two billion times the amount of radiation that is caught by Earth, in other words about 3.86×1026 watts

ALBEDO

The albedo of an object is a measure of how strongly it reflects light from light sources such as the Sun. It is therefore a more specific form of the term reflectivity. Albedo is defined as the ratio of total-reflected to incident electromagnetic radiation. It is a unitless measure indicative of a surface's or body's diffuse reflectivity.

The albedo is an important concept in climatology and astronomy, as well as in computer graphics and computer vision. In climatology it is sometimes expressed as a percentage. Its value depends on the frequency of radiation considered: unqualified, it usually refers to some appropriate average across the spectrum of visible light. In general, the albedo depends on the direction and directional distribution of incoming radiation.

EXAMPLES OF TERRESTRIAL ALBEDO EFFECTS

The tropics

Although the albedo-temperature effect is most famous in colder regions of Earth, because more snow falls there, it is actually much stronger in tropical regions because in the tropics there is consistently more sunlight. When ranchers cut down dark, tropical rainforest trees to replace them with even darker soil in order to grow crops, the average temperature of the area increases up to 3°C (5.4°F) year-round, although part of the effect is due to changed evaporation (latent heat flux).

Small scale effects

Albedo works on a smaller scale, too. People who wear dark clothes in the summertime put themselves at a greater risk of heatstroke than those who wear lighter color clothes.

Trees

Because trees tend to have a low albedo, removing forests would tend to increase albedo and thereby could produce localized climate cooling. Cloud feedbacks further complicate the issue. In seasonally snow-covered zones, winter albedos of treeless areas are 10% to 50% higher than nearby forested areas because snow does not cover the trees as readily. Deciduous trees have an albedo value of about 0.15 to 0.18 while coniferous trees have a value of about 0.09 to 0.15. The difference between deciduous and coniferous is because coniferous trees are darker in general and have cone-shaped crowns. The shape of these crowns trap radiant energy more effectively than deciduous trees.

Studies by the Hadley Centre have investigated the relative (generally warming) effect of albedo change and (cooling) effect of carbon sequestration on planting forests. They found that new forests in tropical and midlatitude areas tended to cool; new forests in high latitudes (e.g. Siberia) were neutral or perhaps warming.

Snow

Snow albedos can be as high as 0.9; this, however, is for the ideal example: fresh deep snow over a featureless landscape. Over Antarctica they average a little more than 0.8. If a marginally snow-covered area warms, snow tends to melt, lowering the albedo, and hence leading to more snowmel.

Water

Water reflects light very differently from typical terrestrial materials. The reflectivity of a water surface is calculated using the Fresnel equations.

At the scale of the wavelength of light even wavy water is always smooth so the light is reflected in a locally specular manner (not diffusely). The glint of light off water is a commonplace effect of this. At small angles of incident light, waviness results in reduced reflectivity because of the steepness of the reflectivity-vs.-incident-angle curve and a locally increased average incident angle.

Although the reflectivity of water is very low at low and medium angles of incident light, it increases tremendously at high angles of incident light such as occur on the illuminated side of the Earth near the terminator (early morning, late afternoon and near the poles). However, as mentioned above, waviness causes an appreciable reduction. Since the light specularly reflected from water does not usually reach the viewer, water is usually considered to have a very low albedo in spite of its high reflectivity at high angles of incident light.

Note that white caps on waves look white (and have high albedo) because the water is foamed up (not smooth at the scale of the wavelength of light) so the Fresnel equations do not apply. Fresh 'black' ice exhibits Fresnel reflection.

Clouds

Clouds are another source of albedo that play into the global warming equation. Different types of clouds have different albedo values, theoretically ranging from a minimum of near 0 to a maximum approaching 0.8. "On any given day, about half of Earth is covered by clouds, which reflect more sunlight than land and water. Clouds keep Earth cool by reflecting sunlight, but they can also serve as blankets to trap warmth."

Albedo and climate in some areas are already affected by artificial clouds, such as those created by the contrails of heavy commercial airliner traffic. A study following the burning of the Kuwaiti oil fields by Saddam Hussein showed that temperatures under the burning oil fires were as much as 10ºC colder than temperatures several miles away under clear skies.

Aerosol effects

Aerosol (very fine particles/droplets in the atmosphere) has two effects, direct and indirect. The direct (albedo) effect is generally to cool the planet; the indirect effect is less certain.

Black carbon

Another albedo-related effect on the climate is from black carbon particles. The size of this effect is difficult to quantify: the IPCC say that their "estimate of the global mean radiative forcing for BC aerosols from fossil fuels is... +0.2 W m^{-2} (from +0.1 W m^{-2} in the SAR) with a range +0.1 to +0.4 W m^{-2}..."

RADIATIVE TRANSFER

Radiative transfer is the physical phenomenon of energy transfer in the form of electromagnetic radiation. The propagation of radiation through a medium is affected by absorption, emission and scattering processes. The equation of radiative transfer describes these interactions mathematically. Equations of radiative transfer have application in wide variety of subjects including optics, astrophysics, atmospheric science, and remote sensing. Analytic solutions to the radiative transfer equation (RTE) exist for simple cases but for more realistic media with complex multiple scattering effects numerical methods are required.

The fundamental quantity which describes a field of radiation is the spectral intensity. If we think of a very small area element in the radiation field, there will be radiation energy flowing through that area element. The flow can be completely characterized by the amount of energy flowing per unit time per unit solid angle, the direction of the flow, and the wavelength interval being considered (polarization will be ignored for the moment)..

In terms of the spectral intensity, I_v, the energy flowing across an area element of area da located at r in time dt in the solid angle $d\Omega$ about the direction $\hat{n}$ in the frequency interval v to $v + dv$ is

$$dE_v = I_v(r,\ \hat{n},\ t)\cos\theta\ dv\ da\ d\Omega\ dt$$

where θ is the angle that the unit direction vector makes with a normal to the area element. The units of the spectral intensity are seen to be energy/time/area/solid angle/frequency. In MKS units this would be $W{\cdot}m^{-2}{\cdot}sr^{-1}{\cdot}Hz^{-1}$ (watts per square-metre-steradian-hertz).

THE EQUATION OF RADIATIVE TRANSFER

The equation of radiative transfer simply says that as a beam of radiation travels, it loses energy to absorption, gains energy by emission, and redistributes energy by scattering. The differential form of the equation for radiative transfer is:

$$\frac{1}{c}\frac{\partial}{\partial t}I_v + \hat{\Omega}\cdot\nabla I_v + (k_{v,s} + k_{v,a})I_v = j_v + \frac{1}{4\pi c}k_{v,s}\int_{\Omega} I_v d\Omega$$

where j_v is the emission coefficient, $k_{v,s}$ is the scattering cross section, and $k_{v,a}$ is the absorption cross section.

SOLUTIONS TO THE EQUATION OF RADIATIVE TRANSFER

Solutions to the equation of radiative transfer form an enormous body of work. The differences however, are essentially due to the various forms for the emission and absorption coefficients. If scattering is ignored, then a general solution in terms of the emission and absorption coefficients may be written:

$$I_v(s) = I_v(s_0)e^{-\tau(s_{0,s})} + \int_{s_0}^{s} j_v(s')e^{-(\tau)s\acute{s}}\quad ds'$$

where $\tau(s_1,s_2)$ is the optical depth of the atmosphere between s_1 and s_2:

$$\tau(s_1, s_2) \stackrel{\text{def}}{=} \int_{s_1}^{s_2} \alpha_v(s)\,ds$$

GREENHOUSE EFFECT

The greenhouse effect is caused by an atmosphere containing gases that absorb and emit infrared radiation. Greenhouse gases trap heat within the surface-troposphere system, causing heating at the surface of the planet or moon.

MECHANISM

The Earth receives energy from the Sun mostly in the form of visible light and nearby wavelengths, largely in the range 0.2– 4 μm, corresponding to the Sun's radiative temperature of 6,000 K. About 50% of the sun's energy is absorbed at the Earth's surface and the rest is reflected or absorbed by the atmosphere. The absorbed energy warms the surface. Simple presentations of the greenhouse effect, such as the Idealized greenhouse model, show this heat being lost as thermal radiation. The reality is more complex: the atmosphere near the surface is largely opaque to thermal radiation (with important exceptions for "window" bands), and most heat loss from the surface is by sensible heat and latent heat transport. Radiative energy losses become increasingly important higher in the atmosphere largely because of the decreasing concentration of water vapor, an important greenhouse gas. It is more realistic to think of the greenhouse effect as applying to a "surface" in the mid-troposphere, which is effectively coupled to the surface by a lapse rate.

Within the region where radiative effects are important the description given by the idealized greenhouse model becomes realistic: The surface of the Earth, warmed to a temperature around 255 K, radiates long-wavelength, infra-red heat in the range 4 - 100 μm. At these wavelengths, greenhouse gasses that were largely transparent to incoming solar radiation are more absorbent. Each layer of atmosphere with greenhouses gases absorbs some of the heat being radiated upwards from lower layers. In order to maintain its own equilibrium, it re-radiates the absorbed heat in all directions, both upwards and downwards. This results in more warmth below, while still radiating enough heat back out into deep space from the upper layers to maintain overall thermal equilibrium. Increasing the concentration of the gases increases the amount of absorption and re-radiation, and thereby further warms the layers and ultimately the surface below.

GREENHOUSE GASES

By their percentage contribution to the greenhouse effect the four major gases are:

- water vapor,
- carbon dioxide
- methane,
- ozone,

The major non-gas contributor to the Earth's greenhouse effect, clouds, also absorb and emit infrared radiation and thus have an effect on radiative properties of the atmosphere

GREENHOUSE GASES & CLIMATE CHANGE

Strengthening of the greenhouse effect through human activities is known as the enhanced (or anthropogenic) greenhouse effect. This increase in radiative forcing from human activity is attributable mainly to increased atmospheric carbon dioxide levels.

CO_2 is produced by fossil fuel burning and other activities such as cement production and tropical deforestation. Measurements of CO_2 from the Mauna Loa observatory show that concentrations have increased from about 313 ppm in 1960 to about 389 ppm in 2010. The current observed amount of CO_2 exceeds the geological record maxima (~300 ppm) from ice core data. The effect of combustion-produced carbon dioxide on the global climate, a special case of the greenhouse effect first described in 1896 by Svante Arrhenius, has also been called the Callendar effect.

Because it is a greenhouse gas, elevated CO_2 levels contribute to additional absorption and emission of thermal infrared in the atmosphere, which produce net warming. According to the latest Assessment Report from the Intergovernmental Panel on Climate Change, "most of the observed increase in globally averaged temperatures since the mid-20th century is very likely due to the observed increase in anthropogenic greenhouse gas concentrations".

Over the past 800,000 years, ice core data shows unambiguously that carbon dioxide has varied from values as low as 180 parts per million (ppm) to the pre-industrial level of 270ppm. Paleoclimatologists consider variations in carbon dioxide to be a fundamental factor in controlling climate variations over this time scale.

SPECIFIC GAS CONSTANT

The gas constant (also known as the molar, universal, or ideal gas constant, denoted by the symbol R or R) is a physical constant which is featured in a large number of fundamental equations in the physical sciences, such as the ideal gas law and the Nernst equation. It is equivalent to the Boltzmann constant, but expressed in units of energy (i.e. the pressure-volume product) per kelvin per mole (rather than energy per kelvin per particle).

Its value is

$$R = 8.314472(15)\frac{\text{J}}{\text{K mol}}.$$

The two digits in parentheses are the uncertainty (standard deviation) in the last two digits of the value. The relative uncertainty is 1.8×10^{-6}.

The gas constant occurs in the ideal gas law, as follows:

$$pV = nRT$$

where p is the absolute pressure, V is the volume of gas, n is the number of moles of gas, and T is thermodynamic temperature. The gas constant has the same units as molar entropy.

SPECIFIC GAS CONSTANT

The specific gas constant of a gas or a mixture of gases (Rspecific) is given by the molar gas constant, divided by the molar mass (M) of the gas/mixture.

$$R_{\text{specific}} = \frac{R}{M}$$

Just as the ideal gas constant can be related to the Boltzmann constant, so can the specific gas constant by dividing the Boltzmann constant by the molecular mass of the gas.

$$R_{\text{specific}} = \frac{k_B}{m}$$

Another important relationship comes from thermodynamics. This relates the specific gas constant to the specific heats for a calorically perfect gas and a thermally perfect gas.

$$R_{\text{specific}} = c_p - c_v$$

where c_p is the specific heat for a constant pressure and c_v is the specific heat for a constant volume.

It is common, especially in engineering applications, to represent the specific gas constant by the symbol R. In such cases, the universal gas constant is usually given a different symbol such as R to distinguish it. In any case, the context and/or units of the gas constant should make it clear as to whether the universal or specific gas constant is being referred to.

ADIABATIC PROCESS

Adiabatic process or an isocaloric process is a thermodynamic process in which no heat is transferred to or from the working fluid. The term "adiabatic" literally means impassable, coming from the Greek roots α′- ("not"), δτ - ("through"), and βαίνετν ("to pass"); this etymology corresponds here to an absence of heat transfer. Conversely, a process that involves heat transfer (addition or loss of heat to the surroundings) is generally called diabatic. Although the two terms can often be interchanged, adiabatic processes may be considered a subset of isocaloric processes; the remaining complement subset of isocaloric processes being processes where net heat transfer does not diverge regionally such as in an idealized case with mediums of infinite thermal conductivity or non-existent thermal capacity.

In an adiabatic irreversible process, dQ=0 is not equal to TdS (TdS>0). dQ=TdS=0 holds for reversible processes only. For example, an adiabatic boundary is a boundary that is impermeable to heat transfer and the system is said to be adiabatically (or thermally) insulated; an insulated wall approximates an adiabatic boundary. Another example is the adiabatic flame temperature, which is the temperature that would be achieved by a flame in the absence of heat loss to the surroundings. An adiabatic process that is reversible is also called an isentropic process. Additionally, an adiabatic process that is irreversible and extracts no work is in an isenthalpic process, such as viscous drag, progressing towards a nonnegative change in entropy.

ADIABATIC HEATING AND COOLING

Adiabatic changes in temperature occur due to changes in pressure of a gas while not adding or subtracting any heat.

Adiabatic heating occurs when the pressure of a gas is increased from work done on it by its surroundings, ie a piston. Diesel engines rely on adiabatic heating during their compression stroke to elevate the temperature sufficiently to ignite the fuel.

Adiabatic heating also occurs in the Earth's atmosphere when an air mass descends, for example, in a katabatic wind or Foehn wind flowing downhill.

Adiabatic cooling occurs when the pressure of a substance is decreased as it does work on its surroundings. Adiabatic cooling does not have to involve a fluid. One technique used to reach very low temperatures (thousandths and even millionths of a degree above absolute zero) is adiabatic demagnetisation, where the change in magnetic field on a magnetic material is used to provide adiabatic cooling. Adiabatic cooling also occurs in the Earth's atmosphere with orographic lifting and lee waves, and this can form pileus or lenticular clouds if the air is cooled below the dew point.

Rising magma also undergoes adiabatic cooling before eruption.

Such temperature changes can be quantified using the ideal gas law, or the hydrostatic equation for atmospheric processes.

It should be noted that no process is truly adiabatic. Many processes are close to adiabatic and can be easily approximated by using an adiabatic assumption, but there is always some heat loss; as no perfect insulators exist.

The definition of an adiabatic process is that heat transfer to the system is zero, $\delta Q = 0$. Then, according to the first law of thermodynamics,

1. $dU + \delta W = \delta Q = 0,$

where dU is the change in the internal energy of the system and δW is work done by the system. Any work (δW) done must be done at the expense of internal energy U, since no heat δQ is being supplied from the surroundings. Pressure-volume work δW done by the system is defined as

2. $\delta W = PdV.$

However, P does not remain constant during an adiabatic process but instead changes along with volume.

It is desired to know how the values of dP and dV relate to each other as the adiabatic process proceeds. For an ideal gas the internal energy is given by

3. $U = \alpha nRT,$

where R is the universal gas constant and n is the number of moles in the system (a constant).

Differentiating Equation (3) and use of the ideal gas law, PV = nRT, yields

4. $dU = \alpha nRdT = \alpha d(PV) = \alpha(PdV + VdP).$

Equation (4) is often expressed as because CV = αR.

Now substitute equations (2) and (4) into equation (1) to obtain

$$-PdV = \alpha PdV + \alpha V\, dP,$$

simplify:

$$-(\alpha+1)P\,dV = \alpha V\,dP,$$

and divide both sides by PV:

$$-(\alpha+1)\frac{dV}{V}=\alpha\frac{dP}{P}.$$

After integrating the left and right sides from V_0 to V and from P_0 to P and changing the sides respectively,

$$\ln\left(\frac{P}{P_0}\right)=-\frac{\alpha+1}{\alpha}\ln\left(\frac{V}{V_0}\right).$$

Exponentiate both sides,

$$\left(\frac{P}{P_0}\right)=\left(\frac{V}{V_0}\right)^{-\frac{\alpha+1}{\alpha}},$$

and eliminate the negative sign to obtain

$$\left(\frac{P}{P_0}\right)=\left(\frac{V}{V_0}\right)^{\frac{\alpha+1}{\alpha}}.$$

Therefore,

$$\left(\frac{P}{P_0}\right)\left(\frac{V}{V_0}\right)^{\frac{\alpha+1}{\alpha}}=1$$

and

$$PV^{\frac{\alpha+1}{\alpha}}=P_0V_0^{\frac{\alpha+1}{\alpha}}=PV^{\gamma}=\text{constant}.$$

ISENTROPIC PROCESS

Isentropic process or isoentropic process is one in which for purposes of engineering analysis and calculation, one may assume that the process takes place from initiation to completion without an increase or decrease in the entropy of the system, i.e., the entropy of the system remains constant. It can be proved that any reversible adiabatic process is an isentropic process.

Second law of thermodynamics states that,

$$\delta Q \le TdS$$

where δQ is the amount of energy the system gains by heating, T is the temperature of the system, and dS is the change in entropy. The equal sign will hold for a reversible process. For a reversible isentropic process, there is no transfer of heat energy and therefore the process is also adiabatic. For an irreversible process, the entropy will increase. Hence removal of heat from the system (cooling) is necessary to maintain a constant internal entropy for an irreversible process in order to make it isentropic. Thus an irreversible isentropic process is not adiabatic.

For reversible processes, an isentropic transformation is carried out by thermally "insulating" the system from its surroundings. Temperature is the thermodynamic conjugate variable to entropy, thus the conjugate process would be an isothermal process in which the system is thermally "connected" to a constant-temperature heat bath.

ISENTROPIC FLOW

An isentropic flow is a flow that is both adiabatic and reversible. That is, no energy is added to the flow, and no energy losses occur due to friction or dissipative effects. For an isentropic flow of a perfect gas, several relations can be derived to define the pressure, density and temperature along a streamline.

Derivation of the isentropic relations

For a closed system, the total change in energy of a system is the sum of the work done and the heat added,

$$dU = dW + dQ$$

The work done on a system by changing the volume is,

$$dW = -pdV$$

where p is the pressure and V is the volume. The change in enthalpy $(H = U + pV)$ is given by,

$$dH = dU + pdV + Vdp = nC_p dT$$

Since a reversible process is adiabatic (i.e. no heat transfer occurs), so $dQ = 0, dS = 0$. This leads to two important observations,

$$dU = -pdV, \text{ and}$$

$$dH = Vdp \text{ or } dQ = dH - Vdp = 0$$

$$dQ = TdS => dS = (1/T)dH - (V/T)dp$$

The heat capacity ratio can be written as,

$$\gamma=\frac{C_p}{C_v}=-\frac{dp/p}{dV/V}$$

For an ideal gas γ is constant. Hence on integrating the above equation, assuming a perfect gas, we get

$$pV^{\gamma} = \text{constant} \quad \text{i.e.}$$

$$\frac{p_2}{p_1} = \left(\frac{V_1}{V_2}\right)^{\gamma}$$

Using the equation of state for an ideal gas,

$$pV = nRT,$$

$$TV^{r-1} = \text{constant}$$

$$\frac{p^{\gamma-1}}{T^{\gamma}} = \text{constant}$$

also, for constant $C_p = C_v + R$ (per mole),

$$\frac{V}{T} = \frac{nR}{p} \quad \text{and} \quad p = \frac{nRT}{V}$$

$$S_2 - S_1 = nC_p \ln\left(\frac{T_2}{T_1}\right) - nR\ln\left(\frac{p_2}{p_1}\right)$$

$$\frac{S_2 - S_1}{n} = C_p \ln\left(\frac{T_2}{T_1}\right) - R\ln\left(\frac{T_2V_1}{T_1V_2}\right)$$

$$= C_v \ln\left(\frac{T_2}{T_1}\right) + R\ln\left(\frac{V_2}{V_1}\right)$$

Thus for isentropic processes with an ideal gas,

$$T_2 = T_1\left(\frac{V_1}{V_2}\right)^{(RC_v)} \quad \text{or} \quad V_2 = V_1\left(\frac{T_1}{T_2}\right)^{(C_v/R)}$$

ENTHALPY-ENTROPY

When a chemical reaction exhibits a linear relationship between enthalpy and entropy, one might observe what is known as an Enthalpy-Entropy Compensation, where the magnitude of change in the Gibbs free energy is less than one might expect. Mathematically, this is because of the Gibbs free energy equation ($\Delta G = \Delta H - T\Delta S$), where the change in enthalpy (ΔH) and the change in entropy (ΔS) have opposite signs-ΔG will change very little if both enthalpy and entropy increase. For instance, in a reaction where the chemical bonds become stronger or where chemical bonds are being formed throughout the course of a reaction a negative ΔH value will result. At the same time, this aforementioned act of forming or even strengthening a bond will limit the movement of the molecule (in terms of the molecule's ability to rotate, vibrate, etc.) and hence decrease the molecule's entropy. This leads to a fairly small ΔG value. This effect is frequently invoked in the discussion of the thermodynamics of proteins, ligands, and nucleic acids.

There are two variations on the usage of enthalpy-entropy compensation in explaining a reaction: the weak, and the strong form of compensation.

- The weak form of compensation is described when ΔH and ΔS have the same sign as a change occurs in some thermodynamic quantity excluding temperature. The weak form of compensation is a result of the rules of thermodynamics. Statistical mechanics shows qualitatively that as a system populates the lower energy levels, the enthalpy and entropy will both decrease.
- Given a regular change in some experimental variable (such as a series of homologous molecules, or a series of experimental conditions excluding temperature), the strong form of compensation occurs when ΔH and ΔS exhibit a linear correlation. In this case ΔG will be small relative to the range of values expected from the experiment.

Athel Cornish-Bowden has argued enthalpy-entropy is probably a statistical artifact, which could result in observing a relationship between two variables which may at first seem to be a trustworthy, but is false because the relationship being observed does not actually exist. Sometimes a graph that is plotted against temperature will be used to attain a value of enthalpy and entropy, when in fact this is not the proper way to measure these values. Assume a linear, Arrhenius plot of the natural log of the rate constant, ln(k), versus inverse temperature T^{-1}. Both the intercept and slope of this plot are used alongside transition-state theory to reveal a linear plot of $\Delta S‡$ versus $\Delta H‡$. This approach is fine for $\Delta H‡$. On the other hand, the ΔS‡ value is derived from an extrapolation that can be as high as twenty times the range of the measured data. One cannot hope for more than a broad idea of the true value of ΔS‡.

Plots of ΔH‡ vs. ΔS‡ have been shown to exhibit an extremely strong linear relationship. Criticism of the enthalpy-entropy compensation arises from this strong correlation, which is "too good to be true." It is believed these plots are a result of looking at the same variable in two different ways, and nothing experimentally significant is being shown.

Ideally, calorimetry experiments can yield the proper measurements of enthalpy and entropy.

CLAUSIUS-CLAPEYRON EQUATION

The Clausius-Clapeyron relation, named after Rudolf Clausius and Benoît Paul Émile Clapeyron, who defined it sometime after 1834, is a way of characterizing a discontinuous phase transition between two phases of matter. On a pressure-temperature (P-T) diagram, the line separating the two phases is known as the coexistence curve. The Clausius-Clapeyron relation gives the slope of this curve. Mathematically,

$$\frac{dP}{dT} = \frac{L}{T\Delta V}$$

where dP / dT is the slope of the coexistence curve, L is the latent heat, T is the temperature, and ΔV is the volume change of the phase transition.

Using the state postulate, take the specific entropy, s, for a homogeneous substance to be a function of specific volume, v, and temperature, T.

$$ds = \frac{\partial s}{\partial v}dv + \frac{\partial s}{\partial T}dT.$$

During a phase change, the temperature is constant, so

$$ds = \frac{\partial s}{\partial v}dv.$$

Using the appropriate Maxwell relation gives

$$ds = \frac{\partial P}{\partial T}dv.$$

Since temperature and pressure are constant during a phase change, the derivative of pressure with respect to temperature is not a function of the specific volume. Thus the partial derivative may be changed into a total derivative and be factored out when taking an integral from one phase to another,

$$s_2 - s_1 = \frac{dP}{dT}(v_2 - v_1),$$

$$\frac{dP}{dT} = \frac{s_2 - s_1}{v_2 - v_1} = \frac{\Delta s}{\Delta v}.$$

Δ is used as an operator to represent the change in the variable that follows it-final (2) minus initial (1)

For a closed system undergoing an internally reversible process, the first law is

$$du = \delta q + \delta\omega = Tds - pdv.$$

Using the definition of specific enthalpy, h, and the fact that the temperature and pressure are constant, we have

$$du + Pdv = dh = Tds \Rightarrow ds\frac{dh}{T} \Rightarrow \Delta s = \frac{\Delta h}{T}.$$

After substitution of this result into the derivative of the pressure, one finds

$$\frac{dP}{dT} = \frac{\Delta h}{T\Delta v} = \frac{\Delta H}{T\Delta V} = \frac{L}{T\Delta V},$$

where the shift to capital letters indicates a shift to extensive variables. This last equation is called the Clausius-Clapeyron equation, though some thermodynamics texts just call it the Clapeyron equation, possibly to distinguish it from the approximation below.

When the transition is to a gas phase, the final specific volume can be many times the size of the initial specific volume. A natural approximation would be to replace Δv with v_2. Furthermore, at low pressures, the gas phase may be approximated by the ideal gas law, so that $v_2 = v_{gas} = RT / P$, where R is the mass specific gas constant (forcing h and v to be mass specific). Thus,

$$\frac{dP}{dT} = \frac{P\Delta h}{T^2R}.$$

This leads to a version of the Clausius-Clapeyron equation that is simpler to integrate:

$$\frac{dP}{dT} = \frac{\Delta h}{R}\frac{dT}{T^2}, \ \ln P = -\frac{\Delta h}{R}\frac{1}{T} + C,$$

or $$\ln\frac{P_1}{P_2} = \frac{\Delta h}{R}\left(\frac{1}{T_2} - \frac{1}{T_1}\right).$$

C is a constant of integration.

These last equations are useful because they relate saturation pressure and saturation temperature to the enthalpy of phase change, without requiring specific volume data. Note that in this last equation, the subscripts 1 and 2 correspond to different locations on the pressure versus temperature phase lines. In earlier equations, they corresponded to different specific volumes and entropies at the same saturation pressure and temperature.

APPLICATIONS

One of the uses of this equation is to determine if a phase transition will occur in a given situation. Consider the question of how much pressure is needed to melt ice at a temperature ΔT below 0°C. Note that water is unusual in that its change in volume upon melting is negative. We can assume

$$\Delta P = \frac{L}{T\Delta V}\Delta T$$ and substituting in

L = 3.34 × 10^5 J/kg (latent heat of water),

T = 273 K (absolute temperature), and

ΔV = -9.05×10^{-5} m^3/kg (change in volume from solid to liquid),

we obtain

$$\frac{\Delta P}{\Delta T} = -13.5\, Mpa/K.$$

To provide a rough example of how much pressure this is, to melt ice at −7 °C (the temperature many ice skating rinks are set at) would require balancing a small car (mass = 1000 kg) on a thimble (area = 1 cm^2).

THERMODYNAMIC DIAGRAMS

Thermodynamic diagrams are diagrams used by scientists and engineers to represent the thermodynamic states of a material (typically fluid) and the consequences of manipulating this material. For instance, a temperature-entropy diagram (T-S diagram) may be used to demonstrate the behavior of a fluid as it is changed by a compressor.

Especially in meteorology they are used to analyze the actual state of the atmosphere derived from the measurements of radiosondes, usually obtained with weather balloons. In such diagrams, temperature and humidity values (represented by the dew point) are displayed with respect to pressure. Thus the diagram gives at a first glance the actual atmospheric stratification and vertical water vapor distribution. Further analysis gives the actual base and top height of convective clouds or possible instabilities in the stratification.

By assuming the energy amount due to solar radiation it is possible to predict the 2 m (6.6 ft) temperature, humidity, and wind during the day, the development of the boundary layer of the atmosphere, the occurrence and development of clouds and the conditions for soaring flight during the day.

The main feature of thermodynamic diagrams is the equivalence between the area in the diagram and energy. When air changes pressure and temperature during a process and prescribes a closed curve within the diagram the area enclosed by this curve is proportional to the energy which has been gained or released by the air.

TYPES OF THERMODYNAMIC DIAGRAMS

There are mainly three different types of thermodynamic diagrams used by the different weather services:

- Skew-T log-P diagram
- Tephigram
- Emagram

These all are derived from the physical P-alpha-diagram which combines pressure and specific volume (alpha) as basic coordinates. The P-alpha-diagram shows a strong deformation of the grid for atmospheric conditions and is therefore not useful in atmospheric sciences. The three diagrams are constructed from the P-alpha-diagram by using appropriate coordinate transformations.

Not a thermodynamic diagram in a strict sense since it does not display the energy - area equivalence is the

- Stüve diagram
  Due to its simpler construction it is preferred in education.

Thermodynamic diagrams usually show a net of five different lines:

- isobars = lines of constant pressure
- isotherms = lines of constant temperature
- dry adiabats = lines of constant potential temperature representing the temperature of a rising parcel of dry air
- saturated adiabats or pseudoadiabats = lines representing the temperature of a rising parcel saturated with water vapour
- mixing ratio = lines representing the dewpoint of a rising parcel

The lapse rate, dry adiabatic lapse rate (DALR) and moist adiabatic lapse rate (MALR), are obtained. With the help of these lines, parameters such as cloud condensation level, level of free convection, onset of cloud formation. etc. can be derived from the soundings.

HYDROSTATIC EQUATION

Hydrostatic Equation or hydrostatic balance occurs when compression due to gravity is balanced by a pressure gradient force in the opposite direction. For instance, the pressure gradient force prevents gravity from collapsing the Earth's atmosphere into a thin, dense shell, while gravity prevents the pressure gradient force from diffusing the atmosphere into space. Hydrostatic equilibrium is the current distinguishing criterion between dwarf planets and other small solar system bodies, and has other roles in astrophysics and planetary geology.

For a volume of a fluid which is not in motion or is in a state of constant motion, Newton's Laws state that it must have zero net force on it - the forces up must equal the forces down. This force balance is called the hydrostatic balance.

We can split the gas into a large number of cuboid volume elements. By considering just one element, we can work out what happens to the gas as a whole.

There are 3 forces: The force downwards onto the top of the cuboid from the pressure, P, of the fluid above it is, from the definition of pressure,

$$F_{top} = P_{top} \cdot A.$$

Similarly, the force on the volume element from the pressure of the fluid below pushing upwards is

$$F_{bottom} = -P_{bottom} \cdot A.$$

In this equation, the minus sign comes from the direction - this force supports the volume element, rather than pulls it down (We are presuming that positive force acts down, if you read "down" as "up" the results are the same for equilibrium).

Finally, the weight of the volume element causes a force downwards. If the density is ρ, the volume is V and g the standard gravity, then:

$$F_{weight} = \rho \cdot\cdot\, g\ V.$$

The volume of this cuboid is equal to the area of the top or bottom, times the height - the formula for finding the volume of a cube.

$$F_{weight} = \rho \cdot g \cdot A \cdot h$$

By balancing these forces, the total force on the gas is

$$F_{total} = F_{top} + F_{bottom} + F_{weight}$$

$$= P_{top} \cdot A - P_{bottom} \cdot A + \rho \cdot g \cdot A \cdot h.$$

This is zero if the gas is not moving. If we divide by A,

$$0 = P_{top} - P_{bottom} + \rho \cdot g \cdot h.$$

Or,

$$P_{top} - P_{bottom} = -\rho \cdot g \cdot h.$$

$P_{top} - P_{bottom}$ is a change in pressure, and h is the height of the volume element - a change in the distance above the ground. By saying these changes are infinitesimally small, the equation can be written in differential form.

$$dP = -\rho \cdot g \cdot dh.$$

Density changes with pressure, and gravity changes with height, so the equation would be:

$$dP = -\rho(P) \cdot g(h) \cdot dh.$$

Note finally that this last equation can be derived by solving the three-dimensional Navier-Stokes equations for the equilibrium situation where

$$u = v = \frac{\partial p}{\partial x} = \frac{\partial p}{\partial y} = 0.$$

Then the only non-trivial equation is the z-equation, which now reads

$$\frac{\partial p}{\partial z} + \rho g = 0.$$

Thus, hydrostatic balance can be regarded as a particularly simple equilibrium solution of the Navier-Stokes equations.

APPLICATIONS

Fluids

The hydrostatic equilibrium pertains to hydrostatics and the principles of equilibrium of fluids. A hydrostatic balance is a particular balance for weighing substances in water. Hydrostatic balance allows the discovery of their specific gravities.

Atmospherics

Hydrostatic equilibrium can explain why the Earth's atmosphere does not collapse to a very thin layer on the ground. In the atmosphere, the pressure of air decreases with increasing altitude. This causes an upward force, called the pressure gradient force, which tries to smooth over pressure differences. The force of gravity, on the other hand, almost exactly balances this out, keeping the atmosphere bound to the earth and maintaining pressure differences with altitude. Without the pressure gradient force, the atmosphere would collapse to a much thinner and denser shell around the earth, and without the force of gravity, the pressure gradient force would diffuse the atmosphere into space, leaving Earth with hardly any atmosphere.

GEOPOTENTIAL

Geopotential is the potential of the Earth's gravity field. For convenience it is often defined as minus the potential energy per unit mass, so that the gravity vector is obtained as the gradient of this potential, without the minus.

For geophysical applications, gravity is distinguished from gravitation. Gravity is defined as the resultant of gravitation and the centrifugal force caused by the Earth's rotation. The global mean sea surface is close to one of the equipotential surfaces of the geopotential of gravity. This equipotential surface, or surface of constant geopotential, is called the geoid.

For the purpose of satellite orbital mechanics, the geopotential is typically described by a series expansion into spherical harmonics (spectral representation). In this context the geopotential is taken as the potential of the gravitational field of the Earth, that is, leaving out the centrifugal potential.

ALTIMETRY

An altimeter is an instrument used to measure the altitude of an object above a fixed level. The measurement of altitude is called altimetry, which is related to the term bathymetry, the measurement of depth underwater.

APPLICATION

Radar altimeter

A radar altimeter measures altitude more directly, using the time taken for a radio signal to reflect from the surface back to the aircraft. The radar altimeter is used to measure height above ground level during landing in commercial and military aircraft. Radar altimeters are also a component of terrain avoidance warning systems, warning the pilot if the aircraft is flying too low, or if there is rising terrain ahead. Radar altimeter technology is also used in terrain-following radar allowing fighter aircraft to fly at very low altitude.

Global Positioning System

Global Positioning System (GPS) receivers can also determine altitude by trilateration with four or more satellites. However, altitude determined using autonomous GPS is not precise or accurate enough to supersede the pressure altimeter for aviation use without using some method of augmentation.

Pressure altimeter

A pressure altimeter (also called barometric altimeter) is the altimeter found in most aircraft. In it, an aneroid barometer measures the atmospheric pressure from a static port outside the aircraft. Air pressure decreases with an increase of altitude-approximately 100 hectopascals per 800 meters or one inch of mercury per 1000 feet near sea level.

The altimeter is calibrated to show the pressure directly as an altitude above mean sea level, in accordance with a mathematical model defined by the International Standard Atmosphere (ISA). Older aircraft used a simple aneroid barometer where the needle made less than one revolution around the face from zero to full scale. Modern aircraft use a "sensitive altimeter" which has a primary needle that makes multiple revolutions, and one or more secondary needles that show the number of revolutions, similar to a clock face. In other words, each needle points to a different digit of the current altitude measurement.

On a sensitive altimeter, the sea level reference pressure can be adjusted by a setting knob. The reference pressure, in inches of mercury in Canada and the US and, visible at the right side of the aircraft altimeter shown here. This is necessary, since sea level reference atmospheric pressure varies with temperature and the movement of pressure systems in the atmosphere.

In aviation terminology, the regional or local air pressure at mean sea level (MSL) is called the QNH or "altimeter setting", and the pressure which will calibrate the altimeter to show the height above ground at a given airfield is called the QFE of the field. An altimeter cannot, however, be adjusted for variations in air temperature. Differences in temperature from the ISA model will, therefore, cause errors in indicated altitude.

The calibration formula for an altimeter, up to 36,090 feet (11,000 m), can be written as:

$$h = \frac{\left(1-(P/P_{ref})^{0.19026}\right)\times 288.15}{0.00198122}$$

where h is the indicated altitude in feet, P is the static pressure and Pref is the reference pressure (use same units for both). This is derived from the barometric formula using the scale height for the troposphere.

CLOUD CLASSIFICATION

Cloud types are divided into two general categories: layered and convective. These names distinguish a cloud's altitude. Clouds are classified by the base height, not the cloud top, and bases may differ depending on the geographical zone.

HIGH CLOUDS (FAMILY A)

High clouds will form between 10,000 and 25,000 ft (3,000 and 8,000 m) in the polar regions, 16,500 and 40,000 ft (5,000 and 12,000 m) in the temperate regions and 20,000 and 60,000 ft (6,000 and 18,000 m) in the tropical region.

- Cirrocumulus (Cc)
- Cirrus (Ci)
- Cirrostratus (Cs)

MIDDLE CLOUDS (FAMILY B)

Middle clouds tend to form at 6,500 ft (2,000 m) but may form at heights up to 13,000 ft (4,000 m), 23,000 ft (7,000 m) or 25,000 ft (8,000 m) depending on the region. Nimbostratus clouds are sometimes included with the middle clouds.

- Altostratus (As)
- Altocumulus (Ac)

LOW CLOUDS (FAMILY C)

These are found up to 6,500 ft (2,000 m) and include the stratus (dense and grey). When stratus clouds contact the ground, they are called fog.

Clouds in Family C include:

- Cumulus (Cu)
  - o Cumulus humilis
  - o Cumulus mediocris
- Stratocumulus (Sc)
- Nimbostratus (Ns)
- Stratus (St)

VERTICAL CLOUDS (FAMILY D)

These clouds can have strong up-currents, rise far above their bases and form at many heights.

Clouds in Family D include:

- Cumulonimbus (associated with heavy precipitation and thunderstorms) (Cb)
  - o Cumulonimbus calvus
  - o Cumulonimbus incus
  - o Cumulonimbus with mammatus
- Cumulus (Cu)
  - o Cumulus congestus (TCu)
- Pyrocumulus

CLOUD CONDENSATION NUCLEI

Cloud condensation nuclei or CCNs (also known as cloud seeds) are small particles (typically 0.2 µm, or 1/100 th the size of a cloud droplet) about which cloud droplets coalesce. Water requires a non-gaseous surface to make the transition from a vapour to a liquid. In the atmosphere, this surface presents itself as tiny solid or liquid particles called CCNs. When no CCNs are present, water vapour can be supercooled below 0°C (32°F) before droplets spontaneously form (this is the basis of the cloud chamber for detecting subatomic particles). In above freezing temperatures the air would have to be supersaturated to around 400% before the droplets could form. The concept of cloud condensation nuclei has led to the idea of cloud seeding, that tries to encourage rainfall by seeding the air with condensation nuclei. It has further been suggested that creating such nuclei could be used for marine cloud brightening, a geoengineering technique.

A typical raindrop is about 2 mm in diameter, a typical cloud droplet is on the order of 0.02 mm, and a typical cloud condensation nucleus (aerosol) is on the order of 0.0001 mm or 0.1 micrometer or greater in diameter. The number of cloud condensation nuclei in the air can be measured and ranges between around 100 to 1000 per cubic centimetre. The total mass of CCNs injected into the atmosphere has been estimated at 2x1012 kg over a year's time. Large concentrations of particulates are also responsible for haze in areas with lower humidity. This dry haze also has an effect on climate by either absorbing or reflecting radiation (see albedo).

There are many different types of atmospheric particulates that can act as CCN. The particles may be composed of dust or clay, soot or black carbon from grassland or forest fires, sea salt from ocean wave spray, soot from factory smokestacks or internal combustion engines, sulfate from volcanic activity, phytoplankton or the oxidation of sulfur dioxide and secondary organic matter formed by the oxidation of VOCs. The ability of these different types of particles to form cloud droplets varies according to their size and also their exact composition, as the hygroscopic properties of these different constituents are very different. Sulfate and sea salt, for instance, readily absorb water whereas soot, organic carbon and mineral particles do not. This is made even more complicated by the fact that many of the chemical species may be mixed within the particles (in particular the sulfate and organic carbon). Additionally, while some particles (such as soot and minerals) do not make very good CCN, they do act as very good ice nuclei in colder parts of the atmosphere.

The number and type of CCNs can affect the lifetimes and radiative properties of clouds as well as the amount and hence have an influence on climate change; the details of this are still not well understood but are the subject of research. There is also speculation that solar variation may affect cloud properties via CCNs, and hence affect climate.

BERGERON PROCESS

The Bergeron-Findeisen process also known as the cold rain or ice crystal process, is the formation of precipitation in the cold clouds of the mid and upper latitudes by ice crystal growth. The equilibrium vapor pressure over water is greater than the saturation vapor pressure over ice, at the same temperature. Therefore in a mixed phase cloud, the liquid water will be out of vapor pressure equilibrium and will evaporate to reach equilibrium. The water droplets will move toward the lower pressure over the ice and diffuse onto the ice crystals. The vapor will be condensed and freeze onto the ice crystal, causing it to grow larger.

In order for the Bergeron Process to occur, supercooled water droplets and ice crystals must be present together in the cloud.

FORMATION OF ICE CRYSTALS

The most common way to form an ice crystal, starts with an ice nucleus in the cloud. Ice crystals can form from heterogeneous deposition, contact, immersion, or freezing after condensation. In heterogeneous deposition, an ice nucleus is simply coated with water. For contact, ice nuclei will collide with water droplets that freeze upon impact. During immersion, an ice nucleus will hit a water droplet and instantly freeze it. Water can also condense onto ice nuclei and then freeze.

Water will freeze at different temperatures depending upon the type of ice nuclei present. Ice nuclei cause water to freeze at higher temperatures then it would spontaneously. For pure water to freeze spontaneously, called homogenous nucleation, cloud temperatures would have to be -42 degrees Celsius

ICE MULTIPLICATION

As the ice crystals grow, they can bump into each other and splinter and fracture, resulting in many new ice crystals. There are many shapes of ice crystals to bump into each other. These shapes include hexagons, cubes, columns, and dendrites.

AGGREGATION

The process of ice crystals sticking together is called aggregation. This happens when ice crystals are slick or sticky at temperatures of -5 degrees Celsius and above, because of a coating of water surrounding the crystal. The different sizes and shapes of ice crystals fall at different terminal velocities and commonly collide and stick.

ACCRETION

When an ice crystal collides with supercooled water its called accretion. Droplets freeze upon impact and can form graupel.

PRECIPITATION

Eventually this ice crystal will grow large enough to fall. It may even collide with other ice crystals and grow larger still through collision coalescence, aggregation, or accretion.

The Bergeron Process often results in precipitation. As the crystals grow and fall, they pass through the base of the cloud, which may be above freezing. This causes the crystals to melt and fall as rain. There also may be a layer of air below freezing below the cloud base, causing the precipitation to refreeze in the form of ice pellets. Similarly, the layer of air below freezing may be at the surface, causing the precipitation to fall as freezing rain. The process may also result in no precipitation, evaporating before it reaches the ground, in the case of forming virga.

INERTIAL FLOW

Inertial flow is not one of the more commonly seen flows in the atmosphere, yet it does exist. The inertial wind is derived from the balance of the following forces in the n equation of motion:

The centrifugal force: $-\frac{V^2}{r_T}$

The coriolis force: $-fV$

Inertial flows are also known as inertial oscillations, since air parcels under the influence of inertial balance follow circular paths in an anticyclonic manner. The following graphic shows the illustration of the forces involved in inertial flow:

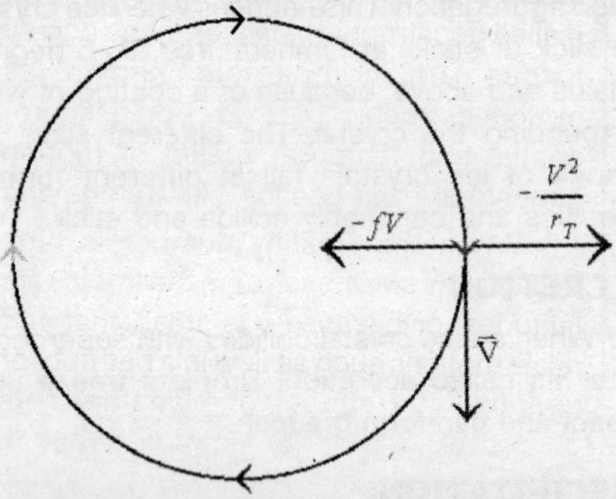

After examining the graphic and applying the inertial flow equation, it becomes apparent that these oscillations are very regular and rotate with a certain period. The period of these oscillations is:

$$P = \frac{\frac{1}{2}\,day}{|\sin\phi|}$$

where:

ϕ is the latitude and P is the period of the oscillation

As stated above, inertial flow is not one of the more commonly seen forces in the atmosphere. The reason is that the pressure gradient force drives most flows in the atmosphere. Since the pressure gradient force is assumed to be zero in inertial flow, this line of reasoning is justified. The only situations where inertial flow may be observed are in the center of large anti-cyclones or cyclones, where pressure gradients are very weak.

Although atmospheric conditions may not be favorable at most times for inertial flow, it is more prevalent in oceanic currents, where transient winds blowing across the surface are more likely to drive the current, as opposed to internal pressure gradients.

GEOSTROPHIC WIND

The geostrophic wind is the theoretical wind that would result from an exact balance between the Coriolis effect and the pressure gradient force. This condition is called geostrophic balance. The geostrophic wind is directed parallel to isobars (lines of constant pressure at a given height). This balance seldom holds exactly in nature. The true wind almost always differs from the geostrophic wind due to other forces such as friction from the ground or the centrifugal force from curved fluid flow. Thus, the actual wind would equal the geostrophic wind only if there were no friction and the isobars were perfectly straight.

GEOSTROPHIC CURRENTS

Flow of ocean water is also largely geostrophic. Just as multiple weather balloons that measure pressure as a function of height in the atmosphere are used to map the atmospheric pressure field and infer the geostrophic wind, measurements of density as a function of depth in the ocean are used to infer geostrophic currents. Satellite altimeters are also used to measure sea surface height anomaly, which permits a calculation of the geostrophic current at the surface. Geostrophic flow in air or water is a zero-frequency inertial wave.

Assuming geostrophic balance, the geostrophic wind components (u_g, v_g) on a constant-pressure surface can be derived as:

$$u_g = -\frac{g}{f}\frac{\partial Z}{\partial y}$$

$$v_g = \frac{g}{f}\frac{\partial Z}{\partial x}$$

where g is the acceleration due to gravity ($9.81\ m.s^{-2}$), f is the Coriolis parameter (approximately $10^{-4}\ s^{-1}$, varying with latitude) and Z is the geopotential height of the constant pressure surface. The validity of this approximation depends on the local Rossby number. It is invalid at the equator, because f is equal to zero there, and therefore generally not used in the tropics.

Other variants of the equation are possible; for example, the geostrophic wind vector can be expressed in terms of the gradient of the geopotential height Φ on a surface of constant pressure:

$$\vec{V}_g = \frac{\hat{k}}{f} \times \Delta_p \Phi$$

GRADIENT WIND

Geostrophic winds exist in locations where there are no frictional forces and the isobars are striaght. However, such locations are quite rare. Isobars are almost always curved and are very rarely evenly spaced. This changes the geostrophic winds so that they are no longer geostrophic but are instead in gradient wind balance. They still blow parallel to the isobars, but are no longer balanced by only the pressure gradient and Coriolis forces, and do not have the same velocity as geostrophic winds.

ROSSBY NUMBER

The Rossby number is a dimensionless number used in describing fluid flow. The Rossby number is the ratio of inertial to Coriolis force, terms $v \cdot \nabla v \sim U^2 / L$ and $\Omega \times v \sim U\Omega$ in the Navier-Stokes equations, respectively. It is commonly used in geophysical phenomena in the oceans and atmosphere, where it characterizes the importance of Coriolis accelerations arising from planetary rotation.

The Rossby number (Ro and not R_o) is defined as:

$$Ro \times \frac{U}{Lf}$$

where U and L are, respectively, characteristic velocity and length scales of the phenomenon and f = 2Ω sinφ is the Coriolis frequency, where Ω is the angular velocity of planetary rotation and φ the latitude.

A small Rossby number signifies a system which is strongly affected by Coriolis forces, and a large Rossby number signifies a system in which inertial and centrifugal forces dominate. For example, in tornadoes, the Rossby number is large (≈ 10^3), in low-pressure systems it is low (≈ 0.1-1) and in oceanic systems it is of the order of unity, but depending on the phenomena can range over several orders of magnitude (≈ 10^{-2} - 10^2). As a result, in tornadoes the Coriolis force is negligible, and balance is between pressure and centrifugal forces (called cyclostrophic balance). This balance also occurs at the outer eyewall of a tropical cyclone. In low-pressure systems, centrifugal force is negligible and balance is between Coriolis and pressure forces (called geostrophic balance). In the oceans all three forces are comparable known as called cyclogeostrophic balance. For a figure showing spatial and temporal scales of motions in the atmosphere and oceans, see Kantha and Clayson

When the Rossby number is large (either because f is small, such as in the tropics and at lower latitudes; or because L is small, that is, for small-scale motions such as flow in a bathtub; or for large speeds), the effects of planetary rotation are unimportant and can be neglected. When the Rossby number is small, then the effects of planetary rotation are large and the net acceleration is comparably small allowing the use of the geostrophic approximation.

RICHARDSON NUMBER

The Richardson number is named after Lewis Fry Richardson (1881-1953). It is the dimensionless number that expresses the ratio of potential to kinetic energy

$$Ri = \frac{gh}{u^2}$$

where g is the acceleration due to gravity, h a representative vertical lengthscale, and u a representative speed.

When considering flows in which density differences are small (the Boussinesq approximation), it is common to use the reduced gravity g' and the relevant parameter is the densimetric Richardson number

$$Ri = \frac{g'h}{u^2}$$

which is used frequently when considering atmospheric or oceanic flows.

If the Richardson number is much less than unity, buoyancy is unimportant in the flow. If it is much greater than unity, buoyancy is dominant (in the sense that there is insufficient kinetic energy to homogenize the fluids).

If the Richardson number is of order unity, then the flow is likely to be buoyancy-driven: the energy of the flow derives from the potential energy in the system originally.

APPLICATION

Thermal convection

In thermal convection problems, Richardson number represents the importance of natural convection relative to the forced convection. The Richardson number in this context is defined as

$$Ri = \frac{g\beta(T_{hot} - T_{ref})L}{V^2}$$

where g is the gravitational acceleration, β is the thermal expansion coefficient, T_{hot} is the hot wall temperature, T_{ref} is the reference temperature, L is the characteristic length, and V is the characteristic velocity.

The Richardson number can also be expressed by using a combination of the Grashof number and Reynolds number,

$$Ri = \frac{Gr}{Re^2}.$$

Typically, the natural convection is negligible when Ri<0.1, forced convection is negligible when Ri > 10, and neither is negligible when 0.1<Ri<10. It may be noted that usually the forced convection is large relative to natural convection except in the case of extremely low forced flow velocities.

Oceanography

In oceanography, the Richardson number has a more general form which takes stratification into account. It is a measure of relative importance of mechanical and density effects in the water column.

$Ri = N^2 / (du / dz)^2$ where N is the Brunt-Väisälä frequency.

The Richardson number defined above is always considered positive. An imaginary N indicates unstable density gradients with active convective overturning. Under such circumstances, N does not have an accepted physical meaning and the magnitude of negative Ri is not generally of interest. When Ri is small (typically considered below 1/4), then velocity shear is considered sufficient to overcome the tendency of a stratified fluid to remain stratified, and some mixing will generally occur. When Ri is large, turbulent mixing across the stratification is generally suppressed.

Aviation

In aviation, the Richardson number is used as a rough measure of expected air turbulence. A lower score indicates a higher degree of turbulence. Values in the range 10 to 0.1 are typical, with values below unity indicating significant turbulence.

REYNOLDS' NUMBER

Instability of airflow may be expressed in terms of the Reynolds Number (Re), which is the ratio of inertial and viscous forces.

$$Re = \frac{D.V.\rho}{\mu}$$

Here, D is the characteristic flow depth, V the wind speed, ρ the air density, and μ the kinematic viscosity. The ratio Re is proportional to the wind speed; viscous forces dominate at low speeds, so that Re is small, whilst inertia is great at high speeds, making Re large. It is observed that fluid flow becomes turbulent when Re exceeds about 1400. This can be seen in cigarette smoke, which accelerates upwards from the burning tip, eventually reaching a speed at which the rising filament breaks into turbulence. Re is important in aeronautical sciences (the airflow around a wing) and in a variety of engineering applications. For instance, an oil pipeline needs to be designed so that Re>1, otherwise frictional retardation gains the upper hand. The viscosity increases as temperature decreases.

FROUDE NUMBER

The Froude number (Fr) is used to describe the flow pattern over an obstacle. In the case of airflow over a mountain ridge (or water over a weir), the current may change accelerate and thin, and then suddenly decelerate, thereby producing a hydraulic jump. This jump is sometimes visible as a rotor cloud in the atmosphere but always visible in water, as a bore. Fr is the ratio of the flow speed (U) to the speed of shallow water waves. If Fr>1, the flow is supercritical: the current is strong and the water shallow. Waves do not travel upstream and the flow thickens when crossing an obstacle. If Fr<1, the flow is subcritical: it thins when it approaches an obstacle.

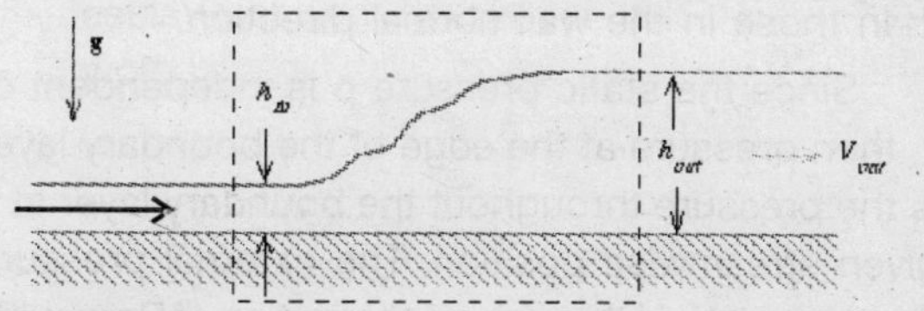

A hydraulic jump, i.e. a discontinuous transition from supercritical flow (left) to subcritical flow (right).

The speed of shallow water waves c= sqrt(gh), where h is the depth of the flow, or, equivalently, the amplitude of the waves (i.e. the height of the obstacle H that triggered the waves). In the case of surface waves, the restoring force is the gravity g, but for waves internal to the atmosphere, the restoring force is the reduced gravity g'

$$F = \frac{V}{\sqrt{ghm}}$$

$$g = \frac{V^2}{F^2 hm}$$

where,

F = froude number

V = flow velocity (m/sec)

g = accelevation of gracity (m/s^2)

hm = mean depth (meter)

MIXING LENGTH THEORY

Mixing length theory is a method attempting to describe momentum transfer by turbulence Reynolds stresses within a fluid boundary layer by means of an eddy viscosity. The theory was developed by Ludwig Prandtl in the early 20th century. Prandtl himself had reservations about the theory, describing it as, "only a rough approximation," but it has been used in numerous fields ever since, including atmospheric science, oceanography and stellar structure.

MATHEMATICAL DERIVATION

To begin, we must first be able to express quantities as the sums of their slowly varying components and fluctuating components.

REYNOLDS DECOMPOSITION

This process is known as Reynolds decomposition. Temperature can be expressed as:

$$T = \overline{T} + T',$$

where $\overline{T}$, is the slowly varying component and T' is the fluctuating component.

In the above picture, T' can be expressed in terms of the mixing length:

$$T' = -\xi' \frac{\partial T}{\partial z}.$$

The fluctuating components of velocity, u', v', and w', can also be expressed in a similar fashion:

$$u' = -\xi' \frac{\partial \bar{u}}{\partial z} \cdot v' = -\xi' \frac{\partial \bar{v}}{\partial z} \cdot w' = -\xi' \frac{\partial \bar{V}}{\partial z}.$$

Although the theoretical justification for doing so is weaker, as the pressure gradient force can significantly alter the fluctuating components. Moreover, for the case of vertical velocity, w' must be in a neutrally stratified fluid.

Taking the product of horizontal and vertical fluctuations gives us:

$$\overline{u'w'} = \overline{\xi'^2} \left| \frac{\partial \bar{V}}{\partial z} \right|.$$

The eddy viscosity is defined from the equation above as:

$$K_m = \overline{\xi'^2} \left| \frac{\partial \bar{V}}{\partial z} \right|,$$

so we have the eddy viscosity, K_m expressed in terms of the mixing length, ξ'.

BOUNDARY LAYER EQUATIONS

The deduction of the boundary layer equations was perhaps one of the most important advances in fluid dynamics. Using an order of magnitude analysis, the well-known governing Navier-Stokes equations of viscous fluid flow can be greatly simplified within the boundary layer. Notably, the characteristic of the partial differential equations (PDE) becomes parabolic, rather than the elliptical form of the full Navier-Stokes equations. This greatly simplifies the solution of the equations. By making the boundary layer approximation, the flow is divided into an inviscid portion (which is easy to solve by a number of methods) and the boundary layer, which is governed by an easier to solve PDE. The continuity and Navier-Stokes equations for a two-dimensional steady incompressible flow in Cartesian coordinates are given by

$$\frac{\partial u}{\partial x}+\frac{\partial v}{\partial y}=0$$

$$u\frac{\partial u}{\partial x}+v\frac{\partial u}{\partial y}=-\frac{1}{\rho}\frac{\partial p}{\partial x}+\nu\left(\frac{\partial^2 u}{\partial x^2}+\frac{\partial^2 u}{\partial y^2}\right)$$

$$u\frac{\partial v}{\partial x}+v\frac{\partial v}{\partial y}=-\frac{1}{\rho}\frac{\partial p}{\partial y}+\nu\left(\frac{\partial^2 v}{\partial x^2}+\frac{\partial^2 v}{\partial y^2}\right)$$

where u and v are the velocity components, ρ is the density, p is the pressure, and ν is the kinematic viscosity of the fluid at a point.

The approximation states that, for a sufficiently high Reynolds number the flow over a surface can be divided into an outer region of inviscid flow unaffected by viscosity (the majority of the flow), and a region close to the surface where viscosity is important (the boundary layer). Let u and v be streamwise and transverse (wall normal) velocities respectively inside the boundary layer. Using scale analysis, it can be shown that the above equations of motion reduce within the boundary layer to become

$$\frac{\partial u}{\partial x}+\frac{\partial v}{\partial y}=0$$

$$u\frac{\partial u}{\partial x}+\frac{\partial v}{\partial y}=-\frac{1}{\rho}\frac{\partial p}{\partial x}+\nu\frac{\partial^2 u}{\partial y^2}$$

and if the fluid is incompressible (as liquids are under standard conditions):

$$\frac{1}{\rho}\frac{\partial p}{\partial y}=0$$

The asymptotic analysis also shows that v, the wall normal velocity, is small compared with u the streamwise velocity, and that variations in properties in the streamwise direction are generally much lower than those in the wall normal direction.

Since the static pressure p is independent of y, then pressure at the edge of the boundary layer is the pressure throughout the boundary layer at a given streamwise position. The external pressure may be obtained through an application of Bernoulli's equation. Let u_0 be the fluid velocity outside the boundary layer, where u and u_0 are both parallel. This gives upon substituting for p the following result

$$u\frac{\partial u}{\partial x}+v\frac{\partial u}{\partial y}=u_0\frac{\partial u_0}{\partial x}+\nu\frac{\partial^2 u}{\partial y^2}$$

with the boundary condition

$$\frac{\partial u}{\partial x}+\frac{\partial v}{\partial y}=0$$

For a flow in which the static pressure p also does not change in the direction of the flow then

$$\frac{\partial p}{\partial x}=0$$

so u_0 remains constant.

Therefore, the equation of motion simplifies to become

$$u\frac{\partial u}{\partial x}+v\frac{\partial u}{\partial y}=\nu\frac{\partial^2 u}{\partial y^2}$$

These approximations are used in a variety of practical flow problems of scientific and engineering interest. The above analysis is for any instantaneous laminar or turbulent boundary layer, but is used mainly in laminar flow studies since the mean flow is also the instantaneous flow because there are no velocity fluctuations present.

SURFACE LAYER

The surface layer is the layer of a turbulent fluid most affected by interaction with a solid surface or the surface separating a gas and a liquid where the characteristics of the turbulence depend on distance from the interface. Surface layers are characterized by large normal gradients of tangential velocity and large concentration gradients of any substances (temperature, moisture, sediments et cetera) transported to or from the interface.

The term is used in boundary layer in meteorology and in physical oceanography. The atmospheric surface layer is the lowest part of the atmospheric boundary layer (typically the bottom 10% where the log wind profile is valid). The ocean has two surface layers: the benthic, found immediately above the sea floor and the marine surface layer, at the air-sea interface.

MATHEMATICAL FORMULATION

A simple model of the surface layer can be derived by first examining the turbulent momentum flux through a surface. Using Reynolds Decomposition to express the horizontal flow in the x direction as the sum of a slowly varying component, $\overline{u}$, and a turbulent component, u';:

$$u = \overline{u} + u'$$

and the vertical flow, w, in an analogous fashion:

$$w = \overline{w} + w'$$

we can express the flux of turbulent momentum through a surface, u_* as the time averaged magnitude of vertical turbulent transport of horizontal turbulent momentum, $u'w'$:

$$u_*^2 = \left|\overline{(u''w\,)s}\right|.$$

If the flow is homogeneous within the region, we can set the product of the vertical gradient of the mean horizontal flow and the eddy viscosity coefficient K_m equal to u_*:

$$K_m \frac{\partial \overline{u}}{z} = u_*^2,$$

where K_m is defined in terms of Prandtl's mixing length hypothesis:

$$K_m = \overline{\xi'^2}\left|\frac{\partial \overline{u}}{\partial z}\right|$$

where ξ' is the mixing length.

We can then express u_* as:

$$\frac{\partial \overline{u}}{\partial z} = \frac{u_*}{\overline{\overline{\xi'}}}.$$

EKMAN LAYER

The Ekman Layer is the layer in a fluid where there is a force balance between pressure gradient force, Coriolis force and turbulent drag.

The mathematical formulation of the Ekman layer can be found by assuming a neutrally stratified fluid, with horizontal momentum in balance between the forces of pressure gradient, Coriolis and turbulent drag.

$$-fv = -\frac{1}{\rho}\frac{\partial p}{\partial x} + K_m \frac{\partial^2 u}{\partial z^2}$$

$$fu = -\frac{1}{\rho_o}\frac{\partial p}{\partial y} + K_m \frac{\partial^2 v}{\partial z^2}$$

$$0 = -\frac{1}{\rho_o}\frac{\partial p}{\partial z},$$

where K_m is the diffusive eddy viscosity, which can be derived using mixing length theory.

BOUNDARY CONDITIONS

There are many regions where an Ekman layer is theoretically plausible; they include the bottom of the atmosphere, near the surface of the earth and ocean, the bottom of the ocean, near the sea floor and at the top of the ocean, near the air-sky interface.

Each of the different regions will have different boundary conditions. We will consider boundary conditions of the Ekman layer in the upper ocean:

$$\text{at } z = 0 : A\frac{\partial u}{\partial z} = \tau^x ; A\frac{\partial v}{\partial z} = \tau^y$$

where τ is the surface stress of the wind field or ice layer at the top of the ocean.

at $z \to \infty : u = u_g, v = v_g,$

where and are the geostrophic flows.

SOLUTION

These differential equations can be solved to find:

$$u = u_g + \frac{\sqrt{2}}{fd} e^{z/d} [\tau^x \cos(z/d - \pi/4) - \tau^y \sin(z/d - \pi/4)]$$

$$v = v_g + \frac{\sqrt{2}}{fd} e^{z/d} [\tau^x \sin(z/d - \pi/4) - \tau^y \cos(z/d - \pi/4)].$$

and by applying the continuity equation we can have the vertical velocity as following

$$w = \frac{1}{f\rho_o}\left[-\left(\frac{\partial \tau^x}{\partial x} + \frac{\partial \tau^y}{\partial y}\right) e^{z/d} \sin(z/d) + \left(\frac{\partial \tau^y}{\partial x} - \frac{\partial \tau^x}{\partial y}\right)(1 - e^{z/d}\cos(z/d))\right]$$

Note that when vertically integrated the volume transport associated with the Ekman spiral is to the right of the wind direction in the Northern Hemisphere.

In the atmosphere, the Ekman solution generally overstates the magnitude of the horizontal wind field because it does not account for the velocity shear in the surface layer. Splitting the boundary layer into the surface layer and the Ekman layer generally yields more accurate results.

PERTURBATION THEORY

Perturbation theory comprises mathematical methods that are used to find an approximate solution to a problem which cannot be solved exactly, by starting from the exact solution of a related problem. Perturbation theory is applicable if the problem at hand can be formulated by adding a "small" term to the mathematical description of the exactly solvable problem.

Perturbation theory leads to an expression for the desired solution in terms of a power series in some "small" parameter that quantifies the deviation from the exactly solvable problem. The leading term in this power series is the solution of the exactly solvable problem, while further terms describe the deviation in the solution, due to the deviation from the initial problem. Formally, we have for the approximation to the full solution A, a series in the small parameter (here called ε), like the following:

$$A = \varepsilon^0 A_0 + \varepsilon^1 A_1 + \varepsilon^2 A_2 + ...$$

In this example, A_0 would be the known solution to the exactly solvable initial problem and $A_1, A_2, ...$ represent the higher-order terms which may be found iteratively by some systematic procedure. For small ε these higher order terms in the series become successively smaller. An approximate "perturbation solution" is obtained by truncating the series, usually by keeping only the first two terms, the initial solution and the "first order" perturbation correction:

$$A \approx A_0 + \varepsilon A_1$$

Perturbation theory is closely related to methods used in numerical analysis. The earliest use of what would now be called perturbation theory was to deal with the otherwise unsolveable mathematical problems of celestial mechanics: Newton's solution for the orbit of the Moon, which moves noticeably differently from a simple Keplerian ellipse because of the competing gravitation of the Earth and the Sun.

Perturbation methods start with a simplified form of the original problem, which is simple enough to be solved exactly. In celestial mechanics, this is usually a Keplerian ellipse. An ellipse is exactly correct when there are only two gravitating bodies (say, the Earth and the Moon) but not quite correct when there are three or more objects (say, the Earth, Moon, Sun, and the rest of the solar system).

The solved, but simplified problem is then "perturbed" to make the conditions the perturbed solution actually satisfies closer to the real problem, such as including the gravitational attraction of a third body (the Sun). The "conditions" are a formula (or several) that represent reality, oftentimes something arising from a physical law like Newton's second law, the force-acceleration equation:

$$F = ma.$$

In the case of the example, the force F is calculated based on the number of gravitationally relevant bodies; the acceleration a is obtained, using calculus, from the path of the Moon in its orbit. Both of these come in two forms: approximate values for force and acceleration, which result from simplifications, and hypothetical exact values for force and acceleration, which would require the complete answer to calculate.

The slight changes that result from accommodating the perturbation, which themselves may have been simplified yet again, are used as corrections to the approximate solution. Because of simplifications introduced along every step of the way, the corrections are never perfect, and the conditions met by the corrected solution do not perfectly match the equation demanded by reality, but even one cycle of corrections often provides a remarkably better approximate answer to what the real solution should be.

PERTURBATION ORDERS

The standard exposition of perturbation theory is given in terms of the order to which the perturbation is carried out: first order perturbation theory or second order perturbation theory, and whether the perturbed states are degenerate (that is, singular), in which case extra care must be taken, and the theory is slightly more difficult.

FIRST-ORDER NON-SINGULAR PERTURBATION THEORY

This section develops, in simplified terms, the general theory for the perturbative solution to a differential equation to the first order. To keep the exposition simple, a crucial assumption is made: that the solutions to the unperturbed system are not degenerate, so that the perturbation series can be inverted. There are ways of dealing with the degenerate (or singular) case; these require extra care.

Suppose one wants to solve a differential equation of the form

$$Dg(x) = \lambda g(x)$$

where D is some specific differential operator, and λ is an eigenvalue. Many problems involving ordinary or partial differential equations can be cast in this form. It is presumed that the differential operator can be written in the form

$$D = D^{(0)} + \varepsilon D$$

where ε is presumed to be small, and that furthermore, the complete set of solutions for $D^{(0)}$ are known. That is, one has a set of solutions $f_n^{(0)}(x)$, labelled by some arbitrary index n, such that

$$D^{(0)} f_n^{(0)}(x) = \lambda_n^{(0)} f_n^{(0)}(x).$$

Furthermore, one assumes that the set of solutions $\{f_n^{(0)}(x)\}$ form an orthonormal set:

$$\int f_m^{(0)}(x) f_n^{(0)}(x)dx = \delta_{mn}$$

with δ_{mn} the Kronecker delta function.

To zeroth order, one expects that the solutions g(x) are then somehow "close" to one of the unperturbed solutions $f_n^{(0)}(x)$. That is, $f_n^{(0)}(x) + O(\varepsilon)$ and $\lambda = \lambda_n^{(0)} + O(\varepsilon)$.

Where O denotes the relative size, in big-O notation, of the perturbation. To solve this problem, one assumes that the solution g(x) can be written as a linear combination of the $f_n^{(0)}(x)$:

$$g(x) = \sum_m c_m f_m^{(0)}(x)$$

with all of the constants $c_m = O(\varepsilon)$ except for n, where $c_n = O(1)$. Substituting this last expansion into the differential equation, taking the inner product of the result with $f_n^{(0)}(x)$, and making use of orthogonality, one obtains

$$c_n \lambda_n^{(0)} + \varepsilon \sum_m c_m \int f_n^{(0)}(x) D^{(1)} f_m^{(0)}(x)dx = \lambda c_n$$

This can be trivially rewritten as a simple linear algebra problem of finding the eigenvalue of a matrix, where

$$\sum_m A_{nm} c_m = \lambda c_n$$

where the matrix elements A_{nm} are given by

$$A_{nm} = \delta_{nm} \lambda_n^{(0)} + \varepsilon \int f_n^{(0)}(x) D^{(1)} f_m^{(0)}(x)dx$$

Rather than solving this full matrix equation, one notes that, of all the c_m in the linear equation, only one, namely c_n, is not small. Thus, to the first order in ε, the linear equation may be solved trivially as

$$\lambda = \lambda_n^{(0)} + \varepsilon \int f_n^{(0)}(x) D^{(1)} f_n^{(0)}(x) dx$$

since all of the other terms in the linear equation are of order $O(\varepsilon^2)$. The above gives the solution of the eigenvalue to first order in perturbation theory.

The function $g(x)$ to first order is obtained through similar reasoning. Substituting

$$g(x) = f_n^{(0)}(x) + \varepsilon f_n^{(1)}(x)$$

so that

$$\left(D^{(0)} + \varepsilon D^{(1)}\right)\left(f_n^{(0)}(x) + \varepsilon f_n^{(1)}(x)\right) = \left(\lambda_n^{(0)}(x) + \varepsilon \lambda_n^{(1)}(x)\right)\left(f_n^{(0)}(x) + \varepsilon f_n^{(1)}(x)\right)$$

gives an equation for $f_n^{(1)}(x)$. It may be solved integrating with the partition of unity

$$\delta(x - y) = \sum_n f_n^{(0)}(x) f_n^{(0)}(y)$$

to give

$$f_n^{(1)}(x) = \sum_{m=(\neq n)} \frac{f_m^{(0)}(x)}{\lambda_n^{(0)} - \lambda_m^{(0)}} \int f_m^{(0)}(y) D^{(1)} f_n^{(0)}(y) dy$$

which gives the exact solution to the perturbed differential equation to the first order in the perturbation ε.

Several important observations can be made about the form of this solution. First, the sum over functions with differences of eigenvalues in the denominator resembles the resolvent in Fredholm theory. This is no accident; the resolvent acts essentially as a kind of Green's function or propagator, passing the perturbation along. Higher order perturbations resemble this form, with an additional sum over a resolvent appearing at each order.

The form of this solution is sufficient to illustrate the idea behind the small-divisor problem. If, for whatever reason, two eigenvalues are close so that difference $\lambda_n^{(0)} - \lambda_m^{(0)}$ become small, the corresponding term in the sum will become disproportionately large. In particular, if this happens in higher-order terms, the high order perturbation may become as large or larger in magnitude than the first-order perturbation. Such a situation calls into question the validity of doing a perturbation to begin with. This can be understood to be a fairly catastrophic situation; it is frequently encountered in chaotic dynamical systems, and requires the development of techniques other than perturbation theory to solve the problem.

INERTIAL WAVE

Inertial waves, also known as inertial oscillations, are a type of mechanical wave possible in rotating fluids. Unlike surface gravity waves commonly seen at the beach or in the bathtub, inertial waves travel through the bulk of the fluid, not at the surface. Like any other kind of wave, an inertial wave is caused by a restoring force and characterized by its wavelength and frequency. Because the restoring force for inertial waves is the Coriolis force, their wavelengths and frequencies are related in a peculiar way. Inertial waves are transverse.

CHARACTERISTICS

Inertial waves are possible only when a fluid is rotating, and exist in the bulk of the fluid, not at its surface. Like light waves, inertial waves are transverse, which means that their vibrations occur perpendicular to the direction of wave travel. (The opposite of a transverse wave is a longitudinal wave, where the vibrations are in the same direction as the wave travel. Sound waves, for example, are longitudinal.) One peculiar geometrical characteristic of inertial waves is that their phase velocity, which tells about the movement of the crests and troughs of the wave, is perpendicular to their group velocity, which tells about the propagation of energy.

Whereas a sound wave or an electromagnetic wave of any frequency is possible, inertial waves can exist only over the range of frequencies from zero to twice the rotation rate of the fluid. Moreover, the frequency of the wave is determined by its direction of travel. Waves traveling perpendicular to the axis of rotation have zero frequency and are sometimes called the geostrophic modes. Waves traveling parallel to the axis have maximum frequency (twice the rotation rate), and waves at intermediate angles have intermediate frequencies. In free space, an inertial wave can exist at any frequency between 0 and twice the rotation rate. A closed container, however, can impose restrictions on the possible frequencies of inertial waves, as it can for any kind of wave. Inertial waves in a closed container are often called inertial modes. In a sphere, for example, the inertial modes are forced to take on discrete frequencies, leaving gaps where no modes can exist.

MATHEMATICAL DERIVATION

Fluid flow is governed by the momentum equation (often called the Navier-Stokes equation) which is essentially a statement of Newton's second law for the fluid. The velocity in a fluid with viscosity under pressure P and rotating at rate Ω changes over time t according to

$$\frac{\partial \vec{u}}{\partial t} + (\vec{u} \cdot \leq \vec{\nabla})\vec{u} = -\frac{1}{\rho}\vec{\nabla}P + \nu\nabla^2\vec{u} - 2\vec{\Omega}\times\vec{u}.$$

To be precise, $\vec{u}$ is the velocity of the fluid as observed in the rotating frame of reference. Since a rotating frame of reference is always accelerating (a so-called non-inertial frame), two additional forces (as mentioned above) must be introduced: the centripetal force and the Coriolis force. In the equation above, the centripetal force is actually part of the generalized pressure P, that is, P is related to the usual pressure p, depending on the distance from the rotation axis r, by

$P = p + \rho r^2\Omega^2.$

The last term on the right side of the momentum equation is the Coriolis term. The first term on the right accounts for pressure, and the second accounts for viscous diffusion.

In the case where the rotation rate is large, the Coriolis force and the centripetal force become large compared to the other terms. Being small in comparison, diffusion and the "convective derivative" (second term on the left) can be left out. Taking a curl of both sides and applying a few vector identities, the result is

$$\frac{\partial}{\partial t}\nabla\times\vec{u} = 2(\vec{\Omega}\cdot\vec{\nabla})\vec{u}.$$

Solutions to this equation are waves that satisfy two conditions. First, if $\vec{k}$ is the wave vector,

$$\vec{u}\cdot\vec{k} = 0,$$

that is, the waves must be transverse, as mentioned above. Second, solutions are required to have a frequency ω that satisfies the dispersion relation

$$\omega = 2\hat{k}\cdot\vec{\Omega} = 2\Omega\cos\theta,$$

where θ is the angle between the axis of roation and the direction of the wave. These particular solutions are known as inertial waves.

The dispersion relation looks much like the Coriolis term in the momentum equation–notice the rotation rate and the factor of two. It immediately implies the range of possible frequencies for inertial waves, as well as the dependence of their frequency on their direction.

EXAMPLES OF INERTIAL WAVES

Any kind of fluid can support inertial waves: water, oil, liquid metals, air, and other gases. Inertial waves are observed most commonly in planetary atmospheres (Rossby waves, geostrophic winds) and in oceans and lakes (geostropic currents), where they are responsible for much of the mixing that takes place. Inertial waves affected by the slope of the ocean floor are often called Rossby waves. Inertial waves can be observed in laboratory experiments or in industrial flows where a fluid is rotating.

ROSSBY WAVE

Rossby (or planetary) waves are giant meanders in high-altitude winds that are a major influence on weather. Their emergence is due to shear in rotating fluids, so that the Coriolis force changes along the sheared coordinate. In planetary atmospheres, they are due to the variation in the Coriolis effect with latitude.

Rossby waves in the atmosphere are easy to observe as (usually 4-6) large-scale meanders of the jet stream. When these loops become very pronounced, they detach the masses of cold, or warm, air that become cyclones and anticyclones and are responsible for day-to-day weather patterns at mid-latitudes.

The special identifying feature of the Rossby waves is its phase velocity (that of the wave crests) always has a westward component. However, the wave's group velocity (associated with the energy flux) can be in any direction. In general: shorter waves have an eastward group velocity and long waves a westward group velocity.

The terms "barotropic" and "baroclinic" Rossby waves are used to distinguish their vertical structure. Barotropic Rossby waves do not vary in the vertical, and have the fastest propagation speeds. The baroclinic wave modes are slower, with speeds of only a few centimetres per second or less.

NUMERICAL WEATHER PREDICTION

Numerical weather prediction uses current weather conditions as input into mathematical models of the atmosphere to predict the weather. Although the first efforts to accomplish this were done in the 1920s, it wasn't until the advent of the computer and computer simulation that it was feasible to do in real-time. Manipulating the huge datasets and performing the complex calculations necessary to do this on a resolution fine enough to make the results useful requires the use of some of the most powerful supercomputers in the world. A number of forecast models, both global and regional in scale, are run to help create forecasts for nations worldwide. Use of model ensemble forecasts helps to define the forecast uncertainty and extend weather forecasting farther into the future than would otherwise be possible.

The atmosphere is a fluid. The basic idea of numerical weather prediction is to sample the state of the fluid at a given time and use the equations of fluid dynamics and thermodynamics to estimate the state of the fluid at some time in the future.

Forecast model for Numerical weather prediction

A model, in this context, is a computer program that produces meteorological information for future times at given positions and altitudes. The horizontal domain of a model is either global, covering the entire Earth, or regional , covering only part of the Earth. Regional models also are known as limited-area models.

GRAVITY WAVE

Gravity waves are waves generated in a fluid medium or at the interface between two media (e.g., the atmosphere and the ocean) which has the restoring force of gravity or buoyancy.

When a fluid element is displaced on an interface or internally to a region with a different density, gravity tries to restore the parcel toward equilibrium resulting in an oscillation about the equilibrium state or wave orbit. Gravity waves on an air-sea interface are called surface gravity waves or surface waves while internal gravity waves are called internal waves.

The phase speed of a linear gravity wave with wavenumber is given by the formula

$$c = \sqrt{\frac{g}{k}},$$

where g is the acceleration due to gravity. When surface tension is important, this is modified to

$$c = \sqrt{\frac{g}{k} + \frac{\sigma k}{\rho}},$$

where σ is the surface tension coefficient, ρ is the density, and k is the wavenumber (spatial frequency) of the disturbance.

DETAILS OF THE PHASE-SPEED DERIVATION

Since $c = \omega / k$ is the phase speed in terms of the angular frequency and the wavenumber, the gravity wave angular frequency can be expressed as

$$\omega = \sqrt{gk}.$$

The group velocity of a wave (that is, the speed at which a wave packet travels) is given by

$$c_g = \frac{d\omega}{dk},$$

and thus for a gravity wave,

$$c_g = \frac{1}{2}\sqrt{\frac{g}{k}} = \frac{1}{2}c.$$

The group velocity is one half the phase velocity. A wave in which the group and phase velocities differ is called dispersive.

MADDEN-JULIAN OSCILLATION

The Madden-Julian oscillation (MJO) is an equatorial traveling pattern of anomalous rainfall that is planetary in scale. The MJO is characterized by an eastward progression of large regions of both enhanced and suppressed tropical rainfall, observed mainly over the Indian Ocean and Pacific Ocean. The anomalous rainfall is usually first evident over the western Indian Ocean, and remains evident as it propagates over the very warm ocean waters of the western and central tropical Pacific. This pattern of tropical rainfall then generally becomes very nondescript as it moves over the cooler ocean waters of the eastern Pacific but reappears over the tropical Atlantic and Indian Ocean. The wet phase of enhanced convection and precipitation is followed by a dry phase where thunderstorm activity is suppressed. Each cycle lasts approximately 30-60 days. Because of this pattern, The MJO is also known as the 30-60 day oscillation, 30-60 day wave, or intraseasonal oscillation.

There are distinct patterns of lower-level and upper-level atmospheric circulation anomalies which accompany the MJO-related pattern of enhanced or decreased tropical rainfall across the tropics. These circulation features extend around the globe and are not confined to only the eastern hemisphere. The Madden-Julian oscillation moves eastward at 5 metres per second (11 mph) across the tropics, crossing the Earth's tropics in 30 to 60 days, with the active phase of the MJO tracked using the degree of outgoing longwave radiation which is measured by infrared-sensing geostationary weather satellites. The lower the amount of outgoing longwave radiation, the stronger the thunderstorm complexes, or convection, is within that region.

EFFECTS

Connection to the monsoon

During the Northern Hemisphere summer season the MJO-related effects on the Indian summer monsoon are well documented. MJO-related effects on the North American summer monsoon also occur, though they are relatively weaker. MJO-related impacts on the North American summer precipitation patterns are strongly linked to meridional (i.e. north-south) adjustments of the precipitation pattern in the eastern tropical Pacific. A strong relationship between the leading mode of intraseasonal variability of the North American Monsoon System, the MJO and the points of origin of tropical cyclones is also present.

A period of warming sea surface temperatures are found five to ten days prior to a strengthening of MJO-related precipitation across southern Asia. A break in the Asian monsoon, normally during the month of July, has been attributed to the Madden-Julian oscillation, after its enhanced phase moves off to the east of the region into the open tropical Pacific ocean.

Influence on tropical cyclogenesis

Although tropical cyclones occur throughout the boreal warm season (typically May-November) in both the north Pacific and the north Atlantic basins, in any given year there are periods of enhanced/ suppressed activity within the season. There is evidence that the MJO modulates this activity (particularly for the strongest storms) by providing a large-scale environment that is favorable (or unfavorable) for development. MJO-related descending motion is not favorable for tropical storm development. However, MJO-related ascending motion is a favorable pattern for thunderstorm formation within the tropics, which is quite favorable for tropical storm development. As the MJO progresses eastward, the favored region for tropical cyclone activity also shifts eastward from the western Pacific to the eastern Pacific and finally to the Atlantic basin.

Link to the El Nino-Southern oscillation

There is strong year-to-year (interannual) variability in MJO activity, with long periods of strong activity followed by periods in which the oscillation is weak or absent. This interannual variability of the MJO is partly linked to the El Nico-Southern Oscillation (ENSO) cycle. In the Pacific, strong MJO activity is often observed 6 - 12 months prior to the onset of an El Nico episode, but is virtually absent during an El Nico episode, while MJO activity is typically greater during a La Nica episode. Strong events in the Madden-Julian oscillation over a series of months in the western Pacific can speed the development of an El Nico or La Nica but do not in themselves lead to the onset of a warm or cold ENSO event.

QUASI-BIENNIAL OSCILLATION

The QBO was discovered in the 1950s, but its cause remained unclear for some time. Rawinsonde soundings showed that its phase was not related to the annual cycle, as is the case for all other stratospheric circulation patterns. In the 1970s it was recognized by Lindzen and Holton that the periodic wind reversal was driven by atmospheric waves emanating from the tropical troposphere that travel upwards and are dissipated in the stratosphere by radiative cooling. The precise nature of the waves responsible for this effect was heavily debated, in recent years however gravity waves have come to be seen as a major contributor.

The QBO (quasi-biennial oscillation) is a quasi-periodic oscillation of the equatorial zonal wind between easterlies and westerlies in the tropical stratosphere with a mean period of 28 to 29 months. The alternating wind regimes develop at the top of the lower stratosphere and propagate downwards at about 1 km per month until they are dissipated at the tropical tropopause. Downward motion of the easterlies is usually more irregular than that of the westerlies. The amplitude of the easterly phase is about twice as strong as that of the westerly phase. At the top of the vertical QBO domain, easterlies dominate, while at the bottom, westerlies are more likely to be found.

EFFECTS

Effects of the QBO include mixing of stratospheric ozone by the secondary circulation caused by the QBO, modification of monsoon precipitation, and an influence on stratospheric circulation in northern hemisphere winter (the sudden stratospheric warmings).

SUNSPOT CYCLE

Sunspots are temporary phenomena on the surface of the Sun (the photosphere) that appear visibly as dark spots compared to surrounding regions. They are caused by intense magnetic activity, which inhibits convection, forming areas of reduced surface temperature. Although they are at temperatures of roughly 3,000-4,500 K, the contrast with the surrounding material at about 5,780 K leaves them clearly visible as dark spots, as the intensity of a heated black body (closely approximated by the photosphere) is a function of T (temperature) to the fourth power. If the sunspot were isolated from the surrounding photosphere it would be brighter than an electric arc. Sunspots expand and contract as they move across the surface of the sun and can be as large as 80,000 km (50,000 miles) in diameter.

The sunspot itself can be divided into two parts:

"The central umbra, which is the darkest part, where the magnetic field is approximately vertical (normal to the sun's surface).

"The surrounding penumbra, which is lighter, where the magnetic field lines are more inclined.

Magnetic field lines would ordinarily repel each other, causing sunspots to disperse rapidly, but sunspot lifetime is about two weeks. Recent observations from the Solar and Heliospheric Observatory (SOHO) using sound waves traveling through the Sun's photosphere to develop a detailed image of the internal structure below sunspots show that there is a powerful downdraft underneath each sunspot, forming a rotating vortex that concentrates magnetic field lines. Sunspots are self-perpetuating storms, similar in some ways to terrestrial hurricanes.

Sunspot activity cycles about every eleven years. The point of highest sunspot activity during this cycle is known as Solar Maximum, and the point of lowest activity is Solar Minimum. Early in the cycle, sunspots appear in the higher latitudes and then move towards the equator as the cycle approaches maximum: this is called Spörer's law.

Wolf number sunspot index displays various periods, the most prominent of which is at about 11 years in the mean. This period is also observed in most other expressions of solar activity and is deeply linked to a variation in the solar magnetic field that changes polarity with this period, too.

SUNSPOT VARIATION

Sunspot populations quickly rise and more slowly fall on an irregular cycle of 11 years. Significant variations of the 11-year period are known over longer spans of time. For example, from 1900 to the 1960s the solar maxima trend of sunspot count has been upward; from the 1960s to the present, it has diminished somewhat. Over the last decades the Sun has had a markedly high average level of sunspot activity; it was last similarly active over 8,000 years ago.

The number of sunspots correlates with the intensity of solar radiation over the period since 1979, when satellite measurements of absolute radiative flux became available. Since sunspots are darker than the surrounding photosphere it might be expected that more sunspots would lead to less solar radiation and a decreased solar constant. However, the surrounding margins of sunspots are brighter than the average, and so are hotter; overall, more sunspots increase the sun's solar constant or brightness. The variation caused by the sunspot cycle to solar output is relatively small, on the order of 0.1% of the solar constant (a peak-to-trough range of 1.3 Wm^{-2} compared to 1366 Wm^{-2} for the average solar constant). Sunspots were rarely observed during the Maunder Minimum in the second part of the 17th century (approximately from 1645 to 1715). This coincides with the middle (and coldest) part of a period of cooling known as the Little Ice Age.

There may be a resonant gravitational link between a photospheric tidal force exerted by the planets and the sunspot cycle.

APPLICATION

Due to their link to other kinds of solar activity, sunspots can predict space weather and the state of the ionosphere. Thus, sunspots can help predict conditions of short-wave radio propagation or satellite communications.

Don Easterbrook, a Professor Emeritus of geology at Western Washington University, claims that there is a cause-and-effect relationship between sunspot activity and measured changes in global temperatures on Earth.

GLOBAL CLIMATE MODEL

A General Circulation Model (GCM) is a mathematical model of the general circulation of a planetary atmosphere or ocean and based on the Navier-Stokes equations on a rotating sphere with thermodynamic terms for various energy sources (radiation, latent heat). These equations are the basis for complex computer programs commonly used for simulating the atmosphere or ocean of the Earth. Atmospheric and Oceanic GCMs (AGCM and OGCM) are key components of Global Climate Models along with sea-ice and land-surface components. GCMs and global climate models are widely applied for weather forecasting, understanding the climate, and projecting climate change.

Climate models use quantitative methods to simulate the interactions of the atmosphere, oceans, land surface, and ice. They are used for a variety of purposes from study of the dynamics of the climate system to projections of future climate.

All climate models take account of incoming energy as short wave electromagnetic radiation, chiefly visible and short-wave (near) infrared, as well as outgoing energy as long wave (far) infrared electromagnetic radiation from the earth. Any imbalance results in a change in temperature.

The most talked-about models of recent years have been those relating temperature to emissions of carbon dioxide (see greenhouse gas). These models project an upward trend in the surface temperature record, as well as a more rapid increase in temperature at higher altitudes.

Models can range from relatively simple to quite complex:

- A simple radiant heat transfer model that treats the earth as a single point and averages outgoing energy
- this can be expanded vertically (radiative-convective models), or horizontally
- finally, (coupled) atmosphere-ocean-sea ice global climate models discretise and solve the full equations for mass and energy transfer and radiant exchange.

This is not a full list; for example "box models" can be written to treat flows across and within ocean basins. Furthermore, other types of modelling can be interlinked, such as land use, allowing researchers to predict the interaction between climate and ecosystems.

MODEL STRUCTURE

Three-dimensional (more properly four-dimensional) GCMs discretise the equations for fluid motion and integrate these forward in time. They also contain parametrisations for processes - such as convection - that occur on scales too small to be resolved directly. More sophisticated models may include representations of the carbon and other cycles.

A simple general circulation model (SGCM), a minimal GCM, consists of a dynamical core that relates material properties such as temperature to dynamical properties such as pressure and velocity. Examples are codes that solve the primitive equations, given energy input into the model, and energy dissipation in the form of scale-dependent friction, so that atmospheric waves with the highest wavenumbers are the ones most strongly attenuated. Such models may be used to study atmospheric processes within a simplified framework but are not suitable for future climate projections.

Atmospheric GCMs (AGCMs) model the atmosphere (and typically contain a land-surface model as well) and impose sea surface temperatures (SSTs). They may include atmospheric chemistry.

- AGCMs consist of a dynamical core which integrates the equations of fluid motion, typically for:
  - o surface pressure
  - o horizontal components of velocity in layers
  - o temperature and water vapor in layers
- There is generally a radiation code, split into solar/short wave and terrestrial/infra-red/long wave
- Parametrizations are used to include the effects of various processes. All modern AGCMs include parameterizations for:
  - o convection
  - o land surface processes, albedo and hydrology
  - o cloud cover

A GCM contains a number of prognostic equations that are stepped forward in time (typically winds, temperature, moisture, and surface pressure) together with a number of diagnostic equations that are evaluated from the simultaneous values of the variables. As an example, pressure at any height can be diagnosed by applying the hydrostatic equation to the predicted surface pressure and the predicted values of temperature between the surface and the height of interest. The pressure diagnosed in this way then is used to compute the pressure gradient force in the time-dependent equation for the winds.

Oceanic GCMs (OGCMs) model the ocean (with fluxes from the atmosphere imposed) and may or may not contain a sea ice model. For example, the standard resolution of HadOM3 is 1.25 degrees in latitude and longitude, with 20 vertical levels, leading to approximately 1,500,000 variables.

Coupled atmosphere-ocean GCMs (AOGCMs) (e.g. HadCM3, GFDL CM2.X) combine the two models. They thus have the advantage of removing the need to specify fluxes across the interface of the ocean surface. These models are the basis for sophisticated model predictions of future climate, such as are discussed by the IPCC.

AOGCMs represent the pinnacle of complexity in climate models and internalise as many processes as possible. They are the only tools that could provide detailed regional predictions of future climate change. However, they are still under development. The simpler models are generally susceptible to simple analysis and their results are generally easy to understand. AOGCMs, by contrast, are often nearly as hard to analyse as the real climate system.

MODEL GRIDS

The fluid equations for AGCMs are discretised using either the finite difference method or the spectral method. For finite differences, a regular grid (i.e. with constant grid spacing) in latitude and longitude is most common. However, variable resolution grids can be used. The "LMDz" model can be arranged to give high resolution over any given section of the planet. HadGEM1 (and other ocean models) use an ocean grid with higher resolution in the tropics to help resolve processes believed to be important for ENSO. Spectral models generally use a gaussian grid, because of the mathematics of transformation between spectral and grid-point space. Typical AGCM resolutions are between 1 and 5 degrees in latitude or longitude: the Hadley Centre model HadAM3, for example, uses 2.5 degrees in latitude and 3.75 in longitude, giving a grid of 73 by 96 points; and has 19 levels in the vertical.

For a standard finite difference model, the gridlines converge towards the poles. This would lead to computational instabilities and so the model variables must be filtered along lines of latitude close to the poles. Ocean models suffer from this problem too, unless a rotated grid is used in which the North Pole is shifted onto a nearby landmass. Spectral models do not suffer from this problem. There are experiments using geodesic grids and icosahedral grids, which (being more uniform) do not have pole-problems.

FLUX CORRECTION

Early generations of AOGCMs required a somewhat ad hoc process of "flux correction" to achieve a stable climate. The danger, however, is that a model may need flux corrections because of unrealistically strong feedback processes that result in a transition to a different climate state. As a result, there has been strong movement away from the use of flux corrections, and the vast majority of models used in the current round of the Intergovernmental Panel on Climate Change do not use them. The model improvements that now make flux corrections unnecessary are various, but include improved ocean physics, improved resolution in both atmosphere and ocean, and more physically consistent coupling between atmosphere and ocean models.

CONVECTION

Moist convection causes the release of latent heat and is important to the Earth's energy budget. Convection occurs on too small a scale to be resolved by climate models, and hence must be parameterised. This has been done since the earliest days of climate modelling, in the 1950s.

OUTPUT VARIABLES

Most models include software to diagnose a wide range of variables for comparison with observations or study of atmospheric processes. An example is the 1.5 metre temperature, which is the standard height for near-surface observations of air temperature. This temperature is not directly predicted from the model but is deduced from the surface and lowest-model-layer temperatures.

CONTOUR ANALYSIS

Interpreting a group of meteorological observations is a great aid to understanding the information from many data points. Meteorologists use a technique called contour analysis to get a better understanding of what information the data is providing. Correct interpretation of the data is crucial in determining atmosphere structure and forecasting its evolution.

Contouring, sometimes called isoplething, is the process of connecting lines of equal valued data. Meteorologists use contouring to create weather maps that connect data taken from weather stations and weather balloons (radiosondes). These measurement sites can be relatively close together (a few kilometers) to great distances apart (hundred of kilometers). The size of the region one analyzes and the time between measurements determines the scale of the analysis.

The most important measurements to weather forecasters are pressure, temperature, moisture, wind, and clouds. All these fields are vital to understanding the current and predicting the future atmospheric state. If a forecaster looks at a map of temperature readings from the entire country, it would take considerable time to get a feeling for which parts of the country are experiencing warm conditions and which are experiencing colder conditions. However, by drawing lines of equal temperature, the meteorologist can quickly see patterns emerge. Contouring is vital in finding the location of fronts, the separation of warm and cold (moist / dry) air masses. Contouring winds can show where the warm and cold air is being advected, the horizontal transport of air, and thus where it might get colder or warmer in the future.

Data is collected at weather stations all around the world (often at airports). The data important to meteorologists includes measurements taken at the surface (surface data) and within the atmosphere (upper air data). Contouring both surface and upper air data is vital to the meteorologist to understand the 'whole story' of how air masses and storms are moving.

Storm systems are usually located where the atmospheric pressure is the lowest, commonly called a Low. Where atmospheric pressure is highest (a High), the weather is usually pleasant. The technique of contouring will make these features readily apparent and of great use not just to the forecaster but also those who plan on this information.

Contours and contour analysis are found everywhere; you see them when you look at the pretty colored temperatures in the weather section of the newspaper, and also when you look to see how steep the mountain is you are about to climb. Every time you look at a map of the Earth you see contours which are the lines of equal latitude and longitude. Nature also creates some of its own contours. When you look at tree stump it is easy to distinguish the tree rings. The age of a tree is easy to identify as each year of its life is represented by a contoured ring of its annual growth.

INTERTROPICAL CONVERGENCE ZONE

The Intertropical Convergence Zone (ITCZ) is the area encircling the earth near the equator where winds originating in the northern and southern hemispheres come together. The ITCZ appears as a band of clouds, usually thunderstorms, that circle the globe near the equator. In the Northern Hemisphere, the trade winds move in a southwestern direction from the northeast, while in the Southern Hemisphere, they move northwestward from the southeast. When the ITCZ is positioned north or south of the equator, these directions change according to the Coriolis effect imparted by the rotation of the earth. For instance, when the ITCZ is situated north of the equator, the southeast trade wind changes to a southwest wind as it crosses the equator.

The ITCZ appears as a band of clouds, usually thunderstorms, that circle the globe near the equator. In the Northern Hemisphere, the trade winds move in a southwestern direction from the northeast, while in the Southern Hemisphere, they move northwestward from the southeast. When the ITCZ is positioned north or south of the equator, these directions change according to the Coriolis effect imparted by the rotation of the earth. For instance, when the ITCZ is situated north of the equator, the southeast trade wind changes to a southwest wind as it crosses the equator.

The ITCZ is formed by vertical motion largely appearing as convective activity of thunderstorms driven by solar heating, which effectively draw air in; these are the trade winds. The ITCZ is effectively a tracer of the ascending branch of the Hadley cell, and is wet. The dry descending branch is the horse latitudes.

EFFECTS ON WEATHER

Variation in the location of the intertropical convergence zone drastically affects rainfall in many equatorial nations, resulting in the wet and dry seasons of the tropics rather than the cold and warm seasons of higher latitudes. Longer term changes in the intertropical convergence zone can result in severe droughts or flooding in nearby areas.

In some cases, the ITCZ may become narrow, especially when it moves away from the equator; the ITCZ can then be interpreted as a front along the leading edge of the equatorial air. There appears to be a 15-25 day cycle in thunderstorm activity along the ITCZ, which is roughly half the wavelength of the Madden-Julian Oscillation, or MJO.

Within the ITCZ the average winds are slight, unlike the zones north and south of the equator where the trade winds feed. Early sailors named this belt of calm the doldrums because of the inactivity and stagnation they found themselves in after days of no wind. To find oneself becalmed in this region in a hot and muggy climate could mean death in an era when wind was the only effective way to propel ships across the ocean. Even today the leisure and competitive sailors attempt to cross the zone as quickly as possible as the erratic weather and wind patterns may cause unexpected delays.

ROLE IN TROPICAL CYCLONE FORMATION

Tropical cyclogenesis depends upon low-level vorticity as one of its six requirements, and the ITCZ fills this role as it is a zone of wind change and speed, otherwise known as horizontal wind shear. As the ITCZ migrates more than 500 km from the equator during the respective hemisphere's summer season, increasing Coriolis force makes the formation of tropical cyclones within this zone more possible. In the north Atlantic and the northeastern Pacific oceans, tropical waves move along the axis of the ITCZ causing an increase in thunderstorm activity, and under weak vertical wind shear, these clusters of thunderstorms can become tropical cyclones.

AIR MASSES AND FRONTS

An air mass is a large body of air of relatively similar temperature and humidity characteristics covering thousands of square kilometers. Typically, air masses are classified according to the characteristics of their source region or area of formation. A source region can have one of four temperature attributes: equatorial, tropical, polar or arctic. Air masses are also classified as being either continental or maritime in terms of moisture characteristics. Combining these two categories, several possibilities are commonly found associated with North America: maritime polar (mP), continental polar (cP), maritime tropical (mT), continental tropical (cT), and continental arctic (A).

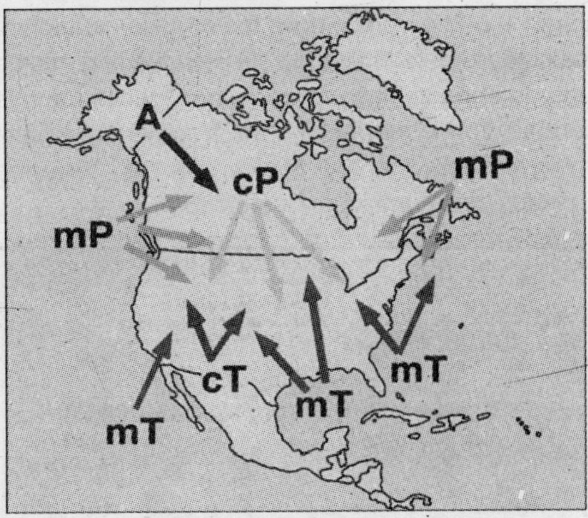

Figure : Source sites and movement patterns for North America's major air masses. Diagram describes the source regions and common patterns of movement for the various types of air masses associated with North America.

Frequently, two air masses, especially in the middle latitudes, develop a sharp boundary or interface, where the temperature difference between them becomes intensified. Such an area of intensification is called a frontal zone or a front. The boundary between the warm and cold air masses always slopes upwards over the cold air. This is due to the fact that cold air is much denser than warm air. The sloping of warm air over the cold air leads to a forced uplifting (frontal lifting) of the warm air if one air mass is moving toward the other. In turn, this uplifting causes condensation to occur and the possibility of precipitation along the frontal boundary.

Frontal zones where the air masses are not moving against each other are called stationary fronts. In transitional areas where there is some air mass movement, cold or warm fronts can develop. A cold front is the transition zone in the atmosphere where an advancing cold, dry stable air mass displaces a warm, moist unstable subtropical air mass. On a weather map, the cold front is drawn as a solid blue line with triangles. The position of the triangles shows the direction of frontal movement. Cold fronts move between 15 to 50 kilometers per hour in a southeast to east direction. The formation of clouds and precipitation at the frontal zone is caused by frontal lifting. High altitude cirrus clouds are found well in advance of the front. Above the surface location of the cold front, high altitude cirrostratus and middle altitude altocumulus are common. Precipitation is normally found just behind the front where frontal lifting has caused the development of towering cumulus and cumulonimbus clouds.

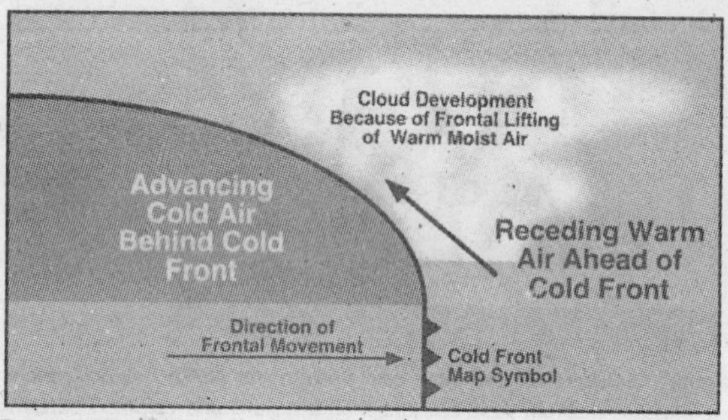

Figure : Atmospheric cross-section of a cold front.

A warm front is the transition zone in the atmosphere where an advancing warm subtropical, moist air mass replaces a retreating cold, dry polar air mass. On a weather map, a warm front is drawn as a solid red line with half-circles. The position of the half-circles shows the direction of frontal movement. Warm fronts move about 10 kilometers per hour in a northeast direction. This is less than half the speed of a cold front. The formation of clouds and precipitation ahead of the frontal zone is caused by gradual frontal lifting. High altitude cirrus, cirrostratus and middle altitude altostratus clouds are found well in advance of the front. About 600 kilometers ahead of the front, nimbostratus clouds occur. These clouds produce precipitation in the form of snow or rain. Between the nimbostratus clouds and the surface location of the warm front, low altitude stratus clouds are found. Finally, a few hundred kilometers behind the front scattered stratocumulus are common in the lower troposphere.

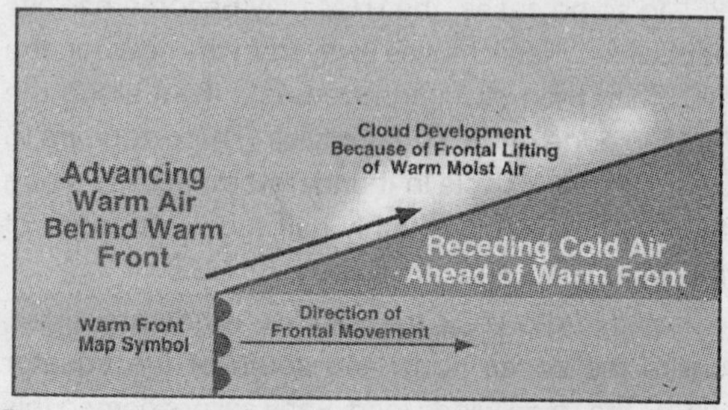

Figure : Atmospheric cross-section of a warm front.

Occluded fronts are produced when a fast moving cold front catches and overtakes a slower moving warm front. Two types of occluded fronts are generally recognized. A cold type occluded front occurs when the air behind the front is colder than the air ahead of the front. When the air behind the front is warmer than the air ahead of the front a warm type occluded front is produced. Warm type occlusions are common on the west coast of continents and generally form when maritime polar air collides with continental polar or arctic air.

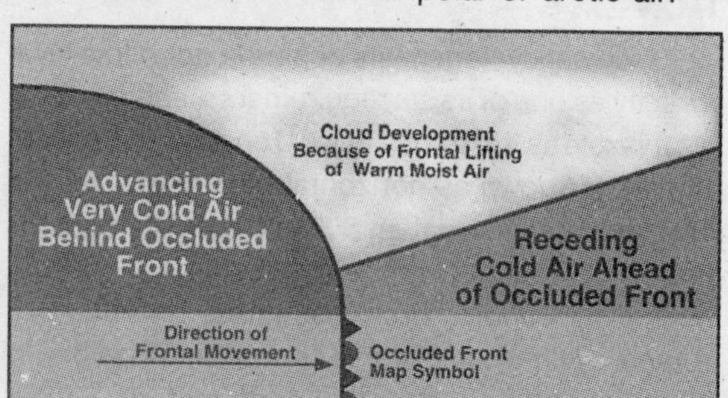

Figure : Atmospheric cross-section of a occluded front.

Finally, the frontal systems described on this page are often associated with a storm system known as the mid-latitude cyclone.

GEOSYNCHRONOUS SATELLITE

Geosynchronous satellite is a satellite whose orbital track on the Earth repeats regularly over points on the Earth over time. If such a satellite's orbit lies over the equator and the orbit is circular, it is called a geostationary satellite. The orbits of the satellites are known as the geosynchronous orbit and geostationary orbit.

If a geosynchronous satellite's orbit is not exactly aligned with the equator, the orbit is known as an inclined orbit. It will appear (when viewed by someone on the ground) to oscillate daily around a fixed point. As the angle between the orbit and the equator decreases, the magnitude of this oscillation becomes smaller; when the orbit lies entirely over the equator, the satellite remains stationary relative to the Earth's surface - it is said to be geostationary.

APPLICATION

Geostationary satellites appear to be fixed over one spot above the equator. Receiving and transmitting antennas on the earth do not need to track such a satellite. These antennas can be fixed in place and are much less expensive than tracking antennas. These satellites have revolutionized global communications, television broadcasting and weather forecasting, and have a number of important defense and intelligence applications.

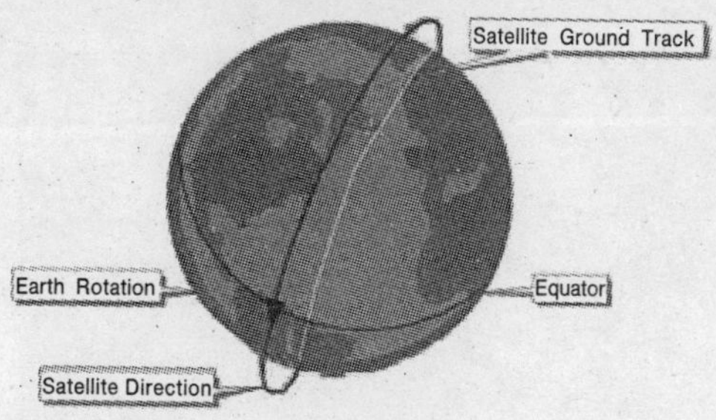

Figure : Orbit of Sun Synchronous Satellites

One disadvantage of geostationary satellites is a result of their high altitude: radio signals take approximately 0.25 of a second to reach and return from the satellite, resulting in a small but significant signal delay. This delay increases the difficulty of telephone conversation and reduces the performance of common network protocols such as TCP/IP, but does not present a problem with non-interactive systems such as television broadcasts. There are a number of proprietary satellite data protocols that are designed to proxy TCP/IP connections over long-delay satellite links – these are marketed as being a partial solution to the poor performance of native TCP over satellite links. TCP presumes that all loss is due to congestion, not errors, and probes link capacity with its "slow-start" algorithm, which only sends packets once it is known that earlier packets have been received. Slow start is very slow over a path using a geostationary satellite.

POLAR ORBITING SATELLITE

Polar orbiting weather satellites circle the Earth at a typical altitude of 850 km (530 miles) in a north to south (or vice versa) path, passing over the poles in their continuous flight. Polar satellites are in sun-synchronous orbits, which means they are able to observe any place on Earth and will view every location twice each day with the same general lighting conditions due to the near-constant local solar time. Polar orbiting weather satellites offer a much better resolution than their geostationary counterparts due their closeness to the Earth.

The United States has the NOAA series of polar orbiting meteorological satellites, presently NOAA 17 and NOAA 18 as primary spacecraft, NOAA 15 and NOAA 16 as secondary spacecraft, NOAA 14 in standby, and NOAA 12. Europe has the Metop-A satellite. Russia has the Meteor and RESURS series of satellites.

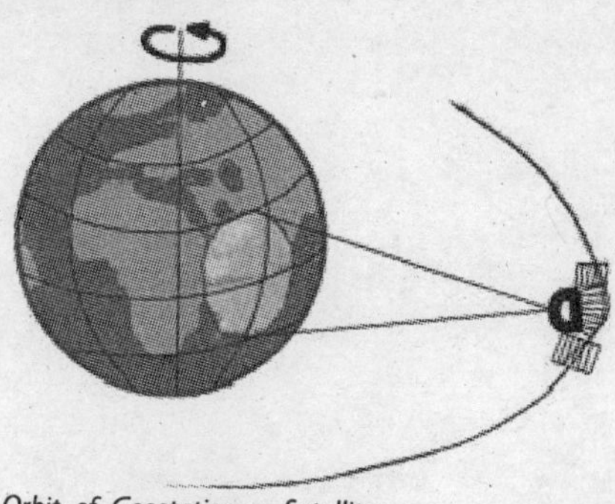

Figure : Orbit of Geostationary Satellites

Comparison between Sun-Synchronous and Geostationary Satellites

Orbital Characteristics	Sun Synchronous Satellites	Geostationary Satellites
Altitude	700 - 900 km	36,000 km
Coverage	81°N to 81°S	1/3rd of the Globe
Orbital period	14 orbits per day	24 hours
Resolution	Fine (182 metre to 1 metre)	Coarse (1 km x 1 km)
Uses	Earth Resources Applications	Telecommunication and Weather monitoring

10. OCEAN SCIENCES

Physical Oceanography

Physical Oceanography

TIDE

Tides are the rise and fall of sea levels caused by the combined effects of the gravitational forces exerted by the Moon and the Sun, and the rotation of the Earth. The tides occur with a period of approximately 12 and a half hours and are influenced by the shape of the near-shore bottom.

Tide changes proceed via the following stages:

- Sea level rises over several hours, covering the intertidal zone; flood tide.
- The water rises to its highest level, reaching high tide.
- Sea level falls over several hours, revealing the intertidal zone; ebb tide.
- The water stops falling, reaching low tide.

Tides produce oscillating currents known as tidal streams. The moment that the tidal current ceases is called slack water or slack tide. The tide then reverses direction and is said to be turning. Slack water usually occurs near high water and low water. But there are locations where the moments of slack tide differ significantly from those of high and low water.

Tides are most commonly semidiurnal (two high waters and two low waters each day), or diurnal (one tidal cycle per day). The two high waters on a given day are typically not the same height (the daily inequality); these are the higher high water and the lower high water in tide tables. Similarly, the two low waters each day are the higher low water and the lower low water. The daily inequality is not consistent and is generally small when the Moon is over the equator.

SPRINGS AND NEAPS TIDES

The semidiurnal tidal range (the difference in height between high and low waters over about a half day) varies in a two-week cycle. Around new and full moon when the Sun, Moon and Earth form a line (a condition known as syzygy), the tidal force due to the Sun reinforces that due to the Moon. The tide's range is then at its maximum: this is called the spring tide, or just springs. It is not named after the season but, like that word, derives from an earlier meaning of "jump, burst forth, rise" as in a natural spring. When the Moon is at first quarter or third quarter, the Sun and Moon are separated by 90° when viewed from the Earth, and the solar gravitational force partially cancels the Moon's. At these points in the lunar cycle, the tide's range is at its minimum: this is called the neap tide, or neaps (a word of uncertain origin). Spring tides result in high waters that are higher than average, low waters that are lower than average, slack water time that is shorter than average and stronger tidal currents than average. Neaps result in less extreme tidal conditions. There is about a seven day interval between springs and neaps.

The changing distance separating the Moon and Earth also affects tide heights. When the Moon is at perigee the range increases, and when it is at apogee the range shrinks. Every 7S lunations (the full cycles from full moon to new to full), perigee coincides with either a new or full moon causing perigean spring tides with the largest tidal range. If a storm happens to be moving onshore at this time, the consequences (property damage, etc.) can be especially severe.

THE TIDAL FORCE

The tidal force produced by a massive object (Moon, hereafter) on a small particle located on or in an extensive body (Earth, hereafter) is the vector difference between the gravitational force exerted by the Moon on the particle, and the gravitational force that would be exerted on the particle if it were located at the Earth's center of mass. Thus, the tidal force depends not on the strength of the lunar gravitational field, but on its gradient (which falls off approximately as the inverse cube of the distance to the originating gravitational body). The solar gravitational force on the Earth is on average 179 times stronger than the lunar, but because the Sun is on average 389 times farther from the Earth, its field gradient is weaker. The solar tidal force is 46% as large as the lunar. More precisely, the lunar tidal acceleration (along the Moon-Earth axis, at the Earth's surface) is about 1.1×10^{-7}g, while the solar tidal acceleration (along the Sun-Earth axis, at the Earth's surface) is about 0.52×10^{-7}g, where g is the gravitational acceleration at the Earth's surface. Venus has the largest effect of the other planets, at 0.000113 times the solar effect.

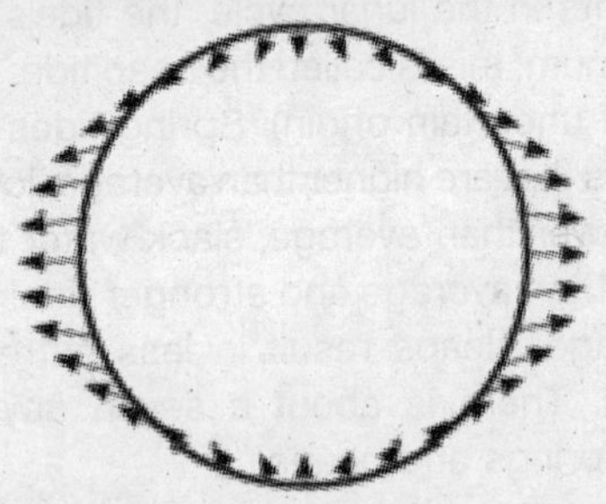

Fig. : The lunar gravity differential field at the Earth's surface is known as the tide-generating force. This is the primary mechanism that drives tidal action and explains two equipotential tidal bulges, accounting for two daily high waters.

Tidal forces can also be analyzed this way: each point of the Earth experiences the Moon's radially decreasing gravity differently; they are subject to the tidal forces of Figure 6, which dominate. Finally, most importantly, only the tidal forces' horizontal components actually tidally accelerate the water particles since there is small resistance. The tidal force on a particle equals about one ten millionth that of Earth's gravitational force.

The ocean's surface is closely approximated by an equipotential surface, (ignoring ocean currents) commonly referred to as the geoid. Since the gravitational force is equal to the potential's gradient, there are no tangential forces on such a surface, and the ocean surface is thus in gravitational equilibrium. Now consider the effect of massive external bodies such as the Moon and Sun. These bodies have strong gravitational fields that diminish with distance in space and which act to alter the shape of an equipotential surface on the Earth. This deformation has a fixed spatial orientation relative to the influencing body. The Earth's rotation relative to this shape causes the daily tidal cycle. Gravitational forces follow an inverse-square law (force is inversely proportional to the square of the distance), but tidal forces are inversely proportional to the cube of the distance. The ocean surface moves to adjust to changing tidal equipotential, tending to rise when the tidal potential is high, which occurs on the part of the Earth nearest to and furthest from the Moon. When the tidal equipotential changes, the ocean surface is no longer aligned with it, so that the apparent direction of the vertical shifts. The surface then experiences a down slope, in the direction that the equipotential has risen.

TIDAL PREDICTION

If tides in the ocean were in equilibrium with the tidal potential, tidal pre- diction would be much easier. Unfortunately, tides are far from equilibrium. The shallow-water wave which is the tide cannot move fast enough to keep up with sun and moon. On the equator, the tide would need to propagate around the world in one day. This requires a wave speed of around 460 m/s, which is only possible in an ocean 22 km deep. In addition, the continents interrupt the propagation of the wave. How to proceed?

We can separate the problem of tidal prediction into two parts. The first deals with the prediction of tides in ports and shallow water where tides can be measured by tide gauges. The second deals with the prediction of tides in the deep ocean where tides are measured by satellite altimeters.

Tidal Prediction for Ports and Shallow Water Two methods are used to predict future tides at a tide-gauge station using past observations of sea level measured at the gauge.

The Harmonic Method This is the traditional method, and it is still widely used. The method typically uses 19 years of data from a coastal tide gauge from which the amplitude and phase of each tidal constituent (the tidal harmonics) in the tide-gage record are calculated. The frequencies used in the analysis are specified in advance from the basic frequencies.

Despite its simplicity, the technique had disadvantages compared with the response method described below.

1. More than 18.6 years of data are needed to resolve the modulation of the lunar tides.
2. Amplitude accuracy of 10^{-3} of the largest term require that at least 39 frequencies be determined. Doodson found 400 frequencies were needed for an amplitude accuracy of 10^{-4} of the largest term.
3. Non-tidal variability introduces large errors into the calculated amplitudes and phases of the weaker tidal constituents. The weaker tides have amplitudes smaller than variability at the same frequency due to other processes such as wind set up and currents near the tide gauge.
4. At many ports, the tide is non-linear, and many more tidal constituents are important. For some ports, the number of frequencies is unmanageable.

When tides propagate into very shallow water, especially river estuaries, they steepen and become non-linear. This generates harmonics of the original frequencies. In extreme cases, the incoming wave steepens so much the leading edge is nearly vertical, and the wave propagates as solitary wave. This is a tidal bore.

ESTUARY

An estuary is a partly enclosed coastal body of water with one or more rivers or streams flowing into it, and with a free connection to the open sea.

Estuaries form a transition zone between river environments and ocean environments and are subject to both marine influences, such as tides, waves, and the influx of saline water; and riverine influences, such as flows of fresh water and sediment. The inflow of both seawater and freshwater provide high levels of nutrients in both the water column and sediment, making estuaries among the most productive natural habitats in the world.

CLASSIFICATION OF ESTUARIES

Estuaries have been classified according to many different schemes. Most commonly, estuaries are classified according to their geomorphology or water circulation.

CLASSIFICATION BASED ON GEOMORPHOLOGY

Drowned river valleys

Many drowned river valley estuaries were formed between about 15,000 and 6000 years ago following the end of the Wisconsin (or 'Devensian') glaciation when a eustatic rise in sea level of 100 m to 130 m, flooded river valleys that were cut into the landscape when sea level was lower, creating the estuarine systems. Additionally, the general subsidence of coastal regions contributed to the development of drowned river valleys. Well developed drowned river valleys are generally found on coastlines with low, wide coastal plains. Their width-to-depth ratio is typically large, appearing wedge-shaped in the inner part and broadening and deepening seaward. Water depths rarely exceed 30 meters. Examples of this type of estuary include the Chesapeake Bay and Delaware Bay, along the U.S. mid-Atlantic coast, and along the U.S. Gulf coast, Galveston Bay and Tampa Bay.

Lagoon-type or bar-built estuaries

These estuaries are semi-isolated from ocean waters by barrier beaches (barrier islands and barrier spits). Formation of barrier beaches partially encloses the estuary with only narrow inlets allowing contact with the ocean waters. Bar-built estuaries typically develop on gently sloping plains located along tectonically stable edges of continents and marginal sea coasts. They are extensive along the Atlantic and Gulf coasts of the U.S. in areas with active coastal deposition of sediments and where tidal ranges are less than 4 meters. The barrier beaches that enclose bar-built estuaries have been developed in several ways: 1) upbuilding of offshore bars from wave action, in which sand from the seafloor is deposited in elongate bars parallel to the shoreline, 2) reworking of sediment discharge from rivers by wave, current, and wind action into beaches, overwash flats, and dunes, 3) engulfment of mainland beach ridges (ridges developed from the erosion of coastal plain sediments approximately 5,000 years ago) due to sea level rise and resulting in the breaching of the ridges and flooding of the coastal lowlands, forming shallow lagoons, 4) elongation of barrier spits from the erosion of headlands, with the spit growth occurring in the direction of the littoral drift due to the action of longshore currents. Barrier beaches form in shallow water and are generally parallel to the shoreline, resulting in long, narrow estuaries. The average water depth is usually less than 5 m, and rarely exceed 10 m. Examples of bar-built estuaries include Barnegat Bay, New Jersey, Laguna Madre, Texas, and Pamlico Sound, North Carolina.

Fjord-type estuaries

Fjord type estuaries are formed in deeply eroded valleys formed by glaciers. These U-shaped estuaries typically have steep sides, rock bottoms, and underwater sills contoured by glacial movement. The shallowest area of the estuary occurs at the mouth, where terminal glacial deposits or rock bars form sills that restrict water flow. In the upper reaches of the estuary, the depth can exceed 300 meters. The width-to-depth ratio is generally small. When estuaries contain very shallow sills, tidal oscillations only affect near surface waters to sill depth, and waters below sill depth may remain stagnant for very long periods of time, resulting in only an occasional exchange of the deep water of the estuary with the ocean. If the sill depth is deep, water circulation is less restricted and a slow, but steady exchange of water from the estuary and the ocean occur. Fjord-type estuaries can be found along the coasts of Alaska, eastern Canada, Greenland, Iceland, New Zealand, and Norway.

Tectonically produced estuaries

These estuaries are formed by subsidence or land cut off from the ocean by land movement associated with faulting, volcanoes, and landslides. Inundation from eustatic sea level rise during the Holocene Epoch has also contributed to the formation of these estuaries. There are only a small number of tectonically produced estuaries; one example is the San Francisco Bay, which was formed by the crustal movements of the San Andreas fault system causing the inundation of the lower reaches of the Sacramento and San Joaquin rivers.

CLASSIFICATION BASED ON HYDROGRAPHY

Salt wedge estuaries

In this type of estuary, river output greatly exceeds marine input and tidal effects have a minor importance. Fresh water floats on top of the seawater in a layer that gradually thins as it moves seaward. The denser seawater moves landward along the bottom of the estuary, forming a wedge-shaped layer that is thinner as it approaches land. As a velocity difference develops between the two layers, shear forces generate internal waves at the interface, mixing the seawater upward with the freshwater. An example of a salt wedge estuary is the Mississippi River.

Partially mixed estuaries

As tidal forcing increases, river output becomes less than the marine input. Here, current induced turbulence causes mixing of the whole water column such that salinity varies more longitudinally rather than vertically, leading to a moderately stratified condition. Examples include the Chesapeake Bay and Narragansett Bay.

Vertically homogenous estuaries

Tidal mixing forces exceed river output, resulting in a well mixed water column and the disappearance of the vertical salinity gradient. The freshwater-seawater boundary is eliminated due to the intense turbulent mixing and eddy effects. The lower reaches of the Delaware Bay and the Raritan River in New Jersey are examples of vertically homogenous estuaries.

Inverse estuary

Inverse estuaries occur in dry climates where evaporation greatly exceeds the inflow of fresh water. A salinity maximum zone is formed, and both riverine and oceanic water flow close to the surface towards this zone. This water is pushed downward and spreads along the bottom in both the seaward and landward direction. An example of an inverse estuary is Spencer Gulf South Australia

Intermittent estuaries

Estuary type varies dramatically depending on freshwater input, and is capable of changing from a wholly marine embayment to any of the other estuary types.

GEOSTROPHIC CURRENTS

Within the ocean's interior away from the top and bottom Ekman layers, for horizontal distances exceeding a few tens of kilometers, and for times exceeding a few days, horizontal pressure gradients in the ocean almost exactly balance the Coriolis force resulting from horizontal currents. This balance is known as Geostrophic Equations

The geostrophic balance requires that the Coriolis force balance the horizontal pressure gradient. The equations for geostrophic balance are derived from the equations of motion assuming the flow has no acceleration, du/dt = dv/dt = dw/dt = 0; that horizontal velocities are much larger than vertical, $w \ll u, v$; that the only external force is gravity; and that friction is small & so the geostrophic balance will be,

$$\frac{\partial p}{\partial x} = \rho f v; \quad \frac{\partial p}{\partial y} = -\rho f u; \quad \frac{\partial p}{\partial z} = -\rho g$$

where $f = 2\Omega \sin \phi$ is the Coriolis parameter. These are the geostrophic equations.

The equations can be written:

$$u = -\frac{1}{f\rho}\frac{\partial p}{\partial y}; \quad v = \frac{1}{f\rho}\frac{\partial p}{\partial x}$$

$$p = p_0 + \int_{-h}^{\varsigma} g(\varphi, z)\rho(z)\,dz$$

where p_0 is atmospheric pressure at $z = 0$, and ζ is the height of the sea surface. Note that we have allowed for the sea surface to be above or below the surface $z = 0$; and the pressure gradient at the sea surface is balanced by a surface current us.

$$u = -\frac{1}{f\rho}\frac{\partial}{\partial y}\int_{-h}^{0} g(\varphi, z)\rho(z)dz - \frac{g}{f}\frac{\partial \zeta}{\partial y}$$

$$u = -\frac{1}{f\rho}\frac{\partial}{\partial y}\int_{-h}^{0} g(\varphi, z)\rho(z)dz - u_*$$

where we have used the Boussinesq approximation, retaining full accuracy for only when calculating pressure.

In a similar way, we can derive the equation for v.

$$v = -\frac{1}{f\rho}\frac{\partial}{\partial x}\int_{-h}^{0} g(\varphi, z)\rho(z)dz + \frac{g}{f}\frac{\partial \zeta}{\partial x}$$

$$v = \frac{1}{f\rho}\frac{\partial}{\partial x}\int_{-h}^{0} g(\varphi, z)\rho(z)dz + v_*$$

Limitations of the Geostrophic Equations

The important limitations of the geostrophic assumption are:

1. Geostrophic currents cannot evolve with time because the balance ignores acceleration of the flow. Acceleration dominates if the horizontal dimensions are less than roughly 50 km and times are less than a few days.

   Acceleration is negligible, but not zero, over longer times and distances.

2. The geostrophic balance does not apply within about 2° of the equator where the

Coriolis force goes to zero because sin $\phi \to 0$.

3. The geostrophic balance ignores the influence of friction.

SEAWATER

Seawater is water from a sea or ocean. On average, seawater in the world's oceans has a salinity of about 3.5%. This means that every kilogram, or every litre, of seawater has approximately 35 grams (1.2 oz) of dissolved salts (mostly, but not entirely, the ions of sodium chloride: Na^+, Cl^-). The average density of seawater at the ocean surface is 1.025 g/ml; seawater is denser than freshwater (which reaches a maximum density of 1.000 g/ml at a temperature of 4°C (39°F)) because of the salts' added mass.

Seawater composition (by mass) (salinity = 35)

Element	Percent	Element	Percent
Oxygen	85.84	Sulfur	0.091
Hydrogen	10.82	Calcium	0.04
Chlorine	1.94	Potassium	0.04
Sodium	1.08	Bromine	0.0067
Magnesium	0.1292	Carbon	0.0028

Although the vast majority of seawater has a salinity of between 31% and 38%, seawater is not uniformly saline throughout the world. Where mixing occurs with fresh water runoff from river mouths or near melting glaciers, seawater can be substantially less saline. The most saline open sea is the Red Sea, where high rates of evaporation, low precipitation and river inflow, and confined circulation result in unusually salty water. The salinity in isolated bodies of water (for example, the Dead Sea) can be considerably greater still.

The density of surface seawater ranges from about 1,020 to 1,029 kg•m^{-3}, depending on the temperature and salinity. Deep in the ocean, under high pressure, seawater can reach a density of 1,050 kg•m^{-3} or higher. Seawater pH is limited to the range 7.5 to 8.4. The speed of sound in seawater is about 1,500 metres/second, and varies with water temperature, salinity, and pressure.

MARINE ENVIRONMENT & ORGANISM

Marine biology is the scientific study of organisms in the ocean or other marine or brackish bodies of water. Given that in biology many phyla, families and genera have some species that live in the sea and others that live on land, marine biology classifies species based on the environment rather than on taxonomy. Marine biology differs from marine ecology as marine ecology is focused on how organisms interact with each other and environment and biology is the study of the animal itself.

Marine life is a vast resource, providing food, medicine, and raw materials, in addition to helping to support recreation and tourism all over the world. At a fundamental level, marine life helps determine the very nature of our planet. Marine organisms contribute significantly to the oxygen cycle, and are involved in the regulation of the Earth's climate. Shorelines are in part shaped and protected by marine life, and some marine organisms even help create new land.

Marine biology covers a great deal, from the microscopic, including most zooplankton and phytoplankton to the huge cetaceans (whales) which reach up to a reported 48 meters (125 feet) in length.

The habitats studied by marine biology include everything from the tiny layers of surface water in which organisms and abiotic items may be trapped in surface tension between the ocean and atmosphere, to the depths of the abyssal trenches, sometimes 10,000 meters or more beneath the surface of the ocean. It studies habitats such as coral reefs, kelp forests, tidepools, muddy, sandy and rocky bottoms, and the open ocean (pelagic) zone, where solid objects are rare and the surface of the water is the only visible boundary.

A large amount of all life on Earth exists in the oceans. Exactly how large the proportion is unknown, since many ocean species are still to be discovered. While the oceans comprise about 71% of the Earth's surface, due to their depth they encompass about 300 times the habitable volume of the terrestrial habitats on Earth.

PLANTS AND ALGAE

Plant life is widespread and very diverse under the sea. Microscopic photosynthetic algae contribute a larger proportion of the worlds photosynthetic output than all the terrestrial forests combined. Most of the niche occupied by sub plants on land is actually occupied by macroscopic algae in the ocean, such as Sargassum and kelp, which are commonly known as seaweeds that create kelp forests. The non algae plants that survive in the sea are often found in shallow waters, such as the seagrasses (examples of which are eelgrass, Zostera, and turtle grass, Thalassia). These plants have adapted to the high salinity of the ocean environment. The intertidal zone is also a good place to find plant life in the sea, where mangroves or cordgrass or beach grass might grow. Microscopic algae and plants provide important habitats for life, sometimes acting as hiding and foraging places for larval forms of larger fish and invertebrates.

MARINE INVERTEBRATES

As on land, invertebrates make up a huge portion of all life in the sea. Invertebrate sea life includes Cnidaria such as jellyfish and sea anemones; Ctenophora; sea worms including the phyla Platyhelminthes, Nemertea, Annelida, Sipuncula, Echiura, Chaetognatha, and Phoronida; Mollusca including shellfish, squid, octopus; Arthropoda including Chelicerata and Crustacea; Porifera; Bryozoa; Echinodermata including starfish; and Urochordata including sea squirts or tunicates.

MARINE MAMMALS

There are five main types of marine mammals.

- Cetaceans include toothed whales (Suborder Odontoceti), such as the Sperm Whale, dolphins, and porpoises such as the Dall's porpoise. Cetaceans also include baleen whales (Suborder Mysticeti), such as the Gray Whale, Humpback Whale, and Blue Whale.
- Sirenians include manatees, the Dugong, and the extinct Steller's Sea Cow.
- Seals (Family Phocidae), sea lions (Family Otariidae - which also include the fur seals), and the Walrus (Family Odobenidae) are all considered pinnipeds.
- The Sea Otter is a member of the Family Mustelidae, which includes weasels and badgers.
- The Polar Bear (Family Ursidae) is sometimes considered a marine mammal because of its dependence on the sea.

BENTHIC ORGANISMS

Benthos are the organisms which live on, in, or near the seabed, also known as the benthic zone.They live in or near marine sedimentary environments, from tidal pools along the foreshore, out to the continental shelf, and then down to the abyssal depths.

Many organisms adapted to deep-water pressure cannot survive in the upper parts of the water column. The pressure difference can be very significant (approximately one atmosphere for each 10 meters of water depth).

Because light does not penetrate very deep ocean-water, the energy source for deep benthic ecosystems is often organic matter from higher up in the water column which drifts down to the depths. This dead and decaying matter sustains the benthic food chain; most organisms in the benthic zone are scavengers or detritivores.

The main food sources for benthos are plankton and organic runoff from land. The depth of water, temperature and salinity, and type of local substrate all affect what benthos is present. In coastal waters and other places where light reaches the bottom, benthic photosynthesizing diatoms can proliferate. Filter feeders, such as sponges and bivalves, dominate hard, sandy bottoms. Deposit feeders, such as polychaetes, populate softer bottoms. Fish, sea stars, snails, cephalopods, and crustaceans are important predators and scavengers.

Benthic organisms, such as sea stars, oysters, clams, sea cucumbers, brittle stars and sea anemones, play an important role as a food source for fish and humans.

CORAL REEF

Coral reefs are underwater structures made from calcium carbonate secreted by corals. Corals are colonies of tiny living animals found in marine waters containing few nutrients. Most coral reefs are built from stony corals, and are formed by polyps that live together in groups. The polyps secrete a hard carbonate exoskeleton which provides support and protection for the body of each polyp. Reefs grow best in warm, shallow, clear, sunny and agitated waters.

FORMATION OF CORAL REEF

Most coral reefs were formed after the last glacial period when melting ice caused the sea level to rise and flood the continental shelves. This means that most coral reefs are less than 10,000 years old. As coral reef communities were established on the shelves, they built reefs that grew upwards, keeping pace with the rise in sea level. Reefs that didn't keep pace could become drowned reefs, covered by so much water that there was insufficient light for further survival.

Darwin predicted that underneath each lagoon would be a bed rock base, the remains of the original volcano. Subsequent drilling has proved this correct. Darwin's theory followed from his understanding that coral polyps thrive in the clean seas of the tropics where the water is agitated, but can only live within a limited depth of water, starting just below low tide. Where the level of the underlying land stays the same, the corals grow around the coast to form what he called fringing reefs, and can eventually grow out from the shore to become a barrier reef. Where the land is rising, fringing reefs can grow around the coast, but coral raised above sea level dies and becomes white limestone. If the land subsides slowly, the fringing reefs keep pace by growing upwards on a base of dead coral, forming a barrier reef enclosing a lagoon between the reef and the land. A barrier reef can encircle an island, and once the island sinks below sea level a roughly circular atoll of growing coral continues to keep up with the sea level, forming a central lagoon. Barrier reefs and atolls don't usually form complete circles, but are broken in places by storms. Should the land subside too quickly or sea level rise too fast, the coral dies as it is below its habitable depth.

In general, the two main variables determining the geomorphology, or shape, of coral reefs are the nature of the underlying substrate on which they rest, and the history of the change in sea level relative to that substrate.

TYPES OF CORAL REEF

The three principal reef types are:

- Fringing reef - a reef that is directly attached to a shore or borders it with an intervening shallow channel or lagoon.
- Barrier reef - a reef separated from a mainland or island shore by a deep lagoon.
- Atoll reef - a more or less circular or continuous barrier reef extending all the way around a lagoon without a central island.

DISTRIBUTION OF CORAL REEF

Coral reefs are estimated to cover 284,300 square kilometers (109,800 sq mi), which is just under one per cent of the surface area occupied by the world oceans. The Indo-Pacific region (including the Red Sea, Indian Ocean, Southeast Asia and the Pacific) account for 91.9% of this total. Southeast Asia accounts for 32.3% of that figure, while the Pacific including Australia accounts for 40.8%. Atlantic and Caribbean coral reefs only account for 7.6%.

Although corals exist both in temperate and tropical waters, shallow-water reefs form only in a zone extending from 30°N to 30°S of the equator. Tropical corals do not grow at depths of over 50 meters (160 ft). The optimum temperature for most coral reefs is 26-27°C, and few reefs exist in waters below 18°C. However reefs in the Persian Gulf have adapted to temperatures of 13°C in winter and 38°C in summer.

Deep water coral is more still exceptional since it can exist at greater depths and colder temperatures. Although deep water corals can form reefs, very little is known about them.

Principal coral reefs and reef areas of the world

- The Great Barrier Reef - largest coral reef system in the world, Queensland, Australia.
- The Belize Barrier Reef - second largest in the world, stretching from southern Quintana Roo, Mexico along the coast of Belize to the Bay Islands of Honduras.
- The New Caledonia Barrier Reef - second longest double barrier reef in the world, with a length of about 1,500 kilometers (930 mi).
- The Andros, Bahamas Barrier Reef - third largest in the world, following the east coast of Andros Island, Bahamas, between Andros and Nassau.
- The Red Sea Coral Reef - located off the coast of Israel, Egypt, Sudan, Eritrea, Djibouti, Somalia, Jordan, Saudi Arabia, and Yemen.
- Pulley Ridge - deepest photosynthetic coral reef, Florida.
- Numerous reefs scattered over the Maldives.

MANGROVE COMMUNITIES

Several major types of mangrove communities are described which result from differences in geological and hydrological processes. Generally, mangroves grow best in depositional environments with low wave energy. Extreme wave conditions: prevent establishment of propagules, destroy relatively shallow root systems, and prevent accumulation of fine sediments. The best sediment conditions are fine-grained muds of silt/clay with lots of organic matter. Primarily, these conditions exist along deltaic coasts or estuarine shorelines. However, all local species can grow on a variety of substrates: sand, mud, rock, and peat. When found on rock surfaces, it appears that they are growing in sediment trapped in cracks rather than directly on the rocky surface.

Riverine forests are tall flood plain forests along flowing waters such as tidal rivers and creeks. Conditions are favorable for extensive growth due to flushing by daily tides. In addition, freshwater runoff and terrestrial nutrient influx enhance this type of mangrove community. Maximum heights of trees in this community are 66 feet (20 m).

Fringing forests exist as a relatively thin fringe along waterways. These forests appear to be flushed daily by tides, but do not receive then amount of terrestrial runoff as the riverine forests. Typically, the classic mangrove zonation pattern of seaward Red-Black-landward White scheme is exhibited in this forest. Maximum heights of trees in this community are slightly over 30 feet (l0 m).

Overwash forests exist as islands frequently washed over by tides. All species are present with the Red mangrove the dominant species. Typically, these islands develop as a Red mangrove propagule strands in a shallow flat. As more and more propagules strand and grow, the "island" begins as a tangle of prop roots. As the island develops the roots eventually trap sediment. Often, bare sand flats are found in the center of these islandsThe maximum height of the community is between 2&emdash; 25 feet (7 m).

Scrub or Dwarf forests are common in the flat coastal fringe of southern Florida and the Keys. All 3 species are present, but height is limited to less than 7 feet (l.5-2 m) except in depressions of mangrove peat. Nutrients appear to be the limiting factors affecting growth, although substrate (marl) is also important.

Two similar forests are the Basin and Hammock communities. Basin forests are inland in depressions channeling terrestrial runoff toward the coast. Trees in this community have maximum heights of almost 50 feet (l5 m). Hammock forests are in depressions but exist on slightly elevated ground. In Florida, these communities exist in the sawgrass communities of the Everglades. Trees rarely growth height in excess of 17 feet (5 m). Tidal flushing of both of the communities is infrequent.

A newer simplified system of mangrove community types is now in use among researchers. It retains the riverine and fringing forest types and omits the overwash forest. Additionally, the scrub or dwarf, hammock, and basin forests are lumped into the category of basin forest. This scheme seems focus on hydrological processes as the dominant influence affecting community types. The fringing forest is along waterways and bays. The riverine forests are along tidal rivers and creeks. Inland of both of these communities are the basin forests.

YOUR SPACE

YOUR SPACE